W9-BKY-466
OTA
MINNESOTA
OTA
Mississippi
IOWA
KA
River
SAS
MISSOURI
LAHOMA
ARKANSAS
S
LOUISIANA
ATLANTIC
OCEAN
GULF OF
MEXICO
0
150
300 Miles
0
150
300 Km.

Encyclopedia
OF THE
AMERICAN WEST

Editorial Board

Charles Phillips
Alan Axelrod
Editors

Macmillan Reference USA
Simon & Schuster Macmillan
New York

SIMON & SCHUSTER AND PRENTICE HALL INTERNATIONAL
London • Mexico City • New Delhi • Singapore • Sydney • Toronto

Produced by ZENDA, INC., Nashville, Tennessee
Design: Gore Studios, Inc.
Proofreading and Index of Professions: John Reiman
General Index: Alexa Selph

Simon & Schuster Macmillan
1633 Broadway, New York, NY 10019

PRINTED IN THE UNITED STATES OF AMERICA

printing number
2 3 4 5 6 7 8 9 10

LIBRARY OF CONGRESS CATALOGING-IN-PUBLICATION DATA

Encyclopedia of the American West / Charles Phillips and Alan Axelrod, editors
p cm.
Includes bibliographical references (p.) and index.
ISBN 0-02-897495-6
1. West (U.S.)—Encyclopedias. I. Phillips, Charles, 1948–
II. Axelrod, Alan, 1952–
F591.E485 1996
978—dc20 96-1685
CIP

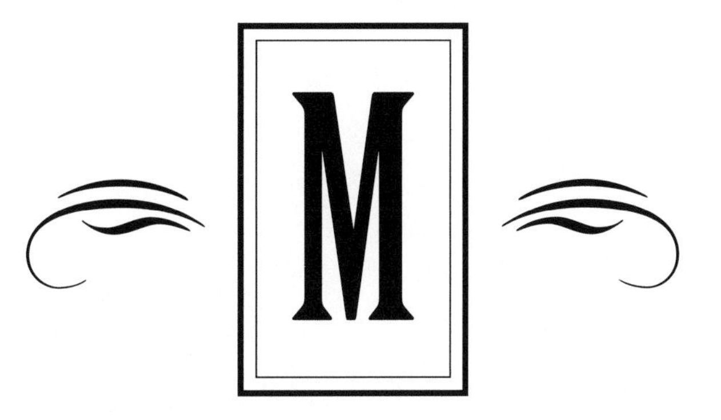

MACKAY, JOHN W.

A leading figure of the "Bonanza Kings" of the COMSTOCK LODE in Nevada, John W. Mackay (1831–1902) was born in poverty in Dublin, Ireland. He rose to great fame and fortune in nineteenth-century Nevada through the combination of perseverance, native intelligence, sound judgment, and honesty.

Mackay's father died in 1842, two years after bringing the family to New York. To help support his mother and sisters, young Mackay left school and began working at a variety of jobs. At the age of sixteen, he was apprenticed to William H. Webb, a builder of steam-wheel ships, and spent the next four years learning to use tools. At the end of his apprenticeship, he sailed to California on one of Webb's ships and went to work in various diggings along the Yuba River near Downieville.

In 1859, Mackay joined the "rush to Washoe" and crossed the Sierra Nevada in hopes of making his fortune on the Comstock Lode. At first, he worked as a pickman in the mines and then moved up to timberman. Eventually, he became a contractor, known for his ability, uprightness, and steady judgment. According to the practice of the day, he often took payment in the form of mining stocks. That led to a number of disappointments, but in 1866, the Kentuck mine across the "divide" in Gold Hill boomed and brought Mackay his first taste of fortune. Two years later, he joined with three friends from California—JAMES GRAHAM FAIR, James C. Flood, and William O'Brien—to buy the Hale and Norcross mine in Virginia City. Mining skill and sound management brought them fabulous wealth. In 1873, they parlayed their financial strength and technical ability into even greater wealth with the Consolidated Virginia mine—dubbed the "Big Bonanza" by writer Dan De Quille.

While Mackay preferred to spend most of his time attending to his affairs in America and living in hotels, his wife, Mary Hungerford Bryant, preferred to live in Europe, first in Paris and then in London. The couple had married in 1866, and Mackay had adopted her daughter Eva. The couple then had two sons—John in 1870 and Clarence in 1874. Mary Mackay was the first of a line of exceptionally wealthy expatriate American women with notable social careers. Her most famous achievement was a splendid ball she gave for Ulysses S. Grant in 1877. Her husband entertained the former president in Virginia City two years later.

By 1880, the Comstock Lode had ceased being productive in a substantial way. Mackay moved on to other endeavors, including a transoceanic and transcontinental telegraph service, which brought him into head-to-head competition with financier JAY GOULD. Mackay won. He also joined in founding the Bank of Nevada to compete with William Sharon's Bank of California.

Always generous to those in need, Mackay donated some $5 million to charities. He was serious about his business, however. When he was told that the Catholic church was on fire during the great Virginia City conflagration of 1875, he was busy sealing up the Consolidated Virginia tunnels. "Damn the church," he said. "We can build another if we can keep the fire from going down these shafts." He contributed generously to the rebuilding of St. Mary's in the Mountains and several other churches.

A man without pretense or guile, Mackay was a solitary figure who was greatly admired. At the time of his death in London in 1902, he was worth between $30 million and $60 million.

—Peter L. Bandurraga

SUGGESTED READING:

Lewis, Oscar. *Silver Kings: The Lives and Times of Mackay, Fair, Flood, and O'Brien, Lords of the Nevada Comstock Lode.* Reprint. Reno, Nev., 1986.

Smith, Grant H. *The History of the Comstock Lode, 1850–1920.* Reno, Nev., 1943.

MACKENZIE, MURDO

Murdo Mackenzie (1850–1939) was one of America's most famous cattlemen in the late nineteenth and early twentieth centuries. He served as manager of three of the largest ranches in the world, including that of the Prairie Land and Cattle Company, the Matador Land and Cattle Company, and the Brazil Land and Cattle Company in South America.

Born near Tain, county Ross, Scotland, Mackenzie immigrated to Trinidad, Colorado, in 1885 to assume management of the vast British-owned Prairie Land and Cattle Company in Colorado, New Mexico, and the Texas Panhandle. After a dispute with the company's board of directors, he went to work for the Scottish-owned Matador Land and Cattle Company, which had extensive holdings in western Texas.

Mackenzie's conservative management and close scrutiny of business allowed the company to show profits, even through the difficult drought years of the 1890s. He refused to carry a gun and prohibited Matador cowboys from card playing and visiting saloons.

By 1912, Mackenzie had expanded the company's holdings to include more than 800,000 acres in two Texas divisions, as well as additional leased ranges in South Dakota and Canada. His success attracted the interest of world-renowned financier Percy Farquhar, who persuaded Mackenzie to assume management of the 2.5 million-acre Brazil Land and Cattle Company. From 1912 to 1917, Mackenzie lived in Sao Paulo, Brazil, and made major contributions to reforming the Brazilian CATTLE INDUSTRY by importing purebred cattle and constructing railroads and packing plants.

Murdo Mackenzie (with full beard, seated) and the officers of the Prairie Land and Cattle Company, 1886. *Courtesy Denver Public Library, Western History Department.*

In 1917, at the age of seventy-two, Mackenzie was appointed as a director of the Matador and resumed management of the ranch after the death of its manager John MacBain in 1922. He remained manager and director of the company until his death in 1939.

Mackenzie's international background gave him a global vision for the cattle business, and he played a large role in the development of the cattle industry. He succeeded in 1906 in persuading Congress to modify the Interstate Commerce Act, which allowed the Interstate Commerce Commission to fix railroad rates. He also served as president of the Texas and Southwestern Cattle Raisers Association and the American National Livestock Association. His son, John Mackenzie, succeeded him as manager of the Matador Land and Cattle Company.

—*David J. Murrah*

SEE ALSO: Matador Ranch, Texas

SUGGESTED READING:

Pearce, William M. *The Matador Land and Cattle Company.* Norman, Okla., 1964.

MACKENZIE, RANALD SLIDELL

Commander of the Fourth Cavalry in Texas and the West, Ranald Slidell Mackenzie (1840–1889) was the oldest son of U.S. Naval Commander Alexander Slidell Mackenzie. Ranald Mackenzie graduated from West Point in 1862. He began his Civil War service in the U.S. Army Corps of Engineers and saw action in the second Battle of Bull Run, Fredericksburg, Chancellorsville, Gettysburg, the Wilderness campaign, and Spotsylvania. Transferred to a combat command in June 1864, he participated in General PHILIP H. SHERIDAN'S Shenandoah Valley campaign and saw action at Winchester, Fisher's Hill, Cedar Creek, Petersburg, Five Forks, and Appomattox. In less than three years, he rose from the rank of second lieutenant to brevet major general of volunteers and reached the rank of brevet brigadier general in the regular army.

Reverting to a lower rank following the war, Mackenzie requested an assignment in the West. He commanded African American troops of the Forty-first Infantry, later reorganized as the Twenty-fourth. In December 1870, he accepted a transfer and became colonel of the Fourth Cavalry.

Ranald Slidell Mackenzie. *Courtesy National Archives.*

From his post at Fort Richardson near Jacksboro, Texas, Mackenzie fought at McClellan's Creek in the Indian Territory on September 29, 1872, to persuade Kwahadi Comanches to submit to reservation life. From Fort Clark on the Rio Grande on May 18, 1873, Mackenzie raided a Kickapoo village and took captives at Remolina, Mexico, because of Indian raids into Texas. He and his Fourth Cavalry fought two engagements in the Red River War on the Texas-Oklahoma border—at Tule Canyon on September 26, 1874, and at Palo Duro Canyon on September 28, 1874. During the latter battle, his cavalry troops destroyed Kiowa and Comanche villages, supplies, and horses in their hideout on the Staked Plains of the Texas Panhandle.

Mackenzie attacked Cheyenne Chief Dull Knife at Willow Creek, Wyoming, on November 25, 1876, to force the Cheyennes to a reservation. After assignments at Fort Sill in the Indian Territory and again on the Rio Grande, he peacefully moved unwilling Utes to their reservation in Utah from 1880 to 1881. On October 26, 1882, while commanding the District of New Mexico in Santa Fe, Mackenzie was promoted to brigadier general. Transferred to command the Department of Texas at San Antonio in November 1883, he suffered a mental breakdown and was given a medical discharge in March 1884. He died at the age of forty-eight.

—*J'Nell L. Pate*

Suggested reading:

Pate, J'Nell L. "Ranald S. Mackenzie." In *Soldiers West: Biographies from the Military Frontier.* Edited by Paul Andrew Hutton. Lincoln, Nebr., 1987.

Pierce, Michael D. *The Most Promising Young Officer: A Life of Ranald Slidell Mackenzie.* Norman, Okla., 1993.

MacLANE, MARY

Writer, bohemian, and actress Mary MacLane (1881–1929) was born in Winnipeg, Canada, and grew up in Butte, Montana. Best known for her two autobiographical books, *The Story of Mary MacLane* (1902) and *I, Mary MacLane* (1917), she also wrote features for newspapers, starred in a motion picture, and became notorious for her outrageous, "unwomanly" behavior.

MacLane's father died when she was eight; after her mother remarried, her stepfather took the family to Butte in search of his fortune. After high school, MacLane, unemployed and feeling restless and trapped, spent her days walking through Butte and recording her thoughts in her diary. In 1902, she sent the handwritten text to a Chicago publisher. *The Story of Mary MacLane* sold eighty thousand copies during its first month in print.

The book challenged the notions of what proper young women were supposed to think and feel. MacLane titillated and outraged readers when she claimed that she wanted not merely romance but seduction. She declared herself "earthly, human, sensitive, sensuous, and sensual" and prayed that she would never become "that deformed monstrosity—a virtuous woman." The Butte Public Library banned the book, and a daily paper denounced it as "inimical to public morality."

Using royalties from book sales, MacLane left Butte and moved to the East Coast. She eventually settled in Greenwich Village where she reveled in the company of other free-spirited women. She wrote about male lovers and her physical attraction to women, but little is really known about her sexual life. In 1909, she returned to Butte where she remained for seven years and haunted gambling dens and roadhouses. There, she wrote another autobiographical book, *I, Mary MacLane.* In 1917, she wrote and starred in a silent film, "Men Who Have Made Love to Me."

MacLane's books and her life offered a feminist critique of Western women's lives in the early twentieth century. However, her own self-absorption prevented her from joining the feminist movement. Little is known about her after 1917. Sales of *I, Mary MacLane* were disappointing; she had no future as an actress; and she never again published. Plagued by financial worries, she appears to have lived quietly until her death in Chicago in 1929.

—*Mary Murphy*

SUGGESTED READING:
MacLane, Mary. *I, Mary MacLane.* New York, 1917.
———. *The Story of Mary MacLane.* Chicago, 1902.
Mattern, Carolyn J. "Mary MacLane: A Feminist Opinion." *Montana: The Magazine of Western History* 27 (Autumn 1977): 54–63.
Wheeler, Leslie. "Montana's Shocking 'Lit'ry Lady.'" *Montana: The Magazine of Western History* 27 (Summer 1977): 20–33.

MADSEN, CHRISTIAN (CHRIS)

Soldier and lawman in Oklahoma, Chris Madsen (1851–1944) was born in Denmark. He joined the Danish Army at the age of fourteen and served in the French Foreign Legion during the Franco-Prussian War in 1870. He came to the United States in 1876, enlisted in the U.S. Cavalry, and served on the Great Plains during the Indian Wars. In 1891, he was appointed a deputy U.S. marshal in Oklahoma where he and fellow lawmen WILLIAM TILGHMAN and HENRY A. ("HECK") THOMAS became known as the "Three Guardsmen." Madsen played a crucial role in breaking up the WILLIAM DOOLIN gang and, in 1911, was appointed U.S. marshal of Oklahoma.

Christian Madsen. *Courtesy Kansas State Historical Society.*

—*John Boessenecker*

SUGGESTED READING:
Croy, Homer. *Trigger Marshal: The Story of Chris Madsen.* New York, 1958.
Shirley, Glenn. *West of Hell's Fringe.* Norman, Okla., 1978.

MAGAZINES AND NEWSPAPERS

The trans-Mississippi West teemed with local periodicals. One scholar has calculated that a total of nearly ten thousand weekly and monthly journals came off presses in the last two-thirds of the nineteenth century. Between 1858 and 1899, some two hundred news journals were launched in Nevada alone. Some newspapers were fleeting affairs, like the *B-B-Blizzard,* published in January 1886 to enlighten and entertain three hundred Atchison, Topeka and Santa Fe line passengers stranded in a snow storm at Kinsley, Kansas. Others, such as San Francisco's *Chronicle,* Denver's *Rocky Mountain News,* and Salt Lake City's *Deseret News,* published for decades and became bastions of the region's freewheeling style of journalism.

One reason for the proliferation of periodicals in the nineteenth-century West was the portability of the flat-bed press. Not much changed since Gutenberg's day, the press was ideal for frontier conditions. "American pioneers," observed a Nevada editor in 1867, "carry with them the press and the type, and wherever they pitch their tent, be it in the wilderness of the interior, among the snow covered peaks of the Sierra, or on the sunny beach of the Pacific, there too must the newspaper appear." The press became one of the earliest marks of a Western community. Cincinnati got its first newspaper in 1793, when the trans-Appalachian region was still considered the Far West and the town had fewer than five hundred citizens. The first newspaper west of the Mississippi was published in 1808 in St. Louis, then a fur-trading outpost of fewer than fifteen hundred people. When a newspaper came to Leavenworth, Kansas, in 1854, the town consisted of four tents.

Would-be Western publishers loaded the presses onto boats or wagons and headed off. In the case of U.S. Navy chaplain Walter Colton and former Kentucky backwoodsman Robert Semple—who began publishing the *Californian* in 1846—they simply discovered a press abandoned in an old Spanish monastery outside Monterey. Once arrived, the newspapermen—and in a few cases, newspaperwomen—set up shop in a tent or a cabin or under a tree. If a town had three buildings, such as Emporia, Kansas Territory, did in 1857, one of them was more likely to house a press than a post office, a school, a church, or even a jail—in this case the *Kansas News*. Denver's *Rocky Mountain News,* first published in 1859, had to settle for a saloon attic. With the first issue to come off the press, the journalists began promoting the local community and printing gossip, rumors, and stale news garnered from new arrivals and aged Eastern papers.

Not only were the presses portable, they were rugged. Judge J. Judson Ames ported his nineteen-hundred-pound Washington Hand Printing Press, Imperial Model No. 3 through the jungles of Panama before it sank in the crocodile-infested waters of the Charges River. He raised the press, dried it off, and published briefly the *Panama Star* before the Imperial Model No. 3 traveled on to California, where it was used to print papers in San Diego and San Bernardino. Carted over the Sierra Madre to the mining camp of Aurora, then back again to Independence, California, Ames's former press churned out, at one time or another, papers called the *Herald,* the *Patriot,* the *Star,* the *Union,* and the *Independent*. The brothers Freeman surely pushed their press to the limits of possibility with their journal, the *Frontier Index*. Starting with the *Kearney Herald* at Fort Kearney in the Nebraska Territory in 1865, the two former Confederate telegraph operators, Legh and Fred, hit upon the notion of traveling west with the construction of the Union Pacific and setting up their press at every new railhead, where thousands of free-spending railroaders and their camp followers turned these head-of-track construction sites into boom towns called generically "HELL-ON-WHEELS." From North Platte to Julesburg to Cheyenne to Laramie City to Fort Benton to Green River to Bear River City, the brothers published their *Frontier Index* and charged an outrageous twenty cents per word for advertising from local merchants, who—eager to unload their wares to the construction crews—paid mostly without complaint. The boom came to a halt for the Freemans when a group of graders rioted and destroyed the press from which the brothers had been publishing calls for a vigilante committee to impose order. The brothers blamed the Union Pacific, with whom they had been feuding, and claimed the attack was a ruse.

Newspapers in the nineteenth century relied on government subsidies, printing contracts, and special postal rates to survive. Local papers could be sent free by post in the publisher's home territory, and editors received exchange papers for free. Especially in the West, these exchanges were essential, since other papers were the source of most news, frequently lifted word-for-word under a general industry understanding that the source would be credited. Circulations in the West, outside San Francisco, where they could run into five figures, were small. As late as 1873, editors made do with minuscule subscription lists: that year, the *Los Angeles Star* had 500 paid-up subscribers; the *Houston Age,* 325; the *Seattle Dispatch,* 144. Even such venerable standard bearers as the *Portland Oregonian* boasted only 1,960 paying customers, and the *Rocky Mountain News,* which had been publishing for fourteen years—an amazing run for a frontier journal—carried only 1,475 subscribers on its roster. However small, the circulation figures did not guarantee that the publisher had been paid in cash. Specie was in short supply out West, and editors frequently courted ruin by accepting payment in trade or—as did a Wichita editor who settled an advertising account for a can of oysters and a barrel of apples—in goods and produce. Editors sometimes despaired, as did one who offered to accept any produce "except babies" from his subscribers, or turned to draconian collection methods, such as the editor who forced a subscriber to settle his bill by threatening to publish his name after catching him kissing one of the editor's "hired girls." "I used to rustle ads for a four-page paper," wrote the former city editor of the Salem, Oregon, *Statesman* in the 1870s, "but it was worse than painful dentistry, and when I tried to collect bills I invited getting shot. So I joined the army and went scouting through three Indian wars, thus getting into the safety zone."

Settlement patterns, government subsidies, and seat-of-the-pants financing probably created the most decentralized press in the world, and the most cantankerous. Hardly surprisingly as the nineteenth century wore on, first scores, then hundreds, then thousands of frontier newspapers vanished into oblivion, although some of those that survived became quite influential despite their—by today's standards—tiny circulations. Not until the middle of the century did mass circulation become a key to a journal's political influence, and all the powerful editors of ANDREW JACKSON's day—Amos Kendall, Thurlow Weed, Thomas Ritchie—owed their influence to their standing in their political parties. Before the 1850s, especially in the West, it was local editors who inspired voters and made electoral politics work, and running a local newspaper or publishing a regional journal not only could make an edi-

In 1869, William Henry Jackson took a photograph of the *Daily Reporter* staff in front of the newspaper's office in Corinne, Boxelder County, Utah. *Courtesy National Archives.*

tor an important figure in the community, which it did almost as a matter of course, but could also serve as a stepping stone to high political appointment or office. Occasionally, too, astute businessmen could make a go of publishing and become wealthy. The *Portland Oregonian* provided an example of both. When president-elect Abraham Lincoln appointed Thomas Dryer, the editor of the near-defunct paper, U.S. Commissioner to the Sandwich (Hawaiian) Islands in 1860, he not only saved Dryer's career but gave the young Henry Pittock, a reporter for the paper, an opportunity to take over the paper in lieu of receiving back pay. The shrewd Pittock turned the paper around; he made it a daily instead of a weekly and hired a brilliant editor named Harvy Scott. Together they made the *Oregonian* a publication that settlers in the Willamette Valley came to rely on more than any other except the Bible.

The potential for such influence attracted thousands of outspoken former lawyers, preachers, politicians, teachers, postmasters, farmers, miners, land speculators, and even a circus clown to try their hands at journalism in the West. Most of them were men, because most of the Anglo population in the West was male, but women, too, participated in the region's journalism, many of them first coming aboard publications as editors' wives and then staying on to publish as their widows. Some women, such as Caroline Romney of the *Durango Record,* launched publishing ventures on their own. Practicing a highly personal—and often vituperative—brand of journalism, Western editors would have accepted, in general, the credo of Legh Freeman, who had gone from the *Frontier Index* to the Ogden *Freeman* in Utah, deep in the heart of Mormon country where, in 1875, he attacked polygamy and referred to plural wives as "concubines": "Independence in All Things, Neutrality in Nothing." Freeman was beaten senseless by a club-wielding Mormon postmaster whom he caught deliberately consigning eastbound copies of the *Freeman* to a train heading west. He then moved on to Montana and Washington to continue publishing newspapers at odds with local authorities. An opinionated, contentious lot, Western editors not infrequently suffered the slings and arrows of outraged readers: angry Republicans sent cannonballs blasting through the front windows of the

Georgetown, Colorado, *Courier,* run by crusading Democrat Jesse Randall; a gang of Denver outlaws kidnapped WILLIAM NEWTON BYERS, editor of the *Rocky Mountain News* after he denigrated their favorite saloon; cattle barons slung Asa Shinn Mercer, publisher of the *Northwestern Live Stock Journal* in a Cheyenne, Wyoming, jail when he began calling them "the Banditti of the Plains." Such outspokenness sometimes paid off, but more often it resulted in libel suits—or, worse, in tar-and-featherings, such as happened to the unpopular editor of the Ogden, Utah, *Morning Rustler.* Dave Day's Ouray, Colorado, *Solid Muldoon* and, later, *Durango Democrat* became so famous for bold barbs that copies sold on newsstands as far away as London, England, but at one point, Day had forty-two lawsuits pending.

Part of the problem may have been that Western editors had little in the way of genuine news to report. Before the telegraph reached the region in the 1860s, fresh news was hard to come by. In February 1846, the *Oregon City Spectator* received a letter mailed six months earlier from a subscriber who mentioned Texas had been annexed by the United States; the newspaper duly reported the news to its own national–expansion-minded readership as a scoop. Not until June 1850 did the shocked residents of Salt Lake City learn, in the *Deseret News,* that San Francisco had burned Christmas Eve the year before. Marriages, deaths, births, social events, prairie fires, lodge meetings, and rumors of gold and silver strikes fought for space in Western papers with stories of local gunfights, if the editor was inclined to give the town a bad name, or peons to local civic virtue, if he was not. Humor and hoaxes were common. Editors were expected to serve the local interests of their communities by agitating for territorial status, or statehood, or the location of the county seat in their town; they also campaigned for railroads, for or against the free coinage of silver, for or against the abolition of slavery, for or against Texas cattle drives, for or against vigilante justice. JAMES BUTLER ("WILD BILL") HICKOK always made good copy if he happened to be in the area. And, on rare occasions, a Western newspaper would come across some real news, or even a genuine scoop, one of the more famous being the *Bismarck Tribune*'s account of GEORGE ARMSTRONG CUSTER's defeat at the Battle of Little Bighorn in 1876—an account based on notes retrieved from the dead body of reporter Mark Kellogg, sent to cover the campaign jointly for the *New York Herald* and Clement A. Loundsberry's *Tribune.*

By then, however, the press had begun to change, and the West itself was a subject of immense interest to big Eastern newspapers and magazines with mass circulations. The mainstream press had not been responsible for the explosion in publishing that hit the country after 1850; instead, evangelists and social activists had pioneered the way. In the 1830s, the American Tract Society alone produced five pages of religious information each year for every adult and child in the country, and by the mid-thirties, the abolitionist press, supported by such organizations as the American Anti-slavery Society, was flooding the mails with its publications. Taking a leaf from such groups, commercial dailies in the larger cities became masters of mass circulation in order to command the kind of capital they needed when technological changes in printing demanded new and large investments. In the 1840s, big-city publications such as James Gordon Bennett's *New York Herald* and Horace Greeley's *New York Tribune* began to take advantage of the railroad and the telegraph to reach audiences of a size hitherto undreamed of. Catering to the varied tastes of a broad readership, they discovered the fascination the "Wild West" held for their readers. By the eve of the Civil War, Bennett's 77,000 and Greeley's 200,000 readers were fed huge doses of information about the trans-Mississippi West. Greeley became a booster of the region as a haven of free—that is, nonslave—labor, and later invested in the utopian community in Colorado that took his name.

Before the Civil War, magazines with a national scope such as the *Nation,* the *North American Review,* and the *Atlantic Monthly* had been grateful for circulations of 10,000. But magazines aimed at a more popular audience, following the lead of the big-city commercial papers, began to develop around mid-century, and by 1860, many of them, such as *Godey's Lady's Book, Peterson's Ladies' National Magazine, Harper's Weekly,* and *Frank Leslie's Illustrated Newspaper,* boasted circulations in the hundreds of thousands and served as true general-interest national journals. After the Civil War, their effect on the trans-Mississippi West, in particular, was immense. In the pages of the Philadelphia-based women's magazines, *Godey's* and *Peterson's,* was born the image of American women that helped develop the cult of domesticity, or true womanhood, which, in turned, formed the role model many women of a certain class followed in the wild and woolly Western towns. At the same time, taking advantage of improvements in printing technology, general-interest rags, such as *Harper's* and *Leslie's,* concentrated on illustration and sent a small army of talented journalist-artists out West to capture the region. Later in the century, they were joined by the *American Mercury, McClure's,* the *Saturday Evening Post, Ladies Home Journal,* and other general-interest magazines, classier than the earlier journals, but just as dedicated to investigating the West and propagating a romanticized image of it to a wide readership.

The growth of readership also meant a growth in influence for the major magazines and commercial dailies; their editors and writers became powerful opinion-makers and spokesmen, and occasionally spokeswomen, for the growing middle class. Indeed, a new breed of mass-circulation commercial daily had appeared in the decades after the Civil War as well, one that appealed to working-class readers, a result, no doubt, of the fact that many of the country's most influential papers came to be controlled by immigrants and their offspring: Adolph C. Ochs ran the *New York Times;* Edward W. Scripps created the first great newspaper chain; Joseph Pulitzer made his mark with the *St. Louis Post-Dispatch* before taking over the *New York World.* And as the power of tabloid journalism and the popular middle-class, general-interest magazines grew, so too grew the power of the press at large. Not only muckraking exposés in *Harper's* and *McClure's* affected Western politics and societies, but also those in the San Francisco, Denver, Los Angeles, and Kansas City papers.

Western editors still occasionally exhibited a strange and quirky independence, as when Moses Harman in Topeka, Kansas, made his *Lucifer, the Light Bearer,* the voice of free love in the region, but a number of Western journalists—WILLIAM ROCKHILL NELSON and FREMONT OLDER among them—were in the forefront of progressive reform. CARRY AMELIA MOORE NATION issued her *Smasher's Mail* in Kansas to trumpet her triumphs for temperance and prohibition in Kansas saloons, and the movement found a welcome home in much of the Western press. Women's suffrage and feminism, in general, found early champions in such papers as the *New Northwest,* launched by ABIGAIL SCOTT DUNIWAY, who became known as the "Mother of Equal Suffrage." The masthead of CAROLINE NICHOLS CHURCHILL's Colorado *Antelope* proclaimed: "The Interests of Humanity, Woman's Political Equality and Individuality"; the paper became so notoriously successful that Churchill made it a weekly, renamed the *Queen Bee,* in which she continued her attacks on liquor and male privilege. In 1897, the *Idaho Woman* came out under the credo of "Equality Before the Law." The late nineteenth century saw the rise of strong establishment papers in the West, such as powerful publisher HARRISON GRAY OTIS's *Los Angeles Times,* but the trans-Mississippi region also was home to the one radical publication in modern America to break through to a mass audience, the *Appeal to Reason.* Published in Girard, Kansas, the weekly had a circulation of 750,000 in 1912 and an "appeal army" of eighty thousand subscription agents combing every state in the nation. The socialist press and the publications of the INDUSTRIAL WORKERS OF THE WORLD found a ready audience in the West. With so well established a radical tradition, perhaps it should come as no surprise that a California millionaire, WILLIAM RANDOLPH HEARST, would follow Pulitzer and Scripps in creating dailies that caught the imagination of working-class Americans, or that one of his more popular writers would be the bitterly iconoclastic AMBROSE GWINETT BIERCE.

Part of that radicalism was the heritage of a strong German-language press that had been publishing newspapers in the trans-Mississippi West in considerable quantity since the failure of Germany's 1848 revolution had sent thousands of Germans across the Atlantic to settle in such areas as West Texas and around Joseph Pulitzer's hometown of St. Louis. Throughout the United States, ethnic newspapers and magazines thrived in the latter half of the nineteenth century, and many newcomers found more newspapers printed in their language in America than in their homeland. For some groups, although larger circulations and the growing numbers of individual titles were something new, ethnic publishing itself predated the Civil War.

Antonio Barreiro had first imported a printing press and started publishing a Spanish-language periodical in 1834. Over the next century and a half, five hundred Hispanic newspapers and *revistas* would be published in the American Southwest, along the Mexican border, and from Colorado to California. These papers provided a means by which the language itself continued to live in a way that, perhaps, oral transmission alone could not have provided. Some were short lived, such as *El Crepusculo,* which published only a few numbers in 1835, but which garnered glory as Taos's first Spanish-language newspaper. Others had considerable runs, such as Santa Fe's *El Nuevo Mexicano.* Owned for a while by Cyrus McCormick, the paper was published continually under the same masthead from 1849 to 1965, and always in Spanish, with an emphasis not only on Santa Fe but also on the traditional lore of the Hispanos. The names of many of the publications reveal their editorial objectives and policies: *El Defensor del Pueblo (The People's Defender)* began publication in Albuquerque in 1882, joining the town's *Opinion Publica* and *Nuevo Mundo.* In the early 1900s, Las Vegas, New Mexico, was home to *El Independiente.* Around the same time, nonindustrial Antonio, Colorado, saw the arrival of *La Via Industrial;* Las Cruces, New Mexico, *Heraldo del Valle;* and Taos, *La Revista.* Even small villages might have a paper, such as the short-lived *El Hispano Americano* in Roy, New Mexico. Spanish-speaking people in San Francisco read *El Eco del Pacifico* and *La Cronica* until 1856, when both ceased publication. One of the Southwest's most widely distributed and influential papers was *La Pensa de San Antonio;* one of its more radical, *El Clamor Público,* or *The Public Outcry,* edited by Francisco P. Ramírez, a young Californio of twenty when he began publishing in 1855.

Asian Americans had established an ethnic press as early as April 1854, when Chinese in San Francisco established *Kim-Shan Jit San-Luk*. By 1855, also in San Francisco, Chinese were publishing *Oriental,* and there, too, in 1891, the first bilingual newspaper among the Chinese in America, the *Chinese World,* appeared. Chinese periodicals were not limited to San Francisco, however—the *Chinese Daily News* appeared in Sacramento in 1856; and the *New China Daily News,* in Hawaii in 1900. The most successful and long lasting of the early twentieth century's Chinese-language newspapers was *CHUNG SAI YAT PO,* founded by Presbyterian minister NG POON-CHEW in 1900; the paper enjoyed a wide circulation until its demise in 1930. Among the earlier Japanese-language newspapers were KYUTARO ABIKO's *Nichibei Shimbun (Japanese American News),* first published in 1898, and thereafter the *North American Times,* the *Japanese American Courier, Nippu Jiji,* and *Hawaii Hochi.* Although the *Korean News,* published in Honolulu between June 10, 1905, and September 1906, was short lived, others followed. On the mainland, San Francisco became home to the *Korean Mutual Cooperation News,* the *New Korean World,* the *United Korean News,* the *United Korean Weekly,* the *Great Unity Information,* and the *New Korea.* Early Filipino newspapers included *Kauai Filipino News,* which changed its name to *Filipino News;* the *Philippine Herald;* the *Philippines Mail;* the *Commonwealth Courier;* and the *Philippine Advocate.* The Asian American press covered the labor-union movement, job opportunities, news from the homelands, information about American culture, the latest on immigration legislation, and developments within the ethnic communities. In general, the papers seem to have undergone three stages: the first, dominated by news from and about home countries reported in the vernacular; the second, by news in English and the vernacular on political and economic conditions in both the homelands and in the United States; and the third, by social, political, and economic news about America frequently written exclusively in English. Few of the Korean or Filipino newspapers lasted long, although the *New Korea* was still being published in Los Angeles and *Philippines Mail* in Salinas, California, at the end of the century. A dozen or more Japanese American newspapers continued into the late twentieth century, most of them either bilingual or featuring a section printed in Japanese, and Chinese American newspapers abounded, both in the West and throughout the country.

In the late nineteenth and early twentieth centuries, the mainstream press in the American West developed a self-conscious regionalism. Literary publications—such as William Gibbe Hunt's *Western Review and Miscellaneous Magazine,* published in Lexington, Kentucky, between 1819 and 1821, and James Hall's Cincinnati-based *Western Monthly Magazine*—argued that the American West was a unique cultural region even when most Americans considered the West itself to be the trans-Appalachian lands. It took a circle of San Francisco writers, which included BRET HARTE and MARK TWAIN, to demonstrate what they were trying to say. In the mid-1860s in such newspapers as San Francisco's *Golden Era* and the literary *Californian,* Harte began to perfect his combination of local color and realism, leavened with humor and a love of talltales, that came to be considered a mark of Western writing. Twain, who began writing for the *Virginia City Territorial Enterprise* in 1862, soon moved to San Francisco, where he learned much from Harte and began contributing pieces to the *Call, The Californian,* and *Alta California,* among others.

In 1868, publisher Anton Roman hired Harte to edit the *Overland Monthly.* With help from INA COOLBRITH, Harte ambitiously tried to turn the monthly into California's answer to Boston's *Atlantic Monthly.* In one way or another, much of the Western press has been trying ever since to do the same kind of thing—compete effectively with the publishing industry and the press, traditionally headquartered in the East. Certainly, one of the more successful attempts was *The Midland: A Magazine of the Middle West,* which John T. Frederick founded in Iowa City, Iowa, in 1915 and edited there and in Chicago until 1933. A journal dedicated to regionalism, *The Midland,* according to H. L. Mencken, writing in the *Smart Set,* "is probably the most influential literary periodical ever set up in America, though its actual circulation has always been small." Even given Mencken's penchant for overstatement, *The Midland* was certainly at the forefront of another trend in magazine publication, both in the West and elsewhere, that began in the early twentieth century and has had a tremendous impact on American life and letters—the "little" magazines, small-circulation, relatively short-lived journals that showcase the best American writing and give talented beginners a place to publish. In that way, little magazines are not unlike Western journalism in its "frontier" period.

—Charles Phillips

SEE ALSO: Art; *Clamor, Público, El;* Literature

SUGGESTED READING:

Bucco, Martin. "The Development of Western Literary Criticism." In *The Literary History of the American West.* Edited by Thomas J. Lyon. Fort Worth, Tex., 1987.

Campa, Arthur L. *Hispanic Culture in the Southwest.* Norman, Okla., 1979.
Leonard, Thomas C. *The Power of the Press: The Birth of American Political Reporting.* New York, 1986.
Lingenfelter, Richard. E. *The Newspapers of Nevada: A History and Bibliography, 1854–1979.* Reno, Nev., 1984.
Miller, Nyle H., Edgar Langsdorf, and Robert W. Richmond. *Kansas in Newspapers.* Topeka, Kans., 1963.
Mott, Frank Luther. *A History of American Magazines.* 5 vols. New York, 1930–1968.
———. *American Journalism: A History.* New York, 1962.
Murrow, Patrick D. "Bret Harte, Mark Twain, and the San Francisco Circle." In *The Literary History of the American West.* Edited by Thomas J. Lyon. Fort Worth, Tex., 339–358.
Reigleman, Milton M. "John T. Frederick." *The Palimpsest* 5 (March-April 1978): 58–65.

MAGNUSON, WARREN GRANT

A congressman and senator, Warren Grant Magnuson (1905–1989) was born in Fargo, North Dakota, and grew up in nearby Moorhead, Minnesota. At the age of nineteen, he moved to Seattle, where he earned his bachelor of law degree at the University of Washington in 1929. He served as special prosecuting attorney for King County, Washington, in 1932; as a member of the Washington state legislature from 1933 to 1934; and as King county prosecutor from 1935 to 1936. In 1936, he won election to the U.S. House of Representatives as a New Deal Democrat and served four terms before successfully running for the Senate in 1944. He remained in the Senate until his defeat in 1980. During his career in the Congress, he supported legislation to advance health and social welfare, to further the cause of organized labor, to strengthen the navy and merchant marine, to develop hydroelectric power, and to protect consumers.

—*Timothy J. McMannon*

SUGGESTED READING:

Redman, Eric. *The Dance of Legislation.* New York, 1973.

MAGOFFIN, JAMES WILEY

Businessman and diplomat James Wiley Magoffin (1799–1868) was born in Harrodsburg, Kentucky. In 1824, he sailed from New Orleans to Tampico, Mexico. After surviving a shipwreck at Matagorda Bay, he resumed his trip. He served as the American consul in Saltillo from 1825 to 1836 and developed a profitable mercantile business in northern Mexico. Leaving Saltillo to avoid involvement in the revolt of Texas against Mexico, he moved to Chihuahua City and became one of the most active traders in the Chihuahua–Santa Fe trade. With the support of his Mexican wife, his command of the Spanish language, and his liberal trading practices, he and his family became prominent in the economic and social life of northern Mexico.

In 1844, he moved his family to Independence, Missouri, raised mules, and, in partnership with his brothers, maintained two wagon trains between Independence and Santa Fe.

In Washington, D.C., in June 1846, Missouri Senator THOMAS HART BENTON introduced President JAMES K. POLK to Magoffin as a man who had accurate knowledge of the affairs and people in northern Mexico. With special instructions from the president, Magoffin joined the Army of the West under General STEPHEN WATTS KEARNY. Magoffin helped pave the way for peaceful occupation of New Mexico by the American forces during a secret conference with Governor MANUEL ARMIJO, a cousin of his wife. Attempting to continue his services as a spy in Chihuahua, Magoffin was arrested and spent nine months in prison.

After his release, Magoffin planned to reenter the Chihuahua trade, but upon reaching El Paso del Norte on his way back to Independence, he found that the high customs duties charged by the Mexican government made profits impossible. In 1849, at the age of fifty, he settled on the United States side of the Rio Grande, at a site first known as Magoffinville and later El Paso. There he built an elaborate hacienda and became a well-known host to army officers and officials passing through town. He established a business empire based on farming, freighting, and merchandising. He also acted as post sutler for Fort Bliss.

Magoffin was a Southern sympathizer and supported the secession of Texas in 1861. When the Confederate forces invaded New Mexico in the CIVIL WAR, he gave them full support. He retreated to San Antonio with the Southern troops in 1862 and maintained his residence there until his death. Magoffin's fortune had been lost through his participation in the Civil War, and he spent his final years seeking and finally obtaining amnesty for his defection to the Confederacy.

—*W. Turrentine Jackson*

SEE ALSO: Santa Fe and Chihuahua Trail

SUGGESTED READING:

Magoffin, Susan Shelby. *Down the Santa Fe Trail and into Mexico.* New Haven, Conn., 1962.
Strickland, Rex W. "Six Who Came to El Paso." *Southwestern Studies* 1 (1963): 1–48.

MAGÓN, RICARDO FLORES

A journalist and political leader, Ricardo Flores Magón (1873–1922) and his two brothers joined the movement against President Porfirio Díaz that led to the Mexican Revolution of 1910. Born into a Mexican family of meager means, Magón studied law as a young adult but switched his interests to journalism in the 1890s. From journalism, Magón entered politics and organized the Liberal Reformist Association at the turn of the century. Within three years, he was forced into exile by the Mexican government. Settling in San Antonio, Texas, Magón and his brother Enrique founded *Regeneracion,* a newspaper with views that led Díaz to send his agents to Texas to harass the brothers. Moving on to St. Louis, Missouri, the Magóns organized the anti-Díaz political group, El Partido Liberal.

As Magón grew older, his politics became more radical and more unpopular. The anarchism he embraced by 1906 or so isolated him from the numbers of Mexican Americans and Mexican refugees who shared his anti-Díaz sentiments. In 1907, he moved to Los Angeles and published a newspaper called *Revolucion.*

When the revolution began, Magón led forces into Baja California, but his campaign failed, and he returned to the United States. During World War I, Magón was arrested and convicted of violating U.S. neutrality laws. He served four years of a twenty-year sentence before he died in federal prison.

—*Patricia Hogan*

SUGGESTED READING:

Cockcroft, James D. *Intellectual Precursors of the Mexican Revolution, 1900–1913.* Austin, Tex., 1968.

MAIL SERVICE

SEE: Adams Express Company; Overland Mail Company; Pacific Mail Steamship; Pony Express; United States Mail Steamship Company; Wells, Fargo and Company

MAJORS, ALEXANDER

Alexander Majors (1814–1900), freighting expert and partner in the company RUSSELL, MAJORS AND WADDELL, was born near Franklin in Simpson County, Kentucky. He grew up on a farm and worked in his father's sawmill and flour mill. To augment the income from his own farming operations, he transported a wagonload of Indian trade goods to the Potawatomi reservation on the Kansas River in 1846. Two years later, he entered the freighting business with six wagons and transported goods from Independence, Missouri, to Santa Fe, New Mexico, on the SANTA FE AND CHIHUAHUA TRAIL. By 1850, Majors was a government contractor who delivered military supplies to Santa Fe. The next year, he supervised a freight train of twenty-five wagons taking merchandise for businessmen to Santa Fe and returned in time to make another trip to Fort Union, the military headquarters for the U.S. Army in New Mexico. Although he continued to deliver for private parties, most of his freighting was done for the War Department. He operated not only in New Mexico but in Colorado and Utah. In his memoirs, *Seventy Years on the Frontier,* Majors is depicted as a strict disciplinarian in the conduct of his freight trains. He refused to travel on Sunday and required his teamsters to take a pledge not to swear, drink, gamble, or mistreat animals, but to behave as gentlemen.

In December 1854, Majors went into partnership with WILLIAM HEPBURN RUSSELL and WILLIAM BRADFORD WADDELL in the freighting business. Majors was responsible for all the road operations, while Russell handled promotion and government contracts, and Waddell dealt with office matters. Russell, Majors and Waddell employed more than four thousand men and used forty thousand oxen and one thousand mules in the business. While the partnership made three hundred thousand dollars in profits in 1855 and 1856, the business was risky. The company overextended itself in making exclusive contracts to deliver supplies to the army during the UTAH EXPEDITION in 1857.

Through the activities of his partner Russell, Majors became involved in stagecoach operations in 1859 and the PONY EXPRESS in 1860, both of which brought him additional financial losses. The firm of Russell, Majors and Waddell collapsed in 1862, and when liquidation failed to provide funds for all the debts, Majors and his former partners paid their obligations from their personal estates.

Majors then purchased the interests of his partners in the freighting business and continued freighting on his own until 1866. Two years later, he worked on the Union Pacific Railroad and later prospected for silver near Salt Lake until 1872. He lived in Salt Lake City until 1879, moved to Kansas City where he resided for several years, and died in Chicago.

—*W. Turrentine Jackson*

SEE ALSO: Overland Freight

SUGGESTED READING:

Bloss, Roy. *Pony Express—The Great Gamble.* Berkeley, Calif., 1959.

Chapman, Arthur. *The Pony Express.* New York, 1932.
Harlow, Alvin. *Old Waybills: The Romance of the Express Companies.* New York, 1934.
Jackson, W. Turrentine. "A New Look at Wells Fargo, Stagecoaches, and the Pony Express." *California Historical Society Quarterly* 45 (1966): 291–324.
———. "Wells Fargo's Pony Expresses." *Journal of the West* 11 (1972): 405–436.
Settle, Raymond W., and Mary L. Settle. *Empire on Wheels.* Stanford, Calif., 1949.
———. *Saddles and Spurs: The Pony Express Saga.* Harrisburg, Pa., 1955.
———. *War Drums and Wagon Wheels.* Lincoln, Nebr., 1966.
Walker, Henry Pickering. *The Wagonmasters.* Norman, Okla., 1966.

MALIN, JAMES CLAUDE

Eminent Kansas historian James Claude Malin (1893–1979) was born on the homestead of his father, Jared Nelson Malin, near Edgeley, North Dakota. In 1903, the Malins moved to Lewis, Kansas, where Jared farmed and later sold farm machinery.

In 1910, James Malin enrolled at Baker University in Baldwin, Kansas, and majored in history, philosophy, and science. After teaching high school for a year, he enrolled in the history graduate program at the University of Kansas in 1915. After more teaching and some army service, he completed his Ph.D. in 1921 and joined the University of Kansas's history department, where he specialized in recent American history, the trans-Mississippi West, and the history of Kansas. While the doctoral program was small in his time, he advised many masters' candidates. He retired in 1963.

Malin excelled in research. He published seventeen books and many articles and book reviews. Among his studies of the settlement and territorial processes in the Kansas-Nebraska region, his doctoral dissertation examined the factors shaping federal Indian policy during the mid-nineteenth century. In writing about John Brown, he convincingly described the self-seeking land grabbing and lawlessness that characterized the activity of both free- and slave-state supporters in Kansas. Subsequently, he showed that Stephen A. Douglas's efforts to provide territorial government for the Kansas-Nebraska region were intended to encourage economic development, particularly railroad building, and mirrored much Western public opinion.

Malin explored human adaptation to the North American grassland and used census manuscript data, local newspaper sources, and concepts from other disciplines including ecology. The settlers were mobile, he argued, and adaptation was a folk process that included experimentation with crops, technology, and cultural practices. He believed that New Deal policies for the Great Plains inadequately reflected environmental imperatives. Malin criticized Frederick Jackson Turner because his theories emphasized the loss of opportunity in postfrontier America, and he found Walter Prescott Webb's regionalism unduly restricted in perspective. Rejecting relativism, Malin argued that historians should analyze unique events within open systems and suggested that their task paralleled the work of ecologists. In later years, he studied the folk culture of Kansans in detail.

Malin served as president of the Agricultural History Society and of the Kansas State Historical Society and held other important posts in learned societies.

—*Allan G. Bogue*

Suggested reading:

Bogue, Allan G. "James C. Malin: A Voice from the Grassland." In *Writing Western History: Essays on Major Western Historians.* Edited by Richard W. Etulain. Albuquerque, N. Mex., 1991.
Malin, James C. *The Grassland of North America: Prolegomena to Its History with Addenda and Postscript.* 1947. Reprint. Gloucester, Mass., 1967.
———. *History and Ecology: Studies of the Grassland.* Edited by Robert P. Swierenga. Lincoln, Nebr., 1984.
———. *Indian Policy and Westward Expansion.* Lawrence, Kans., 1921.
———. *John Brown and the Legend of Fifty-Six.* Philadelphia, 1942.
———. *The Nebraska Question, 1852–1854.* Ann Arbor, Mich., 1953.
———. *Winter Wheat in the Golden Belt of Kansas: A Study in Adaptation to Subhumid Geographical Environment.* Lawrence, Kans., 1944.

MAMMY PLEASANT

See: Pleasant, Mary Ellen ("Mammy")

MAN-AFRAID-OF-HIS-HORSE (SIOUX)

An Oglala tribal leader, Man-Afraid-of-His-Horse (1802–1893) participated in the negotiations to end the War of the Bozeman Trail, culminating in the Fort

Laramie Treaty of 1868. Born on the Northern Plains, Man-Afraid-of-His-Horse (whose native name is actually translated "Man-of-Whose-Horse-They-Are-Afraid) was a member of the Payabya ("push ahead" or "head of the circle") Oglala band. Oglala leaders traditionally came from his family, and Man-Afraid-of-His-Horse continued this tradition. He became a "shirt wearer" (a tribal executive), and in 1850, he emerged as one of the leading Oglalas due to his ability as a military leader. In 1854, he tried to negotiate a peaceful conclusion to the Mormon cow crisis to no avail, but he did succeed in keeping the Oglalas out of the ensuing conflict, known as the GRATTAN MASSACRE.

At the time of the Bozeman Trail controversy, Man-Afraid-of-His-Horse realized that his advanced age prevented him from being an aggressive leader. He divided his duties between RED CLOUD, whom he advanced from soldier to war leader, and his son, YOUNG-MAN-AFRAID-OF-HIS-HORSE, to whom he abdicated his civil leadership. The division of duties reflected Man-Afraid-of-His-Horse's desire to preserve his family's prominence and Lakota tradition and to ensure strong military leadership. Red Cloud refused to relinquish power at the end of the crisis, and because of his large following, he was able to hold his position, thus creating a conflict between him and Man-Afraid-of-His-Horse.

Man-Afraid-of-His-Horse signed the Fort Laramie Treaty, and many Oglalas and a large number of northern Lakotas considered him the Oglala spokesman because of his tribal status. He also supported the 1876 Black Hills cession as an appeal to reason. He spent his last years near Pine Ridge.

—Richmond L. Clow

SEE ALSO: Sioux Wars

SUGGESTED READING:

Grinnell, George Bird. *The Fighting Cheyennes.* Norman, Okla., 1956.

Hyde, George. *Red Cloud's Folk: A History of the Oglala Sioux.* Norman, Okla., 1937.

———. *Spotted Tail's Folk: A History of the Brulé Sioux.* Norman, Okla., 1961.

McGillycuddy, Julia B. *McGillycuddy, Agent.* Palo Alto, Calif., 1941.

Olson, James C. *Red Cloud and the Sioux Problem.* Lincoln, Nebr., 1965.

MANDAN INDIANS

SEE: Native American Peoples: Peoples of the Great Plains

MANGAS COLORADAS (APACHE)

The greatest Eastern Chiricahua chief, Mangas Coloradas ("Red Sleeves," ca. 1795–1863) may have been known as Chief Fuertes before 1842. His people lived in southern New Mexico and conducted persistent raids into Chihuahua and Sonora, Mexico. Even when not fighting the Mexicans, Mangas Coloradas, a huge man for an Apache, standing about six feet, four inches tall, was aloof toward them. He observed brief periods of peace only to accept the rations that Mexican authorities provided to his people to mollify the fierce warriors and keep them off the warpath. Mangas Coloradas probably was not involved in the 1837 Juan José Compá massacre by scalp hunters, but he immediately succeeded Juan as chief of the Eastern Chiricahuas, a merger of the Mogollon and Mimbres bands. He remained chief the rest of his life.

On October 20, 1846, Mangas Coloradas met Brigadier General STEPHEN WATTS KEARNY near the Gila River, after the United States took over Apache country during the United States–Mexican War. Mangas tried to persuade Kearny to join him in forays south of the border, but the officer declined and went on the California.

In 1852, Mangas Coloradas encountered JOHN RUSSELL BARTLETT, who was conducting a survey of the border between Mexico and the United States. Later that year, the Apache chief "signed" a treaty at Acomas, New Mexico. The treaty provided for the end of Indian attacks on the Mexicans, but it was not lasting. An astute leader, Mangas Coloradas refused to endorse further treaties that would provide for the dominion of the United States over his people.

The 1860 discovery of gold at Pinos Altos, north of present-day Silver City, attracted a horde of rough, combative gold-seekers. Since the site of the discovery lay in Apache territory, trouble immediately erupted. The Apaches were accused of thefts and depredations. Miners, exasperated by the incidents, seized Mangas Coloradas, tied him to a tree, and flogged him. From that time on, the relationships between the Apache leader and Americans was hostile.

Mangas Coloradas joined COCHISE, the leader of the Central Chiricahuas, in attacks on parties of Anglo-Americans traveling through Apache country. The Indian warriors burned stage stations and killed many whites. Cochise and Mangas Coloradas jointly laid the ambuscade that touched off the Battle of Apache Pass, where the latter was severely wounded. He was taken by his followers to Janos in Chihuahua, where his followers told a physician attending the chief that if he died, the physician would die as well.

Mangas Coloradas recovered from his wounds. Soon, however, he was captured by white mountaineers and turned over to the U.S. Army. While he slept, a soldier laid a heated bayonet across his stomach, and when Mangas Coloradas started in pain, he was shot. An officer reported that he was killed "while trying to escape."

—*Dan L. Thrapp*

SEE ALSO: Apache Wars

SUGGESTED READING:

Griffen, William B. *Apaches at War and Peace: The Janos Presidion, 1750–1858.* Albuquerque, N. Mex., 1988.

Thrapp, Dan L. *Encyclopedia of Frontier Biography.* Glendale, Calif., and Spokane, Wash., 1988 and 1989.

MANIFEST DESTINY

John L. O'Sullivan, editor of the *New York Post,* first used the term *manifest destiny* to describe America's restlessness and passion for new land in a political discussion about the potential annexation of Texas and its effect on NATIONAL EXPANSION published in the July-August 1845 issue of the *United States Magazine and Democratic Review.* "It is our manifest destiny," he wrote, "to overspread the whole of the continent which Providence has given us for the development of the great experiment entrusted to us." O'Sullivan's rhetoric appeared to be high-minded, but what it described was something less abstract, something almost visceral. The hungering for riches, the longing to possess land, the search for a good life—in short, what historian Patricia Nelson Limerick calls the peculiar American transformation of the profit motive into a passion—had been going on since THOMAS JEFFERSON substituted the phrase *pursuit of happiness* for *property* in the trinity of man's natural rights that he borrowed from philosopher John Locke when writing the American Declaration of Independence.

Not all Americans believed in the nation's manifest destiny to conquer the continent. Many thought

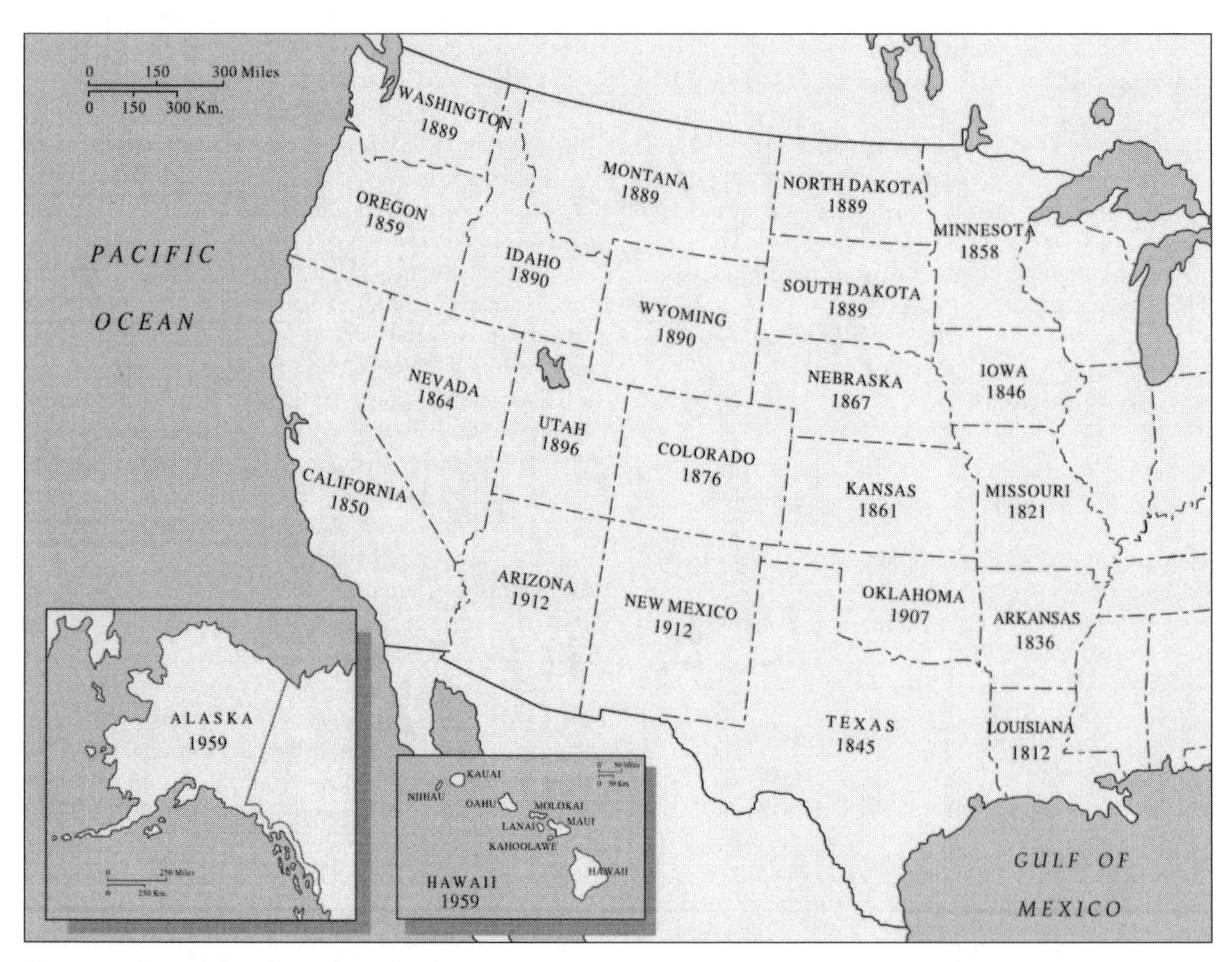

Western states and their dates of statehood.

the United States should not even accept Texas. But the acquisition of land itself was historically central to an American's understanding of life, liberty, and the pursuit of happiness, and *land* had become the central concept in the ideology of the westward movement. From the beginning, the leaders of the American republic had been determined to avoid the fate of Europe, with its small elites addicted to luxury and its huge, murderously miserable majorities of people without property. Not just a Thomas Jefferson, who idealized the independent and hard-working farmer and became the patron saint of the West, but also federalists such as John Adams, who declared bluntly that "power always followed property," understood what happened when populations grew, as in the Old World, out of balance with the supply of land.

Cheap credit and a small plot of land somewhere was ever the dream of the West's common man, whose political ideal was Mr. Jefferson's "empire of liberty" and whose political party was ANDREW JACKSON's Democratic party. Even many among the privileged class in America, at least before the Civil War, argued that the U.S. "experiment" in government depended on the prosperity of individual property-holders and thought widely distributed land ownership was the best safeguard against dangerous concentrations of power and a disgruntled mass of humanity. It was hardly surprising, then, that Americans developed what Drew McCoy called "a vision of expansion across space—the American continent—as a necessary alternative to the development through time that was generally thought to bring both political corruption and social decay." Little did it matter that the land was already occupied by Native American tribes and Hispanic villagers. Americans' visions was one of innocence as well as manifest destiny, and one could hear the romantic longing for the lost purity of Eden in *New York Tribune* editor Horace Greeley's battle cry of expansion: "Go West, young man, and grow up with the land."

There was something of the missionary's zeal for domination as well as the settlers' longing for security wrapped up in this vision of the West as a potential social Eden. And it was no accident that the senior U.S. senator from Missouri, THOMAS HART BENTON, who for thirty years was Congress's most vociferous advocate of free land for the homesteader and America's national spokesman for the West, also talked loftily of the holy Anglo-Saxon mission to remove the "Red Man" from the "wilderness" and civilize the continent. Benton, among others, adopted O'Sullivan's phrase and made it the clarion call of Western expansion. For manifest destiny was not the banner behind which to build a nation, as Jefferson and others had persuaded themselves they were doing east of the Mississippi and in the LOUISIANA PURCHASE; manifest destiny was the American mask for a true empire.

John Gast's nineteenth-century *American Progress* shows trains, stagecoaches, and men advancing civilization across the Great Plains while an angelic woman, stringing telegraph wire as she goes, hovers overhead. Americans enthusiastically embraced the notion of manifest destiny as an obligation of conquest and settlement. *Courtesy Library of Congress.*

In 1836, Benton and his fellows in Congress had passed the Wisconsin Organic Act, modifying the NORTHWEST ORDINANCE to get rid of the first administrative stage of government entirely, make both houses of territorial assemblies elective, and create universal male suffrage in the territories. Once the political events—Texas annexation, the UNITED STATES–MEXICAN WAR, the settlement of OREGON BOUNDARY DISPUTE with England, the growing sectional crisis over extending slavery—associated with the adoption of manifest destiny as a national stance toward expansion had unfolded, and the civil war they helped cause was over, the Wisconsin Organic Act would be used, as Richard White notes, like a "political cookie cutter" to stamp out identical governments across the West. This was the ultimate accomplishment of manifest destiny, the creation of what Patricia Nelson Limerick calls an "empire of innocence." As the *Whig Intelligencer* proudly proclaimed after the United States had defeated Mexico and paid $15 million for vast lands in the Southwest once belonging to the defeated nation: "[W]e take nothing by conquest. . . . Thank God."

—*Charles Phillips*

SUGGESTED READING:

Hietala, Thomas R. *Manifest Design: Anxious Aggrandizement in Late Jacksonian America.* Ithaca, N.Y., 1985.

Horseman, Reginald. *Race and Manifest Destiny.* Cambridge, Mass., 1981.
Limerick, Patricia Nelson. *The Legacy of Conquest: The Unbroken Past of the American West.* New York, 1987.
Merk, Frederick. *Manifest Destiny and Mission in American History: A Reinterpretation.* New York, 1963.
White, Richard. *"It's Your Misfortune and None of My Own": A New History of the American West.* Norman, Okla., 1991.

MANSFIELD, MICHAEL JOSEPH (MIKE)

Montana politician Mike Mansfield (1903–) was born in New York City and moved with his family to Great Falls, Montana, in 1906. He served in the army, navy, and marines, worked in the copper mines in Butte, and taught history at the University of Montana in Missoula. In 1940, he ran for Congress against JEANNETTE RANKIN and lost. Two years later, he won the congressional election. He served five terms in the House of Representatives and four in the Senate. From 1961 to 1977, he was Democratic majority leader, a position he held longer than any other person in Congress. From 1977 to 1989, under Presidents Jimmy Carter and Ronald Reagan, he served as ambassador to Japan.

—*Harry W. Fritz*

MANUELITO (NAVAJO)

A Navajo chief who was also known as Bullet or Pistol Bullet, Manuelito (ca. 1818–1893) was a strong opponent to the government's efforts to relocate his tribe. He was born probably near Bear Ears Peak in southeastern Utah. Very little is known about his early life. After achieving some prominence as a warrior, he married the daughter of the war chief NARBONA. Later, in a raid on a Mexican settlement, he acquired a second wife. When U.S. forces occupied New Mexico in 1846 during the United States–Mexican War, Missouri volunteers under Colonel ALEXANDER WILLIAM DONIPHAN were assigned to punish the Indians for stealing livestock. Led by Manuelito, the Navajos consistently evaded Doniphan by holing up in Canyon de Chelly, their traditional stronghold.

During the 1850s, the Navajo Indians and the soldiers of Fort Defiance fell into a dispute over pasture land at the mouth of Canyon Bonito. The soldiers wanted the land to graze their horses, whereas the Navajos had held the land for many generations. The dispute developed into combat, in which Manuelito played a key leadership role. In 1859, troops destroyed his home, crops, and livestock. The following year, Manuelito and BARBONCITO led an attack on Fort Defiance, narrowly failed to overrun the fort, and evaded Colonel EDWARD RICHARD SPRING CANBY who pursued them.

Manuelito. Photograph by E. A. Burbank. *Courtesy National Archives.*

In January 1861, Manuelito and other prominent Navajos, including Barboncito, Delgadito, Armijo, and Herrero Grande, parleyed with Canby and agreed to work out peace terms. For several months, an uneasy peace endured, until a dispute erupted in September 1861 over a horse race between Manuelito and an army lieutenant just outside Fort Defiance. The Navajos claimed that a soldier had sabotaged the race by cutting Manuelito's bridle rein. The army judges, hardly impartial, refused to run the race again. Soldiers brutally put down the ensuing riot by using artillery that killed ten. The incident renewed Navajo raiding under Manuelito and others.

Manuelito achieved his greatest prominence in 1864 as one of the war leaders who refused to surrender to CHRISTOPHER HOUSTON ("KIT") CARSON, who, acting under orders from General JAMES H. CARLETON, rounded up the Navajos for removal to the hated reservation known as the Bosque Redondo. Manuelito held out longer than the other chiefs but finally reported to Fort Wingate in September 1866 with a mere twenty-three warriors—the remnants of his forces.

The Bosque Redondo was indeed a terrible place, and the Navajos endured disease and chronic shortages of provisions and supplies. The alkaline soil of the reservation supported few crops. Manuelito was one of a delegation of chiefs who traveled to Washington, D.C., to plead for permission to return to their land, which was finally granted in a treaty of June 1, 1868. Manuelito served as principal chief of the tribe from 1870 and was chosen by reservation authorities as chief of the Navajo police in 1872. He made a second trip to Washington, D.C., to meet with President Ulysses S. Grant in 1876. Manuelito stepped down as principal chief in 1885 and died on the Navajo Reservation in the New Mexico Territory in 1893.

—*Alan Axelrod*

SEE ALSO: Navajo Wars

SUGGESTED READING:

McNitt, Frank. *Navajo Wars: Military Campaigns, Slave Raids, and Reprisals.* Albuquerque, N. Mex., 1972. Reprint. 1990.

Thompson, Gerald. *The Army and the Navajo: The Bosque Redondo Reservation Experiment.* Tucson, Ariz., 1976.

Underhill, Ruth. *The Navajos.* Norman, Okla., 1956.

MAP MAKING

SEE: Cartography

MARCOS DE NIZA, FRAY

An explorer whose early life remains obscure, Fray Marcos de Niza (?-1558) is remembered for a controversial expedition in 1539 that led to full-scale exploration of southwestern North America. A Frenchman (apparently from Nice, hence "de Niza") who served Spain as a Franciscan in Peru and Central America in the 1530s, Marcos was in Mexico City in 1538 when Viceroy Antonio de Mendoza needed a seasoned explorer for a delicate mission. ÁLVAR NÚÑEZ CABEZA DE VACA, having recently returned from his extraordinary journey across North America, raised hopes that a wealthy civilization existed north of Mexico. In an effort to stave off powerful rivals Hernán Cortés and Hernando de Soto, Mendoza reasoned that a reconnaissance led by a priest would draw little attention, and he put Marcos in charge of a small preliminary expedition. To guide Marcos, the viceroy turned to the black slave, Esteban, who had previously accompanied Cabeza de Vaca. Esteban was killed by Indians in the course of his scouting for Marcos.

Within a year, Marcos returned to Mexico and reported the existence of seven wealthy cities in the north. The smallest, called Cíbola, was itself "bigger than the city of Mexico." Marcos claimed only to have seen Cíbola from a prudent distance rather than to have entered it, since he feared the Cíbolans might kill him as they had Esteban.

On the strength of Marcos's reports, Mendoza launched the costly expedition of FRANCISCO VÁSQUEZ DE CORONADO and sent Marcos along as a guide. In July 1540, Marcos and Coronado stood before Cíbola—one of the modest villages of the Zuni Indians in what is today western New Mexico. Appalled that the town, numbering perhaps one hundred families, bore no resemblance to the great city Marcos had described, Coronado pronounced Marcos a liar.

Ever since, scholars have remained divided. Did Marcos see Cíbola on his 1539 journey and allow his imagination to play tricks on him? Or upon learning of the death of Esteban, did he turn back well before reaching Cíbola and fabricate that portion of his report to avoid the shame of not fulfilling his mission? Geographic landmarks and distances are recorded vaguely in Marcos's written report to the viceroy, and they sustain multiple interpretations of his route and his destination.

—*David J. Weber*

SEE ALSO: Cíbola, Seven Cities of; Exploration: Spanish Expeditions

SUGGESTED READING:

Hallenbeck, Cleve. *The Journey of Fray Marcos de Niza.* Rev. ed. Dallas, Tex., 1987.

MARCY, RANDOLPH BARNES

Soldier, trail-blazer, and map-maker, Randolph Barnes Marcy (1812–1887) was born in Greenwich, Massachusetts. After graduating from West Point in 1832, he served in Michigan and Wisconsin for the next thirteen years except for two short periods of recruiting duty in the East. During the United States–Mexican War, he participated in the battles of Palo Alto and Resaca de la Palma.

During the twelve years following the war with Mexico, Marcy was in the Southwest, most of the time in the field. In 1849, while escorting emigrants from Fort Smith to Santa Fe, he reconnoitered and opened a

An illustration entitled *Wichitaw Village on Rush Creek* accompanied Randolph Barnes Marcy's report on his 1852 Red River Expedition. *Courtesy Library of Congress.*

new trail. Based on his travels, he drafted a reasonably accurate map of the Southwest. In 1851, he was an escort to General W. G. Belknap and advised him on where to locate a chain of forts, including Fort Sill, from eastern Oklahoma to western Texas. In 1852, Marcy led an expedition that traced the Red River to its source, a feat that had escaped both ZEBULON MONTGOMERY PIKE and STEPHEN HARRIMAN LONG. Two years later, he located and surveyed several small Indian reservations in Texas, and for a short time in 1857, he was involved in the campaign against the Seminole Indians in Florida.

Marcy returned to the Southwest to accompany Colonel Albert Sydney Johnston during the UTAH EXPEDITION against the Mormons to establish federal authority in Utah. The expedition had to winter at Fort Bridger where there was great suffering from lack of supplies. Marcy led a winter march over six hundred miles of snow-covered mountains to obtain supplies and animals for the isolated post.

Named inspector-general of the Department of Utah, he was soon ordered to New York to prepare a semiofficial guidebook, *The Prairie Traveler,* published in 1859 by authority of the War Department. An excellent compendium for travelers on numerous overland trails, the book confirmed Marcy's reputation as an outstanding explorer and trail-blazer.

During the Civil War, Marcy's son-in-law, General George B. McClellan, appointed him chief-of-staff. He served through the Peninsular and Antietam campaigns. When President Abraham Lincoln removed McClellan as commander of the Army of the Potomac, Marcy's role in the war naturally diminished. He remained a professional soldier and held the rank of colonel and inspector-general until 1863. For the next fifteen years, he served as inspector in various departments and, in 1878, was appointed inspector-general of the army with the rank of brigadier general. He served in that capacity until his retirement in 1881.

Even in retirement, he was an outdoor man who made big-game hunting trips. He had great facility at writing and published two volumes of recollections: *Thirty Years of Army Life on the Border* and *Border Reminiscences.*

—*W. Turrentine Jackson*

SEE ALSO: Exploration: United States Expeditions

SUGGESTED READING:

Foreman, Grant. *Adventures on Red River.* Norman, Okla., 1937.

———. *Marcy and the Gold Seekers.* Norman, Okla., 1939.

Hollon, W. Eugene. *Beyond the Cross Timbers: The Travels of Randolph B. Marcy.* Norman, Okla., 1955.

Marcy, Randolph Barnes. *The Prairie Traveler.* Salt Lake City, 1859. Reprint. 1928.

MARQUETTE, JACQUES

Jesuit priest and explorer Jacques Marquette (1637–1679) was born in Laon, France. After training as a priest, he went to New France (Canada) in 1666. Marquette studied Indian languages and assisted in the establishment of missions at Sault Ste.-Marie in 1668 and St. Ignace in 1671, both in present-day Michigan. His next assignment was far different from mission building: he explored the Mississippi in company with trapper and explorer LOUIS JOLIET.

Commissioned by Comte de Frontenac, governor of New France, the two explorers were to find the mouth of the Mississippi River. They left the mission at St. Ignace and traveled to Green Bay. There they ascended the Fox River in Wisconsin and, making use of a map based on Indian lore, portaged to the Wisconsin River. Entering the Mississippi near Prairie du Chien, they traveled south to the mouth of the Arkansas. Along the way, they were greeted hospitably by the Indian tribes. Learning that to travel farther would place them in possible danger from the Spanish, they returned by way of the Illinois River. Marquette, exhausted by the trip, remained at Green Bay, while Joliet continued on to report to the governor.

In 1674, Marquette set out to establish a mission among the Illinois Indians, but caught by the winter weather with two companions, he camped near the site of present-day Chicago. Marquette reached the Indians near present-day Utica, Illinois, but illness forced him to return to St. Ignace. While en route, he died on May 18, 1679, near the mouth of the river now known as Pere Marquette.

—*Patrick H. Butler, III*

SEE ALSO: Exploration: French Expeditions; Missions: Early Franciscan and Jesuit

SUGGESTED READING:

Donnelly, Joseph P. *Jacques Marquette, S.J., 1637–1675.* Chicago, 1968.

MARRIAGE AND FAMILY

SEE: Child Rearing; Community Property; Cult of True Womanhood; Divorce; Domestic Service; Fertility; Homesteaders; Intermarriage; Native American Cultures: Family Life, Kinship, and Gender; Picture Brides; Pioneer Life; Polygamy; Women on the Spanish-Mexican Frontier; Women in Wage Work; Working-Class Women

MARSH, GEORGE PERKINS

The author of *Man and Nature; or, Physical Geography as Modified by Human Action,* George Perkins Marsh (1801–1882) was among the earliest writers to recognize the environmental hazards posed by lumbering and sheep grazing. Marsh was born and raised at the base of a mountain along the Quebec River in Woodstock, Vermont, and it was there that he first personally witnessed the consequences of reckless sheep-grazing and lumbering practices. He saw how the mountainside was denuded and how the resulting run-off from snow and rain caused the Quebec River to flood each spring.

Marsh studied law, was elected to the Vermont legislature, and later received an appointment as ambassador to the Ottoman sultan. In the course of his diplomatic career, he traveled widely, and much of what he saw in France and the Mediterranean reminded him of the kind of environmental damage he had seen during childhood. After returning to the United States, he temporarily left politics and diplomacy for a career in the management of natural resources. He was appointed Vermont's fishery commissioner and published his *Report on the Artificial Propagation of Fish* in 1857. In this document, he carefully explored the negative impact of logging and sheep grazing as well as farming and other industry on streams and rivers.

Returning to his diplomatic career in 1861, Marsh accepted an appointment as U.S. ambassador to Italy, a post that left him plenty of time to complete *Man and Nature.* The work included chapters on wildlife, waters, sands, and forests and examined the impact of industry, agricultural, and engineering projects on each. Marsh's work was often cited by naturalists concerned about environmental damage in the American West during the latter half of the nineteenth century; the problems he exposed—particularly with regard to soil-eroding agricultural practices, clear-cut lumbering, and hydraulic-mining projects—were particularly large beyond the Mississippi. His book, which was translated into Italian in 1869, was also highly influential in Europe, where it was used as the basis for much early environmental policy.

—*Alan Axelrod*

SUGGESTED READING:

Lowenthal, David. *George Perkins Marsh: Versatile Vermonter.* Burlington, Vt., 1958.
Marsh, George Perkins. *Man and Nature.* New York, 1864.

MARSH, JOHN

California rancher John Marsh (1799–1856) first journeyed westward in 1823 with a Harvard degree and a job to teach the children of army officers stationed at Fort Snelling. Married for a time to a woman of French and Sioux ancestry, he served as an Indian agent, but the death of his wife and an indictment for illegal dealings with the natives caused him to flee to Independence, Missouri. By 1835, he had settled in Santa Fe. The stories he heard of California's pastoral paradise, however, lured him westward the following year.

Marsh had studied some medicine while at Harvard and had learned a little more from the post surgeon at Fort Snelling; when he settled in the San Joaquin Valley, he had a monopoly on available medical services. He built up a herd on his ranch by charging his patients exorbitant fees, payable in cattle, for his advice. In later years, he constructed a monument to his success, a mansion named the Stone House. In the early 1840s, Marsh wrote a series of letters, published in the Eastern press, praising the virtues of California and encouraging settlement. He meant to attract enough migrants to the region to raise the value of his own lands. Thought of as an embittered, miserly man, Marsh was murdered by a ranch hand in a disagreement over wages.

—*Patricia Hogan*

SUGGESTED READING:
Lyman, George D. *John Marsh: Pioneer.* Chautauqua, N.Y., 1931.

MARSHALS

SEE: Federal Marshals and Deputies

MARSTON, HELEN

See: Beardsley, Helen Marston

MARTIN, ANNE HENRIETTA

Nevada WOMEN'S SUFFRAGE leader and politician, Anne Henrietta Martin (1875–1951) was born in Nevada. She received a B.A. degree from both the University of Nevada and Stanford University. In 1897, she completed an M.A. in history at Stanford. Following college, she went to England and worked with the militant branch of the British women's suffrage movement between 1909 and 1911.

Anne Henrietta Martin championed the cause of women's suffrage, an issue that was better received in the West than in the Eastern states. *Courtesy Kansas State Historical Society.*

Martin returned to the United States in 1911 and spent the next several years working for women's suffrage. In 1912, she became president of the Nevada Equal Franchise Society; her efforts led to the state victory for women's suffrage in 1914. As president of the Women's Party of Western Voters, she coordinated an unsuccessful effort to promote national women's suffrage by asking Nevada women voters to defeat the candidates of "the party in power" (the Democrats) in the presidential election. In 1917, Martin served as vice-chair of the newly formed NATIONAL WOMAN'S PARTY and participated in the group's picket line in front of the White House. In 1918 and 1920, she ran for the U.S. Senate as an independent from Nevada. She lost, but drew 20 percent of the vote.

During the 1920s and 1930s, Martin dedicated her energies to pacifist activities and worked with the Women's International League for Peace and Freedom.

—*Joanne L. Goodwin*

SUGGESTED READING:
Anderson, Kathryn. "Anne Martin and the Dream of Political Equality for Women." *Journal of the West* 27 (1988): 28–34.
Cott, Nancy F. *The Grounding of Modern Feminism.* New Haven, Conn., 1987.

MARTÍNEZ, ANTONIO JOSÉ

A Catholic priest in New Mexico, Antonio José Martínez (1793–1867) grew up in northern New

Mexico. He studied to become a priest in Durango, Mexico, and after graduation was assigned the parish in Taos, New Mexico.

When the United States took possession of New Mexico in 1848 after the war with Mexico, the local Catholics were severed from their diocese centered in Durango. A new diocese led by JEAN BAPTISTE LAMY, who came to the area from France via the United States, was centered in Santa Fe.

Martínez, in his late fifties when Lamy arrived in New Mexico, continued to work at the parish in Taos where he had been working for more than thirty years. His industry, intelligence, and strong will had made him a favorite among the locals. At a time when New Mexico did not have many schools, he began educating local children, many of whom later attended the seminary in Durango and became priests. He bought the first printing press in New Mexico and used it to print books and New Mexico's first newspaper.

Martínez's personality, intelligence, and popularity set him on a course of conflict with Lamy and, especially, with Lamy's assistant Joseph Machebeuf. The differences were cultural rather than ecclesiastical or theological. "Padre" Martínez, as he was commonly called, became Lamy's most vocal, but by no means only, antagonist. Always a champion of his own people, Martínez criticized Lamy's condescending attitude and the practices of his French American administration. As a result of Martínez's opposition, Lamy stripped the Taos cleric of his priestly duties and started excommunication proceedings against him. Nonetheless, Martínez continued to perform his duties among a close-knit group of family and friends until his death in 1867.

Although novelist WILLA CATHER maligned Padre Martínez in her novel, *Death Comes for the Archbishop,* his reputation has withstood misinformation and bias, and he stands today as somewhat of a folk hero among New Mexicans.

—Thomas E. Chávez

SUGGESTED READING:

Chávez, Fray Angélico. *But Time and Change: The Story of Padre Martinez of Taos, 1793–1867.* Santa Fe, N. Mex., 1981.

De Aragon, John Ray. *Padre Martinez and Bishop Lamy.* Las Vegas, N. Mex., 1978.

MARTINEZ, MARIA MONTOYA

A Native American born at the San Ildefonso Pueblo in northern New Mexico, Maria Montoya Martinez (1886–1980) was an exceptionally talented potter, whose ceramic works caused a revival of Indian pottery among the pueblos of the Southwest and advanced an appreciation among Anglos of Native Americans arts. One of five daughters of a Catholic family, Poveka, or Yellow Pond Lily, as she was called, attended St. Catherine's Indian School in Santa Fe. As a young girl, she learned to make pottery from a maternal aunt. In 1904, she married Julian Martinez, and the two spent their honeymoon demonstrating Pueblo arts and culture at the St. Louis World's Fair. When Julian joined the archaeological excavations of a cave at Rito de los Frijoles in 1908, he copied designs found on prehistoric ceramics found in the diggings. Maria incorporated the ancient designs into her pots and experimented with other designs and techniques. By 1919, the two had perfected the techniques of producing their famous black matte designs on a lustrous black body.

Maria and Julian Martinez devoted much of their lives to promoting and popularizing Native American pottery. The honeymoon trip to St. Louis was the first of countless demonstrations before Anglo audiences. From 1909 to 1912, the couple lived and worked at the MUSEUM OF NEW MEXICO, where they demonstrated their work and produced their ceramics in programs design to record and preserve traditional Indian crafts. Maria's works encouraged a major revival of Pueblo pottery, bringing fame and respect to her own pueblo and improving the economic circumstances of many Pueblo Indians. She won national and international prizes and honors for her works, and the pots she produced command the highest prices on the art market. She is generally recognized as the best of modern Pueblo potters.

When Julian Martinez died in 1943, Maria continued making pots first with Santana, her daughter-in-law, and later with her son, Tony or Popovi Da. The family tradition continued through six generations of potters; by the late twentieth century, Maria's grandson, Tony Da, and her great-granddaughter, Barbara Gonzales, had become most famous for their exceptional works.

—Patricia Hogan

SEE ALSO: Native American Pottery, Southwestern

SUGGESTED READING:

Marriott, Alice. *Maria, the Potter of San Ildefonso.* Norman, Okla., 1945.

McGreevy, Susan Brown. *Maria: The Legend, the Legacy.* Santa Fe, N. Mex., 1982.

Nelson, Mary Carroll. *Maria Martinez.* Minneapolis, Minn., 1974.

MASON, BIDDY

Born a slave in Georgia, Biddy Mason (1818–1891) became the most prominent African American woman in post–Civil War Los Angeles. Mason was the property of a Mormon planter who brought her and her three children to Salt Lake in 1848 and then to San Bernardino, California, in 1851. Five years later, she successfully petitioned for the freedom of her thirteen-member extended family. Mason subsequently settled in Los Angeles, where she became a successful midwife. She assisted in the births of hundreds of Anglo, Chicano, Native American, and African American children between 1856 and 1891.

Using $250 she had saved, Mason purchased a parcel of land between Spring Street and Broadway, just beyond the city limits, in November 1866. Her purchase made her one of the first black female property owners in the Los Angeles area. Six years later, she founded the First African Methodist Episcopal Church, the oldest African American church in Los Angeles. As downtown Los Angeles expanded, the value of her property grew. In 1884, Mason sold part of her homestead for $1,500 and constructed a two-story commercial building to house a nursery, bakeries, a restaurant, and furniture and carpet stores. The upper floor was the residence of her extended family. With the proceeds from the sale of part of the homestead, rents, and sales of other town lots, Mason generated considerable wealth. For the rest of her life, she donated regularly to charities, homeless families, and stranded settlers and became renowned for her philanthropy.

—*Quintard Taylor*

SUGGESTED READING:

Hayden, Dolores. "Biddy Mason's Los Angeles, 1856–1891." *California History* 68 (Fall 1989): 87–99.

MASON VALLEY RANCH, NEVADA

The largest cattle ranch in Nevada in the late nineteenth century, the Mason Valley Ranch was established by Henry N. A. Mason in Lyon County, near Yerington. Mason had first driven a herd of cattle from California to the Great Basin region in 1854 and had returned with another herd in 1869 to the Walker River region, later known as Mason Valley. Between 1871 and 1880, he expanded his holdings. On his more than ninety thousand acres, he raised more than thirty thousand head of cattle. The drought of 1889 and the severe winter of 1990 pushed him far into debt and compelled him to sell his ranch to HENRY MILLER, whose holdings spread through California, Oregon, and Nevada.

—*Candace Floyd*

SEE ALSO: Cattle Industry

MASTERSON, BARTHOLOMEW (BAT)

Farmer, buffalo hunter, lawman, gambler, and journalist, Bat Masterson (1853–1921) was born in Quebec, Canada. (He later changed his name to William Barclay Masterson.) His family moved from Canada to New York, then to Illinois, and finally, in 1871, to Kansas. Leaving the family farm in 1872, he and his older brother Ed worked as graders for the Santa Fe Railroad as well as skinners for buffalo hunters. It was in this period that he met Wyatt Earp.

Masterson then turned to buffalo hunting and was at Adobe Walls in 1874 when Comanche, Kiowa, and Cheyenne warriors attacked. Later, Masterson worked as a civilian scout under General NELSON APPLETON MILES for a couple of months. Then he worked as a teamster.

In 1876, Masterson was involved in a gun battle with a soldier over a woman. After the smoke cleared, both his opponent and the woman were dead, and he was seriously wounded. Settling in DODGE CITY, KANSAS, he purchased a saloon and, for a time, served as a policeman. He was elected sheriff of Ford County in 1877.

Masterson's term as sheriff was eventful: his brother Ed was killed; Masterson arrested James Kenedy for the accidental shooting of Dora Hand; and the Northern Cheyenne Chief MORNING STAR led a raid near Dodge. During his tenure as sheriff, Masterson also worked for the Santa Fe Railroad in its fight with the Denver and Rio Grande over control of Raton Pass.

Defeated for reelection, Masterson moved to Colorado. He was called on to save Billy Thompson, the younger brother of gambler and gunman BENJAMIN F. THOMPSON, from a Nebraska lynch mob. In 1881, he went to Tombstone, Arizona. He returned to Dodge City in 1881 and again in 1883, when he helped LUKE SHORT in the DODGE CITY WAR settle his differences with the town administration.

In his forties, Masterson, on occasion, served as a peace officer, but mainly he gambled and was active in promoting sporting events, especially prize fights.

In 1902, Masterson moved to New York City from Denver. He was appointed deputy U.S. marshal by

Bartholomew (Bat) Masterson. *Courtesy National Archives.*

President THEODORE ROOSEVELT. Masterson became a friend of writer Alfred Henry Lewis, and with his encouragement, Masterson decided to be a writer. A series of his articles was published as *Famous Gunfighters of the Western Frontier.*

Masterson was made sports editor of the *New York Morning Telegraph.* Still quick to anger, Masterson drank heavily and occasionally got into trouble. In October 1921, while writing a column at his desk, he suffered a fatal heart attack.

—*Richard A. Van Orman*

SEE ALSO: Earp Brothers; Gunfighters

SUGGESTED READING:

DeArment, Robert K. *Bat Masterson: The Man and the Legend.* Norman, Okla., 1979.
O'Connor, Richard. *Bat Masterson.* New York, 1957.
Thompson, George G. *Bat Masterson: The Dodge City Years.* Topeka, Kans., 1943.

MATADOR RANCH, TEXAS

Founded in 1878 by A. M. Britton and H. H. Campbell at Ballard Springs in West Texas, the Matador Ranch became one of the largest, longest-lived, and best-known cattle empires in North America. Around 1880, S. W. Lomax joined the operation, forming the Matador Cattle Company, with the Matador *V* brand.

In 1882, the Matador Land and Cattle Company, Limited, a joint-stock venture organized in Dundee, Scotland, bought the ranch, which included some 100,000 acres and 40,000 head of cattle. Under manager MURDO MACKENZIE, the operation, by 1916, held 880,000 acres in Texas, leased land in South Dakota, Montana, and Saskatchewan, Canada, and supported 70,000 head of cattle and horses.

The "Matadors" was broken up in the 1950s. In 1993, Koch Industries of Wichita, Kansas, continued to operate a greatly reduced Matador Ranch around the old division headquarters in Motley County, Texas.

—*Richard C. Rattenbury*

SEE ALSO: Cattle Industry

SUGGESTED READING:

Lincoln, John. *Rich Grass and Sweet Water: Ranch Life with the Koch Matador Cattle Company.* College Station, Tex., 1989.
Pearce, W. M. *The Matador Land and Cattle Company.* Norman, Okla., 1964.

MATHER, DAVE

Frontier peace officer, gold-seeker, gambler, and thief, Dave Mather (1845?–?) claimed to be a lineal descendant of Cotton Mather, the celebrated eighteenth-century New England Puritan. Born in Connecticut, Mather, who carried the nickname "Mysterious Dave," first came to public attention in early 1879, when newspapers mentioned he was riding with one of the West's most noted horse thieves, Dutch Henry Brown, in Trinidad, Colorado. Later that year, Mather was in Las Vegas, New Mexico, where he served as constable. As a city policeman, he shot and killed Joseph Costello in the line of duty and was absolved of wrongdoing by a coroner's jury.

Mather hunted for gold in the Gunnison country and then turned up in Texas, first in San Antonio and then Fort Worth, where he was arrested for stealing a gold ring from his paramour.

On June 5, 1883, Mather was appointed assistant marshal of DODGE CITY, KANSAS. His record there brought him severe criticism from both citizens and newspapers. Probably because of his reputation, he was defeated for Dodge township constable, and when the city administration changed in the spring of 1884, he was fired.

Dave Mather. *Courtesy Kansas State Historical Society.*

In July 1884, an old feud between the new assistant marshal, Thomas C. Nixon, and Mather erupted; Nixon shot at Mather, and three days later, Mather killed Nixon. Mather was granted a change of venue to another county where he was acquitted; the jury decided that Nixon had been the aggressor and Mather had acted in self-defense.

Less than a year after the Nixon affair, Mather and his brother Josiah were accused of killing David Barnes in Ashland, Kansas. Barnes and Dave Mather had been playing cards when a dispute over the winnings arose. A general shooting began, and Mather was wounded and Barnes killed. The brothers were freed on bail, which they promptly jumped.

Mather next was appointed city marshal of New Kiowa, Kansas, in August 1885, but nothing is known of his exploits there or, with certainty, of his later life and death.

—*Joseph W. Snell*

SEE ALSO: Gunfighters

SUGGESTED READING:

Miller, Nyle H., and Joseph W. Snell. *Why the West Was Wild.* Topeka, Kans., 1963.

O'Neal, Bill. *Encyclopedia of Western Gunfighters.* Norman, Okla., 1979.

MATHER, STEPHEN TYNG

Conservationist and first director of the NATIONAL PARK SERVICE, Stephen Tyng Mather (1867–1930) routinely sought great challenges to absorb his abundant reserves of energy and enthusiasm. Born in California and graduated from the state's fledgling university in 1887, Mather soon found his niche in the booming borax industry. Gifted with a shrewd sense of marketing and an unlimited capacity for hard work, he achieved great success in the promotion of the once-obscure mineral. In the process, he accumulated a small fortune.

Mather's business triumphs, however, did not quell his restless temperament. Long an avid outdoorsman and conservationist, he had grown increasingly distressed at the federal government's lackluster management of the national parks. When invited by fellow Californian FRANKLIN KNIGHT LANE, Woodrow Wilson's

Stephen Tyng Mather (right), first director of the National Park Service, pictured at Yosemite National Park with Secretary of the Interior Albert B. Fall, 1921. Photograph by F. P. Farquhar. *Courtesy National Archives.*

secretary of the interior, to take responsibility for the parks, Mather accepted his greatest challenge.

From his arrival in 1915 until his departure in 1929, Mather devoted himself to the establishment, promotion, and development of a national park system. Drawing upon his vast array of political, journalistic, and business contacts, he and his able young assistant, HORACE MARDEN ALBRIGHT, rallied support for measures to designate new parks, to improve public services throughout the parks, and to create a National Park Service to manage all these reserves. Appointed director of the National Park Service after Congress passed its enabling legislation on August 25, 1916, Mather struggled to defeat frequently proposed encroachments onto park lands by irrigationists, mining companies, or stock-raisers and to protect the inviolability of park boundaries.

Disabled by a massive stroke in November 1928, Mather resigned as director in January 1929 to resounding public acclaim. His remarkable flair for promotional tactics and his deep-seated preservationist instincts had entrenched the national parks in the public consciousness and ensured the permanent protection of many of America's great scenic treasures. Mather's ready acceptance, however, of ever-increasing numbers of visitors set the Park Service on a course that would collide with the preservationist movement in later years as visitation reached astronomical proportions.

—Peter J. Blodgett

SUGGESTED READING:

Albright, Horace M., as told to Robert Cahn. *The Birth of the National Park Service, The Founding Years, 1913–33.* Salt Lake City, 1985.

Shankland, Robert. *Steve Mather of the National Parks.* 3d ed. New York, 1971.

Swain, Donald. *Wilderness Defender: Horace M. Albright and Conservation.* Chicago, 1970.

MAURER, KATHERINE R.

A Methodist missionary to the Chinese in California, Katherine R. Maurer (1881–1962) was a native of Milmay, Ontario. She spent her adult years in San Francisco and devoted most of her life to missionary work among immigrants passing through the U.S. Immigration Station at Angel Island in San Francisco Bay. In 1912, the WOMAN'S HOME MISSIONARY SOCIETY of the Methodist Episcopal Church appointed Maurer to serve as Deaconess at Angel Island, a position she held for almost forty years.

Both immigration officials and immigrants thought highly of Maurer and called her the "Angel of Angel Island." She provided a range of services aimed primarily at Asian women detained at the island. She gave advice and reassurance to immigrants awaiting investigation, brought them supplies from the city, taught English, and organized recreational activities through the San Francisco Chinese Young Men's Christian Association. Although sponsored by the Methodist Episcopal church, Maurer perceived her work to be nondenominational and geared toward serving the daily needs of immigrants, rather than toward actively converting them.

—Lucy E. Salyer

SUGGESTED READING:

Lai, Him Mark, Genny Lim, and Judy Yung, eds. *Island: Poetry and History of Chinese Immigrants on Angel Island, 1910–1940.* San Francisco, 1980.

MAXWELL, MARTHA ANN DARTT

Martha Ann Dartt Maxwell (1831–1881), naturalist and taxidermist, was born in Dartt's Settlement, Pennsylvania. She attended Oberlin College in Oberlin, Ohio, and Lawrence University in Appleton, Wisconsin, before marrying Wisconsin businessman James A. Maxwell in 1854. Their daughter Mabel was born in 1857. Between 1860 and 1862, the couple prospected in the Colorado gold fields, and Martha Maxwell bought a ranch near Denver. There, she encountered a claim-jumper who was a German taxidermist and who became the inspiration for her life work. In Boulder, she opened the Rocky Mountain Museum (1874), which featured birds and mammals mounted in a re-creation of their natural habitat. A similar, larger exhibit in the Kansas-Colorado Building at the 1876 Philadelphia Centennial Exposition brought her national fame.

Modern scientists recognize Maxwell as the first woman ornithologist to have a subspecies she herself discovered named for her ("Mrs. Maxwell's Owl," *Otus asio maxwelliae*), while museum historians give her credit for her work as an early proponent of habitat exhibits in natural-history museums. Few of her specimens have survived, but numerous photographs document her accomplishments.

—Maxine Benson

SUGGESTED READING:

Benson, Maxine. *Martha Maxwell, Rocky Mountain Naturalist.* Lincoln, Nebr., 1986.

MAXWELL LAND GRANT COMPANY

After the United States–Mexican War, the American Southwest became an internal empire of the United States, and the lands of this empire were subject to American laws and land policy rather than those of Spain and Mexico. The complicated history of the Maxwell Land Grant became a classic example of the problems associated with land ownership in the conquered region, problems connected with the grandiose dreams of American empire-builders and the aspirations of poor squatters seeking the cheap land traditionally associated with a move westward into "unsettled" regions. As a result both of the often legally ambiguous nature of Spanish and Mexican land grants and of conflicts between rich American lawyers or territorial politicians and land-hungry American settlers, wild speculation in Southwestern lands became rampant in the second half of the nineteenth century and reached a fevered pitch in the 1870s and 1880s. The shady dealings, political intrigue, and violence that characterized America's post–Civil War empire building, in general, and the story of the Maxwell Land Grant, in particular, was part and parcel of the attempt by Americans to disinherit the Hispanic landowners of the Southwest, *ricos* (the wealthy) and Californios and poor villagers and farmers alike, whom the Americans considered foreigners, in favor of Anglo entrepreneurs and homesteaders.

The Spanish empire and Mexico had approached land ownership differently than the United States. Land titles—under Mexican law—were held by families and their lineages, not by individuals, but under American law, lands were subdivided among heirs, who could sell without regard to the family. Land, like everything the Americans touched, became a commodity, and Hispanic landowners fell prey to coercion and fraud, in part, because of their reluctance to transform their ranchos into ranches, their ancestral estates into capitalist enterprises. Three years after the Treaty of Guadalupe Hidalgo that ended the United States–Mexican War, Congress passed a new land law that allowed Americans to contest Mexican land titles. It set up a commission to review the validity of dozens of Spanish land grants plus the hundreds more made by the Mexican government. Neither Spain nor Mexico had ever taken many legal pains in granting land. Both had drawn up the grants without surveying equipment and loosely marked them on often inaccurate maps. On the maps, one border might be indicated as marked by a notch in a tree, another as "between the hills at the head of a running water," a third by a pile of stones. Anglo squatters often settled on the fringes of these large, ill-defined land grants. Operating under a long-standing American tradition that unimproved or "idle" land belonged to those who settled on it and made productive use of it, squatters enjoyed a quasi-legal status under American land policy and were hard, if not impossible, to get rid of once they moved in. In the end, it often hardly mattered if Hispanic landowners won or lost their claims to big land grants or even communally held village property in court, the land itself was already gone. In the second half of the nineteenth century in California, in Texas, in New Mexico Territory, many rancheros were losing their lands in the U.S. courts to lawyer-speculators and to American squatters.

It was in this atmosphere that the history of the Maxwell Land Grant unfolded. The grant was originally awarded in 1841 by Mexican governor MANUEL ARMIJO, himself a major speculator in land grants, to a prominent Taos merchant named CARLOS BEAUBIEN and Guadelupe Miranda, secretary of the New Mexican government. A year later, American Fur Trade Company trapper Lucien Bonaparte Maxwell, who had become a friend of CHRISTOPHER HOUSTON ("KIT") CARSON while serving with JOHN CHARLES FRÉMONT and trapping in the Sangre de Cristo Mountains, settled in Taos, a town much beloved by Carson. There, Maxwell married Beaubien's daughter and, following a trend among Western fur traders, acquired interest in his father-in-law's lands under Mexico's Colonization Law of 1824, which had been passed to encourage American settlers to become Mexican citizens and landholders with a stake in the future of Mexico rather than the United States. Meanwhile, the grant itself was challenged by some Taos citizens, led by a local priest ANTONIO JOSÉ MARTINEZ, who felt that Beaubien and Miranda were misrepresenting the extent of their grant and encroaching of communal village properties. Although Padre Martinez succeeded in having a new Mexican governor void the grant, Beaubien and Miranda held out for their rights through a series of legal actions, ultimately maintaining control of the grant. When Beaubien died in 1864, long after the United States had acquired the region, Maxwell bought out the claims of his relatives as well as the land owned by Miranda, who had decided to return to his native El Paso del Norte, today's Cuidad Juárez.

Maxwell, the second largest individual landowner in the United States, treated his extensive holdings as a principality and acted the part of a great lord in the Taos region. In 1867, gold was discovered on Maxwell's land, and prospectors, swarming onto his estate, ignored his claims to ownership. Conscious of both the former legal challenges and the increased value of the grant, Maxwell sought to have his ownership validated by the U.S. land courts, which, in 1869, confirmed his title to some 97,000 acres east of the Sangre de Cristo Mountains under the 1824 Mexican law. Secure in his ownership of what was now officially the Maxwell Land Grant, Maxwell sought to realize a fortune by selling off his land. Soon thereafter, he had attracted four groups of major investors, two American groups, one out of Denver, the other Santa Fe, and two European companies. Heading the Colorado group was JEROME BONAPARTE CHAFFEE, a wealthy mine owner. STEPHEN BENTON ELKINS led the New Mexican investors. In 1869, Maxwell gave Chaffee and Elkins an option to buy, and a year later, they paid him $1.3 million and formed the Maxwell Land Grant and Railroad Company.

Understanding well the vagaries of land-grant titles, Chaffee and Elkins had the grant resurveyed in an attempt to increase the land they had bought from the 97,000 acres the land office had already confirmed to some 2 million acres and, on that basis, resold the grant to English investors, who, in turn, mortgaged the land to financiers in Amsterdam. The British investors made William Jackson Painter, superintendent of the Kansas Pacific Railroad, president of the Maxwell Land Grant company and issued stock for $5 million. Then, Secretary of the Interior Columbus Delano ruled that the company was only entitled to the original 97,000 acres, which sent officials scurrying to Congress for help. Chaffee had become the Colorado Territory's U.S. delegate in 1871, and Elkins New Mexico's in 1872, forming part of a loosely connected group of business leaders and politicians that folks called the "SANTA FE RING." Despite the ring's best efforts, the company faced bankruptcy by 1875, and the Dutch bankers took control from the New Mexico gang. Meanwhile, squatters had begun settling in the Cimarron area, unaware that the land was claimed as private property by the company; prospectors were staking claims to company holdings in booming Elizabethtown; Texas ranchers were lusting for the area's rich grazing lands; and local investors, led by Richard Springer, opposed the influence of the Santa Fe Ring, led by Colfax County probate judge Robert Longwill, over the company and the land grant. Ultimately, the broiling conflicts spilled over into the Colfax County War.

More a string of assassinations than a war, the conflict began when thugs hired by Longwill murdered a Methodist minister who supported the local settlers. Over the next two years, there were lynchings, ambushes, and murders; at one point, Texas gunman [ROBERT] CLAY ALLISON killed one of Longwill's associates, Pancho Griego, and in the long run, Longwill fled Colfax County to safe haven in Santa Fe. The feuding and mob violence, which lasted almost a decade, represented, according to historian Howard Lamar, a deep-rooted conflict based on different notions of the frontier. Settlers, ranchers, and miners, believed that the Southwestern lands taken from Mexico were part of the public domain, just as the Louisiana Purchase lands had been; the financiers and capitalists of the Maxwell Land Grant Company, as overseers of a colonial economy, saw a business opportunity based on the integrity of the Spanish and Mexican land grants as inviolable private property. Ultimately, the federal government in the form of U.S. Land Commissioner James A. Williams called for a new survey, which, this time, gave the company 1.7 million acres, and the company's patent was upheld by the U.S. Supreme Court based on that survey. Controlled by Dutch bankers, the Maxwell Land Grant Company transformed its land, cattle, and mining investments into the vast empire of profit first imagined by Elkins and Chaffee. Thriving well into the twentieth century, the company was bought out in the 1960s by a group of diverse investors, including Texas oil men, the Phelps-Dodge mining interests, and even the Boy Scouts of America.

—*Charles Phillips*

SUGGESTED READING:

Grassham, John W. "Carlos H. Beaubien, 1800–1864." Masters thesis. New Mexico State University, Las Cruces, N. Mex., 1983.

Keleher, William A. *The Maxwell Land Grant.* Santa Fe, N. Mex., 1975.

Pearson, Jim Berry. *The Maxwell Land Grant.* Norman, Okla., 1961.

MAY, KARL FRIEDRICH

The popular German writer Karl Friedrich May (1842–1912) wrote more than twenty volumes of German American westerns. May (pronounced *Mai)* emerged from serving two prison terms (for theft and fraud) to create three fictional worlds—mystical fantasy; Islamic adventures (featuring Karl May/Old Shatterhand in his Arabian guise as Kara ben Nemsi); and German American westerns, primarily starring two superheroes, Old Shatterhand, an indomitable German *Westmann,* and Winnetou, a noble chief of the Apaches.

Set in an American Southwest of the 1870s and 1880s and grounded in "authentic" detail gleaned from reference books, May's enormously popular three-volume *Winnetou* (1893) features the German greenhorn Scharlie (an alterego for May), who enters the West as part of a railroad survey crew. Kidnapped by the Kiowas, whom he at once amazes and subdues through powerful karate chops (thus the nickname "Old Shatterhand"), Scharlie becomes blood brother to Winnetou, the *Hiawatha*-reading Apache chief. Together, the pair undertake a series of adventures. Roaming the West, Winnetou (in whom May glorifies the Native American) and Old Shatterhand (in whom May idealizes the German character) right wrongs, punish desperadoes (usually Yankees, Mormons, or half-breeds), and futilely attempt to forestall the *Götterdämmerung* of the Indian nations.

The long-standing "Karl May controversy," focusing on whether German youth should be exposed to the violence and imagination in May's westerns, has not hindered the spread of Karl May Festivals, Winnetou Clubs and puzzles, and Old Shatterhand water pistols, as well as dozens of dramas and feature films. Since 1969, the Karl-May-*Gesellschaft* (Society) has promoted serious literary study of May's writings as repositories of German character, psychology, nationalism, and ideology. May has been a major influence in shaping Germany's idealized image of a mythic American West, which, though alien to the American mind, has inspired millions of German readers.

—*Richard H. Cracroft*

SEE ALSO: Literature: The Western Novel

SUGGESTED READING:

Billington, Ray Allen. *Land of Savagery Land of Promise.* New York, 1981.

Cook, Colleen. "Germany's Wild West Author: A Researcher's Guide to Karl May." *German Studies Review* 1 (February 1982): 67–86.

Cracroft, Richard H. "World Westerns: The European Writer and the American West." In *A Literary History of the American West.* Edited by Thomas J. Lyon, et al. Fort Worth, Tex., 1987.

"Karl der Deutsche." *Der Spiegel* 16 (September 12, 1962): 54–74.

MAYBECK, BERNARD RALPH

One of California's premier early twentieth-century architects, Bernard Maybeck (1862–1957) was born in New York City. He received his training in Europe at the École des Beaux-Arts in Paris from 1880 to 1886. After working briefly in New York and in Kansas City, Missouri, he settled in San Francisco. In 1894, he joined the faculty of the University of California at Berkeley as a drawing instructor; four years later, he was appointed the university's first professor of architecture, a post he held from 1898 to 1903.

Along with his academic career, Maybeck developed a thriving private practice in architecture. He designed the university's Hearst Hall (1899; destroyed by fire in 1929), which incorporated an innovative laminated-wood arch motif; the Town and Gown Club (1899); the Men's Faculty Club (1900), a striking variation on the Spanish mission style prevalent in California; the First Church of Christ, Scientist (1910, Berkeley), a free-Gothic adaptation; and the Palace of the Fine Arts (1915), designed for San Francisco's PANAMA-PACIFIC INTERNATIONAL EXPOSITION. Maybeck's last major work was the campus of Principia College in Elsah, Illinois, completed in 1938.

—*Alan Axelrod*

SEE ALSO: Architecture: Urban Architecture

McBETH, SUE AND KATE

Susan Law McBeth (1830–1893) was born in Scotland. When she was two years old, her family immigrated to the United States and settled on the Ohio River in Wellsville, Ohio, where Kate McBeth (1833–1915) was born. Both girls were imbued with a sense of equality and kindness and were influenced by the family's strong religious underpinnings and Wellsville's status as a way station on the Underground Railroad. Both girls were educated, although Kate's schooling is unclear; Sue graduated with honors from the Steubenville Female Seminary in 1854 and began a teaching career, first in Wellsville, then in Iowa.

In 1860, the Presbyterian Board of Foreign Missions called Sue to work with the Choctaw Indians in the Indian Territory. She hesitantly agreed, only to find her mission interrupted by the outbreak of the Civil War. In 1873, she was offered the chance to resume her work, this time in Idaho with the Nez Percés. Moving to the Kamiah Agency, Sue prepared Indian men for the ministry. Her main objectives were, first, to break the power of the old chiefs, thereby fostering an individual relationship with God and assimilating the Nez Percés into white society, and, second, to offer a moral example that contrasted sharply with the un-Christian–like influence of the soldiers who surrounded the mission.

In 1879, Kate joined her sister Sue at Kamiah. Kate was responsible for educating and ministering to the women, while Sue continued her work with the men. In 1885, the sisters moved to Mount Idaho and continued teaching there when the DAWES ACT was passed in 1887. Although the Dawes Act was later discredited, implementation of its land-allotment system in Idaho was largely due to the work of the McBeth sisters. After suffering a stroke, Sue died in 1893. Kate continued her work with the Nez Percés until she died in 1915.

—*Kurt Edward Kemper*

SEE ALSO: Missions: Nineteenth-Century Missions to the Indians; United States Indian Policy

SUGGESTED READING:

Coleman, Michael. *Presbyterian Missionary Attitudes toward American Indians, 1837–1893.* Jackson, Miss., 1985.

McCARRAN, PATRICK A.

Nevada politician Patrick A. McCarran (1876–1954), born near Reno, began his ascent to the leadership of Nevada's Democratic machine when he was elected to the state's assembly in 1902. Stints as a district attorney and state supreme-court judge and two defeats in elections for the U.S. Senate (1916 and 1926) preceded a successful campaign in 1934. An ardent opponent of New Deal legislation—unless his home state benefited—McCarran opposed President Franklin D. Roosevelt's attempts to pack the U.S. Supreme Court, a stance that won favor among his constituents. By 1940, he had solidified his control over Nevada's Democrats and, in the process, earned a reputation as a lone wolf in the party.

In the Senate, McCarran shepherded the Civil Aeronautics Act and the Internal Security Act of 1950. His McCarran-Walter Immigration and Nationality Act of 1952 allowed—for the first time under the quota system—immigration of peoples from Asia and the Pacific islands and permitted their becoming naturalized citizens. McCarran's lifelong hatred of communism was manifest in legislation that blocked the admission of "politically undesirable" aliens and called for the deportation of "politically undesirable" naturalized citizens.

McCarran died in Hawthorne, Nevada, shortly after delivering a speech on communism.

—*Patricia Hogan*

SEE ALSO: Immigration Law: Immigration Law after 1900

McCARTY, HENRY

SEE: "Billy the Kid"

McCOY, JOSEPH G.

Joseph G. McCoy (1837–1915), originally from Sangamon County, Illinois, promoted the use of the Chisholm Trail, along which millions of head of cattle were driven from Texas to ABILENE, KANSAS, for shipment by rail to Eastern packing companies. (The trail across the Indian Territory had been originally opened by JESSE CHISHOLM after the Civil War.) McCoy negotiated rates with railroad lines for cattle shipment and received informal permission from the Kansas governor to ignore the ban on importing Texas cattle—a ban instituted because of TEXAS FEVER, a tick-borne disease carried by Texas longhorns and deadly to other cattle. McCoy bought 250 acres in Abilene to use for corrals and loading pens, and within two months time, his facilities were prepared to process, weigh, and load cattle into forty cars in two hours. He sent handbills to Texas to promote the Abilene facilities, and the marketing effort was a success. During the 1867 cattle droving season, 35,000 head were brought to Abilene for shipment. By 1871, the total was about 190,000. During this time, Abilene was transformed from a hamlet with a dozen families to a boom town, and McCoy was elected its first mayor.

In 1869, McCoy fell on hard times when the cattle market collapsed, due, in part, to the state's enforcement of the cattle quarantine. He had purchased cattle on credit, and when the railroad refused to pay him his fee for processing shipments from Abilene, he was penniless. The courts finally ruled in his favor, and he paid off his debts. While he remained in the cattle business, he was never again the major operator in Abilene. In 1873, he moved to Kansas City, Missouri, and established a livestock commission company. The following year he wrote *Historic Sketches of the Cattle Trade of the West and Southwest.*

Throughout his life, McCoy was engaged in a wide range of enterprises: groceries, real-estate, a flour and feed store, and wrought-iron fences sales. He also worked as a stockman, cattle inspector, livestock broker, and narcotics agent for the U.S. Treasury Department.

—*Candace Floyd*

SEE ALSO: Cattle Industry; Cattle Towns; Cattle Trails and Trail Driving

SUGGESTED READING:

Dykstra, Robert R. *The Cattle Towns.* New York, 1968.
Walker, Don D. *Clio's Cowboys: Studies in the Historiography of the Cattle Trade.* Lincoln, Nebr., 1981.
Worcester, Donald Emmet. *The Chisholm Trail: High Road of the Cattle Kingdom.* Lincoln, Nebr., 1980.

McCULLOCH, HARTNELL AND COMPANY

McCulloch, Hartnell and Company was formed in Lima, Peru, on March 21, 1822, by Hugh McCulloch, a Scotsman, and William E. P. Hartnell, an Englishman, both clerks in the employ of John Beggs and Company, an English firm headquartered in Santiago, Chile. The two young men persuaded Beggs to finance their plan to exchange English and South American goods for Mexican California's products, especially hides and tallow. The pioneering venture laid the foundation for systematic commerce with Alta California. Within two years, a number of competitors who imitated the firm's business practices challenged McCulloch, Hartnell and Company. It was dissolved on May 1, 1828, due to losses incurred from rival traders and Beggs's disaffection with results. However, the company's legacy to California was the formation of the hide and tallow trade, which dominated the region's economy until the 1840s.

—*Doyce B. Nunis, Jr.*

SUGGESTED READING:

Dakin, Susanna Bryant. *The Lives of William Hartnell.* Stanford, Calif., 1949.

Ogden, Adele. "Hides and Tallow: McCulloch, Hartnell and Company, 1822–1828." *California Historical Society Quarterly* 6 (September 1927): 254–264.

McFARLAND, JOHN HORACE

John Horace McFarland (1859–1948) pioneered the printing of horticultural catalogues in color and was a leading advocate of the "city-beautiful" movement. Born near Harrisburg, Pennsylvania, he first became well known as a photographer and writer. Between 1900 and 1914, he contributed numerous articles on and photographs of gardens and plants, especially trees, to major periodicals. Eventually, McFarland gained renown as a printer, gardener, parks enthusiast, city beautifier, and rosarian.

He helped found the American Civic Association in St. Louis in 1904, served for twenty years as its president, and turned it into a powerful parks and civic-betterment organization.

At the 1908 White House Governor's Conference on Conservation, McFarland alone spoke for the "preservation" of scenery as a "national resource." He then vigorously pushed the campaign that led to the establishment of the NATIONAL PARK SERVICE in 1916.

Often quarreling with GIFFORD PINCHOT over the "fair use" conservation ideas he espoused in the UNITED STATES FOREST SERVICE, McFarland became the SIERRA CLUB's chief congressional strategist during its battle against damming Yosemite's Hetch Hetchy Valley, which Pinchot supported.

As the nation's "switchboard" for the "city-beautiful" movement, McFarland worked closely with local citizens to clean up dozens of American cities, notably Dallas, Texas. Beautifying highways by removing billboards was another McFarland campaign.

Largely through his efforts, the American Rose Society was transformed from a small commercial growers' organization into a nationwide public association devoted to private rose culture.

Even into his eighties, McFarland continued traveling throughout Western communities in Texas, Oklahoma, and Iowa, and speaking on civic-improvement, park, and rosarian concerns.

—*Ernest J. Morrison*

SEE ALSO: Hetch Hetchy Controversy

SUGGESTED READING:

Jones, Holway R. *John Muir and the Sierra Club: The Battle for Yosemite.* San Francisco, 1964.

Morrison, Ernest J. *Horace McFarland: A Thorn for Beauty.* Harrisburg, Pa., 1994.

Wilson, William H. *The City Beautiful Movement.* Baltimore, 1989.

McGEE, WILLIAM JOHN

A pioneer American anthropologist, geologist, and hydrologist, William John McGee (1853–1912) was largely self-taught. He walked his native state of Iowa to collect information for his first scientific work, "On the relative position of the forest bed and associated formations in northeastern Iowa." He followed that paper, which was published in 1878, with more than one hundred books and scientific articles.

On the strength of McGee's independent work, JOHN WESLEY POWELL invited him to join the UNITED STATES GEOLOGICAL SURVEY in 1883. Ten years later, McGee moved to the newly created Bureau of American Ethnology. There, he issued numerous studies on Native American peoples, many of which involved comprehensive, unique anthropological work.

A keen observer, McGee was attentive to details. These traits were balanced with concern for treating problems in large contexts. He felt, as a hydrologist, that most Mississippi River engineering works were "little more than feeble temporizing with a mighty power." He believed flood control, canalization, WATER power, and IRRIGATION must be considered as a whole. He was convinced, too, that restoring upstream forests and grasses—to eliminate sedimentation—was the key to harnessing the Mississippi.

In promoting his integrated forest-water concept with GIFFORD PINCHOT of the UNITED STATES FOREST SERVICE and President THEODORE ROOSEVELT, McGee sowed the seeds that led to the White House Governor's Conference on Conservation. Pinchot claimed that McGee "was the scientific brains of the conservation movement."

McGee died of cancer in Washington. His last article was on the "Symptomatic Development of Cancer." According to Gifford Pinchot, "It was always the *application* of knowledge that appealed to him."

—*Ernest J. Morrison*

SUGGESTED READING:

Pinchot, Gifford. *Breaking New Ground.* New York, 1968.

McKENZIE, ALEXANDER ("BIG ALEX")

Alexander ("Big Alex") McKenzie (1851–1922) was the most important political leader in North Dakota in the late nineteenth century, even though he never held a major public office. Born in Ontario, Canada, McKenzie moved to the Dakota Territory in 1868 and settled in Bismarck five years later. After working on a construction crew for the Northern Pacific Railroad, he was elected sheriff of Burleigh County in 1874 and held that position for twelve years. During this time, he also served as the political agent for the Northern Pacific Railroad, which—along with other Minneapolis and St. Paul railroad interests and the banking and grain industries—controlled nearly every aspect of political and economic life in the territory.

McKenzie dispensed patronage to his supporters and aid to incoming settlers, thus building a huge political machine—called the "Old Gang"— in the Republican party. He used his power to ensure the election of senators who would protect the interests of the railroads, banks, and grain industry. Through his efforts, the territorial capital of the Dakotas was moved from Yankton to Bismarck.

In 1900, McKenzie was convicted and imprisoned for his attempt to take control of disputed mining claims in Alaska. His railroad magnate friend, JAMES J. HILL, and the chairman of the Republican National Committee, Mark Hanna, persuaded President William McKinley to pardon McKenzie due to his ill health. The political boss was not too ill, however, to take part in a heated state campaign in 1906 in which the state's first Democratic governor, John Burke, was elected. With the growth of the Progressive movement and the founding of the Good Government League, McKenzie's power came to an end.

—*Candace Floyd*

SUGGESTED READING:

Robinson, Elwyn B. *History of North Dakota.* Lincoln, Nebr., 1966.

Wilkins, Robert P. *North Dakota: A Bicentennial History.* New York and Nashville, Tenn., 1977.

McKENZIE, DONALD

An original partner in the Pacific Fur Company, Donald McKenzie (1783–1851) was largely responsible for the company's abandonment of ASTORIA during the War of 1812. Born in Inverness, Scotland, McKenzie moved to Canada at the age of seventeen and, within a year, joined his brothers in the FUR TRADE as a clerk with the North West Company. Never happy with this employer, McKenzie was recruited by JOHN JACOB ASTOR and became a founding partner of the Pacific Fur Company in 1810. McKenzie proved his mettle as a member of the company's ill-fated overland expedition to Fort Astoria from 1810 to 1812 and quickly earned a reputation on the Pacific Coast as a tough trader. When war erupted between the United States and Great Britain in 1812, however, he believed a British attack on Astoria was imminent and used his position and influence to oversee the sale of the Pacific Fur Company to the North West Company in 1813. Astor looked upon the actions of his Canadian partner as nothing less than a betrayal.

With the demise of the Pacific Fur Company, McKenzie returned to the service of the North West Company as a partner and continued his trade activities in the Columbia region. After the North West Company and the HUDSON'S BAY COMPANY merged in 1821, he headed the Bow River expedition in 1822 to investigate the trade prospects of present-day southern Alberta. In 1825, he was named governor of Assiniboia and was responsible for overseeing the well-being of the Red River Colony (Winnipeg, Manitoba). He retired to Mayville, New York, in 1833 and died there as the result of a riding accident eighteen years later.

—*W. A. Waiser*

SUGGESTED READING:

Mackenzie, C. W. *Donald McKenzie: "King of the Northwest."* Los Angeles, 1937.

Ronda, J. R. *Astoria and Empire.* Lincoln, Nebr., 1990.

McKENZIE, KENNETH

Fur trader and founder of the Columbia Fur Company, Kenneth McKenzie (1797–1861) was labeled by a contemporary as "the ablest trader that the American Fur Company ever possessed." Born in Scotland, McKenzie learned the fur trading business as a clerk for the North West Company and worked briefly for HUDSON'S BAY COMPANY before moving to St. Louis in 1822. There, he allied with other former North West and Hudson's Bay men to form the Columbia Fur Company. Quickly McKenzie's outfit established a formidable presence on the Minnesota, Red, and Missouri rivers, a region also coveted by JOHN JACOB ASTOR'S AMERICAN FUR COMPANY.

Astor's much larger company first attempted to drive McKenzie out of business. When this effort failed, Astor proposed a confederation of the two companies. In 1829, McKenzie established FORT UNION at the confluence of the Yellowstone and Missouri rivers, where he created the headquarters for a profitable Indian trade that reached to the Rocky Mountains.

Pioneering the advance of steamboats to the farthest reaches of the Missouri, McKenzie induced Astor to supply Fort Union by boat. Living regally at the fort, McKenzie earned the name "king of the Missouri" but soon ran afoul of government officials. When McKenzie could not obtain necessary quantities of liquor for trade, he began making whiskey from Indian corn. Government officials learned of McKenzie's whiskey making in 1834 and threatened to revoke the American Fur Company's trade license. He accepted responsibility and retired to St. Louis.

McKenzie thereafter dabbled in the FUR TRADE but never again so prominently. He occasionally traveled to the upper Missouri country and, in later life, amassed a substantial fortune from importing and commission businesses and land and railroad investments.

—Paul L. Hedren

SUGGESTED READING:

Mattison, Ray H. "Kenneth McKenzie." In *The Mountain Men and the Fur Trade of the Far West.* Vol 2. Edited by LeRoy R. Hafen. Glendale, Calif., 1965.

McLAUGHLIN, JAMES

Indian agent and SITTING BULL'S nemesis, James McLaughlin (1843–1923) was born in Ontario, Canada, worked as a blacksmith, and engaged in a variety of business ventures before heading the Devils Lake Indian Agency in the Dakota Territory in 1876. After compiling a record of competence in agency management, McLaughlin took over the larger agency at Standing Rock in 1881. Married to a Dakota woman, McLaughlin was bettered versed in the Sioux language and customs than most agents, and he genuinely believed that the federal policies of education and agriculture would improve the lives of the Indians in his care. Authoritarian in his ways, he had little truck with Indians who resisted his ideas of Indian progress.

Sitting Bull, leader of the Hunkpapa Sioux, had arrived at the Standing Rock Agency in 1883 and, in his attempt to cleave to the old ways, immediately came into conflict with the Indian agent. Throughout the remainder of the 1880s, the two fought for the souls of the reservation Indians, but little that McLaughlin did diminished Sitting Bull's influence over his people. When the Sioux embraced the GHOST DANCE religion in the summer of 1890, McLaughlin saw the movement as a serious threat to the peace of the reservation. Convinced that Sitting Bull was one of the "fomenters of disturbance" caused by the Ghost Dance, McLaughlin ordered the chief's arrest, an order that resulted in the Sioux leader's death.

McLaughlin continued to work for the BUREAU OF INDIAN AFFAIRS after the WOUNDED KNEE MASSACRE that followed Sitting Bull's death. The agent published recollections of his career in 1910, entitled—without irony—*My Friend the Indian.*

—Patricia Hogan

See also: United States Indian Policy

SUGGESTED READING:

McLaughlin, James. *My Friend the Indian.* Lincoln, Nebr., 1989.

Pfaller, Rev. Louis L., O.S.B. *James McLaughlin: The Man with the Indian Heart.* New York, 1978.

McLOUGHLIN, JOHN

Chief factor for the HUDSON'S BAY COMPANY in the Oregon territories from 1824 to 1846, John McLoughlin (1784–1857) was born in Rivière-du-Loup, Quebec. At the age of fourteen, he began the study of medicine and was licensed to practice in 1803. He worked for a time as company physician at Kaministikwia for the North West Company, founded in Montreal in 1783, but he soon turned his attention from medicine to the FUR TRADE. When the North West Company merged with the Hudson's Bay Company, he secured the position of chief factor in charge of the Las La Pluie district. In July 1824, he became general superintendent of the Columbia District, a position he retained for twenty years.

John McLoughlin. *Courtesy Library of Congress.*

Headquartered at Fort Vancouver, a huge stockade including warehouses, stores, offices, a schoolhouse, dormitories, and a powder magazine, McLoughlin was in control of a territory jointly occupied by Great Britain and the United States. Thwarting his efforts to make the region highly profitable to the Hudson's Bay Company were the American fur traders, who legally were not under his control. To combat the American competition, McLoughlin persuaded the company to increase the attractiveness of company employment, and he encouraged some American traders to sell their interests to the company.

Methodist missionaries led by Jason Lee and Marcus Whitman were not so easily dealt with as the American fur traders. While Lee's party settled on the Willamette River, south of the Columbia River, Whitman's group settled in the interior of the territory. Both groups sent back East reports of Oregon's bounty, and within a few years, massive numbers of emigrants had settled in the territory. The Hudson's Bay Company then decided to remove its headquarters to the north to Vancouver Island, and McLoughlin retired in 1846 and settled on land he owned in Oregon City.

—*Candace Floyd*

See also: Whitman, Marcus and Narcissa

Suggested reading:

Holman, Frederick V. *Dr. John McLoughlin: The Father of Oregon.* Cleveland, Ohio, 1907.

McNELLY, LEANDER H.

Captain in the Texas Rangers, Leander H. McNelly (1844–1877) was born in Brooke County, Virginia, the son of P. J. and Mary (Downey) McNelly. In 1860, after residing briefly in Missouri, McNelly migrated to Washington County, Texas, where he herded sheep for rancher T. J. Burton. On September 13, 1861, he enlisted in the Texas Mounted Volunteers of General Henry Hopkins Sibley's Confederate brigade. Over the following two years, he won distinction at Val Verde in the New Mexico campaign and then at the Battle of Galveston on July 4, 1863. McNelly was promoted to captain of scouts on December 19 with orders to recruit his own company. He enlisted a group of mounted Texas troopers for a Confederate campaign in Louisiana. In March 1864, they participated in the capture of Brashear City; in April, at the Battle of Mansfield; and late in May, against federal troops, who were known as the "Texas Traitors" and commanded by future Texas governor E. J. Davis. Upon his discharge in 1865, McNelly took up farming west of Brenham, Texas, married Carrie Cheek, and had two children. In 1870, for some inexplicable reason, he accepted Republican Governor Davis's offer to be one of the four captains in the state police; during the next four years, he became known as a fearless and incorruptible law officer.

Late in the spring of 1874, after the election of Democratic Governor Richard Coke, McNelly was appointed captain of the Special Force of Rangers; his orders were to "clear out" badmen from the state. He and his men first went to DeWitt County, where, for the remainder of the year, they were partially effective in curbing lawlessness engendered by the Sutton-Taylor Feud. They dampened terrorist activities between the two factions and thereby paved the way for a peaceful accord. McNelly then proceeded to his next assignment in the Nueces Strip (between the Nueces River and the Rio Grande), where Mexican bandits were rustling cattle, burning ranchos and villages, and murdering the inhabitants with impunity. For two years, the McNelly Rangers were extremely effective. Two actions were memorable. On June 12, 1875, they killed twelve Mexican marauders and stacked their bodies "like cord wood" in the Brownsville square; on November 19, 1875, McNelly led his thirty-one Texas Rangers south of the Rio Grande in a successful attack on Mexican rustlers at their Las Cuevas headquarters.

Because of a tubercular condition, McNelly resigned his command on January 26, 1877. He died on his plantation in Washington County, Texas, on September 4, 1877, and was buried at Burton. Texas Rangers still revere him today for his statement: "You can't lick a man who just keeps on a comin' on."

—*Ben Procter*

SUGGESTED READING:

Procter, Ben. *Just One Riot: Episodes of Texas Rangers in the 20th Century.* Austin, Tex., 1991.

Webb, Walter Prescott. *The Texas Rangers: A Century of Frontier Defense.* Austin, Tex., 1965.

McPHERSON, AIMEE SEMPLE

Founder of the Foursquare Gospel church, Aimee Semple McPherson (1890–1944) was born in Ontario, Canada. She reigned as one of Pentecostalism's foremost EVANGELISTS during the early twentieth century. At the time of her death, her church had branches around the world.

Raised in the Salvation Army church, she was baptized into the Pentecostal faith at the age of seventeen. In 1908, she married Pentecostal minister Robert Semple and joined him on the revival circuit. In 1909, Pentecostal leaders ordained her as a preacher. The Semples then traveled as missionaries to China, where Robert died of typhoid. She returned to the United States to work for the Salvation Army but quit in 1912 to marry Harold McPherson. Soon, however, she developed an illness that she interpreted as God's punishment for her abandonment of evangelism. In 1915, she left her husband and embarked on a career as an itinerant preacher, advocating speaking in tongues, premillennialism (the notion that Christ's second coming will precede his thousand-year reign on earth), and Biblical fundamentalism. Appearing in a white dress, white shoes, and a blue cape, she became famous for her preaching and faith healing.

Her popularity soaring, Aimee McPherson settled in Los Angeles and, in 1923, opened the Angelus Temple, headquarters of the Foursquare Gospel church. Her elaborate theatrical worship services drew large crowds. Hiring a musical director and orchestra, she dramatized her sermons with costumed actors and live animals. She established a Bible college and a radio station to broadcast her sermons.

Yet scandals haunted her, the most sensational occurring in 1926, when she disappeared while swimming in the ocean. Although most believed that she had drowned, a month later she reappeared, claiming she had been kidnapped. Rumors circulated that she had joined an Angelus Temple radioman for a tryst. A grand jury indicted her for perjury, but the district attorney dropped the case due to lack of evidence.

Meanwhile, her churches expanded nationally and internationally. During the Great Depression, she established an employment agency and a soup kitchen. But she suffered through illnesses, estrangement from family members, and a third failed marriage. In 1944, she died of an accidental drug overdose during a revival tour. Foursquare Gospel churches endured and continued to grow into the 1990s.

—*Jill Watts*

SUGGESTED READING:

Epstein, Daniel Mark. *Sister Aimee: The Life of Aimee Semple McPherson.* New York, 1993.

Thomas, Lately. *Storming Heaven: The Lives and Turmoils of Minnie Kennedy and Aimee Semple McPherson.* New York, 1970.

McSWEEN, ALEXANDER A.

SEE: Lincoln County War

McWHIRTER, MARTHA WHITE

Founder and leader of the WOMAN'S COMMONWEALTH, a celibate utopian society, Martha White (1827–1904) was born in Gainsboro, Tennessee. She married George McWhirter in 1845 and moved with him to Bell County, Texas, in 1855. McWhirter bore twelve children between 1846 and 1867; five survived to adulthood.

As she matured, McWhirter increasingly objected to women's economic subservience to men in conventional marriage; she also objected to the sectarianism of conventional religious denominations. Her conflicts were resolved in 1867, when she received a divine vision. She was inspired to "sanctify" herself through a commitment to ecumenism (a unified Christian church) and celibacy (disavowing sexual relations). The women who followed McWhirter in her commitment to these values, including three generations of women in her own family, became known as Sanctificationists. They formed the nucleus of the Woman's Commonwealth, which McWhirter led, first in Belton, Texas, and then in Washington, D.C., for thirty years.

McWhirter's charismatic leadership style is evident in her many letters, necessitated by the group's varied businesses. In her letters, she often denounced worldliness, by which she meant materialism, sex, and unbridled familial affection. In 1892, McWhirter wrote a petition to the Texas legislature demanding married women's property rights. Her business acumen earned her recognition as the first female member of the Belton Board of Trade in 1894. After 1900, she participated in suffrage and socialist organizations.

—*Sally L. Kitch*

SUGGESTED READING:
James, Eleanor. "Martha White McWhirter (1827–1904)." In *Women in Early Texas.* Edited by Evelyn M. Carrington. Austin, Tex., 1975.
Kitch, Sally L. *This Strange Society of Women: Reading the Letters and Lives of Woman's Commonwealth.* Columbus, Ohio, 1993.

MEAD, ELWOOD

IRRIGATION and RECLAMATION pioneer Elwood Mead (1858–1936) was born near Patriot, Indiana. Enrolling in the new land-grant institution, Purdue University, he received a degree in agriculture and worked for a time for the UNITED STATES ARMY CORPS OF ENGINEERS in surveying and building levees on the Wabash River.

He followed his Purdue mentor, Charles L. Ingersoll, to the Colorado State Agricultural College at Fort Collins in 1882. There, he first came into contact with irrigation enterprises diverting water from Colorado's eastern slope. Mead received a degree in civil engineering from the Iowa Agricultural College at Ames and, for a time, read law. In 1885, he returned to Colorado, where he was appointed assistant state engineer and professor of irrigation engineering, the first such position in the United States. In 1888, Mead was appointed the first territorial engineer of Wyoming where he played an influential role in mapping irrigation enterprises and passing water laws.

Mead became influential in the irrigation movement in the West, moving from regional to national to international prominence. In 1899, he was designated head of the Office of Irrigation Investigation within the United States Department of Agriculture. He accepted a visiting appointment as professor of institutions and practice of irrigation at the University of California at Berkeley in 1901. His lectures were published in 1903 as *Irrigation Institutions.*

In 1907, Mead moved to Australia, where he worked for eight years helping the state of Victoria create irrigation works in the Murray-Darling-Murrumbidgee river system, enact water laws, and create an irrigation-colony settlement system. He subsequently became an international consultant to a number of foreign governments.

When Mead returned to the United States, he rejoined the Berkeley faculty, worked as cost consultant on federal reclamation projects for the Department of the Interior, and helped design a scheme to create agricultural colonies for veterans of World War I. He also worked with California officials to establish irrigation colonies at Durham and Delhi.

In 1924, Mead was named United States commissioner of reclamation. He played a significant role in planning and constructing several reclamation projects including the erection of Boulder Dam (now HOOVER DAM). He suffered a stroke shortly after celebrating his eighty-seventh birthday and died on January 16, 1936. The reservoir impounded by Boulder Dam was named Lake Mead in his honor.

—*Donald E. Green*

SUGGESTED READING:
Conkin, Paul. "The Vision of Elwood Mead." *Agricultural History* 34 (1960): 88–97.
Kluger, James R. *Turning on Water with a Shovel: The Career of Elwood Mead.* Albuquerque, N. Mex., 1992.

MEARS, OTTO

Merchant and toll-road and railroad builder Otto Mears (1840–1931) was born in Russia. Orphaned at the age of three, Mears arrived in San Francisco eight years later and began working as a teamster. He served with a California infantry regiment in the New Mexico Territory and was discharged at Las Cruces in 1864. After working for a Santa Fe trading firm, he moved to Conejos and then to Saguache in the Colorado Territory as a storekeeper. Eventually, he owned stores in Saguache and in Ouray. He supplied flour to area miners and soldiers, and, learning the Ute language and making friends with Chief Ouray, he delivered staples to the Los Pinos Agency of the Utes. Following the massacre of NATHAN COOK MEEKER in the White River Massacre, Mears helped rescue the captured women and served on the commission that negotiated the Ute removal.

Mears spent one term in the Colorado House of Representatives and thirty-four years on the Board of Capitol Managers.

He has been called the "pathfinder of the San Juan" because of the toll roads he built in southwestern Colorado between 1867 and 1886. Later, he constructed three railroads in the San Juan area. After the 1893 economic crash, Mears moved to the East where he attempted unsuccessfully to establish a resort in Mary-

Otto Mears pictured with Ouray, chief of the Ute Indians. *Courtesy Denver Public Library, Western History Department.*

land and then worked with the early Mack truck firm. He returned to live in Colorado in 1906. In 1917, he moved to Pasadena, California, where he spent the rest of his life.

—*Liston E. Leyendecker*

SUGGESTED READING:

Hafen, LeRoy R., "Otto Mears, 'Pathfinder of the San Juan.'" *The Colorado Magazine* 9 (March 1932): 71–74.

Kushner, Ervan F. *Otto Mears: His Life and Times with Notes on the Alferd Packer Case.* Frederick, Colo., 1979.

MEDICINE

Frontier medicine

In the nineteenth-century trans-Mississippi West, as in the rest of the United States, the treatment of disease was often rooted in local custom, not necessarily in professional training or scientific knowledge. Laypeople on the frontier combined folk medicine with information gleaned from do-it-yourself manuals, medical dictionaries, and popular books, such as Alexander Thomas's *Family Physician,* William Buchan's *Domestic Medicine,* the anonymous *House Surgeon and Physician: Designed to Assist Heads of Families, Travelers, and Sea Faring People,* or—perhaps the most prominent—Dr. John C. Gunn's *Domestic Medicine, or Poor Man's Friend.* The American Medical Association was not formed until 1847, and even then, it was criticized for its lack of standardization; doctors, not yet part of a professional group, were trained through an eclectic combination of private study, formal schooling, and apprenticeships; medical schools, businesses run by local practitioners for profit, catered to the lower-middle class and working class, poor students who paid to attend lectures of dubious value when it came actually to treating illness or injury.

Few on the frontier agreed about what constituted legitimate practice, and suspicious pioneers, as well as some doctors themselves and many educated Westerners, remained skeptical of those attempting to unify medicine under one, universally accepted form of therapy. Common folk and political leaders viewed calls for uniformity as a ploy by this or that medical-interest group to claim an unjustified measure of legitimacy, and thus a proliferation of groups promoted a variety of therapies, the tenets and training of which differed. Urban doctors did not offer the same medicine practiced by rural doctors, and both competed with homeopaths, allopaths, eclectics, Thomasonians, and a host of others, including druggists and medicine-show salesmen hawking a range of patent medicines, which were often addictive or outright dangerous to the user's health. All medical men and women adjusted their treatments to the market and prescribed differently for different classes and ethnic groups.

Most rural doctors relied on herbal treatments, and botanically minded groups such as the Thomasonians, and later the eclectics, who incorporated local folk medicine into their therapeutics, were popular in the West. Cities saw a wider range of family practitioners competing for patients, although most tended to be "family" or "community" doctors engaged in general practice with only a few specializing in surgery, ophthalmology, and other areas. The bulk of the medical profession consisted of family doctors who lived in the communities where they practiced, made house calls or treated patients in home offices, joined the same churches and clubs as their patients, presided at such significant events in their patients' lives as births and deaths, and, not uncommonly, moved into their patients' homes for the duration of an illness. Compared to the often brutal therapies of medical doctors, based on the age-old theory of the human body's "humors," the milder therapies of homeopathy, with a perhaps more elegant rationale, appealed strongly to merchants and rich urbanites.

The frontier army proved a training ground for many doctors, especially surgeons, that more than rivaled the medical schools of the day. In the U.S. Army Medical Department, the young practitioner was likely to see duty in every aspect of frontier medicine. During the five years after the United States–Mexican War, when the army's troop strength averaged 10,000, the Medical Department treated 134,708 cases, with some 1,835 of its patients dying. In 1849 alone, 700 soldiers came down with cholera, and half of them died from it. That same year, the army, as historian Robert M. Utley says, was "prostrated" by 7,000 cases of dysentery, which killed 151 men. Fevers traveling the Isthmus route through Panama, respiratory ailments and venereal diseases, scurvy from a diet lacking in fresh vegetables, all debilitated thousands each year and killed hundreds, so that, on average, each soldier had to be hospitalized three times a year, and every year, one in 33 of them died of some disease. Indian hostilities and war, of course, increased the number and type of cases an army doctor handled, adding to a "curriculum" described thus by one doctor: "The surgery was amputations for frost-bite, gunshot wounds, fractures and dislocations."

On the other hand, the army was not well served by frontier medicine, which was primitive, nor by its medical officers, since low pay and the discomforts of service in the West discouraged able practitioners from seeking a career in the military. Although every post and fixed detachment rated a surgeon or assistant surgeon, Utley notes that the "medical department never attained a strength or competence commensurate with the need" for effective medicine in the army. To close the gap between such a need and the lack of supply resulting from the army's perennial difficulty in attracting qualified doctors, the surgeon general sometimes contracted with civilian doctors. Whether regular or contract, "most army surgeons lacked the competence of their brethren in civil life," which, in any case, was not all that high. Not surprisingly, rude medicine practiced by a poorly trained corps of physicians too small to meet its responsibilities added up to an excessively ill army with a high mortality rate. The chances of recovery for a wounded man amounted to less that 50 percent, and if he happened to be shot in the abdomen, the recovery rate was closer to zero. Abdominal operations were so dangerous that few army surgeons attempted them, and after simple amputations, performed quickly without anesthesia, patients frequently died from shock and loss of blood.

Civilians did not fare much better. Surgeons and physicians were often feared, and many common folk set their own sprains or broken bones or had them set by friends who were good at that sort of thing. Stories abounded in the West of mountain men and pioneers performing self-amputation or amputating the limbs of a companion. Even the practice of everyday medicine involved draconian measures. Until at least the Civil War, bloodletting was popular, with physicians drawing of a pint or two at a time by cutting into a vein or scoring the skin. Leeches accomplished the same goal more slowly. Doctors used strong purgatives and emetics and applied heated cups to the bodies of their patients. Since illness was frequently equated with moral failing, doctors told themselves and their patients that the cruelty of the treatment was an appropriate consequence of transgression. It is little wonder that many turned when they could to home remedies, local herbalists, Native American healers, and Hispanic folk-medicine practitioners or bought the promises of patent-medicine salesmen and faith healers common to medicine shows or camp meetings.

Folk medicine

Lacking knowledge of or even fearing the era's medical arts, Westerners saw folk medicine as a viable health-care alternative and responded to injury and illness with a pharmacopoeia of what they sometimes called "old wives'" remedies. They applied poultices of elm bark or flaxseed to bullet wounds, gave pewter spoon shavings with sugar to those suffering from worms, fed children with hives or the "croup" (cough) garlic or roasted onions, cut open snake bites with sharp knives and packed the wound with gunpowder, and drained the blood of black cats from amputated ears and tails to treat skin inflammations (often caused by erysipelas, or "St. Anthony's fire"). The strong survived the treatment as well as the disease; the weak more often died. Pioneer women, in particular, often improvised better home treatments. They mashed onions in sugar to create an effective cough syrup, dissolved gunpowder in water to produce a serviceable eyewash, wrapped onions in tobacco and baked them in the hearth before squeezing out juice to serve as a cure for earache. European folk-wisdom and local materials served as the basis for most home remedies. Goose grease and turpentine became a standard salve for colds and, indeed, almost any disorder. Pioneers with dandruff washed their hair with coal oil. Asthmatics drank buttercup tea. Those with snakebites sometimes applied warm manure to the swelling, while those with earaches sometimes poured warm urine in their ears. Some drank sassafras tea to get rid of spring fever and ate well-done roasted mice to cure measles. Those with boils sometimes carried nine pellets from a shotgun shell around in their pockets; those with warts threw beans over their left shoulders; those suffering from rheumatism stuffed a potato in their pants.

In many Indian tribes, shamans acted not only as ceremonial priests and soothsayers but as healers on call to treat any member of the tribe who fell ill or was wounded in the hunt or in battle, a function reflected in the Euro-American use of the term *medicine men* to describe such healers. Native American healers carried bags of secret conjures and talismans to aid them in their work and often performed ritual chants during the healing process. Among the tools of the trade, the shaman might number dried fingers, deer tails, rattles, and a small sack of curative herbs—black nightshade, which the Comanches used to treat tuberculosis; Indian turnip, a Pawnee headache powder; yarrow, which the Utes used as a salve for cuts and bruises. Many herbs carried what physicians today would admit were genuine curative powers. The Dakotas effectively treated asthma with powdered skunk-cabbage roots, the Kiowas prevented dandruff with a plant called soaproot, the Cheyennes drank a tonic of boiled wild mint for nausea, and the Crees chewed spruce-tree cones to soothe sore throats. Some herbal cures were probably of no more value than today's over-the-counter cold medicines, and some were based on understandings as equally incorrect about the nature of the illness being treated or the cure desired. But Prince Maximilian, dying of scurvy at Fort Clark in 1834, was cured by the Indian remedy of eating raw bulbs of wild onion, and a Cheyenne saved William Bent from choking to death from an inflamed throat by removing the infected membrane with a hunk of sinew strung with sandburs and buffalo fat. Eventually the Euro-American medical profession would recognize Native American medicine by accepting hundreds of Indian drugs as having intrinsic medicinal value in its official pharmaceutical journals.

Among the Spanish-speaking population of the Southwest, the acceptance of folk medicine was widespread, an attitude generally referred to as *curanderismo.* Several classes of folk healers shared in common an extensive knowledge of herbs and their curative powers: *curanderos, medicos, parteras, arbolarios,* and *sobadores.* Called in general *curanderos,* the various healers formed a group of specialists, often more specialized in the past than their descendants are today, whose services varied, depending on the ailment.

The *arbolarios* (or *herbolarios)* began as dispensers of herbs but, in time, extended their practices to the more lucrative casting out of evil spirits and the undoing of hexes, or *embrujos.* In attempting to reverse the mischief of witches, *arbolarios* often had to establish family histories and come up with rough mental diagnoses in order to find the causes of the curses, and inadvertently, they came to act as something like folk psychiatrists helping to relieve the anxieties of their patients. *Pateras* once functioned solely as midwives, who might occasionally prescribe home remedies connected with their trade. But they knew what was good for *empacho,* a common ailment among infants suffering from indigestion, and all sorts of rubefacients and brewings to recommend for growing children. Particularly as the need for MIDWIFERY declined, they expanded their practices to advising young wives in the care of their offspring and to prescribing herbs, occasionally even for adults, although men still preferred male *curanderos. Medicos* were often more than mere folk healers. Especially the women among them combined religion with healing by calling on God and various saints when dispensing their brews. They made the sign of the cross over their concoctions and might utter a benediction, thus giving the patient greater faith in the medicine. Sometimes these faith healers were called *sanadores,* which literally means "healer," and a few traveled all over the Southwest in toned-down, more religious versions of the spectacular medicine shows staged by their more flamboyant Anglo counterparts. Finally there were the *sobadores* (masseurs), who could set a dislocated joint with a slight turn or single jerk, give good rubdowns for aching bones and muscles, or provide the weary and ailing teamsters on the Santa Fe Trail with an *apreton de arriero,* a "driver's hug." A combination folk osteopath and chiropractor, the *sobadore's* therapy was immediate and on-the-spot.

Some of the herbs (and their uses) peddled by the *curanderos* became proverbial, familiar to every Hispanic housewife, just as some European folk remedies appeared in the medicine chests of nearly all Anglo pioneer homes. Combining curing and Catholicism, more miracle workers than showmen, *curanderos,* nevertheless, did a brisk business and traveled about the region replenishing the *alacenas,* or "cupboards," of folks, who kept a basic supply of herbal remedies in the days when doctors were rare. Most *curandero* prescriptions called for teas, brewings, and compresses, with animal oils and fats such as skunk oil, coyote salve, and snake oil high on the lists of ingredients. Healers rubbed a newborn pig on epileptics, prescribed ground badger—baked and mixed with magpie soup—for asthma and cat's flesh for tuberculosis, suggested wearing underwear around the neck for cramps, stanched open wounds with compresses made from cobwebs, stamped Bull Durham and Tuxedo tobacco labels on the foreheads of those suffering migraines, and helped young men win the hearts of young women by giving them dried jackrabbit bones to toss in the longed-for maidens' soup or coffee. One of the more popular healing brews in the Southwest was *Te de la Abuela,* or "Grandma's Tea," which many families used at regular intervals. A healer named Benigno Romero did a brisk business in Albuquerque with Sanadora, a bottled salve widely advertised in local Spanish papers, until 1919 when the U.S. Post Office stopped its sale on a legal technicality. Many almanacs printed in Spanish carried long advertisements for *curandero* folk medicines and herbs.

Folk medicine provided both Anglos and Hispanics with a degree of comfort, security, and peace of mind in a region of the country that lacked effective health care. And even after the turn of the century and the rise of modern medicine, folk remedies and home cures continued to appeal to the poor and the Spanish-speaking, who could neither afford doctors nor communicate their symptoms and ailments effectively to them. Indeed, many Mexican Americans were all but excluded from modern health-care systems. Throughout the 1920s, for example, the infant mortality rate among Mexican Americans in Los Angeles was three times higher than that of Euro-Americans, and in a city where Mexican Americans made up one-tenth the population, they suffered from 25 percent of the cases of tuberculosis. Based on mimetic and sympathetic magic, folk medicine attempted to explain and control the vicissitudes of daily life, to influence the course of the future, and to direct the workings of nature. Folk medicine functioned for common folks much as did the proverbs, maxims, beliefs, omens, and other expressions of folk wisdom on which folk medicine's cures often depended.

Modern medicine

Around the turn of the century, reforms in medical education, standardized training for physicians, control of entry to the profession and the licensing of doctors, the rise of public-health departments in big cities, and the increased use of hospitals for medical care as well as confinement led to improvements in medical practices in the West as they did in the rest of the country. Long enjoying a reputation for its salubrious climate, the region early on became a haven for health farms and sanitariums in California, Colorado, and Arizona, where "consumptives" and "invalids," two euphemisms for those suffering from tuberculosis, sought climate-based cures. As a region traditionally strong in public colleges and universities and government-funded research, the West held its own in the scientific revolution that transformed medicine in the twentieth century. By the late twentieth century, for example, Texas hospitals were known for open-heart surgery; the University of Iowa (which created buffered painkillers), for experimental medicine; Stanford University, for major advances in organ-transplant operations and therapy. The region also pioneered in health insurance and modern health-care delivery systems (courtesy of shipbuilding magnate HENRY J. KAISER's creation of company-sponsored employee insurance programs and health-maintenance organizations, or HMOs). Hawaii and Oregon also led the country in health-care reform, the former for its introduction of the first universal health-care insurance program, the latter for its capitation of payments for fee-for-service charges and its rankings for "rationing" procedures reimbursed by public funds.

—*Charles Phillips*

SEE ALSO: Disease; Doctors; Native American Cultures: Disease, Spiritual Life; Nursing

SUGGESTED READING:

Ashburn, P. M. *A History of the Medical Department of the U.S. Army.* New York, 1929.

Campa, Arthur A. *Hispanic Culture in the South West.* Norman, Okla., 1979.

Flexner, James T. *Doctors on Horseback.* New York, 1969.

Shikes, Robert H. *Rocky Mountain Medicine: Doctors, Drugs, and Disease in Early Colorado.* Boulder, Colo., 1986.

Starr, Paul. *The Social Transformation of American Medicine: The Rise of a Sovereign Profession and the Making of a Vast Industry.* New York, 1982.

Vogel, Virgil J. *American Indian Medicine.* Norman, Okla., 1970.

Weiner, Michael A. *Earth Medicine—Earth Foods.* New York, 1972.

MEDICINE LODGE TREATY OF 1867

When the Civil War ended in 1865, Americans and European immigrants resumed their westward migration across the continent for settlements in California, Colorado, and other areas. Between the Western settlements and the Easterners lay the Great Plains. For some pioneers, the region was only a flat expanse between them and their new lives farther west. Others, however, saw in the vast terrains of places like Kansas and Nebraska possibilities for settlement and successful ventures in farming. The problem for the sojourners and the settlers of Great Plains was, as the federal government saw it, that Native American tribes inhabiting region threatened lines of communication and transportation as well as new and fragile settlements. Violent conflict between Indians and whites, the government realized, would only intensify as more settlers moved west.

A *Harper's Weekly* illustration shows Comanche Indians making their way to Medicine Lodge Creek for the council with the U.S. government's "peace commission." October 16, 1867. *Courtesy Library of Congress.*

In the summer of 1867, the federal government formed a "peace commission" to secure an agreement with leaders of the Southern Plains tribes: Cheyennes, Arapahos, Kiowas, Comanches, and Plains Apaches. The commission's charge was to convince the tribes to give up the lands they lived and hunted on and move immediately onto reservations in present-day Oklahoma. In exchange for their removal, the United States government would supply the Indians with schools, cattle herds, and instruction in farming.

Before the Medicine Lodge Treaty, the government had viewed the Great Plains as "one big reservation," where tribal peoples could live their traditional way of life. The treaty, however, signaled the beginning of the federal policy of assimilation and tribal annihilation that the government continued to enforce for the next three-quarters of a century.

The tribal leaders who signed the treaty on October 21 and 28, 1867, likely saw it merely as a means of ending years of sporadic hostilities. When the council ended, most tribes simply returned to their hunting grounds, and the conflicts between Indians and whites continued. The Native Americans who moved to the reservations found that the U.S. Congress was unwilling to appropriate funds for their support and that military patrols attacked them when soldiers could not find the hostile Indians they were ordered to subdue.

Although the implementation of the Medicine Lodge Treaty faltered, the Indian policies it embodied endured. These policies were enforced by peaceful means when adequate, but the wars between Indians and whites that continued for the next two decades suggest the price at which "peace" was bought.

—Patricia Hogan

SEE ALSO: Central Plains Indian Wars; Native American Peoples: Peoples of the Great Plains; United States Indian Policy

SUGGESTED READING:

Brown, Dee. *Bury My Heart at Wounded Knee: An Indian History of the American West.* New York, 1970.

Fritz, Henry E. *The Movement for Indian Assimilation, 1860–1890.* Philadelphia, 1963.

MEDILL, WILLIAM

Commissioner of Indian Affairs from 1845 to 1849 and governor of Ohio, William Medill (1802–1865) was born in New Castle County, Delaware. He studied at Newark Academy and, in 1830, began working for the law office of Philemon Beecher in Lancaster, Ohio. Medill was admitted to the Ohio bar in 1832.

Three years later, he was elected to the state legislature. In 1838, he was elected to the United States Congress as a Democrat.

In 1844, Medill was appointed second assistant postmaster general and, the following year, became commissioner of Indian affairs. Although his appointment was based on politics rather than knowledge of Indian policy, he was determined to educate himself regarding past policies and problems of Indian-white relations. He concurred with his predecessor, T. Hartley Crawford, that the future of Native Americans depended on their assimilation into white culture, and he administered Indian affairs on this premise.

Having concluded a treaty with the Cherokees in 1846, Medill argued that they were not entitled to compensation related to their removal westward as provided for in the Treaty of New Echota in 1835. The Senate Indian Committee reached a different conclusion in 1850, leading to an appropriation to settle the Cherokee claim in 1851. Medill also refused to intervene to protect the landed interests of Choctaws who remained in Mississippi by the Treaty of Dancing Rabbit Creek in 1830. He argued that they were entirely under the jurisdiction of the state.

Medill rejected the idea of educating young Native Americans in the East and opted instead for a system of using Christian missionaries to teach them agricultural and mechanical arts, basic academic skills, and Christian values. Medill concentrated on restructuring the Indian Office and reforming Indian trade practices (Intercourse Act of 1847). He proposed that Indian lands west of the Mississippi be consolidated by creating two large reservations—one in the north and one in the south—with a corridor between to allow safe passage for settlers moving to the West.

With the election of Zachary Taylor as president in 1848, Medill's days in the Indian Office were numbered. His efforts to curb corruption in the Indian trade had created many enemies in Washington, and he was replaced by Orlando Brown in 1849.

Despite a bitter end to his years as commissioner of Indian affairs, Medill's political career was far from over. He presided over the Ohio state constitutional convention in 1850 and became lieutenant-governor of Ohio in 1852 and governor from 1853 to 1856. Under President James Buchanan, he served as comptroller of the United States Treasury from 1857 to 1861.

—*Henry E. Fritz and Marie L. Fritz*

SEE ALSO: United States Indian Policy

SUGGESTED READING:

Harmon, George Dewey. *Sixty Years of Indian Affairs: 1789–1850.* Chapel Hill, N.C., 1941.

Kvasnicka, Robert M., and Herman J. Viola, eds. *The Commissioners of Indians Affairs, 1824–1877.* Lincoln, Nebr., 1979.

Trennert, Robert A., Jr. *Alternative to Extinction: Federal Indian Policy and the Beginnings of the Reservation System, 1846–51.* Philadelphia, 1975.

MEEK, JOSEPH LAFAYETTE

A distinguished mountain man and early settler of the Oregon Territory, Joseph LaFayette Meek (1810–1875) was born in Virginia. He left home while still a teenager and traveled to Missouri where his brother Stephen worked for William Sublette. Meek took a job with Sublette and left for the mountains on March 17, 1829. After the RENDEZVOUS in July of that year, he and his trapping party were joined by David Jackson and JEDEDIAH STRONG SMITH.

Meek rapidly learned the beaver business and became a "free trapper," working primarily for the ROCKY MOUNTAIN FUR COMPANY. In 1833, he accompanied JOSEPH REDDEFORD WALKER's party to California and later joined JAMES (JIM) BRIDGER's group. Meek had several Indian wives.

Joseph LaFayette Meek. *Courtesy Oregon Historical Society.*

In the summer of 1840, Meek and Robert Newell gave up trapping and drove wagons from Fort Hall to the Willamette Valley in Oregon. In 1843, Meek was elected sheriff and, in 1846, won a seat in the legislature.

After the attack by Indians on the mission of Marcus and Narcissa Whitman, the Oregon legislature elected Meek to travel to Washington to solicit aid and protection. With no financing, he left the territory in January 1848, and after arriving in Washington, he lobbied Congress to pass a territorial bill and give him a commission as U.S. marshal.

Meek continued to operate his farm and lived to see the story of his life, Frances Fuller Victor's *River of the West,* published in 1871.

—*Charles E. Hanson, Jr.*

See also: Fur Trade; Mountain Men; Trappers

Suggested reading:

Tobie, Harvey E. "Joseph L. Meek." In *The Mountain Men and the Fur Trade of the Far West.* Edited by LeRoy R. Hafen. Glendale, Calif., 1965.

Vestal, Stanley. *Joe Meek the Merry Mountain Man.* Lincoln, Nebr., 1963.

Victor, Frances Fuller. *The River of the West.* Hartford, Conn., 1871.

MEEKER, NATHAN COOK

Utopian, communitarian, and Indian agent Nathan Cook Meeker (1817–1879) was born in Euclid, Ohio. After attending school in Oberlin and Hudson, Ohio, Meeker became a wanderer, moving about the country and changing jobs many times in the years before 1870. Among his activities were newspaper work in New Orleans, teaching in Euclid and in Allentown, Pennsylvania, and owning small businesses in Euclid. A student of Fourier, the French utopian thinker who advocated a society based on communal associations known as "phalanxes," Meeker lectured on utopian ideas, and in 1846, he joined the Trumbull Phalanx at Braceville. He also developed his ideas in a novel, *The Adventures of Captain Armstrong,* which described the education of savages on a desert island.

After three years at Braceville, Meeker moved to southern Illinois, where he worked as a storekeeper and newspaper correspondent. In 1865, he became the agricultural editor of Horace Greeley's *New York Tribune.* In 1868, he published *Life in the West,* which dealt with the utopian community of Oneida and life in the Mississippi Valley. Sent West to study the Mormons, he found cooperative emigrant colonies and wrote about them instead. In 1869, Greeley and Meeker organized a cooperative settlement on the Platte River north of Denver on the Denver Pacific Railroad, By May 1870, Meeker had acquired 12,000 acres from the railroad and expected another 110,000. The cooperative settlement, based in the town of Greeley, recognized private ownership of land and individual rights but did not permit saloons or billiard halls; its settlers were regarded as cranks. Meeker stayed eight years in Greeley, where he ran the town's paper, until he became the Indian agent among the Utes at White River, Colorado.

Although apparently sympathetic to the Indians in some ways, Meeker sought to end their roving and buffalo hunting and attempted to teach them farming. In the fall of 1879, unable to persuade the Utes to change, Meeker sent for cavalry. Before the troops arrived, he and six assistants were killed on September 29, 1879, and the troops were ambushed in what was later called the White River Massacre. The event provided the government with the excuse to limit the Utes to new, small reservations in Utah.

—*Patrick H. Butler, III*

See also: Pacific Northwest Indians Wars

Suggested reading:

Sprague, Marshall. *Massacre: The Tragedy at White River.* Lincoln, Nebr., 1957. Reprint. 1980.

MERCER, ASA

See: Johnson County War

MESQUAKIE INDIANS

See: Native American Peoples: Peoples Removed from the East

MESQUITE

Present in the American Southwest for at least four thousand years, mesquite *(genus Prosopis)* appears in two major variations: the honey-mesquite *(Prosopis glandulosa juliflora)* and the screw-pod variety

(Strombocarpo odorata). In the era before permanent settlement, stands of this thorny, short-trunked shrub appeared mainly along watercourses. Periodic prairie fires limited its spread and maturity.

Native Americans ground nutritious mesquite beans into a meal or flour or used them to brew a slightly alcoholic beverage. They also rendered gum from the mesquite into glue.

Wild horses and cattle consumed the leaves and beans produced by the shrub's low branches. Dropped in fertilizing manure far from their point of origin, some undigested pods took root in new regions. The spread of cattle ranching and trail driving after the Civil War also abetted its export and introduced the shrub into the southern Great Plains.

Once established, the plant's deep, radiating root system robbed water from the surrounding land, suppressed grass, and sometimes dried up wells and springs. Mesquite flourished amid overgrazing and drought, grew denser and more impenetrable with time, and made the gathering of cattle difficult.

Fencing and farming further assisted its propagation, and by 1900, mesquite posed a serious threat to the Southwestern range. Ranchers fought its encroachment with fire and labor gangs. Tractors and other machinery later joined the battle. Despite these expensive and ongoing efforts, the tough, resilient, and aggressive mesquite continues to plague the ranchers and agricultural economy of the Southwest.

—B. Byron Price

SUGGESTED READING:

Byrns, Robert E. "The Ubiquitous Mesquite." *West Texas Historical Association Year Book* 14 (1969): 176–182.

Dobie, J. Frank. *A Vaquero of the Brush Country.* Dallas, Tex., 1929.

Inglis, Jack M. *A History of Vegetation on the Rio Grande Plain.* Bulletin 45, Texas Parks and Wildlife Department, 1964.

Watt, Peter. *Dictionary of the Old West 1850–1900.* New York, 1994.

METHODIST EPISCOPAL WOMAN'S HOME MISSIONARY SOCIETY

SEE: Woman's Home Missionary Society

METHODISTS

SEE: Protestants

MÉTIS PEOPLE

Canadians called people of mixed Indian and French or Scottish ancestry descended from local Indian women and European fur traders in the Red River region of what is now the province of Manitoba "Métis." Some scholars, studying the nature and origin of Métis communities, have argued that the "mixed-blood" heritage central to Métis culture was a widespread phenomenon that arose naturally, in the Canadian FUR TRADE, from the social and economic interaction between Indians and Europeans. Other, more recent work suggests that, to the contrary, Métis communities were the rare, if not unique, product of particular events and special historical circumstances. Despite the occasional discovery by researchers of new mixed communities connected to the fur trade, regardless of whether some scholars accept the Peace-Athapascan Iroquois (in northwestern Alberta) or the "Hudson Bay English" as true "Métis," most historians agree that, in at least two areas, Métis communities flourished—in the Great Lakes region and on the western plains of Canada. Certainly, the Métis played an important role in the fur trade of the Old Northwest and in the history and development of the Canadian West.

St. Lawrence–Great Lakes Métis

From the earliest contact with Native Americans, French, Dutch, and English traders set up factories to warehouse goods for barter and furs for transshipment when Indian hunters arrived from the interior loaded with beaver and buckskin. Participating in a ritual and commercial exchange with the natives, the Europeans called the traffic both the *fur trade* and the *Indian trade.* Both the Indians and the Europeans formed alliances; both played their partners off against possible rivals. The alliance between the French and the Huron Confederacy led the former to extend their factories, first established at Quebec in 1608, up to Montreal in 1641. French factory representatives, known as *coureurs de bois,* or "runners of the woods," sometimes traveled illegally between Montreal and the Indian villages. Seeking to smooth the path of commerce between Huron traders and French merchants, the *coureurs* served as brokers in the trade. They played up to their Indian hosts, joined them in war, and married women from the leading native families. Children from these unions raised in the villages became Hurons. The few raised in New France were considered Canadian. The factory system, bound to the shores of rivers and lakes, left little room for "mixed-blood" communities to develop. Then, in the winter of 1648 to 1649, the Iroquois Confederacy, armed with Dutch guns, launched the first attack of a decades-long trade war that saw the eventual destruction of Huronia and altered forever the St. Lawrence–Great Lakes trading system. Although the French tried to reestablish the Indian trade through the Ottawa tribes, the Five Nations of the confederated tribes, who allied with the English in New York when the Dutch left, continued to harass the traffic. In the half-century following the destruction of Huronia, Indians ceased to deliver furs directly to the French.

Instead Euro-Canadians (and some non-French Europeans, and even a few nonlocal Indians) took their place, traded with hunting bands in the interior, and transported furs to Montreal. In this new *en derouine* (itinerant peddling) system, which replaced the coast-bound factory system, individual *bourgeois,* or "merchants" (under the command of a royally appointed military officer) dispatched from the principal posts around the Great Lakes trading parties led by *commis,* or "clerks." As the *coureurs de bois* of old had done, *commis* served as brokers in the trade and frequently found it advantageous to join their Indian suppliers on war junkets, to participate in the Indians' spoils and profits, and to take "country wives" from among Indian women. For those *commis* who succeeded in creating lasting households, native wives were critically important. As John E. Foster points out, not only did the Indian wives supply vital social connections to the hunting bands, they also displayed economic skills in trading and household management that frequently kept the *commis* to whom they were married safe in their roles as middlemen. The more successful *commis* sometimes became *bourgeois* themselves, and they established large households and commanded key positions in the extended network of families living throughout the Great Lakes region. Some of their sons became hunters or trappers like their Indian cousins; the more talented became brokers and succeeded their fathers as *commis.* Others, hoping to forge alliances and improve their positions, gave their own daughters in marriage to successful *commis* and *bourgeois.* Thus developed the Great Lakes Métis communities. Consummate realists, they survived Britain's conquest of New France in 1763 by accepting the British merchants who replaced the French *bourgeoisie* into their ranks as new kin. Not until Americans arrived fifty years later determined to take the land and settle the region rather than simply to continue the trade did the Métis decline and their communities on the Great Lakes disappear.

Origins of the Plains Métis

The French fur trade had penetrated the interior to Canada's Great Plains by 1680, but it took fifty years for the industry firmly to establish operations in the region. Part of the difficulty had been logistics. The fur brigades could carry a supply of side pork and Indian corn sufficient to get them out on the plains, but not adequate to sustain them on the return to Montreal. French voyagers solved the problem by establishing a series of provisioning posts and trading for wild rice harvested by Indians in the shallows of the lakes west of Lake Winnipeg. When British peddlers took over after the Seven Years' War, the provisioning-post and brigade system became an effective weapon in the stiff competition between the HUDSON'S BAY COMPANY and its new rival, the North West Company.

In effect, by hiring the experienced French voyagers, the North West Company came to dominate the Montreal trade, wresting high profits based on its labor-intensive canoe brigades. One group paddled cargoes of fur from Athabasca country to Grand Portage and, later Fort William; another canoed trade goods up from Montreal. The members of the latter brigade, unable to make a round trip in a single season before the waters froze, had to hunt and fish their way across a vast stretch of the continent. They relied on food caches at strategic forts along the route, and during at least part of each winter, they—as well as the hunting brigades along the Saskatchewan and Red rivers with whom they made exchanges—had to be fed. The North West Company encouraged its partners wintering in the area to supply small parties of *engagés,* or "hired hands," to take goods and go on buffalo hunts with the Indians. Some of the older of these *engagés,* who had taken country wives from the bands with whom they wintered, chose to live out their lives free on the plains primarily as buffalo hunters. The local *bourgeois* were happy to see them go, since most were past their prime and had large families the *bourgeois* would no longer have to feed. The local Cree and Assiniboin Indians put up with their aggressive buffalo hunting because they were kin.

The origins of the Plains Métis lay in the appearance of *les gens libres,* or "the free men," around the outposts of the St. Lawrence–Great Lakes fur trade along the Red, Assiniboine, and North Saskatchewan rivers of the Canadian Northwest. French and Scottish *engagés* who had left their employment in the trade not at Montreal, but in the Canadian interior, they came together in bands of two or three households and supplied provisions and furs to the local forts. Their survival and their soon flourishing way of life depended on the historical developments that led company traders at the posts to cooperate actively with them and that persuaded the Indian bands with whom they shared the prairie to tolerate their presence. Earlier historians tended to consider them "failed" Euro-Canadians who had "gone native" and become "Indianized." Associating Euro-Canadians who set up

Métis households with the wild outlawry of the old *coureurs de bois,* these historians believed *les gens libres* had chosen what they considered Indian licentiousness over the family values and citizenship of their true ethnic heritage. Later scholars, however, saw in their actions the ethos of the late eighteenth-century fur trade and in the men themselves individualists who tolerated company work only until they could become their own masters. In any case, the freemen who put down roots gave birth to a generation of buffalo hunters called the Métis.

Some Métis may also have descended from those engaged in company service but who did not quit their jobs; instead, they set up households among the "house" Indians, bands who lived near the various posts and were a feature of the fur trade throughout its history. Sent from post to post, these young voyagers sometimes took a succession of Indian wives at posts six hundred to one thousand miles apart. For these men, work lay at the center of their social world, fellow *engagés* were their true lifelong companions, and masculinity came to define their sense of self. How much they contributed to the Plains Métis tradition is the subject of debate, and in several cases, their offspring identified themselves as Indians under the treaties of the 1870s.

Red River Settlement

The heart of the Red River Settlement was the junction of the Assiniboine and the Red rivers in today's downtown Winnipeg. Home, some claim, to the majority of Canada's Métis people, the settlement split in two where the rivers met. Along the south and west forks on narrow river lots lived around 55 percent of the population—Plains Métis and a few Canadians. Along the Red River to the north lay the riverside farms of another group of Métis, the so-called Hudson Bay English, scions of Scottish-Indian unions who made up another 30 percent of the settlement. Nearby resided the Highland Scots (some 8 percent of the populace), who had been sent by Lord Selkirk to settle the town in 1812, and the Saulteaux and the Swampy Crees of the Indian village (7 percent). The Catholic Plains Métis spoke French, and the Protestant Métis spoke English, although both could communicate in either Cree or Saulteaux when they chose. The divisions between the two Métis communities had been etched as much by recent history as by ethnic ancestry.

At first, the Métis hunting the land along the Red River and the Assiniboine had cheered the arrival of the Highlanders, whom they saw as ready consumers for their surplus buffalo meat, pemmican, fish, and fowl. Assisted by the "anglais" agents of Selkirk and the Hudson's Bay Company (which, since 1773, had been following its nor'wester competitors into the interior), the Scots were rivals of the North West Company. Company agents sought to convince the Plains Métis that the Scots were usurping Métis land. Caught up in the commercial competition, the Red River Settlement polarized around ethnic divisions of "French and Catholic" and "British and Protestant," especially after a Métis party killed twenty settlers and Hudson's Bay Company servants in June 1816. The Battle of Seven Oaks poisoned the atmosphere for a century. Even when the two companies merged in 1820, the resentments lingered. Although Hudson's Bay, with its stricter management style, had triumphed over the more freewheeling North West Company, the majority of its officers were drawn from the ranks of former nor'westers, Highland Scots merchant-adventurers who had provided the North West Company with its élan. The Hudson's Bay Company, which loomed over the economy of the Canadian Northwest, would not take official control of the Red River settlement until 1835. But the settlement received company support and depended on its commerce. Meanwhile, throughout the 1820s, Plains Métis drifted into the settlement and squatted, mostly with company approval, down by the water on the south and west forks of the Red River.

Late in spring each year, the Métis hitched oxen or horses to their screeching RED RIVER CARTS and set off for a rendezvous in the south near Pembina on the United States–Canadian border to launch a buffalo hunt. They left behind only the old, the ill, and the crippled. Households boasting a skilled buffalo hunter or two hired company *engagés,* to whom they were probably related, to drive extra carts and help in the skinning and processing of buffalo robes. At Pembina, they held an assembly and organized the hunt, electing ten *captaines* who each chose ten *soldats*. They selected ten hunters past their prime to serve as guides. During the hunt, each captain and each guide commanded for a day, and the day's hunt started at dawn when the day guide raised a flag above his cart. The Métis then struck camp, packed their carts, harnessed and herded their livestock, and rolled out at least two abreast. The captain of the day posted his soldiers to the front, rear, and sides of the column, and they, following the direction set by the guide, looked for buffalo and kept their eyes out for Dakotas, who claimed the prairies hunted by the Métis as hunting grounds. At the least sign of trouble, the Métis drew their carts in a circle; if buffalo were spotted, they pulled up in a single line and awaited the commands of the hunt leader for the day.

The line advanced toward a herd slowly until it was perhaps a quarter-mile away, at which point the captain shouted *"allez,"* and the hunt exploded into a frenzy of gunfire, galloping horses, curses, and dust, as hunters leaped astride their mounts, charged into the herd, and fired their weapons. In a matter of minutes, it was all over for the day. Each hunter might have killed anywhere from two to five bisons, and immediately after his final kill, he began butchering the animals in preparation for the women's work of drying the meat and producing pemmican. The women hung the meat, cut into strips, out in the sun or over fires to dry, then pounded it into a coarse powder and mixed it with melted fat and berries. Once the pemmican had cooled, they sewed it into ninety-pound buffalo-hide bags for transportation back to the settlement and easy storage there. The company's relatively nearby posts on the North Saskatchewan, the Red, and the Assiniboine rivers bought the bags of pemmican and dried meat, took what they needed, and delivered the rest to Norway House to provision boat brigades or for transshipment to more northerly posts.

The risk of injury in the hunt or of attack from the Dakotas made the work dangerous, and social and political authority among the Métis was, in part, determined by one's accomplishments in the field and reputation as a hunter. In general, however, the Métis established time limits to the exercise of any power and restricted the scope of all authority, both of which were determined by the community. After the hunt, the Métis returned to the Red River Settlement in the summer, where the prominent hunters negotiated the sale of their pemmican and dried meat, and others harvested crops grown in the river-front gardens and back fields of their homes. Some scholars have suggested that the troubles to come for the Red River Settlement were basically the result of a conflict between the hunting culture of these Plains Métis and the more advanced agricultural economy of the Scots settlers; others have more recently argued that all the Métis at Red River depended on agricultural goods to round out their incomes and that the major differences between the Métis households with French heads and those with Scottish heads were in the size of their fields rather than in the uses to which they put them, with the Scots Métis owning larger plots. According to this latter view, it was a change in the nature of the buffalo trade to a proto-industrialized activity, a series of crop failures, the collapse of markets for agricultural goods, and new employment practices of the Hudson's Bay Company that led the Plains Métis to turn almost exclusively to hunting in the 1840s, a move that ultimately led to their decline.

Canadian expansion and the Red River Settlement

Certainly, the buffalo trade heated up in the 1840s. After 1820, the Hudson's Bay Company, having swallowed its major competitor, made little real effort to stifle illicit trade. The geographical isolation of the Northwest traffic worked to the company's advantage, and almost any exchange between the Indians and their Métis kinsmen, however clandestine, would result in the furs finding their way into company warehouses in any case. Other than tying the Métis directly to company interests by offering their leader, Cuthbert Grant, a sinecure of £300 annually as "Warden of the Plains," Hudson's Bay maintained its monopoly mostly because of the difficulty of establishing commercial links to the world outside the territory. Meanwhile, the company had slashed its expenses in the decades after 1820, reduced its purchases of "country provisions," and set a standard price that varied little year by year. By the 1830s, the market for Métis pemmican and dried meat had become saturated as the Métis population at Red River doubled between 1820 and 1840 and the number of Red River carts used in the hunt increased from 540 to 1,210. The company dealt only with established hunters, and young Métis men found it increasingly difficult to raise their political status, their social prestige, and their incomes in the traditional ways associated with the hunt.

In 1844, Norman Kittson, a Canadian, opened a trading post for the AMERICAN FUR COMPANY on the Red River at Pembina, a few yards south of United States–Canadian border. An experienced trader related to the Métis, Kittson not only knew what he was doing but, with backing from the Americans, could also stand up to the kind of competition that Hudson's Bay had used in the past to destroy his predecessors. Kittner's post was a beacon for ambitious young Métis hunters, and as they flocked to trade with the American Fur Company, Cuthbert Grant's influence over the Red River Métis declined. Soon, young Métis challenged the company's hegemony over the Canadian Northwest. Seeking to stanch the wounds inflicted by the new challengers, Hudson's Bay underscored its official, but hitherto generally unenforced, opposition to free traders. In 1849, the company accused Guillaume Sayer and three other Métis of trafficking in furs in violation of the Hudson's Bay charter. During the trial, the father of four-year-old LOUIS DAVID RIEL, who would become the best-known Métis leader in Canadian history, headed a committee of ten Métis who assembled a mob outside the courtroom to make sure their views were heard. Despite the "courthouse revolt," the jury found Sayer guilty. But satisfied with legal vindication and mindful of the volatility of Métis-company relations, company officials requested that the courts drop all additional charges. French-speakers, either misunderstanding what was said in court or assuming the request revealed the company's weakness, interpreted the outcome as a victory for free trade. At any rate, they continued to trade with the Americans and strengthened commercial ties with St. Paul in the Minnesota Territory and with the established fur-trading firms in Missouri. Hudson's Bay never again challenged them with the legal canons of its charter.

In the long run, however, matters did not work out as well for the Métis as they imagined in the days of the free-trade controversy. The new traffic went both ways. Corporations other than Hudson's Bay grew interested in the Northwest they once thought fit only for nomadic tribes and fur traders. During the 1850s and 1860s, commercial agents and missionaries, both Catholic and Protestant, put in appearances in the region, and overland travelers crossed the plains on their way to British Columbia. Upper-class British tourists sought excitement and adventure in carefully organized hunting slaughters in the wilds of the Canadian West. Government-sponsored expeditions gathered data on the region. As the strangers came in greater numbers, the BUFFALOES began to disappear. Before 1820, buffaloes occasionally wandered near the settlement itself, but by 1840, the Métis sometimes had to travel three hundred miles to hunt them. By 1860, the distance required to find a herd had doubled. As they followed the diminishing herds to the west and south, the Métis encroached on the hunting grounds of the Blackfoot, Dakota, and Crow Indians, who considered them allies of their Cree and the Assiniboin cousins and, therefore, enemies. Some Métis became *hivernants,* or "winterers," who organized hunting bands that spent the winter on the prairies rather than return to the Northwest settlements. Riverside gardens fell into disuse, and livestock roamed on many Métis properties as their owners came to rely solely on hunting, trapping, and fishing. In the late 1860s, the Red River Settlement's summer hunt itself sometimes failed, which, combined with declines in crop production, led the colony to seek relief supplies from both Canada and the United States.

As a people whose life centered around the hunt, the Métis were already anxious about the future when London created the Dominion of Canada in 1869, and the Hudson's Bay Company announced that it was transferring Rupert's Land, its vast holdings in the Canadian Northwest, to the new Canadian federal government. Having developed a distinctive way of life in the course of the past half-century and considering themselves a nation with rights in the Northwest, the Métis resisted the Canadian takeover. Fearing that a wave of settlers from Ontario would follow the transfer, they established a provisional government under the leadership of Louis Riel, and in 1870, their government negotiated a union with Canada that led to the creation of the province of Manitoba. Shortly thereafter, Riel was incarcerated and then banished. In 1874, four years after signing the treaty, the Métis witnessed the departure of the last hunt from the Red River Settlement. A few Métis had already begun migrating west to the Qu'Appelle Valley and north to Saskatchewan; now they were joined by ever-growing numbers from Red River. Others trekked south to the Dakota Territory and settled temporarily at St. Joseph before heading on to Montana. Following their defeat on the battlefield in the 1885 Saskatchewan Rebellion, led by a messianic Riel who had returned to Canada, the Métis faced the close of a half-century search for national identity.

Over the next fifty years, many, if not most, of the Métis dispersed from Red River, frequently to the fringes of the dominant Anglo-Canadian society. A few in Winnipeg, by emphasizing their French and Catholic heritage, carved out a separate identity and defined a corporate role for themselves in the new settler's West; others sought out their kinsmen on Indian reservations as Ontarians and Upper Canadians poured onto the plains and reshaped the nature of the economy, society, land, and government of the region. Those Métis left on the "Half-Breed Scrip" land grants established by the 1879 Manitoba treaty attempted to adjust to these changes by turning from a hunting culture to sedentary agriculture, much as the Plains Indians to the south were being forced to do. Before 1900, when Marquis wheat became widely available in the Canadian West and offered some chance of success, the Métis raised livestock and emphasized mobility with as much success as any other ethnic group. After 1900, the major obstacle to taking up wheat farming became a lack of capital. Without social connection and inexperienced in Canadian politics, many of them lost their lands and headed north and west "into the woods."

In Canada, as in the United States, the Great Depression of the 1930s saw a rise in interest in the fate of ethnic groups. Efforts to resurrect *la nation métisse* led the Alberta Provincial Government to create a Royal Commission to investigate conditions among the "half-breeds." The result was the Métis Betterment Act of 1938, which established eight Métis colonies spread around northern Alberta. The colonies were supposed to be protected environments where the Métis could be instructed in "the intricacies of modern society." Although large numbers of Métis in Alberta never moved to the colonies, they did serve to rekindle a sense of identity among the Métis that spread into other areas in western, northern, and central Canada throughout the rest of the century.

—*Charles Phillips*

SEE ALSO: Intermarriage: Marriage Between Euro-Americans and Native Americans

SUGGESTED READING:

Brown, J. S. H. *Strangers in the Blood: Fur Trade Families in Indian Country.* Vancouver, British Columbia, 1980.

Burley, David V., Gayel A. Horsfall, and John D. Brandon. *Structural Considerations of Métis Ethnicity: An Archaeological and Historical Study.* Vermillion, S. Dak., 1992.

Cox, Bruce Alden, ed. *Native People, Native Lands: Canadian Indians, Inuit and Métis.* Ottawa, Ontario, 1988.

Faragher, John Mack. "Americans, Mexicans, Métis: A Community Approach to the Comparative Study of North American Frontiers." In *Under an Open Sky: Rethinking America's Western Past.* Edited by William Cronon, George Miles, and Jay Gitlin. New York, 1992.

Flanagan, Thomas. *Riel and the Rebellion: 1885 Reconsidered.* Saskatoon, Saskatchewan, 1983.

Foster, J. E. "The Country-born in the Red River Settlement, 1820–1850." Ph.D. diss., University of Alberta, 1973.

Macleod, R. C., ed. *Swords and Ploughshares: War and Agriculture in Western Canada.* Winnipeg, Alberta, 1993.

Peterson, Jacqueline. "Prelude to Red River: A Social Portrait of the Great Lakes Métis." *Ethnohistory* 25 (1978): 41–67.

———. "Women Dreaming: The Religiopsychology of Indian-White Marriage and the Rise of a Métis Culture." In *Western Women: Their Land, Their Lives.* Edited by Lillian Schlissel, Vicki L. Ruiz, and Janice Monk. Albuquerque, N. Mex., 1988.

Ray, A. J. *Indians in the Fur Trade: Their Role as Trappers, Hunters, and Middlemen in the Lands Southwest of Hudson Bay, 1660–1870.* Toronto, Ontario, 1974.

Sawchuk, Joe, Patricia Sawchuk, and Thersea Ferguson. *Métis Land Rights in Alberta: A Political History.* Edmonton, Alberta, 1981.

Sprenger, Herman. "The Métis Nation: Buffalo Hunting vs. Agriculture in the Red River Settlement (circa 1810–1870)." *The Western Canadian Journal of Anthropology* 3 (1972): 158–170.

Stanley, G. F. C. *The Birth of Western Canada: A History of the Riel Rebellions.* Reprint. Toronto, Ontario, 1992.

Van Kirk, Sylvia. *"Many Tender Ties": Women in the Fur Trade in Western Canada, 1670–1870.* Winnipeg, Alberta, 1980.

MEXICAN BORDER CONFLICTS

Mexican border conflicts in the nineteenth and early twentieth centuries had their origins in the ill-defined nature of the international boundary between the two nations and in the vast expanse of desert that created havens for Indian raiders, outlaws, and revolutionaries. The debate over whether the Nueces River or the Rio Grande marked the true boundary between Texas and Mexico sparked the UNITED STATES–MEXICAN WAR of 1846 to 1848. After the war, the border controversies continued once the Mexican cession lands of the Southwest became part of the United States. JOHN RUSSELL BARTLETT's heralded boundary survey of 1850 to 1853 extended the line from El Paso, Texas, to San Diego, California, but the demarcation existed only in legal documents and theory, for local Hispanic and Anglo settlers viewed the area as one geographically unified region.

Racial problems also inflamed the borderlands as newly arrived Anglos threatened the political and economic power of Hispanics. South Texas especially became a troublesome area at mid-century, beginning with the 1855 raid of Captain James H. Callahan and TEXAS RANGERS on Piedras Negras. Although ostensibly directed against Indians, the expedition seemed more intent upon recovering runaway slaves who had escaped from Texas. Even before the rancor of the Callahan Raid had subsided, a larger issue exploded at Brownsville, Texas, on September 29, 1859, when JUAN NEPOMUCENO CORTINA occupied the town with a large force of Mexican militiamen and civilians to proclaim the Republic of the Rio Grande. Reacting against blatant racism and double standards of justice dealt to Hispanics, Cortina became a popular Robin Hood figure in the Rio Grande Valley. After his army was forced to flee back into Mexico, Cortina remained a constant source of irritation along the border because his followers occasionally seized American-owned cattle and freight wagons in retaliation for specific acts of racial injustice.

During the 1860s, lawlessness increased along the border as American troops were withdrawn to fight in the Civil War and Mexican forces were simultaneously locked in their own War of the Reform and efforts to oust the foreign occupation of Emperor Maximilian. Outlaw groups, many of them posing as revolutionaries, pillaged both sides of the border with impunity, and the United States indirectly supplied weapons to Benito Juárez in hopes that he could oust French influence from the Western Hemisphere.

During the 1870s and early 1880s, the border remained a troublesome area mostly due to Indian attacks. The United States government worked toward reciprocal crossings agreements with President Porfirio Díaz and achieved notable success. The agreements allowed military forces from both nations to cross the border "when in hot pursuit" of raiders, so long as they did not remain long or disturb innocent civilians. Colonel RANALD SLIDELL MACKENZIE initiated the largest operation in May 1873 when his Fourth Cavalry attacked Kickapoo, Lipan, and Mescalero camps at Remolino, Coahuila. But at that point, the reciprocal crossing agreement had not been finalized, so

Mexican irregulars at the international bridge in Matamoros, opposite Brownsville, Texas, 1913. *Courtesy Archives Division, Texas State Library.*

Mackenzie had to operate secretly; he barely escaped confrontation with Mexican troops. More fortunate were the several brief incursions undertaken by Lieutenant Colonel William R. Shafter and Lieutenant John Bullis, who pursued Indians east of the Big Bend area of Texas into Coahuila during the 1870s. The same kinds of operations were undertaken against Apaches in New Mexico, Arizona, Chihuahua, and Sonora during the late 1870s and early 1880s. During the final pursuit of GERONIMO in 1886, Captain Emmett Crawford had the permission of the Mexican government to lead a large group of loyal Apache scouts into the Mexican Sierra Madre. Just before negotiating Geronimo's surrender, Crawford was killed by Mexican militiamen who contended that they had mistaken his scouts for "hostiles." The end of the APACHE WARS in 1886 settled the vexing Indian question along the border, but military units and civilian law officers continued to remain active against cattle rustlers, smugglers, and other outlaws who found that skipping back and forth across the border provided a fair measure of protection.

By 1910, an element of revolution was introduced into the borderlands. Francisco Madero rose against the government of Porfirio Díaz in October 1910, and his outcry mobilized northern revolutionaries under the banners of men such as Pascual Orozco and FRANCISCO ("PANCHO") VILLA. Their April 1911 seizure of the border town of Ciudad Juárez alarmed Americans across the river in El Paso, but the victory hastened the resignation of Díaz. In the early stage of the Mexican Revolution, Villa's control over the northern Mexican states increased, and his friendship with Americans ensured him a continuous flow of weapons and other supplies across the border. This situation changed dramatically on October 19, 1915, when President Woodrow Wilson granted recognition to the de facto government of Venustiano Carranza and cut off further aid to Villa.

Responding to this change in the balance of power, and perhaps hoping to provoke war between the United States and Carranza's government, five hundred Villista soldiers attacked the New Mexico border town of Columbus on March 9, 1916, where they killed seventeen people and burned many buildings. Six days later, General JOHN JOSEPH PERSHING led soldiers into Chihuahua with orders to drive the Villistas away from the border. Initially, Carranza showed a willingness to cooperate with Pershing's Punitive Expedition, and representatives worked out a reciprocal crossings agreement similar to those of the 1880s. Yet, when it became clear that the Americans were augmenting their forces to more than fourteen thousand men and were preparing to stay in Chihuahua for an indefinite time, Carranza balked at finalizing the understanding. He warned the Americans to advance no farther south than Colonia Dublán and ultimately instructed his commanders to resist the advance if it continued. On April 12, 1916, during a confrontation between American troops and citizens of Parral, forty Mexicans were killed. A new level of hysteria was broached on June 21 at Carrizal, where twelve American soldiers were killed and twenty-four were captured amid an even higher number of Mexican fatalities. Fearing further confrontations and also concerned with the growing likelihood that his country would soon enter World War I, President Wilson withdrew all American forces in February 1917.

Even though direct intervention was now over, the United States maintained relatively large garrisons in the Southwest until 1922 in case revolutionary activities again spilled across the border. Soldiers pursued Mexican attackers from the Indio Ranch near Del Rio, Texas, in December 1917; Texas Rangers executed innocent Hispanics at Pilares during March 1918; and troops reinforced Presidio and El Paso, Texas, and Nogales, Arizona, at various times when their sister cities below the border came under rebel attack. After all the years of violence and misunderstanding, the high level of distrust did not immediately dissipate after the frontier and revolutionary eras.

—Michael L. Tate

SUGGESTED READING:

Clendenen, Clarence C. *Blood on the Border: The United States Army and the Mexican Irregulars.* New York, 1969.

———. *The United States and Pancho Villa.* Ithaca, N.Y., 1961.

Tompkins, Frank. *Chasing Villa: The Story behind the Story of Pershing's Punitive Expedition into Mexico.* Harrisburg, Pa., 1934.

Utley, Robert M. *Frontier Regulars: The United States Army and the Indian, 1866–1891.* New York, 1973.

MEXICAN CESSION

Under the terms of the Treaty of Guadalupe Hidalgo, which ended the UNITED STATES–MEXICAN WAR (1846 to 1848), Mexico ceded to the United States the area of the present-day states of New Mexico, Arizona, Utah, Nevada, and California plus parts of present-day Colorado and Wyoming. Eastern New Mexico became part of the United States by Mexico's acceptance of the Rio Grande as the border with TEXAS. The Republic of Texas, whose independence and annexation by the United States were now formally recognized, had claimed but never exercised authority over eastern New Mexico.

With the additional land purchased under the Gadsden Treaty of 1853, the present southern boundaries of Arizona and western New Mexico were established. The boundaries of the contiguous forty-eight states were thus established with the acquisition of almost one million square miles including Texas, a land acquisition comparable only to the LOUISIANA PURCHASE in the history of American expansion.

NICHOLAS TRIST, chief clerk in the Department of State (the equivalent in rank to a present-day undersecretary), conducted long and difficult negotiations before concluding the Treaty of Guadalupe Hidalgo on February 2, 1848. President JAMES K. POLK had lost confidence in Trist and had recalled him to Washington. Polk accepted Trist's work, however, and asked Congress to ratify the treaty because the terms included substantially all he had hoped to achieve in the war. Following ratifications by the United States in March and by Mexico in May, American troops ended their long occupation of Mexico City.

The Mexican and Native American inhabitants of the area of the Mexican cession were few and widely scattered, and there were very few other inhabitants of any race or culture except in Texas. Most Indians subsisted off the land and moved according to seasonal availability of food, with the notable exception of agricultural village (pueblo) Indians in present-day New Mexico and northern Arizona.

Spanish-Mexican-Indian people arrived in New Mexico near the end of the sixteenth century and settled along the Rio Grande. The first lasting Spanish settlement in present-day Texas came more than a century later. Catholic missionaries in many places worked early among the Indians, by 1690 in southern Arizona, for example. San Diego was the first Spanish population center in present-day California.

Anglo-Americans entered the Mexican cession area early by varied routes. Mormons arrived in the Great Salt Lake region in 1846 and opened a flood of international settlement. Mountain men were first into New Mexico, and seafaring Yankees in the hide-and-tallow trade were first in California. Overland emigrants first used the OREGON TRAIL to enter California, and in much smaller numbers, the SANTA FE AND CHIHUAHUA TRAIL to enter New Mexico and Arizona.

Civil governments under the American territorial system were established in New Mexico and Utah in 1850, Colorado and Nevada in 1861, and Arizona in 1863. California jumped directly into statehood in 1850, having received a huge surge in population with the start of the gold rush.

Mexican cession, 1848.

The first of the governmental establishments were delayed until 1850 largely because of the national debate over the extension of slavery, a debate which surfaced in Congress when Missouri had applied for statehood in 1820. Westward extension of the dividing line of 36° 30' set in the MISSOURI COMPROMISE was unacceptable to the North and to California, which would have been split in two. Texas was a slave state, but antislavery feeling clearly seemed predominant not only in California but also in the only other centers of significant population, New Mexico and Utah.

The COMPROMISE OF 1850 contained proslavery elements: enactment of a harsh federal fugitive slave law, agreement that the people of New Mexico and Utah should decide for themselves whether or not to allow slavery (subject to veto by Congress or their appointed governors), and a $10 million payment to Texas for relinquishing its claim to eastern New Mexico. The main antislavery elements of the compromise were admission of California as a free state and prohibition of slave trading in the District of Columbia.

Viewed from an 1850's perspective, the effects of the compromise were unknown. New Mexico's territorial legislature did enact proslavery laws at one point, evidently for political advantage. California's support of the North in 1861 was opposed by powerful voices, which were suppressed only with difficulty.

Another problematic legacy of the Treaty of Guadalupe Hidalgo lay in its provision that Mexican citizens who continued to live in the cession area would automatically receive the full rights and privileges of United States citizenship. Those who wished to move from the area were to have ample time to relocate without suffering any loss of property or rights. It was a paper promise. Those who left for Mexico were often compelled to sell their land and property at reduced value or to abandon them. In addition, they were harassed as they fled for the border like refugees. If they sought recourse through the legal system, rudimentary as it was in most locales, they faced every possible impediment, formal or not. To the insults and psychological depression they suffered as a defeated people stranded among the victors was added the injury of sudden poverty.

Most Mexicans did not leave, however. Many were the products of families who for several generations had been Texan, New Mexican, or Californian. The *ricos* (affluent) among them often accommodated to, mixed with, and even married the newcomer *gringos* (Anglo-Americans). This mixing of cultures took place early in Texas, where some leaders of the 1836 independence struggle were Mexican Texans. There was less of it in California.

The process may have been most evident, within the Mexican cession area, in New Mexico. There, the opening of commerce on the Santa Fe Trail in 1821 had produced two-way exchanges of people as well as of goods. Sons of *rico* families traveled to schools in Missouri and the Eastern states. The adjustment by the *ricos* under the American regime after 1846 was relatively easy, and, in fact, some used their knowledge and status to take advantage of *peon* compatriots who were illiterate and inexperienced in American customs, law, and commerce. J. Francisco Chavez and Antonio Joseph, for example, were associated with the SANTA FE RING that dominated New Mexican economic activities and politics. Stripping ordinary grant holders of their property was bad enough, but even more regrettable were the takeovers of land held in common by the especially vulnerable New Mexican villages and Indian pueblos.

After World War II, the American public became more sensitive to the property and cultural losses suffered everywhere in the Mexican cession area by native Mexican-Americans, in violation of the spirit and often the plain language of the Treaty of Guadalupe Hidalgo. Mexican Americans of the "GI generation" were better educated, more affluent and sophisticated than their predecessors, and less willing to submit to racist insults and oppression. Many called themselves "Chicanos," and under leaders such as Reyes Tijerina in New Mexico, they worked to reclaim as much as possible of their lost heritage. Their struggle continues, bearing close comparison in many ways with the struggle of Native Americans to maintain their heritage, but confused in some ways with the long-standing controversies over the rights of illegal immigrants from Mexico and elsewhere.

—*John Porter Bloom*

SEE ALSO: Gadsden Purchase; Spanish Settlement; National Expansion; Tejanos

SUGGESTED READING:

Griswold del Castillo, Richard. *The Treaty of Guadalupe Hidalgo: A Legacy of Conflict.* Norman, Okla., 1990.

MEXICAN IMMIGRATION, 1900–1935

Mexicans are often regarded and treated as recent arrivals to the United States, but they are actually part of a well-established community. Mexicans have resided in the American Southwest since settlement under Spanish and Mexican rule. However, the number of Mexican nationals increased dramatically when immigrants began pouring into the area at the beginning of the twentieth century. An increasing number of Mexicans also moved to areas other than the Southwest. By the 1920s, Mexicans were laying railroad track in Montana, harvesting sugar beets in Wisconsin, assembling cars in Detroit, canning fish in Alaska, making steel in Chicago, and sharecropping in Mississippi.

Historians and demographers have concluded that more than 10 percent of Mexico's entire population came to the United States between 1910 and 1930. Recent research indicates that that figure is probably misleading, because many people entered without documentation. There were seldom more than sixty Bureau of Immigration agents stationed along the nearly two-thousand-mile border from California to Texas.

Mexican immigrants usually took on unskilled, backbreaking jobs and menial occupations. There was also a castelike employment pattern that effectively denied Mexican nationals as well as American citizens of Mexican descent any opportunity to attain better jobs. The Spanish-language press in Mexico and the United States frequently reported cases of ill treatment. The reports ranged from discrimination in Texas and shanghaiing workers in Alaska to complaints over low wages in Minnesota and school SEGREGATION in California.

Mexican immigrants endured these insults because they had no choice. Their only hope for gainful employment and opportunity for their children lay north of the border. A combination of socio-economic and political factors motivated Mexicans to journey to the United States. As Mexico's population increased dramatically, the size of farms and homesteads in the countryside shrank. The cost of basic food stuffs increased significantly while wages remained low. Hunger and malnutrition therefore became accepted facts of life.

Although pressing economic need compelled Mexicans to cross the border, some immigrants were also refugees of the political turmoil sweeping the Mexican nation. The chaos reached its climax in the

Mexican Revolution from 1910 to 1920. A vicious civil war, the revolution claimed one-tenth of Mexico's population.

Immigration therefore provided a safety-valve for relieving political and economic pressures. Each Mexican leaving the country lessened the burden on the nation's economy. Moreover, Mexicans remembered their homeland and usually sent money home on a regular basis to their families. Yet the Mexican government never recognized the benefit of immigration and its financial impact on the Mexican economy.

While political problems south of the border were important factors, most Mexican immigrants also based their decisions to move to the United States on economic factors. U.S. companies conducting business in Mexico frequently transported their Mexican employees across the border to their facilities. Railroad companies and agricultural bureaus also played key roles in bringing Mexicans to the United States. Those companies regularly sent agents as far south as Mexico's central plateau to recruit workers, even though such actions violated American law. Mexican immigration was truly a key factor in the spectacular economic growth of the American Southwest. In addition, the first massive immigration wave also brought about the establishment of Mexican communities throughout the United States. Mexicans harvesting crops or laying railroad track frequently traveled beyond the American Southwest to other regions of the country in search of better paying jobs in a variety of industries such as machine shops, steel mills, and meat packing. Consequently, sizeable Mexican communities emerged by the 1920s in Chicago, Omaha, Gary, Pittsburgh, Detroit, and other major cities of the Midwest and East.

The number of Mexican workers in the United States increased significantly because industry's and agriculture's need for cheap labor coincided with the government's restriction of immigration from Asia and Europe. Despite their vital role in the U.S. economy, Mexicans were regarded as an exploitable labor force imported to perform short-term jobs. They were therefore viewed as temporary rather than permanent residents. That attitude, together with differences in language and culture, created a tense relationship between the Mexican community and the Anglo-American society.

It is therefore not surprising that the outbreak of the Great Depression unleashed a massive deportation and repatriation movement against Mexican Americans as well as Mexican nationals. About one million people—one-third of the Mexican population in the United States—were deported or repatriated during the depression. Deporting those without papers and repatriating others was regarded as a way to create jobs for "real Americans." Industrialists and agriculturalists led the way by firing their Mexican workers and shipping them to the border. Local or county charities sought to control growing welfare costs by forcibly repatriating Mexicans. Even though Mexican workers had contributed significantly to the prosperity of the United States, American society saw them as convenient scapegoats for the ills of the Great Depression.

—*Francisco E. Balderrama*

SEE ALSO: Borderlands Theory; Migrant Workers

SUGGESTED READING:

Balderrama, Francisco E. *In Defense of La Raga: The Los Angeles Mexican Consulate and Mexican Community, 1929–1936.* Tucson, Ariz., 1982.

Cardoso, Lawrence A. *Mexican Emigration to the United States, 1897–1931; Socio-Economic Patterns.* Tucson, Ariz., 1980.

Garcia, Mario T. *Desert Immigrants: The Mexicans of El Paso, 1880–1920.* New Haven, Conn., 1981.

Reisler, Mark. *By the Sweat of Their Brow: Mexican Immigrant Labor in the United States, 1900–1940.* Westport, Conn., 1976.

MEXICAN SETTLEMENT

The Mexican presence in Western North American dates to the Spanish colonial period when racially diverse groups colonized the region called the Spanish borderlands. *Criollos,* mixed-blood *castas,* Hispano-Mexican Africans, and Christian and non-Christian tribal groups of central and northern Mexican origin accompanied the Spanish-born clergy, officials, and military leaders moving northward. Nonwhites frequently outnumbered the Spaniards and *criollos*. New Mexico's pioneer families in 1598 included groups of European and American-born settlers and larger groups of Mexica, Otomi, and Tlaxcalan tribal auxiliaries. The central Mexicans later settled at Santa Fe in the barrio of Analco, the first such enclave on the far northern frontier of Mexico. A pastoral life along the RIO GRANDE evolved on ranches and other tiny communities and remained essentially unchanged into the Mexican era.

To the east, similarly diverse groups permanently occupied the Gulf Coast and eastern and southern Texas in the 1710s and 1720s at strategic outposts to deter French encroachments that had threatened Spanish claims to the region in the late seventeenth century. By 1731, the pueblo later known as San Antonio had been founded by Canary Islanders who proved disappointing as colonists. In their efforts to colonize the lower Rio Grande Valley, the Spaniards turned to *castas,* blacks, and central Mexican auxiliaries in the 1740s and 1750s. Nearly six thousand of these settlers accompanied colonial authorities to establish a string of ranches and towns, such as Laredo and Mier. This enterprise represented the first land rush into the present-day borders of the United States. Recruits received free land, exemption from taxes for ten years, and stipends for relocating to the lower Rio Grande area. In the process, they firmly planted the CATTLE INDUSTRY, the legendary vaqueros (or COWBOYS), and subsistence agriculture as hallmarks of Texas life.

Jesuit colonization of southern Arizona beginning in 1687 produced a missionary frontier that, with the exception of the presidio at Tucson, remained isolated well into the American period. More important as a settlement area was Alta California as a Pacific outpost of Spain and later Mexico. The strategic occupation beginning in 1769 brought Franciscan missionaries, soldiers, and artisans to Christianize the local Indians and thwart Russian and other foreign challenges. By the close of the eighteenth century, four military garrisons and three civilian towns stretched along the coast with *casta* military recruits joined by multiracial civilian families. The towns of SAN JOSE, LOS ANGELES, and briefly the Villa of Branciforte were primarily inhabited by recruits from the Pacific Slope of New Spain. SAN DIEGO, SANTA BARBARA, Monterey, and SAN FRANCISCO were Mexican towns carved out of missions and forts. But limited immigration and geographical distance from the rest of Mexico restricted population. Only two thousand Mexicans lived in Alta California in 1800; by the beginning of American conquest, their numbers had grown to only seventy-five hundred.

Characteristics of Hispano-Mexican settlements before 1848 included isolation between provinces that generated regionalism among inhabitants and the importance of cultural values best manifested in family life, religious traditions, and customs, such as *Las Posadas* and Passion plays, annual patron saints day fiestas, and celebrations honoring the virgin of Guadalupe. From a political perspective, the Mexican period retained the colonial administrative practice of appointed governors for frontier territories. But the reluctance of Mexico City to permit greater political autonomy for TEJANOS, Californios, or residents of New Mexico met with considerable protest among frontier leaders who espoused a federalist ideology rooted in self-governance for distant regions. The 1835 Texas War, 1836 Alvarado Revolt in Alta California, and the 1837 New Mexico uprising resulted mainly from philosophical disputes over the most suitable system of government for the north. With the exception of Texas, which revolted and declared independence with the aid of Americans, the government in Mexico City answered other regional protests by appointing local leaders as governors. Town governments maintained many Spanish practices. Local magistrates, for example, functioned as administrators, and judicial officials were empowered to settle an assortment of legal disputes—from domestic marital discord to indebtedness.

Economically, frontier life in Mexican settlements revolved around the cattle industry in Texas and Alta California and SHEEP RANCHING in New Mexico. In California, the emergence of the hide and tallow industry generated a barter system in the 1830s and 1840s through which the ranchero class swapped their cattle hides and tallow for luxuries imported by American trading companies. The opening of the Santa Fe trade in 1822 launched two decades of lucrative merchant activities between Anglo-American and New Mexican traders; however, MINING ventures in these regions proved less profitable than in the earlier Spanish or later American periods. In Alta California, secularization of the mission system led to the proliferation of more than seven hundred land grants. The prosperity of the rancheros eroded, however, as Americans began confiscating Mexican-owned property in the 1850s.

After 1848, Mexican institutions yielded to American ones as political and socio-economic displacement of the general populace shifted power in Southwestern communities away from rancheros and merchants. Laredo, Texas; TUCSON, ARIZONA; and Santa Barbara, California, proved exceptions; these towns remained isolated Mexican settlements until the late nineteenth century when Western railroads opened them to non-Mexicans. Immigrants from Mexico from the 1880s onward increased the Mexican presence in SAN ANTONIO, ALBUQUERQUE, and Los Angeles. Broadening their geographic presence in the West, Mexicans were also drawn outside the Southwest—into Oklahoma, Kansas, Nebraska, and Wyoming—through their search for jobs in agriculture, mining, ranching, and on railroads.

—*Gloria E. Miranda*

SEE ALSO: Barrios; Borderlands Theory; Catholics; Missions: Early Franciscan and Jesuit Missions; *Posadas, Las*; Spanish and Mexican Towns; Spanish Settlement; Texas Revolution

SUGGESTED READING:

Gutierrez, Ramon. *When Jesus Came, the Corn Mothers Went Away: Marriage, Sexuality, and Power in New Mexico*. Stanford, Calif., 1991.

Jones, Oakah L. *Los Paisanos: Spanish Settlers on the Northern Frontier of New Spain*. Norman, Okla., 1979.

Miranda, Gloria E. "Hispano-Mexican Childrearing Practices in Pre-American Santa Barbara." *Historical Society of Southern California Quarterly* 65 (Winter 1983): 307–320.

Weber, David J. *The Mexican Frontier, 1821–1846: The American Southwest under Mexico.* Albuquerque, N. Mex., 1982.

MEXICAN WAR

SEE: United States–Mexican War

MIDDLETON, "DOC" (RILEY, JAMES M.)

Outlaw and showman in WILD WEST SHOWS, James M. Riley (1851–1913) was born in Bastrop, Texas. In 1875, he was sent to the Texas penitentiary for horse theft. A year later, he escaped and fled to Nebraska, where he assumed the alias of "Doc Middleton." After killing a soldier in a dance hall fight, he became one of the most celebrated horse thieves in the West. During the next few years, he and his band were suspected of stealing two thousand head of Indian and government horses. Imprisoned in 1879, he reformed and, after his release, occasionally performed in Buffalo Bill's Wild West show.

—*John Boessenecker*

SUGGESTED READING:

Hutton, Harold. *Doc Middleton: Life and Legends of the Notorious Plains Outlaw.* Chicago, 1974.

MIDWIFERY

A midwife is a person who assists women in childbearing, especially by providing care during the process of labor and delivery. Midwifery has been practiced in white settlements of America since the first colonists arrived on the Atlantic seaboard, and the practice was carried west with the earliest settlers. Gradually, however, the custom declined as the medical establishment initiated a vigorous campaign, which peaked between 1910 and 1920, to force midwives out of business. At least two motives prompted that activity. First, DOCTORS found that the maternal and infant mortality rates were about the same for births attended by midwives and those attended by physicians. That finding prompted medical schools to recognize obstetrics-gynecology as a specialized field of study. A second motivation was that physicians feared the competition from midwives. Doctors quickly took steps to end that competition by moving into the business of delivering babies and providing all the services the process required.

As in the South, where black "grannies" presided at the majority of births, the use of midwives in the West was slow to disappear. Cultural preference, economics, and distance from professional medical care combined to keep midwives in demand.

Among Native Americans, certain ritual ceremonies governed childbirth—ceremonies that were not meant to be shared with non-Indians. Among some groups, such as the Navajos and some of the Pueblos, birth was a family affair in which the woman's mother attended the delivery. If complications arose, a midwife was called in.

The role of the midwife, or *partera,* was central to Mexican and Hispanic women's lives, and the birthing process was a woman-only affair. The *partera* was an important person within the community; she had learned birthing skills from her mother, grandmother, or other female relative. She served as counselor and confidante to many and took a lifelong interest in the babies she delivered.

One result of the debate over the use of midwives was the rise of nurse-midwifery, a compromise between the lay midwife and the obstetrician. The first nurse-midwifery program, the Maternity Association of New York City, was established in 1918. In 1925, Mary Breckinridge, a graduate nurse trained in England, established the Frontier Nursing Service in the mountains of Kentucky on the premise that if a successful nurse-midwifery program could be established in the remote and poverty-stricken mountain areas of Kentucky, similar programs could be established anywhere in the United States. The service flourished and served as an important training center for nurse-midwives; many of those who provided midwifery services in the Western states trained at the Frontier Nursing Service.

After the 1920s, deliveries attended by midwives declined nationally until the 1970s, when demand for female birth attendants triggered a slow but steady increase in the number of midwife-attended births.

—*Sandra Schackel*

SEE ALSO: Medicine; Nursing

SUGGESTED READING:

Buss, Fran Leeper. *La Partera: Story of a Midwife.* Ann Arbor, Mich., 1980.

Deutsch, Sarah. *No Separate Refuge: Culture, Class, and Gender of an Anglo-Hispanic Frontier in the American Southwest, 1880–1940.* Oxford, Eng., 1987.

Litoff, Judy Barrett. *American Midwives, 1860 to the Present.* Westport, Conn., 1978.

Schackel, Sandra. *Social Housekeepers: Women Shaping Public Policy in New Mexico, 1920–1940.* Albuquerque, N. Mex., 1992.

MIGRANT WORKERS

The phenomenal growth of FARMING, MINING, railroad construction, commercial fishing, and other enterprises in the West during the late nineteenth and twentieth centuries created an unprecedented need for inexpensive, unskilled, seasonal laborers. While laborers of Anglo-American descent dominated many enterprises in the 1800s, at the turn of the century and after, as operations grew in scale and work became more menial, Asian, southern European, and, especially, Mexican immigrants characterized the work force.

Working for low wages in conditions of extreme heat, discomfort, and danger, rushing from one "island" of employment to the promise of work at the next, and living temporarily in rude housing provided by employers, migrant families eked out an existence by employing all available hands—husband, wife, and children. As difficult as migrant labor was, many workers felt they were better off than in their homelands, an opinion held strongly by Mexican workers particularly as revolution in Mexico between 1910 and the 1920s created economic turmoil. Increasingly after immigration laws in 1924 limited the entry of Asians and southern Europeans, Mexican and Mexican Americans increasingly swelled the ranks of migratory labor. In fact, between 1900 and 1930, the Mexican population in the Southwest increased from about 375,000 to nearly 1.2 million. All told, about 10 percent of Mexico's population crossed the border.

Mexican agricultural workers, perhaps, had the hardest lot. They took jobs digging, picking, and stooping in fields of sugar beets, cantaloupes, fruits, vegetables, and cotton. Laborers were recruited by labor contractors, who, in concert with farm owners, fixed wages so that no laborer would quit his or her job for better pay elsewhere. In 1903, for example, workers in Texas earned fifty to seventy-five cents a day. Farmers withheld a portion of these wages, or "borrowed" their shoes each night, to ensure that the workers stayed until the job was completed. Workers lived in farmer-supplied housing sometimes made of nothing more than burlap, canvas, or palm leaves. For such shelter and for food and supplies, workers were charged fees often in excess of what the commodities would have cost at the local grocery store.

Recruiters gathered huge numbers of laborers to harvest crops quickly, but when the harvest was in, the Mexicans were out of work until they moved on to another crop. Families often lived in five places in a single year and spent as much as four months of the year just searching for work. When jobs were available for women and children, families of necessity ignored child-labor laws and compulsory-school laws. At the end of the growing season, some families returned to Mexico; others searched for work in the usually poor and dilapidated BARRIOS in American cities where Mexicans gathered strength from being with people of their own culture.

Farm owners felt no obligation to improve the lot of their work force. In fact, owners saw the status quo as the very salvation of their enterprises. They wanted Mexican workers precisely because, as the owners saw it, they seemed to accept working conditions that other laborers did not. Mexican workers, reported the *California Fruit Grower* in 1907, "are plentiful, generally peaceable, and are satisfied with very low social conditions."

Actually, Mexican laborers were not as docile as their employers wanted to believe. During the Great Depression, when farm owners in California attempted to cut wages, their workers staged strikes in the Imperial and San Joaquin valleys. In the latter strike of 1933, workers were not intimidated by the arrests and harassments of their leaders, nor by the farm owners who evicted laborers from their camps. In the end, the workers accepted a compromise wage—less than they wanted but more than the owners intended to pay. In spite of the *bracero* system, which allowed laborers from Mexico to cross the border for the duration of the Southwest's growing season, trade unions and social organizations of Mexican laborers gained numbers throughout the following decades, and farm owners were forced to make concessions to them.

—Patricia Hogan

SEE ALSO: Railroads; Industrial Workers of the World; Labor Movement; Mexican Immigration, 1900–1935

SUGGESTED READING:

Daniel, Cletus E. *Bitter Harvest: A History of California Farm Workers, 1870-1941.* Ithaca, N.Y., 1981.

McWilliams, Carey. *Factories in the Field: The Story of Migratory Farm Labor in California.* Boston, 1939.

Reisler, Mark. *By the Sweat of Their Brow: Mexican Immigrant Labor in the United States, 1900–1940.* Westport, Conn., 1976.

MILES, NELSON APPLETON

Civil War hero and captor of CHIEF JOSEPH and GERONIMO, Nelson Appleton Miles (1839–1925) was the last commanding general of the United States Army. Miles was born in the rural township of Westminster, Massachusetts. In October 1861, he raised a company of volunteers and joined the Union Army of the Potomac. He participated in every subsequent major battle on the eastern front except the second battle of Manassas and Gettysburg. Wounded four times, he won a series of promotions culminating in a brevet major generalship. With the collapse of the Confederacy, Miles was assigned command of the Military District of Fort Monroe, Virginia, where he was responsible for holding ex-Confederate President Jefferson Davis prisoner. In 1866, Miles was promoted to full colonel in the Fortieth Infantry Regiment; from late February 1867 through March 1869, he was engaged in Reconstruction duties in North Carolina.

After securing a transfer to the Fifth Infantry, Miles joined his new regiment in Kansas. In August 1874, he led a column south from Fort Dodge during the Red River War. A determined campaigner, Miles won a minor skirmish at Tule Canyon, Texas, and kept troops in the field through most of the winter. After the Battle of Little Bighorn, he and his regiment established the Tongue River Cantonment (later Fort Keogh) in Montana in the fall of 1876. Launching several campaigns that winter, his victories against SITTING BULL's coalition at Cedar Creek (from October 19 to 20, 1876), CRAZY HORSE and the Oglalas and Cheyennes at Wolf Mountains (January 8, 1877), and Lame Deer's Minneconjous at Muddy Creek (May 7, 1877) were instrumental in breaking the military power of the Northern Plains tribes. From the Tongue River Cantonment, Miles also joined the chase against Chief Joseph and caught the Nez Percés just short of the Canadian border in the Bear Paw Mountains. The bluecoats' initial assault having failed, Miles settled in for a siege; Chief Joseph and most of his followers surrendered in early October 1877. Miles also assisted in the following year's Bannock campaigns.

In 1881, Miles was appointed brigadier general. Following commands of the Departments of the Columbia and the Missouri, he was transferred in 1886 to the Department of Arizona, where he directed the campaigns resulting in Geronimo's surrender. After a two-year stint as head of the Division of the Pacific, Miles was awarded his second star and command of the Division of the Missouri in 1890. Directing military operations during the GHOST DANCE outbreak, Miles angered civilian and military superiors by pressing for strong disciplinary action against Colonel James W. Forsyth, who had commanded troops at Wounded Knee.

In 1892, Miles received the Medal of Honor for his gallantry at the Battle of Chancellorsville during the Civil War. In October 1895, he was named commanding general of the United States Army. During the Spanish-American War, he led the invasion of Puerto Rico. Although his opposition to substantive army reforms and his propensity to speak too freely with the press antagonized Presidents William McKinley and THEODORE ROOSEVELT, Miles was appointed lieutenant general in June 1900. He retired from the army at the age of sixty-four. In 1904, he unsuccessfully sought the Democratic presidential nomination.

Nelson Appleton Miles. *Courtesy National Archives.*

Although Miles lacked a formal military education, he was a talented, brave combat leader whose tenacious pursuits made him one of the nation's finest Indian fighters. Ambitious, jealous of the success of others, and egotistical enough to publish two autobiographies and a book-length account of his 1897 military tour of Europe, he had many conflicts with civilian superiors and fellow officers. Miles criticized the corruption within the BUREAU OF INDIAN AFFAIRS and supported that agency's transfer back to the War Department. He rejected tribal values and believed that Indians were inferior to "civilized" societies.

Miles married Mary Hoyt Sherman, niece of Senator John Sherman and General WILLIAM TECUMSEH SHERMAN, in 1878. While escorting his grandchildren to the circus, he died in Washington, D.C., of a heart attack and was buried at Arlington National Cemetery.

—*Robert Wooster*

SEE ALSO: Apache Wars; Central Plains Indian Wars; Little Bighorn, Battle of; Pacific Northwest Indian Wars; Sioux Wars; Wounded Knee Massacre

SUGGESTED READING:

Personal Recollections and Observations of General Nelson A. Miles. 2 vols. 1896. Reprint. Lincoln, Nebr., 1992.

Utley, Robert M. "Nelson A. Miles." In *Soldiers West: Biographies from the Military Frontier.* Edited by Paul Andrew Hutton. Lincoln, Nebr., 1987.
Wooster, Robert. *Nelson A. Miles and the Twilight of the Frontier Army.* Lincoln, Nebr., 1993.

MILLER, ALFRED JACOB

Artist Alfred Jacob Miller (1810–1874) made a lifelong career of painting the scenes he witnessed on one extraordinary expedition to American West. Born in Baltimore, Maryland, Miller developed his artistic talents under the tutelage of Thomas Sully and, beginning in 1833, as a student at the École des Beaux-Arts in Paris. After Paris, he studied at the English Life School in Rome. Returning to the United States, Miller opened a studio in Baltimore, but when it failed, he moved to New Orleans.

In Louisiana, he met Sir William Drummond Stewart, a Scottish sportsman and veteran of several hunting excursions into the Far West. Stewart invited Miller to accompany his next expedition and sketch the scenes and settings of the mountain men and Native Americans they met. In the summer of 1837, Stewart, Miller, and men of the American Fur Company embarked from present-day Kansas City, headed along the Oregon Trail to Fort William on the Laramie River, and made their way to the fur trappers' rendezvous on the Green River in present-day Oregon. Miller sketched images of the Shoshone, Nez Percé, Bannock, Flathead, and Crow Indians he encountered and spent a month sketching scenes of the rendezvous.

Returning to New Orleans, Miller produced eighteen oil paintings from his sketches. In 1840, he traveled to Stewart's Murthly Castle in Scotland, where he produced a series of paintings for the nobleman's hunting lodge. Miller presented Stewart nearly one hundred sketches and water colors of their Western journey.

Back in the United States in 1842, Miller settled in Baltimore and spent his remaining years producing a large number of oils and water colors of Western themes for sale to the public.

Miller's one excursion into the West occurred at a time—for the most part—before the Native Americans were altered by contact with large numbers of whites and before the mountain man and his trade became obsolete. Miller's works are valued for his depictions of a West very few people ever saw.

—*Alan Axelrod*

SEE ALSO: Art: Western Art

SUGGESTED READING:

Axelrod, Alan. *Art of the Golden West.* New York, 1990.
Rossi, Paul, and David C. Hunt. *The Art of the Old West.* New York, 1971.

MILLER, GEORGE

Nebraska editor George Miller (1831–1920) devoted much of his life to the promotion of Nebraska and Omaha. After practicing as a physician for several years, Miller moved to Omaha in 1854. Abandoning his practice, he became involved in Nebraska politics and real-estate development. He was elected to the territorial House of Representatives in 1855 and served on the territorial council from 1857 through 1859. In 1865, Miller founded the *Omaha Herald,* which he used to proclaim the agricultural wonders of Nebraska, as well as to provide technical advice to Nebraska farmers. In the 1890s, he was largely responsible for persuading farmers to plant Turkey Red winter wheat, a move that helped make Nebraska a leading producer of wheat. Miller also persuaded Union Pacific officials to build a railroad bridge across the Missouri River in Omaha, rather than at another site downstream, thus ensuring the city's continued growth. Miller sold the *Herald* in 1887; several years later, it merged with the *Omaha World.* The *Omaha World-Herald* remained a major regional paper throughout the twentieth century.

—*Mark A. Eifler*

SEE ALSO: Magazines and Newspapers

SUGGESTED READING

Brown, Wallace. "George L. Miller and the Boosting of Omaha." *Nebraska History* (Fall 1969).
———. "George L. Miller and the Struggle over Nebraska Statehood." *Nebraska History* (December 1960).
Morton, J. Sterling, and Albert Watkins. *History of Nebraska, from the Earliest Explorations of the Trans-Mississippi Region.* Lincoln, Nebr., 1918.

MILLER, HENRY

Henry Miller (1827–1916) established a ranching empire that covered more than eight hundred thousand acres in California, Oregon, and Nevada. Born in Württemberg, Germany, Miller immigrated to New York and worked as a butcher. During this time, he used his family name, Kreiser. Deciding to move to San Francisco, he bought a ticket from a man named Henry Miller and used not only the man's ticket but also his name.

Henry Miller. *Courtesy National Cowboy Hall of Fame and Western Heritage Center.*

Once in San Francisco, Miller built a successful butcher business. He soon took on his chief competitor, Charles Lux, as a partner. Miller bought his first ranch in the San Joaquin Valley of California in 1857, and during the drought of 1862 to 1863, he expanded his holdings. From this beginning, the company of Miller and Lux eventually grew to become the largest ranching business on the Pacific Coast. The company's land holdings stretched into Oregon and Nevada and were home to more than one million head of cattle. In addition, the partners expanded into sheep raising.

The partners were also interested in farming and water rights. They constructed storage dams and irrigation systems and grew crops on five hundred thousand acres. When the San Joaquin and Kings River Canal and Irrigation Company fell on hard times, Miller purchased it and made large profits running the business. Subsequent battles with local residents over water set many important precedents for the water laws of California.

After Lux died in 1887, Miller fought Lux's heirs for twenty years in court. Once the case was settled, he reorganized his company as the Pacific Livestock Company. He died at the age of eighty-nine.

—*Candace Floyd*

SEE ALSO: Cattle Industry

SUGGESTED READING:

Paul, Rodman W. *The Far West and the Great Plains in Transition, 1859–1900.* New York, 1988.

MILLER, JAMES B. ("DEACON JIM")

Noted Texas gunfighter and hired killer, James B. Miller (1866–1909) was born in Van Buren, Arkansas. He was arrested at the age of eight for killing his grandparents but was never prosecuted. At seventeen, he killed his brother-in-law with a shotgun, but once again he escaped punishment. Quiet and temperate and dressing in clothing more suitable to a Methodist preacher, he became known as "Deacon Jim" or sometimes as "Killing Jim." In 1894, he feuded with Sheriff Bud Frazer in Pecos, Texas. In two gunfights, Frazer wounded the gunman, but Miller was saved from death by a steel bulletproof vest. In 1896, the vengeful Miller killed Frazer in a saloon in Toyah. He was acquitted of murder, but in 1899, he ambushed and killed one of the witnesses who had testified against him. By then the word was out that Miller's gun was for hire. He boasted, "I have killed eleven men that I know about; I have lost my notch stick on sheepherders I've killed out on the border." In 1904, he murdered a lawyer, James Jarrott, and a real-estate man, Frank Fore. Two years later, Miller was hired to kill a deputy U.S. marshal in Oklahoma. In 1908, he was suspected of ambushing the noted lawman PATRICK FLOYD JARVIS (PAT) GARRETT in New Mexico, but historians disagree whether the killer was Miller or Wayne Brazel. After ambushing a rancher near Ada, Oklahoma, Miller and the three men who had hired him were lynched in a livery stable.

—*John Boessenecker*

SEE ALSO: Gunfighters

SUGGESTED READING:

Shirley, Glenn. *Shotgun for Hire.* Norman, Okla., 1970.

MILLER, JOAQUIN (HEINE [HINER], CINCINNATUS)

Joaquin Miller (ca. 1839–1913) was a poet and novelist as well as a gold-seeker, lawyer, judge, and newspaper editor. Most sources put the exact place of his birth at Liberty, Union County, Indiana. Miller's farmer parents wandered throughout the middle border region until 1852, when the family moved to Oregon. Leaving home in 1856, young Miller struck out for the Klamath River area below the Oregon-California border. He worked odd jobs for local gold miners and prospected for gold himself. Resolutely anticonventional, Miller also adopted the name Joaquin in honor of the California social bandit JOAQUIN MURIETA. Miller's earliest literary enterprise was a stint as editor of the *Democratic Register* in Eugene, Oregon, in 1863, but his abrasively secessionist views made him highly unpopular, and he left Eugene for San Francisco that year. He asserted himself as a man of letters, but San Francisco's literary circles scoffed at him as a harmless eccentric and a figure of fun. He returned to Oregon and lived there until 1870, when he set off for Europe and settled in London. There his outlandish manners and Western costume—sombrero and cowhide boots—persuaded many that he was indeed an American genius, a diamond in the rough, or, more accurately, a raw nugget from the far Western gold fields. He was lionized in particular by the members of the Pre-Raphaelite Brotherhood, who saw him as a frontier incarnation of the Byronic wanderer.

After returning briefly to the United States in 1871, Miller went back to Europe the following year by way of South America and the Near East. He returned to the States again in 1876 and lived in various locations until 1886, when he settled in San Francisco again. There he enjoyed acceptance in literary circles and was commissioned by the *New York Journal* to cover the Klondike gold rush of 1897 to 1898.

Miller's literary output may be divided into three broad periods. His early works include *Specimens* (1868), personal, highly melodramatic narrative verse, and *Songs of the Sierras* (1871), the Byronic flavor of which helped win him acclaim in England. Miller's middle period began with *Songs of the Sunlands* (1873), which reflected his reading of the English poets Algernon Charles Swinburne, Elizabeth Barrett Browning, and Dante Gabriel and Christina Rossetti. In 1873, Miller also wrote the quasi-autobiographical and sentimental prose work, *Life amongst the Modocs,* which was followed by two romantic novels: *The One Fair Woman* (1876) and *First Fam'lies of the Sierras* (1875). Miller returned to verse in 1877 with *The Baroness of New York,* a protracted romantic narrative poem, then *Songs of Italy* (1878), lyric verse inspired by Elizabeth Barrett Browning. His *Shadows of Shasta* (1881) was an inept novel but is worth examining for its impulsive and impassioned defense of the Indians. Also revelatory is *The Danites in the Sierras* (1882), a dramatic narrative, which reflected popular sentiment against the Mormons. Closing out the middle period is *In Classic Shades* (1890), lyric verse on American themes.

It was in his final period that Miller wrote his best work. *The Building of the City Beautiful* (1892) is a prose romance, which advocates a community of peace, equality, tolerance, and brotherhood. *Songs of the Soul* (1896) contains the author's best poetry, including two widely reprinted and anthologized verses, "The Passing of Tennyson" and "Columbus." *A Song of Creation* (1899) presents dramatic nature portrayals of Miller's travels. His final work, *Overland in a Covered Wagon,* was published posthumously in 1930. Intended as a grand introduction to his collected poems, it is a highly effective, colorful, and moving evocation of settler life in the Middle West and the trek to Oregon and California.

—*Alan Axelrod*

SUGGESTED READING:

Miller, Joaquin. *The Complete Poetical Works of Joaquin Miller.* San Francisco, 1897.

———. *Overland in a Covered Wagon: An Autobiography.* New York, 1930.

Peterson, Martin S. *Joaquin Miller: Literary Frontiersman.* Palo Alto, Calif., 1937.

MILLER BROTHERS 101 RANCH WILD WEST SHOW

The Miller Brothers 101 Ranch Wild West Show was a successful and flamboyant Wild West show during the early twentieth century in Oklahoma. In 1870, Colonel George Washington Miller sold his plantation in Kentucky and moved to the West in search of new business opportunities. While wintering in Missouri, he butchered and processed two thousand pounds of hog meat. The following spring, he traveled to Texas, sold the meat, and returned to Oklahoma Territory with four hundred longhorns.

Miller's three sons, Zack, Joseph, and George, expanded leasing arrangements with the Indian tribes from their father's fifty thousand acres to ninety thousand acres and purchased an additional forty-five thousand acres. The panic of 1893 bankrupted their cattle empire and forced the Millers to diversify into farming. Bumper wheat crops funded an expansion into the profitable raising of horses, mules, hogs, geese, ducks, and buffaloes. As cash flow increased, the brothers opened a tannery, meat processing plant, a feed-lot operation, a refinery, and fourteen other independent operations on the ranch.

Cowgirls and their horses rest at water's edge on the 101 Ranch. *Courtesy Western History Collections, University of Oklahoma Library.*

Zack Miller's flamboyant nature turned profits from many ventures that at first appeared to be foolhardy investments. While on a trip to the Mexican border to buy mules during the Mexican Revolution, he witnessed a rebel attack on the federal troops. The Federales's wagon train was forced across the international border, and Zack offered to buy the entire contents of the wagon train for forty thousand dollars in gold. The deal was struck, and the Millers became the owners of all of the wagons, mules, horses, clothing, small arms, frying pans, machine guns, hogs, and chickens needed to supply a Mexican army of five thousand men. Zack sold five acres filled with wagons for five hundred dollars per acre. He shipped the military accouterments back to the Miller Ranch to be used as props and costumes in the 101 Wild West Show.

The Miller ranching and farming operation had become a public attraction for those who lived or traveled near Ponca City, Oklahoma. The Miller brothers, being opportunistic businessmen, staged a RODEO that included an appearance of GERONIMO and the originator of bulldogging, BILL PICKET. The crowd, estimated at thirty thousand, was enough to persuade them to organize a traveling Wild West show. Before World War I, the show reflected a stylized, symbolic West without the boredom, dirt, and hard work of everyday ranching. During the war years, the Millers joined with Ringling Brothers Circus in a partnership that ended with the disbanding of the show. It reemerged as an independent operation in 1924.

Operating under the title "101 Ranch Real Wild West and Great Far East," the Millers gave up their pure frontier theme and introduced elephants, camels, circus cars, and exotic costumes. For five years, the show operated at a loss, and declining oil revenues and a general economic malaise, resulting from the stock market crash of 1929, compounded the financial drain. Joe's accidental death in 1927 was followed two years later by George's death. Zack, whose explosive entrepreneurial style had been supported by the expertise of Joe and George in agriculture and corporate management, was forced to sell the 101 Ranch at bankruptcy auction in 1931. The headquarters, the White House, remains in public trust as a monument to one of the more successful of the ranching empires of the cattle-trailing era.

—*James H. Thomas*

SEE ALSO: Wild West Shows

SUGGESTED READING:

Skaggs, Jimmy M., ed. *Ranch and Range in Oklahoma.* Oklahoma City, Okla., 1978.

MILTON, JEFF DAVIS

The son of a Florida governor, lawman Jeff Davis Milton (1861–1947) arrived in Texas in 1877 and worked briefly as a cowboy before enlisting in the TEXAS RANGERS in 1880. After three years of service, Milton drifted into New Mexico, where he became a deputy sheriff, cowboy, and range detective before migrating to Arizona. Again, he became a sheriff's deputy but soon accepted a position as a customs inspector on the Arizona-Mexico border.

After leaving the Customs Service about 1890, Milton fired locomotive boilers and was a Pullman conductor before becoming chief of police in El Paso, Texas, in 1894. By 1897, he was back in Arizona, serving first as deputy U.S. marshal and then signing on as a Wells Fargo agent on the Southern Pacific Railroad. In 1900, he was severely wounded in an attempted express robbery at Fairbanks, Arizona.

After a few years as a prospector, Milton joined the U.S. Immigration Service in 1904 and served that agency until his retirement in 1932. He died in Tucson.

—*B. Byron Price*

SUGGESTED READING:

Chesley, Hervey E. *Adventuring with the Old-Timers: Trails Travelled and Tales Told.* Edited by Byron Price. El Paso, Tex., 1979.

Haley, J. Evetts. *Jeff Milton: A Good Man with a Gun.* Norman, Okla., 1948.

Price, B. Byron. "When a Good Man with a Gun Met a Good Man with a Pen: Writing Jeff Milton's Biography." *Journal of Arizona History* 33 (Spring 1992): 1-26.

MINERAL LANDS LEASING ACT OF 1920

Passed by the U.S. Congress in 1920 to facilitate the development of natural fuel resources in the public domain, the Mineral Lands Leasing Act applied to gas, coal, oil, oil shale, phosphate, and sodium deposits. The act, which provided for competitive and noncompetitive mineral leases on federal lands, is generally regarded as a victory for Western business interests, but interpretation of its priorities has been in flux ever since its passage. Problems arose when claims of mineral deposits were made on federal lands where the surface rights were owned by the states, thus causing endless interpretation by Congress and the courts.

—*Kurt Edward Kemper*

SEE ALSO: Coal Lands Act of 1873; Coal Mining; Oil and Gas Industry

SUGGESTED READING:

Paul, Rodman. *Mining Frontiers of the Far West, 1848–1880.* New York, 1963.

MINERS

SEE: Mining: Miners

MINIMIC (CHEYENNE)

A Cheyenne tribal leader who favored diplomacy to armed resistance on the southern Great Plains from 1865 to 1875, Minimic was incarcerated at Fort Marion, Florida, after the surrender of his tribe. His name first surfaced in federal records during the year of the SAND CREEK MASSACRE (1864), when, for a reason that is unclear, U.S. Agent Edward W. Wynkoop briefly placed him in the guardhouse at Fort Lyon. Minimic became influential after the successful 1868 campaign orchestrated by Major General PHILIP H. SHERIDAN, through which the balance of power between tribal and non-Indian forces shifted to favor the U.S. Army. The following year, Minimic and Little Robe negotiated with an officer at Camp Supply for peace for their 46 lodges and, on April 7, 1869, for their settlement at Fort Sill. Thereafter, the Cheyenne leaders stood out as a minority often shunned by some 500 armed Dog Soldiers, who, in defiance of federal officials, led 165 lodges to the Republican River in western Kansas.

Joining Minimic and Little Robe in cooperation with federal negotiators were Medicine Arrows and Buffalo Head. The four leaders brought their followers together with peace-seeking Kiowas under the supervision of the kindly U.S. Agent Brinton Darlington. With Darlington, they moved their bands from Camp Supply to the North Canadian River near present-day El Reno, which then became known as the Cheyenne-Arapaho or Darlington Agency.

Subsequently, many Cheyennes drifted away from the agency to hunt, while the Dog Soldiers roamed northward to mingle with Sioux. By the winter of 1871 to 1872, however, most of the Southern Cheyennes reunited around Darlington Agency, where they lived in relative harmony.

The death of Brinton Darlington during April 1872 brought almost immediate trouble. Whiskey traders and Texas cattlemen created mischief, and the new agent, John D. Miles, reacted to the disturbances by withholding annuities to force compliance with agency rules.

Soon angry Cheyenne Dog Soldiers killed four in a party of surveyors and took refuge on the Washita River. This action revived a rift between the "peace" and "war" factions in Southern Cheyenne bands. Little Robe, Big Jake, and Stone Calf worked beside Minimic to negotiate with the federal authorities in 1873, while 160 Dog Soldiers raided settlements in Colorado.

By the spring of 1874, Cheyennes, Arapahos, Comanches, Kiowas, and Plains Apaches acted in concert to expel white intruders from hunting ranges on the southern Great Plains. The war faction was clearly in charge, and General Sheridan assumed a posture of attack. During the protracted war, ever-increasing numbers took refuge at Darlington Agency. GREY BEARD, Medicine Arrows, and White Antelope were the last to surrender, when on March 6, 1875, they brought in 821 people.

U.S. Army leaders decided to incarcerate the most dangerous Cheyenne leaders at a distant place. Almost at random, they chose thirty-one men and one woman, placed them in chains, and shipped them to Fort Marion, Florida. Grey Beard was shot while attempting to escape. General NELSON APPLETON MILES acknowledged that Minimic, Heap of Birds, and Bear Shield were not criminals and should be released. Nevertheless, they traveled as prisoners to incarceration in Florida.

—*Herbert T. Hoover*

SEE ALSO: Central Plains Indian Wars

SUGGESTED READING:

Berthrong, Donald J. *The Southern Cheyennes.* Norman, Okla., 1963.

National Archives. Record Group 75, Cheyenne-Arapaho Agency.

MINING

HISTORICAL OVERVIEW

California

"Boys, I believe I have found a gold mine!" James Marshall's January 24, 1848, announcement changed the course of American history. That morning, while looking into a mill tailrace under construction on the South Fork of the AMERICAN RIVER, Marshall saw yellow flakes. It was gold, and within a year, a worldwide rush would be on its way to California.

As the news spread, the first impact was felt in SAN FRANCISCO. A *California Star* article on May 27, 1848, described the town: "Stores are closed and places of business vacated; a large number of houses tenantless." The reporter explained why this had happened: "[a] motley assemblage, composed of lawyers, merchants, grocers, carpenters, cartmen and cooks all possessed with the desire of becoming suddenly rich" had rushed to the gold fields. Soon others joined them from Oregon and Washington. Then Central and South Americans arrived, bringing mining skills and techniques the Yankees lacked.

The idea of becoming suddenly rich motivated hundreds of thousands of people over the next sixty years to endure hardships and to travel to places they never expected to go. Mining seemed to offer the opportunity of getting rich without working; still as one dismayed miner noted, "I never worked so hard in my life to get rich without working."

It was hardly that way in 1848. Placer gold—free gold obtained by separating it from sand and gravel—was found almost everywhere in California's Sierra Nevada. A fortunate individual with a pick, shovel, and strong back might make thousands of dollars from one claim. When such news reached the Eastern states, Europe, and Asia, the great rush of 1849 took shape.

Back in the diggings, the Forty-eighters established the pattern Western mining followed for the next generation. Mining camps grew near the diggings as people hurried to "mine the miners." Transportation routes spread like a web through the mountains. Miners had gold dust, but the high cost of living, freighters, saloonkeepers, and others worked to ensure it would not burden them long. The miners meanwhile developed a body of mining law to handle such questions as claim size and ownership rights. Eventually, they developed rudimentary WATER law. Their mining techniques evolved from gold panning to building sluice boxes and water ditches to work more gravel and find more gold. When the Forty-niners arrived, they found an urban world awaiting them and fewer opportunities than a year before.

The world caught gold fever, and the "sordid cry of Gold, Gold, Gold" echoed everywhere. Perhaps one

Major mining sites in the West, 1848–1900.

hundred thousand people reached California in 1849, producing instant statehood; the gold they mined ignited American and European economies. By the end of the year, ounce-a-day diggings (roughly $20) replaced dreams of hundreds of dollars. Some mining camps already had become GHOST TOWNS, surrounded by the remains of mining and a land ripped by the gold-seekers' frenzy. Stories of rich discoveries and the strange "goings-on" in the camps fascinated readers throughout the world. A legend was born, a legend that would not die.

While less public attention was focused on later years, California continued to produce gold. The $81,294,000 production of 1852 was the record; it would not be until 1862 that the yearly total dipped under $40 million. California dominated the first decade of mining in the Far West. Placer mining would always predominate, and hydraulicking and dredging were pioneered there, yet Californians, by the early 1850s, were digging into the ground and starting hard-rock mining. Grass Valley and Nevada City remained mining centers for the next century.

California was a training ground for placer and hard-rock mining and mining law; as Californians rushed elsewhere, they took their experience and knowledge with them. San Francisco rebounded from near abandonment to become the West Coast's wealthiest, most cosmopolitan community, thanks to its mining neighbors. California developed an industrial and agricultural economy, as well as a transportation network, to support its miners, and they became the basis of the state's growth once mining started its inevitable decline.

The days of the independent Forty-niner and the "poor man's diggings" in placer mines were soon replaced by companies, corporate control, and miners working for someone else. It took money now to make money in mining. By the mid-1850s, restless miners looked anxiously for the new mother-lode country. In 1858, many futilely stampeded to British Columbia's Fraser River, then came news of silver discoveries east across the Sierra Nevada.

Nevada

The year 1859 proved even a more bountiful year than 1849. Not one but two rushes opened Nevada and Colorado; one came east to the silver-ribbed Comstock, the other westward to the better-known Pikes Peak country. Two of America's greatest mining states burst on the scene, repeating the story of California.

Because of its location, the COMSTOCK LODE attracted Californians in large numbers once the discovery of silver had been confirmed. For nearly a decade, miners worked the area without striking success. Then in 1859, the "blasted blue stuff" assayed out to be silver, and Californians rushed eastward. The Comstock Lode, named for an early prospector, ran two and a half miles below the two mining communities that came to symbolize the district—Gold Hill and VIRGINIA CITY. They became mining towns—larger, wealthier, and more permanent than the camps of the Forty-niners. The urban nature of the mining in the West continued unabated.

Once the magnitude of the Comstock's wealth became known—and these mines made millionaires—the rush to the "new Comstocks" began. Later arrival MARK TWAIN explained, "I confess, without shame, that I expected to find masses of silver lying all about the ground. I expected to see it glittering in the sun on the mountain summits." So did many others, and as a result, they rushed off to Aurora, Austin, Eureka, Pioche, White Pine, and other new strikes in some of Nevada's more isolated and desolate regions. They did find gold and silver districts; none, however, would equal the Comstock.

Top: Hydraulic gold mining near Virginia City, Montana, 1872. Photograph by William Henry Jackson. *Courtesy National Archives.*

Bottom: Ore from a nearby mine being transported for processing in Pima County, Arizona Territory, ca. 1898. *Courtesy National Archives.*

From 1860 to 1880, the Comstock's enormous production of $300 million in silver and gold (its ore proved almost as rich in gold as in silver) benefited California nearly as much as Nevada. San Francisco's *Daily Alta California* declared on February 3, 1872, "Nevada is the child of California." Californians assumed control of the Comstock, particularly San Francisco investors and industrialists. They ventured into a new world. Mining historian Rodman Paul wrote: "Technologically, economically, and sociologically the Comstock Lode represented a big and abrupt stride beyond the farthest limits reached in California during the 1850s."

The Comstock went through two periods of bonanza. The first, 1860 to 1864, helped underwrite the Northern states' effort during the Civil War. Following a period of borrasca (barren rock), the Big Bonanza lasted from 1873 into 1878. Both displayed an orgy of speculation with nearly seventeen thousand claims located along the lode. So uneven were the rewards of mining that half the Comstock's total production came from two pairs of adjacent mines: the Crown Point and Belcher and the Consolidated Virginia and California.

Individual fortunes took wing. Californian GEORGE HEARST, an early arrival, laid the basis for his wealth with the Ophir Mine. During the Big Bonanza, JOHN MACKAY, JAMES GRAHAM FAIR, James Flood, and William O'Brien rose from penniless origins to win the fight for the Consolidated Virginia and emerge as the Comstock's greatest Bonanza Kings.

Significantly, the Comstock provided a training ground for miners, mining engineers, and smeltermen and for a variety of equipment and technological advancements. Comstock owners and stockholders lavishly spent profits to develop new milling processes and introduce equipment, for instance, compressed-air drills, dynamite, and square-set timbering to stabilize the soft, crumbling rock.

Comstock miners were some of the best in the world, and they came from throughout world. Irish, Cornish, and English dominated. Among the difficulties the miners faced were heat, humidity, and hot water—170 degrees by the time the shafts went down to three thousand feet. Their strong union became a model for miners throughout the West, as did their standard four-dollar-a-day wage for underground work.

By 1880, ore values and production were declining sharply. While mining at the Comstock continued, the bonanza days receded into history. No other late-nineteenth-century Nevada district replaced the "queen," and by the turn of the century, Nevada's mining had slipped into the doldrums. Mining's heritage of abandoned machinery, camps, mine dumps, and litter could be seen everywhere. With eternal optimism, old-timers awaited the new boom.

Colorado

The Pikes Peak rush was the second largest in American history. If one California mother lode existed, there might be others; and Americans stood ready. When they read in newspapers, such as the *New York Times* on September 28, 1858, that "late news" from Pikes Peak left no doubt "the scene from California would be repeated," they caught gold fever. A few arrived that fall; many more followed the next year.

A little gold had been found that summer, but not until the late winter of 1858 to 1859 were discoveries made that gave a substantial basis for the rush. About one hundred thousand people started out for Colorado, but many turned back because they feared a humbug. It was not. John Gregory's discovery near today's Central City gave solid foundation to Colorado's mining. Unlike California, Colorado's placer deposits quickly gave out. Hard-rock mining emerged by the summer of 1859 and dominated after 1860. Nor did California investors go beyond the Comstock; Colorado would rely on Easterners and Europeans for money and machinery. DENVER developed as a regional smelting center and manufacturing center for mining equipment and as the urban heart of the Rocky Mountains, its hinterland full of mines, camps, farms, and ranches.

Prospectors quickly scurried across the Snowy Range and explored the Western Slope. New discoveries were trumpeted as having "leads, gulches and bars, [that] beat California out and out." Hopes outran reality; by 1863, Colorado appeared to have passed its peak as a mining region. Placer mining played out, and the mills could not save the gold from the "refractory" ore mined in the territory's mining heart, Gilpin County. Unfortunately for Colorado's later reputation, Eastern investors, flush with profits from the Civil War, were seeking new investment opportunities at that moment. Coloradans responded with mines and stocks; for a glorious half year, Colorado proved the hit of the stock market. The gold bubble collapsed in April 1864 amid accusations, expenses, and none of the promised profits. For a dozen years, investors shunned the mining pariah.

To make matters worse, Idaho and Montana challenged Colorado's Rocky Mountain mining dominance. Idaho mining discoveries erupted on the scene in 1862; however, Montana's new placer diggings, which came into their own in 1863 and 1864, provided the real threat. Colorado lost population and its reputation as a "poor man's diggings." None of the three territories, however, developed as their boosters had hoped—isolation, rapidly declining placer deposits, and little outside investment killed expectations.

Colorado became the first of the three to rebound, starting with the silver discoveries at Caribou in Boulder County in 1869 and 1870. Silver had been mined earlier at Georgetown, but the complex ore and the territory's reputation kept investors away. With better smelting capabilities and transportation, silver held out new promise. The great discoveries at LEADVILLE in 1877 and 1878 put Colorado back on the mining map. "All roads lead to Leadville. Everybody was going there!" observed author MARY HALLOCK FOOTE, whose husband Arthur was among the hopeful. Leadville boomed just as the Comstock declined, and it too made millionaires, the most famous, HORACE AUSTIN WARNER TABOR. Leadville challenged Denver for state dominance; its silver riches, however, eventually underwrote

Denver's growth and prosperity. Suddenly, investors fell over themselves to buy Colorado properties and stocks. Not only did Leadville thrive, but within a decade, the San Juans (Silverton, Ouray, and Telluride) and Aspen rivaled the silver queen. To help overcome isolation and high elevations, Colorado mining pioneered in the use of electricity and trams. Its narrow-gauge trains opened a new era of railroading.

Colorado's mineral treasure box seemed bottomless. Oil and coal had been found in 1859 and 1860, and they were joined by lead, copper, zinc, and eventually tungsten, molybdenum, natural gas, oil shale, and uranium. Coloradans witnessed one rush after another for more than a century.

Montana

Montana meanwhile struck its own bonanza—copper. The once gold and silver camp of BUTTE emerged as one of the world's great copper districts. This could not have happened at a better time to meet the growing needs of an industrial nation. Yet, it was not without cost. The bitter and epic struggle between WILLIAM ANDREWS CLARK and MARCUS DALY to control Butte's enormous deposit involved nearly the entire state and lasted two decades. Finally, Daly's ANACONDA MINING COMPANY emerged triumphant, then defeated another challenge from FREDERICK AUGUSTUS HEINZE, and for a generation dominated Montana's political and economic life. Clark, who finally achieved his goal of becoming a United States senator, shifted his attention to Arizona's copper.

Industrial Butte also witnessed the first major environmental crisis. The smoke from open-air heap-roasting copper ore gave off suffocating smoke, filled with sulphur and arsenic fumes. Cattle eating grass on adjacent hillsides plated their teeth with copper, and cats licking the grime from their whiskers risked arsenic poisoning. People with respiratory problems faced death in Butte. The issue was not easily resolved because Butte's existence depended on copper. Finally in late 1890, an unusually high number of deaths attributed to respiratory diseases aroused Butte to action. The result stopped heap roasting and shifted the smelters to the nearby town of Anaconda. The fight did not end, however; ranchers and farmers, as well as the federal government, took the Anaconda Company to court over the impact of the smelter smoke on the land, forests, and animals. The fight dragged on into the 1920s.

Similar "smoke cases," as they were called, were contested in California, Utah, and Colorado. California additionally saw a celebrated struggle between farmers and townspeople against hydraulic miners, whose debris washed down into the Marysville region. Mining lost the *WOODRUFF* v. *NORTH BLOOMFIELD, ET AL.* case in which the United States Circuit Court "perpetually enjoined and restrained" the companies from discharging or dumping into the rivers. Such court rulings should have warned the industry; sadly, they did not. The days of rape and run were coming to a close, but the industry continued environmentally to sow the wind.

Strip mining, a form of surface mining, left huge pits in the earth's surface. Laws passed in the 1970s compelled mining companies to fill in the gashes their operations made. In this image, miners load coal from a pit near Wilburton in the Indian Territory, ca. 1898. *Courtesy National Archives.*

Mining in the 1870s and 1880s spread throughout the Rocky Mountains, Great Basin, and Southwest. The gold rush into South Dakota's Black Hills forced a classic confrontation between miners and Indians over use of the land and resources with the government caught in the middle. Within two years, the removal of the Sioux and Cheyennes, following the Battle of Little Bighorn (June 1876), ended the struggle. Meanwhile, life went on in Deadwood and the surrounding camps. George Hearst and partners purchased the HOMESTAKE MINE, one of the West's best and definitely the longest operating property. The Homestake Company came to dominate the district from its town of Lead.

Arizona and Idaho

Far to the south in Arizona, Tombstone's silver mines opened in the late 1870s, gained nonmining-related notoriety, and, within a decade, collapsed because of low-grade ore. Tombstone, Deadwood, and Leadville however captured the public's attention and became the yardsticks against which a "real" mining community must be measured. Arizona's copper proved more lasting and significant. So too did Utah's copper centered on Bingham Canyon, and the Kennecott Company came to rival Butte in the twentieth century.

Idaho started as a placer-mining region, which, like neighboring Montana, included many Chinese miners. In many Western mining areas, racism prevented the Chinese from working in mining. The Coeur d'Alene district in northern Idaho brought Idaho back into mining prominence in the 1880s. Unfortunately, like other Western districts, it became a center of labor strife in the 1890s and following decade. The WESTERN FEDERATION OF MINERS attempted to unionize the hard-rock miners with some success after its 1892 organization in Butte. For the next dozen years, the union and the owners fought it out across the Rocky Mountains, the latter finally triumphant.

Late nineteenth- and early twentieth-century mining

Colorado and Nevada provided the last hurrahs for the initial era of Western mining. In the early 1890s, CRIPPLE CREEK drew national attention. Colorado's greatest gold district lay at the southwest corner of Pikes Peak, the goal of so many Fifty-niners. For more than a decade, its production averaged $15 million a year, despite vicious labor disputes in 1894 and 1903 to 1904. Trains, electricity, stock exchanges, corporate control, and all the "modern" conveniences arrived almost with the first miners. So did tourists to "see the elephant" before this epoch disappeared. Nevada's last excitements came with Tonopah (1901) and Goldfield (1904), ending a twenty-year mining depression. Ely and its copper mines added further excitement; Nevada surged back into the mining news. By the time of America's entry into World War I, Cripple Creek, Goldfield, and Tonopah had slipped into decline. No new discoveries grabbed headlines. The era that had started in 1848 came to a close; mining had opened and developed what once had been an unsettled, unknown land.

The familiar cycle of discovery, boom, bust, and abandonment was repeated hundreds of times in the West. Abandoned buildings, mine dumps, ghost towns, and lingering environmental problems marked the land where the prospector and miner toiled. If that delimited mining's heritage, the era would have been a historical footnote. Mining, however, had explored, publicized, and helped settle the West, given birth to states, created permanent transportation networks, and developed an enduring economy. Its profits supported a host of endeavors from medicine to theater. Major regional cities, such as Helena, Denver, and San Francisco, owed their prominence to mining. Mining left behind major tourist attractions and a legend of an era that will not come again. MARK TWAIN summarized its sway over people: "We were stark mad with excitement—drunk with happiness—smothered under mountains of prospective wealth."

—*Duane A. Smith*

SEE ALSO: Alaska Gold Rush; Arizona Mining Strikes; Black Hills Gold Rush; Booms; California Gold Rush; Coal Mining; Colorado Gold and Silver Rushes; Copper Kings, War of the; Copper Mining; Cripple Creek Strikes; Disease; Gambling; Gold Mining; Industrial Workers of the World; Klondike Gold Rush; Lead Mining; Labor Movement; Montana Gold Rush; Silver Mining; Socialism; Violence

SUGGESTED READING:

Brown, Ronald. *Hard-Rock Miners: The Intermountain West, 1860–1920.* College Station, Tex., 1979.

Elliott, Russell R. *Nevada's Twentieth-Century Mining Boom.* Reno, Nev., 1966.

Fell, James E., Jr. *Ores to Metals: The Rocky Mountain Smelting Industry.* Lincoln, Nebr., 1979.

Greever, William. *The Bonanza West.* Norman, Okla., 1963.

Paul, Rodman. *Mining Frontiers of the Far West, 1848–1880.* New York, 1963.

Smith, Duane A. *Mining America: The Industry and the Environment, 1800–1920.* Manhattan, Kans., 1987.

Smith, Grant H. *The History of the Comstock Lode 1850–1920.* Revised. Reno, Nev., 1980.

Twain, Mark. *Roughing It.* Various editions since 1872.

Young, Otis. *Western Mining.* Norman, Okla., 1970.

PROSPECTORS

Most Americans who migrated to the American West in the second half of the nineteenth century were dreamers. Perhaps no profession better typifies the image of the successful dreamer than the prospector who found his vein of gold. Only a few such prospectors ever existed, but the possibility of becoming one of them drove tens of thousands of dreamers to Western "diggings." News of gold in California in 1848, for example, caused a stampede of between eighty and one hundred thousand gold-seekers.

A prospector's job is to find natural deposits of gold and other precious metals. Technically, he is a specialist trained in the topographical features and geological formations that signal the presence of mineral deposits. In common usage, the term refers to the trained and untrained hordes who were lured west by reports of gold in California at mid-century and to the thousands of fortune-seekers who later responded to gold and minerals discoveries in Nevada, Colorado, Montana, and other states. A miner, on the other hand, is a wage worker hired by a mining company to extract minerals from the deposits the prospector has discovered. For the prospector, there was an infinitesimal chance of striking it rich; for the miner, there was none.

Prospectors began their search with the simple technology of placer mining, methods of extracting miner-

The news of the discovery of gold and other minerals in the West lured thousands of prospectors from all over the world. A nineteenth-century magazine illustration depicts fortune-seekers heading to Colorado. *Courtesy Library of Congress.*

als from the earth's surface. Erosion caused particles of minerals to break from deposits and flow to stream beds or catch in crevices. The prospector traced the nuggets and particles back to their source and assessed the deposit in terms of the profitability of mining the find. When the prospector found a feasible deposit, he staked a claim to it and sold his interest to a syndicate with the capital to develop and operate the mine.

The work was solitary or involved, at most, three to six prospectors placering a series of locations. In the boom days, however, crowds of prospectors working the same area resembled "bees around a hive." The job involved bending, stooping, shoveling, and hauling, and often, prospectors labored for hours in the middle of a river or stream. The muddy ground that had been worked over looked as if it were "literally turned inside out."

The first arrivals to a promising site lived in tents, in "housing" made of canvas cast over the branches of a tree, or in the open. As word of mineral discoveries spread, more prospectors, or "desert rats," crowded the area. Crude little camps developed offering laundries and services, saloons and bawdy houses. Suppliers moved in, and the cost of food and other commodities soared. Liquor, GAMBLING, a few women, traveling theater troupes, lying contests, and mock trials provided entertainment.

These male-dominated communities were remarkably democratic. By general consent, the inhabitants formed rules for staking and protecting claims, using WATER and other resources, and behaving agreeably. Such codes, formulated simply so prospectors could get along with each other, later became the basis for territorial, state, and federal mining laws.

Democracy, however, sometimes lapsed. Violence and vigilantism characterized some settlements, and towns dominated by Easterners and European immigrants showed little tolerance for prospectors of Chinese and Mexican ancestry.

Probably the most skilled prospectors migrating west came from Georgia's gold fields, in operation since the beginning of the nineteenth century. Trained Irishmen, Germans, Swedes, and Australians rushed to the Western mountains too. Prospectors came from all walks of life; what they had in common was a penchant for dreaming and a propensity for gambling.

Prospectors who failed to find the motherlode returned to their homes or stayed in the growing mining towns to operate stores, saloons, boarding houses, hotels, liveries, and restaurants. A significant minority became career prospectors, chasing another rumor of riches in Nevada, or Colorado, or Alaska.

—*Patricia Hogan*

SEE ALSO: California Gold Rush; Gold Mining

SUGGESTED READING:
Greever, William. *Bonanza West: The Story of the Western Mining Rushes, 1840–1900.* Norman, Okla., 1963.
Marks, Paula Mitchell. *Precious Dust: The American Gold Rush Era, 1848–1900.* New York, 1994.
Parker, Watson. *Gold in the Black Hills.* Norman, Okla., 1966.

MINERS

In the nineteenth century, the West's first, easy surface pickings or placer mining of gold and other metals quickly gave way to the more difficult and arduous tasks of quartz mining, digging beneath the earth's surface for ore-rich rock. Processes for separating the mineral from the rock became more sophisticated, required huge milling and smelting systems, and consumed larger outlays of capital as the century wore on. As quartz mining replaced placer operations, workers hired for a wage—miners—provided the labor for extracting and processing gold, silver, copper, and other minerals. For much of the second half of the nineteenth century, the mining industry employed the largest nonagricultural labor force in the West.

Miners as a group were a varied lot, represented by Irish, Cornish, German, Scandinavian, Chinese, and southern European immigrants, native-born Americans, and laborers of Hispanic descent. Job assignments often reflected a caste system. Chinese laborers were hired to haul ore and rubble, prepare meals, and wash laundry. Hispanic workers also were consigned to positions that required less skill and received smaller wages. Top-paying jobs down in the shafts were reserved for native-born Americans and immigrants from western and northern Europe. Immigrants from the southern and eastern regions of Europe loaded and pushed carts of ore. In some mines, Hispanics did exactly the same jobs as Euro-Americans but still received less pay. Single and young for the most part, miners were an itinerant group, working one mine until it played out, then moving on to the next promise of employment.

Some employers provided their workers room and board in company houses, supplied goods through the company store, and tended the injured in company

Top: Miners at the head frame of a mine shaft of the U.S. Treasury Mine. *Courtesy Center for Southwest Research, General Library, University of New Mexico.*

Bottom: This image of the Cliff Mine, New Mexico, taken about 1880, shows the equipment of simple hand mining. *Courtesy Center for Southwest Research, General Library, University of New Mexico.*

A mine cave-in, photographed by Timothy H. O'Sullivan, 1867. *Courtesy National Archives.*

hospitals. In other mining communities, workers found lodging in the hastily assembled towns constructed to serve the mining enterprise. Such towns teemed with ways to separate a hard-rock miner from his hard-earned money. Saloons, gambling dens, brothels, and dance halls thrived in rough communities composed mostly of males.

Work in the tunnels was often dangerous, unhealthy, and, always, strenuous. Blasts of dynamite, the presence of poisonous gases, and the threat of cave-ins and floods occurred daily, but the pay was better than miners could expect in other industries or in farming.

If employers were willing to pay decent wages, they seemed reluctant to take responsibility for making the mining tunnels safer for their workers. It was miners' concerns for their own safety on the job that led, in part, to the first organized labor action. In 1864, workers at Nevada's Comstock Lode formed the Miner's Protective Association and struck for higher wages, shorter hours, and better working conditions. Similar concerns at the turn of the century provided the WESTERN FEDERATION OF MINERS, the INDUSTRIAL WORKERS OF THE WORLD, and other unions the issues they needed to gather members. Strikes, some violent, a few murderous, checkered the history of mining in the West.

—*Patricia Hogan*

SEE ALSO: Arizona Mining Strikes; Coal Mining; Copper Mining; Cripple Creek Strikes; Disease; Gambling; Labor Movement; Lead Mining; Ludlow Massacre; Violence

SUGGESTED READING:

Brown, Ronald C. *Hard-Rock Miners: The Intermountain West, 1860–1920.* College Station, Tex., 1979.

Lingenfelter, Richard E. *The Hardrock Miners: A History of the Mining Labor Movement in the American West, 1863–1893.* Berkeley, Calif., 1974.

Smith, Duane A. *Rocky Mountain Mining Camps: The Urban Frontier.* Bloomington, Ind., 1967.

Wyman, Mark. *Hard Rock Epoch: Western Miners and the Industrial Revolution, 1860–1890.* Berkeley, Calif., 1979.

MINING CAMPS AND TOWNS

Outside a few exceptions in Georgia and Appalachia, mining boom towns were a phenomenon of the trans-Mississippi West. After they heard about gold discoveries in the area, miners found their way to camps with names like Poverty Bar, Angels Camp, Coyote Diggings, Cuteye Foster's, Drunkards Bar, Dead Man's Bar, Gouge Eye, Mad Mule Gulch, Rough and Ready, Murderers Bar, Whiskytown, and Rattlesnake Bar. There was Dry Bar, which boasted twenty-six saloons. Few were more than camps, and most clung to arid and bleak, windswept mountain spots, parched by sun in summer, buried in snow throughout the winter, deep in mud whenever it rained, and always, it seemed, huddled under smoke billowing up from smelters.

Men came to make their fortunes, and in such mining towns, newcomers heard fabulous stories about others who had struck it rich both nearby but more often somewhere else in the West. Some of the stories were more or less true. There were prospectors who, indeed, struck it rich and with little effort. But they were few. By the time most of the miners arrived at a camp in California, the Rocky Mountains, or the Southwest, the easy pickings and the rich claims had all been staked and were being worked. For some, there was still a living to be made, but it was hard labor for niggardly wages—a few ounces of gold worth a few dollars a day at most, and even that was irregular. Working a mine near Hangtown, one group of prospectors averaged three dollars a day; another netted a penny a day. For those who did not simply give up, it was obvious that their fortunes would not be made quickly. They would have to find a claim, stake it, work it, and live from day to day, week to week, month to month. At first, a claim consisted of whatever area a man could work. He proved possession by keeping his tools on the site and by continually working it. Soon, individual camps established bylaws governing claims more formally. Limits to size were established; in rich camps, a claim might be as small as one hundred square feet—the size of a modern bathroom—and the principal of one man, one claim prevailed.

Disputes were settled by ad hoc juries. As to living, the camps offered food at inflated prices (potatoes one dollar a pound; a chicken, four dollars; apples, two for seventy-five cents), liquor, GAMBLING (a shrewd three-card monte dealer made more in a night than most miners made in a month of heartbreaking work), and laundry service (eight dollars to wash a dozen shirts—some miners actually sent their shirts to China for washing; it was cheaper). The camps also purveyed DISEASE, including dysentery and scurvy.

Women were, it seemed, a million miles away. One camp entrepreneur offered a peek at a lady's bonnet and boots for the admission price of one dollar. Women were recruited for the camps; to be sure, the first were not Sunday-school teachers:

> Hangtown gals are plump and rosy,
> Hair in ringlets, mighty cozy,
> Painted cheeks and jossy bonnets—
> Touch 'em and they'll sting like hornets!

Deadwood, in the Dakota Territory, mushroomed when rumors of gold finds drew thousands. Photograph by Timothy H. O'Sullivan. *Courtesy National Archives.*

While some Eastern employment agencies scouted professional prostitutes for the camps—calling them "domestics"—other women did come with less directly commercial intentions. Early in 1849, a Mrs. Eliza W. Farnham, widow of an Oregon Trail pioneer and formerly a matron at New York's Sing Sing Prison, attempted to recruit "100 to 130 intelligent, virtuous and efficient" women for marrying into the camps. She managed actually to find a grand total of 3. Later, a Miss Pellet attempted to recruit 5,000. She, too, had few takers. By 1850, less than 8 percent of California's population was female. Nevertheless, mining camps were quick to establish schools—lacking only teachers and students.

Some of the more "civilized" institutions were hurriedly established in the larger camps. The camps supported an astounding wealth of newspapers, more per capita than anywhere else in the United States. A greater surprise was the early presence and tremendous popularity of the THEATER, with Shakespearean companies in particular favor. The great Booth dynasty—in the persons of Junius Brutus, father and son, and Edwin—performed regularly in the camps. Actresses, of course, were even more in demand, the most famous of whom was LOLA MONTEZ. She had made her act into a hit in San Francisco, but even in the entertainment-starved Far West, her success was brief. A performance in Sacramento was rewarded with a barrage of rotten eggs and apples. The actress at last retired to Grass Valley, west of Lake Tahoe, where she befriended a Mrs. Mary Ann Crabtree. Boarding-house keeper and wife of a failed prospector, Mrs. Crabtree had theatrical ambitions for her daughter, Lotta, and Lola obligingly taught the girl a repertoire of songs and dances. It so happened that, about this time, child performers were enjoying a tremendous vogue in the mining camps—"Fairy Stars," they were called—and LOTTA CRABTREE debuted, with great success, in a camp named Rabbit Creek. She, at least, struck it rich, earning more money that night than her father had in four years of prospecting. As an adult, she became the nation's most celebrated comedienne.

The existence of such a luxury as "theater" was amazing considering the moral and physical squalor of the mining camps. Given the strain and hazard of mining and the isolation of mining camps, the carousing and violence to which they were prone seemed inevitable. Much of the time spent "in town" was spent drunk. "Town" usually consisted of a collection of tents and a few ramshackle wooden structures. Mrs. Louise Amelia Knapp Smith Clappe, who came to the gold fields with her husband (he wisely set up not as a prospector, but as a physician), described the town of Rich Bar in 1851. She wrote under the nom de plume "DAME

Virginia City, Nevada, in its glory days at the height of the silver boom in 1867. Photograph by S. J. Morrow. *Courtesy National Archives.*

SHIRLEY" and published a regular column in a California magazine. Rich Bar, she wrote, had only one street, which was lined with "round tents, square tents, plank hovels, log cabins &c, varying in elegance from the palatial splendor of 'The Empire' down to a 'local habitation' formed of pine boughs and covered with old calico shirts." The Empire was a quintessential mining town saloon–dance-hall–general-store. Its two stories made it the tallest building in town, and its glass-paned windows were the town's only specimens of the glazier's art. Part of the interior was "fitted up as a bar-room. A really elegant mirror is set off by a back-ground of decanters, cigar vases and jars of brandied fruit." On a table covered with a green cloth was deployed the ubiquitous pack of monte cards. "The remainder of the room does as a shop where velveteen and leather, flannel shirts and calico—the latter starched to an appalling state of stiffness—lie cheek by jowl with hams, preserved meats, oysters and other groceries in hopeless confusion." Four steps up from the barroom-store was the hotel parlor, "carpeted in straw matting and draped with purple calico." Another four steps led to four eight-by-ten bedrooms. "It is," concluded Dame Shirley, "just such a piece of carpentering as a child two years old, gifted with the strength of a man, would produce. . . . And yet this impertinent apology for a house cost its original owners more than eight thousand dollars."

Another feature of mining towns was crime and punishment, and a good deal of both. Drunken brawling was routine and, as the placer gold disappeared and fortunes proved increasingly elusive, thievery also became a fixture of life. One institution most mining towns lacked was a jail, so penalties for violating the law included banishment and whipping. Grand larceny—theft of more than one hundred dollars in gold, cash, or goods—was punishable by hanging.

Legal institutions executed justice—as well as those judged guilty—with lightning dispatch. The rule of the twelve-man jury prevailed, and sentences included banishment, flogging, and hanging. Often, however, sentence was passed without benefit of trial. Malefactors were captured, accused, found guilty, and executed by informally assembled vigilante bands. These groups frequently extended their ad hoc jurisdiction beyond the prosecution of criminals by indulging themselves in the persecution of immigrants. For, while some grew rich in the camps, most grew disillusioned. And when they realized that their high hopes for improved personal fortunes were doomed, Westerners looked for someone to blame. They blamed the "foreigners": Indians, South Americans, Frenchmen, Germans, and Irishmen were subjected to various restrictions, even on occasion mob VIOLENCE; the Mexicans and Chinese were subjected to much more elaborate persecution.

Anglo miners thought of all Hispanos, including those who were native Californians, as foreigners. Seven years before James Marshall discovered gold in Sutter's millrace, Francisco Lopez struck a far smaller lode on his ranch in the hills of Los Angeles. Mexican miners from the state of Sonora came up to work in these gold fields and, after the 1848 strike, headed north to work in the vicinity of Sutter's mill. Vigilantes relentlessly harassed the Sonorans, ejected them from their claims, evicted them from the camps, and even lynched them. In this, they were abetted by the California legislature, which passed in 1850 the Greaser Act—the law's official title—and a tax on "foreign" miners. From California, Mexicans and Mexican Americans, like their Anglo counterparts, followed new strikes and new camps, where they faced similar treatment. JUANITA OF DOWNIEVILLE, hanged after killing an Anglo in a dispute in one of the camps, became a martyr for the Hispanic miners. Cast out by mining-town society, some Mexicans and Mexican Americans became bandits, social outlaws against the community at large, the most famous being the semimythical JOAQUIN MURIETA, the first in the West's gallery of legendary desperadoes.

While the Irish and Germans, despite the social discrimination against them, were generally anxious to integrate themselves into the West's mainstream, the Chinese tended to keep apart (indeed, the Euro-Americans gave them little choice) and maintained in the camps much of the dress and some of the traditions of their ethnic homeland, including an allegiance to "tongs," fraternal organizations transplanted from China. Sometimes in the camps, rival tongs engaged in gang fights. When Weaverville's two tongs decided to clash, two thousand townspeople came out to watch. More often the Chinese faced the violence of the Euro-American miners, who called the traditional queues of the Chinese "pigtails" and bragged of beatings administered to the Asian-born miners. Perhaps not surprisingly, many camps had opium dens and separate gambling rooms and houses of prostitution patronized by the Chinese, although both opium and Chinese prostitutes proved popular with other miners as well.

BOOMS typically lasted from one to six years, and in the busts that inevitably followed, mining camps and towns either pulled themselves out of economic depression through technological advances and new investments of capital in revivals that sometimes extended their existences for decades or they declined into GHOST TOWNS. The towns that survived quickly industrialized, witnessing all that entailed: corporate ownership and management of the mines, the unionization of labor, the predominance of foreign-born immigrant workers. Their social structures resembled industrial counterparts in the East: an elite of mine owners, managers, engineers, and supervisors; a merchant and professional class of storekeepers, doctors, lawyers, editors, and ministers; and a core population of ethnically diverse skilled and unskilled laborers. Not a few, particularly those mining coal and copper, became "company" towns owned or dominated by one large corporation. Especially in the late nineteenth and early twentieth centuries, labor strife was not uncommon, and both the WESTERN FEDERATION OF MINERS and the INDUSTRIAL WORKERS OF THE WORLD were active in the mining communities of the West. A few, such as BUTTE, MONTANA, survived into the late twentieth century as major cities, while others, such as Aspen, Colorado, became destinations for tourists and vacationers with economies far removed from the booms that originally gave birth to the mining camps and towns.

—*Alan Axelrod*

SEE ALSO: Alaskan Gold Rush; Black Hills Rush; California Gold Rush; Chinese Wars; Colorado Gold and Silver Rushes; Denver, Colorado; Gold Mining; Coal Mining; Copper Mining; Klondike Gold Rush; Labor Movement; Lead Mining; Leadville, Colorado; Montana Gold Rush; Silver Mining; Social Banditry; Urban West; Vigilantism; Virginia City, Nevada

SUGGESTED READING:

Emmons, David M. *The Butte Irish: Class and Ethnicity in an American Mining Town, 1873–1925*. Urbana, Ill., 1989.

Goldman, Marion S. *Gold Diggers and Silver Miners: Prostitution and Social Life on the Comstock Lode*. Ann Arbor, Mich., 1979.

Mann, Ralph. *After the Gold Rush: Society in Grass Valley and Nevada City, California, 1849–1870*. Stanford, Calif., 1982.

Marks, Paula Mitchell. *Precious Dust: The American Gold Rush Era: 1848–1900*. New York, 1994.

Paul, Rodman W. *Mining Frontiers of the Far West, 1848–1880*. New York, 1963.

Petrik, Paula. *No Step Backward: Women and Family on the Rocky Mountain Mining Frontier*. Helena, Mont., 1987.

Reps, John W. *Cities of the American West: A History of Frontier Urban Planning.* Princeton, N.J., 1969
———. *The Forgotten Frontier: Urban Planning in the American West before 1890.* Columbia, Mo., 1981.
Rohrbough, Malcolm J. *Aspen: The History of a Silver-Mining Town, 1879–1893.* New York, 1989.
Smith, Duane A. *Rocky Mountain Mining Camps: The Urban Frontier.* Bloomington, Ind., 1967.
Wells, Merle W. *Gold Camps and Silver Cities.* 2d ed. Moscow, Idaho, 1983.

MINING ENGINEERS

Mining in the American West began with the simple washing of gravels and rapidly expanded into forms of complex industrial enterprise. Initially in California and Nevada and later throughout the American West and into Alaska, mining relied on skilled *technicians,* a term that became synonymous with *mining engineers.* Before the 1870s, mining engineers were either Europeans or Americans trained in Europe, mainly at German universities. The first and most important American school was the Columbia University School of Mines; after the turn of the century, the Colorado School of Mines and the University of California at Berkeley were important centers of mining education.

From their first appearance, mining engineers were all-purpose professionals, trained with specific skills but involved in enterprises that demanded a multitude of different talents. At a typical claim site, the mining engineer might locate the ore bodies, assess prospects for profitability, supervise construction of a mining works, oversee the raising of the ore, make arrangements for assays and shipping, and, in some cases, manage the construction and operation of a mill. Toward the end of the century, the larger scale of mining enterprise meant more specialization on the part of its engineers.

In pursuit of his trade, the mining engineer (and often his family) traveled to remote places in the American West and Alaska and later to mining sites around the world. As a public figure, the mining engineer served as a bridge between the on-site mining operations and the investors who financed them. Throughout the last third of the nineteenth and well into the twentieth centuries, the mining engineer was one of the West's first and most universally recognized professionals.

—*Malcolm J. Rohrbough*

SUGGESTED READING:

Rickard, Thomas A. *Retrospect: An Autobiography.* New York, 1937.
Spence, Clark C. *Mining Engineers and the American West.* New Haven, Conn., 1970.
Stegner, Wallace. *Angle of Repose.* New York, 1971.

MINING LAW

SEE: Caminetti Act of 1893; Coal Lands Act of 1873; Foreign Miners' Tax of 1850; Mineral Lands Leasing Act of 1920; Mining; Mining Law of 1872; Multiple-Use Doctrine; *Woodruff* v. *North Bloomfield, et al.*

MINING LAW OF 1872

Far into the twentieth century, the Mining Law of 1872 remained the basic piece of legislation regulating the extractive industries of the trans-Mississippi West in their exploitation of mineral resources on public lands. Also called the Apex Law, the act codified the practice generally accepted among miners since California gold-rush days of basing placer claims on the top, or "apex," of a vein. Since few seemed able to agree precisely where this apex lay, the law stimulated some expensive and confusing legislation, but more importantly to later developments, it also provided for the sale of mineral lands in the West and established for miners the unrestricted right to prospect and mine on federal lands. This, in effect, put mining outside public control and left mining operations free to respond to market forces. Although coal mining and later oil production fell outside the law, following the lax attitudes toward mining, the federal government did not exercise much control over their exploitation on public lands until the early twentieth century. The Apex Law, says historian Richard White, represented a tremendous gift by the federal government of public resources to private enterprise.

—*Patricia Hogan*

MINNESOTA

Minnesota is bordered on the east by Wisconsin, the south by Iowa, the west by North Dakota and South Dakota, and the north by the Canadian provinces of Manitoba and Ontario. The Northwest Angle in Lake of the Woods is the northernmost point in the contiguous United States. With an area of 84,068 square miles, including 4,059 square miles of inland water, Minnesota is the twelfth largest state. St. Paul, the state capital, was also the territorial capital. Minnesota's nickname, the "Gopher State," was derived from an 1857 cartoon that lampooned railroad promoters as striped gophers, a small rodent abundant on the state's prairies.

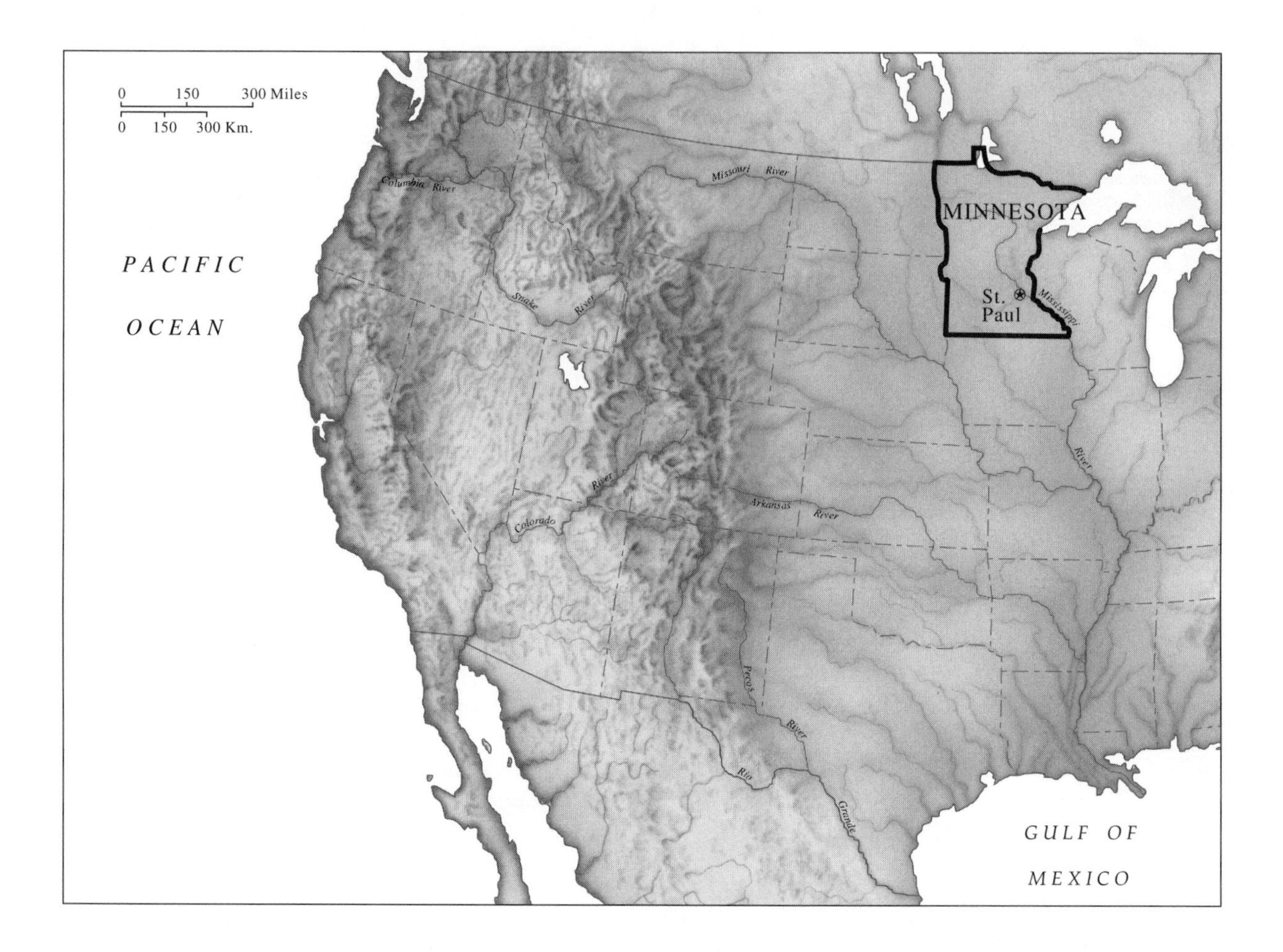

Population

The 1990 census reported that Minnesota's population was 4,375,099, composed of 3,056,474 urban and 1,318,625 rural inhabitants. The greatest concentration is in the Minneapolis–St. Paul metropolitan area with 2,413,873 people. The four largest cities are Minneapolis (368,883), St. Paul (272,235), Bloomington (86,335), and Duluth (85,493). Minnesotans are 94.4 percent white, with blacks, at 2.2 percent, constituting the largest minority. Asians, Hispanics, and Native Americans are other significant minorities. During the decade of the 1940s, Minnesota made the transition from a mainly rural to a predominantly urban state. Since 1945, especially, rural Minnesota has been losing population, and the fastest growing area is the suburban belt around Minneapolis and St. Paul.

Physical features

Minnesota is roughly rectangular in shape. Its longest north-south distance is 408 miles, and the east-west distance averages about 225 miles. With the exception of hilly terrain in the northeastern part, southeast area, and the Coteau des Prairies—a long prominent ridge in the Southwest—the land is generally flat. The highest elevation, 2,230 feet, is Eagle Mountain in the northeast near Grand Marais, and the lowest is 602 feet on the western shore of Lake Superior. Minnesota's topography shows the effects of glaciation, which leveled most of the land and formed thousands of lakes.

Before settlement, about two-thirds of Minnesota was forested, and the remainder was prairie. The coniferous forest lay mainly in the north and northeast, and the deciduous forest was to its west and south. Most of southern and western Minnesota is part of the eastern Great Plains.

Minnesota has three distinct drainage systems, all of which flow out of the state. Most of the drainage is by way of the Mississippi River, which rises in Lake Itasca near Bemidji and flows to the Gulf of Mexico. It and its main tributary, the Minnesota, drain much of the agricultural land. The watershed of the northwest, which flows northward to Hudson Bay, is dominated by the Red and Rainy rivers. The St. Louis River is the main stream in the northeast. Its waters run into Lake Superior and ultimately through the Great Lakes and the St. Lawrence River to the Atlantic.

Climate

Climate has been the most important geographic factor in shaping Minnesota. Continental in type, it features, long, cold winters; hot summers; and great fluctuations in precipitation with an overall tendency toward semiaridity. In the Twin Cities of Minneapolis and St. Paul, January, the coldest month, has an average temperature of 11.2° F and in July, the warmest month, the average is 71° F. The normal growing season in southern Minnesota is 160 days and in the northwest about 100 days. Farmers in the state have had to make extensive adaptations in the raising of animals, crops, and fruit trees because of the relatively brief frost-free period.

Natural resources

The greatest natural resources are fertile agricultural land, forests, and iron ore. The rich glaciated soils of the south and west are among the nation's best. Lumbering in the coniferous forest, which produced quality building materials in the frontier period, was succeeded by a pulpwood-products industry. The three iron ranges—the Vermilion and Mesabi in the northeast and the Cuyuna in the central region—have been the United States's main iron source in the twentieth century. Since about 1960, most of the iron has been extracted from taconite, a low-grade ore underlying the Mesabi Range.

History

French explorers, who were extending their fur trade westward and trying to discover the fabled NORTHWEST PASSAGE—a supposed all-water route to the Pacific through a temperate zone—first claimed Minnesota in the European conquest of the American subcontinent. Pierre Esprit Radisson and his brother-in-law Médard Chouart, Sieur des Groseilliers, reached Minnesota in 1660. Before losing that part of Minnesota east of the Mississippi to Great Britain in 1763, French voyageurs established a FUR TRADE and explored much of the area.

During the French period, the two main Native American groups were the Dakotas (or Sioux) and Ojibwas (or Chippewas). The Dakotas, who controlled the area early in the French period, were descended from Woodland people who had occupied the area for hundreds of years. The Ojibwas, whom the French first encountered in the vicinity of Sault Ste. Marie, moved

"Junction of the Mississippi and Minnesota Rivers near Fort Snelling, Minnesota," ca. 1886. *Courtesy National Archives.*

Since 1872, northern Minnesota's Mesabi Range yielded a high-grade iron ore. A panorama view of the Shenango iron mine, 1910. *Courtesy National Archives.*

into the area about 1680. They intensified their advance after 1736 and, by the late eighteenth century, had pushed the Dakotas into the southern half of the state.

The British followed the French and engaged in the fur trade and seeking the Northwest Passage. British traders stubbornly clung to the region despite the transference in 1783 of the area east of the Mississippi to the United States when Great Britain recognized its independence. Two years after the United States acquired the area west of the Mississippi as part of the LOUISIANA PURCHASE of 1803, the United States pressured British traders by sending a small military expedition headed by ZEBULON MONTGOMERY PIKE into the area. Despite Pike's reconnaissance, the British did not finally abandon the area until after the end of the War of 1812.

A summer parade through the center of town in Ortonville, Minnesota, ca. 1880. *Courtesy National Archives*

Determined to occupy the area, the Americans established Fort Snelling in 1819 at the confluence of the Mississippi and Minnesota rivers in the present-day Minneapolis–St. Paul area. Fur traders mainly of the American Fur Company and an agency for the Dakota Indians at Fort Snelling augmented the military post. The first major Indian treaties were in 1837 when the Dakotas and Ojibwas ceded land between the Mississippi and St. Croix rivers. These treaties opened the way for the establishment of Minnesota's first towns—St. Paul, which became the most important steamboat port on the Upper Mississippi; Stillwater on the St. Croix, which became the first major center of Minnesota's burgeoning LUMBER INDUSTRY; and St. Anthony (merged with Minneapolis in 1872) on the east side of the Mississippi at the Falls of St. Anthony.

After Wisconsin was admitted to the Union in 1848, the territory of Minnesota was organized. An assemblage of fur traders and lumbermen, who had formerly lived in the Wisconsin Territory, convened the Stillwater Convention on August 26, 1848. They elected HENRY HASTINGS SIBLEY, the area's chief fur trader, to represent the "Minnesota area" in Congress. Although Sibley had no legal standing, STEPHEN A. DOUGLAS of Illinois and other prominent Democrats won him a courtesy seat in the House of Representatives. Early in 1849, the Democrats achieved the formation of the Minnesota Territory, which extended westward to the Missouri and White Earth rivers, an area about twice the size of the later state. By 1849, approximately five thousand Americans were living in the territory. To encourage settlement, the federal government negotiated major cession treaties with the Dakotas and Ojibwas.

The Dakota treaties of Traverse des Sioux and Mendota in 1851 opened the most desirable agricultural lands, but over the next twelve years, most of the lands within the state had been relinquished by the natives.

Following a territorial population boom, Minnesota was admitted to the Union as the thirty-second state on May 11, 1858. For a time, its admission was jeopardized because of the congressional debate over granting statehood to Kansas. Despite the bitter sectional feelings of the time and the sharp controversy between the Democrats and the newly formed Republican party, Congress finally agreed to admit Minnesota while deferring the question of Kansas's statehood.

The panic of 1857, the Civil War, and the war of 1862 with the Dakota Indians dominated Minnesota's early statehood period. Because of an action taken by Governor Alexander Ramsey, Minnesota had the distinction of volunteering the first Union troops in the Civil War. While contributing heavily to the war effort, Minnesotans were further stressed by an Indian war in 1862. The Dakotas, confined to reservations on the upper Minnesota River and resentful of the federal government's failures to honor treaty provisions, launched attacks in the Fort Ridgely–New Ulm area in August 1862. Nearly five hundred settlers and soldiers were killed in the conflict, whose Minnesota phase was ended in about five weeks when troops led by Henry Hastings Sibley forced most of the Dakotas to retreat into the Dakota Territory.

From the end of the Civil War in 1865 to the turn of the century, Minnesota boomed. Its agricultural frontiers were essentially filled by 1885, and the Twin Cities emerged as one of the nation's major metropolitan areas. St. Paul, a major transportation center, was larger than its rival Minneapolis until 1890. Minneapolis, which was founded on land that was originally part of the old Fort Snelling military reservation, developed as a lumbering and flour-milling center. Strategically located on the west side of the Falls of St. Anthony and between the vast wheat fields of the Great Plains and Eastern markets, Minneapolis was recognized as the nation's and the world's flour-milling center by 1890. Aided by Minnesota-based railroads, Minneapolis developed a vast, essentially rural hinterland westward across the Great Plains. In the nonagricultural parts of the state, lumbering in the coniferous forest reached its zenith in 1905, and the first iron ore was shipped from the Vermilion Range in 1884.

During the first generation of the West's post–Civil War Industrial Revolution, Minnesotans were actively involved in farm protest organizations including the Grange, the Farmers Alliance, and the Populist party. The nationally known orator and writer IGNATIUS DONNELLY was especially active in the protest movement. Minnesota's tradition of protest politics continued into the twentieth century. During the Progressive era, the state acquired a national reputation for its liberal stances on economic, political, and social issues. During the World War I era, the newly formed Farmer-Labor party challenged both Democrats and Republicans. With their socialistic tendencies, the Farmer-Laborites enjoyed their greatest success from 1931 to 1939, when they held the governorship and dominated the legislature. In 1944, the Farmer-Labor party merged with the Democrats to form the Democratic-Farmer-Labor party. Mainly because of the DFL and its most successful politicians—Hubert H. Humphrey, Eugene McCarthy, and Walter Mondale—Minnesota is nationally regarded as one of the most liberal states.

Ethnicity and culture

Although Minnesota is known for its Scandinavian heritage, Germans constitute its single largest ethnic group, followed by Swedes and Norwegians. Only by combining Swedes, Norwegians, and Danes do Scandinavians outnumber Germans. Religiously, Minnesota is dominated by Lutherans and Roman Catholics, who composed 25.8 and 25.4 percent of the 1990 population, respectively.

Mainly because of its many lakes, central and northern Minnesota is famous for tourist attractions and activities including fishing and recreational boating. The state is well publicized nationally because of its three major league professional sports teams—the Minnesota Twins (baseball), the Minnesota Timberwolves (basketball), and the Minnesota Vikings (football). The Guthrie Theater in Minneapolis, the Minnesota Orchestra, and the St. Paul Chamber Orchestra contribute to the Twin Cities' role as one of the nation's ranking cultural centers.

—*William E. Lass*

SEE ALSO: Agrarianism; Populism; Progressivism

SUGGESTED READING:

Blegen, Theodore C. *Minnesota: A History of the State.* Minneapolis, Minn., 1963.

Clark, Clifford E., Jr., ed. *Minnesota in a Century of Change: The State and Its People since 1900.* St. Paul, Minn., 1989.

Folwell, William Watts. *A History of Minnesota.* 4 vols. St. Paul, Minn., 1921–1930.

Holmquist, June Drenning, ed. *They Chose Minnesota: A Survey of the State's Ethnic Groups.* St. Paul, Minn., 1981.

Lass, William E. *Minnesota: A Bicentennial History.* The States and the Nation. New York and Nashville, Tenn., 1977.

Schwartz, George M., and George A. Thiel. *Minnesota's Rocks and Waters: A Geological Story.* Rev. ed. Minneapolis, Minn., 1963.

Upham, Warren. *Minnesota Geographic Names: Their Origin and Historic Significance.* Rev. ed. St. Paul, Minn., 1969.

MINNESOTA SIOUX UPRISING

SEE: Sioux Wars

MISSIONS

EARLY FRANCISCAN AND JESUIT MISSIONS

Both the soldier and the priest arrived in the trans-Mississippi West as agents of the global Spanish empire. Ultimately, the model for the Spanish mission system in the American Southwest was the "holy experiment" of the Jesuits in the Central Highlands of South America, where, during the seventeenth century, the order began establishing a string of thirty *reducciones,* from the Spanish word *reducir,* "to bring together." These communities were centered around a market square and a plaza and consisted of several thousand Indians managed by only a handful of clerics, who taught the natives European agriculture, music, architecture, and religion. The communities would be replicated in modern-day Texas, New Mexico, Arizona, and California, but, as it turns out, it was not the Jesuits, but the Franciscans who first arrived in the northern reaches of New Spain—today's Mexico—with JUAN DE OÑATE's colonizing expedition in 1598.

In the seventeenth century, Oñate and his successors established no military garrisons or presidios in New Mexico, which is what they called Spain's northernmost frontier. More than eight hundred miles beyond the edges of New Spain's mining district, the isolated region attracted few immigrants. The number of Spaniards probably never exceeded three thousand. While the king expected his *encomendaros* (those rewarded for their service with a specified number of natives "in trust," or in *encomienda)* to serve as soldiers as well as settlers, the *encomienda* system itself was justified as facilitating the Christianization of the Indians. During the fifteen years of Oñate's initial enterprise, a small army of Franciscan padres baptized thousands of Indians, thereby creating a population of Christian souls, so the padres argued, who must not be abandoned. Although a colonist could extract labor as well as tribute from "his" Indian families—sometimes the inhabitants of several villages—when he ignored his spiritual duty to see to their salvation, he fell afoul of the missionary, who operated as sort of combination guilty conscience and imperial spy. Indeed, "for much of the seventeenth century," says scholar David J. Weber, "New Mexico endured largely as a missionary outpost."

The missionaries launched a program to eradicate the Pueblo religion and replace it with Catholicism. Unable to imagine that people could become Christians without also becoming European, the Franciscans tried to reshape native life by teaching Indians to dress, eat, and live like Spaniards. The friars, no doubt, succeeded in completely converting some natives, but in most cases, the Pueblos simply adopted those features of Catholicism they found compatible with their traditional spiritual beliefs despite the public floggings meted out by the Franciscans in a vain effort to discourage "pagan" religious dances and other evidence of "devil worship." The Franciscans commonly relied on military force to prevent converts from slipping back into apostasy, but it was not merely their guns, their goods, or their horses—better weapons, more wealth, faster transportation—that allowed them to stay in the area. They survived, too, because some of the Indians wanted them there. While the Spanish had horses and weapons, they also brought with them sheep, plows, tools, and new crops—peaches, wheat, oats, plums, and apricots. Their military might was evidence of their god's power, and the friar was a ritual specialist, a good consultant on ways to appease that god. All this the Indians found beneficial and put to their own use. Indeed, the Spanish made powerful allies. The Pueblos were not one people, not simply "Indians," but tribal members of independent villages, each village eager for strong friends to help defend it against, perhaps even defeat, its rivals.

By the middle of the seventeenth century, after some fifty years of the Spanish occupation, the Pueblos seem to have reached the conclusion that the benefits of the alliance no longer outweighed its costs, and they joined their hereditary enemies, the Apaches, in resisting the empire in the PUEBLO REVOLT. These series of resistances were the first steps in the expulsion of the Franciscans, which the Hopis completed in 1680. Unlike with the earlier revolt, Spain did not attempt a reconquest after the Hopi attacks, most likely because, by the late seventeenth century, defense—not conversion—had become Spain's major concern in western North America. Spain, which had opened the New World to Europe and, for a time, had dominated it, was a bankrupt nation unable to defend its American holdings against the Indians or incursions by other European colonists. In 1699, when the French established their first enduring colony in Louisiana, the Spanish

The way to salvation. Images from the eighteenth century show the process by which Indians converted to Christianity. Indians present themselves for baptism (top left); accept punishment for past sins such as witchcraft (lower left); sit for instruction in Christian ways (top right); and follow a Spanish official to the baptismal ceremony. *Courtesy New York Public Library, Manuscripts and Archives Section.*

colonial government in Mexico City decided it could no longer depend on the royal government in Madrid and, on its own authority, gave the Jesuits permission to build a series of missions in what is today the American Southwest.

The Jesuit missionaries were effective empire-builders. By persuasion or force, they convinced the Indians of the Southwest to help build missions across a frontier that ultimately stretched from the Pacific Ocean to the Red River valley. The church provided each new mission with money from a special fund to buy beads, vestments, tools, the necessities of life, and—of course—seeds. Older, established missions were expected to contribute as well, offering whatever they could spare in the way of grain, cuttings, breeding stock, chickens, and wine. A couple of padres would arrive on a spot, throw up a temporary chapel and a few rude log cabins, and launch immediately into proselytizing. They believed they had purchased the Indians' faith with a few glass beads, clothing, blankets, and, most especially, food, and they sought to enforce this faith with a detachment of musket-armed soldiers. Once converted, the Indians were not allowed to leave the mission grounds without permission of the clergy. When converts fled, and many of them did, they were given eight days to come back of their own volition. When the "grace" period lapsed, a friar and loyal converts, often accompanied by royal troops, chased them down. Inside the mission, converts spent their days tilling the fields and replacing temporary structures with the distinctive architecture of the Spanish West. Not precisely slaves, the Indians, nevertheless, provided a stable source of semiforced labor and were the economic heart of the mission. Over the years, they expanded and developed the compound, and by stages, the mission grew into a thriving complex, part multiple dwelling, part workshop, part grain bin, all dominated by the church itself, which sometimes took a half-century to complete.

Best known among the Jesuit missionaries was EUSEBIO FRANCISCO KINO, an extraordinary man by any measure. Trained as an astronomer and mathematician, Kino traveled some twenty thousand miles—often as much as seventy-five miles a day on horseback—and founded twenty-four missions in Mexico and the Southwest during the quarter-century of his missionary work. He drew the most accurate maps of the Spanish frontier empire, proving—among other things—that California was not an island, as many believed. At least twenty Western cities owe their origins to his work, as does the region's great cattle industry—for it was Kino who first introduced varieties of livestock into the country. Few New World Jesuits were as beloved or beneficent as Father Kino. The Jesuits were hard taskmasters, and, especially in the older portions of the Spanish colonial empire—central Mexico, Paraguay, and Uruguay—they imposed a cruel military discipline on the Indians. The Spanish government found this less objectionable, however, than the degree of autonomy the Jesuits abrogated to themselves. When, in a sudden and devastating move, the Spanish crown expelled all Jesuits from New Spain in 1767, the missions, in many parts of the colonial empire, fell into rapid decay.

But in the American Southwest, the Franciscans quickly stepped in to fill the vacuum left by the departure of their Jesuit rivals. The mission system reached its apotheosis under the Franciscans in California, who, at their peak, numbered only thirty-eight souls, all told. The padres were patient colonizers, however, who assumed from the start that it would take a decade from the time they arrived in an area until they had "pacified" the local Indians and got the mission functioning properly. Best known among this second round of Franciscan missionaries was Father JUNÍPERO SERRA. When Russian fur traders menaced Spain's hold on Northern California, the enfeebled Madrid government turned to the church and attached Serra to General José de Gálvez's expedition in 1769 to occupy Alta California. Although Serra suffered from chronic ill health aggravated by his zeal for public self-mortification (flagellation, beating his breast with a stone, burning himself with candles), he founded nine of the twenty-one Franciscan missions that stretched in an unbroken chain from SAN DIEGO to Sonoma along a dirt path graciously dubbed El Camino Real, the Royal Highway. By the time the Franciscans were done, the mission, accompanied by a presidio, was the standard settlement of the Spanish frontier.

The product of empire, the missions were themselves miniature empires. Farming was the principal industry of SAN JOSE, with staple crops raised at the mission itself, and animal products—meat, hides, wool—coming from the mission rancho some twenty-five miles away. Within the mission compound was, of course, the church, a graveyard, workshops, a communal oven and well, and a granary. The space between the compound's double walls was divided into Indian apartments. Measuring 11 by 14 or 16 1/2 feet, furnished with bedsteads, buffalo-hide mattresses, cotton sheets, and wool blankets, the accommodations offered a higher material standard of living than many Indians might find outside the mission. Even clothes were provided: a workday set and a Sunday set.

The day began at sunrise with prayer and hymns, followed by a breakfast of *atole,* roasted corn gruel. Some Indians worked on the church; some fashioned arrows for defense against hostile Apaches and Comanches; others, protected from hostiles by armed guards, farmed just outside the mission walls. Women wove baskets, spun wool, made pottery, and baked bread in the communal oven. The tolling of Angelus summoned the Indians to prayer and lunch, followed by a siesta. Work was resumed until Vespers, a time for prayer and religious instruction. After an evening meal of roasted corn gruel, there was brief time for recreation, and bedtime came at sunset.

Neophytes not only labored for the church but also displayed considerable talents, for example, in music; they formed choirs and orchestras, which performed at the weddings and fiestas of the rancheros and farmers who trekked into a region on the heels of the missionaries. But make no mistake about it: the missions were coercive and dictatorial institutions intended to be a divisive force in Indian society. Where the friar went, so went the soldier; what the friar decreed, the soldier enforced. The Spanish established missions for judicial and military reasons, not merely religious ones. The missions succeeded in entrenching Spanish authority along the stretches of the New World empire while using only a smattering of troops and at almost no cost, since labor was performed as the padres directed by unpaid Indians. The missions grew rich off this labor, and the friars understood that their purpose was never especially to make the Indians happy, only to make them Catholic.

When it came down to choices, the friars ensured that the Crown's interest came before the Indian's welfare, and they had—and often, took—recourse to shackles, stocks, and the barbed lash; they punished their charges not only with hobbling and whipping, but also with solitary confinement, mutilation, branding, and even execution. When a California missionary protested such treatment to Mexico City, he was seized by Spanish soldiers, declared insane, and rushed out of the province under armed guard. Worse yet—as Francis Jennings, among others, has calculated—the rate of death within the missions was much greater than outside them, just the opposite of what, Jennings says, one might expect. But the Mission Indians were undernourished and extremely vulnerable to new forms of European-spawned disease, especially given their cramped, poorly heated, badly ventilated living quarters. Jennings notes that the entire Indian population of the missions fell from a high of seventy-two thousand to only some eighteen thousand by the time the system was shut down.

Despite all that, the friars did not consider themselves vicious brutes, as they did some of the conquistadors. Men of their era, as David Weber points out, they inflicted punishments on their charges that were no different than those Spanish officials meted out to lower-class Spaniards. For that matter, given the right circumstances, the Indians could be quite as harsh as the Spanish. But unlike the Indian tribes, the Spanish colonial empire, as whole, had been historically rapacious with a reputation not only for greed but also for cruelty. The so-called BLACK LEGEND, says Jennings, may have been born of a propaganda war between empires, but it was in many ways a reality for the native peoples of the Southwest, one the missionaries in the long run did little to alleviate. If they protected the Indians from their native enemies, they, nevertheless, subjugated them, coerced them into accepting an alien religion, and nearly destroyed their cultures. In winning the implacable enmity of the Navajos, Comanches, and Apaches, soldier and missionary alike would leave a legacy of hatred for ethnic Europeans that survived long after the empire had fallen and the revolutionary government of Mexico had secularized the missions in the mid-1830s. For better or worse, the Jesuits and Franciscans "settled" much of the Southwest and California. Exploitative though they were, they became the far-flung nuclei around which the settlements, towns, and cities of the region developed. Historically, culturally, and architecturally, the early Spanish missions left an indelible mark on the American West.

—*Charles Phillips and Alan Axelrod*

SEE ALSO: California Ranchos; Catholics; Slavery and Indenture in the Spanish Southwest

SUGGESTED READING:

Archibald, Robert. *Economic Aspects of the California Missions.* Washington, D.C., 1978.

Cook, Warren L. *Flood Tide of Empire: Spain and the Pacific Northwest, 1543–1819.* New Haven, Conn., 1973.

Gerhard, Peter. *The North Frontier of New Spain.* Princeton, N.J., 1982.

Gutierrez, Ramon A. *When Jesus Came, the Corn Mothers Went Away: Marriage, Sexuality, and Power in New Mexico, 1500–1846.* Stanford, Calif., 1991.

Jennings, Francis. *The Founders of America: How Indians Discovered the Land, Pioneered in It, and Created Great Classical Civilizations; How They Were Plunged into a Dark Age by Invasion and Conquest; and How They Are Now Reviving.* New York, 1993.

Hall, Thomas D. *Social Change in the Southwest, 1350–1880.* Lawrence, Kans., 1989.

Kissel, John L. *Kiva, Cross, and Crown: The Pecos Indians and New Mexico, 1540–1840.* Washington, D.C., 1979.

Simmons, Marc. *The Last Conquistador: Juan de Oñate and the Settling of the Far Southwest.* Norman, Okla., 1991.

Spicer, Edward H. *Cycles of Conquest: The Impact of Spain, Mexico, and the United States on the Indians of the Southwest.* Tucson, Ariz., 1962. Reprint. 1981.

Weber, David J. *The Spanish Frontier in North America.* New Haven, Conn., 1992.

NINETEENTH-CENTURY MISSIONS TO THE INDIANS

In the nineteenth century, Anglo-Protestant missions to the Indians in the United States were, in their own way, as involved in the building of an empire as missions of the Jesuits and Franciscans had been in the seventeenth and eighteenth centuries. There was something of the missionary's zeal for domination, as well as the settler's longing for security, wrapped up in the vision of the West as a potential social Eden shared by Americans who began asserting that it was their MANIFEST DESTINY to inhabit the continent around the middle of the century. This vision drew westward men and women, among them JASON LEE, MARCUS AND NARCISSA WHITMAN, and HENRY HARMON AND ELIZA HART SPALDING, who talked about converting the Indians while dreaming of founding a great new state, to the Oregon Country in the 1830s. As the fur trade fell into decline with the introduction of silk from the East and cheap nutria fur from South America, their missions became the outposts of the new Western migration. Lee's settlement, at least, was quite cognizant of its role. Its fifty-one inhabitants petitioned the U.S. Congress in 1838 to establish jurisdiction over the territory, flattering themselves that they were "the germ of a great state," despite the fact that the HUDSON'S BAY COMPANY believed the area might well belong to England.

Indeed, it was in an Oregon territory dominated by the Hudson's Bay Company that the missionaries' story really began. Hudson's Bay had brought Iroquois Indians—employed as trappers—across the Rockies to the Columbia River region shortly before the War of 1812. The Iroquois, who had been converted to Catholicism in Canada, introduced some aspects of the religion to the Nez Percés and Flatheads and, in particular, talked up the "black robes," who had great and powerful wisdom to impart—a knowledge, the implication ran, that would make an Indian as powerful as a white man. But it was not until 1831 that the Nez Percés and Flatheads sent a party east to seek missionaries. They reached St. Louis, where they met with WILLIAM CLARK, superintendent of Indian affairs. With difficulty, he deciphered their talk of "black robes" and sent the delegation to a group of St. Louis Catholics, who, however, had neither the authority nor the resources to organize a missionary venture. Meanwhile, as so often happened when Indians ventured into white settlements, two of the delegates fell ill and died—though not before having been baptized. The other two delegates set off for home aboard the steamboat *Yellowstone.* One of the delegates died on board the *Yellowstone;* the other was ambushed and killed by Blackfoot Indians as he was making his way through the mountains. "The seemingly inconsequential request," write historians Ferenc and Margaret Szasz of the ill-fated delegation, "would help to determine the course of the history of the Northwest. It opened the door for missionaries and migrants and thus became the basis for America's claims to the Oregon Country."

For the Native Americans, whose traditional life was centered around spiritual concepts, the appeal of "white religion" probably lay in their desire to understand the workings of the obviously powerful culture they saw encroaching on their societies. Perhaps not surprisingly, in 1833 and 1837, other groups of Salishan and Sahaptian natives traveled the same path to St. Louis. But for the Euro-Americans, the Indians' request fired the growing competition among religions and denominations for American souls. The mainline Protestant churches, having drummed the Mormons into the "wilderness" of Utah, congratulated themselves, according to the Szaszes, for having saved the trans-Appalachian region from "barbarism" through their "benevolent empire" of Bible, tract, Sunday School, and education societies and were looking for new fields to conquer. The Catholic church, often under attack as a "foreign" institution because of it vast influence over Mexico's Southwest, could hardly afford to abandon the Northwest Indians to Protestants, who were eager to establish God's "New Israel" and carry their mission to both whites and Indians west of the Mississippi.

Shortly after the Nez Percé–Flathead delegation left, William Walker arrived in St. Louis. A chief of the northern Ohio Wyandots born of a white father, who had been adopted into the Wyandot tribe, and a mother, who was one-quarter Indian, Walker had been educated at the Methodist Kenyon College academy and even served Michigan's territorial governor as private secretary. He went to Missouri to discuss with Superintendent of Indian Affairs William Clark suitable tracts of the Indian Territory on which his tribe—like the other Eastern tribes, subject to "removal"—might settle. He had little success on this front (the Wyandots finally moved west, though not until 1842), but he did learn from Clark about the recent delegation in search of missionaries. Walker dashed off a letter to Methodist churchmen in Ohio, a letter zealous to the point of fabrication. Walker reported that he had interviewed the Nez Percé and Flathead representatives himself. He even invented dialogue to prove it. The letter was published in the March 1833 number of the *Christian Advocate and Journal* and created a sensation. Here were wretched savages yearning for the light of religion! Walker, who had never seen a Flathead, even made reference to what he imagined was the tribe's characteristic deformity. Despite their name, the tribal members, in fact, did not flatten their heads, any more than the Nez Percé pierced their noses, but Walker's inclusion of this detail served to make the Indians' plight seem perhaps more poignant. The Wyandot's letter launched a generation of Methodist missions to Oregon.

Jason Lee came first. After he had read Walker's letter in the *Methodist Christian Advocate,* Lee enticed a Massachusetts schoolteacher named Cyrus Shepard to join him, and the two applied to Boston merchant NATHANIEL JARVIS WYETH (who, in his own mind at least, had recently become a major supplier to the Western FUR TRADE) for help in establishing a mission in the Pacific Northwest. Wyeth, an atheist, who had already intruded upon Hudson's Bay country in 1832, was just then planning his second expedition, and he got the Methodists to the Northwest aboard his ships in 1834. But when the missionaries reached Flatheads and Nez Percés by the hundreds at Ham's Fork, Jason Lee decided not to accompany them back to their villages. Quite contrary to the mandate of his mission, he chose instead to continue with Wyeth to FORT VANCOUVER.

Headquarters of the Hudson's Bay Company, Fort Vancouver was presided over by Dr. JOHN MCLOUGHLIN, who had inherited from his predecessors the company's "mission" of honoring, in public, the United States–British detente in Oregon, while seeking, behind the scenes, always to advance the interests of the great monopoly, thereby also serving the British Foreign Office's designs to delay American access to the Pacific as long as possible. So when Jason Lee sought McLoughlin's advice on where to establish a mission, McLoughlin, who wanted to keep the newcomers as far as possible from Fort Vancouver, steered Lee to the Willamette Valley, which was at a remove from Hudson's Bay Company trapping grounds. Lee probably never realized that McLoughlin had helped him set up his mission among the valley farms of old French voyageurs and their Indian wives partly to keep the Methodists from moving farther into the interior and upsetting the company's Indian suppliers. In fact, the valley was far more fertile and inviting than the more arid region of the Flatheads and Nez Percés, and McLoughlin, with the typical company man's blindness to the potentials for settlement, failed to realize that he had recommended more than a mission site. He had inadvertently shown Jason Lee the seed bed of an American colony.

The next year, the Hudson's Bay Company compounded the mistake by helping two other missionary parties open stations in the area—one east of the Cascades at Waiilatpu on the Walla Walla River, and the other at the Clearwater Fork of the SNAKE RIVER, deep in the heart of Nez Percé country. Actually, the two teams—Marcus and Narcissa Whitman and Henry and Eliza Spalding—had arrived together, but they did not get along. In 1835, Marcus Whitman, a physician and

Presbyterian minister, had toured the Pacific Northwest with Samuel Parker, scouting a location for an Oregon mission. After finding a site, he returned east briefly and married Narcissa Prentiss. Although she had married Whitman in order to serve the cause, the thing seemed hastily done, since Henry Spalding, who traveled with them, had been her former suitor back in New York. The four, including Eliza, had the strong-willed contentiousness—and, one suspects, the sexual repressions—of self-appointed agents of God. Bickering all the way across country, when they arrived in Oregon, according to Patricia Nelson Limerick, they divided up Indian tribes and locations much as traveling salesmen might stake out merchandise and sales territories.

There was more than a little jealously between Narcissa Whitman and Eliza Spalding, who were the first two white women to cross the American continent, and they created quite a stir among Indian and trapper alike. Narcissa's blonde, buxom, wide-eyed beauty was especially celebrated among the small fraternity of MOUNTAIN MEN who wandered into Whitman's Cayuse Indian mission near Walla Walla in present-day Washington. Marcus Whitman and Henry Spalding were the envy of most of the male-dominated Far West, including Jason Lee and Cyrus Shepard, until a ship bearing five women reached the Methodist mission on the Columbia River during the winter of 1836 and a quick ceremony in a grove of fir trees gave two of the women new last names.

The indefatigable Whitman had to fight his own mission board to continue his work, while ministering both spiritually and as a physician to Indians and emigrants alike. In a short time, his mission became a vital way station for mountain men and incoming settlers, who came to rely on his courage and medical skill. Legendary mountain man JAMES (JIM) BRIDGER, who had taken a Gros Ventre arrow in the back during a fight at Pierre's Hole in 1832, came to Whitman in 1835 to have the long-imbedded arrowhead removed and, one suspects, to see Narcissa again.

Narcissa's letters to friends and family in the East reveal a lonely, frustrated, overworked woman, severely tested by the daily trials of cooking three meals a day for twenty people, including the eleven orphans duty demanded she adopt as well as anyone who might wander in off the OREGON TRAIL, which ran past her front doorstep. She quarreled with the other missionary wives and despaired over the death of her only naturally born child by drowning at the age of two. Caught up in the tangled race relations of missionary work, ministering to the spiritual needs her church had invented for those she considered savages, she probably did not think about how God's work might appear to the Indians of the Northwest. For what they saw was an ever-growing stream of white settlers passing through the mission onto their lands east of the Cascades. And what they—the Nez Percés and the Cayuse Indians—heard, from a firebrand Delaware named Tom Hill, was how the Algonquian tribes had suffered under just such a tide of migration in the East and had ultimately lost their freedom and their homes as a result. There, just as here, angry clashes had resulted when whites trampled crops or poached game; there, just as here, sporadic fighting had broken out when braves stole horses or pilfered camps.

Meanwhile the CATHOLICS had not ignored the potential for Northwest missions. In June, 1840, Jesuit PIERRE-JEAN DE SMET made a brief journey from St. Louis to the lands of the Flatheads and the Pend d'Oreilles, and he returned the following year with two more Jesuits, Nicholas Point and Gregory Mengarini. Following in the footsteps of their missionary ancestors in South America and the American Southwest, the Jesuits hoped to persuade the Indians to give up their nomadic life and settle down to become European-style yeoman farmers. Dreaming of creating, as they said, "a new Paraguay," they established St. Mary's Mission in the Bitterroot Valley of Montana in 1841, followed by the Coeur d'Alene Mission of the Sacred Heart on the St. Joe River, the St. Ignatius Mission to the Flatheads, the St. Paul Mission to the San Polis, and the St. Michael Mission to the Spokans. The missions never truly worked as had the old Jesuit *reducciones,* but they did boast such facilities as a hospital, a sawmill, a flour mill, and a printing shop. Mission schools taught the Indians theology, English, and some skills. De Smet played on the romantic appeal of the American West to encourage European novices and priests to cross the Atlantic Ocean and serve in the northern Rocky Mountain and Plateau missions. Some two hundred did so, and rumor claimed that each mission had its resident genius. Without imperial troops to enforce conversions, however, the nineteenth-century Jesuits could do little when the Indians made it clear that, despite their curiosity about the white man's religion, they preferred their traditional ways to settled mission life. It was the missionaries, not the Indians, who adapted to the situation, and the Sacred Heart Mission, for example, moved three times in thirty-six years to follow the tribe.

Missionaries for both the Catholics and the PROTESTANTS were adept at counting the number of souls they saved. And evidently a number of Nez Percés did indeed become Presbyterians, while, in 1890, a Catholic writer pointed out that nearly seven thousand out of ten thousand Montana Indians were Catholics. The counts, however, were not all that accurate, and some twentieth-century historians have concluded that the missions were a general failure. Certainly many natives—and many European immigrants to the region—were indifferent to the missionaries. In St. Louis during the fur-trade days, folks liked to observe that "God would never cross the Mississippi" and that there was "no Sunday west of St. Louis." Recent historians have echoed these beliefs by calling the Pacific Northwest "the least churched region" in the country.

The missions did, however, tie the region to the United States. In 1842, when the AMERICAN BOARD OF COMMISSIONERS FOR FOREIGN MISSIONS decided to close the Northwest missions to the Plateau tribes, Marcus Whitman undertook a dangerous midwinter trip back East to argue his case. Many credited him with having "saved Oregon," but as the Szaszes point out, his greater contribution to the American cause may have come a bit later. In November, both Marcus and Narcissa Whitman, along with others, were brutally murdered by Indians whose families had been decimated by measles introduced to their tribe through the Waiilatpu Mission. When news of the "Whitman Massacre" reached Congress, it responded by creating a government for the Oregon Territory, the first official American government west of the Rockies. It was as national martyrs, not as Protestant missionaries, that the Whitmans made their mark on the American West.

After the Civil War, the federal government reduced the Indian tribes to living not in Jesuit-style religious communities, but on reservations. And there, after they had lost their mobility, Native Americans became truly vulnerable to Protestant missions, determined, as always, both to convert and to "civilize" them. Especially the Quakers, who figured prominently in the BUREAU OF INDIAN AFFAIRS' handling of the Indians in the wake of GRANT'S PEACE POLICY, urged the Indians to give up their tribal ways, accept individual allotments, and become Christian citizens of the United States. However well intentioned, this reform movement, in the course of time, proved not to be so much a means to the salvation of Native American souls as it became, like the very first Spanish missions, a way to grab more Indian land.

—*Charles Phillips and Alan Axelrod*

SEE ALSO: United States Indian Policy

SUGGESTED READING:

Berkhofer, Robert F., Jr. *Salvation and the Savage: An Analysis of Protestant Missions and American Indian Response, 1787–1862.* New York, 1972.

Bowden, Henry Warner. *American Indians and Christian Missions: Studies in Cultural Conflict.* Chicago, 1981.

Burns, Robert Ignatius. *The Jesuits and the Indian Wars of the Northwest.* New Haven, Conn., 1966.

Drury, Clifford M. *Marcus and Narcissa Whitman and the Opening of Old Oregon.* Glendale, Calif., 1973.

Milner, Clyde A., II. *With Good Intentions: Quaker Work among the Pawnees, Otos, and Omahas in the 1870s.* Lincoln, Nebr., 1982.

Prucha, Francis Paul. "Two Roads to Conversion." *Pacific Northwest Quarterly* 79 (October 1988): 30–37.

Schoenberg, Wildred P. *A History of the Catholic Church in the Pacific Northwest, 1743–1983.* Washington, D.C., 1987.

Szasz, Ferenc M. *The Protestant Clergy in the Great Plains and Mountain West, 1865–1915.* Albuquerque, N. Mex., 1988.

———, ed. *Religion in the American West: Historical Essays.* Lanham, Md., 1987.

———, and Margaret Connell Szasz. "Chapter Ten: Religion and Spirituality." In *The Oxford History of the American West.* New York, 1994.

MISSIONS IN HAWAII

In 1819, the first Protestant mission to HAWAII was organized by the AMERICAN BOARD OF COMMISSIONERS FOR FOREIGN MISSIONS (ABCFM), a coalition of Congregational, Presbyterian, and Dutch Reformed churches formed in 1810. The immediate initiative for the mission was the death in 1818 of HENRY OBOOKIAH (OPUKAHAIA). A Hawaiian youth, Obookiah had attended the ABCFM's Foreign Mission School in Cornwall, Connecticut, and while there had converted to Christianity and made plans to return to Hawaii to spread the gospel.

The first mission included seven couples, led by the Reverends Hiram Bingham and Asa Thurston, five children, and four Hawaiian boys who had attended the Foreign Mission School. Six of the seven couples had married, and, in some cases, met only a month or less before their departure in October 1819 from Boston aboard the brig *Thaddeus.* The wives, who shared the mission charges with their husbands, instilled a sense of Christian family and provided links to female members of the Hawaiian royal family—links that were crucial to the success of the mission.

Shortly before the missionaries left their homeland, King Kamehameha I had died, and the traditional Hawaiian religious system based on a set of taboos or *kapus* collapsed only months before they arrived in March 1820. The new king, Kamehameha II or Liholiho, had some misgivings about the mission but allowed the group to land with one year's probation.

Over the next twenty-five years, the ABCFM mission made rapid gains in converting Hawaiians and establishing schools. In 1825, several members of the royal family, particular Kaahumanu, the dowager queen of Kamehameha I, converted to Christianity. The missionaries created an alphabet for the Hawaiian language to promote literacy and established schools that enrolled fifty-two thousand native students, two-fifths of Hawaii's population by 1831. By the 1840s, more than twenty thousand Hawaiians had joined the church.

Although ABCFM policy specifically prohibited missionaries from engaging in political activity, the mission exerted its influence over public policy by enacting blue laws to regulate trade and outlaw prostitution largely in response to the rowdiness and drunkenness brought on by the arrival of the American whalers in the 1820s. In the 1830s and 1840s, King Kamehameha III called on missionaries to strengthen Hawaii's political organization. While some missionaries encouraged the creation of fee-simple land ownership, others—notably the Reverend William Richards—devised a constitutional monarchy with a representative assembly.

The ABCFM mission held a virtual monopoly on the Christian religion in Hawaii from 1820 until 1839, when the monarchy decreed religious toleration and allowed French Catholic priests to remain. After the ABCFM dissolved the mission in 1853, the Congregational church in Hawaii existed independently.

American mission activity broadened its base when eight Mormon elders arrived in 1850. The Mormons set out to minister throughout the islands but soon concentrated their activities at a settlement on Lanai. They gained four thousand converts by the time the first mission ended in 1857. The mission was revived in 1861 with the arrival of Walter Murray Gibson, who soon quarreled with church officials over the disposition of property on Lanai and was excommunicated. Although no longer a part of the mission, Gibson later served as Hawaiian prime minister under King David Kalakaua from 1882 to 1887. The mission was again reorganized in 1864 and 1865 with a sugar plantation established at Laie on Oahu. Despite economic problems, the Laie mission survived. Church membership rebounded to nearly five thousand by the 1890s; in 1919, a temple was completed at Laie.

No subject arouses more controversy in Hawaii than the impact of the Congregational (ABCFM) missionaries. While most commentators praise the missionaries for bringing literacy to the native Hawaiians, they condemn them for repressing various aspects of native Hawaiian culture, including the hula. While many of the missionaries returned to the United States, a substantial number remained in Hawaii as did their children. Several missionaries, particularly Samuel N. Castle and Amos S. Cooke, entered mercantile businesses and planted sugar. Their later economic success, as well as that of their descendants, led to the expression that the "missionaries came to do good and ended doing well." In the political arena, Lorrin A. Thurston, the grandson of missionary couple Asa and Lucy Thurston, is considered the leader of the Hawaiian Revolution of 1893. SANFORD B. DOLE, the first president of the Republic of Hawaii, was also the son of a missionary. The dominance of missionary descendants in the political and economic life of Hawaii continued into the twentieth century. As late as the 1950s, descendants of forty missionary couples lived in the islands. Although their dominance diminished in the years after World War II, missionary descendants still form the base of many older established Caucasian families in modern-day Hawaii.

—*John S. Whitehead*

SEE ALSO: Bingham, Hiram and Sybil

SUGGESTED READING:

Britsch, R. Lanier. *Moramona: The Mormons in Hawaii.* Laie, Hawaii, 1989.

Grimshaw, Patricia. *Paths of Duty: American Missionary Wives in Nineteenth-Century Hawaii.* Honolulu, Hawaii, 1989.

Kuykendall, Ralph S. *The Hawaiian Kingdom, 1778–1854.* Honolulu, Hawaii, 1938.

Zwiep, Mary. *Pilgrim Path: The First Company of Women Missionaries in Hawaii.* Madison, Wis., 1991.

MISSISSIPPI RIVER

The largest river in North America, the Mississippi drains a region of some 1.2 million square miles, nearly one-eighth of the continent, including some thirty-one states. With its headwaters in Minnesota at Lake Itasca, the Mississippi flows almost due south through the interior of the continent to the Gulf of Mexico. Half way there, its waters mix with those of the Missouri and the Ohio rivers, its two principal tributaries. The river enters the Gulf after flowing 2,340 miles into a vast delta southeast of New Orleans. From its headwaters to St. Paul, Minnesota, the river runs clear, twisting through low country dotted with lakes and marshes; from St. Paul, the Mississippi grows into the powerful "Father of Waters," as the Indians called it, gathering water from the streams and rivers of Minnesota, Wisconsin, Illinois, and Iowa, until it hits the turbulent, sediment-filled, once utterly unpredictable Missouri. There, it turns into the muddy Mississippi. Below its junction with the Ohio at Cairo, Illinois, the Mississippi swells to the kind of grandeur that perhaps a MARK TWAIN could do justice in describing. A brown, decep-

Mississippi River.

tively quiet-flowing flood, one-mile wide from bank to bank, the Mississippi dumps more than six hundred thousand cubic feet of water into the Gulf of Mexico a year.

For Native Americans and the early Euro-American explorers, voyageurs, missionaries, conquerors, and trappers, the Mississippi was a broad brown road into the interior, one they traveled by canoe, raft, bateau, and boat. The first Europeans to set eyes on the river were Spaniards, who found it an impediment to their explorations in the Southwest. In 1673, two Frenchmen, JACQUES MARQUETTE and LOUIS JOLIET, put their birch-bark canoes in the waters and explored the river as far as they dared, mistaking it for a tributary of the Missouri. SIEUR DE LA SALLE, who was essentially a fur trader, although he tried his hand at a number of enterprises, more fully explored the Mississippi and envisioned a series of trading posts along its banks and a fleet of boats to carry trade goods and furs up and down the river. French traders and missionaries, following in his wake, established a loose European hegemony over the region with the sufferance of their Indian partners in the FUR TRADE and set up a trading post in ST. LOUIS, MISSOURI, and a port of call in New Orleans. Even after Louisiana fell under Spanish control in 1763, and after it was bought by the United States in 1803, the nonnative residents remained French in language and life style. For a while, finding the headwaters of the Mississippi became an obsession for the Europeans. The North West Company's DAVID THOMPSON thought the headwaters lay at Turtle Lake in Minnesota, which he found in 1798. ZEBULON MONTGOMERY PIKE braved a cruel Minnesota winter to find the river's origin in 1805, declaring Leech Lake the Mississippi's "main source" and Red Cedar Lake (Cass Lake) its "upper source." Lewis Cass agreed with Pike after checking out the region on a government-sponsored expedition in 1820. Finally a mineralogist fascinated by the Indians, HENRY ROWE SCHOOLCRAFT, unlocked the mystery. With Cass in 1823, Schoolcraft returned on his own well-equipped expedition in 1832, when an Ojibwa at Cass Lake guided him to the actual spot, which he and a missionary dubbed "Itasca," from the Latin for "true head" *(veritas caput)*.

For the Americans, the Mississippi became the main north-south avenue of travel, and it remains one of the busiest commercial waterways in the world. As early as 1837, the UNITED STATES ARMY CORPS OF ENGINEERS began to tinker with the river, and in 1879, a Mississippi River Commission was established, but not until the great flood of 1929 did the federal government launch a massive flood-control program. Straightened, shored up with levies and flood ways, its navigability improved, the Mississippi River of the late twentieth century is plied by pleasure boats and barges, the latter carrying oil, coal, coke, iron, steel, chemicals, sand and gravel, and sulfur, among other products. Once the haven of steamboat casinos and river-boat gamblers, the Mississippi has witnessed, in recent years, a returned to games of chance, sponsored by several state governments and played on *faux* steamers meant to recapture the atmosphere of risk and adventure the river once represented for generations of settlers headed west.

—*Charles Phillips*

SEE ALSO: River Transportation

MISSOURI

Missouri, the "Show Me State," is the nation's seventeenth largest state, containing 69,686 square miles. Located near the nation's geographic center, it is also the United States's population center. In 1994, Missouri's population was 5,278,000, ranking it sixteenth. It is the nation's environmental crossroads as well, situated between the humid East and the arid West, the Eastern forest and the Western prairie, the long growing season of the Cotton Belt South and the rich glacial and loessial soils of the Corn Belt North, and possessing the Coastal Plain's low elevation and the Ozark Uplands' highlands. The state's two major cities, ST. LOUIS and KANSAS CITY, are located on the eastern and western borders, respectively. The capital, Jefferson City, is located at the state's center.

Until the late nineteenth century, Missouri was physically defined by its rivers. The wide MISSOURI RIVER, running south, forms a portion of the state's northwestern boundary before turning west at present-day Kansas City and racing across the state to just north of St. Louis where it meets the Mississippi River, which forms the eastern boundary. From agricultural hamlet to burgeoning metropolis, it was upon this river system that the state of Missouri was built.

Native Americans

The ancestors of the North American Indians who first inhabited the land we know as Missouri came to live in the Missouri and Mississippi River valleys in about 10,000 B.C. A number of distinct cultural periods followed, the most creative being the "Mississippi Period" (900 to 1500 A.D.) in which the people lived in towns along the Mississippi River banks and are best remembered for the large, flat-topped temple mounds where they performed religious ceremonies.

As the Mississippian culture declined, another, called the "Oneota," arose, from which Missouri's two main historical tribes, the Missouri and Osage descended. The Missouri Indians, who first gave their name to the river and later to the state, were once a vigorous and thriving tribe but fell victim to smallpox and relentless persecution by their Sac (Sauk) Indian enemies until the surviving remnant merged with their Oto kinsmen. The most important Indians in the region were the Osage Indians. The Osage men were avid hunters and presided over a patriarchal society in which the women performed domestic labors and took responsibility for child rearing. After years of uneasy relationship with European then American invaders, the Osage tribe gradually retreated until the last of the tribe left the state in 1825.

European exploration and settlement

European penetration into the region had its origins in the French quest for empire in the seventeenth century. In 1673, Father JACQUES MARQUETTE and LOUIS JOLIET—in search of Indian souls, furs, and the Pacific source of the Mississippi River—were the first white men to stand on what is now Missouri soil. The first permanent white settlement was Ste. Genevieve on the western banks of the Mississippi in about 1750. In 1764, St. Louis became Missouri's second permanent white settlement just south of the confluence of the Missouri and Mississippi Rivers.

In 1762, France gave the territory known as Louisiana to Spain in exchange for assistance in the Seven Years' War against England. Spain split the territory into two administrative units near the northern border of what is now the state of Louisiana. Upper Louisiana, which included all of present-day Missouri, was ruled by a lieutenant-governor in St. Louis.

In 1795, the Spanish began allowing Americans into the region on the condition that they would adopt

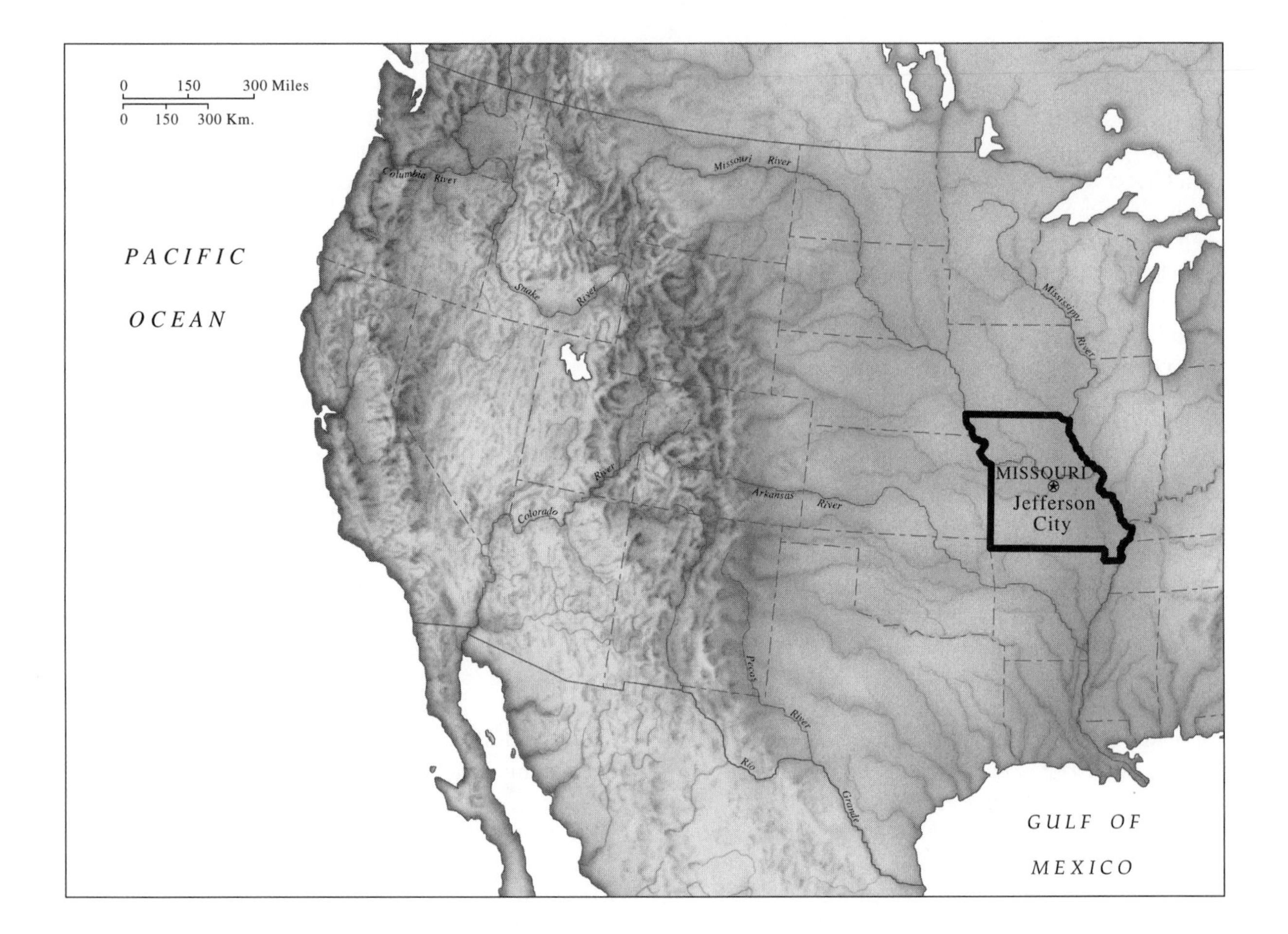

Spanish citizenship and Catholicism. Two American settlers who did were New England native MOSES AUSTIN, who came to mine lead in Potosi in 1796, and the frontiersman DANIEL BOONE who, in 1798, accepted a Spanish land grant in the Femme Osage district.

Transfer to the United States

In 1800, Spain secretly transferred Louisiana to Napoleon Bonaparte, in exchange for Tuscany. Upon learning of the deal, in 1802, U.S. President THOMAS JEFFERSON sent envoys to negotiate with the French leader. They arrived at a propitious moment. Napoleon, having suffered unexpected reverses in Santo Domingo and needing cash to continue his European struggle against Great Britain, agreed to sell Louisiana to the United States. On March 9, 1804, control of the Upper Louisiana formally passed to the United States. Under American dominion, the region quickly established a reputation for political factiousness and lawlessness that continued after Missouri became a territory in 1810.

Following the WAR OF 1812, the state underwent its first major immigration as land-hungry settlers from Kentucky, Tennessee, Virginia, and North Carolina poured into the fertile Missouri "Boonslick," running through central Missouri along the Missouri River.

During the first half century, Missouri became the "mother of the West," serving as the nation's base camp for America's explorers, fur traders, and voyagers on the overland trails. Among the very first to venture west was the LEWIS AND CLARK EXPEDITION (from 1804 to 1806), which set out to explore the Louisiana Territory. While this and other expeditions added significantly to knowledge of the West, so did the experiences of Missouri fur traders such as MANUEL LISA, JAMES (JIM) BRIDGER, CHRISTOPHER HOUSTON ("KIT") CARSON, and WILLIAM HENRY ASHLEY, who kept the men of Europe in beaver-fur hats until the market collapsed in the 1840s.

If the FUR TRADE helped establish the early Missouri economy, it was later sustained by overland trade that began with Santa Fe in 1821. By 1830, Independence, Missouri, had become established as the main jumping-off point for trails west. The organization and methods first pioneered by the Santa Fe traders would later serve as the model for the pioneers stricken with

"Oregon fever" in the 1840s and "gold fever" after the start of the California rush in 1849. In 1861, ST. JOSEPH's fabled PONY EXPRESS, with its team of fast relay riders, began mail service to California.

Territory to state

While Missouri served as the springboard for the creation of states farther west, its acquisition of statehood in 1821 was problematic. Missouri was founded by emigrants from the Upper South, who brought their slaves and proslavery attitudes with them. When Missouri applied for statehood in 1819, it threatened to undo the national balance between free and slave states, and it won statehood only after two national compromises: the balancing entry of the free state of Maine and the forbidding of slavery in any other portion of the LOUISIANA PURCHASE north of Missouri's southern border.

Upon achieving statehood, the territorial capital at St. Louis was moved to nearby St. Charles and then to a centrally located site selected in 1822, named the City of Jefferson in honor of the purchaser of Louisiana.

Initially, Missouri's state politics were a fractious contest between the old French elite (with their American allies) and the ambitious champions of more recent arrivals. In the end, the newcomers easily routed the old elite, and THOMAS HART BENTON, who won election as one of Missouri's first two senators, came to dominate Missouri's politics and served as a prominent national spokesman for Western interests during the next thirty years.

Between 1830 and 1860, Missouri's population increased more than 1,000 percent, climbing to nearly 1.2 million by 1860. The long strands of population following the Mississippi and Missouri rivers now expanded to fill out the state. The make-up of Missouri's population underwent a radical change, with foreign- and Northern-born outnumbering the emigrants from the Upper South who had originally settled the state. While people from Tennessee and Kentucky continued to arrive, they were now "hill folks" settling in the thinly populated Ozarks. More than half of the foreign-born immigrants to Missouri during that period were Germans, who established themselves primarily along the Missouri River valley between St. Louis and Jefferson City. Although much smaller in number, the Irish composed the second largest immigrant group. Generally poor, they tended to congregate principally in St. Louis.

A small but significant group that came to the state was systematically oppressed and lived and worked under the continual threat of violence. In 1860, Missouri's black slaves numbered approximately 115,000, making up a little less than 10 percent of the population. Slave life was hard in Missouri but not impossible. Most field slaves worked from sunup to sundown raising tobacco or hemp, lived in shanties behind their masters' houses, kept gardens for food, and wore shifts and cast-off clothing from whites. Household slaves and those in urban areas usually had lighter work and sometimes more freedom but often longer hours. Only a handful of the state's slaveholders owned more than a few slaves. Abolitionist sentiment in the state was slight, usually confined to a small number of evangelical Northern emigrants such as Maine's Elijah Lovejoy, whose abolitionism and anti-Catholicism led to the mob destruction of his St. Louis newspaper and his subsequent "martyrdom" across the river in Alton, Illinois, in 1837.

White Missourians would pay a fearful price for allowing slavery within the state's borders, but the cost only gradually became apparent after the UNITED STATES–MEXICAN WAR. Missouri volunteers had played an enthusiastic and conspicuous role in wresting the northern third of Mexico away from the country, but the national quarrels over permitting slavery's spread into the new territories rent the fabric of Missouri's domestic peace. In 1856, Missouri "border ruffians" marched into "Bleeding Kansas" to intimidate Free-Soil settlers from the North. The following year, the United States Supreme Court in the *DRED SCOTT* DECISION, a slave-freedom suit arising out of St. Louis, declared the MISSOURI COMPROMISE an unconstitutional infringement on the rights of slaveholders. Still, Missouri made clear it wanted both slavery and union. Of all the states, only Missouri gave all of its 1860 electoral votes to STEPHEN A. DOUGLAS, the moderate Democratic candidate in a polarized nation.

Civil War and Reconstruction

When sectional tension burst into civil war, the Missouri legislature called a special constitutional convention to consider secession, but not a single secessionist was elected. After an aborted attempt to seize the federal arsenal in St. Louis, pro-Southern Governor Claiborne Jackson fled Missouri and eventually set up a secessionist government in Texas. A pro-Union government was organized by the constitutional convention, and in August 1861, the federal government declared martial law. The first major battle in Missouri took place at Wilson's Creek that month, resulting in a Confederate victory. A second battle at Pea Ridge, Arkansas, in March 1862, however, resulted in a Union victory and secured Missouri for the North. Vicious guerrilla warfare characterized much of the subsequent fighting in the state, engendering hatreds and lawlessness—best represented by Confederate bushwacker Jesse James's career—that long outlasted the war.

In 1864, pro-Union voters put members of the Radical Union party firmly in power. The new legislature called a constitutional convention that abolished slavery on January 1, 1865, and brought a number of progressive reforms to state government. Yet, it also sought to repress former Confederates and their sympathizers—barring them from political life and certain professions. Radical Republicanism reached its peak in 1868 but soon fragmented. Appalled by party corruption, Liberal Republicans doubted the wisdom of repressive measures and broke away from Republican regulars. The division led to the return of Democrats to state power in 1872.

As elsewhere, the transition to freedom was not easy for Missouri's African Americans. The Freedmen's Bureau, set up by the U.S. Congress, provided help, as did the Missouri Equal Rights League, which labored to bring formal education to former slaves. The league's secretary, James Milton Turner, emerged as one of the more significant black leaders of the period.

From 1860 to 1900, Missouri underwent a transportation revolution as antebellum dreams of crisscrossing the state with railroads came true. Another dream was realized when, in 1874, James B. Eads mastered the unique problems involved in bridging the Mississippi River. Ironically, these successes would signal the decline of the steamboat trade that had originally given St. Louis so much of its economic importance.

Missouri continued to attract immigrants during the years following the CIVIL WAR. Between 1860 and 1890, the state's population doubled. Kansas City was an urban phenomenon of the late nineteenth century. Barely more than a village in 1860, it became one of the country's great agricultural processing centers and home to more than 160,000 people by 1900. Although St. Louis, with ill-grace, surrendered Midwestern economic leadership to CHICAGO, ILLINOIS, during the period, the Missouri city grew impressively, becoming the third most important manufacturing center in the United States and producing shoes, chemicals, beer, clothing, iron, and brick, among other products.

Late nineteenth-century development

Missouri's rural complexion changed too. In some ways, Missouri farmers fell victim to their own success. In the late nineteenth century, the number of acres of land brought under cultivation tripled, while technological advances made these acres more productive than ever before. The resulting fall in agricultural prices unfortunately coincided with a severe period of deflation. The result was an extended period of agrarian protest from the 1870s to the turn of the century. The most important agrarian protest in Missouri was associated with the Populist party in the 1890s.

Rural and urban dwellers alike had a growing concern about political corruption and fear of economic centralization in business trusts. St. Louis circuit attorney Joseph Folk gained fame in 1902, when he broke the power of city boss Edward Butler and propelled himself into the governor's office. Folk was followed by Attorney General Herbert Hadley, who won national attention by pressing the antitrust suit that broke up Standard Oil. Hadley then became the first Republican governor in thirty-eight years.

Cultural life

By the time of the Progressive era, Missouri had matured and ceased to be a Western state in some ways, but some of its earlier Western sensibility continued in its art. From its earliest days of statehood, Missouri had attracted talented painters. One of America's most important nineteenth-century painters was GEORGE CALEB BINGHAM, called the "Missouri artist" and known particularly for his antebellum river scenes and election paintings. An echo of Bingham's interest in the commonplace is found in the work of regionalist Thomas Hart Benton, Missouri's best twentieth-century painter. In literature, the same frontier sentiments are best represented in the work of Samuel Clemens or, MARK TWAIN, whose masterpiece, *The Adventures of Huckleberry Finn* (1884), and children's book, *The Adventures of Tom Sawyer* (1876), drew on his childhood in Hannibal. Other Missouri writers of particular interest include Kate Chopin, whose works, particularly *The Awakening* (1899), have found special interest in a generation of feminist readers; and best-selling author Harold Bell Wright, whose *Shepherd of the Hills* (1907) helped popularize Missouri's Ozarks. Missourian Scott Joplin is best remembered today for his ragtime tunes such as "The Maple Leaf Rag" (1899) and "The Entertainer" (1902).

Once the nation's "gateway to the West," as memorialized by the St. Louis Arch, Missouri is losing its distinctiveness. In the 1990s, Branson, Missouri, became the nation's favorite tourist destination by playing on its Ozark regional flavor. Yet over the course of the twentieth century, national chain stores, radio and television, highways, and integration into a global economy gradually made Missouri's story and the nation's one and the same.

—*Kenneth H. Winn*

SEE ALSO: Guerrillas; James Brothers; Santa Fe and Chihuahua Trail

SUGGESTED READING:

Foley, William E. *The Genesis of Missouri: From Wilderness Outpost to Statehood.* Columbia, Mo., 1989.

Kirkendall, Richard S. *History of Missouri. Vol. 5. 1919–1953.* Columbia, Mo., 1986.

Kremer, Gary R., and Antonio F. Holland. *Missouri's Black Heritage.* Rev. ed. Columbia, Mo., 1993.
McCandless, Perry. *History of Missouri. Vol. 2. 1820–1860.* Columbia, Mo., 1972.
Parrish, William E. *History of Missouri. Vol. 3. 1860–1875.* Columbia, Mo., 1973.
———. *Missouri: The Heart of the Nation.* 2d ed. Arlington Heights, Ill., 1992.
Rafferty, Milton. *Historical Atlas of Missouri.* Norman, Okla., 1982.
Thelen, David. *Paths of Resistance: Tradition and Democracy in Industrializing Missouri.* New York, 1986.

MISSOURI COMPROMISE

In February 1819, Missourians petitioned Congress for admission into the Union as a slave state. The request touched off a two-and-a-half year quarrel that threatened the Union itself. French colonists had established slavery in Missouri in the eighteenth century, and they were subsequently assured of their property rights by the terms of the LOUISIANA PURCHASE. Although the first American settlers, coming primarily from Kentucky and Tennessee, thought of themselves as Westerners rather than Southerners, they brought to Missouri the proslavery attitudes of their native states. In asking for Missouri's entry into the Union, they threatened to undo the balance of free states to slave states—a balance that stood at eleven apiece—and to push the wedge of slavery into the same northerly latitude as the free states of Ohio, Indiana, and Illinois.

The "Missouri crisis" was formally ignited by New York Congressman James Tallmadge, Jr., who proposed adding to the enabling bill permitting Missouri to form a state government an amendment that provided for the gradual abolition of slavery within its borders. It soon became clear that Tallmadge's amendment had larger implications touching on a host of fundamental issues, including the limits of Congress's constitutional power, the character of Western development, sectional identity, and the morality of slavery. As a result, the normal operation of politics broke down; the Northern-dominated House passed Tallmadge's amendment, and the Southern-dominated Senate rejected it.

At that critical juncture, the residents of Maine, who had been living under the governance of Massachusetts, applied for statehood. A group of conciliatory politicians then sought a way through the impasse by tying the admission of the free state of Maine to that of the slave state of Missouri, thereby keeping the balance between free and slave states the same. Even though the balance was maintained, Southerners regarded the successful extension of slavery into the West as a victory. In an additional attempt to allay Northern fears, Illinois Senator Jesse Thomas proposed that after Missouri's entrance into the Union, slavery would not be permitted in any other state formed out of the vast unincorporated area of the Louisiana Territory north of 36° 30'—the latitude of Missouri's southern border. When Congress agreed, Missouri's enabling legislation was passed and signed into law in March 1820. The Missouri crisis seemed at last over.

The sectional deal, however, nearly came unraveled when Missouri subsequently submitted to Congress a state constitution that forbade the settlement of free blacks in the state. Since the United States Constitution outlawed the discrimination of the citizens of one state by those of another and since many Northern states recognized free blacks as citizens, antislavery opponents again sought to bar Missouri's entrance into the Union. In a second compromise, forged by Kentucky Congressman HENRY CLAY, Congress declared that the president would recognize Missouri's statehood only if its legislature solemnly declared that it would never enforce its constitutional proscription against free blacks' settling within its borders. Although greatly irritated by having its internal affairs tampered with in a manner never required of any other state, the Missouri legislature passed the required proclamation. President James Monroe declared Missouri's official entrance into the Union on August 10, 1821.

The Missouri Compromise of 1820 became the rock on which nineteenth-century American nationalism was built. When it crumbled in the 1850s, so did the Union.

—*Kenneth H. Winn*

SEE ALSO: National Expansion: Slavery and National Expansion

SUGGESTED READING:

Moore, Glover. *The Missouri Controversy, 1819–1821.* Lexington, Ky., 1953.
Remini, Robert. *Henry Clay: Statesman for the Union.* New York, 1991.
Shoemaker, Floyd C. *Missouri's Struggle for Statehood, 1804–1821.* Jefferson City, Mo., 1916.

MISSOURI FUR COMPANY

In early 1809, MANUEL LISA, Pierre Menard, William Morrison, Pierre Chouteau, Auguste Chouteau, Jr., Sylvestre Labbadie, Benjamin Wilkinson, Reuben Lewis, Andrew Henry, and WILLIAM CLARK came together to form the St. Louis Missouri Fur Company for the purpose of hunting furs in the northern Rocky

Mountains. Their initial expedition, sent upriver that spring, was a disappointment, for while it showed a profit, the difficulties of finance, transportation, hostile relations with the Indians, and the impending WAR OF 1812 proved too daunting for most of the partners. The company reorganized in 1812 into a limited partnership with three directors—Lisa, Labbadie, and Clark—and changed its name to the Missouri Fur Company, but continuing problems put it out of business by 1814. Using new sources of American money, Manuel Lisa created another Missouri Fur Company in 1819, and, although it survived his death in 1820, it failed four years later because of Indian hostility, increased competition, and inadequate financing. In its brief existence, the Missouri Fur Company introduced white civilization to the natives along the Missouri River and in the Rocky Mountains, maintained peace with the various tribes during the War of 1812, and paved the way for later, more successful fur companies.

—*Richard E. Oglesby*

SEE ALSO: Chouteau Family; Fur Trade

SUGGESTED READING:

Oglesby, Richard E. *Manuel Lisa and the Opening of the Missouri Fur Trade*. Norman, Okla., 1963. Reprint. 1984.

MISSOURI INDIANS

SEE: Native American Peoples: Peoples of the Great Plains

MISSOURI RIVER

The western river of the MISSISSIPPI RIVER system, the Missouri is the longest river in the United States. It flows 2,741 miles through a basin of six hundred thousand square miles, about half the size of the Mississippi River basin. The Missouri River basin drains parts of ten states and two Canadian provinces. From its headwaters 4,000 feet above sea level, it falls 3,630 feet before discharging 69,300 cubic feet of water per second into the Mississippi seventeen miles above St. Louis. The Missouri is one of the most significant geographical determinants in the history of the westward movement, in the growth of population, and in the economic development of the trans-Mississippi West.

On August 12, 1805, in southwestern Montana, the American explorers MERIWETHER LEWIS and WILLIAM CLARK came upon a tiny mountain creek that was "the remotest water of the Missouri." One member of the expedition, with one foot on either side of the stream, thanked God he had lived to straddle the headwaters of the great river. The stream flows north into the channel of the Jefferson, which continues toward its confluence with the Madison and Gallatin rivers at Three Forks, Montana. From there, the Missouri runs through the Big Belt Mountains and the Lewis Range, passes through Helena, Montana, where it descends into a narrow gorge—the Gates of the Mountain—and turns into a swift flowing river of cataracts and falls. North of Great Falls, Montana, the river bends on its way across upper Montana. Fed by the Teton, Marias, Milk, and Sun rivers, the Missouri increases in current and volume. Flowing through rocky areas, which serve as a natural filter, the water remains clear. As the river rolls across the Great Plains, the concentration of silt and sediment increases, and the water changes to a muddy color. The Yellowstone, one of its principal tributaries, joins the river as it enters North Dakota. The Missouri flows southeast through Lake Sakakawea and then south past Bismarck through Lake Oahe and into South Dakota. The Grant, Morea, White, and Cheyenne rivers feed the Missouri before it reaches Pierre, South Dakota, where it runs to the Nebraska boundary and curves east, forming the boundary between the southeastern tip of South Dakota and northeastern Nebraska to Sioux City, Iowa. There it moves south between Nebraska and Iowa. The Platte drains into the Missouri a few miles below Omaha, Nebraska, and Council Bluffs, Iowa. The river then forms the boundary between Kansas and Missouri and joins with the Kansas or Kaw River at Kansas City, Missouri. There it bends and meanders east 577 miles across Missouri, drawing waters from the Grand, Osage, Gasconade, and Chariton rivers as it flows toward the Mississippi.

Many Indian tribes inhabited the regions of the river before the arrival of the Europeans. In Missouri, the Osages lived south of the Missouri River near its confluence with the Osage. Farther upriver, the Kansa (also known as the Kaw) inhabited the land west of the great bend at present-day Kansas City. The Omahas of northern Nebraska and the Pawnees ranged over the prairie between the Platte and Republican rivers one hundred miles from the Missouri. In the winter of 1804 to 1805, Lewis and Clark wintered with the Mandans, a sedentary tribe that lived in stockaded earthen lodges on the Upper Missouri. As they explored the river to its headwaters, the explorers encountered the Sioux, Dakota, Yankton, Cheyenne, Shoshone, and many lesser tribes who lived on both sides of the river.

The French, ambitious in their plans to expand the FUR TRADE and spread Christianity into the Mississippi

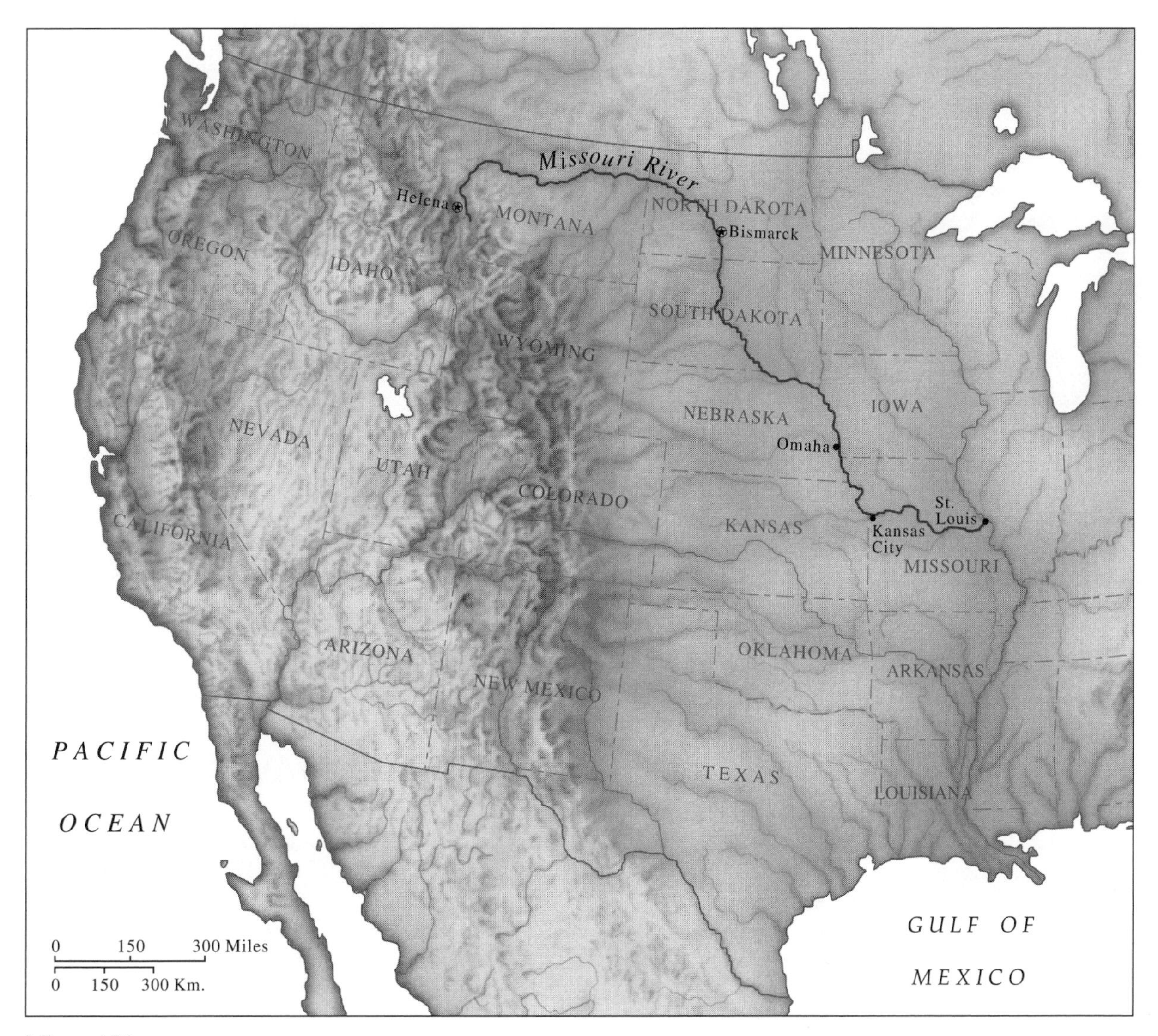

Missouri River.

River valley, sent Father Jacques Marquette and Louis Joliet in 1673 to explore the Mississippi. They reported when they reached the mouth of Pekitanoui (the Indian name of the Missouri that means "muddy waters") that along the banks of the Missouri were villages of the Missouris ("people of the big canoes"). From this Indian tribe came the name of the river, the territory, and the state.

French traders followed Marquette and Joliet into Louisiana west of the Mississippi. Etienne Veniard de Bourgmond reached the mouth of the Platte River in Nebraska and built Fort Orleans in 1723 on the north bank of the river near the mouth of the Grand. By 1738, Pierre Gaultier de Variennes had contacted the Indians on the Upper Missouri. In 1769, a French trader, Louis Blanchette, established St. Charles, the first permanent settlement on the Missouri, twenty-three miles northwest of St. Louis.

After the Louisiana Purchase (1803), the Lewis and Clark Expedition explored Upper Louisiana and returned with journals filled with geographical and scientific information about the river, including its first map. By the time the journals were published in 1814, the vanguard of fur traders and pioneer settlers had begun to use the river as a highway into the trans-Missouri West. Forts, trading posts, and towns appeared along its course as far as northern Montana in the decades before the Civil War.

In 1819, the *Independence* steamed upriver and demonstrated that steamboats could navigate the strong current and dangerous waters of the Missouri. Vital to the economic development and growth of settlements

A view of the Missouri Valley, east of Benton, ca. 1889. *Courtesy Montana Historical Society.*

along the river, steamboats became the major carriers of people and commerce, until the railroad replaced them after the Civil War.

The great overland migration across the OREGON TRAIL to the Far West began in the 1840s. Towns on or near the river in western Missouri and Iowa actively competed for the business of supplying the pioneers with provisions for their journeys. Although more emigrants probably started from Independence, Missouri, other Missouri towns—WESTPORT LANDING, Weston, and ST. JOSEPH—and Atchison, Kansas, also profited from the trade. The Mormons used Kannesville (now Council Bluffs, Iowa) for their departure point across the MORMON TRAIL to the valley of the Salt Lake in the late 1840s.

The first great effort to control flooding of the river was the construction of Fort Peck in Montana. Started in 1933, the dam was completed in 1937 and is one of the largest earthen dams in the country. In 1944, Congress passed the Flood Control Act (Missouri Basin Project), which authorized the UNITED STATES ARMY CORPS OF ENGINEERS and the BUREAU OF RECLAMATION to build a series of dams and reservoirs for flood control, crop IRRIGATION, and navigation improvements on the Missouri. By the mid-1950s, five of the main-stream dams were completed—Garrison in North Dakota; Oahe, Big Bend, and Fort Randall in South Dakota; and Gavin's Point on the border between South Dakota and Nebraska. The Water Resources Act of 1965 funded irrigation and hydroelectric-power projects in the upper basin, while in the lower basin, flood-control projects were planned and constructed. The army engineers also deepened the channel from Sioux City, Iowa, to St. Louis to keep the river open for navigation between these points from mid-March to November.

Although much has been done to improve the river and control flooding, destructive floods occurred in 1973, 1984, and 1986. In 1993, heavy early summer rains drenched the Midwest and filled the branches and tributaries of the Mississippi and Missouri below the flood-control dams and reservoirs in the upper basin. By mid-July, the two great rivers rampaged through the Midwest, caused an estimated $17 billion in damage, and devastated an area the size of Texas. As the floodwaters receded and the painful tasks of clean-up and rebuilding began, many economic problems and environmental issues remained as to how to control the unpredictable river.

—*Charles T. Jones, Jr.*

SEE ALSO: River Transportation

SUGGESTED READING:

Biddle, Nicholas, ed. *The Journals of Lewis and Clark*. New York, 1962.

Merk, Frederick. *History of the Westward Movement*. New York, 1978.

Munro, David, ed. "Missouri River." In *Chambers World Gazetteer*. New York, 1988.

Nasatir, Abraham P. *Before Lewis and Clark*. St. Louis, Mo., 1952.

Vestal, Stanley. *The Missouri*. Lincoln, Nebr., 1945.

MITCHELL, DAVID DAWSON

Fur trader and superintendent of Indian affairs, David Dawson Mitchell (1806–1861) was born in Louisa County, Virginia. He became a clerk in 1828 for the AMERICAN FUR COMPANY, headquartered in St. Louis, and was stationed with the Ioway Outfit. In 1830, he was transferred to the Upper Missouri Outfit where he supervised the building of Fort Mackenzie in 1832. In 1833, Mitchell traveled up the Missouri River with Prince Maximilian of Wied-Neuwied and Swiss artist KARL (OR CARL) BODMER to visit the Blackfoot Indians. Five years later, he witnessed the smallpox epidemic among the Arikara, Assiniboin, Blackfoot, Mandan, Minnetarie, and Sioux tribes. In 1835, he became a partner in another fur-trading venture on the upper Missouri at a post built by Narcisse Leclerc in 1833 and renamed Fort Mitchell.

A member of the Whig party, Mitchell used his political connections in 1841 to attain the position of superintendent of Indian affairs. From his headquarters in St. Louis, he reported on the large quantity of liquor that flowed to the Indian Country by way of the Missouri River and was an advocate of the suppression of the liquor trade.

During the United States–Mexican War, he served in the army holding the rank of lieutenant colonel and took control of Chihuahua before marching to join forces with Zachary Taylor at Saltillo.

After the Whigs regained power, Mitchell returned to St. Louis and resumed his work as superintendent of Indian affairs in 1851. During his two-year tenure in office, he helped negotiate the first FORT LARAMIE treaty and promoted the concept of allotment of reservations in severalty. In 1855, he helped organize, and became president of, the Missouri and California Overland Mail and Transportation Company.

—*Henry E. Fritz and Marie L. Fritz*

SUGGESTED READING:

DeVoto, Bernard. *Across the Wide Missouri.* Boston, 1947.

Harmon, George D. *Sixty Years of Indian Affairs, 1789–1850.* Chapel Hill, N.C., 1941.

Kvasnicka, Robert M., and Herman J. Viola, eds. *The Commissioners of Indian Affairs, 1824–1877.* Lincoln, Nebr., 1979.

Sunder, John E. *The Fur Trade on the Upper Missouri, 1840–1865.* Norman, Okla., 1965.

MIWOK INDIANS

SEE: Native American Peoples: Peoples of California

MIX, TOM

Born Thomas Hezikiah Mix in Mix Run, Pennsylvania, the cowboy movie star Tom Mix (1880–1940) appeared in more than 250 motion pictures from his debut in *Ranch Life in the Great Southwest* (1910) to his final starring role in the serial *The Miracle Rider* (1935). His silent films of the 1920s, featuring daredevil stunts often astride Tony, his "wonder horse," established him as America's favorite for two decades.

Mix's prominence in the 1920s belied his humble origins. Reared in poverty and unschooled after the fourth grade, Mix enlisted in the army in 1898, was promoted to first sergeant in 1900, and reenlisted in 1902, the year in which he married the first of his five wives. He was listed as AWOL in 1902 and was carried on army rolls for years as a deserter. During his enlistment, he was assigned to an artillery battery on the East Coast. Subsequent claims that he had fought in the Spanish-American War, the Philippine Insurrection, the Boxer Rebellion, and the Boer War were fabrications by Hollywood publicists and Mix himself.

Moving to Guthrie in the Oklahoma Territory in 1902, Mix became drum major for the Oklahoma Cavalry Band and later worked as a bartender. The MILLER BROTHERS' 101 RANCH WILD WEST SHOW hired him to greet guests in 1905, and there his film career began. He signed with the Selig Polyscope Company in 1910, Fox in 1917 (his seventy-eight feature films for Fox established his reputation), and Film Booking Office (a forerunner of RKO) in 1928. After suffering through the Wall Street crash of 1929, he joined the Sells-Floto Circus and toured through 1931. Beginning in 1932, he made nine films for Universal Studios, and

Tom Mix. *Courtesy National Cowboy Hall of Fame and Western Heritage Center.*

in 1933, he reached agreement with the Ralston-Purina Company for the use of his name for a radio program. In 1934, he joined the Sam B. Dill Circus, which he bought and renamed the Tom Mix Circus, touring the county until 1938. He reprised a successful 1925 European tour in 1938 and resumed a schedule of personal appearances in the United States in 1939. The following year, driving alone between Tucson and Phoenix, Mix swerved to avoid highway construction and died in an automobile wreck. Although it was estimated that he had earned more than $6 million during his thirty-year career, he left an estate valued at only $115,000. He is buried in Forest Lawn Memorial Park, Glendale, California.

—*William W. Savage, Jr.*

SUGGESTED READING:

Mix, Paul E. *The Life and Legend of Tom Mix*. South Brunswick, N.J., 1972.
Ponicsan, Darryl. *Tom Mix Died for Your Sins*. New York, 1975.

MODOC INDIANS

SEE: Native American Peoples: Peoples of California; Peoples of the Pacific Northwest

MODOC WAR

SEE: Pacific Northwest Indian Wars

MOFFAT, DAVID HALLIDAY

David Halliday Moffat (1839–1911), banker, mining entrepreneur, and railroad builder, was born in Washingtonville, New York. He arrived in Denver on March 17, 1860, as representative of C. C. and S. B. Woolworth, owners of a chain of book and stationery stores. As an investor in Colorado mining camps and railroads and, after 1880, as president of the First National Bank of Denver, Moffat achieved financial and social success and contributed to Colorado's development and growth. His concluding venture was the attempted construction of the Denver, Northwestern and Pacific Railway, whose proposed route extended west from Denver to the Pacific. From 1902 until his death, Moffat devoted his fortune, plus many

David Halliday Moffat, Jr. *Courtesy Denver Public Library, Western History Department.*

assets of the First National Bank, to that project, which business associates finished many years later.

—*Liston E. Leyendecker*

SUGGESTED READING:

Mehls, Steven Frederick. "David H. Moffat, Jr.: Early Colorado Business Leader." Ph. D. diss., University of Colorado at Boulder, 1982.

MOGOLLON, NEW MEXICO

SEE: Ghost Towns

MOJAVE DESERT

Located in southern California and stretching east into Nevada, Arizona, and Utah, the arid lands of the Mojave Desert occupy some twenty-five thousand square miles. It encompasses one-sixth of California's land area. Confined by the Sierra Nevada and the Colorado Basin at its northwest reaches, the desert stretches into the arid lands of the Great Basin to its north and into the Sonoran Desert at its extreme southern and southeastern parts. The San Gabriel–San Bernardino Mountains border its southwestern regions.

The Mojave Desert receives about five inches of rainfall each year. Daily temperatures fluctuate as much as eighty degrees Fahrenheit, and winter frosts are common. The desert's terrain includes broad basins, eroded mountains, fault blocks, and alluvial surfaces, much of them 2,000 feet above sea level. A notable exception, however, is DEATH VALLEY, a stretch of desert on the California-Nevada border. Death Valley marks the lowest point (at 287 feet below sea level) on the North American continent. The Mojave Desert supports some vegetation—creosote bush, Joshua trees, burroweed, and some cactus.

Home to native peoples of the Yuman language group, the desert was first traversed by an American when, in 1826, mountain man JEDEDIAH STRONG SMITH, loaded up a supply of water from the Colorado River and headed across the desert to Mission San Gabriel (present-day Los Angeles). Smith tried to follow the intermittent Mojave River, which he called the "Inconstant," but the journey was grueling. Smith characterized the desert as "a complete barren," and "a country of starvation."

Other trappers, eager to do business with Mexican California, followed Smith's route across the Mojave Desert. JOHN CHARLES FRÉMONT skirmished with Indians in the desert during his 1844 Western expedition. Some hardy or foolish Forty-niners attempted to cross the desert in their rush to reach the California gold fields.

The desert held little appeal to the thousands of Easterners headed for California's coast and fertile interior farm lands. Later in the nineteenth century, the excavation of salts, borax, and potash drew teams of workers into the desert. The desert also yielded silver, tungsten, gold, and iron. By the beginning of the twentieth century, engineer WILLIAM MULHOLLAND's plan to move water from the Colorado River across the desert to the city of Los Angeles defied nature itself.

Today the Mojave Desert supports some cattle grazing in its northern reaches. Military installations, taking advantage of the flat terrain and isolation, conduct space landings and aviation tests and stock ordinance. Death Valley National Park and Joshua Tree National Monument attract thousands of tourists each year. The desert's population is concentrated in small towns in its the southwestern corner.

—Patricia Hogan

MOJAVE INDIANS

SEE: Native American Peoples: Peoples of California

MOMADAY, N. SCOTT

SEE: Literature: Native American Literature

MONTANA

In Spanish, *Montana* means "mountain" or "mountain region," but of all the so-called mountain states, Montana has the lowest average elevation, 3,400 feet. Canada—British Columbia, Alberta and Saskatchewan—borders Montana on the north, North and South Dakota on the east, Wyoming on the south, and Idaho on the south and west. Larger than all but three states—Alaska, Texas, and California—Montana has a population density lower than all but two, Alaska and Wyoming. With 147,138 square miles of territory and only 799,065 people as of 1990, Montana was three times larger in area than Pennsylvania, which had sixteen times as many people.

Today, most Montanans trace their ancestry to western and northern Europe, to Great Britain, Ireland, Germany, France, and the Netherlands; a goodly number of them came from eastern Europe as well, particularly from Poland. The state's only large racial minority is made up of Indians from various tribes, two-thirds of whom live on the state's seven reservations. Most of the rest live in cities near the reservations—notably Missoula, Great Falls, and Billings. Few African Americans are permanent residents. Like the small numbers of Asian Americans and Hispanics, most of the state's African Americans live in Montana temporarily to work or attend school. In the early years of the twentieth century, families from northern Europe settled on homesteads, while other European immigrants came to work in the mines. Montana's cities, relatively few in number and small in population, developed from mining camps, trading centers, and railroad towns. Since 1970, in fact, Montana's rural regions have grown faster than its towns, but overall growth itself, rapid in the 1970s, declined to half the national average in the 1980s.

Distant from markets, manufacturing centers, and supply and service industries, Montana plays to its strength—the outdoors. Winter sports, HUNTING, fishing, and long trips are all characteristic of life in the state, which—despite its northern location—is resolutely Western. The main street in Helena, the state capital, is Last Chance Gulch, which was the city's original name, just the kind of name prospectors invading Montana's high country in the 1880s to pan for gold might be expected to give a town. The territory boomed into existence on the backs of copper miners and cow-

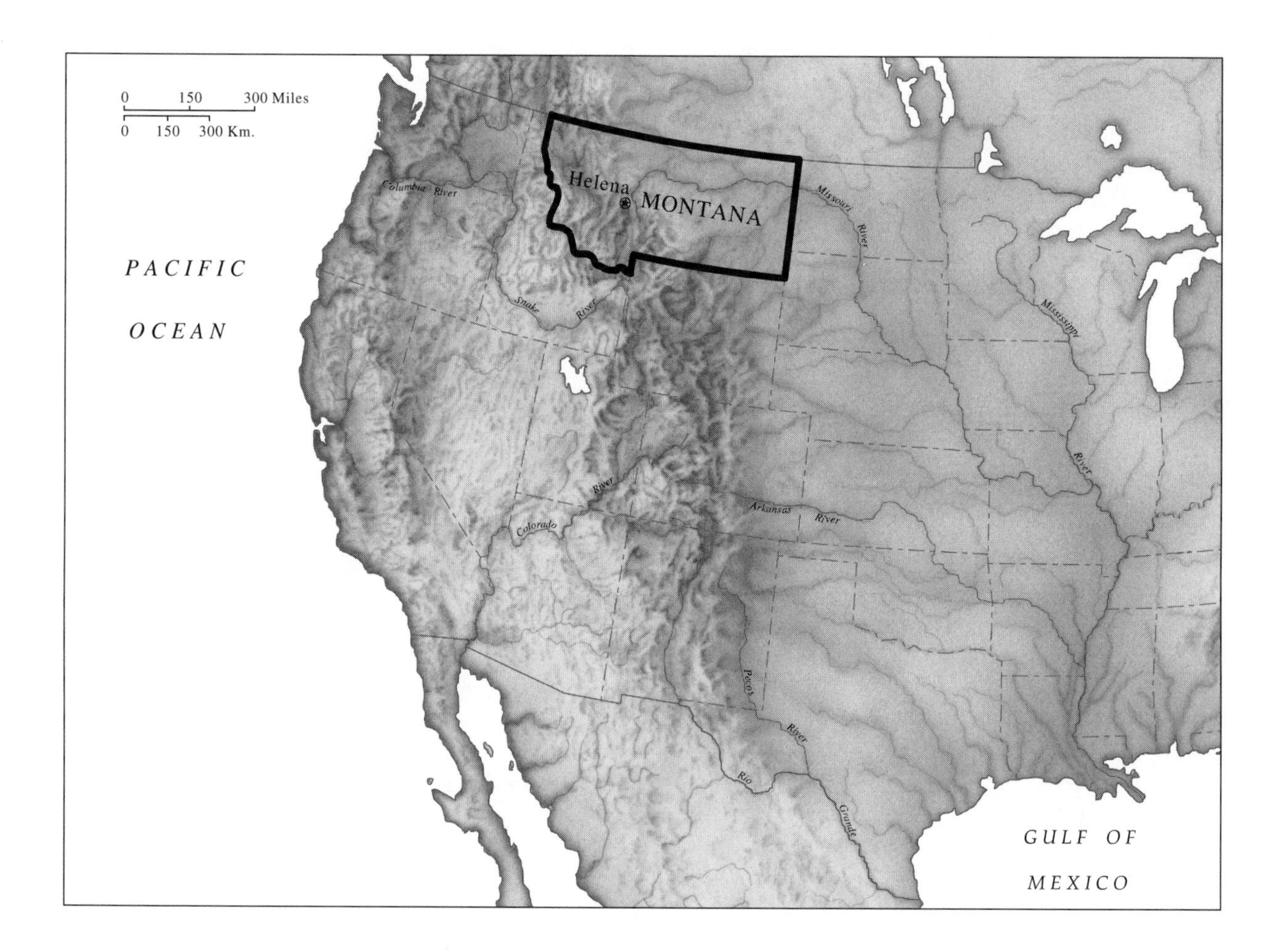

boys, and its earliest towns were run by copper kings and cattle barons. The cattle drive was an institution before Montana became a state; the company town became one shortly thereafter. For much of its history, Montana's frontier ethic meant that, as historian Clark C. Spence writes, "Montanans and outsiders alike," convinced nature was inexhaustible, "plundered the earth with too little concern for the environment itself or for future generations." Still, says Spence, proud of their wide-open spaces, their freedom, and their relative isolation, many Montanans think something of the "pioneer spirit" clings to the state and shapes their existence.

Geography and climate

The Rocky Mountains and the two dozen or so kindred ranges that make up the system sprawl across the western two-fifths of Montana. John Steinbeck described the Rockies, sweeping down from British Columbia, as "a great splash of grandeur," and the high country of Montana is a region of rugged, snow-capped peaks, dramatic glacier-carved valleys, mountain meadows, treeless ridges, sharp crags, ice-cold, fast-flowing streams, and deep, blue lakes. The highest mountain, Granite Peak in the Beartooth range, at 12,788 feet above sea level, towers over a region that includes the Mission Range, Flathead Lake, and two national parks, Yellowstone and Glacier. Lying along the Continental Divide, the mountains are covered with trees—white pine, Douglas fir, larch, lodgepole pine, western red cedar, and ponderosa, the state tree. Thirteen million acres of timber stretch west of the Divide; nine million, to the east. Glaciers carved the mountains in the last Ice Age, and small glaciers remain, although they hardly approach the past's great cold tongues of ice. The floors of the mountains' spectacularly rugged, narrow northwestern and south-central valleys are humid and wooded; those of the broad, panoramic west-central and southwestern valleys are wide, dry, and grassy. Montana's mountains are home to some rare and imposing animals, grizzly bears, Rocky Mountain goats, bighorn sheep, and moose, plus most of those common—or once common—to other areas as well, such as American elks, mule deer, black bears, mountain lions, bobcats, and forest grouse.

Montana is the only state in the Union whose waters flow into three oceans. Rising in Glacier National Park and in Teton County, mountain streams feed the Belly, St. Mary's, and Waterson rivers, which run across Canada to Hudson Bay and the Arctic Ocean. The Clark Fork, with headwaters near BUTTE and fed by such rivers as the Blackfoot, the Bitterroot, and its major tributary, the Flathead, winds its way to the Pacific via the Columbia River. The Flathead flows into and out of Flathead Lake, the state's largest. The Kootenai, rising from the lowest elevation—1,820 feet—of any river in the state, also drains into the Columbia. And then there is the Missouri, the highway of frontier Montana, beginning in the southwestern mountains, then looping its way north before plunging toward its junction with the Mississippi, which carries the Missouri's sediment-filled waters to the Gulf of Mexico. Ranging in color from mud-brown to "badly made pea-soup" green, historically irascible and irregular, the MISSOURI RIVER—its navigable stretches sometimes called "Montana's seacoast"—provided a commercial link with fur-trading St. Louis, a point of entry for westering Americans to overland trails, a dammable source of irrigation water for bottomland farmers and hydroelectric power for twentieth-century residents.

The Great Plains cover the eastern three-fifths of Montana. Made up of high, rolling prairies filled with blue gamma, bunch, bluestem, needle, and other grasses suitable for grazing buffaloes and cattle, the plains are punctuated by hills, buttes, wide river valleys, and isolated mountains. WALTER PRESCOTT WEBB called the vast sweep of yellowish range land, golden grain fields, and fallow stretches of brown "the burnt right flank of the desert." If nature made the Great Plains, the early Indians probably extended them, using controlled PRAIRIE fires to increase the grasslands and, therefore, the range of buffalo and other large game. Indeed, the sharp contrast between Rocky Mountain west and Great Plains east constitutes the most powerfully and immediately obvious geographic division of Montana. Out on the plains live pronghorns, mule deer, coyotes, badgers, and plains grouse, and near water in both the plains and mountain meadows reside white-tailed deer, beavers, muskrats, minks, bald eagles, ring-necked pheasants, ducks, geese, and swans.

Montana's Great Plains are semiarid, but in the mountains, the climate varies. At the lower reaches, the dry valley bottoms have a climate not unlike the plains. Up the mountains, the weather grows cooler, wetter, and snowy in zones corresponding to altitude. Little snow falls on the plains, where sometimes a warm winter wind, the chinook, blows along the foothills of the Rockies and interrupts the bitter cold. Montana's winters, cold and raw, are infamous, with temperatures averaging 18° F. In January 1954, thermometers at Roger's Pass, a bit northwest of Helena, read 70° below zero. Summers, especially out on the plains, can be hellishly hot. At Glendive in 1893 and again at Medicine Lake in 1937, temperatures rose to 117° F. Montana's average rainfall is 15.48 inches, but western Montana gets 18 inches a year, while in the east only 13 inches fall. The Great Plains, harsh and open in the winter, sweltering in the summer, tend to extremes. The mountainous west enjoys greater protection from the winds, although in the Madison Valley, the wind blows four ways at once, and even May can often be chancy in the shadows of the mountains.

Native peoples

Montana was once peopled by the Assiniboin, Blackfoot, Cheyenne, Crow, Flathead, Gros Ventre, Kalispel, Kutenai, Nez Percé, and Pend d'Oreille Indians, who lived primarily by hunting and gathering. By the nineteenth century, the Crows occupied the south-central areas of present-day Montana. The Cheyennes lived and hunted the southeastern corner of the state. The Assinboins and Gros Ventres shared the central and north-central portions of the region. The Blackfoot Indians controlled and jealously guarded Montana's northwestern corner. The area around Flathead Lake was Pend d'Oreille territory, and the mountains west of the lake were home to the Kalispels. The Flatheads claimed the Clark Fort and Bitterroot valleys. After the Euro-American conquest of the region, the United States forced the Flatheads to move to their present-day location in the Flathead River valley and, eventually, confined most of the other tribes to reservations carved from their respective homelands.

Territorial period

Most of Montana became part of the United States when THOMAS JEFFERSON's administration negotiated the LOUISIANA PURCHASE in 1803, although the western reaches in the Rocky Mountains, as part of the Oregon Country, remained the subject of dispute with Great Britain until 1846, when the British relinquished their claim as the result of diplomatic negotiations. Members of the LEWIS AND CLARK EXPEDITION were probably the first people of European descent to set foot in Montana. They were followed quite soon by fur trappers and traders, some of whom came to be called MOUNTAIN MEN, who set up forts along the Upper Missouri to trade with the Indians. One of the earliest, FORT BENTON, was established in 1846; it grew into an important port on the Missouri River and survives today. By the time Fort Benton was founded, Catholic missionaries had already arrived in the area. In response to a delegation of Flatheads seeking spiritual advice in

St. Louis in the early 1830s, Father PIERRE-JEAN DE SMET led the Catholics to Montana and, in 1841, established Saint Mary's Mission—widely believed to be the first permanent settlement in Montana—near present-day Stevensville. By the mid-1840s, trail-blazers had carved the northern Overland Trail through Montana from the east, the BOZEMAN TRAIL led to the territory from the south, and Mullan Road ran west from Fort Benton, which had become the terminus of the steamboat traffic up the Missouri.

In the early 1860s, prospectors discovered rich placer deposits of gold, and the rush that followed contributed to the establishment of the Montana Territory in 1864, with Bannack, on Grasshopper Creek, serving as its capital. Soon thereafter, however, the capital was transferred to Virginia City, in Alder Gulch. As gold-seekers and settlers arrived and pressed onto Indian lands, the Montana tribes fought to protect their hunting grounds. Allied Dakotas and Cheyennes won a major victory in the SIOUX WARS when they defeated the brash GEORGE ARMSTRONG CUSTER and his Seventh Cavalry at the Battle of Little Bighorn in 1876. The next year, a band of Nez Percé under CHIEF JOSEPH won a battle in the Big Hole Basin, then fled toward Canada, where SITTING BULL and some of the Sioux had gone to try a fresh start free of harassment from the U.S. Army. Met and defeated by U.S. troops a few miles south of the Canadian border, Chief Joseph surrendered to General NELSON APPLETON MILES at the foot of the Bear Paw Mountains late in 1877.

Top: "A Montana ranch, comfortable if not elegant, and the home of many well-to-do persons engaged in mining or stock-raising." Photographed in 1872 by William Henry Jackson. *Courtesy National Archives.*

Bottom: The Montana town of Gardiner in Park County, 1887. The town's main street abuts the foothills in the background. *Courtesy National Archives.*

Montana's livestock industry had origins similar to those in the Spanish Southwest—Catholic missions. De Smet and his followers introduced some forty head of cattle to St. Mary's Mission in 1846. The very next year, Philip Poindexter and William C. Orr undertook a cattle drive to the territory, where they registered the first cattle brand in Montana's history. Their ranch, called sensibly enough the P&O, became one of the better-known operations in Montana. They also pioneered the Canadian CATTLE INDUSTRY, launching one of the earliest large trail drives onto the prairies of Alberta. The first Texas cattlemen arrived in 1866, the year Nelson Storey drove his herd up the Texas Trail into the Yellowstone River valley. Sheep, too, initially came to Montana courtesy of the Catholic missionaries, who wintered three hundred of the creatures near St. Peter's Mission in 1867. In 1869, John Bishop trailed fifteen hundred sheep from The Dalles in Oregon to Montana's Beaverhead River valley, and since—like Bishop—a number of the territory's prominent stockmen, Robert Ford, CONRAD KOHRS, James and Andrew Fergus, raised both sheep and cattle, there was none of the conflict between the two so dear to western novels and movies. By 1870, Montana's western valleys teemed with herds, whose owners hoped to make a killing by selling beef to hungry miners in mountain camps. After January 23, 1870, when the U.S. Army set upon an undefended Piegan Blackfoot camp on the Marias River and massacred some two hundred men, women, and children, cattlemen quickly moved onto the vast plains east of the mountains that had served the tribe as a hunting range. The defeat of the Nez Percés and the surrender of the Cheyennes and Sioux to reservations "opened" the Yellowstone as a popular range. Fantastic profits attracted investors from the East and from Scotland and England, too. By 1886, the money boom had led to a dangerous overcrowding and overgrazing of the range, During the long dry summer, the grass was depleted. With the arrival of the "Hard Winter of 1886 to 1887," the industry collapsed, as cattlemen lost 75 percent of their stock. Foreign investment vanished, and Montana cattlemen took charge of the industry and began, more soberly, to rebuild.

Hard-rock MINING also first boomed in the 1880s, when the railroads at last began coming to Montana and bringing with them the capital and the transport necessary for the industry to thrive. It was no accident that the first came to Butte, which began as a gold camp but turned to shaft mining when copper was discovered there. MARCUS DALY organized the ANACONDA MINING COMPANY in 1880, and Thomas Edison electrified New York City in 1882. Edison needed Daly's copper to conduct his electricity; Daly needed Edison's electricity to make himself a wealthy man and Butte the "Richest Hill on Earth." In 1883, the Northern Pacific Railroad, the town's second rail line, arrived, and Butte flourished as a boisterous, swaggering company town. Like cattle, copper would become a mainstay of the industrializing economy in what was about to become the forty-first state in the Union.

Statehood and modern Montana

Twenty-five years after Montana had become a territory, it was admitted into the Union. Although it

An official of the AAA Good Roads program on a lonely Montana road near Glendive, July 1912. Photograph by A. L. Westgard. *Courtesy National Archives.*

held its first constitutional convention in 1866 and a second one in 1884, not until November 8, 1889, did Montana become a state. Like a number of other Western states in what some historians have called the United States "internal colony," Montana grew both dependent on and resentful of the FEDERAL GOVERNMENT during its extended territorial period, a heritage that remained evident in the late twentieth century with the rise of a number of survivalist groups in the state. A more immediate effect of the delay in becoming a state became evident in the viciousness of partisan politics following Montana's admission into the Union. Montana's Democrats and Republicans fought over everything, and so severe was the party conflict that the new state failed to organize its first legislature. Instead, the parties each sent two senators to the U.S. Congress, and since the Republicans were the majority that year in Washington, they recognized the Republican senators from Montana and sent the Democrats packing. Next, the parties wrangled over where the state capital should be located. The state's constitutional convention required the question to be put to the voters, and seven cities entered the race in 1892, with Anaconda receiving the most votes. The matter did not rest there, however, mainly because it got caught up in the growing contests between Montana's leading mining magnates—Marcus Daly, WILLIAM ANDREWS CLARK, SAMUEL THOMAS HAUSER, AND CHARLES ARTHUR BROADWATER—for control of the state's economy and its political offices that became known as the "War of the Copper Kings."

The war kept the state in turmoil from the mid-1880s until 1906. Two years after Anaconda, whose bid was backed by Marcus Daly, had won the election for state capital, a new election was held, and Helena, backed by William Andrews Clark, retained the honor of housing the state's government after a hot contest. Clark had won a battle, but he would ultimately lose the war to Daly (whose Anaconda Mining Company became one of the largest mining conglomerates in the world), while Clark was denied the seat in the U.S. Senate he so burningly desired. Both Clark and Daly were Democrats; so was FREDERICK AUGUSTUS HEINZE, a dynamic young mining engineer whose abrupt rise in popularity and influence threatened both Daly and Clark. The various rivalries thoroughly confused party politics in Montana and created a situation in which the narrow political balance between the two major parties opened the possibility of sudden political victory at any time by Progressives, Fusionists, special corporation interest groups, cattlemen, anybody, really, with clout or a political following. Daly died in 1900; Clark finally went to the Senate in 1901; Anaconda, taken over by a New York holding company named Amalgamated Copper in 1901, bought out Heinze's interest in 1906. The war was over, but the tense nature of Montana politics continued as the president of Anaconda, JOHN DENNIS RYAN, consolidated a group of small electric companies in the Butte area into the Montana Power Company in 1912. As Montana Power grew in wealth and influence, Ryan—who controlled the majority of the press in the state because Anaconda, from 1894 to 1959, owned most of its newspapers—could exercise the kind of clout that had once belonged to Daly to control Montana's economy and bedevil its politics.

Perhaps it should be no surprise, then, that the state's first major Progressive, John M. Dixon, had begun his political career as a Republican arch-conservative but became a liberal leader during his term in the U.S. Senate after he was elected in 1906. Defeated for a second term because he bolted the party to join the Bull Moose campaign to elect THEODORE ROOSEVELT president for a third time, Dixon ran for governor in 1920, won, and proceeded, over the next four years, to introduce one of the most Progressive state programs in the country. Nor should it come as a shock that Montana came within five votes of being the first state to adopt WOMEN'S SUFFRAGE in 1899 and sent the first woman, JEANNETTE RANKIN, to the U.S. Congress in 1916. The War of the Copper Kings itself had led to the adoption of the eight-hour workday, well ahead of other states, and Montana became the first state to institute an old-age pension in 1923. It continued to send such Progressive leaders as Thomas Walsh, BURTON K. WHEELER, and MICHAEL JOSEPH (MIKE) MANSFIELD to Washington. Meanwhile, Montana's powerful corporate interests kept close watch on the statehouse and made sure that no liberal programs truly interfered with their profit making or plundering of the state's natural resources. The political schizophrenia of sending liberals to Washington and conservatives to the state capital is not unique to Montana, but in few other states has the contrast been so marked.

Montana's economy would remain essentially extractive. Oil and natural-gas production began on the Great Plains of Montana in 1915, expanded immensely in the 1950s, and peaked in the 1960s. COAL MINING, a feature of Montana's industrializing since the days of coal stoves and steam engines, boomed in the 1970s. Big lumbering concerns and manufacturers of forest products became vital to western Montana in the twentieth century, and since two-thirds of the state's more than fourteen million acres of commercial forest land belongs to either the federal or the state government, Montana's corporate interests long depended on the complacency of elected officials in order to keep pumping out plywood, and pulp, and paper.

Not until the closing of the copper mines at Butte, the smelter in Anaconda, and the copper refinery at Great Falls in the early 1980s did Montana begin to free itself, to some degree, from its heavy reliance on the primary economic sector. Today, two-thirds of all jobs in Montana are in the service sector with a major emphasis placed on TOURISM, which has become a significant component of Montana's economy. To be sure, Montanans pay a high price for the wide-open spaces they both enjoy and tout to the world. A growing number of communities have no dentists, no physicians, no hospitals. Sparse populations mean a small tax base and relatively low incomes, and Montana's politicians are caught between pressures from taxpayers to curb programs and from low-income groups to provide wider services, while Montana's large Indian population means special programs are, in many cases, mandated. But Montana seems determined, now that the copper century has apparently come to an close, marking a turning point in the state's history, to push for new, innovative businesses that provide jobs without further destroying its majestic mountains, polluting its crystal waters, cluttering its wide-open spaces, or darkening its big Western skies.

—Charles Phillips

SEE ALSO: Copper Kings, War of the; Copper Mining; Labor Movement; Lumber Industry; Missions: Nineteenth-Century Missions to the Indians; Oil and Gas Industry; Progressivism

SUGGESTED READING:

Alwin, John A. *Eastern Montana.* Helena, Mont., 1982.
———. *Western Montana.* Helena, Mont., 1983.
Farr, William E., and K. Ross Toole. *Montana: Images of the Past.* Boulder, Colo., 1978.
Fritz, Harry W. *Montana: Land of Contrast.* Woodland Hills, Calif., 1984.
Malone, Michael, and Richard B. Roeder. *Montana: A History of Two Centuries.* Seattle, Wash., 1976.
Spence, Clark C. *Montana: A Bicentennial History.* The States and The Nations. New York and Nashville, Tenn., 1978.
Toole, K. Ross. *Twentieth-Century Montana: A State of Extremes.* Norman, Okla., 1972.

MONTANA GOLD RUSH

The first Montana placer-gold strike of consequence occurred in July 1862 when John White discovered gold on Grasshopper Creek (Bannack). Within months, thousands of itinerant miners from the West joined pilgrims from the East, all scrambling into Montana's gulches to strike it rich. Three other major strikes followed quickly: Alder Gulch (Virginia City) in May 1863, Last Chance Gulch (Helena) in July 1864, and Confederate Gulch (Diamond City) in December 1864. Hundreds of additional, smaller strikes occurred between 1862 and 1872 in Montana's foothills and mountains.

The rush first brought young, single, rugged, transient men. Successful strikes, however, drew to the camps a secondary population of merchants, lawyers, craftsmen, gamblers, newspapermen, farmers, and prostitutes—all eager to accumulate gold dust without mining. The camp society that evolved included Chinese, Spanish, Irish, Germans, French, Mexicans, ex-Union soldiers, and ex-Confederate militia—potentially a volatile mix.

In a relative wilderness, these placer miners created pragmatic local governments—usually including a mining-district president, a claims recorder, a sheriff, and a miners' court. In late 1863, when faced with a corrupt sheriff, HENRY WILLIAM PLUMMER, and his band of thirty "Innocents," the mining-camp inhabitants became vigilantes and eradicated the criminals. They also united to petition Congress for territorial status, and the Montana Territory was established in 1864.

Montana's placer-gold rush produced an estimated $100 million from 1862 to 1872. The growing population spawned by the rush developed enduring overland routes to handle its commerce, as well as a temporary Missouri River steamboat system that terminated in Fort Benton. The gold rush also launched Montana into its first industrial age, complete with ridges denuded of pines, pristine creeks fouled by tailings, and moonscapes caused by hydraulic mining. To men with a "git it and git out" attitude, such ruthless treatment of the environment proved common in the West.

By the 1870s, as Montana mining evolved to the quartz stage, more stable communities succeeded the temporary mining camps. Immigrant families transplanted their "stateside" social, cultural, institutional, and political patterns in Montana. As transient as were the gold-rush miners, as fleeting as was their "frontier," they composed the first significant wave of white migration to Montana—for better or worse.

—David A. Walter

SEE ALSO: Gold and Silver Rushes; Mining

SUGGESTED READING:

Barsness, Larry. *Gold Camp: Alder Gulch and Virginia City, Montana.* New York, 1962.
Burlingame, Merrill G. "The Great Gold Camps." In *A History of Montana,* Vol. 1. Edited by Merrill G. Burlingame and K. Ross Toole. New York, 1957.
Cushman, Dan. *Montana: The Gold Frontier.* Great Falls, Mont., 1973.

Dimsdale, Thomas. *The Vigilantes of Montana [1866]*. Norman, Okla., 1953.
"Territorial Gold Mines in 1869." *Montana: The Magazine of Western History* 1 (Spring 1951): 35–57.
Wolle, Muriel. *Montana Pay Dirt.* Chicago, 1963.

MONTEZ, LOLA

Entertainer Lola Montez (1818–1861) was born in County Limerick, Ireland, to British army officer Edward Gilbert and the former Miss Oliver, who, according to Montez, was of Moorish-Spanish descent. She was baptized Maria Dolores Eliza Rosanna Gilbert.

In 1822, Gilbert moved his family to India. After her father's death in a cholera epidemic and her mother's remarriage to Captain John Craigie, Lola was sent to live with her stepfather's Calvinist relatives in Scotland. Her education included schooling in Paris and training at a young ladies' finishing school in Bath.

In 1837, Lola's mother returned from India in the company of Lieutenant Thomas James with the intention of arranging a marriage between her daughter and a wealthy and elderly Calcutta judge. Lola escaped to Ireland with James. Eight months after their elopement, the couple returned to India; James then left her for another woman. Lola's stepfather arranged for her return to the British Isles to live with relatives. Following a shipboard relationship and an official separation from James, she remained in London to study acting. After a period of training in Spain, from which she emerged as "Lola Montez," she made her London debut on June 3, 1843.

In subsequent performances, Montez met with acclaim. While on the continent, her name was linked with pianist Franz Liszt, novelist Alexandre Dumas, the liberal Paris journalist Dujarier, and Ludwig I, King of Bavaria, who named her Baroness Rosenthal and Countess Landsfeld. Concerted political opposition resulted in her banishment and the king's abdication. In Switzerland on July 19, 1849, Montez married George Trafford Heald, who had recently acquired a substantial inheritance. Amid charges of bigamy against Montez, the couple fled to Spain and later separated.

On December 29, 1851, Montez made her New York debut before a largely male audience. She then appeared in the East, the Midwest, and even the California gold-mining region, where she performed the provocative "Spider Dance," an adaptation of the Italian "Tarantella" in which she incorporated elements of the polka, waltz, mazurka, and jig.

On July 2, 1853, Montez married Patrick Purdy Hull, an Irish journalist and part owner of the *San Francisco Whig*. The couple settled in Grass Valley in a cottage, which Montez accented with an imported bathtub, a marble fireplace, an aviary, and a menagerie—including a pet bear. Following her rejection of Purdy, the cigar-smoking Montez entertained at frolicsome salons. Ever attentive to her neighbors—including the future stage star LOTTA CRABTREE, she was honored by local miners who christened a nearby Sierra peak "Lola Montez."

In 1856, Montez liquidated much of her estate to assist the children orphaned by the apparent suicide of her manager, Charles Folland. Back East, she joined the Episcopal church and delivered several lectures that detailed her life and which had been written by the retired Reverend C. Chauncey Burr. Taking the name "Fanny Gibbons," she lived in a simple New York boarding house on West 17th Street until 1860 when she suffered a paralytic stroke. She died on January 17, 1861.

—*Gloria Ricci Lothrop*

SUGGESTED READING:

Foley, Doris. *The Divine Eccentric: Lola Montez and the Newspapers*. Los Angeles, 1969.
Goldberg, Isaac. *Queen of Hearts*. New York, 1936.
Wyndham, Horace. *The Magnificent Montez*. New York, 1935.

MONTEZUMA, CARLOS

Indian physician, editor, and political reformer Carlos Montezuma (1865?–1923), a Yavapai Indian, was born in Arizona. In 1871, he was captured by the Pima Indians who sold him to Carlos Gentile, a photographer. After traveling to New York with Gentile, Montezuma was raised by a series of white foster parents and eventually enrolled in the medical school at the University of Illinois. Following his graduation in 1889, he engaged in private practice and then joined the Indian Health Service. He worked in North Dakota, at the Western Shoshone Agency in Nevada, and finally at the Colville Agency in Washington. From 1894 to 1896, he served as the physician at Carlisle Indian School in Pennsylvania.

Montezuma resigned from the Indian Health Service to return to private practice in Chicago. He devoted much of the remainder of his career to social and political reform. Considerably influenced by the Progressive movement, he believed that the reservation system prevented Native Americans from acculturating and that residency on reservations isolated Indian people from the mainstream of American life. Along with other Native American Progressives, he blamed United States Indian Policy and the Bureau of Indian Affairs for the Indians' failure to assimilate and charged that the BIA was staffed by "generally incompetent and broken-down white derelicts" who "squeezed the life-blood out of the Indians." He further asserted that only the abolition of the bureau and the reservation system would guarantee that Indian people would achieve an equitable position in American society.

Gertrude Simmons Bonnin, Charles Daganett, and other Indian Progressives formed the Society of American Indians in 1911; Montezuma waited two years before joining the group because of his fears that the Bureau of Indian Affairs had too much influence on the organization. In 1916, he began the publication of *Wassaja,* a journal advocating the abolition of the BIA and the integration of Indian people into the mainstream of American life. He continued to edit and publish *Wassaja* until 1922, when he became disenchanted with the society and charged that its leadership had lost its militancy and had acquiesced to the BIA.

Disillusioned by political fragmentation among the ranks of Indian Progressives and suffering from tuberculosis, Montezuma moved from Chicago to the Yavapais' Fort McDowell Reservation in central Arizona in 1922. Although he previously had condemned the reservation system, he spent the final months of his life defending the Yavapais' residency at Fort McDowell. When the Bureau of Indian Affairs urged the Yavapais to join the Pimas on the Salt River Reservation, Montezuma opposed the move and championed the Yavapais' claims to water from the Verde River. He died of tuberculosis at Fort McDowell.

Montezuma's life mirrored the hopes and frustrations of acculturated, educated Native American during the first quarter of the twentieth century. Influenced by the Progressive movement, they hoped to implement reform through the federal government but were thwarted by a federal bureaucracy reluctant to make any meaningful changes. Although the Society of American Indians proved ineffective at promoting reform, it did provide the foundation for other pan-Indian political movements that developed later in the century.

—*R. David Edmunds*

Suggested reading:

Clark, Neil M. "Dr. Montezuma, Apache Warrior in Two Worlds." *Montana: The Magazine of Western History* 23 (1973): 56–65.

Iverson, Peter. *Carlos Montezuma and the Changing World of the American Indian.* Albuquerque, N. Mex., 1982.

Larner, John William, Jr., ed. *The Papers of Carlos Montezuma, M.D.: Including the Papers of Maria Keller Montezuma Moore and the Papers of Joseph W. Lattimer.* Wilmington, Del., 1983.

MONTGOMERY WARD AND COMPANY

See: Trade Catalogs

MONTOYA, JOSEPH

Born in Pena Blanca, New Mexico, Joseph Montoya (1895–1978) became one of the major Hispanic American political leaders of the mid-twentieth century. After completing law school, Montoya became active in state Democratic politics and served as the state representative from Sandoval County from 1937 to 1940. He served in the New Mexico senate from 1940 to 1946. He was elected lieutenant-governor and served from 1947 to 1951 and again from 1955 to 1957. He was elected congressman-at-large from New Mexico and served from 1957 to 1964. In 1965, he was elected senator. During his two terms, he was a member of the Select Committee to Investigate Campaign Practices.

—*Patrick H. Butler, III*

MOONEY, THOMAS JOSEPH

Born in Chicago, labor organizer and activist Thomas Joseph Mooney (1882–1942) came from a coal miner's family. His father died when Mooney was ten years old, and the youngster began working as an iron molder's apprentice at the age of fourteen. He joined the iron molder's union shortly thereafter, but work was not steady. After several trips through Europe, Mooney embraced the Socialist party, joined the Industrial Workers of the World (IWW), helped in the publication of *Revolt,* a socialist newspaper, and worked for Socialist Eugene V. Debs's 1908 run for the U.S. presidency. Two years later, Mooney returned to Europe to attend the International Socialist Congress in Copenhagen.

Mooney settled in San Francisco and actively participated in a variety of labor groups and leftist organizations: the San Francisco Socialists, the Industrial Workers Defense League, the Syndicalist League, and the IWW. He ran as a Socialist candidate—unsuccessfully—for supreme court judge in 1910 and for sheriff in 1911.

From 1913 to 1914, Mooney and a drifter from New York, Warren Knox Billings, became involved in the electrical workers' long and violent strike against the Pacific Gas and Electrical Company. Billings was arrested for carrying dynamite, convicted, and spent time in prison; Mooney faced similar charges but was acquitted.

Meanwhile as the United States appeared to be headed into World War I, the conflict between labor and management took on a different cast as the public responded with greater concern to the tensions, growing over the past several years, between companies and workers and to labor's generally increasing radicalism. Labor's strikes and interferences with production seemed to many an impediment to the nation's preparedness for war. Some—especially management—called labor unpatriotic. The city's businessmen used the war to campaign for open shops (in which workers need not be members of a union) under the guise of national preparedness. A showdown was, perhaps, inevitable.

On July 22, 1916, San Francisco and many cities held Preparedness Day events to rally support for America's likely entrance into the war. At the intersection of Market and Steuart streets, a bomb exploded in the midst of the parade, killed ten people, and injured another forty. Mooney and Billings, Mooney's wife, and several other individuals were arrested for the bombing.

At the ensuing trial, the state's case against Mooney and the others rested on the testimony of an Oregon rancher, Frank Oxman, who told the court that he had seen a group of people, including Mooney and Billings, deposit a battered suitcase at Market and Steuart streets. Mooney countered that he was elsewhere at the time of the explosion. The jury, however, convicted the two. Billings got life in prison; Mooney was sentenced to die.

Predictably, labor partisans charged that Mooney had been railroaded by capitalists' puppets, but even dispassionate observers saw the convictions as a travesty. Protesters demanded redress, and no less a personage than President Woodrow Wilson urged the state to reconsider. California's Governor Stephens responded by commuting Mooney's sentence to life in prison.

Subsequent investigations unearthed a photograph of Mooney on a rooftop some distance from the bombing. A clock, also pictured in the image, fixed the exact time the photograph was taken. It was impossible for Mooney to have traveled from the scene of the photograph to the scene of the bombing in the time available. As the case received more attention, investigations revealed that Oxman was not in San Francisco on the day of the bombing. His testimony, so important to the state's case against Mooney, was perjured. Repeated motions for a retrial were denied. The judge and jury retracted their decisions. Three of the prosecutors recommended pardon. None of it made a difference; Mooney spent twenty-two years behind bars, while his case became labor's most cherished cause célèbre.

By 1939, tensions between management and labor and the public's fears of socialists, communists, the IWW, and all manner of prolabor organizations had become less intense. After Culbert L. Olson became governor of California that year, he granted Mooney an unconditional pardon. Billings, as a second offender (stemming from his 1914 conviction) was not eligible for a pardon, but nine months later, his sentence was commuted to time served, and he too was released.

In fragile health from his life in prison, Mooney died three years later.

—Patricia Hogan

SEE ALSO: Labor Movement; Socialism

SUGGESTED READING:

Frost, Richard H. *The Mooney Case.* Stanford, Calif., 1968.

Ward, Estolov Ethan. *The Gentle Dynamiter: A Biography of Tom Mooney.* Palo Alto, Calif., 1983.

MOOSE

The numbers and range of moose, the largest land animal found in North America in historic times, were always more limited than other members of the deer family, *Cervidae.* Greater in size than any other member of the deer family living or extinct, a moose *(Alces alces)* may stand almost seven feet high at the shoulders, with legs up to four feet long. A moose may reach more than nine feet from nose to tail and may weigh up to one ton. Its palmated antlers may extend for more than six feet and weigh more than seventy-five pounds. Seven subspecies of moose may be found in the northern conifer forests of the globe.

With their long, spindly legs, three- to six-inch long, coarse, purplish gray hair, long neck, mulelike ears, and extended nose and muzzle, moose function effectively in a wet forest environment in almost all weather conditions. As browsers, they consume large quantities of bark, twigs, leaves, moss, lichen, and water lilies. In the winter, after packing down the snow around a tree, their stiltlike legs and necks allow them to reach branches up to fourteen feet high. When searching for water lilies, their favorite food, they often totally submerge their heads in lakes and ponds seeking the roots and bulbs of the plant.

The moose of the American West are primarily the Alaska-Yukon species, which is found in this region, and the Shiras moose, which is found in the Yellowstone and Grand Teton area and other locations in the Rocky Mountains. Shiras moose have been transplanted with modest success to other Western areas. While they are a very visible part of the ecosystems of the parks of the northern Rocky Mountains, their numbers in these areas began to grow only after 1880. They were never a major food source for either Native Americans or settlers.

—*Phillip Drennon Thomas*

SUGGESTED READING:

Bauer, Erwin A. *Horned and Antlered Game.* New York, 1986.

Peterson, Randolph. *The North American Moose.* Toronto, Ont., 1955.

MORAN, THOMAS

With his engravings, water colors, and oils of Yellowstone and the Grand Canyon, Thomas Moran (1837–1926) created an indelible record of two of the West's most distinctive natural areas. His published illustrations appeared in government reports and the major periodicals of his era. They created a romantic perception of distant Western lands and generated a national interest in preserving a unique region that lacked easily definable economic value.

Born in Bolton, England, Moran moved with his family to America in 1844. His extended family had such a commitment to and talent for art that a dozen of them became known as "The Twelve Apostles of Art." At the age of sixteen, Moran was apprenticed in an engraver's shop and began to develop skills and techniques that contributed to his growth as a painter. In his free time, he worked in water colors. An avid reader, Moran was deeply moved by the poetry of Wordsworth, Shelley, and Coleridge and artistically impressed by the wood and steel engravings, mezzotints, aquatints, and lithographs he found in the magazines of the period. He was essentially self-taught in art. While realistic, his landscapes would always have a strong romantic element in them.

From 1861 to 1862, Moran studied the works of John Constable and others in England. While in London, he fell under the influence of J. M. W. Turner. Turner's influence was to remain part of Moran's artistic and intellectual heritage, although he always sought to be a distinctly American painter. Despite his never having traveled to the West, he was asked to prepare illustrations for two articles on Yellowstone for *Scribner's Monthly* in 1871. Invited to join FERDINAND VANDEVEER HAYDEN's exploration of the Yellowstone region in 1871, the frail Moran quickly agreed. His water colors and sketches, along with WILLIAM HENRY JACKSON's photographs, were instrumental in persuading Congress to make Yellowstone America's (and the world's) first national park. His *Grand Canyon of the Yellowstone* hangs today in the Senate Corridor in the U.S. Capitol. In 1873, Moran made two pack trips into the Grand Canyon with the aid of John K. Hillers and JOHN WESLEY POWELL. While twenty-nine of Moran's sketches appeared as illustrations in Powell's *Exploration of the Colorado River of the West,* his most monumental work based on the 1873 journey was the massive *Chasm of the Colorado,* which Congress acquired as a complementary piece to his earlier Yellowstone painting.

Although Moran is remembered for his large oil canvases of these regions, most of his work was smaller in scale and more restrained in topography. He devoted more than a half century to pursuing the most artistically interesting sites in the American West.

—*Phillip Drennon Thomas*

SEE ALSO: Art: Western Art

SUGGESTED READING:

Clark, Carol. *Thomas Moran: Watercolors of the American West.* Austin, Tex., 1980.

Heald, Weldon F. "Thomas Moran: Depicter of Western Grandeur." *Montana: The Magazine of Western History* 15 (1965): 42–54.

Kinsey, Joni. *Thomas Moran and the Surveying of the American West.* Washington, D.C., 1992.

Wilkins, Thurman. "Major Powell and Thomas Moran in Canyon Country." *Montana: The Magazine of Western History* 19 (1969): 16–31.

MORE, J. MARION

Idaho miner J. Marion More (1827?–1868) moved to the Pacific Northwest around 1850. After prospecting for gold during the Clearwater gold rush in present-day Idaho, More served as a delegate to the Washington Territory legislature in 1861. When a major gold deposit was discovered in the Boise Basin in 1862, More decided to promote the establishment of a new territory, separate from the Washington Territory. The discovery also prompted him and others to found Idaho City in October 1862. With interests in several mining companies, More soon faced financial setbacks. He had overextended himself, and he saw his empire collapse in August 1866. Early in 1868, he faced another disaster when one of his properties was contested in the Owyhee "war." While peace was restored in April, More was a casualty—not of the war itself but of a drunken brawl. He was fatally wounded when shooting broke out during the celebration that marked the end of the conflict.

—*Candace Floyd*

SUGGESTED READING:
Gray, Dale M. "War on the Mountain." *Idaho Yesterdays* 29 (Winter 1985): 24–32.

MORENO, LUISA

Trade union and civil rights activist, Luisa Moreno (1906–1992) was born in Guatemala. Her elite parents christened her Blanca Rosa Rodríguez López. (When she began organizing in the United States, she took the name Luisa Moreno). As a teen-ager, Moreno moved to Mexico where she worked as a journalist and pursued her talents as a poet. At the age of twenty-one, she published her critically acclaimed collection of poems, *El Venedor de Cocuyos (Seller of Fire-flies),* in Mexico City. That year, she married artist Angel De León, and the couple moved to New York City. In 1928, Moreno gave birth to her only child, a daughter Mytyl.

During the Great Depression, Moreno struggled to support her infant daughter and unemployed husband by bending over a sewing machine in Spanish Harlem. She organized her *compañeras* into La Liga de Costureras, a Latina garment workers' union. In 1935, the American Federation of Labor hired her as a professional organizer. Leaving her abusive husband behind, Moreno, with Mytyl in tow, boarded a bus for Florida where she unionized African American and Latina cigar rollers. Within two years, she joined the Congress of Industrial Organizations (CIO), and in 1938, she became affiliated with the United Cannery, Agricultural, Packing, and Allied Workers of America (UCAPAWA-CIO).

From 1938 to 1947, Moreno organized Mexican farm and food-processing workers throughout the Southwest. Her most notable success was among southern California cannery workers, 75 percent of whom were women. Under UCAPAWA, Mexican, Jewish, and Anglo women secured higher wages and innovative benefits including equal pay for equal work. During the 1940s, Moreno became the first Latina vice-president of a major U.S. labor union and the first Latina member of the California CIO Council.

Moreno also served as the principal organizer for the first national civil rights assembly among Latinos, El Congreso de Pueblos de Habla Española (Spanish-speaking Peoples' Congress). Meeting in Los Angeles in April 1939, Congreso delegates drafted a comprehensive platform. Many of its planks (for example, political representation, immigrant rights, and bilingual education) resonate with as much force today as they did more than a half century ago. El Congreso also called for an end to segregation in public facilities, housing, education, and employment. The projected national network of local chapters never developed, however, and the organization was further weakened by red-baiting.

From 1945 to 1950, UCAPAWA, which had become a target of conservative politicians and trade unionists, slowly disintegrated. Marrying former labor organizer Gray Bemis, Moreno retired from public life in 1947. A year later, she faced deportation proceedings. Journalist Carey McWilliams and newspaper editor Ignacio López headed her defense committee. She was offered citizenship in exchange for testifying at the deportation hearing of labor leader Harry Bridges, but she refused to be "a free woman with a mortgaged soul." She left the United States in 1950 under terms listed as "voluntary departure under warrant of deportation" on the grounds that she had once been a member of the Communist party. After four decades of political activism in Guatemala, Cuba, and Mexico, she died in her native Guatemala on November 4, 1992.

—Vicki L. Ruiz

SEE ALSO: Labor Movement

SUGGESTED READING:
Camarillo, Albert. *Chicanos in California.* San Francisco, 1984.
García, Mario T. *Mexican Americans: Leadership, Ideology, and Identity, 1930–1960.* New Haven, Conn., 1989.
Ruiz, Vicki L. *Cannery Women, Cannery Lives: Mexican Women, Unionization, and the California Food Processing Industry, 1930–1950.* Albuquerque, N. Mex., 1987.

MORES, ANTONIO MARQUIS DE

Dakota rancher and businessman Antonio Marquis de Mores (1858–1896) was born in Paris, France, to a prominent French and Spanish noble family. A graduate of St. Cyr, he was commissioned in the French army but resigned in 1882. He then met and married Medora von Hoffman, the daughter of a wealthy New York banker, in Cannes. In 1883, the couple moved to the Dakota Badlands, and backed by von Hoffman, established Medora (Y Cross Ranch) as their headquarters to slaughter cattle in the Great Plains and ship beef to Eastern markets in refrigerated cars. De Mores established the Northern Refrigerated Car Company, the Northwest Dressed Beef and Land Company, retail outlets, and freight and stage lines. Unable to compete with the beef trust, de Mores left the Dakotas in 1887 after an estimated financial loss of $1.5 million.

—Harmon Mothershead

SUGGESTED READING:
Dresden, Donald. *The Marques de Mores: Emperor of the Bad Lands.* Norman, Okla., 1970.

MORGAN, JULIA

Architect Julia Morgan (1872–1957) was born in San Francisco. In 1890, she enrolled in the program in civil engineering at the University of California at Berkeley. In her senior year, she began attending informal classes on architecture held by BERNARD RALPH MAYBECK and went to work for him following her graduation in 1894. Two years later, she went to Paris planning to attend the École des Beaux-Arts. Since the school was not yet accepting women students, she first worked and studied in Paris and then finally entered the school in 1898. The first woman to complete the program, she received her certificate in architecture in 1902.

She returned to San Francisco to work in the office of John Galen Howard, a New York architect engaged in a major building program for the University of California's campus in Berkeley. During this period, Morgan designed the Hearst Mining Building and Greek Theater for the campus and developed a professional relationship with philanthropist PHOEBE APPERSON HEARST.

In 1904, Morgan left Howard's firm to open her own office in San Francisco. Following the SAN FRANCISCO EARTHQUAKE OF 1906, she was put in charge of rebuilding the Fairmont Hotel. That year, she also built Berkeley's first residence of reinforced concrete.

In her forty-seven-year career, Morgan designed nearly seven hundred buildings. Among her most notable projects were the Asilomar YWCA Conference Center in Pacific Grove; the Berkeley Women's City Club; YWCA buildings in Honolulu and numerous cities in California; the Hearst compound at Wyntoon, California; the campanile, library, gymnasium, and social hall at Mills College; and the Hearst Mining Building, Greek Theater, and Phoebe A. Hearst Women's Gymnasium at the University of California at Berkeley. Her interest in structure, attention to detail, passion for quality, and use of structural materials as an integral part of the design resulted in an extraordinary body of work. She preferred to design from the inside out, and she carefully considered scale, space, color and light. Her success was based on her style; she mixed historicism, the arts and crafts movement, and classical training with flexible concern for the appropriateness of materials and sensitivity to the site, all while meeting the demands of her clients. Morgan received an honorary Doctor of Laws degree from the University of California at Berkeley in 1929 and retired in the early 1950s.

—Waverly B. Lowell

SEE ALSO: Architecture: Urban Architecture

SUGGESTED READING:
Boutelle, Sara Holmes. *Julia Morgan: Architect.* New York, 1988.
Longstreth, Richard W. *Julia Morgan: Architect.* Berkeley, Calif., 1986.
Olson, Lynne. "A Tycoon's Home was His Petit Architect's Castle." *Smithsonian Magazine* (December 1985): 60–71.

MORMON, BOOK OF

SEE: *Book of Mormon*

MORMON MANIFESTO

The Manifesto of 1890 has been called Mormonism's "watershed" event. Written by WILFORD WOODRUFF, fourth president of the CHURCH OF JESUS CHRIST OF LATTER-DAY SAINTS (commonly called MORMONS), the proclamation officially ended the practice of plural marriage. Members of the church accepted Woodruff's manifesto as official doctrine in October 1890.

The events that led to the issuing of the manifesto were complex. Publicly announced in 1852, the practice of plural marriage had actually existed within the Mormon church since at least the 1840s. It had become an institution entrenched not only in Mormon theology but also Mormon society, although only about 20 percent of the Mormon membership practiced plural marriage. While bigamy had been illegal since 1862, intense judicial prosecution of Mormon polygamists did not occur until the 1880s with the EDMUNDS ACT OF 1882 and the EDMUNDS-TUCKER ACT OF 1887. Increased prosecution of polygamists disrupted Mormon families as men and even some women went into hiding to avoid arrest. A large number eventually served time in prison. Even more problematic were the lost rights of polygamists as the laws denied them the right to vote or to sit on juries and other rights. Further worsening the situation, Idaho passed the Test Oath, which denied the right to vote as well as other rights to anyone believing in the divinity of *celestial marriage* (the Mormon term for *plural marriage).* The United States Supreme Court upheld the constitutionality of the Test Oath in 1890. The Cullom-Strubble Bill, legislation patterned on the Idaho Test Oath, was introduced into Congress to take away voting and other rights from all Utah Mormons.

Public opinion across the country was against the Mormon church and its practice of plural marriage. News stories, polemical tracts, and novels containing fantastical descriptions of Mormon misery and depredation were published, thus fanning the flames of public anger against Mormons. While church leaders fought to stem the antipolygamy tide, government officials and a disapproving American populace fought to stop Mormonism's peculiar institution.

While these events were occurring, church leaders and their representatives in Washington, D.C., were pressing for statehood for Utah. Leaders of the Mormon church believed that statehood would enable them to pass state laws protecting their religious practices, including plural marriage. Unfortunately for the Mormons, Congress would not grant statehood to the people of Utah for the very reasons they desired it.

It was within this setting that Woodruff realized that the Mormon church would probably be destroyed by the antipolygamy legislation and subsequent judicial prosecution. After discussing the situation with fellow church leaders, Woodruff announced that he had been inspired to stop the practice of plural marriage in order to avoid the destruction of the church.

Reaction among the members of the church was mixed. While some met the decision with joy, most were shocked and even saddened by the manifesto. At the time a vote was taken by church members, many refused to vote for or against making the manifesto official doctrine, thus showing a painful ambivalence toward the manifesto. A number of women in the congregation cried as the vote was taken, and there was a noticeable somberness throughout the congregation.

For polygamist and monogamist Mormons alike, the social and doctrinal implications were significant. While most members of the church accepted the manifesto, it took more than a decade and at least one other official statement in 1904 to end completely the Mormon practice of taking new plural wives. Because most men refused to abandon their families, it was decades before the formerly approved Mormon polygamous unions ceased to exist.

However, there were those who refused to accept the Mormon church's cessation of polygamy. A number of polygamist groups exist throughout Utah and other parts of the West. Most of the groups have their theological foundations in nineteenth-century Mormonism but believe that mainstream Mormonism has gone astray by ceasing to practice plural marriage. The LDS church, for its part, does not accept polygamists as members in good standing. Thus, modern polygamists are not members of the LDS church.

While ending the practice of plural marriage was difficult for many and impossible for some, the results of Woodruff's manifesto were immediate and significant. The proposed Cullom-Strubble Bill was not passed by Congress, and measures were taken to alleviate some of the suffering on the part of Mormon families. In 1893, U.S. President Benjamin Harrison issued a general amnesty for all people who had entered into polygamous relationships before November 1890.

Most satisfying for the residents of Utah was statehood, which it received in January 1896. Before this time, the Mormon church had begun its entry into the social, political, and economic mainstream of American life. Without the manifesto, it is questionable as to when, if ever, these changes would have taken place.

—*Craig L. Foster*

SEE ALSO: Polygamy: Polygamy among Mormons

SUGGESTED READING:

Alexander, Thomas G. "The Manifesto: Mormondom's Watershed." *This People* 11 (Fall 1990): 20–27.

_____. *Things in Heaven and Earth: The Life and Times of Wilford Woodruff, a Mormon Prophet.* Salt Lake City, 1992.

Hardy, B. Carmon. *Solemn Covenant: The Mormon Polygamous Passage.* Urbana, Ill., 1992.

Van Wagoner, Richard S. *Mormon Polygamy: A History.* Salt Lake City, 1986.

MORMON MASSACRE

SEE: Mountain Meadows Massacre

MORMONS

Historical Overview
Ronald W. Walker

Far West Settlements
Newell G. Bringhurst

HISTORICAL OVERVIEW

The CHURCH OF JESUS CHRIST OF LATTER-DAY SAINTS, one of America's most successful native-born religious institutions and a major force in the settlement and development of the West, was established on April 6, 1830, at Fayette in upstate New York. Its first leader or "prophet," JOSEPH SMITH, JR. (who served as president from 1830 to 1844), said that he had received visions calling him to restore primitive Christianity. He also claimed to have translated, by divine aid, a set of golden plates containing a religious history of a people living in the Western Hemisphere. That translation became the *BOOK OF MORMON*, which members of the LDS church, or Mormons, regarded as a companion to the Bible.

The church's bold, millennial claims, its startling growth, and its close-knit social, economic, and political practices excited persecution from its neighbors and thus motivated the Mormon flight to the West. From New York State, the church moved first to the Western Reserve of Ohio, then to western Missouri, then to NAUVOO, ILLINOIS, where the church established its headquarters, and finally to Utah.

The last leg of the "exodus" was led by BRIGHAM YOUNG, who assumed leadership of the church after Joseph Smith's assassination, and served as president until 1877. A man of little formal education, Young merged religious zeal with an extraordinary executive skill. If the first stages of the Mormon migration from Nauvoo in February 1846 were uncertain, Young quickly imposed discipline. Companies were formed in a semimilitary organization of "tens," "fifties," and "hundreds," which closely looked after the religious and secular needs of the emigrants. Young also ordered temporary communities to be built on the Iowa plains, complete with cabins and newly sown crops, for the companies that would soon follow.

Leaving "Winters Quarters" near Omaha in the Nebraska Territory in April 1847, Young led a pioneer vanguard to the Great Basin. After three months of travel, he arrived at the southeast strand of the Great Salt Lake, then in Mexican territory, where he established the main Mormon settlement, Great Salt Lake City. It was, he said, "a good place to make Saints." Isolated from the more promising lands of California and Oregon, this neglected, semiarid territory gave the Mormons a place to gather their converts in relative peace and seclusion. Young had chosen wisely.

Thousands of settlers soon followed, and Young used several means to aid them. In 1849, he established the PERPETUAL EMIGRATING FUND, which allowed poor converts to borrow funds for their trips with the promise of repayment after settling in Utah. During its thirty-seven year existence, the PEF played a major role in bringing many of the Nauvoo diaspora to Utah, and, perhaps more importantly, it assisted twenty-six thousand foreign-born immigrants as well. By 1856, Young had a new plan. For the next five years, he urged converts to "walk and draw their luggage" in handcarts rather than use costly teams and wagons. About three thousand did so. And in the 1860s, he began a "down-and-back system." Each spring, hundreds of Utah volunteers filled their wagons with supplies, met needy emigrants at staging areas in Nebraska and present-day Wyoming, and returned with a new supply of citizens. When the railroad reached Utah in 1869, fifty thousand had already traveled the MORMON TRAIL.

The Mormons were engaged in Zion building, or constructing an ideal community. Like other religious communities, they had personal and community observances. They embraced the ideals of Christian piety, Sabbath observance, tithe paying, and obedience to a health code called the "Word of Wisdom," which, during the pioneer period, was usually defined as the moderate use, not abstinence, of tobacco and alcohol. Religious fervor was probably best expressed by the Mormons' community spirit. By accepting the "restored Gospel" and being baptized, by "gathering" to the distant Zion and settling in one of its new communities, and finally by subordinating themselves to the Mormon theocracy, the nineteenth-century Saints showed their religious devotion. For them, community building was a sacred experience.

The Mormon Zion was utopianism on a large scale. Young hoped his State of Deseret might spread throughout the West. Under his administration and that of his nineteenth-century successors, JOHN TAYLOR (president from 1877 to 1887) and WILFORD WOODRUFF (president from 1887 to 1898), five hundred Mormon communities were founded in eight states, reaching from the borders of Mexico to Canada. Some sites on the "Outer Cordon"—Las Vegas, Nevada; San Bernardino, California; and Carson Valley, Nevada—were soon abandoned to non-Mormons, but LDS influence was lasting in Arizona, southern Idaho, western New Mexico, and the San Luis region of Colorado. During the nineteenth century, the main concentration of LDS settlements remained in Utah. There, in the Cache and Sanpete valleys and, more importantly, along the north-south, one hundred mile Wasatch Front of Provo, Salt Lake City, and Ogden, the Mormon population became an economic hub for Great Basin West.

Many of Zion's first residents were foreign-born, young, and mobile. The 1870 census showed three or four of every ten Utahns were descended from northern Europeans, mainly the British and Scandinavians. The statistic actually understated things. With 50 percent of Utah's population under fifteen years of age and born in the United States, more than half of the territory's adults in 1870—a better gauge of foreign influence—had come from abroad. These men and women were often on the move. Studies suggest that between 75 and 80 percent of Utah's pioneer town dwellers moved on within ten years. Some sought better land and flowed with the outward tide of Mormon

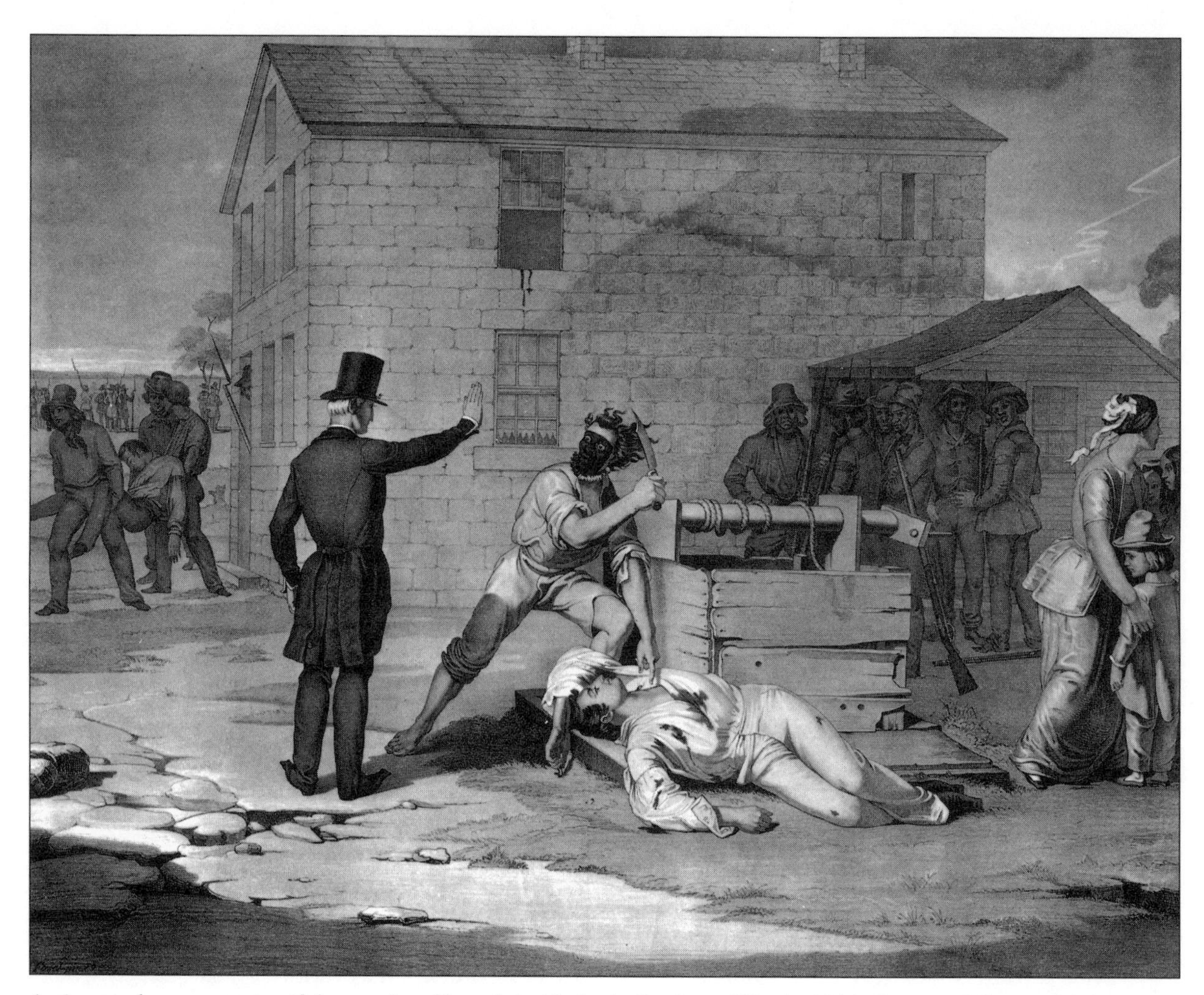

A nineteenth-century print of the murder of Joseph Smith, Jr., in Carthage, Illinois, 1844. *Courtesy Library of Congress.*

expansion. Others grew tired of Zion's demands and left Utah and Mormonism entirely.

Those who remained became grist for Brigham Young's social and cultural mill. He advised them to avoid such vocations as mining and merchandising, which he regarded as spiritually unrewarding or premature. Instead, he hoped his people would settle in what twentieth-century sociologists called the "Mormon village." There, in farm-based, small communities, the Saints became the first Euro-Americans to practice widespread irrigation and, later, dryland farming. They also worshipped, went to school, held their lyceums, and perhaps attended the community drama. After 1870, they even shopped together. When the Union Pacific Railroad reached the region and brought a massive influx of new goods and ideas, Young established, in most villages, a branch of the ZION'S CO-OPERATIVE MERCANTILE INSTITUTION. The stores, he hoped, would lower prices and maintain the Saints' cooperative and egalitarian ways.

Young's social order gave women an important role. While women were barred from the LDS priesthood and therefore were unable to perform church ordinances or preside over congregations, they nevertheless were encouraged to prophecy, heal, and speak in tongues. Moreover, from the church's first years, they voted in their congregation and later were among the first American women to secure the civil ballot and hold elective office. Leading Mormon women EMMELINE BLANCHE WOODWARD WELLS and Emily S. Richards took part in the national suffrage movement.

The RELIEF SOCIETY (LDS) provided more typical activity. First started in Nauvoo and reinstated in the late 1860s, the organization taught the ladies of "Mormondom" practical as well as spiritual improvement. Under the initial leadership of ELIZA ROXCY SNOW and her turn-of-the-century successors, Zina D. H. Young, Bathsheba W. Smith, and Emmeline Blanche Woodward Wells, Relief Society women managed cooperative stores, raised silk, stored grain, ran the

Deseret Hospital, held women's meetings, and ideally set a good example by "retrenching" against extravagance and style. Relief Society women championed their concerns through the independently published *Women's Exponent*. Mormon plural marriage or polygamy (the practice by which a man takes more than one wife at a time) made special demands on Mormon women. Polygamy was inaugurated by Joseph Smith but not publicly announced until 1852. While probably no more than 20 to 25 percent of the church's adults yielded to its requirement, women who were part of polygamous marriages faced the daunting task of raising children whose fathers were often absent.

The Saints had arrived in the Great Basin with badly fractured political loyalties. Their religion told them to idealize American tenets, and they soon raised the United States flag and sought statehood. But their earlier persecutions caused them to be deeply suspicious of non-Mormons, a sentiment that their fellow citizens reciprocated. Non-Mormons were especially troubled by the Mormons' plural marriages and by the economic, political, and religious power that the Mormon theocracy placed in church leaders' hands.

The tension between Mormon and "Gentiles" (or non-Mormons) was always close to the surface and at times flared openly. Responding to rumors of a Mormon rebellion against the central government, President James Buchanan ordered the Utah Expedition and dispatched twenty-five hundred troops to Utah in 1857 and 1858. The specter of the army kindled the fear of a new pogrom against Mormons. In southern Utah, such fears helped bring about the Mountain Meadows Massacre, in which local settlers, acting independently of Salt Lake City, joined in an Indian attack that killed more than one hundred California-bound emigrants.

The Utah Expedition failed to settle the question of sovereignty within the territory, and in the 1880s, federal officials once more asserted their authority. Several antipolygamy court decisions and congressional acts—most importantly the Edmunds-Tucker Act of 1887—stripped the church of most of its property, imprisoned or forced polygamist men to go "underground," and denied ordinary members the rights to vote and to sit on juries. In 1890, faced with unrelenting pressure, Wilford Woodruff announced the revelation that halted new polygamous unions. His "Manifesto" was made still more binding by another declaration on the topic of polygamy by Joseph Fielding Smith (president from 1901 to 1918) fourteen years later.

The 1890s were a watershed. Setting aside the old practices of plural marriage, the "gathering," and a theocracy based on the control of an exclusively Mormon political party, the church placed itself within the American mainstream, and Utah finally received statehood in 1896. If "old Mormonism" had successfully gathered and "raised" a pioneering, religious society, the transformed, twentieth-century faith had its own success. Under such leaders as Heber J. Grant (president from 1818 to 1945), David O. McKay (president from 1951 to 1970), and Spencer W. Kimball (president from 1973 to 1985), Mormonism greatly expanded and coordinated its religious programs and gradually shed its rural-Utah, polygamous image. Mormonism changed on a personal level as well. During the twentieth century, men and women left their farms and businesses in the West for careers in the wider world. They were particularly drawn to public service.

The title page of a travel book for Mormons heading west. *Courtesy Library of Congress.*

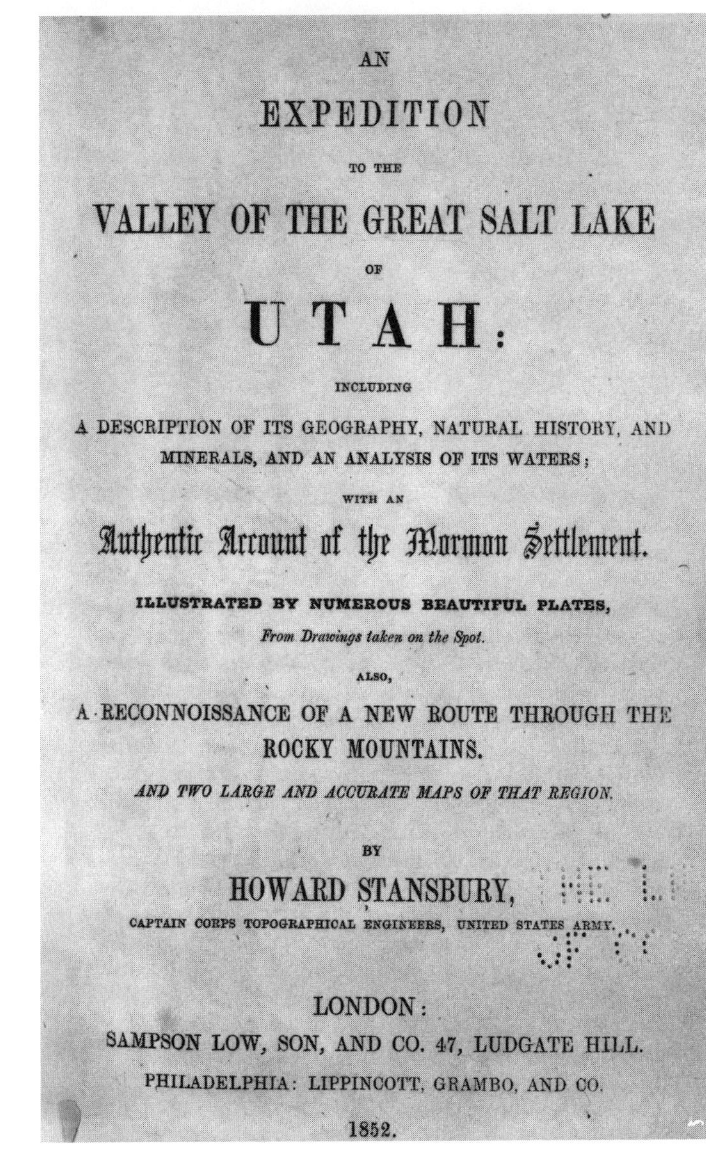

AN

EXPEDITION

TO THE

VALLEY OF THE GREAT SALT LAKE

OF

UTAH:

INCLUDING

A DESCRIPTION OF ITS GEOGRAPHY, NATURAL HISTORY, AND MINERALS, AND AN ANALYSIS OF ITS WATERS;

WITH AN

Authentic Account of the Mormon Settlement.

ILLUSTRATED BY NUMEROUS BEAUTIFUL PLATES,

From Drawings taken on the Spot.

ALSO,

A RECONNOISSANCE OF A NEW ROUTE THROUGH THE ROCKY MOUNTAINS.

AND TWO LARGE AND ACCURATE MAPS OF THAT REGION.

BY

HOWARD STANSBURY,

CAPTAIN CORPS TOPOGRAPHICAL ENGINEERS, UNITED STATES ARMY.

LONDON:

SAMPSON LOW, SON, AND CO. 47, LUDGATE HILL.

PHILADELPHIA: LIPPINCOTT, GRAMBO, AND CO.

1852.

"Mormons in a Kanyon *[sic]* of the Rocky Mountains," from the *Illustrated London News,* April 18, 1857. *Courtesy Library of Congress.*

Workers in Cottonwood Canyon cut granite for the Mormon temple in Salt Lake City, 1872. *Courtesy National Archives.*

REED SMOOT, who sat in the U.S. Senate for thirty years, set the precedent for a stream of twentieth-century LDS congressmen, cabinet members, and government officials.

Church demographers charted these developments. At the start of the century, church membership stood at 268,331. By 1945, it had risen to almost one million, and forty-five years later, in 1990, it exceeded seven million. At the middle of the twentieth century, the church had 180 stakes (roughly similar to Protestant church dioceses), half of them located in Utah. Forty years later, there were 1,700 stakes, with fewer than one-quarter located in Utah. During the same time span, the percentage of membership living outside the United States had grown dramatically from 8 percent to about 35 percent. The church was rapidly becoming international.

Mormonism left its old regionalism behind but kept many of its values intact. It continued to stress education. At the end of the twentieth century, its high-school "seminaries" and higher education "institutes" offered part-time religious instruction to almost one-half million rank-and-file students, while the church's flagship Brigham Young University became the largest private institution of higher education in the United States. Attendance at LDS congregational worship increased rapidly in the twentieth century and revealed the vitality of Mormon community life. The church's welfare system, started during the 1930's Great Depression, preached self-reliance and gave members the chance to help each other, while the Saints' historical evangelizing fervor continued with more than forty-seven thousand full-time missionaries spreading the Mormon word. And in politics, church leaders no longer played their old, activist role but nevertheless reserved the right to speak, usually conservatively, on the moral and social issues of post–World War II society: abortion, disarmament, divorce, feminism, family life, gambling, homosexuality, pornography, sexual promiscuity, and military service in the secular state.

Modern Mormonism's centralized, traditionally minded leadership struggled to manage an increasingly diverse membership. Could Mormonism admit members from new cultures and still retain its identity? How successfully could secularism and the growing discomfort of some intellectuals be handled? Likewise, a number of Mormon women labeled the leadership a patriarchy and demanded a larger role within the church. But this unusual church with its varied and unusual past, has survived challenges of similar magnitude in its history.

—*Ronald W. Walker*

SEE ALSO: Deseret, State of; Handcart Companies; Mormon Manifesto; Polygamy: Polygamy among Mormons

SUGGESTED READING:

Allen, James B., and Glen M. Leonard. *The Story of the Latter-day Saints.* Salt Lake City, 1976.

Arrington, Leonard J., and Davis Bitton. *The Mormon Experience: A History of the Latter-Day Saints.* New York, 1979.

Ludlow, Daniel H., ed. *Encyclopedia of Mormonism.* 5 vols. New York, 1992.

O'Dea, Thomas F. *The Mormons.* Chicago, 1957.

Roberts, B. H. *A Comprehensive History of the Church of Jesus Christ of Latter-Day Saints.* 6 vols. Salt Lake City, 1930.

Shipps, Jan. *Mormonism: The Story of a New Religious Tradition.* Urbana, Ill., 1985.

FAR WEST SETTLEMENTS

The Mormon church (or the CHURCH OF JESUS CHRIST OF LATTER-DAY SAINTS, as it is formally known), in addition to establishing numerous settlements in Utah, promoted dozens of settlements in other parts of the Far West during the latter half of the nineteenth century. The settlements were a major priority of BRIGHAM YOUNG and other Mormon leaders from the beginning of the mass Mormon migration, in 1846, from Illinois to the Great Basin.

Young vigorously promoted Far Western Mormon settlements in various ways. In early 1846, he hoped to establish Vancouver Island, then relatively unoccupied and part of British America, as a major gathering place for Mormons from Great Britain. English converts, who had been joining the Latter-day Saints movement since the late 1830s, constituted an ever-larger percentage of total church membership. Plans for such a Mormon settlement, however, never materialized.

More significant was the Mormon leader's instructions to SAMUEL BRANNAN, a New York-based Mormon newspaper editor and Mormon official on the East Coast. Young ordered Brannan to gather a group of East Coast Mormons, outfit a ship, and take it around the Horn of South America to San Francisco. Brannan took his group of 238 Mormons aboard the *Brooklyn,* left New York on February 4, 1846, and arrived in San Francisco (or Yerba Buena as it was then known) on July 31, 1846. Shortly thereafter, Brannan founded an agricultural settlement, named New Hope, on the Stanislaus River in the fertile San Joaquin Valley. This Mormon settlement never flourished due mainly to conflict that developed between Young and Brannan, a conflict that culminated in the latter's excommunication from the Mormon church. But New Hope was the first Mormon settlement in the Far West. It was established one year before the Mormon migration to and settlement of Salt Lake City.

Young's plans for extensive Far West settlement were most dramatically evident in his proposal for a Mormon-dominated state. His plan was drawn up shortly after his arrival in Utah and submitted to the United States Congress in March 1849. The Mormon leader's State of Deseret (derived from a *BOOK OF MORMON* term meaning "honey bee") would encompass a vast region of some seven hundred square miles bordered by Oregon on the north, the Rockies on the east, the Sierra Nevada on the west, the Pacific Ocean on the southwest, and Mexico on the south. The region included the present-day state of Utah, along with northern Nevada and Arizona; much of Wyoming, Colorado, New Mexico, and southern California; and portions of Oregon and Idaho. The State of Deseret would cover one-sixth of the total land mass of the continental United States. Government officials rejected Young's proposal and approved an alternative plan that established the Territory of Utah, a considerably smaller region, consisting of present-day Utah and Nevada.

Young continued to promote the establishment of Mormon settlements throughout the Far West. Among the earliest and most important was San Bernardino founded in 1851 under the leadership of Mormon Apostles Amasa Lyman and CHARLES COULSON RICH. Young viewed the southern California settlement as a crucial link in a line of settlements, or "Mormon corridor," stretching from the Salt Lake Valley to a seaport on the Pacific Ocean. Mormon control of a Pacific seaport in either San Pedro or San Diego would serve as a point of disembarkation for Saints arriving from Great Britain in ever increasing numbers. Exceeded in size only by Salt Lake City, San Bernardino flourished initially, numbering some three thousand settlers by 1855.

Shortly thereafter, the Saints established a second settlement at Las Vegas Springs. Founded in 1855 by William Bringhurst and Nathaniel V. Jones, the settlement was a vital link along the "Mormon corridor." It was also a center for Mormon missionary efforts among the local Indians. Neither San Bernardino nor Las Vegas, however, was successful, due to a combination of conflict with local non-Mormons, internal dissension among Mormon settlers, and difficulty in maintaining adequate contact with Mormon leaders in Salt Lake City. Thus, in 1857, Young ordered his followers to abandon both settlements.

More successful were Mormon settlements established in present-day Wyoming and Idaho. In Wyoming, the Mormons gained control over two outposts along the OREGON TRAIL. The first, Fort Supply was founded in 1853 as a rest and resupply center for Mormon overland emigrants making their final push into the Great Salt Lake Valley. The second outpost, FORT BRIDGER, was located twelve miles east of Fort Supply. The Mormons purchased the fort in 1855 from its namesake, the mountain man JAMES (JIM) BRIDGER. In Idaho, the Mormons established a settlement at Fort Limhi in 1855, primarily as a center for Mormon missionary activity among the local Indians.

From the late 1850s until the early 1870s, there was a marked decline in the number of Mormon settlements established outside of Utah. The few settlements founded were located in Nevada, which was detached from the territory of Utah and granted statehood in 1864. Three major areas in Nevada were settled by the Mormons beginning in 1864. The first was at Panaca, in Meadow Valley, 350 miles southwest of Salt Lake City. The second was Call's Landing, on the Colorado River at the extreme southern tip of Nevada. The third was along the Muddy River in southeastern Nevada, where settlers founded a series of Mormon communities.

The failure to establish settlements elsewhere during this period was due mainly to increased difficulties with the federal government—difficulties which culminated in the UTAH EXPEDITION of 1857 and the dispatch of federal troops to Utah. Although the troops were withdrawn in 1861 at the beginning of the Civil War, President Abraham Lincoln sent a second armed detachment, the California Volunteers, to Utah to keep an eye on the Mormons and their practice of polygamy, a practice coming under increased attack by federal officials. Congress enacted a series of laws to curb Mormon plural marriage, beginning with the Morrell Anti-bigamy Act in 1862.

Federal antipolygamy actions, notwithstanding, Young and other Mormon officials renewed their efforts to establish settlements throughout the Far West in the 1870s and 1880s. In the Salt River valley of western Wyoming (later known as Star Valley), the Mormons founded a settlement in 1878 under the direction of Moses Thatcher and Brigham Young, Jr. Mormons also settled in the Snake River valley of southeastern Idaho during the 1880s. To the south, the Mormons organized settlements in Bunkerville and Mesquite, Nevada, in 1879 and 1880. And in the San Luis Valley of south central Colorado, the Mormons founded a community at Manassa in 1879—best known, perhaps, as the birthplace of Jack Dempsey, one-time Mormon and future heavyweight boxing champion.

Church leaders, increasingly alarmed over the growing antipolygamy campaign of the United States government, influenced Mormon colonization efforts. Seeking a more secure place of refuge for his followers, Young looked south to Mexico. He directed the founding of several settlements along the Little Colorado River in present-day Arizona under the direct supervision of Lot Smith, WILLIAM J. FLAKE, and Erastus Snow, and those settlements were firmly established by the mid-1870s. The Little Colorado settlements were intended to serve as connecting links of a new "Mormon corridor" between Utah and Mexico. Young ultimately hoped to establish Sonora Valley, Mexico, as a Mormon gathering place, securely out of reach of United States government officials determined to end the practice of Mormon polygamy. Although Young died before realizing this goal, his successor, John Taylor, supervised the founding of three major Mormon settlements in Mexico—Colonia Juarez, Colonia Dublan, and Colonia Diaz, all established during the 1880s. The Mexican settlements grew and were encouraged by the presence of such important Mormon leaders as apostles Moses Thatcher and Brigham Young, Jr. By the 1890s, the Mexican settlements boasted more than three thousand Saints. As such, they represented isolated but significant centers of American culture in a Mexican environment.

During the mid-1880s, JOHN TAYLOR supervised the establishment of a second Mormon sanctuary beyond the boundaries of the United States. The Mormon leader directed Charles Ora Card to lead a group of Saints north into Alberta, Canada. The resulting settlements grew and flourished. By the 1890s, the Mormons had established settlements throughout the region, the most important being Cardston, named for its Mormon founder.

Mormon settlements outside of Utah during the course of the late nineteenth century covered the length and breadth of the American Far West and beyond. Although they enjoyed a record of mixed success, the settlements that endured—particularly those in southeastern Idaho, northern Arizona, eastern Nevada, western Wyoming, and southern Alberta—attracted significant numbers of Mormon settlers and continued to grow. The Mormons who lived in the Far West settlements exerted significant influence in the economic, political, and social affairs of their various regions—and continue to do so today.

—Newell G. Bringhurst

"Mormon emigrants," in a caravan of covered wagons, 1879. Photograph by C. W. Carter. *Courtesy National Archives.*

SEE ALSO: Deseret, State of

SUGGESTED READING:

Allen, James B., and Glen M. Leonard. *The Story of the Latter-day Saints.* 2d ed., rev. and enlarged. Salt Lake City, 1992.

Arrington, Leonard J. *Great Basin Kingdom: An Economic History of the Latter-Day Saints.* Cambridge, Mass., 1958.

———, and Davis Bitton. *The Mormon Experience.* New York, 1979.

Bolton, Herbert E. "The Mormons and the Opening of the Great West." *Utah Genealogical and Historical Magazine* 17 (1926): 40–72.

Campbell, Eugene E. *Establishing Zion: The Mormon Church in the American West, 1847–1869.* Salt Lake City, 1988.

Hunter, Milton R. *Brigham Young the Colonizer.* Independence, Mo., 1940.

Ricks, Joel E. *Forms and Methods of Early Mormon Settlement in Utah and Surrounding Regions, 1847 to 1877.* Logan, Utah, 1964.

MORMON TRAIL

Mormons moving from NAUVOO, ILLINOIS, to the Salt Lake Basin in present-day Utah used a 1,297-mile-long trail, known as the Mormon Trail. The trail ran across southern Iowa and generally followed primitive territorial roads and Indian traces to present-day Council Bluffs. From there, the trail continued across Nebraska north of the Platte River (on a trail previously blazed by trappers and Oregonian missionaries) through present-day Grand Island and Scottsbluff into Wyoming, along the Platte to Fort Laramie. At the fort, the Mormon Trail crossed the Platte and followed the OREGON TRAIL for 397 miles, partly along the Sweetwater River, to the Continental Divide at South Pass. After turning southwest to FORT BRIDGER, the Mormons left the Oregon Trail and picked up the California-bound Reed-Donner Party trace (Hastings Cutoff) through the Wasatch Range of the Rocky Mountains into the valley of the Great Salt Lake.

The Mormon Trail was used from February 1846, when the Mormons left Nauvoo, through the immigrant season of 1868; thereafter, Mormons were able to ride the Union Pacific Railroad to Utah.

Up to seventy thousand Mormons used the trail. Contrary to popular belief, the Mormons did not blaze the trail; instead they wove together earlier trails and traces. The trail bears their name because of the improvements they made and because they used it so extensively for twenty-two years. Parts of the trail were subsequently used by other travelers and businesses: gold rushers; Pony Express riders; the transcontinental telegraph; stage, freight, and mail lines; the U.S. Army; and the Union Pacific Railroad.

—Stanley B. Kimball

SEE ALSO: Church of Jesus Christ of Latter-day Saints; Handcart Companies; Mormons

SUGGESTED READING:
Kimball, Stanley B. *Historic Sites and Markers Along the Mormon and Other Great Western Trails.* Urbana, Ill., 1988.
———, and Hal Knight. *111 Days to Zion.* Salt Lake City, 1978.
Stegner, Wallace. *The Gathering of Zion: The Story of the Mormon Trail.* New York, 1971.

MORNING STAR (NORTHERN CHEYENNE)

Morning Star, or Dull Knife (1808?–1883) as Euro-Americans later called him, was an Ohmeseheso who emerged during the mid-nineteenth century as a great Northern Cheyenne Old Man Chief and Sweet Medicine Chief. During his younger years, Morning Star distinguished himself for bravery in battle and for his even greater diplomacy.

During a clash between the U.S. Army and the Northern Cheyennes at the Upper Platte River bridge, Morning Star sought peace and reconciliation rather than conflict. His quest for peace between his people and Euro-Americans reflected his political obligations and role in Cheyenne society. In 1854, the Cheyenne Council of Forty-Four renewed itself and selected him as an Old Man Chief for the Ohmeseheso or Northern Eaters band.

During the 1860s and 1870s, despite the continual loss of Northern Cheyenne lands and resources, Morning Star advocated peaceful relations with the U.S. military, governmental officials, and immigrants. His advocacy of peace and coexistence with Euro-Americans would cost the Northern Cheyenne leader, when in 1866, Dakota soldiers whipped him. When he negotiated with military officials on the construction of new forts on Northern Cheyenne lands and in the Dakota Territory, many angry Northern Cheyennes threatened him for his actions. Although losing some political prestige, he realized that conflict was inevitable and necessary for the Northern Cheyennes to survive.

In an effort to quell the growing Cheyenne and Dakota resistance, the U.S. military launched a series of military campaigns in 1876. On several occasions, U.S. military forces attacked Morning Star's camps. One of the most devastating attacks came in 1876 at the hands of United States troops commanded by Colonel RANALD SLIDELL MACKENZIE. The army troops destroyed Morning Star's village, leaving his people destitute. After his 1876 winter camp on Rosebud Creek was captured and his starving people were relentlessly harassed by U.S. military forces following GEORGE ARMSTRONG CUSTER's annihilation, Morning Star and his people surrendered in 1877 at the Red Cloud Agency in Nebraska. On May 28, 1877, 937 Northern Cheyennes, including Morning Star's band, were removed to the Darlington Agency in the Indian Territory. During their stay, Morning Star repeatedly pleaded with Agent John D. Miles that malarial fever, the distribution of rations, and Southern Cheyenne hostility made conditions impossible for his people. On September 9, 1878, Morning Star and other Northern Cheyenne leaders led 353 Northern Cheyennes north to their homeland. Captain L. B. Johnson's troops discovered Morning Star's band, who had crossed the Platte River, and escorted them to Fort Robinson. The fort's commander locked Morning Star's people in a guarded barracks to force their return to the Indian Territory. They were denied food, water, and fire for warmth. On January 9, 1879, Morning Star and his people escaped from their prison. U.S. troops searched for them for twelve days and murdered 61 Northern Cheyennes, most of whom the soldiers buried in mass graves. (Some of the remains of Northern Cheyennes, however, found their way into Eastern scientific museums.) The survivors temporarily resided at the Pine Ridge Agency but eventually transferred to Fort Keogh, where they worked as scouts. In 1883, the seventy-five year old Morning Star died, one year before the Northern Cheyennes received their reservation in southeastern Montana. Morning Star's tenacity of purpose to create a homeland for all Northern Cheyennes was realized on October 16, 1993. That day, the remains of 24 murdered Northern Cheyennes were brought home.

—*Gregory R. Campbell*

SUGGESTED READING:
Campbell, Gregory R. "Memoir 23." *Plains Anthropologist* 34 (124): 85–97.
Grinnell, George Bird. *The Fighting Cheyennes.* Norman, Okla., 1977.
Hoig, Stan. *The Peace Chiefs of the Cheyennes.* Norman, Okla., 1989.

MORRILL ACT OF 1862

Named for its creator and chief sponsor, Representative Justin S. Morrill (1810–1898), a Vermont Republican, the Morrill Act is officially known as the Land Grant Act of 1862. Morrill's object was to provide grants of land to state colleges whose "leading object [would be to teach subjects] related to agriculture and the mechanic arts," yet without excluding general sciences and classical studies. The act had a profound effect on American higher education. State universities in Alaska, Arizona, Arkansas, California, Colorado, Hawaii, Idaho, Iowa, Kansas, Louisiana, Minnesota, Montana, Nebraska, Nevada, New Mexico, North Dakota, Oklahoma, Oregon, South Dakota, Texas, Washington, and Wyoming benefited from the Morrill Act, which provided each state with thirty thousand acres of federal lands for each of its senators and representatives. Money from the sale of these land funded the establishment and growth of public universities all through the West and Midwest. In 1890, in order to address the inequality of grants from state to state, Congress passed a second Morrill act, providing annual cash allotments of up to twenty-five thousand dollars for what were by then called the "land-grant" colleges.

—*Alan Axelrod*

SEE ALSO: Colleges and Universities

MORRIS, ESTHER HOBART MCQUIGG SLACK

Wyoming suffragist and the first woman justice of the peace in the United States, Esther Hobart McQuigg Slack Morris (1814–1902) was born in New York, the eighth of eleven children. Her first husband died in 1845, leaving land in Illinois.

Esther Hobart McQuigg Slack Morris. *Courtesy Denver Public Library, Western History Department.*

She married a storekeeper, John Morris, in Peru, Illinois, and in 1869, the family moved to South Pass City, Wyoming, a remote mining boom town. In this mostly male village of fewer than five hundred, Morris, nearly six feet tall and an outspoken advocate of women's rights, stood out from the crowd. Although reports of her lobbying tactics differ, she clearly influenced William H. Bright, representative to Wyoming's territorial government. Bright introduced legislation granting Wyoming women the vote, and in 1869, Wyoming became the first territory or state to enfranchise its women citizens. The legislature also passed laws granting married women control of their own property and mandating equal pay for women teachers.

In 1870, Morris was appointed justice of the peace of South Pass City. She tried more than seventy cases in eight and one-half months on the bench. She remained active in the women's rights movement throughout her life. Feminist historian Grace Raymond Hebard immortalized Morris as the "mother of woman suffrage."

—*Virginia Scharff*

SEE ALSO: Women's Suffrage

SUGGESTED READING:

Chapman, Miriam G. "The Story of Women's Suffrage in Wyoming, 1869–1890." M.A. thesis, University of Wyoming, 1932.

MORTON, J. STERLING

Nebraska promoter Julius Sterling Morton (1832–1901) was born in Adams, New York. He spent his boyhood in Michigan and attended the University of Michigan. In 1854, he moved to the newly established territory of Nebraska, where he became active in politics and in the promotion of settlement. He developed a large orchard near Nebraska City and worked to improve agriculture. He served as secretary of agriculture in Grover Cleveland's second administration. He is best known as the promoter of Arbor Day.

—*James C. Olson*

SUGGESTED READING:

Olson, James C. *J. Sterling Morton.* Lincoln, Nebr., 1942. Reprint. 1972.

MOSES, PHOEBE ANN

SEE: Oakley, Annie

MOSHER, CLELIA DUEL

Trained as a physician, Clelia Duel Mosher (1863–1940) devoted her life to the study of female physiology and behavior. Her innovative research shattered some of America's long-held notions of women's physical inferiority. Born in Albany, New York, Mosher completed high school in 1881, but her physician-father discouraged her from attending college out of concern for her health, weakened by tuberculosis as a child. To encourage her to stay home, he built her a greenhouse, which Mosher turned into a profitable floral business. Using money from the sale of her flowers, she began college in 1889 and, although, indeed, near collapse after the first year, continued on and graduated from Stanford University in 1893, at the age of twenty-nine.

Mosher remained at Stanford as an assistant in hygiene and soon embarked on her mission of debunking myths about female physiology. She first attacked the notion that physiology caused women to breathe differently from men. Not physiology, but constraining undergarments worn by fashionable women made them breathe the way they did. Mosher's research earned her a master's degree from Stanford, and her conclusions were validated two years later by a (male) Harvard doctor.

From breathing, Mosher moved on to research "functional periodicity," at the time used as the rationale for keeping women out in the working world. Mosher's approach was novel. Most of the literature on female physiology (most of it grim) had been based on observations of the sickly women whom male doctors encountered in their practices. Mosher determined to study healthy women, and to that end, she devised a questionnaire for her women students and directed them in keeping monthly records of their menstrual experiences. Her data comprised records of four hundred healthy women and the results of their physical examinations. But before she got far in her analysis, she enrolled in medical school at Johns Hopkins University to give herself a better perspective on her research and to give her conclusions more credibility. She earned her degree in 1900 and, shortly thereafter, resumed the analysis of the menstrual study. Her report identified four factors that led to women's discomfort during their periods, all of which an informed woman could modify.

After medical school, Mosher returned to California and established her own medical practice. In 1910, she went back to Stanford University as an assistant professor of personal hygiene and medical advisor for women. From the head of the classroom, Mosher urged her students to understand and appreciate their own physiology and to give up conventional notions about their bodies and their limitations. She advocated deep-breathing exercises (dubbed "moshering" by the students who swore by them) to strengthen abdominal muscles and minimize menstrual cramps; erect posture to avoid an unhealthy realignment of internal organs; and sensible clothes, regardless of fashion.

Mosher combined her years of medical research with an awakening feminism in a book published in 1915, *The Relation of Health to the Woman Movement.* Her work at the university was interrupted during World War I, when she served in the Red Cross and oversaw the evacuation of children from Paris. In Europe, she saw women assume physical labors previously believed unsuitable for their "delicate" natures. Back in California after the war, Mosher produced *Woman's Physical Freedom,* in which she debunked some of the myths of menopause; she found that most symptoms were psychological, not physiological, and some were associated with social changes (such as children leaving home, what today is called "empty-nest syndrome") common to women of middle age.

Mosher's most extraordinary research, "Statistical Survey of the Marriages of Forty-Seven Women," was never published. While still a student in college, Mosher began collecting questionnaires from women about their marriages, their sex lives, and their attitudes toward both. To the initial responses, she added other questionnaires from her patients and students. Although her sample of subjects was self-selected (limited to women willing to reveal such intimate details of their lives) and too small to be truly representative of all American women, her survey predated the Kinsey studies by a half-century. It suggested that some women did not behave according to the passionless, Victorian stereotype of the times.

Clelia Mosher retired to a home of her own design in 1929 and died in 1940.

—*Patricia Hogan*

SUGGESTED READING:

Degler, Carl N. "What Ought to Be and What Was: Women's Sexuality in the Nineteenth Century." *American Historical Review* 75 (1974): 1467–1490.

MOSSMAN, BURTON C.

Ranch manager and captain of the ARIZONA RANGERS, Burton C. Mossman (1867–1956) was born near Aurora, Illinois. He attended common schools in Minnesota and, in the mid-1880s, became a cowboy and range boss in southern New Mexico. Moving to Arizona, he supervised the liquidation of the Bloody Basin properties and the breakup of the Aztec Land and Cattle Company. In 1901, he was appointed the first captain of the Arizona Rangers, created by the territory to combat stock thieves. His capture in Mexico of the celebrated killer Augustine Chacon received widespread publicity. In 1903, Mossman took over management of the Hansford Land and Cattle Company's grazing leases on the Pecos River in New Mexico and on the Sioux Reservation in South Dakota. In 1907, he acquired the Sioux lease and annually ran fifty thousand feeders. Mossman organized and ran the Diamond A, a ranching pool in New Mexico, from 1925 to 1944. His career mirrored the changing role of the ranch manager during the shift from open- to closed-range ranching in the West.

—Harwood P. Hinton

SEE ALSO: Cattle Industry

SUGGESTED READING:

Hunt, Frazier. *Cap Mossman: Last of the Great Cowmen.* New York, 1951.

O'Neal, Bill. *The Arizona Rangers.* Austin, Tex., 1987.

"MOTHER" JONES

SEE: Jones, Mary Harris ("Mother")

MOTION-PICTURE INDUSTRY

From the beginning, movies made money, even in the early days when the motion-picture industry consisted of a number of small, undercapitalized storeroom operations showing short "flickers" to working-class stiffs and their families in New York, Chicago, and Philadelphia. Mostly immigrants or the sons of immigrants, like many of those in their audiences, movie-makers somehow got hold of a camera and film, shot moving images of anything that moved, and charged a nickel to watch the products of their labors. Their biggest worry was that Thomas Edison, who had invented some of the equipment they used, claimed he had patents on the entire process of producing pictures and took draconian measures against those who made films and did not work for him. By 1903, Edwin S. Porter had shown the producers something of the narrative possibilities of the new medium with his film, *The Great Train Robbery,* an instant success. Before long, the audiences were growing, and growing more sophisticated, as Edison's agents got rougher. The "nickelodeons" needed more movies; New York, Chicago, and Philadelphia were not good towns in which to shoot films during the winter; and audiences were hungry for new scenery. Stock companies, including a director, a cameraman, an actor, and actress, and others who played bit parts, carried equipment, wrote titles, did whatever needed doing, and traveled the United States, and sometimes northern Mexico, looking for places to make pictures and get away from Edison.

That was how Francis Boggs, a director for the Selig Polyscope Company, happened to be passing through California in 1907. He shot some water scenes for *The Count of Monte Christo,* before returning East, where his boss and company owner William Selig and a number of other production companies were about to come to an understanding with Edison. Rather than fight a losing battle against the revolution in entertainment he had launched, Edison now tried to organize the industry by joining with the other film-making companies to form a joint distribution operation, the Motion Picture Trust. Those coming late to the business, or too inconsequential to be included in the negotiations, or otherwise excluded, ignored the Motion Picture Trust and continued to make flickers on the fly. Boggs told Selig about California's cloud-free skies and its cheap real estate. In March 1909, Boggs arrived in LOS ANGELES to look for a spot to set up a permanent studio. Producers wanted realistic scenery; they wanted long shooting days; and ever since the *Great Train Robbery,* they wanted to make "westerns," which made Los Angeles ideal. For the independents, who hated the Trust, the town offered two additional benefits—it was a long way from Thomas Edison in New York, and it was close to Mexico. When the authorities showed up to serve papers or Trust goons appeared on the scene to break up sets, they loaded up their equipment and slipped across the border.

Other companies followed Selig and the independents, and by 1910, movie-makers from Biograph (whose D. W. Griffith was destined to become one of the industry's great directors), Lubin, Kalem, Pathé, and New York Motion Picture—indeed, almost every major production company—arrived in the area to rent studios in downtown Los Angeles, Glendale, Pasadena, and Santa Monica. In the early days, some searched for cheaper and more removed space in Orange, San Diego, and Santa Barbara. In 1911, Nestor's David Horsley ran across an abandoned tavern in a little temperance town founded in 1887. Located at the corner of Sunset Boulevard and Gower Avenue, the tavern had been long closed under the town's prohibition ordinances, and the town itself, faced with a problem endemic to the West—the lack of an adequate supply of water—had been forced to disincorporate and become part of the patchwork city of Los Angeles in 1909.

No longer independent, the town could not harass the movie-makers with local laws aimed at discouraging movie-making, as some of the other suburbs that had wearied of the studios and their disruptive business and loose-living personnel had done. On hard times, the place was also cheaper than high-rent downtown Los Angeles. The name of the place was Hollywood, and when Horsely rented the tavern, it became Hollywood's first movie studio.

Quick to see Hollywood's advantages, the independents moved in. William Fox established Fox Films on Sunset Boulevard in 1912. Carl Laemmle and his Imp Company bought out Nestor. Even Vitagraph, a Trust company, moved down from Santa Monica. Over night, quiet suburban Hollywood disappeared, and the locals watched in amazement as the production companies constructed barnlike studios for interior shots and filmed exteriors in the middle of the streets. The irreverent comics from Mack Sennett's studio seemed to be everywhere, upstaging the locals by pushing their way into patriotic parades and other public events, driving fast race cars and even faster women through the town, and carousing and drinking at all hours. As much as the production crews in Hollywood were disrupting the town's life, Hollywood's independents were disrupting the life of the industry. By 1912, the center of production had shifted from New York to Hollywood, and that year, Fox sued the Trust for restraint of trade and later settled out of court. Among the independents, perhaps Carl Laemmle was the most troublesome.

Laemmle, who would go on to found Universal Pictures, took on Edison directly by publicly protesting the Trust's way of doing business, making films in secret far from its thugs and spies in New York, and creating what became the Hollywood star system. One of the more odious of the Trust's prohibitions was its ban on giving credit to those playing in its nickelodeon melodramas. Before 1910, the movie-going public had no idea who they were watching on the screen, and as audiences developed favorites, they began to refer to them by the names they used in the pictures. Petite, golden-haired Gladys Smith was called "Little Mary" long before she adopted the stage name Mary Pickford, while cowboy star G. M. Anderson was known simply as "Bronco Billy." Fans knew some actors only by their studios—"The Biograph Girl," "The Vitagraph Girl," "The Imp Girl." To break the hold the Trust consequently exercised over film players, Laemmle seduced Florence Lawrence, the popular "Biograph Girl," away from the studio that along with Edison held the vast majority of shares in the Trust. He promised her more money and—for the first time in motion-picture history—her name up in lights, the old Broadway dream translated into a new medium. Laemmle quickly discovered that Lawrence's devoted fans could be counted on to show up in sufficient numbers at the box office to justify increased rental fees for his pictures. He had spawned a star, and the lust for such stars would dominate Hollywood ever afterward.

Vitagraph became the first Patent Company to follow suit and break the Trust ban, making stars of the good-looking Maurice Costello and "The Vitagraph Girl" herself, Florence Turner. The studio's globular John Bunny became the first movie comedian known by name to the public; and Arthur Johnson, the first "matinee idol." But for sheer popular appeal, none of these could hold a candle to Mary Pickford, whom Laemmle made a star when he swooped down on Biograph again to carry off both her and her hard-drinking husband, Owen Moore; nor could they hope to match the public's adoration of the "Little Tramp," Charlie Chaplin, who worked his way to stardom from the ranks of vaudeville slapstick through Mack Sennett's Keystone comedies. Immediately, a sensational rise to fame and riches came to those who became stars. In 1910, Mary Pickford may have made $5 a day; by 1914, she was pulling down a cool $1,000 a week. A year later she signed a contract for $104,000 a year. Mack Sennett paid Charlie Chaplin $150 a week. Essanay took him on, in 1914, for $1,250 a week. The next year, Mutual upped the price to $10,000 a week plus a $150,000 signing bonus. In 1917, at age twenty-seven, Chaplin signed a contract with the First National Film company to deliver eight films in eighteen months for $1 million.

Underwritten by the growing popularity of its contract celebrities and the wealth they had begun to generate, Hollywood used its stars to break Edison and the Trust. By 1915, the year the federal government invoked the Sherman Anti-Trust Act to dissolve the combine altogether, it was already falling apart because not only was it unable to enforce its edicts and collect its fees, Trust studios had stuck with the short one-reel flickers, while the more innovative independent Hollywood studios captured the market with feature-length films, many showcasing the stars the movie-going public now demanded. The audience itself had changed and now included middle-class viewers willing to pay increased ticket prices to see their favorite stars.

As individual players grew obscenely rich, the conspicuous consumption and loose living that typically attend fast-made fortunes began to be reported in the press to fans hungry for a glimpse at the private lives of their idols. Gossip became a prime Hollywood commodity, just as it had in New York's vaudeville days, when Walter Winchell had invented the Broadway gossip column. Local columnists grew quite powerful within the "colony," as they honed the art of innuendo, hired studio publicists, and fed rumors and lies to an audience fascinated by romanticized rags-to-riches stories like that of Mary Pickford. The high-living Gloria Swanson, who vamped that, while Pickford "may have been the first woman to make a million, I am the first woman to spend one," actually married a marquis. Shorn of the tawdry demands for casting-couch sex and the desperate pandering of the "talent" or—in some cases—their mothers, such stories offered a glamorous alternative to dull and oppressive Main Street respectability. The stories also prompted young women to leave home and head for Hollywood, where their dreams mostly collapsed into unfulfilled longing. Tens of thousands of women, between the ages of nineteen and twenty-five, came to Tinsel Town between 1919 to 1929, and a frantic Hollywood chamber of commerce, worried about the image of its municipality, posted notices in railway stations as far away as Calcutta, India, warning young women that there was no work in the movies.

Warnings had little effect, however, since stars such as Pickford and Swanson were so obviously successful, as successful as any women in history. They had "star quality"—an odd ability to project on film (or, for that matter, on stage) not just the character one happens to be playing at the moment, but some ineffable essence, made up of looks, manner, presence, and style, that strikes a cord with a broad public—and they had "it" at the right point in history. The attention paid Pickford and Chaplin fit neatly into a general cult of celebrity that arose from the new consumer-driven society of the 1920s—a society based on the mass market stitched together by revolutions in transportation and by commercialized communications. Based on charisma rather than accomplishment, modern celebrity was a slave to image, and a star's success was totally dependent on the studio's ability to sell this image to an audience that was tyrannical in its demands, fickle in its loyalties, and subject to abrupt changes in its tastes—as Gloria Swanson, Mary Pickford, and Charlie Chaplin were to learn.

Many reacted not with fascination but with moral outrage. Mary Pickford's divorce, Fatty Arbuckle's arrest for manslaughter in the death of actress Virgian Rappe, and the murder of director William Desmond, coming fast on the heels of one another, gave studios pause. Since they could control what they showed on screen much easier than what their famous hired hands did behind closed doors, they formed a censorship board as a kind of preemptive strike against more formal public measures. Creating the Motion Picture Producers and Distributors of America, the moviemakers hired former U.S. Postmaster General Will Hays as its president, and the Hays board (as it became known) imposed a kind of mindless, if naive, code on motion pictures that did, indeed, cut out some of the movies' salaciousness. The code also led to a hypocritical purity few but the most gullible took at face value. The better directors became adept at getting around the code in any case.

Just as destructive to the old style movie making was the institution of the studio system by a rapidly consolidating industry. Hollywood's big profits attracted Wall Street investors who merged and consolidated companies, reigned in the talent with draconian studio contracts, assigned business managers and efficiency experts to trim budgets and cut wasteful expenditures, and put strong-willed studio heads in charge to produce money-making films that ensured good returns on investment. When Louis B. Mayer, a former junk dealer, small theater owner, and film distributor, who had come to Hollywood in 1918 to launch his own studio, took over the newly created giant Metro-Goldwyn-Mayer in 1924, the day of the Hollywood movie mogul and the vertically integrated motion-picture industry had arrived.

Mayer, the Warner brothers, and a handful of others, often tyrannical, sometimes vulgar, always with their fingers on the pulse of popular taste, made the motion-picture industry into a major force in American culture, politics, and life. The advent of sound at almost the same time as the arrival of the studio system thinned the ranks of silent-film directors, stars, and producers, and the moguls took all but complete control of Hollywood—always with the acquiescence of the money men in New York—and stamped the national psyche with an imprint of their own. Many of them Jewish with origins in eastern Europe, the moguls were insecure in their social standing and lacking, ultimately, in self-confidence, argues Neal Gabler. Perhaps only within the fairly fluid social structure of the newly evolving California life style could these men have risen to such prominence so quickly, and they were, by turns, grateful to and resentful of the dominant culture, bold and ruthless in business, domineering towards their employees and associates, submissive and reticent toward political authority and the economic and cultural elite. They hired, for example, the best and most talented writers they could find—William Faulkner, Dorothy Parker, F. Scott Fitzgerald, Dashiell Hammett, Lillian Hellman—and paid any price to get them to come to Hollywood, but once they had the writers on the payroll, they treated them like factory hands. They produced movies that reflected America and life as they wanted it to be—a morally good land, full of promise and happy endings, with citizens who acted decently and courageously—yet they were themselves morally lax, cynical about the motives of others, and often lacking in conviction and courage. They made a movie of John Steinbeck's *Grapes of Wrath* but buckled under to Joe McCarthy and the House Un-American Activities Committee. The apotheosis of the studio system, in this sense, was the Disney Studio, whose founder, Walt Disney, was incessantly positive in his animated productions but suspicious and paranoid enough in his private life to spy for the FBI. At the same time, these men created immensely successful enterprises that produced films cherished by broad segments of the American public and made Hollywood the center of the world's entertainment industry.

In the 1950s, with the advent of television and the death of many of the moguls, the studios fell into decline, and Hollywood soon passed its heyday of power and influence. Los Angeles remained a center of media entertainment; and the motion-picture industry, a mainstay of the state's and the country's economy. But the studios themselves were broken up and sold off. Hollywood's legacy, however, in at least one sense, remained strong. Three-quarters of a century after the first studio opened at the corner of Sunset and Gower, Hollywood-style celebrity so dominated contemporary culture—and the commercial electronic media that had grown ubiquitous in the daily lives of Americans—that an ability to appeal to wide audiences, to create a consistent and charismatic "image," regardless of that image's relation to anything resembling reality, to make oneself admired and beloved whatever one's achievement, had itself become both a qualification for high political office and almost a definition of success in American culture.

—*Charles Phillips*

SUGGESTED READING:

Brownlow, Kevin. *The Parade's Gone By. . . .* New York, 1968.

Gabler, Neal. *An Empire of Their Own: How the Jews Invented Hollywood.* New York, 1988.

Garth, Jowett. *Film: The Democratic Art.* New York, 1976.

Marx, Samuel. *Mayer and Thalberg: The Make Believe Saints.* Hollywood, Calif., 1975.

Schatz, Thomas. *The Genius of the System: Hollywood Filmmaking in the Studio Era.* New York, 1988.

Sklar, Robert. *Movie-Made America: How the Movies Changed American Life.* New York, 1975.

MOUNTAIN LIONS

With the largest range of any native mammal found in the Western Hemisphere, mountain lions may be found from the Atlantic to Pacific oceans and from the Yukon to Patagonia. Mountain lions are found in the United States primarily in Texas, New Mexico, Arizona, Colorado, Wyoming, Montana, Idaho, Utah, Nevada, Oregon, and Washington. In Florida, limited numbers of mountain lions exist as endangered species. The population of mountain lions has always limited by their primary prey species—the deer.

Known scientifically as *Felis concolor,* the mountain lion is also called puma, cougar, *león americano, tigre,* the long tail, catamount, painter, and panther. It is venerated in the traditions and mythologies of many Indian tribes for its stealth, grace, and prowess as a hunter. In these cultures, it was called upon to aid in the hunt and in war and to dispel disease and bring good health.

Mountain lions, the world's second largest plain-colored cat and the fourth largest species of all the great cats, are the only native, unspotted cats found in North America. The color of the their fur ranges from grizzled gray to shades of fawn, cinnamon, rufous or ferruginous tan or rust. Generally, mountain lions that live in a forest habitat are darker than those living in more open country. Their under parts are white in color.

Although they have been known to reach nine feet four inches in length and weigh more than 276 pounds, the average mature lion is between six and eight feet in length and weighs between 100 to 200 pounds. Its long, fur-covered, cylindrical tail is a characteristic feature and is approximately half the length of its head and body. Its head is small and rounded with short, furred, rounded ears. Heavily muscled, it moves with remarkable agility on slim, supple legs and may stand up to two feet at the shoulders. Maturing between the ages of two and three years, they produce litters that may contain from one to four kittens. In captivity, they have lived for up to twenty-five years, but in the wild, they seldom exceed eighteen years.

The mountain lion is noted for its short bursts of speed rather than for sustained speeds over longer distances. Among the most graceful of all predators, it is praised for the elegance with which it runs, jumps, and climbs.

In search of food, a male mountain lion may develop a home range of fifteen to thirty square miles. Females may occupy a range of five to twenty-five square miles. They prefer fresh meat, and while deer are their food of choice, they will also eat bighorn sheep, elks, beavers, rabbits, squirrels, marmots, bobcats, peccaries, and porcupines. As their habitat decreased and became fragmented through settlement and as deer populations declined, mountain lions began to prey on domestic animals—horses, steers, colts, calves, sheep, goats, chickens, and pigs. Efficient at stalking their prey, mountain lions make most of their kills at dusk or at night. They usually kill prey by jumping onto its back and breaking its neck as they hold the victim with their front paws. During the winter months, mountain lions take a deer a week and thus serve as major checks on deer populations. When preying on domestic animals, they often kill more than they will consume. In 1980, a mountain lion in Ely, Nevada, killed fifty-nine sheep in one night. Between 1977 and 1981, Nevada ranchers annually lost an average of 375 colts, calves, ewes, and lambs. Sheep-raisers had an average loss of 0.29 percent of their flocks to this predation. Since World War II, in Colorado, mountain lions rank below the coyote, bear, bobcat, dog, and eagle in sheep predation. Although they generally avoid humans, there are indisputable nineteenth- and twentieth-century records of attacks on humans. State and federal governments have attempted to limit their populations by developing bounty systems and hiring professional hunters. In California, hunters have received as much as $629 for each lion. Excessive hunting and trapping of lions, as well as other predators, so reduced their numbers that both on the Kaibab plateau on the north rim of the Grand Canyon and in Yellowstone and the Tetons deer and elk herds exceeded the carrying capacity of their ranges and died in large numbers from starvation in the first three decades of this century.

—*Phillip Drennon Thomas*

SEE ALSO: Wildlife

SUGGESTED READING:
Tinsley, Jim Bob. *The Puma, Legendary Lion of the Americas.* El Paso, Tex., 1987.
Young, Stanley P., and Edward A. Goldman. *The Puma: Mysterious American Cat.* Washington, D.C., 1946.

MOUNTAIN MEADOWS MASSACRE

In September 1857, Utah Indians and local Mormon settlers ambushed and killed some one hundred California-bound emigrants, known as the Fancher Company, in a remote area of southern Utah. There were several interrelated factors that precipitated the incident, known as the Mountain Meadows Massacre. First, the doomed emigrant company, composed entirely of non-Mormons, arrived in Utah at an extremely tense time. In 1857, during what became known as the Utah War, the MORMONS anticipated armed conflict with the federal government and U.S. Army troops then traveling into the region. Second, the Fancher Company's members were from Missouri and Arkansas and made no secret of their intense dislike for Mormons. Some emigrants actually bragged of direct involvement in earlier anti-Mormon violence in Missouri and Illinois. In response, the Mormons refused to trade with the emigrants or sell them badly needed food and supplies.

Further aggravating the situation was a third factor stemming from ongoing difficulties with the Indians of southern Utah. The Indians, after years of tense relations and some armed conflict with Mormon settlers, had finally established a reasonably good relationship with their new neighbors. In this relationship, the Indians believed (or wanted to believe) that the MORMONS had given them tacit approval to raid and steal from non-Mormon emigrant companies passing through the region. To make matters worse, the Indians accused the Fancher Company, itself, of killing their livestock and poisoning their wells.

Thus, when the Fancher Company reached southern Utah, the situation had become critical, particularly after local Mormons refused to sell the emigrants food. The angry emigrants retaliated by destroying Mormon property and vowing to return to Utah with an armed force to wipe "every damn Mormon off the earth." The alarmed Mormons, in conjunction with their Indian allies, decided to take a drastic course of action. On September 11, 1857, at Mountain Meadows, some fifty Mormon militiamen and two hundred local Indians surrounded and killed all the Fancher Company members, except for eighteen small children.

When news of the massacre first reached church leader BRIGHAM YOUNG in Salt Lake City, he did not believe that local Mormons were involved and initially viewed the incident as an Indian affair. As details of direct Mormon involvement were revealed following a federal investigation, Young moved to punish those responsible, in particular, JOHN D. LEE, the primary local Mormon leader involved.

Mormon involvement in the Mountain Meadows Massacre contributed to a highly negative image of the entire Latter-day Saints movement. That image persisted among many non-Mormon Americans for years to come.

—*Newell G. Bringhurst*

SEE ALSO: Church of Jesus Christ of Latter-day Saints; Utah Expedition

SUGGESTED READING:
Brooks, Juanita. *John Doyle Lee: Zealot-Pioneer-Builder-Scapegoat.* Glendale, Calif., 1962.
———. *The Mountain Meadows Massacre.* 1962. Reprint. Norman, Okla., 1991.

Irwin, Ray W. "The Mountain Meadows Massacre." *Arkansas Historical Quarterly* (Spring 1950).
Shirts, Morris. *The Mountain Meadows Massacre: Another Look*. Cedar City, Utah, 1992.

MOUNTAIN MEN

When MANUEL LISA died in 1820, the lieutenant-governor of the new state of Missouri, WILLIAM HENRY ASHLEY, decided to take over where Lisa had left off. In 1821, he teamed up with ANDREW HENRY, Lisa's former partner, and organized a new fur-trading company to tap the Upper Missouri. In February 1822, he placed a call in the *St. Louis Gazette and Public Advertiser* for "Enterprising Young Men . . . to ascend the Missouri to its source, there to be employed for one, two, or three years." Promising to pay them "$200 per annum," he got what he asked for. The men he assembled included those destined to be remembered as some of the West's boldest and most colorful explorers, including JEDEDIAH STRONG SMITH, JAMES (JIM) BRIDGER, THOMAS FITZPATRICK, EDWARD ROSE, HUGH GLASS, JAMES CLYMAN, and the SUBLETTE BROTHERS, Milton and William. Ashley's enterprising young men and other trappers in the Rocky Mountain FUR TRADE were the first who came to be called "mountain men."

Ashley himself "invented" the RENDEZVOUS system used by the mountain men. In the winter of 1824 to 1825, he led an expedition out of Fort Atkinson and headed for the Rocky Mountains. Ashley's winter march across prairie and mountain was daring. Pounded by wind and snow north of the PLATTE RIVER, Ashley's men abandoned their wagons; their horses nearly starved until they found a stand of cottonwood, whose bark made life-saving forage; fortunately, the Indians were friendly. At length, Ashley's men crossed the Rockies west of South Pass at Morrow Creek and reached the Green River on April 15. There, Ashley split his party of twenty-five into four groups: one to explore the Green; one to trap its tributaries; one to find the source of the river today known as the Colorado; one to trap beavers in the mountains west. As he sent his men in all directions, Ashley made plans to meet them fifty miles downriver at a "place of randavoze for all our parties on or before the 10th of July next." It was the first rendezvous in fur-trade history, if one ignored the meetings of DONALD MCKENZIE and his SNAKE RIVER Brigades and the trading fairs the Spanish had been holding with the Utes and Shoshones for decades. In typically Western fashion, what started out as a makeshift and temporary solution became a new, more effective way of doing business: the rendezvous became the major economic institution of the American Rocky Mountain fur trade and the major social institution for the mountain men.

Each year, Ashley moved men, supplies, and fur between the mountains and the lower MISSOURI RIVER by pack trains and wagons. To keep in touch with his wandering brigades, he designated a spot in the heart of the mountains for the annual rendezvous. There, the mountain men met a company trader—soon to be Ashley himself, who went into the supply end of the business—to exchange whiskey, guns, knives, and the like for the yearly take in beaver. Soon, the trader became the main beneficiary of the Rocky Mountain system. A good trapper arrived at the rendezvous with three or four hundred pelts; a lucky one, sometimes with twice that many. The mountain men sold the pelts to Ashley, his successor Bill Sublette, or whomever, in later years, happened to hold the concession. Before the trade began its decline, pelts brought between $2 and $4 each and could be resold in St. Louis at a 200-percent markup.

The mountain men seemed satisfied enough with the $2,000 or so they cleared at a time when skilled labor earned perhaps $1.50 a day. The trappers, however, tended to spend much of what they made during the month-long rendezvous on liquor, Indian women, GAMBLING, and, most of all, the goods and supplies they needed for the coming year—all offered at outrageous prices by the same merchants who bought their furs. In effect, the trappers worked eleven months for a single debauch at the rendezvous. WASHINGTON IRVING described these men as they arrived at the rendezvous or, sometimes, in St. Louis. They had, he wrote, "the manners, habits, dress, gesture and even walk of the Indian." The mountain man, said Irving, plaited his hair, grown long below the shoulders, and tied it with otter skins or "party-colored ribands." His knee-length hunting shirt was of ruffled calico brightly dyed or of ornamented leather, and his legs were wrapped in leggings "ornamented with strings, fringes, and a profusion of hawks' bells," while his feet were shod in "a costly pair of moccasins of the finest Indian fabric, richly embroidered with beads." A scarlet blanket hung from his shoulders, "girt around his waist with a red sash, in which he bestows his pistols, knife, and the stem of his Indian pipe." As to the mountain man's horse—"selected for his speed and spirit, and prancing gait"—it was decked out as fantastically as its rider, with beaded and embossed bridles and crupper, the head, mane, and tail "interwoven with abundance of eagles' plumes," and its coat "bestreaked and bespotted with vermilion, or with white clay, whichever presents the most glaring contrast to his real color." But despite their appearance and sometimes crude manners, William Goetzmann argues that the mountain men were not a "backwoods proletariat enslaved and exploited by ruthless company masters"; they were, at the least, small businessmen in a cottage industry, who shared the values of "men of enterprise" but who garnered little of the wealth their risky work produced.

They seemed, at least on some level, to love danger, or at least adventure, which they courted year-long and paid dearly to brag about at the rendezvous. Hugh Glass, for example, could talk of being mauled nearly to death by a grizzly bear and being nursed back to health by the Sioux. Jim Bridger might boast that he was the true discoverer of the Great Salt Lake. The African American JAMES PIERSON (JIM) BECKWOURTH, a former blacksmith known far and wide as the greatest liar in the West, no doubt sometimes recounted how he became a war chief of the Crows, while Jeremiah "Liver-eating" Johnson could have spoken, if he chose, of the one-man war he carried on with the same Crows. William Sublette's repertoire might have included the winter of 1824, when the Crows, naked to the waist and contemptuous of the subzero weather, had made two tremendous buffalo hunts and slaughtered more than one thousand animals—so many that entire villages stayed out all night guarding the individual carcasses from wolves. ETIENNE PROVOST could brag about the time he ran into PETER SKENE OGDEN and his Snake River Brigade in Weber Canyon in the winter of 1825. Thirty-four-year-old JOSEPH REDDEFORD WALKER, in fact, chose the rendezvous at Green River in 1833 to announce that he was undertaking an expedition all the way to the coast of California.

The work was dangerous; some five hundred mountain men were killed by Indians over the three decades when the trade was in its heyday—a 25 percent mortality rate. When perhaps the most renown of all Ashley's mountain men, Jedediah Smith, was killed by Comanches on May 19, 1831, the *Illinois Magazine* eulogized the intrepid explorer, dead at the age of thirty-two, in its June 1832 issue: "Though he fell under the spears of savages, and his body has glutted the prairie wolf, and none can tell where his bones are bleaching, he must not be forgotten." Already the historical romanticizing of the mountain men had begun.

They would come to be seen as rude Lord Byrons, outcast banditti of the plains and mountains, loving the hunt and the chase, spurning the comforts of civilization, infatuated with the wildness of the West. From Washington Irving, who hailed their "wild, Robin Hood kind of life" to BERNARD DEVOTO, who christened them "Odysseus Jed Smith and Seigfried Carson and wingshod Fitzpatrick," historians as well as dime novelists would take these remarkable men and place them in a "province of fable" born of a then-current literary movement in Europe founded by Johann Wolfgang von Goethe, who built on the cultural heritage of France's Jean Jacques Rousseau. The Romantics made an exotic Eden of the American wilderness, noble savages of the now hard-pressed Plains Indians, and "nature's" heroes of the hard-bitten American trappers. For the Europeans, the trappers' distance from the effeminate culture of the East was a mark of their authenticity: it was what made them "real men."

But the mountain men did not want to be authentic; they did not want to be "real men" in the wilderness; they wanted to be landed gentry. And for that reason, they saw the West as a place to live, once they had made their fortunes, and they viewed the exploring they did in search of that fortune also as a means to triumphant American enterprise and—sooner or later—American settlement. In other words, the mountain man was, according to Goetzmann, one of the new common men, a citizen of ANDREW JACKSON's America, whom Richard Hofstadter described as "an expectant capitalist, a hardworking ambitious person for whom enterprise was a kind of religion . . . the master mechanic who aspired to open his own shop, the planter, or farmer who speculated in land, the lawyer who hoped to be a judge, the local politician who wanted to go to Congress, the grocer who wanted to be a merchant." The mountain men, implies Goetzmann, were not Robin Hoods but civilization's reluctant heroes. They also shared Jackson's dark frontier metaphysics. They justified the economic plunder of the West's natural wealth as part of the advance of American civilization; they—unlike the British—almost instinctively looked for emigrant routes over the mountains to Oregon and California and, having found them, joined in the demand for federal protection of the citizens who would use them.

They had the ear of government; they were, in fact, its friends and advisors. They knew Governor WILLIAM CLARK and Senator THOMAS HART BENTON. They would even become officials of the government themselves, as when Ashley joined Benton in Congress. And whenever JOHN CALDWELL CALHOUN, DANIEL WEBSTER, or others stood up in the senate to question Western expansion, these former mountain men, like all Westerners, were shocked, since such expansion was the basic assumption under which they operated and hoped to achieve success. To them, the West was not a wilderness or a desert, not an Indian refuge, not a large-game preserve, but their future hometown. Charles Keene, himself a erstwhile mountain man, summed it up in the *Missouri Herald and St. Louis Advertiser:*

> The recent expedition of General Ashley to the country west of the Rocky Mountains has been productive of information on subjects of no small interest to the people of the Union. It has been proved, that overland expeditions in large bodies may be made to that remote region. . . . The whole route lay through a level and open

> country, better for carriages than any turnpike road in the United States. Wagons and carriages could go with ease as far as General Ashley went, crossing the Rocky Mountains . . . and descending . . . towards the Pacific Ocean.

Such was the "public policy," says Goetzmann, with which the mountain men, for almost two decades, fought off the British claims to the Far Northwest. The irony was that, not the British, but the AMERICAN FUR COMPANY ran the mountain men out of business. In the 1820s, JOHN JACOB ASTOR put his immense financial resources to work buying up the Upper Missouri commerce. Calling his outfit in Missouri his Western Department, he destroyed his rivals in one of two ways: he negotiated with them, in which case they were invariably incorporated into the American Fur Company; or, he undersold them, easily taking short-term losses to win his long-term victory. By 1827, the American Fur Company had a virtual monopoly on the Upper Missouri. Astor's string of posts and experienced traders laid the foundation for a production system that endured until the 1860s.

Astor's competitive methods drove up the price of pelts and recklessly depleted the population of beavers, but in economic terms, they were sound, rational policy, since he could operate at a loss seemingly forever, and the mountain men could be bankrupted in a season. Indeed, William Sublette and ROBERT CAMPBELL, trying to run the hated Astor out of the mountains, had brashly established trading posts on the Missouri in direct competition with him. But it did not work, and within a year, they had had enough. In January 1834, Sublette's and Astor's lawyers, reaching an accommodation in New York, partitioned the West. Sublette and Campbell sold their interest on the Upper Missouri to Astor; Astor got out of the Rocky Mountains.

But it was too late. As one historian wrote, the competition had "finally ruined the fur trade for the American companies in the Rocky Mountains." There were not enough beavers left. The new owners dissolved the Rocky Mountain Fur Company at the 1834 rendezvous, and a reorganized American Fur Company moved into the mountains the same year and extended its monopoly over all of the American West.

In many ways, the mountain men were the midwives for a new wave of migration into the American West. Their exploits encouraged others to engage in another round of exploration. The mountain men's "discovery" of new lands for settlement and the blazing of paths to those new lands also gave pioneers a goal: for even the heartiest of emigrants did not simply load up their Conestogas and head west unless they had some place to go and a reason to go there.

—*Charles Phillips*

SUGGESTED READING:

Goetzmann, William H. *Exploration and Empire: The Explorer and the Scientist in the Winning of the American West.* New York, 1966.

Hafen, LeRoy R., ed. *The Mountain Men and the Fur Trade of the Far West.* 10 vols. Glendale, Calif., 1965–1973.

Wishart, David J. *The Fur Trade of the American West, 1807–1840.* Lincoln, Nebr., 1979.

MOUNTIES

SEE: North West Mounted Police

MOURNING DOVE

A Native American novelist, Mourning Dove (Christine Quintasket McLeod Galler, 1884?–1936) led a double life—as a migrant laborer and as a writer, lecturer, and politician. The oldest child of Joseph and Lucy Quintasket, Native American leaders and ranchers, Christine Quintasket was born on the Colville Reservation of the Confederated Tribes in north-central Washington. She attended boarding schools at the Goodwin Catholic Mission in Kettle Falls, Washington, and at Fort Spokane. After her mother died, she returned home to care for her siblings. She joined the staff of Fort Shaw School near Great Falls, Montana, after her father remarried. She herself then married Hector McLeod, a Flathead.

Eventually estranged from McLeod, she moved to Portland in 1912, adopted the name "Morning Dove" (Humis-humish), and launched her writing career. Her first novel, *Cogewea,* conveyed the emotional depth and range of native peoples to counter the stoic "Indian" stereotype she found offensive. To improve her writing style, she enrolled in a Calgary business school. About a year later, in 1914, she met Lucullus Virgil McWhorter, a Yakima businessman, who edited her novel and arranged for its publication in 1927.

In the meantime, while teaching on the Inkameep Okanagan Reserve in British Columbia, she began to record stories from the Salishan elders. In 1919, she married Fred Galler of the Colville Reservation and moved to East Omak, Washington, on her home reservation. There she encouraged native craftswomen and intervened during legal difficulties between the local Native Americans and whites. She also began preparing a collection of bedtime stories with the help of McWhorter and Hester Dean Guie. In 1921, she changed the spelling of her pen name to "Mourning Dove."

During the early 1930s, a white official angered her by belittling her literary abilities. As a response, she drafted several versions of an autobiography, *Mourning Dove: A Salishan Autobiography,* which provides a superb overview of the history of the interior Salishan tribes and female life. It was published in 1990.

During her lifetime, Mourning Dove became a Colville leader (she was the first woman elected to the Colville tribal council) and writer who overcame great odds to achieve fame. She left behind a string of publications that continue to help natives and whites understand each other. In addition to *Cogewea,* her works include *Coyote Studies* (1990), *Tales of the Okanogans* (1976), and *Mourning Dove's Stories* (1991). Overextending herself, she complained of a "nevrous" disposition. She became disoriented and died while in a state hospital.

—*Jay Miller*

SEE ALSO: Literature: Native American Literature

SUGGESTED READING:

Miller, Jay. "Mourning Dove: The Author as Cultural Mediator." In *Being and Becoming Indian: Biographical Studies of North American Frontiers.* Edited by James Clifton. Chicago, 1989.

John Muir. *Courtesy Library of Congress.*

MUIR, JOHN

The most influential conservationist in America, John Muir (1838–1914) first explored the wilderness as an escape from the grim and austere home of his fanatically Calvinist father. His experiences in the schools of his native Scotland were no better, although his teachers recognized him as exceptionally bright. The educational system, he later wrote, was "founded on leather." Muir's escapes into the out-of-doors germinated lifelong habits. "When I was a boy in Scotland," his autobiography revealed, "I was fond of everything that was wild, and all my life I've been growing fonder and fonder of wild places and wild creatures."

His family's move to Wisconsin, in 1849, placed Muir beyond the reaches of public schools, but he taught himself advanced mathematics and developed a passion for reading, especially the travels of Western explorer Alexander von Humboldt. A tinkerer and an inventor, Muir won first place in a science competition in Madison, Wisconsin, in 1860. He caught the attention of a University of Wisconsin professor, who invited Muir to take classes. At the university, he discovered the Transcendentalist writings of Ralph Waldo Emerson and HENRY DAVID THOREAU and the scientific writings of Louis Agassiz and Asa Gray, all of which had a profound impact on his thinking. Muir left school in his junior year to begin a series of "wanderings"; the first trek took him through southeastern Canada and the north-central United States. Supporting himself with odd jobs that allowed time for his wilderness studies, Muir next traveled, in 1867, from Indiana to Cedar Key, Florida, a journey he recorded along with his environmental observations as "A Thousand-Mile Walk to the Gulf."

Muir moved to California and its Yosemite Valley in 1868, where he lived intermittently for several years, traipsing the mountains and recording his observations of their geology and botany. Recalling the glaciology lessons of his college days, Muir concluded that the Yosemite Valley was a product of glacial actions, not the result of cataclysmic convulsions as many believed. The articles he published on his theories earned him the scorn of some (he was labeled an "ignoramus" by leading geologists), but twentieth-century seismic explorations of the valley proved him correct.

In the mid-1870s, Muir began studies of the great sequoias. He concluded that rather than seeking out wet areas, the giant trees actually created such areas by capturing water that would otherwise roar on to lower regions in destructive floods. In practical terms, Muir saw the destruction of the Sierra forests by lum-

John Muir and Theodore Roosevelt in Yosemite National Park, 1903. *Editors' collection.*

ber companies as a threat not only to the region's beauty but also to the maintenance of the region's watershed. His long campaign for a federal forest-conservation policy resulted from his studies.

Throughout the late 1870s, Muir explored Washington, Oregon, and Utah. The lure of unknown Alaska, purchased by the United States in 1865, was so great that Muir postponed his engagement to his future wife, Louie Wanda. He headed off for his first of five trips to Alaska in May 1879.

Muir became a successful farmer in the 1880s, but in his prosperity, he continued his writing on and advocacy of environmental causes. He fought for the establishment of YOSEMITE NATIONAL PARK, created in 1890. Two years later, Muir and friends founded the SIERRA CLUB. Originally an alpine club encouraging camping and climbing, the new organization was dedicated to the preservation of the Yosemite and Sierra wilderness areas. Muir served as its first president and led the fight against big businesses' designs on Yosemite's lumber, mining, and grazing resources.

The Sierra Club's success, however, was short lived. By 1900, San Francisco began casting about for more water for its growing population. The city settled on the Hetch Hetchy Valley, northeast of Yosemite Valley. The dam the city proposed would create a reservoir that fluctuated 240 feet each season, turning the beautiful valley into a monstrous eyesore. Preservationists initially blocked court applications for the use of the valley, but by 1905, GIFFORD PINCHOT announced that President THEODORE ROOSEVELT's administration would support the dam's construction. The Sierra Club continued the battle against the "Hetch Hetchy Steal," as it was called, but the dam was built in 1913.

Muir, however, had other successes. President Grover Cleveland established thirteen forest reserves in 1897 to protect the lands from commercial exploitation. After President Roosevelt joined Muir in a camping trip through Yosemite in 1903, the president began his conservation programs in earnest. Muir's work and his Sierra Club influenced the creation of the NATIONAL PARK SERVICE in 1916, but Muir, himself, had died two years before.

John Muir ardently believed that a nation of increasingly urbanized people—"tired, nerve-shaken, over-civilized"—required wilderness areas as a respite from their city lives. His writings, more than sixty-five magazine articles and four books, as well as his advocacy sparked tremendous growth in the environmental field in the late 1800s and early 1900s. His leadership of the Sierra Club helped turn the organization into a powerful lobby for the protection of the environment and wilderness lands. His influence was hardly diminished a century later.

—*Patricia Hogan*

SEE ALSO: Hetch Hetchy Controversy

SUGGESTED READING:

Clarke, James M. *The Pathless Way.* Madison, Wis., 1984.

Fox, Stephen. *John Muir and His Legacy: The American Conservation Movement.* Boston, 1981.

Jones, Holway R. *John Muir and the Sierra Club: The Battle for Yosemite.* San Francisco, 1965.

Muir, John. *The Mountains of California.* New York, 1901.

———. *My First Summer in the Sierra.* Boston, 1911.

———. *Our National Parks.* Boston, 1901.

———. *The Story of My Boyhood and Youth.* Boston, 1913.

Smith, Herbert F. *John Muir.* Boston, 1965.

Wolfe, Linnie Marsh. *Son of the Wilderness: The Life of John Muir.* Boston, 1945.

MULES AND MULE TRADE

The hybrid offspring of a male donkey and a female horse, the mule has faithfully served generations of Westerners as pack animals and draft-farm animals. The mule generally stands as tall as a horse and resembles the latter in the uniformity of its coat and the shape of its neck and croup. The mule's short and thick head, long ears, thin limbs, small hooves, and short mane more resemble those of the donkey. Mostly brown or bay in color, mules are usually sterile.

Mules have been around for at least three thousand years. Evidence suggests that the animals were bred in Asia Minor a millennium before Christ. From there, mules spread into western Europe, and by the fifteenth century, France, Spain, and Italy supported their own breeding centers. Mules arrived on the North American continent with Spanish explorers. In fact, Spain had quite a surplus of mules at the time of Spanish explorations because its people preferred riding the hybrids rather than horses.

The earliest mules in Spanish Mexico were used in mining operations. Horses (also brought to North America from Spain) carried Spain's first explorers into the present-day southwestern United States. Within a century after mule breeding was well established in Mexico, however, JUAN DE OÑATE's settlement in New Mexico included more than one hundred mules as well as some donkeys and mares brought along for future breeding.

Spain did not transport mules to North America simply to remove a surplus from the motherland. Mules were better suited to hauling, harnessing, and transporting duties than horses. In spite of its well-entrenched reputation for being an ornery animal, the mule was a more dependable species than his glamorous half brother. The hybrid was sure footed in rugged terrain, survived on less grain, carried heavier loads, was more durable in hot and cold weather, had the stamina to haul its burden over long distances, and had the longest working life (eighteen years) of any draft animal. The Spanish, and later the Mexicans and Americans, discovered to their own advantage that to Native Americans, mules were less desirable than horses, and therefore Indians were less likely to steal them.

Even compared to oxen, mules were better at hauling. Although oxen in numbers equal to mules could haul heavier loads, especially in muddy or sandy terrain, they tired sooner than the hybrids. And oxen, unlike mules, became weakened on a diet of the short grasses available on the Western terrain.

Mules became the chief draft animals of the Spanish settlements in the New World. They hauled coaches and carriages, and many Spanish Americans also preferred riding the animals. The Spanish missions became the chief mule breeders of the region, and sometimes, when striking out to establish new missions far removed from other settlements, missionaries took along mules as a hedge against starvation.

With the establishment of trade systems between Mexico's Santa Fe and the United States's Missouri, American traders brought back Mexican mules. Selling the mules in the South was nearly as profitable as trading with the Mexicans, but it left the settlers just west of the Mississippi River without a sufficient supply of the draft animals. As a consequence, Missourians began breeding mules for their own use and for sale to a demanding regional market. Missouri mules, bred of large Mexican jackasses and big draft mares, produced a superior animal and commanded high prices.

A common feature of overland travel and freighting, mules increasingly replaced horses as draft animals. Major freight companies made use of the hybrids too, and many families heading west arrived at their homesteads courtesy of the mules that pulled their CONESTOGA WAGONS across the country. Into the twentieth century, mules continued to carry supplies into communities removed from rail lines.

The United States Army stationed at far-flung Western outposts relied on mule-drawn wagons to deliver supplies to forts and to follow troops on expeditions.

"Cinching and loading pack mule with flour during starvation march of Gen. George Crook's expedition into the Black Hills." Photograph by S. J. Morrow, 1876. *Courtesy Denver Public Library, Western History Department.*

An army wagon train consisted of thirty-six men, 112 wagon mules, six riding mules, and twenty-eight wagons. In campaigns against Indians, the army used mule pack trains, made up of sixty-four mules and fourteen men traveling at the end of a column. The army's ability to move quickly on Indians and their fleet-footed ponies often determined the success or failure of a campaign. But moving too far in advance of accompanying supplies could also mean disaster if troops and horses had no provisions in the field. General GEORGE CROOK gambled on having adequate supplies on his so-called starvation campaign against the Sioux in the summer and fall of 1876. Intending a speedy attack on the Indians, Crook ordered his troops to abandon all wagons, tents, and extra clothing. There was, however, no quick engagement, and Crook's men chased the Indians for weeks through Wyoming, into Montana, and east to the Dakota Territory until supplies ran out.

Crook, himself, rode to war on a favorite mule and made a science of mule-borne logistics and supply. His use of the mule trains was usually effective. One of GERONIMO's warriors attested to the effectiveness of Crook's mobility: "It was only when Gen. George Crook chased the Indians with a column supplied by mule pack trains that the Apaches had a hard time staying out of reach."

As draft animals, mules had a significant impact on Western agriculture. Pulling steel plows, mules cultivated millions of square miles of farm lands; teams of up to thirty mules powered the huge combines and harvesters of wheat farming. Hauling produce to market and doing the farmers' strenuous chores, mules earned the respect and affection of their masters even as they cussed at the animals for their stubbornness.

—*Patricia Hogan*

SUGGESTED READING:

Gregg, Josiah. *Commerce of the Prairie* (with a biographical sketch by Max L. Moorhead). Norman, Okla., 1954.

Steele, James W. *Frontier Army Sketches*. Albuquerque, N. Mex., 1969.

Walker, Henry Prickering. *The Wagonmasters: High Plains Freighting from the Earliest Days of the Santa Fe Trail to 1880*. Norman, Okla., 1969.

MULHOLLAND, WILLIAM

At the time of his death, few people mourned the loss of William Mulholland (1855–1935); yet he had made Los Angeles, California, the premier city of the American West. Born in Dublin, Ireland, Mulholland worked during his late teens as a seaman. In 1874, he landed in New York and eventually took work with a relative in Pittsburgh. There he read Charles Nordhoff's accounts of California and was inspired to seek his fortune in the West.

In 1877, he arrived in southern California and began working on artesan wells. For a time, he prospected for gold in the Arizona mountains without success and then worked as a ditch tender for the Los Angeles City Water Company. One day, the president of the company asked Mulholland what he was doing. Without looking up from his digging, Mulholland replied, "None of your damn business!" When called to the president's office, Mulholland expected to be fired but instead received a promotion. He rose rapidly within the company and became its superintendent in 1880.

While Mulholland lacked the formal education of an engineer, he studied hydraulics and mastered and memorized the details of the Los Angeles water system. In 1902, the city bought the company and hired Mulholland, who knew the system better than anyone else.

In 1910, he realized that an ever-increasing water supply would ensure the growth of Los Angeles. He planned and led the acquisition of water from the Owens Valley, more than 250 miles to the east of the city. He then supervised the building of a $25 million conveyance system, one of the largest public-works projects of the time. With the completion of the aqueduct came problems. The residents of Owens Valley fought a highly publicized battle against the exportation of water and even dynamited segments of the aqueduct. Moreover, Mulholland's lack of formal engineering training cost the city dearly in repeated failures of concrete ditches and siphons. In March 1928, the Saint Francis Dam failed costing the lives of four hundred to five hundred people. A formal inquiry pinned the blame on Mulholland's poor engineering. His career ruined, he lived out an embittered and secluded life.

—*James E. Sherow*

SEE ALSO: Owens Valley War

SUGGESTED READING:

Kahrl, William L. *Water and Power: The Conflict over Los Angeles' Water Supply in the Owens Valley*. Berkeley, Calif., 1982.

Matson, Robert William. *William Mulholland: A Forgotten Forefather*. Stockton, Calif., 1976.

MULLER V. OREGON (1908)

During the Progressive era, the state of Oregon enacted a law that limited women to a ten-hour workday. In 1905, Curt Muller, the owner of a Portland laundry, challenged the statute by demanding that his laundresses work beyond the legal limit. He was arrested and fined. After losing his case before the Oregon Supreme Court, Muller appealed to the U.S. Supreme Court. Attorney Louis D. Brandeis, a self-styled "people's lawyer," was hired to defend the Oregon statute. In his preparation, Brandeis departed from traditional defense practices by applying environmental and sociological views to the needs of a changing society. His staff obtained data from libraries, labor unions, social workers, and other experts. The "Brandeis Brief," considered to be the prototype of "sociological jurisprudence," generally implied, among other issues, that women were weaker than men and needed special treatment. In 1908, the Supreme Court supported the "Brandeis Brief" and upheld the Oregon law. The *Muller* decision has been debated recently by those who assert that the case patronizes women and weakens their argument for social justice. Others support the sociological impact on jurisprudence as in the decision of *Brown* v. *Board of Education of Topeka,* which ended the segregation of public schools across the nation.

—*Fred L. Koestler*

SUGGESTED READING:

Mason, Alpheus T. "The Case of the Overworked Laundresses." In *Quarrels That Have Shaped the Constitution.* Edited by John A. Garraty. New York, 1964.

MULTIPLE-USE DOCTRINE

Multiple use is a public-lands management doctrine. The Forest Organic Act of 1897 gave two clear purposes for the management of the millions of acres of forest reserves created in the 1890s: to provide for a continuous supply of timber and to promote favorable conditions of water flow. The law also permitted the use of other forest resources that remained unnamed, except for mining, which was explicitly mentioned. The new UNITED STATES FOREST SERVICE within the Department of Agriculture received its instructions regarding the use of forest resources in a 1905 letter from Secretary of Agriculture James Wilson, who emphasized what amounted to a multiple-use, utilitarian approach to resource management.

The chief of the Forest Service, GIFFORD PINCHOT, and his assistants enthusiastically accepted the mandate, which the Forest Service in retrospect termed "multiple use." While the Forest Service pursued multiresource development, the NATIONAL PARK SERVICE embraced aesthetic preservation and recreational uses and highlighted nonutilitarian values. In 1933, the Forest Service's Copeland Report outlined the modern concept of multiple use. Congress passed the Multiple-Use and Sustained Yield Act in 1960; the new law officially named the multiple resources of the national forests—timber, water, range, wildlife, recreation, and minerals. The Forest Service's multiple-use policies created controversy as dominant users resisted new policies that made way for a variety of other public-land uses. The public-range lands that came under jurisdiction of the BUREAU OF LAND MANAGEMENT after 1946 permitted grazing use to dominate. But even the BLM, by the 1960s, moved slowly toward multiple use, and by the last decades of the twentieth century, it joined the Forest Service in multidimensional ecosystem management.

—*William D. Rowley*

SUGGESTED READING:

Muhn, James, and Hanson R. Stuart. *Opportunity and Challenge: The Story of the BLM.* Washington, D.C., 1988.

Steen, Harold K. *United States Forest Service: A History.* Seattle, Wash., 1976.

MUNDT, KARL E.

Congressman and senator from South Dakota, Karl E. Mundt (1900–1974) was born in Humbolt, South Dakota. He taught school at Eastern State Normal School before he was elected to the U.S. House of Representatives in 1938. Ten years later, he was elected to the Senate. He wrote the Endangered Species Act, was involved in the passage of the U.S. Information and Education Act, and played a crucial role in establishing the Food for Peace program.

These actions would suggest that Mundt was an internationalist. He was a "new isolationist," however, or what diplomatic historians call a "unilateralist" (someone who believes the United States should go its own way in foreign policy). He was an ardent anti-Communist and served diligently on the House Un-American Activities Committee. In the Senate, he assisted his good friend Joseph McCarthy on the Committee on Government Operations and chaired the Army-McCarthy hearings. He was also instrumental in the enactment of the Internal Security Act of 1950.

Mundt suffered a debilitating stroke on November 22, 1969, but refused to retire until his Senate term ended in 1972.

—*R. Alton Lee*

SUGGESTED READING:

Heidepriem, Scott. *A Fair Chance for a Free People: A Biography of Karl E. Mundt.* Madison, S. Dak., 1988.

Lee, R. Alton. "New Dealers, Fair Dealers, Misdealers and Hiss Dealers: Karl Mundt and the Internal Security Act of 1950." *South Dakota History* 10 (Fall 1980): 277–290.

MURIETA (OR MURRIETA), JOAQUIN

Legendary Mexican bandit of the gold-rush years in California, Joaquin Murieta (?–1853?) is most often identified simply as "Joaquin." He was immortalized by Cherokee writer and politician, JOHN RIDGE in *The Life and Adventures of Joaquin Murieta, the Celebrated California Bandit* (1854). Ridge's fiction embellished on the many brief accounts of, and even "interviews" with, the notorious Joaquin. According to Ridge, Joaquin went to California from Mexico after fighting in the United States–Mexican War; he lived in Los Angeles in 1849 and made his way to Murphy Flat in the Sierra mines. There he entered a scene of rising racial tension against foreign miners, especially Mexicans. Joaquin tried mining, was forced off a claim, and took up gambling to earn a living. But, Ridge asserted, when Yankees raped Joaquin's wife, Rosita, he formed a band of outlaws to seek revenge.

Joaquin Murieta. *Courtesy Bancroft Library.*

Accounts do exist about one or more bandits known as Joaquin—surnamed Muriati, Murieta, Ocomorenia, Valenzuela, Boteller, Botello, and Carrillo—who from 1851 to 1853 ravaged the state. The bandit seemed to be everywhere at all times, from Stockton to Los Angeles, stealing cattle, holding up gamblers at gun point, waylaying stagecoaches, intimidating miners (particularly in Chinese camps, for reasons unknown), and wantonly killing victims or witnesses. The legislature authorized a one-thousand-dollar reward for his capture or death. Taking up the charge, Captain Harry Love and his California Rangers tracked down Mexican bandits in Mariposa County in July 1853 and killed their leaders. As proof of their exploits, the rangers severed the head of one dead leader and the hand of his lieutenant, Three-Finger Jack; pickled the remains in whiskey; and claimed the reward money. These grizzly souvenirs later earned fifty thousand dollars at freak shows and disappeared in the rubble of the SAN FRANCISCO EARTHQUAKE OF 1906.

One can never know whether or not the dead bandit leader was the real Joaquin, nor can one take much stock in the biographical details provided by Ridge. Yet the Native American novelist, who used the pen name "Yellow Bird," wrote about racial matters with deep conviction. He had grown up in a tumultuous time when whites were pressing against the Indian nation of Georgia. He experienced anti-Indian discrimination, had witnessed the murder of his father in Oklahoma, and was a fugitive in California from murderous personal enemies. Ridge's yarn had emotional impact and hit a cultural nerve. So many others pirated it that the tale became a popular romantic legend, and Ridge earned no money from his novel.

The Joaquin story symbolized the Mexican-Yankee clash in the West and had great literary appeal regardless of historical truth. It was told and retold throughout Latin America even in the twentieth century. As recently as 1967, the great Chilean poet, Pablo Neruda, published a drama about the bandit, entitled *Fulgor y Muerta de Joaquin Murieta.* Some historians cite Joaquin as a classic example of SOCIAL BANDITRY. He personifies the brigand who, in a time of rapid social change or modernization, forms a band of semiorganized rebels to protect an older way of life or to undo a perceived evil. Robin Hood is the best known example. The bandit-hero, sometimes vicious and crude and sometimes tinged with nobility, has been a popular figure throughout Europe, Asia, and America.

—*Leonard Pitt*

SUGGESTED READING:

Parins, James W. *John Rollin Ridge: His Life and Works.* Lincoln, Nebr., 1991.

Pitt, Leonard. *The Decline of the Californios: A Social History of the Spanish-Speaking Californians, 1846–1890.* Berkeley, Calif., 1968.

MURPHY, LAWRENCE G.

SEE: Lincoln County War

MURRAY, WILLIAM ("ALFALFA BILL")

Democratic politician, president of the Oklahoma Constitutional Convention, and governor of Oklahoma, William ("Alfalfa Bill") Murray (1869–1956) was born in the community of Toadsuck in Grayson County, Texas. He attended public schools before leaving home and later attended College Hill Institute in Springtown, Texas. While dabbling in teaching, journalism, and politics, he also read law. He was admitted to the Texas bar in 1895 and practiced law in Fort Worth.

In 1898, Murray moved to Tishomingo, the capital of the Chickasaw nation, where he married Mary Alice Hearell, the niece of the nation's governor. The dissolution of Chickasaw tribal properties brought him both economic and political prominence. The first he parlayed into a sizable farm near Tishomingo; the second culminated in his service as president of the Oklahoma Constitutional Convention from 1906 to 1907.

After Oklahoma became a state, Murray served as Speaker of the first legislature from 1907 to 1909 and as a United States Representative from 1913 to 1917. In the 1920s, he left politics and Oklahoma to lead a band of settlers to Bolivia.

With the failure of the Bolivian colony, Murray returned to Oklahoma and launched a political comeback. In 1930, he surprisingly won the Democrats' gubernatorial primary and the general election by a then-record margin. His governorship, though colorful, yielded little in the way of substantive achievement.

Ineligible for reelection in 1934, Murray returned to politics in 1938 but lost in the Democratic primary. Several other attempted comebacks failed dismally, and Murray spent his declining years writing a series of books that ranged from the unusual to the bizarre. He died in Oklahoma City.

—Danney Goble

SUGGESTED READING:

Bryant, Keith L. *Alfalfa Bill Murray.* Norman, Okla., 1968.

MUSEUM OF NEW MEXICO

Composed of four state museums in Santa Fe and five state monuments throughout the state, the Museum of New Mexico was established in 1909 when the Territory of New Mexico converted the PALACE OF THE GOVERNORS into a museum.

Today, the Palace of the Governors is a history museum and includes a complex of four buildings, the most important of which is the old palace built in 1610.

The Museum of Fine Arts was established in 1917 in a building modeled after the mission-church of San Esteban at the Acoma Pueblo. The collections, emphasizing Southwestern art, include paintings, illustrations, sculptures, and photographs. The museum carries out programs on music, dance, and art and houses a fine-arts library.

The Museum of Indian Art and Culture/Laboratory of Anthropology began with the laboratory in 1931. The "lab" became a center for anthropological work throughout the Southwest and Mexico. The Indian Art and Culture Museum opened in 1986 to exhibit the collections of the lab. The museum consists of two buildings, which house galleries, educational facilities, a research library, collections, and an auditorium.

The Museum of International Folk Art was built in 1953 and contains folk-art collections from all over the world. The galleries include space dedicated to the famous Girard Collection and Spanish folk life. Programs include a strong education department, a research library, demonstrations, lectures, and dances. The collections reflect an emphasis on New Mexico.

The five state monuments included in the Museum of New Mexico's holdings are Fort Sumner where members of the Navajo and Comanche nations were gathered in a failed government farming experiment in the 1860s; a seventeenth-century mission and pueblo ruin at Jemez Pueblo; Kuaua, a sixteenth-century pueblo ruin outside of Albuquerque; Fort Seldon, a nineteenth-century U.S. Army fort north of Las Cruces; and a majority of the historical structures in the town of Lincoln where people such as "BILLY THE KID," PATRICK FLOYD JARVIS (PAT) GARRETT, and John Tunstall left their legacy.

In addition, the Museum of New Mexico has a traveling exhibition service, publishes books through its own press, and issues a museum magazine entitled *El Palacio* three times a year.

—Thomas E. Chávez

SUGGESTED READING:

Chauvenet, Beatrice. *Hewett and Friends: A Biography of Santa Fe's Vibrant Era.* Santa Fe., N. Mex., 1983.
El Palacio (Special anniversary issue). Vol. 90, no. 2 (1984).

MUSEUMS AND CULTURAL ORGANIZATIONS

SEE: Amon Carter Museum; Arizona Historical Society; Autry Museum of Western Heritage; Buffalo Bill Historical Center; DeGolyer Library; Hearst San Simeon State Historical Monument; Huntington Library, Art Collections, and Botanical Gardens; Joslyn Art Museum; Los Angeles County Museum of Natural History; Museum of New Mexico; National Cowboy Hall of Fame and Western Heritage Center; Newberry Library; Oakland Museum of California; Palace of the Governors (New Mexico Museum); Thomas Gilcrease Institute

MUSIC, WESTERN

The music that has come to be called "western music" is a mixture of popular, country, and folk styles that grew out of themes from the songs of the cowboys.

Cowhands on the trail drives of the mid- to late 1800s and on the ranches of the late 1800s and early 1900s produced an extensive body of job-related folk songs drawn from their experiences and reflecting their lives—the work they did on the roundups and trail drives, the food they ate, and the dangers they faced. There was little room on the cattle trails and in the cow camps for musical instruments, and although cowboys occasionally brought along a fiddle, harmonica, or banjo, they did most of their singing unaccompanied. While many cowboy songs were parodies or reworkings of earlier traditional or popular songs, most were original compositions of cowboy poets, often set to the tune of old, familiar songs. "Oh, Bury Me Not On the Lone Prairie," for example, was a cowboy version of the old sailor's song "The Ocean Burial (Oh, Bury Me Not in the Deep Deep Sea)." The well-known "Tying Knots in the Devil's Tail (The Sierry Petes)," written by northern Arizona cowboy Gail Gardner, was set to the familiar tune of "Polly Wolly Doodle."

During the 1920s, the fledgling media of radio and phonograph recording discovered cowboy singers, who then began to perform on local radio stations and to make records. In 1925, Texan Carl T. Sprague recorded "When the Work's All Done This Fall" for the Victor label, and its spectacular sales of some nine hundred thousand copies sparked a boom in the recording of "authentic" old-time cowboy singers, including Jules Verne Allen and Harry ("Haywire Mac") McClintock.

By the end of the decade, the cowboy was also a mainstay of the motion picture western. In 1929, cowboy and actor Ken Maynard strummed his guitar and sang in the film *The Wagon Master;* this performance ushered in the era of the movies' singing cowboy. He was followed in the 1930s by GENE AUTRY, Roy Rogers, Tex Ritter, and a herd of other "B" western crooners who became national heroes.

While these "stars" sang some traditional cowboy songs, they increasingly performed numbers composed by professional Tin Pan Alley songwriters, such as "The Last Round-Up," by Billy Hill, and "Don't Fence Me In," by Cole Porter—a composition introduced by Roy Rogers in the 1944 Warner Brothers movie *Hollywood Canteen.* Unlike traditional cowboy songs, which were often starkly realistic in their portrayal of cowboy life, the professional compositions were highly romantic and pictured a carefree, adventurous life on the range.

As performers moved from traditional cowboy songs to professionally composed "western" songs, changes occurred as well in instrumentation and musical style. Most of the early cowboy recording artists, such as Sprague and Allen, played simple guitar music, sometimes accompanied by a fiddle or a harmonica. The movies' singing cowboy had begun to use "hot," polished instrumental ensembles, including such instruments as fiddle, bass, and accordion in addition to the guitar. They drew heavily on contemporary influences like jazz, popular music, and "western swing."

Texas Bob Wills developed and popularized western swing, a hybrid of country fiddling, jazz, blues, Mexican music, and big-band swing. His big bands employed drums, piano, and horns, and they pioneered the use of electrically amplified standard and steel guitars. Wills and his band, The Texas Playboys, enjoyed tremendous popularity from the 1930s to the 1950s, often drawing crowds that rivaled those of the big bands of Benny Goodman, Glenn Miller, and Tommy Dorsey. As western swing became established, other band leaders, such as Spade Cooley, who became known as "the king of western swing," followed Wills's lead. The style and repertoire of western swing had a tremendous influence on western music in general.

The best-known western singing group, The Sons of the Pioneers, founded in 1933 by Roy Rogers (who at the time went by the name Leonard Slye), Tim Spencer, and Bob Nolan, combined intricate close-harmony singing with sophisticated instrumental backup. Songs such as "Tumbling Tumbleweed," "When Payday Rolls Around," and "Cool Water" made the Sons of the Pioneers the most popular and influential western singing group of all time. Their style and repertoire influenced essentially every western singing group that followed.

Western music combined the familiar image of the cowboy with romantic songs, sophisticated instrumentation, and harmony singing and became a very popular cultural phenomenon. Country music performers from the Southeast, including Jimmie Rodgers and

Patsy Montana (Rubeye Blevins) began to dress in western-style stage clothes and adopt names like The Golden West Cowboys and The Prairie Ramblers. Eventually, record companies and dealers combined the two genres into "country and western music," which was easier to promote and merchandise. The term stuck for years, but although the two kinds of music shared much in common, they were really two separate and distinct strains of American music.

In the late 1970s, a strong revival of interest in western music began, spearheaded by performers such as Riders in the Sky and Michael Martin Murphey. This interest was spurred on by the resurgence during the following decades of public enthusiasm for things western and cowboy, as reflected in the popularity of television shows and movies like *Lonesome Dove* and *Dances with Wolves*. Western music once again recaptured the imagination of a large audience and flourished as a distinct and important style of folk-based American music.

—*Charlie Seemann*

SEE ALSO: Cowboy Songs; Film: The Western; Folk Music; Rogers, Roy, and Dale Evans

SUGGESTED READING:

Green, Douglas B. "The Singing Cowboy: An American Dream." *Journal of Country Music* 7: 2 (May 1978): 4–62.

Griffis, Ken. *Hear My Song: The Story of the Celebrated Sons of the Pioneers*. Los Angeles, 1977.

Malone, Bill C. *Country Music USA*. Austin, Tex., 1985.

Tinsley, Jim Bob. *For a Cowboy Has to Sing*. Orlando, Fla., 1991.

Townsend, Charles. *San Antonio Rose: The Life and Times of Bob Wills*. Urbana, Ill., 1976.

MUSTANG AND HORSE TRADE

The FUR TRADE was a dominant force behind the exploration and imperial control of North America. Bearing the metalwares and textiles of their respective home industries, traders representing Russia, Spain, France, Great Britain, the Netherlands, and, ultimately, the United States, Mexico, and Canada probed the interior of the continent in search of untapped reservoirs of wild animals. In the larger context, the traders were pawns in an imperial chess game for control of North America. But they were also private entrepreneurs who evolved a distinctive frontier life style. And the economy whose profits they sought was a transformative agent in New World history. It brought the native peoples into the worldwide market economy, in the process often disrupting them and infecting them with disease epidemics. In some instances, participation in trade overhauled entire societies. The animal trade brought many disparate ethnic and cultural groups together. It served as a magnet to draw Euro-Americans into the Indian lands and provided much of the impetus for wars and migrations of native peoples that lasted for 350 years.

Mustanging (the catching of wild horses) and the horse trade between Indians and Euro-Americans was, in some ways, merely another variation of the fur trade. Until late in the nineteenth century, the trade in wild horses was not the organized business that the pelt and robe trade was. Yet it must have commenced on a considerable scale soon after the PUEBLO REVOLT of 1680 made large numbers of horses available. Until the twentieth century, the horse trade differed, too, in that it involved securing living animals. But mustangers and horse traders essentially played the same role in frontier life that employees of fur companies did.

During the half-century after the Pueblo Revolt, trade was the chief agent of transfer of horses from one Indian tribe to another. The Black Hills region was a major center of this trade and dispersal on the Northern Plains, which had placed horses in the hands of groups as far from present-day New Mexico as the Great Lakes by 1730. Alluring to both Indians and Euro-Americans was the knowledge that horses had gone feral across the plains surrounding the New Mexican settlements of the upper Rio Grande. Horses not only became the magnet that drew many tribal groups onto the Great Plains, they also bent tribal migrations southward. As horse traders, the Southern Plains tribes, especially, evolved extensive contacts with both native and Euro-American groups interested in horses. Agricultural villages of prairie Sioux and Caddo peoples, located in fixed sites along the major rivers, became middlemen trading citadels, funneling horses to Eastern markets.

The Spanish and mestizo colonists in Texas early on learned the fine art of catching *mestenos* (wild horses), employing a technique of impounding, or chasing the animals into spiral-shaped corrals hidden into the topography. By 1778, the capture of mustangs had become so important to the Texas economy that it was taxed and regulated; revenues were slated for a Mustang Fund for Indian gifts and ransom money. A typical year was 1785, when *mesterneros* around San Antonio caught and paid taxes on 828 mustangs. The presence of huge herds of feral horses running wild in the Spanish borderlands ultimately became a serious problem for Texas and New Mexico officials trying to control the trade. French traders operating out of Louisiana and St. Louis established the patterns. In an effort to cut off this illegal trade, the Spanish government granted trading monopolies to some traders and allowed them to export horses into Louisiana. This was only partially successful. Officially, Spanish records show 1,187 horses going from Texas to New Orleans in 1802; an American Indian agent in Louisiana figured the volume was closer to 7,300 horses that year.

The monopolies failed to stop the contraband trade. The market even for unbroken horses (average price $20) on the advancing American frontier was a strong one; outstanding animals brought $100 or more in St. Louis, Natchez, and Lexington. Until the opening of the Santa Fe trade in 1821, the horse trade was the most important economic exchange in the Southwest. In the first three decades of the nineteenth century, scores of little-known American horse traders probed the Southern Plains, returning mustangs to the American frontier, making geographical discoveries, and extending American interests among the Plains Indians.

The horse and mule trade continued to be an important part of the Western economy after 1821. New Mexican burros acquired in Santa Fe became the cornerstones of the Missouri mule industry. Horses also were a key item in the trade of the BENT BROTHERS, whose 1830's posts on the Arkansas River siphoned horses, via Indian traders, from the wild herds and from Spanish herds as far away as California and to the Horse and Mule Market in St. Louis.

Wars created good markets. Texas mustangers supplied both sides with remounts during the TEXAS REVOLUTION. The American military seems never to have regarded wild horses very highly and acquired few of them for use in the United States–Mexican War, the Civil War, or the Indian Wars, although both sides in the Civil War put more than 300,000 mules into service. During the Spanish-American War and particularly during England's Boer War and World War I, however, the market for wild American horses was very strong. Miles City, Montana, produced at least 32,000 wild horses, which were sold to army buyers for $145 to $185. Horse exports from the United States were reckoned at 51,500 in 1898, 103,000 in 1903, and a crest of 357,553 in 1916. After World War I, most of the wild horse capture and trade in the West was conducted by mustangers under contract by pet-food companies, a practice that was ended with the passage of the Wild Horse and Burro Conservation acts of 1959 and 1971.

—*Dan Flores*

SUGGESTED READING:

Dobie, J. Frank. *The Mustangs.* New York, 1934.

Flores, Dan, ed. *Journal of an Indian Trader: Anthony Glass and the Texas Trading Frontier.* College Station, Tex., 1985.

Wishart, David. *The Fur Trade of the American West, 1807–1840.* Lincoln, Nebr., 1979.

NAHL, CHARLES

See: Art: Book and Magazine Illustration

NAICHE (APACHE)

The last Chiricahua chief and the son of Cochise and grandson of Mangas Coloradas, Naiche (ca. 1856–1921) was born probably in southeastern Arizona. In 1861, he was captured with his mother at Apache Pass, and the subsequent Bascom Incident, in which his father was accused of kidnapping a white boy and was held by U.S. authorities, ignited twenty-five years of hostilities. He attended the 1872 meeting between Cochise and General Oliver Otis Howard—a meeting that briefly ended war between the Chiricahuas and the army. Naiche became chief in 1876 and was in command of his warriors during the U.S. Army's campaign to capture Geronimo. After the campaign, Naiche and his people were sent to the East in exile. He married three times and fathered fourteen children. He died at Mescalero, New Mexico.

—*Dan L. Thrapp*

Suggested reading:
Debo, Angie. *Geronimo: The Man, His Times, His Place.* Norman, Okla., 1976.
Lockwood, Frank C. *The Apache Indians.* Lincoln, Nebr., 1987.

Naiche, son of Cochise. Photograph by Ben Wittick. *Courtesy School of American Research Collections in the Museum of New Mexico.*

NANA (APACHE)

A Mimbres war leader but never a chief, Nana (ca. 1800–1896) was born in southern New Mexico. His known wife, Nah-dos-te, was a sister of Geronimo. General George Crook called Nana "the brains of the hostile bands" and an inveterate raider. A companion of Victorio, Nana escaped the Tres Castillos Massacre, and then across the Southwest, he led a spectacular raid, in which he killed forty Americans. He surrendered to Crook in 1883, broke out of the Apache res-

Nana. Photograph by Ben Wittick. *Courtesy National Archives.*

ervation with Geronimo in 1885, again surrendered in 1886, and was exiled to the East. He died at Fort Sill, Oklahoma.

—*Dan L. Thrapp*

SUGGESTED READING:

Lekson, Stephen H. *Nana's Raid: Apache Warfare in Southern New Mexico, 1881.* El Paso, Tex., 1987.

NARBONA (NAVAJO)

Navajo chief, peace advocate, and father-in-law of MANUELITO, Narbona (ca. 1776–1849) lived in the turbulent years of the eighteenth and nineteenth centuries when relations between Navajo Indians and Spanish, then Mexican, then American soldiers and settlers were characterized by an endless series of raids and counterraids for plunder, livestock, and captives. As a warrior still in his twenties, he could not stop the massacre of Navajo women, children, and elderly men led by the Spanish governor of New Mexico at Canyon de Chelly in January 1805. As settlers increasingly encroached on Navajo lands in the first decades of the nineteenth century, Navajo retaliation intensified. By 1835, Narbona had risen to the position of chief of the Navajos, and he attempted to end the wars by approaching New Mexico's governor for peace. Perhaps an exchange of captives resulted from the chief's appeal, but it brought no lasting results. A continuation of hostilities motivated Narbona to make a similar appeal to Mexican officials in 1841. Narbona agreed to the Martinez Treaty in 1844.

Relations between the Navajos and the New Mexicans hardly improved when, in August 1846, General STEPHEN WATTS KEARNY seized the region in the United States–Mexican War and promised American troops would protect settlers from Indian attacks. Kearny ordered troops into Navajo territory two months after taking control. After a few weeks of fighting, Narbona signed an agreement with the Americans in November, although it was soon rejected by other Navajo leaders and the U.S. Congress. Narbona attempted to secure peace for his people again in May 1848. The raids and retaliations, however, continued.

The Navajo chief still had peace on his mind when he and other Navajos encountered New Mexico's military governor Colonel John M. Washington and his forces in August 1849. In a dispute over the ownership of a horse, American troops fired on the Navajos. Narbona was hit several times and died. A trophy hunter "ripped off the scalp of nearly white shoulder-length hair." The NAVAJO WARS continued for two more decades.

—*Patricia Hogan*

SUGGESTED READING:

McNitt, Frank. *Navajo Wars.* Albuquerque, N. Mex., 1972.

NARVÁEZ, PÁNFILO DE

Spanish-born explorer Pánfilo de Narváez (ca. 1478–1528) first arrived in the Western Hemisphere in 1498 and spent most of his early years in the West Indies. By 1511, he had become chief lieutenant to Diego Velazquez and participated in the Spanish conquest of Cuba. Narváez's treatment of the Arawak Indians during the campaign brought him a reputation for cruelty and the condemnation of the Spanish church.

In 1520, Velazquez sent Narváez to Mexico to arrest Hernan Cortés, whose conquest of Mexico lacked royal authority. Narváez's troops confronted Cortés's soldiers on May 23, 1520. In the conflict, Narváez lost an eye before being captured and imprisoned at Zempoala. Released in 1521, Narváez returned to Spain.

Charles I sent Narváez back to the American continent in 1527 with a commission to explore and conquer the lands between Rio de las Palmas in northeastern Mexico and the Cape of Florida. Named captain general and governor of the new realm by the king, Narváez sailed with five ships and more than six hundred colonists. A hurricane that struck while the ships were harbored in Cuba killed a number of settlers and disheartened others, who then deserted the expedition. Another storm blew the ships north of Cuba along the western coast of Florida. Landing near present-day Tampa Bay in May 1528, Narváez claimed the land for Spain and devised a plan to split his forces: his ships were to ply the coast while a land force searched Florida's interior for the fabled cities of gold reported by Juan Ponce de León some years before. The expedition's treasurer, Álvar Núñez Cabeza de Vaca vigorously protested Narváez's plan, but the governor of the new realm prevailed.

With about three hundred men, Narváez explored the region, fought with natives, and lost track of his ships, which searched the Gulf Coast fruitlessly for a year for some trace of the Spaniard and his forces. Narváez constructed five makeshift barges to replace the vessels and planned to follow the Gulf Coast to Mexico with a company much depleted by Indian hostilities and illness. Narváez launched his barges in September 1528. Wanting water and rest, he put ashore after a week and skirmished with Indians, a pattern that was repeated for several weeks. Separating himself from the slower barges, Narváez and the men in his vessel pressed on to Mexico. His barge was apparently lost in a storm. Other barges reached a coastal island, perhaps Galveston, where the Spaniards were enslaved by Indians. Of the three hundred men of Narváez's land party, only Cabeza de Vaca and three other men eventually reached Mexico, and the four survivors stumbled into Mexico after years of wandering through the present-day American Southwest.

—*Patricia Hogan*

See also: Exploration: Spanish Expeditions

Suggested reading:

Bishop, Morris. *The Odyssey of Cabeza de Vaca*. 1933. Reprint. Westport, Conn., 1971.

NATAWISTA (BLOOD)

Natawista (or Natawista Iskana or Madame Culbertson, ca. 1825–1895), a Blood Indian woman, combined the roles of hostess, diplomat, and interpreter in trading posts of the upper Missouri River. In 1840, Natawista traveled with her father, Men-Es-To-Kos, on a trading expedition from Canada to Fort Union at the mouth of the Yellowstone near the present-day Dakota-Montana border. There she married—in an Indian ceremony—the head of the fort, Major Alexander Culbertson. She impressed such diverse visitors to the fort as the missionaries Pierre-Jean de Smet and Nicolas Point and the artist John James Audubon.

But Natawista was more than an officer's wife and hostess. In 1845, when Culbertson journeyed farther up the Missouri to establish a new fort—which later became Fort Benton, Montana—Natawista served as a diplomat, negotiator, and interpreter to the Blackfoot, Blood, Piegan, and Gros Ventres Indians. In 1847, Isaac Stevens, governor of the Washington Territory, appointed Culbertson special agent to the tribes of the Blackfoot Confederacy during the 1847 survey of routes for the right-of-way of a transcontinental railroad. Traveling with her husband, Natawista served as interpreter and peacemaker while the "special agent" made the governor's case among the various Indian camps.

In 1858, Culbertson retired to Peoria, Illinois, where he built an impressive mansion. In 1859, he and Natawista were married in a Catholic ceremony and then spent the next decade living in high style on the profits from a variety of investments. When his investments finally faltered, Culbertson returned to trading in the upper Missouri. Sometime in the early 1870s, Natawista left her husband to live with the Bloods in Alberta, Canada.

—*Alan Axelrod*

Suggested reading:

Waldman, Carl. *Who Was Who in Native American History*. New York, 1990.

NATION, CARRY AMELIA MOORE

Carry Nation (1846–1911), temperance and women's rights champion, was born in Garrard County, Kentucky. Her family moved to Missouri in 1856 and Texas in 1867. There she married Charles Gloyd, a young physician and an alcoholic. After their marriage failed, she returned to Missouri and became a schoolteacher. In 1877, she married David A. Nation, preacher, editor, lawyer, and Civil War veteran. The couple moved to Texas, and after her husband failed at farming, the family moved to Medicine Lodge, Kansas, in 1889, where she and other members of the Woman's Chris-

TIAN TEMPERANCE UNION rallied antialcohol residents to close Medicine Lodge's illegal saloons in 1899. Nation blamed alcohol for destroying marriages and family life and believed that she was divinely ordained to wipe out strong drink.

After passive methods of preaching and confronting saloon customers failed, she used a hatchet for the first time to smash saloons in Kiowa, Kansas, in 1900. Later that year, she wrecked the bar at the Carey Hotel in Wichita, Kansas. She described her actions as "hatchetations," but police called them "disturbing the peace." Late in 1901, her husband David Nation was granted a divorce.

Between 1901 and 1908, Carry Nation took her crusade across Kansas and into Missouri, Texas, Michigan, Montana, and Washington, D.C. She appeared at Chautauqua gatherings, county fairs, and even burlesque shows. During this period, she wrote her autobiography and started several publications, including the *Hatchet, Smasher's Mail,* and *Home Defender.* By 1909, these publications had failed, and her own health was declining. She moved from Washington, D.C., to Arkansas. In 1911, after suffering a stroke, she was admitted to a sanitarium in Leavenworth, Kansas, where she died. She was buried in the family plot at Belton, Missouri, not far from the town of Peculiar. Nearly forgotten when national prohibition became law in 1920, she is today remembered as a larger-than-life figure who promoted TEMPERANCE AND PROHIBITION and the rights of women.

—*David Dary*

SUGGESTED READING:

Asbury, Herbert. *Carry Nation: The Woman with the Hatchet.* New York, 1929.

Nation, Carry A. *The Use and Need of the Life of Carry A. Nation.* Topeka, Kans., 1904.

NATIONAL COWBOY HALL OF FAME AND WESTERN HERITAGE CENTER

The National Cowboy Hall of Fame and Western Heritage Center, located in Oklahoma City, Oklahoma, was founded in 1965. The museum maintains important collections of art and artifacts reflecting the history and cultures of the trans-Mississippi West. Its art collection includes important works by FREDERIC REMINGTON, CHARLES MARION RUSSELL, ALBERT BIERSTADT, CHARLES SCHREYVOGEL, and members of the TAOS SCHOOL OF ARTISTS, among others. The museum's contemporary Western art holdings, headed by five monumental landscapes by artist Wilson Hurley, is unrivaled.

Broad-based historical collections, anchored by the Joe Grandee Museum of the Frontier West, contain particularly significant artifacts related to cowboy and military life. The West of myth and legend is represented by the personal memorabilia of such notable performers as JOHN WAYNE, Barbara Stanwyck, Bob Wills, and TOM MIX.

The Cowboy Hall of Fame also maintains a research library and archives and possesses an especially important collection of rodeo photography. Since 1970, the museum has published *Persimmon Hill* magazine, a quarterly devoted to the historic and contemporary American West.

The institution annually recognizes significant contributions to the history and culture of the West through inductions into its Hall of Great Westerners, Rodeo Hall of Fame, and Hall of Great Western Performers. Since 1961, the Cowboy Hall of Fame also has sponsored the annual Western Heritage Awards, recognizing the year's best films, television, literature, and music with Western themes.

The Cowboy Hall of Fame is home to Westerners International, the Rodeo Historical Society, the Western Chuck Wagon Association, and the Howdy Pardner Club for children.

—*B. Byron Price*

SUGGESTED READING:

Persimmon Hill 18 (Summer 1990). Silver Anniversary Issue devoted to the history of the National Cowboy Hall of Fame and Western Heritage Center.

NATIONAL EXPANSION

NATION BUILDING AND EARLY EXPANSION

In the nineteenth century, the trans-Mississippi region was transformed by the expansionist initiatives of the

United States into the "American" West. A mass migration changed what had been, for the most part, an Indian and Hispanic land of small villages and tribal communities into a colonial dependency dominated by a growing capitalist economy and peopled by a work force of millions of Anglo-Americans, African Americans, European immigrants, Mexican immigrants, and Chinese immigrants. The migration took place under the political imprint of the American nation, which rearranged the social and physical landscape of the West. The domination—some historians call it the "conquest"—of the West by the United States and its incorporation into the American empire implied both a form of political and military control. But neither the lands nor their peoples were totally subjected to a monolithic power, nor did the domination proceed seamlessly from East to West. Instead, a new political entity spread willy-nilly by trade, treaty, purchase, and violent conquest during periods of financial BOOMS and busts that were, in turn, frequently spawned by chance discoveries and the uneven development of natural resources. Although gains in territory at the expense of Mexico, France, Great Britain, and various Indian tribes was perhaps the most obvious characteristic of American expansion into the trans-Mississippi region, expansion also involved the growth of federal power, the imposition of a national political definition on the region, and the gradual creation of a bureaucratic state to administer the newly designated American lands. In all, the "winning of the West" was a tale not of steady triumphs and absolute successes, but of fits and starts, of native resistances and political controversies, of enterprises launched and abandoned, which only in the retelling became an account of progressive victory and national glory.

The ideas, politics, and institutions that governed the expansion of the United States into the trans-Mississippi West, however, were born and developed east of the river before 1800. The very concept of a peculiar region considered uniquely "Western," for example, had a political pedigree stretching back to colonial times. In fact, the American West itself was a political and cultural construction before it was ever a landed reality. As such, the American West had been invented by Virginia planters who feared it was too dangerous to allow the indentured servants they had previously preferred to slaves to remain in their seaboard colony. Part of a vast underclass of miserably poor whites, many of them dispossessed by the British enclosure laws of the 1500s and 1600s, servitors and indentured workers made up more than half the colony. According to such scholars as Howard Zinn, they were beginning to find common cause with African slaves. Since every free white man was required by law to carry a gun to defend the colony, much of the "rabble" was armed. Not trusting the poor, especially after Bacon's Rebellion in 1676 revealed their revolutionary potential, the landed elite hit on a happy expedient: monopolize the good land in the east, force the landless whites west into the wilderness where they would run up against Indian "savages," and make them into a buffer for the seaboard rich against Indian troubles. In 1705, the Virginia assembly passed a law giving every freed indentured male ten bushels of corn, thirty shillings, and a gun. Every freed woman got fifteen bushels of corn and forty shillings. And all freed servants got fifty acres of land west of the Tidewater.

Beginning as a politically expedient solution to Virginia's turbulent class problems, the West became the place where poor Europeans, so recently displaced from their homeland, found a plot of earth that they felt conferred dignity and distinguished them from the enslaved and the savage. Before the century was out, they were pressing beyond the Appalachians into the Ohio Valley. There, in large measure to secure the Ohio lands for settlement, American colonials would start a conflict that sparked a worldwide conflagration known in the New World as the French and Indian War and in Europe as the Seven Years' War. Fought for a number of reasons—many of them far removed from the American West—the Seven Years' War clearly indicated that American expansion was, from the start, part of an international nexus of events, and it would remain so throughout the eighteenth and nineteenth centuries. During the conflict, the French used the Indians as instruments of deliberate terror, and the British used their "beastly" backwoodsmen as a sacrificial advance guard. The roots of the seemingly implacable hatred between Indian and pioneer, suggests Francis Jennings, lay in the mutual depredations of the long and bloody French and Indian War. After it was over, King George issued the Proclamation of 1763, which declared a boundary line at the mountains beyond which the English colonists were not permitted to settle. The proclamation line itself was not a *border* in the usual sense of a demarcation between two sovereign powers, nor a *frontier* as the Old World used the word. For political reasons, the king defined the border as a line behind which he would allow "civilization" (a word just then coming into common usage) to flourish and beyond which "savagery" would be contained.

The proclamation line, as Jennings points out, was the reality behind the legendary American frontier. In time, the king's definition gave the word *frontier* a new American meaning as the advancing edge of white settlement and the march of civilization into the wilderness. There would be many future boundaries declared, and each would be broached by white settlers just as they defiantly crossed this one, although the movement was not inexorably westward, but sometimes to the west, sometimes south, sometimes north, wherever Indian lands were officially demarcated. Settlers violating the proclamation line were subject to raids from resentful Indians. Since they were breaking the law, when they turned to royal colonial officials for aid, it was not always forthcoming, which widened the gap between the frontier settlements and Tidewater civilization and between colonists and mother country. The proclamation line also encouraged American pioneers to flout royal authority. In 1774, when the border erupted, the British could not hold the line. Troops, sent initially to patrol the frontier, removed to the East and were billeted in American homes, which caused more resentment. Taxes passed to pay for increased troop strengths in America were among the factors that eventually led to open rebellion in 1776.

Colonial politics shaped the frontier pattern of Western settlement in which settlers moved onto Indian lands without the sanction of—and often against the wishes of—official government policy and then demanded the protection of the government against Indian reprisals, thereby establishing a Western legacy of both dependence on centralized authority and resentment of it. Post-Revolutionary politics, however, provided the legal means by which national expansion would be accomplished. After the Revolution, Americans poured into the trans-Appalachian West. Some Revolutionary soldiers were granted lands in the Ohio Valley for service in the rebellion; others were representatives of Eastern land companies seeking quick profits from speculative booms in Western real estate; still others were poor commoners after cheap land or a new living as long hunters and fur trappers. The mostly Algonquian tribes of the Old Northwest—the triangle of land bounded by the Ohio and Mississippi rivers and the Great Lakes—fought for forty years against such encroachments, from Pontiac's Rebellion just after the French and Indian War until their defeat by "Mad" Anthony Wayne at the Battle of Fallen Timbers in 1792. During this period, at the height of the Indian resistance, Congress, urged on by the Ohio Company, had passed the NORTHWEST ORDINANCE in 1787. An effort to appease discontented frontiersmen and to impose some order on them, it was one of the most important pieces of legislation passed under the Articles of Confederation.

The Northwest Ordinance specified how territories and states were to be formed from land "gained" by the United States as a result of the Revolution. The law called for the land of what was then considered the Northwest to be divided into three to five territories. Congress would appoint a governor, a secretary, and three judges to administer each territory. When the adult population of a territory reached five thousand, elections would be held to form a legislature and to select a nonvoting representative to Congress. A territory could write a constitution and apply for statehood when the adult male population reached sixty thousand. In other words, the ordinance established goals for and encouraged westward expansion. Such expansion was an invasion of Indian land, the occupation of which now had a political purpose—statehood. While the ordinance placed certain restrictions on the constitutions of new states and banned slavery from the newly occupied region (a ban that would have dire political consequences), it also called for religious freedom, trial by jury, and state government-supported education, all of which would ensure that any new territory politically and institutionally resembled the states. This, in turn, allowed pioneers, once they had settled in sufficient numbers to create a state with a voice in Congress equal to that of the original thirteen colonies. And it was precisely here that the new country displayed the genius of its revolution-spawned republicanism. The Northwest Ordinance was, in fact, a document for the political handling of colonized land. The "mother country" east of the Appalachians, understanding the psychology of colonial peoples, declared that it would treat its Western lands not as colonies but, in the long run, as full partners in a single nation. Alone among the expansive imperial powers of the eighteenth and nineteenth centuries, the United States established an orderly method, at least on paper, for creating a coherent polity from conquered land. The ordinance served as a model for the transition from territory to statehood in the trans-Mississippi West as the U.S. population expanded westward.

The nation's first venture west of the Mississippi came in 1803 with President THOMAS JEFFERSON's purchase of France's vast holdings in North America. The LOUISIANA PURCHASE and its aftermath was an early, if nearly accidental, form of imperialism that served as a long prelude to a more vigorous and self-conscious imperial expansion that began in the 1840s. The federal government's purchase of the land, for exigent geopolitical reasons, far in advance of its settlement by U.S. citizens was one of the attributes distinguishing trans-Mississippi expansion from early expansion into the trans-Appalachian West. If national expansion's frontier ideology was a legacy of colonial times, if its legal machinery was the child of post-Revolutionary land speculation, then its agent in the trans-Mississippi West was the federal government. The federal government taking these first, tentative steps west of the Mississippi River was not the highly centralized state of a powerful young nation hungry for empire, but the decentralized republican government of a weak and disorganized new country, struggling to survive in a world filled with strong empires, each with a stake in North America. Indeed, it was more the weakness of the United States government, its fears and worries, than its strength that led it westward.

At the end of the eighteenth century, Britain, Spain, and France continued to push their New World interests even as they fought among themselves. The United States, despite its official reluctance to enter into European alliances, remained caught up in the centuries-old struggle for empire. England, deeply involved in the fur trade with the Native Americans, encouraged Indian resistance movements in the Old Northwest and continued to do so even after Anthony Wayne's victory at Fallen Timbers and the subsequent Treaty of Greenville (1794) "secured" the region for the United States. A source of anxiety for the Westerners moving into the Ohio Valley, Kentucky, and Tennessee, Indian troubles were not a concern for New Englanders, who engaged in a lively trade with the British. Spain, fearful that the United States would throw its small but strategic weight behind the British, then threatened to cut off trade along the Mississippi and conspired with Kentuckians and Tennesseans to leave the union they had only recently joined (Kentucky became the first "Western" state in 1792; Tennessee, the second in 1796). Thomas Pinckney, the American envoy to Spain, negotiated a treaty in 1796 to keep the Mississippi open, which alleviated the danger of secession by Kentucky and Tennessee. But Americans occupying the Ohio and Mississippi river valleys continued to worry both about English perfidy with the Indians and Spain's possession of New Orleans. For all the voraciousness they would eventually show toward trans-Mississippi lands, Americans, at the time, were not much interested in the region. They were infinitely more concerned with the American West of the day, which included the states of Kentucky and Tennessee as well as the territories of present-day Ohio, Indiana, Illinois, Michigan, Alabama, and Mississippi.

In 1800, Thomas Jefferson was elected president. That same year, Spain gave Louisiana back to France by secret treaty, and Napoleon Bonaparte made plans to make it the footstool of a New World empire just as soon as he had reclaimed Santo Domingo (present-day Haiti), which France had lost in a recent slave rebellion. About the time the United States became aware of the transfer, Spain—which still retained formal possession of Louisiana—closed the port of New Orleans to American trade. The two events—the Treaty of San Ildefonso and the Spanish proclamation of October 16, 1802, revoking the U.S. right of deposit in New Orleans—shocked and angered Western settlers and worried Jefferson, who feared he might be forced to change his basic foreign policy and ally the United States with Great Britain if this was a foretaste of Napoleon's future policy. Believing that only England, with its mighty navy, could stand up to Napoleon, many Americans—and Westerners in particular—were also convinced that British fur traders continued to agitate the Indians in the West, including Ohio, which became a state in 1803. Clearly, Britain, almost as a matter of course, treated its former colonies with great diplomatic disdain.

Jefferson sent envoys to Paris to negotiate a treaty with France, and Napoleon, bogged down in his adventure in Haiti, offered the United States one of the greatest real-estate deals in history. In the Louisiana Purchase, Jefferson's Democratic-Republican administration bought an empire, although no one knew exactly, or agreed upon, its true extent. Federalist-dominated New England, not at all happy with the purchase, argued that the region was useless because it was too vast to be governed and was, therefore, a threat to republican government; New Englanders worried that if the nation survived an expansion into these lands, the West and the South would combine to dominate government at the expense of New England. Jefferson and the Republicans responded that the Louisiana Purchase ensured that plenty of land would be available to future generations, especially to the yeoman farmers they considered the true backbone of the republic.

The political and philosophical arguments surrounding the Louisiana Purchase produced two additional characteristics of national expansion into the trans-Mississippi West. On the one hand, each official step westward threatened to break apart the political balance between North and South upon which national unity had been based. On the other hand, each official step was justified by the Jeffersonian claim that the country was establishing an "empire of liberty," which would ensure the future prosperity and progress of the nation as a whole. Thus, even as Jefferson was planning—and the Congress was (sometimes secretly) funding—the LEWIS AND CLARK EXPEDITION into Louisiana and ZEBULON MONTGOMERY PIKE's exploration (which most historians agree was a spy mission into Spanish territory), some Federalists were conspiring with Jefferson's ambitious Democratic-Republican vice-president Aaron Burr to detach New England and New York from the Union. When the plan went awry, Burr blamed Federalist Alexander Hamilton and killed him in a duel. Fleeing into the trans-Appalachian lands to escape arrest, Burr hatched another plot, one that included approaches both to Spain and Britain as well as to disgruntled French-speaking residents of Louisiana, to establish an independent empire in the West.

While the BURR CONSPIRACY was something of a comic opera, it did reveal the dangers of a weak and faction-ridden government when it came to administering a Western empire, although a relatively weak central government was precisely the kind of government presumed by Jefferson's "empire of liberty." A plot that threatened to make the point far more seriously than Burr's skullduggery, however, was brewing in the region around the same time. About 1805, Shawnee sachem TECUMSEH began building, with British encouragement, a pan-tribal Indian alliance that he hoped would result in an Indian confederacy—a Native American state—stretching from the Great Lakes to the Gulf of Mexico. The young republic's vulnerability was further underscored when Great Britain and Napoleonic France went to war. Although the United States declared itself neutral, both of the belligerents ignored the neutrality and disrupted at will American trade on the high seas. Even more odious to Americans, the English navy arrogantly impressed U.S. sailors into service on its own ships. By 1811, a full-scale Indian uprising was again under way in the Ohio and Mississippi river valleys, and Westerners were calling for another war with England.

Jefferson had been drawn into the Louisiana Purchase because he hoped to avoid becoming embroiled in European disputes, but in many ways, his action only hurried such entanglement. The purchase increased internal and sectional conflicts, highlighted the federal government's weaknesses, and made the country more a target of international concern and manipulation. Americans fought the WAR OF 1812 officially to protect U.S. sovereignty—the nation's right to remain neutral and engage in foreign trade at sea. But New England—the section of the country most involved in the international trafficking—did not support the war, resisted raising troops, and sometimes refused to do so, and, toward the end of the conflict, held a convention that resolved to secede from the Union unless the United States withdrew from the war. In contrast, as scholar Donald R. Hickey has pointed out, the Republican War Hawks who took control of Congress in 1812 and pushed James Madison's new administration into battle, were led by a Westerner, Kentuckian HENRY CLAY, and were, for the most part, Westerners or the product of recent "Indian frontiers." Extreme nationalists, the War Hawks also talked of taking Canada from the British, which antiwar Virginian John Randolph claimed was always the bellicose young West's true goal.

In general, the war went badly for the United States. The Americans failed to achieve any of the official war aims and actually lost ground diplomatically at the peace talks in Ghent. At best, they managed to settle for what the Treaty of Ghent (1814) claimed was a return to the "status quo antebellum." Still, Tecumseh was killed, his Indian confederacy destroyed, and British influence over the tribes greatly diminished, which—along with ANDREW JACKSON's defeat of the Creeks at Horseshoe Bend and his victory in New Orleans—helped to explain the feeling, especially in the West, that the United States had essentially won the war. Certainly, the war created a much stronger sense of an American nation and bound the trans-Appalachian West, formerly a seething cauldron of sedition, firmly to the republic.

In the war's wake, writes historian Merrill D. Peterson, "a country that had hugged the Atlantic seaboard and sought its prosperity in foreign trade was about to spill into the Transappalachian West." In the next six years, five "Western" states—Louisiana (1812), Indiana (1816), Mississippi (1817), Illinois (1818), Alabama (1819)—entered the Union. In Congress, Henry Clay launched an economic program he called the "AMERICAN SYSTEM." A combination of government-sponsored internal improvements and government protection of infant industry, the program presaged the central role the federal government would later play in the economy of the trans-Mississippi West. And, as Peterson notes, "the rise of the West as a self-conscious section added a disturbing new element to the [nation's] political balance." The war had given the country a Western hero, Andrew Jackson, who undertook a renegade campaign against Florida, which led to the 1819 ADAMS-ONIS TREATY with Spain—a treaty that more clearly established the Western and Southwestern boundaries of the country. More popular in the West than ever, Jackson eventually became the first president from the region, elected in 1828 by its "common men" who had begun to participate in large numbers in national elections. Once in office, Jackson completed the conquest of the trans-Appalachian West by removing the Indian tribes east of the Mississippi to the "surplus" lands of the Louisiana Purchase. In the process, he opened up the old Southwest of Alabama, Mississippi, and Louisiana to the slave-based seacoast economy of the plantation South.

The Indians in the trans-Mississippi West would not remain "free from the mercenary influence of White men" as President Jackson promised, but the very fact that he made such a promise says something about American attitudes toward the region. As Clyde A. Milner, II, has pointed out, "a flood of white settlers did not immediately follow the high tide of Indian removal in the 1830s." In fact, says Milner, "the bulk of the Louisiana Purchase, not just the area of present-day Oklahoma, could still be viewed as 'Indian Territory' until after the Civil War." Indeed, the decades following the War of 1812 were not characterized so much by expansion as by consolidation, not by imperial adventures but by nation building. For European imperialists, the distinction between mother country and colony remained clear, but in the United States, the colonies became—by law—the mother country. The war had created the circumstances under which the United States was willing to make the trans-Appalachian lands into an American West, a regional partner in a single nation. Expanding that nation beyond the Mississippi—even into U.S. territory—however created serious political problems, which became clear when Missouri tried to join the nation in 1819.

When the United States did begin to settle the Louisiana Purchase lands in earnest and to expand elsewhere into the trans-Mississippi region, the mold for that expansion had already been cast. Like earlier expansions, it would be characterized by a frontier ideology, by the treatment of Indians as savages, by the promotion of agrarian values, by the justification that Americans were creating a unique "empire of liberty," by the dispossession of many of those inhabiting the region, by the introduction of social, legal, and political models established in the East, by the attempt to incorporate conquered lands into the American polity, by subsequent sectional clashes that threatened the union, and by a federal government that served as the general agent of expansion and the major promoter and protector of the region's economy.

—Charles Phillips

SEE ALSO: Financial Panics; Land Policy: Land Companies; Missouri Compromise; Native American Peoples: Peoples Removed from the East; Trail of Tears

SUGGESTED READING:

Billington, Ray Allen, and Martin Ridge. *Westward Expansion: A History of the American Frontier.* 5th ed. New York, 1982.

Blum, John M., et al. *The National Experience.* 2 vols. New York, 1968.

Hickey, Donald R. *The War of 1812: A Forgotten Conflict.* Chicago, 1990.

Jennings, Francis. *Empire of Fortune: Crowns, Colonies and Tribes in the Seven Years War in America.* New York, 1988.

Merk, Frederick. *History of the Westward Movement.* New York, 1978.

Milner, Clyde A. II, "Chapter Five: National Initiatives." In *The Oxford History of the American West.* New York, 1994.

Peterson Merrill D. *The Great Triumvirate: Webster, Clay, and Calhoun.* New York, 1987.

White, Richard. *"It's Your Misfortune and None of My Own": A New History of the American West.* Norman, Okla., 1991.

Zinn, Howard. *A People's History of the United States.* New York, 1980.

TEXAS AND NATIONAL EXPANSION

Expansionist activities by the United States or its citizens focused frequently on Texas throughout the first half of the nineteenth century. These efforts included the promotion of Texas independence from Spain and later Mexico, the annexation of Texas by the United States, expansion of the area claimed by Texas, and use of Texas as a base for expansion farther west.

Texas first became an area considered for expansion by some people in the United States before that nation even bordered Texas. JAMES WILKINSON, a United States Army officer in the Mississippi Valley region, secretly sold information to Spanish officials while he and his former clerk, Philip Nolan, became involved in trade between United States and Spanish territories. In the 1790s, Nolan gathered horses in Texas for sale in Spanish Louisiana and in the United States with Spanish approval. Yet some Spanish officials suspected him of spying. When Nolan and twenty-five men returned to Texas in 1800, Spanish soldiers moved to intercept them the next spring. Nolan died in a skirmish on March 21, 1801, in north-central Texas. Spanish authorities hanged one of Nolan's men and imprisoned the others for several years.

Interest on the part of the United States and some of its citizens increased in 1803 after the LOUISIANA PURCHASE. Because of the unclear boundary of that territory acquired by the United States from France, President THOMAS JEFFERSON used the short-lived French settlement on the Texas coast in the seventeenth century to argue a claim to the region. Spain denied this view based on its settlements and control of Texas through the eighteenth century. When Jefferson sent expeditions to explore the Louisiana Purchase territory, a group led by Thomas Freeman and Peter Custis moved up the Red River in 1806, until Spanish soldiers halted them as they reached Texas.

That same year, United States and Spanish troops moved to face each other near the Sabine River. The commanders, Generals James Wilkinson and Simon Herrera, found a peaceful solution, however, which became the Neutral Ground Agreement. United States troops would advance no farther west than Arroyo Hondo, while Spanish soldiers would not move east of the Sabine River, thus leaving a neutral ground between the streams until the two nations resolved the boundary.

United States citizens showed renewed interest in Texas during the Mexican war for independence that began in 1810. Bernardo Gutierrez de Lara traveled to the United States to seek support for the revolution. While the government offered no official aid, leaders encouraged him to recruit Americans to fight for the cause. In Louisiana, an ambitious United States Army lieutenant, Augustus W. Magee, resigned to become the military commander of the new force. The soldiers included Mexicans who favored independence as well as American men who sought adventure, land, and the possibility of transferring Texas to United States control. The army of about one hundred filibusters captured Nacogdoches without a fight in August 1812. That fall, Magee led three hundred men against La Bahia, where he became sick and died. Spanish troops surrounded the town in November but retreated to San Antonio during February 1813. Led by Samuel Kemper, the still-growing invasion army defeated one thousand Spanish soldiers at the battle of Rosillo near Salado Creek and San Antonio. Political and personal disputes within the revolutionary army brought changes in command, followed in August 1813 by defeat at the battle of the Medina. Most of the fourteen hundred men died fighting against almost two thousand Spanish troops under Joaquin de Arredondo, who harshly cleared the territory of all opposition.

A new group of rebels gathered on Galveston Island during 1816. It included Mexican and South American revolutionaries as well as Henry Perry, a former officer under Magee. Perry unsuccessfully invaded Texas in 1817 with fifty followers and died attempting to capture La Bahia.

Two years later, the United States and Spain agreed to the Sabine and Red rivers as the boundary between their territories in the ADAMS-ONIS TREATY, which also transferred Florida to the United States. Some citizens of the United States opposed the decision and formed new filibustering efforts aimed at conquering Texas. James Long put aside his trading activities in Natchez during 1819 to gather three hundred men including some veterans of the Magee-Gutierrez expedition. They captured Nacogdoches in June, but Spanish troops forced them back into Louisiana while Long tried to form an alliance with Jean Laffitte, who operated privateering vessels from Galveston Island. Long created a new base on Bolivar Point across from Galveston Island in 1821 but was taken prisoner when he attacked La Bahia that fall. He died in a Mexican prison during that year as Mexico gained its independence.

While the Mexican war for independence ebbed and flowed, Anglo-Americans in the region that later became Arkansas pushed west to the Red River and began to establish themselves on the south side at Jonesborough in 1815 and Pecan Point in 1816. When Arkansas became a territory in 1820, the legislature formed Miller County to provide government for the area. By the 1830s, settlers there began to request from Mexico titles to their lands in what became Red River County, Texas.

A more organized colonization effort developed in 1820 under the leadership of MOSES AUSTIN, who had settled in Missouri during the 1790s when it was Spanish territory. Despite some early reluctance, Spanish officials in 1821 approved his proposal to bring three hundred families to Texas because the region had declined in population during the revolution. When Moses Austin died that year his son, STEPHEN FULLER AUSTIN, assumed direction of the project. The younger Austin began to gather colonists at a time when the depression of 1819 had cost some people their lands in the United States, while land in Texas could be acquired more cheaply and in larger amounts. In 1822, he traveled to Mexico City to convince the newly independent Mexican government that it should confirm his contract, which he accomplished in 1823. The following year, the Mexican Congress adopted a general colonization law that allowed state control of settlement. From 1824 to 1830, the state of Coahuila and Texas authorized additional colonies by Austin and twenty-four other EMPRESARIOS, who primarily promoted immigration from the United States, although a few focused on Mexican or European settlers. Besides Austin, the most successful colony became that of Green De Witt. Each family that came to Texas received more than four thousand acres of land for minimal fees.

In 1826, Haden Edwards, an empresario in East Texas, stirred conflict over land grants with Mexican settlers already in the region and led a brief rebellion against Mexico; he and his followers were then expelled. During the late 1820s, the United States made offers to purchase Texas from Mexico, which refused. These events, combined with the growing number of Anglo-American settlers, led the Mexican government in 1830 to halt immigration from the United States.

Several companies of land speculators in the United States, especially the Nashville Company of Tennessee and the Galveston Bay and Texas Land Company of New York City, continued illegally to sell land scrip despite the Mexican law of 1830. Representatives of these companies, including Sterling C. Robertson and DAVID GOUVENEUR BURNET who had been active in the late 1820s, lobbied both the United States and Mexican governments in the early 1830s and resumed legal efforts in 1834 when the decree of 1830 was repealed. By 1834, probably twenty thousand Anglo-Americans had settled in Texas with more arriving each day. Competition among land speculators in Texas and the United States for grants from the Mexican government contributed to unrest in Texas. This situation—joined with a move to a more centralized government in Mexico, resistance in Texas to new customs duties, and Texans' fear that Mexico might abolish slavery—led to revolt in 1835.

When fighting began in October 1835 between Texas settlers and Mexican soldiers, the Texans formed a Permanent Council to provide political leadership. The council called for support from the United States in the form of volunteers, supplies, and funds to finance the uprising. A Consultation, or convention, became the government in November and promised land to volunteers who fought for the cause, which still focused on individual and states' rights under the Mexican Constitution of 1824. The General Council and governor chosen by the Consultation fought over power and whether to move toward independence. That idea seemed strongest in the highly democratic army, which included increasing numbers of volunteers from the United States.

In the spring of 1836 at the ALAMO and at Goliad, the Mexican regulars defeated and destroyed the small Texas armies, which consisted primarily of new immigrants from the United States. When SAM HOUSTON gathered another force to oppose the advance of the Mexican army, his men included a combination of prewar Texas settlers and new recruits arriving from across the Sabine River. The Convention of March 1836 that declared Texas's independence also promised land for new soldiers. At least fifty-five of the men who fought at San Jacinto had been in the United States Army within the previous two years; some probably were absent without leave for the purpose of service in Texas. After the decisive battle, almost two thousand additional volunteers arrived from the United States and provided a disruptive force in Texas government until disbanded in the fall of 1836.

The new Republic of Texas claimed as its southern and western boundary the Rio Grande, as a result of the Treaty of Velasco signed by President ANTONIO LÓPEZ DE SANTA ANNA after his defeat and capture at San Jacinto. Santa Anna may have saved his life by signing the treaty, but the Mexican Congress rejected the Texas claim of independence and the boundary. The traditional boundary of Texas under Spain and Mexico had been the Nueces River north of the Rio Grande.

In the first election held by the republic, its voters chose Sam Houston as president and overwhelmingly agreed that he should seek annexation to the United States. Texas diplomats pursued this goal with the administration of ANDREW JACKSON but found the United States reluctant to stir conflict with Mexico. Jackson, in a final decision as he left office in 1837, did recognize the Republic of Texas, with the agreement of the Congress. Annexation faced opposition during 1838 in the United States Congress, however, primarily because Texas would be a slave state.

The focus in Texas shifted away from annexation and toward expansion when MIRABEAU B. LAMAR became president of the republic in 1838. Lamar negotiated with Mexico, without success, for recognition of independence and the Rio Grande boundary. At the same time, he spoke for a greater republic with ports on the Pacific Coast and sent an expedition in 1841 to assert authority over and to open trade with towns along the upper Rio Grande in what had always been New Mexico under Spain and Mexico. Mexican troops captured the starving members of the Texan Santa Fe expedition and imprisoned them until 1842; neither side fully controlled the region between the Nueces and the Rio Grande.

While the republic struggled with Mexico as well as the United States and its own aspirations, settlers poured in from the United States causing the population, including slaves, to increase from 40,000 in 1836 to 142,000 by 1847. With the republic facing continued internal and external conflicts as well as a considerable debt, Houston, who had been reelected president, played British and French interests in Texas trade and continued independence against the United States's desire to expand and limit European influences. Renewed interest in annexation resulted in a treaty that failed in the United States Congress because of sectional issues during 1844. Then, after the election to the presidency of JAMES K. POLK who favored expansion, outgoing President JOHN TYLER, in 1845, pushed through Congress a joint resolution of annexation, which Texas accepted.

Mexico refused to recognize the annexation of Texas to the United States and withdrew its ambassador. President Polk sent John Slidell to offer Mexico payment for accepting annexation and the Rio Grande border and for the purchase of California and New Mexico. Fear of continued American desire for expansion at the expense of Mexico caused the Mexican public and government to oppose any loss of territory. Polk then sent ZACHARY TAYLOR with United States troops into the disputed area between the Nueces and the Rio Grande early in 1846. Using a skirmish near the Rio Grande in April as justification for a declaration of war he already planned, Polk received from Congress official approval for military action in May.

In the war that followed between the United States and Mexico, Texas provided several regiments for the armies that captured northern Mexico and later Mexico City. As a result of the United States's successes, the two nations signed the Treaty of Guadalupe Hidalgo in early 1848. By its terms, the Rio Grande became the Texas boundary, and Mexico transferred California and

New Mexico to the United States in return for fifteen million dollars and the payment, by the U.S. government, of debts owed by Mexico to U.S. citizens.

After the war, the United States government faced a conflict between the Texas claim of the Rio Grande as its state boundary and the reality that settlements in New Mexico had never been controlled by Texas. Debate in Congress over whether slavery should be allowed in the new territories acquired from Mexico further complicated the problem. U.S. officials in New Mexico refused to accept Texas's authority over the region, while the citizens of New Mexico organized to seek recognition as a state. Texas leaders threatened military action to assert their claim in the territory. After lengthy debates, Congress adopted the COMPROMISE OF 1850 that settled several issues including the boundary question. Congress agreed to pay Texas ten million dollars for reduction of the state debt inherited from the republic, while the state accepted a new western boundary. The role of Texas as a focal point of expansionist activities throughout the first half of the nineteenth century had come to a close.

—*Alwyn Barr*

SEE ALSO: Mexican Border Conflicts; Texas Revolution; United States–Mexican War

SUGGESTED READING:

Binkley, William C. *The Expansionist Movement in Texas.* Berkeley, Calif., 1925.

Chipman, Donald E. *Spanish Texas, 1519–1821.* Austin, Tex., 1992

Colton, Ray C. *The Civil War in the Western Territories.* Norman, Okla., 1959.

Haynes, Sam W. *Soldiers of Misfortune: The Somervell and Mier Expeditions.* Austin, Tex., 1990.

Lack, Paul D. *The Texas Revolutionary Experience: A Political and Social History, 1835–1836.* College Station, Tex., 1992.

Reichstein, Andreas V. *Rise of the Lone Star: The Making of Texas.* College Station, Tex., 1989.

Warren, Harris G. *The Sword Was Their Passport: A History of American Filibustering in the Mexican Revolution.* Baton Rouge, La., 1943.

THE ELECTION OF 1844 AND NATIONAL EXPANSION

"As late as 1844," writes historian Richard White, "the federal government . . . continued to play a largely reactive role in [national] expansion." This was true, despite the fact that American filibusters, settlers, missionaries, and merchants actively undercut attempts by both Mexican and British authorities to maintain sovereignty over major stretches of the North American continent, the former in present-day Texas, the Southwest, and California, the latter in what is now Washington and Oregon. Like Texas, the Oregon region had not been included in the LOUISIANA PURCHASE, although under a series of agreements beginning in 1818, the United States and Great Britain had established a joint occupation of the Far Northwest. Despite these diplomatic successes and the sympathy elected officials felt for pioneers headed to the area, the federal government—foundering on sectional issues and incapable of forging a national consensus on expansion—in the long run proved both unwilling and unable to acquire the Oregon Territory just as it could not manage to annex Texas after its Anglo revolution.

During the decade that Congress first debated, then ignored, then debated again the annexation of Texas, American settlers—many of them Christian EVANGELISTS attracted by the possibility of Indian converts and whose missionary zeal had been fired by the Second Great Awakening sweeping through much of the Northeast—began to settle in the Oregon Country. JASON LEE, MARCUS AND NARCISSA WHITMAN, HENRY HARMON AND ELIZA HART SPALDING, Protestant missionaries bent for the Willamette Valley in search of Nez Percé, Cayuse, and Flathead souls, sparked the "Great Emigration" that began around 1842. Although the numbers—around five thousand by 1844—were small, they were sufficient to disrupt the lives of the eight hundred British subjects farming land granted them by the HUDSON'S BAY COMPANY and the several thousand Native Americans in the region. The continuing overland migration to Oregon supported American claims in the region, and perhaps it was no accident that it came at a time—the mid-1840s—when the country was witnessing a resurgence of republican imperialism, justified by an expanded political rationale, fed by new religious convictions, and taking as its point of departure old Jeffersonian arguments about the West representing an "empire of liberty."

The new expansionists responded to what was clearly a reluctance on the part of many, perhaps most, Americans at the time to push the nation beyond its existing borders by claiming that not only did an empire west of the Mississippi represent a triumph for liberty, it was also ordained. Not merely Texas and Oregon, but Canada, Mexico, Cuba, and, in fact, all the lands of North America belonged to the United States because of the moral superiority of its dominant Anglo-Saxon race. Not until after the presidential election of 1844 would the term *MANIFEST DESTINY* pop up in the writings of New York journalist John O'Sullivan during the final debate over Texas annexation, but it was clearly the idea toward which the powerful coterie of expansionists, led by Senator Robert Walker,

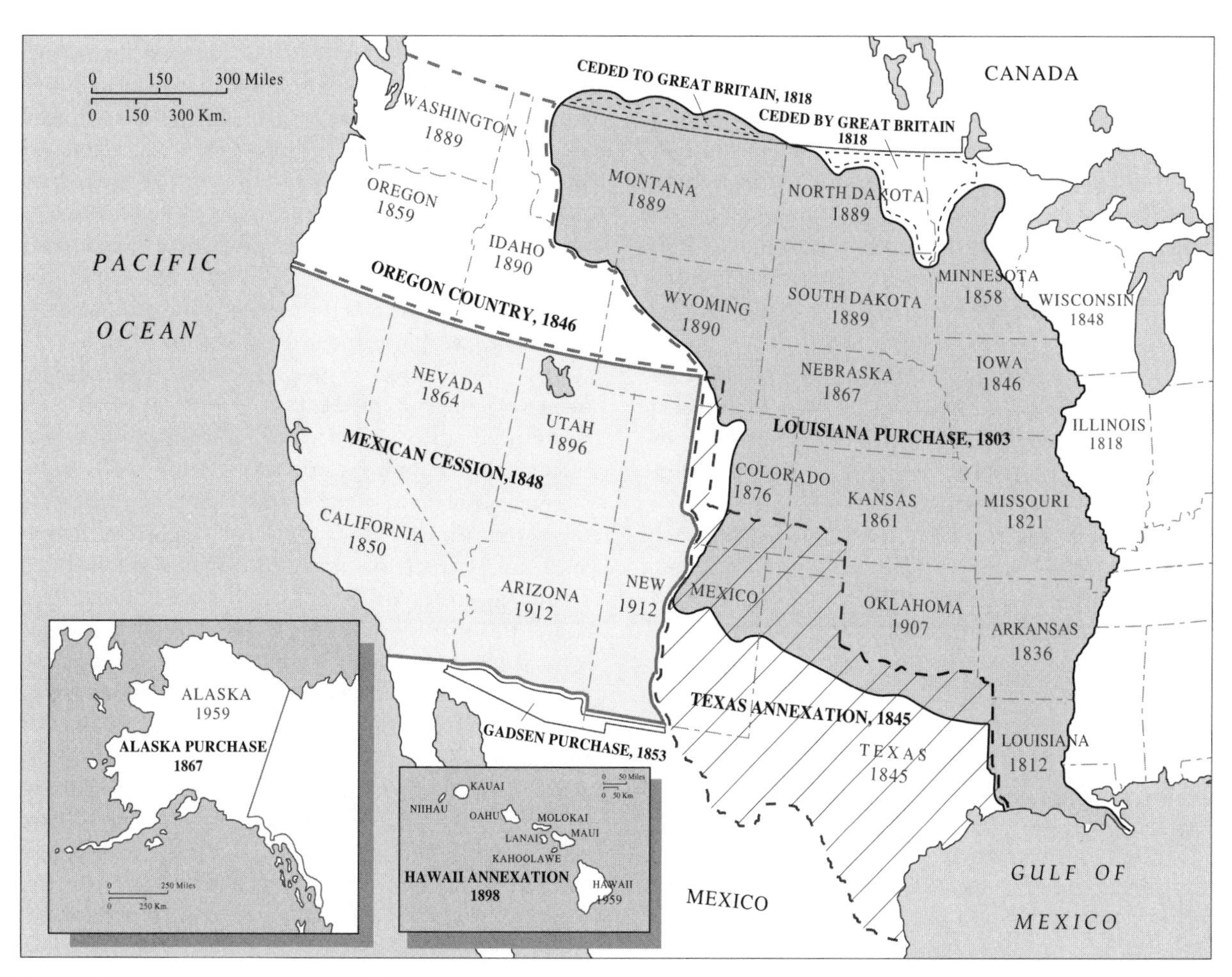

National expansion into the trans-Mississippi West.

within the administration of JOHN TYLER were working toward when they tried to make national expansion the central issue of the election. Concentrating first on Texas, the expansionists tried to persuade Southerners that an independent Texas would inevitably come under British influence, abolish slavery, become a mecca for runaway slaves, and totally undermine the Southern way of life. To those Northerners adamantly opposed to any annexation that would allow another slave state into the Union, the expansion lobby advanced another argument, one that played on Northern racism. Walker and his cronies knew that, while Northerners disliked slavery on principle and feared increased political power for the South, they dreaded even more the consequences of emancipating slaves who might migrate north. So, they argued that annexing Texas would stop just such a migration. Blacks did not like the cold, they said, and they would naturally shun the "uncongenial" North. As both free blacks and slaves moved south, they would drain the border states of their race and undermine slavery there as an institution. Sooner or later, all Africans, lured by tropical climates and "kindred" races south of the new border would pass on through Texas and settle in Latin America, emptying the United States of black people. If most Northerners did not buy the notion that Texas would serve as a "safety valve" to protect the United States from racial turmoil, enough Northern Democrats were entranced by the idea—containing slavery by expanding it—that Walker succeeded in turning the annexation of Texas from a sectional issue into a partisan one in time for the 1844 presidential election.

Walker's triumph came as a total surprise to the two leading candidates. In fact, HENRY CLAY and Martin Van Buren—both of whom fully expected to receive the presidential nomination from their respective parties—found the Texas question a source of embarrassment precisely because it had become so wrapped up in the controversy over slavery. After apparently consulting in private, they tried to remove the issue from the campaign entirely by making separate, but quite similar, statements opposing the annexation of Texas without prior consent from Mexico. The statement did not hurt Clay's bid for the nomination. There was never any question whom the Whig convention in Baltimore would declare as the party's hopeful. The Tyler administration was Whig party in name only, and its close ties to expansionist Southern Democrats had left Henry Clay more popular with Whigs than ever. They endorsed Clay's candidacy unanimously by public acclamation. The Baltimore convention adopted a platform that avoided taking any stand whatsoever on Texas, or indeed, on most of the other major national issues of the day.

Van Buren was not so lucky. He arrived at the Democratic party conclave, also held in Baltimore, certain he had enough delegates to win the prize on the first ballot and make his long-awaited political comeback. The "Little Magician" felt comfortable with his declaration that to make Texas officially a territory of the United States would divide the Union, North and South, over the slavery issue. Not until he actually got to the convention had he any inkling of the grip annexation fever had on his party and some of his country. True, Michigan's Lewis Cass, former secretary of war and hero of 1812, one of a number of expansionists who had cut their teeth politically on ANDREW JACKSON's Indian policies, rabidly advocated annexing Texas. Supposedly Van Buren's strongest challenger, Cass seemed not much more a threat than South Carolina's JOHN CALDWELL CALHOUN, the former War Hawk turned "sleepless guardian of slavery." Also on the ballot would be Kentucky's Richard Mentor Johnson, the former vice-president whose followers claimed he had been the man who killed Shawnee chief TECUMSEH during the War of 1812 and chanted about the convention halls, "Rumpsey-dumpsey, rumpsey-dumpsey, Colonel Johnson killed Tecumseh." And when JAMES K. POLK from Tennessee had his name put up for nomination, the political wits in the gallery shouted: "James Who?" That was the field: a blustering war horse from Michigan, the ancient old man from South Carolina who had first argued that slavery was an absolute good, a Kentucky Indian-killer married to a mulatto, and a political nobody from Tennessee. Van Buren seemed unbeatable.

But then the atmosphere began to change in the smoke-filled rooms of Baltimore hotels. Not unaware of the growing sentiment for expansion among many Americans, the local party bosses and the backers of various candidates began to make deals, and soon a "Stop Van" movement was in full swing. The Little Magician's floor managers were the first to realize what was happening. Aware that their hold on their own delegates was eroding, they tried to get the two-thirds of the convention's 266 votes they needed for nomination by creating a stampede for Van Buren on the first ballot. It did not work. Instead of the 177 votes he needed, Van Buren got 146. And that was his high point. By the seventh ballot, Cass had garnered a little more than 100 votes, and the convention was deadlocked. That night most delegates, drunk on adrenaline and cheap whiskey, did not go to bed, but instead engaged in the horse swapping, the character assassination, the rumor-mongering, and the late-night debate of party politics. Moving among the factions was a historian named George Bancroft, who would become the Homer of manifest destiny, working the delegates for Polk.

Despite the jibes of the gallery wits, Polk was far from a political unknown. Born in North Carolina, he had moved to Tennessee as a young man and became successful as both a lawyer and a planter. Naturally, he entered politics as a Jacksonian Democrat and served seven terms in the House of Representatives, two as Speaker. After his one term in office as governor of Tennessee, the good citizens of the state had twice declined to return him to the office, which accounted some for his political exile at the time. But, as Bancroft carefully pointed out again and again that night, he was, after all, a protégé of Andy Jackson, just like Van Buren, only unlike Van Buren he was a fervent annexationist. And that, Bancroft argued, was just what the party needed—someone whose commitment to expansion was clear and unqualified. The next morning, the eighth ballot found Van Buren with 104 votes, Cass with 114, and Polk with 44. Polk's tally started a stampede away from the stalemate between the two leading candidates, which had only grown worse overnight. On the tenth ballot, the dour little man from Tennessee had become the Democratic party's nominee for president and history's first "dark-horse" candidate.

To avoid the accusation of sectional favoritism, the Democrats constructed a platform that cleverly combined a demand for annexing Texas with a demand for the acquisition of Oregon. The latter demand grew from Senator Walker's and the expansionist lobby's attempt to link the Texas SAFETY-VALVE THEORY with commercial arguments for expansion. Most Americans were still enthralled by Andrew Jackson's gloss on THOMAS JEFFERSON's ideal republic: a country primarily of farmers that also offered ample commercial opportunity to the common man. North and South, they agreed that the United States needed foreign markets to absorb the large agricultural surpluses American farmers, South and West, could produce. Without such markets, they believed, the economy would shrivel, as it had after the panic of 1837. Given the depression that followed, politicians—including Polk—saw the struggle for markets in apocalyptic terms. They proclaimed that America could dominate world markets by controlling raw materials even as they fretted incessantly about other countries, especially England, developing other sources of supply or choking off the markets American merchants needed. (Hence, they argued, England wanted Texas as an alternate source of raw cotton in order to ruin the American South.) The logic of the economic argument could be exported beyond Texas. It had taken deep root in the Western farm states (today's Midwest), which had sent aggressive expansionists of their own, mostly Democrats such as THOMAS HART BENTON, to Congress. The agrarian imperialists insisted that Oregon was a key to the entire trade of the Far East. "The great point at issue," declared Congressman STEPHEN A. DOUGLAS of the dispute with England over Oregon, "is the freedom of the Pacific Ocean, . . . the trade of China and of Japan, of the East Indies, and. . . maritime ascendancy."

The same argument could be applied to California and New Mexico. The Mexican territories were important sources of raw materials for America's ongoing market revolution. New Mexico, of course, had the long-established Santa Fe trade, but California also exported hides to New England, where Irish factory workers manufactured boots and shoes. Through California's strategic harbors came whale oil, which lubricated the American economy as a crucial fuel, and the U.S. whaling industry plied the Pacific from the California ports they needed for repair and supply. Polk, of course, was aware of this. Like the expansionists whose standard-bearer he was about to become, he wanted to promote American trade with the Pacific Rim. Later, when he came to outline the objectives of his administration for his secretary of the navy, George Bancroft, the acquisition of California would be second only to the settlement of the Oregon question (Texas having by then been annexed). And, also later, in explaining his imperialism to Congress, Polk argued that California's harbors "would afford shelter for our navy, for our numerous whale ships, and other merchant vessels employed in the Pacific Ocean, and would in a short period become the marts of an extensive and profitable commerce with China, and other countries of the East." Thus would California and Santa Fe become key objectives in the UNITED STATES–MEXICAN WAR. But for during the election, nobody talked much about California or New Mexico. At the moment, the expansionists were content to hammer together a Democratic platform containing the dubious assertion that the United States had clear title to both Texas and Oregon; thus, it followed "that the *re-occupation* of Oregon and the *re-annexation* of Texas [emphasis added] at the earliest practicable period are great American measures, which this convention recommends to the cordial support of the Democracy of the Union."

By combining the expansionist desires of the South and West, the Democrats not only managed to dangle territory out West as a solution to the economic problems and class conflicts obscured by tense racial issues, they also found a winning formula for the election. As historian John S. D. Eisenhower noted, many Northerners also bought the market argument for annexing Texas or went along with the rising tide. *The Pennsylvanian* remarked: "We are just beginning to awake to the vitality of the Texas question"—that is "the loss of a market for Northern manufacturers which the possession or control of [Texas] by England would entail." Throughout the campaign, the issues surrounding America's manifest destiny transcended all others, and even Henry Clay began to shift his position. He said he would favor annexation after all if it could be achieved without war and upon "just and fair terms." Such halfhearted endorsements paled in the face of the spread-eagle oratory and the bellicose slogans of the Democrats. Polk won by a small plurality—thirty-eight thousand popular votes—and by a margin of 170 to 105 in the electoral college.

The election was so close that when the tally from Tennessee was counted giving Clay—a Whig—the contest, most Tennesseans assumed Polk had lost, period. A shocked Andrew Jackson—dying at the Hermitage—was almost moved to tears of rage, rather than mere rage itself, but candidate Polk, at home in Columbia, though unpleasantly surprised by Tennessee's defection, was more sanguine. He had in his hands the latest returns, delivered by courier on horseback from his friend General Robert Armstrong, the U.S. postmaster in Nashville. Nationally, the vote was even; it all depended on New York. Soon came the sound of hoof beats followed by a pounding on the door, which Polk opened to hear the courier cry: "Glorious News! New York is yours!" Polk took the messenger's bulletin, nodded politely, closed the door, and went about his business. All day he strolled about Columbia, met friends and neighbors, chewed the fat, and smiled affably. To none of them did he once mention he was now president-elect of the United States of America.

Polk came into office a dark-horse candidate elected by a slim margin. He was determined to follow an aggressive imperial policy that enjoyed only weak support from the American people. While voters may have approved narrowly the idea of adding Texas and Oregon to the United States, few wanted a war with Britain or Mexico in order to do so. Almost certainly, any hint of American military action to acquire New Mexico and California would have reversed the results of the election. And in any case, both of the northern provinces of Mexico were already drifting toward some kind of political and economic accommodation with the United States. Perhaps a truly inspired leader could have risen above the sectional pressures of the moment, made the bare majority who had voted for expansion into a true consensus, and pulled off the kind of diplomatic coup Thomas Jefferson had with the Louisiana Purchase. Polk was not that leader, and instead, America found itself launched on what would generally come to be considered one of the more shameful episodes in its history, a series of events that in their perfidy rivaled the country's treatment of the Indians. The United States–Mexican War was, according to Eisenhower, a criminal rape by a powerful and predatory nation of a weak and hapless neighbor.

On the surface, Polk appeared a hard-working, bland, mediocre, affable man, but he was, in fact, both quite stubborn and what today we would probably loosely label paranoid. He confided in few men, trusted none, and received little trust from others. As president, he isolated himself from the public and from daily life, and his isolation made him both personally unpopular and easy prey for political enemies, whose attacks only increased his secretiveness and his distrust of others. He was obsessed with politics, not with issues. "Polk's religion," according to biographer Charles Sellers, "was politics, and the Democratic Party was his church." All his adult life, Polk had lived and breathed politics. He never joined a church, never took up a hobby, never played a sport; instead, he made his self-denial a source of pride as he bragged in his diary about spending his days occupied by his office "in the discharge of my public duties." As president, he would be more concerned with the political disagreements between himself and his secretary of state, James Buchanan, than with those between himself and the new president of Mexico, José Joaquin Herrera; he worried more about the impact of his foreign policy on those powerful senators within his own party, such as Thomas Hart Benton, John C. Calhoun, and chairman of the Foreign Relations Committee, William Allen, than he did about their impact on other countries, such as England, France, and Mexico; he wanted more to avoid a party squabble than a brutal war; and when war came, he would rather frustrate the political ambitions of his generals than win battles. At the same time, his obsession with politics also meant that he was determined to fulfill every pledge his party had made during the campaign. Polk was dedicated to the platform that got him elected when no one thought he could be, and so he was committed to geographic expansion regardless of cost.

Because he was so committed, as Clyde A. Milner, II, points out, the new president "articulated the major theme of his era—national expansion." He partly achieved his expansionist ends even before his inauguration. Texas was annexed in the last days of the Tyler administration via a joint resolution of Congress. Mexico immediately severed diplomatic relations with the United States. A Texas convention accepted the offer made by Congress in the summer of 1845, and—as Eisenhower points out—in the four months before Texas voters ratified the resolution in October, Polk did everything he could to ensure that war with Mexico would follow fast on the heels of Texas's joining the Union in February 1846. As war loomed with Mexico, Polk moved to resolve the Oregon issue with Britain. Having backed the expansionist political slogan of "Fifty-four Forty or Fight" (calling for a boundary between the United States and Britain at 54° longitude and 40' latitude that would have given Polk the vast area he coveted between Mexico's Alta California and the southern border of Alaska), Polk maintained in public a belligerent tone. But behind the scenes, he compromised and accepted a division of Oregon along the forty-ninth parallel. The English, for their own reasons, did not wish to push the issue to war, and Polk could not afford to fight both England and Mexico. And while the government had once more followed in the footsteps of its citizens in acquiring Oregon, the acquisitions of California and the Southwest in the war with Mexico would mark a new stage in Western expansion, a stage in which expansion would be the conscious policy of an imperial-minded federal government.

Immediately after Congress passed the joint resolution on Texas, Irish workers in New York, Boston, and Lowell, Massachusetts, demonstrated against annexation. Adamantly opposed to the spread of slavery and black labor, the Irish—who made up the bulk of the common soldiers in the small American army—were sensitive to the cant of colonial conquest amid the rhetoric of expansion and manifest destiny. After Polk took office and called for war against Mexico on the slimmest of pretenses, Congress passed a declaration of war on May 13, 1846, the Senate by a vote of 40 to 2, the House by 174 to 14. Congress appropriated $10 million to the war effort and authorized Polk to recruit an army of fifty thousand volunteers. The country was probably not so united as the vote indicated. The vote itself, as historian Frederick Merk points out, was stampeded through Congress. Whigs, who felt they had no choice but to support military measures, were far less enthusiastic than Democrats. Young Abraham Lincoln, after his election in 1846 to Congress, would introduce his "spot resolutions" that demanded the administration show him the exact spot where American blood had been shed during the incidents that the president used to justify the war. Irish workers did not buy Polk's argument from the beginning, staged a demonstration in New York, and called the war a plot by slave owners. Soon, they were joined by the New England Workingmen's Association. Some newspapers, like Horace Greeley's *New York Tribune*, loudly opposed the war from the start. Whig opposition grew throughout the war, and ultimately the war's unpopularity snowballed after it became clear that Polk had deliberately provoked a fight and that, despite his protestations, the Mexican war was a war of conquest. Abolitionists and antislavery Whigs, calling themselves "Conscience Whigs," accused Polk of launching a war of aggression to enhance the "Slave Power" South. In 1847, the Massachusetts legislature resolved that the war was "unconstitutionally commenced by order of the President" and that it was waged for the "dismemberment of Mexico." "Only Vietnam," wrote Robert Leckie ". . . would exceed Mexico in public disapproval." Almost as soon as the first shots were fired in earnest, a new sectional crisis of great proportion was brewing.

As Richard White has pointed out, just because John O'Sullivan had contributed the phrase *manifest destiny* to American politics, that did not mean that he—or the expansionists who took up the phrase as a clarion call to glory—had convinced most Americans that they had an inherent right to the entire continent. Otherwise, why did it take so long for the nation to annex Texas, whose people repeatedly sought admission between 1836 and 1844, and why was the war with Mexico the source of such bitter divisions in the country? Instead, White suggests, national expansion was less the outcome of a widely shared belief in manifest destiny and more the result of a compromised achievement by expansionists who, for a few years, persuaded Americans that expansion was the means to solve problems that, if left unchecked, would destroy the republic. The government, and James K. Polk, White says, acted more from fear and anxiety than from confidence. Certainly, once Mexico was defeated, Americans had second thoughts, and Polk found that sectional splits prevented him from gaining all the territory he wanted. It was a furious president who accepted the Treaty of Guadalupe Hidalgo negotiated by NICHOLAS TRIST, whom Polk considered an unauthorized agent, under the direction of General WINFIELD SCOTT, whom Polk considered a political rival. But accept it he did, because he was convinced that the antiwar sentiment rampant in the United States allowed him no room to reject it.

For $15 million and the assumption of claims from U.S. citizens against Mexico, the federal government acquired all of present-day California, Nevada, and Utah, most of New Mexico and Arizona, and a good deal of Colorado. It was perhaps the greatest land grab in all human history, except for Ivan the Terrible's subjugation of Siberia in 1581, and still it was not enough. Five years later, the government would buy the rest of the present-day continental United States from Mexico in the $10 million GADSDEN PURCHASE. The empire failed to match the dreams of the expansionists, who wanted Canada, Mexico, Central America, and the Caribbean, but it was certainly enough land to fuel the unsettled question of whether the West should be slave or free to a white-hot intensity. As Ralph Waldo Emerson remarked, the nation may have swallowed the territory, but inevitably the territory would consume the nation.

—*Charles Phillips*

SEE ALSO: Mexican Cession; Oregon Boundary Dispute; Oregon Trail; Texas Revolution

SUGGESTED READING:

Eisenhower, John S. D. *So Far from God: The U.S. War with Mexico, 1846–1848.* New York, 1989.

Hietala, Thomas R. *Manifest Design: Anxious Aggrandizement in Late Jacksonian America.* Ithaca, N.Y., 1985.

Horsman, Reginald. *Race and Manifest Destiny.* Cambridge, Mass., 1981.

Leckie, Robert. *From Sea to Shining Sea: From the War of 1812 to the Mexican War, the Saga of America's Expansion.* New York, 1993.

McCormac, Eugene I. *James K. Polk: A Political Biography.* New York, 1965.

Merk, Frederick. *History of the Westward Movement.* New York, 1978.

———. *Manifest Destiny and Mission in American History: A Reinterpretation.* New York, 1963.

Pletcher, David. *The Diplomacy of Annexation: Texas, Oregon, and the Mexican War.* Columbia, Mo., 1973.

Schroeder, John H. *Mr. Polk's War: American Opposition and Dissent, 1846–1848.* Madison, Wis., 1973.

Sellers, Charles. *James K. Polk, Continentalist, 1843–1846.* Princeton, N.J., 1966.

White, Richard. *"It's Your Misfortune and None of My Own": A New History of the American West.* Norman, Okla., 1991.

SLAVERY AND NATIONAL EXPANSION

As settlers from the United States pushed beyond the Mississippi in the early nineteenth century, they took with them the institutions they had known at home. The most controversial was slavery, and the debate over the role of slavery in the trans-Mississippi West played an important part in the national crisis over slavery that led to the CIVIL WAR. By 1820, the issue of slavery in the newly acquired Western lands was dividing the nation and affecting the entry of new states and the development of transportation networks. The issue eventually led to bloodshed in Kansas and Missouri in the 1850s.

The first overt evidence of the tension over slavery appeared in 1820 with the debate on the entry of Missouri and Maine into the Union. Admitting Missouri

An 1838 illustration of the proslavery riot of November 7, 1837, in Alton, Illinois. *Courtesy Library of Congress.*

as a slave state and Maine as a free state, forbidding slavery in the Louisiana Territory north of the 36° 30' line, and reaffirming the principle that Congress could prohibit slavery in the territories if it chose to do so, the MISSOURI COMPROMISE appeared to settle the issue of slavery in the West for a generation, although statesmen, such as THOMAS JEFFERSON and John Quincy Adams, saw it as a preamble to national tragedy.

The debate over the annexation of Texas brought the issue of slavery in the West back to the fore. Although Texans had hoped for annexation after their victory over the Mexican army in 1836, they remained an independent nation for almost a decade because of the opposition of abolitionists. Only fears of Texas becoming a British satellite led President JOHN TYLER to reopen the issue in 1843. The election of JAMES K. POLK in 1844 was due to his support for annexation, although HENRY CLAY lost critical support among abolitionists by saying that he would rather be right than president in the same election. Annexation was completed in 1846 and set the stage for the UNITED STATES–MEXICAN WAR and further legislative activity concerning slavery in the West. In 1846, the WILMOT PROVISO was offered to amend a bill appropriating funds to facilitate negotiations with Mexico over land acquisition. According to the proviso, which was passed twice by the House but defeated in the Senate, none of the new territory was to be open to slavery.

In 1850, after the conquest of the Southwest and West Coast in the war with Mexico, the issue of slavery in the new territories returned to the scene and dominated the legislative developments leading to the Civil War through the 1850s. The COMPROMISE OF 1850 included a provision permitting the settlers of the New Mexico and Utah territories to decide whether they would be slave or free, although California was admitted as a free state at the same time. Four years later, STEPHEN A. DOUGLAS introduced legislation that would permit the residents of the Kansas and Nebraska territories the same right, thus effectively nullifying the Missouri Compromise. The success of this legislation led to the fighting between pro-slavery and abolitionist forces that earned Kansas the name "Bleeding Kansas" and set JOHN BROWN on the path to Harper's Ferry and to execution. The 1857 *DRED SCOTT* DECISION, which permitted the recapture of escaped slaves in free states and voided the Missouri Compromise, further heightened the sectional tensions.

At the same time, other aspects of life in the West were shaped by the debate over slavery as politicians attempted to use issues of transportation and settlement to support the interests of their regions. During the 1850s, Jefferson Davis advocated the development of the Butterfield stage line and plans for rail lines from the South to California through Texas as a means of improving the slave region's ties to the West. The 1853 GADSDEN PURCHASE, adding a portion of land in southern New Mexico and Arizona, facilitated this development. At the same time, Southern politicians opposed the homestead legislation that would have granted 160 acres to settlers because they feared an influx of Free-Soilers into the West.

Southerners also supported further expansion by the United States in Latin America. Filibusters, such as WILLIAM WALKER and George W. L. Bickley, hoped to bring new land to the United States and to strengthen the slave-state position with the addition of Central America, Cuba, and other territories to form a slave Union. George Bickley's Knights of the Golden Circle attempted to organize an invasion of Mexico from Texas in 1860 but were blocked by SAM HOUSTON; the era of the filibusters came to a close with the coming of the Civil War.

—*Patrick H. Butler, III*

SUGGESTED READING:

Buenger, Walter L. *Secession and the Union in Texas.* Austin, Tex., 1984.

Freehling, William H. *The Road to Disunion: Secessionists at Bay, 1776–1854.* New York, 1990.

Josephy, Alvin M., Jr. *The Civil War in the American West.* New York, 1991.

May, Robert E. *The Southern Dream of a Caribbean Empire.* Baton Rouge, La., 1973.

THE IMPERIAL IMPULSE

During the UNITED STATES–MEXICAN WAR, a FEDERAL GOVERNMENT that had previously followed the lead of its citizens—filibusters, settlers, missionaries, merchants, and traders—in acquiring an empire in the West adopted, for the first time, a consciously imperialist policy that marked a new stage in national expansion. Claiming the entire continent for itself as part of an inherent right, the United States—during a conflict provoked by federal officials—took control of lands that were formerly ruled by Mexico and Britain. During the war with Mexico, the FEDERAL GOVERNMENT grew stronger in the trans-Mississippi West. Its relatively new strength, however, would not become readily apparent until after the Civil War, when the government helped develop the colonial economy of those lands it had previously conquered by opening them to Eastern markets.

Having acquired the trans-Mississippi lands and laid claim to a region in which there already lived a variety of native peoples, a distinct Hispanic population, and a few hundred fur trappers of various nationalities, the federal government saw to the occupation of the land: it used its powers to make treaties in order to reduce Indian holdings and open the West to its citizens; it promoted settlement by publishing the reports of federally sponsored explorations that frequently indicated routes for migration and pointed out the best areas for cultivation; it protected OVERLAND TRAVEL and helped to supply trading groups and emigrant parties; it sought to develop the region economically by building roads, subsidizing stagecoach lines, and promoting the construction of railways. Finally, the federal government imposed on the land the social, political, and legal models that had been established east of the Mississippi. In many ways, the United States's handling of those trans-Mississippi lands not fully settled and incorporated into the national polity before the Civil War more closely resembled the treatment meted out by nineteenth-century European powers to their colonial empires than it did the treatment of earlier U.S. territories by the central government. Certainly, the economy of the region remained a colonial-style economy through much of the century. Indeed, the U.S. Congress prolonged the political apprenticeship of much of the West, sometimes well into the twentieth century, before granting statehood.

Late in the nineteenth century, the "imperial impulse," born of the conquest of the region in the 1840s and sustained by the administration of the American West as an internal empire, led the country to continue expanding beyond its continental boundaries. Using the ideology it had developed in westward expansion, the country justified its imperial adventures abroad. In many ways, the severe depression that began in 1893 and so adversely affected the Western economy merely fired a fever already growing in the elite political and financial circles of American society. To the ruling class, it seemed that overseas markets for American goods might relieve the problem of underconsumption at home and that overseas sources of raw materials might weaken the position of an increasingly hostile labor force. In short, overseas colonies might prevent the kind of economic crisis that was bringing something resembling class war to America in the 1890s. As one prominent editor, Henry Watterson, pointed out, America could "escape the menace and peril of socialism and agrarianism" by means of "a policy of colonization and conquest."

Young expansionists such as THEODORE ROOSEVELT could be fairly explicit in their private views that foreign adventures should divert farmers and laborers from their preoccupation with economic ills, although for public consumption they dressed these views in the racist and "manly" theories that had been the heritage of the American West since John O'Sullivan coined the phrase *MANIFEST DESTINY*. When the United States failed to annex Hawaii in 1893 after local plantation owners and missionaries put down the last resistance of the native peoples, Roosevelt called such pussyfooting "a crime against white civilization." And he told the Naval War College: "All the great masterful races have been fighting races. . . . No triumph of peace is quite so great as the supreme triumph of war." Roosevelt wrote a friend in 1897: "In strict confidence . . . I should welcome almost any war, for I think this country needs one."

But even the cautious "stand-patters" of the Republican party, such as William McKinley, understood the appeal of foreign adventures. Some years before he became president, McKinley had remarked that "we want a foreign market for our surplus products." True, once in office and faced with widespread public opposition to imperial adventures, he called the forced annexation of foreign lands "criminal aggression," but when it came down to taking control of occupied territories or letting them become independent, he simply claimed that the matter was "in the hand of Almighty God" and gobbled up the real estate. As Walter Lafeber noted: "[A]lthough he did not want war, he did want what only a war could provide; the disappearance of the terrible uncertainty in American political and economic life, and a solid basis from which to resume the building of a new American commercial empire."

In Congress, too, the consensus was growing. In 1897, Indiana's U.S. Senator Albert Beveridge declared: "American factories are making more than the American people can use; American soil is producing more than they can consume. Fate has written our policy for us; the trade of the world must and shall be ours." His economics were correct, at least. Farm products, especially tobacco, cotton, and wheat, had long depended on international markets for prosperity. By then, American trade in general exceeded every country in the world but England. In the two preceding decades, new overseas investments by American capitalists had reached one billion dollars. In 1885, the *Age of Steel* wrote that internal markets were insufficient and the overproduction of industrial products "should be relieved and prevented in future by increased foreign trade." Oil, too, had become a big export. By 1891, John D. Rockefeller's Standard Oil Company produced 90 percent of America's kerosene export and controlled 70 percent of the world market, and oil had grown to become second only to cotton as the leading product shipped overseas.

Not merely the industrialists, but large commercial farmers—including some of the West's Populist leaders—were demanding expansion. Congressman JERRY SIMPSON of Kansas told Congress that farmers, with their huge agricultural surplus, "must of necessity seek a foreign market." What they had in mind, he made clear, was not necessarily foreign conquest, but an open-door trade policy such as the United States—along with the major European powers—was then imposing on China: in other words, what William Appleman Williams called an "informal empire." Of course, as Westerners knew well from the occupation of Texas and California, informal empires had a way of feeding true expansion, especially if that expansion could be made to look like an act of generosity—for example, helping a rebellious group overthrow foreign rule, as in, for example, Cuba.

By 1898, Cuban rebels had been fighting for independence from Spain for three years. American businessmen had been interested in the Cuban revolt from the start because of its commercial possibilities. They had already made substantial economic investment in the island, $50 million or so in sugar plantations, railroads, and mining. Throughout 1898, the opinion began to grow among them that it would be best to force Spain out of Cuba and increase these investments, which could not be done without war, and the war could not be left to the Cuban rebels, since they would not necessarily protect American interests. That left intervention. At first, the fever for war with Spain, whipped up by the American "yellow press" as part of a continuing circulation war between Joseph Pulitzer's *New York World* and WILLIAM RANDOLPH HEARST'S *New York Journal,* played to American patriotism and the "foundation myth" of the Revolutionary War—the idea that the Cubans, like the Americans of 1776, were fighting a war for their own liberation. Pulitzer and Hearst eagerly fed their readers sensationalist—if sometimes incidentally true—stories of the atrocities carried out by Cuba's Spanish rulers. But as Spain failed to quell the rebellion, and the fighting and rioting in Cuba continued, McKinley did not recognize the insurgents officially as belligerents, since such recognition would have allowed the United States, under international law, to give aid to the rebels without sending troops. Instead, he ordered the battleship *Maine* to Havana in order "to protect American citizens" (that is, American plantations and businesses), and the war rhetoric took a decided turn toward Western-style nationalism. Now, the pundits claimed, Americans should fight as part of the country's unique manifest destiny to bring true civilization to a savage land. The outgoing Cleveland administration had mentioned that a Cuban victory might lead to "the establishment of a white and black republic" in which the blacks might dominate. In 1896, Winston Churchill—half American, half English—had sounded a similar warning in a *Saturday Review* article: "A great danger represents itself. Two-fifths of the insurgents in the field are negroes." The Spanish minister to the United States, hoping to play on American racial phobias, had been hitting the same note all along. Instead of discouraging Americans leaders, however, such "scare" tactics merely led them to assert that the racially "inferior" Cubans could not be trusted to run their country themselves. Annexation was in the air along with the whiff of gunpowder when the *Maine* exploded in Havana harbor, and the cry of "Remember the *Maine!*" went up in conscious imitation of the Texas Rebellion and the United States–Mexican War.

The anti-imperialists in America, led by WILLIAM JENNINGS BRYAN and CARL SHURZ, certainly read the political subtext of the *Maine* "incident" (actually the ship's own powder magazines had caused it to blow up, although a court of inquiry, at the time, found that it had hit a submerged mine). Rallying their forces in Congress against the imperialists (led by Roosevelt and Henry Cabot Lodge), Bryan, Shurz, and others engineered passage of legislation introduced in Congress by HENRY M. TELLER prohibiting annexation of Cuba as the result of any U.S. action. Meanwhile, the business community had also begun to rally. Pittsburgh's iron industrialists let it be known that the possibility of war "has decidedly stimulated the iron trade." Shippers also noted that "actual war would very decidedly enlarge the business of transportation." Banker Russell Sage intoned that should war come, "There is no question as to where the rich men stand." John Jacob Astor, great grandson of the fur trader, and William Rockefeller said they were "feeling militant." J. Pierpont Morgan believed further talk with Spain would lead nowhere. According to Washington, D.C., press reports a "belligerent spirit" inhabited the Navy Department, egged on "by contractors for projectiles, ordnance, ammunition and other supplies, who have thronged the department since the destruction of the *Maine.*"

The belligerent spirit was Teddy Roosevelt, McKinley's under-secretary of navy. From deep within the administration, Roosevelt kept up a steady pressure on the president for intervention in Cuba, turned his frontier metaphysics to the cause, and argued that foreign adventure could renew the virility of the ruling Anglo-Saxon class just as the frontier once had done. Borrowing an idea from WILLIAM F. ("BUFFALO BILL") CODY's Wild West show, he formed a unit of "Rough Riders," drawn primarily from the ranks of those who played supporting roles in his book, *The Winning of the West*—cowboys, hunters, sheriffs, Texas Rangers, a few outlaws, and a large number of former vigilantes (but no mechanics, sodbusters, sharecroppers, clerks, factory hands, or immigrants). He did accept some Indians from Buffalo Bill's show. They wanted to learn soldiering in order to become "civilized," he said later. In time, he would even come to praise the bravery of a "half-breed" among them as coming "of soldier stock on both sides and through both races," but for now, the Indians were segregated into their own company. There were no bankers, brokers, or businessmen nor their employees among the Rough Riders, in fact, nothing of the "modern" America—whose economics were leading to intervention—at all. This was to be Roosevelt's fantasy, a fantasy of Western adventure in which he played a successful GEORGE ARMSTRONG CUSTER, or at least a militarized, aristocratic version of JAMES FENIMORE COOPER's character Hawkeye: a frontier hero, destined to lead.

On March 21, 1898, Henry Cabot Lodge informed McKinley that he had talked with "bankers, brokers, businessmen, editors, clergymen and others" in Boston and that "everybody," including "the most conservative classes," wanted the Cuban question—which was, in short, what to do about the "succession of spasms" that were disrupting commerce—"solved." On March 25, an adviser in Cuba wired the White House a telegram saying: "Big corporations here now believe we will have a war. Believe all would welcome it as a relief to suspense." Two days later, McKinley presented Spain with an ultimatum that demanded an armistice but which mentioned nothing about Cuban independence. Cubans took McKinley's pronouncement to mean that the United States planned simply to replace Spain, and, indeed, when McKinley asked Congress for a declaration of war on April 11, he made no mention of recognition for Cuba or of its independence. After Congress, by joint resolution nine days later, gave McKinley the power to intervene, American forces invaded Cuba, and the American military ignored the rebel army. General William Shafter told rebel leaders to stay out of the Cuban capital, Santiago, which he would put in the hands of a defeated Spain's civil authorities. Roosevelt's Rough Riders staged a charge up San Juan Hill to little military benefit for the United States but to much political benefit for Teddy Roosevelt. When two African American units served with honor and considerable bravery, Roosevelt, ignoring that soldiers are supposed to listen to officers in combat, pointed out that they were "peculiarly" dependent on their white officers, unlike his Rough Riders, whose noncommissioned officers could carry the day themselves. At any rate, it was all over in three months.

The United States did not annex Cuba, but it occupied the island. Fast on the heels of the army came American capital. According to Eric Foner:

> Even before the Spanish flag was down in Cuba, U.S. business interests set out to make their influence felt. Merchants, real estate agents, stock speculators, reckless adventurers, and promoters of all kinds of get-rich schemes flocked to Cuba by the thousands. Seven syndicates battled each other for control of franchises for the Havana Street Railway, which were finally won by Percival Farquhar, representing the Wall Street interests of New York.

The lumber industry, too, immediately set up shop in this new Western-style bonanza-addicted economy. "The moment Spain drops the reigns of government in Cuba," wrote the editors of *Lumberman's Review*, "the moment [will have arrived] for American lumber interests to move into the island. . . . Cuba still possesses 10,000,000 acres of virgin forest abounding in valuable timber . . . nearly every foot of which would be saleable in the United States and bring high prices." Then came more railroads, more mines, more plantations. United Fruit moved into the Cuban sugar industry, the American Tobacco Company onto its tobacco lands. By 1901, an additional $30 million had been invested, and 80 percent of Cuba's mineral exports were in American hands, mostly those connected to the wrists of Bethlehem Steel. Naturally, the U.S. army had to stay to protect such interests. The Cubans went out on a series of strikes in 1899 and 1900 and were brutally suppressed. By the time the Cuban Constitutional Convention met in 1901, the United States simply informed the new government that the army would stay unless and until it included the Platt Amendment, passed by the U.S. Congress in February of 1901, in its new constitution. The amendment gave the United States "the right to intervene for the preservation of Cuban independence" and "for the protection of life, property, and individual liberty," plus a few naval coaling stations. There was no need actually to annex Cuba; the United States already controlled the island.

Where there was a Western-style economy, there was also a frontier ideology. The Spanish-American War did lead to a series of annexations of countries not covered under the Teller Amendment. The new colonies were: Puerto Rico, Guam, and the Philippines, for which the U.S. paid Spain $20 million. The Hawaiian Islands, already penetrated by American missionaries and sugar-plantation owners who were able to oust the recently crowned QUEEN LILIOUKALANI, cost nothing since it was taken from the natives themselves. Explaining his decision to annex the Philippines to a group of ministers visiting the White House, McKinley said he had looked at all the options and decided he could not give the islands back to Spain, which would be "cowardly and dishonorable"; nor could he turn them over to Germany or France, America's "rivals in the Orient," because that would be "bad business and discreditable"; nor could he leave the Filipinos to themselves, since "they were unfit for self-government" and would soon "have anarchy and misrule worse than Spain's."

> [T]here was nothing left for us to do but take them all and to educate the Filipinos, and uplift and civilize and Christianize them, and by God's grace do the very best we could by them, as our fellow men for whom Christ also died. And then I went to bed and went to sleep and slept soundly.

Teddy Roosevelt, after his return from Cuba, ran for governor of New York, making the Philippine "question" the centerpiece of his campaign. The most famous of his many speeches and writings about the Spanish-American War was the campaign talk he gave to the wealthy conservatives of Chicago's Hamilton Club called "The Strenuous Life." There, Roosevelt flattered these "men who pre-eminently and distinctly embody all that is most American in the American character," comparing their role in contemporary society to that of the earlier frontiersmen, who had "formed the kernel of that distinctive and intensely American stock . . . the vanguard of the army of fighting settlers." He wanted to preach to these men "not the doctrine of ignoble ease, but the doctrine of the strenuous life, the life of toil and effort, labor and strife." He was talking, of course, not about life in a factory, but life out on the wide-open spaces of the world. To such men he would argue, both here and in another speech entitled "Expansion and Peace," that imperialism was the logical, the necessary extension of the frontier, of the country's "westering" course, the fulfillment of the destiny of the "fighting races" of the globe. Foreign adventure, like the advancement of the wild frontier, was a means to personal and to racial regeneration. He called Filipinos "Apaches" and anti-imperialists "Indian lovers," and he suggested that the latter were traitors not merely to their race, but also to their sex. They emasculated America's manhood.

Not only did Roosevelt win the gubernatorial contest, but the next year—1900—he was nominated as McKinley's running mate in the president's bid for a second term. As in 1896, Populist sentiment ran strong throughout the Democratic party, and its candidate—yet again William Jennings Bryan—was in good shape going into the election because of the party's critique of big business as opposed to Republican support of the hated banking interests and industrial trusts. As a "Progressive," Roosevelt was nominated, perhaps, to attract some of the liberal Democrats amid the party's angry farmers and militant workingmen. But the real key to the election was Bryan's anti-imperialism. With unremitting, even gleeful demagoguery, Roosevelt lashed out at Bryan by focusing on his unpopular foreign-policy positions. Aided by the Republican press, Roosevelt identified Bryan as a backer of Emilio Aguinaldo, leader of the Filipino opposition to annexation, and in cartoon after cartoon, editorial after editorial, speech after speech, Bryan was denounced as a coward and a sissy.

In February 1899, the Filipinos rose in revolt against American colonial rule. Their leader, Aguinaldo, had earlier been brought back from exile in China by U.S. warships to lead his countrymen against Spain. Now, Aguinaldo and his *insurrectos* were demanding Filipino independence within a U.S. protectorate, which sparked outrage "back home" where, as Howard Zinn notes, "talk of money mingled with talk of destiny and civilization" in a country that had acquired a taste for empire. McKinley claimed the fighting began when the insurgents attacked American forces, although U.S. troops later testified that the occupying army fired the first shot. At any rate, the rebellion was under way, and the same *Harper's Weekly* that had hailed Aguinaldo as a hero in January, excoriated him as a savage in March. This "beast" had ordered his men, according to the magazine, to "exterminate . . . without compassion" or distinction of age or sex all "the civilized race" in the islands.

Harper's had merely sounded the clarion call for a propaganda war that would treat the Philippine insurrection as a replay of *The Winning of the West,* with appropriate historical irony, since before it was over, McKinley would be dead and the chief Rough Rider himself in the saddle of the presidency. Albert Beveridge took up the battle cry in the Senate. He began by invoking the frontier, which justified American seizure of the Philippines because it "means opportunity for all the glorious manhood of the republic—the most virile, ambitious, impatient, militant manhood the world has ever seen." Anti-imperialists were wrong, Beveridge argued, when they insisted that it was unjust for America to rule the Filipinos without their consent, because it is not a question of political philosophy: "[It] is elemental. It is racial." To be American means not to be beholden to some set of universal principles, like those extolled in the Declaration of Independence, but to belong to a superior race privileged by nature to understand and exercise true democracy. The nation, Beveridge asserted, had always recognized this fact in governing without their consent such "dependent" classes as children, lunatics, even whites living in unorganized territories, and especially the Indians. If Americans had not subjugated and dispossessed the Indian, there would be no America. If an American argued for Filipino independence, he was arguing that savages had a right to self-government, which was the same as saying that "the patriots of 1776" were nothing but "a swarm of land pirates." In taking the Philippines and crushing the natives, Americans were not violating their most basic principles at all. "We do but what our fathers did—we pitch the tents of liberty farther westward . . . we only continue the march of the flag." Dissenters were "infidel[s] to American power and prestige." And by January 9, 1900, when the troops were knee-deep in slaughter, Beveridge extolled the new manifest destiny:

> Mr. President, the times call for candor. The Philippines are ours forever. . . . And just beyond the Philippines are China's illimitable markets. We will not retreat from either. . . . We will not renounce our part in the mission of our race, trustee, under God, of the civilization of the world.

Harper's, realizing the key the notion of "savages" held for the revived frontier metaphysics, developed the Indian-war analogy at length over the course of the insurrection. In "Filipino Leaders," Frank Millet compared *insurrecto* tactics to those of the Indians and Filipino religion to the Ghost Dance; in Marion Wilcox's "Philippine Ethnology," the author claimed that North American Indians were so much like Filipinos that Americans might discover "that some of our present hostiles are blood-relations to the poor foes of the Pilgrims and the Puritans." But it was not just a matter of journalist lackeys and their ideological "reporting." The army high command was riddled with old Indian fighters. Generals Otis, Merrit, Lawton, Bell, Jacob Smith, and Chaffee had each learned their trade fighting in the Plains and Apache Wars. They adapted what they had learned to defeat Moro tribesmen and hired Filipino scouts. When it came to setting up refugee camps or "pacifying" districts, they had picked up the tricks of the trade on Indian reservations, or perhaps worse yet—some of them—during the CIVIL WAR in the antiguerrilla campaigns of Missouri, where the laws of civilized warfare were suspended by decree and anything was possible. It was as second nature for them to talk of Filipino casualties as "400 Indians" as it was for the press to trumpet the "Success of the Moment Against Filipino Braves." It should come as no surprise that *Harper's Weekly* quoted one "regular," supposedly a former scout for Custer, suggesting that the best way to beat the Filipinos was to find the Asian version of the buffalo and kill it.

As with the Indian Wars, then, so with the Filipino revolt. As in frontier metaphysics, so in imperial ideology. Once foreign adventures became savage wars, the logic of massacre took over. To prevent the savage from exterminating "civilization," the United States had to exterminate the savage, at least until he was pacified. American firepower overwhelmed all the Filipinos could throw together. Before it was all over, America sent seventy thousand troops, four times as many as it sent to Cuba, and they inflicted many more times the casualties. In the opening battle, Admiral George Dewey steamed up the Pasig River and fired five-hundred-pound shells into Filipino trenches, creating so many dead natives that the Americans used their bodies for breastworks. A British witness mourned: "This is not war; it is simply massacre and murderous butchery." And that was only the beginning. The *insurrectos* held out for three long years, and to do so against such odds, they had to have had the support of the population. General Arthur MacArthur, commander of the war, was reluctant to accept this fact. "I believed," he said, "that Aguinaldo's troops represented only a faction. I did not like to believe that the whole population of Luzon . . . was opposed to us." He was "reluctantly compelled," however, to accept that Filipino guerrilla tactics "depended upon almost the complete unity of action of the entire native population," which meant, of course, that every Filipino was the enemy.

Despite what American newspapers and magazines were reporting quite openly, however, public officials responded to charges of brutality with typical dissimulation. Said Secretary of War Elihu Root: "The war in the Philippines has been conducted by the American army with the scrupulous regard for the rules of civilized warfare . . . with self restraint and with humanity never surpassed." Some were sickened by the slaughter and hated the war. In the four African American regiments serving in the Philippines, many of the black soldiers established a rapport with the natives, and an "unusually large number" of them deserted. "I was struck," wrote William Simms, "by a question a little

Filipino boy asked me . . . 'Why does the American Negro come . . . to fight us where we are much friend to him and have not done anything to him. . . . Why don't you fight those people in America who burn Negroes, that make a beast of you . . . ?" The Philippine "situation" aroused many prominent blacks and black congregations in the United States to militant opposition to the war. And they were not the only ones. Invocations to savage war were one thing, actual atrocities another. William James cursed: "God damn the U.S. for its vile conduct in the Philippine Isles!" And MARK TWAIN wrote in the *New York Herald:* "I bring you the stately matron named Christendom, returning bedraggled, besmirched, and dishonored from pirate raids in Kiao-Chou, Manchuria, South Africa, and the Philippines, with her soul full of meanness, her pocket full of boodle, and her mouth full of pious hypocrisies."

Eventually, even Secretary Root was forced to admit that there had been "Marked Severities," severities that became notorious when several officers involved in the activities at Samar were court-martialed. Roosevelt and his allies were able to turn the Samar massacres from an embarrassment into renewed public support for the war by insisting even more vehemently than they had before on the "savage" nature of the Filipino rebels. Congress held investigations following the unsuccessful trials, and testimony that should have been damaging about freely employed water torture and similar "inhuman conduct" not within "the ordinary rules of civilized warfare" was vitiated by General J. Franklin Bell's observation that he had never been dressed down for taking the same or similar measures against the Indians and by General MacArthur's contention that he had simply been fulfilling the destiny of America's "Aryan ancestors." They used the myth of the Indian Wars to justify the Philippine slaughter and, in doing so, fully resuscitated frontier metaphysics to produce a new domestic ideology. By 1904, Teddy Roosevelt could employ the Philippine "question" yet again to defeat William Jennings Bryan in the presidential elections.

The new imperial frontier had performed well in derailing the agrarian revolt and labor's class war. Eric Foner observed that after the Spanish-American War was declared, "the majority of trade unions succumbed to war fever." The United Mine Workers, for example, pointed to higher prices due to the war and said: "The coal and the iron trades have not been so healthy for some years past as at present." Although the socialists and the more radical unionists opposed the war, the workers, like the farmers, abandoned, for the moment, their struggles to cash in on the promised new markets. But when the smoke cleared, it was not they who had made the money. By 1904, more than one thousand railroad lines had been consolidated into six huge combinations, each allied with either the House of Morgan or the Rockefeller family. As Thomas Cochran and William Miller noted, the imperial leaders of the new oligarchy were: the House of Morgan, run by J. P. Morgan; the First National Bank of New York, directed by George F. Baker; and the National City Bank of New York, presided over by James Stillman, agent of the Rockefeller interests. "Among them," write Cochran and Miller, "these three men and their financial associates occupied 341 directorships in 112 great corporations. The total resources of these corporations in 1912 was $22,245,000,000, more than the assessed value of all the property in the twenty-two states and territories west of the Mississippi River." Clearly, land was no longer the measure of wealth and power in the United States, and America's empire had moved off shore, beyond the trans-Mississippi West.

—*Charles Phillips*

SUGGESTED READING:

Beiser, Robert. *Twelve against Empire: The Anti-Imperialists, 1892–1902.* New York, 1968.

Dyer, Thomas. *Theodore Roosevelt and the Idea of Race.* Baton Rouge, La., 1980.

Foner, Philip. *A History of the Labor Movement in the United States.* 4 vols. New York, 1947-1964.

———. *The Spanish-Cuban-American War and the Birth of American Imperialism.* 2 vols. New York, 1972.

Gatewood, Willard B. *"Smoked Yankees" and the Struggle for Empire: Letters from Negro Soldiers, 1898–1902.* Urbana, Ill., 1971.

Healy, David. *U.S. Expansionism: The Imperialist Urge in the 1890s.* Madison, Wis., 1970.

Hobsbawm, Eric. *The Age of Empire, 1875–1914.* New York, 1980.

Lafeber, Walter. *The New Empire: An Interpretation of American Expansion.* Ithaca, N.Y., 1963.

Linderman, Gerald F. *The Mirror of War: American Society and the Spanish American War.* Ann Arbor, Mich., 1974.

Linn, Brian McAllister. *The U.S. Army and Counterinsurgency in the Philippine War, 1899–1902.* Chapel Hill, N.C., 1989.

Miller, Stuart Creighton. *"Benevolent Assimilation": The American Conquest of the Philippines, 1899–1903.* New Haven, Conn., 1982.

Slotkin, Richard. *Gunfighter Nation: The Myth of the Frontier in Twentieth-Century America.* New York, 1992.

Williams, William Appleman. *The Roots of Modern American Empire.* New York, 1969.

———. *The Tragedy of American Diplomacy.* New York, 1972.

Young, Marilyn. *The Rhetoric of Empire.* Cambridge, Mass., 1968.

Zinn, Howard. *A People's History of the United States.* New York, 1980.

NATIONAL FARMERS ORGANIZATION

SEE: Agrarianism

NATIONAL PARK SERVICE

Founded in 1916, the National Park Service resulted from the need for some kind of comprehensive administration of the growing number of national parks and monuments. Before 1916, national park areas had been stepchildren of the Department of the Interior, with officials devoting spare time to management issues. The U.S. Army had physical responsibility for most major national parks, with cavalry stationed in places such as Yellowstone and Sequoia national parks.

While the system was never adequate, it passed for administration until the enactment of the ANTIQUITIES ACT OF 1906. The legislation encouraged the proliferation of national park areas; it allowed the president to use unchecked executive discretionary power to proclaim "national monuments" from the public domain. National parks were few in number. Their establishment required congressional approval, a long and often difficult process. But following 1906, the proclamation of new national monuments became a regular feature of the Roosevelt and Taft administrations. By 1911, there were more than thirty national parks and monuments under the administration of the Department of the Interior.

By then, efforts to establish an agency to administer national parks had a long history. In 1910, Secretary of the Interior Richard Ballinger advocated the idea; in 1912, President William Howard Taft added his voice to a growing clamor. Woodrow Wilson's Secretary of the Interior, FRANKLIN KNIGHT LANE, and public-spirited leaders such as HORACE MCFARLAND of the American Civic Association pressed Congress to create a new agency. By 1913, there was an assistant secretary of the interior responsible for national park matters, the only person in Washington, D.C., with any direct responsibility for the burgeoning park system.

In 1915, the individuals who would be most closely associated with the National Park Service got their first taste of government service. During a summer trip in 1914, Borax millionaire STEPHEN TYNG MATHER was angered by the poor management of Sequoia and Yosemite national parks. He wrote Lane to complain and was told in reply: "If you don't like the way the parks are being run, come on down to Washington and run them yourself." Mather accepted the challenge and took on the task of inventing an identity and image for the national parks. Helping him was HORACE MARDEN ALBRIGHT, who was supposed to shield his boss from red tape.

The creation of the agency in 1916 was both a first step in this process and a foregone conclusion. In the aftermath of the failure to protect the Hetch Hetchy Valley from development, the idea of preservation received a boost. Coupled with existing sentiment that favored a parks bureau, the signing of the National Park Service Act into law on August 25, 1916, gave Mather and Albright the base from which to fashion a national park system worthy of nature's nation.

The agency experienced a difficult beginning. Initially a small bureau with few resources, the National Park Service was forced to grapple with larger land-management agencies within the federal government to create a position of its own. The Park Service also received a multifaceted set of obligations. It was to guard the parks and preserve them for the future while simultaneously making them available for use. This seeming contradiction lay at the heart of many of the policy problems of the agency.

Mather and Albright made a formidable duo. Mather had excellent conservation credentials and came from the right social circle in which to promote national parks. Albright, an aggressive young man with an eye on law school, was a fine complement. Endowed with piranhalike instincts for land acquisition, Albright

The National Park Service maintains a vast number of park areas throughout the West, such as Mount Rainier National Park in Washington State. *Courtesy The Bettmann Archive.*

fought battles in the cloakrooms of Congress while Mather lobbied the public. Together they developed an extraordinary promotional program: they built ties with railroads, which brought most of the visitors to national parks, conveyed political and civic leaders to national parks on catered recreational and constituency-building tours, engineered funding programs for activities in national parks, placed more than one thousand articles about national parks in American publications between 1917 and 1919 alone, and generally built an audience where one had not previously existed. By the end of the 1910s, just three years after its founding, the Park Service had a clearly established mission and a concrete image in the eyes of the American public.

The 1920s were pivotal for the new agency. With its emphasis on promotion and leisure, the National Park Service was ideally suited for the cultural revolution sweeping the United States. The world of delayed gratification gave way to one of indulgence, and Americans reveled in the individual freedom spawned by technology and prosperity. More and more people could afford automobiles, and many had the time to travel in them. Mather and Albright recognized the value of highways as a way to allow them to tap in to this new constituency. Mather's representatives lobbied governors in nearly every Western state, and a number of highways to national parks were built.

During the 1920s, significant changes also occurred within the agency. National parks developed a primacy in the system that resulted from the difficulty associated with their establishment. National monuments, much easier to establish, were clearly relegated to lesser status, and areas in the monument category with the attributes of national parks were considered for admission among these "crown jewels" of the system. Beginning with the transfer of the Grand Canyon from monument to park status in 1919, a decade-long procession followed. Zion, Bryce Canyon, and Carlsbad Caverns were among the former monuments that enjoyed newly enhanced status. Mather and Albright also initiated plans for national parks in the East, both as a means to build a national constituency and as a way to differentiate the National Park Service from agencies with similar missions such as the United States Forest Service. As a result, national parks such as Lafayette (now Acadia) in Maine, Shenandoah, Great Smoky Mountains, and Mammoth Cave became part of the primary category of federally reserved parks.

By the beginning of the New Deal, the National Park Service had become a formidable agency. With a domain that extended from Florida to Alaska, the Park Service administered a wide array of scenic, historic, and prehistoric sites. A well-developed infrastructure and an agency self-image tied to the culture of consumption helped the Park Service straddle the bifurcated mission given it at its inception. Charged with ensuring both the preservation of the parks and their use, the Park Service ever after faced the prospect that any of its decisions could alienate a part of its constituency. That reality has made policy making a difficult exercise ever since.

—*Hal Rothman*

SEE ALSO: Hetch Hetchy Controversy

SUGGESTED READING:

Foresta, Ronald. *America's National Parks and Their Keepers.* Washington, D.C., 1984.

Rothman, Hal. "A Regular Ding Dong Fight: Agency Culture and Evolution in the NPS–USFS Dispute, 1916–1937." *Western Historical Quarterly* 20 (April 1989): 141–161.

Shankland, Robert. *Steve Mather of the National Parks.* 3d ed. New York, 1970.

NATIONAL POPULAR EDUCATION BOARD

The National Popular Education Board, founded in 1847, recruited and trained single, Protestant evangelical women from New England and upper New York State to teach in schools in the West, primarily in the Mississippi Valley. Founded by Catharine Beecher, the board trained nearly six hundred women and placed them in teaching positions throughout the West. Although the board urged the women to teach for a minimum of two years and then to return to their homes, a study of the future lives of the pioneer teachers revealed that two-thirds of them became permanent settlers in the West.

After recruiting sixty-eight teachers during the first year, Beecher turned the administration of the board's activities over to William Slade, former governor of Vermont. During the board's most active period, a spring and fall class of between twenty and twenty-five women each gathered for six weeks in Hartford, Connecticut, for an institute before traveling to their Western assignments. In 1851, 5 teachers journeyed across the Isthmus of Panama to Oregon, and in 1852, 3 teachers moved to California. The Ladies' Society for the Promotion of Education in the West in Boston sponsored 109 teachers before merging with the National Board in 1852.

During the institute at Hartford, the women were supervised by Nancy Swift, who had been principal of the Middlebury (Vermont) Female Seminary and had taught in Huntsville, Alabama. Slade recruited candidates through lecturing, circulars, and personal contacts at academies and female seminaries, and a committee of voluntary women assisted Swift in selecting the teachers from those candidates. The National Popular Education Board also included ministers and community leaders who searched for communities with teaching positions or the desire to start schools. The board continued its operations until 1858.

—*Polly Welts Kaufman*

SEE ALSO: Public Schools; Teachers

SUGGESTED READING:

Kaufman, Polly Welts. *Women Teachers on the Frontier.* New Haven, Conn., 1984.

NATIONAL WOMAN'S PARTY

The National Woman's party, best known today as the group that first proposed the Equal Rights Amendment, evolved from the militant wing of the early twentieth-century women' suffrage movement by way of a little-known attempt to take advantage of the power of Western women voters. Although votes for women had first been proposed in 1848, decades of state-by-state campaigns had met with limited success. By 1916, women had full suffrage in eleven states, all but one of them in the West. That was the situation when Alice Paul and Lucy Burns set out to rejuvenate the campaign for WOMEN'S SUFFRAGE by calling for a federal constitutional amendment.

Paul and Burns met in England in 1909 while working with a militant branch of the English suffrage movement. The two committed themselves to revitalizing the American movement with the lessons learned in England. On their return to the United States, they became members of the Congressional Committee of the National American Woman Suffrage Organization and began to organize political activities and attract attention from the media. One event, a mass march of five thousand suffrage supporters, occurred the day before Woodrow Wilson's inauguration as president in March 1913. The march nearly upstaged the presidential ceremonies. The following year, the committee became independent of the National American Woman Suffrage Organization and adopted the name Congressional Union.

In 1916, the Congressional Union implemented the strategy of "punishing the party in power." Democrats received the brunt of the group's attacks because a federal suffrage bill had not passed under their administration. The group held a convention in Chicago to form a Woman's party and made plans to organize women voters in the Western states where women could vote. If women voters and suffrage supporters could defeat Democratic candidates in states where women held the vote, it would prove their political strength. Nevada's ANNE HENRIETTA MARTIN led the Western campaign.

The Woman's party sent organizers to each Western state. Mabel Vernon and Maud Younger went to Nevada, Katherine Morey to Kansas, Lucy Burns to Montana, and Margaret Whittemore to Washington. Despite the fact that Wilson won the election, the Woman's party maintained that its strategy put the issue of suffrage in the forefront of politics and encouraged women to see their potential as a voting bloc. The campaign also represented a shift toward aggressive tactics by part of the suffrage movement.

In 1917, the Woman's Party of Western Voters merged with the Congressional Union to form the National Woman's party (NWP). The group retained its strategy of punishing the party in power but shifted its attention to Congress and President Wilson. Following a series of unsatisfactory interviews with the president, the NWP began to picket the White House. Eventually, the demonstrators were arrested, fined, and jailed. In August, they received long sentences to the Occoquan Workhouse. Some went on hunger strikes in prison and were force-fed. Although the NWP lost some members over the "militant" strategy, the brutality of the arrests garnered tremendous publicity for suffrage. The NWP kept up the pressure until the suffrage amendment was ratified. In 1923, the group decided to move the issue of sexual equality forward and proposed an Equal Rights Amendment to the Constitution.

—*Joanne L. Goodwin*

SUGGESTED READING:

Cott, Nancy F. *The Grounding of Modern Feminism.* New Haven, Conn, 1987.

Ford, Linda G. *Iron-Jawed Angels: The Suffrage Militancy of the National Woman's Party, 1912–1920.* Lanham, Md., 1991.

NATIVE AMERICAN BASKETRY

Natives of nearly all tribes of the trans-Mississippi West used vessels of woven or coiled grasses, sticks, tree bark, and leaves for a variety of activities—utilitarian and ceremonial. Baskets were fashioned into platters, bowls, jars, mats, and many other shapes and decorated with dyes, applied beads, shells, animals hairs and quills, and feathers. Although all native groups used baskets of some form, the technological and aesthetic development of baskets was more refined in some tribes than in others. Some tribes of the California region developed a wide variety of superb baskets. Peoples of the Salish tribe and their neighbors of the Northwest interior produced baskets distinctive for their applied decorations by a technique called "imbrication" made

Top: Photographer Henry Peabody recorded an image of a Hopi women making a basket in 1900. *Courtesy National Archives.*

Bottom: Papago basketmaker at work, Arizona, 1916. Photograph by H. T. Cory. *Courtesy National Archives.*

A collection of Apache basketwork belonging to Lieutenant L. P. Davidson of the Eleventh Infantry, 1893. *Courtesy National Archives.*

with porcupine quills. Hopi Indians made the most elaborate wicker baskets. And baskets made by Apaches, who perhaps learned the craft from the Indians of the Southwest pueblos, were sought after by the Zunis, Yavapais, and other tribes. Basketry, however, was not a craft highly developed by the Yuma Indians, for example, nor by the Indians of the northern Great Plains, where vessels of animal hides served gathering, transporting, cooking, and storing functions.

In addition to the baskets made for utilitarian purposes, many tribes made baskets for their rituals and ceremonies. A Hopi woman, for example, made a basket of special design for her husband-to-be. The basket became a treasured keepsake and was buried with the husband when he died. Indians of the Northern Plains produced baskets especially for agricultural ceremonies and adoption rituals. Ceremonial baskets were less affected by the influences of Indian contacts with European and American traders and settlers than the functional baskets were.

In all Indian cultures, women made the baskets for everyday use. Baskets embodied the symbolic connection between women and their responsibilities for gathering, cultivating, and preparing food for the family. Taught by their mothers, female Indians learned all the steps involved in basketry: where to find and when to gather the raw materials; which plants and minerals produced the dyes; how to dry and shred the sticks or grasses; how to ply the materials into the warp and weft or coil; and how to fashion the intricate patterns of geometric designs or representational plants, animals, birds, and deities.

Archaeologists have discovered evidence of baskets made more than nine thousand years ago, and many tribes apparently engaged in basketry up to the time European and American explorers recorded their observations of the making and use of baskets among the natives they encountered. The first European traders among Indians tribes often brought new tools and materials that led to changes in the technology and design of Indian baskets. Metal needles, for example, improved the stitching in coil baskets, and aniline dyes increased the colors available to the basket-makers. Indians who traded furs for food and other essentials from Euro-Americans often had more time to devote to their crafts, and initially, in nearly every native society, the times of first contact with whites coincided with the production of lavishly decorated baskets and other crafts.

The settlement of the West by Europeans and Americans in the eighteenth and nineteenth centuries disrupted traditional Indian ways of life, evidenced by the decline in native crafts, including basketry. As Indians were pushed off their lands, tribal women were distanced from familiar sources of the materials used in making baskets. In addition, trade with Euro-Americans supplied native peoples with manufactured goods, which replaced the utilitarian functions of handmade vessels. The first major decline in basketry, for example, occurred after the United States gained control of the Southwest in the mid-1800s and built the railroads that tied the region to the rest of the country.

Even as Native Americans ceased making baskets for their own use in the later nineteenth and early twentieth centuries, they discovered a market for their crafts among Euro-Americans tourists—brought West by the same railroads—eager for inexpensive mementos of their travels. Many Indians, sometimes entire families, engaged in the production of cheaply made baskets. Other natives used the demand for native-made baskets to try nontraditional designs and techniques. Bright colors, innovative designs, and new forms satisfied the tastes of fashionable Easterners and captured the attention of museums and serious collectors.

After the turn of the century, many Indian tribes and non-Indians became alarmed that traditional basketry skills (those needed to make baskets for tribal use) would die with the last elders practicing the craft. Several tribes and organizations, such as the Sequoya League and the Southwest Society, encouraged the perpetuation of basketry. The American Indian Art League served as a exchange for the sale of baskets and other crafts. The federal government established the Indian Arts and Crafts Board in 1935 to act as an informational, promotional, and advisory clearinghouse for the development of authentic Native American arts. Interest in Indian arts increased again in the 1960s and continued well into the last years of the twentieth century.

—*Patricia Hogan*

SUGGESTED READING:

Feest, Christian F. *Native Arts of North America.* Updated ed. London, 1992.

Porter, Frank W., III, ed. *The Art of Native American Basketry: A Living Legacy.* Westport, Conn., 1990.

NATIVE AMERICAN BEADWORK

Applied decoration to clothing, weapons, baskets, and utilitarian and ceremonial objects, beadwork ornament was common to most tribes of the trans-Mississippi West in the nineteenth and twentieth centuries. Native women traditionally used naturally available materials to make beads: shells, stone, deer hoofs and toes,

A string and belt of wampum, 1890. *Courtesy National Archives.*

animal teeth and bones, nuts, and seeds. Transforming such materials into beads required labor-intensive cutting, grinding, rolling, and perforating. Early beadwork designs often were borrowed from quillwork patterns that decorated clothing and other objects of everyday use. Among Eastern tribes, and the tribes of the Great Plains in contact with them, wampum was a common display of beadwork. A string or belt of shell beads, wampum was originally used in ceremonies as a record of the importance of an agreement between two tribes or as a tribute from one tribe to another. With the arrival of European traders in the seventeenth century, wampum became money, valued in an exchange for European manufactured goods.

When Europeans perfected a machine for making glass beads in the mid-eighteenth century, Indians traded their furs and other goods for the cheap glass ornaments. Freed from having to make their own beads, native women had more time to design and stitch elaborate beadwork. The introduction of European beads marked the flowering of beadwork among many tribes.

Various tribes became known for their particular styles and techniques of beadwork. In spot stitching, or overlay, a string of beads was anchored to the base material by stitching a second thread over the string at short intervals. Spot stitching permitted the native women flexibility in design, shapes, and color, and the technique was prevalent from the East Coast to the Northwest. In lazy stitching, identified with the Indians of the Plains, native women used a single string for threading the beads and anchoring them to the base fabric. Lazy stitching is distinctive for its straight lines, solid bead applications, and rectangular forms. Crow stitching, named for the tribe with which it is closely associated, combined both the overlay and the lazy stitch.

A Chippewa (Ojibwa) vest and sash of exquisite beadwork worn by One-Called-From-A-Distance, White Earth Reservation, Minnesota, 1894. *Courtesy National Archives.*

A young Havasupai girl adorned with a beaded necklace. Photograph by Henry Peabody, about 1900. *Courtesy National Archives.*

The Indians of the Great Plains produced some of the most outstanding beadwork. Cultures that valued warfare and the horses that made war more efficient, Plains Indians beaded elaborate patterns on their weapons, horse blankets and bags, and other accouterments. As contact with white traders and settlers increased in the nineteenth century, Plains beadwork took on new developments. Images in beadwork became less representational and more realistic, much like the drawings in the ledgers Plains natives used to document the major events in their lives. After the 1870s, some beadwork reflected the designs and patterns of oriental rugs white settlers brought to the region.

To some extent, contact with whites facilitated the exchange of beadwork styles and techniques among tribes of different traditions. For example, the realism characteristic of the Plains Indians beadwork spread to the Yakima and Plateau tribes in the late nineteenth century. The floral designs of the Kiowas, however, most likely came directly from the Delawares when they removed to the Indian Territory. In other instances, similar styles developed independently. The beaded collars among the Southwest Indians had much in common with the collars made by some Arctic tribes, but it is unlikely that one influenced the other.

The heyday of Indian beadwork occurred during the late 1800s, but the craft continued well into the last half of the twentieth century.

—Patricia Hogan

SEE ALSO: Native American Ledger Drawings

SUGGESTED READING:

Feest, Christian F. *Native Arts of North America.* Updated ed. London, 1992.

Orchard, William C. *Beads and Beadworks of the American Indians.* Contributions from the Museum of the American Indian, vol. 11, 1929.

NATIVE AMERICAN CHURCH

The peyote religion, now known as the Native American church (NAC), is the most enduring and significant of Native American religious movements and revitalization efforts. The NAC has been active for more than a century. It combines elements of traditional Native American religion and Christianity to create a new form of worship that both speaks to Native Americans and helps resolve questions of faith arising from the conversions achieved by Christian missionaries.

Mexican Indians had used peyote, a hallucinogenic cactus, since prehistoric times, mostly for religious purposes, such as producing the visions and trances necessary for group dancing in ceremonies. Peyote was introduced to the Kiowas and Comanches of the Southern Plains around 1870, and its use spread slowly but steadily across the Great Plains and into neighboring regions.

The diffusion was deliberate, the result of peyote leaders traveling through the West as missionaries for the visionary religion and the drug's sacred power. QUANAH PARKER, a Comanche, and John Wilson, a Delaware-Caddo, were two such leaders, both of whom joined the peyote religion in the early 1880s.

The decades that witnessed the growth of the peyote religion also saw the introduction of the GHOST DANCE, first in 1870 and then again in 1890. Ghost dancing was an attempt to revitalize Native American cultural spiritualism by promising resurrection and harmony among Indians. Although the peyote religion lacked the fervor of the Ghost Dance movements, it demonstrated a greater stamina as its membership continued to grow and it gained widespread acceptance among a variety of tribes.

Like the 1890 Ghost Dance, the peyote religion incorporated an accommodation with the dominant Euro-American culture, mostly by blending various traits of Christianity and remnants of traditional Indian spirituality. That blend helped bridge the gap between Indian culture and that of the increasingly ubiquitous American settlers. The late nineteenth and early twentieth centuries, during which the peyote religion gained a lasting foothold, was a dark and dismal period in Native American history, one during which Indians suffered and endured warfare, relocation, starvation, disease, and depopulation. The shared difficulties, together with a growing interaction among resettled tribes, helped spawn pan-Indian characteristics for tribes that had lost much of their individual cultural identity. Many elements of the peyote religion—such as the visionary effects of peyote and the use of fetishes and other paraphernalia—were appealing to Native Americans precisely because they were not tribal, but "Indian."

In 1918, the peyote religion was institutionalized as the Native American church in order to create an "official" religion that could counter attacks on its practitioners for using what would otherwise have been an illegal drug.

In 1944, the name was changed to the Native American Church of the United States, and in 1955, it was further modified to the Native American Church of North America to recognize the church's inclusion of Canadian Indians, a testimony to the movement's ever-growing popularity.

NAC ceremonies take place on such holidays as Christmas Eve, New Year's, Easter, Independence Day, and Armed Forces Day. The rites, held before a crescent-shaped altar, last through the night, during which practitioners eat peyote buds or ingest dried peyote, often brewed into tea. The ceremonies include drumming, weeping, and the burning of sage and juniper, along with Christian-influenced prayer and confessionals.

Although state legislatures and the Supreme Court rulings from the late 1950s and early 1960s permit Native American church members to consume peyote as an exercise of their religious freedom, many nonnatives and some tribal members still consider its use an abomination. Nonnatives usually abhor the practice as immoral, while Indians more often claim that the taking of peyote has little to do with genuine Native American traditions.

—*Melissa A. Davis*

SUGGESTED READING:

Dutton, Bertha P. *Indians of the American Southwest.* Englewood Cliffs, N.J., 1975.

Gill, Sam D. *Native American Religions: An Introduction.* Belmont, Calif., 1982.

NATIVE AMERICAN CULTURES

DEMOGRAPHY

Many factors have contributed to the population, location, and movement of Native Americans. For the last several centuries, chief among them was the dramatic impact European colonization had on Indian populations. Native American populations gradually declined throughout the seventeenth and eighteenth centuries and plummeted during the nineteenth century, particularly between 1890 and 1900. At the turn of the century, the decline stopped. Indian populations rose slowly until World War II; since then, they have grown quite rapidly.

Estimates of native populations and of the migrations of natives before 1600 are speculative and involve various assumptions about the origins of native inhabitants. One theory—the land-bridge theory—holds that during the later stages of the Pleistocene or Ice Age, Asian peoples followed large animals across a stretch of land called Beringia not yet covered by the waters of the Bering Strait into modern-day Alaska. Over the course of 20,000 years, they dispersed throughout Canada and the Americas. Critics of the theory claim that it encompasses a period of time too short to explain the biological, linguistic, and geographical variation among Indians. The critics support the idea of trans-Pacific contacts during prehistory or of migrations taking place sporadically beginning as many as 155,000 years ago. Other demographers date the migrations in three waves: the first occurred between 40,000 and 16,000 years ago; the second, approximately 12,000 years ago; and the last, nearly 9,000 years ago. Each migration period resulted in distinct Indian populations, including the Paleo-Indians, the Na-Dene, and the Eskimo-Aleut.

Certainly, within the forty-eight contiguous United States, the settlement of various regions occurred at different times. The Northeast was settled between 10,000 and 6,000 years ago. Settlement in the Midland region has been tentatively dated at 19,000 to 10,000 years ago. The Southwest and the Northwest settlement dates back more than 12,000 years, while California and the Great Basin settlements occurred approximately 10,000 years ago.

During prehistory, glacial activity influenced migration and settlement. For thousands of years, the Wisconsin glacier covered much of the continent, and natives probably lived only in southern areas or along the Pacific Coast. As glaciers receded northward, groups located in the tundra along its edge also moved to the north. While woodlands appeared across the north, other regions, such as the Great Basin and the Central Plains, grew increasingly arid. Eventually, the water from the melting glaciers disappeared, which in turn drove out large mammals and much wild flora and made the semiarid regions even less hospitable to human inhabitants.

Climate obviously affected the geography and the subsistence resources available to humans across the continent. The migration patterns of Indians varied according to which areas afforded land that could be farmed. West of the Mississippi, Indians found arable land on some of the Eastern Plains and in parts of the Southwest. Populations grew dense in the Pacific

"Brigadier General Nelson A. Miles and Buffalo Bill viewing hostile Indian camp near Pine Ridge Agency, South Dakota," site of the Wounded Knee Massacre. Photograph by Grabill, January 16, 1891. *Courtesy National Archives.*

Northwest and California, however, because the ocean provided a better subsistence year round than either farming or foraging. Indeed, the coastal regions became home to more than five people per ten square miles. The Plateau region and much of the Plains area—unsuitable for subsistence, particularly before the introduction of the horse with which to hunt bison—supported fewer than one person per ten square miles.

The population estimates of aboriginal North America at the time Columbus arrived in the West Indies in 1492 range from 900,000 to several millions. Most twentieth century scholars place the number between 1.2 million and 5 million. Of this population, they estimate that approximately 680,000 lived west of the Mississippi River. However, long before the Europeans arrived, the population of Paleo-Indians may have been much larger; data suggest the rise and fall of several complex settlements before contact.

Demographic factors, such as life expectancy and death rates, played an important role in the overall population and well-being of aboriginal North America. Life expectancy was two to three years longer for agricultural groups than for foragers. Epidemic diseases were rare on the continent, and in any case, it was difficult for any one disease to ravage native populations because they were so sparse and had relatively few domesticated animals to serve as hosts. Warfare, accidental death, childbirth and its attendant maternal complications, and some malnutrition contributed to the death rates among early inhabitants.

European contact devastated the Indian populations. By 1900, the number of Native Americans was roughly 150,000 individuals—7 percent of its former size. The depopulation stemmed directly from European-spawned diseases and warfare. Euro-American Indian policy, sometimes publicly proclaimed, sometimes covert, included warfare, relocation, and assimilation and led not merely to a steep rise in death rates but also to the decimation of Indian culture.

From 1520 until 1900, the Native Americans suffered through more than ninety epidemics of Old World diseases, including smallpox, typhus, measles, bubonic plague, cholera, and scarlet fever. Viruses spread relentlessly through populations with no immunological defenses and afflicted large groups simultaneously. Traditional Native American medical practices were useless against the quick-spreading European diseases,

The extermination of buffaloes, source of food, clothing, and shelter for the Plains Indians, subdued native resistance to their relocation onto reservations in the second half of the nineteenth century. *Courtesy National Archives.*

and the epidemics returned every few years to attack subsequent generations of Indians.

Epidemic diseases also helped depopulate the native North American peoples by lowering their fertility or birth rate. In the presence of widespread illness, Indians had fewer children for both physical and sociological reasons; serious illness delayed marriages, lessened sexual desire, decreased the number of conceptions, and increased the number of miscarriages. Many diseases struck individuals between the ages of fifteen and forty, the years in which humans usually reproduce, and smallpox and other diseases, in fact, physically impaired their ability to reproduce.

The arrival of the Europeans brought both an increased number of wars and wars of a different scale than the Native Americans were used to fighting, which greatly contributed to American Indian depopulation. Not only did the Europeans fight Indians, but they encouraged intertribal warfare and joined in alliances with certain tribes specifically to fight others. Wars of differing severity embroiled tribes in every region of the trans-Mississippi West, beginning with the appearance of the Spanish in the sixteenth century and ending with the Sioux and Apache wars of the late 1800s. The federal government waged more than forty wars against the Indians. In 1894, the United States Bureau of the Census estimated that more than 50,000 Indians had perished in battles and individual conflicts since 1775, and this official estimate was probably low. Although the deaths from epidemics were certainly greater than the fatalities of war, a number of the conflicts nearly decimated tribes in particular regions. The South Dakota battle at Wounded Knee, the Sand Creek Massacre of the Cheyenne, and the decimation of a Nootka village of the Pacific Northwest were all characterized by the relentless slaughter of Native Americans. Nineteenth-century gold miners reduced the Indian population of Northern California from 250,000 to 20,000. Many tribes in Texas were virtually extinguished by both the Spanish and the Americans.

The military events that contributed to the decline of the American Indian population were associated with Indian removal and relocation and with the overall destruction of Indian culture. Through the Indian Removal Act of 1830, which legitimized forced migration, the United States government relocated tribes to designated regions throughout the West. The process was characterized by incidents of warfare, starvation, physically destructive "walks" to reservations, and epidemics compounded by densely packed tribes on small areas of land. The systematic relocation resulted in a tremendous redistribution of Indian populations; most Southern and Southeastern groups became part of the trans-Mississippi West. In the most famous of these relocations, the Cherokees lost one half of their population in transit on the Trail of Tears to the Indian Territory in present-day Oklahoma. But the Cherokees were by no means unique, even among the five so-called Civilized Tribes of the Southeast that were "removed" in the late 1820s and early 1830s. And tribes such as the Navajos, too, suffered tremendous loss of life on their march to Bosque Redondo in New Mexico more than a decade later.

Traditional culture and means of survival were also destroyed before, during, and after removal. Usually, campaigns to subdue the Indians included the purposeful destruction of subsistence practices. In addition to burning crops, Western settlers slaughtered buffaloes and reduced their population from perhaps sixty million before European contact to fewer than one thousand by 1895. The buffalo met the fundamental needs of an enormous number of Indians, particularly in the Plains regions; its near extinction collapsed the Indians' economies and their ability to sustain themselves. Although part of the relocation agenda called for making farmers out of foragers, it was no coincidence that the reservations were concentrated in regions unsuitable for European agricultural techniques. In effect, the Indians were stripped of their survival methods and deprived of the means to compensate for such devastating losses. The effects of reservation life still echo today; the suicide rate among Native Americans on reservations is far greater than that of Indians off the reservation.

Following the government's successful subjugation of tribes, the Native American population experienced a slow but steady recovery. After the turn of the twentieth century, many of the factors contributing to a dismal demographic situation subsided. Death rates fell, and birth rates increased substantially. In addition, the first two decades of the twentieth century saw attitudes towards Indians change for the better. The Bureau of the Census began tabulating the number of individuals with any substantial amount of Indian "blood." A greater acceptance of the Native American presence, coupled with less restrictive census definitions, resulted in many more reports of Native American individuals. Between 1950 and 1980, the Indian population rose by 281 percent—a total of almost two million people.

Much of the recovery can be attributed to census self-identification, which began in the 1960s, and the increasing migration of Native Americans from reservations to urban areas, where alcoholism and suicide are less likely to occur. The spread of many diseases was checked following the 1955 transfer of health-care responsibility from the Bureau of Indian Affairs to the Public Health Service. And in conflicts between natives and nonnatives, formal litigation has replaced genocidal warfare.

Estimates point to the years between 2000 and 2020 as the period of total "recovery," when the Indian population may reach the level it was at before any Native American had ever laid eyes on a European.

—*Melissa A. Davis*

SUGGESTED READING:

Eliades, David K. "Two Worlds Collide: The European Advance into North America." In *A Cultural Geography of North American Indians.* Edited by Thomas E. Ross and Tyrel G. Moore. Boulder, Colo., 1987.

Jaffe, A. J. *The First Immigrants from Asia: A Population History of the North American Indians.* New York, 1992.

Thorton, Russell. *American Indian Holocaust and Survival: A Population History since 1492.* Norman, Okla., 1987.

DISEASE

The introduction and spread of Old World diseases among Native Americans was one of history's greater tragedies. Between the 1520 and 1900, an estimated ninety-three epidemics and pandemics raged through Indian populations across the continent. Colonists and explorers brought smallpox, measles, the bubonic plague, scarlet fever, mumps, dysentery, malaria, and diphtheria, among other diseases. The Indians had few if any natural immunities to those illnesses, and traditional Indian medicine—adequate for pre-contact maladies—proved ineffective against them. Inexorably, European-spawned microbes led to a historically unprecedented depopulation of the natives. Indeed, Old World diseases apparently accounted for more North American Indian deaths than four centuries of warfare.

Although there exist no precise records from the sixteenth century regarding the number of deaths caused by disease, parallel situations documented in other areas of the world indicate that the highest number of fatalities most likely occurred during first hundred years following the arrival of Europeans on American shores. In that first century, mere transient contact, rather than permanent relationships, was sufficient for many diseases to become epidemic, since the immunological virginity of the population attacked by the exotic new viruses and bacteria facilitated their ability to take hold and spread.

During the sixteenth and seventeenth centuries, Indians of the trans-Mississippi West experienced several epidemics. Smallpox, the leading cause of death, reached the American Southwest in 1528, following a Spanish shipwreck on the coast of Texas. Cholera killed an estimated half of the Texas Indians who came into contact with subsequent expeditions. In addition, FRANCISCO VÁSQUEZ DE CORONADO introduced the bubonic plague to the Pueblo tribes, who suffered an epidemic from 1545 to 1548. From 1709 to 1710, one-quarter of California's Indians died from smallpox; another smallpox epidemic raged along the West Coast from 1729 to 1730, and yet a third hit in 1763. From 1719 to 1778, tribes throughout the Southwest experienced a series of smallpox epidemics that decimated the San Antonio mission, Apache groups in West Texas, and the Pueblos. The Pueblo populations also endured two later smallpox epidemics—one in the early 1780s, another later in the decade.

Smallpox and other diseases also swept through the tribes of the Great Plains, such as the Kiowas and the Sioux, during the mid-1730s and the early 1780s. The Indians of the Pacific Northwest suffered similar epidemics at about the same time. The tribes of the Northwest were also exposed to many sexually transmitted diseases via seafarers from Russia, who also introduced them to liquor. Alcoholism became one of the leading causes of death among Indians, and it still poses a threat on many reservations. Malaria was probably brought to North America on the slave ships plying the Atlantic Coast from Africa, and the disease spread quickly across Southern lands toward the West. For three centuries, epidemic diseases ravaged Native American populations, but only occasionally was there a European present to record for history the devastation and suffering they caused.

By the nineteenth century, record keeping had improved. According to the many more detailed records of North American Indian epidemiology, the century witnessed some twenty-seven epidemics, including, among others, thirteen of smallpox, five of measles, three of cholera, two of influenza, and one each of diphtheria, scarlet fever, tularemia, and malaria. In addition, there were a number of more localized but particularly devastating smallpox epidemics. One of those—in 1830—caused the Pawnees to lose half of their population. In another, lasting from late 1815 into early 1816, 4,000 Comanches died in a total population that numbered 10,000. There were two particularly devastating smallpox pandemics, from 1801 to 1802 and from 1836 to 1840. The first began in the Central Plains and infected the Omahas, Sioux, Crows, and Iowas among others. It soon spread to the Pacific Northwest groups, infecting the Flatheads, Salish, Spokans, and others, then made its way through the Texas groups of the Kiowas, Wichitas, and Caddos. The second pandemic struck in the Northern Plains when a fur-trading company refused to dump its infected cargo of trading goods being delivered by river boat. As Indians traded for the tainted goods, the disease took hold, killing more than 10,000 Indians immediately, then traveling the well-established fur-trade network to claim the lives of an additional 215,000 Indians across the Great Plains, along the Pacific Northwest, and into Alaska.

The enormous loss of life resulting from the epidemics created social and emotional havoc among the Indians. Many illnesses struck segments of the native population between the ages of fifteen and forty, when individuals traditionally took responsibility for subsistence and when most of them married and reproduced. High mortality rates caused family life to dwindle and hampered the ability to procure food, clothing, and shelter. Despair often accompanied the material hardships. When smallpox ravaged the Omahas in 1801 and 1802 and their population fell from around 3,500 to fewer than 300, the tribe not surprisingly believed it was doomed. Seeking a more honorable end to their enfeebled existence, they formed a war party and attacked their traditional enemy, the Cheyennes. By the time the Omahas stopped fighting and returned home, most of their lands had been occupied by other tribes. Over time, the Omahas recovered at least in number, and today they reside on a small portion of their ancestral home in Nebraska. The Mandans of the Northern Plains also sank into despair when they were exposed to smallpox by the arrival of the infested steamboat cargo on the upper Missouri River in 1837. Their numbers fell from around 2,000 to fewer than 100 people within the course of a few short weeks. So few Mandans were left that they could not even bury the abundant dead, and the forlorn survivors grew suicidal. Their beloved Chief Four Bears starved himself to death.

The Kiowas and the Sioux recorded their debilitating losses in tribal history by winter counts and drawings depicting important occurrences from the previous year. Their counts for the winters of 1779 to 1780 and 1780 to 1781 detailed the number of people infected with smallpox, and they referred to the plague years as "Smallpox Used Them Up Winter."

Native American medicine was no match for the deadly, infectious germs that attacked the vulnerable immune systems of the Indians. Not only were traditional medical practices highly ineffective in curing or preventing illnesses such as smallpox, the exotic new viruses and bacteria struck with such speed that they immobilized entire tribes and prevented many groups from devising new treatments. Native Americans sometimes considered the new diseases to be evil spirits, and they tried to subdue them with ritual prayer or sacrifices. Other methods—particularly those calling for Indians to spend time in sweat houses and then take cold baths—frequently worsened the condition of infected individuals.

In 1800, Americans began using a smallpox vaccine, and some Indians were vaccinated during the nineteenth century. President THOMAS JEFFERSON directed explorers to inoculate Indians, and later, President ANDREW JACKSON invested the burgeoning BUREAU OF INDIAN AFFAIRS with the responsibility for Indian vaccinations. However, in the midst of intense conflict, many Indians distrusted vaccination, and many officials seemed indifferent to the enterprise altogether. As the United States expanded westward throughout the century, epidemics continued to rage while many tribes were relocated to reservations. Once placed on reservations, the Indians were more easily vaccinated. In addition, many treaties began providing for health care, medicine, and doctors for relocated groups.

Although the vaccinations lowered the Native American mortality rate from disease, for decades health-care appropriations for Indians were minimal. During the early twentieth century, the focus shifted from curing the sick to revitalizing the population. In July 1955, the federal government transferred responsibility for Indian health care from the Bureau of Indian Affairs to the Public Health Service, a move that marked the beginning of a genuine recovery among Native Americans decimated by nearly five centuries of epidemic diseases.

—Melissa A. Davis

SUGGESTED READING:

Jackson, Curtis E., and Marcia J. Galli. *A History of the Bureau of Indian Affairs and Its Activities among Indians.* San Francisco, 1977.

Mails, Thomas E. *The Mystic Warriors of the Plains.* New York, 1991.
Thorton, Russell. *American Indian Holocaust and Survival: A Population History since 1492.* Norman, Okla., 1987.

FAMILY LIFE, KINSHIP, AND GENDER

Native American societies are based on the concept of interdependence. Interdependence means that all things in the universe are dependent on one another. The idea is that everything in the universe works together to achieve a balance in oneself, the community, and the universe. In Native American societies before their contact with European culture, relationships intertwined both animate beings and inanimate beings (for example, trees and water). The philosophical and sacred notion of interdependence produced a well-defined kinship system.

Precontact Native Americans lived in kinship societies, and extended family groups formed their communities. The extended family, made up of blood and nonblood relatives, had at its core the nuclear family. The nuclear family consisted of a woman, her husband, and their children. Many tribes practiced polygamy, in which a man had two or more wives, while other tribes were monogamous. Both men and women initiated divorce, which was common and not considered immoral.

Some tribes, including the Navajo, Crow, Iroquois, and the Cherokee, were (and are) organized around the clan system. A *clan* may be defined as a group of relatives who share an identity, hold property in common, and trace their descent from a common ancestor. The clan includes several extended families. Clan systems of social organization define boundaries or relationships, responsibilities, and obligations. All kinship networks have rules for appropriate behavior. For instance, it is inappropriate for clan relatives to marry each other even though they may not be blood relatives. Moreover, all kinship systems work to ensure the orderliness and survival of the tribe, which encompasses the nuclear families, the extended families, and the clans.

Many tribes from the Northeast, Southeast, and Southwest were matrilineal or matrilocal. In these tribes, married couples lived near the wife's family, the mother was the center of the family, and her children received their identity from her family. Additionally,

Christian Barthelmess, in 1890, photographed Stump Horn, a Southern Cheyenne Indian, and his family beside his home and horse-drawn travois. *Courtesy National Archives.*

A Ute warrior and his bride, northwestern Utah, 1874. Photograph by John K. Hillers. *Courtesy National Archives.*

A Navajo papoose, 1936. A Navajo mother, by securing her child on a cradleboard, could work nearby, confident that her offspring was safe from harm. Window Rock, Arizona. Photograph by H. Armstrong Roberts. *Courtesy National Archives.*

the wife was an equal to her husband and his family, not a dependent. Other tribal groups, such as the tribes of the Great Plains, were patrilineal or patrilocal. In them, the father was the center of the family, the newly married couple moved near the husband's family, and descent was passed through the husband's family.

In addition to the kinship systems, tribes have informal and formal methods of organizing the community and ensuring conformity. For example, among the Crow Indians, there exists the idea of "teasing cousins." Teasing cousins could ridicule other teasing cousins into proper behavior. The teasing, often conducted in public, resulted in the person being teased adopting appropriate behavior and humility. The Navajos, as well as other tribal groups, have a similar relationship system, which is used to control behavior.

Another way to achieve order was through a division of labor based on gender and aimed at ensuring that tasks essential to the well-being of the tribe were accomplished. Each tribe had its own system for assigning roles to women and men—a system that was based on the tribe's beliefs and the cultural values. While division of labor by gender was well defined, the divisions could be crossed; that is, males might perform female tasks and vice versa without the individual's being labeled "deviant."

Given the notion of interdependence, it is not surprising that many precontact Native American societies were egalitarian. Although groups maintained a division of labor by gender, they had economic, political, and social freedom for both women and men. The sexes remained different, yet equal, and female and male roles complemented each other. Each role was seen as important and necessary for the survival and enrichment of the community. Women's and men's responsibilities were thought of and institutionalized as parallel rather than hierarchical. In the egalitarian native societies, authority was dispersed and decisions were made by those who would be carrying them out. People contributed according to their abilities and interests.

Within the family, Native American children learned cultural and societal values. While the tribal groups varied in their traditional child-rearing beliefs and practices, Native American children modeled and imitated the behaviors of important people in their lives. In the extended family network, which was the foundation of tribal societies, many people other than biological relatives were included in child rearing. Although child rearing was predominantly a female task, men and women of all ages worked together to raise children. In tribal societies, children were valued members; they represented the renewal of life. Traditional education of children involved the use of stories, humor, and theater; experience as a primary tool for learning was emphasized. Children were taught a deep appreciation for the meaning of community. Although seen as individuals, children were reared to be responsible to the community and to understand that the community was only as strong as its individual members.

From the beginning of contact with Europeans, Native American societies began to change. By the 1800s, the federal government had in place two overlapping approaches regarding the treatment of Native Americans, and both were implemented through various policies. One was to "civilize" Native Americans through a policy of assimilation; the other was to control them. By 1871, most Native American groups had signed treaties and were placed on reservations, where they lived in abject poverty. After being displaced from their original homelands, Native Americans found that the government had banned many spiritual ceremonies. The bans made it increasingly difficult for Native Americans to balance their world. A once sacred world had become unsacred, unholy. Moreover, many Native Americans (for example, the Salish and Kootenai tribes in Montana) were subjected to the pass system; in order to leave the reservation boundaries, they needed a form, or pass, signed by the Indian agent.

Assimilation and control tactics are key in understanding the transformation in Native American family life. Economic changes, racial and cultural conflicts, and gender relations interacted to produce altered family systems. Indeed, forced colonization disrupted the traditional roles of Native Americans. The fur trade had an impact on the family as well. Men were involved in trapping and trading, while women became more dependent on men for survival. Egalitarian arrangements gave way to patriarchal systems.

Extended family networks found in contemporary tribal societies differ from those in native societies before contract with European cultures. Native families have suffered because of federal policy mandates, including removal of children from their homes and communities to boarding schools primarily in the 1800s to mid-1970s; adoption and foster care, especially seen in the 1950s to 1978; and removal to other institutional settings (for example, orphanages or reform schools). The removal of children was instrumental in the alteration of child-rearing practices. Many children reared in oppressive environments find it difficult as adults to be parents, and they sometimes are incapable of developing loving relationships. In 1978, Congress passed the Indian Child Welfare Act to prevent the unwarranted removal of children from their homes and communities.

In the late twentieth century, many social ills still plagued reservation and urban life. Alcoholism directly or indirectly affected most Native American families,

An Eskimo mother shows a method of transporting her child. Nome, Alaska, about 1915. Photograph by H. G. Kaiser. *Courtesy National Archives.*

A Hopi woman demonstrated a method of dressing the hair of an unmarried women for photographer Henry Peabody, about 1900. *Courtesy National Archives.*

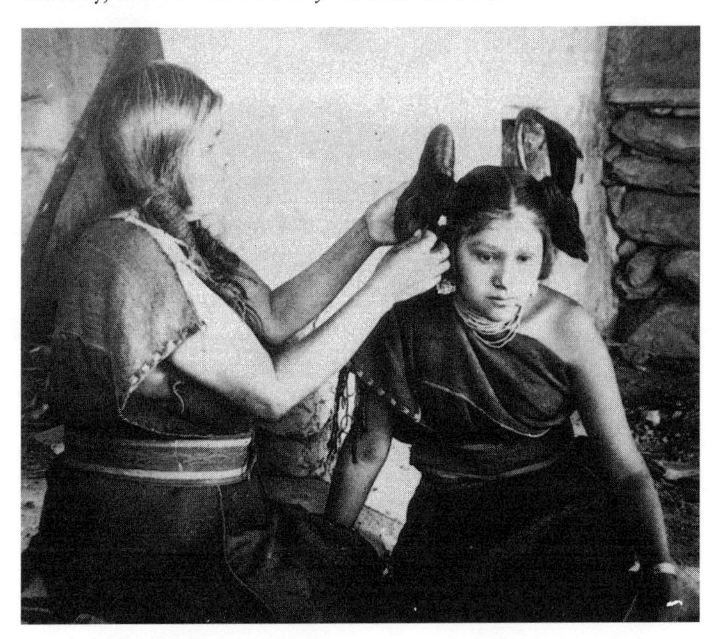

Family traditions and native cultures were disrupted when Indian children were separated from their parents and sent to boarding schools to learn "American" ways. At the Indian School in Carlisle, Pennsylvania, students conduct experiments in the physics laboratory, about 1915. *Courtesy National Archives.*

and some reservations had exceedingly high rates of homicide and suicide. Compounding these problems was a high unemployment rate on most Indian reservations and a large number of families living below the poverty level. Moreover, many Native Americans suffered from various forms of discrimination.

The structure of Native American families must be understood in terms of racism, sexism, and economics. Native American families are molded for survival in the midst of oppression. Despite the hardships, they have survived. Clearly, the endurance of the extended family in the face of assaults by the federal government is a sign of its strength. Many Native Americans still maintain strong beliefs in themselves as native peoples and in their tribal communities. Most importantly, there still remain strong feelings of Indian identity that instill pride in themselves and in their culture.

—*Luana Ross*

SEE ALSO: Child Rearing: Native American Child Rearing; Indians Schools; Polygamy: Polygamy among Native Americans; United States Indian Policy: Civilization Programs

SUGGESTED READING:

Albers, Patricia, and Beatrice Medicine, eds. *The Hidden Half: Studies of Plains Indian Women.* Lanham, Md., 1983.

Allen, Paula Gunn. *The Sacred Hoop: Recovering the Feminine in American Indian Traditions.* Boston, 1986.

Bachman, Ronet. *Death and Violence on the Reservation: Homicide, Family Violence, and Suicide in American Indian Populations.* New York, 1992.

Beck, Peggy V., and Anna L. Walters. *The Sacred: Ways of Knowledge, Sources of Life.* Tsaile, Ariz., 1977.

Blackwood, Evelyn. "Sexuality and Gender in Certain Native American Tribes: The Case of Cross-Gender Females." *Signs: Journal of Women in Culture and Society* 10 (1984): 27–43.

Buffalohead, Priscilla K. "Farmers, Warriors, Traders: A Fresh Look at Ojibway Women." In *The American Indian: Past and Present.* Edited by Roger L. Nichols. New York, 1986.

Devens, Carol. *Countering Colonization: Native American Women and Great Lakes Missions, 1630–1900.* Berkeley, Calif., 1992.

Etienne, Mona, and Eleanor Burke Leacock, eds. *Women and Colonization: Anthropological Perspectives.* New York, 1980.

Leacock, Eleanor Burke. *Myths of Male Dominance.* New York, 1981.

Thorton, Russell, and Melissa L. Meyer. "Special Issue: American Indian Family History." *American Indian Quarterly* 15 (Summer 1991): 285–367.

Unger, Stephen, ed. *The Destruction of American Indian Families.* New York, 1977.

SPIRITUAL LIFE

Native American spirituality manifested itself in many forms of religious practice and belief systems. It fundamentally defined the world view, customs, and social institutions of the Indians. While religious beliefs were passed down through ancestors, native religions were not static but changed throughout Native American history, according to prevailing forces and cultural influences.

A number of Indian tribes in the Southwest shared beliefs about creation. They believed that the location of life could be found in several different worlds, through which the believers had passed or were passing; the present plane was but one of many where they might find themselves. They conceived of creation as an emergence or birth from darkness to light.

For many Indians, what Euro-Americans called the "cardinal points" of the compass were important. Zunis, for example, believed their ancestors first lived underground, deep in the earth. Creation figures led the Zunis to the surface with rainbows and lightning bolts. The ancestors were then instructed to find the "middle place," where they finally settled. Zuni village and social organization was based on a seven-part cosmological structure: the four cardinal directions, north, south, east, and west; zenith (the sky); nadir (underground); and the center. Clans were organized into seven groups that corresponded to each direction. In addition, the directions were associated with seasons and events. Each Zuni in turn came to assume a dominant role in village life, depending on his clan and its direction in relation to a given season and a set sequence of village, individual, and spiritual actions revolving around the middle place. When the individual's time came round, his and his clan's point in space and time was the center of the universe for all clans, directions, seasons, and events. The complexity of the Zuni universe required much communal solidarity and organization, which was made possible by their sedentary subsistence pattern. In contrast, the more nomadic Plains groups and many Pacific Northwest peoples for whom cardinal directions were also significant and powerful—associated as they were with sacred wildlife, with the seasons, and with the material objects on which they depended—followed a less ritualistic cycle.

Native Americans had a variety of symbolic artifacts and actions to help them engage their spirituality or create a bridge between two different worlds, typically that of their ancestors—or the place where deities reside—and their own. Such artifacts and actions were usually associated with rituals and ceremonies. Navajos believed that illness was caused by unbalanced forces associated with holy beings who had to be appeased for the illness to subside. To appease these beings, Navajos drew on the floor of their hogans circular "sand paintings" that depicted the cardinal directions associated with the holy beings. The patient was placed in the center of the painting, which represented the state of order at the time of creation. So placed, the patient's perspective was centered on cosmic wholeness and unity, which reestablished the individual's position within the balance of life. The painting was destroyed following the rite because its religious significance was spent; in essence, it disappeared as a part of the patient's renewal.

Through dances, celebrations, feasting, physical and emotional sacrifice, offerings, and storytelling, native peoples showed their reverence to their deities. Hopi women perform a ritualistic dance for the camera of John K. Hillers, 1879. *Courtesy National Archives.*

Brave Buffalo, a Sioux medicine man. Photograph by Frank B. Fiske, Fort Yates, North Dakota. *Courtesy State Historical Society of North Dakota.*

Many religious and ceremonial objects—such as the Navajo sand paintings—that struck Euro-Americans as works of art, achieved their true power and beauty for the Native Americans only in conjunction with ritual action. Sioux shamans commonly called on the bear to cure and to bless war parties by smoking a tobacco pipe, its bowl carved in the effigy of a bear. The true orientation of the effigy—with the bear facing the smoker—only became apparent when the pipe was being used in ritual. Thus, the effigy's religious significance, like that of the sand painting, was inseparable from the action performed with it. Similarly, medicine or prayer bundles gained their power over time through their histories of ownership. Common in many tribes, from the Northern Plains to the Southwest, the bundles contained feathers, stones, hides, and bones, and their uses and associated rituals were quite diverse from family to family. Ceremonial masks were another example of symbolic objects whose meaning became clear only in conjunction with their ritual use. Kwakiutls of the Pacific Northwest used masks as a clan crest to designate fixed and eternal positions within their social organization. Kwakiutl creation belief held that the ancestors of the clans came down to earth, took off their animal masks, and became human. To don a mask associated with a clan's ancestor was to animate the reality from which the clan was born. Unworn, the masks had no such meaning.

The Indian tribes of the West revered the natural world, its elements, and the deities responsible for the way nature operates. Hopi kachinas could bring rain. Ute Bear Dances ensured the animal's longevity. The Pacific Northwest raven totem represented a creature who had created the world. Thus, native peoples, submissive and grateful to nature, widely believed that humans did not hold dominion over life or over the environment. Agricultural groups—such as the Navajos—prayed to deities who controlled the order of nature, while the hunting and gathering tribes—such as the Sioux, with their reliance on the bear—invoked nonhuman creatures to meet their spiritual needs.

Through ritual actions using sacred objects, Native Americans not only paid respect to their ancestors, but also honored the origins of knowledge and materials. They showed their reverence through physical and emotional sacrifice, celebration, feasting, offerings, dances, storytelling, and many other forms of homage. Many groups attributed ill fortune to the mismanagement of attitudes toward reverential objects or to the malicious endeavors of powerful peers. Thus, to restore order or health, the Indians invoked higher powers to counteract ill wishes or to appease offended deities.

Shamans—magico-religious healers, medicine men and women—were often the Indians' vehicles to the divine. The Plains Indians had holy men, doctors, war chiefs, bundles, dreams, visions, and sacred wildlife, all acting when need be as intermediaries to the gods. When illness struck, individuals looked first to their medicine bundles. If they needed further help, they turned to the services offered by doctors or herbalists—many of whom not only tended to the sick but also aided in tribal hunts by blessing arrows and shields. If herbalists failed to bring relief from illness, the Indians ultimately consulted a holy man. Generally, more nomadic tribes relied heavily on the individual and personal visions, whereas sedentary groups engaged in more elaborate communal endeavors.

When an Indian turned to a doctor, the herbalist first made himself worthy of providing aid through ritual purification that cleansed him of his "self" and thus made him a useful receptacle for divinity. Having gained his knowledge of medicine through dreams and

A tree burial for an Oglala Sioux Indian near Fort Laramie, Wyoming. *Courtesy National Archives.*

visions sent by higher beings, the herbalist rewarded his deities by sharing with them his fee—a kind of payment for the herbs he dug up to effect his cures. Since the herbalist only knew whatever a higher being was willing to share, he tended to specialize in one area, such as internal medicine, minor surgery, or the setting of broken bones.

Herbalists first cleansed their patients with coal smoke and then sang to them accompanied by drums. Plains Indian healers often eradicated the evil from patients with various sucking techniques. Some employed paraphernalia such as tubing; others simply attached their mouths to the afflicted part of the body. The Shoshones believed ghosts took possession of an ill person and caused the sickness. They used incantations, sweat baths, and drums to help exorcise the apparition. The doctor would then cover the patient's mouth with his own, suck out the unwanted spirit, and spit it on the ground. Similar methods were employed by the Cheyenne, Ute, Kiowa, and Blackfoot Indians.

Many native groups held beliefs associated with journeys through transitional worlds either in the past or to come. For the Indians, life on earth was marked by a series of transitions—birth, puberty, marriage, and death. They tended to view death not as an end, but as a transition to the ancestral world. Some Native Americans believed that at death an individual moved to a world replete with ancestors, deities, and forces of nature that must be accommodated for survival, a world they revered and celebrated during their earthbound existence. Many believed, for example, that those who had passed beyond life might become clouds.

The Indian deities responsible for Native American survival included natural elements and figures that controlled nature. The different planes of existence were peopled with figures of knowledge, power, and heroic exploits. In the original world—the Indian underworld—these figures bestowed life-giving guidance and knowledge that allowed the Indians to emerge on the earth and live as they did at present. Coming to light and alighting on the earth were cosmic events continuously recounted in a tremendous range of Indian lore. By keeping such tales close at hand, by repeating them incessantly, Indian societies were able to maintain order and balance, develop strategies, make decisions, and resolve conflicts, thus holding intact the daily face-to-face interaction that was the basic fabric of Indian culture. Many native ceremonies centered around the underworld figures and their teachings. Often ceremo-

A Dakota Sioux scaffold burial. Artwork by H. C. Yarrow, 1880. *Courtesy National Archives.*

nies—particularly those scholars call "clowning"—were replete with humorous and frightful performances. The antics of sacred clowns demonstrated exactly the opposite of what should be done, exaggerated human foibles, or grossly depicted taboos and perverse behavior. The performance of sacred clowns—considered the result of divine knowledge and absolutely necessary to the survival of life on earth—reinforced balance and order by contrasting with Indian definitions of and Indian teachings about what was normal.

Like all aspects of Indian life, the traditional religious practices of the Native Americans suffered from contact with the Europeans and Christianity. The onslaught of European diseases, rapid and unexpected, overwhelmed most Native American healing systems and undercut the beliefs that sustained them. Some natives converted to the "more powerful" Christian god; others attacked the new religion as the cause of the infections that were destroying them. Many native groups took their traditional practices underground to protect them from abolition first by the Spanish padres, then by the Euro-American Protestant missionaries. This was how the Pueblo Indians preserved their ceremonialism, which they still practice today in addition to Christian ritual. The Yaquis of Arizona incorporated into their religion elements of the teachings by the Jesuit missionaries who came to their villages; they now have four cults associated with Biblical characters surrounding the death and resurrection of Jesus. In a process scholars call "syncretism," the Yaquis fully integrated Christianity and their traditionally elaborate ceremonial dances. Other tribes, particularly those of the Plains, have laced the teachings of Christian missionaries with continual innovations. Others, especially in the late nineteenth century, tired of the efforts to accommodate a foreign religion. Native American despair over the loss of their lands and culture spawned the Ghost Dances of 1870 and 1890—the latter being a particularly widespread phenomenon. Both movements involved the resurrection of dead ancestors and restoration of life as they lived it before contact with the Europeans, and both movements were tolerated by federal authorities only provided that the Indians maintained peace. But each attempt to regain true native spirituality ultimately led to violence.

Throughout the twentieth century, Indians grew increasingly assimilated into the dominant culture. As late as the 1920s, Native American ceremonies were being outlawed by the federal government. As assimilation spread, intertribal contact also grew apace. The introduction of cash economies led many natives to seek work off the reservation. English became a language commonly spoken by Indians, who used it to communicate with other tribes. From these trends, a pan-Indian identity began to emerge side by side with tribal affiliations. The NATIVE AMERICAN CHURCH (NAC) came into being and addressed the tribal, pan-Indian, and assimilated roles of the Native Americans. Known in the sensation-addicted American press for its religious use of the hallucinogen peyote, the NAC included among its practices the seeking of visions and ritual drumming, as well as prayers and confessionals. Clearly, as Native American populations began to recover from nearly five centuries of decimation by European and Euro-American viral, cultural, and military attack, many Indians were attempting to forge a new religious life for themselves in a modern world hostile to their traditional beliefs and religions.

—Melissa A. Davis

SEE ALSO: Ghost Dance; Missions; United States Indian Policy

SUGGESTED READING:
Dutton, Bertha P. *Indians of the American Southwest.* Englewood Cliffs, N.J., 1975.
Gill, Sam D. *Native American Religions: An Introduction.* Belmont, Calif., 1982.
Mails, Thomas E. *Mystic Warriors of the Plains.* New York, 1991.
Wherry, Joseph H. *The Totem Pole Indians.* New York, 1974.

SUBSISTENCE PATTERNS

Subsistence patterns refer to the customary methods by which people obtain, produce, and prepare the items essential to survival, such as food, clothing, and shelter. As a vital part of basic existence, these patterns often have a tremendous impact on many other aspects of daily life, including religion, social systems, and material culture. The subsistence patterns of Native American cultures were greatly altered by the coming of the Europeans—at first through the spread of diseases, the introduction of new domestic animals (especially the horse), and the outbreak of armed conflict; later by the attempt to integrate Indians into budding European markets, by wars of conquest and attrition, and ultimately by the Euro-American defeat, diffusion, and domination of the Indians.

Originally, Indian subsistence patterns grew out of their practices in farming, hunting, and gathering. The more agriculturally inclined groups led sedentary lives in villages, while hunters and gathers were nomadic, roaming their territory in search of food and materials. In particularly harsh environments, the nomadic peoples often followed game as it migrated, and they traveled to various locations looking for wild plants as they bloomed or matured, a search for subsistence scholars call a "seasonal round." In more prosperous locations, hunters and gatherers had access to a variety of animal and plant life year round, which meant they tended to wander less. Usually, the more sedentary a group was, the more complex its religious, so-

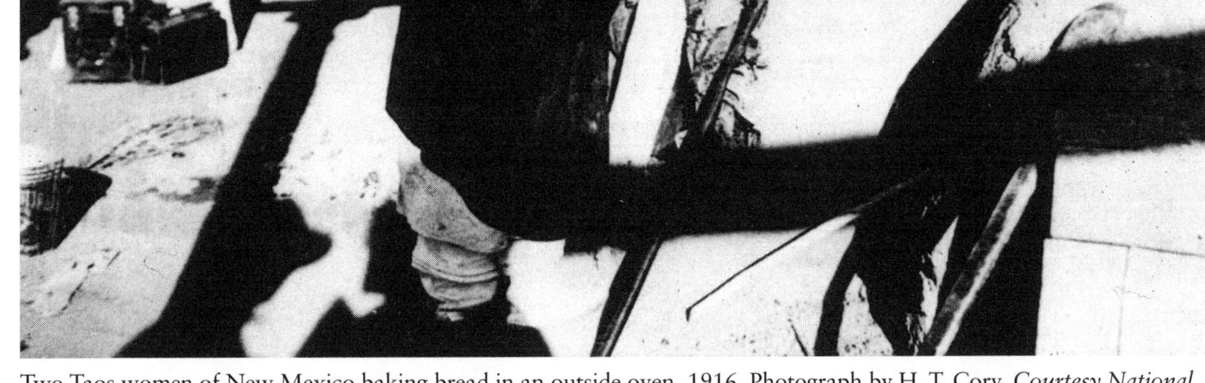

Two Taos women of New Mexico baking bread in an outside oven, 1916. Photograph by H. T. Cory. *Courtesy National Archives.*

Top: Salmon, a major portion of the Aleuts' diet, hangs from drying racks in a village in Old Harbor, Alaska, 1889. Photograph by N. B. Miller. *Courtesy National Archives.*

Bottom: Swinomish Indians display a skate caught in a fishtrap, Tulalip Indian Agency, Washington. Photograph by Andrew T. Kelley, 1938. *Courtesy National Archives.*

cial, and material life. Because nomadic peoples often broke into small bands for many months of the year, they found it harder to maintain centralized political structures and elaborate communal rituals. Constantly relocating, nomadic bands carried only the essential material goods. In contrast, sedentary farmers built permanent housing, gathered together for socializing and trade, engaged in many communal ceremonies (often requiring elaborate dress and instruments), and accumulated aesthetic as well as utilitarian objects.

Before the eighteenth century, the Plains tribes were few in number. They lived along rivers and streams in houses of earth. They subsisted basically on fish and small-scale horticulture but also gathered plants and nuts, hunted small game, and perhaps engaged in an annual bison hunt. Sometime between 1700 and 1750, Plains Indians acquired the horse, which led to dramatic changes in their subsistence patterns and culture. Although some tribes remained sedentary, others became full-fledged nomads, hunting BUFFALOES—also known as American bisons—as a primary means of subsistence and replacing their dirt lodges with portable tepees. As the skillful hunters procured most of what a tribe ate, wore, and used to make material goods, the Plains Indians not only increased in population, they became patriarchal.

Many tribes in the Southwest practiced intensive agriculture as a primary means of subsistence well before their first contact with Spanish explorers. The Pueblo Indians, for example, raised corn, beans, and squash without irrigation. The Spanish found Pimas raising turkeys and the Yumas irrigating their crops. Centuries of subsistence farming led Pueblo groups to develop complex cultural institutions and populous, integrated societies. Other groups, such as the Navajos and Apaches, subsisted by hunting and gathering. Over time, the Navajos adopted farming from the Pueblo tribes and acquired peach trees and sheep from the Spanish. After the Navajos began producing wool, they eventually ceased to grow cotton, which had formerly been a widespread staple. Although they became pastoralists as well as farmers, and although they spread across vast grazing lands, they continued to maintain their communal beliefs and engage in their elaborate communal rituals. The Apaches, on the other hand, remained nomads until modern times, and those Apaches living farthest east developed a hunting and raiding culture much like that of the Great Plains horsemen. The Apaches roamed and raided in small bands, owned few material possessions, and kept their religion simple.

The peoples of the Great Basin subsisted on many fewer sources of food and materials. Surrounded by an arid landscape, they dug roots and grub worms for food; hunted small game, such as rabbits; gathered some wild plants; and lived in thatched wickiups. Because of the scarcity of resources, the Basin Indians lived in very small groups of fewer than one dozen nuclear families. Often, they broke apart during the summer months and reconvened—mostly for communal hunting—during the winter season. A headman, whose authority was largely charismatic, loosely directed the seasonal band. The Basin Indians did not develop a centralized political structure. Even within families, authority shifted according to activity. Their ceremonial life was no more elaborate than their political one; all gatherings were social, and rituals were limited to those that directly aided survival.

The damp forests of the Pacific Northwest provided the region's tribes with an abundance of wild plants and large game. Coastal Indians enjoyed the bounty of the Pacific Ocean. Living in the midst of cedar forests, the Pacific Northwest tribes naturally used wood as a primary source for their material culture. They built elaborate longhouses and fashioned highly decorated, ocean-going ships. These tribes had the luxury of leisure time; they devoted many hours to everything they produced and created complex and beautiful objects for both utilitarian and aesthetic ends. Agriculture, a time-consuming occupation no matter how crudely practiced, played little role in their subsistence.

The prosperous and sedentary culture of the Pacific Northwest Indians was reflected in their social and political organization. Their society was based on clans, whose totems they carved on tremendous cedar poles. Chiefs made important decisions and played primary roles in potlatching ceremonies, which were the basis of much of the ceremonial practice in the region. The potlatch involved the ritual distribution and—indeed—the ritual destruction of material goods, a practice that only underscored how rich the area was in resources.

Farther inland, Native Americans shared some subsistence patterns in common with their Coastal neighbors to the west, but also others with the Plains tribes to the east and the Basin Indians to the south. The inland tribes fished, hunted small game and bisons, and grubbed for roots. Their houses were usually permanent; yet they often used tepees. Tribes in present-day Nebraska were particularly skilled farmers, who often found themselves engaged in battling drought and grasshopper infestations and who adapted corn to their environment.

The Indians in the trans-Mississippi West shared a number of subsistence patterns. Tribes used suitable resources and adapted to their environmental economy in the most advantageous ways. Completely dependent on the resources of the earth, the sky, and the local rivers, they shared a very conservative attitude toward nature and restricted the number of plants and animals they harvested and the uses to which they put them in farming, hunting, and gathering. For example, Plains tribes, such as the Cheyenne and Osage Indians, often did not kill the first buffalo they saw. Instead, they asked it to tell its herd of their needs so that some of the bisons might come and be killed. Likewise, the Navajos and other tribes limited the use of some plants to healers with special knowledge of the appropriate rituals to be used when first coming across those plants in gathering.

Arrow Maker and his daughter, Paiute Indians, pose before their home made of materials at hand, 1872. Photograph by Clement Powell. *Courtesy National Archives.*

Tribes hunting buffaloes, bears, and MOOSE usually procured a number of necessary materials from a single kill—food, fuel, clothing, and bone for weapons. Because large game was so important to the survival of hunting groups, they revered the animals, and often entire tribes engaged in ritual prayer to the big game before a hunt and in a ceremonial apology afterward. Rituals also focused on the hunters and their weapons. Pueblo women, whose power differed from that

Plains Indians used animal skins in constructing their lodges, such as the one pictured here beside Little Big Mouth, a medicine man photographed by William S. Soule, 1869 or 1870. *Courtesy National Archives.*

of the men, stayed away from hunters to avoid interfering with the spirit of their weapons.

Shared attitudes regarding matters of subsistence led the Native Americans to make various land-tenure agreements both within and among tribes. These agreements provided for individual land use but emphasized group needs over personal ones. Indians were far too culturally diverse to accomplish absolute tenure; however, in many areas, the tribes operated very efficient systems of land use, transfer, and acquisition.

Unlike the Eastern tribes, many groups west of the Mississippi were initially spared the encroachment of Euro-American settlers because their land was considered marginal at best. Except in the Spanish Southwest, most Indians dealt primarily with trappers and traders. The Euro-American frontiersmen introduced the Indians to such items as hoes and traded for crops and buffalo-related goods. As the trade networks grew, the Indians turned more and more to Euro-American farming techniques and equipment. Eventually, the ever-increasing numbers of settlers and the great buffalo hunts that they encouraged and in which they participated caused the near extinction of an animal central to the life of the Plains groups, many Basin tribes, and the Eastern Apaches.

In 1887, the General Allotment Act (often called the DAWES ACT) dramatically changed the nature of Native American subsistence patterns. Designed to promote individual ownership and farming among all tribes, the act stripped Indians—particularly nomadic tribes—of their autonomy, land, efficiency, and means of survival. The farming groups were often relocated to infertile plots and suffered through inadequate instruction and appropriations. Although the lands allotted were much more suitable for grazing, the government promoted agriculture—and what officials presumed was its more "civilizing" effect—rather than livestock raising.

In addition, Congress disregarded Indian culture when setting its Western agenda, ignored the native system of land tenure, and rejected the traditional Indian division of labor. For example, many tribes—particularly those "removed" to the West from the Southern states—regarded farming as women's work, but the U.S. government ignored women in the transition to new lands, an action that not only greatly reduced women's traditional rights of inheritance, in keeping with European notions of primogeniture, but also "shamed" Indian men by forcing hunters and warriors to cross often rigid boundaries of gender.

By the 1930s, the government recognized the destructiveness of its attempts to institutionalize subsistence. Admitting that its policy of turning hunters into farmers had failed—and observing the success of the more traditional communal farmers still practicing in the Southwest—the United States introduced the Indian New Deal, allowing—at least in principle—more autonomy to the individual tribes. But after nearly five decades, the subsistence strategies of the Native Americans had been thoroughly redefined in ways that no longer supported their religious, social, or material culture.

—*Melissa A. Davis*

SEE ALSO: Corn Growing; Fishing; Hunting

SUGGESTED READING:

Ballas, Donald J. "Historical Geography and American Indian Development." In *A Cultural Geography of North American Indians.* Edited by Thomas E. Ross and Tyrel G. Moore. Boulder, Colo., 1987.

Dutton, Bertha P. *Indians of the American Southwest.* Englewood Cliffs, N.J., 1975.

Hughes, J. Donald. *American Indian Ecology.* El Paso, Tex., 1983.

Hurt, R. Douglas. *Indian Agriculture in America.* Lawrence, Kans., 1987.

Jackson, Curtis E., and Marcia J. Galli. *A History of the Bureau of Indian Affairs and Its Activities among Indians.* San Francisco, 1977.

Mails, Thomas E. *The Mystic Warriors of the Plains.* New York, 1991.

ECOLOGY

As with other cultural categories such as art or politics, the notion of ecology as a set of beliefs or practices separate from the other aspects of daily life was foreign to the Native American peoples of North America. Similarly, there was no single "ecology" practiced by "American Indians" as members of a unified culture. The various tribal and language groups had their own ways of life, their own attitudes toward nature, their own methods of hunting and farming, all of which had different impacts on the natural environment. To say, as many scholars have, that, in general, the American Indians adapted themselves to their various environments and lived in harmony with nature is not to say that they did not make changes in their surroundings or affect entire ecosystems.

Everywhere humans live, their social and cultural activities have an effect on the natural environment. Whereas an observer might marvel at the way the Great Plains tribes adapted their culture to the movement of the great herds of grazing animals that fed on the massive grasslands, the tribes themselves constantly increased those grasslands at the expense of forests by burning away at the edges of the woods. Similarly, corn-growing peoples cleared land for planting by FIRE, and in some areas of the South, planted fields stretched from village to village. Northern woods had been so fully cleared of scrub to facilitate hunting that they resembled woodland parks, broken by artificially created meadows or "barrens," by the time Europeans arrived, and their more intensive agriculture, which allowed marginal or exhausted lands to lie unattended, actually encouraged the regrowth of many of the continent's "forest primeval." The "wilderness," in many ways, followed European settlement rather than stood in its way. Where native peoples established permanent towns, they tended to use up nearby trees for firewood, material goods and utensils, and housing. FRANCISCO VÁSQUEZ DE CORONADO, for example, noted that the Zuni Indians had to travel some distances from their villages to find junipers to cut. The ecological impact of Indian cultures was also indirect as well as immediate. The moose of North America, for example, had for thousands of years been culled by skillful hunters until they were different animals—faster, maybe even more alert—than they would otherwise have been. The Indians evidently hunted some species to extinction, such as the woolly mammoth. And their subsistence practices favored certain species (such as the American buffalo, which had spread from its natural habitat on the Great Plains to the wooded areas far east of the Mississippi by the time of European contact) over others.

But for all the variations in tribal practices and regardless of the impact Native Americans had on the North American environment (an impact that compared to that of Western industrial society was relatively minor in any case), Indians, in general, lived in a careful, if rough, balance with nature because doing so was necessary to their survival. Should they make serious ecological mistakes, they immediately felt the consequences. Acting in ways that destroyed a tribe's balance with the local ecosystem, which provided them with food, clothing, and shelter, meant that the natural environment on which they so depended could no longer provide for their needs. As a result, Native American peoples developed an attitude toward nature that Euro-Americans would characterize as spiritual or religious, an attitude that lay at the heart of most Indian cultures. Of course, the cultural category of *religion* no more corresponded to Native American thinking than did that of *ecology.* Most Indian words for *religion* more closely resembled the Isleta Pueblo term *lifeway* or *life-need,* and for the Hopis, what Euro-Americans called *religion,* the Indians dubbed simply the *Hopi way.* For native tribes, raw nature was not a wilderness but something tame, something that was part of their lifeway and life-need, and their experiences with nature almost always involved a spiritual dimension. Their notions of the environment were part and parcel of their religious world view, and they explained their attitudes toward nature in religious terms.

Indian beliefs about nature, then, were not attempts to explain the world, but a way of expressing their involvement with the world. Native Americans did not approach a bear, a tree, a corn plant, or a mountain as a phenomenon to be studied but as a sentient presence that one could feel, hear, and talk to. Often misunderstood as a form of animism, Indian religion was, at once, an ecology and a way of being in the world; although it was simple in its general outline and highly complex in its detail, which varied from tribe to tribe, it carried with it no systematic theology. Knowing that human actions were basically a response to nature and that everything an individual did created a response in nature, Native Americans tended to see the response as anything but impersonal: everything in nature was alive, not merely animate. A star, a hill, a flower, an eagle, the ground itself was as conscious and living as a human, and the Zunis, for example, called each of these "things" in nature *ho'i*, or "a living person." Things in nature were imbued with the sacred power—what the Dakota called *wakan*—that permeated all natural forms and movements. Things in nature—"the wingeds, the two-leggeds, and the four-leggeds"—were really gifts of the Wakantanka (the Sioux word Euro-Americans translate as "Great Spirit") who was the one who breathed in every living thing. The Apaches called this supreme being "Life Giver"; the Cherokees, "Giver of Breath"; the Papagos, "Earthmaker"; the Crows, "The One Who Made All Things." Still another great power was Mother Earth herself, or sometimes Grandmother Earth, who supported the people by providing fruits, roots, fish, and animals. For most Indians, then, animals themselves were powerful beings, with the same claim to existence that humans enjoyed, and plants were frequently considered people.

Since the world and the things in nature were, like man himself, a gift, Indians did not, in general, consider humans the lords of the universe, placed here to despoil forest and field, but beings inside nature and equal with a rabbit or a deer or a young corn plant. Humans could be tricked by such beings, by Rabbit, Bluejay, or Coyote, and certainly hunters could kill nothing but out of necessity and with apologies to the prey and offerings to the Life Giver for having done so. As Frank G. Speck pointed out, for the Indians, hunting was "not a war upon the animals, not a slaughter for food or profit, but a holy occupation." Similarly, Native Americans believed that ritual was as vitally important for growing crops as physical toil in the field. Many tribes had a Corn Dance, and Southwestern Indians described such rituals as "singing up the corn." A large number of Indian ceremonies—the Sun Dance, the Buffalo Dance, the Deer Dance, the Eagle Dance—were, in fact, ways of speaking directly with nature, of practicing Indian ecology in hunting and agriculture. Such oneness with nature was often reflected in the clan structure of Indian society, where the clans took names such as Turtle and Eagle. A cooperation with nature, rather than a competition against it, formed the essence of Indian ecology.

This ecological cooperation also extended to land ownership. Although it is not accurate to say, as scholars did for many years, that land, in the Indian view, was not "owned," it is, in fact, generally true that land ownership was subject to communal needs. Many Indians did have a sense of "property" rights, especially those who lived along the Northwest Coast, where each family owned a stretch of beach and whatever drifted ashore was theirs to use or bestow as gifts. Precisely where property rights were strongest, so was the injunction to share one's wealth with others, and the peoples of the Northwest held elaborate social gatherings called "potlatches," which were, in effect, competitions in gift giving, contests promoting communal goals. More generally, however strongly an individual's attachment might be to land he or she cultivated, once that individual ceased to occupy or use the land, it returned to the community, became again part of the natural environment, a gift to be used by another.

The coming of white culture had a major impact on Indian ecology just as it did on Indian culture in general. Notions of land use changed, as Euro-Americans insisted that the earth was a thing and, as such, alienable from nature—something that could be sold and passed along like a favorite weapon or artifact. Some Indians took up hunting as a commercial profession, trapping beavers and killing deer and buffaloes for their exchange value. For a period, many Indians did not fully understand that land on which they continued to hunt and fish no longer was truly theirs in the old sense. Once they came to understand that the earth they thought belonged to the past and future instead was the property of speculators and settlers, many felt they had fallen out of harmony with nature and the sacred universe. Few Navajos, for example, were ever comfortable outside their homeland between the sacred mountains that they felt, in their souls, was the "place" for them. Whatever else it was, the rounding up of Native Americans on reservations disturbed the ecological balance at the heart of many of their cultures, and in most cases, this, in itself, was enough to create an abiding despair. Ironically, as Americans, in general, became more sensitive to ecology in the twentieth century, they came to appreciate, respect, and, in some case, emulate traditional Native American attitudes toward nature.

—*Charles Phillips*

SEE ALSO: Corn Growing; Fishing Industry; Hunting

SUGGESTED READING:

Hughes, J. Donald. *American Indian Ecology.* El Paso, Tex., 1983.

Hurt, R. Douglas. *Indian Agriculture in America.* Lawrence, Kans., 1987.

Jordan, Terry G., and Matti Kaups. *The American Backwoods Frontier: An Ethnic and Ecological Interpretation.* Baltimore, 1989.

Pyne, Stephan J. *Fire in America: A Cultural History of Wildland and Rural Fire.* Princeton, N.J., 1982.

Ross, Thomas E., and Tyrel G. Moore, eds. *A Cultural Geography of North American Indians.* Boulder, Colo., 1987.

Washburn, Wilcomb E. *The Indian in America.* New York, 1975.

POLITICAL ORGANIZATION

Euro-American assumptions about the political structure of Indian society have ranged from the widespread belief that the Native Americans were totally autocratic to assertions by some observers and scholars that the Indians had no politics at all and lived in a state of virtual anarchy. The truth is not only that the reality of everyday Indian life was more complex than early Europeans realized, nor is it merely that Indian political organization lay somewhere between the two poles, but that there were any number of different political structures among the wide variety of NATIVE AMERICAN PEOPLES, that Indian political organizations developed and changed over time, and that tribal politics changed according to varying conditions, such as drought or the availability of game, special circumstances, such as extended wars, or historical events, such as the rise of a new leader or contact with new peoples and cultures. Not only did the Aztecs, first observed by Spanish explorers, appear to European eyes the subjects of ruler-gods, they had, in fact, only relatively recently risen to glory through a long campaign of conquest that may have invested their leaders with unusual authority. The appearance of European adventurers in Peru exacerbated civil unrest among the Incas and led to significant changes in their political organization. Exotic diseases introduced by Europeans decimated many North America tribes long before the Europeans ever arrived to observe that some Indians seemed to live without laws or religion, a condition to which the new epidemics may well have contributed. Such developments or changes, however, were not solely related to the Old World's invasion of the New. The Iroquois Confederacy evolved as a kind of mutual defense pact long before the arrival of the whites; the evidently complex political structures of certain Mississippi River valley tribes probably resulted from conquests by peoples fleeing political unrest and war in Mexico and Central America; the rudimentary political structures of California tribes may well have had much to do with their centuries-long geographical isolation from contact with any other native peoples.

The reintroduction of HORSES into North America by early Spanish explorers, for example, had a profound effect on the political organization of many Native American peoples in the trans-Mississippi West. Many Plains tribes who had formerly been pedestrians become mounted nomads. Some tribes, adapting horses to domestic use, moved onto the Great Plains at least part of the year in search of BUFFALOES, which brought them into conflict with others already in the region. Gender roles changed in some tribes, which occasionally moved from matriarchal societies dependent on farming to patriarchal ones looking toward the hunt for sustenance. Newly nomadic peoples frequently raided the stores of those tribes who retained some form of agriculture. The Lakota (Sioux) culture, Robert M. Utley points out, was hardly a generation old when SITTING BULL was born. Around the beginning of the nineteenth century, the nomadic Lakotas had ridden on to the High Plains and occupied the region between the Missouri River and the Bighorn Mountains, ranging north to the Canadian prairies and south to the Platte and Republican rivers. Their migration brought them into conflict with the Assiniboins to the north and with the Crows, who conducted a fighting retreat in the west as Sioux and Crow hunting grounds merged into a "zone of conflict" along the Powder River. Like many Plains tribes, the Lakotas' social organizations and political institutions were shaped by the war and the hunt, and these organizations were loose and constantly changing in response to the movement of game, the activities of allies and enemies, and their own highly developed sense of individual freedom.

Their very names reflected these influences: Eastern Sioux called themselves *Dakota* (ally); in the western dialect the word became *Lakota; Sioux,* the name used by whites and to which all the tribes eventually responded, was a corruption of the Ojibwa word for *enemies.* Originally, the Sioux had been made up of seven autonomous but related groups who shared a culture, history, and language. The semisedentary four eastern tribes, sometimes labeled Santees, lived along the Minnesota River, which in the eighteenth century was the Dakota heartland, and hunted—mostly on foot—on the prairie and in the forests, fished in local rivers, and cultivated and harvested wild rice. A middle range of Sioux tribes, the Yankton and Yanktonai, having abandoned the woodlands for the prairies east of the Missouri, retained many customs of the Eastern Dakota, although they also followed buffaloes on horseback and served as a kind of cultural bridge between Eastern Sioux and the Western Sioux, or Lakota. These latter, also called collectively the Teton, had further divided into seven tribes and transformed themselves into the horse-and-buffalo Indians that became celebrated by Euro-Americans, especially WILLIAM F. ("BUFFALO BILL") CODY in his Wild West show, as "true" Indians.

Each of the Lakota tribes claimed its own hunting ground, although the tribe did not jealously guard the hunting ground against other Sioux. Family served as the basis for the bands—the *tiyospaye*—that stood at the core of Lakota tribal society. Fiercely independent, these bands—consisting of relatives by blood, marriage, adoption, or simply declaration—did not, except under special circumstances, feel bound by tribal decisions or a leader's commands. Dissenting bands were free to leave the tribe at any time; they might join with other like-minded bands or merely wander alone onto the plains. No chief ruled by virtue of social position but led by personal example and demonstrated wisdom under the advice and consent of a council of elders. All council decisions represented a consensus, sometimes reached after long deliberation, since unanimity, not majority vote, was the goal. The Lakota deferred any ruling on which not everyone agreed, which could produce drift, paralysis, or heated factionalism on important issues. During war, formal camp migrations, communal hunts, or any event involving the entire tribe and affecting its common welfare, every Lakota was expected to obey council decisions. At these times, tribal leaders—men of experience in war, hunting, civil matters, and spiritual affairs—relied on men's societies, fraternal groups that produced the *akicita* (tribal policemen), who enforced council decisions and tribal rules and regulations. With backing by the *akicita,* four executive officers—called "shirt wearers"—carried out tribal policies, and for a people who rarely came together as a tribe outside the annual hunt, these shirt wearers—their abilities and temperaments—proved especially important to Sioux politics.

The independence and looseness of Sioux politics were typical of many Native Americans groups, and not merely those on the Plains, although details of organization varied widely. For some, like the Apaches, individual bands and their charismatic leaders were even more dominant, and there was little political authority outside the band. For many of the California Indians and Great Basin tribes, political organizations—beyond basic family relationships—simply did not exist. On the other hand, Pacific Northwest tribes tended to be highly structured socially, with set castes or classes, including a slave class, answering to autocratic chiefs invested with great authority if not something approaching dictatorial powers. Even some Plains Indians were more rigidly structured than the Sioux. The Kiowas, for example, had six subtribes or bands—the Kata (or Biters and Arikaras), the Kogui (or Elks), the Kaigwu (or The People—that is, the Kiowas proper), the Kingep (or Big Shields), the Semat (or Thieves, Kiowa-Apaches), and the Kongtalyui (or Black Boys). There may once have been a seventh, the Kuato, who had been exterminated by the Dakotas about 1780. A political division unrelated to clans and not based on marriage, each band had its own leader, who was subject to the authority of a head chief, and some of the bands had their own "medicine" or religious ceremonies. Kiowa society was ranked by social class, the ranking being based on military exploits, religious power, and wealth, with some room made for social mobility. Wealth alone did not ensure high ranking, but when combined with prowess in war or spiritual accomplishment, it was a powerful consideration affecting both the great and the common people. Perhaps 10 percent of the Kiowas belonged to the aristocracy, or Onde; 40 percent, to a second rank of wealthy people, the Ondegup'a—warriors, medicine men, people of limited property, even some captives climbing up the ladder of success; half the Kiowas belong to a third rank of poor people, the Kaan; and a few Kiowas were no-accounts or misfits, lazy and unambitious, sometimes simply crazy people called Dupom. War leaders exercised absolute control and military discipline over their bands; positions of authority were reserved for full-blooded tribal members, although captives and mixed-bloods might become notable warriors or be adopted by prominent families; and rank and honor generally fell to the sons of important men.

It was tribes whose politics resembled those of the Kiowas that led Europeans first to use words such as *king* or *emperor* when describing Indian political leaders, although extended contact with the various tribes soon led European settlers to replace those labels with *chief* or *headman,* especially after some of the powers of many Indian leaders had been undercut, neutralized, or even destroyed. Some scholars have rightly pointed out that such concepts as *king, prince,* or *princess* bear little relation to political power in Native American cultures, although to dismiss the exercise of a kind of power equivalent to that of a European ruler as "a white man's fiction," goes too far, as Wilcomb Washburn points out. While it is true that many Indian political leaders made decisions affecting tribal policies first in council and by talking matters over until a consensus was reached, much the same could be said about most European monarchs, even the absolute kings who came to power in the sixteenth and seventeenth centuries. If many tribal leaders lacked the coercive powers commonly held by European kings, the latter also could hardly have ruled effectively without demonstrating the same ability to lead by example and persuasion as Indian leaders. And whites were no better at controlling their ordinary citizens than Indian chiefs were at restraining their youthful tribal members. The fact that Indian women often, as a matter of course, played a role in and exercised influence over Native American politics may have persuaded some Europeans that Indian male leaders lacked the kind of authority held by European rulers, but in truth, however Indian leaders assumed positions of authority, by whatever process Indian leaders were replaced, they performed much the same leadership functions that Europeans of power or influence performed for their society. Since, as Bernard Mishkin has pointed out, horse, rank, and warfare were so inextricably interwoven in Plains society, Plains leaders may have been easier for European eyes to identify, but native leadership was evident even among those native peoples in the Arctic, Great Basin, northeastern Mexico, and California, whose largest political unit, at the time of European contact, was the family and whom anthropologists have claimed had no "true political organization."

William T. Hagan compared North American Indian bands or villages to autonomous Greek city-states, and Wilcomb Washburn took the analogy a step further to point out that the city-states, like many Indian bands, joined together for some peaceful pursuits—communal hunts on the one hand, Olympic games on the other—and in times of crisis or war to form joint military defenses against invaders. Just as in Greece, such circumstances also sometimes called forth great Indian political leaders, such as TECUMSEH or Sitting Bull. The unremitting white pressure on Native American tribes could sometimes distort Indian politics, as when KEOKUK, a mixed-blood who would normally not have been admitted into the council of the Sac (Sauk) and Fox (Mesquakie) Indians, came to exercise great authority over the two tribes after Black Hawk's defeat by dint of his relationship to the whites, as well as his own bravery in battle and his eloquent use of the Algonquian language. With Tecumseh, white encroachments led to a transtribal political alliance that, before it collapsed under the pressures of military reversals and deeply ingrained notions of tribal political independence, seemed to promise just the kind of mutual defense the Greeks once mounted against the Persians. Certainly, the Sioux and Cheyennes, who fought the U.S. Army under such leaders as Sitting Bull, CRAZY HORSE, GALL, and others, forged an effective military and political alliance. Never suffering defeat on the battlefield, they were undone, instead, by the extended nature of the conflict, which Indian political organizations, whose powers lay vested in the band and the tribe, were not well equipped to sustain. Tribal political organizations continued to characterize Indian life on the reservation, even given the assault on tribal authority under the Indian reform movement and its insistence on individual assimilation, and they continue to play a major role for Native Americans even today.

—*Charles Phillips*

SUGGESTED READING:

Hagan, William T. *American Indians.* Chicago, 1961.

———. *The Sac and the Fox.* Norman, Okla., 1958.

Hassrack, Royal B. *The Sioux: Life and Customs of a Warrior Society.* Norman, Okla., 1964.

Jennings, Francis. *The Founders of America: How Indians Discovered the Land, Pioneered It, and Created Great Classical Civilizations; How They Were Plunged into a Dark Age by Invasion and Conquest; and How They Are Now Recovering.* New York, 1993.

Josephy, Alvin M. *The Indian Heritage of America.* New York, 1970.

Mails, Thomas E. *The Mystic Warriors of the Plains.* New York, 1991.

Mayhall, Mildred P. *The Kiowas.* Norman, Okla., 1971.

Utley, Robert M. *The Lance and the Shield: The Life and Times of Sitting Bull.* New York, 1993.

Washburn, Wilcomb E. *The Indian in America.* New York, 1975.

WARFARE

Upon arriving in the American West, Europeans and Americans found native peoples engaged in widespread tribal wars. The tribes adjusted their fighting to geography and climate and made their weapons from available materials. Unique tribal cultures—along with the impact of the whites' actions, guns, and horses—also determined styles of warfare.

Despite its tribal basis, a number of similarities characterized all Indian warfare. Feelings of tribal superiority and spiritual beliefs encouraged the conflicts. The small size of most bands and the requirement that men hunt to support their people meant that raiding had limited objectives, and heavy casualties were unacceptable. Being formal and ceremonial, most conflicts contained considerable amounts of bravado and religious ritual. Because tribes migrated in search of fish, game, and edible plants, a constant source of intertribal conflict was land—seen as communal rather than as individual property. While territory was a cause of war, typically it was less important as an individual motive than either plunder, which provided wealth, or winning social prestige.

Among the Pacific Northwest Coast tribes, prestige and wealth motivated warriors. Often villages, rather than tribes, fought each other. Their chiefs led raids in huge war canoes to capture prized trapping grounds or fishing areas. War parties, operating secretly, also acquired plunder and captured women and children for slaves. A problem arose in this culture of very complex social structures of families and clans when men from one village inadvertently fought or enslaved people of their own clan, an unacceptable cultural taboo.

Northwest Coast warriors used war clubs and elaborately carved bone daggers, but with the coming of Europeans, firearms became the most important weapons. Victors in battle often strung enemy heads on ropes as trophies. But violent death inevitably

Karl Bodmer's drawing of Four Bears, a Mandan chief, holding a lance and wearing a painted and quilled shirt, ca. 1833. *Courtesy National Archives.*

brought revenge, and so the cycle of war continued. Eventually white officials, traders, and missionaries brought the tribal wars to an end in the 1800s. In part, the famous giveaway ceremony, the potlatch, was a substitute for the earlier exchange of property through war.

Unlike the Pacific Northwest Coast tribes who waged wars for prestige and wealth, the California tribes tended to be less aggressive. Surviving from hunting, fishing, and gathering over terrain with rather specific tribal boundaries, the numerous small bands fought most often over encroachment and poaching. Rival shamans often complicated these motives with accusations of witchcraft against their enemies. Wars most often consisted of ambushes but also could be more formal engagements. Because war was not common, war honors were not of great importance, and tribes required purification after battle. Fighting with primitive weapons like spears, bows and arrows, and even stones, the California Indians were no match for the invasion of Euro-American miners in the 1850s. The influx of whites to the region soon brought the intertribal warfare to an end.

The Yuma and Mojave tribes of the lower Colorado River valley of present-day southern California were an exception to the relative pacifism of California tribes. Warriors were part of a distinct class. They did not marry. Instead, they devoted their lives to raiding and revenge. Commonly armed with bows and arrows, parties of ten to forty men roamed far and wide to attack enemy camps. The purpose of these raids was more to seek revenge or glory and to annihilate the enemy than to secure economic gain.

To the east of the California tribes, Great Basin Indians survived in a harsh environment on small game, insects, and roots and seeds. The Great Basin peoples did not fight over land and food but in defense and retaliation. Men only occasionally raided their enemies. Then, once the goal was accomplished, they returned to the more important task of survival.

South of the Great Basin, a variety of cultures in present-day New Mexico and Arizona fought each other. Beginning in the sixteenth century, the presence of the Spanish—with their guns and horses—complicated intertribal warfare in that arid land. Pueblos, Navajos, and Apaches vied with the Spanish and later the Mexicans and the Americans as enemies, allies, and participants engaged in raiding, warfare, and a profitable slave trade.

Although often depicted as a peaceful people, the Pueblo Indians actually have a long history of warfare. In 1680, the Pueblo Indians rebelled against the Spanish and drove them from the area for more than ten years. After the Spanish returned, the Pueblos often cooperated with them as auxiliaries against the Navajos, Apaches, and Comanches. Although not as diligent in raiding as their opponents, the Pueblos sometimes did invade enemy territory. The social importance of warfare was illustrated by the Women's Scalp Association, made up of Tewa Pueblo women who greeted returning warriors and ceremonially chewed on enemy scalps.

With the Pueblos and Apaches, the numerous Navajos had an ambiguous relationship that consisted of both raiding and trade. The Navajos also raided the Spanish and counted the Ute tribe, in Colorado, as a major enemy. Navajo culture, based on herding sheep, hunting, and some farming, had to adapt to counter numerous Ute raids for horses.

The Navajos used their captives in the growing Southwest slave trade. Thousands of slaves changed hands among the Spanish, Navajos, Apaches, Pueblos, Utes, and Comanches. In all this, Navajo culture developed a special place for warfare. The "Enemy

Way" ceremony remains to this day an important part of Navajo spiritual tradition.

While Navajo raiding declined after the tribe's forced exile to Fort Sumner in the 1860s, Apache warfare continued into the 1880s. Members of several tribes spread through southern New Mexico and Arizona, inveterate Apache warriors adapting their fighting techniques to desert and mountain terrains. Some Eastern Apaches had lived on the plains before the Comanches drove them out in the early 1700s. This disaster, together with long wars with the Spanish, led the Apache hunters and gatherers to live partially from their raiding proceeds, valuing especially plunder in guns and animals. They traveled in small groups and "harvested" the peasants of northern Mexico, always leaving their victims with some property so that the raiding party could return at a later date to steal again.

Revenge war parties were different from raids. Warriors in Apache war parties used special ambush techniques to annihilate the enemy. To be successful in battle, Apaches used spiritual power—wearing a "medicine cord" and carrying pollen. But, unlike the Plains Indians, the Apaches did not have specific war honors. Success was determined, instead, by plunder and captives, mutilation of dead enemies, and sometimes the torture, by women, of a male captive in order to avenge a dead relative.

Southwestern tribal warfare created problems for the Spanish, Mexicans, and Americans, who, accordingly, adopted policies of using Indian allies to end the wars. Ultimately, the whites recruited Pueblo, Ute, Navajo, and Apache warriors against their own people or enemy tribes in order to end the Indian Wars.

Despite the extensive conflicts in the Southwest, nowhere in the West was warfare more sophisticated than on the Plains. Supported by huge buffalo herds and, by the 1700s, guns and horses, Plains Indians lived a relatively easy existence that allowed men time for raiding. Nearby cultures, also rich in horses, engaged in warfare like that of the Plains Indians. These cultures included the tribes of the Rocky Mountains, the Columbia River plateau, and the Prairie Indians east of the Great Plains.

Plains warfare existed long before the acquisition of horses, but the animals provided infinite mobility and were viewed as highly valuable. Tribes of the Plains and the bordering areas migrated to follow buffalo herds, and conflicts over territory were common. The large Sioux and Comanche nations were particularly successful in conquering new lands.

Inevitably, war acquired strong cultural meanings. A warrior searched for spiritual power in order to be successful. More important than fighting over hunting lands, war determined a young man's social prestige as well as his wealth, counted in horses. Warfare resulted in losses of life, but more often than not, it was limited and individualistic, consisting of stealing horses and enemy weapons and proving one's courage by charging to engage an enemy. Tribes judged men's successes by war honors like rescuing a friend and "counting coup," or striking the enemy in close combat. Tribal society supported this warfare, waged legitimately against anyone who was perceived as inferior or not part of the tribe. Women encouraged the fighting; they mutilated dead enemies, mourned dead relatives until revenge was accomplished, and married only men who were warriors.

On the Plains, intertribal warfare became such a disruption to the economic and expansion policies of Europeans and, later, Americans that the whites worked to end it. In the late 1800s, the United States Army defeated the Sioux and other hostile bands by using their tribal enemies, the Pawnees and Crows, as allies. By the 1890s, the government ended intertribal conflict by military conquest and extensive white domination of the land. The essence of Indian warfare, based on tribalism, prestige, and plunder, was incompatible with the advanced technology and national purposes of the United States.

—Anthony R. McGinnis

SEE ALSO: Apache Wars; Navajo Wars; Pacific Northwest Indian Wars; Pueblo Revolt; Texas Frontier Indian Wars; United States Army: Scouts; Yuma Revolt

SUGGESTED READING:

Calloway, Colin G. "The Inter-tribal Balance of Power on the Great Plains, 1760–1850." *Journal of American Studies* 16 (1982): 25–47.

———. "Sword Bearer and the 'Crow Outbreak' of 1887." *Montana: The Magazine of Western History* 36 (1986): 38–51.

Dunlay, Thomas. *Wolves for the Blue Soldiers: Indian Scouts and Auxiliaries with the U.S. Army, 1860–1890*. Lincoln, Nebr., 1982.

Ewers, John C. "Intertribal Warfare as a Precursor of Indian-White Warfare on the Northern Plains." *The Western Historical Quarterly* 6 (1975): 397–410.

McGinnis, Anthony. "A Contest of Wits and Daring: Plains Indians at War with the U.S. Army." *North Dakota History: Journal of the Northern Plains* 48 (1981): 24–32.

———. *Counting Coups and Cutting Horses: Intertribal Warfare on the Northern Plains, 1738–1889*. Evergreen, Colo., 1990.

Roscoe, Will. "'That is My Road': The Life and Times of a Crow Berdache." *Montana: The Magazine of Western History* 40 (1990): 46–55.

White, Richard. "The Winning of the West: The Expansion of the Western Sioux in the Eighteenth and Nineteenth Centuries." *Journal of American History* 65 (1978): 319–343.

WEAPONS

Indians of the American West used a variety of weapons in almost constant tribal wars. While individual cultures, indigenous materials, and even religious significance determined the weapons used, a number of weapons were common to all tribes: bows and arrows, lances, clubs, and knives. When the Spanish, French, English, and finally the Americans entered the West, they greatly influenced both tribal warfare and weaponry. Metal for knives and arrowheads, firearms, and horses gave warriors new and powerful weapons. But these trade items also created a dependence on the white man's technology, a dependence that ultimately had a great impact on Native Americans.

Along the Northwest Coast, while guns furnished new power, warriors also used weapons they had produced for centuries—clubs and knives, made of wood, stone, and whalebone. Warriors, especially the Tlingits who were noted for their weapons, often carved on the handles of weapons intricate designs to resemble ravens or other sacred animals. Men also used cedar bark to make body armor.

John K. Hillers photographed a Paiute Indian drawing his bow and arrow while his companions, in festive dress, look on. October 1872. *Courtesy National Archives.*

San Juan, chief of the Mescalero Apaches, photographed with a spear and shield. *Courtesy National Archives.*

The more peaceful California Indians used their hunting weapon, the bow and arrow, for their occasional wars, although short spears and clubs and even stones were also common. Men constructed bows from yew wood and used sinew to reinforce them and make bowstrings. Flint was most desirable for knives, arrowheads, and spearheads.

To the south, the Mojaves and Yumas, more warlike than other California tribes, had a larger array of weapons. Willow and mesquite, from the desert terrain, provided wood for bows. Arrows often had only fire-hardened ends instead of points. Some warriors also used small shields and five-foot spears for lethal fighting.

In the Southwest, more than in California and the Northwest, whites influenced Native American warfare and weapons. Spanish policy kept weapons out of Indian hands, but the Pueblos, important Spanish allies, were exceptions to the rule. The Spanish outfitted the Pueblos with horses and guns. The Navajos and

Guns, which Native Americans received from Europeans traders, altered warfare among Indians tribes and made them dependent on white man's technology. *Courtesy National Archives.*

Apaches had more difficulty acquiring firearms. It was not long before they owned many horses through raids and breeding, and their dependence on firearms became so great that a significant portion of Apache raiding was undertaken to procure ammunition. When ammunition was not available, Apaches used small stones as bullets.

As inveterate raiders, the Navajos used a variety of weapons: bows and arrows, clubs, shields, and eight-foot lances. Although only partially nomadic, the Navajos avidly embraced the use of horses, both for warfare and herding sheep.

The Apaches used horses more for travel and for food than for waging war. Apaches preferred to fight on foot and created a variety of appropriate weapons long before the introduction of the gun. Warriors spent their time in the rancheria, or village, constructing bows from the wood of mulberry, locust, or mountain oak; war clubs, called "stone carriers"; and sometimes shields and small lances.

The Plains warriors also devoted hours to making weapons, but, unlike the Apaches, they focused their fighting around the use and acquisition of horses. Nearby Plateau and Prairie cultures and the Nez Percés of Idaho and Pawnees of Nebraska also used horses extensively in war, as well as weapons distinctive to their regions.

A nineteenth-century magazine offers its Eastern readers an illustration of an Indian luring a snake for its venom to be used for poison arrows. *Courtesy Patrick H. Butler, III.*

Plains warriors straightened ash or birch limbs for arrows and shaped bows from ash, elm, or other available wood. They applied sinew to the back of the bow, and the Crows who were noted for their bows, often added laminated horns from mountain sheep for strength. The coup-stick, shaped like a shepherd's staff, was essential for the courageous feat of striking an enemy. Highly decorated shields, made small to use on horseback, were considered to have spiritual powers. Lances, war clubs, and knives completed the arsenal of the Plains warriors. The importance of arms to the culture was demonstrated by the fact that taking an enemy's weapon was a war honor; among the Blackfoot Indians, it was the most important honor.

To the Plains warriors, European guns became valued weapons. Early single-shot rifles, especially muzzle-loaders, were not always as effective as bows and arrows, but they were powerful and frightening to the enemy. Repeating rifles, available by the late 1860s, were even more valuable and increased the Indians' overall firepower. In the 1860s and 1870s, the United States Army tried to limit the availability of guns and ammunition to Native Americans.

Indian warriors, using traditional weapons made from indigenous material, carried on effective warfare against other tribes as well as against American soldiers. Metal and guns added to the effectiveness of tribal war, while making Indians dependent on white culture. However, with the possible exception of horses, European and American products did not revolutionize tribal war.

—*Anthony R. McGinnis*

SUGGESTED READING:

Haley, James L. "He Makes Weapons." In *Apaches: A History and Culture Portrait.* Garden City, N.Y., 1981.

Hofsinde, Robert (Gray-Wolf). *Indian Warriors and Their Weapons.* New York, 1965.

Mails, Thomas E. *The Mystic Warriors of the Plains.* Garden City, N.Y., 1972.

McGinnis, Anthony. *Counting Coups and Cutting Horses: Intertribal Warfare on the Northern Plains, 1738–1889.* Evergreen, Colo., 1990.

ACCULTURATION

Before the arrival of European explorers, the geographic region later designated as the United States was home for at least five million indigenous people. Those Native Americans were subdivided into groups separated by geography, language, and culture. Interactions among the groups resulted in exchanges of material culture as well as mixings of ideas, concepts, and spiritual beliefs. When native groups moved to different geographic locations, their cultures were often vitally affected by climate, topography, and new neighbors. Even the most cherished and respected traditions continually underwent modifications and adaptations to changed circumstances, both environmental and human. When external factors create change within a group, the process is called "acculturation."

Human interchanges generally result in adaptations on the part of the participating cultures. When one of the cultures proves militarily, economically, demographically, and politically dominant, the altered living patterns of the subordinate group are most noticeable. That is especially true when the dominating culture writes the evaluative texts describing the processes of acculturation experienced by the other group. Until the 1970s, nearly all descriptions of Native American acculturation stemmed from studies and observations done by Europeans and Euro-Americans. Those studies have tended to blur tribal group distinctions and characterize cultural changes monolithically as Indian acculturation.

Social scientists and historians, aware of the horrific population losses suffered by Native Americans (the numbers of U.S. natives had dwindled to less than two hundred thousand by 1900) and the accompanying loss of political control, have generally emphasized the degrees of cultural loss. These scholars concentrated on the alterations they saw as leading toward assimilation, that point at which a culture loses its separate identity within the mainstream of another, presumably more advanced, culture. No one can argue that Native American groups have not been substantively affected by continuous contact with Euro-Americans; however, despite many predictions of inevitable assimilation, Indian tribes have maintained their "otherness" within a non-Indian nation. Thus cultural persistence is as remarkable as acculturation.

Since the 1970s, scholars have modified the acculturation model in which the "primitive, less advanced" Indian more or less passively adapts to "the white man's road." In these studies, scholars point out differences in the effects of culture change on individual tribal histories, and they generally accord tribespeople an active role in adapting the majority culture's ways to fit their own. Scholars more often describe resistance to acculturation as understandable, even admirable, rather than simply mindless stubbornness.

Part of this changed attitude reflects a rethinking of the history of the European subjugation of indigenous America. There is a recognition that the Indian policies of European and U.S. governments originated in ethnocentrism. Finding little worth in Native American "savagery," policy-makers generally assumed for themselves a cultural superiority that led to programs designed to "civilize" the Indian. Their enthusiasm fre-

"Blacksmithing at the Indian training school, Forest Grove, Oregon, 1882." *Courtesy National Archives.*

quently ended in coerced change or forced acculturation that they hoped would then lead to assimilation, the disappearance of a despised or undesirable other. Scholars continue to debate the motives and moralities of the acculturation policy-makers. Did the agents of acculturation have the best interests of Indians in mind? Should they only be accused of excessive zeal or was their policy making more cynically derived? Did they hope to effect "cultural genocide" to achieve dominance over indigenous peoples and their lands?

Culture change within the hundreds of Native American groups before European contact can only be dimly and imprecisely explained. While physical evidence of Indians living in North America over thousands of years is not lacking, it scarcely provides a complete record. Social scientists endlessly speculated about the motivations behind the movements of ancient Americans, their varying expressions of culture, and their internal structures and patterns of living. Excavations that yield sea shells hundreds of miles from either coast would indicate continental trading and, by extension, cultural exchange. The degree and nature of those interminglings can only be speculated on except for the periods around the time of the European invasion.

Unconsciously, the first Europeans brought enormously significant change in the form of diseases previously unknown and consequently devastating to Native Americans. Traditional healing practices failed and led directly to spiritual disillusionment along with demographic disaster. Tribes afflicted with smallpox epidemics sometimes lost as much as 90 percent of their populations; the remnants often joined surviving tribes. Europeans benefited from the new living spaces these population losses provided.

European and Euro-American trade goods, especially furs, made available to Native Americans in commercial dealings wrought cultural changes of all kinds. Firearms were so obviously potent weapons to the many war-oriented tribes that they were widely coveted by Indians. They came to replace the bow and arrow just as the tomahawks manufactured by the white man gradually replaced the Indians' war clubs. Warriors adopted these weapons easily. The acculturative aspect of these replacements would have been minimal except that the Indians became more dependent on the white man for weapons. Indian trade rifles were designed to entice the eye but required frequent repair. As the only gunsmiths existed inside the Euro-American community, tribes became necessarily tied to the newcomers. Often treaties would promise the services of a gunsmith for signatory tribes, an indication of the Indians' desire to maintain their muskets and rifles.

The spiritual belief system that guided each Indian group through ritual and ceremony was also vitally affected by European contact. Astonishment and dismay at the invaders' military successes caused many

"Indian team hauling 60 miles to market the 1,100 bushels of wheat raised by the school. It brought four cents more than wheat raised by white farmers near by and was sold for seed." Seger Colony, Oklahoma Territory, 1900. *Courtesy National Archives.*

Native Americans to seek new ways to hold their tribal universes together. Not uncommonly, they nominally accepted Christianity and often incorporated its teachings in the observance of traditional ways not always appreciated by missionaries. Once forced into reservation life, which in itself was sometimes alienating and dispiriting, some tribes readily accepted the promises and prophecies of men offering relief. The GHOST DANCE movement of the 1890s was only one of several religious expressions of discontent with changed circumstances and hope for a revitalization of the old ways. Often individual Indians adopted multiple spiritual beliefs: belonging to a Christian denomination, attending a road man's peyote meetings, and observing parts of their tribal customs.

Occasionally, a traditional ritual was so integral to the life of a tribe that the people would go to great lengths to continue its observance. Before the Osage Indians were moved from their homes in Missouri to a reservation in Kansas and later, in the early 1870s, to the Indian Territory, they practiced an ancient war mourning ceremony. It stipulated four full days of lamentations for a dead warrior after which a war party would ride out of camp to take the scalp of an old enemy—a Cherokee, a Pawnee, or perhaps an Arapaho. The government agent for the Osage Indians ordered an end to the scalping part of the ceremony as it stirred up revenge raids against the Osage people, who would then naturally organize retribution. Desperate to claim the scalp needed to complete the mourning ritual, the Osage tribe would hire a man from a neighboring tribe to hide out in a designated spot and allow a "war party" to "scalp" him, symbolically by cutting off his hair. Volunteers for this duty grew scarce because the Osages tended to get carried away in cutting the hair. The Osage "war party" was then reduced to visiting farms in Kansas to buy the long tresses of a farm wife to symbolize a captured scalp.

Much attention has been given by scholars to the U.S. government's "civilization" program in which Indians were to be acculturated to the white man's ways. Essentially the concept was simple: remove all vestiges of tribal life to produce an English-speaking, God-fearing, hard-working, patriotic farmer who wore "citizen's clothes" rather than breechcloth and blanket. Government agents, agency farmers, missionaries, and educators combined efforts to effect these changes. During the last part of the nineteenth century, tribalism itself was attacked as the communal land bases of many tribes were divided into individual land holdings, or allotments.

Many tribes resisted these attempts at forced acculturation. Children of school age were hidden from truant officers. Forbidden ceremonies were carried on in private. Traditional forms of governance were continued beneath a facade of the white man's majority rule. Some Native Americans accepted parts of the acculturation and "Indianized" them to fit old patterns; others embraced as much as they could, believing it the wave of the future. A few were adamantly opposed to any deviation from the traditional and expressed disapproval whenever possible. Upon returning home, one boarding-school student announced to his relatives as he exchanged his school uniform for tribal dress: "It took Father Schoenmakers fifteen years to make a white man out of me, and it will take just fifteen minutes to make an Osage out of myself."

Indian people continued to cling to their traditions and modify their ceremonies to meet the demands of a changing world. They believe that they remain intrinsically Native American regardless of adaptations. They believe that geographic relocation, government policy, altered custom, mixed blood, and the majority culture's attitudes—be they hostile, romantic, or paternalistic—cannot deny the persistence of their several cultures.

—*Terry P. Wilson*

SEE ALSO: Dawes Act; U.S. Indian Policy: Civilization Programs

SUGGESTED READING:

Crosby, Alfred W., Jr. *The Columbian Exchange: Biological and Cultural Consequences of 1492.* Westport, Conn. 1972.

Prucha, Francis Paul, ed. *Americanizing the American Indians: Writings by the "Friends of the Indian," 1880–1900.* Cambridge, Mass., 1973.
———. *The Great Father: The United States Government and the American Indians.* Lincoln, Nebr., 1984.
Spicer, Edward H. "Persistent Cultural Systems." *Science* 174 (1971): 795–800.
Thornton, Russell. *American Indian Holocaust and Survival: A Population History since 1492.* Norman, Okla., 1987.

NATIVE AMERICAN LEDGER DRAWING

Ledger drawing maintained the Native American tradition of storytelling through art, yet it continued an art form in a medium influenced by Indians' contacts with Anglo-Americans. Traditional forms of Native American art used large animal skins as canvases on which were portrayed detailed stories. Often these canvases contained hundreds of images including scenes of war, hunts, ceremonies and rituals, and other incidents of traditional life. The drawings portrayed either a single event in an individual's life or sometimes one person's entire life. Around 1860, Plains Indians, particularly the Sioux peoples, began using crayon and ink on paper in small ledgers they had received from white traders. These ledgers replaced the scarce supply of animal hides caused by the Anglo-Americans' extermination hunts.

Because of the small size of the ledgers, the stories of ledger drawings were not as fully developed as those found on animal skins. In place of several scenes detailing one life, an entire book would be filled with individual scenes to tell a chronological story, a biography in art. This reduction to single-scene composition caused a stylistic change. The artists supplied greater detail in the ledger drawings by adding facial features, frontal sketches of animals, and spatial depth through overlapping features and horizons. The portability of the ledgers and the refinements in their images created a market for the art form among white people. At the same time, Indian artists began signing their works, just as contemporary Anglo artists did. This practice gave celebrity to some accomplished artists such Oglala Sioux artist Amos Bad Heart Bull, Kiowa artist Silverhorn, and Cheyenne artist Howling Wolf. As the precontact life of the Plains Indians gave way to military defeat, reservation confinement, and near cultural genocide, however, the ledger-art tradition faded in the early twentieth century. Quite simply, Indian artists felt that there was no glory worth recording.

—*Kurt Edward Kemper*

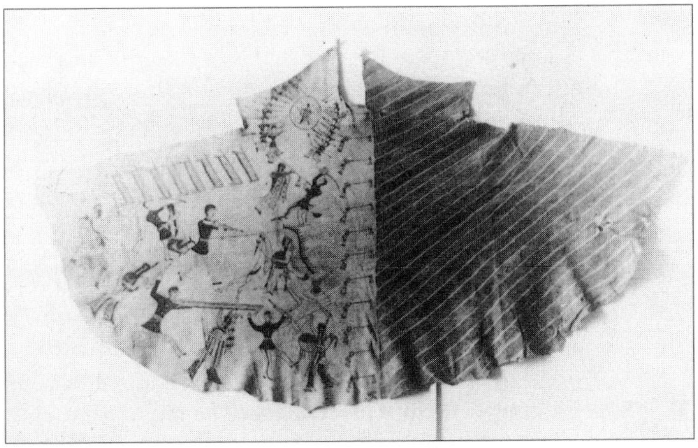

Ledger paintings continued a tradition of recording significant events and biographies of individuals on large canvasses of animal skins. The images that decorate this tepee depict the battles between Kiowa Indians and the U.S. Army. *Courtesy National Archives.*

SEE ALSO: Native American Peoples: Peoples of the Great Plains

SUGGESTED READING:

Feest, Christian. *Native Arts of North America.* New York, 1980.
Szabo, Joyce. *Howling Wolf and the History of Ledger Art.* Albuquerque, N. Mex., 1994.

NATIVE AMERICAN PEOPLES

PRE-COLUMBIAN PEOPLES

Archaeologists and other scholars disagree on much about the pre-Columbian peoples of North America. Much speculation and several theories have been advanced to explain the scant archaeological record of the ancestors to those Europeans came to call "Indians." Most likely the Indians migrated from Asia toward the rising sun in three great waves. The first were the Paleo-Indians, who probably passed through Beringia at least fourteen thousand years ago, perhaps as many as fifty thousand, when glaciers had lowered the sea levels. They moved across much of present-day Canada and the United States, some continuing a twenty-five-hundred-year journey ultimately to establish settlements in South America as well. Some believe their culture was neolithic, and that they used stones they found in nature (or perhaps crudely worked) as tools and weapons before, a bit later, developing the fluted points Euro-Americans call "arrowheads" or "spearheads." The Paleo-Indians were most likely followed by a second wave of migration around ten thousand years ago by a people who chipped and ground their tools and ornaments using stones or other tools and employed a spear-thrower. Perhaps these were the ancestors of the Northwest Coast and Athapascan peoples of North America. Almost at the same time came a third wave of migrants, the forbears of the Inuits, or Eskimos, and Aleuts who settled along the coasts of Alaska and the chain of islands today known, appropriately enough, as the Aleutians.

By the time the Paleo-Indians began to arrive in the new lands, the great masses of glacial ice that had allowed them to set out on their long trek had melted, leaving in their wake rivers and lakes of all sizes. In North America, even some of those areas that today are deserts were then swamps or grasslands. Plant life abounded, game was abundant, and life was no doubt comparatively grand given where they had started. The good climate and lavish food supply led the Indians to multiply rapidly, and by one thousand years ago, settlements existed all across North America. The Paleo-Indians hunted big game—deer, elk, and many species now extinct, such as giant beavers and buffaloes, camels, and the famous woolly mammoths. Some of the Indians were nomads, others more sedentary, depending on how far the game they hunted ranged. Large grazing herds roamed the vast plains, and the hunters followed them. But in the thickly forested land toward the Atlantic, a stable population of smaller game allowed hunters and their families to establish more or less permanent homes.

The Clovis people were among the most successful of the hunters. They produced excellent fluted flint points that easily pierced the hides of the great North American mammals. The Clovis people also used the *atlatl,* or "spear-thrower," a device made up of a short shaft with a hook at the end that held the butt of the spear, thus lengthening and strengthening the arm of the hunter and improving the accuracy, the speed, and the power of every toss. Nevertheless, it took teams to bring down the mammoths and other big game. From the start, the big prey served as more than food—their hides became garments and tent walls; their bones were used as tools, weapons, and jewelry. Around fifty-five hundred years ago, bows and arrows appeared, revolutionizing hunting. Whether the new technology was brought over in a new wave of migration or was invented by indigenous hunters remains a subject of debate, but it arrived none too soon since by at least 5000 B.C. the great beasts had all been hunted to extinction, and better weapons were sorely needed for the swifter, smaller game. As the climate grew gradually warmer, a wealth of new marine life appeared offshore, and the Indians took to fishing in stretched-hide and birch-bark canoes on sea as well as on lakes and rivers. The warmer weather meant also that they could expand their source of food to a greater variety of berries, seeds, fruits, and nuts and move now here, now there according to the harvest seasons of the wild plants.

As the Paleo-Indian period drew to a close, the Cochise people in southeastern Arizona were gathering and foraging for seeds and nuts, which they began to grind on millstones to produce something not unlike flour. They also honed their weaving skills and made rude pottery. Near Bat Cave, in modern-day New Mexico, at least one group related to the Cochise people had begun to grow corn, which they either domesticated themselves by developing a hybrid grain out of wild grass or borrowed from another tribe farther south for their own gardens. At about the same time, another culture—later called the Eastern Woodlands people—spread eastward from present-day Missouri into Kentucky, south to Alabama and Florida, and north to New England and southern Canada. During this period, too, a group of metalworkers, belonging to what is now called the Old Copper culture, cropped up in the Great Lakes region of Wisconsin; they traded their copper goods as far south as Florida and as far east as New York.

All of these people, and others, began settling down and, around 1000 B.C., took to residing in the same location and became rudimentary farmers. This new agricultural life style created permanent communities in which relatively large numbers of people lived in substantial shelters. Villages, towns, even cities emerged; regional trade flourished; pottery came into use; tobacco was cultivated; smoking pipes were produced; ceremonies were developed along with religious objects and implements; and several of the new agricultural peoples began constructing burial mounds. The oldest were built along the Atlantic Coast from Florida to South Carolina. On an island off the coast of Georgia appeared ring-shaped structures that looked suspiciously like those one might find down in Colombia, meaning, perhaps, that the Indians were taking long boat trips up the coast as early as 2400 B.C. The Adena, who built mounds one-quarter mile long in the twisting shape of a snake, lived in the Ohio Valley from about 1000 B.C. to 200 A.D., and at Indian Knoll, Kentucky, there were mounds dating back to 3000 B.C.

The peoples of this elaborate society, gradually spreading throughout the valley of the Ohio, down to the Gulf of Mexico, up to Wisconsin, and from New York in the East to Kansas in the West, are generally called the Mound Builders, after their burial mounds and earthwork systems, and their culture is often referred to as the Hopewell, after an archaeological site in southern Ohio. The period of greatest development for the Hopewell culture was between 400 B.C. and 400 A.D. Their mounds should not be confused with the structures that were built much later by probable descendants of these people along the Mississippi River. These "temple mounds," flat-topped pyramids—the most spectacular of which were found at a site near Cahokia, Illinois—resembled the great Meso-American pyramids, especially those of the Mayas. Dating from the tenth century and later, the "temple mounds" may well have been built by colonizers pushed north by the great Toltec civilization or other invaders.

And it was in the south, in Meso-America—modern-day Mexico and Central America—that some have speculated lay the genesis of the agricultural revolution. For there, in the lowlands around the modern city of Veracruz and in the lowlands sheltered by the hills around Lake Texcoco, which is now oversprawled by Mexico City, sprang up highly complex ceremonial societies, great civilizations, which—to quote historian Edwin F. Walker—"developed an agriculture far above that of any European country" of their day.

It was a people called the Olmecs who settled in the Veracruz area, and by about three thousand years ago, they had established a lively, far-reaching, and sophisticated trade in jade and obsidian. The jade was prized for its assumed spiritual qualities and apparently used in worship. The obsidian was also used in decorative and perhaps religious objects, but even more importantly, it was a valued material for the manufacture of razor-sharp and steel-hard pointed weapons. Propelled by agriculture and commerce, the Olmec civilization built tremendous and elaborate buildings, almost certainly using a form of slave—or forced—labor. As their numbers swelled and their principal city of Teotihuacan grew, the Olmecs developed large-scale agricultural techniques, including terracing and irrigation, technologies entirely unknown in Europe. As for the sacred city of Teotihuacan, the center of the people's religion, nothing like it existed in the Old World. About 300 A.D., the city harbored a population of some 50,000. Paris had 10,000, and London's population had yet to be established. At its height, about 650 A.D., Teotihuacan was populated by more than 125,000.

During this same period, in the Yucatan, the civilization of the Mayas grew and prospered, though not as spectacularly as that of the Olmecs. However, in addition to various artifacts, they created a system of hieroglyphics and their famous calendar, which, based on extraordinarily precise astronomical observations, was far more accurate than the Gregorian calendar in use today.

The civilizations of Meso-America flourished while that of Rome rose and fell and the Dark Ages engulfed the Old World. What the Meso-Americans failed to develop, however, was an alphabetical language and significant labor-saving technologies based on the wheel. Likely, these theocratic cultures were built on the backs of slaves, and in the presence of abundant human labor, great works were accomplished, but technology lagged. Even domestic animals were largely unknown.

During the eighth century A.D., some unknown cataclysm swept Meso-America. Teotihuacan was abandoned by mid-century, and the Mayan cities were similarly abandoned during the next century and a half. Most scholars believe that this abandonment was related to an invasion from the north by a people called the Toltecs, possibly allied with the Otomi, who overran Teotihuacan—or what was left of it—and, by the tenth century, came to dominate the Mayas as well. The Toltecs, whose very name means *artificer,* were great architects, who created a new, even mightier empire in the Mayan and Olmec regions as well as in the Texcoco area. Tradition also holds that it was the Toltecs who introduced human sacrifice on a large scale in a religion based on two eternally warring gods: Tezcatlipoca—the black Lord of the Sky, the North, and the Night—and Quetzalcoatl—the white birdlike deity of the Morning Star. The Aztecs, who later displaced the Toltecs and built their new capital of Tenochtitlan in Texcoco, clung even more fiercely to the religion centered around these two gods.

The Toltecs developed a far-reaching commercial culture more elaborate than that of the Olmecs. The Toltecs exported metalwork, salt, rubber, cacao, fabric, paints, dyes, and a host of other goods. Some of this commerce was likely carried north into present-day New Mexico and Arizona, and, although the issue is subject to scholarly dispute, it is also likely that this period, beginning roughly in 700 A.D., saw the colonization of the U.S. Southwest and, up the Mississippi, colonization into the Ohio and Great Lakes region. Many scholars believe that colonizers also pushed eastward into Alabama, Georgia, and Florida, as well as up the Appalachian chain into the Carolinas. Some of the colonizers may have been the Toltecs themselves; some may have been Olmecs and others who, displaced by the Toltecs, fled northward. Natchez Indian traditions weave a myth of origin that suggests the latter. The Toltec influence also spread south into South America.

It is likely, then, that the Toltecs were the first significant invaders not of the Western Hemisphere but in the Western Hemisphere, and what must be recognized is that much of what we think of as the lands of the American Indian were, in fact, the continent's earliest zones of percolating influence, zones of advancing colonization, and zones of interaction between the colonizers and the indigenous people already in place, the kind of areas that the sons and daughters of European colonizers would call for their own political reasons "frontiers."

Who were these indigenous people? Navajo tradition called them the Anasazi, "the ancient ones," a term that modern scholars apply to the Basket Maker-Pueblo continuum of Native American civilization in New Mexico and northern Arizona. But these "ancient ones" themselves were preceded by two earlier cultures, the Mogollon and the Hohokam. The Mogollon emerged around 100 B.C. in the southern uplands along the present-day border of New Mexico and Arizona. An agricultural people who lived in pithouse villages, they produced distinctive ceramics and may have developed from an even more ancient people, the Cochise culture, whose origins date back at least to 8000 B.C., when agriculture seems to have been introduced to the area.

The influence of the later Mogollon was broadcast into the deserts of southern Arizona, where it probably combined with cultural influences transmitted from Mexico to produce the Hohokam people—a Pima word meaning "those who have vanished." Like the Olmecs and others in Meso-America, the Hohokam practiced advanced forms of agriculture and transformed the drainages of the Salt and Gila rivers by building a system of canals and irrigation works.

The Anasazi seem to have developed from the Mogollon and the Hohokam. Since the earliest evidence of this people are elaborate woven baskets preserved in dry caves, the early Anasazi—or, perhaps, immediate precursors of the Anasazi proper—are called the Basket Makers. Around 700 to 900 A.D., the Basket Makers began a transition from the cave and pit house to multiroom masonry structures above ground and, even more characteristically, apartmentlike cliff dwellings dubbed by the Spanish "pueblos." It is this period, an era of great turmoil in Meso-America, that may well have coincided with the beginnings either of an invasion or a colonization effort from Mexico, perhaps by the Toltecs or peoples driven northward by them.

The transition to life above ground promoted the development of an increasingly complex agricultural society between 800 and 1100 A.D., which scholars call the beginning of the Classic or Great Pueblo Period. During the eleventh through the thirteenth centuries, farming methods became steadily more sophisticated, employing elaborate and effective irrigation systems, and market culture developed, along with religion and ceremony associated with agriculture and weather control. Three great Pueblo population centers grew up during these years, one at Mesa Verde, Colorado; another at Chaco Canyon, New Mexico; and the third at Kayenta, Arizona. Chaco Canyon, in particular, is rich with fascinating ruins that often suggest the Meso-American roots of the area's inhabitants.

At the apogee of the Classic period, between 1276 and 1299, natural disaster—apparently a severe drought combined with an epidemic of infectious diarrhea—and attacks by other, probably nomadic, tribes brought a sudden decline to the three centers of Pueblo population. Some of the Pueblo Indians fled south, establishing new towns from which the modern Zuni and Hopi cultures developed. Others migrated east to the Pajaritop Plateau and the valleys of the Rio Grande and its tributaries. These groups seem to have rebuilt their civilizations rapidly; for when the conquistadors encountered them in 1581, they were highly impressed by the architecture, agriculture, crafts, and what one Spaniard described as the "very remarkable . . . neatness . . . they observe in everything."

By the time the fourth great migration to the North American continent began in 1492, the land was inhabited by a variety of natives with cultures far more numerous and diverse than those of the so-called European Old World. As late as the start of the sixteenth century, between five hundred and one thousand distinct and mutually unintelligible languages were spoken in North America. In Central and South America, the languages likely numbered closer to two thousand.

—*Charles Phillips and Alan Axelrod*

SEE ALSO: Archaeology

SUGGESTED READING:

Ceram, C. W. *Gods, Graves, and Scholars: The Story of Archeology.* New York, 1952.

Cordell, Linda S. *Prehistory of the Southwest.* Orlando, Fla., 1984.

Cressman, L. S. *Prehistory of the Far West: Homes of the Vanquished Peoples.* Salt Lake City, 1977.

Fitzhugh, William W., and Aron Crowell, eds. *Crossroads of Continents: Cultures of Siberia and Alaska.* Washington, D.C., 1988.

Frazier, Kendrick. *People of Chaco: A Canyon and Its Culture.* New York, 1986.

Haury, Emil W. *The Hohokam, Desert Farmers and Craftsmen: Excavations at Snakestown, 1964–1965.* Tucson, Ariz., 1976.

Jennings, Francis. *The Founders of America: How the Indians Discovered the Land, Pioneered in It, and Created Great Classical Civilizations; How They Were Plunged into a Dark Age by Invasion and Conquest; and How They Are Now Reviving.* New York, 1993.

Josephy, Alvin M. *The Indian Heritage of America.* New York, 1968.

———. *America in 1492: The World of the Indian Peoples before the Arrival of Columbus.* New York, 1993.

Kroeber, A. L. *Cultural and Natural Areas of Native North America.* Berkeley, Calif., 1939.

PEOPLES OF ALASKA

Alaska was the original point of entry for Native Americans into the Western Hemisphere from Asia. Today, it is home to a variety of native peoples. About 23,000 years ago, the last glaciation exposed a land bridge linking Siberia and Alaska. The bridge lasted until about 14,000 years ago. Some disputed archaeological evidence points to human presence in Alaska 20,000 to 25,000 years ago or earlier. Other evidence points to occupation around 11,700 years ago. Cultural remains in Alaska that appear to be ancestral to the Na-Dene (interior Athapascans and Northwest Coast Indians) date to around 9,000 years ago. Some archaeological evidence suggests the arrival of the ancestors of the Aleut-Eskimo peoples at about the same time or a little later.

Environment and distribution

Except for the temperate coastal strip of southeastern Alaska, the Northwest Coast, Alaska has an arctic to subarctic climate. The nine-hundred-mile-long Aleutian chain—home to native Aleuts—is characteristically foggy, damp, windy, and rich with maritime resources. Coastal Alaska is tundra, with little vegetation and cold winters, but with abundant food. This region is home to the coastal Eskimos. There are also some inland caribou-hunting Eskimos (Nunamiuts) north of the Brooks Range. Interior Alaska south of the tree line is taiga—the northern boreal evergreen forest—with long, cold winters and brief, hot summers. Here, food resources are fewer, and populations are smaller. This is the territory of the Athapascan Indians of the subarctic forests. The Indians of the Northwest Coast (southeastern Alaska) lived in an area possessing rich stores of sea mammals and salmon.

The native peoples of Alaska shared a number of cultural traits. Groups tended to be mobile—interior and northern groups more so than others—shifting to exploit varied resources at different times of the year. Most depended on combinations of land or sea-mammal hunting, together with ocean or river fishing. Shared features included the use of tailored skin clothing, skin or bark tents, semisubterranean dwellings, skin- or bark-covered boats, fish traps and weirs, or fish dams, for salmon, and the fence and game surround in hunting caribou. The Aleuts and Eskimos used the spear-thrower, while the Indians used the bow and arrow. With the exception of groups on the Northwest Coast, all had relatively simple social and political structures. Their religious beliefs were based on a world inhabited by spirits and the need to placate them. All groups had shamans—religious specialists who treated illness and dealt with the supernatural. Where known, the bear was often sacred. Most groups engaged in occasional feuds and warfare. All areas of Alaska had well-established trade networks, with periodic trade fairs along the coasts and at strategic inland locations.

The Aleuts

The Aleuts split from a common Aleut-Eskimo stock about 4,000 years ago and adapted to life on the coast. They may have numbered 15,000 or more at the time of white contact. The Aleuts lived in large,

A Knik chief and his family posed for photographer J. G. Kaiser in Anchorage, Alaska, ca. 1910. *Courtesy National Archives.*

In 1935, Stanley Morgan photographed an elderly Eskimo woman in front of her summer tent, Point Barrow, Alaska. *Courtesy National Archives.*

communal houses in permanent villages. They used skin kayaks for hunting and larger open boats for travel. They exploited all the resources available, including sea mammals, birds, shellfish, and fish. They also used poison-tipped spears to hunt whales and employed nets and weirs in fishing. In some areas, they hunted caribou. Aleut social organization was simple, and leadership was informal. Social rankings included nobles, commoners, and slaves. They traced their kinship through both mothers and fathers and placed equal importance on both.

The Eskimos

Derived from inland hunting peoples, by 2000 B.C., the Eskimos had a complex culture emphasizing land and sea-mammal hunting and fishing. By 1000 B.C., all essential aspects of Eskimo culture were present, including pottery, oil lamps, permanent houses, and whaling. The Eskimo language has several dialects, with a western and southern Yuit population and a more northerly Inuit one. At the time of white contact, the Eskimos in Alaska numbered 26,000 to 30,000.

In western and southern Alaska, the Eskimos occupied the major rivers, where their culture was similar to the Athapascans. In winter, Eskimos in the more northern areas fished through the ice and hunted seals at breathing holes. More southerly groups hunted in open water much of the year. In summer, the Eskimos used skin-covered kayaks to hunt seal, walrus, and whales. They used the larger umiaks for travel and, in some areas, for whaling. Weapons included harpoons, three-pronged leisters, and nets. In some areas, the Eskimos also caught salmon in stone weirs and hunted caribou. Archaeological evidence indicates that the Eskimos used dog sleds for travel quite early. The Eskimos normally moved between winter villages and other locations for fishing and hunting. Villages consisted of rectangular family dwellings, with a larger *kazigi,* or ceremonial men's house. During periods of travel, the Eskimos used skin tents. Community size ranged from 50 to 300 individuals or more, with informal leadership. Although Eskimos traced kinship through both parents, they emphasized the line descended through the father. Eskimo religious life stressed belief in a world of spirits. The shaman and observation of taboos were important. The southern

An Eskimo spear- and lance-maker displays his wares for the camera, 1935. Point Barrow, Alaska. Photograph by Stanley Morgan. *Courtesy National Archives.*

Eskimos also observed an annual cycle of ceremonies and ritual feasts.

Athapascans of the interior

The thinly distributed Athapascan Indians consisted of groups speaking different dialects, and at white contact totaled perhaps 10,000 to 12,000. Groups included the Tanana, Tanaina, Ingalik, Kolchan, Kutchin, Han, Koyukon, and Ahtna. The Athapascans appear to have separated from the Northwest Coast groups some 5,000 to 9,000 years ago. Athapascan material culture included tailored skin clothing, the bow, snowshoes, toboggans, bark-covered canoes, and snares and fish weirs. Caribou hunting involved the use of fences and surrounds. Dwellings included skin and bark tents, and semisubterranean dwellings. The Athapascans were more nomadic than coastal groups. From spring through fall, they engaged in the pursuit of caribou and collection of salmon. They hunted waterfowl in the fall months and pursued moose and hares all year. Late winter and spring were often times of hunger. Groups closer to the coast, with heavy salmon runs, were more sedentary. Residential groups consisted of bands of 50 to 100 members, usually related to several other bands in the same region. Individuals belonged to one of three matrilineal clans, and groups practiced exogamy (marrying outside their mothers' clans). Leadership was informal, most often evident in cooperative efforts during caribou and salmon migrations. Religious life stressed control of animal and nature spirits; shamans were important.

Top: The members of an Eskimo dance orchestra used drumheads made from whale stomachs. Point Barrow, Alaska. Photograph by Stanley Morgan. *Courtesy National Archives.*

Bottom: Eskimos of Point Barrow, Alaska, with a boat made of skin—called a *umiak*. Photograph by Stanley Morgan. *Courtesy National Archives.*

The Indians of the Northwest Coast

The major groups of natives in the southeastern Alaska included the Eyak, Tlingit, and northern Haida. These Indians lived in a temperate rain forest with abundant resources. They totaled 10,000 to 12,000 at the time of white contact. Earliest signs of occupation date about 7,000 to 8,000 years ago.

The Northwest Coast Indians developed a rich material culture and complex social life. Prolific salmon runs provided an abundant harvest, which people preserved for later use. The Indians used canoes to hunt sea mammals and caught a wide variety of fish. The Tlingit in the north also hunted caribou. The Northwest Coast groups were superb woodworkers who constructed gabled plank houses, and large dugout cedar canoes. In their villages, they erected totem poles for commemoration and status. Clothing was minimal in the milder climate, although they wove blankets for ceremonial use and made body armor of slats

Two women of the Tlingit tribe with several children, photographed by the Miles brothers, near the Kotsina River, Alaska, 1902. *Courtesy National Archives.*

or hides for warfare. Ranked matrilineal kin groups existed. Men inherited property from their mother's brother. The potlatch, an elaborate gift-giving feast, validated status and inheritance. Religious life focused on animal spirits, particularly in connection with the annual salmon migrations. The concept of a personal protective or guardian spirit—often revealed in a vision quest or dream—was widespread. This was particularly true of shamans, who were often powerful individuals.

Recent history

While Russian trade goods reached Alaska by the late 1600s, the discovery of Alaska by VITUS BERING in 1741 began the period of sustained white contact. During the early Russian occupation, the fur trade, particularly along the southern coast, was important. Beginning in 1841, commercial whaling by Americans in the Bering Sea resulted in extensive contact with Eskimos. Missionary efforts started in 1794 and continued after the United States purchased Alaska in 1867. Together with the gold rushes starting in the late 1800s, missions and American occupation led to rapid social and cultural change. Americans introduced reindeer herding along the coast in the 1890s, but it was largely unsuccessful. Change proceeded rapidly after World War II and the completion of the Alaskan Highway.

Beginning in the 1830s with virulent smallpox epidemics and continuing into the early twentieth century, disease caused major population declines. From the late 1880s to the 1950s, Christian missions and schools became widespread, health care improved, and native populations grew rapidly. The 1990 census listed the total number of Eskimo, Aleuts, and Indians in Alaska at 85,698. Perhaps 70 percent reside in 178 native communities. Although some still hunt, fish, and trap, many also seek seasonal employment. Most natives do not have full-time jobs, and public assistance is a significant source of income.

In 1967, increased political awareness led to the establishment of the Alaska Federation of Natives, and twelve native corporations pressed aboriginal land claims. In 1971, the Alaska Land Claims Settlement Act allotted forty million acres and more than $962 million to these regional corporations, which use these resources for development and investment in commercial enterprises. By 1993, these efforts had mixed success.

—*Edward H. Hosley*

SUGGESTED READING:

Fagan, Brian M. *The Great Journey: The Peopling of Ancient America.* New York, 1987.

Greenberg, Joseph H., Christy G. Turner, II, and Stephen L. Zegura. "The Settlement of the Americas: A Comparison of the Linguistic, Dental, and Genetic Evidence." *Current Anthropology* 27 (1986): 477–497.

Helm, June, ed. *Handbook of North American Indians, Vol. 6: Subarctic.* Washington, D.C., 1981 (see also *Vol. 5: Arctic* and *Vol. 7: Northwest Coast).*

Van Stone, James W. *Athapascan Adaptations: Hunters and Fishermen of the Subarctic Forests.* Chicago, 1974.

———. *Point Hope: An Eskimo Village in Transition.* Seattle, Wash., 1962.

PEOPLES OF CALIFORNIA

California Indians are remarkably diverse and numerous. Before the arrival of Europeans, there were more than 300,000 people living in present-day California, making it one of the most populated native areas north of the valley of Mexico. More than one hundred tribes, practicing many life ways and speaking scores of languages, were scattered from the dense rain forests of the north to the arid deserts of the south. Anthropologists have identified six cultural areas throughout the state: northwest, northeast, central, Great Basin, southern, and Colorado River. Within these broad geographical regions, Indians followed similar ways of life. In the northwest part of California, the Yuroks, Karoks, Hupas, and other tribes fished for salmon, hunted, and gathered acorns and other plant products. They lived in long-established villages and built plank houses. Shrewd traders, these Indians worked to accumulate wealth that was measured in dentalium shell beads and other precious items. In northeastern California, which was much drier and had less vegetation than the northwestern part, the Pit River and Modoc Indians hunted and gathered seeds and roots and periodically moved their camps to take advantage of seasonally available resources. The central California Indians hunted, fished, and gathered acorns that grew in abundance throughout the state. The central region was wetter and richer than the northeastern region, and the Indians were more sedentary. Their communities consisted of small round houses built of local materials, a large round house for meetings and rituals, and sweat lodges. The Miwoks, Nisenans, Yokuts, and Patwins were among the tribes that lived in the central area. The southern California tribes included the Chumashes, Cahiullas, Diegueños, and others. Near the ocean, these people relied on fish, mollusks, and sea mammals for food, as well as plant products and the ubiquitous acorn. In the interior deserts, they ate rabbits, mountain sheep, and other small animals. The Colorado River tribes—Yumas, Halchidomas, and Mojaves—were the only California Indians who customarily farmed before the arrival of Europeans. They made use of the annual floods of the Colorado River to irrigate their fields of beans and maize. The Indians of the Great Basin, such as the Chemehuevis and Washos, lived in the blistering deserts east of the Sierra Nevada. They followed a seasonal round that enabled them to hunt and gather animals and plants as they became available in the sparse environment. All of these peoples had deeply held religious beliefs, which they expressed in rituals and stories.

California Indians first encountered Europeans in the sixteenth century when Spanish maritime expeditions sailed up the Pacific Coast from Mexico. Under Spain's aegis, Catholic missionaries founded missions in Baja California (now part of Mexico), but no permanent Spanish settlements were made in the present-day state of California until 1769 when Franciscan

A Modoc woman, Winema or Tobey Riddle, her husband, an agent, and four other Modoc women posed for photographer Eadweard Muybridge, 1873. *Courtesy National Archives.*

missionaries under the direction of JUNÍPERO SERRA established a few missions along the coast. Eventually there were twenty-one missions located from San Diego to just north of San Francisco Bay. In theory, the missions were intended to convert Indians to Catholicism and to educate them in European language, culture, and skills so that they would become useful members of Spanish colonial society. From the Spanish perspective, the missions had humane goals, but the practical results for the Indians were dire.

Franciscans gathered thousands of Indians into these large institutions, which raised cattle and agricultural crops on lands that Indians formerly had depended on for sustenance. Simultaneously, the missions became nurseries for diseases that Indians had not been previously exposed to, and thousands of them perished. Between 1769 and 1848, the Indian population fell from about 300,000 to perhaps 175,000. Not surprisingly, many Indians rejected the missions and resisted Spanish authority. There were intermittent revolts within the missions and frequent attacks from without. Often these offensives took the form of small-scale livestock raids, but there were general uprisings as well. In 1781, Quechan Indians killed priests, soldiers, and settlers and forced the Franciscans to abandon two missions on the Colorado River. In 1824, Indians rebelled at the missions near Santa Barbara, fortified one, and held it until troops dislodged them. While population decline, dispossession, and resistance were important factors in the story of the Mission Indians, many Indians voluntarily entered the missions and were loyal to the priests who instructed them.

Photographer Timothy H. O'Sullivan took an image of two Mojave braves while on one of his Western expeditions, 1871. *Courtesy National Archives.*

After Mexico established its independence from Spain, the new government embarked on a program of dismantling the missions. Liberal lawmakers intended that Indians would receive individual parcels from mission holdings, but California rancheros quickly appropriated those lands for themselves. Most Indians either worked on private ranches or moved away from the settled areas.

In the meantime, Indians in the interior and northern parts of California had remained free of permanent non-Indian settlements, although American fur traders and those from the British-owned HUDSON'S BAY COMPANY began to exploit the region in the late 1820s. In the early 1840s, American settlers began to gather around Sutter's Fort in the Sacramento Valley. As their Mexican counterparts had done, the American ranchers, including JOHN AUGUST SUTTER, relied on Indian labor. When the UNITED STATES–MEXICAN WAR erupted, these men sided with the United States, and some of their Indian employees fought with U.S. forces against Mexican Californians. At the end of the war, California became a part of the United States.

In 1848, a gold strike on the American River set off a worldwide rush that brought hundreds of thousands of newcomers to California. The immigration proved to be a disaster for the Indians; miners rapidly dispersed throughout the state, expropriated Indian land, and killed Indians at will. By 1860, only about 30,000 Indians remained in

Salvadora Valensuelo, a Mission woman, making lace at Pala Mission, California, 1936. Photograph by Walter D. Wilcox. *Courtesy National Archives.*

California. The survivors faced difficult choices. In 1851 and 1852, federal agents negotiated eighteen treaties that provided for Indian reservations throughout the state. However, the U.S. Senate refused to ratify the treaties, and the reservations were not established. Instead, in the 1850s, the government established on federal land a few temporary Indian reservations, which could be abandoned whenever it was expedient. These reserves were inadequate to maintain the Indian population. The federal government abandoned most of the reservations, leaving only the Round Valley, Hoopa Valley, and Tule River reservations to serve the Indian population. Eventually, the government gave these reservations permanent status. Most Indians, however, lived elsewhere, either working for farmers and ranchers or eking out a precarious existence on isolated and marginal lands that were not claimed by whites.

The poor conditions of California Indian life attracted the attention of reformers such as HELEN HUNT JACKSON, CHARLES FLETCHER LUMMIS, and Charles Kelsey, who lobbied Congress to obtain land for Indians. In the 1870s and 1890s, the federal government set aside about a dozen small reservations for southern California Indians. In the early twentieth century, Congress funded the purchase of land for northern California Indians so that there were more than one hundred small parcels reserved for Indians in addition to the three large reservations that were left from the gold-rush era. Yet, most California Indians remained poor, working-class people, who labored in the state's towns, forests, fields, and vineyards.

In the twentieth century, Indians began to work within the legal system to improve their conditions. They joined organizations—such as the Indian Board of Cooperation, Society for Northern California Indians, Mission Indian Federation, and the California Indian Brotherhood—fought school segregation, and sued to obtain citizenship rights. In 1944, after sixteen years of litigation, a federal court of claims awarded California Indians $17 million for the reservations that were called for by the treaties of 1851 and 1852 but never established. After the courts deducted the amount of money the federal government had spent on California Indian reservations, the Indians received only $150 each. The case covered only a fraction of the lands that Indians had lost. In 1946, Congress authorized American Indians to present claims before the Indian Claims Commission. After long, difficult, and contentious litigation, California Indians were awarded more than $29 million in 1964, which resulted in per capita payments of $668. While the California claim was being decided, the federal government embarked on a policy of terminating federal responsibility for reservations and turning them over to the Indians. In the 1950s, Indians on more than forty small reservations voted for termination, and the federal government withdrew health, welfare, and educational services and left the Indians to rely on the state government and their own resources. Whatever benefits the Indians may have expected from termination, they were worse off than they had been before.

In 1969, California became a focal point for Indian political activism when a group called Indians of All Tribes occupied Alcatraz Island for two years and made various demands of the federal government. While such events gained headlines, they failed to accomplish anything substantial for the state's Indians. More importantly, tribal councils systematically defended their rights in court. While Indians were not always successful in court, they managed to secure important civil, land, and water rights. Most Indians, however, do not reside on reservations, but in California's large cities, where most of them are part of the working-class and working-poor urban population. Since the 1960s, many California colleges and universities have established Indian studies programs to encourage Indian education and provide a source of information about Indians for all of the state's citizens.

—Albert L. Hurtado

SEE ALSO: United States Indian Policy

SUGGESTED READING:
Castillo, Edward D. "Twentieth Century Secular Movements." In *Handbook of North American Indians, Vol. 8: California*. Edited by Robert F. Heizer. Washington, D.C., 1978.
Heizer, Robert F. *The Natural World of the California Indians*. Berkeley, Calif., 1980.
Hurtado, Albert L. *Indian Survival on the California Frontier*. New Haven, Conn., 1988.
Phillips, George Harwood. *Chiefs and Challengers: Indian Resistance and Cooperation in Southern California*. Berkeley, Calif., 1975.
———. *The Enduring Struggle: Indians in California History*. San Francisco, 1981.
———. *Indians and Intruders in Central California, 1769–1849*. Norman, Okla., 1993.
Rawls, James L. *Indians of California: The Changing Image*. Norman, Okla., 1984.

PEOPLES OF THE GREAT BASIN

While the harsh environment of the Great Basin limited the complexity of social and political structures, Basin Indians had rich traditions that sustained them through the pressures of contact with Europeans and Americans. Their story is one of resiliency.

Aboriginal culture

The Great Basin is a natural area with distinctive features in its surface water (hydrography), its plant life (flora), and its physical geography (physiography). The hydrographic basin—consisting of most of present-day Nevada, western Utah, the southeastern corner of Oregon, and the southeastern corner of Idaho—is an area of interior drainage where rivers and streams drain into Ice Age or Pleistocene lakes rather than into the ocean. The term *Great Basin* also refers to the larger plateaus—the region between the Rocky Mountains on the east and the Pacific Coast mountains on the west and including the Columbia Plateau on the north and the Colorado Plateau on the south. The region between the mountain ranges has a semiarid to arid climate. The region's vegetation typically is sagebrush and piñon-juniper woodland, but the area also contains several eco-niches—from alpine in the high mountains rimming the Basin to hot and cold deserts in the low-lying regions. The flora regions affect the distribution of Native American populations in the Great Basin, whose numbers were estimated at about forty thousand in the sixteenth century.

Although there is dispute among ethnographers as to which groups belong in the Great Basin culture area, there are general agreements as to the common cultural and linguistic traits of the peoples. With the exception of the Washo (who speak Hokan but are included on the basis of historical links and material culture), Great Basin tribes spoke one of three branches of Numic languages—a division of the Uto-Aztecan language family—and practiced a hunting-and-gathering subsistence based on seasonal migrations.

The tribes living in the Great Basin had distinct historical territories that sometimes extended beyond the boundaries of the Great Basin itself. In the north-central region, across Idaho and the southwestern corner of Montana, lived the Northern Shoshones and Bannocks. Western Wyoming and northern Utah were the home of the Eastern Shoshones. The Ute Indians ranged across most of Colorado, from the Wyoming border to New Mexico and from near Kansas to Utah. Southern Paiute territory covered southeastern Utah, northwestern Arizona, southeastern Nevada, and southwestern California. The Kawaiisu Indians resided in eastern California. Farther north, spilling over into Nevada, were the Owens Valley Paiute and the Washo Indians. The Western Shoshones claimed the central part of the Great Basin, from eastern Nevada extending into California and from northwest Utah into the southeastern corner of Idaho. Finally, the Northern Paiutes lived in southeastern Oregon, western Nevada, and a corner of northwestern California.

Great Basin flora and fauna are diverse but not abundant. Tribes made use of a wide variety of resources. Women gathered roots, herbs, nuts, berries, seeds, and native fiber plants and used an assortment of poles, baskets, and hand stones to process them into food and medicine. Men netted birds, fish, and rabbits and hunted game animals (either communally or alone) by killing them with poisoned arrows or driving them into pits or under deadfalls. A man reputed to have spiritual power to summon and incapacitate animals directed communal hunts. Women processed the products of the hunt by roasting or drying meat and making clothing, shelters, and implements out of skins, bones, and sinews. Some Southern Paiutes and Western Utes grew corn and beans, and Owens Valley Paiutes cultivated tobacco.

The quest for food shaped the social structure of Great Basin peoples. Resources were scarce, and before the introduction of the horse, the environment could not support social groups larger than one to ten households. While some married couples preferred to live with the family of the wife, most newly married couples either established their own households or lived with relatives who most needed their labor. Families traced descent through both parents—there were no lineages or clans. Most marriages were monogamous, but polygamous unions occasionally occurred. Serial monogamy appears to have been common, and people often shifted residence groups from year to year.

Similarly, the environment influenced the political arrangements of Great Basin peoples. Native peoples in areas of relatively abundant resources, such as the Owens Valley Paiutes in eastern California and the Utes and Northern and Eastern Shoshones in the Rocky Mountain valleys, were organized into bands of several hundred people for several months of the year. In Owens Valley, families foraged individually in the winter and summer but lived as a community in the spring and fall. Similarly, the Utes and Northern and Eastern Shoshones gathered into camps during the summer when resources were plentiful. A headman directed band activities, but he led only by persuasion and example. He had no authority to coerce band members to behave in a particular way. Seasonal bands existed, then, as a loose collection of families without centralized political structures.

Throughout most of the Great Basin, however, the limited carrying capacity of the land discouraged any political organization beyond the family or cluster of families camping together. The residence camps were also without a hierarchy or political power. Elders, male or female, were respected for their greater experience and wisdom but could not impose their wishes on others. Family leadership was temporary and specific to the task at hand. The environment of the Great Basin simply could not support the sedentary life style needed to develop elaborate political structures.

The spiritual beliefs and practices of Great Basin peoples also reflected the demands of the subsistence quest. All groups viewed the natural world as endowed with supernatural power, and all groups had shamans—both male and female—who would tap into that power to perform healing rituals, manipulate the hunt, or control the weather. Hunting and gathering were spiritual matters. The remains of game animals were treated with respect, and gathering was often accompanied by prayers. Subsistence activities and animals were also prominent in myths. Birth, puberty, and death rites were widespread but were the province of the extended family; there were no priesthoods, no formal dogmas, no elaborate ceremonies. Whenever resources permitted, Great Basin peoples gathered to dance and visit each other, but these occasions were more social than ritual in nature.

Aboriginally, then, Great Basin cultures adapted to a harsh environment. Social structures were flexible, and political structures were nearly nonexistent. People identified themselves as members of distinct groups joined by language, kinship, and world view and by inhabiting specific territories. These traditions and ties of kinship sustained Great Basin peoples as distinct cultural entities throughout the period of conquest by Euro-Americans.

Postcontact culture

Contact with Europeans drastically altered Great Basin cultures; however, the situation of the peoples was somewhat different from that of other cultures. Because of their isolated location, Great Basin peoples were shielded from the more devastating consequences of contact until the late nineteenth century. Nevertheless, the initial impact of contact was tremendous for groups who adopted the horse.

By 1776, some Great Basin peoples already had horses. While groups in the interior of the region did not use them (because the environment would not support them), the Northern Shoshones, and Bannocks, and the Eastern Utes quickly adopted horses. The culture of the mounted groups rapidly changed as they began raiding—both for horses and for slaves to barter for horses—and as the easternmost groups moved onto the plains to hunt bisons.

The equestrian groups organized into bands led by men who were successful hunters and warriors. These men directed hunting and raiding parties but arrived at decisions only though consultation with a band council. The council had no coercive authority, and anyone unhappy with its planned course of action could withdraw from the group. Women participated in the council, and they followed men on raids to scalp and gather loot. The chiefs and councils did not replace the family as the primary source of social control, for the family still settled most disputes.

The presence of mounted bands also changed the configurations of intergroup relations in the Great Basin and its immediate vicinity. Previous associations between groups had been peaceful, but now equestrian groups raided nonmounted native peoples to capture slaves for barter. Relations with Hispanics, who moved into the region south of the Great Basin in 1598, and with Indians surrounding the Great Basin, such as the Navajos and Comanches, were characterized by shifting alliances, confrontations revolving around horse and slave raids, and conflicts over resources.

Intermittent warfare continued in the Great Basin during the period of Anglo settlement. The Mormons, arriving in the region of the Great Salt Lake in 1847, initially clashed with Indians over resources and slave trading. By 1854, however, the Indians had been defeated, and the Mormons kept them quiet by supplementing native subsistence activities with food and wage labor and by attempting to teach them farming. Native peoples remained at peace with Anglo settlers until the 1860s. At this time, growing numbers of miners pouring into the area of the Comstock Lode in Nevada and increased traffic along the overland trails in the central Great Basin completely disrupted native subsistence strategies. Conflict once again broke out.

The federal government intervened in the hostilities. The BUREAU OF INDIAN AFFAIRS (BIA) had already negotiated several treaties and agreements, promising to supply Great Basin peoples with annuities and presents in return for peace. In 1855, the government also tried to establish reservations in Utah, where the Indians could, with the help of the bureau, learn farming, ranching, or trade skills. With an increase in confrontations in the 1860s, the U.S. government pursued its reservation policy more vigorously.

The establishment of reservations throughout the Great Basin in the late nineteenth and early twentieth centuries was an uneven process. The federal government relocated Indians it perceived to be in the way of settlement while leaving those in undesirable locations alone. A few scattered bands of Western Shoshones and Paiutes managed to evade relocation by living in remote places and following a seasonal cycle of hunting, gathering, and wage work in agriculture or mining. The rest of the Great Basin tribes, however, moved to reservations.

Indians on the reservations were subjected to forced culture change. The Bureau of Indian Affairs attempted to force them to farm, raise stock, or work for wages. While Indians living on reservations did adopt some subsistence farming and wage labor, they also continued to hunt and gather, frequently leaving the reservations in seasonal cycles. These subsistence patterns continue today. The acculturation plans of the Bureau of Indian Affairs failed because of Indian resistance, the marginal quality of much Great Basin land, and the incompetence of many administering agents.

Beginning in the 1930s, the Bureau of Indian Affairs shifted from its policy of forced acculturation and established elected tribal councils to conduct reservation business. Although council plans were always subject to governmental approval, the councils pursued their own economic and educational strategies. In the late twentieth century, tribal governments struggled with economic underdevelopment and the resulting social problems of poor health, alcoholism, and violence. Great Basin peoples also worked to control their mineral and water resources and to regain lost lands. The ability of tribal governments to solve their problems has been limited by lack of funds, tensions with states and federal bureaucracies, and tribal conflicts over development strategies.

Despite centuries of struggle—first against an austere environment and then against European and American encroachment—native peoples persisted in the Great Basin.

—*Katherine M. B. Osburn*

SEE ALSO: United States Indian Policy

SUGGESTED READING:

d'Azevedo, Warren L., ed. *Handbook of North American Indians, Vol. 11: Great Basin.* Washington, D.C., 1986.

———, Wilbur A. Davis, Don D. Fowler, and Wayne Suttles, eds. *The Current Status of Anthropological Research in the Great Basin.* Reno, Nev., 1966.

Clemmer, Richard O. "Differential Leadership Patterns in Early Twentieth-Century Great Basin Indian Societies." *Journal of California and Great Basin Anthropology* 11 (1989): 35–49.

Cline, Gloria Griffen. *Exploring the Great Basin.* Westport, Conn., 1963.

Fowler, Don D., and Catherine S. Fowler, eds. *Anthropology of the Numa: John Wesley Powell's Manuscripts on the Numic Peoples of Western North America.* Washington, D.C., 1971.

Malouf, Carling, and A. Arlene Malouf. "The Effects of Spanish Slavery on the Indians of the Intermountain West." *Southwestern Journal of Anthropology* 1 (1945): 378–391.

Steward, Julian H. *Basin-Plateau Aboriginal Sociopolitical Groups.* Salt Lake City, 1970.

Washburn, Wilcomb E. *Handbook of North American Indians, Vol. 4: History of Indian-White Relations.* Washington, D.C., 1988.

PEOPLES OF THE GREAT PLAINS

Thirty-seven Native American tribes are indigenous to the Great Plains, which begin where the Mississippi River alluvial basin meets the prairie that reaches west to an irregular line along the ninety-eighth meridian. Beyond it lie two elongated provinces that extend from the Edwards Plateau of Texas to southern Manitoba, Saskatchewan, and Alberta: semiarid Low Plains and largely arid High Plains. Indigenous peoples in the region established rights of residence, use, and jurisdiction between the twelfth and seventeenth centuries. Archaeologists suppose they entered the region from the four directions and replaced prehistoric occupants who had vanished. Tribal philosophers insist that they "were always here." Historians shrink from the controversy and settle for an identification of prehistoric placement, roughly from north to south: Plains Cree; Plains Ojibwa (called Saulteaux in Canada); Assiniboin (also called Stoney in Canada); Crow; Blackfoot; Gros Ventre; Hidatsa; Mandan; Arikara; a federation of thirteen Dakota, Nakota, and Lakota tribes named Sioux (by neighboring Ojibwas); Ponca, Pawnee; Omaha; Iowa; Oto; Missouri; Arapaho; Cheyenne; Kansa; Quapaw; Osage; Wichita; Comanche; Kiowa; and Plains Apache. The federation of Sioux tribes comprises three subdivisions plus the related Assiniboin. In Anglicized spellings, Dakotas include the Mdewakanton and Wahpekute (Santee) plus Sisseton and Wahpeton. Nakotas are Yankton and Yanktonai. Lakotas include

Oglala, Brulé, Hunkpapa, Sans Arc, Minneconjou, Two Kettles, and Blackfoot Sioux.

Recent demographic studies suggest an aggregate Great Plains population of approximately 400,000 when non-Indians first appeared during the sixteenth century. The land mass controlled by Great Plains tribes included slightly more than one-half billion acres—43 percent of the land in the forty-eight continental states plus 100 million acres in southwestern Canada. Overall, they claimed approximately 1,500 acres per capita.

Population figures

Fragmented information exists to suggest great variations in population trends among the thirty-seven tribes—variations that, in turn, affected their capacities to retain control of the land. Statistics for the Sioux federation illustrate that some tribal groups experienced little reduction in size during the nineteenth century and grew substantially during the twentieth. Fairly reliable observers placed the aggregate population of Sioux people at approximately 32,000 in 1700; 25,000 in 1780; 28,000 in 1807; 28,100 in 1823; 25,400 in 1841; 30,200 in 1857; and 27,765 (plus 2,640 Assiniboins in the United States) in 1868. These reports were the products of guesswork by observers who estimated the average numbers of persons per lodge (from 8 to 10), reported the number of lodges (from hearsay evidence), and multiplied the results. From about 28,500 people in 1870, the total population of Sioux living on or near the reservations grew to approximately 74,600 in 1991.

A similar profile exists in fragmented demographic studies of Cheyennes: 2,000 in 1816; 2,500 in 1847; 3,351 in 1907; 6,674 in 1968 (total enrollment); and some 5,400 in 1985 (reservation residents). Oto-Missouri population went from an estimated 800 in 1804 to 1,358 on or near reservation in 1991, Ponca from 800 in 1876 to 2,482 on or near reservation in 1991, and Pawnee from 1,000 in 1804 to 2,273 on or near reservation in 1991.

Other tribes endured losses that account for an aggregate decline of 42 percent across the Great Plains. For example, Quapaw numbers dropped from an estimated 1,000 in 1800 to 215 in 1893 and then recovered to 984 by 1991. Kansa population declined from about 1,500 in 1700 to 250 by 1900 and then grew to 581 by 1991.

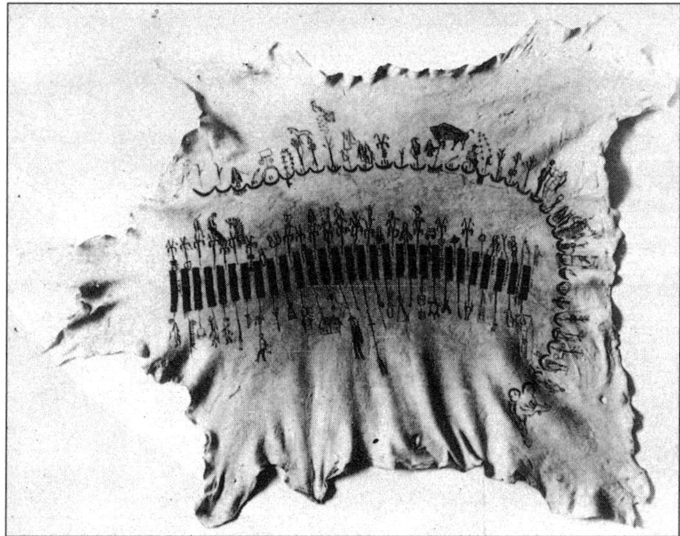

Top: Karl Bodmer's illustration of a Blackfoot Indian camp near Fort McKenzie, Montana, 1833. *Courtesy National Archives.*

Bottom: Anko, a Kiowa Indian, used a large animal skin to make his calendar of thirty-seven months, ca. 1895. *Courtesy National Archives.*

For half a century or more, tribes situated near major waterways in use for transportation and settlement suffered alarming losses of population from cholera, measles, influenza, pneumonia, venereal disease, and smallpox, especially during epidemics that broke out in 1780, 1833, 1837, and 1853. Epidemics had limited impact among the tribes with opportunities to flee, such as the Cheyenne and Sioux peoples. After

the mid-nineteenth century, the populations of all the tribes were decimated by pneumonia, tuberculosis, venereal disease, malnourishment, poor housing, and the consumption of alcoholic beverages. At the same time, variations in the census figures for some tribes resulted from movements of groups from agency to agency in search of suitable places for permanent location.

Top left: A group of Minneconjou Sioux, in costume for a dance ritual, Cheyenne River, South Dakota, August 9, 1890. Photograph by John C. H. Grabill. *Courtesy National Archives.*

Top right: A council of Cheyenne and Arapaho Indians meet with an agent at Segar Colony, Oklahoma, 1900. *Courtesy National Archives.*

Bottom: Quanah Parker, a Comanche chief, in front of his tent. Photograph by Lanney. *Courtesy National Archives.*

Between 1900 and 1940, the numbers of Indians enrolled at agencies fell because of relocation and intermarriage in addition to high mortality rates. Thereafter, pronounced recovery in tribal census figures came not only due to improved health-care delivery and living conditions, but also to reidentification. Following the establishment of the Indian Claims Commission in 1946, many of Great Plains heritage sought enrollment to share in payments authorized by Congress. Since the 1960s, others have applied for tribal membership to participate in a cultural renaissance on reservations across the Great Plains.

Tribal land bases

Differences in demographic trends among Sioux and Cheyenne peoples, on one hand, and Quapaw and Kansa peoples, on the other, reflect the correlation between population loss and exposure to non-Indians. A similar relationship exists between distance from areas substantially populated by white people and tribal success in the retention of land. All prairie peoples south of Minnesota sustained enormous losses by the end of the nineteenth century. Quapaws started with 32 million acres but retained only 18,522 acres by 1857. Kansa people saw their 20 million acres diminish to 100,137 acres by 1872. Oto-Missouri people endured a decline from 1.16 million to 29,000 acres by 1906. Moreover, these tribes and all of their prairie neighbors, except the Omahas and a few families of Iowas, were removed from their homelands to crowded reservations in Oklahoma.

The Dakotas on Minnesota prairie land suffered an even greater loss. After giving up nearly 20 million acres by treaties and war, they were landless after 1865. Most scattered on five reservations west of Minnesota or on seven tiny reserves in Canada. The few who drifted back lived by assignment on federal property until the 1930s, when they recovered 3,389 acres to support an aggregate population of 556 on four reservations, or 6.1 acres per capita.

Nakotas and Lakotas, situated farther west along the Missouri River valley in South Dakota, initially surrendered a vast acreage yet retained a more suitable land base. When first encountered by non-Indians, Nakotas and Lakotas shared with Dakotas at least 100 million acres to sustain an aggregate population of some 28,500, or 3,500 acres per capita. By 1950, middle and western tribal members enrolled at seven reservations retained ownership of more than 6 million acres for an aggregate enrolled population of 29,717, or 207.2 acres per capita.

At the northwestern fringe of the High Plains, Blackfoot people fared better than most. They retain 4 million tribal trust and allotment acres for an enrolled membership of 14,111, or some 285 acres per capita.

According to statistics compiled from 1985 to 1993, Native Americans in the Great Plains retained 17,692,903 acres, or approximately 3.5 percent of the region their forbears claimed before non-Indians arrived. For the number of members enrolled in 1993, this amounted to about 74.97 acres per capita.

Linguistic networks

Archaeological evidence, tribal memory, and reports by early non-Indian observers bear evidence about the relationships among tribes through linguistic networks. In the north, those of Algonquian heritage included the Blackfoot, Cheyenne, Arapaho, Gros Ventre, Plains Cree, and Plains Ojibwa; of Caddoan heritage were the Wichita, Pawnee, and Arikara who came to the Great Plains from the south; of Siouan heritage were the three subdivisions of Sioux—plus the related Assiniboin—the Crow, Hidatsa, Mandan, Iowa, Missouri, Oto, Omaha, Osage, Ponca, Kansa, and Quapaw who penetrated at the east; of Numic-Shoshonean heritage were the Comanche and the Plains Shoshone from the west; of Puebloan heritage were the Kiowa, and of Athapascan heritage the Plains Apache, both of whom had relatives in the Southwest.

Cross-cultural linguistic traits suggest frequent contacts among the networks, which belie an assumption that common linguistic heritage was the key to diplomatic accord. Siouan Assiniboin and Crow peoples acted in concert with Algonquian Cree and Ojibwas, for example, to preserve a military line against all subdivisions of Sioux.

Changing relationships are better explained as the products of the natural conditions that influenced territorial arrangements. Notably, Assiniboins withdrew from the Yanktonai Sioux tribe to scatter as a discrete society in alliance with Saulteaux and Crees on sparsely occupied land along the northern perimeter of Sioux country. Caddo Indians from the Texas-Louisiana border scattered to settle as Arikaras along the upper Missouri Valley, as Pawnees below the Poncas and Sioux in Nebraska, and as Wichitas on unoccupied territory west of the Texas-Oklahoma cross-timbers.

Intertribal conflicts

The potential for carnage existed among the thirty-seven tribes, who were well schooled in big-game hunting, but records of aggression are easily misconstrued. In *Tribal Wars of the Southern Plains,* Stan Hoig implied extensive bloodshed on the southern Great Plains until the larger tribes unified midway through the nineteenth century to expel unwanted intruders. Scores of publications about the Sioux country suggest similar devastation. A paucity of casualties on record raises doubt about the intention of one tribe to eliminate another, however, and indicates probable goals of war and diplomacy among the tribes similar to those in pre-Napoleonic Europe.

Subsistence patterns

Three general patterns of existence were followed by the thirty-seven tribes. Those who lived east of the ninety-eighth meridian enjoyed by far the greatest variety of natural resources to support an enviable, semisedentary way of life. Tribes situated along the one-hundredth meridian applied woodland horticultural techniques to sustain the most sedentary existence. Tribes of the High Plains and northern perimeter relied most heavily on big game in the most nomadic pattern of existence.

The Sioux people

For semisedentary residents of the prairie-plains, the federation of Sioux tribes makes an irresistible model. Strength of numbers, civilian governance, military organization, material advantage, and suitable alliances all contributed to their dominance from the northeastern edge of the prairie westward between the Platte River basin and the present-day Canadian border to the land of the Crows and Shoshones, at the outer edge of the Missouri River drainage basin.

On at least 100 million acres, Sioux leaders defined tribal boundaries along rivers, trails, and navigational landmarks. They negotiated with neighboring groups for privileges to enter their lands for purposes of hunting, gathering, or settlement. Along the border zones, neighboring tribes shared space and natural bounty without fear of attack. In general, the occasional conflicts between the tribes were caused by violations of territorial boundaries fixed through diplomacy. Sioux people confronted Ojibwas to the east, Pawnees to the south, and Crows to the west. At the same time, Sioux spokesmen permitted the Cheyennes rights of passage and settlement. In return, Cheyennes allowed Sioux people to range unmolested as far west as the Rocky Mountains. Limited conflict existed among the tribes over rights of occupancy and use until non-Indians appeared. Crowded conditions, competition for access to fur trade, and muddled diplomacy thereafter led to wars between the tribes as well as between the races and eventually to reallocations of space by treaties.

The Sioux sustained semisedentary lives by economic diversification. Like other Plains peoples, they depended on great herds of bison, comprising as many as 60 million head, but the bison represented only a part of the bounty they claimed by hunting and fishing. As buffaloes grew scarce, they shifted their attention to different animals—deer, antelopes, and elks. As those animals grew scarce because of non-Indian settlement, tribal hunters placed greater emphasis on the pursuit of smaller game—mourning doves, fox squirrels, rabbits, beaver, muskrats, mink, skunks, badgers, weasels, raccoons, coyotes, grouse, prairie chickens, ducks, and geese plus Chinese pheasants and Hungarian partridges. They also caught catfish, buffalo fish, and other species in large quantities.

While living on the Minnesota woodland-prairie border, Sioux people wintered in band-sized groups and used valleys and breaks as hunting areas and as shelters from wind and blowing snow. From spring to fall, they assembled at the southern perimeter of Mille Lacs. En masse, tribal groups made hunting expeditions in the spring, when bison calves and yearlings drifted with cows near scattered herds of bulls, and late in the summer, when cows and bulls gathered in rut. Observers counted groups of Sioux as large as 2,500 en route to the High Plains buffalo pasture, where they broke into parties of 100 or less to hunt. Although individual freedom and extended family autonomy were hallmarks of the culture, the authority of soldiers' societies superseded that of civilian leaders during the hunt. Spiritual leaders constructed sweat lodges along the way and invited general participation in prayers for safety and guidance. Camp criers sounded reveille and determined directions and distances of travel by

A camp of Wichita Indians, ca. 1904. Photograph by Henry Peabody. *Courtesy National Archives.*

the angles of sticks they placed in the ground. Women, teen-agers, and elders managed baggage and looked after meat, while soldiers scouted the horizon for game.

A panoramic view of the Rocky Boy Agency, home to Ojibwa (Chippewa) Indians, 1936. Photograph by Walter D. Wilcox. *Courtesy National Archives.*

Back in Minnesota, the chase after scattered buffaloes continued, but hunters took a variety of other animals and fish; some Sioux people gathered natural bounty and gardened. Mainly women and youngsters gathered salt from deposits and sap from maple and box elder trees to season natural products that included wild rice (grain), turnips, potatoes, various berries and fruits, and vegetables cultivated in gardens. With conservationist techniques, they took shares of eggs from migratory birds in the spring and divided caches of nuts with rodents who had packed them away in the fall. Hunters traded meat and other items with gardening specialists, among whom none were more proficient than the Missouri Valley Arikaras and Hidatsas on the northern Great Plains.

Sioux people lived in cabins made of poles and bark or grass at permanent encampments. While on the move or on hunting trips, they used portable tepees, transported by dog or horse travois. Every summer, they met with neighboring tribes at rendezvous or Sun Dances, where they found spiritual renewal and prayed for success in the harvest of natural bounty. At massive gatherings, diplomacy, cross-cultural communication, and intermarriage regulated Great Plains culture and diminished the probability of intertribal warfare over the use of land.

Most of the time, Sioux people remained in place as a federated society subdivided into occupational groups by gender, age, and choice. Some specialized in politics, soldiering, and hunting. Some farmed, gathered, maintained housing and travel baggage, or did sentry duty. Others attended to religion, historical memory, and the arts. A prevailing philosophy surrounding the Sacred Pipe religion guided hunters, provided protection, and brought order in human relationships with natural forces of Mother Earth under one Grandfather God, Wakantanka Tunkasila. A complex social structure protected individual freedom and ensured domestic order and diplomacy by the inclusion of soldiers' societies and civilian leaders.

During the eighteenth century, Sioux tribes left Mille Lacs to scatter across their massive area. Pressure from Ojibwas, direct access to fur trade, space for a growing population, and possibly a desire for a better climate were the principal reasons for their move. Dakotas at the east, Nakotas near the middle, and Lakotas at the west modified social mores long in use while they adjusted economic and cultural practices to accommodate increasing reliance on the trade of furs and robes with non-Indians.

Tribes on the prairie-plains

Southward on the prairie-plains, a similar pattern prevailed. Omaha, Iowa, Ponca, Oto, Missouri, Kansa, Quapaw, and Osage peoples lived in bark or earthen lodges; raised crops, fished, and gathered natural bounty; and once or twice a year, hunted bisons and other big game. Like the Sioux, they cooperated with some and competed with other neighbors for space.

Meanwhile, tribes situated along the one-hundredth meridian applied techniques earlier refined by woodland peoples to sustain more sedentary lives. In the main, Arikaras, Hidatsa, Mandans, Pawnees, and Wichitas lived in towns of sod-covered lodges. They combined hunting and gathering with horticulture but emphasized farming as the mainstay of economy. Caddoan Arikaras serve as a model. On plots of approximately one acre per family—separated by brush rows, grassy patches, or willow fences—women practiced crop rotation, fertilization, and fallowing in the production of corn, beans, squash, pumpkins, and tobacco. Their tools included hoes made of bison scapula, rakes of sticks tied by natural fiber, and miscellaneous bone instruments. The gardeners stored produce in bottle-shaped caches, six to eight feet deep. Lined with grass and covered with buffalo hides, grass matting, and earth, the caches were camouflaged and watertight enough to preserve vegetables for years without spoilage.

The principal crop was corn: flint corn, which had a high protein content; flour corn, which was ground; and sweet corn, which had a high sugar content and was used "in the milk." The importance of corn was indicated by its inclusion in the Arikara creation story and ceremonial practices and also by its abundance as an item of trade. The Arikaras, Hidatsa, Mandans, Pawnees, and Wichitas, all heavily committed to crop production, possessed the only reliable agricultural surpluses for exchange between upper Mississippi and upper Rio Grande Native American settlements.

Tribes on the High Plains

High Plains residents relied most heavily on bisons, deer, elks, antelopes, and small game; they also gathered some foods on slopes and valleys. Those in the southern and central areas also practiced casual farming. After planting and weeding, they abandoned their fields for the hunt with the intention of harvesting their crops in the fall.

Spanish horses brought them speed and agility for the pursuit of game as well as for defense and raids on neighboring tribes. Plains Shoshones ranged eastward into Wyoming and Montana. Comanches competed with Jicarilla Apaches for game in eastern New Mexico, exercised control over the Staked Plains and eastern Colorado, and traded for produce among Wichitas and Pawnees. Kiowas roamed among Plains Apaches and Comanches and also ranged northward as far as the forks of the Missouri River in Montana. Selectively, they allied with Apaches and Crows, intermittently befriended and competed with Comanches, and maintained a line of defense against the Sioux.

The most flexible among residents of the High Plains were the Cheyenne people. Tribal memory harkens back to the consolidation of four bands of prairie settlers into three villages separated by ecological necessity until the prophet Sweet Medicine cemented them into a single unit, bonded by language, philosophy, military societies, and citizenship under a single council. Because civilian and military leaders maintained land-use rights and jurisdiction under agreements with neighboring groups, until the mid-nineteenth century, the Cheyenne people were free to range more extensively than most others to satisfy their needs for wood, water, shelter, food, and grass for ever-growing herds of horses. The grasslands became increasingly important because the Cheyennes' herd of horses reached an average of four head per lodge.

Through an abiding alliance, Cheyenne people were the only outsiders allowed to reside in Sioux country without disturbance. After Lakotas marked new areas for tribal settlement west of the Missouri River, Cheyennes moved on, and between 1828 and 1838, they divided into southern and northern contingents. Among High Plains residents, they were unusual for their range of movement and diversity of culture yet typical for their reliance on buffaloes, deer, elks, and antelopes. They planted crops but left them unattended from seedling stages to gather and hunt until harvest time.

Nomadic life faltered for Southern Cheyennes after their successive massacres by Colonel JOHN M. CHIVINGTON at Sand Creek in 1864 and GEORGE ARMSTRONG CUSTER on the Washita River in 1868. Survivors joined Kiowas, Comanches, and Arapahos in an unsuccessful attack on Adobe Walls and stood with Comanches in their Red River War. The surrender of more than 800 Southern Cheyennes on March 6, 1875, foretold the end of nomadic existence.

Northern Cheyennes followed a similar course in an alliance with Lakotas that led to a victory at the Battle of Little Bighorn in the summer of 1876. The placement of Cheyenne people on two High Plains reservations in 1884, followed by a division through council vote in 1895, represented an end to their nomadic way of life.

The Kiowas, Apaches, and Comanches, allied defensively with the Southern Cheyennes after the 1840s, similarly saw their resistance end in confinement. By treaty in 1868, Kiowas accepted reservation life in southwestern Oklahoma. Quanah Parker's Comanches acted in concert with Eastern Apaches and Southern Cheyennes in the Red River War until 1874, after which they settled near Kiowas in Oklahoma. Arapahos shared the fate of Southern Cheyennes in Oklahoma and of Plains Shoshones on the eastern slope of the Rocky Mountains.

Northern Great Plains peoples

Along the northern perimeter, Crow, Blackfoot, Assiniboin, Plains Cree, and Plains Ojibwa peoples lived the most tenuous nomadic existence on semiarid lands. By varying degrees, all five groups were gravely affected by the competition of robe and fur traders. From the establishment of a station by Hudson's Bay Company near the confluence of the Assiniboine and the Red rivers in 1817 to the founding of the Dominion of Canada in 1867, company operatives prevailed over most of the region. Many Saulteaux, Crees, and Stoneys intermarried and raised Métis children, who grew up to take occupations as buffalo hunters and hide traders, shippers, and producers of vegetables and travel food known as pemmican.

After 1867, the northern tribes scattered by treaties on small reserves, including eight set aside in Canada for Sioux refugees from the United States. Below the boundary, Crow and Blackfoot people settled at reservations on the Missouri River plateau. Nearby, some Plains Crees and Saulteaux accepted a small reservation. Assiniboins joined the Gros Ventre people at Fort Belknap and Yanktonais at Fort Peck Reservation. At Turtle Mountain Reservation, in north-central North Dakota, the Mechif tribe included mainly Plains Cree and MÉTIS PEOPLE with a minority of Plains Ojibwas. A new language—a mixture of Cree, Ojibwa, and French—emerged, and Roman Catholic influence prevailed.

Nowhere were the intrusions of fur traders and missionaries more prevalent than in the northern Great Plains, but all across the region, merchants and denominational representatives became forces as strong as U.S. and Canadian Indian policy-makers. After the fur trade ended, a majority of Native Americans embraced Catholicism for its similarities in ceremonial forms and spiritual assumptions, and a lesser number accommodated Episcopal philosophies for the same reason. The greatest discord existed among the tribes primarily subjected to Presbyterian, Congregational, Methodist, Baptist, and other Protestant teachings.

Reservation life

An attitude no worse than guarded suspicion prevailed as long as natural resources were abundant. Armed confrontations such as the Arikara War of 1823 mainly represented conflicts of interest provoked by traders. In the main, the tribes welcomed explorers, federal employees, missionaries, tourists, and fur traders of good deportment. Together, tribal members and non-Indian hunters harvested animal resources to the commercial advantage of non-Indians. Native Americans exchanged a part of their natural bounty and labor for manufactured items that added comfort to life and embellished ceremonial activities and the arts.

The depletion of wildlife, the forfeiture of land by war or treaty, and most of all the influx of non-Indian settlers finally riled many Great Plains peoples. Near mid-century, federal treaty-makers sought first to arrange safe passage for overlanders and then to concentrate tribal groups on reservations. For more than a decade, the larger tribes held their ground. Horses, guns, and cavalry tactics brought victories to the Sioux in the GRATTAN MASSACRE, FETTERMAN MASSACRE, and Battle of Little Bighorn, for example, and to the Comanches in the Red River War. Gradually, the force of numbers coupled with industrial products and efficient transportation gave an advantage to non-Indians. Such leaders as SITTING BULL and Quanah Parker called off the fight to prevent a blood bath. Some Northern Plains peoples fled to Canada, but the majority surrendered arms and ponies to accept reservation life.

No confrontation over land was more dramatic than the one affecting middle and western Sioux plus neighboring tribes over the Black Hills region. Responding to defeat in the Fetterman Massacre, federal spokesmen capitulated in the 1868 Fort Laramie Treaty, which gave native claimants exclusive control over the Great Sioux Reservation—some 60 million acres—until three-fourths of the adult males in all signatory tribes acceded to encroachment. Yet after the demise of George Armstrong Custer and the Seventh Cavalry, by the Agreement of February 28, 1877, Congress illegally reduced that expansive reservation to 21.7 million acres. By the Agreement of March 2, 1889, Congress further diminished its size to 12.7 million acres divided into six reservations.

On the Sioux reservations, as elsewhere across the Great Plains, the underlying purpose of federal policy was detribalization through Christianization, social acculturation, family farming and ranching, relocation for integration, and federal citizenship. Tribes with the greatest experience in horticulture were the most successful with family farming and ranching. Those who relied on hunting and gathering struggled the most. West of the ninety-eighth meridian, High Plains peoples adopted cultural changes. The GHOST DANCE, introduced by the Paiute WOVOKA, instilled hope for a return to a hunting existence, from western Oklahoma to southern Saskatchewan, until the movement faltered after the death of Sitting Bull and the WOUNDED KNEE MASSACRE. The Peyote religion (NATIVE AMERICAN CHURCH) brought comfort to scattered groups as far north as the Canadian border. The Grass Dance gave expression to soldiers' lodges, many of whose members relinquished their functions in the social order to agency staff members but retained vital responsibilities for elders and invalids as well as cultural activities by the formation of dance-hall societies. At isolated places, intertribal Sun Dances, ceremonies, and other activities were sustained, mainly underground.

Cultural activities gained federal sanction when John Collier became U.S. Indian commissioner and the Indian New Deal went into effect. After survival in relative secrecy for a generation, both social and spiritual practices came back into public view during the 1950s, and thereafter, with encouragement by the civil rights movement, became a stimulus for revival in tribalism. Christian churches fell into disuse, sweat lodges appeared, and Sun Dances flourished. Medicine men served burgeoning communities and counseled, with others, traditional training at tribally controlled community colleges, high schools, and elementary schools. Powwows, great feasts, giveaways, and other ceremonies became more numerous, and traditional arts flourished.

On reservations created in the nineteenth century, ancient systems of governance had succumbed to federal usurpation; groups of leaders selected by traditional means had relinquished authority to business committees. Through the preparation of claims, at the invitation of Congress, and with the passage of the Indian Reorganization Act of 1934, elected and appointed tribal leaders have labored under the supervision and protection of the secretary of the Department of the Interior. They have worked to accomplish three objectives: defense against political encroachment by state and local governments, the supply of services for tribal members, and coordination of economies sufficient to sustain growing communities of reservation residents.

Tribes indigenous to the Great Plains region live on reservations situated mainly in Oklahoma, South Dakota, North Dakota, and Montana. Slowly, their aggregate land base grows through the judicious use of tribal resources. Steadily, their aggregate population draws closer to its estimated total of two centuries ago, with tribal governance, essential services, and economic independence as primary goals. Manifestly, Great Plains tribal cultures have survived through continuous protection against erosion from external influences to flourish in renaissance at the end of the twentieth century.

—Herbert T. Hoover

SEE ALSO: Central Plains Indian Wars; Little Bighorn, Battle of; Quanah Parker; Sand Creek Massacre; Sioux Wars; United States Indian Policy

SUGGESTED READING:
Cash, Joseph H. *The Sioux People (Rosebud).* Phoenix, Ariz., 1971.
Davis, Mary, ed. *Native America in the Twentieth Century.* New York, 1994.
Hoig, Stan. *Tribal Wars of the Southern Plains.* Norman, Okla., 1993.
Hoover, Herbert T. *The Yankton Sioux.* New York, 1988.
———, and Karen P. Zummerman. *The Sioux and Other Native American Cultures of the Dakotas: An Annotated Bibliography.* Westport, Conn., 1993.
Kehoe, Alice B. *North American Indians.* Englewood Cliffs, N.J., 1992.

PEOPLES OF HAWAII

Native Hawaiians, the *kanaka maoli,* are descendants of Polynesians who migrated to Hawaii on ocean-going double-hulled canoes as early as 300 A.D. from the Marquesas Islands. By 1100 A.D., the early settlements had expanded to the eight major inhabitable islands in the Hawaiian archipelago—Hawaii, Maui, Kahoolawe, Lanai, Molokai, Oahu, Kauai and Niihau. From 1100 to 1650, the kanaka maoli developed a distinctive Hawaiian society, characterized by extensive taro and aquaculture production and rank stratification. The linguistic, mythological, and family systems of the kanaka maoli shared an ancient Polynesian origin with Tahitians, Maori, and Samoans, but Hawaiian civilization was unique in many aspects of its socio-economic organization, religious rituals, hula (dance), *mele* (song), *oli* (chant), and arts.

Hawaiian society was organized around the *ahupua'a,* the basic pie-shaped unit of land into which all major islands were divided from the shore to the mountain top. In the inland regions, the farmers cultivated taro, which was pounded into poi, a staple of the Hawaiian diet. Farmers built extensive terraces with irrigation ditches that brought water over great distances. Sweet potatoes, yams, and bananas were also grown in the upland areas. People who lived along the shoreline were skilled at fishing or collecting seaweed and shellfish. Stone-walled fishponds were constructed along the shoreline so that an abundance of fish was always available. The people who lived within the *ahupua'a* formed an *'ohana,* or extended family system, by which upland farmers exchanged their produce freely with coastal residents who gathered protein-rich foods from the sea.

Social stratification among ancient native Hawaiians similarly stressed interdependency and reciprocity. The people, or *maka'ainana,* composed the great majority of society; they were responsible for the productivity of the land and the sea. The skilled experts and priests were the *kahuna,* who specialized in a variety of areas including canoe building, medicine, navigation, house construction, and divination. The *ali'i* were the exalted chiefs and chieftesses who derived their *mana* (divine power) from the *akua* (gods). As symbols of their divinity, the chiefs wore elaborate feather capes and helmets, considered the finest example of featherwork in the world.

The four main gods were Kane, Kanaloa, Ku, and Lono. Along with thousands of other deities, four *akua* were found in all aspects of the natural world. From the *akua* flowed *mana,* the supernatural power that infused all things animate and inanimate with life. The *ali'i* traced their lineage directly to the *akua,* and thus they were imbued with great *mana.* Their power always needed to be protected through extensive *kapu* (sacred laws), which were strictly enforced. *Pu'uhonua* (places of refuge) were provided to lawbreakers who safely reached those sacred havens.

Tributes were offered to the gods who were represented in stone and wooden images placed within stone-platform *heiau* (temples) erected throughout the islands. The nature of the offerings varied according to the god being honored but included food, fish, flowers, and sometimes human sacrifice. Sacred dance, music, and chants were also performed in tribute to *akua* and *ali'i.* During the annual *makahiki* (harvest season), peace prevailed throughout the islands. During this time period, athletic competitions including surfing, boxing, wrestling, and bowling were widespread.

The people also regularly gave offerings of food, feathers, and other valuables to the chiefs. A *konohiki* (overseer) made certain that the required tributes were set aside for the chiefs of that district or island. Rivalries for these "taxes" sometimes resulted in warfare and the expansion of political control by victorious chiefs. By the late eighteenth century after an extended period of warfare, the island of Hawaii was controlled by one *mo'i* (king), and a single chief ruled over Kauai and Niihau, and another over the islands of Maui, Kahoolawe, Molokai, Lanai, and Oahu.

European contact

European contact first took place in 1778 and 1779 with the arrival of Captain JAMES COOK. The size of the native population was estimated by Cook to be more than 300,000. Recent scholarship suggests that the native population may have been as high as 800,000 to 1 million. The immediate result of European contact was the introduction of foreign diseases and the rapid decline of the native population. By the first census of 1831, the native population had dropped to 130,000. Venereal diseases caused infertility, and epidemics of virulent disease—dysentery, whooping cough, and smallpox—decimated the population until only 40,000 native Hawaiians survived in 1890.

Western contact also introduced iron and modern weapons to native Hawaiians. Kamehameha, a young chief on the island of Hawaii, used foreign guns and military advisors to launch several wars of conquest against rival chiefs in the 1790s. By 1810, he had successfully united all eight Hawaiian islands under his control, thereby establishing the Hawaiian Kingdom. Over the next eighty years, eight Hawaiian monarchs ruled the Hawaiian Islands: Kamehameha I (reign, 1810–1819), Kamehameha II (1819–1824), Kamehameha III (1825–1854), Kamehameha IV (1855–1863), Kamehameha V (1863–1872), Lunalilo (1873–1874), Kalakaua (1874–1891), and LILIOUKALANI (1891–1893).

Religious changes also occurred in Hawaiian society with western contact. The *kapu* system was overthrown in 1819, and temples and images were destroyed. In March 1820, the first American Protestant missionaries arrived in the islands. Converting several prominent chiefs to Christianity in 1825, the missionaries were soon able to exert their influence through the promotion of churches and schools. Since Hawaiians had no written language, American missionaries with native advisors translated their religious texts into Hawaiian with an English alphabet of twelve letters (*a, e, i, o,* and *u* and *h, k, l, m, n, p,* and *w*). By 1830, common schools were established throughout the islands, and eventually 75 percent of the native population was able to read and write the Hawaiian language.

Political, social, and economic control over the kingdom increasingly shifted into the hands of foreigners throughout the nineteenth century. Sandalwood traders stripped the Hawaiian forests of the fragrant tree between 1810 and 1830. Whaling fleets replenished their supplies in the islands between 1840 and 1860. The Great Mahele, or land division, in 1848 abolished the *ahupua'a* system of land stewardship and established private ownership of land. Acquiring large tracts of the private lands, sugar planters, in the 1860s, started an industry that eventually dominated the islands' economy and displaced the native farmers from their taro terraces and fishponds.

On January 17, 1893, American sugar interests, with the assistance of United States officials in HONOLULU and military troops from the U.S.S. *Boston,* overthrew Queen Lilioukalani, thus ending the independent reign of the Hawaiian monarchy. With the annexation of the Hawaiian Islands by the United States in 1898, the Hawaiian language was no longer used in public schools. Tens of thousands of sugar-plantation laborers were imported from China, Japan, Okinawa, Portugal, Puerto Rico, and the Philippines.

Twentieth-century developments

By 1900, the declining native Hawaiian population had become a dispossessed minority group in its own homeland. Concern for the survival of the remaining indigenous people led the U.S. Congress to pass, in 1920, the Hawaiian Home Commission Act, which set aside some public lands for native Hawaiian homesteads. By 1990, the Department of Hawaiian Home Lands regulated more than 187,000 acres, although only about 5,770 leases were granted to qualifying Hawaiians to homestead 32,700 acres of land in various places throughout the islands.

With the shift of the island economy from sugar production to tourism in the 1960s, many native Hawaiians found employment in the tourism industry, in which commercial "Hawaiianness" in music and dance was valued. The continued growth of tourism created many challenges for the native Hawaiians who saw many of their traditional values such as *aloha 'aina* (love of the land), *aloha kanaka* (love of people), and their ancient arts, hula, and song diluted for visitors. Large-scale resort development in rural areas encroached upon the few remaining Hawaiian communities where modified *'ohana* family systems struggled to survive.

In 1976, the successful Hawaii to Tahiti voyage of *Hokule'a,* a replica of a double-hulled canoe, instigated a renewed effort to preserve Hawaiian language, culture, and lands. Hawaii became the first bilingual state in the nation in 1978 when both Hawaiian and English were recognized as official languages. The Office of Hawaiian Affairs (OHA), an elected representative body of native Hawaiians from various districts in the islands, was established to address the many social, economic, and cultural challenges still facing native Hawaiians who continued to have the lowest median income of the state's ethnic groups and the highest health and social welfare risks. In 1986, John Waihe'e became the first native Hawaiian to be elected governor of the state.

The educational needs of the native Hawaiian community have been partially met by the Kamehameha Schools, a private educational institution for native Hawaiian children stipulated in the will of Princess BERNICE PAUAHI BISHOP and established after her death in 1884. Her extensive landholdings, composing a ninth of the total area of the islands, were held in trust by the Bishop Estate. Proceeds from leasing these lands go to a school for Hawaiian boys and girls. The Kamehameha Schools today provide thousands of native Hawaiian children an outstanding general curriculum and Hawaiian studies in one of the best educational facilities in the state.

Through extensive intermarriage with the Asians, Spanish, and Caucasians who settled in Hawaii during the expansion of the sugar industry, the native Hawaiian population by 1990 had grown to 12.5 percent of the population or about 125,000 people. Fewer that 2,000 Hawaiians can claim a full-blooded native ancestry. Community organizations and royal societies—such as the Hawaiian Civic Clubs, the Kaahumanu Society, the Sons and Daughters of Hawaiian Warriors, and the Order of Kamehameha—represent the various interests and needs of Hawaii's indigenous community.

On January 17, 1993, tens of thousands of native Hawaiians and their supporters throughout the state met in public gatherings, vigils, and ceremonies to mark the one-hundredth anniversary of the overthrow of the Hawaiian monarchy and to voice their right of sovereignty. The models of sovereignty that have been proposed range from independence for the Hawaiian Islands to the setting aside of native lands as a "nation within a nation." In December 1993, President Bill Clinton recognized the illegality of the 1893 overthrow of the Hawaiian monarchy in a formal apology to native Hawaiians. The acknowledgment heightened native Hawaiians' expectations that by the end of the century some form of sovereignty would be implemented for the kanaka maoli of Hawaii.

—*Glen Grant*

SEE ALSO: Missions: Missions in Hawaii

SUGGESTED READING:

Fuchs, Lawrence H. *Hawaii Pono: A Social History.* San Diego, Calif., 1961.
Kamakau, Samuel M. *Ka Poe Kahiko: The People of Old.* Honolulu, Hawaii, 1964.
———. *Ruling Chiefs of Hawaii.* Honolulu, Hawaii, 1992.
Kameeleihiwa, Lilikala. *Native Land and Foreign Desires: How Shall We Live in Harmony.* Honolulu, Hawaii, 1992.
Kirch, Patrick V. *Feathered Gods and Fishhooks: An Introduction to Hawaiian Archaeology and Prehistory.* Honolulu, Hawaii, 1985.
Kuykendall, Ralph S. *The Hawaiian Kingdom.* 3 vols. Honolulu, Hawaii, 1938–1967.
Lilioukalani. *Hawaii's Story by Hawaii's Queen.* Honolulu, Hawaii, 1992.
Linnekin, Jocelyn. *Sacred Queens and Women of Consequence: Rank, Gender and Colonialism in the Hawaiian Islands.* Ann Arbor, Mich., 1990.
Stannard, David. *Before the Horror: The Population of Hawaii on the Eve of Western Contact.* Honolulu, Hawaii, 1989.

PEOPLES OF THE PACIFIC NORTHWEST

Geographically, the Pacific Northwest extends from the coast along Oregon, Washington, British Columbia, and the islands of southern Alaska eastward across the Columbia River plateau, northern Idaho, and northwestern Montana. The Indians of the region, although originating from diverse language families, shared a number of characteristics in their material culture, in their craft specialties, and in their kinship patterns, most of them attributable to the region's environment. Yet, differences did appear, especially when it came to an individual tribe's contact with Euro-American settlers.

The native peoples of the Pacific Northwest included tribes distantly related to various major language families—Algonquian, Peutian, Nez Percé, and Na-Dene. The Algonquian family of Pacific Northwest Indians included the Nootka and the Kwakiutl and Salish tribes. The Nootkas and Kwakiutls lived along the coast of British Columbia and Washington. The Salish Indians were divided into two groups: the Coastal Salish and the Interior Salish. Among the Coastal Salish, who lived in northwestern Washington on the Puget Sound and in British Columbia, were the Chehalis, Nisqualli, Cowlitz, Squamish, Comox, Tillamook, and

Bella Coola tribes. The Interior Salish, who spread from inland British Columbia and Washington to northern Idaho and northwestern Montana, included the Coeur d'Alene, Kalispel, Spokan, Okinagon, Pend d'Oreille, and Flathead tribes. The Peutian language family included the Klamath, the Modoc, and the Chinook tribes. The Klamaths and Modocs lived along the present-day border between California and Oregon. The Chinooks lived farther north, near the mouth of the Columbia River. The Nez Percé language family, whose tribes spoke variations of Shaphaptin, included the Klikitat, Umatilla, Yakima, Walla Walla, and Nez Percé tribes. They inhabited the Columbia Plateau, an area covering eastern Washington, northeastern Oregon, northern Idaho, and northwestern Montana. Finally, the Na-Dene language family included the southern Alaskan tribes—the Tlingit, the Ank, the Chilkat, and the Sitka—as well as some Athapascan speakers and the Kwalhioqua, Tlatskanai, Chasta-Costa, Tolowa, Hupa, and Wailaki tribes who lived in Washington, Oregon, and northern California.

Around 1750, the population of all the Pacific Northwest tribes numbered at least 70,000, and probably many more. By the beginning of the twentieth century, their population had dropped to fewer than 30,000. Their depopulation followed the 1830 Indian Removal Act, a federal law that spawned warfare, displacement to unfamiliar and often undesirable land, and a general decline in the quality of Native American life. The increased contact with white settlers that characterized the late nineteenth century also created epidemics of European diseases among the tribes.

Many tribes in the Pacific Northwest were among the most prosperous and densely populated of American Indians. The coastal tribes took full advantage of the bountiful sea, while the inland groups enjoyed rich vegetation and a variety of game. Coastal tribes depended on fish, seals, sea otters, and beached whales for food and materials, which they procured with nets and clubs. To travel and fish, they used canoes, hollowed out from the trunks of the tremendously tall cedar trees that lined the Pacific shore. Some ornately decorated canoes, holding as many as seventy people, made impressive warships.

Cedar was, in fact, the basis for most of the Coastal tribes' material culture. Working only with tools of stone and bone, they used cedar not only to make canoes, but also to build enormous multifamily

Photographer Lee Muck recorded the home of Gabe Gobin, an Indian logger, at the Tulalip Reservation, Washington, 1916. *Courtesy National Archives.*

Johnnie Saux, a Quinielt Indian of Washington State, displays his prize salmon, 1936. Photograph by Walter D. Wilcox. *Courtesy National Archives.*

longhouses, in which forty or fifty people could live. Built side by side along the shore facing the sea, each with canoes moored in the front, the houses had one shore-side entrance and, along the long edge of the gabled roof, an opening that allowed the smoke from the various family fires to escape. Cedar planks formed the siding for the homes, and cedar tree trunks—spaced evenly from front to rear—served as support posts. Inside, a central area for family fires was surrounded by three or four ascending tiers, or deep steps, that reached the outside walls, allowing more space for numerous residents.

The Plateau Indians used construction techniques similar to those of their neighbors along the coast, and their permanent settlements consisted of planked longhouses. Not as sedentary as the Coastal Indians, the inland tribes hunted such game as deer, elks, and even buffaloes in the eastern reaches of the plateau; they gathered edible roots—cama, kouse, bittersweet, and carrot; and they followed seasonal salmon runs in the tributaries of the Columbia River. Since their subsistence required greater mobility than that of the Coastal Indians, tribes such as the Nez Percé depended on the horse instead of the canoe, and they developed characteristics typical of some Plains Indians. For example, like the Plains tribes, the Plateau Indians slept in tepees during their equestrian hunting trips. Also unlike the Coastal Indians, who dressed in seal skin and hewn cedar bark, the peoples of the Plateau wore the hides of the game they killed, as did Plains Indians.

Construction technology was not the only characteristic of material culture shared by all tribes of the Pacific Northwest. All of them, for example, used stone boiling, a method of cooking in which stones are placed in a fire and then removed to a wooden box or a woven basket for heating food. Stone boiling was one reason Pacific Northwest Indians never developed pottery; instead, the utilitarian objects of daily life that for them became the artistic expressions of nonmaterial culture were baskets, blankets, and wooden products. For example, boiled and twined basketry was the chief craftwork of the Klikitats, who became especially esteemed for the soft bags they created with woven material such as spruceroot. The Chilkats were known for the extraordinary woven fringed capes (often referred to as blankets) that bore geometrical representations of animals, representations that mimicked those they painted on the fronts of their houses. Not only the Chilkat, but most Na-Dene and Coastal Algonquian tribes used animals in their decorative artwork. And Pacific Northwest Indians were master lumbermen and woodworkers, who used the abundant and pliable cedar to carve elaborate animals, or clan totems, into many utilitarian items, including canoes, support posts, and house fronts.

Fashioned in the form of an animal, the totem represented the ancestors of the matrilineal clans—kinship groups who traced their lineage through their mothers—that dominated the social organization of the Pacific Northwest Indians. The tribes did not regard the totems as deities, but as heroic, somewhat mythical, protectors of clan members. The clans themselves were exogamous, meaning a member born into one group—say, the Eagle clan—had to marry someone born into a different group—perhaps the Raven clan. Not surprisingly, one house might be home to members of numerous clans, each of whose clan heroes would be displayed on the totem pole in front of the longhouse. The household's predominant clan, however, was represented by the totem at the top of the pole, and the clan chief—who always lived in the rear of the longhouse—had a special wood screen elaborately decorated with his clan's totem in front of his sleeping area.

Such clan-based social organization characterized most Pacific Northwestern groups except a few in northern California. The tribes did not consider one clan to be inherently better or worse than one another, and their social structure reflected that belief. This is not to say that the tribes had no class system; indeed, they even engaged in slave trade. The slaves, however, could belong to any tribe or clan. They were normally wartime captives who had become part of a complex economic system known as potlatch.

Potlatches were competitions for prestige that involved the exchange of enormous amounts of material goods, including slaves. Clans or tribes gathered for potlatch ceremonies, during which the host bestowed as many blankets and as much fish as possible. The more he gave away, the more prestige he earned for himself, his clan, and his protective totem. Every clan and tribe reciprocated with a later potlatch. Because the clans made surplus goods for use as gifts during the potlatch, they created an economic safety net in the event of unforeseen disaster. Among the Coastal Indians, then, the meaning of wealth was prestige, a prestige garnered by generosity, and material goods themselves were merely a means to an end.

The search for prestige, however, often escalated potlatch generosity into the ostentatious destruction of materials—blankets were frequently burned, fish were sometimes tossed back into the sea, occasionally a slave might even be clubbed. And because almost every ritual—weddings, births, funerals—were accompanied by potlatches, such destructive behavior mortified European missionaries and Euro-American settlers. The federal government began discouraging the practice in the early 1900s and eventually banned it altogether. The last potlatches were held in the 1940s, but following the cultural revitalization many tribes experienced in the early 1970s, some of the rituals of the potlatch were reintroduced. By the early 1990s, thousands of tribal members attended biannual gatherings where younger generations performed traditional Pacific Northwest dances and displayed the woodworking techniques of their ancestors.

The Euro-Americans not only attacked the potlatch; they also attacked some of the Pacific Northwest tribes themselves. The Modoc War of 1872 to 1873 resulted from the Modocs refusal to join the Klamaths on their reservation. The Modocs first came into conflict with Euro-American culture around 1830, as Oregon was settled, and over the following decades Euro-American settlement threatened the very existence of many tribes. Both the Klamaths and the Modocs participated in the GHOST DANCE of 1870, a Native American religious revival that began in western Nevada. The movement involved traditional aspects of ritual and included a new message: all dead Indians would be resurrected and live in harmony with their people. Two hundred Modocs left the Nome Cult Indian Farm, where they had been placed in 1858. They also refused to stay with the Klamaths, with whom they had never been friendly, on the reservation in Oregon. Led by Kintpuash, or CAPTAIN JACK, the Modocs defeated U.S. troops sent to force relocation and killed several peace commissioners deployed to negotiate with them. The Modocs retreated to the California Lava Beds. There, Captain Jack and several other leaders were captured and hanged for the murders of the peace commissioners. The surviving 153 Modocs were sent to the Indian Territory (Oklahoma), where their numbers declined rapidly. In 1909, the 53 remaining Modocs were returned to Oregon.

In 1877, the Nez Percés were forced from their land in eastern Washington and northern Idaho. En route to Fort Lapwai Reservation, the Nez Percés fought with U.S. troops and were victorious at White Bird Canyon, where CHIEF JOSEPH led seven hundred Nez Percés on an ingenious retreat that spanned over one thousand miles. But trapped in Montana, they were defeated, and the captives were sent to Oklahoma. While living in the Indian Territory, the Nez Percés became ill and many died, mostly from malaria. In 1885, most of the surviving 287 Nez Percés were permitted to go to Fort Lapwai. The U.S. government decided, however, that Chief Joseph was subversive and exiled him to the Colville Reservation in Washington where he died in 1904.

The Nez Percés were also affected by the Native American religious revivals of the late nineteenth century. A dream dancer named Smohalla, who preceded the 1870 Ghost Dance movement by a decade, also taught resurrection, a belief that may have helped sustain the Nez Percés during their grueling retreat. When the Ghost Dance itself was revived in the 1890s, em-

At Taholah, Washington, Frank Tlyasman, a Quinielt Indian, in his new dugout canoe, 1936. Photograph by Walter D. Wilcox. *Courtesy National Archives.*

phasizing cooperation with the "whites" as the condition of resurrection and peace to come, the Nez Percés joined with the Sioux and others in the revival that ultimately led to the tragedy at Wounded Knee.

Unlike the Plateau Indians, the Coastal tribes never experienced the kind of warfare with the Euro-Americans that so decimated the Modocs and the Nez Percés, nor did they participate in the Ghost Dances. That, however, did not prevent the federal government from moving them onto reservations and attempting to destroy their Native American cultures in the name of assimilation.

—*Melissa A. Davis*

SEE ALSO: Pacific Northwest Indian Wars; United States Indian Policy

SUGGESTED READING:
Benedict, Ruth. *Patterns of Culture.* Cambridge, Mass., 1934.
Brown, Dee. *Bury My Heart at Wounded Knee.* New York, 1970.
Thorton, Russell. *American Indian Holocaust and Survival: A Population History since 1492.* Norman, Okla., 1987.
Wherry, Joseph H. *The Totem Pole Indians.* New York, 1974.
White, John Manchip. *Everyday Life of the North American Indian.* New York, 1979.
Williams, Maria. "Contemporary Alaska Native Dance: The Spirit of Tradition." In *Native American Dance, Ceremonies, and Social Tradition.* Edited by Terence Winch. Washington, D.C., 1992.
Wissler, Clark. *Indians of the United States.* Rev. ed. Garden City, N.Y., 1966.

PEOPLES OF THE SOUTHWEST

The cultural region designated as the Southwest includes the present-day states of Arizona and New Mexico; the point at which those states meet Utah and Colorado, known as Four Corners; and the area of western Texas bordering New Mexico. Geographically, the region features a diverse terrain: mountains, canyons, rivers, deserts, and fertile valleys. The native peoples were equally diverse, descending from a variety of parent language families: Aztec-Tanoan, Hokan-Sioux, Keresan, Peutian, and Na-Dene.

The Aztec-Tanoan family consisted of Uto-Aztec and Tanoan language branches. The Uto-Aztec included the Shoshonean-speaking Hopis of northern Arizona, and the Piman-speaking Pima-Maricopas and Papagos of central and southern Arizona. Many Southern Paiute peoples, who also spoke a branch of Shoshonean, were native to northwestern Arizona and southwestern Utah. The Ute Mountain and Southern Ute groups of southwestern Colorado spoke a Shoshonean language of the Uto-Aztec family as well.

The Tanoan branch of the Aztec-Tanoan family included most Pueblo tribes of Arizona and New Mexico, further divided as speakers of Tiwa, Tewa, and Towa. Tiwa speakers included the Sandia, Isleta, Taos, and Picuris Pueblos of the northern Rio Grande Valley. The Tewa speakers consisted of Santa Clara, San Ildefonso, San Juan, Tesuque, Nambe, Hano, and Pojoaque groups located north of Santa Fe. The Jemez Pueblo tribe, west of Santa Fe, spoke Towa. The remaining Pueblos of San Felipe, Acoma, Laguna, Santo Domingo, and Cochiti of west-central New Mexico, spoke Keresan, a relatively isolated language. The Zuni Pueblo of western New Mexico spoke a derivation of the Peutian language family called Zunian.

The Southwest was also home to members of the Yuman language group, a branch of the Hokan-Sioux linguistic family. The language group included River

A man and woman of the Laguna Pueblo in New Mexico display the garments, jewelry, and some pottery of their tribe. Photograph by Ben Wittick. *Courtesy National Archives.*

Left: A group of Zuni men posed for John K. Hillers's camera in 1879. *Courtesy National Archives.* Right: A Navajo family in Canyon de Chelly, New Mexico Territory, 1873. The wife sits at her loom, her husbands displays his bow and arrow. Photograph by Timothy H. O'Sullivan. *Courtesy National Archives.*

Yumans (Mojaves and Yumas) located in western Arizona along the lower Colorado River; Upland Yumans, or Pai Indians—Havasupai and the Hulapai (Walapai)—in northwest-central Arizona, along the upper Colorado River; and the Yavapai Yumans in south-central Arizona.

The Na-Dene language family extended into the region with the coming of the Navajo and Apache tribes, who spoke a derivation of Athapascan. The Apaches were divided into the Apaches and the Western Apaches. The former included the Jicarillas of northern New Mexico, the Lipans along the New Mexico-Texas border, the Warm Springs Apaches to the west, and the Chiricahuas in southeastern Arizona. The Western Apaches, located along the southern Arizona-New Mexico border, included the San Carlos, White Mountain, Cibeque, and Tonto tribes. The Navajos occupied a large portion of northeastern Arizona, and their population spilled over the current borders of New Mexico, Colorado, and Utah.

Like many Indian groups across the continent, the native tribes of the Southwest became severely depopulated during the last half of the nineteenth century. Warfare, relocation, disease, starvation, and the loss of cultural autonomy reduced an enormous population (more than 100,000 Navajos alone, and about half as many Pueblos) by nearly two-thirds.

The Pueblos, who made up a large part of the Southwest's native population, had a very highly developed life style, even during prehistory. Their famous dwellings were elaborate apartment-style structures built into and around cliffs. When the Spanish encountered them in 1540, the Pueblos lived in sixty to sev-

Henry Peabody photographed Supai Charlie and his Havasupai *ha-wa,* or "dwelling, " in Havasu Canyon, Arizona, 1900. *Courtesy National Archives.*

enty autonomous villages, some home to as many as 2,000 people. Even to the early Spanish explorers, it was evident that the Pueblos were already in a period of decline from a grander past.

The Pueblos were primarily a horticultural society. They grew squash, corn, and pumpkins and sometimes maintained fruit orchards. An estimated 25 percent of their subsistence came from crops; thus they were largely sedentary and were able to build large villages and develop complex social institutions.

Pueblo cosmology consisted of a sequence of worlds leading from past to present. Previous planes of existence were peopled by figures of power and knowledge and characterized by heroic exploits. By recounting stories about the eras of creation, Pueblos maintained social order—resolving conflicts, accounting for misfortunes, sustaining harmony. Their spirituality, manifested in ritual and ceremony, permeated every aspect of their daily life. Pueblo ceremonies featured religious dances revolving around kachinas—spiritual entities who bestowed upon the Pueblos the knowledge and materials necessary for their survival, including the rain that allowed them to grow crops. During the religious dances, the dancers wore masks that united them spiritually with a particular kachina. The Pueblos also made KACHINA CARVINGS for their children to help teach the kachina pantheon. The Zuni Pueblos engaged each fall in a ceremony for the Shalako, or rain god messengers, during which they reenacted the Zuni migration to their contemporary home—the middle world. Both religious dances and the Shalako ritual reflect the Pueblos' long struggle to forge an existence in the arid Southwest.

The Navajos, too, believed in eras of creation that spawned a knowledge of balance and order. Although the Navajos occasionally raided other tribes, they—like the Pueblos—lived mainly by agriculture, raising sheep as well as crops. Corn (called by scholars "maize") was the Navajos' primary source of food. They considered maize the foundation of life and celebrated it as such in their legends, songs, and ceremonies. Navajo cosmology, like that of the Pueblos, evidenced a reverence toward most everything in the natural world, and like those of the Pueblos, Navajo deities were anthropomorphic—that is, they had human form. The Navajo gods were responsible for creating and controlling natural forces, such as thunder and lightning.

Navajo dwellings, or hogans, were the center of Navajo ceremonial life. Shaped not unlike a tepee, the conical huts were made with mud and featured long entrance ways attached to their eastern sides. Because the Navajos needed broad ranges to raise sheep, families were spread over large areas, and the great distances between clan members only made religious ceremonies, extended ritual, and careful attention to clan genealogy that much more crucial to maintaining their tribal identity.

Both the Navajos and the Pueblos made pottery and worked in silver. Both crafts had initially been utilitarian, their designs often of Mexican origin but with motifs reflecting the Navajo and Pueblo reverence for nature. By the twentieth century, Indian artisans were making from pottery and from silver decorative and ornamental works of art to satisfy the demand of a large commercial market.

Some native Southwestern cultures—especially those in the eastern and northern reaches of the region—were heavily influenced by the Plains Indians. Apaches to the east and Utes and Paiutes to the north, like the natives on the Great Plains, grew to depend on horses for hunting, for gathering, and for raiding their more sedentary neighbors. They dressed in hides, dwelled in tepees (or brush shelters in the mountains), foraged for wild plants, grew some corn, and hunted buffaloes. As seminomads, their social organization and rituals were less structured than those of the natives living in permanent settlements to the west.

Like many Indians, the Apaches incorporated their children into every aspect of culture. They trained both boys and girls to fight; children attended most adult functions; they were sheltered from neither knowledge about nor the experience of adult sexual relations. Apache women participated in raiding parties and were highly respected in Apache society provided they remained chaste until marriage. Apache society was matrilineal—the Apaches traced their descent from their mother, and a husband would set up a household with his wife's band. Although Apache bands were semipermanent, spending time both on the plains and in the mountains, they were loosely organized, and membership in a band often shifted during movement. As was the case with most Indians who traveled in bands, the Apaches valued items for their usefulness, and their pottery was utilitarian. Because the Apaches often abandoned their horses to scale mountains, they placed an exceptionally high worth on moccasins; individual Apaches included extra soles among their small caches of valuables.

The Plains Indians influence was particularly evident in the ritual focus of the tribes living in the northern reaches of the Southwest—for example, in the Ute Bear Dance, which coincided with the end of the animal's hibernation period each spring. Considering the bear to be among the wisest of creatures, the Utes believed their nearly five-day-long ceremony helped the bear recover from its long winter's rest. Each summer, the Utes also performed the Sun Dance, which they

borrowed directly from the Plains tribes. The Sun Dance commemorated the day, generations before, when the buffalo first appeared—as a gift from a god to a wandering Indian—and put an end to famine. Both the Bear Dance and the Sun Dance symbolized rebirth—of nature and of Ute ancestors. The Utes, like the other tribes of the Southwest, revered nature in their ceremonies, but whereas the Pueblo invoked rain through their kachinas, the Utes celebrated and invoked the game they hunted.

Those Apache bands living farther west were not as greatly influenced by the culture of the Plains tribes. Instead, their culture more closely resembled that of their linguistic brethren, the Navajos. While the Jicarilla Apaches, for example, performed a Bear Dance, it resembled the Ute ceremony mostly in name. The Jicarilla Bear Dance was a holiness rite very similar to a Navajo ceremony, except that the Apaches replaced Navajo drumming with a rhythmic stick rubbing taken from the Utes to create a dance unique to the Jicarillas.

Those Southwestern tribes living in the desert and along the Colorado River were neither sophisticated horticulturists nor nomadic hunters on horseback. The desert peoples—the Pima and the Papago Indians—had little choice: their lands were no good for raising crops. They gathered whatever plants and hunted whatever small game happened to be available; they went without clothes; they had little use for material goods of any kind. The River Yuman people—including the Pai and the Mojave tribes—lived a bit more abundantly since they could do some farming on the fertile strips along the Colorado, and a few Pai groups near the Grand Canyon even managed to irrigate crops successfully. Most of the desert and river bands centered around the family unit, although they had no formal clans and did not officially observe marriage and divorce. Their religion was not highly ritualized, although they did have practicing shamans, or religious healers. They traced their descent and determined ownership through their fathers, but although theirs was a patrilineal society, females owned the products they created, including pottery and baskets.

The Indians of the Southwest were among the first North American tribes to come into contact with Europeans, and early conflicts with the Spanish abounded. The Apaches have a particularly lengthy list of war leaders whose exploits are well known. Expert raiders, particularly after they acquired horses and firearms, Apaches plundered Pueblo and Spanish settlements for centuries. From 1837 to 1877, they engaged in ongoing warfare with Mexican troops, and for thirty years beginning in the 1860s, Apaches—COCHISE, MANGAS COLORADAS, VICTORIO, Choto, Loco, NANA, Ulzana, GERONIMO—resisted the U.S. government's attempts to settle them on reservations. Geronimo's final surrender in 1886 marked the end of the country's Indian Wars.

Top: The rancheria of an Apache Indian photographed by Camillus S. Fly. *Courtesy National Archives.*

Bottom: The interior of a Navajo hogan located on a reservation in the New Mexico Territory, 1903. Photograph by D. Griffiths. *Courtesy National Archives.*

The Pueblos, too, were famous for one of the more successful defiances in American history, the PUEBLO REVOLT of 1680, which forced the Spanish to retreat from their lands for twelve years. After the Spanish returned and reconquered the region, the Pueblos suffered massive depopulation and did not take up arms again. Instead, they continued their revolt silently and passively: they conformed outwardly, allowing their traditions to go underground. By avoiding contact, secretly resisting change, and being overtly dutiful, the Pueblos managed cultural preservation during the eighteenth and nineteenth centuries, even after the United States took control of their lands in 1848. Today, although they have adopted some Euro-American institutions, the Pueblos remain ceremonially and socially very traditional. They have gained worldwide recognition for the revitalization of traditional pottery, made possible by Nampeo of the Hopis in the 1890s and MARIA MONTOYA MARTINEZ of the San Ildefonso Pueblo in the early 1900s.

An Apache bride. *Courtesy National Archives.*

Apache infants secure in their cradleboards. *Courtesy National Archives.*

In 1868, the Utes were resettled west of the Continental Divide, where miners and trappers steadily continued to encroach upon their lands in the San Juan Mountains. In 1879, a confrontation between the Utes and the U.S. military resulted in the deaths of twenty-five settlers and soldiers. By 1882, two-thirds of the Colorado Utes were exiled to Utah and forced to give up their nomadic way of life in favor of agriculture.

The Pima peoples of central Arizona were resettled along the Gila and Santa Cruz rivers in 1871 without violent incident, despite their refusal to move to the Indian Territory in present-day Oklahoma and despite the U.S. government's numerous modifications to the Pima reservation boundaries. The Papagos, whose lands in southwestern Arizona accumulated as few as four inches of rainfall annually, experienced little aggression from settlers or the military, even after the 1853 Gadsden Purchase, which put their territory in the hands of the U.S. government. Early in the twentieth century, a number of executive orders established more than two million acres of Papago reservations, mostly along the Mexican border.

The Yuman territory also came under the control of the United States through the Gadsden Purchase, and Fort Yuma was established in the center of their region. The Yumas had fairly friendly relations with the Euro-Americans. In contrast, the Mojaves, just north of the Yumas, were almost destroyed by soldiers in 1859. The Fort Mojave Reservation was established in 1880 and included parts of Arizona, California, and Nevada. By the turn of the century, the Mojave population had decreased from 3,000 to fewer than 1,000.

The Pai Indians' contact with Euro-American settlers was marked by numerous violent incidents. As early as 1826, the Pais engaged in hostilities with trappers and raiders. Throughout the century, the Pais took military action to protect their lands and traditions. In 1866, a growing number of mining settlements precipitated the Walapai War, which lasted through 1869. In 1871, the Western Pais were forced to relocate to the Colorado River Indian Reservation, although they escaped to their homeland, which by 1875 was occupied by ranchers and their cattle herds. The Pais were granted reservations on an ancestral plateau in the 1880s.

At the end of the twentieth century, the Southwest remained home to a relatively large number of native peoples when compared to other regions of the United States. Population estimates included more than 35,000 Pueblos, 140,000 Navajos and Apaches, 3,000 Utes, 11,000 Pimas and Papagos, 1,200 Southern Paiutes, and 22,000 Yumas, Mojaves, and Pais. Many of these peoples, such as the Pueblos and the Navajos, have managed to preserve much of their traditional culture and to maintain tribal autonomy.

—Melissa A. Davis

SEE ALSO: Apache Wars; Native American Pottery, Southwestern; Native American Silverwork, Southwestern; United States Indian Policy; Yuma Revolt

SUGGESTED READING:
Dutton, Bertha P. *Indians of the American Southwest.* Englewood Cliffs, N.J., 1975.
Waldman, Carl. *Encyclopedia of North American Tribes.* New York, 1988.
Waters, Frank. *Book of the Hopi.* New York, 1963.
———. *Masked Gods: Navaho and Pueblo Ceremonialism.* New York, 1950.
Weigle, Marta, and Peter White. *The Lore of New Mexico.* Albuquerque, N. Mex., 1988.
Wissler, Clark. *Indians of North America.* Rev. ed. Garden City, N.Y., 1966.

PEOPLES REMOVED FROM THE EAST

During the 1820s through the 1840s, the federal government negotiated or compelled the mass removal of native peoples from lands east of the Mississippi primarily to Western lands known as the Indian Territory. At the time of its greatest extent, the Indian Territory encompassed present-day Oklahoma and parts of Kansas, Nebraska, and the Dakotas. The Indian Removal Act of 1830 accelerated the removal program by giving policy the force of law and authorizing military means to conduct and enforce removal.

The principal targets of removal were the so-called Five Civilized Tribes—the Cherokee, Creek, Choctaw, Chickasaw, and Seminole Indians—but numerous smaller, less well-known groups were also removed.

The Alabamas

The Alabama Indians were members of the Creek Confederacy. Some Alabama Indians accompanied the Creeks to the Indian Territory during the 1830s and settled near the town of Weleetka, Oklahoma. The tribe had been located primarily on the upper Alabama River. Eighteenth- and nineteenth-century estimates put their number well below 1,000 people.

The Apalachees

A portion of the small Apalachee tribe lived for a time with the Lower Creeks in Alabama. Others lived in Western Florida, Georgia, and Louisiana. The Apalachees were a prominent tribe during the seventeenth century and figured importantly in early Spanish accounts, especially that of ALVAR NÚÑEZ CABEZA DE VACA. However, a major war with the Creeks, who were apparently assisted by English traders in 1702, and a 1704 campaign waged by South Carolina colonists all but destroyed the Apalachees. The population of this group in 1650 has been estimated at about 7,000. By the mid-eighteenth century, their number had dwindled to a few hundred, and by the early nineteenth century, below 100. A few individuals were reported to have removed to the Indian Territory.

The Biloxis

The Biloxi Indians, whose name apparently derived from a word signifying "first people," were based primarily along the lower Pascagoula River in present-day Mississippi and part of Louisiana. Their numbers were always small, probably never more than 1,000 individuals. A few Biloxi Indians removed to the Indian Territory and settled among the Choctaws and Creeks.

The Cherokees

The Cherokees suffered the most infamous fate of the tribes removed under authority of the Indian Removal Act of 1830. Persecuted by the governments of the states in which they lived—the western Carolinas, northern Georgia, and eastern Tennessee—the tribe was victimized by a series of fraudulent treaties and land grabs. By the Treaty of New Echota (1835), a small Cherokee faction sold seven million acres of Cherokee land and agreed to removal westward within three years. The overwhelming majority of the Cherokee Nation repudiated the treaty, but the federal government chose to enforce it. General WINFIELD SCOTT was dispatched to administer removal by force. During 1838 and 1839, more than 15,000 Cherokees were driven along the TRAIL OF TEARS and were marched to Arkansas and the Indian Territory. Through a combination of deliberate cruelty and sheer incompetence on the part of the U.S. Army, some 4,000 Cherokees died en route of disease and exposure.

The removal of 1838 and 1839 was not the first dislocation the Cherokees had endured. An Iroquoian-speaking people, they had originally lived near the Great Lakes. Following defeat at the hands of Iroquois and Delaware tribes during the late sixteenth century, the Cherokees migrated to the Southeast, where they became a most numerous and most powerful group. After the American Revolution—in which they aided the British—the Cherokees increasingly adopted white culture and developed extensive plow agriculture as well as cotton and wool industries. They also adopted the institution of slavery as well as a written, syllabic alphabet (developed by SEQUOYAH during the early 1820s) and a constitutional form of government modeled after that of the United States.

Once they were settled in the Indian Territory, the Cherokees joined the Chickasaws, Choctaws, Creeks, and Seminoles to form the Five Civilized Tribes. During the CIVIL WAR, the Five Civilized Tribes openly sided with the Confederacy, which gave the federal government a pretext for seizing tribal lands after the war. During the early 1880s, when the government formally abolished tribal ownership of lands, and after the Indian Territory became the state of Oklahoma in 1907, all tribal lands were opened for white settlement.

A substantial number of Cherokees avoided the removal of 1838 by taking refuge in the Great Smoky Mountains. They subsequently resettled in North Carolina, where they formed a tribal corporation in 1889. At the time of the last tribal census in 1987, Cherokees living on or near the reservation in North Carolina number 6,110. Some 43,000 persons of Cherokee descent lived in eastern Oklahoma; of this number, perhaps 15,000 were considered full-blooded Cherokees.

The Chickasaws

The Chickasaws, a tribe of the Muskogean linguistic stock, primarily ranged throughout most of present-day Mississippi, Alabama, southwestern Kentucky, and western Tennessee. By the late seventeenth century, their population numbered about 4,000 and was concentrated along the Tombigbee River drainage in northern Mississippi and Alabama. The Chickasaws lived as much by hunting and fishing as they did by farming, and they were skilled and enthusiastic warriors, who frequently fought against neighboring Cherokees, Choctaws, Creeks, and Shawnees. In their first clash with Europeans, against the forces of Hernando de Soto in 1541, they came close to victory, and during the early eighteenth century, they joined forces with the Natchez to resist the encroachments of the French.

By a series of treaties, the Chickasaws ceded most of their lands to the United States during the early 1800s. Most of the tribe was removed to the Indian Territory in 1837. Once settled in the West, they became members of the Five Civilized Tribes.

In 1856, the Chickasaw Nation was established in the Indian Territory, and many members of the tribe enjoyed considerable prosperity in agricultural and lumbering industries. The Five Civilized Tribes's espousal of the Confederate cause during the Civil War resulted in federal seizure of some tribal lands after the war, and the postwar influx of white settlers further disrupted tribal life. When Oklahoma statehood was approved in 1906 (it joined the Union the following year), the Chickasaw Nation was dissolved. In the 1990s, approximately 12,000 Chickasaws lived on or near their reservation in Oklahoma.

The Choctaws

During the eighteenth century, the Choctaws, a Muskogean-speaking people, lived in many villages scattered throughout central and southern Mississippi. Despite the profusion of villages, the Choctaws were a highly cohesive group, roughly organized into three regional divisions, which met annually to discuss common problems. An agricultural people, the Choctaws had a highly developed ritual culture, which included a ritual ball game that was the object of fascination for white visitors, ritual head deformation of infants, and deposition of the bones of the dead in ossuaries.

The Choctaws frequently warred with Spanish and English colonists as well as with the neighboring Chickasaw and Creek tribes. By the early nineteenth century, American settlers had penetrated deeply into Choctaw lands, and by the Treaty of Dancing Rabbit Creek (1830), the tribe ceded all of its territory east of the Mississippi River to the federal government. The major phase of Choctaw removal was accomplished in 1834, when some 13,000 had moved to the Indian Territory. There, they joined the Five Civilized Tribes, prospered as farmers and merchants, and established the Choctaw Republic. Unlike the Cherokees and Chickasaws, the Choctaws largely favored the transformation of Oklahoma from Indian Territory to statehood. Large numbers of Choctaws still lived in the state at the close of the twentieth century.

The Creeks

At their height in the mid-eighteenth century, the Creeks were a powerful, though loose, confederacy of some fifty towns comprising perhaps 20,000 individuals along the waterways of present-day Georgia and Alabama. For the most part, the Creek tribes were Muskogean-speaking and had a highly developed agricultural social structure. Their towns characteristically included a public square, where such rituals as the annual Corn Dance were performed. Creek men played *chunkey,* a ritual ball game. Most agricultural labor was performed by women, while the men hunted and fished.

By the middle of the eighteenth century, French and British traders had established a lively commerce with the Creeks. During the French and Indian War and again during the Revolution, most of the Creeks allied themselves with the British. The War of 1812 split the Creeks into so-called White Sticks, who were neutral or allied to the United States, and the Red Sticks, who allied themselves with the British. Troops under ANDREW JACKSON devastated the Red Stick forces at the Battle of Horseshoe Bend (Alabama) on March 27, 1814. Surrender terms included the cession of much of their finest land to the United States. Indeed, Jackson imposed equally harsh terms on his own allies, the White Stick Creeks. By 1832, in the wake of the Indian Removal Act, all Creek factions had ceded their remaining land east of the Mississippi. From 1836 to 1840, the Creeks were removed to Indian Territory, where they became one of the Five Civilized Tribes. The Creek Nation was formed in 1839, very soon after resettlement in the Indian Territory, but was dissolved in 1907 after Oklahoma entered the Union. In the mid-1990s, some 55,000 Creek people lived on or near their Oklahoma reservation.

The Delawares

In the seventeenth and eighteenth centuries, the Delawares, a Algonquian-speaking confederacy, were very powerful and ranged throughout all of present-day New Jersey as well as parts of adjacent New York, Pennsylvania, and Delaware. The name was bestowed by English colonists. The confederacy consisted of three major tribes—the Munsee, Unalachtigo, and Unami, which collectively referred to themselves as the Lenni-Lenape.

The Delawares suffered early incursions by European settlers during the seventeenth century, and by 1720, the Five Nations of the mighty Iroquois League had pushed the Delawares even farther westward. By the middle of the century, they had established villages in eastern Ohio, where they united with the Wyandots and Shawnees to resist post–Revolutionary American expansion. In 1795, by the Treaty of Greenville, the Delawares at last ceded their Ohio lands to the federal government. This brought about a diaspora, with bands settling in Ohio, Missouri, Arkansas, Texas, and Ontario.

In 1835, many of the bands were gathered at the direction of the federal government and removed to a reservation in Kansas. In 1867, the majority of the Delawares were resettled in the Indian Territory, where they lived among the Cherokees. The Delawares were highly valued by the U.S. Army as scouts during the Indian Wars in the West. Today, Delaware bands in Ontario and Oklahoma consist of some 11,000 people, a population significantly greater than the 8,000 or so individuals who made up the confederacy during the mid-eighteenth century.

The Foxes

See Sac (Sauks) and Foxes (Mesquakies).

The Hitchitis

The Hitchitis, a significant subtribe of the Creek Confederacy, moved with the Creeks to the Indian Territory.

The Illinois

During the seventeenth century, the Illinois Indians, a large and powerful confederation of Algonquian-speaking groups—including the Cahokia, the Kaskaskia, the Michigamea, the Moingwena, the Peoria, and the Tamaroa tribes—dominated most of present-day Illinois, southeastern Wisconsin, and adjacent parts of Iowa and Missouri. They lived by agriculture supplemented by hunting and were fierce warriors, who nearly destroyed the Winnebago Indians before the middle of the seventeenth century. The Illinois tribes were themselves under continual attack from the Iroquois tribes as well as the Santee Sioux and the Potawatomis. This, combined with diseases introduced by European settlers, brought a sharp drop in population. After a Kaskaskia man assassinated the great Ottawa chief Pontiac in 1769, warfare virtually annihilated the Illinois groups.

The few surviving Illinois people were removed to the Indian Territory in 1868. By 1885, they numbered no more than 150.

The Iroquois

The Iroquois League was a powerful and highly influential union of Iroquoian-speaking tribes—

originally the Seneca, Cayuga, Onondaga, Oneida, and Mohawk tribes; the Tuscarora tribe became the sixth member of the league in the early eighteenth century. At the height of its influence, the league ranged over territory from New York's Mohawk Valley and Finger Lakes region and was bordered on the north by Lake Ontario and the Adirondacks and on the south by the Catskills and by the Pennsylvania state line. The league, which enjoyed extensive trading relationships with other tribes as well as with European colonists, continually pressed westward in search of beavers, which were prime articles of commerce. At one point, the league's influence extended as far west as the Mississippi.

The Iroquois League seems to have endured from the sixteenth through much of the eighteenth centuries and then eroded during divisions caused by the American Revolution.

Although the Iroquois League still existed at the end of the twentieth century, by the nineteenth century, when the Senecas and Tuscaroras, together with the Wyandots (an Iroquois "client" tribe), were removed to the Indian Territory, the league had long since ceased to exercise real power.

The Kickapoos

An Algonquian-speaking Indian tribe, the Kickapoos were originally based in central Michigan. By 1670, the tribe had migrated to the portage of the Fox and Wisconsin rivers in southwestern Wisconsin, where it became loosely allied with the Sac and Fox tribes. The Kickapoos suffered great losses at the hands of the Ojibwa, Ottawa, and Potawatomi tribes during the Fox Wars of the early eighteenth century but enjoyed a resurgence after participating in the conquest of the Illinois tribe, whereupon they settled near Peoria, Illinois.

By the early nineteenth century, the Kickapoos were broadcast across the prairie from central Illinois to northern Mexico. Although the tribe supported the Shawnee leader TECUMSEH against the Americans in the War of 1812, it sided with the federal government against the Seminoles in Florida a decade later. During the early 1820s, warfare with the Osage Indians was intense, and in 1852, a large Kickapoo faction migrated to Texas and then to Mexico. Some returned to the United States in 1873 and settled in the Indian Territory.

A Kickapoo wickiup in the Indian Territory, ca. 1880. *Courtesy National Archives.*

The Koasatis

Part of the Creek Confederacy, the Koasati tribe removed from Alabama and Louisiana and settled with the Creeks in northwestern Indian Territory.

The Mesquakies

See Sac (Sauk) and Foxes (Mesquakies).

The Miamis

During the eighteenth century, the Miami Indians, an Algonquian-speaking tribe, were very influential in the Ohio Valley. Originally from what is now northern Illinois and Indiana, the Miami tribe was driven out of its homeland by the Iroquois League during the 1640s and moved westward into present-day Wisconsin, Michigan, and Ohio before returning to Indiana early in the 1700s. The Miamis were active during the Ohio Valley Indian Wars, but their population was greatly reduced by the War of 1812, after which they ceded most of their lands to the federal government. In the 1840s, the surviving Miamis, about 1,000 individuals, were moved to Kansas and later to Oklahoma. In the mid-1990s, fewer than 600 Miamis lived on or near their reservation in Oklahoma.

The Mikasukis

A small Hitchiti-speaking tribe, the Mikasuki people lived in Florida and were associated with the Seminoles, whom they accompanied to the Indian Territory during the 1830s.

The Munsees

The Munsee tribe was closely associated with the Delawares. A very small number of Munsee Indians accompanied the Delawares to the Indian Territory. Early in the twentieth century, only 21 Munsees were reported in Oklahoma.

The Muskogees

The Muskogees were one of the principal Creek tribes and were removed to the Indian Territory with the Creeks.

The Natchez

The Natchez Indians occupied the east side of the lower Mississippi River and developed a remarkably stratified social organization. Speaking a Muskogean language, they lived in five towns and numbered 4,000 during the eighteenth century. In 1713, the French set up a trading post near Grand Village and three years later built Fort Rosalie. Friction quickly developed and escalated into full-scale warfare, in which French forces chased the Natchez Indians across the Mississippi. They withstood a protracted siege at Sicily Island, Louisiana, many of them dying from disease. While some joined the Chickasaws and others fled to the Coosa River, most of the surviving Natchez Indians moved to the Indian Territory in 1832.

The Okmulgees

A Hitchiti Creek tribe, the Okmulgees removed to the Indian Territory with a large group of Creeks in the 1830s.

The Ottawas

The Ottawas were a group of five independent Algonquian-speaking clans who were grouped by the French—with whom they traded—under a single name. During the seventeenth century, they were closely allied with the Huron Confederacy of Ontario and, later, with the Ojibwa and Potawatomi Indians. Ottawa groups were scattered throughout much of Michigan, Wisconsin, Illinois, and Indiana and in Ontario and Manitoba in Canada. In 1763, their extraordinary leader, Pontiac, unsuccessfully attempted to unite several tribes in an effort to drive out the English. Although some Ottawa Indians remain in Canada, Michigan, and Wisconsin, many migrated to Kansas and were subsequently removed to the Indian Territory in 1868.

The Peorias

The Peoria tribe was associated with the Illinois Indians and was removed to the Indian Territory along with them.

The Piankashaws

A tribe associated with the Miami Indians, the Piankashaws came to the Indian Territory with the larger group.

The Potawatomis

The Potawatomi Indians, an Algonquian tribe, were closely related to the Ojibwas and Ottawas but split from these groups by 1500 and migrated to western Michigan. By the late 1640s, warfare had driven them to seek refuge in northeastern Wisconsin. From there, they expanded into much of present-day Wisconsin, Michigan, Illinois, and Indiana. Following defeat in the War of 1812, the Potawatomis suffered many encroachments of white settlement and finally surrendered their Great Lakes lands to the federal government in the 1830s. With this, the tribe divided, some moving into northern Wisconsin and Michigan and others migrating west to Iowa, Kansas, and the Indian Territory. Approximately one-third of the population moved to Ontario, Canada. Recent census figures put the

Potawatomi population on or near U.S. federal reservations at more than 6,000.

The Sacs (Sauks) and Foxes (Mesquakies)

The Sac and Fox tribes of Michigan, Illinois, and Iowa were always closely associated. Their economy was based on a combination of agriculture and hunting, and they had a highly organized society, with a great deal of power being invested in a council of chiefs.

In 1804, factions of the Sac and Fox tribes began ceding lands to the United States. The charismatic Black Hawk, a Sac leader from northern Illinois, repudiated and resisted the cessions, igniting BLACK HAWK'S WAR in 1832, which resulted in much suffering among the tribes.

In 1854, the Sac and Fox peoples were formally divided. The Sacs settled on reservations in the states of Iowa and Kansas and in the Indian Territory, and the Foxes, with some exceptions, remained in the upper Midwest.

The Seminoles

The Seminole and Creek tribes lived together in Georgia during most of the eighteenth century, and then the Seminoles left to settle in Florida. Speakers of the Muskogean language, they lived by agriculture, hunting, and fishing. During the early nineteenth century, the Seminoles fell afoul of white settlers, both by refusing to vacate lands and by declining to return the fugitive slaves they harbored. Troops under the command of Andrew Jackson drove them farther south away from white settlement in the First Seminole War (1817 to 1818). In 1819, the United States purchased Florida from Spain, and more settlers came into the region. The Treaty of Payne's Landing, concluded in 1832, called for the removal of the Seminoles. When most of the tribe repudiated the treaty and refused to move, the Second Seminole War (1835 to 1842) was ignited under the leadership of Osceola and, later, Wildcat and Halek. Although the U.S. Army was unable to defeat the Seminoles in military terms, protracted hostilities wore the resisters down, and all but some 300 of the approximately 4,300 Seminoles moved to the Indian Territory, becoming one of the Five Civilized Tribes. The Seminoles who remained in Florida lived primarily on three reservations near Lake Okeechobee. The Third Seminole War from 1855 to 1858 was concluded when the Seminoles who had been removed to the Indian Territory were brought back to Florida to negotiate on behalf of the government.

The Senecas

The westernmost of the Iroquois League, Seneca Indians were among those who were removed to the Indian Territory with other members of the league. Whites often labeled as "Seneca" all Iroquois who were relocated in the West.

—Alan Axelrod

SUGGESTED READING:

Axelrod, Alan. *Chronicle of the Indians Wars: From Colonial Times to Wounded Knee.* New York, 1993.

Bailey, Lynn R. *The Long Walk.* Los Angeles, 1964.

Brown, Dee. *Bury My Heart of Wounded Knee.* New York, 1970.

Cokran, David H. *The Cherokee Frontier.* Norman, Okla., 1969.

Debo, Angie. *A History of the Indians in the United States.* Norman, Okla., 1971.

Ehle, John. *Trail of Tears: The Rise and Fall of the Cherokee Nation.* New York, 1988.

Fleischmann, Glen. *The Cherokee Removal.* 1838. Reprint, New York, 1971.

Gibson, Arnell. *The Chickasaws.* Norman, Okla., 1971.

Tyler, Lyman. *A History of Indian Policy.* Washington, D.C., 1973.

NATIVE AMERICAN POTTERY, SOUTHWESTERN

The Native American craft of pottery making was first introduced to the peoples of the American Southwest from Mexico, perhaps as early as 350 B.C. From the recovery of ancient potsherds, scholars not only have traced changes in techniques and design, but also have deduced that the craft itself first appeared among the

Pottery in the interior of an Acoma dwelling, New Mexico, about 1900. Photograph by Henry Peabody. *Courtesy National Archives.*

Nampeo, a Hopi potter, displays examples of her work, about 1900. Photograph by Henry Peabody. *Courtesy National Archives.*

Pueblo peoples, then spread throughout the Southwest to the Navajos and other tribes.

Decorative patterns were traditional and characteristic of particular Pueblos. Hopi designs favored birds and masks; the Zias preferred birds and clouds. The Santo Domingo Indians used bold, geometric representations, in contrast to the realism of Cochiti flora and fauna. Serpents and water symbols were also popular motifs in Pueblo designs. For example, a sky loom—a band design symbolizing rain between the sky and earth—appeared on many Pueblo wares. The Santa Clara Indians were known for plain black pottery. Other Pueblo groups produced polished ware of red, black and red, and black and cream, forms that remained prevalent from the nineteenth century through the 1920s.

Like the designs and patterns, pottery-making techniques were a carefully transmitted tradition. The craft was chiefly women's work, and tools, such as stones for smoothing clay, were often passed from mother to daughter for many generations. Potters first collected clay and tempered it with a fortifying material such as water. They made paints from local plants and chewed yucca leaves until they were stiff enough to serve as paintbrushes. Without the aid of a potter's wheel, craftswomen made each piece by coiling, stacking, and smoothing strips of clay. After allowing a piece to dry in the open air, they decorated it and then fired it upside-down on a grate over an open fire.

In the late nineteenth and early twentieth centuries, many Pueblo Indians stopped manufacturing pottery or produced only utilitarian pieces. Archaeological discoveries inspired some young Pueblo artisans to continue the practice as an art form. In the 1890s, Nampeo, a Hopi potter, created pieces based on potsherds recovered from the period before European contact. Beginning in 1908, MARIA MONTOYA MARTINEZ of San Ildefonso based her work on potsherds discovered by archaeologists from the American School of Research, garnering over time worldwide recognition for her art. But most Navajo and Apache potters had abandoned the craft, although groups in southern Arizona—the Pima-Maricopas are one example—continued to make utilitarian items such as bean pots and water-cooling jugs well into the last years of the twentieth century.

In recent years, commercial manufacturers have begun producing "Indian" pottery in direct competition with native craftspeople. In the attempt by Native American artists to maintain an important source of

N. T. Corey photographed potters of the Santa Clara Pueblo, New Mexico, at their craft in 1916. *Courtesy National Archives.*

income in the face of such competition, the quality of some native pottery has declined. Poor quality pottery—especially mass-produced pottery—is marked by its garish color, by decoration that is applied after firing, by its smaller size, and by the poor execution of its design.

—*Melissa A. Davis*

SUGGESTED READING:

Dutton, Bertha P. *Indians of the American Southwest.* Englewood Cliffs, N.J., 1975.

Weigle, Marta, and Peter White. *The Lore of New Mexico.* Albuquerque, N. Mex., 1988.

NATIVE AMERICAN SILVERWORK, SOUTHWESTERN

The Navajos began working with silver around 1868, after they returned from exile at Fort Sumner, New Mexico. First melting American dollars, they soon came to favor the Mexican peso for its malleability and high silver content, but by the twentieth century, they had turned to wire and sheet silver. Among the first items made by the Navajos were tobacco tins, bridles, bow guards, and other utilitarian objects. Their tools were simple—a pair of scissors, a file, a hammer.

Gradually, the Navajos shifted toward objects of personal adornment. They produced primarily jewelry—such as the well-known pendant necklace depicting an old Spanish design of young pomegranates—and an array of conchas, bracelets, and hatbands. Some scholars believe Navajo designs for the conchas were borrowed from Southern Plains tribes, others from European Old World sources. Before 1880, most Navajo silver jewelry lacked settings. While the Navajos had treasured and cut turquoise for centuries, they did not use settings for the semiprecious stone until 1890.

The Zunis, who picked up silverwork from the Navajos in the 1870s, gradually abandoned other metalwork. Their designs were primarily flat-relief work depicting Zuni people, animals, and butterflies. Beginning in 1890, the Zunis created increasingly complex turquoise settings, which came to distinguish their jewelry from that of the Navajos, who emphasized the silver rather than the setting. Many Pueblo tribes adopted silverwork in the late nineteenth century and imitated Navajo designs. These tribes included the Hopis, the Acomas, Isletas, and Lagunas, the Santo Domingos, and the Jemezes, Santa Annas, and Santa Claras.

Indians first traded silver products within tribes before expanding that trade to other tribes. In the early

A Navajo silversmith with examples of his work and tools, about 1880. Photograph by Ben Wittick. *Courtesy National Archives.*

twentieth century, commercial traders, such as the Fred Harvey Company, bought Indian jewelry to sell to tourists. As the jewelry's popularity spread to the East, its production grew to become a tremendous enterprise. Today, Navajo and Pueblo traders market their silverwork in cities throughout the Southwest. Commercial manufacturers imitate Indian silverwork and provide stiff competition to Native American artisans who depend on sales as an important source of income. Although the imitators are required by law to label their wares as such, the laws are weakly enforced.

—*Melissa A. Davis*

SUGGESTED READING:

Dutton, Bertha P. *Indians of the American Southwest.* Englewood Cliffs, N.J., 1975.

Weigle, Marta, and Peter White. *The Lore of New Mexico.* Albuquerque, N. Mex., 1988.

NATIVE AMERICAN WEAVING

The origins of weaving among Native Americans are lost in the centuries prior to Indian contact with Euro-

John K. Hillers's photograph of a Hopi man weaving a blanket, 1879. *Courtesy National Archives.*

peans. Evidence of textiles made of yucca leaves and apocynum fibers dating from the fourth century exist among the archaeological findings of the Anasazi peoples of the Southeast. A craft common to most all cultures, weaving among native peoples varied in materials, technology, and design. Within most tribes, women became weavers, although, among the Pueblo Indians, the men were responsible for producing textiles, blankets, mats, and similar woven objects. The arrival of Europeans on the North American continent altered Indian textiles and their uses.

Native Americans of the Pacific Northwest interior made a twined bag of apocynum decorated with bear grass using techniques that resembled basketry. During the nineteenth century, cotton twine and corn husks were used to make bags of similar construction. Later, textile-makers used wool to add geometric and abstract decoration. Tribes such as the Salish produced blankets made of vegetable fibers. Mountain-goat hair and the hair of a species of dog now extinct were spun into thread—sometimes softened with bird down or cattail fluff—and woven into textiles. Highly decorated blankets were reserved for tribal nobility. The introduction of commercial yarns in the early nineteenth century replaced dog hair and added colors to the blankets. A number of Northwest Coast tribes used cedar bark combined with mountain-goat wool to fashion distinctive blankets, capes, cloaks, skirts, and other garments. The rare Chilkat blankets are the most prized of all.

On the Northern Plains, tribal peoples wove mats of bulrushes or cedar for use in the construction of dwellings and as floor coverings and as screens for drying foods. Barks, roots, and, later, European yarns supplied the materials for bags made by Ojibwa women. Strips of rabbit hide, sometimes woven with cotton twine, offered warmth against the cold.

In the Southwest, where true loom weaving was practiced, tribes developed sophisticated looms around the eighth century when peoples of the Anasazi pueblos domesticated cotton for use in making garments, bags, bands, and straps. When Spaniards arrived from Europe in the sixteenth century, their introduction of sheep offered natives of the Southwest wool fibers for blankets and other textiles. Among the Pueblo tribes, men were usually the weavers; the Zuni people, however, left most of the textile making to the women. Weaving among the Pueblo peoples diminished as European cloths replaced the woven textiles natives used for their garments.

Perhaps the legacy of Pueblo weavers best known to nonnatives is that they taught their craft to Navajo peoples near the end of the seventeenth century. The Navajos quickly mastered the art of weaving, and their distinctive blankets, belts, women's dresses, rugs, and other textiles have found markets among native and nonnative peoples ever since. The Navajos introduced the color red to their traditional designs of natural whites and browns by unraveling and then respinning the red threads of *bayeta,* an English flannel cloth they received in trade from the Spanish.

The variety of designs in Navajo textiles was limited only by the weaver's skill and imagination. Traditionally, her tasks began with the sheared wool of the sheep herded and tended by her tribesmen. The weaver was responsible for carding, washing, spinning, and dyeing the wool; the latter task involved gathering native plants from which the dyes were made. The Na-

A Navajo weaver demonstrates the spinning of yarn used on the loom behind her. Photograph by Milton Snow. *Courtesy National Archives.*

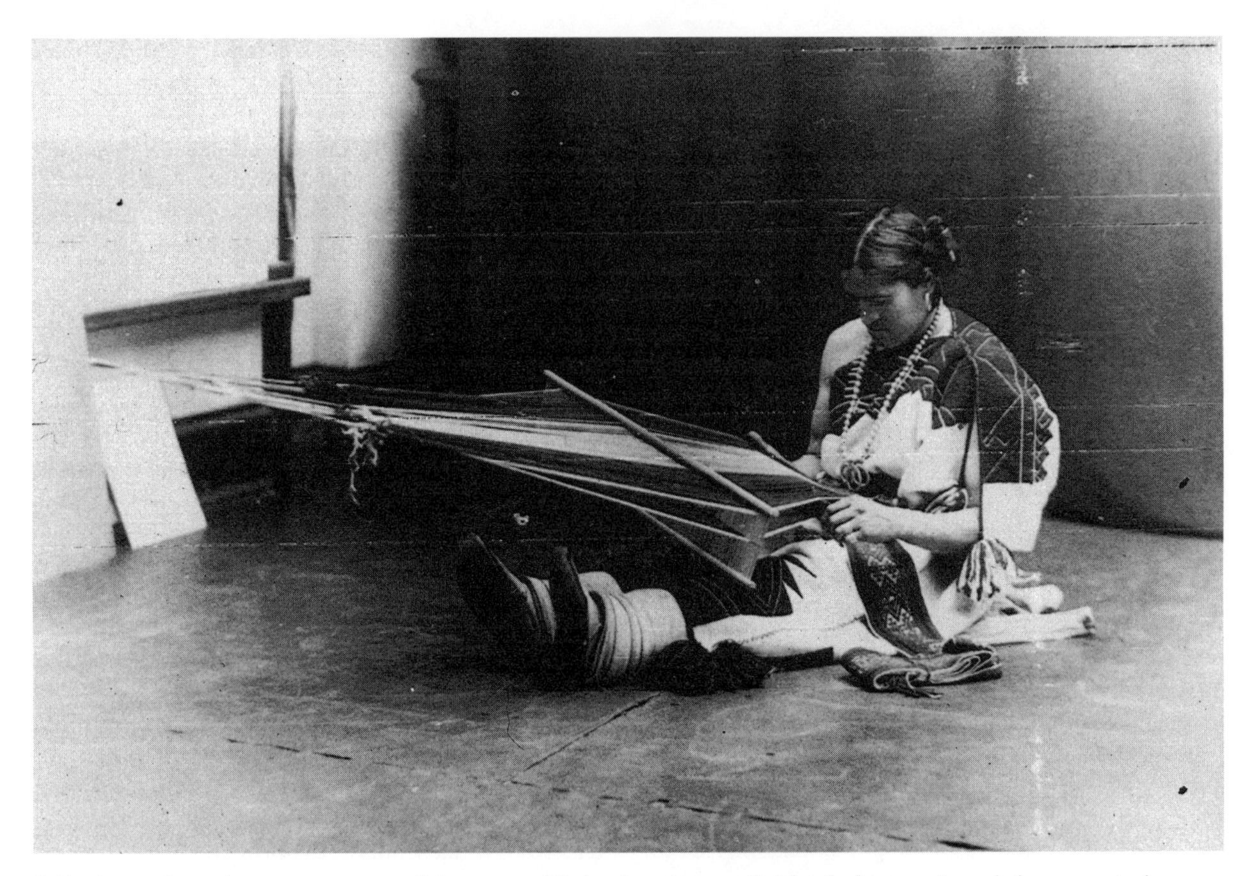

A Zuni man dressed as a woman, a tradition among Native Americans called *berdache,* weaving a belt on a waist loom. Photograph by John K. Hillers, 1879. *Courtesy National Archives.*

vajo blankets and, later rugs, of the mid-nineteenth and twentieth centuries evolved from striped designs to zig-zag bands, to diamonds and triangles, evidence of the weavers's skill and, in part, her contact with design motifs from beyond her village. Serape-style blankets of the mid-nineteenth century represent the apex of the weaver's craft. The introduction of commercial yarn after 1850 increased the weaver's productivity and added colors to her works. Navajo products of this era were traded over much of the trans-Mississippi West, as far away as the Northern Plains.

As tribal use of Navajo textiles declined at the end of the nineteenth century, weavers adapted their products for sale to whites. Making fewer blankets for native use and more rugs for commercial use, Navajo weavers allowed their designs to be influenced by the middlemen who sold their textiles to white customers. Designs similar to oriental rugs appeared, for example, and the influence of the white trader led to designs of distinctive regional styles named for the trading posts that handled the rugs. Two Gray Hills, a design of two triangles whose peaks meet in the center, was usually made of natural browns, grays, blacks, and whites. The Ganado design incorporated black, white, and red geometric designs.

Commercial success, however, also produced some inferior rugs bearing little resemblance in quality or taste to the more traditional weavings. Images of airplanes, cars, and swastikas and the use of aniline dyes and cotton string for hand-spun wool marked the hastily made, garishly designed rugs for the tourist trade. Such excesses led Navajo weavers and traders alike to encourage the use of older styles, designs, and traditional materials. The result, since about the middle of the twentieth century, has been a revival of the fine craft and quality of the traditional Navajo weavings.

—*Patricia Hogan*

SEE ALSO: Native American Peoples: Peoples of the Southwest

SUGGESTED READING:

Blomberg, Nancy. *Navaho Textiles: The William Randolph Hearst Collection.* Tucson, Ariz., 1982.

Feest, Christian. *Native Arts of North America.* 1880. London. Rev. ed. 1992.

Fox, Nancy. *Pueblo Weaving and Textile Arts.* Santa Fe., N. Mex., 1978.

NATURALIZATION LAW OF 1790

Passed by the U.S. Congress, the Naturalization Law of 1790 enumerated qualifications required of individuals hoping to become naturalized citizens of the United States. Individuals born on U.S. lands were automatically citizens of the United States, but the immigration of many individuals from foreign lands forced Congress to consider the incorporation of new members into the republic.

The law specified that prospective citizens reside in the United States for two years, using the time to learn republican principles and their role in the political process and to demonstrate that they were individuals of "proper and decent behavior." Most important, however, for a nation of immigrants, the law required that naturalized citizens had to be "white."

The law prohibited Native Americans from becoming citizens, even though they were born in lands that were or would become the United States. (Free African Americans were sometimes granted citizenship in Northern states before the Civil War; slaves, universally freed under the Reconstruction era's Thirteenth Amendment to the U.S. Constitution, were given the franchise of citizens by the Fourteenth Amendment.) The DAWES ACT of 1867 gave Indian peoples their U.S. citizenship. In the nineteenth and twentieth centuries, immigrants from China, Japan, Korea, and India also were denied citizenship based on the 1790 law, a condition finally remedied by the McCarran-Walter Act of 1952.

—*Patricia Hogan*

SEE ALSO: Alien Land Laws; Chinese Exclusion; Immigration Law

SUGGESTED READING:
Takaki, Ronald. *A Different Mirror: A History of Multicultural America.* Boston, 1993.

NATURAL RESOURCES CONSERVATION SERVICE

See: Soil Conservation Service

NATURE FAKERS

Nature fakers were early twentieth-century nature writers (including Ernest Thompson Seton, Charles G. D. Roberts, JOHN GRIFFITH (JACK) LONDON, and especially William J. Long) charged with fabricating natural-history "facts" and overly dramatizing animal behavior in order to sell their books to an eager and gullible public. The nature-fakers (sometimes spelled "fakirs") controversy began in 1903, when *Atlantic Monthly* published JOHN BURROUGHS's scathing attack, "Real and Sham Natural History." Most of the writers he attacked in the article chose not to defend themselves in public and emerged with their reputations intact. Long, though, launched an aggressive defense and became the focus of the controversy. The battle, waged on the pages of popular magazines and in private letters to publishers, continued until THEODORE ROOSEVELT publicly supported Burroughs and trounced Long in 1907.

The debate was sometimes humorous and asked such questions as can a woodcock set and apply a cast to its own broken leg and can a wolf kill a caribou with a single bite. On a more serious level, it was a debate about whether animals are instinctive machines or reasoning beings. It also weighed the merits of science versus empathy as methods of understanding and interpreting animal behavior. The controversy helped set standards of accuracy in nature writing.

Although the controversy has been largely forgotten, *nature faker* has become a term of humorous derision applied to supposed nature sentimentalists. The term was used against opponents of the Hetch Hetchy Dam, and park rangers involved in law enforcement have also used it to characterize interpretive naturalists.

—*Ralph H. Lutts*

SUGGESTED READING:
Burroughs, John. "Real and Sham Natural History." *Atlantic Monthly* 91 (March 1903): 298–309.
Lutts, Ralph H. *The Nature Fakers: Wildlife, Science and Sentiment.* Golden, Colo., 1990.
Roosevelt, Theodore. "Nature Fakers." *Everybody's Magazine* 17 (September 1907): 427–430.

NAUVOO, ILLINOIS

In the winter of 1838 to 1839, a group of Mormon refugees, fleeing an extermination order issued against them by the governor of Missouri, moved to Illinois. They settled in Nauvoo for seven years and built a town of perhaps twelve thousand inhabitants. Although modest by later standards, Nauvoo was then the largest town in Illinois. The MORMONS left Illinois in 1846, refugees again, headed this time for a no-man's land in the Great Basin.

Nauvoo is on the east bank of the Mississippi River some 240 air kilometers north-northwest of St. Louis and 230 east-northeast of the earlier Mormon settlements in Missouri. Today, Nauvoo is between Keokuk, Iowa, twelve miles downstream, and Fort Madison, Iowa, upstream a lesser distance. The town site is a peninsula jutting into the river about a mile from base to point and some three miles across at the base. The peninsula, formed by a shelf of limestone rising above the adjoining bedrock, causes the river to make a great bend. Extending into the river, the shelf formed the Des Moines Rapids, an infamous barrier to river navigation. Thus the location was a portage site, attractive for commercial possibilities. Indeed, it had been given the name "Commerce" by its Eastern speculator-owners. The Mormons tried to cut a canal across the peninsula but were thwarted by the hard limestone. The cut then became a quarry for building stone.

Above the peninsula rises a bluff, the characteristic escarpment that separates the river's flood plain from adjoining upland prairies. Nauvoo rose both on the lowland peninsula, called "the Flat," and the upland, known as "the Hill." These two areas came to have political significance. Church leaders and most Mormons lived on the Flat. Non-Mormons, or Gentiles, had businesses and residences on the Hill.

Nevertheless, the hill was to be the site of a great temple projected by the Prophet JOSEPH SMITH, JR. Nauvoo, he said, meant "City Beautiful." The temple rose as a crown on the bluff, overlooking the town below. The scene was magnificent and romantic, as reported by many curious visitors who came both to marvel at it and to speculate about its meaning.

From the first, Nauvoo was a boom town, its society and economy supplied by a growing stream of converts. Mormonism was a "mission miracle," and thousands were baptized. At first they came from New England, the Middle Atlantic states, and the Old Northwest states. During the years that the Mormons lived in Nauvoo, missionaries to England reaped a great harvest of converts there. Nauvoo was the "Gathering Place," said Joseph Smith. Converts must come and bring their wealth, their skills, and their devotion. From Nauvoo, said the prophet, the latter-day kingdom of God would roll forth to fill first the United States, then the Western Hemisphere, and finally the whole earth. Converts did come, and so many moved to Nauvoo from England that the society had something of an international character.

The economy was built on the construction industry. The swelling population must be housed; places of business, built; outlying farms, opened. Nauvoo was not an exporting economy. It consumed its own production.

The largest building projects by far were the temple on the Hill and the Nauvoo House hotel on the Flat. The former was intended for new and unique religious purposes. The latter was a joint-stock enterprise, although its financing was intermingled with that of the church and of the prophet himself. Both were costly buildings and consumed large amounts of resources. (Much of the labor for building the temple, however, was contributed by the faithful.) The temple was completed after Smith's assassination in 1844. The hotel remained unfinished.

Joseph Smith's vision and intent were to combine the secular and religious lives of his followers into a literal kingdom of God on earth, the consummation of which was necessary to prepare for the Second Coming. The task must be accomplished quickly, so Nauvoo's brief history exhibited a kind of forced-draft spirit. Nothing was casual or unhurried. Smith even prophesied God's condemnation if the work of kingdom building were not accomplished "in time." Time was ending; history was closing. The Saints were called to a most demanding, but most glorious, task.

Central to Smith's enterprise was the introduction of sacred rites that would bind past to future, earth to heaven, and the living to the dead: "sealings" of family members for eternity, proxy baptisms for dead ancestors, and endowments of special powers on the Mormon lay priesthood. The temple was to be the unique and essential locus of these rites. Into that religious context, the concept of plural marriage was secretly introduced, with Smith himself providing the personal model as well as the supporting doctrine.

The political problems created by Nauvoo both for Mormons and for Illinois proved insurmountable. The Saints were a corporate religious body apparently controlled by one man. They were so numerous that they could be a deciding factor in statewide elections. As such, they were courted by both political parties but were trusted by neither.

Smith used a liberal city charter granted by the state to make Nauvoo a self-governing, quasi-independent city-state of which he was mayor. It had its own "army," the Nauvoo Legion, mustered under the state's militia law. Smith made himself lieutenant general, a rank not occupied since George Washington. He then declared himself a candidate for the U.S. presidency in the spring of 1844 and sent Mormon elders to enter him on the ballots of the various states. All of these moves augmented the neighbors' anxiety and hostility.

A fatal crisis developed when a faction within the church itself charged Smith with exceeding both his spiritual authority and his legal powers. His characteristic pugnacity gave way to seeming fatalism, and he surrendered to law officers at the county seat of Carthage. Incarcerated in the county jail, he and his brother Hyrum were shot by a mob on June 27, 1844.

A succession struggle ensued in which Mormonism ultimately broke into numerous sects. BRIGHAM YOUNG, president of the Quorum of Twelve Apostles, emerged as leader of the great majority of Saints, including most of the population of Nauvoo.

Nauvoo proved to be a kind of dress rehearsal for the Mormon kingdom Brigham Young later fashioned in the Great Basin. Precedents were set: theocratic government with control vested in a priestly hierarchy; a powerful presidency; a corporative church, combining sacred and secular aspects of life into a single whole; the concept of a place-specific, earthly kingdom that was also the kingdom of God; temple-centered "work" as the heart of religious observance; and a polygamous family system intended for eternity.

At the outset of the Nauvoo experience, Mormonism was a millenarian and apocalyptic sect drawn around a charismatic, quixotic prophet. The Nauvoo experience provided outlines of doctrinal and political schema that would propel it into a long future.

—*Robert Flanders*

SEE ALSO: Church of Jesus Christ of Latter-day Saints

SUGGESTED READING:

Allen, James B., and Glen Leonard. *The Story of the Latter-day Saints*. Salt Lake City, 1976.

Arrington, Leonard J., and Davis Bitton. *The Mormon Experience: A History of the Latter-Day Saints*. New York, 1979.

Flanders, Robert. "Dream and Nightmare: Nauvoo Revisited." In *The New Mormon History*. Edited by D. Michael Quinn. Salt Lake City, 1992.

———. *Nauvoo: Kingdom on the Mississippi*. Urbana, Ill., 1965.

Hansen, Klaus J. *Quest For Empire: The Kingdom of God and the Council of Fifty in Mormon History*. East Lansing, Mich., 1967.

NAVAJO INDIANS

SEE: Native American Peoples: Peoples of the Southwest

NAVAJO RUGS

SEE: Native American Weaving, Southwestern

NAVAJO STOCK-REDUCTION PROGRAM

During President Franklin D. Roosevelt's first term in office, the program for allotting Indian land was brought to an abrupt halt by the Indian Reorganization Act of 1934. The act was based on a policy devised by John Collier, whom FDR had appointed commissioner of Indian affairs, and it was designed (Collier said) to offer the Indians a "New Deal." A critic of rugged individualism like many New Dealers, Collier admired what he considered the "sense of community" he found among the Indians, especially the Navajos of New Mexico, whom (Collier said) defined "the individual and his society as wholly reciprocal." Only the Indians, he argued, still possessed a "fundamental secret of human life—the secret of building great personality through the instrumentality of social institutions." There was much that whites could learn from the Indian way of life, which should be appreciated "as a gift for us all." Indeed, according to Collier:

> *Assimilation*, not into our culture but into modern life, and *preservation and intensification* of heritage are not hostile choices. . . . If the Indian life is a good life, then we should be proud and glad to have this native culture going on by the side of ours.

To Collier's way of thinking, allotment—breaking tribal lands into individual plots—had been "much more than just a huge white land grab; it was a blow, meant to be fatal, at Indian tribal existence." Believing that "the role of government was to help, but not coerce, the tribal efforts" of the Indians and that the goal of Indian policy should not be the absorption of Native Americans into the white populations, but the maintenance of Indian cultures on their communally owned lands, Collier proposed to do away with allotment, establish Indian self-government, and preserve Indian civilization, its arts, its crafts, its traditions. FDR thought this was, as he said, "great stuff," and the law was passed, reversing a policy dating back to 1607. The new law, however, would only apply to tribes who voted to accept it, a further effort to give back to the Indians "control over their own destinies."

The next year, 172 tribes voted in favor of the law; 73, against it. Among the Indians who rejected the law were the Navajos, who saw in Collier another in a long of line of American leaders, beginning with Thomas Jefferson, who talked about Indian autonomy while telling Indians how to run their lives. The Navajos had not forgotten that whites had been telling them what was good for them and what they should do for centuries. One of the most hated figures in their history was Christopher Houston ("Kit") Carson, who had come close to causing the Navajos as a people to disappear during the American Civil War. After they had surrendered to him, Carson's troops destroyed their orchards and the sheep herds they had been raising since they first acquired the creatures from the Spanish during the seventeenth century. Carson marched the Indians on what they called the "Long Walk" to Bosque Redondo, where they were to take up life as farmers rather than sheepherders. But in 1858, this first experiment in social engineering having failed, the government resettled the Navajos on a reservation in their original homeland and gave them sheep to replace those Carson had slaughtered.

Now came Collier, a New Deal liberal, telling them they could have self-rule but suggesting at the same time that it was best for them to reduce their stock of sheep. In what Collier called his "ethnic laboratory," new government studies had determined that the Navajos were raising on their reservation one-half million more animals than their range could support, thereby causing overgrazing and severe soil erosion. Unless the Navajos faced the problem soon, Collier warned, this native sheep-raising people would encounter great hardship and much suffering. The federal government had to intervene for the tribe's own good.

The drama of the Navajo stock-reduction program would play out against the backdrop of the Great Depression's Dust Bowl, for it was in 1935, the year the Navajos rejected the Indian New Deal, that the black blizzards began to roll across the Great Plains. According to Donald Worster, the roots of the Dust Bowl lay not completely in nature but, at least in part, in what some historians have called the "Great Plow Up" of the 1920s. Shortly before World War I, agricultural entrepreneurs had begun to turn millions of new acres of prairie to wheat, so that by the time the long droughts of the early 1930s started, 33 million acres lay naked, denuded of grass, and open to the winds. Lewis Cecil Gray—the principal author of the 1936 New Deal government report, *The Future of the Great Plains*—was one of those who blamed the Dust Bowl not just on nature nor on an imperfect understanding of Great Plains agriculture but also on destructive forces in American culture promoted by the greedy ethics of runaway capitalism. Instead of profit-seeking, the New Deal trumpeted collective action toward broad social goals and—as Gray's report and dozens of other such documents indicated—came to distrust individual effort, local initiative, and traditional wisdom.

At the same time, it seemed to many—and to some in government—as if nature itself were taking revenge for American greed and hubris. Not only year after year of drought, but also swarms of locusts and mercilessly cold winters, plagued the West of the 1930s. Much New Deal planning seems now like a massive counterattack, as if those who could engineer and perfect a complex capitalist society were not about to be undone by mere nature. Out West, as Worster points out, nothing so stirred the contemporary imagination and renewed the American people's faith in their ability to conquer nature than the building of Boulder Dam (now called Hoover Dam). The largest of its kind ever planned, the dam fired the dreams of Los Angeles's William Mulholland and his fellow civic salesmen, who had drained dry the Owens Valley and now were turning to the Colorado River as the major source of water for their burgeoning city and the big agricultural interests of California's Imperial Valley. There were also the Bureau of Reclamation professionals, whose very job description called for them to undo nature wherever possible. These bureaucrats, whom Worster calls "pharaonic administrators" grown bold on New Deal power, wanted at the least to build "the biggest dam ever built by anyone anywhere." All of them, says Worster—the bureaucrats, the Imperial Valley farmers, the Los Angeles promoters—were filled with dreams and desires beyond imagining. Those dreams, the very future itself it seemed, the Navajo were threatening by herding their sheep.

Collier had received reports that silt from the erosion on Navajo land was filling up the Colorado River and threatening to clog Boulder Dam, then under construction, thus hurting the important attempts to supply the Imperial Valley with irrigation and Los Angeles with electricity. The United States Geological Survey had determined:

> Briefly, in the main Colorado system, the Little Colorado and the San Juan are major silt problems, while within each of these basins the Navajo Reservation's tributaries are the major silt problem. The fact is the . . . Navajo Reservation is practically "Public Enemy No. 1" in causing the Colorado Silt problem.

Just as it complained to Midwestern farmers about the problems created by their heedless plowing, the federal government warned the Navajo that, unless they stopped overgrazing their sheep, the erosion would continue, the silt would build up, and economic development in the Southwest would be blocked entirely.

At first, the government had come to the reservation talking about the Navajos' future, but the Navajos understood well enough that it was the future of white man's civilization and not their own that was causing concern. What worried them was that they depended on sheep for their livelihood. Raising sheep, points out Ronald Takaki, was a way of life for the Navajos, one steeped in their history, one they knew and understood better than the Indian Affairs bureaucrats. The animals were a part of their world. Navajo boys grew up caring for the flocks. For them, sheep and survival were synonymous. As one Navajo father explained to his son, "Remember what I've told you. . . . Everything comes from the sheep."

When the Navajos tried to explain that their sheep were not the problem, nature was, with her dry ground, big winds, and refusal to drop rain in the last few years, the bureaucrats stopped talking about the Navajo economy and the Navajo future and talked about their own. No doubt, to New Deal ears the Navajos' assertions sounded like the complaints of farmers, blaming the problems they created on the weather. In any case, Navajo truculence stood in the way of social progress. Collier told the Navajo council:

> Down there on the Colorado River is the biggest, most expensive dam in the world, the Boulder Dam now being built which will furnish Southern California with water and with electric power, and the Boulder Dam will be filled up with your fine agricultural soil in no great number of years if we do not stop erosion on the Navajo reservation. This reservation, along with the other Indian reservations on the Colorado River, is supplying much more than half the silt that goes down the Colorado River, which will in the course of a comparatively few years render the Boulder Dam useless and thereby injure the population of all Southern California and a good deal of Arizona too.

Expressing concerns about Navajo survival but driven by the need to protect Boulder Dam and the economic interests of the United States, Collier created a stock-reduction program on the Navajo reservation, under which the New Deal government would purchase four hundred thousand sheep and goats and then compensate the Indians for any loss of future income with employment in federal projects.

Collier came to the Navajos seventeen times in five years trying to explain his program. He complained that never in his "long life of social effort and struggle" had he ever "experienced among any other Indian group, or any group whatsoever" the kind of "anguished hostility" that he experienced with the Navajos. Why, they would not even listen to his experts. Collier had brought in A. C. Cooley, an economist one assumes, to explain how losing livestock would actually increase their livelihood. Cooley showed them a chart. The blue line stood for the sheep; the yellow line, for wages from federal projects; the red line, for income derived from the stock. Now, because of improved grazing, better breeding, and more careful management, when the blue line and the yellow line fall over the next few years, the red line actually rises. To the Navajos this was truly voodoo economics; believing that less was more took a leap of faith they could not make. One of them asked why all three lines could not simply rise together.

When paternal suasion and financial double talk failed, Collier turned—as men with his job had been doing for centuries—to the tactics of divide and conquer. He struggled to identify and manipulate those on the council sympathetic to his arguments or anxious to ingratiate themselves with the New Dealers. "We elected the council, but they couldn't do anything," complained one Navajo. "And we think they are just put in to try to get us to listen to Collier." Despite a bitter, sometimes wild, always angry opposition, the council voted for Collier's program. Now, the U.S. government *ordered* the Navajos to reduce their stock. Angry Navajos wrote to their agent, Jacob C. Morgan, and at the council meetings, Collier and his experts refused to let the dissenters do much talking. When they did manage a hearing, Collier simply would not listen. Instead, he proceeded to carry out government policy. He brought in local police to enforce the orders from Washington. As the Navajos watched agents take their animals, they worried aloud about how they would live without their stock and expressed especial bitterness at the loss of goats. "The poorest people owned goats—the easiest people to take away from," explained one Navajo. One herder called Collier's program a "war" against his people.

By 1935, Collier's agents had reduced Navajo stock by four hundred thousand sheep and goats, but he decided that was not enough. Announcing that there were still 1.2 million Navajo animals grazing on land capable of supporting only one-half million, Collier decreed: "This means a further reduction of 56 percent [will] be necessary in order to reduce the stock to the carrying capacity of the range." Meanwhile, the Navajos were fast becoming dependent on wages—making up 40 percent of their pitiful per capita annual income of $128—that came from temporary government jobs. Stock reduction reduced the Navajos to relief workers on the federal dole in makeshift New Deal jobs programs. Little wonder the Navajos denounced Collier's project as "the most devastating experience in Navaho history" since Kit Carson imprisoned them at Bosque Redondo in the 1860s.

As it turned out, the Navajos were right all along about the overgrazing and the soil erosion. Scientists who did further research on silt settlement determined that overgrazing was not the source of the problem. Nature was perfectly capable of silting up the Lake Mead reservoir without any help from the Navajos. From the beginning, the Navajos had tried to explain to the government experts how their fathers and grandfathers had talked about erosion and how even government reports had documented the run-off as early as the 1890s. Dry weather came in cycles, and a certain amount of erosion was related more to drought than to overgrazing, unless you did what the white cattlemen and the farmers did to the land. But the Navajos were not agribusinessmen but traditional sheepherders, and consequently, they did not overgraze. They had pointed out to Collier what was obvious—the early 1930s were dry years—and they predicted that their range would recover when the drought ended. "We know something about that by nature," they told the bureaucrats, "because we were born here and raised here and we knew about the processes of nature on our range." Generation after generation, says Takaki, the Navajos had searched the skies for dark clouds at dawn and dusk and prayed to their gods for rain and understood the grass always came again when their prayers were answered.

Perhaps the mistake the Navajos made was trying to describe the real West to men for whom land was an abstraction, weather always a surprise, and time money. These men did not, could not, see the Indians as experts on nature but, essentially, as children who understood little about the ways of the world—that is, the New Dealers' own administered and calibrated society. To the Navajos, the real West was wind, water, earth, and sky, not the surveyed lines and squares of real estate, arid lands begging for "reclamation," or the buried treasure of raw materials waiting to be unearthed Collier and others imagined. The tragedy of the Navajo Stock-Reduction Program was that its conception resulted from the very clash between cultures the Indian New Deal hoped to overcome.

—*Charles Phillips*

SEE ALSO: Federal Government; Native Peoples: Peoples of the Southwest; Reclamation; Owens Valley War

SUGGESTED READING:

Dippie, Brian W. *The Vanishing American: White Attitudes and U.S. Indian Policy.* Lawrence, Kans., 1982.

Iverson, Peter. *The Navajo Nation.* Westport, Conn., 1981.

Kelley, Lawrence C. *The Navajo Indians and Federal Indian Policy, 1900–1935.* Tucson, Ariz., 1968.

Parman, Donald L. *Navajos and the New Deal.* New Haven, 1976.

Takaki, Ronald. *A Different Mirror: A History of Multicultural America.* Boston, 1993.

Taylor, Graham D. *The New Deal and American Indian Tribalism: The Administration of the Indian Reorganization Act, 1934–45.* Lincoln, Nebr., 1980.

White, Richard. *The Roots of Dependency: Subsistence, Environment, and Social Changes among the Choctaw, Pawnees, and Navajos.* Lincoln, Nebr., 1983.

Worster, Donald. *Under Western Skies: Nature and History in the American West.* New York, 1992.

NAVAJO WARS

At the time of their first contact with Spanish colonists in the late sixteenth or early seventeenth century, the Navajos, or Apaches de Nabaju ("Strangers of the Cultivated Fields"), lived in scattered bands and cultivated small plots in the San Juan River basin in the present-day Four Corners region of Arizona and New Mexico. Adept assimilators, these Athapascan-speaking hunter-gatherers were recent arrivals in the Southwest, along with their Apache kinsmen. They learned farming techniques from their Pueblo and Ute neighbors, with whom they traded and engaged in warfare. Pueblos, who hid out among the tribe following the 1680 PUEBLO REVOLT, taught the Navajos the fundamentals of horsemanship and sheep raising.

Navajo raiding evolved after the Spaniards introduced sheep and horses into New Mexico around 1600. The horse revolutionized Navajo society, giving the Indians mobility, status, and wealth. On horseback, they attacked Spanish settlements, as well as Hopi, Zuni, Ute, and Pueblo villages, and carried off sheep, captives, and more horses. Spanish enslavement of women and children to work on ranches and missions gave rise to a pattern of raids and counterraids, with the Navajos at times the victims of slave hunters and at other times acting as middlemen in the sale of captives to the Spaniards in exchange for horses. At first, the Navajos were little more than a nuisance to the New Mexicans who were preoccupied with forming alliances against the Apaches, Utes, and Comanches. By 1775, however, raids had become so destructive of livestock that officials were forced to import horses from Spain. New Mexicans launched a series of ineffectual military campaigns. Typically, the Navajos came to the treaty table in time for the spring planting of crops and then resumed raiding in the fall and winter.

Relatively peaceful relations ended around 1800. Reacting to Spanish encroachment on Navajo grazing lands, on August 3, 1804, nearly one thousand warriors attacked Cebolleta. In retaliation, Lieutenant

Colonel Antonio Narbona launched a winter campaign that culminated on January 17 and 18, 1805, with the apparent massacre of women, children, and old men in Canyon de Chelly.

The pattern of slave raids and reprisals continued after Mexican independence, with the Navajos holding the upper hand. In 1823, Governor José Antonio Vizcarro and fifteen hundred soldiers conducted the largest campaign to date in Navajo country but with little effect. Navajo raids intensified during the 1830s, as New Mexico settlers pushed westward, seized slaves, and usurped Navajo land. In a final effort at peacemaking, New Mexicans and Navajos signed the Martinez Treaty at Jémez on March 18, 1844. Like most earlier agreements, it required the Navajos to surrender their captives, while placing the New Mexicans under no similar obligation. Of an estimated three thousand to six thousand slaves in New Mexico at this time, as many as 75 percent were Navajos. The treaty was quickly broken, and the countryside slipped into anarchy, as roving bands of Hispanic settlers conducted slave-hunting expeditions and waged guerrilla warfare. In desperation, officials in Santa Fe forged an alliance with Sandoval and the Dine Ana 'aii ("Enemy Navajo"). Living north of Cebolleta, this group had declared allegiance to Spain in the early 1800s. Outcasts from the rest of the tribe and viewed with suspicion by Hispanics and Anglos, members of the group often served as guides and auxiliaries on Navajo campaigns.

The Americans who seized control of New Mexico in 1846 perpetuated old customs of dealing with the Navajos. On October 6, General STEPHEN WATTS KEARNY ordered Colonel ALEXANDER WILLIAM DONIPHAN into Navajo country. At Ojo del Oso (Bear Spring, near present-day Gallup) on November 21, Zarcillos Largos and other headmen agreed to halt their attacks and return captives. Congress, and the majority of Navajos, rejected the treaty.

Colonel John M. Washington's arrival as military governor in October 1848 signaled the beginning of conflict between the military and civilians over how to deal with the Navajos. As settlers cried out for extermination, Washington and Indian agent James S. Calhoun concluded a treaty on September 9, 1849, that annexed Navajo lands to New Mexico and obligated tribesmen to turn over captives and stolen property. Although the U.S. Senate eventually ratified the Washington Treaty, once again most Navajos refused to abide by its terms. As a prelude to the conference, soldiers killed NARBONA, a prominent Navajo advocate of peace, in a dispute over a horse.

Antagonism between civilians and the military deepened with the appointment in July 1851 of Colonel EDWIN V. SUMNER as army commander in New Mexico. Stubborn and abrasive, Sumner clashed with Calhoun, the newly appointed governor, and citizens who called for arming volunteers against the Navajos. Undermanned and instructed to economize, Sumner preferred peaceful coercion to warfare. He withdrew garrisons from settlements and established Fort Defiance in Navajo country. The post curbed raiding for a time, but its presence was a festering thorn to the Navajos.

The relative calm in the relations between Indians and whites through the mid-1850s was due in large measure to the efforts of Indian agent Henry Dodge. Known as "Red Shirt" to the Navajos, he worked tirelessly to mediate disputes until his death at the hands of Apaches in 1856.

In the meantime, Governor David Meriwether tried a new method of dealing with the Navajos. On July 16 and 17, 1855, two thousand warriors assembled at Laguna Negra, near Fort Defiance. The resulting treaty, which was not ratified by the Senate, would have deprived the Navajos of two-thirds of their land and settled them on a seven-thousand-acre reservation. The conference was notable for the emergence of MANUELITO as a spokesman for Navajo dissidents.

Dissatisfaction grew as Navajos reacted to renewed Ute attacks and increasing New Mexican encroachment on grazing lands. Many wealthy and powerful Navajos believed they could defeat the Americans in a fight to preserve their homeland, but the severe drought in 1857 and imminent starvation rallied young warriors behind Manuelito.

A dispute over grazing rights near Fort Defiance ignited a half-decade of bitter fighting. After soldiers ran off Indian stock and Navajos murdered Captain William Brooks's black slave, in the fall and winter of 1858 and 1859, Lieutenant Colonel Dixon S. Miles led a punitive expedition into Canyon de Chelly. The resulting treaty was ineffectual. Despite the calming influence of Zarcillos Largos and GANADO MUCHO during the spring of 1860, Navajos raided New Mexican settlements. On April 30, one thousand warriors unsuccessfully attacked Fort Defiance. In September and October, New Mexico volunteers under Colonel Manuel Chaves invaded Canyon de Chelly, destroyed crops, seized livestock, and took captives. Zarcillos Largos was killed in the fighting. That attack began the period of warfare and exile that Navajos remember as Nahondzod—"The Fearing Time."

Navajos, Utes, and Apaches raided freely as the army prepared to meet the Confederate invasion of New Mexico. The massacre of Navajos by Chaves's volunteers at Fort Fauntleroy on September 13, 1861, enraged tribesmen, who struck out with renewed fury.

Union commander General Edward Richard Spring Canby proposed a firm policy for dealing with the Navajos. Those who agreed to settle on a reservation would be protected by the government; those who refused would be considered enemies and hunted down. Canby's successor, General James H. Carleton, set the plan in motion.

A veteran of Navajo campaigns in the 1850s, Carleton was a humanitarian who envisioned the wholesale transformation of native culture and the eventual assimilation of Indians into Anglo-Christian society. He selected Bosque Redondo, a barren flat on the Pecos River in eastern New Mexico, as the site for his grandiose experiment. Carleton first turned his attention to the Mescaleros, who were quickly subdued and resettled at Bosque Redondo. He then unleashed Colonel Christopher Houston ("Kit") Carson to round up the Navajos. Apart from its modest military results, Carson's sweep through Canyon de Chelly in the winter of 1863 and 1864 enabled him to persuade a large number of Navajos that his intentions were peaceful. Meanwhile, Delgadito had even greater success in persuading his tribesmen near Fort Wingate to surrender.

On February 26, 1864, the first of six contingents of Navajos began the Long Walk into exile on the Pecos. Many died of cold and hunger along the way. By the spring of 1865, more than nine thousand Indians (slightly more than eighty-five hundred of them Navajos) were crowded onto forty square miles in the shadow of Fort Sumner.

Greed, bickering, and nature itself doomed Carleton's herculean efforts at Bosque Redondo. Civilian contractors defrauded the Indians and the government; the army and the Indian Bureau quarreled constantly over policy and responsibility; insects and floods destroyed the crops; disease ravaged the Indian population; and Comanche raids decimated the reservation herds. The Mescaleros fled the reservation on the night of November 3, 1865. Conditions eventually became so intolerable that the Navajos pleaded to be returned to their former homes. Following an inspection, General William Tecumseh Sherman and Lewis Tappan signed a treaty on June 1, 1868, that restored the Navajo homeland.

Although the Bosque Redondo was a tragic failure, it affected the Navajos in fundamental ways. By bringing them into close contact with whites, it fostered mutual understanding and started the tribe on the road to assimilation. Farming techniques learned at Bosque Redondo increased crop production and made raiding less attractive. Introduced to metalsmithing, the Navajos refined the craft to an art form and became some of the finest silversmiths in the Southwest. Introduction of the wagon enabled families to travel long distances and, thereby, fostered tribal cohesion. The seeds of justice and government sewn along the Pecos eventually blossomed into a sophisticated tribal political structure. Most important, for the first time, the vast majority of Navajos were gathered together in one place at Bosque Redondo. They emerged from the experience with a heightened sense of tribal unity. The Bosque Redondo experience brought down the curtain on centuries-old patterns of raids and reprisals. For good and ill, the Navajos who returned to the Four Corners region in 1868 were a changed people.

—*Bruce J. Dinges*

See also: Native American Peoples: Peoples of the Southwest

Suggested reading:

Kelly, Lawrence. *Navajo Roundup: Selected Correspondence of Kit Carson's Expedition against the Navajo, 1863–1865*. Boulder, Colo., 1970.

McNitt, Frank. *Navajo Wars: Military Campaigns, Slave Raids, and Reprisals*. Albuquerque, N. Mex., 1972. Reprint. 1990.

Thompson, Gerald. *The Army and the Navajo: The Bosque Redondo Reservation Experiment*. Tucson, Ariz., 1976.

Underhill, Ruth M. *The Navajos*. Norman, Okla., 1956.

NAVARRO, JOSÉ ANTONIO BALDOMERO

A leader in the Texas Revolution against Mexico, José Antonio Baldomero Navarro (1795–1871) was born in San Antonio, Texas, the son of Angel Navarro and Maria Josefa Ruiz y Peña.

Following his father's trade, Navarro became a merchant in San Antonio. An avid reader, he embraced freedom while opposing colonial tyranny. At the age of eighteen, he joined adventurer Augustus Magee, a graduate of the U.S. Military Academy, and Bernardo Gutierrez de Lara, a supporter of Miguel Hidalgo, in an early attempt for Mexican independence. Spanish forces crushed their efforts, and Navarro fled to Louisiana.

In 1816, following three years of exile, Navarro returned to San Antonio. In 1821, he met Stephen Fuller Austin, and the two men maintained a lifelong friendship. Navarro was elected representative to the legislature of Coahila and Texas in 1821. Certain of the inevitability of Texas's independence from Mexico, Navarro eventually sold his business interests to help the Texans' cause. He was one of the signers of the Texas Independence Proclamation on March 2, 1836.

José Antonio Baldomero Navarro. *Courtesy Archives Division, Texas State Library.*

In 1841, MIRABEAU B. LAMAR, president of the Republic of Texas, appointed Navarro to lead an expedition to New Mexico. He was captured by the Mexican army, taken to Mexico City, and sentenced to death by General ANTONIO LÓPEZ DE SANTA ANNA. His sentence was later commuted to life. He escaped and eventually landed in Galveston, Texas. In 1845, he was appointed to serve as a delegate to the Texas Constitutional Convention, which ultimately voted for annexation to the United States.

Navarro served as U.S. senator from Texas from 1846 to 1848. He supported the cause of slavery and, in 1861, championed Texas's secession from the Union.

—*Fred L. Koestler*

SUGGESTED READING:
Dawson, Joseph M. *José Antonio Navarro: Co-creator of Texas.* Waco, Tex., 1969.

NEBRASKA

Located near the center of the Great Plains, Nebraska has defied easy description for nearly two hundred years. Travelers often described the state as flat, monotonous, or boring. Yet the state's gently rolling topography rises from its eastern tall-grass prairies to the short-grass High Plains of the western Panhandle. River valleys, especially those of the Platte, Loupe, Niobrara, and Republican, and the awesome Sandhills, which dominate the north-central portion of the state, also provide variety. Nebraska's weather is also far from monotonous; while average temperatures range from roughly 10° F in January to 86° F in July, seasonal extremes, droughts, floods, blizzards, and tornadoes belie any notion of "normal" conditions.

Geography and environment

Variety also characterized reports of the Nebraska environment throughout the nineteenth century. In 1823, Major STEPHEN HARRIMAN LONG described the region as the "GREAT AMERICAN DESERT." Later nineteenth-century land promoters, however, portrayed the state as the "Garden of the World." Both images had some basis in truth during the nineteenth century. Nebraska's soils are among the most productive in the world, but an adequate water supply—the key to unlocking the state's agricultural bounty—remains elusive. Although twentieth-century agricultural production has been aided by the OGALLALA AQUIFER, a vast reservoir of underground water, the technology required to make extensive use of the reservoir did not exist during the nineteenth century.

Native Americans

Nebraska's earliest peoples, nomadic hunters who roamed the plains twelve thousand years ago searching for mastodons and mammoths, adapted their life style to the environment. Climatic changes brought droughts, and the hunters abandoned the plains for several thousand years. About twenty-five hundred years ago, as conditions on the plains improved, the hunters returned, this time supplementing their diets by raising corn, beans, squashes, and sunflowers. Once again climatic changes drastically changed the environment and led to a population decline. However, by about 1500, conditions on the plains again improved, and Native American tribes once more lived along the river valleys on the plains.

Of all of Nebraska's native inhabitants, the Pawnees were the most powerful. Living in earthen lodge villages along the Loupe, Platte, and Republican rivers, the Pawnees dominated a vast territory covering nearly all of Nebraska and Kansas and participated in

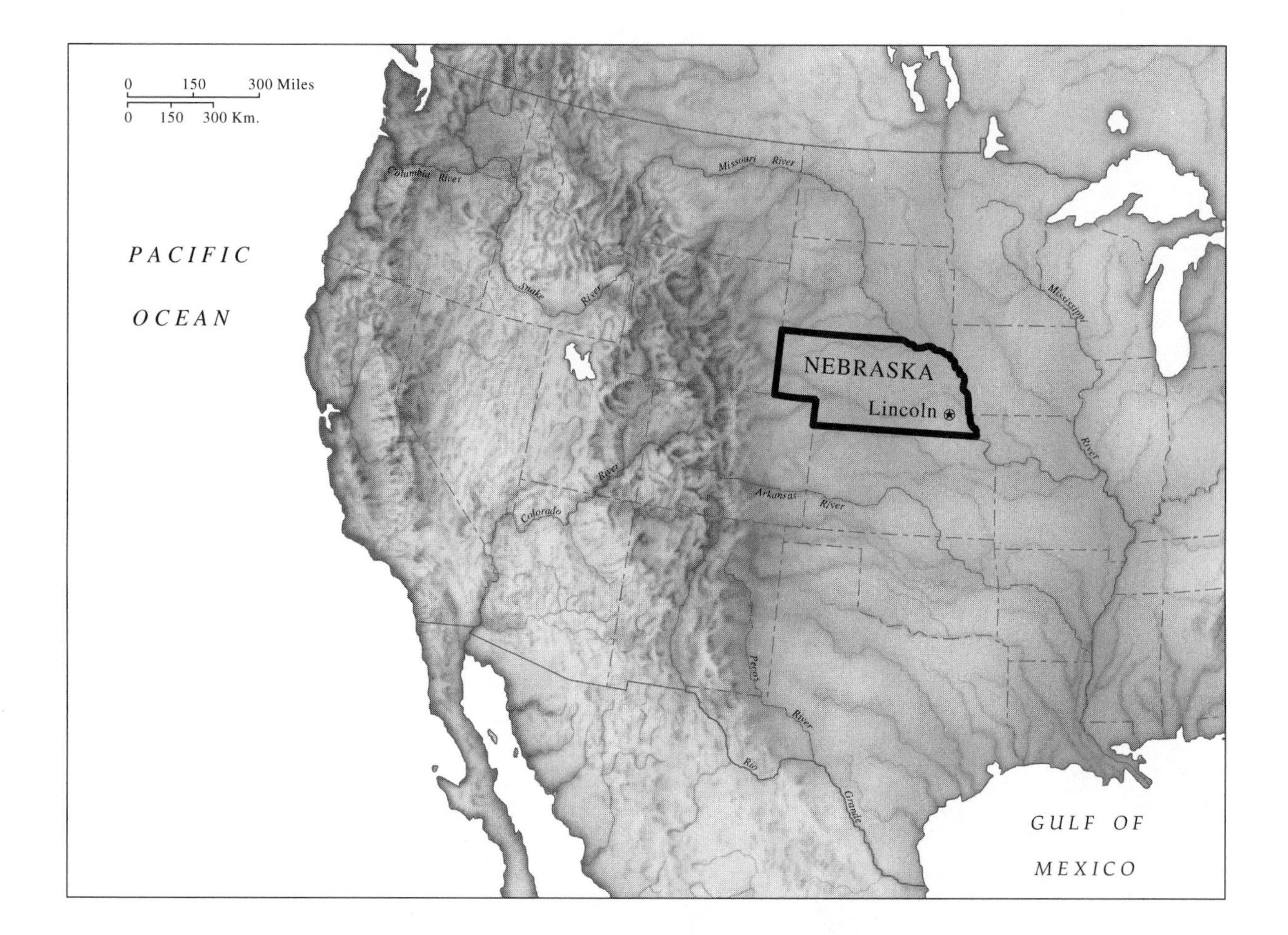

a large trade network that included the Arikaras, Mandans, and Hidatsas on the upper MISSOURI RIVER, the French and Americans in St. Louis, the Caddoan-speaking Indians of Texas and Oklahoma, and Spanish and Mexicans in Santa Fe. By the 1820s, the Pawnees numbered about ten to fifteen thousand and were the most powerful tribe on the Central Plains. In the early 1500s, other tribes to the east—the Otos, Missouris, Omahas, and Poncas—moved into Nebraska, settled along the Missouri River, and embraced Pawnee customs, especially the use of earthen lodges.

Exploration

In the eighteenth and nineteenth centuries, Nebraska was a meeting ground on the edge of several different North American frontiers. Foremost among the expanding European empires were New Spain and New France. Spanish interest in the Great Plains peaked with FRANCISCO VÁSQUEZ DE CORONADO, who in 1541 set off to find the mythical Seven Cities of Cíbola. His expedition reached only as far north as present-day Kansas. In the centuries that followed, French fur traders explored the rivers of the plains. Those traders were the first whites to explore and name the PLATTE RIVER; *Platte,* meaning "flat," was the French equivalent of *Nebraska,* the Oto word for "flat water." French activity on the plains, especially the 1714 expedition of Etienne Veniard de Bourgmont to explore the lower reaches of the Missouri, finally provoked a Spanish response. In 1720, Pedro de Villasur led an expedition from Santa Fe northward to the Platte River. The Pawnees, who were engaged in extensive trade with the French, attacked the expedition and nearly wiped out the party.

To both the French and Spanish, however, the Great Plains were only the periphery of their North American empires. In 1763, when France was expelled from North America following the Seven Years' War, title to the Great Plains passed from France to Spain. In 1800, Spain secretly deeded the region back to France, ostensibly so that the region would act as a buffer zone between New Spain and the United States. But in 1803, France sold the Great Plains to the United States as part of the LOUISIANA PURCHASE.

Nineteenth-century developments

The Americans originally viewed the Great Plains as a vast Indian reservation. Yet fur-trade profits quickly drew the new nation's interest to the region. Nebraska tribes already had long traditions of trade with the French, and following the LEWIS AND CLARK EXPEDITION (from 1804 to 1806), American fur traders rushed up the Missouri River to take advantage of the Indian trade. Traders quickly built Fort Lisa (1812) and Fort Atkinson (1820) along the Missouri River, and from the 1830s on, the AMERICAN FUR COMPANY operated a post near present-day Bellevue (near Omaha). Those outposts also served as a staging ground for missionary activity, Indian agents, and early settlers.

American fur traders also discovered the natural advantages of the Platte River valley. Although the Platte River is too shallow for navigation, its broad, gravel-banked valley seemed to be a nearly perfect "natural highway" that led to South Pass, the most important passageway through the Rocky Mountains. In 1824, fur trader WILLIAM HENRY ASHLEY and a party of twenty-five men traveled from Fort Atkinson to the trapping grounds of the Rocky Mountains. Newspaper accounts of the trip described the ease of travel in the Platte Valley. In 1830, fur traders JEDEDIAH STRONG SMITH, David Jackson, and William Sublette drove the first wagons from St. Louis to a trade RENDEZVOUS in the Rockies along the Platte Valley route. The Great Platte River Road soon became the nation's major highway of westward expansion.

Americans were not the last of the frontiersmen to push into Nebraska. Beginning in the 1830s, nomadic hunters, led primarily by the Oglala and Brulé bands of the Teton Sioux, also swept into the region. This movement of nomadic tribes had roots in the seventeenth century, when horses were reintroduced onto the plains from settlements in northern New Spain. Over the next century, horses spread over the plains, allowing tribes to travel farther in search of buffaloes and to store and carry greater quantities of dried meat through the winter. Although some tribes, like the Pawnees, used horses to enrich their semisedentary existence, others turned completely to nomadism and became dependent on the buffalo hunt for their bold life style. Tribes hunting buffaloes in western Nebraska included the Arapahos and Cheyennes. The most powerful nomadic tribes on the Northern Plains, however, were the various bands of the Teton Sioux, who began invading Pawnee homelands in the 1830s.

Conflict between the Teton Sioux and Pawnees at first caused Americans little concern. In the 1840s, Americans seemed more interested in crossing the Great Plains than in settling there. As early as 1841, California-bound settlers took the long trail along the Platte River. During his 1842 expedition, JOHN CHARLES FRÉMONT compiled and published the first accurate map and guidebook of the Platte route. The following year the first large wagon train of settlers left Independence, Missouri, for the Oregon Country, traveling along the now famous trail. The Platte route also proved popular with the Mormons, who followed the valley to reach the Great Salt Lake beginning in 1847.

The discovery of gold in California (in 1848) and Colorado (in 1858) suddenly put thousands of transient "argonauts" on the trail. Soon freight companies were regularly shipping goods between the Denver mining area and terminuses along the Missouri River in eastern Nebraska. Between 1841 and 1866, when the transcontinental railroad essentially ended wagon travel on the trail, approximately one-quarter to one-half million people traversed Nebraska.

Although white migration through the Platte Valley intruded on rich Pawnee agricultural lands, conflicts between the Pawnees and Americans were minimal. The Pawnees, who were dependent on white trade goods, welcomed American help in their increasing struggles with the Sioux. Endemic diseases—smallpox in 1831 and cholera in 1849—and constant attacks by the Sioux, significantly weakened Pawnee power. By 1857, the Pawnees had given up all claims to lands north of the Platte, opening nearly the entire eastern two-thirds of the territory to white settlement. In 1873, a large party of Sioux slaughtered a hunting party of Pawnees, including women and children, in the valley of the Republican River, near present-day Trenton. Two years later, the Pawnees ceded their remaining lands in Nebraska and accepted a reservation in Oklahoma.

Conflict between Americans and the nomadic tribes, however, was more violent. In the summer and fall of 1864, Cheyenne, Arapaho, and Sioux warriors attacked travelers and settlers throughout the Platte Valley. Although most of the fighting on the plains took place outside Nebraska, the Sioux and Cheyennes, led by CRAZY HORSE, continued to threaten Nebraska settlements well into the 1870s. However, largely because of the disappearance of the buffalo, the Oglala and Brulé tribes surrendered their hunting rights in western Nebraska in 1875. Following the Great Sioux War of 1876 and 1877, Crazy Horse brought his starving followers to Fort Robinson in northwestern Nebraska. In a scuffle that broke out when Crazy Horse surrendered, however, the great Indian leader was killed.

Territorial years

Travel along the Platte River Road pointed out its practicality as a transcontinental railroad route. In 1854, Illinois Senator STEPHEN A. DOUGLAS, in order to clear the way for a transcontinental railroad, intro-

Top: When the Union Pacific Railroad reached the one hundredth meridian in its construction of the transcontinental line, photographer John Carbutt recorded the festivities. The photograph was taken about 275 miles west of Omaha, Nebraska. *Courtesy National Archives.*

Bottom: Near Big Springs, Nebraska, a covered wagon meets an automobile, 1912. Photograph by A. L. Westgard. *Courtesy National Archives.*

duced a bill to create the Nebraska Territory on the Central Plains. Southern politicians altered the Nebraska bill by providing for two new territories in order to preserve the balance between slave states and free states in Congress; as a result the central plains were divided between Nebraska and Kansas.

Nebraska's growth was steady but not rapid; by 1860, its population had reached 28,841. The passage of the HOMESTEAD ACT OF 1862, the conclusion of the Civil War in 1865, and the construction of the UNION PACIFIC RAILROAD through the Platte Valley from 1865 to 1867 spurred further growth. In 1864, Congress authorized Nebraska to form a state government, but Nebraskans rejected the measure because they feared an increase in taxes. They finally passed the measure in June 1866, and Nebraska was formally recognized as a state on March 1, 1867. The legislature voted to locate the state capital in Lancaster (renamed Lincoln) in 1867.

Construction of the Union Pacific and the Burlington and Missouri River Railroad (later the Chicago, Burlington and Quincy) in the late 1860s provided Nebraska settlers with access to Eastern markets. As a subsidy for building the RAILROADS, these two companies were given more than 7 million acres of land; ultimately 16 percent of all Nebraska's acreage was given to the dozen or so railroads that crisscrossed the state. Nearly every town west of Omaha and Lincoln owed its existence to railroads, whose officials designated towns six to ten miles apart along the routes—the distance at which a farmer could drive his wagon, loaded with produce, and return home on the same day.

During the 1870s, Nebraska's population doubled. "Boomers" (promoters), many of them employed by the railroads, hailed the region as an agricultural paradise. Pseudo-scientific promoters popularized the idea that "rain follows the plow." According to this theory, the thick plains sod was impervious to rain, which merely ran off the land after a storm. By breaking the sod, farmers were allowing the ground to absorb the water needed to sustain intensive agricultural development. Land could be easily acquired in many ways, especially through homesteading or from a railroad land agent. In 1873, the TIMBER CULTURE ACT allowed homesteaders to acquire an additional section (160 acres) by planting part of that land with trees and tending it for ten years.

Early settlers at first used local materials to build their homes and outbuildings. Although wood could be obtained easily in eastern Nebraska, settlers in the central and western parts often had to live in soddies, or SOD HOUSES, and cook with buffalo chips while getting their farms established.

The panic of 1873 and plagues of locusts in 1874 and 1876 ruined many farmers who had not yet built up the financial reserves needed to weather hard times. Most Nebraska farmers, in the 1870s, learned to diversify their crops; they planted wheat as well as corn to hold off ruin. In the 1880s, however, that lesson was forgotten or ignored by the rush of newcomers. Nebraska's population expanded quickly, from 452,402 in 1880 to 1,058,910 in 1890, the biggest jump in the state's history. Fortunately, the early 1880s were wet years, so the struggle of the starting years was easier for the newly arrived farmers.

Many of these newcomers came from Europe, predominantly Germany, Sweden, Ireland, and Bohemia. The railroads sold their Nebraska land in major Eastern cities and in Europe, transported recently arrived Europeans to the plains cheaply, and counted on making lasting profits by shipping Nebraska agricultural goods to distant markets. Much of the railroads' lands was sold in large blocks, through colonization schemes, to European immigrants. This practice created ethnic enclaves that remained relatively intact well into the twentieth century.

Meanwhile, western Nebraska's economy boomed with the CATTLE INDUSTRY. As early as the 1860s, cattlemen, lured by the Union Pacific's offer of low shipping rates, began driving their herds of Texas longhorns to Nebraska. From 1873 until the mid-1880s, Ogallala was the terminus of those trails; it became famous as a rowdy cowboy's town. When farmers in Kansas and Nebraska petitioned for herd and quarantine laws, the great cattle drives ended. But by then, ranching was well established in western Nebraska. Other ranchers soon discovered that the grass-covered dunes of the Sandhills also held good range lands. When James S. Brisbin's *The Beef Bonanza; or How to Get Rich on the Plains* was published in 1881 with its description of the quick and easy profits of the cattle business, Eastern and European investors responded enthusiastically. The great blizzards of 1885 to 1886 and 1886 to 1887, however, ended the heyday of the cattle bonanza.

Ranching revived twenty years later, although as a more carefully managed industry. Pure-blooded stock—

A family poses beside a covered wagon in Loup Valley, Nebraska. *Courtesy National Archives.*

such as Hereford, shorthorn, and Angus—were bred instead of the Texas longhorns; fenced lands maintained cattle breeds; and hay supplemented the standard grass diet, especially in the harsh winters.

In the 1880s, Nebraska's corn production tripled, and oat yields increased sixfold. Cattle output tripled, and Omaha emerged as a major packing center. But as the 1880s drew to a close, farm prices decreased, while grievances against the railroads increased. Demanding regulation of railroad rates and a drastic increase in the currency supply, debt-ridden, Midwestern farmers formed the People's Independent (Populist) party in 1890. The Depression of 1893, accompanied by drought and crop failures, further fueled the agrarian revolt. Realizing the power of the Populist movement, Democrats and Republicans slowly began to change their platforms. In 1896, WILLIAM JENNINGS BRYAN, who called for the free and unlimited coinage of silver as a solution to the limited money supply, took control of the Nebraska Democratic organization, and Populists and Democrats cautiously joined forces. Although the combined Populist-Democratic legislature in 1897 failed to pass railroad regulation, it did manage to secure regulation of grain-elevator company combines, telephone and telegraph firms, and stockyards. With the return of prosperity, POPULISM faded. But Nebraska PROGRESSIVISM, most likely a refection of the earlier Populist activity, was very strong. In 1907, a Progressive Republican legislature finally passed railroad regulation, as well as laws to regulate child labor, a primary-election law, and other reforms.

Twentieth-century Nebraska

By the beginning of the twentieth century, when only semiarid tracts of land remained available for homesteaders, Nebraska farmers turned in new directions. They grew alfalfa, sugar beets, and winter wheat in addition to corn. Dryland FARMING and IRRIGATION increased. The Kinkaid Act (1904) permitted homesteaders to obtain 640 acres in the arid Sandhills after five years tenancy. "Kinkaiders," as the Sandhills dryland farmers were called, struggled with the land while living in tarpaper shacks or soddies. Ranching, rather than farming, remained the dominant industry of the region.

Kearney, Nebraska, hosted a parade of the U.S. Infantry, 1880. *Courtesy National Archives.*

World War I spurred inflated commodity prices and created a golden age for Nebraska agriculture, but it also increased mortgage indebtedness. After the war, the bonanza ended and then completely collapsed in the 1930s. Drought, dust storms, and heat added to the economic problems. President Franklin D. Roosevelt's New Deal programs, particularly the Rural Electrification Administration and the Public Works Administration, helped somewhat. Meanwhile state government, aided by Senator GEORGE W. NORRIS, established a one-house, nonpartisan state legislature. The Unicameral first met in 1937 and has generally functioned well. As the Depression passed, state politics became increasingly conservative.

After World War II, both urban and rural Nebraskans enjoyed unparalleled prosperity. Population growth has been slow but steady, reaching 1,606,000 in 1990. The population reflects its Midwestern heritage; nearly 60 percent of Nebraskans born outside of the state are from other Midwestern states. Nebraska's leading ethnic groups are (in order): German, Czechoslovakian, Swedish, Russian, Danish, British, Polish, Canadian, Italian, and Mexican. The population remains very homogeneous: 93.8 percent white, 3.6 percent black, 2.3 percent Hispanic, 0.8 percent Native American, and 0.8 percent Asian. Although ethnic enclaves remain today, ethnic identities have generally been muted by restrictions on the use of foreign languages (particularly in German communities during World War I), loss of isolation through increased mobility and communications in the United States generally, and intermarriage of second- and third-generation immigrant children.

Nebraskans consider themselves Midwestern, rather than Western, and in population, religion, culture, and economy, they are. There has been a population shift away from farms toward cities. Mechanized agriculture, increasing job opportunities in Omaha and Lincoln, and a highway system that provides easy access to city employment opportunities have further depopulated small towns and farms. Agriculture remains vital to the state's economy, but Nebraskans find themselves increasingly a part of urban America.

—*Mark A. Eifler*

SEE ALSO: Agrarianism; Central Plains Indian Wars; Kansas-Nebraska Act; Railroad Land Grants; Sioux Wars; Sublette Brothers

SUGGESTED READING:

Baltensperger, Bradley H. *Nebraska: A Geography.* Boulder, Colo., and London, 1985.

Dick, Everett. *The Sod House Frontier.* New York, 1937.

Hicks, John D. *The Populist Revolt.* Minneapolis, Minn., 1931.

Jenkins, Allan, ed. *The Platte River: An Atlas of the Big Bend Region.* Kearney, Nebr., 1993.

Mattes, Merrill J. *The Great Platte River Road.* Lincoln, Nebr., and London, 1969.

Olson, James C. *History of Nebraska.* 2d ed. Lincoln, Nebr., and London, 1966.

Sheldon, Addison E. *Land Systems and Land Policies in Nebraska.* Lincoln, Nebr., 1936.

NELSON, AVEN

Botanist, educator, and university president Aven Nelson (1859–1952) was born near Summitville, Iowa, to Norwegian-immigrant parents. Nelson became the preeminent botanist in the Rocky Mountain area. First, however, he was a teacher. As his biographer wrote, Nelson "put teaching first among his duties and accomplishments." Educated in public schools in his native state, he graduated from Missouri State Normal School in Kirksville even though he had not obtained a high-school diploma. After his marriage, he accepted a teaching position at Drury College in Missouri, where he stayed for two years. In the spring of 1887, he was hired to teach English at the University of Wyoming, which was to open later that fall. After he arrived and it was found that another faculty member was more qualified to teach English, Nelson was assigned classes in calisthenics and biology. He set out to learn about botany along with his students. Over the years, he assembled the Rocky Mountain Herbarium, the foremost collection of plants between St. Louis and the West Coast. Following research expeditions to Yellowstone and elsewhere in the Rocky Mountain region in the late 1890s, he was granted a master's degree from Harvard in 1902 and a doctoral degree from Denver University in 1904. Over the next decade, he wrote important botanical papers and gained national prominence in the field. Recognition from his peers gained him the presidencies of the Botanical Society of America, the American Society of Plant Taxonomists, and the national honorary society Phi Kappa Phi. When the president of the University of Wyoming resigned in 1917, the trustees selected Nelson as interim president. He served until 1922, when he resigned to return to his career in botany. He retired from the University of Wyoming in 1942 but remained active in the field as teacher, author, and researcher.

—*Phil Roberts*

SUGGESTED READING:

Hardy, Deborah. *Wyoming University: The First 100 Years, 1886–1986.* Laramie, Wyo., 1986.

Williams, Roger L. *Aven Nelson of Wyoming.* Boulder, Colo., 1984.

NELSON, WILLIAM ROCKHILL

Newspaper editor and publisher William Rockhill Nelson (1841–1915) was born in Indiana and spent his early years in various vocations before settling on journalism and moving to KANSAS CITY, MISSOURI. In September 1888, he launched the *Kansas City Evening Star,* a politically independent, family newspaper that became one of the leading journals of PROGRESSIVISM. A pioneer in muckraking coverage of local corruption, Nelson helped make the reporter an employee central to journalism. Intrepid foe of the Pendergast machine that controlled the city's politics and made the city an underworld haven with a thriving, alcohol-laced nightlife, Nelson used the *Star* to push for prohibition and public improvements, from parks to paved streets. Nelson modestly claimed to have "pulled Kansas City out of the mud."

—*Kurt Edward Kemper*

SEE ALSO: City Government; Pendergast, James; Pendergast, Tom

SUGGESTED READING:

McCorkle, William L. "Nelson's Star and Kansas City, 1880-1898." Ph.D. diss. University of Texas at Austin, 1968.

NEVADA

Nevada, known as the "Silver State," encompasses some 110,000 square miles. Once described as "geology by day and astronomy by night," much of Nevada is an area of interior drainage, known as the Great Basin, with parallel mountain ranges running north to south. Las Vegas, in the southern tip of the state, lies outside the Great Basin drainage system. Explorer JOHN CHARLES FRÉMONT remarked that this land of interior basins "excites Asiatic, not American ideas." For many years, Nevada, although geographically larger than New England, had the smallest population of any state.

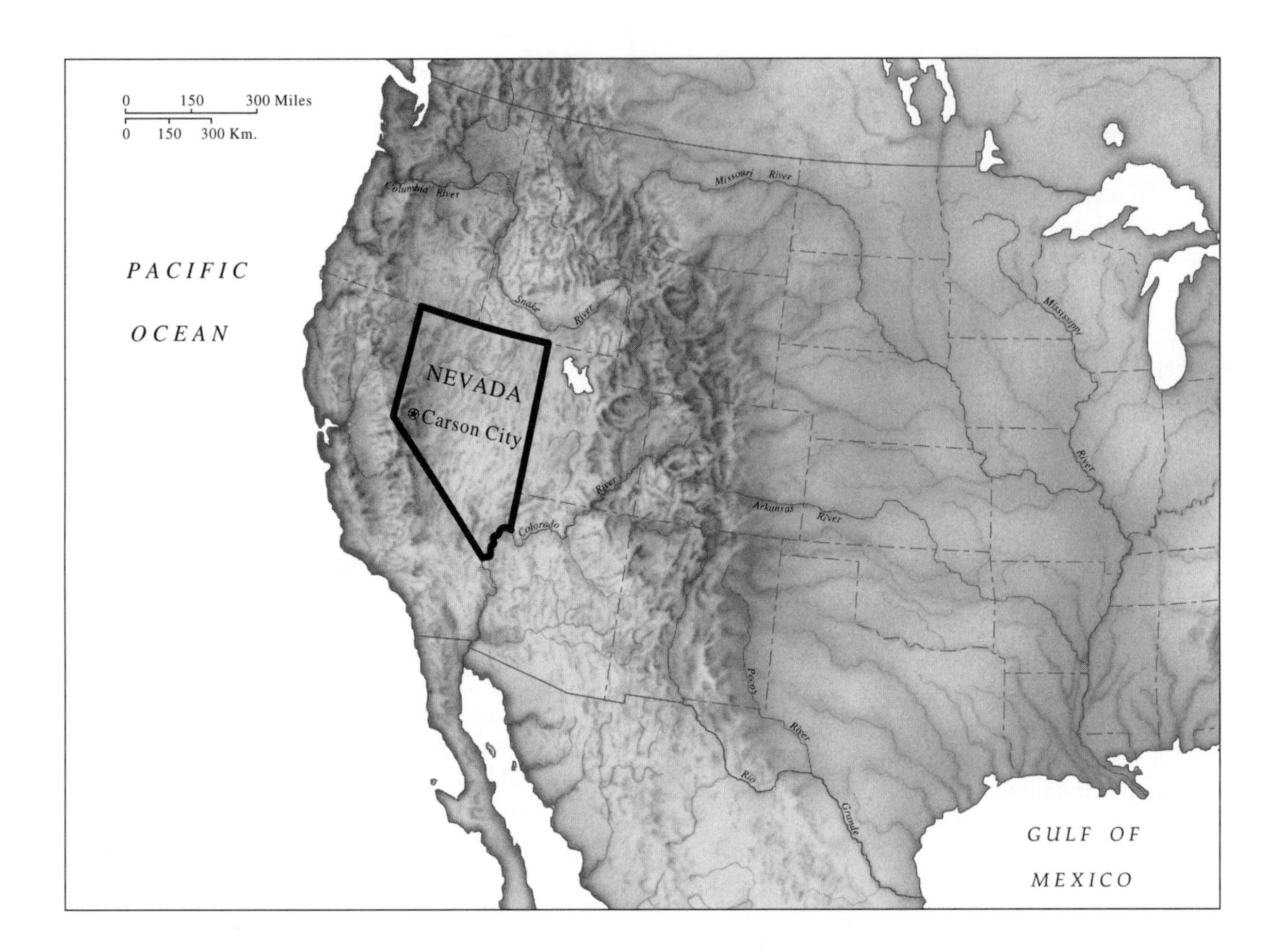

Geography and climate

Aridity prevails in Nevada with fewer than ten inches of rainfall per year, but many of the high mountain ranges accumulate considerable snow pack, which provides water for the lower valleys. In the north, the seasons are those of the high desert country with warm summers and cold winters (on occasion 50° F below zero in northeastern Nevada) and with a distinct lack of humidity. The difference between day and night temperatures is often 50°. In southern Nevada's MOJAVE DESERT, temperatures above 100° F prevail from June through September. Occasional freezes in late December and January give way to the warmth of a prolonged spring. Lack of moisture in the growing season, intense summer heat, and winter freezes challenge the survival of flora and fauna, make large-scale agriculture difficult, and require that livestock-raisers maintain vast acreages to support relatively few animals.

Exploration and Native Americans

The Spanish failed to explore or settle in the Great Basin. Friars probed the peripheries by 1776 but returned to Santa Fe with tales of a river they called the San Buenaventura flowing from the central Rockies toward California. Stories of that mythical river persisted into the fur-trade era of the 1820s and 1830s as trappers tried to find a water route from the Rockies across the intervening desert to the coast. Crisscrossing the region from 1825 to 1831, JEDEDIAH STRONG SMITH from the ROCKY MOUNTAIN FUR COMPANY in St. Louis and PETER SKENE OGDEN from the HUDSON'S BAY COMPANY dispelled the myth of the San Buenaventura and made contact with native people.

Native peoples of the Great Basin were in four major groupings during the period of contact with Europeans: the Northern Paiutes from Walker Lake north to Pyramid Lake and into the northern Black Rock Desert; the Southern Paiutes south from Walker Lake into the Las Vegas Valley; Western Shoshones from south-central Nevada to the Idaho border well north of the Humboldt River; and the Washos from Lake Tahoe into the Truckee Meadows south to the Carson River along the leeward side of the Sierra Nevada.

Fur and mule traders, including EWING YOUNG, Antonio Armijo, and WILLIAM WOLFSKILL, traveled through southern Nevada from New Mexico. Like George C. Yount, they followed the Old Spanish Trail north to the Ute country and then south through the Las Vegas Springs into California. Across northern Nevada came Joseph Reddeford Walker from the central Rockies over the Bonneville flat desert toward Ogden's River, which he followed, in 1833, to its sinks in western Nevada. On this route, he clashed with Indians and moved south along the Sierra Nevada, until he crossed the mountains near Yosemite or Walker's Pass. His return from the San Francisco Bay took him again along Ogden's River, but this time, he turned north to Thousand Springs Creek and into the Goose Creek and Raft River, which provided a connecting water route between the trail to California and the Oregon Trail to the north.

In 1844, Frémont entered the northwestern corner of present-day Nevada from Oregon and explored south to a body of water he named Pyramid Lake. He made a dangerous midwinter crossing of the Sierra Nevada and sighted a beautiful lake, later named Tahoe. On a second trip to the Great Basin in 1845, Frémont saw Ogden's River from a distance and named it the Humboldt after the famed German scientist, Alexander von Humboldt.

The Humboldt River marked the route of the developing California Trail across Nevada in the 1840s. In 1846, the Donner party, after suffering the delays along the ill-advised Hastings Cutoff, came across the trail and attempted to take the Truckee River Pass over the mountains. When early snow trapped them, forty-one out of eighty-seven emigrants perished in a winter of starvation and cannibalism. The spread of the news about the tragedy slowed migration, but gold discoveries in California sparked the 1849 gold rush over the trail. Further encouragement to migration came with the end of the United States–Mexican War and the 1848 Treaty of Guadalupe Hidalgo, which secured the Southwest for the United States. The Compromise of 1850 extended civil government to the region; California became a state, and Utah was made a territory governing most of the Great Basin.

While California-bound travelers used Nevada as a land bridge, the Mormon migration to the Salt Lake Valley, beginning in 1847, established a permanent community in the Great Basin. Mormon outposts reached the base of the Sierra Nevada by 1850 at Mormon Station (or Genoa) and Las Vegas with the building of the Mormon Fort there in 1855. The Mormons abandoned their outposts in Nevada during the Utah Expedition of 1857, and internal problems spurred the collapse of the Las Vegas mission. Meanwhile placer miners, working their way up the canyons leading to Mount Davidson above the Carson River, discovered the Comstock Lode in 1859.

The sleepy ranching and mining enterprises on the eastern slope of the Sierra Nevada gave way to a full-fledged mining boom in the communities that formed along the Comstock Lode—Virginia City, Gold Hill, and Silver City—during the winter of 1859 to 1860. The "Rush to Washoe" brought more than six thousand miners to the region; the rush caused tensions with local Paiute Indians—tensions that culminated in the Pyramid Lake Indian War of May and June 1860.

Territory to state

With no civil government to deal either with miners or Indians, local residents demanded that Congress form a new territory. Because Southern congressmen had abandoned their seats after the election of Abraham Lincoln and the secession of the South from the Union, Congress was able to move quickly, in early 1861, to create the Nevada Territory from the lands of western Utah Territory. Three years later, as the end of the Civil War approached, Nevada voted on statehood but rejected a proposed state constitution in January 1864 only to approve a revised document nine months later. Nevada came into the Union on October 31, 1864, in time to vote for Lincoln's reelection and to help ratify the Thirteenth Amendment to the U.S. Constitution banning slavery.

The development around the Comstock Lode moved to new heights after the war until the lode failed in 1877. But during the mining heyday, Virginia City was "queen" of the Comstock, a bustling center of activity in the region between the mountains of the West. The silver and gold ores of the Comstock commanded huge investments from the Bank of California. Its agent in Nevada, William Sharon, monopolized the rich mines, ore processing, and rail transportation to the lode. In 1868, he used Chinese laborers to build the Virginia and Truckee Railroad, which connected the Comstock with Reno on the overland Central Pacific Railroad by 1872. When Adolph Sutro proposed a seven-mile tunnel from the Carson River to the mines to supply them and remove ore, Sharon objected because it threatened the bank's power. Much to his satisfaction, the tunnel's completion was delayed until 1878, too late to serve the Comstock.

John W. Mackay, James Flood, James Graham Fair, and William O'Brien of the "Bonanza crowd" were the most successful competitors to Sharon and the "Bank crowd." In 1873, they struck a bonanza that shook the confidence of the Bank of California. The few who grew rich on the Comstock or defended the mining and railroad interests joined the plutocracy that commanded the political life of the state and its U.S. senatorships. Comstock-era senators included lawyer William M. Stewart, servant to the mining and rail-

At the Comstock Mine, Virginia City, Nevada, Timothy H. O'Sullivan photographed cars filled with ore coming out of the mine shaft. *Courtesy National Archives.*

road interests; William Sharon of the "Bank crowd"; William Fair of the "Bonanza crowd"; and finally John Jones, a mining superintendent who became a Comstock millionaire.

Twenty years of mining depression followed the Comstock's demise. By 1900, Nevada's population fell to 42,000, probably half its former figure. The state tried to find panaceas for its ailing economy by adopting the causes of free silver and IRRIGATION. The Silver party, which emerged on the local level in the 1890s, sought the free and unlimited coinage of silver in the hopes that government purchases of the metal would raise prices, spur prospecting, and encourage the discovery of new bonanzas. The Silver party denounced Congress for demonetizing silver in the Mint Act of 1873, referred to by Nevadans and others as the "Crime of '73." Likewise, irrigation attracted interest, but local and state efforts to launch large enterprises failed in the depressed economy of the 1890s. It was not until a decade later that Nevada Congressman FRANCIS G. NEWLANDS, with backing from President THEODORE ROOSEVELT, pushed through the NEWLANDS RECLAMATION ACT OF 1902 that committed the federal government to Western water and irrigation projects.

Twentieth-century development

Federal RECLAMATION in Fallon, east of Reno, quickened economic life in Nevada during the first decade of the new century. Discoveries of gold and silver ore in Goldfield, Tonopah, and Rhyolite in southern Nevada brought a twentieth-century mining boom that resembled the excitement of the Comstock era. By 1910, the state's population reached its highest recorded mark at 81,875, but it still remained predominantly a male population by two to one. By 1910, Reno had gained a national reputation as a thriving DIVORCE center. Two new trans-Nevada railroads appeared: the Western Pacific in the north and the Salt Lake–Los Angeles Railroad built through southern Nevada. With the growth of the latter railway, Las Vegas emerged in 1905. Finally COPPER MINING and smelting in McGill and Ruth in White Pine County added industrial metals to Nevada's mining wealth. These communities attracted immigrants from across the oceans just as the Comstock had done in an earlier era. The "new immigration" came mostly from southern and eastern Europe. Italians, Greeks, Serbs, Croats, and Japanese worked in the copper pit at Ruth and in the smelter at McGill.

During the upsurge in economic life, a Progressive-reform movement sought to bring a new day to Nevada. By expanding direct democracy, regulating corporations, and passing morality legislation, Progressives tried to rid Nevada of the political influence of mining barons and railroad interests. Nevadans voted to include the initiative, referendum, and recall in the state constitution. In 1914, women won suffrage in a campaign led by ANNE HENRIETTA MARTIN, who later ran unsuccessfully for the U.S. Senate. State government undertook the regulation of private utilities and inspection of mines for safety; in the matters of moral uplift and reform, the legislature declared GAMBLING illegal and tried to discourage the divorce trade but did not prohibit PROSTITUTION.

From the southern mines came the new political leaders of the state. Key Pittman, Tasker L. Oddie, and PATRICK MCCARRAN came into political prominence. GEORGE WINGFIELD, most successful of all the mining entrepreneurs, made his fortune in Goldfield. He chose to stay in Nevada and invest in its various banking and business opportunities. He avoided high political office but exercised great power through an alleged bipartisan political machine. He frowned on the morality of reform implicit in PROGRESSIVISM and pushed the state toward a vice-related economy. Recognizing what was already occurring in the 1920s as the automobile made the state and its wide-open towns accessible, Nevadans voted to legalize gambling again in 1931. Residency requirements for obtaining a divorce under Nevada law fell from six months, to three months, and then to six weeks by 1931. With the longstanding acceptance of legalized prostitution, until the federal government demanded its cessation near new military bases at the onset of World War II, the national press denounced Nevada for its moral depravities.

The collapse of Wingfield's banking empire during the Great Depression opened the way for Democrat Pat McCarran's election to the U.S. Senate in 1932 and the rise of the McCarran machine that dominated Nevada until his death in 1954. While many other states and the federal government funded New Deal services, sometimes with deficits, to meet the crisis of the Depression, Nevada declared a policy of "One Sound State." It advertised itself as a state whose budgets were balanced and whose taxes were low or nonexistent, all in an effort to attract private wealth. The state did not tax gambling revenues until after World War II. Consequently, its small tax base allowed few public expenditures and services. Helping to stabilize and strengthen its economy were a number of Depression-era federal programs, including the construction on the Colorado River of the gigantic Boulder Dam (now Hoover Dam) that eventually supplied power for the growth of southern Nevada and its air-conditioned casinos.

After World War II, Nevada grew rapidly as its resort-based gambling economy appealed to the consumer appetites of an America that enjoyed leisure time and increased income and, to a greater extent, accepted gambling as a tolerable vice in society. From a state of barely 100,000 in 1940, Nevada grew by century's end to a population of 1.5 million. As with World War II, the Cold War with the Soviet Union brought defense dollars to the state. In that new struggle, Nevada welcomed the Atomic Energy Commission's test site north of Las Vegas but later resisted the placement of MX missiles in the state and the building of a repository for the nation's nuclear wastes.

Las Vegas became conspicuous and notorious in Nevada's post–World War II growth when underworld money financed the building of large casinos. Among the rumors and realities of the presence of a crime syndicate in Nevada and after congressional investigations, the state imposed regulations and background investigations on all future gaming applicants through a state gaming board in 1955. As federal threats to intervene in the gambling industry waned, Nevadans congratulated themselves on the continuing growth in gaming revenues and the taxes collected for support of state government—taxes that, in some years, made up more than 60 percent of state revenues. Gaming income quickly outstripped both mining and agricultural income with gross revenue from gambling growing to just over $800 million in 1972 to almost $5 billion in 1990. In gaming, Nevada found its economic viability, which, in a sense, finally legitimized its political existence.

Las Vegas grew rapidly. Ongoing reapportionment of the seats in the legislature shifted political power from Reno to the new colossus in the south. Known for its wide-open spaces and as a home to the nation's largest wild horse population and Basque sheepherders, Nevada ironically became one of the most highly urbanized states with most of its inhabitants concentrated either in Reno or Las Vegas. The new urban population reflected the growing diversity of American life, particularly with a dramatic increase in the Hispanic population. U.S. Census figures for 1990 indicated 6.6 percent of the population was African American; 1.6 percent, American Indian; 3.2 percent, Asian; and 10.4 percent, Hispanic.

In the sparsely populated interior of the state, gold mining assumed greater importance by the 1980s, and Nevada became one of the major gold-producing areas of the world. Yet wilderness areas and a Great Basin National Park encompassing Mount Wheeler and the Lehman Caves in eastern Nevada became a part of the Nevada recreational scene. With 86 percent of its land owned by the federal government, Nevada is second only to Alaska as the state with the largest percentage of public lands.

With the immense "theme casinos," sprouting from the desert floor in Las Vegas, a Disney theme-park era came to Nevada gambling by the end of the century and produced what Las Vegas's prominent gaming entrepreneur Steve Wynn termed "The New Las Vegas." In addition, a "new" Nevada featured what some term a "postindustrial" economy based on service and entertainment. If the new Nevada represented the future of a society that embraced gaming, the social-overhead costs of a gaming economy should be noted in Nevada's highest rate of alcoholism in the nation and in its rates of suicide, divorce, child abuse, and teenage pregnancies. While its experiment with building a gaming economy has been widely hailed as the enterprise that finally brought financial stability to the

Theodore Roosevelt (third from left) campaigning in Reno, Nevada, 1910. *Courtesy National Archives.*

state, the social costs of a gaming society were mostly ignored or considered to be justified because of the inherent resource deficiencies of the Nevada environment.

—*William D. Rowley*

SEE ALSO: Booms; Currency and Silver as Western Political Issues; Ghost Towns; Gold Mining; Sliver Mining

SUGGESTED READING:

Angel, Myron, ed. *History of Nevada.* 1881. Reprint. Oakland, Calif., 1958.
Elliott, Russell R. *History of Nevada.* Rev. ed. Lincoln, Nebr., 1987.
Hulse, James W. *The Silver State: Nevada's Heritage Reinterpreted.* Reno, Nev., 1991.
Lillard, Richard G. *Desert Challenge: An Interpretation of Nevada.* New York, 1942.
Moehring, Eugene P. *Resort City in the Sunbelt: Las Vegas, 1930–1970.* Reno, Nev., 1989.
Titus, A. Contandina. *Bombs in the Backyard: Atomic Testing and American Politics.* Reno, Nev., 1986.

NEWBERRY LIBRARY

The Newberry Library is an independent research library in the humanities, with particularly strong collections in Western Americana, indigenous American cultures, and American frontiers. With a general focus on the history and culture of Europe and the Americas from the Middle Ages through the mid-twentieth century, the library has several notable collections, encompassing the history of printing, music history, the history of cartography, Renaissance literature, genealogy, local history, and American sheet music.

Founded in Chicago in 1887, the Newberry Library owes its existence to a clause in Walter Newberry's will, leaving half of his estate to establish a "free public library" if both of his daughters died without heirs. Thus, unlike such comparable institutions as the HUNTINGTON LIBRARY, ART COLLECTIONS, AND BOTANICAL GARDENS, the Newberry began not with an individual's collection but with a sum of money amassed through real-estate speculation. Shaped by the trustees of Newberry's will and founding Librarian William F. Poole, the initial collecting policies reflected the world of Chicago's late nineteenth-century Protestant elite. The collection looked to the East, toward New York, New England, and western Europe. It was the twentieth-century donation of Edward Ayer's substantial collection of materials on indigenous Americans (North and South) and their encounters with Europeans that enabled the Newberry to emerge as a center for research on American Indians and the American West.

The Newberry's extensive research and educational programs, which include fellowships, publications, adult education, lectures, and exhibits, form an essential part of the library's mission. Three of its four research centers, focusing on family and community history, the history of cartography, and the history of American Indians, play a significant role in generating scholarship on the American West, in addition to disseminating research to a broad audience.

—*James Grossman*

SUGGESTED READING:

Achilles, Rolf, ed. *Humanities Mirror: Reading at the Newberry, 1887–1987.* Chicago, 1987.

NEWELL, FREDERICK HAYNES

Instrumental to the founding the BUREAU OF RECLAMATION, Western irrigation engineer Frederick Haynes Newell (1862–1932) was born in Bradford, Pennsylvania, and, after his mother's death, was raised by his aunts in Newton, Massachusetts. Receiving a degree in mining engineering from the Massachusetts Institute of Technology in 1885, he worked as a surveyor for three years before taking a job as assistant hydraulic engineer in the UNITED STATES GEOLOGICAL SURVEY. Under the direction of JOHN WESLEY POWELL, Newell headed the hydrographic branch of the agency, a corps of engineers charged with measuring and surveying streams and mapping river basins in the Western states. Newell held the position for fourteen years, and his experience in the arid West led him to work on drafts of IRRIGATION legislation like the NEWLANDS RECLAMATION ACT OF 1902 and to lobby Congress for their passage. The Newlands law established the Reclamation Service and gave it authority to develop a complex of dams and irrigation networks to supply water for Westerners who settled and developed public lands. Newell became chief engineer of the service, and when it became independent of the Geological Survey in 1907, he was named director.

During Newell's tenure at the agency, the Reclamation Service spent nearly $100 million on twenty-two RECLAMATION projects in eighteen states. Not every project fulfilled the original intent of the law. The scope and location of some projects were dictated more by politics and the influence of powerful land owners than by the needs of family farmers intent on improving public lands, which occasionally led to such events as the OWENS VALLEY WAR.

Newell stepped down from the Reclamation Service in 1914 but continued to consult with the agency.

In the next year, he became head of the department of civil engineering at the University of Illinois and rose to prominence in several professional organizations and government commissions and advisory boards. Newell also wrote several books on irrigation and engineering. In 1920, he retired from teaching and founded the Research Service, an organization of engineering consultants. He died suddenly of heart failure in his Washington, D.C., home.

—*Kurt Edward Kemper*

SUGGESTED READING:

Dawdy, Doris Ostrander. *Congress in Its Wisdom: The Bureau of Reclamation and the Public Interest.* Boulder, Colo., 1989.

NEWELL, ROBERT

Mountain man and OREGON politician, Robert Newell (1807–1869) began a career in fur trading in his early twenties, when he headed to St. Louis from his Butler County, Ohio, home. The diary he kept while trapping beavers in the Rocky Mountains documented trapping details and trading operations from 1829 until his move to Oregon in 1840. He led the first group of settlers and missionaries along the full length of the OREGON TRAIL to Walla Walla and Fort Vancouver and on to the Willamette Valley. Newell settled in Oregon with his Nez Percé wife and their five sons. He became a leader of the Champoeg community, held public office, and eventually served two terms as the Speaker of the House for Oregon's legislature.

—*Patricia Hogan*

NEWLANDS, FRANCIS G.

A Nevada congressman and senator noted for his work in support of IRRIGATION programs for the arid West, Francis G. Newlands (1848–1917) was born in Natchez, Mississippi. After two years at Yale and law school in Washington, D.C., Newlands moved to San Francisco in 1870. There in 1874, he married Clara Adelaide Sharon, the daughter of William Sharon, a wealthy magnate of the Comstock Lode and Bank of California. When his wife died in 1881 and his father-in-law died in 1885, Newlands became the trustee for his three daughters of Sharon's entire estate of nearly thirty million dollars.

After a stab at a political career in California, he turned his eyes toward NEVADA. He arrived in the state with his new wife, Edith McAllister of San Francisco, in late 1888. When it became clear that a Senate seat was not available, Newlands settled for a congressional seat while he identified himself with the irrigation and silver causes. Congressman Newlands became a major force in the passage of the RECLAMATION legislation in 1902. By 1903, the newly elected Senator Newlands emerged as a leading Western Progressive in the Democratic party. He stood for increased power of the FEDERAL GOVERNMENT and bureaucracy, especially in areas of resource conservation and use. The beneficial use of water became a major theme when he advocated river control through flood prevention, production of power, WATER storage for irrigation, and improved navigation from the head waters to sea. All of this was part of his program for the New West—rationalization of the uses of Western resources and improved waterway transportation.

—*William D. Rowley*

SUGGESTED READING:

Darling, Arthur B., ed. *The Public Papers of Francis G. Newlands.* Boston, 1932.

Hays, Samuel P. *Conservation and the Gospel of Efficiency: The Progressive Conservation Movement, 1890–1920.* Cambridge, Mass., 1959.

Rowley, William D. *Newlands, Nevada, and the Nation: Of Reclamation and Reform.* Bloomington, Ind., 1995.

NEWLANDS RECLAMATION ACT OF 1902

Passed by the U.S. Congress, the Newlands Reclamation Act of 1902 established a federal program of reservoir and dam construction throughout the West. Named for its principal author, Nevada Congressmen Francis G. Newlands, the legislation created a Reclamation Fund to finance IRRIGATION projects. The first money for the fund came from the sale of public lands served by the WATER projects. Land parcels of 160 acres were available for settlers who claimed title to their lands after working them for three years. Water users were to pay fees and the cost of project construction in ten annual payments, and after the FEDERAL GOVERNMENT had been paid for construction, control of the water projects would transfer to the users. The law created the Reclamation Service, charged with selecting project sites and construction. FREDERICK HAYNES NEWELL served as the agency's first director. In the first five years of its existence, the service initiated twenty-one irrigation projects.

As President THEODORE ROOSEVELT's first piece of Progressive legislation, the Newlands Act launched a new era of federal involvement in the American West.

Attempts by private concerns and local and state governments had failed to produce irrigated lands of any sizeable amount. (Efforts by the Mormons of Utah were a noticeable exception.) Roosevelt, ascending to the presidency when William McKinley was assassinated, liked the RECLAMATION act for several reasons: It opened up new, improved lands to homesteaders; it fit in with his notions of conservation of—meaning, the use of—natural resources such as water; and it helped populate the West, vulnerable to Japan's expansionism and its need for lumber, metals, and other Western riches. Roosevelt signed the Newlands Reclamation Act into law on June 17, 1902.

The reclamation law, however, had its detractors, the most vocal of which protested federal control of so important a resource as water within Western states. To some, federal control of reclamation smacked of the SOCIALISM then threatening the political order of American life. When the implementation of the law failed to match the plans on paper, the law's detractors had even more ammunition. Water users were unable to repay the Reclamation Fund within the ten years specified by the law. Later amendments allowed farmers and other users twenty years—still later up to forty years—to meet their obligations, but the result was that reclamation was not the self-supporting enterprise imagined by the law's architects. The selection of dam sites and project construction occasionally became the victim of politics and pressures from influential water users rather than the small farmers developing new lands. In other areas, irrigation could not improve poor soils, inadequate drainage of crop fields, or a lack of markets for the crops produced. Some earnest homesteaders had little knowledge of irrigation farming. They overwatered their fields and allowed their irrigation ditches to silt up. Many filed claims on more acres than they had water to irrigate, and thus, they faced economic ruin in trying to hang onto unproductive fields.

In spite of these drawbacks, the Newlands Reclamation Act of 1902 boasted some striking achievements. Its first projects, for example, on the Salt River in Arizona, the Carson-Truckee rivers in NEVADA, and the Milk River in Montana, were clearly engineering marvels, and the accompanying rail lines built to serve water construction sites, the development of nearby towns and service centers, and the productivity of previously useless lands fueled the growth of some Western areas. Some historians rank the Newlands Reclamation Act as significant as the HOMESTEAD ACT OF 1862 in the development of America's West.

—*Patricia Hogan*

SEE ALSO: Climate; Progressivism

SUGGESTED READING:

Lilley, William, and Lewis L. Gould. "The Western Irrigation Movement, 1872–1902: A Reappraisal." *The American West: A Reorientation.* Edited by Gene M. Gressley. Laramie, Wyo., 1966.

Robinson, Michael. *Water for the West.* Chicago, 1979.

Warne, William. *The Bureau of Reclamation.* New York, 1973.

NEW MADRID EARTHQUAKE OF 1811

On December 15, 1811, the first of three earthquakes occurred in New Madrid County, Missouri Territory. Earthquakes followed on January 23 and February 7, 1812; all three caused more than eighteen hundred aftershocks. The first quake of the series was the most severe within the United States. Scientists have estimated that the 1811 earthquake would have measured between 8.4 and 8.8 on the Richter scale (the SAN FRANCISCO EARTHQUAKE OF 1906 was estimated to be 8.3; the San Francisco earthquake of 1989 measured 6.9). The quakes occurred along the New Madrid fault line, forty miles wide and two hundred miles long, running from the Missouri-Illinois border south to Memphis, Tennessee.

The 1811 earthquake caused the town of New Madrid to drop more than ten feet in elevation, and the community was flooded by the Mississippi River. Homes were torn apart, trees were uprooted, and the banks of the Mississippi were destroyed. The quake also changed the channel of the Mississippi River, which actually ran northwards for several hours following the disaster. In the aftermath of the quakes, river boats and other water traffic were detoured and delayed for months. When the floor of the Mississippi River buckled and caused its waters to rise, the flooding formed Reelfoot Lake in Kentucky. The principal quakes were reportedly felt as far away as Canada and the Gulf Coast.

Some Missourians who lost their homes and lands fled the region after the quake. Others remained, hoping federal aid would allow them to rebuild their homes and communities. Congress did not respond to their calls for assistance until 1815, however, because the federal government was preoccupied with a war with England. In 1815, Congress passed an act allowing residents to relocate to other public lands of equal acreage. Land acquisition for the victims of the quake was limited to 640 acres. Speculators rushed to New Madrid to purchase damaged properties at extremely low prices from original landholders who were unaware of the congressional action. In turn, the speculators traded their property titles for government land of much greater value. Missourians, by 1820, were angered by their losses and demanded federal remedy. In the same year, Congress passed a law to disallow the claims that had been transferred from victims of the earthquakes.

Historians record Shawnee Chief TECUMSEH's prediction of the New Madrid earthquake. It is said that he and Big Warrior, a Creek chief, argued shortly before the disaster. After Big Warrior dismissed Tecumseh's call for an intertribal confederation, the Shawnee chief predicted that upon his return to Tippecanoe, he would stomp his foot and the earth would shake. The earthquake occurred while Tecumseh was traveling to Tippecanoe and led Big Warrior to believe that Tecumseh, indeed, had supernatural powers.

—*Barbara Harper*

SUGGESTED READING:
Foley, William E. *A History of Missouri: Volume 1, 1673 to 1820.* Edited by William Parrish. Columbia, Mo., 1971.
Phillips, Charles. *Missouri: Mother of the American West.* Northridge, Calif., 1988.

NEWMAN, ANGIE

Angelia Louise French Thurston Kilgore Newman (1837–1910) was an anti-Mormon reformer best known for her pet project, the INDUSTRIAL CHRISTIAN HOME FOR MORMON WOMEN in Salt Lake City. Born in Montpelier, Vermont, she spent much of her childhood in Wisconsin, and after her marriage to merchant David Newman, she settled in Lincoln, Nebraska.

After a visit to Salt Lake City alerted her to the existence of Mormon polygamy, the practice whereby church leaders took more than one wife at a time, she persuaded several women's organizations to back her campaign to establish a refuge for Mormon wives. Newman regarded Mormon polygamy as "the substitution of the Harem for the Home," and she and other Protestant reformers believed women in polygamous marriages were eager to leave them. Traveling to Washington, D.C., she presented dramatic accounts of Mormon women's suffering to the U.S. Senate Committee on Education and Labor and persuaded the senators to fund the Industrial Christian Home. The home opened to much fanfare in 1886 but closed its doors only seven years later.

A popular lecturer and frequent contributor to Methodist missionary periodicals, Newman worked for temperance, social purity, and the establishment of charitable institutions all her life. She died in Lincoln at the age of seventy-two.

—*Peggy Pascoe*

SUGGESTED READING:
James, Edward T., ed. *Notable American Women: A Biographical Dictionary.* Vol. 2. Cambridge, Mass., 1971.
Pascoe, Peggy. *Relations of Rescue: The Search for Female Moral Authority in the American West, 1874–1939.* New York, 1990.

NEW MEXICO

Sharing its southern border with the Mexican state of Chihuahua, New Mexico, the "Land of Enchantment," lies between Arizona and Texas. With its capital in SANTA FE, New Mexico encompasses 121,563 square miles. The state has four main regions: the Great Plains; the Rocky Mountains; the Basin and Range region; and the Colorado Plateau. The Great Plains of New Mexico are part of the large interior plain that stretches across North America from Canada to Mexico. In New Mexico, the western edge of the Great Plains covers nearly one-third of the state. The ROCKY MOUNTAINS extend into the north-central area of New Mexico from Colorado southward to Santa Fe. Snow melt from the mountains provides irrigation water in the spring along the fertile Rio Grande valley. The RIO GRANDE, which rises in southern Colorado, flows north-south through the center of the state before it enters Texas at El Paso where it continues southeastward until it empties in the Gulf of Mexico. In the southern Rockies, Wheeler Peak (13,161 feet) is the highest point in New Mexico. Other mountain ranges in northern New Mexico include the Sangre de Cristo, north of Santa Fe, and the Nacimiento and Jemez ranges west of the Rio Grande. The Basin and Range cover about one-third of the state. The Basin and Range region extends south and west from the Rockies toward the Arizona–New Mexico border. This region includes the Guadalupe, Mogollon, Organ, Dacramento, and San Andres ranges. Broad, low-lying basins, where streams have no outlets, lie between the mountain ranges. The Jornada del Muerto (Deadman's Journey) and the Tularosa are the largest basins in the state. The Colorado Plateau is a broken region composed of wide valleys and plains, deep canyons, sharp escarpments, and rugged, windswept plateaus, or mesas.

New Mexico's economy is based on MINING (63 percent), agriculture and ranching (22 percent), and manufactured products (15 percent). Federal uses of the land include national forests, defense installations, grasslands, and Indian reservations.

Since the founding of New Mexico in 1598, most New Mexicans have lived in villages surrounding a larger town, particularly those centered around Santa Fe, which was established in 1610, and ALBUQUERQUE,

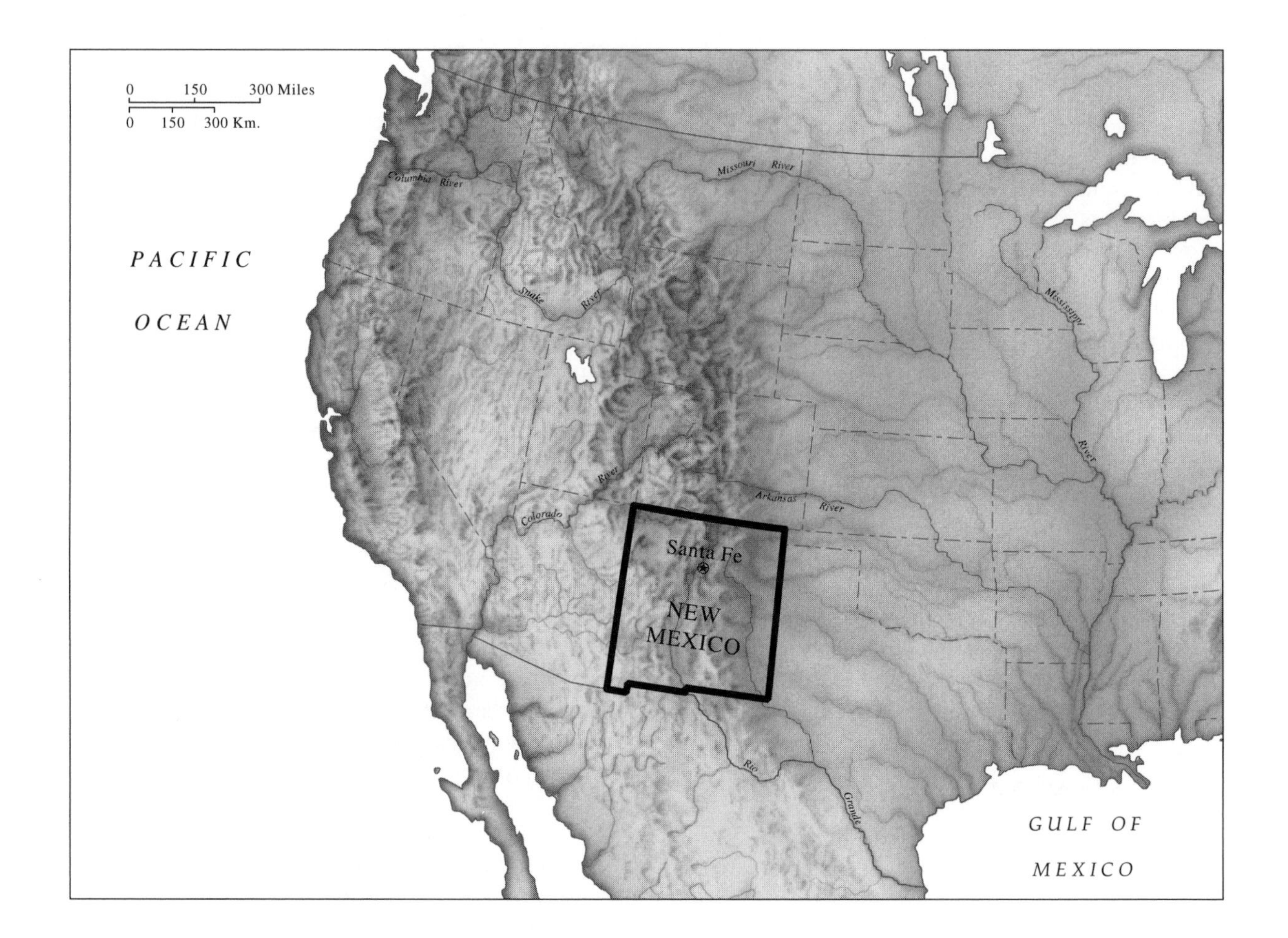

which was founded in 1706. Urban growth exploded during and after World War II, when defense installations and airbases caused other centers of population to grow, principally around Alamogordo, Clovis, Albuquerque, and Roswell. In the last half of the twentieth century, New Mexico moved from an extractive economy dominated by mining, ranching, and farming to an economy driven by light manufacturing, TOURISM, and services. This transformation has changed the barriers of race and gender in the state, permitting more women and ethnic minorities access to education, housing, and jobs. Still, profound political and economic inequalities reflect New Mexico's past as well as its Sunbelt present, resulting in low-paying service jobs. Nonetheless, dominant Anglo-American ethnic groups share with the Hispanic culture in the daily economic life of New Mexico as well as in the arts, in politics, and in education. According to the 1990 census, New Mexico's population numbered 1,515,069. Hispanics compose the largest ethnic minority (38 percent), followed by Native Americans (.08 percent), and African Americans (.02 percent).

Native Americans

American Indians have probably lived within the area of New Mexico for more than twenty thousand years. Lithic spearheads found at Folsom and other places indicate the presence of Indian forebears in northeastern New Mexico some ten thousand years ago. From about 500 B.C. to 1200 A.D., the Mogollon Indians inhabited the valleys along the New Mexico–Arizona border. Their early homes were pit houses, hovels that were partially dug in the ground. Later, as village patterns emerged, structures were built above ground. Another ancient people, the Anasazi, who originated in the Four Corners area of New Mexico, Arizona, Utah, and Colorado, gradually moved southwestward toward the Rio Grande. The Anasazi society was among the more complex of North American Indians. The Anasazis raised corn and cotton, tamed wild turkeys, traded with their counterparts in present-day Chihuahua and other parts of Mexico, and built elaborately constructed pueblos. They were cliff dwellers as well as villagers who built multistoried pueblos along arid lands and river valleys in New Mexico. The

Navajo and Apache tribes entered New Mexico about 1500 A.D. from the north. Utes and Comanches arrived in the region after them.

The Indian cultures in New Mexico changed with the coming of Europeans. Early Spanish explorers in the sixteenth century were the first Europeans to make contact with Indians in New Mexico. The first Spanish explorers to reach southern New Mexico did so by accident. ÁLVAR NÚÑEZ CABEZA DE VACA, a member of the ill-fated PÁNFILO DE NARVÁEZ expedition to Florida in 1528, was among the few survivors of a shipwreck near the Texas coast. For eight years, Cabeza de Vaca and three other survivors wandered west of Texas, probably passing through southern New Mexico south of Las Cruces, until they reached the Spanish settlements on the Pacific Coast in Sonora. Although he did not see them, in his report to the viceroy, Cabeza de Vaca was the first to make mention of Indians who lived in pueblos and grew cotton north of where he had passed. Later, between 1538 and 1542, two Spanish expeditions entered New Mexico and left descriptions of land and people. Fray Marcos de Niza left a controversial description of Zuni Pueblo in 1539, and FRANCISCO VÁSQUEZ DE CORONADO established a base camp along the Rio Grande near present-day Albuquerque during the winter of 1540 to 1541. De Niza explored as far north in New Mexico as the Taos Pueblo and as far south as present-day Socorro. The farthest reach of the Coronado expedition was central Kansas. The expedition made contact with both Pueblo Indians and Plains Indians and noted their cultures, economies, and abilities to wage war.

Between 1580 and 1582, two other expeditions entered New Mexico. One was led by Francisco Sanchez Chamuscado (1580) and the second by Antonio de Espejo (1581). The attempts of these expeditions to evangelize the Pueblo Indians met with little success. They did, however, document what they saw, leaving an ethnographical record of sedentary, semisedentary, and nomadic groups they had encountered at first contact. The significance of these early Spanish expeditions is that they began a written tradition, thereby initiating the historical period of the Pueblo tribes. Today, Tiwa-, Tewa-, Tano-, and Keresan-speaking Pueblo Indians inhabit the Rio Grande valley from Isleta to Taos. The desert Pueblo Indians live in the region from Acoma to Zuni, Zia, and Jemez. Athapascan-speaking descendants of the Navajos and Apaches live on reservations located in western and south-central New Mexico.

Spanish colonial period

The Spanish colonial period in New Mexico is divided into two major periods. The pre–PUEBLO REVOLT period, from 1598 to 1680, and the post–Pueblo Revolt period, from 1692 to 1821, are separated by a twelve-year hiatus during which refugee Spanish camps were located at El Paso del Norte. The arrival of Spanish settlers and Franciscan missionaries in 1598 set in motion a profound cultural change in New Mexico. In January 1598, JUAN DE OÑATE led a wagon caravan of more than three hundred settlers from Santa Barbara in present-day Chihuahua to New Mexico. His mission, which had the blessing of the viceroy, was to establish a permanent settlement among the Pueblos of New Mexico. By July, the wagon train had reached an Indian settlement called Caypa near the San Juan Pueblo in northern New Mexico. Dispossessing the natives there of their homes, Oñate moved his colony to a new capital at San Gabriel at the confluence of the Rio Grande and Rio Chama. Exploration of New Mexico continued as Oñate visited every pueblo in the area and sent out expeditions eastward to the Great Plains and westward to the Colorado River in Arizona.

Displeased with the Spanish presence in the area, the people of Acoma decided to expel the invaders. They conspired to assassinate Oñate but failed in their attempt. Instead, they later killed his nephew, Juan de Zaldívar, and thereby triggered a series of events that led to the capture of Acoma and the severe punishment of its people. By 1609, Oñate had fallen out of favor and was tried and exiled from New Mexico by royal officials for his abuse of the Indians. In 1609, a new governor, Pedro de Peralta, arrived in New Mexico with instructions to establish a new capital for the province at Santa Fe.

Throughout the seventeenth century, New Mexico was fraught with disagreements between civil authorities and missionaries about control of Indian subjects. Complicating relationships within the Spanish colony, the Holy Office of the Inquisitio—introduced into New Mexico in 1626—was used by clergymen to intimidate settlers and officials and force them to conform to the clergy's demands. The political struggle among Spanish settlers and clergymen, exacerbating issues of Indian religious practices, labor, and punishment, resulted in injustices against the natives. Particularly, labor systems like the tribute-collecting regiment of the *encomienda* and the labor-inducing *repartimiento,* produced inequalities between the colonials and the natives. The native corrective to abuses in the colonial system was revolt. Finally, a series of rebellions led to the Pueblo Revolt of 1680, during which Santa Fe was captured by Pueblo warriors, and the Spanish settlers were forced to flee the widespread sack and plunder of New Mexico.

The second Spanish period, following the "Reconquest of New Mexico" in 1692 by DIEGO DE VARGAS,

Surveyors of the Jornada Range Reserve, New Mexico, at camp, 1912. *Courtesy National Archives.*

ushered in a new relationship between Pueblo Indians and Spanish settlers. Santa Fe was reestablished as the capital of New Mexico. Warfare between Apache, Navajo, Comanche, and Ute tribes against Spanish settlers and their Puebloan allies characterized the period. The exploration of Utah by New Mexicans in 1765 and 1776 opened up trade routes as far northwest as the Great Basin and an eventual route to California. The establishment of the Villa de San Felipe de Alburquerque in 1706 and present-day Cuidad Chihuahua in 1709 had created other opportunities for trade. The rest of the century saw the development of new towns and industries throughout New Mexico. The Spanish empire eventually gave way to an independence movement in 1821.

Throughout the colonial period (from 1598 to 1821), New Mexico was linked with Mexico City through the long immigration and trade route known as El Camino Real de Tierra Adentro, the Royal Road of the Interior. Via the Camino Real, the Spaniards introduced into New Mexico many Old World products such as fruit trees, vegetables, and wheat. Domesticated animals—HORSES, cattle, goats, sheep and others—were also introduced by Spanish colonials. Ironworks, including tools, weapons, and household utensils, were likewise brought to New Mexico by Spanish settlers. A new language—Spanish—a new religion—Catholicism—and new legal customs and traditions such as the land and water principles and laws on COMMUNITY PROPERTY introduced in the colonial period have continued to influence culture in New Mexico.

After Mexican independence in 1821, a new order resulted in the creation of Mexico as a nation-state. Between 1821 and 1848, New Mexico existed as a territory of Mexico. During that period, Anglo-Americans from Missouri expanded their trade interests toward Santa Fe. Initiated by WILLIAM BECKNELL in 1821, the Santa Fe Trail provided new and lasting trade opportunities for New Mexico. During this period, in 1829, Antonio Armijo blazed the OLD SPANISH TRAIL connecting Santa Fe with Los Angeles in California. With the resulting trade along the Santa Fe Trail, the Camino Real, and the Old Spanish Trail, Santa Fe began to prosper economically.

As Anglo-American traders and settlers moved west into Texas and New Mexico, trouble developed between the United States and Mexico. In 1846, after the United States's annexation of Texas, war broke out between the two countries. U.S. forces under General

Stephen Watts Kearny quickly took control of New Mexico before invading California. The Treaty of Guadalupe Hidalgo ended the war in 1848, and the United States took possession of New Mexico and the region. By dint of the treaty, New Mexico became a territory of the United States, and its Spanish-speaking population became American citizens. Despite Mexico's liberal granting of citizenship to peaceful tribes, New Mexico's Indian population was denied citizenship in accordance with U.S. Indian policy.

Territorial years

In 1850, New Mexico was organized into a territory of the United States. The New Mexico Territory included Arizona and southern Colorado as well as parts of Utah and Nevada. In 1853, the Gadsden Purchase expanded New Mexico's territorial boundaries to include land south of the Gila River as well as the land between Mesilla and El Paso. New Mexico's boundary ran along its present southern border as far west as the Colorado River.

During the territorial period, New Mexico experienced war on several fronts. In 1861, the Civil War broke out, and Confederate troops from Texas under Henry Hopkins Sibley invaded New Mexico. The short-lived invasion was repelled by Union forces and territorial militia before Albuquerque, Santa Fe, and Tucson had fallen to Confederate forces. One significant result of the Civil War in the West was that Congress declared Arizona a separate territory in 1863. As they had against Spain and Mexico, Apache and Comanche tribes waged war against the United States throughout the nineteenth century. In the end, on September 4, 1886, Geronimo, one of the last of the great Apache chiefs, surrendered. New Mexico's territorial period also witnessed the Lincoln County War in the late 1870s as cattlemen and other groups fought for political control of the area. The bitter feud burst into open violence with the murder of rancher John G. Tunstall. "Billy the Kid" and other outlaws played a leading role in the fighting. Finally, General Lew Wallace, appointed territorial governor in 1878, declared martial law and used troops to end the bloodshed. (Wallace later gained fame as the author of *Ben Hur.)* At century's end, in the Spanish-American War of 1898, some New Mexicans saw service as members of Theodore Roosevelt's Rough Riders in Cuba.

In the late nineteenth century, the railroads reached New Mexico. Linking the territory with the rest of the nation, the railroads created an economic boom in mining and the cattle industry. A new technology followed as telegraph wires influenced the system of communication in New Mexico.

The territorial period of New Mexico served as a transition from Mexican sovereignty to U.S. sovereignty, during which Spanish-speaking New Mexicans fought for their citizenship rights in the territorial courts. The Court of Private Land Claims examined more than three hundred land-grant cases but verified fewer than one-third of them, most of them in New Mexico. Similarly, Native Americans sought to gain citizenship rights under the terms of the Treaty of Guadalupe Hidalgo in a series of cases that reached the U.S. Supreme Court but failed.

Early statehood

The main political issue for the New Mexico Territory was its quest for statehood, which it achieved on January 6, 1912, when it became the forty-seventh state of the Union. By then, New Mexico's population was about 330,000.

Border problems, resulting from the Mexican Revolution of 1910, manifested themselves when Francisco ("Pancho") Villa raided the town of Columbus in 1916 and killed several Americans. The U.S. Army sent an expedition under General John Joseph Pershing to catch the elusive Villa but failed. Almost simultaneously, New Mexico—along with the rest of the nation—was drawn into World War I. More than seventeen thousand New Mexicans served in the armed forces.

In the early 1920s, New Mexico's economy waned due to a harsh drought that spread throughout the Southwest. As the ranching industry floundered, banks closed, and the onset of the Great Depression began to takes its toll. In the midst of the economic downturns, oil was discovered in New Mexico, and the large potash industry near Carlsbad opened. By 1930, the tourism industry began to grow, especially after Carlsbad Caverns became a national park.

New Mexico ushered in the Atomic Age during World War II. The world's first atomic bomb was tested at Trinity Site near Alamogordo on July 16, 1945. The two atom bombs dropped on Japan in August 1945 by the United States were produced at Los Alamos, a town and laboratory secretly built in the mountains northwest of Santa Fe. Following World War II, New Mexico prospered as its population rapidly grew. Federal monies provided funds for work on nuclear-energy development and rocketry. Federal airbases and research installations helped spur economic growth.

In 1950, the discovery of uranium in northwestern New Mexico gave new impetus to the state's boom-and-bust economy. By the late 1950s and early 1960s, the rate of growth in Albuquerque and Roswell had slowed. The military base at Roswell was closed, and Albuquerque suffered from a reduction in federally employed personnel. By 1970, both cities had recovered their losses by attracting nongovernment industries. Other New Mexico cities underwent similar crises. In the 1960s, a large coal mine opened near Raton; coal-burning electric generating plants were constructed near Farmington; and, a molybdenum mine near Questa began operation. Meanwhile, the potash industry at Carlsbad received serious competition from Canada.

New Mexico ranks as a leading center for scientific and nuclear research. Although Sandia Laboratories in Albuquerque and Los Alamos Labs had been among the largest employers conducting research in nuclear engineering involving thousands of people working in military and nonmilitary uses of nuclear energy, their influence began to wane in the mid-1990s as a result of government downsizing.

New Mexico's vast mineral reserves continue to play a role in solving energy problems faced by the nation since the 1970s. Despite the completion of the San Juan-Chama project in the 1980s, lack of water, however, continues to be a problem for New Mexico. Environmental degradation, overpopulation, and the continued exploitation of dwindling natural resources all affect New Mexico and cause concern for the future of the state.

—*Joseph P. Sanchez*

SEE ALSO: Apache Wars; Camino Real, El; Santa Fe and Chihuahua Trail; Spanish and Mexican Towns; Spanish Law

SUGGESTED READING:

Beck, Warren A., and Ynez D. Haase. *Historical Atlas of New Mexico*. Norman, Okla., 1969.

Chávez, Thomas E. *An Illustrated History of New Mexico*. Niwot, Colo., 1992.

Simmons, Marc. *New Mexico: A Bicentennial History*. New York and Nashville, Tenn., 1977.

Twitchell, Ralph Emerson. *The History of the Military Occupation of the Territory of New Mexico*. 1909. Reprint. New York, 1976.

Williams, Jerry L., and Paul E. McAllister, eds. *New Mexico in Maps*. Albuquerque, N. Mex., 1979.

NEWSPAPERS

SEE: Magazines and Newspapers

NEW THOUGHT

Although much diversity exists among groups who adhere to the movement labeled "New Thought," generally adherents believe that mind power can alter an individual's circumstances and that positive thinking can conquer adversities. While the philosophy first appeared in the northeastern United States, it has attracted many ardent supporters in the West.

New Thought originated in New England in the 1840s. Hypnotist Phineas P. Quimby, convinced that sickness resulted from negative thoughts, established a mental-healing practice through which he taught the sick to cure themselves through positive thinking. After his death, some of his patients revised and expanded his teachings. One of the most famous was Mary Baker Eddy, founder of Christian Science. Eddy contended that sickness resulted from sin and could only be eradicated through a psychic link to Christ's spirit. Other advocates insisted that mind power produced not only good health but also prosperity, and some embraced elements of Eastern religions and mysticism.

By the late nineteenth century, New Thought had spread to the American West. While many subscribers to mind power became affiliated with the movement through the study of its publications, others joined New Thought denominations or formed new ones. The Unity School of Christianity and Christian Science established branches throughout the region. In 1899, advocates of mental healing, Nona Brooks and Malinda Cramer, founded the Church of Divine Science in Colorado. In Los Angeles in 1917, two brothers from New England, Ernest and Fenwicke Holmes, organized the Church of Religious Science. Both of these groups maintained that mental healing derived from God's spirit, which they claimed dwelt in all people. By the mid-twentieth century, a variety of New Thought sects flourished in the West, and disciples hosted conferences, forged a national alliance, and published books, newspapers, and magazines promoting mind power.

While members of the formal New Thought organizations were predominately Euro-American, many African Americans joined Christian Science and the Unity churches. During the 1930s, Father Divine, a Harlem minister, attracted both African American and Euro-American followers in the West. Divine insisted that those who tapped into his spirit could conquer disease, poverty, and racism; his disciples believed he was God.

Much of New Thought's appeal derived from the uniqueness of the Western experience. Recent migrants, searching for security in an unfamiliar and sometimes hostile new environment, composed much of the region's population. New Thought empowered these people and gave them confidence and a sense of control over their destinities. Additionally, many new arrivals suffered from illnesses that had driven them to warmer climates. Undoubtedly, Western health-seekers found encouragement in the notion that positive thinking could overcome diseases and disabilities.

New Thought continued to be popular in the West during the late twentieth century. In the 1980s, it appeared in a updated form known as "New Age" philosophy. Like early New Thought advocates, New Agers stressed self-mastery through positive thinking and the channeling of spiritual energy. With the economic downturn of the 1980s and 1990s, many Westerners found solace in New Age sects that promised success through mind power.

—Jill Watts

SUGGESTED READING:

Braden, Charles S. *Spirits in Rebellion: The Rise and Development of New Thought.* Dallas, Tex., 1963.

Frankiel, Sandra Sizer. *California's Spiritual Frontiers: Religious Alternatives in Anglo-Protestantism, 1850–1910.* Berkeley, Calif., 1988.

Watts, Jill. *God, Harlem U.S.A.: The Father Divine Story.* Berkeley, Calif., 1992.

NEW WESTERN HISTORY

The new Western history was officially born in September 1989 at a symposium sponsored by the National Endowment for the Humanities in the picturesque town of Santa Fe, New Mexico. The symposium's title, "Trails: Toward a New Western History," was chosen by Western historian Patricia Nelson Limerick, who also distributed a one-page statement to the Santa Fe participants and audience entitled "What on Earth Is the New Western History?" The media picked up on this declaration of a new approach to studying the Western past, and articles appeared in numerous newspapers and magazines, including: the *Washington Post, New York Times, Los Angeles Times, Denver Post, New Republic, U.S. News and World Report,* and *The Chronicle of Higher Education.*

Limerick's statement declared that the new Western history emphasized the West as a place, namely that area west of the one hundredth meridian or the Mississippi River. She noted that new Western historians rejected the old term *frontier,* which emphasized the West as a process, not a place, and was "nationalistic and racist." To describe the means by which the West was shaped, Limerick suggested terms such as *invasion, conquest, colonization,* and *exploitation.* Furthermore, she stressed the theme of continuity in Western history and thus rejected the commonly held idea that 1890—the date of the Census Bureau's declaration of the end of a distinct frontier line that was emphasized by FREDERICK JACKSON TURNER in his famous frontier thesis—marked a significant point of departure in Western history. The Turnerian model, she insisted, suggested an artificial break in Western history and deemphasized the importance of the twentieth-century West.

Limerick rejected the old notion that the settlement of the West was a story of national "progress" and "improvement," and pointed to the presence of "failure" and "injury." "[H]eroism and villainy, virtue and vice, and nobility and shoddiness," she insisted, "appear in roughly the same proportions" in the history of the West. Finally, Limerick stressed that neutral history was impossible and that the new Western historians cared about the subjects they studied and that concern showed in their work.

Why the explosion of media interest in the new Western history after the "Trails" symposium? These historians, revising previous accounts of Western history (Western revisionists), became the subject of the kind of attention normally reserved for political scandals and big sports events. The media even coined a catchy label for the most renowned of the Western revisionists—Patricia Nelson Limerick, Richard White, Donald Worster, and William Cronon—the "Gang of Four." Images of four superhero scholars saving the Western past from the injustices of traditional interpretations, or of four renegade writers trashing the cherished Western American heritage, may have sprung to readers' minds. The media helped define for the public what was at stake in revising the Western past. Unfortunately, in doing this, the media also oversimplified the story of how the West was being rewritten and helped construct an adversarial arena in which scholars were expected to exchange barbed comments. The *Washington Post*'s headline, "Shootout in Academia over History of U.S. West," was indicative of the trend. Even the "Gang of Four" label was somewhat misleading, since William Cronon's work was quite different from that of Limerick, White, and Worster.

The new Western historians were reacting to the vitality of romantic notions of the Old West in both scholarly writing and the public imagination. Frederick Jackson Turner's 1893 essay, "The Significance of the Frontier in American History," became an important focal point of the media coverage because it was Turner's century-old idea of a triumphal process of white frontier settlement to which the revisionists were reacting. Turner stressed the rugged independence, heightened democracy, and strident nationalism of the frontiersman. The new Western historians, on the other hand, emphasized the conquest of Native Americans and other peoples of color, the subjugation of women and the laboring classes, and the despoliation of the environment.

The media attention was hardly surprising. Turner's frontier thesis presented the settlement of the Western frontier as the proudest chapter in the nation's past. His West was the most American part of America. Revisionists, however, called for a major reassessment that emphasized the murky underside of Western history. But casting a shadow on the Western past called into question the whole national heritage, it seemed. The new Western history struck a raw nerve and sparked a media reaction because Western imagery is such an important element of American national mythology.

The new Western history met with a spirited response. Renowned Western novelist Larry McMurtry may have expressed the sentiments of many others when he wrote in the *New Republic* that the new Western history amounted to "Failure Studies," because it was obsessed with stressing the downside of Western history. Western revisionists responded to the charge of overnegativity by arguing that their critics were unable to see the realities of the Western past because their vision was clouded by the mists of myth and misperception. Revisionists contended that the Western past of their writings was a less attractive place, but it was a far more realistic one. Western historian Elliott West aptly described the new Western history as a "longer, grimmer, but more interesting story."

Heightened media coverage of the "Showdown at the Politically O. K. Corral," as one journalist called it, lasted for more than a year, and the media did not abandon the story in the early 1990s. When the Smithsonian Institution hosted a controversial art exhibit, "The West as America: Reinterpreting Images of the Frontier, 1820–1920," from March to July 1991, media interest in Western revisionism was reignited. The exhibit designers, heavily influenced by the work of the new Western historians, took the heroic images of westward expansion and recast them as mere justifications for imperialism and conquest, as fundamentally racist and materialist images. More than seven hundred visitors to the exhibit wrote down their reactions in the comment books provided, and their responses were mixed and quite emotional. Some praised the exhibit's effort to present a less romantic Western past. Others viewed it as "a mean-spirited and cynical attack on Western art and artists." As the exhibit designers noted, the heated public reactions may have been, in part, a reflection of public reaction to the Gulf War (the final phase of which coincided with the exhibit) and to the issue of political correctness.

A second major art exhibit, "Discovered Lands, Invented Pasts: Transforming Visions of the American West," was on view at various museums and art galleries from mid-1992 to mid-1993 and helped sustain media interest in Western revisionism. The year 1993 also marked the one-hundred-year anniversary of Turner's frontier thesis. Another wave of articles and books on Turner helped keep media interest focused on the volatile field of Western history. Media coverage raised the stakes and intensified the debate. Western history—all too often relegated to basement status in academia and subjected to the pejorative label "Cowboy and Indian history"—had once again become a promising field for scholars.

Unfortunately, the debate became increasingly ugly as it entered the public sphere. In March 1993, Western historian Gerald Nash, launching a particularly virulent attack on the new Western history, charged that it was not scholarship but leftist propaganda. Nash's comments sparked another round of charges and countercharges among Western historians. Older scholars argued that the new Western historians (who are generally in their early forties) are suffering from "post-Vietnam depression syndrome" and are merely using the West as a dumping ground for their intellectual disillusionment. Revisionists countered that many older scholars were simply incapable of picturing a West that is not weighed down with mythic baggage.

The West had become a regional battleground in the academic war over political correctness and multiculturalism. New Western historians, emphasizing the history of women, peoples of color, the environment, and the laboring classes, appeared to be a clear example of the ascendancy of leftist theories centered on the themes of race, class, and gender.

These themes—race, class, and gender—along with an emphasis on the environment, were the product of social changes in the 1960s and 1970s. These changes, which resulted from the civil rights movement, Vietnam War protests, women's rights movement, the gay and lesbian rights movement, and a widespread disillusionment with mainstream culture, helped shape the thinking of Western revisionists. New fields of study, such as women's history, African American history, environmental history, Chicano history, Native American history, and labor history have developed since the 1960s, and these developments were bound to affect Western history.

While officially born in 1989, important examples of the new Western history began to appear a few years earlier. In 1985, Donald Worster's sweeping account of the West's dependence on a limited resource—WATER—was published. *Rivers of Empire: Water, Aridity, and the Growth of the American West* described the massive ecological damage that had resulted from the large-scale efforts to redirect water resources to

Western cities and farms. There was little to glory about in Worster's story of bureaucratic and economic elites controlling a vital commodity at the expense of the great mass of ordinary Westerners.

In 1987, the most influential work of new Western history, Patricia Nelson Limerick's *Legacy of Conquest: The Unbroken Past of the American West,* was published. Limerick began her book with an urgent plea to Western historians to get beyond the erroneous notion of a frontier closing in 1890, and to get on with the task of opening up a hugely important chapter in the West's history—the twentieth century. In a superbly structured and finely written narrative, Limerick summarized the findings of recent revisionist writings on the West. She countered Turner's romantic, triumphant story with a tragic, painfully ironic account centered around the theme of conquest. While Turner's thesis dealt at great length with rugged Euro-American frontiersmen taming the wilderness, Limerick's account included coverage of the many groups that Turner left out—women missionaries and prostitutes, miners, failed farmers, Mexicans, Chinese, and Japanese.

Turner's canvas was a rosy, romantic landscape; Limerick's picture is bleaker, its focal points are dried up rivers, abandoned mines, and nuclear test sites. The cover of *The Legacy of Conquest,* featuring a crowded land office, emphasized Limerick's argument that the pursuit of profit was the prime motivating factor behind Western settlement, not the agrarian dream of self-sufficiency and appreciation of nature's beauty.

The year 1991 saw the publication of *Trails: Toward a New Western History,* an important collection of essays about the new revisionism, some of which had been presented at the Santa Fe symposium. That year also marked the appearance of an important revisionist textbook by Richard White. *"It's Your Misfortune and None of My Own": A New History of the American West.* White did not mention Frederick Jackson Turner or use the term *frontier.* The book was a reaction to the late RAY ALLEN BILLINGTON's frontier-centered text, *Westward Expansion* (first published in 1949, and most recently in 1982). White centered on the West as a region with geographic boundaries—the Missouri River and the Pacific Ocean. He emphasized race relations, urban growth, the West's dependency on the federal government, and the transformation of the Western environment.

Also in 1991, William Cronon published his ground-breaking study of the special relationship between the city of Chicago "and the vast region lying to its west." *Nature's Metropolis: Chicago and the Great West* demonstrates how this close relationship between a city and its "hinterland" reshaped the landscape. Whether Cronon should be categorized as a revisionist or not, *Nature's Metropolis* was certainly reflective of the new Western history's emphasis on urban history and on hierarchical relationships among people, companies, governments, and regions. Another important collection of revisionist essays, *Under an Open Sky: Rethinking America's Western Past,* edited by William Cronon, George Miles, and Jay Gitlin, appeared in 1992.

Another influential revisionist book, William G. Robbins' *Colony and Empire: The Capitalist Transformation of the American West* (1994) examined the effects of global capitalism on the West. Robbins emphasized the themes of industrial violence and exploitation, racism, urban growth, and federal influence and produced perhaps the grimmest, starkest, most depressing major work of new Western history.

In addition to the sweeping studies of Worster, Limerick, White, Cronon, and Robbins, Western revisionism has proved an important catalyst to the fields of environmental history, urban history, women's history, Native American history, Chicano history, African American history, and, most recently, gay and lesbian history. The revisionists' emphasis on previously excluded groups has helped illuminate the West's diversity. Their insistence on moving beyond Turner's closed frontier has sparked excellent work on the recent Western past. The new Western historians' emphasis on the West as a geographically definable region, characterized by its aridity, has led to fascinating discussions about "Where the West Is." Elliott West seems to have been correct in characterizing the new Western history as a longer, grimmer, but more interesting story.

However, as is generally the case with most sweeping exercises in scholarly revisionism, the new Western history has had its excesses. Critics have charged that the new scholarship is actually not so new; that the revisionists fail to adequately define the West as a region; that they are too polemical; and that they focus too exclusively on Western failure. Perhaps the new Western historians worked too hard to present a framework that was 180 degrees removed from the old Turnerian model. Eager to promote their new approach, the revisionists (along with the media, eager to promote a good story) probably exaggerated the gulf between the "new" and the "old" history. Indeed, the term *old Western history,* was created for the purposes of contrast with *new Western history;* no school of old Western historians existed. Generations of Western historians, whose work was quite varied, were lumped together as examples of the old-fashioned, triumphal Turnerian approach. But, Turner had long been subject to criticism before the new Western history appeared on the scene. Furthermore, by emphasizing the West as a defined place—a region—in contrast to the notion of a frontier process, the revisionists placed a little too much emphasis on banishing the frontier concept from Western history.

However, in 1994, key revisionists Limerick and White themselves wrote about the significance of the frontier concept in connection with an exhibit entitled "The Frontier in American Culture," held at Chicago's Newberry Library. This was an indication that the new Western history had achieved ascendancy and become the mainstream. Revisionists were comfortable analyzing the frontier theme. Limerick even wrote an important, and in some ways complimentary, essay about the previously scorned Frederick Jackson Turner, and White was also elected to the presidency of the Western History Association.

The new Western history has indeed transformed the study of the American West, bringing it up to speed with the broader field of U.S. history, which had, for some decades, been emphasizing the themes of race, class, and gender. As more women and people of color write Western history, the old story of heroic white settlement seems destined to receive increasingly less attention. Studies of the Western past are likely to become richer, more inclusive, more reflective of the diversity of the West and its population. And, one hopes, the excessive polemics that have characterized the field during the last decade, will subside as Western historians follow the advice of the *Trails: Towards a New Western History* editors and write about a Western past that includes "failure as well as success; defeat as well as victory; sympathy, grace, villainy, and despair, as well as danger, courage, and heroism; women as well as men; varied ethnic groups and their differing perspectives as well as white Anglo-Saxon Protestants." Works that follow these guidelines will tell a very complex, interesting, and realistic story.

—David M. Wrobel

SEE ALSO: Frontier: Frontier Thesis

SUGGESTED READING:

Cronon, William. *Nature's Metropolis: Chicago and the Great West.* New York, 1991.

———, George Miles, and Jay Gitlin, eds. *Under an Open Sky: Rethinking America's Western Past.* New York, 1992.

Faragher, John Mack. "The Frontier Trail: Rethinking Turner and Reimagining the West." *American Historical Review* 98 (1993): 106–117.

Gressley, Gene, ed. *Old West/New West: Quo Vadis?* Worland, Wyo., 1994.

Horn, Miriam. "How the West Was Really Won." *U.S. News and World Report* (May 21, 1990): 56–65.

Limerick, Patricia Nelson. *The Legacy of Conquest: The Unbroken Past of the American West.* New York, 1987.

———. "Turnerians All: The Dream of Helpful History in an Intelligible World." *American Historical Review* 100 (1995): 697–716.

———, Clyde Milner, and Charles Rankin, eds., *Trails: Toward a New Western History.* Lawrence, Kans., 1991.

McMurtry, Larry. "Westward Ho Hum: What the New Historians Have Done to the Old West." *New Republic* (October 9, 1990): 32-38.

Nash, Gerald D. *Creating the West: Historical Interpretations, 1890–1990.* Albuquerque, N. Mex., 1991.

Ridge, Martin, Gerald Thompson, Gerald D. Nash, and William H. Goetzmann. "Symposium: The New Western History." *Continuity* 17 (1993): 1–32.

Robbins, William G. *Colony and Empire: The Capitalist Transformation of the American West.* Lawrence, Kans., 1994.

White, Richard. *"It's Your Misfortune and None of My Own": A New History of the American West.* Norman, Okla., 1991.

Worster, Donald. *Rivers of Empire: Water, Aridity, and the Growth of the American West.* New York, 1985.

———. *Under Western Skies: Nature and History in the American West.* New York, 1992.

NEZ PERCÉ INDIANS

SEE: Native American Peoples: Peoples of the Pacific Northwest

NEZ PERCÉ WAR

SEE: Pacific Northwest Indian Wars

NG POON-CHEW

Born in the Guangdong province of China, Ng Poon-Chew (1866–1931) was the publisher of the influential Chinese-language daily *CHUNG SAI YAT PO (Chinese American Daily Paper)* and a strong defender of Chinese civil rights in America.

He arrived in the United States in 1881 and worked as a house boy in San Jose. He attended the local Sunday school where he learned English and embraced Christianity. He converted around 1883 and began working for the Chinese Presbyterian mission in San Francisco under the direction of the Reverend Augustus Loomis.

Ng later enrolled in the San Francisco Theological Seminary and was ordained the first Chinese Presbyterian minister on the West Coast in 1889. In 1892, he married a Chinese Christian convert, and the couple had four daughters and one son. The family moved to Los Angeles in 1894 to head the Chinese mission there but returned to San Francisco in 1898 after the mission burned down.

In 1900, Ng began publishing *Chung Sai Yat Po,* one of the more successful Chinese-language newspapers in the country until it ceased publication in 1951. Through editorials, Ng advocated a strong modern China and equal rights for Chinese living in America. In addition to working as a publisher, he frequently spoke in defense of the Chinese. He addressed the House of Representatives, met with THEODORE ROOSEVELT, received an honorary doctorate from the University of Pittsburgh, and was a regular speaker in the Chautauqua movement in the Western states.

—*K. Scott Wong*

SEE ALSO: Chinese Americans

SUGGESTED READING:

Hoexter, Corinne K. *From Canton to California: The Epic of Chinese Immigration.* New York, 1976.

NICOLET, JEAN

Born in Cherbourg, France, Jean Nicolet (sometimes spelled Nicollet) de Belleborn (1598–1642) was a fur trader and explorer in New France (Canada). In 1818, he joined the Compagnie des Marchands de Rouen et de Saint-Malo and came to New France. Operating with the better-known Samuel de Champlain, he became not only an explorer but an official liaison between the French and various Indian tribes. Nicolet centered his headquarters among the Algonquins on Allumette Island in the Ottawa River from 1618 to 1620. He also lived with the Nipissing Indians for nine years and was appointed their official interpreter in 1633. Nicolet visited the Iroquois, Hurons, and Winnebagos (who took him for a god) as well. His goal was to further French influence among the Indian tribes to ensure that furs they collected would be traded with the French instead of with the English on Hudson's Bay or to the Dutch in New York.

Nicolet traveled west in 1634 in search of a NORTHWEST PASSAGE, or "the China Sea." During that trip, he explored Lake Michigan, Green Bay (in present-day Wisconsin), and the Fox River and moved southward toward Illinois. He was the first white explorer in the Old Northwest. Nicolet ultimately settled at Trois Rivieres on 160 acres of wooded land granted him by the French monarchy. There he died by drowning during a severe storm.

—*Andrew Rolle*

SEE ALSO: Fur Trade

SUGGESTED READING:

Butterfield, C. W. *History of the Discovery of the Northwest by John Nicolet in 1634, with a Sketch of His Life.* Cincinnati, Ohio, 1881.

Gosselin, Auguste. *Jean Nicolet et le Canada de Son Temps.* Quebec, 1905.

"Notes on Jean Nicolet." *Collections of the Wisconsin Historical Society* 7 (1879): 188–194.

NISENAN INDIANS

SEE: Native American Peoples: Peoples of California

NISQUALLI INDIANS

SEE: Native American Peoples: Peoples of the Pacific Northwest

NOBLE-SAVAGE THEORY

The idea of the "noble savage" predates the first contacts between Europeans and American Indians in the fifteenth century. The concept flourished among the Greeks and may even have had an earlier origin. In each succeeding age of Western civilization until the present, the concept has appeared with varying degrees of prominence. In truth, the noble savage is only one aspect of the larger idea of the savage. The notion assumes an original state or at least a state that precedes the one that now exists. In its ignoble version, the savage's movement away from that original condition has been wholly salutary. But for the *noble* savage, any movement has been a process of degeneration. The noble savage enjoyed a world of innocence, free of the trials and complexities of life, before history and culture imposed their burdens on pristine nature. For Europeans, the noble savage offered an ideal against which to measure their own world. Although supposedly existing in the past, with a minor switch in perspective, the noble savage could serve as an example of a goal to be achieved.

Thus when American natives appeared in the European consciousness, there was a ready-made conception that would incorporate them into European modes of thinking. Columbus began the process in the Caribbean by describing the Taino people he met in largely noble terms and the Caribs he did not meet as representatives of the ignoble side of formulation. The English took their ideas about Indians from the Spanish and French accounts published in England by such anthologizers as Eden, Hakluyt, and Purchas. Experience did little to change the basic conceptions, although circumstances of Indian-European relations did seem to dictate whether the native people should be seen as noble or ignoble. Indian warriors who resisted white settlement were likely to be ignoble; defeated or vanishing natives could be more plausibly portrayed as noble.

Michel Eyquen de Montaigne had offered the starkest definition of the noble savage in the late sixteenth century, a figure devoid of any social attachments, virtuous because he represented the antitheses of a corrupt world. The conception has remained serviceable into the present age, although other times have supplied their own special vision. In the late eighteenth century, for example, the rational savage who exhibited a certain pristine wisdom was replaced by the sentimental savage, a figure that would persist into the twentieth century. That rendition of the noble savage was particularly united to an age in the throes of economic and social turmoil, an age that yearned for the supposed tranquility of the natural condition. In the novels of JAMES FENIMORE COOPER, in Henry Wadsworth Longfellow's *Hiawatha,* in the paintings by CHARLES BIRD KING, GEORGE CATLIN, and SETH EASTMAN, and even in the photography that became prominent in the latter part of the nineteenth century, the Indian appeared as a creature of noble character, worthy of the nostalgic interest of a society deeply in doubt of its own integrity. Despite the development of a realistic anthropology in the first half of the twentieth century, the noble savage continued to flourish. After the 1960s, with the rise of a counterculture and the development of a new conception of the physical environment, the noble savage took on a new life.

The noble savage has been a perennial expression of the Europeans' and their descendants' search for self-definition, a search they have carried on at the expense of a realistic portrayal of native people.

—*Bernard W. Sheehan*

SUGGESTED READING:

Baudet, E. H. P. *Paradise on Earth: Some Thoughts on European Images of Non-European Man.* Middletown, Conn., 1988.

Berkhofer, Robert T., Jr. "White Conceptions of Indians." In *Handbook of North American Indians.* Edited by William C. Sturtevant and Wilcomb E. Washburn. Vol. 4. Washington, D.C., 1988.

———. *The White Man's Indian: Images of the American Indian from Columbus to the Present.* New York, 1978.

Sheehan, Bernard W. *Savagism and Civility: Indians and Englishmen in Colonial Virginia.* Cambridge, Mass., 1980.

NONPARTISAN LEAGUE

Agrarian anger against corporate domination of the national economy and the high-handed treatment of Western farmers by powerful political machines serving the interests of railroads and grain trusts led to the establishment of the Nonpartisan League in North Dakota in 1915. The brainchild of ARTHUR CHARLES (A. C.) TOWNLEY, who had previously worked with the Socialist party, the league sought to remedy the grievances of farmers by political means. Its agenda was especially attractive in North Dakota, virtually a one-crop state, where farmers were subjected to the wild fluctuations of the international wheat market. Townley's high-pressure campaign to found the organization called for state-owned banks, grain elevators, and mills, state-sponsored farm-insurance programs, tax breaks for farmers for improving their operations, and state inspection of grains, weights, and measures, as well as a slew of progressive reforms including women's suffrage, the introduction of an inheritance tax, and universal public education. The league's avowedly socialistic program stirred up immense controversy, and its right-wing enemies denounced the organization as a bastion of atheism, anarchism, and free love. Its flamboyant leadership, which included William Lempke and Lynn Frazier, however, attracted some 30,000 members within a year.

Adamantly opposed to America's entry into World War I, a position that played well in the isolationist West, the NPL insinuated itself into the dominant Republican party. Capturing the state House of Representatives in 1916, the league placed Frazier in the governor's seat and made Lempke his attorney general. In 1918, the league swept state elections and enacted much of its program the following year. At its zenith, the league attracted some 250,000 members, and its influence spilled over into neighboring Minnesota, Canada, and the wheat-growing areas of the Northwest. Once in power, personality conflicts rather than disagreements over policy prompted defections from its ranks, and other reform and farm movements chipped away at the league's following as charges of disloyalty and mismanagement directed at some of its leaders began to appear in the press. Much more damaging, however, was the United States's entry into the war and the wave of patriotism, fed by federal propaganda organizations, that rolled over the country. Having, like the INDUSTRIAL WORKERS OF THE WORLD, come to prominence courtesy of SOCIALISM's antiwar gospel, the league now found itself the victim of conservative reaction. In the elections of 1920, it lost its hegemony in North Dakota, and in 1921, Frazier and Lempke were removed from office in the first recall election of state officials in U.S. history, an ironic turn of events given that the recall itself was a favorite reform of POPULISM and PROGRESSIVISM. Defeat in North Dakota led to the swift decline of the league, which was replaced by the Farm-Labor party as the champion of wheat farmers and agrarian revolt. After 1932, the NPL itself became a rigid political machine, and in 1956, it affiliated officially with the Democrats.

—*Charles Phillips*

SEE ALSO: Agrarianism

SUGGESTED READING:

Morlan, Robert L. *Political Prairie Fire: The Nonpartisan League, 1915–1922.* Minneapolis, Minn., 1955.

NOOTKA INDIANS

SEE: Native American Peoples: Peoples of the Pacific Northwest

NOOTKA SOUND CONTROVERSY

In 1790, a dispute arose between Britain and Spain—after the latter, in 1789, had seized four trading vessels owned by Captain John Meares in Nootka Sound—that nearly caused the two countries to go to war. In April 1790, Meares and his associates appealed to the British government for redress. When Spain, claiming possession of the entire Northwest Coast of America by right of a 1493 papal grant, refused to come to terms and confirmed that their explorers had formally taken possession of not just Meares's ships but of the region itself, the British threatened war. Contending that rights of sovereignty could be established only by the actual occupation of the land, the British turned to Prussia for diplomatic support and received it. A militarily weakened and nearly bankrupt Spanish empire backed down and signed the Nootka Sound Convention on October 28, 1790. Acknowledging that both nations were free to navigate Pacific waters, fish in the ocean, and establish trading posts and settlements on land unoccupied by other Europeans, the convention ended Spain's claim to a monopoly over America's West Coast and cleared the way for the expansion, eventually, of Canada's provinces to the Pacific.

—*Charles Phillips*

NORBECK, PETER

Governor and U.S. senator from South Dakota, Peter Norbeck (1870–1936) was born in Clay County in the Dakota Territory to a Swedish-Norwegian family. One of South Dakota's more successful politicians, he was elected state senator in 1908, lieutenant-governor in 1914, and governor in 1916. From 1921 to 1936, he served as a U.S. senator.

As a state and national political leader, Norbeck worked to bring government help to struggling farmers. He also had a strong interest in conservation. He was the "father" of Custer State Park in the Black Hills and a major fundraiser for Mount Rushmore National Memorial.

—*Gilbert C. Fite*

SUGGESTED READING:

Fite, Gilbert C. *Peter Norbeck: Prairie Statesman.* Columbia, Mo., 1948.

NORRIS, BENJAMIN FRANKLIN, JR. (FRANK)

Along with MARK TWAIN, JOHN GRIFFITH (JACK) LONDON, and OWEN WISTER, Frank Norris (1870-1902) ranks as a major literary interpreter of the American West. A native of Chicago, Norris moved with his family to Oakland, California, in 1884. He studied painting and drawing in San Francisco in 1886 and in Paris at the Académie Julian the following year. Returning to San Francisco, he entered the University of California in 1890 and in the next year published *Yvernelle,* a medieval romance in verse. From 1894 to 1895, he studied writing and French literature at Harvard, where he began to discover the materials and voice of his mature fiction. Turning away from an earlier effete aestheticism, Norris began to refashion himself as the "boy Zola."

Back in San Francisco, he wrote for *The Wave,* a local magazine. In 1897, he traveled to South Africa. The following year, he covered the war in Cuba for a

New York–based syndicate. Upon returning to California, he published his first novel, *Moran of the Lady Letty* (1898), a bizarre adventure novel of the sea. Drawing upon work completed two years earlier, he then published *McTeague* (1899), the novel generally regarded as his masterpiece. A classic of naturalism, *McTeague* told the story of a dim-witted dentist who murdered his avaricious wife. In a completely different vein, *Blix* (1899) offered a charming contemporary romance set, like *McTeague,* in San Francisco. Norris's versatility dazzled contemporary reviewers.

In 1900, Norris published *A Man's Woman,* his weakest novel, but rebounded the following year with *The Octopus,* a seminal Western novel of enormous scope and ambition that ranks near the top of his accomplishments. The first in a projected "Epic of the Wheat" trilogy, *The Octopus* drew upon the Mussel Slough Affair of 1880, a bloody and tragic clash between wheat farmers and railroad operatives. *The Pit,* the second volume, published posthumously in 1903, extended the story to the Chicago Board of Trade. Early death from a ruptured appendix kept him from writing *The Wolf,* the projected third volume. Other posthumously published works include *The Responsibilities of the Novelist* (1903), a collection of newspaper articles on writing, and *Vandover and the Brute* (1914), a grim naturalistic study of the degeneration of a young San Francisco artist and sensualist.

—*Don Graham*

SUGGESTED READING:

Graham, Don. *The Fiction of Frank Norris: The Aesthetic Context.* Columbia, Mo., 1978.

McElrath, Joseph R., Jr. *Frank Norris Revisited.* New York, 1992.

Pizer, Donald. *The Novels of Frank Norris.* Bloomington, Ind., 1966.

Walker, Franklin. *Frank Norris: A Biography.* Garden City, N.Y., 1932.

NORRIS, GEORGE W.

Nebraska politician George W. Norris (1861–1944) was born in Sandusky County, Ohio. In 1883, he received an LL. B. degree from Northern Indiana Normal School, and he started his law practice in Beatrice, Nebraska, in 1885. He later moved to Beaver City and then to McCook. In 1895, he was elected a district judge, serving until 1902, when he was elected to the U.S. House of Representatives. He served five terms in the House before winning a seat in the Senate in 1912. He served from 1913 to 1943.

In Congress in 1910, Norris, the "fighting liberal," first came to national prominence when he led efforts to lessen the power of the Speaker of the House, Joseph G. Cannon, who had blocked legislation to regulate big business and institute economic policies favorable to farmers. In the Senate, Norris opposed American intervention in World War I and the subsequent Versailles Treaty. He championed agriculture, especially programs that directly benefited farmers. He was instrumental in securing passage of federal support of river development, and in the 1930s, his work culminated in the creation of the Tennessee Valley Authority and a similar, but smaller version of this program in Nebraska. He sponsored the Rural Electrification Administration and the Farm-Forestry Act. He coauthored the Norris–La Guardia Act of 1932, which limited the use of injunctions in labor disputes and promoted collective bargaining by labor. He called for direct election of presidents and wrote the Twentieth Amendment to the Constitution, which abolished the "lame-duck" session of Congress and provided for newly elected presidents to take office in January rather than March. In 1936, he was elected as an Independent for his final term in the Senate. He was defeated in 1942 and returned to McCook.

While he labeled himself a Republican for most of his career, his political views were more akin to those of the Progressives—and sometimes were even more liberal, especially in the area of governmental control of resource development. He supported Democratic presidential candidates Alfred E. Smith in 1928 and Franklin D. Roosevelt in 1932, 1936, and 1940. His autobiography, *Fighting Liberal,* was published in 1945.

—*Candace Floyd*

SUGGESTED READING:

Lowitt, Richard. *George W. Norris.* 3 vols. Urbana, Ill. 1963–1978.

NORTH DAKOTA

North Dakota, the "Sioux," "Flickertail," or "Peace Garden State," is located in the center of the North American continent, in the northern part of the Great Plains region. It is bounded by the American states of Minnesota on the east, South Dakota on the south, and Montana on the west and by the Canadian provinces of Manitoba and Saskatchewan on the north. With 70,702 square miles, North Dakota is the seventeenth largest state in terms of area, but with only 635,000 people, it ranks forty-seventh in population. Until 1990, when the census showed that a small majority of the state's residents were urban, the population had been predominantly rural. The major cities,

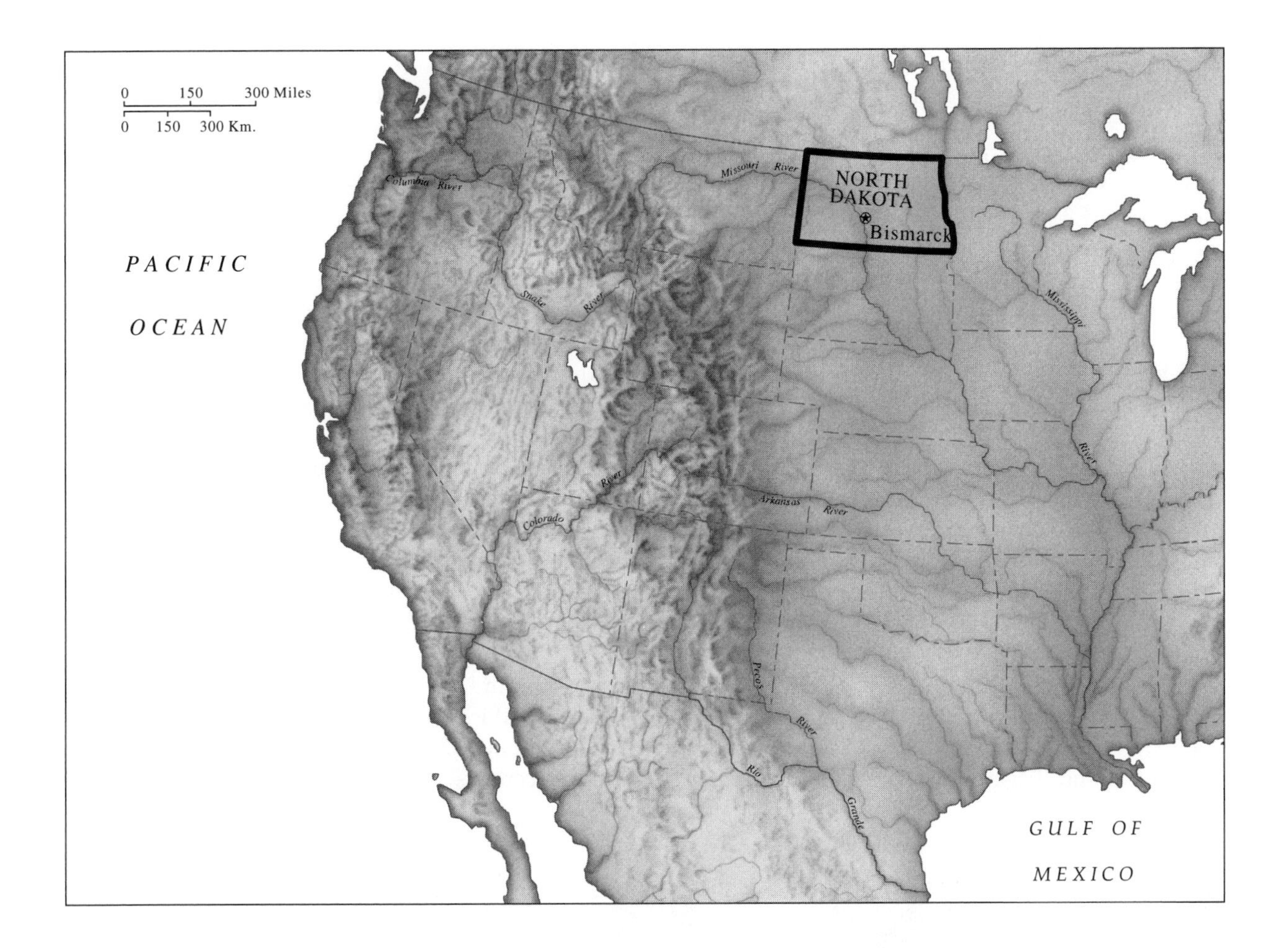

in declining order of population, are Fargo, Grand Forks, Bismarck (the capital), Minot, Jamestown, Dickinson, Mandan, and Williston.

Climate and geography

North Dakota's terrain is characterized by three major physiographic regions. Along the Minnesota border is the Red River valley, a remarkably flat area that was formed as the bed of a prehistoric lake left by melting glaciers. As this body of water—named Lake Agassiz for Louis Agassiz, who hypothesized its existence—retreated to the north, it left a tall-grass prairie of extraordinary fertility. West of the Red River valley is the Drift Prairie region, an area of gently rolling hills formed by glacial action. The rich chernozem soils of the Drift Prairie supported a tall- or short-grass regime, depending on available moisture. The Missouri Slope region dominates southwestern, west-central, and south-central North Dakota. The glaciated portion of the slope resembles the short-grass portions of the Drift Prairie. The unglaciated portions include the Badlands, the state's most remarkable natural wonder, as well as rugged bluffs and buttes.

The state is drained by two major rivers, the Missouri, which flows south and east, and the Red, which flows north into Lake Winnipeg. The state has one large natural lake, Devils Lake, and one large artificial one, Lake Sakakawea, formed when Garrison Dam on the Missouri River was completed in 1953. The state also has dozens of small lakes, as well as thousands of natural sloughs and potholes, especially in the Drift Prairie region.

North Dakota's climate is emphatically continental. Farther from any moderating body of water than any other state, North Dakota has cold winters, in which temperatures regularly fall below 20° F below zero, and hot summers in which the temperature often exceeds 90° F. Distance from the Gulf of Mexico, the major moisture source, holds annual precipitation under twenty inches for nearly all of the state and under fifteen for most of the western part. Seventy percent of the moisture falls during the growing season.

North Dakota's most valuable natural resource is its land, the basis of agriculture, its dominant industry. The state is a major producer of wheat, barley, beef, sunflowers, dry edible beans, sugar beets, potatoes, and a number of other crops and animal products. Much of the Missouri slope is underlain by lignite coal, which is burned for electrical generation, as well as oil, which has been pumped commercially since 1950. In the late twentieth century, North Dakota was the nation's seventh leading oil state, producing about 35 million barrels per year. Substantial quantities of limestone and brick- and ceramic-quality clay are also available and are exploited commercially.

Native Americans

Although a number of Paleo-Indian sites have been identified in North Dakota, the first modern inhabitants were the Mandans, who settled in agricultural villages along the Missouri River beginning about 1300 A.D. In the mid-seventeenth century, they were joined by Arikaras and Hidatsas, driven west by population pressures. Shortly thereafter, Sioux and Ojibwas also entered the state and developed an economy by exploiting buffalo herds.

The first known European visitor to North Dakota was the Sieur de la Vérendrye, who came to the Mandan villages in 1738. He was followed by French fur traders and, beginning in the 1780s, representatives of the HUDSON'S BAY COMPANY. In 1801, trader Alexander Henry erected a post at Pembina, which became the first permanent European settlement in the state. Many traders intermarried with the Ojibwas, and their offspring, called Metís, dominated the FUR TRADE and carried their goods by cart as far as St. Paul, Minnesota.

The United States bought the Upper Missouri country from France in 1803 in the LOUISIANA PURCHASE, and MERIWETHER LEWIS and WILLIAM CLARK wintered at the Mandan villages in 1803 to 1804. Eastern North Dakota came to the United States as a result of the Convention of 1818, which extended the Canadian border along the 49th parallel from the Lake of the Woods to the crest of the Rockies.

Territorial period

In 1861, Congress created the Dakota Territory, but settlement was slow in its northern part because of the intense hostility of the Sioux, difficulty of transportation, and the forbidding climate. The Sioux were slowly subdued in a series of wars between 1862 and 1876, and in 1872, the Northern Pacific, a land-grant railroad, crossed the Red River at Fargo. In later years,

George Armstrong Custer (standing center) and hunting and camping party, Little Heart River, Dakota Territory, 1875. *Courtesy National Archives.*

it was followed by the Great Northern, the Soo Line, and other carriers. The 1870s also revealed some of the state's economic potential. Oliver Dalrymple produced hundreds of thousands of bushels of premium quality wheat on his "bonanza" farm west of Fargo; and on the Missouri Slope, cattlemen established open-range ranches. The ensuing population boom seemed to justify the division of the Dakota Territory, and in 1889, North and South Dakota entered the Union as separate states.

Early statehood

The early European settlers of North Dakota were mostly Canadians of French or Scottish extraction or Yankees from Minnesota and Wisconsin. But the late-nineteenth and early twentieth centuries also saw a flood of European immigrants, especially Norwegians, Germans, and Germans from Russia. By 1910, North Dakota led the nation in the percentage of its population composed of immigrants or the children of immigrants. Scandinavian and German immigrants imparted a number of important characteristics to North Dakota, including its wariness of outsiders, its tendency to display a siege mentality, and its intense isolationism before both world wars.

The young state to which these immigrants came was fated to have a boom-and-bust existence for its first fifty years. The surge of population and economic activity in the 1880s was followed by a sharp downturn in the 1890s. The decade before World War I saw another boom, followed by a sag in the 1920s and a near-collapse in the 1930s. Part of the problem was weather, as droughts in the 1890s and 1930s showed, but more serious was economic overdependence on wheat, a commodity that fluctuated wildly in price. Exacerbating North Dakota's problems was distance from financial and commercial centers, which meant that North Dakotans paid high interest rates when they borrowed, high freight rates when they shipped, and high prices when they bought.

The major political debate in the young state involved the best path to economic development. The major faction of the dominant Republican party, led by railroad lobbyist ALEXANDER ("BIG ALEX") MCKENZIE, argued that the state must create an attractive environment for outside capital. Populists, socialists, and members of such farm groups as the American Society of Equity and the Farmers Union contended that North Dakotans must protect their resources from predatory outside interests and develop them themselves.

The debate reached a tumultuous climax in 1916, when the NONPARTISAN LEAGUE (NPL), an agrarian protest organization created by former socialist ARTHUR CHARLES (A. C.) TOWNLEY, seized control of the Republican party and elected a slate of state officers and legislators headed by farmer Lynn Frazier. In the five years that followed, Governor Frazier and the NPL enacted a number of reform measures, most notably the creation of a state-owned bank and a state-owned grain elevator and flour-milling complex, both of which still exist. Scandals and a determined and often unscrupulous opposition succeeded in turning Frazier and the NPL out in 1921, but the league continued to operate as a faction in the Republican party.

The economic and climatic disaster of the 1930s plunged the state into the depths of despair. The Farmers Holiday Association, led by Usher Burdick, urged farmers to withhold crops from market until prices rose, and "penny auctions" to thwart farm sales became common, but one-third of farmers still lost their farms. William Langer revived the NPL and turned it into a personal political machine that helped him seize the governorship in 1932. As governor, the demagogic "Wild Bill" embargoed grain shipments from the state and declared a moratorium on farm foreclosures. Temporarily derailed by a felony conviction in 1934, Langer bounced back to be elected governor again in 1936; in 1940, he was sent to the Senate where he joined isolationist Gerald Nye.

World War II marked a major turning point in the history of the state. In the short run, the war witnessed a much-welcomed period of prosperity resulting from high agricultural prices and good yields. In the long run, it marked the beginning of a sustained period of relative economic stability. Federal agricultural programs launched under Franklin Roosevelt's New Deal stabilized prices, pumped capital into farm lending institutions, encouraged farmer-owned cooperatives, and stimulated rural electrification. Another effect of federal programs, agricultural and nonagricultural alike, was redistribution of income from rich to poor states. As one of the latter, North Dakota regularly received three or four dollars from the federal treasury for every one it sent in.

Post–World War II period

After the war, the state was less isolated from the rest of the country. North Dakotans traveled more and had broader experiences; they purchased more products from national chain stores in their towns; and they were more influenced by national media. They got in step with international politics, now that Germany was no longer the enemy. The commitment of North Dakota to the Cold War cause of the United States was heightened by the construction of major U.S. Air Force bases at Grand Forks and Minot.

As North Dakota became more the government's ward and less its antagonist, the state's politics became less idiosyncratic. As the "sons of the wild jackass" who dominated the state's congressional delegation—men such as Bill Langer, Usher Burdick, and Bill Lemke—died out, they were succeeded by people who were more conciliatory and less colorful. The state's party system also took on a more conventional cast. Pushed by the conservative Republican Organizing Committee and pulled by Democratic liberals, the NPL shifted, beginning in 1956, giving the state a true two-party system for the first time in history. Enjoying great success statewide, the Democratic-NPL party occupied the governorship for all but four years between 1961 and 1993 and held the entire congressional delegation beginning in 1987. Vigorous two-party competition has helped the state's dominant minority—American Indians—and women play a more active role. In 1992, women won the offices of lieutenant-governor, attorney general, and agriculture commissioner.

Other aspects of North Dakota's political life have not changed. Citizens continue to follow the commonwealth political tradition, and North Dakota encourages broad participation in public affairs. The state has election-day voter registration and very permissive initiative and referendum laws that encourage citizen legislation. North Dakota also leads the nation in elected officials per capita.

Although it was more stable, the postwar North Dakota economy continued to be relatively undiversified. While energy development and public-sector spending provided some diversification, the state continued to be overwhelmingly dependent on agriculture. After World War II, agriculture was revolutionized as a range of farm chemicals, improved crop varieties, and bigger and better machines dramatically increased productivity. One result of this revolution was a remarkable shrinkage in the number of farms and the on-farm population. In 1940, there were nearly 80,000 farms in the state, and the farm population stood at about 330,000. By 1990, there were fewer than 30,000 farms, and the farm population was barely 100,000. A shrinking rural population especially devastated local social institutions and trade centers, which were further harmed by increased farmer mobility. While the manufacturing and service sectors grew in the major towns, they could not provide employment for all the surplus labor. The result has been steady out-migration. North Dakota was the only state in the Union with a smaller population in 1990 than it had in 1920.

North Dakota's isolation and its shrinking population give many people in the state the sense that the nation has passed them by. Adding to this feeling is the reality that the state usually lies outside of national consciousness, except when some disaster strikes or a humorist needs a synonym for *nowhere*. Indeed, North Dakota is a place where nothing of national significance happens and where nobody of national importance lives. Certainly, important people have been born there—authors Maxwell Anderson, Louise Erdrich, Louis L'Amour, and Larry Woiwode, journalist Eric Severeid, statesman Warren Christopher, and musician Lawrence Welk come readily to mind—but they all became important somewhere else.

North Dakota lies outside of the mainstream of the region and the country. While the West and the nation are diverse, North Dakota is relatively homogenous. Most people have a European background, with American Indians, the largest non-European group, composing 4 percent of the population. The state thus has relatively little racial variety but also little conflict.

North Dakotans display generally admirable character traits. They work hard and are people of integrity. They are neighborly and generally tolerant without being obtrusive. North Dakotans behave. The state's crime rate is consistently among the nation's lowest. Like their northern and central European forbears, they tend to be low-keyed, diffident, and fatalistic. They try to avoid conflict and like to adjust to new ideas slowly, by half-steps and mutual accommodation. They also tend, like their peasant ancestors, to be conservative and to avoid risks. Unlike most of the West, North Dakota has punished risk-takers more often than it has rewarded them.

North Dakotans are strongly tied to families, communities, and institutions. The divorce rate is low, a relatively high percentage of children live in two-parent households, and people retain strong and caring relationships with kin. The state consistently ranks among the nation's leaders in church membership, with the Catholic and Lutheran churches of immigrant forbears predominant. North Dakotans value schooling and have made great sacrifices to support an elaborate and, some argue, overbuilt educational system. The state leads the nation in the percentage of the population that has graduated from high school and in the percentage of people attending college. Community pride and loyalties are very strong. North Dakota towns are clean, neat, and well maintained. Town celebrations are well attended and draw back residents who have migrated. Major focuses of town pride, such as participation in high-school sports, are so compelling that sometimes an entire town will attend a game, thus necessitating the borrowing of a policeman from nearby to keep an eye on property.

While much of the West is in the mainstream, North Dakota is a backwater, and most of the state's people are comfortable with that status.

—David B. Danbom

SEE ALSO: Booms; Bonanza Farming; Métis People; Red River Carts; Sioux Wars

SUGGESTED READING:
Danbom, David B. "North Dakota: The Most Midwestern State." In *Heartland: Comparative Histories of the Midwestern States.* Edited by James H. Madison. Bloomington, Ind., 1988.
Robinson, Elwyn D. *History of North Dakota.* Lincoln, Nebr., 1966.
Wilkins, Robert P., and Wynona H. Wilkins. *North Dakota: A Bicentennial History.* New York and Nashville, Tenn.: 1977.

NORTHERN PACIFIC RAILROAD

SEE: Burlington Northern Railroad

NORTHERN SECURITIES COMPANY

SEE: Burlington Northern Railroad

NORTHFIELD RAID

On September 7, 1876, Northfield, Minnesota, was the site of a bank robbery by the James-Younger gang. The determination of the people of Northfield to protect their property resulted in the deaths or capture of six of the eight-man gang.

Jesse James had originally planned to rob the First National Bank of Mankato, Minnesota, rather than the First National Bank of Northfield. When James, and his brother Frank; Cole, Jim, and Bob Younger; Clell Miller; Samuel Wells (also known as Charlie Pitts); and William Stiles (also known as William Chadwell) arrived at Mankato, a group of people was gathered in front of the bank. Jesse James decided to abort his plan and instead rob the bank in Northfield, some forty miles away.

When the eight horsemen entered Northfield, Jesse James, Bob Younger, and Samuel Wells entered the bank while the others remained outside. Inside the bank, Joseph L. Heywood, the cashier, refused to open the vault. His throat was slashed, and he was then shot. A teller, A. B. Bunker, who tried to escape, was shot and wounded. Outside, a Swedish boy of seventeen, who spoke little or no English, was killed by outlaw gunfire for not obeying an order to stop. A few of the townsfolk, aware of the robbery, came to the rescue.

The Northfield Tragedy, by Joseph H. Hansen. *Courtesy Minnesota Historical Society.*

Armed with rusty shotguns and antique rifles, they began to fire at the desperados. The shooting from both sides was intense. Gun smoke and panic ruled over Northfield during the afternoon. William Stiles and Clell Miller were killed. Samuel Wells was killed after the largest manhunt in Minnesota. Jim, Bob, and Cole Younger were captured. Jesse and Frank James escaped.

—*Fred L. Koestler*

SEE ALSO: James Brothers; Younger Brothers

SUGGESTED READING:

Settle, William A., Jr. *Jesse James Was His Name.* Columbia, Mo., 1966.

NORTHWEST COAST INDIANS

SEE: Native American Peoples: Peoples of the Pacific Northwest

NORTH WEST COMPANY

SEE: Hudson's Bay Company

NORTH WEST MOUNTED POLICE

The Royal Canadian Mounted Police were called the North West Mounted Police, popularly known as the Mounties, until 1920. Today, the RCMP is Canada's federal police force, responsible for the country's internal security and serving as a provincial and criminal police organization in all of Canada but Ontario and Quebec. The Mounties remain the only police in the Yukon and the Northwest Territories, where the organization was founded in 1873 as the North West Mounted Rifles. The United States reacted badly to the idea of an armed force patrolling its northern borders, so the politic Canadians changed the name of the organization to the North West Mounted Police. First installed in Alberta's Fort McLeod, the Mounties were responsible for policing nearly three hundred thousand square miles of the Canadian West, home to Native American tribes, some fur traders, and, soon, a horde of gold-rush prospectors from the south. Originally numbering some three hundred men, the Mounties first dealt with U.S. traders who were causing troubles among Canada's Indians by trading cheap whiskey for buffalo hides. The tact and dogged persistence with which they pushed the traders back across the border and pacified the Indians became a hallmark of the Mounty style. In 1877, after a series of successful actions against American outlaws operating across the border, the Fort Benton, Montana, *Record* observed with some admiration that the Mounties "fetched their man every time." Over time, the notion that the Mounties "always got their man" became a part of Western folklore that, like most legends, played better in the press than in reality. Certainly, the North West Mounted Police's evenhanded and just treatment of native tribes was a key factor in keeping the strong Blackfoot confederacy from joining in the rebellion staged by LOUIS DAVID REIL among the MÉTIS PEOPLE in 1885. The only authority in Canada's vast Western wilderness, the Mounties were forced to take up a wide variety of duties, including guarding the extension of the Canadian Pacific Railway to the ocean in 1885, keeping careful watch during the Yukon gold rush over the activities of prospectors (when the number of Mounties were increased to around eight hundred), and, after the turn of the century, providing assistance and advice to help the more than three hundred thousand settlers who poured into the Canadian West survive in the extremely rugged region. The prefix "Royal" was added to their name in 1904. In 1920, when the Royal North West Mounted Police was expanded into a nationwide, federal organization, the Mounties moved their headquarters from Regina to Ottawa.

—*Charles Phillips*

NORTHWEST ORDINANCE

Adopted by the Confederation Congress on July 13, 1787, the Ordinance for the Government of the Territory of the United States North West of the River Ohio set forth the basic framework for the American territorial system. Provision for government for the new national domain became imperative after the United States gained title to the trans-Ohio region—including present-day Ohio (admitted to the Union in 1803), Indiana (1816), Illinois (1818), Michigan (1837), Wisconsin (1848), and part of Minnesota (1858)—through the cession of conflicting state claims in the region.

After Virginia ceded its claim to Western lands on March 1, 1784, the stage was set for adoption of the first territorial-government ordinance, drafted by a committee headed by THOMAS JEFFERSON, and an ordinance for the survey and sale of federal lands. The land ordinance of May 20, 1785, established the rectilinear grid for state boundaries and immediately took effect.

The 1784 government ordinance, however, never took effect, although its provision for the admission of new states "on an equal footing with the . . . original states" was incorporated in the 1787 ordinance. Between 1784 and 1787, successive congressional committees extended the boundaries of projected new states, raised the population threshold for statehood (from approximately 20,000, or as many "free inhabitants . . . as shall then be in any one the least numerous of the thirteen Original states," to 60,000 free inhabitants), and elaborated provisions for temporary congressional rule during the prestatehood, or territorial, phase.

Because the Northwest Ordinance limited the scope of self-government in the territorial period while delaying the onset of statehood, many scholars have concluded that it constituted a conservative reaction to the liberal provisions of Jefferson's earlier ordinance. Congress recognized, however, that settlement would be retarded if the Confederation government failed to remove squatters, pacify Native Americans, and preserve law and order in the territories. The strongest pressure for effective congressional rule came from the Ohio Company of Associates, a New England land company whose representative, Manasseh Cutler, played an important role in the final stages of the revision process.

The committee that drafted the ordinance included Virginians Edward Carrington and Richard Henry Lee, John Kean of South Carolina, Melancton Smith of New York, and Nathan Dane of Massachusetts, lead author and Cutler's prime contact. Endorsed by all seven state delegations then in attendance, the final version of the ordinance reflected a broad consensus on the need to regulate expansion and to recruit industrious, market-oriented farmers from the Northeastern states as settlers. Agreement between the Northern and Southern states was remarkable, especially in the ban on slavery. That agreement anticipated the more complicated compromises on the slavery issue—compromises then being negotiated at the Philadelphia convention and incorporated into the federal Constitution.

The completed ordinance consisted of two major parts: provisions for temporary TERRITORIAL GOVERNMENT and "articles of compact between the original States and the people and States in the said territory." Beginning with a crucial section on private property and inheritance rights, the government provisions then defined the responsibilities of the territorial governor, secretary, and judges. As soon as there were five thousand "free male inhabitants of full age," the governor was to authorize the election of representatives to the general assembly by property owners holding at least fifty acres. By the time of the Wisconsin organic act in 1836, Congress had liberalized suffrage requirements, hastened the formation of territorial legislatures, and made most territorial officials elective. The compact articles, by contrast, were designed to "remain unalterable, unless by common consent." Compact guarantees of civil liberties proved generally uncontroversial; the injunctions to support "religion, morality, and knowledge"—and to treat Native Americans with "the utmost good faith"—were meaningless and unenforceable. The interests of the FEDERAL GOVERNMENT, most notably with respect to distribution of the national domain, were specified in Article 4. Over the years, Articles 5 (laying out new state boundaries) and 6 (the slavery ban) generated considerable controversy. Ultimately, Congress ignored Article 5, most conspicuously in the cases of the boundaries between Michigan, Ohio, and Indiana and between Wisconsin and Illinois. The outcome of the conflicts over the slavery prohibition was more ambiguous. Although no Northwest Ordinance state legalized slavery, its illegality depended on action—or inaction. For example, in Illinois in 1823 and 1824, some leaders argued that Illinois was entitled, according to the principle of state equality, to decide on the slavery issue itself, regardless of the ordinance prohibition.

The U.S. Supreme Court confirmed in *Strader* v. *Graham* (1850) that the Northwest Ordinance did not have any authoritative constitutional standing. Yet, through congressional revision and negotiation with embryonic new states, the framework for territorial government and the creation of new states proved durable. Settlers in frontier regions continued to look forward to admission to the Union "on an equal footing with the original states" according to the ordinance's promise.

—*Peter S. Onuf*

SEE ALSO: Land Policy; National Expansion

SUGGESTED READING:

Onuf, Peter S. *Statehood and Union: A History of the Northwest Ordinance.* Bloomington, Ind., 1987.

NORTHWEST PASSAGE

The myth of the Northwest Passage, a short navigable water route connecting the Atlantic to the Pacific through the North American continent, drove generations of Spanish, French, and English explorers of North America to search the continent and its coasts. As the explorers following Columbus began mapping the coasts of North America, they sought a water route that would permit them to pass through the barrier of the continent and make a short voyage to the wealth of the Far East. Only in the twentieth century was the dream of a passage by ship realized when a few strong hulled vessels made their way through the Arctic ice and when the Arctic Ocean became a passageway for nuclear submarines.

Interest in a passage around the American continent from the north preceded the discovery of the Pacific by Hernando Cortés in 1513. John Cabot, in his two voyages of 1497 to 1498, appears to have been searching for a passage, particularly during his second voyage, which ended with his disappearance. His son, Sebastian Cabot, while concealing his belief in the viability of a passage from the Spanish in 1536, attempted to interest the English crown in an effort to find the passage until his death. At first following his father's route, Sebastian Cabot, in a voyage dating approximately from 1508 to 1509, cruised down the East Coast of North America searching for another route after his crew turned mutinous off the coast of Labrador. Cabot's backing appears to have come primarily from merchants in London and Bristol rather than the crown. With the accession of Henry VIII to the throne, further voyages were stopped, and Cabot gained employment in Spain.

The Spanish, who employed Cabot, were not greatly interested in a northwest passage route above 60° north latitude because it would place it in the sphere of English, French, and Portuguese influence. In 1523, the Spanish did send Estevio Gomez, rather than Cabot, in search of a passage but he failed to find one. Spanish interest in a passage continued in different ways, as the explorers of North America, including JUAN DE OÑATE, sought to find the Strait of Anian somewhere in the North American continent. Even in the eighteenth century, when a true understanding of the geography of North America was still incomplete, there is evidence of Spanish fears that the English would find the passage.

As English interest in the New World grew, efforts to find a passage were revived under the auspices of merchants and the crown. The maps prepared by Giovanni da Verrazzano in 1524 led the English to assume that a passage existed. Over the remainder of the century, a variety of navigators, including John Rut in 1527, Richard Hore in 1536, Martin Frobisher from 1576 to 1578, and Sir Humphrey Gilbert in 1583, received a mix of support. Even as settlement at Jamestown began in 1607, there was hope that the Chesapeake Bay might contain the elusive passage. A few years later, in 1611, Henry Hudson sought the passage, first along what became known as the Hudson River and then, in 1612, into Hudson's Bay where he was marooned.

Later efforts to find a passage included one supported by Benjamin Franklin from 1753 to 1754 and several in the nineteenth century, including the ill-fated expedition of Sir John Franklin from 1845 to 1848. Commander Robert McClure of the Royal Navy actually made the passage from west to east in 1854, but partially on foot. Finally, from 1903 to 1905, Roald Amundsen in the Norwegian fishing sloop *Gjoa* successfully traveled through Arctic waters around the North American continent. In 1944, the Canadian Mounted Police schooner *St. Roch* made the passage in about four months from east to west after having taken almost two years to go from west to east. In 1969, the Standard Oil tanker *Manhattan* made the voyage in an effort to demonstrate it was commercially feasible, but nothing followed. Today, nuclear submarines follow the track of the *USS Nautilus,* which cruised to the North Pole beneath the ice in 1958.

Beyond the demonstrations of bravery and heroism of those who attempted to find the passage over the centuries, the importance of the Northwest Passage was its role in luring explorers and settlers along the coast of North America as well as in the Spanish Southwest. The notion of an inexpensive route to the Far East through the barrier of the North American continent prodded explorers and governments to map and then settle the continent and was an important element of the pattern of Western expansion that led to the European settlement of North America.

—*Patrick H. Butler, III*

SEE ALSO: Exploration

SUGGESTED READING:

Morison, Samuel Eliot. *The European Discovery of America: The Northern Voyages.* New York, 1971.

Quinn, David Beers. *England and the Discovery of America: 1481–1620.* New York, 1974.

Weber, David J. *The Spanish Frontier in North America.* New Haven, Conn., 1992.

NORTON, JOSHUA

Self-proclaimed Norton I, emperor of the United States and protector of Mexico, Joshua Norton (1818 or 1819–1880) cut quite a figure on the mid-nineteenth-century streets of San Francisco. Bedecked in a ratty coat of military design, scuffy boots, a rusty sword on his belt, and a top hat decorated with rooster feathers, Norton I plied the hills of the city, broadcast his imperial proclamations in the local newspaper, paid for his meals and lodgings with scrip issued in the name of his em-

Joshua Norton, or Norton I, emperor of the United States and protector of Mexico. *Courtesy Bancroft Library.*

pire, and basked in the indulgent affections of his fellow San Franciscans.

Born in London of Jewish parents, Norton migrated with his family to South Africa as a youngster. He arrived in San Francisco during California's gold-rush days, engaged in successful land speculation in the 1850s, and amassed a fortune reported at one-quarter million dollars. In a risky attempt to corner the rice market, however, Norton lost all his real estate and his wealth. He apparently lost his reason, too, but in his imperial posturings, the city found a boost to tourism and commerce. Merchants discovered that their business increased when they advertised their establishments operated by "appointment to His Majesty, Norton I." Plays and operas were written about him; travel books prepared tourists for their encounters with him; and street vendors grew rich from the sale of Norton I dolls, cigars, postcards, and other souvenirs. The Emperor of the United States and Protector of Mexico was the city's most popular tourist attraction.

Norton I collapsed unceremoniously in the street on a rainy January night and died. Some ten thousand mourners paid homage to him in death. News of his demise appeared in papers in Cleveland, Philadelphia, Seattle, New York, and Denver. The city of San Francisco still honors its emperor. Each year it holds a parade for Norton I.

—*Patricia Hogan*

SUGGESTED READING:

Drury, William. *Norton I: Emperor of the United States.* New York, 1986.

NOVELS, WESTERN

SEE: Literature: The Western Novel

NURSING

The history of nursing in the West begins with human habitation of the region: for centuries, the care of the sick and disabled was the responsibility of women in the tribe or family. Nursing was a domestic art passed down from mother to daughter. Nursing as Westerners know it today, a largely female profession employing specially trained care-givers, is a much more recent phenomenon. It dates from the establishment of the first nurses' training schools in the West in the late 1880s. Reflecting nursing's history, the schools were designed for women; contemporary social attitudes dictated that they be segregated by race as well.

From the beginning, white and black Western women saw the new profession of nursing as an attractive career alternative to teaching or DOMESTIC SERVICE. The numbers of nursing schools—all too many in small and poorly equipped hospitals—nursing students, and graduates multiplied rapidly. In Kansas alone, thirty schools opened between 1900 and 1910. Ten nursing schools for black students were founded in four Western states between 1890 and 1920. By 1920, there were 41,560 trained nurses in the West; there had been 11,119 in all of the United States in 1900. That dramatic increase reflects not only nursing's appeal but also the recognition by hospital administrators that the promise of care by trained nurses was likely to draw patients from home to hospital. Without nurses, hospitals in the West and elsewhere would not have grown as they did.

The hospital was the principal site of a Western nurse's training; although the University of Minnesota founded its School for Nurses in 1909, collegiate education for nursing did not become significant until the 1930s. The training—two years in the beginning, expanded to three in the twentieth century—consisted largely of apprenticeship work on the wards. In addition to caring for patients, student nurses cleaned, cooked, and mended. Student nurses were the primary care-givers, and they typically worked ten to twelve hours a day, six or six and a half days a week. In 1913, the California legislature mandated an eight-hour day for student nurses, but its example was not widely followed until the 1930s. For the nursing service they provided the hospital, students received room and board; some schools also paid monthly stipends of $5 to $10.

Perhaps as befits modern American nursing's origins in war—Florence Nightingale in the Crimea and volunteer nurses in America's Civil War—the atmosphere in nursing schools was militaristic: order and discipline were of foremost importance, and students were required to give unquestioning obedience to authority. Some of the Western students of the 1880s and 1890s—mature women aged twenty-five to thirty-five—found the strict regimen difficult and failed to complete the course; the eighteen- to twenty-year-olds who entered nursing schools in the twentieth century were even more inclined to withdraw.

The vast majority of nursing students who completed their training entered private-duty nursing; opportunities in the fields of supervision and visiting nursing were limited, and students provided the bulk of nursing service for hospitals. Private-duty nurses typically practiced in homes where they remained with their patients twenty-four hours a day until care was no longer needed. Private duty offered special challenges in many areas of the West where isolation, poor transportation, and primitive living conditions made care-giving extremely difficult. Nurses who traveled miles on horseback or in wagons to attend a birth or care for a typhoid patient at home in a tent, crude cabin, or sod house contributed significantly to the public health of the region.

Initially, private-duty nurses were reasonably well compensated for their labors—as long as they were regularly employed. The proliferation of nursing schools, however, sharply increased the number of graduate nurses, the competition for cases, and the waiting time between them. There was a depression in private-duty practice by the 1920s, and graduate nurses willingly accepted employment as hospital staff nurses when the Great Depression led many hospitals to close their nursing schools. By the end of the 1930s, hospital-staff nursing had become and remains the largest field of employment for graduate nurses.

—*Judith M. Stanley*

SEE ALSO: Disease; Doctors; Medicine; Midwifery

SUGGESTED READING:

Kalisch, Philip A., and Beatrice A. Kalisch. *The Advance of American Nursing.* 2d ed. Boston, 1986.

Reverby, Susan M. *Ordered to Care.* Cambridge, Mass., 1987.

Writers' Program of the Work Projects Administration. *Lamps on the Prairie.* Edited by Susan Reverby. New York, 1984.

NYE, EDGAR WILSON (BILL)

Humorist Bill Nye (1850–1896) wrote newspaper columns in Laramie, Wyoming, from 1876 to 1883. A native of Maine, Nye was raised in Wisconsin. Moving west, he settled in Laramie and set out on a career that would gain him a reputation as a rural philosopher. First working for the *Laramie Sentinel,* he then edited the *Laramie Boomerang,* a newspaper named for his mule. His columns often revolved around local and national news. Others portrayed colorful characters from Wyoming's rural communities. Along with his newspaper work, Nye mined for gold and practiced law. He served as justice of the peace, United States commissioner, and postmaster between jobs on the *Sentinel* and the *Boomerang.* In 1883, Nye returned to Wisconsin and later moved to New York and North Carolina. Continuing his newspaper work, he wrote syndicated columns for the *New York World.* He published fourteen books, including *Bill Nye and Boomerang* (1881), *Forty Liars and Other Lies* (1882), *Baled Hay* (1884), and *Remarks by Bill Nye* (1886). His most popular work was *Bill Nye's History of the United States* (1894), which sold five hundred thousand copies. He died of a heart attack at the age of forty-five.

—*Candace Floyd*

SUGGESTED READING:

Kesterson, David B. *Bill Nye.* Boston, 1981.

Larson, T. A., ed. *Bill Nye's Western Humor.* Lincoln, Nebr., 1968.

O

OAKLAND, CALIFORNIA

Founded on the *contra costa* (opposite shore) of the San Francisco Bay in 1852 by lawyer and land speculator Horace W. Carpentier, Oakland, CALIFORNIA, was incorporated on May 4, 1852. Oakland was promoted as a stable, family-oriented community in contrast to overwhelmingly male and often lawless San Francisco. The first public school in Oakland was opened in 1853 as was Henry Durant's private academy, which eventually became the University of California. By 1860, the town had six churches, even though its population numbered only 1,543.

Oakland seemed destined to remain a quiet suburb of San Francisco until Carpentier negotiated with the CENTRAL PACIFIC RAILROAD to make the town the western terminal of the transcontinental rail line. On November 8, 1869, the first train arrived in Oakland after a seven-day journey from New York. Laden with passengers and freight, the train symbolized the transformation of both Oakland and California.

By 1870, Oakland had 10,500 residents. Ten years later, the population was 34,555, making it the second largest city on the Pacific Coast. Although hardly a rival to San Francisco, Oakland was nonetheless growing out of the shadow of the larger city. During the 1870s, it became a major transshipment point for goods coming to or leaving San Francisco. Hides, sugar, salmon, redwood, fruits and vegetables, and cotton all numbered among the processed products from Oakland; new factories produced carriages and furniture. With industrialization came child labor and hazardous working conditions. JOHN GRIFFITH (JACK) LONDON, employed by an Oakland Cannery in the 1890s, declared "I knew no horse in the City of Oakland that worked the hours I worked." Not surprisingly, organized labor attempted to make Oakland a union town. Oakland railroad workers participated in the Pullman strike of 1894, and American Federation of Labor-affiliated locals soon emerged in a variety of industries.

Oakland's population was always multiethnic and multiracial. Of the 1,543 people in the city in 1860, 96 were Asians, 7 were black, and 4 were Indian. Of the Euro-American residents, 617 were foreign-born. Nineteenth-century Oakland continued to attract a diverse population. Black Pullman porters settled near the depot and created an African American community in what is now West Oakland. Chinese immigrants settled in Oakland in the 1850s, and by 1870, there was a Chinatown. Prevented from competing for industrial jobs, the Chinese became cooks, laundry workers, and vegetable peddlers.

By the beginning of the twentieth century, Oakland's future as a major metropolis was ensured. The growth in West Coast shipping after the opening of the Panama Canal generated a demand for port facilities beyond San Francisco's capacity. By World War I, a shipbuilding industry evolved on the waterfront, and in the 1920s, Oakland became known as the "Detroit of the West" as General Motors, Willys, and Caterpillar Tractor opened plants in the city. Other Eastern firms relocated in Oakland including Western Electric and General Electric. By 1929, the city's fifteen hundred manufacturing plants employed sixty-two thousand workers. No longer simply a suburb of San Francisco, Oakland had finally emerged as a major industrial and financial center.

—*Quintard Taylor*

SUGGESTED READING:

Bagwell, Beth. *Oakland: The Story of a City.* Novato, Calif., 1982.

Crouchett, Lawrence P., Lonnie G. Bunch, III, and Martha Kendall Winnacker. *Visions toward Tomorrow: The History of the East Bay Afro-American Community, 1852–1977.* Oakland, Calif., 1989.

OAKLAND MUSEUM OF CALIFORNIA

A consolidation of three cultural institutions, the Oakland Museum of California presents the environment, history, and art of the Golden State. The museum, a municipal agency that enjoys generous private support, opened its doors in 1969 at its present site, an internationally renowned, three-tiered complex of exhibition galleries, interior gardens, courts, and an expanse of lawn located on 5.91 acres in the heart of the city.

The Hall of California Ecology features the interrelated lives of plants and animals within each of California's eight biotic zones. Exhibit cases and dioramas allow visitors to take a simulated walk from the Pacific seashore to the Sierra Nevada crest and beyond. The Aquatic California Gallery exhibits the state's oceanic, fresh water, and estuarine environments as well as hot springs and snow banks. Informing the installation is the theme of California environmentalism, the use and misuse of water, and Californians' interdependent relation to aquatic life. All told, the natural history collections number 90,000 objects and specimens.

The Cowell Hall of California History emphasizes the mixing of cultures and the dreams of the disparate groups that peopled the state's history: Native Americans, Spanish settlers, American emigrants, and, in an innovative installation, people of the twentieth century. The exhibit galleries are supported by the history department's 160,000-item collection of craft works, tools, costumes, furniture, machines, graphic and printed materials, games, decorations, and vehicles. Multidimensional programs, interactive computers, and department activities focus on the social, political, economic, and technological influences that characterize California's past and present. The history department has major holdings in the ethnography of Native Americans and peoples of the Pacific. The department maintains a photographic collection of one million images including the Andrew J. Russell Collection of Union Pacific Railroad construction.

The museum's Gallery of California Art exhibits paintings, crafts, graphics, sculpture, and photography spanning the days of the earliest explorers to the present. Among the 80,000 works of art are paintings and sketches by explorers, gold-rush genre pictures, massive panoramic landscapes, examples of the California decorative style, impressionists, post-impressionists, abstract expressionists, Bay Area figurative, pop, and funk. Several galleries feature one-person and group shows of California artists, in addition to prints, photographs, and decorative arts. Items from the museum's sculpture collection are featured throughout the exterior gardens. Other areas of the museum present traveling exhibitions and special exhibits of California themes.

In addition, the museum owns the world's most extensive archive of the work of documentary photographer Dorothea Lange and a library of natural sounds—featuring species and environmental sounds recorded live in natural habitats. A variety of innovative programs and activities highlight the museum's community-based approach to understanding the state's multicultural composition.

—Patricia Hogan

SUGGESTED READING:
Frye, Melinda Young, ed. *Natives and Settlers: Indian and Yankee Culture in Early California.* Oakland, Calif., 1979.
Jurmain, Claudia K., and James J. Rawls, eds. *California: A Place, a People, a Dream.* San Francisco, 1986.
Orr-Cahill, Christina. *The Art of California: Selected Works from the Collection of the Oakland Museum.* Oakland, Calif., 1984.

OAKLEY, ANNIE

Born Phoebe Ann Moses near Woodland, Darke County, Ohio, Annie Oakley (1860–1926) was a world-renowned sharpshooter, popularized by her seventeen years with WILLIAM F. ("BUFFALO BILL") CODY's Wild West exhibition. One of five children of Jacob and Susan Moses, she was raised on a farm in rural Ohio. How she taught herself to shoot with her father's rifle, at age eight, is a part of the myth surrounding her phenomenal skill and success. By Oakley's own accounts, her first shot killed a squirrel by neatly piercing its head.

Oakley's father died in 1866, leaving the family destitute. In 1870, she went to the county poor farm and then to work for a farm family who mistreated and virtually enslaved her. She escaped, returned to her mother in 1875, and began market hunting and contest shooting.

Oakley married exhibition marksman Frank Butler in 1882 after beating him in a shooting contest the year before. Why she then chose the stage name Oakley is unknown. The couple toured as a stage act and with the Sells Brothers Circus until 1884, when Oakley secured employment with Buffalo Bill's Wild West. She was a star attraction and became a popular symbol of the American West to audiences in North America and Europe.

Oakley's adoption by SITTING BULL, who dubbed her "Little Sure Shot," has been considered a fabrication by some biographers, but the two met after a shoot-

A poster produced for Buffalo Bill's Wild West in about 1890 by the A. Hoen and Company of Baltimore, Maryland, featured Annie Oakley, world-renowned sharpshooter. *Courtesy Buffalo Bill Historical Center.*

ing exhibition in St. Paul, Minnesota, in 1884. Proximity to Oakley was, reputedly, what finally influenced Sitting Bull to join Cody's Wild West Show in 1885.

Although women sharpshooters were not a rarity, Oakley distinguished herself by her fast, accurate shooting, athletic stunts, and her petite and feminine appearance and demeanor. She won twenty-seven medals from prestigious shooting clubs and matches in the United States and Europe, including the London Gun Club. An unverified story is that she shot the ashes off German Crown Prince Wilhelm's cigarette. She later claimed regretting her opportunity to avert World War I.

Oakley left Buffalo Bill's Wild West in 1901. A train wreck allegedly caused a hip injury and severe trauma that turned her hair white. The sudden change in her youthful appearance has also been attributed to an accident in a health spa.

In 1903, ever mindful of her public image, Oakley pursued and won nearly all of fifty-five libel suits against newspapers that published an erroneous article that called her a thief and cocaine user.

Oakley's later career included a short stint in a play, *The Western Girl,* three seasons with Young Buffalo Wild West, exhibition and tournament shooting, and exhibitions for charities. She also taught shooting skills at a resort in Pinehurst, North Carolina. During World War I, she gave exhibitions in army camps. At the age of sixty-two, she broke a world's record for women's shooting. She retired to Ohio in 1926.

Oakley's legend has been the subject of popular novels, movies, and television programs.

—*Sarah Wood-Clark*

SEE ALSO: Wild West Shows

SUGGESTED READING:

Havighurst, Walter. *Annie Oakley of the Wild West.* Reprint. Lincoln, Nebr., 1992.
Kasper, Shirl. *Annie Oakley.* Norman, Okla., 1992.
Sayers, Isabelle S. *Annie Oakley and Buffalo Bill's Wild West.* New York, 1981.

OATMAN, OLIVE

As a young girl, Olive Ann Oatman (1837 or 1838–1903) spent five years as a captive among the Apache and Mojave Indians. In August 1850, Oatman and her family headed west from Fulton, Illinois. Although the family of nine began the journey with fifty other wagons, the Oatmans left the wagon train with some eight other families to follow the Rio Grande and Gila River. When a crippled wagon stopped the rest of the migrants, the Oatmans pressed on to California alone. On March 18, 1851, the family was attacked by Yavapai or Mojave Apache Indians. Six family members were killed. Olive Oatman's brother, Lorenzo, was severely wounded but survived. Olive and her seven-year-old sister, Mary, became captives.

The Oatman girls served as slave laborers for their captors and suffered beatings. After about a year, the sisters were sold to Mojave Indians and walked north to an Indian village on the Colorado River. Treated less harshly, they were given a plot of land on which to grow their own wheat, corn, and melons. Neither sister was sexually molested, a constant if unwarranted fear among Euro-American pioneers. Both girls, however, wore the tattoos of Mojave women. Olive Oatman wore her tattoos for the remainder of her life.

During a drought in 1853, frail Mary Oatman died of starvation along with many Mojaves. Lorenzo Oatman had begun searching for his sisters soon after the attack on his family. After several years, he learned that one of them might still be alive. A Yuma Indian named Francisco facilitated Olive Oatman's release, and on February 22, 1856, she arrived at Fort Yuma. For several months, Oatman seemed dazed and refused to speak, having nearly forgotten the English language. She eventually recovered, although one friend observed that she always remained "quiet and reserved."

Oatman and her brother proceeded to California, studied for a time in Santa Clara Valley, and came to the attention of the Reverend Royal B. Stratton, who wrote *Life among the Indians: Being an Interesting Narrative of the Captivity of the Oatman Girls* (1857). The book enjoyed huge sales and went through several editions. Of interest as a captivity narrative—always popular among the American reading public—Oatman's account also detailed the culture of Mojave Indians before contact with white people.

In 1858, Olive Oatman moved near Rochester, New York, and, the following year, began lecturing with Stratton about her captivity and the customs of the Indians with whom she lived. She married John B. Fairchild in 1865 and moved with him to Michigan before settling in Sherman, Texas, where she remained until her death.

—Kelly L. Lankford

Olive Ann Oatman. Oatman wore the tattoos of her captivity for the rest of her life. *Courtesy Arizona Historical Society.*

SEE ALSO: Literature: Indian Captivity Narratives

SUGGESTED READING:

Namias, June. *White Captives: Gender and Ethnicity on the American Frontier.* Chapel Hill, N.C., 1993.

Stratton, Royal B. *Life among the Indians: Being an Interesting Narrative of the Captivity of the Oatman Girls among the Apache and Mohave Indians.* San Francisco, 1857.

OCHOA, ESTEBAN

Businessman and freighter Esteban Ochoa (1831–1888) was born in Chihuahua, Mexico. As a young man, he went to Kansas City to study English and to receive training in the mercantile houses there. After becoming a naturalized U.S. citizen, he established a firm in Mesilla, Arizona, became a spokesman for Mexican Americans, and worked to bridge the gap between the Mexican and Anglo populations.

Forming a partnership with Pinkney R. Tully, Ochoa opened stores throughout New Mexico and Arizona and engaged in freighting. Tully and Ochoa profited immensely from their alliance with the "federal ring" of political insiders who helped them obtain government contracts to supply merchandise. Ochoa hauled goods from Kansas City on his own freighting outfits and operated a stage line from Yuma and Tucson to Santa Fe.

During the Civil War, Ochoa was expelled from his Tucson headquarters when he refused to take an oath of allegiance to the South when Confederates invaded Arizona, but at the end of the war, he returned to Arizona and recovered his property.

The freighters suffered constant attack from Apache raiders and operated under harsh conditions. On one occasion, Indians drove off the company's draft oxen, slaughtered them, and dried the meat on a bluff along the Salt River, since known as Jerked Beef Butte. Despite those challenges, the firm of Tully and Ochoa was the most extensive in Arizona and New Mexico for twenty years. With the arrival of railroads in the early 1880s, however, Ochoa's freighting business collapsed, and he was reported to have lost one hundred thousand dollars.

Ochoa actively encouraged public education in Arizona; he donated the land for the establishment of the first public school in Tucson. He served a term as mayor of the city and represented it in the territorial legislature between 1868 and 1871 and in the House of Representatives in 1877. Throughout his career, he was recognized as a leading spokesman for the Mexican American community in southern Arizona and New Mexico.

—*W. Turrentine Jackson*

SUGGESTED READING:

Farish, Thomas Edwin. *History of Arizona.* Vol. 2. San Francisco, 1915.

Lamar, Howard. *The Far Southwest, 1846–1912.* New York, 1977.

Wagoner, Jay J. *Arizona Territorial History, 1863–1912: A Political History.* Tucson, Ariz., 1970.

O'DONEL, CHARLES

SEE: Bell Ranch, New Mexico

OGALLALA AQUIFER

The Ogallala Aquifer is a vast ground-water formation underlying much of the High Plains. It lies at depths ranging from about 50 to 300 feet beneath 174,000 square miles in Texas, New Mexico, Oklahoma, Kansas, Colorado, Nebraska, Wyoming, and South Dakota.

The aquifer, with three billion acre-feet of WATER, is one of the largest deposits of fresh water in the world. The thickness of the formation ranges from 150 to 300 feet or more. The most extensive and thickest area

lies beneath the Sandhills of Nebraska. The headwaters of several Texas rivers, including the Red River, were originally fed from springs of Ogallala origin. Much of the water in the forks of the Loup and the Dismal rivers of Nebraska originates from the aquifer bubbling up through the sandy bottoms of those streams. The formation consists of fresh water lying in a matrix of sand and gravel. The floor of the matrix is an impervious red clay, sometimes called the "red beds," of the Cretaceous era.

Through the use of WINDMILLS, the aquifer supplied water to settlers, ranchers, townspeople, and railroads as early as the 1870s. During drought years, settlers used windmills to irrigate small acreages of garden vegetables and fruit trees. By 1910 in Hereford, Texas, nearly every house in town had its own windmill, drawing water from depths of 25 to 35 feet. In 1908 near Portales, New Mexico, a number of shallow wells with pumps powered by a single electrical generating plant demonstrated that the Ogallala could yield hundreds of gallons per minute for irrigating commercial crops. By 1917, a few pumping plants, powered primarily by hot plug, oil-burning engines, dotted the South Texas plains and western Kansas. Most of the pumping plants were installed by land speculators who used the IRRIGATION works to enhance their land values. Generally, farmers could not afford the costly pumping machinery.

During the 1930s, in the worst years of the DUST BOWL, irrigation on the Southern Plains began to expand for a number of reasons: cheaper power plants, more efficient pumps, more promising cash crops, credit from New Deal agencies and pump companies, and desperate, indebted farmers. During the 1940s and 1950s, pump irrigation proliferated across the Canadian River into the northern part of the Texas Panhandle, the Oklahoma Panhandle, and western Kansas. By the 1960s, pumps began to appear in the Nebraska Sandhills. Irrigation in the Sandhills was made possible by the invention of the center-pivot sprinkler system, which the Valmost Company of Valley, Nebraska, began marketing in the previous decade.

The very success of irrigation on the High Plains has led to the depletion or threatened depletion of the Ogallala in several areas, especially the older irrigated regions, and every High Plains state has passed some kind of law to regulate or monitor ground-water withdrawal for irrigation.

—*Donald E. Green*

SUGGESTED READING:

Baker, T. Lindsay. "Irrigating with Windmills on the Great Plains." *Great Plains Quarterly* 9 (Fall 1989): 216–230.

Bowden, Charles. *Killing the Hidden Waters.* Austin, Tex., 1977.

Green, Donald E. *Land of the Underground Rain: Irrigation on the Texas Plains, 1910–1970.* Austin, Tex., 1973.

Kromm, David E., and Stephen E. White, eds. *Groundwater Exploitation in the High Plains.* Lawrence, Kans., 1992.

Opie, John. *Ogallala: Water for a Dry Land.* Lincoln, Nebr., 1993.

OGDEN, PETER SKENE

Explorer, fur trader, chief factor for the North West Company, Peter Skene Ogden (baptized February 12, 1790–1854) was the son of Isaac Ogden, judge, and Sarah Hanson.

Ogden rejected the family tradition of the law and joined the Montreal-based North West Company (NWC) in 1809 to follow the FUR TRADE. The climax of the long, bitter struggle of the company with its powerful rival, the HUDSON'S BAY COMPANY (HBC), was at hand, and Ogden played an often violent role in the contest. In 1818, he was indicted for murdering an Indian who had been trading with the HBC and fled to the Columbia department.

When the companies finally merged in 1821 under the banner of the Hudson's Bay Company, Ogden was excluded from the agreement as punishment. He went to London to plead his case. On the advice of George Simpson, the Hudson's Bay Company's local governor who feared Ogden as a potential competitor, the company relented and Ogden was appointed chief trader in 1823 and dispatched to Spokane House. His assignment was to trap the little-known Snake River country south of the Columbia, a region beset by difficult terrain, inhospitable Indians, and encroaching American traders. Over the next six years, his annual forays were splendidly recorded in his journals. There was no attempt at resource management; the country was to be denuded of beaver to reduce its attractiveness to the Americans. Ogden vigorously pursued that strategy to the gratification and commendation of his superiors.

By 1830, no white trader knew the country south of the Columbia as well as Ogden. He traveled east to Wyoming; opened up and trapped in the Humboldt River area in Nevada; saw the Great Salt Lake; and, on his last trip, visited the lower Colorado and perhaps reached the Gulf of California. Each year, he returned substantial profits in beaver, although often at a high cost in men and horses.

Ogden was transferred in 1831 to Fort Simpson on the northwestern coast of British Columbia. There he spent three years competing with the Americans who traded by sea and the RUSSIAN-AMERICAN COMPANY op-

Peter Skene Ogden. *Courtesy Library of Congress.*

erating out of Sitka, Alaska. He was promoted to chief factor in 1834 and given command of the New Caledonia district in the interior, where for the first time he encountered no competitors. Over the next nine years, the country was trapped bare, and returns declined steadily. He took leave in 1844 and spent the year in England.

The resolution of the OREGON BOUNDARY DISPUTE in 1846 meant the end of joint occupation of the region by Britain and the United States, and the Hudson's Bay Company became a foreign concern on the Columbia River. Incoming American settlers disrupted the trade and often provoked the local Indians. The most serious incident occurred in 1847 when the Cayuse Indians attacked a mission near Walla Walla, killing twelve and detaining forty-seven others. Because the new provisional government for the Oregon Territory lacked the means to respond effectively, Ogden quickly intervened and persuaded the Indians to release their captives. Provisional Governor George Abernethy expressed the gratitude of the territory, and the Hudson's Bay Company continued its trading activities with the blessing of the authorities.

A man of some wealth and considerable reputation, Ogden stayed on at Fort Vancouver until 1854 when he fell ill, retired, and died in Oregon City.

—J. E. Rea

SUGGESTED READING:

Binns, Archie. *Peter Skene Ogden: Fur Trader.* Portland, Oreg., 1967.

Cline, G. G. *Peter Skene Ogden and the Hudson's Bay Company.* Norman, Okla., 1974.

Elliott, T. C. "Peter Skene Ogden, Fur Trader." *Oregon Historical Quarterly* (1910).

Hudson's Bay Record Society (HBRS), vol. 13, *Peter Skene Ogden's Snake River Journals, 1824–25.*, and vol. 23, *Peter Skene Ogden's Snake River Journals, 1828–29.*

O'HARE, KATE RICHARDS

Kate Richards O'Hare (Carrie Kathleen Richards O'Hare Cunningham, 1876–1948) was a leader of the Socialist party of America, labor activist, World War I-era prison inmate, and penal reformer. She was a leader of the international Socialist movement, and she helped pass the Hawes-Cooper Bill of 1929 to prevent the transportation of prison-made goods across state lines.

Kate Richards was born to homesteaders in Ottawa County in central Kansas. Uprooted in 1887 by depression and drought, her family settled in Kansas City, Missouri. She taught school, undertook rescue work for the Florence Crittenton Mission, and was one of the first women machinists. She became an organizer for the Socialist Party of America and a national and international Socialist leader. After marrying a colleague, Frank Patrick O'Hare, she moved to Kansas City, Kansas, rural Oklahoma, and St. Louis, where the couple combined party activism with rearing four children. They edited the agrarian socialist monthly, *The National Rip-Saw,* while Kate O'Hare toured as one of the most popular orators on the socialist lecture circuit and drew huge crowds especially in the Southwest. She lectured on behalf of democratic SOCIALISM, labor reform, and WOMEN'S SUFFRAGE and ran for the U.S. Congress twice. For campaigning against American involvement in World War I, she was convicted of violating the Espionage Act and served fourteen months in the Missouri State Penitentiary. Upon her release in 1920, she became a zealous crusader for prison reform. She worked in labor education, served on the staff of UPTON SINCLAIR'S EPIC campaign, and was appointed in 1939 to the staff of the California Department of Penology to reform prison conditions.

—Sally M. Miller

SUGGESTED READING:

Foner, Philip S., and Sally M. Miller, eds. *Kate Richards O'Hare: Selected Writings and Speeches.* Baton Rouge, La., 1982.

Miller, Sally M. *From Prairie to Prison: The Life of Social Activist Kate Richards O'Hare.* Columbia, Mo., 1993.

OIL AND GAS INDUSTRY

Oil, in the form of animal tallow and whale oil, had been used in America since colonial days for lubricating wagon axles, for medicine, and in oil lamps. Rock oil, a kerosene product distilled from surface shale rocks, was also used for illumination. In early nineteenth-century America, the preferred oil for lighting came from whales, but by mid-century, the whaling industry was in decline, as whales were hunted to the brink of extinction, and the price of whale oil became increasingly prohibitive. Around the same time, a New York businessman named John Austin learned of a new Austrian lamp that burned kerosene cleanly and effectively. Austin perfected the Austrian prototype and marketed it in the United States, thus creating a greater need for kerosene refined from shale oil.

Various oil companies went into the business during the late 1850s, among them the Pennsylvania Rock Oil Company of Connecticut, founded by George H. Bissell, a New York attorney, and James Townsend, a businessman from New Haven. Learning that large amounts of oil were floating on water near Titusville, Pennsylvania, the two men secured a sample and took it to Benjamin Silliman of Yale University, who declared that it would make a very good illuminating substance. Bissell and Townsend purchased some Titusville property, set up their company, and hired Edwin L. Drake to find the oil. Drake, in turn, hired a drilling expert named William Smith, who urged his boss to sink a well; at a depth of sixty-nine feet, they struck oil. Drake's Titusville well was the first to tap oil at its source, and the find touched off a boom that created the American oil industry. Cheap petroleum products quickly ousted expensive whale oil as the illuminant of choice. Titusville and other Pennsylvania towns sprouted dozens and then hundreds of wells.

Entrepreneurs rushed to grab their pieces of the action, most notably and most successfully John D. Rockefeller, who loomed over the development of the oil industry and in the American imagination as the first of the great post–Civil War "robber barons." A twenty-three-year old living in Cleveland at the time of the Titusville strike, Rockefeller decided his city was ideally situated for oil refining, and determined to go into the oil business, he built a refinery there in 1862. As the company grew, Rockefeller sought to control all aspects of the new industry, from exploration and drilling through refining and pricing to transportation and distribution. In 1870, amid widely fluctuating oil prices, Rockefeller, Henry Flagler, and others created the Standard Oil Company, the first and the largest of the big postwar trusts, which over the next decade came to control 90 percent of the U.S. oil industry. Investing in railroads as well as oil companies, Rockefeller intentionally created bottlenecks in both transportation and refining to drive his competitors out of business, and—as he reaped ever larger profits—he launched ruinous rate wars, sustained by preferential rates and rebates from the railroads, to kill off independent producers. In many quarters, Rockefeller's name became synonymous with ruthlessness and corruption as he moved his headquarters to New York, incorporated in New Jersey, and employed a massive network of information gatherers and decision-makers who helped him achieve a nearly complete monopoly over oil transportation and refining.

During the twentieth century, oil would become without doubt the most important mineral in the trans-Mississippi West, far and away more valuable and significant than the region's legendary gold and silver. The oil industry contained powerful new corporations that dominated the West in the twentieth century much as the railroads, hard-rock mining, and cattle industries had in the nineteenth century. Yet at the turn of the century, oil production in the Western states was fairly inconsequential. Except in California, where some had been trying seriously to exploit oil reserves since the mid-1860s, crude-oil production proved meager, despite Standard Oil explorations on the High Plains beginning in the 1890s. In 1900, the oil industry was dominated by first Ohio, then West Virginia, and third Pennsylvania, with California ranked fifth. But along with California, the entire rest of the West—Louisiana, Texas, Colorado, Kansas, Oklahoma Territory, Wyoming—produced less than 10 percent of the nation's total oil output. By 1911, the year the Supreme Court broke up the Standard Oil Trust, the West was producing more than 72 percent of the country's oil, four of the top six oil states lay west of the Mississippi—California, Oklahoma, Louisiana, Texas. In the last half of the twentieth century, the West was responsible for more than 95 percent of U.S. oil production.

The change was abrupt and had many causes, chief among them being, naturally enough, major new oil finds. In early 1901, Standard Oil rejected as pointless drilling a hill known as Spindletop just outside Beaumont, Texas. But a bullheaded, independent Texas driller named Patillo Higgens went ahead with the exploration and proved himself right by conjuring up a tower of thick, dark liquid that spewed skyward through hundreds of feet of sand. Spindletop Hill became perhaps the most desirable piece of real estate in the world, and the backwater South Texas town grew almost overnight from fewer than ten thousand to nearly fifty thousand residents. Spindletop gushed two hundred feet and blew out 110,000 barrels of Texas crude a day for nine days before the oil men could cap it. The discovery touched off a new boom soon fed by other finds outside Tulsa, Oklahoma, and in Louisiana. The business was volatile, and the army of wildcatters, roughnecks, roustabouts, and fortune-seekers who swelled the boom towns and oil camps of the midcountry and the Southwest lost their shirts as frequently as they made their piles amid wildly speculatively booms and busts. A thriving town's swelled population could deflate instantly when a well ran dry or when there was a new find, sometimes just a few miles down the road.

The sheer amount of new oil alone would not have worked the major changes in the oil industry at the turn of the century, for there were only so many kerosene lamps in the world. A few of the sharper new oil capitalists—men such as Frank Phillips and Henry Sinclair—by the early years of the twentieth century, had begun to explore the use of oil as a fuel for heating homes and businesses and powering ships and locomotives. There had always been some oil, left over from refining, that was used as fuel, but after the turn of the century, the discovery of huge crude-oil fields in the West, much of it not all that suited to refining, meant that there was a plentiful and inexpensive alternative to the costly coal imported into the region. Even before 1900, wine-makers, power companies, sugar-beet refiners, cement companies, iron and steel factories, and brick and clay kilns in California looked to local oil companies as a source of fuel, and now railroads and big ocean-going ships joined the customer list. By World War I, the federal government was proving a major customer: during the war, railroads and steamships, moving men and materiel, bought and burned half California's annual oil output. In Kansas and Oklahoma, the oil was too light and rich to be "wasted" on fuel, but the Gulf Coast's heavy crude, like California's, was perfect for fuel, which became its primary use.

Increasingly, too, after 1900, oil men found a market for one of oil's distillations, gasoline, to power the internal-combustion engines of the new horseless carriages. Some eight thousand automobiles were pinging and banging their way along dusty roads the year Spindletop first spewed its black gold; by 1905, there were perhaps one hundred thousand motor vehicles in America. Then, in 1908, Henry Ford introduced the Model-T and mass production to the automobile industry and turned what had been a toy of the wealthy into a necessity for the middle class. By 1910, there were five hundred thousand cars in the country, and their number increased some twenty times in the coming decade. Crude oil, sold directly as fuel before 1910, was afterward "topped" in rude refineries to save gasoline, and in California, where Los Angeles had already developed as a sprawling town of inter-urban railway stops, the combination of a crude oil exceptionally high in octane and a local good-roads movement helped create a car culture that would profoundly influence life in the new century. As Texas oil geologist Everette Lee De Golyer put it, the "age of illumination" was replaced in 1900 by the "age of fuel," which, in turn, was replaced in 1910 by the "age of motor fuel."

The oil fields of Saratoga, Texas, in 1908.
Courtesy Library of Congress.

Rich as the oil industry had become from developing lighting, heating, and lubricating oils and other products, the rapid emergence of the automobile as a pervasive feature of American life early in the twentieth century made it far richer. The companies the Texas oil men and others formed—Gulf, Sunoco (originally Sun Oil Company), Texaco (originally Texas Oil Company)—made their shareholders, if not as rich as John D. Rockefeller, at least rich enough to take on Standard Oil. In part, the number of major new finds offered so many opportunities for investment that even the Standard Oil Trust could not cover them all, although it tried. In 1900, Standard bought a pioneering firm called Pacific Coast Oil and, in 1906, renamed it the Standard Oil Company of California (later Chevron). By 1911, Standard Oil had become the leading oil company in the state, controlled 30 percent of the industry, and engaged in every aspect of the business but overseas production and sales. In Kansas and Oklahoma, the trust acquired productive leases to oil fields and transferred them, in 1900, to a new subsidiary, the Prairie Oil and Gas Company, which produced, bought, stored, piped, and refined the bulk of the highly prized midcontinent "light" petroleum. In Louisiana, too, the trust set up a Standard Oil Company at Baton Rouge in 1909 that soon controlled the business from start to finish. In Texas, however, with its powerful Populist tradition and antitrust sentiments, Standard Oil ran into trouble.

It was not that the original investment in Texas oil came from within the state. Indeed, Texas's Sun Oil Company—controlled by the Pew family of Philadelphia and western Pennsylvania—had been active in Ohio and Indiana before it transferred its energy southward. Pittsburgh's Mellon family, well acquainted with the industry in western Pennsylvania, dominated the Texas company that became Gulf Oil. Another Pennsylvania family, the Laphams (who controlled the U.S. Leather Trust), joined maverick capitalist John W. Gates to become the major investors in the company that was the predecessor of Texaco. Instead, it was the state's antimonopoly laws—passed by Texas Populists—that foiled John D. Rockefeller. Those laws prevented any one corporation from dominating the production, transporting, refining, and wholesaling of oil, as Standard Oil was want to do, and although Standard Oil of New Jersey became a major stockholder in Humble Oil of Texas, which would later be called Exxon, it never managed to break the tradition of "Texas independents"—large companies specializing in one aspect of the oil industry and, thereby, competing effectively with the trust.

What was more, the trouble for Standard Oil spread from Texas. When production declined sharply after 1905, Gulf Oil and Texas Oil sought to offset their losses by building pipelines to the midcontinent fields in Kansas and Oklahoma, where they went head to head with Prairie Oil and Gas, quickly reduced the trust's market share, and paved the way for a new group of rivals in the next decade—Sinclair Oil and Refining Corporation, Phillips Petroleum Company, Cities Service Company, Skelly Oil Company, and others. Long before the Supreme Court began to review Standard Oil's monopoly status, Texas courts had handed the trust serious setbacks. In addition, the series of events that led to the antitrust suit against Standard Oil came out of the West. Embattled Kansas oil men forced themselves on the state's attorney general, who hauled Prairie Oil and Gas into court. This action emboldened some in Congress to call on the federal Bureau of Corporations to investigate Standard Oil's methods of operation in the Kansas industry. The bureau's voluminous reports led directly to the filing of the government's suit in federal district court in Missouri in 1905. After the Circuit Court ruled, three years later, against the trust, the Rockefeller interests appealed to the U.S. Supreme Court, which, in 1911, declared Standard Oil of New Jersey an illegal monopoly.

Not only did the flush new oil fields of the American West and the new markets opened up for oil in the twentieth century lead to the breakup of the Standard Oil monopoly that had dominated so much of the nineteenth century's economic development, they also put an end to the belief—common among many scientists before World War I—that the oil resources of the United States would be quickly exhausted and that oil itself would be a mineral of scarce interest except historically by the middle of the new century. It was this opinion, for example, that had led the government, in 1912, to set up federal oil reserves in Elk Hills and Buena Vista, California, and shortly thereafter at TEAPOT DOME, Wyoming, to protect the navy against possible future shortages. As oil boomed in the wildcat atmosphere after the fall of the trust, speculation in federal oil leases also flourished, ultimately creating a major scandal. The cheap new fuel also drove the engine of urbanization, especially in cities such as Los Angeles and Houston, located near major new finds. Boasting broad boulevards and stretches of suburban homes, the automobile-friendly Western cities sprawled out along landscapes that often featured hundreds of miles of oil derricks.

Texas, after Standard Oil was defeated, repealed its antimonopoly laws in 1917, and Texaco went on to become a major vertically integrated company reminiscent of the Rockefeller operation. It never completely displaced the independents, however, in large measure because of the growing number and the extent of new discoveries. Although amid the 1920s boom, a few, such as Henry L. Doherty, crusaded for more sound conservation practices, and some attempts at limiting production were introduced throughout the region, they had little effect. In Oklahoma in 1927 and 1928, the full-throttle production at the massive new Seminole and Oklahoma City finds produced a generation of instant millionaires before the Oklahoma Corporation Commission took the then apparently draconian step of trying to limit production statewide to fewer that seven hundred thousand barrels a day. But greedy operators ignored the legal rulings of a commission whose powers to regulate the industry they and many others openly questioned. There is little doubt the wide-open industry brought spectacular, if sometimes fleeting, prosperity. One result of independent oil production was that goodly percentages of the revenues from oil remained within in a state. In Oklahoma, even the Indians grew rich off oil leases, with the Osages becoming the wealthiest per capita ethnic group in the country. In Texas, through a combination of wages, leases, taxes, equipment sales, and services incomes, the industry pumped huge amounts of money into the local economy. Leases on state lands, for example, provided the money to create the Texas university system.

In California, too, after 1911, oil money underwrote the regional economy. There, despite Standard Oil's early entry into the industry, other companies also set up shop. The Union Oil Company was a Ventura County enterprise that initially drew, as had operators in Texas, on the skills and capital of Pennsylvania. Fuel oil turned out to be lucrative early on in California because it needed little refining and the state lacked coal reserves. Cheap oil quickly replaced expensive imported coal on locomotives, on ships, and in factories. The Associated Oil Company, formed by a big group of investors from the San Joaquin Valley in 1901, soon came under the control of the Southern Pacific Railroad, which also ran the Kern Trading and Oil Company to produce oil on the land granted to the railroad. The Santa Fe Railroad also used its land grants to enter into the oil business. Because new oil discoveries lay near the big oil markets in Los Angeles and San Francisco, transportation costs were low, and it took less capital to enter the industry. At the same time, California was far enough away from the Eastern oil fields that any attempt to import oil incurred prohibitively high transportation costs. All of which meant that Standard Oil, although it owned a much larger share of the California market than it ever did that of Texas, could neither create the bottlenecks in transportation and obstacles to refining that drove out competitors as it had in the East nor glut the local market with imported oil to drive down prices and stifle smaller companies. Shortly before the 1911 break up of the trust's monopoly, a group of prominent Western entrepreneurs in shipping and utilities put together another competitor called the General Petroleum Company. And such independents continued to flourish even after the fall of the trust allowed the giant Royal Dutch Shell Petroleum Company to invade the California industry by buying up rich oil lands in the San Joaquin Valley and by selling gasoline on the West Coast imported from Sumatra.

California, selling its oil regionally to Washington, Oregon, Arizona, Nevada, Alaska, and Hawaii, became the largest oil-producing state in the country before 1926, when midcontinent and East Texas finds began to change the equation. California was the first of the Western states to invest in its higher education system. The oil profits that helped fund the University of California system produced many returns from the engineers, chemists, and geologists who were trained by its schools. They discovered new oil fields, helped to make oil production more effective and efficient, and invented new uses for petroleum in everything from asphalt to plastic. Colleges and universities in Oklahoma and Texas soon came to rival California in the training of geologists and engineers, although as a whole, perhaps, the schools in the former states did not compete as well with California's ever-growing and broad-based system. As automobiles grew more prominent in California, the refining of petroleum expanded as well until, by 1929, it had become the state's largest industry. Although California's market share fell steadily after 1923, the state invested oil profits in new industries that quickly made it a manufacturing center.

In Texas, on the other hand, the percentage of the state's overall revenue that depended on the petroleum industry continued to increase in ways that, in the long run, might prove detrimental. Just how vulnerable Texas in particular, but also a West whose fortunes in general were too closely tied to oil, was became alarmingly clear during the early 1930s, when a reckless boom spawned by the mammoth East Texas field, the largest find in the nation's history, finally led to overproduction and a major bust. In a single year, prices plummeted from $1.30 to three cents a barrel. For every barrel shipped, ten more oozed back into the Texas dirt. Texas imposed limits on production, and other Western states followed suit. Under the Market Demand Act of 1932, Texas granted the authority to regulate the industry to the Texas Railroad Commission, which tried to restrict production by an equitable "prorationing" system, but it took the imposition of martial law and the Texas National Guard to enforce compliance with the new rules. And even though wildcatters grew choosier about picking sites, roustabouts drifted to steadier jobs, and oil wells were tapped for a few barrels a day a few days a month, the commission's work was undercut by a black market in "hot oil" that some Texans produced in violation of the law to sell in markets outside the state.

During the summer of 1933, the New Deal government in Washington acted through the National Recovery Administration to close the black market in Texas crude by drawing up a federal code for government-issued drilling permits and federally imposed production quotas. The Interior Department's Bureau of Mines began issuing monthly forecasts of refinery demand as a basis for establishing quotas. By the authority delegated to the NRA, Secretary of the Interior Harold L. Ickes stanched the seepage of illegal oil under an executive order. Oil men grew fearful that Franklin D. Roosevelt's administration intended to nationalize the petroleum industry and convert oil production into a public utility, and they began to look around for some other means of control. Talk of an interstate agreement of some kind was already widespread when the U.S. Supreme Court declared the NRA unconstitutional. The New Dealers in Washington threw their support behind the idea of interstate regulation. In February of 1935, Congress passed the Connally "Hot Oil" Act to stop interstate shipments of oil that exceeded quotas based on the Bureau of Mines monthly forecast and set by state regulatory boards or commissions. Six major oil-producing states came up with an Interstate Oil Compact, and most other Western states, except for California, joined the compact after it was ratified by Congress in August 1935. Yet one among many examples of the growing private-public partnership between Western industries and the FEDERAL GOVERNMENT that increasingly characterized the region, the compact was perhaps overly protective of the domestic oil industry, but it, nevertheless, brought some order and efficiency to a chaotic enterprise in the throes of a major collapse.

The demand for oil not only rebounded from its 1930's slump but seemed to become insatiable after World War II (which in itself, naturally, proved a huge boost for the industry), as scientists and consumers continued to find uses for oil in an increasing number of products—petrochemicals, diesel fuels, jet propulsion. New finds cropped up throughout the West, not only in California, Texas, Louisiana, Kansas, and Oklahoma, but also in New Mexico, Arkansas, Montana, Wyoming, Colorado, North Dakota, and Alaska. Since the Great Depression, the industry has grown increasingly fond of offshore drilling, especially off the coasts of Louisiana, Texas, California, and Alaska. Although oil explorations had occurred in Alaska before the turn of the century, only a modest commercial production had developed around Cook's Inlet in the south before 1968. That year, industry explorations discovered a vast new field on the state's isolated and frozen North Slope, and nine major oil companies, acting alone and in various combinations, soon paid the Alaskan government in excess of $900 million to explore the slope. Plans for a trans-Alaska pipeline to pump the black gold from the North Slope to the ice-free port at Valdez fell victim to environmental protests until the Arab oil embargo of 1973 sparked a panic over energy. National legislation swept doubts aside, and the 789-mile Alaska Pipeline was ready for operation in 1977.

The so-called energy crisis affected far more than the construction of the pipeline. On October 17, 1973, when the Arab Organization of Petroleum Exporting Countries (OPEC) declared an embargo on oil exports to nations that had supported Israel in its war against Egypt, the declining oil industry in the American West got a new lease on life. Big oil companies and independents in Texas and Oklahoma, who for years had sought and won federal protection from foreign oil imports, suddenly rediscovered the timeless virtues of free trade. If freed by Congress from federal regulations, they promised, they would, in turn, save the country from the kind of energy shortages that had begun to haunt the American imagination, as commuters lined up for hours at gas pumps around the country. At the same time, the Texas Railroad Commission and other such state regulatory agencies continued to protect small producers with regulations as arcane as any the federal government had ever devised. When Northern energy companies and consumer groups complained about the inefficiencies and high costs associated with the smaller, marginal, stripper wells, Texans plastered their cars with bumper stickers inviting outsiders to go "freeze in the dark."

Under national energy policies first developed by President Richard Nixon and brought to fruition under President Jimmy Carter, the favorable investment atmosphere not only encouraged these small producers to take the risks involved in a renewed search for gas and oil or in finding ways to improve recovery of oil from marginal fields, it also created a new boom in oil and natural gas in Texas and Oklahoma. The boom generated immense profits, which big oil companies and Texas oil men began to invest in new energy ventures. Denver, with little oil or gas reserves of its own, became the corporate headquarters for coal and shale-oil developments across the Western interior. Salt Lake City boomed as well when new energy companies moved in and set up shop. Indeed, Montana, Wyoming, and the entire mountain West was swept up in the enthusiasm for new energy sources, alternative energy sources, and synthetic fuels.

But grand plans to strip-mine the High Plains and make Wyoming or Utah another Pennsylvania fell apart as the distillation of oil from shale proved economically prohibitive even with high oil prices. Also, various energy conservation measures turned out to be surprisingly effective, and a worldwide recession sharply cut demand. The member nations of OPEC responded to falling prices by stepping up production and arguing among themselves. By the early 1980s, OPEC had lost the ability to dictate oil prices, and the energy crisis had turned into a energy glut that brought development plans in Utah and Montana and Wyoming to an abrupt halt and that devastated the oil and gas industries in Texas and Oklahoma, where the economy went into a sharp downward spiral. The industry's woes were also exacerbated by a growing number of oil spills from ocean-going oil tankers and offshore drilling—spills that caused extensive environmental damage to the Alaska and California coasts, the most infamous being the wreck of the Exxon *Valdez*. By the late twentieth century, despite a "sagebrush rebellion" in favor of renewed Western development and an increasingly probusiness Congress, the U.S. oil industry—in large measure a Western industry—had fallen into a general disrepute as great as any in its often checkered, sometimes glorious history.

—*Charles Phillips*

SUGGESTED READING:

Andreano, Ralph. "The Structure of the California Petroleum Industry, 1895–1911." *Pacific Historical Review* 39 (May 1970): 171–192.

Davidson, Art. *In The Wake of the Exxon Valdez: The Devastating Impact of the Alaska Oil Spill.* San Francisco, 1990.

Franks, Kenny A. *The Oklahoma Petroleum Industry.* Norman, Okla., 1980.

Guilliford, Andrew. *Boomtown Blues: Colorado Oil Shale, 1885–1985.* Niwot, Colo., 1989.

Johnson, Arthur M. "California and the National Oil Industry." *Pacific Historical Review* 39 (May 1970): 155–170.

Prindle, David F. *Petroleum Politics and the Texas Railroad Commission.* Austin, Tex., 1981.

Rister, Carl Coke. *Oil! Titan of the Southwest.* Norman, Okla., 1949.

White, Gerald T. "California's Other Mineral." *Pacific Historical Review* 39 (May 1970): 135–154.

———. *Formative Years in the Far West: A History of Standard Oil Company of California and Its Predecessors through 1919.* New York, 1962.

Williamson, Harold F. *The American Petroleum Industry.* 2 vols. Evanston, Ill., 1959, 1963.

OJIBWA INDIANS

SEE: Native American Peoples: Peoples of the Great Plains

O. K. CORRAL, GUNFIGHT AT

In the early afternoon of October 26, 1881, the three EARP BROTHERS, Virgil, Wyatt, and Morgan, along with JOHN HENRY ("DOC") HOLLIDAY, confronted Joseph Isaac (Ike) Clanton, William (Billy) Claiborne, William (Billy) Clanton, Robert Finley (Frank) McLaury, and Thomas Clarke McLaury in a vacant lot facing Fremont Street in Tombstone, Arizona. In the point-blank shootout that followed, an estimated thirty shots were fired in twenty to thirty seconds. Tom and Frank McLaury and Billy Clanton were killed; Ike Clanton and Billy Claiborne ran; and Virgil and Morgan Earp received leg and shoulder wounds. The gunfight at the O. K. Corral was a tragic bloodletting, celebrated in song, motion pictures, television shows, and documentaries and in books, articles, and stories beyond number. The fight did not occur in the O. K. Corral, however. Instead, it occurred in an empty lot between the home of City Councilman W. A. Harwood and the boarding house of photographer Camillus Fly. The O. K. Corral, nearly a hundred feet east, opened on Allen Street. The question remains whether the error in naming the gunfight is attributable to faulty memories of old-timers and is perpetuated out of habit or whether, as biographer Paula M. Marks suggests, it is attributable to the fact that O. K. Corral "has a ring to it."

The causes of the shootout are varied. Earlier, Wyatt Earp pistol-whipped, or "buffaloed," outlaw leader "CURLY" BILL BROCIUS over the accidental shooting of Tombstone's first city marshal, Fred White. Then, in an unrelated affair, Earp proposed to rustler Ike Clanton that he betray three outlaws who had attempted to hold up a Wells Fargo stage and had killed the driver. Wells Fargo had posted a "dead or alive" reward of thirty-six hundred dollars. As a candidate for sheriff of the newly formed county of Cochise, Earp wanted the glory of capturing the bandits. He told Clanton to

Bird's eye view of Tombstone, Arizona, where the Earp brothers faced the Clantons and their cohorts in the legendary gunfight at the O. K. Corral. *Courtesy Arizona Historical Society.*

set the killers up; Earp would then see that Clanton received the reward. Clanton agreed and enlisted the aid of Frank McLaury. The plot miscarried, through no fault of Earp's, but Clanton claimed betrayal and swore revenge.

Recent scholarship has presented more compelling causes for the shootout. Wyatt and Virgil Earp were successful businessmen in Tombstone. They owned property, held mining claims and water rights, and made money gambling. They had everything to lose by a shootout. Probably, they intended only to arrest and disarm the cowboys. But Morgan Earp and "Doc" Holliday were loose cannons. They owned no property or other interests in Tombstone, and they had problems with Ike Clanton and Frank McLaury. A number of witnesses testified that Morgan Earp and "Doc" Holliday fired the first shots. Morgan was reported to have said, "Let them have it." Wyatt and Virgil Earp were left with no choice but to fight.

Although the gunfight had no social or political impact, the gunfight at the O. K. Corral has become the prototype for unfocused Western VIOLENCE, and it helped create the enduring myth of Western GUNFIGHTERS.

—Jack Burrows

SUGGESTED READING:

Marks, Paula Mitchell. *And Die in the West: The Story of the O. K. Corral Gunfight.* New York, 1989.

Martin, Douglas D. *Tombstone Epitaph.* Albuquerque, N. Mex., 1951.

Turner, Alford E. *The O. K. Corral Inquest.* College Station, Tex., 1981.

———, ed. *The Earps Talk.* College Station, Tex., 1980.

O'KEEFFE, GEORGIA

Best known for her paintings of Western subjects, Georgia O'Keeffe (1887–1986) was one of the twentieth century's most critically acclaimed—and certainly one of its most popular—modernists. Born near Sun Prairie, Wisconsin, O'Keeffe first studied at the Art Institute of Chicago and later at the Art Students League of New York. Following her training, she supported herself as a commercial artist and a teacher of art in Texas and South Carolina.

In 1916, she caught the attention of Alfred Stieglitz, a New York photographer and arbiter of art. Stieglitz exhibited O'Keeffe's work at "291," his avant-garde gallery, and the two became lovers. They married in 1924.

O'Keeffe's early works have been called imitative, but a summer vacation in Santa Fe, New Mexico, in 1917 changed all that. She found in the region a spiritual home, and "from then on," she later commented, "I was always on my way back." By the early 1920s, she had developed her own representational style of the natural land forms, hills, rocks, flowers and plants, tiny churches and buildings, and bleached animal bones of the region. In works of brilliant colors, she extracted from the natural forms before her their gently rhythmic outlines and imbued them with a powerful, impersonal sensuality. It was her genius to transform biomorphic forms into stark, abstract beauty.

Seeking breathing room from her marriage, in the late 1920s, she headed west again, staying for a time in Taos with the wealthy art patron MABEL DODGE LUHAN. She worked alone, separated by choice from the colony of artists that had invaded Taos since the turn of the century. She returned to New Mexico for many summers thereafter and produced her most popular works, including the bleached bones series and *Black Iris* in the 1920s, thirties, and forties.

After Stieglitz died in 1946, O'Keeffe moved permanently to a New Mexico that energized her life and her art. She resided in two homes—one a hillside retreat near the village plaza of Abiquiu, the other close to the Ghost Ranch. She continued to paint into her eighties, although she required assistants to read the colors on her tubes of paint. Of the New Mexico she so brilliantly portrayed on canvas, she said: "Sometimes I think I am half mad with love for this place."

—Patricia Hogan

SEE ALSO: Art; Taos School of Artists; Women Artists

SUGGESTED READING:

Lisle, Laurie. *The Portrait of an Artist: A Biography of Georgia O'Keeffe.* New York, 1980.

Robinson, Roxana. *Georgia O'Keeffe.* New York, 1989.

OKINAGON INDIANS

SEE: Native American Peoples: Peoples of the Pacific Northwest

OKLAHOMA

Oklahoma, the "Sooner State," is located in the south-central United States. It shares borders mainly with Texas, Arkansas, and Kansas but also touches New Mexico, Colorado, and Missouri. The state consists of 69,919 square miles and had a population of

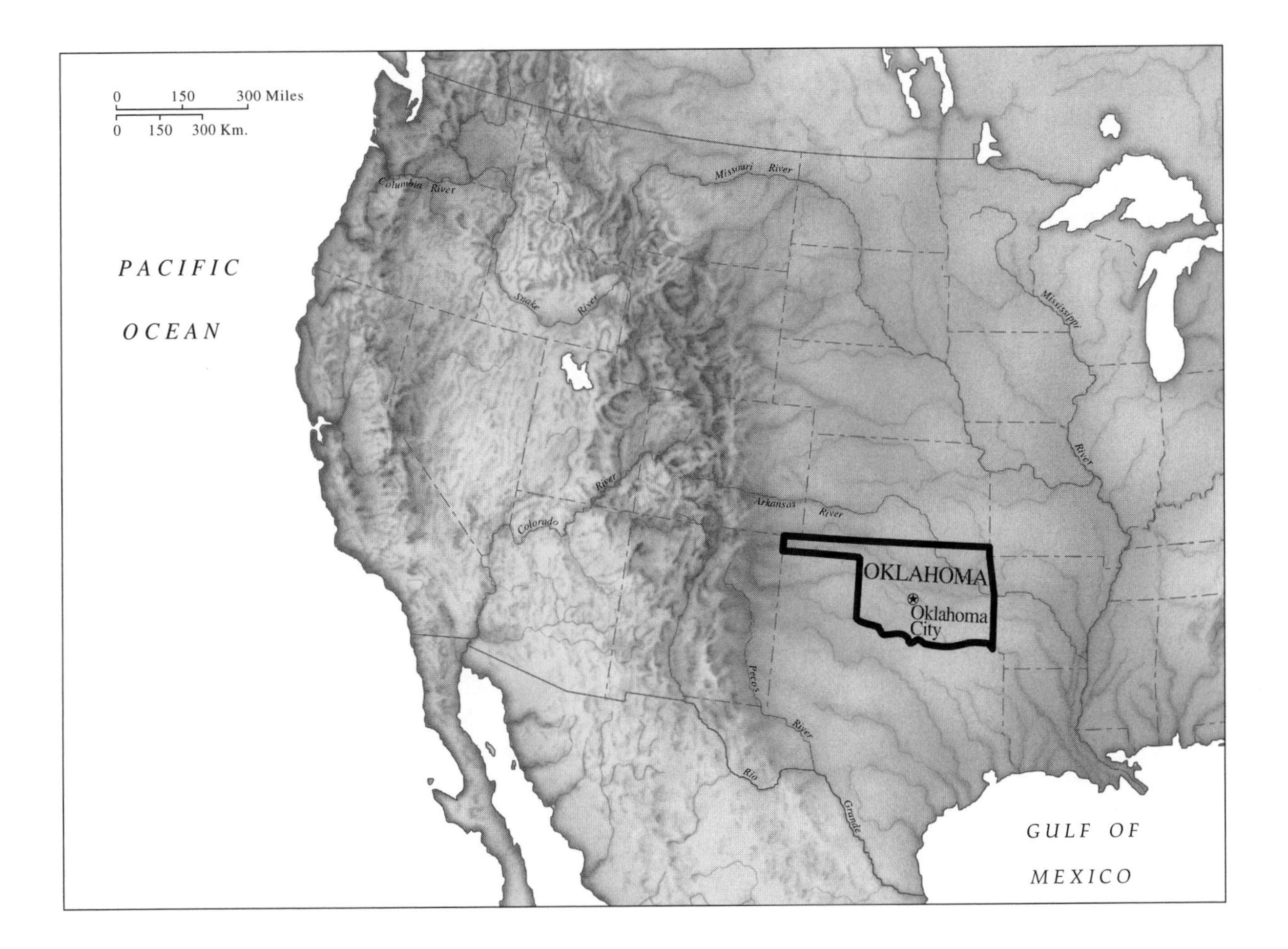

3,145,585, according to the 1990 census. Relatively few minorities reside in Oklahoma; its population includes 7.4 percent African Americans, 1.1 percent Asians, and 2.7 percent Hispanics. Even the American Indian population amounts to only 8 percent of the total; although with 252,420 Native Americans, Oklahoma has the largest number of Native Americans of all states. A large proportion of the Native Americans, however, have less that one-half Native American blood. Slightly below the national average, Oklahoma is 70 percent urban, with almost half of the population residing in the metropolitan areas of the capital—Oklahoma City—and Tulsa.

Geography and climate

Level plains and prairies prevail throughout much of Oklahoma, but four systems of mountains or hills break the terrain: the Ozarks in the northeast; the Ouachita Mountains in the southeast; the Arbuckle Mountains, an ancient worn system of hills in the south-central area; and the more formidable granite peaks of the Wichita Mountains in the southwest. From the lava-capped Black Mesa—about five thousand feet above sea level—in the northwestern corner of the Oklahoma Panhandle, the elevation generally slopes downward to the southeastern corner of the state, where the lowest spot is less than three hundred feet above sea level.

The eastern half of Oklahoma is largely wooded, with oak and hickory forests common in the Ozarks and with oak and pine stands covering much of the Ouachitas, where a large pulp mill is a major industry. Most of the remainder of eastern Oklahoma is covered with small post oak and black jack oak trees, with larger species in the river bottoms. The western fringe of those small oak forests, known as the Cross Timbers, marks the transition into increasingly treeless prairies and plains that dominate the western part of the state. In flora and fauna, Oklahoma is a crossroads with both Eastern and Western species of plant and animal life.

Oklahoma lies largely in the humid, subtropical zone. Rainfall in the southeastern corner totals almost sixty inches annually, but the majority of the state receives between twenty-five and forty inches per year. The far northwestern sections are characterized by the semiarid features of the High Plains, where ten to fourteen inches of rainfall annually is the norm. Farmers at first attempted to grow corn in Oklahoma, but the rainfall and related soil conditions made the crop unprofitable. Cotton once dominated the southern half of the state and is still important in the southwestern section. For decades, however, wheat and cattle have been the principal agricultural products, and Oklahoma consistently is among the top five in production. Oklahoma also ranks high in growing pecans, peanuts, grain sorghum, and hay.

Outsiders often visualize Oklahoma as a source of oil wealth—an image strengthened by postcards showing oil derricks on the grounds of the state capitol. Actually, drillers have depleted many of the once enormous oil fields. Natural gas, however, is still abundant and will remain a major source of income for years. The once great lead and zinc mines also have been nearly depleted in northeastern Oklahoma, which was part of the tri-state lead and zinc district (with Kansas and Missouri). In western Oklahoma, several companies have tapped large underground layers of gypsum, a product so abundant that mining it could last for centuries. Coal mining, however, has declined steadily since Oklahoma became a state, when eight thousand miners worked the coal veins. Now, some strip mining occurs in the northeast. In various locations, limestone, granite, and several types of clay provide materials for buildings, road surfaces, bricks, and pottery. Confounding the stereotypical image of Oklahoma created by the DUST BOWL, the eastern half of the state contains several large lakes, which were the result of New Deal reservoir-making programs and the Arkansas River navigation project in the 1950s and 1960s. Those reservoirs provide recreation, drinking water, hydroelectricity, and flood control.

Native Americans

Ironically, when the first Europeans arrived in the region, few tribes inhabited Oklahoma, which literally means "red people" in the Choctaw language. Small numbers of Wichitas, Caddos, Pawnees, Quapaws, and Plains Apaches occupied the state when, in 1541, FRANCISCO VÁSQUEZ DE CORONADO passed through in search of Gran Quivira, purportedly a city of great wealth but really a village of meager grass huts in southern Kansas. Immediately following Coronado, Andre do Campo, a Portuguese national in the Spanish army, wandered through the area, and in the early 1600s, JUAN DE OÑATE, the governor of Nuevo Mexico, mapped a route through the region. A few missionaries may have drifted into present-day Oklahoma later, but Spanish influence remained minimal. By the early 1700s, French trappers and traders entered eastern Oklahoma, while other French adventurers traveled through in attempts to establish trade with Santa Fe. Bernard de la Harpe, by far the most important of these Frenchmen, received a franchise for trapping northwest of Natchitoches, toured the area in 1719, and recorded his experiences in a detailed journal. The French intrusion made Oklahoma a region of colonial rivalry with the Spanish, but their confrontations ended when France ceded the entire Louisiana area to Spain in 1763.

During the 1790s, Auguste and Pierre Chouteau, the well-known merchants of St. Louis who lost their rights to trade on the upper Missouri River, persuaded a large segment of the Osage tribe to settle at the Three Forks area (the juncture of the Arkansas, Verdigris, and Grand rivers). Shortly after the LOUISIANA PURCHASE, American trappers and traders, most notably Nathaniel Pryor, also began entering eastern Oklahoma. From 1819 to 1824, parts of Oklahoma came under the jurisdiction of the Territory of Arkansas, and a few farming families began settling in the eastern part of the region. Meanwhile, American explorers moved through present-day Oklahoma: JAMES WILKINSON in 1806 as part of ZEBULON MONTGOMERY PIKE's expedition, Indian Agent George C. Sibley in 1811, STEPHEN HARRIMAN LONG and John Bell in 1820, and naturalist Thomas Nuttall in 1819 and 1820. Long's mislabeling of the region as part of the GREAT AMERICAN DESERT had a significant impact. His assessment reinforced the emerging governmental policy that the area would be the ideal for the resettlement of Indian tribes from east of the Mississippi.

During the 1820s and 1830s, thousands of Choctaws, Chickasaws, Creeks, Seminoles, and Cherokees moved to present-day Oklahoma, first voluntarily and later forcibly, from their homelands in several Southeastern states. Combined, the Five Civilized Tribes had constituted the largest Indian population east of the Mississippi River. Except for the Seminoles, the tribes had developed governments based on both their native traditions and the governments of their white neighbors. SEQUOYAH, a Cherokee unable to read or write English, created a written form of his tribe's language, and the other nations, aided by Christian missionaries, developed written versions of their own languages. Diplomatically and militarily, the Five Civilized Tribes had played a major role in the history of the southeastern United States, and their removal to Oklahoma became a major issue during ANDREW JACKSON's presidency. The removal also exacerbated tribal factionalism and caused the loss of thousands of lives as they traveled to their new homes.

In particular, the Cherokees, Choctaws, and Chickasaws intermarried with whites and adopted much of their culture and economic system. Before the

Civil War in the Indian Territory (as Oklahoma was called), all five of the tribes eventually established their own separate governments and remained largely independent of the federal government, which provided oversight through Indian agents. Under this system, the Indians prospered and, to a large extent, recreated societies and economies much like those they had in their former homelands. Some even owned African American slaves. The major difference between the Indian cultures and the culture of the Southern states was communal land ownership. Each tribe produced leaders of great political skill, such as JOHN ROSS and Stand Watie (Cherokees), the McIntosh family and OPOTHLEYAHOLA (Creeks), Micanopy and Wildcat (Seminoles), Edmund Pickens and Cyrus Harris (Chickasaws), and Peter Pitchlynn and the Folsom family (Choctaws). Missionaries—predominately Baptists, Methodists, and Presbyterians—continued the activities they had begun in the Southeast with these tribes.

The Civil War shattered the societies of the Five Tribes and caused old factional animosities to return, especially among the Cherokees, Creeks, and Seminoles. Because all the tribes aligned themselves officially with the Confederacy, the federal government punished them by taking away about half of their lands and settling the Plains Indians and woodland tribes from Kansas and Nebraska on them. Eventually, almost seventy tribes resided in Oklahoma, although the Kiowas, Comanches, Kiowa-Apaches, Cheyennes, and Arapahos settled on their reserves only after costly warfare and the destruction of the buffalo.

The land-rush years

The new arrangement lasted only a few years. By 1879, DAVID L. PAYNE, a minor Kansas politician, began leading land-hungry whites to demand the opening of unused Indian lands in the central and western parts of the Indian Territory. Payne's dramatic forays into the area, combined with the aid of powerful congressional allies and railroad officials, helped force the opening of the unassigned lands in central Oklahoma in 1889. The next year, Congress combined the central area with the Panhandle to form the Territory of Oklahoma. After the initial dramatic land rush, the government allotted lands to various tribes, and those adjacent areas were added to the territory in piecemeal fashion. Additional land rushes opened the Sac (Sauk) and Fox (Mesquakie), Iowa, and Potawotami-Shawnee lands in 1891, the Cheyenne and Arapaho area in 1892, the Cherokee Outlet in 1893, and the small Kickapoo reservation in 1895. The government used a unique, massive land lottery to open the Kiowa-

Guthrie, Oklahoma Territory, on April 27, 1889. This image shows Oklahoma "Avenue." *Courtesy Western History Collections, University of Oklahoma Library.*

Federal marshals enforced prohibition laws in Guthrie, Oklahoma Territory, May 28, 1889. *Courtesy Western History Collections, University of Oklahoma Library.*

Comanche and Wichita lands in 1901. Mostly from the Midwest, the newcomers to the Oklahoma Territory also included several thousand Europeans; Germans, German Russians, and Czechoslovakians were the most numerous and concentrated mostly in the north-central part of Oklahoma.

Meanwhile, in the eastern half of present-day Oklahoma (still called the Indian Territory), the Five Tribes continued to hold their lands, but their sovereignty gradually eroded. Powerful economic forces dramatically altered the Indian Territory as several railroads entered the lands of the Five Tribes and, in turn, led to the opening of coal mines, the establishment of non-Indian cities, and an influx of businessmen and merchants. Also, landless farmers from the South inconspicuously drifted into the Indian Territory to rent land from the Indians, usually mixed-bloods. When the non-Indian population far exceeded the population of the Five Tribes in the 1890s, Congress moved to abrogate its agreements with the Indians, an action heartily endorsed by the citizens of adjacent states. The Dawes Commission, created by Congress in 1893, facilitated the transition from communal to individual ownership, but due to the large population of the Five Tribes, almost no surplus was left for the non-Indians. After the Dawes Commission completed the process in 1906, white speculators gained control of most of the allotted land through often fraudulent purchases and leases.

Statehood

As the government dispossessed the tribes and abolished their governments, the vast majority of residents of both the Oklahoma Territory and the Indian Territory clamored for either separate or combined statehood. Leaders in the Indian Territory unsuccessfully attempted to form the state of Sequoyah, separate from the Oklahoma Territory, in 1905, but Congress passed the Enabling Act in 1906, which combined the two territories and called for a constitutional convention at Guthrie. WILLIAM ("ALFALFA BILL") MURRAY of Tishomingo, CHARLES NATHANIEL HASKELL of Muskogee, Robert L. Williams of Durant, and Henry S. Johnston of Perry—all Democrats—held important positions at the convention in 1906 and 1907, and they dominated politics in the state for almost three decades.

Most observers miscalculated by assuming that the Republican party would control state politics because of its favored position in the Oklahoma Territory, yet the Democrats held 99 of the 112 positions at the constitutional convention. They fashioned an organic document notable for its length and its provisions for a weak executive branch and for direct democracy devices. Indicative of the influence of the Oklahoma Farmers Union and the Twin Territories Federation of Labor, the constitution restricted corporations and favored labor and agriculture. Responding to a requirement of the Enabling Act, the convention drew up a prohibition amendment for the constitution to be ratified simultaneously. Despite tremendous lobbying, the delegates refused to allow women's suffrage. The public overwhelmingly endorsed the constitution and elected a slate of officers, with Democrats holding all statewide positions. Among them was social justice advocate CATHERINE ANN (KATE) BARNARD, who served as commissioner of charities and corrections, even though women could not vote and could hold no other offices.

State government and politics experienced much turbulence in the first few decades. Leaders quickly came to depend on oil-production taxes as a principal source of revenue when the Glenn Pool and Cushing-Drumright fields began leading the nation in production. Despite this prosperity, from 1910 to 1917,

Oklahoma had the strongest Socialist party in the United States, bolstered by desperately poor tenant farmers. The rabid patriotism of World War I and the hysteria of the Red Scare destroyed the Socialists' influence and ushered in the disruptive 1920s, during which the KU KLUX KLAN thrived. Indicative of this trend, one of the nation's worst race riots erupted in Tulsa in 1921. Later in the decade, the state legislature ousted Governors Jack Walton and Henry S. Johnston in part due to the opposition of the Klan. In 1930, "Alfalfa Bill" Murray returned to Oklahoma after a colonization attempt in Bolivia and won the governorship. The state's most colorful politician, Murray entertained the nation with his use of the national guard and martial law in such incidents as the dispute with Texas over the opening of free bridges in competition with toll bridges.

An adversary of Franklin D. Roosevelt, Murray opposed many New Deal initiatives, but his successor, Ernest W. Marland, aligned himself with the New Deal and tried to develop similar programs at the state level. Conditions during the Great Depression required such efforts because of the severe suffering of the large number of tenant farmers and because of the extreme drought conditions, which were most severe in the counties of the Panhandle—the heart of the Dust Bowl. Following the national trend, Oklahoma recovered from the Depression during World War II, when Governor Robert S. Kerr, a "self-made" oil man, began leading the state in new directions. Kerr originated several policies and programs that subsequent governors followed. He actively sought to diversify the state's economy and encouraged the development of private industry and the location or expansion of large government installations (such as Tinker Air Force Base near Oklahoma City and Fort Sill at Lawton). Kerr and his successors also emphasized road construction and tourism development.

During the late 1940s, two African American students, Ada Louis Sipuel and George McLaurin, successfully challenged SEGREGATION in landmark cases involving the law school and graduate college at the University of Oklahoma. Like many Southern states, Oklahoma made cosmetic changes in the public schools until forced to desegregate fully in the 1960s. In 1959, Governor J. Howard Edmondson succeeded in repealing prohibition and establishing the state's first civil-service merit system. He and others also tried to attract a variety of new industries to the state, and Tulsa and Oklahoma City both grew partially because of their efforts. Politicians elected by Oklahomans to national office aided in this development. Robert S. Kerr, the wealthy and powerful "uncrowned king of the Senate," and former Speaker of the U.S. House of Representatives Carl Albert, among others, brought federal projects and employment on a large scale to the state. Yet, during the last years of the twentieth century, Oklahoma's economy remained overly dependent on agriculture, mining, and defense industries. Development of the economy and the dilemma of paying for governmental services dominated Oklahoma politics. Especially after the 1960s, Oklahomans increasingly turned to Republican politicians to solve those problems, electing the first two Republican governors and voting for Republican presidential candidates. Voters also began electing women to state offices, although not with the frequency found in other states.

At the close of the twentieth century, Oklahomans looked back over their history with a mix of pride and dissatisfaction. Born at the end of the frontier era, Oklahoma suffered through high farm tenancy, a struggling agriculture, and erratic prosperity in the oil industry. The 1930s brought humiliation caused by images of the Dust Bowl migration and the frequent use of the epithet "Okie." Since then, Oklahomans have preferred to emphasize the state as a place of cowboys and Indians, as movies and literature often depicted it. To be sure, Oklahomans contributed to "high" culture with its Indian ballerinas (Maria Tallchief and Yvonne Chouteau) and its writers (playwright Lynn Riggs, short-story writer George Milburn, and historians John Hope Franklin and Daniel Boorstin). Following World War II, however, citizens of the state self-consciously took even greater pride in athletics (Mickey Mantle, University of Oklahoma football, and gymnast Shannon Miller). Also, country-music artists Garth Brooks, Reba McIntyre, and Vince Gill, among others, elicited pride from most modern-day Sooners. And, at last, state leaders seemed intent on capitalizing on the international interest in American Indians by labeling the state "Native America" in tourism advertisements. Conservative, yet erratic, Oklahoma displays many cultural and economic contradictions found elsewhere in the American West.

—*Kenny L. Brown*

SEE ALSO: Chouteau Family; Native American Peoples: Peoples Removed from the East; Socialism

SUGGESTED READING:

Bryant, Keith L., Jr. *Alfalfa Bill Murray.* Norman, Okla., 1968.

Debo, Angie. *And Still the Waters Run: The Betrayal of the Five Civilized Tribes.* Princeton, N.J., 1940.

———. *Oklahoma: Foot-Loose and Fancy-Free.* Norman, Okla., 1949.

Gibson, Arrell, M. *Oklahoma: A History of Five Centuries.* Norman, Okla., 1981.

Goble, Danney. *Progressive Oklahoma: The Making of a New Kind of State.* Norman, Okla., 1980.

Joyce, Davis D., ed. *"An Oklahoma I Had Never Seen Before": Alternative Views of Oklahoma History.* Norman, Okla., 1994.

Morgan, H. Wayne, and Anne Hodges Morgan, eds. *Oklahoma: New Views of the Forth-Sixth State.* Norman, Okla., 1982.

Scales, James R., and Danney Goble. *Oklahoma Politics: A History.* Norman, Okla., 1982.

Stein, Howard F., and Robert F. Hill, eds. *The Culture of Oklahoma.* Norman, Okla., 1993.

Strickland, Rennard. *The Indians in Oklahoma.* Norman, Okla., 1980.

Wright, Muriel H. *A Guide to the Indian Tribes of Oklahoma.* Norman, Okla., 1951.

OKLAHOMA LAND RUSH

At noon on Monday, April 22, 1889, between forty and fifty thousand eager home-seekers invaded the unassigned lands of the Indian Territory in the present-day state of Oklahoma. Also known as the Oklahoma District, the approximately two million acres opened to settlement by the land run included ten thousand parcels of 160 acres each, located in the center of the Indian Territory. Drawn by the promise of free land and opportunities offered by an area largely devoid of non-Indian settlement, participants quickly staked their claims. By evening, every homestead had been taken, and the towns of Guthrie, Kingfisher, Norman, and Oklahoma City had been established.

Agitation for opening the Oklahoma District began a decade before the land rush. In 1879, two attorneys, ELIAS BOUDINOT, a mixed-blood Cherokee, and T. C. Sears, an employee of the Missouri, Kansas and Texas Railroad, released to newspapers information indicating that treaties signed in 1866 removed several million acres from the domain of the Creek and Seminole tribes. That land qualified for public entry. Their discovery provided the impetus for the "Boomer" movement. Boomers advocated the immediate opening of the unassigned lands to non-Indian settlement. DAVID L. PAYNE, a Kansan and Civil War veteran, became the movement's principal leader. Supported in part by the St. Louis and San Francisco Railroad, Payne recruited settlers and led numerous illegal intrusions into the Oklahoma District during the early 1880s. Federal troops expelled Payne and his colonists, but he used these escapades to gain favorable publicity for settlement of the area. When Payne died in 1884, others, including William L. Couch and Samuel Crocker, continued the Boomer incursions.

The activities of the Boomers and their influential supporters eventually secured action by Congress. Early in 1889, William M. Springer, a congressman from Illinois, introduced an amendment to the Indian appropriations bill providing for the opening of the unassigned lands. Before leaving office in March, President Grover Cleveland signed into law the Indian Appropriations Act of 1889, which included the Springer Amendment. Cleveland's successor, Benjamin Harrison, subsequently issued a proclamation ordering the Oklahoma District open to settlement on April 22, 1889. No evidence exists to indicate that federal officials planned a land rush, but weeks before the opening, eager home-seekers flocked to the region. Three

On September 16, 1893, the United States government opened lands on the Cherokee Outlet for settlement. This illustration by H. Worrall portrays the settlers' mad dash to stake their claims. *Courtesy Library of Congress.*

days before the run, they were permitted to cross surrounding Indian land in order to camp on the border of the Oklahoma District.

When participants flooded into the unassigned lands, they found many claims already taken. "Sooners," settlers who illegally entered the district before the designated time, preempted much of the best farm land or prime locations for town sites. Many Sooners had participated in the Boomer movement or had worked for the Atchison, Topeka and Santa Fe Railroad, which bisected the Oklahoma District. The presence of the Sooners and the problem of claim jumpers prompted confrontations, and current scholarship indicates that incidents of violence occurred more frequently than previously reported. Moreover, many Sooner cases—lawsuits arising from claims and counterclaims to the same tract of land—clogged the courts of the Oklahoma Territory for years. Four more land runs followed the land rush of 1889, opening more of the Indian Territory to permanent non-Indian settlement.

—*William P. Corbett*

SUGGESTED READING:

Agnew, Brad. "Voices from the Land Run of 1889." *Chronicles of Oklahoma* 68 (Spring 1989): 4–29.

Gibson, Arrell M. *Oklahoma: A History of Five Centuries.* Norman, Okla., 1981.

Green, Donald E. "The Oklahoma Land Run of 1889: A Centennial Re-Interpretation." *Chronicles of Oklahoma.* 67 (Summer 1989): 116–149.

Hoig, Stan. *The Oklahoma Land Rush of 1889.* Oklahoma City, Okla., 1984.

Miner, H. Craig. "Cherokee Sovereignty in the Gilded Age: The Outlet Question." *Chronicles of Oklahoma* 71 (Summer 1993): 128.

OLDER, FREMONT

A crusading journalist of the Progressive era, Fremont Older (1856–1935) used his mighty pen to attack corporate excesses and political corruption. Born in Appleton, Wisconsin, Older headed to San Francisco in 1873 and thereafter moved frequently from one newspaper job to the next. After nine years as a nomad newsman, he settled in San Francisco in 1884 working for the *San Francisco Bulletin.* Within a decade, he was named managing editor.

Older attacked his first target, the SOUTHERN PACIFIC RAILROAD, for its policy of paying kickbacks to high-volume freighters while charging exorbitant fees to small farmers. Older's biting editorials spurred Progressive politicians in Washington, D.C., to regulate railroad fees and outlaw price fixing.

The editor then turned to corruption in San Francisco's city government. City boss ABRAHAM (ABE) RUEF controlled all levels of municipal government and, by some estimates, pocketed five hundred thousand dollars in bribes from corporations eager to do business in the city on favorable terms. Older, former mayor JAMES DUVAL PHELAN, and Rudolph Spreckels led the attack on Ruef and his ring, until Older held a secret meeting with President THEODORE ROOSEVELT, who sent his ablest prosecutor FRANCIS JOSEPH HENEY and detective WILLIAM J. BURNS to investigate. The *Bulletin*'s pages reported every indiscretion Heney uncovered, kept the investigation in the public's eye, and lobbied for funds to continue the inquiry. The four-year probe into San Francisco corruption ended with Ruef's conviction on charges of accepting bribes, not from corporate bosses, but from purveyors of prostitution.

Older continued to use his position at the *Bulletin* and later at the *San Francisco Call* to promote his leftist causes. He spent twenty years, for example, trying to get radical labor leader THOMAS JOSEPH MOONEY released from prison. In the end, Older had a kind of epiphany, deciding that the whole system—including the reformers—was corrupt, not just Abe Ruef and his ilk. When Ruef went to jail, Older worked for his release and asked Ruef for forgiveness. Thereafter, the two became lifelong friends.

—*Patricia Hogan*

SUGGESTED READING:

Davenport, Robert Wilson. "Fremont Older in San Francisco Journalism: A Partial Biography, 1856–1918." M.A. thesis, University of California, Los Angeles, 1969.

Starr, Kevin. *Inventing the Dream: California through the Progressive Era.* New York, 1985.

OLD SHASTA, CALIFORNIA

SEE: Ghost Towns

OLD SPANISH TRAIL

The first direct connection between northern New Mexico and southern California, the Old Spanish Trail was first mentioned in historical records in 1833 when Antonio Armijo followed the route. The "Old Spanish Trail" is a misnomer for a Mexican trail that extended from Santa Fe, New Mexico, up the Chama River valley, through the Four Corners area and southern Utah, to the present-day site of Las Vegas, Nevada. From there, the trail extended into California, crossed the MOJAVE DESERT to Cajon Pass through the

San Bernardino Mountains, and on to the mission of San Gabriel and Los Angeles.

Primarily used to take sheep to the West Coast, the trail reached its apex when gold was discovered in California and New Mexican sheepherders used the opportunity to feed the gold rushers. Probably the most famous of the sheepherders was Chávez, for whom the ravine next to the present-day site of Dodger Stadium was named.

Some emigrants did use the trail, and it is important to note that William Workman's expedition of 1841 traveled over the trail and arrived in San Gabriel within a week after the first emigrant party successfully traversed the more popular OREGON TRAIL that entered California to the north.

The Old Spanish Trail was abandoned for the Whipple route, a more direct, easier, and warmer route to the south. By the 1860s, the Old Spanish Trail was no longer in use.

—Thomas E. Chávez

SUGGESTED READING:

Hafen, LeRoy R., and Anne W. Hafen. *Old Spanish Trail: Santa Fe to Los Angeles.* Glendale, Calif., 1954.

OLIVE, ISOM PRENTICE ("PRINT")

Isom Prentice, or "Print," Olive (1840–1886) was an adventurous cowboy and, at times, a gunfighter. Born in Louisiana, he moved with his family to Williamson County, Texas, at the age of three. During the Civil War, he fought with the Confederate Army at the battle of Shiloh and was captured by the Union Army at Vicksburg. He was eventually set free and settled in Galveston, Texas.

At the end of the Civil War, he worked as a cowhand at his father's place—the Jim Olive Ranch. He drove several large herds of cattle—numbering up to ten thousand—north to markets. The "Olive Pens" became famous in the region. Some, as large as twenty acres, were near Taylor, Texas.

In 1870, Olive killed Dave Fream in a gunfight and was himself seriously injured. The following year, he was again badly wounded in a saloon dispute with Jim Kennedy. In 1875, he and his brother Jay were arrested for trapping a cattle rustler and wounding him.

Olive moved north in search of a better life. He could not escape, however, his life as gunfighter. Wounded in 1876, he witnessed the death of his brother Jay while chasing rustlers. He avenged his brother's death by killing one man and seriously wounding another. In 1879, he was indicted and sentenced to life in prison for second-degree murder in Hastings, Nebraska. Years later, he was released.

Olive had plans to settle in Trail City, Colorado, but was killed in 1886 by Joseph Sparrow, his trail boss, in a dispute over money.

—Fred L. Koestler

SUGGESTED READING:

Chrisman, Harry E. *The Ladder of Rivers: The Story of I. P. (Print) Olive.* Denver, 1962.

OLLOKOT (NEZ PERCÉ)

A war chief among the Nez Percés during the Nez Percé War of 1877, Ollokot (or Ollikut, Ollokut, Ollicot, Olikut, or Alokut ["Frog"], ca. 1845–1877) was the brother of CHIEF JOSEPH (the Younger) and the younger son of Chief Joseph the Elder, leader of the so-called nontreaty Nez Percés, who were effectively dispossessed of their lands by an 1863 treaty revision unilaterally redefining the reservation boundary. The nontreaty Nez Percés repudiated the original treaty and refused to vacate the lands coveted by gold-seeking whites. Armed conflict was nevertheless avoided during the life of Joseph the Elder. On his death, in 1871, Ollokot became war chief among the nontreaty Nez Percés, while Young Joseph, who favored maintaining peaceful relations, concerned himself with civil matters.

While Ollokot and the younger warriors agitated for war, Young Joseph's point of view prevailed until June 1877, when young Nez Percés killed four white settlers and provoked war. Joseph and Ollokot led their people on a six-month, seventeen-hundred-mile flight from the pursuing forces of the U.S. Army and managed to best the army in encounter after encounter. Ollokot particularly distinguished himself by leading successful charges at the battles of White Bird Canyon on June 17, 1877, and Camas Creek on August 19.

The Nez Percés were just forty miles south of the safety of the Canadian border when, exhausted, they decided to camp on the northern edge of the Bear Paw Mountains. It was there on September 30 that forces under the command of NELSON APPLETON MILES attacked. Ollokot was among the first to fall in the Battle of Bear Paw Mountain, which lasted until October 5.

—Alan Axelrod

SEE ALSO: Pacific Northwest Indians Wars

SUGGESTED READING:
Brown, Mark J. *The Flight of the Nez Percé*. Lincoln, Nebr., 1967.

OLMSTED, FREDERICK LAW

Known as the founder of landscape architecture in the United States, Frederick Law Olmsted (1822–1903) was instrumental in the establishment of Yosemite and other Western national parks.

Born in Hartford, Connecticut, Olmsted studied at Yale University but was forced to interrupt his education because of a severe eye ailment. In 1850, he traveled to Europe, a trip that inspired his first book, *Walks and Talks of an American Farmer in England* (1852). Impressed by English public parks, Olmsted used his book to point out the social and humanizing role parks might play in the burgeoning cities of the United States. New York City's politicians were convinced by his argument, and in 1857, Olmsted was appointed superintendent of the embryonic Central Park. His partner, architect Calvert Vaux, won the design competition and Olmsted took on the role of landscape architect-in-chief, modeling Central Park after the informal English gardens of the eighteenth century but ingeniously adapting the design to allow for extensive public use.

Frederick Law Olmsted. *Editors' collection.*

After working as general secretary of the United States Sanitary Commission during the Civil War, Olmsted traveled to California to head the Mariposa Mining Estate in the Sierra Nevada and was particularly impressed by the Yosemite Valley. In 1864, the state appointed him manager of the valley, which had been granted by the federal government to California "for public use, resort, and recreation." In his 1865 influential report on the new state park, Olmsted promoted its value to the people of California and to the nation as a whole. He put forth a cogent exposition and defense of what was at the time a newly emerging idea: the preservation of tracts of great scenic beauty as public property forever protected from private ownership. He bolstered his position with the same arguments he had used to promote urban parks—the scenic beauty of nature was necessary to promote and preserve "the health and vigor of man" and was nurturing, in particular, to the intellect. Moreover, Olmsted argued, if scenic tracts were not preserved, the denizens of modern civilization would have no place to go for relief from the many pressures of this civilization, and the result might well be grave and widespread emotional disorders.

In 1865, Olmsted returned to the East to complete work on Central Park. Its success led to several other important commissions for urban parks, including Prospect Park in Brooklyn, the city parks of Boston, Mount Royal Park in Montreal, major parks in Chicago (as well as the entire suburban community of Riverside near that city), the grounds of the U.S. Capitol in Washington, D.C., the vast Biltmore estate outside of Asheville, North Carolina, and the plan of Stanford University's campus in California.

In 1879, Olmsted resumed his activities in the field of nature preservation. Through his efforts to restore Niagara Falls, which was threatened by erosion and the effects of unregulated tourism, the Niagara Falls State Reservation was established in 1888. Two years later, Western naturalist JOHN MUIR solicited his support in the national park movement. Olmsted was an enthusiastic and eloquent supporter, and he was often quoted in defense of Yosemite and other national parks.

—*Alan Axelrod*

SUGGESTED READING:
Fein, Albert. *Frederick Law Olmsted and the American Environmental Tradition*. New York, 1972.
Roper, Laura Wood. *F. L. O.: A Biography of Frederick Law Olmsted*. Baltimore, 1974.

OLSON, FLOYD BJERSTERNE

Born in Minneapolis, Floyd B. Olson (1891–1936) served as governor of Minnesota from 1931 to 1936—years of the Great Depression, farm protest, and labor unrest. Although nominally a radical Socialist, he drew broad support for his pragmatic policies that paralleled those of the New Deal.

The child of working-class Scandinavian immigrants, Olson studied law and became Hennepin County attorney in 1919, twice winning reelection. The Farmer-Labor party nominated him for governor in 1924 and again—with success—in 1930. Despite controversy surrounding his administration, he was personally popular with voters, and his early death from cancer was widely mourned.

—*Rhoda R. Gilman*

SUGGESTED READING:

Gieske, Millard L. *Minnesota Farmer-Laborism: The Third-Party Alternative.* Minneapolis, Minn., 1979.

Mayer, George H. *The Political Career of Floyd B. Olson.* Minneapolis, Minn., 1951.

OMAHA INDIANS

SEE: Native American Peoples: Peoples of the Great Plains

OMAHA, NEBRASKA

In 1854, promoters established Omaha at a ferry crossing on the Missouri River in the brand-new Nebraska Territory. Omaha owed its rise to the construction of the first transcontinental railroad system, the settlement of the Great Plains, and the building of an agribusiness industry. Throughout Omaha's history, outside decisions had a significant impact on the community. Local interests consistently welcomed outside public and private capital, while at the same time formulating policies designed to achieve economic independence and freedom of action.

Initially, Omaha had trouble competing with other Missouri River towns. Omaha freighting firms suffered serious losses following the panic of 1857, but outfitting for the Pikes Peak gold rush of 1859 brought a change in fortunes. Omaha began to prosper after Eastern interests holding property in the community in 1863 made it the eastern terminal of the UNION PACIFIC RAILROAD's segment of the first transcontinental line. The railroad base was so firm that, despite the national financial panics of 1873 and 1893, Omaha grew from a frontier transportation center into a regional metropolis. Then, the settling of NEBRASKA provided Omaha with a commercial hinterland. A large meat-packing industry, centered in suburban South Omaha and primarily financed by Chicago capital, flourished. A political boss, Thomas Dennison, created a wide-open town with a favorable climate for business.

The population of Omaha grew from 30,518 in 1880 to 214,066 in 1930. For many decades, the leaders of Omaha were native-born Roman Catholics and Protestants. Members of the Roman Catholic Creighton family were important community benefactors. South Omaha became part of Omaha in 1915. The city had a small African American community and a large number of immigrants. Racial tension culminated in the anti-Greek riot of 1909 and the anti-African American courthouse civil disorder of 1919. By the end of the 1920s, however, Omaha had achieved a measure of stability and what local leaders believed was an unlimited future.

—*Lawrence H. Larsen*

SUGGESTED READING:

Chudacoff, Howard P. *Mobile Americans: Residential and Social Mobility in Omaha, 1880–1920.* New York, 1972.

Larsen, Lawrence H., and Barbara J. Cottrell. *The Gate City: A History of Omaha.* Boulder, Colo., 1982.

OÑATE, JUAN DE

Born in Nueva Galica in western Mexico, Juan de Oñate (ca. 1549–1626) capped the efforts of the Spanish to establish a permanent settlement on the upper RIO GRANDE.

Under the Comprehensive Orders for New Discoveries issued by the Spanish crown in 1573, investigation of frontier territories could be undertaken only with official credentials. The orders also specified that, except for the costs of missionaries, explorations would not receive financial support from the government. Oñate, determined to explore the upper Rio Grande, was forced to spend approximately one-half million pesos, a substantial part of his personal fortune, on the expedition. He received permission to establish the expedition in 1595 but was unable to begin his trip until January of 1598.

Moving north in the spring of 1598, Oñate's expedition followed the track of FRANCISCO VÁSQUEZ DE CORONADO and later explorers. Oñate's group crossed the Rio Grande at the site of what would become El Paso in April. Two months later, at a settlement (still extant) of Keresan-speaking Indians near present-day Albuquerque, Oñate claimed the territory for Spain and effected the submission of the Indians. He established his headquarters at the Tewa-speaking pueblo, called San Juan by the Spanish, and then moved across the Rio Grande to Yunge, which he named San Gabriel. That was the only Spanish settlement in New Mexico until 1608, when, after Oñate's departure, settlers moved to the site of Santa Fe, a less crowded and more defensible location.

Oñate had hoped to find access to a strait through North America and a seaport. In addition, he sought treasure in a city known as Quivira, which was in the territory of the Wichita Indians. Oñate's settlers soon became mutinous, and the Indians became hostile. Although Oñate crushed one Indian revolt, the viceroy lost confidence and recalled him in 1606. Acquitted of some allegations regarding his leadership in 1614, Oñate was nonetheless prohibited from returning to New Mexico. He rebuilt his fortune in the mines and returned to Spain in 1621 after the death of his wife. Vindicated by the king, he received a knighthood and became the king's mining inspector.

—Patrick H. Butler, III

SUGGESTED READING:

Hammond, George P., and Agapito Rey, eds. and trans. *Don Juan de Oñate: Colonizer of New Mexico: 1595–1628.* 2 vols. Albuquerque, N. Mex., 1953.

Simmons, Marc. *The Last Conquistador: Juan de Oñate and the Settling of the Far Southwest.* Norman, Okla., 1991.

101 RANCH

SEE: Miller Brothers 101 Ranch Wild West Show

O'NEILL, WILLIAM OWEN ("BUCKEY")

Pioneer Arizonan and hero of the First U.S. Volunteer Cavalry Regiment ("Rough Riders") in the Spanish-American War, William Owen ("Buckey") O'Neill (1860–1898) moved to the Arizona Territory in 1879. In Phoenix, Tombstone, and principally in Prescott, where he ultimately married and made his home, he worked as a newspaper reporter and editor, circuit and probate judge, sheriff, mining and real-estate speculator, developer of the Bright Angel Trail in the Grand Canyon, and Populist party congressional candidate. He was elected sheriff of Yavapai County in 1888 and mayor of Prescott and adjutant general of the Arizona Territory in 1897.

O'Neill was influential in organizing the Arizona contingent of the First U.S. Volunteer Cavalry Regiment, in which he served as a troop captain. In Cuba, he took part in the confused action at Las Guasimas on June 24, 1898, and was killed by a sniper's bullet on July 1, in front of his troops at Kettle Hill, a secondary ridge of the San Juan Hill complex. He is buried at Arlington National Cemetery.

In 1907, a bronze statue "To the Memory of Captain William O. O'Neill" and honoring the Rough Riders was unveiled in front of the Yavapai County Courthouse in Prescott.

—Dale L. Walker

SUGGESTED READING:

Walker, Dale L. *Death Was the Black Horse: The Story of Rough Rider Buckey O'Neill.* Austin, Tex., 1975. (Reprinted as *Buckey O'Neill, The Story of a Rough Rider.* Tucson, Ariz., 1983.)

OPERA

Throughout the period of white settlement of the West, towns of distinction boasted opera houses, although, in most instances, more drama and minstrel shows were performed there than grand opera. While the management's stage offerings depended on the community's proximity to a waterway or railroad, the construction of an opera house was viewed as a crowning achievement in a town's social and cultural maturity, symbolic of its bond with civilization. In San Francisco during the 1850s, impresario Thomas Maguire built a series of opera houses named the Jenny Lind, although the Swedish soprano herself never sang west of the Mississippi River. HORACE AUSTIN WARNER TABOR built an opera house in Leadville, Colorado, in 1879, with money from his Matchless Mine and, two years later, opened a more elaborate opera house in Denver. Less imposing houses were often included on the second floor of a two- or three-story building, with a hotel or other place of business below. Interiors of opera houses were consistently described by the local press as the most lavish in the area, and by early Western standards, they were dazzlingly ornate and, at times, bordered on gaudy.

Itinerant opera companies had limitations, but among the better troupes to play in the early West were the Emma Abbott Grand English Opera Company, the Emma Juch Opera Company, Her Majesty's Opera Company (managed by British impresario James Henry Mapleson), and a number of companies originating in Mexico. Troupes usually offered a good voice or two;

Adelina Patti, Emma Nevada, and Minnie Hauk rank among the famous singers to perform in the West.

The most celebrated opera with a Western setting is Giacomo Puccini's *The Girl of the Golden West,* which premiered at the Metropolitan Opera House in New York on December 10, 1910, with Arturo Toscanini conducting, Emmy Destinn and Enrico Caruso in leading roles, and the composer present for final rehearsals. Of the American operas set in the West, Douglas Moore's *The Ballad of Baby Doe* has been the most popular.

—*Ronald L. Davis*

SUGGESTED READING:

Davis, Ronald L. "Opera Houses in Kansas, Nebraska, and the Dakotas: 1870–1920." *Great Plains Quarterly* 9 (Winter 1989): 13–26.

———. "Sopranos and Six-Guns: The Frontier Opera House as a Cultural Symbol." *The American West* 7 (November 1970): 10–17, 63.

MacMinn, George R. *The Theater of the Golden Era in California.* Caldwell, Idaho, 1941.

Zivanovic, Judith K., ed. *Opera Houses of the Midwest.* Manhattan, Kans., 1988.

OPHIR, UTAH

SEE: Ghost Towns

OPOTHLEYAHOLA (CREEK)

A leader of the Creek Indians, Opothleyahola (1798–1863) was born into the Wind Clan in the Upper Creek town of Tuckabatchee on the Tallapoosa River near its junction with Coosa. He married once and had at least two daughters and one son.

The Upper Creeks, in the early nineteenth century, generally supported the traditionalist side in the factional division over the spread of European civilization among the native people. Although Opothleyahola favored formal education (his son attended the Choctaw Academy), he was a traditionalist who remained illiterate and spoke only Creek. He never converted to Christianity. At the time of TECUMSEH's visit to the South in 1811, Opothleyahola was influenced by the prophets who appeared in the Creek towns. As a result, he fought with the Red Sticks on the British side of the WAR OF 1812 and was among the defeated at Horseshoe Bend (1814).

After the war, Opothleyahola became the speaker for Big Warrior, the leader of the Upper Creeks, and in the 1820s, he opposed the policies of William McIntosh, the mixed-blood leader of the Lower Creeks. When McIntosh, who favored the transfer of Creek lands and removal, was deposed in 1824, Opothleyahola became speaker of the Creek Nation. At the illegal Treaty of Indian Springs (1825), he warned McIntosh of his impending execution.

By 1834, Opothleyahola saw that removal was the only choice, and in 1836, he moved with his people to the Indian Territory, where he settled on the Canadian River.

Although he became a prosperous farmer and slave owner in the West, Opothleyahola continued to champion the old ways. At the outbreak of the Civil War, he favored neutrality but was forced into the conflict by the McIntosh faction of the Lower Creeks who supported the Confederacy. In 1862, in an attempt to bring his supporters safely to the Union lines in Kansas, Opothleyahola fought a brilliant but unsuccessful campaign against Lower Creeks and Confederate troops. He died in Kansas in 1863, defeated and destitute.

—*Bernard W. Sheehan*

SEE ALSO: Native American Peoples: Peoples Removed from the East

SUGGESTED READING:

Bearess, Edwin C. "The Civil War Comes to Indian Territory, 1861: The Flight of Opothleyahola." *Journal of the West* 11 (1972): 9–42.

Green, Michael D. *The Politics of Indian Removal: Creek Government and Society in Crisis.* Lincoln, Nebr., 1982.

White, Christine Schultz. "Opothleyahola, Nationalism, and Creek Politics." Ph.D. diss., Texas Christian University, 1986.

OPUKAHAIA, HENRY (OBOOKIAH)

A native Hawaiian orphaned during the island unification wars of Kamehameha I, Henry Opukahaia (before 1800–1818) sailed to the United States on an American ship in 1809. Taught some English by a American traveler, Opukahaia settled in New Haven, Connecticut, where he studied American subjects and Christian ways. An apt pupil, he attracted the attention of Samuel J. Mills, a leader among Protestants eager to send missionaries overseas. Mills urged Opukahaia to acquire a proper Christian education and then return to his home and preach among his people. The young Hawaiian spent several years perfecting his English and then enrolled in a school run by the AMERICAN BOARD OF COMMISSIONERS FOR FOREIGN MISSIONS at Cromwell, Connecticut.

Opukahaia was an enthusiastic missionary convert, and his teachers were pleased with his devotion. He translated the Book of Genesis into the Hawaiian language and had begun working on a Hawaiian grammar, dictionary, and spelling book. Before he could return to Hawaii, however, Opukahaia died of typhus in 1818. His death inspired the American Board of Commissioners to send missionaries to the Hawaiian Islands as quickly a possible. The first group, which included Hiram and Sybil Moseley Bingham and four American-schooled Hawaiian natives, sailed the following year. Their arrival, and those of the hundreds of missionaries who followed in the next half-century, changed Hawaii forever.

—Patricia Hogan

See also: Missions: Missions in Hawaii

Suggested reading:

Daws, Gavan. *Shoal of Time: A History of the Hawaiian Islands.* Honolulu, Hawaii, 1968.

OREGON

Known as the "Beaver State," Oregon is bounded by Washington, Idaho, Nevada, and California. It is the tenth largest state in geographical size, with an area of 97,073 square miles. Its population in 1990 was 2,853,733 people, making it the twenty-ninth largest state in population. The capital city is Salem. For most of the region's history, Oregonians have depended on its physical features for their livelihood. Among the most important physical features are the Columbia River to the north and the Pacific Ocean to the west, both of which have provided shellfish and floating fish, especially the six species of Pacific salmon; the fertile Willamette Valley between the Coast and the Cascade ranges of mountains; the Coast and Cascade mountain ranges, which are a source of timber; and the Columbia-Deschutes Plateau of central and eastern Oregon, a region that has proved useful for wheat, sheep, and cattle industries. The Rogue River valley to the south has been a mining, fishing, and fruit-raising area.

Oregon's climate varies widely east and west of the Cascade Mountains. On the coast of the Pacific Ocean, the climate is mild, humid, and equable, with an average rainfall of sixty to eighty inches annually. The Willamette Valley has a comparable climate, although the annual rainfall is less: from fifteen inches in the south to between thirty and fifty inches in the north. East of the Cascade Mountains, the climate is drier and colder than in the west, with an annual precipitation ranging from five to fifteen inches.

Native Americans

The aboriginal peoples of Oregon arrived from Siberia at least twelve to fifteen thousand years ago. They eventually disbursed into more than one hundred bands and tribes, each with its own government, social organization, and language. The principal language groups were Athapascan, Salishan, Shastan, Uto-Aztecan, and Penutian. The population of Oregon before the arrival of the Europeans is estimated to have been at least 45,000 people. They were divided into six cultural areas: Lower Columbia River, Pacific Coast, Inland Valley, Klamath Lake, Columbia Plateau, and Great Basin.

Exploration period

The first Europeans to glimpse what is present-day Oregon were Spaniards under the command of Juan Rodríguez Cabrillo and Bartolomeo Ferrelo in 1542. The Spanish were seeking gold and silver and a passageway into the interior of North America. The English privateer Sir Francis Drake may have been off the Oregon coast in 1579, but the evidence is debatable. After 1600, the Spanish sent another expedition to the region, but they temporarily abandoned their explorations because of fears that the English might exploit any passageway to the interior to invade northern Mexico and its valuable silver mines. In the late eighteenth century, there were many explorations of the Oregon Country. By then, Oregon was defined as the entire region between the Rocky Mountains and the Pacific Ocean between 42° and 54° 40' (the northern boundary of Spanish California and the southern boundary of Russian Alaska, respectively). The Spanish continued to search for an interior passageway and to make territorial claims to the region to keep out potential competitors: Russia and Great Britain. Spain carried on a fur trade at Nootka Sound on the western coast of Vancouver Island and established a settlement at Neah Bay. The British government sent Captain James Cook on a naval expedition in 1778 to search for a Northwest Passage, a waterway linking the interior of America to the Pacific Coast. Cook spent only a few weeks in the Oregon Country before sailing on to Alaska and Hawaii. After Cook's death at the hands of the native people of Hawaii, his expedition continued to China, where his men found that the sea-otter furs acquired at Nootka Sound commanded a high price. After a report of the Cook expedition was published in 1784, the "fur rush" to the Oregon Country began. In 1788 and 1792, the American Robert Gray visited the region. During his first trip, he landed on the coast of present-day Oregon at Tillamook Bay before continuing northward on a voyage that would eventually make him the first American to cir-

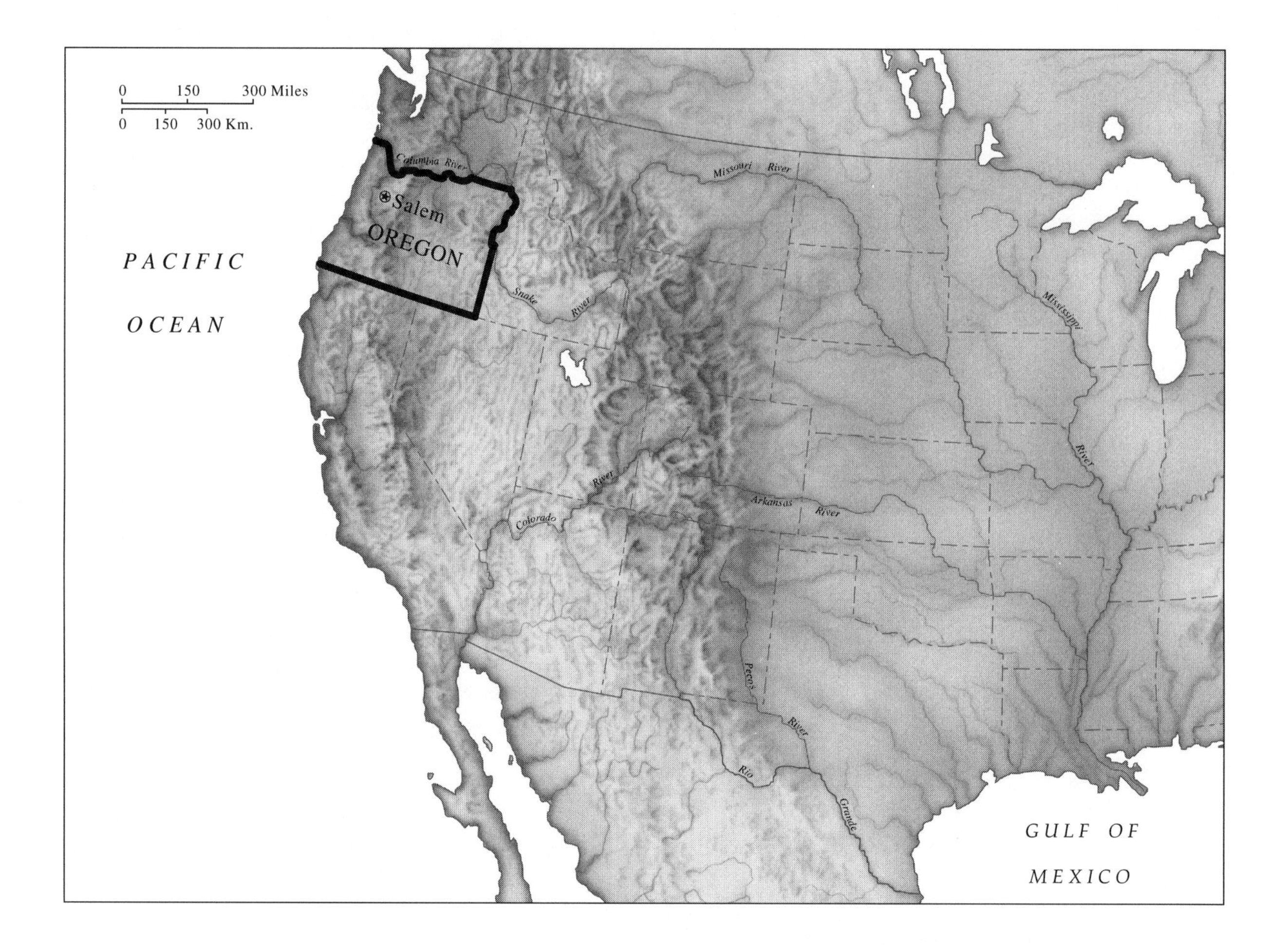

cumnavigate the globe. In 1792, Gray became the first Caucasian to cross the bar of the Columbia River, a feat that helped established a United States territorial claim to the Pacific Northwest. In the same year, George Vancouver, a British naval officer, began a three-year visit to the Oregon Country. What brought him was an incident of three years earlier, when the British and the Spanish almost came to blows over the rights of trade and possession at Nootka Sound. The two governments settled their problems, and Vancouver was dispatched to the Oregon Country to handle the local arrangements of the settlement. He was also commissioned to search again for the Northwest Passage. By 1795, he had thoroughly explored Vancouver Island and its surrounding waters and had laid to rest the idea of a transcontinental water route. The maritime fur trade lasted for only a short time. By the early nineteenth century, the sea otter had been almost exterminated. Traders then trapped the inland beaver.

THOMAS JEFFERSON, as president of the United States, created a large-scale American interest in the region. In 1804, he dispatched MERIWETHER LEWIS and WILLIAM CLARK on an overland military expedition to the mouth of the Columbia River. The thirty-three members of the expedition who completed the journey (including Clark's slave, York; SACAGAWEA, an Indian woman, and her baby; two French Canadian civilians; and twenty-eight soldiers) had four objectives: to find the best commercial route to connect the Missouri and Columbia rivers; to record the main features of the natural environment; to establish economic and political relations with the Native Americans; and to give the United States a claim—by way of an overland expedition—to the Oregon Country to counter those of Britain. All but the first objective were gained to some degree, but Lewis and Clark had to report that the Columbia River route was not adequate to market the furs of the Great Plains and the Rocky Mountains.

By the 1820s, the London-based HUDSON'S BAY COMPANY dominated the beaver trade in the Northwest. In time, many of the French Canadian employees of the company retired to farm in the Willamette Valley where they were joined by America's former mountain men leaving the Rocky Mountains.

Oregon pioneers

Missionaries were also among the first Americans to settle permanently in Oregon. Methodists under JASON LEE came to the Willamette Valley in 1834; Congregationalists and Presbyterians led by MARCUS AND NARCISSA WHITMAN established themselves in southern and eastern Washington and eastern Idaho in 1836; and the first Catholic missionaries came to the Pacific Northwest in 1838. Although enthusiastic and hardworking, the missionaries were not very successful in converting the Indians to Christianity or to Euro-American civilization. The Methodists gave up in 1844, and the Whitman mission at Waiilatpu (near present-day Walla Walla, Washington) was destroyed by the Cayuse Indians in 1847. The Congregationalists and Presbyterians never returned, and the Catholics concentrated their missionary endeavors thereafter in present-day Idaho and Montana. Regardless of the degree of their success, the missionaries did publicize the agricultural and commercial attractions of the Oregon Country to their fellow countrymen in the East. The men and women they influenced came to stay.

Those pioneers were the American farmers who first crossed the OREGON TRAIL from the Missouri River valley to the WILLAMETTE RIVER valley in 1841. Their motives in migrating were varied. Some sought a new beginning after financial ruin during the national depression that began in 1837; others were fleeing personal problems; still others sought adventure; and many were attracted to the mild climate and splendid soil of the Willamette Valley. Their four-to-six-month journey over the two-thousand-mile trail to Oregon necessitated solving many problems: getting along with the other pioneers in the face of boredom and fatigue; facing disease, especially the dreaded cholera; and mastering a natural environment of dusty, treeless, semiarid plains, dangerous rivers, and difficult mountains. To solve their problems, the pioneers relied on faith in God, their own qualities of persistence, and their conservatism. They maintained, as far as possible, their legal systems, gender roles, and elective form of government during their long journey to their new homes. Although the pioneers were worried that the Native Americans would cause difficulties, the tribes, in fact, proved to

Wheat harvesting in Pendleton, Oregon, 1916. *Courtesy National Cowboy Hall of Fame and Western Heritage Center.*

A railway portage near Cehilo on Oregon's Columbia River allowed freight and passengers to travel even where the river was unnavigable. *Courtesy Oregon Historical Society.*

be helpful as guides, suppliers, and ferrymen. The pioneers also had assistance from the U.S. Army, whose forts provided shelter and supplies and whose soldiers patrolled the trails.

Once settled in the new land, the pioneers passed through three forms of government. In 1843, the farmers, missionaries, and some of the French Canadian fur trappers created an informal governmental structure, the Provisional Government, to maintain law and order until the sovereignty question with Great Britain was settled. The government was traditional in form with judicial, legislative, and executive branches. In 1846, the United States and Great Britain drew the present-day boundary of the United States and Canada along the forty-ninth parallel between the crest of the Rocky Mountains and Puget Sound. Two years later, responding to the American settlers in Oregon who feared Indian attacks after the Whitman Massacre, Congress created the Oregon Territory and gave the region's residents limited powers of self-government. However, many soon found the restrictions of territorial status galling, and in 1857, they chose delegates to a convention that drew up a constitution similar in its provisions to those of the constitutions of the Midwestern states. The document prohibited both slavery and the residence of free African Americans, provisions respectively alienating Southerners and Northerners in Congress. At last, however, Congress admitted Oregon as the thirty-third state.

Early statehood

Oregonians voted narrowly in favor of Abraham Lincoln in the presidential election of 1860 and supported the Union cause during the Civil War, although there was a small minority of Confederate sympathizers in the state. Oregon was the state probably least touched by the Civil War. There were no military battles within hundreds of miles of its borders, and few Oregonians went East to serve in either army. One notable exception was United States Senator Edward Baker who died as a member of the Union Army at the Battle of Ball's Bluff.

During the pioneer period, Oregon's economy was based on the export of lumber and wheat. The principal city—because it was located at the confluence of the Columbia and Willamette rivers—was PORTLAND, which has remained the metropolis of the state. Culturally, Oregon has been conservative, with the forms of its cultural institutions such as schools and churches modeled on those of the East and Midwest. Throughout the nineteenth century, the state produced no notable or innovative writers or artists. The ethnic composition of the new state included French Canadians, northern Europeans, Hawaiians, African Americans, and Native Americans, although the last three groups were denied citizenship by the state constitution, and most of the Indians had been forced onto reservations by 1864. Family life was marked by separate spheres of work for most men and women, with women being excluded from the political realm.

After the Civil War, Oregon's economy remained dependent on the export of natural resources. Salmon canning and livestock raising joined lumbering and farming as principal industries. The arrival of the transcontinental Northern Pacific Railroad in Portland in 1883 facilitated commerce and helped diversify the population somewhat, with an increase in numbers of African Americans and Chinese and the introduction of Japanese and peoples from eastern and southern Europe. Politics—marked by keen competition between the Republican and Democratic parties—was controlled by large corporations, especially the SOUTHERN PACIFIC RAILROAD. Cultural life continued to be conservative.

Twentieth-century development

In the twentieth century, Oregon moved forward reluctantly into the modern world. In 1902, voters amended the state constitution to incorporate the initiative and referendum, and shortly afterwards, they added the direct primary, recall of elected officials, and women's suffrage to the constitution. Oregon remained a Progressive state until the 1920s when the reactionary spirit of the postwar years resulted in a law prohibiting Chinese and Japanese from owning land; the temporary rise of the KU KLUX KLAN; and passage of the COMPULSORY SCHOOL BILL (declared unconstitutional by the United States Supreme Court in 1925) that outlawed private and parochial schools. Most Oregonians in the 1930s supported Franklin D. Roosevelt, but Republicans won most of the federal and state elections until after World War II. From then on, the state's politics were bipartisan.

World War II had a great effect on Oregon. Government contracts stimulated the shipbuilding industry under the leadership of HENRY J. KAISER. Many women got their first taste of employment outside the home by working in the shipyards and other wartime industries. The state received thousands of immigrant war workers, including its first sizable contingent of African Americans. Large numbers of Mexican nationals worked in the harvest fields. Japanese and Japanese Americans were sent to relocation camps away from a "war zone" west of the Cascade Mountains. And the financial problems of the Great Depression were swept away.

After the war, the Oregon economy entered into several decades of fluctuating prosperity. Farming, ranching, and forestry remained the major resource-based industries. Economic changes included the new electronics industry and a strengthened tourism industry made possible by postwar affluence. Oregon's exports to foreign nations were also an important factor in its economic prosperity.

Oregonians continued to be concerned with the natural environment and with taxation. Under the leadership of Governor Tom McCall (1967 to 1975), the state adopted a system of statewide land-use planning, the first such system in the country. In addition, the state passed a bottle-deposit law and created the Willamette River Greenway. In the Portland area, which in the 1990s contained about one-half the population of the state, the city acquired improved public transportation, participated in a metropolitan service district, and revitalized neighborhoods. Further efforts to maintain and develop public services have been frustrated by a voter tax revolt that resulted in the defeat of several new tax referenda since 1944 and the passage of a property-tax limitation measure in 1990. Culturally, Oregon has produced one of America's most distinguished architects, Pietro Belluschi; a Pulitzer Prize–winning novelist, H. L. Davis; a nationally acclaimed poet, William Stafford; and an internationally renowned writer of science fiction, Ursula Le Guin. After World War II, the population of Oregon soared and became more diverse ethnically with increasing numbers of Hispanics (who make up the largest minority in the state), African Americans, and Southeast Asians.

Oregon's history has been a quiet one. The state has had little influence in national political affairs; until recently, it depended on a resource-based colonial economy; and it has only produced a handful of nationally recognized cultural figures. Its citizens have been content with an average standard of living, the opportunity to enjoy the natural environment, and a modest level of public services. By and large, the state's residents have placed few demands on themselves and have been content to make a modicum of changes (provided they cost few tax dollars) to preserve their conservative way of life.

—Gordon B. Dodds

SUGGESTED READING:
Beckham, Stephen Dow. *The Indians of Western Oregon: This Land Was Theirs.* Coos Bay, Oreg., 1977.
Dodds, Gordon B. *The American Northwest: A History of Oregon and Washington.* Arlington Heights, Ill., 1986.
———. *Oregon: A History.* New York, 1977.
Faragher, John M. *Women and Men on the Overland Trail.* New Haven, Conn., 1979.
Johansen, Dorothy O. *Empire of the Columbia: A History of the Pacific Northwest.* 2d ed. New York, 1967.
Johnson, David Alan. *Founding the Far West.* Berkeley, Calif., 1992.
Moynihan, Ruth Barnes. *Rebel for Rights: Abigail Scott Duniway.* New Haven, Conn., 1983.
Pomeroy, Earl. *The Pacific Slope.* Lincoln, Nebr., 1992.
Schwantes, Carlos. *The Pacific Northwest: An Interpretive History.* Lincoln, Nebr., 1989.
Zucker, Jeff, Kay Hummel, and Bob Hogfoss. *Oregon Indians: Cultural History and Current Affairs.* Portland, Oreg., 1983.

OREGON BOUNDARY DISPUTE

In the 1840s, the Oregon Country, a vast region west of the Rocky Mountains, played a major role in the diplomatic history of the United States. The Oregon Treaty with Britain on June 15, 1846, settled what had become known as the "Oregon Question." Pending for more than half a century, the dispute originally involved conflicting claims of ownership of this extensive area by Spain, France, Russia, Great Britain, and the United States.

One by one, all but two of the competing powers gave up their claims to the Oregon Country. Spain was there first, and it was a Spaniard, Bruno Hezeta, who sighted the mouth of a mighty river but failed to probe the bay and thus missed making the effective discovery of the Columbia River. In a confrontation at Nootka Sound in 1790, Spain and England abjured settlement

The Oregon Treaty of June 15, 1846, settled the dispute over the United States–Canadian border.

on the Northwest Coast and opened the area to international trade. Spain later surrendered her claims to the Pacific Northwest above 42° north latitude to the United States through the ADAMS-ONIS TREATY of 1819.

The Dane VITUS BERING, sailing for Russia, reached the Aleutians in 1741, a voyage that spawned a lucrative sea otter trade with northern China. From Fort Sitka, in 1796, Russia expanded her influence and, by 1812, had established FORT ROSS on Bodega Bay, a move that revealed Russian designs on San Francisco Bay. Responding to a *ukase* from the czar in 1821 proclaiming Russian sway as far as the 51° north latitude, John Quincy Adams incorporated his noncolonization principle into the Monroe Doctrine, warning Russia off, and the next year a treaty established 54° 40' north latitude as Russia's southern boundary in North America.

JAMES COOK, seeking a Pacific entry to the fabled NORTHWEST PASSAGE, was at Nootka Sound in 1778, and he claimed the Northwest Coast for Britain. Reports from his journal launched the maritime sea-otter fur trade with China. About the same time that George Vancouver was surveying Puget's Sound, Alexander MacKenzie, a Scot, surmounted the Canadian Rockies and reached the Pacific in July 1793, the first white man to cross the continent north of Mexico.

In 1778, lured by the promise of profits from the sea-otter fur trade, ROBERT GRAY was in the vanguard of American approaches to the Northwest Coast. Four years later, on May 11, 1792, Gray discovered the "Great River of the West" and named it Columbia after his ship. Gray did not go up the Columbia, nor did he claim the area for the United States. A few months later, Vancouver's lieutenant, William Broughton, sailed 120 miles up the Columbia and claimed its drainage for Britain.

In 1803, Napoleon sold Louisiana, with its vague western border, to the United States thereby eliminating France as a contender for any part of the Oregon Country and freeing President THOMAS JEFFERSON to dispatch the LEWIS AND CLARK EXPEDITION to the Pacific.

By 1824, Spain, France, and Russia could no longer lay claim to any part of the Oregon territory, and the contest was narrowed to the British and the Americans, who, through a spin-off from the Treaty of Ghent, agreed that the Oregon Country was to be "free and open" to nationals of both countries for ten years.

President John Quincy Adams, in 1824 and again in 1826, sought to negotiate with the British on the basis of extending the boundary at the forty-ninth parallel to the sea but had no success. In 1827, so-called joint occupation was continued indefinitely, subject to termination by either nation with a year's notice.

In the election of 1844, JAMES K. POLK, running on an expansionist platform, defeated his Whig opponent HENRY CLAY. The new president probably wanted all of Oregon, but he followed his predecessors and offered to settle along the forty-ninth parallel. The British ambassador turned down the offer without consulting his superiors. Polk then reasserted his country's right to the whole of Oregon in his annual message to Congress in December 1845. Congress hotly debated the question for five months, and "fifty-four forty or fight" became the expansionist's shibboleth. In point of fact, on the bases of population and use, the British had the stronger position north of the Columbia; the Americans were superior south of the river.

By the spring of 1846, both nations, eager to avoid war, were inclined to compromise. Britain faced the crisis of potato famine in Ireland, and the powerful HUDSON'S BAY COMPANY had moved its headquarters from the northern bank of the Columbia to Vancouver Island in the face of a rising tide of American migration into the Willamette Valley. Americans were anxious to settle the issue because the United States and Mexico were at war.

The Oregon Boundary Treaty of June 15, 1846, extended the boundary along the forty-ninth parallel to the main channel between Vancouver Island and the mainland and through Juan de Fuca Straits to the sea with free navigation of the Columbia and possessory rights to the Hudson's Bay Company honored and paid for. In 1872, thanks to arbitration by Germany, the final boundary line ran down the Canal de Haro to the sea, giving the San Juan Islands to the United States.

A combination of Britain's distresses, the pressure of increasing population in Oregon, and an aggressive president resulted in a resolution of the Oregon boundary dispute favorable to the United States.

—*Edwin R. Bingham*

SUGGESTED READING:

DeVoto, Bernard. *Year of Decision: 1846.* Boston, 1943.

Merk, Frederick. *The Oregon Question.* Cambridge, Mass., 1967.

Miles, Edwin A. "Fifty-four Forty or Fight: An American Political Legend." *Mississippi Valley Historical Review* 44 (1957–1958): 291–300.

OREGON STEAM NAVIGATION COMPANY

Founded in 1860, the Oregon Steam Navigation Company dominated the transportation of goods and gold-seekers along the Columbia and Snake rivers to the gold fields of Idaho. Begun by John C. Ainsworth, SIMEON GANNETT REED, Robert E. Thompson, and others, the company was financed by Western capital and, in its nineteen years of operations, proved to be hugely successful. Not only did it pay out some $4.6 million in profits, it contributed to the development of the community of PORTLAND, OREGON, as a dominant commercial center of the Northwest.

—*Kurt Edward Kemper*

SUGGESTED READING:

Dodds, Gordon. *Oregon: A History.* New York, 1977.

Paul, Rodman W. *The Far West and the Great Plains in Transition, 1859–1900.* New York, 1988.

OREGON TRAIL

Scholars generally consider 1843 the year that marked the opening of the Oregon Trail for emigrant traffic to the Northwest. That year, some 875 settlers trundled along the trail, but it had already been more or less in use for more than three decades. Years before families began moving across the plains, over the Rocky and Blue mountains, and down into the Willamette Valley, explorers, merchants, clergy, and lay missionaries traveled basically the same route west. By 1810, fur trappers and traders had determined and broadcast the geography of the northern Rockies. ANDREW HENRY, trapping alone, may have found and used the South Pass across the Continental Divide in 1811. Late that year and in early 1812, part of JOHN JACOB ASTOR's exploring party under WILSON PRICE HUNT followed the OREGON portion of the trail. In 1818, the British and United States governments agreed to open the Oregon Country to settlement by both nations. Beginning in 1827, they renewed their agreement year-by-year. Meanwhile, traders steadily traveled from the Missouri westward on the route.

Oregon City, the western terminus of the trail, was established in 1829 by JOHN MCLOUGHLIN, chief factor of the British HUDSON'S BAY COMPANY. With his encouragement, a few settlers (many retired fur trappers) soon made their homes in the Willamette Valley. In 1840, the first emigrant families arrived from the east, and in 1843, the Americans in the area met at nearby Champoeg to form a provisional government, despite the fact that the Oregon Country was still open for settlement by both England and the United States.

The first great American promoter of settlement in Oregon, HALL JACKSON KELLEY, organized The American Society for Encouraging the Settlement of Oregon Territory in 1829 in Boston. Among those who joined were NATHANIEL JARVIS WYETH and BENJAMIN LOUIS EULALIE DE BONNEVILLE, both of whom would be instrumental in making the Oregon Trail possible. Although the Hudson's Bay Company's settlements in the Oregon Country demonstrated the feasibility of Kelley's ideas, many who had some practical experience with overland travel (chiefly traders and trappers) were less sure that a major domestic migration was feasible.

Ironically, Native American interests influenced settlement. In the summer of 1834, Methodist minister JASON LEE and his nephew, Daniel, set out for the Oregon Country. Their journey was in response to a visit to St. Louis by three Nez Percés and a Flathead. Evangelical Protestants assumed that the Indians wished to learn the whites' religion. Jason Lee established his mission at Salem, in the Willamette Valley. Samuel Parker—representing the AMERICAN BOARD OF COMMISSIONERS FOR FOREIGN MISSIONS—arrived in St. Louis six weeks after the Lees' departure. With no other parties that he might accompany heading west, Parker went home to upstate New York to drum up support and colleagues for his proposed trip. He recruited Marcus Whitman, a physician eager to enter the mission field, who joined him on an expedition the next summer. In 1836 Whitman, his bride, Narcissa, and the Reverend HENRY HARMON AND ELIZA HART SPALDING set out for the Oregon Country. They had wagons with them, the first to cross the Rockies, and Narcissa Whitman and Eliza Spalding were the first white women to do so.

Geographically, the Oregon Trail began in "jumping-off" communities on or near the MISSOURI RIVER. The earliest, Independence and WESTPORT LANDING, MISSOURI, were already used to supplying parties taking the Santa Fe Trail. As settlement moved northwestward on the river, so did the start of the Oregon trek. The route ran for twelve hundred miles along the Platte and North Platte rivers to Fort Laramie, then up the Sweetwater to the Continental Divide at the almost imperceptible South Pass, then west and northwest to FORT HALL. Most emigrants went south to Raft River, where the California Trail split off, and Oregon-bound emigrants headed west and northwest again.

About eight hundred miles lay ahead. Some emigrants stayed on the north side of the SNAKE RIVER west of Fort Hall; others crossed the Snake at Three-Island Crossing. Both options involved crossing the Snake again after the river turned north. Emigrants could stay on the south side of the river—an alternate lacking much potable water—to join the main route west of the Snake. A single route led past Farewell Bend of the Snake and across dry country to the Blue Mountains. Early emigrants turned north from the Blues to MARCUS AND NARCISSA WHITMAN's mission at Waiilatpu and arrived at the Columbia River near Fort Walla Walla.

As new starting points developed, the eastern end of the route began to resemble the unbraided end of a rope. The western half of the Oregon Trail came to look more like a cat's cradle. At first it looped as far north as the Whitman mission; but some travelers, and all of them after the Whitmans' deaths in 1847, remained further south and reached the Columbia about twenty miles upstream from The Dalles. Early emigrants found some way to get down the Columbia from either Fort Walla Walla or The Dalles—at the head of the narrowest, sheerest part of the Columbia Gorge—to FORT VANCOUVER and to Oregon City on the WILLAMETTE RIVER.

Various efforts were made to find alternatives to the dangerous boat ride. In 1845, one thousand or more emigrants followed Stephen Meek on a route that was supposed to lead them straight across the middle of Oregon to the Willamette. Unfortunately, Meek was unfamiliar with most of that country. When his party crossed the dry, dusty, and unmarked high desert to the eastern slopes of the Cascades, its members were forced to turn north, and they regained the Oregon Trail at The Dalles. Also in 1845, at least two parties decided to take substantial quantities of livestock cross country rather than on the scarce and expensive boats downriver. One party was led by the enterprising Samuel Barlow, who, the next year, turned his carved-out route into a toll road that allowed emigrants a passage across the Cascades around Mount Hood. It was really no easier a trip, but at least it did not require finding or building boats. Its use picked up steadily despite the tolls. Reverse migrations into central Oregon, the Columbia Plateau, and Idaho beginning in the 1860s gave Barlow's road new life, and it remained in use as a toll road until 1919.

An alternative to both boats and tolls was created by JESSE APPLEGATE, who had brought livestock west in the Great Migration of 1843, and other early settlers in the Willamette Valley. In 1846, they laid out a route up that valley and then southeastward into the Nevada Desert, where it joined the California Trail. Emigrants were thus offered an easier passage across the Cascades to enter the Willamette Valley at its head. Farther inland, in 1857 a federal survey under Frederick Lander began the serious process of establishing (and improving) the best route west. His namesake road links South Pass to Fort Hall. Goodale's Cutoff, first used by emigrants in 1862, stretches from Fort Hall north of the main Oregon Trail and the Snake on a higher plateau, touches the main route around Boise, and then strikes northwestward to the Snake and overland to Baker City, Oregon. In some places following ancient Native American trails, it became a significant alternate as well as an access route to mining areas.

As the CENTRAL PACIFIC RAILROAD and the Oregon Short Line grew across the landscape, freighters and stage operators developed routes from the railroad to the Oregon Trail. The Kelton Road, which ran northwestward from Kelton, Utah, was the most successful. As settlers moved eastward from the Willamette Valley to eastern Oregon and to Idaho, other routes were developed to supply them from both east and west.

From the beginning of migration, several forts offered emigrants advice, provisions, and simple links to their previous world. Fort Laramie and FORT BRIDGER in present-day Wyoming, Fort Hall and Fort Boise in present-day Idaho, and Fort Walla Walla in present-day Washington were places to "recruit" livestock and resupply wagons, leave messages that might be taken east, and talk with people who had spent more time on the trail. Other sources of information included the guidance provided by such people as former MOUNTAIN MEN and Marcus Whitman, on his return from the east in 1843, and the written information (with maps) available in such sources as JOHN CHARLES FRÉMONT's report of his expeditions in the early 1840s and Samuel Parker's journal, published in 1842.

It is impossible to estimate how many settlers used the Oregon Trail. By 1860, about 53,000 had traveled overland to Oregon—10,000 of them in 1852. Shortly thereafter, gold strikes in Idaho and the beginnings of settlement in central and eastern Oregon created an eastward migration that followed the same routes (though by commercial vessels on the Columbia and Snake). Even into the twentieth century, emigrants who could not afford to use the railroad used historic wagon routes to reach the Northwest.

—*Judith Austin*

SEE ALSO: California Overland Trails; Overland Travel

SUGGESTED READING:

Lavender, David. *Westward Vision: The Story of the Oregon Trail.* New York, 1963.

Unrah, John D., Jr. *The Plains Across: The Overland Emigrants and the Trans-Mississippi West, 1840-1860.* Urbana, Ill., 1979.

ORPHANS

Cholera, accidents, armed conflicts, blizzards: in the American West, the event leaving a child orphaned was only as limited as the possibility for human calamity. Care of orphans varied. First responsibility fell to the extended family, but when an Indian group or Spanish village or Euro-American settlement was decimated by disease or armed attack, traditional patterns collapsed, and outsiders stepped in. Catholic missions provided care for orphans in some instances, and on the Overland Trail, a family or entire wagon train took in orphans. At journey's end, the children were often turned over to those judged more capable or charitable. For example, the seven Sager children, orphaned in 1833, were deposited at the mission of MARCUS AND NARCISSA WHITMAN, and after 1851, some trail orphans went to the San Francisco Orphanage Asylum Society.

In newly settled areas, local relief organizations provided care. These organizations were replaced later with church, state, and private institutions. A few, such as the Cherokee Orphan Asylum in the Indian Territory or San Francisco's Pacific Hebrew Orphan Asylum, served a specific group. Others, such as the State Orphans' Home in Carson City, Nevada, or St. Mary's Orphanage in Galveston, Texas, were less exclusionary. Institutions multiplied with Western settlement after the Civil War. By 1876, Western states had institutions for war orphans and war widows. These women, and their children, were "dependents" who shared an orphan status.

Orphanages differed in outlook. Most state and private orphanages provided education, but those for Native Americans also stressed acculturation. Some orphanages kept children until they were adults. Others sought home placement with early forms of foster care and with indenture (a legal contract binding a minor to a family or employer until the child reached adulthood). Less popular was adoption; French or Spanish codes recognized adoption, but foundations of English common law in most states emphasized guardianship. Into the twentieth century, some states had no adoption laws.

Whites who became guardians of Native American orphans often realized economic gains. Beginning with the allotment treaties of the early 1800s, orphans received individual reserves or trusts sold for their benefit. Taking on the guardian role, whites gained controlling interests of minors' allotments, annuities, and rights to raise cattle on reservations and or rent pasture.

To the West's orphan population were added children and teen-agers from Eastern states. Beginning in the 1850s, New York and Boston charities sent minors to the West. By the late 1860s, the activity (today called the "orphan trains") reached into Kansas, Nebraska, Iowa, Oklahoma, and Texas. By the 1890s, it extended to the West Coast. Of the thousands brought to the West (most of them males), the majority had at least one living parent. Nevertheless, they were labeled "orphans" and treated accordingly. Some were indentured or adopted, but most lived with families without any legal contract. State officials worried that the Eastern children took homes away from orphans housed in state-operated institutions, and partly because Western states protested, orphan trains ended in 1929.

—*Marilyn Irvin Holt*

SUGGESTED READING:

Bremner, Robert H. *The Public Good: Philanthropy and Welfare in the Civil War Era.* New York, 1980.

Holt, Marilyn Irvin. *The Orphan Trains: Placing out in America.* Lincoln, Nebr., 1992.

Mattes, Merrill J. *The Great Platte River Road.* Lincoln, Nebr., 1969.

Schlissel, Lillian. *Women's Diaries of the Westward Journey.* New York, 1982.

OSAGE INDIANS

SEE: Native American Peoples: Peoples of the Great Plains

O'SULLIVAN, TIMOTHY H.

An outstanding field photographer who pioneered the photographic documentation of the Western landscape, Timothy H. O'Sullivan (1840–1882) was born probably in Ireland. As a teenager, he worked in Mathew B. Brady's New York City and Washington, D.C., galleries. During the Civil War, O'Sullivan documented the conflict for both Brady and Alexander Gardner and quickly gained a reputation for battlefield creativity and daring. Dozens of his pieces, including his famous Gettysburg shot, *Harvest of Death,* appeared in Gardner's *Photographic Sketchbook of the Civil War.*

CLARENCE KING selected O'Sullivan in 1867 to serve as the official photographer for the Geological Exploration of the Fortieth Parallel. During several field seasons (from 1867 to 1869 and in 1872), O'Sullivan covered the Great Basin by wagon and horseback, taking hundreds of memorable eleven-by-fourteen-inch and stereopticon photographs. During the winter of 1867 and 1868, he executed the first magnesium-flare photographs underground, in mines beneath Carson City in the Nevada Territory.

In 1870, O'Sullivan photographed the Isthmus of Panama for the Darien Expedition, but the next year he returned to the Southwest with George W. Wheeler's military surveys. Over the next several years, he shot enduring images, particularly in the Grand Canyon, DEATH VALLEY, and Canyon de Chelly. O'Sullivan left the West in 1875 to establish a private photography business in Washington, D.C., and, in 1880, he became the official photographer for the U.S. Treasury Department. A deteriorating tubercular condition forced him to retire from that office in 1881; he died the next year, at the age of forty-one.

O'Sullivan's images of the American West remain distinctive for their stark contrasts of light and dark, for their complex compositions, and for their depictions of the landscape's texture and contour. He produced all of his work with the bulky, time-consuming, and awkward wet-collodion process. His photographs convey the austere vastness of the Great Basin.

Major collections of O'Sullivan's work are held by the Bancroft Library at the University of California, Berkeley, and by the Still Picture Branch of the National Archives and Records Administration in Washington, D.C. Approximately twenty repositories across the nation retain smaller, yet important collections of his photography.

—*David A. Walter*

In 1867, Timothy H. O'Sullivan took the first photographs of underground mines, showing the life of silver miners beneath Carson City in the Nevada Territory. In this image, a miner loads ore onto a cart at the foot of an elevator shaft. *Courtesy National Archives.*

SUGGESTED READING:

Dingus, Rick. *The Photographic Artifacts of Timothy O'Sullivan.* Albuquerque, N. Mex., 1982.

Gardner, Alexander. *Photographic Sketchbook of the Civil War.* New York, 1959.

Horan, James D. *Timothy O'Sullivan: America's Forgotten Photographer.* Garden City, N.Y., 1966.

Paddock, Eric. "One Man's West: The Photography of Timothy H. O'Sullivan." *Colorado Heritage* 2 (1986): 42–47.

Snyder, Joel. *American Frontiers: The Photographs of Timothy H. O'Sullivan, 1867–1874.* New York, 1981.

OTERO, MIGUEL ANTONIO, SR.

New Mexico's third territorial delegate to Congress, Miguel Antonio Otero (1829–1882) was one of the founders of Gross, Kelly and Company, a leading wholesale-merchandising firm in the Southwest, and an early promoter of railroad construction in New Mexico. He was born in the village of Valencia, New Mexico, to Vicente Otero and Gertrudis de Otero, both of Spanish ancestry. Otero attended private and parochial schools as a child and was one of the first native New Mexicans to travel east to the United States for an education. He studied at St. Louis University and graduated from Pingree College in Fishkill, New York. After returning to St. Louis, he studied law and was admitted to the Missouri bar.

In early 1851, Otero returned to New Mexico and entered law practice in Albuquerque. The next year, he was elected to the second New Mexico Territorial Assembly. In 1854, Otero, a Democrat and newly appointed attorney general for the territory, ran for a delegate's seat in the U.S. House of Representatives. Defeated in the election, Otero contested the results before Congress and was selected over José Manuel Gallegos.

Otero was reelected to Congress in 1856 and 1858. While serving his second term, he married Mary Josephine Blackwood of Charleston, South Carolina. The couple had four children, one of whom, Miguel Antonio Otero, Jr., would become governor of the New Mexico Territory.

In 1861, Otero became involved in the mercantile business in Westport Landing (Kansas City), Missouri, and was one of the organizers of Otero, Sellar and Company in 1867. The company followed the expansion of the railroad west from Missouri and later became Gross, Kelly and Company. In the 1870s, Otero was one of the chief promoters of railroads in New Mexico. He became associated with and eventually was a director of the Atchison, Topeka and Santa Fe Rail-

ROAD, which laid thousands of miles of track in New Mexico. Otero was also one of the organizers of the San Miguel National Bank in Las Vegas, New Mexico, and served as its president until his death.

—Maurilio E. Vigil

SUGGESTED READING:

Otero, Miguel Antonio, Jr. *Otero: An Autobiographical Trilogy.* New York, 1974.

Vigil, Maurilio E. "Miguel Antonio Otero." In *Los Patrones: Profiles of Hispanic Political Leaders in New Mexico History.* Edited by Maurilio E. Vigil. Washington, D.C., 1980.

OTERO, MIGUEL ANTONIO, JR.

New Mexico's longest serving territorial governor, Miguel Antonio Otero, Jr. (1859–1944), was born in St. Louis, Missouri. His equally famous father, Miguel A. Otero, Sr., was New Mexico's delegate to Congress and a pioneer industrialist. After attending private schools, the Naval Academy, and Notre Dame University, Otero joined his father's mercantile firm, Otero, Sellar and Company, a leading Southwestern merchandising firm, which became Gross, Kelly and Company. Otero served as clerk, bookkeeper, and cashier for the company. In 1880, he became cashier at the San Miguel State Bank in Las Vegas, New Mexico, where his father was director and president.

Between 1880 and 1890, Otero held several elected and appointed offices in San Miguel County. In 1888, he attended the Republican National Convention and met William McKinley. When McKinley was elected president, he appointed Otero as territorial governor of New Mexico in 1888. Otero held that position under President THEODORE ROOSEVELT and established a reputation as an able executive. His administration of eight years is regarded as the most effective in the sixty-year period of territorial status.

After Otero stepped down as governor, his successor, George Curry, appointed Otero territorial treasurer, a post he held from 1909 to 1911. When New Mexico became a state in 1912, Otero was appointed to the Board of Penitentiary Commissioners and Parole Board and served as its president from 1913 to 1917. From 1917 to 1921, he was U.S. marshal for the Canal Zone District in Panama. A Republican, Otero joined the Progressive coalition that bolted from the Republicans to form the Bull Moose Progressive party. He attended its national convention and was on its central committee. He then joined the Democratic party, served on its national committee from 1920 to 1924, and attended the national conventions in 1920 and 1924. Otero's last public position was as president of the Board of Regents at New Mexico Normal (now Highlands) University from 1923 to 1925.

—Maurilio E. Vigil

SUGGESTED READING:

Coan, Charles F. *A History of New Mexico.* Chicago, 1925.

Otero, Miguel Antonio, Jr. *Otero: An Autobiographical Trilogy.* New York, 1974.

Twitchell, Ralph Emerson. *The Leading Facts of New Mexican History.* Cedar Rapids, Iowa, 1912.

Vigil, Maurilio E. "Miguel A. Otero, Jr." In *Los Patrones: Profiles of Hispanic Political Leaders in New Mexico History.* Edited by Maurilio E. Vigil. Washington D.C., 1980.

OTERO-WARREN, MARIA ADELINA EMILIA (NINA)

Maria Adelina Emilia (Nina) Otero-Warren (1881–1965) was the first Hispanic and the first woman to run for the U.S. House of Representatives. Born in Las Lunas, New Mexico, to an upper-class family, she was educated by tutors and attended an all-girls school and Maryville College of the Sacred Heart in St. Louis, Missouri. Leaving college before graduation, she married Lieutenant Rawson Warren in 1904. She lived in New York City from 1912 to 1914 and worked with the settlement-house movement in the inner-city.

After her mother's death in 1914, Otero-Warren returned to New Mexico to help care for her six half sisters and two brothers. She became involved with the suffrage movement in New Mexico and rose to lead the state chapter of the Congressional Union, the Women's Division of the Republican State Committee for New Mexico, and the Legislative Committee of the New Mexico Federation of Women's Clubs. Typical of Progressive-era women, Otero-Warren served and presided over many state committees on health and welfare reform. With her women's rights activism and her experience in social-welfare work, she gained the support of her politically powerful relatives for appointment as school superintendent in Santa Fe in 1917. She won election to the post in 1918 and remained in office until 1929.

Nominated as the Republican candidate for the U.S. House of Representatives in 1922, Otero-Warren ran a vigorous statewide campaign emphasizing her social activism and Hispanic bilingual heritage. Her candidacy received attention and publicity from many newspapers in the East and the Southwest. During the later days of the campaign, Otero-Warren was accused of misrepresenting her marital status to the public; she was not a widow but had been divorced from Rawson Warren before her political campaign. It seems hard to gauge whether this damaging information caused her to lose the election to Democrat John Morrow; no Republicans were elected in what turned out to be a Democratic sweep.

Otero-Warren decided not to seek higher office after 1922. Instead, she focused on educational and social-welfare issues. In 1936, she wrote *Old Spain in the Southwest,* a collection of romanticized vignettes of the lives and traditional customs of upper-class Hispanics in New Mexico. She worked as a state and federal government appointee and as a real-estate broker in Santa Fe until her death.

—*Elizabeth Salas*

SUGGESTED READING:

Jensen, Joan M. "Disfranchisement Is a Disgrace: Women and Politics in New Mexico, 1900–1940." *New Mexico Historical Review* 56 (1981): 14–19.

Rebolledo, Tey Diana. "Hispanic Women Writers of the Southwest: Tradition and Innovation. In *Old Southwest, New Southwest.* Edited by Judy Nolte Lensink. Tucson, Ariz., 1987.

OTIS, HARRISON GRAY

Conservative publisher of the *Los Angeles Times* newspaper, Harrison Gray Otis (1837–1917) was born near Marietta, Ohio. Descended from the colonial rabble-rouser James Otis, Harrison Gray Otis had scant formal education. After learning the printer's trade as an apprentice and taking some course work at a business college in Columbus, Ohio, he moved to Kentucky. Becoming a member of the newly formed Republican party, he was a delegate to its national convention in 1860.

Otis served with distinction during the Civil War and rose to the rank of lieutenant colonel. He lived in Ohio and Washington, D.C., after the war. In 1876, he moved to Santa Barbara, California, as editor of the *Santa Barbara Press.* Moving to Los Angeles, he acquired part interest in the *Los Angeles Times* in 1882 and then full control of the paper four years later. He remained in this position for the rest of his life. He used the paper as a pulpit of ultraconservative Republicanism and gave frequent voice to his antiunion sentiments. On October 1, 1910, the offices of the newspaper were bombed and twenty employees were killed. Predictably, Otis was a keen supporter of the United States's declaration of war against Spain in 1898 and even served briefly in Cuba as a major general.

In 1914, Otis transferred his interest in the *Times* to his daughter and son-in-law, Marian and Harry Chandler, but continued to function as publisher until his death.

—*Alan Axelrod*

OTO INDIANS

SEE: Native American Peoples: Peoples of the Great Plains

OURY BROTHERS

Virginians by birth, William Sanders Oury (1817–1887) and Granville H. Oury (1825–1891) both made names for themselves in the Arizona Territory of the late nineteenth century. William headed west in the mid-1830s and settled first in Texas. In 1836, he was a volunteer at the ALAMO, but WILLIAM BARRET TRAVIS had sent him to Gonzales, Texas, for reinforcements just before the deadly battle began. After Texas gained its independence, William joined the Texas Rangers and later saw action in the United States–Mexican War. Moving to the Arizona Territory, he worked as a newspaperman and as an overland-stage agent. He served as Tucson's first mayor in 1864. Later, as a rancher, William improved local stock by breeding them with shorthorn cattle.

Granville Oury, although often overshadowed by his older brother, enjoyed success in Arizona politics. He served as a territorial judge and Speaker of the House in the legislature in the mid-1870s. Forgiven for his Confederate sympathies during the Civil War, he served in the U.S. Congress from 1880 to 1884.

—*Patricia Hogan*

OUTLAWS

SEE: Cattle Rustling; Film: The Western; Guerrillas; Gunfighters; Horse Theft and Horse Thieves; Jayhawkers; Law and Order; Literature: Dime Novels, The Western Novel; Lynching; Northfield Raid; O. K. Corral, Gunfight at; Radio and Television Westerns; Social Banditry; Vigilantism; Violence

OVERLAND FREIGHT

Overland freight was the business of transporting goods by wagons prior to the coming of the railroads. Missouri River towns were the starting points for the longest hauls, and overland-freight carriers included large

In the days before the railroads arrived, wagons transported goods to towns and settlements throughout the West. Pictured here are wagons on an old freight road in Montana in 1883. *Courtesy National Cowboy Hall of Fame and Western Heritage Center.*

companies with hundreds of wagons, small operators that ran only several wagons, merchants hauling their own goods, and farmers working in the business part-time.

History

Overland freighting on the Great Plains was pioneered in 1822 by William Becknell, the "father of the Santa Fe trade," when he moved goods from Missouri to Santa Fe, New Mexico. For two decades after Becknell's first trip, the business on the 800-mile Santa Fe Trail from Independence and Westport Landing (Kansas City), Missouri, averaged about eighty wagons and 150 men annually. Traversing much of present-day Kansas, the trail followed the north bank of the Arkansas River to a point about 20 miles upstream from where Dodge City later developed. Whenever adequate water for men and animals was available, freighters forded the Arkansas at that point and worked their way southwestward across the Cimarron Desert. In dry years, they followed the mountain branch of the trail, which crossed the Arkansas at present-day La Junta, Colorado, and then ran southward through Raton Pass.

The Santa Fe trade was eclipsed by a burst of activity on the Platte River route. The federal government's decision to fortify the Platte River Trail (commonly called the Oregon Trail) and the initial movement of Mormons to Utah during the United States–Mexican War created new business for overland freighters. Until the opening of the Kansas and Nebraska territories in 1854, Fort Leavenworth was the usual base for Platte River Trail freighters, who followed the Oregon Trail to Fort Kearny on the Platte.

Settlement in eastern Kansas enabled Atchison to become a major rival of Fort Leavenworth, and the government's decision to send several thousand troops to occupy Utah from 1857 to 1858 made Nebraska City, Nebraska, the most important freighting site. In the spring of 1858, Russell, Majors and Waddell, the army's transportation contractor, moved its depot to Nebraska City, where the shortest route to the Platte began. The company, owned by William Hepburn Russell, Alexander Majors, and William Bradford Waddell, dispatched about nine hundred wagons from Nebraska City to the Salt Lake City vicinity in 1858.

The Colorado gold rush beginning in 1859 proved to be a boon to overland-freight companies. During the Civil War, Indian hostility on the Platte River route stimulated military freighting, and the discovery of gold in Montana as well as the necessity of supplying stagecoach and Pony Express stations added important civilian markets. Overland freighting peaked in 1864 and 1865. Atchison and Leavenworth, Kansas, and Nebraska City and Omaha, Nebraska, were all sources of branch trails leading to the Platte River valley, while Kansas City, Missouri, dominated the Santa Fe trade. With the settlement of Utah, an important freighting trail was developed southwestward to the head of navigation on the Colorado River. Freighting on the Platte River route was doomed by the completion of the Union Pacific line in 1869, but freight wagons were sent northward from Corinne, Utah, to Montana's gold-mining area until the Utah and Northern Railway joined the Northern Pacific Railroad in 1884. The Black Hills gold rush, which opened in 1875, stimulated freighting from Sidney, Nebraska; Cheyenne, Wyoming Territory; and Fort Pierre and Bismarck, Dakota Territory. This wagon trade ended when a railroad from the east reached the Black Hills in 1886.

Nature of the trade

Goods of all types were transported by overland freighters. The wagons used were modeled after the famed Conestoga wagons of southeastern Pennsylvania. They were finished in the typical Conestoga colors—blue box, red wheels, and white canvas or osnaburg cover—but their boxes were flatter than those of the classic Conestogas. The most famous Western freight wagons were those of Espenchied and Murphy, manufactured in St. Louis; the Studebaker, made in South Bend, Indiana; and Schuttlers, produced in Jackson, Michigan. Large wagons usually had a sixteen-foot-long box and a capacity of about two tons, although three-ton loads were sometimes successfully hauled in them.

A full wagon train consisted of twenty-six wagons, the number judged suitable for rapid corralling and other trail maneuvers. Each train was commanded by a wagon master and an assistant, who also served as the unit's clerk. Depending on the animals used—mules or oxen—wagons were driven by muleskinners or BULLWHACKERS. Trains normally had several night herders, so the average crew complement of full trains was about thirty men. The cumbrous wagons advanced about fifteen miles a day—if the trail was dry and firm. The freighting season ordinarily started about May 1, when the grass was long enough to sustain the animals, and lasted until winter, although wintertime freighting was sometimes conducted in terrain without mountains, such as the 525-mile trail from Omaha to Denver.

Compared to steamboating, overland freighting was expensive. In the 1850s and 1860s, new wagons cost about $200 to $300 each, mules another $200 to $300 a span, and oxen about $75 to $150 a yoke. Each wagon usually required three spans of mules or six yokes of oxen. Most freighters used oxen because they were cheaper than mules and could be sustained by grazing, but mules were better for moving fast and for freighting in winter.

Freighting heritage

While they lack the broad appeal of cowboys and stagecoach drivers, overland freighters have figured in shaping the popular image of the West. In 1844, JOSIAH GREGG introduced many Americans to the hardships and drama of freighting with the publication of his *Commerce of the Prairies,* the classic account of the Santa Fe trade. Later, the famous New York journalist Horace Greeley vividly described the immense scope of Russell, Majors and Waddell's operations. Good firsthand accounts of freighting on the Platte River route were written by bullwhackers Julius C. Birge, John Bratt, and WILLIAM HENRY JACKSON.

—*William E. Lass*

SUGGESTED READING:

Birge, Julius C. *The Awakening of the Desert.* Boston, 1912.
Bratt, John. *Trails of Yesterday.* Lincoln, Nebr., 1921.
Greeley, Horace. *An Overland Journey from New York to San Francisco in the Summer of 1859.* New York, 1860.
Gregg, Josiah. *Commerce of the Prairies.* 2 vols. New York, 1844.
Jackson, William Henry. *Time Exposure: The Autobiography of William Henry Jackson.* New York, 1940.
Lass, William E. *From the Missouri to the Great Salt Lake: An Account of Overland Freighting.* Lincoln, Nebr., 1972.
Madsen, Betty M., and Brigham D. Madsen. *North to Montana: Jehus, Bullwhackers, and Mule Skinners on the Montana Trail.* Salt Lake City, 1980.
Settle, Raymond W., and Mary Lund Settle. *War Drums and Wagon Wheels: The Story of Russell, Majors and Waddell.* Lincoln, Nebr., 1966.
Walker, Henry Pickering. *The Wagonmasters: High Plains Freighting from the Earliest Days of the Santa Fe Trail to 1880.* Norman, Okla., 1966.

The business of overland freighting proved a boon to the development of many Western towns. *Courtesy National Cowboy Hall of Fame and Western Heritage Center.*

OVERLAND MAIL COMPANY

Persistent demands for a through mail service to the Pacific Coast culminated in Congress's authorizing a semiweekly overland service in March 1857. With a government subsidy of $600,000 a year, the Overland Mail Company was awarded the contract by the postmaster general. Organized by men having substantial financial and managerial interests in the major express companies—American, National, ADAMS EXPRESS COMPANY, and WELLS, FARGO AND COMPANY—the company included directors JOHN BUTTERFIELD, WILLIAM GEORGE FARGO, and William B. Dinsmore.

The route of the Overland Mail Company started at St. Louis and Memphis. The two routes converged on Fort Smith, Arkansas, and then circuitously arrived at Preston and El Paso, Texas; Tucson and Yuma, Arizona; and Los Angeles and San Francisco, California. The route was almost twenty-eight hundred miles in length. The first stages left from opposite ends of the line on September 25, 1858, and made the trip in just over twenty days.

Frank Leslie's Illustrated Newspaper of October 28, 1858, featured an image of passengers of the Overland Mail Company changing from a stagecoach to a "celebrity wagon." *Courtesy Library of Congress.*

The Overland Mail Company had invested more than $1 million before the first mail was delivered. The aggressive spokesman for the company was its president, John Butterfield, and the line was often referred to in the early years as the "Butterfield Overland Mail," although his name was never incorporated in the official company title, nor did it appear on the side of the Concord coaches making the run.

Other companies developed stagecoach services on a more central route from Missouri to Denver and Salt Lake City and on to the California border. The competing operations had hoped to obtain the overland mail contract. RUSSELL, MAJORS AND WADDELL introduced the PONY EXPRESS to publicize the superiority of the central route to the southerly route used by the Overland Mail Company. Butterfield proposed to meet the challenge by establishing a rival pony express, but Wells Fargo directors who also served on the board of the Overland Mail Company blocked the action to prevent competition. Dissension had already developed because the Overland Mail Company could not repay the start-up loans advanced to it by Wells Fargo. To forestall foreclosure, the board of directors of the Overland Mail Company was reorganized in April 1860 to give the directors and large shareholders in Wells Fargo the majority of seats. Butterfield, weary and ill, was removed from the presidency, and William B. Dinsmore, of Adams Express Company, was elected.

With the outbreak of the Civil War, the Overland Mail Company abandoned its route through Texas and began using the central route. In March 1861, the company received a contract for delivery of a daily overland mail both by stagecoach and by Pony Express. Russell, Majors and Waddell was given a subcontract whereby the Central Overland California and Pike's Peak Express Company operated the stage and Pony Express line east of Salt Lake City. A year later, BEN HOLLADAY, to protect loans he had made, purchased the assets of Overland Mail Company at a foreclosure sale, and from 1862 to 1864, he fulfilled the mail contract.

In 1865, the contracts for the overland-mail service were divided between Holladay's Overland Stage Line, which carried the mail from St. Joseph, Missouri, to Salt Lake City, and the Overland Mail Company, which operated from Salt Lake City to Carson City and Virginia City, Nevada. Continuing an arrangement that had been in effect since 1861, the Overland Mail Company made a subcontract with the Pioneer Stage Company to deliver the mails from western Nevada to Folsom, California.

In 1866, Wells, Fargo and Company took on the responsibility of all transportation and mail service west of the Missouri River. The company had consolidated the interests of the express companies, the Holladay lines, the Pioneer Stage Company, and the Overland Mail Company. The transcontinental railroad was under construction, and Wells Fargo continued to carry the mails between the terminals of the railroad. The completion of the railroad on May 10, 1869, automatically canceled the last overland-mail contract.

The overland-mail service was a great factor in binding the nation together. It ensured the loyalty of the Pacific Coast during the Civil War and was a facilitator of business and commerce on a national scale.

—*W. Turrentine Jackson*

SEE ALSO: Pike's Peak Express Company

SUGGESTED READING:

Conkling, Roscoe P., and Margaret B. Conkling. *The Butterfield Overland Mail, 1857–1869*. Glendale, Calif., 1947.

Jackson, W. Turrentine. "A New Look at Wells, Fargo, Stagecoaches, and the Pony Express." *California Historical Society Quarterly* 45 (1966): 291–324.

OVERLAND STAGE LINE

SEE: Holladay, Ben

OVERLAND TRAVEL

Early overland Euro-American emigrants wandered into California by way of the Southwestern deserts. After 1833, however, they followed a route blazed by

JOSEPH REDDEFORD WALKER, a mountain man from Tennessee. He set out due west from Missouri, took the South Pass through the Continental Divide, proceeded west across the Great Basin, then climbed the Sierra Nevada, and descended into California. By doing so, he blazed the California fork of what would soon be generally called the "Overland Trail" and thereby established the principal overland route gold-seekers and later settlers would follow to the Pacific.

As mobile communities, members of wagon trains elected leaders and assigned tasks according to the skills of each emigrant. They traveled in wagons that varied from hastily modified farm equipment to sturdily built and highly prized prairie schooners—the "covered wagons" destined to become a popular icon of Western migration. The prairie schooner evolved from the CONESTOGA WAGONS, which were originally developed in the Conestoga River valley of Lancaster County, Pennsylvania, and had been conveying settlers and their belongings since the eighteenth century. The prairie schooner could carry a load weighing a ton and a half yet was light enough to be pulled efficiently by a team of oxen. Little more than a simple box on wooden wheels that were fitted with iron tires, the prairie schooner was hardly an elegant conveyance. The design did not include springs. Hickory bows, over which a canvas or cotton cover was stretched, were fitted to the sides of the box and afforded meager but welcome protection for cargo and passengers. However, the wagons were often so full of belongings and provisions that passengers spent much of the journey walking beside the vehicles rather than riding in them.

The key to survival on the trail was the discipline of the wagon-train community. A typical day on the

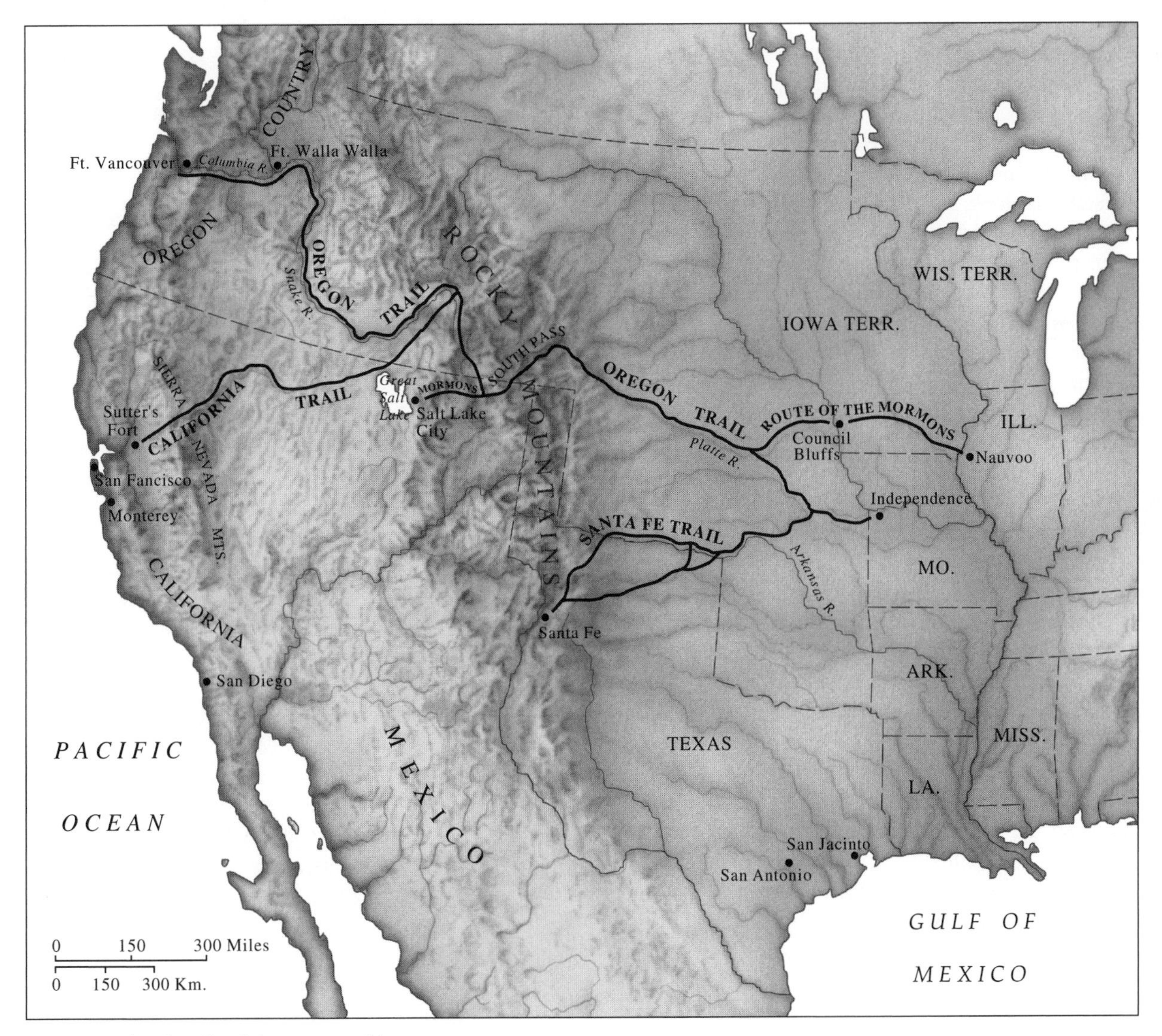

Major overland trails of the westward journey.

The overland journey was more rugged than portrayed in this romanticized illustration of emigrants heading west. *Courtesy Library of Congress.*

trail began with reveille—the discharge of sentinels' rifles at four o'clock in the morning. The stock, which had been set out to graze, was gathered, and teamsters selected their teams of oxen and drove them into a corral—formed by the circled wagons—to be yoked. By seven o'clock, the train was on the move, led by a mounted pilot and his guards. On a good day, over even terrain, the train might progress about fifteen miles.

At nightfall, the drivers made a circle with their wagons to form a stockade, unyoked their oxen teams, and drove them out to pasture. By eight o'clock, there was time for some diversion and then sleep. If the travelers were tempted to grumble about the regimentation, they had only to look along the trail for the hastily dug and rudely marked graves of those who succumbed to one of the many hazards of the journey.

The most immediately formidable hazard was the climate. The plains, reasonably hospitable in every season but winter, were nevertheless subject to severe storms. The deserts, with their merciless heat, were killing grounds. Insects, especially on the prairie, were likewise a plague; the swarms of mosquitoes sometimes made life all but unbearable. While Indians were occasionally hostile, few violent conflicts erupted. The worst killer of all was disease, primarily cholera, which haunted the Overland Trail as it did all the other westering routes. In 1849 alone, it claimed at least fifteen hundred victims on the trail. Other dire ailments included dysentery and scurvy.

Surviving the three- to seven-month journey took discipline, strength, luck, and an ability to endure hard work and tedium. During the years of the California gold rush from 1849 to 1850, most travelers along the trail were men. Perhaps as few as 2 percent of those making the journey were women. As the dream of gold faded, more families, including women and children, used the trail. Women, as might be expected, did the cooking and washing. Just how arduous these activities were on the trail can be gauged by the complaints of the men who had to assume these duties during the gold-rush years, when women were conspicuous by their absence.

Most of those who undertook the overland trek survived, and those who lived through the ordeal were transformed by it: haggard, worn, some reduced to skin and bones. It was enough to persuade many would-be emigrants to choose the sea route around Cape Horn or sea-and-land routes to and across the Isthmus of Panama or to and across central Mexico in order to avoid the overland ordeal.

—*Alan Axelrod*

SEE ALSO: California Overland Trail; Oregon Trail

SUGGESTED READING:

Schlissel, Lillian. *Women's Diaries of the Westward Journey.* New York, 1982. Reprint. 1992.

OWENS, COMMODORE PERRY

Born in Tennessee on the anniversary of Commodore Perry's victory on Lake Erie during the War of 1812, Commodore Perry Owens (1852–1919) lived in Indiana as a child. In the 1870s, he moved to Texas and then drifted through the Southwest. In 1881, he entered Apache County, Arizona, as an experienced gunman with a reputation for honesty, courage, and a deadly aim. Working first as a cowboy and as a manager of a stagecoach station, he was elected sheriff of Apache County in 1886. He was then drawn into the feud between the Grahams and the Tewksburys. Owens attempted to arrest stock thief Andy Blevins, known as Andy Cooper, in Holbrook. A gunfight ensued, leaving Blevins and two others dead. While the Holbrook citizens admired Owens's courage in the incident, they came to fear him and to connect him with the community's bloody history. In 1895, he was elected sheriff of Navajo County and was later named deputy U.S. marshal. He eventually retired from his career as a lawman and spent the remainder of his life running a saloon.

—*Candace Floyd*

SEE ALSO: Graham-Tewksbury Feud

SUGGESTED READING:

Ball, Larry D. *Desert Lawmen: The High Sheriffs of New Mexico and Arizona, 1846–1912*. Albuquerque, N. Mex., 1992.

OWENS-ADAIR, BETHENIA ANGELINA

A physician, feminist, and advocate of eugenical sterilization, Bethenia Angelina Owens-Adair (1840–1926) was born in Van Buren County, Missouri. Her parents moved the family to Roseburg, Oregon, in 1843. One of nine children, Bethenia Owens married farm laborer Legrand Hill when she was only fourteen years old. The marriage failed by 1859, and Owens insisted on making her own living by taking in washing, ironing, and sewing work as well as nursing. By 1861, she had begun teaching and had earned enough money to build her own house in Astoria, Oregon. Subsequently, she returned to Roseburg, where she opened a millinery shop, which developed into a thriving business.

After her son by her marriage to Hill had entered college, Owens embarked on a new career: medicine. In 1873, she traveled to Philadelphia, where she enrolled in the Eclectic School of Medicine—a disreputable institution, but one of the very few in the nation that would accept women as students. After a year of study, which included work with a private tutor and attendance at lectures in Philadelphia's Blockly Hospital, she graduated and returned to Oregon, where she established a practice in Portland. Despite resistance from the male medical establishment, Owens's hydrotherapy (or water cure) practice flourished among women and children. She used a portion of her earnings to finance a full medical education at the University of Michigan, an excellent institution that accepted women. She returned to Portland with a medical degree in 1881 and practiced in Oregon and Washington for the next twenty-five years.

Owens married Colonel John Adair on July 24, 1884, and hyphenated her last name. In addition to her pioneering medical work, Owens-Adair was a leading feminist, an advocate of women's suffrage, and an activist in temperance movement. More controversial was her advocacy of eugenical sterilization. In part through her efforts, legislators of the states of Washington and Oregon adopted bills permitting state-sanctioned sterilization of criminals, epileptics, the insane, and the "feeble-minded." Oregon's bill was vetoed by the governor after the state legislature passed it in 1909 but was reintroduced and enacted in 1925.

—*Alan Axelrod*

SUGGESTED READING:

Owens-Adair, Bethenia. *Dr. Owens-Adair: Some of Her Life Experiences*. Portland, Oreg., 1906.

OWENS VALLEY WAR

Sometime after midnight on May 21, 1924, more than forty residents of California's Owens Valley dynamited the aqueduct some miles north of Lone Pine, one link in the Owens Valley's elaborate waterworks that drained the Owens River to feed water across the Mojave Desert to LOS ANGELES. The Owens Valley War, sometimes called "California's Little Civil War," that they launched had its roots in a dream first envisioned three decades before by Los Angeles's erstwhile Progressive mayor, Fred Eaton, to use the river to quench what he knew, even then, would be the city's thirst for growth in a new century.

As a native-born Los Angeleno, as a chief engineer of the Los Angeles City Water Company in the late nineteenth century, as city engineer, and as mayor, Eaton was the man most responsible for municipalizing the city's water. Eaton's urgings put Los Angeles in the forefront of the nationwide Progressive good-government movement when it created a Board of Water Commissioners that answered to the City Council, which held jurisdiction over commission funds and set municipal water rates. Los Angeles had placed water use, the key to its future, beyond the vagaries of electoral politics, and the water board quickly became a shadow government within the City of Angels. Around Eaton there grew a cabal of Los Angeles movers and shakers who conspired to divert water from the Owens Valley, which lay two hundred miles north of Los Angeles on the other side of the Sierra Nevada.

Chief among Eaton's cohorts in the scheme was WILLIAM MULHOLLAND, a Dublin-born immigrant, who came to the United States as a merchant seaman in 1874 and took a job tending ditches for the Los Angeles City Water Company before working his way up through hard labor and study to become the supervising water engineer for Los Angeles when it municipalized his company. Launching a number of Los Angeles water projects, including the Elysian Reservoir, the Solano Reservoir, the Buena Vista pumping plant, and a tunnel bored directly into the bedrock below the river to collect more ground water, Mulholland was, by early in the twentieth century, arguing publicly that Los Angeles needed a new source of water if the city wanted to keep developing.

Another key player in the Owens Valley controversy was Joseph B. Lippincott, a former employee of Eaton. By 1903, Lippincott had gone to work for the new federal Reclamation Service (later the BUREAU OF RECLAMATION) as its chief of operations in California. The service, an outgrowth of the same Progressive water policies—developed by President THEODORE ROOSEVELT and GIFFORD PINCHOT—that had led to the passage of the NEWLANDS RECLAMATION ACT OF 1902, targeted the Owens Valley as a logical site for one of its earliest and major IRRIGATION projects. The valley's excellent soils and abundant water had attracted many settlers, who brought over forty thousand acres into cultivation in cereals and fruit. It seemed, at first blush, to be a perfect testing ground for the Reclamation Service.

In April 1903, the service's first director, FREDERICK HAYNES NEWELL told Lippincott to survey the valley for a possible RECLAMATION project. In July 1903, Lippincott reported back that the Owens Valley was indeed an ideal spot to launch a major reclamation project and prove the worth of the agency. The Reclamation Service featured the potential Owens Valley Project in its 1903 annual report, and Lippincott himself penned an article on the proposal for the April 1904 issue of *Forestry and Irrigation* magazine. The only trouble was that as an engineering consultant for the Los Angeles area in the 1890s, Lippincott had become fully aware of Frank Eaton's dreams of diverting the water of the Owens River to feed the urban growth of Los Angeles. By 1902, Los Angeles had completed the municipalizing of its water company, which, in turn, allowed the city to issue bonds and raise the kind of public sums that Eaton, now a private investor, hoped would finance an aqueduct from the Owens Valley across the desert to Los Angeles and the southern coast. In Eaton's ambitious scheme, half the water would go to the city for domestic consumption, half would be distributed to irrigation districts and other clients. Los Angeles would grow bigger; Eaton would grow richer.

In August 1904, Lippincott invited Eaton to the Owens Valley on a Reclamation Service–sponsored tour of the site he had selected as the best possible spot for a major dam and reservoir: Long Valley just north of Bishop, where Inyo, Fresno, and Maderia counties intersected. The real purpose of the visit, however, was to warn Eaton that he had better move quickly by laying out the Reclamation Service's plans for the upper valley. Eaton got the point and rushed back to Los Angeles to find William Mulholland and give him a tour of the Owens Valley. During a buckboard ride across the desert from Los Angeles to the Sierra Nevada, Eaton explained the Reclamation Service's designs on the valley to Mulholland and swore him to secrecy. After Mulholland saw the valley, the river, and the reservoir site at Long Valley, he was converted to Eaton's cause. He returned to Los Angeles and met secretly with the Board of Water Commissioners and won its support for what became both his own and Eaton's grand scheme. Board members spread the word to Los Angeles's tight-knit elite, also sworn to secrecy on the theory that Los Angeles needed room to maneuver without alarming valley residents, which might have led to public protests, and without sparking outside interest in the Owens Valley itself, which could set off speculation among others than those in the know. The cabal held, as Lippincott, covering his backside, confidentially informed Newell, in November 1904, that Los Angeles was considering the Owens Valley as a potential water source.

A month later, Newell, Lippincott, Eaton, Mulholland, and William B. Matthews, an attorney for the city, met in Los Angeles to discuss the situation. The Los Angelenos let it be known that they were indeed interested in the Owens Valley but claimed they needed more information. Lippincott offered to turn over all the Reclamation Services studies. Newell made it clear that his service would step aside only on the condition that the Los Angeles Aqueduct be publicly financed, owned, and managed, since the new agency was not about to give up ground unless it was to another public project. Some agreement was obviously reached, since work of the Reclamation Service ceased in the Owens Valley and no mention of the project, so highly touted the year before, appeared in its new annual report.

When Lippincott went on the Los Angeles city payroll as a special consultant to William Mulholland in March of 1905 at half his government salary, Newell reprimanded him, but Lippincott blandly responded that he had the backing of California's U.S. Senator George C. Perkins. Perkins supposedly claimed that since the federal agency was supported by federal funds, it owed whatever consulting services the state and local government wanted. Not only did Lippincott provide Mulholland and company with strategic surveys of the Owens Valley, he gave Eaton a letter of introduction that left the impression the former mayor was buying up property on behalf of a public project. Instead, Eaton, whose plans to participate directly in the finances and revenues of the aqueduct had been dashed by Newell's conditions, needed to purchase options on critical sites for later resale to the city if he was going to realize any kind of profit at all from the deal.

On money advanced him by the city, Eaton operated in secret to purchase lands for the project, making money off the direct resale of some properties to the city and off commissions as agent in other sales. From an initial cash investment of perhaps $15,000, Eaton realized something over $550,000 in a few months, and the elite Los Angeles cabal even had to raise $300,000 from private sources to indemnify the city against its payments to its former mayor. As the Board of Water Commissioners found itself paying out such huge sums from the public treasury in June 1905, reality set in, and they realized they could not keep the matter secret much longer. For the project to work, the interested parties decided, the Reclamation Service would have to cede its claims in the valley publicly to Los Angeles, a bond issue would need to be passed to cover money already paid to Eaton and for future purchases, the aqueduct would have to be planned and designed, and a second bond issue would need floating to cover construction costs.

When the Reclamation Service, in June 1905, announced its intention to withdraw from the valley and the *Los Angeles Times* went public with the entire story, angry Owens Valley ranchers—feeling betrayed by the government and defrauded by Eaton—went looking for the former mayor, who was still in the area purchasing land options. Immediately, however, he fled to San Francisco. As the *Times,* whose owners were part of the cabal, launched a campaign in favor of the bond issues, WILLIAM RANDOLPH HEARST—who was not among those in the know—set his *Examiner* on a crusade to expose the corruption involved in the affair. Mulholland tried to conjure a water crisis in Los Angeles by talking about a ten-year drought that no one else seemed to have noticed. Not only did the *Examiner* dispute Mulholland claims, but it also disclosed that HARRISON GRAY OTIS, owner of the *Times,* and Edwin T. Earl, publisher of the *Los Angeles Express,* were both involved in the syndicates that included a number of prominent citizens (HENRY EDWARDS HUNTINGTON and EDWARD HENRY HARRIMAN among others) who had surreptitiously been buying up land in the San Fernando Valley under the assumption its value would soar once the aqueduct was built. So open were the conflicts of interest that even Water Commissioner Moses Sherman would join one of the two syndicates. After some calls for a full investigation of the whole matter, Los Angeles solved the problem by inviting Hearst into the inner circle and agreeing to submit Mulholland's plans to an independent outside board of review. Hearst personally drafted the editorial in which the *Examiner* endorsed the new bond issues.

By the time the residents of Owens Valley managed to band together to fight the Los Angeles raid on their water, the deal was pretty much done. The Reclamation Service could hardly back out, and since Los Angeles had its support, it also had the support of the Roosevelt administration. Washington touted the project as a great example of Progressive government, one creating public works that offered the greatest good for the greatest number of people. Valley residents, led by the registrar of the U.S. Land Office in the Owens Valley, Stafford W. Austin, and by a U.S. congressman from Bakersfield named Sylvester C. Smith, tried to contain the damage. They tried to introduce federal legislation that allowed Los Angeles access to Owens River water for domestic use but banned its diversion for the irrigation of the San Fernando Valley. Roosevelt intervened personally to have the no-irrigation legislation killed and then declared a stretch of land in the valley—not a single acre of which supported even one tree—a federal forest preserve in order to prevent residents from filing homestead or private claims against land to be used for the aqueduct.

In the long run, however, the panel of outside engineers that convened in 1906 to review Mulholland's elegant designs did far more damage to the residents of Owens Valley than Teddy Roosevelt. Ignoring Mulholland's life-time of study of the Los Angeles River watershed and his years of experience, the experts slashed Mulholland's plans in the name of cost savings. They eliminated three reservoir sites—one at Long Valley in the Owens Valley, the others in the San Fernando Valley—and scratched the municipal railroad Mulholland had planned that would have connected the Owens Valley directly with a growing Los Angeles market.

Instead, they rerouted the aqueduct into the San Fernando Valley by going through the San Francisquito Canyon, which, the experts pointed out, would create three major drops generating enough hydroelectric power to serve Los Angeles, Long Beach, Pasadena, and Santa Monica, thus also generating new public revenues. Mulholland responded that by eliminating the three reservoirs, they had destroyed the storage he considered crucial to maintaining the system year after year, regardless of rainfall, in effect, making the Los Angeles Aqueduct little more than a gigantic diversionary ditch that siphoned the Owens Valley directly. Mulholland blamed Fred Eaton for the loss of the Long Valley reservoir, because Eaton was asking $1 million for twelve thousand strategic acres he owned there. Mulholland reasoned that even if he had persuaded the review board that the storage was essential, members would never have voted to pay Eaton that much money.

Their friendship foundered, and Mulholland built the Los Angeles Aqueduct according to the redesign. He personally supervised the construction from horseback and presided over the opening ceremony on November 5, 1913. As the crowd, ignoring the official program, rushed to taste the water when the spill gates were thrown open, Mulholland quipped, "There it is. Take it." And take it they did—for about a decade. Just as Mulholland had warned the review committee, the Los Angeles Aqueduct had, by the summer of 1923, used up it resources in the Owens River. When, after a long dry spell, it became clear that the aqueduct could no longer serve both urban Los Angeles and the agricultural empire it had annexed in the San Fernando Valley, Mulholland suspended irrigation in the valley and went to work expanding the water sources in the Owens Valley.

Mulholland dug wells and bought water rights from farmers located upriver from the intake point. As those in the Big Pine area began to reap profits, other farmers, looking for a similar windfall and hoping to force Los Angeles to make another major purchase, began to divert water from the Owens River into their own canals before it reached the aqueduct. When desperate San Fernando Valley farmers visited the area to meet with Owens Valley leaders—two local bankers who were brothers, Wilfred and Mark Watterson—they were shocked by the offers they received. Los Angeles, said the Owens Valley farmers, could have the entire upper valley for $8 million. Later accounts would paint the coming conflict as a battle between imperial Los Angeles and local farmers, but that was a war already long lost back in the teens when the city and the federal government had joined forces to create the initial project and suppress local discontent. Now Owens Valley residents wanted to make the best deal they could while they still had enough water to make any deal at all.

Los Angeles rejected the Wattersons' offer, and the Owens Valley War got underway. Los Angeles refused to budge after residents dynamited the aqueduct north of Lone Pine in May 1924. Owens Valley farmers and townspeople, led by Mark Watterson, struck next in the fall. On November 16, 1924, one hundred or so residents descended on the Alabama Gates at Lone Pine and, with the help of a renegade employee, seized the aqueduct and shut off the water, which sent the Owens River flowing back into its dry bed. Over the next four days, the local crowd swelled to fifteen hundred, and a tent city sprang up. Equal parts festival, social protest, and conspiracy, the "war" became a matter of speeches, hymns, and folk songs. As cowboy star Tom Mix, shooting on location, hired a *mariachi* band to entertain the crowd, Wilfred Watterson headed to Los Angeles to hawk the sale of the entire district.

At first the talks went well, and residents called off the occupation at the Alabama Gates. The Owens River once again changed course toward Los Angeles, and the Owens Valley folk celebrated with a barbecue. Then negotiations broke down, and the dynamiting started all over again. Los Angeles sent a private army of perhaps one hundred men into the valley to guard the aqueduct and place the residents under an unofficial and illegal martial law. Despite such measures, valley residents managed to dynamite the aqueduct some ten times over the next two months. Not until a Los Angeles–backed audit of the Wattersons' books by the state banking commissioner revealed that the brothers had evidently embezzled nearly $800,000 did the tide turn against the Owens Valley locals. Five local banks owned by the brothers failed, many residents were ruined, the Wattersons were convicted and sent to prison, and the resistance collapsed.

The next year, 1926, Los Angeles voters passed a $12 million bond issue to buy out the Owens Valley, which also included the purchase from Fred Eaton—who himself had been bankrupted by the local bank failures—of his Long Valley property. The Owens Valley was finished as an agricultural community, and a Los Angeles made skittish by the civil war began increasingly to seek water elsewhere, most notably from the Colorado River. Not quite twenty years later, after a local Roman Catholic priest had helped to revitalize the area as a tourist and recreation center for Los Angeles, the city finally constructed the dam and reservoir at Long Valley that, had it come on line in 1913 instead of 1941, might well have created a project to match the one first imagined by the Reclamation Service in 1903 and the one first designed by William Mulholland in 1907.

—*Charles Phillips*

See also: City Government

Suggested reading:

Kahrl, William. *Water and Power: The Conflict over Los Angeles' Water Supply in the Owens Valley.* Berkeley, Calif., 1982.

Reisner, Marc. *Cadillac Desert: The American West and Its Disappearing Water.* New York, 1986.

Starr, Kevin. *Material Dreams: Southern California Through the 1920s.* New York, 1990.

OXNARD AGRICULTURAL STRIKE

In a unique moment in race and labor relations, the Oxnard Agricultural Strike of 1903 joined Mexican and Japanese laborers in a united, successful stand against their employers and the bosses of the Western Agricultural Contracting Company.

In the midst of Japanese-exclusion movements on the West Coast, Issei (first-generation Japanese immigrant) workers first labored in the sugar-beet fields of Oxnard, California, in 1899. Initially, the workers were hired by Japanese labor contractors, but in 1902, several Oxnard businessmen formed the Western Agricultural Contracting Company (WACC). The company attempted to drive the independent labor contractors out of business and to lower the wages paid to the field workers. It took the company only a year to gain control of about 90 percent of the labor contracts in the sugar-beet industry. At the same time, the WACC cut the wages of workers from $5 per acre to $3.75 per acre.

The workers of Oxnard responded to the wage cuts by organizing the Japanese-Mexican Labor Association (JMLA) in February 1903. The JMLA membership included five hundred Japanese workers and two hundred Mexican workers; they elected a president and a secretary to represent the Mexican branch and another secretary for the Japanese branch. Union meetings were conducted in Spanish and Japanese. In March, the JMLA led its members and about five hundred additional workers in a strike. The strikers demanded increased wages and the right of independent l bor contractors to contract directly with the growers. he strike was a success. Because the strike involved about 90 percent of the labor force, the farmers agreed to increase wages for union members to $5 per acre, and the WACC canceled all but one of its labor contracts. The strike ended after one month.

The Oxnard Agriculture Strike enjoyed the support of organized labor. The JMLA had organized farm laborers, something that had not been done before successfully. The union also was unique in that it brought together workers of different ethnic identities who defined their struggle in terms of the working class against the owner class. The Los Angeles County Council of Labor, for example, supported the union and, specifically, its inclusion of Japanese workers.

When the Mexican secretary of the union petitioned the American Federation of Labor to charter the JMLA as the Sugar Beet Farm Laborers' Union of Oxnard, it was the very unity of the union that became a problem. Samuel Gompers, president of the federation, placed one condition on issuing the union's charter: "Your union will under no circumstances accept membership of any Chinese or Japanese." The JMLA rejected the federation's terms. J. M. Lazarras, secretary of the Mexican branch, responded to Gompers: "We will refuse any other kind of charter, except one which will wipe out race prejudice and recognize our fellow workers as being as good as ourselves." The JMLA continued for a few more years, but in part because it lacked a charter and the support of organized labor, it foundered.

—*Patricia Hogan*

SEE ALSO: Japanese Americans; Labor Movement

SUGGESTED READING:

Almaguer, Tomáas. *Racial Fault Lines: The Historical Origins of White Supremacy in California.* Berkeley, Calif., 1994.

Takaki, Ronald. *Strangers from a Different Shore: A History of Asian Americans.* New York, 1989.

OZAWA V. UNITED STATES

The Supreme Court case *Ozawa* v. *United States* concerned Takao Ozawa, a Japanese immigrant who, after living in California and Hawaii for more than twenty years, sought to become a U.S. citizen. U.S. law limited the right of naturalization to "free white persons" and "to aliens of African nativity and to persons of African descent." Holding that the phrase *white persons* must be interpreted to include only those of the "Caucasian race," the Supreme Court, in its 1922 decision, upheld the lower court, which had denied Ozawa's application. In lower courts, Chinese had been denied the right of naturalization beginning in 1878, and Japanese beginning in 1894. In confirming these precedents, the *Ozawa* decision revealed the racist assumptions that permeated turn-of-the-century U.S. immigration and citizenship policy.

—*Peggy Pascoe*

SEE ALSO: Immigration Law

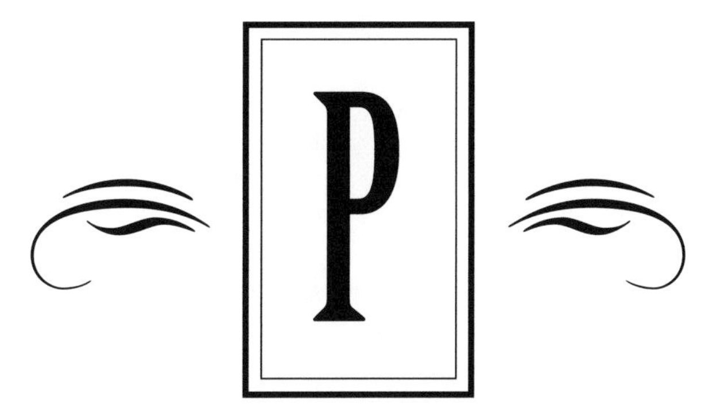

PACIFIC MAIL STEAMSHIP COMPANY

The isolation of the North American Pacific Coast had often proved troublesome for European empires that had established outposts in the region. By the mid-1840s, the United States—whose foreign policy seemed increasingly bent on fulfilling what it considered its manifest destiny to occupy the continent—had begun to look for better and faster means of communication and supply for its fledgling Pacific Coast communities than the overland trails from Missouri or the sea routes around Cape Horn. As international relations grew tense with Britain (over the Oregon settlements) and with Mexico (over U.S. incursions in California and the Southwest), commercial steamship operations that sailed off both the Caribbean and Pacific coasts of Panama and which, in a crisis, could be converted to military uses seemed an attractive solution to many U.S. opinion-makers and politicians.

In 1845, and again in 1847, Congress passed legislation authorizing the U.S. Department of the Post Office to develop mail service to the Far West across the Isthmus of Panama, but the government could find no contractors willing to brave the swampy, pestilence-ridden jungles, despite successful diplomatic negotiations with Britain and an imperial war against Mexico that made both the Oregon and California territories officially part of the United States. Then, in 1848, news that gold had been discovered in California spread rapidly throughout the East, and the isthmus route suddenly seemed worth the risk. Charged by Congress to develop the traffic, the U.S. Navy did better than the Post Office, contracting with William H. Aspinwell to carry passenger and mail service between Panama and Oregon on a monthly basis. Incorporating the Pacific Mail Steamship Company in New York in April 1848, with a capital investment of $500,000, Aspinwell negotiated an annual federal subsidy of nearly $200,000, which was $100,000 less than what the United States Mail Steamship Company got for delivering mail and passengers from New York and New Orleans to Panama.

The Pacific Mail Steamship Company ran three boats out of Panama, the *California,* the *Panama,* and the *Oregon,* all of which became nefarious during the gold rush for their complete inability to handle adequately the crush of Forty-niners who arrived at the isthmus port of Charges demanding passage to the mushrooming metropolis of San Francisco. Tickets, whose prices had been set at $250 for cabin passage and $100 for steerage, brought scalpers huge windfalls. On the maiden voyages of both the *Oregon* and *Panama,* passengers paid $1,000 to suffer in steerage. The prices reflected the draconian choices left to the Forty-niners: long, arduous, weather-plagued, obstacle-ridden, dangerous trips overland or around the Horn or shorter, arduous, weather-plagued, obstacle-ridden, dangerous trips across Panama. Those opting for the latter sometimes found the ocean passage from New York to Charges—depending on how much they paid—comfortable enough. Often, however, the U.S. Mail Steamship Company pressed all-but condemned vessels into service and overbooked even those. But it was at Charges that real hardship began. Argonauts had to bargain with the inhabitants of the mud-hut town for canoe transportation up the Charges River to a point in the middle of the jungle, where the gold-seekers then began a two-day tropical march to Panama City, there to await transportation to California. It was always a long wait, as hundreds of travelers clamored for limited space on the Pacific Mail Steamship Company's limited number of ships. And waiting in a disease-infested tropical city was no picnic; many considered themselves lucky to pay the $1,000 "bribe" for a berth in steerage.

Aspinwell could hardly keep pace with business. He bought the *Tennessee* and a British steamer named the *Unicorn* and put them in service trundling folks to

San Francisco, added the *Fremont* and the *Columbia* to the Oregon run, and built an entirely new steamboat, the *Golden Gate.* During 1849, the company began offering fortnightly sailings to and from both San Francisco and Astoria. By 1850, the company was worth some $2 million and had paid out a 50 percent dividend to stockholders. Not surprisingly, such profits soon led the U.S. Mail Steamship Company to compete for the Pacific leg of the trade. The company's Atlantic service was bad, and it was never much of a financial success, mainly because it had not only to unload the mail at Charges but to transport it laboriously across the isthmus for shipment north via the Pacific Mail Steamship Company.

For a while, the competition was intense and bitter between the two government contractors, but ultimately they reached an agreement to share the business equally as long as they each held on to their mail contracts. Indeed, they were well on the way to establishing a monopoly when railroad magnate "Commodore" Cornelius Vanderbilt decided to enter the business. In 1851, Vanderbilt set up his competing service through Nicaragua, where a picnic atmosphere did prevail as passengers arriving at Greytown from New York and New Orleans were rowed up the San Juan River in light-draft boats to Lake Nicaragua, steamed across to Virgin Bay, carted by carriage and stage over a macadam road to the Pacific Ocean, and then steamboated up the coast. Within a year, Vanderbilt began selling off his Nicaraguan holdings to an American enterprise in which he held part interest, the Accessory Transit Company, which had been constructing the Panama Railroad across the isthmus. When Accessory installed a notorious Tennessee-born filibuster from California named WILLIAM WALKER as president of Nicaragua, Vanderbilt became agitated by Walker's attempts to take control of the railroad, which was completed in 1855, as well as the transit business. Vanderbilt organized the Independent Line, started a rate war against the Nicaraguan Transit Company, and fomented his own local revolution to unseat Walker.

Walker was, indeed, expelled from the presidency in 1857 (he was eventually executed by unfriendly Hondurans), but meanwhile the Nicaraguan Transit Company cooperated with the Pacific Mail Steamship Company and the U.S. Mail Steamship Company to rid themselves of Vanderbilt and his trouble making. They did so by paying him directly to stay out of the business, some $40,000 a month beginning in 1856. By 1859, when U.S. Mail Steamship's original mail contract expired and it withdrew from the isthmus, Vanderbilt's monthly fee had increased to $56,000. Then, Vanderbilt went head to head with Pacific Mail for the new contract and won, which in turn inspired the Panama Railroad to hook up with Pacific Mail in order to compete with Vanderbilt by running steamers on the Atlantic route between New York and Aspinwall, Panama (renamed Colón, Panama). The competition proved expensive for everybody, and within a year, all parties were ready for a truce. After Pacific Mail had agreed to limit its operations to the Pacific and Vanderbilt his business to the Atlantic, the commodore, in late 1860, purchased a huge interest in the Pacific Mail Steamship Company and consolidated his various other interests into a corporation he called the Atlantic and Pacific Steamship Company.

For a decade after the California gold rush, Pacific Mail—unlike U.S. Mail Steamship—had run its passenger and mail service with relative efficiency and had satisfied its government contracts. The company continued to be reasonably prosperous, and in 1865, it bought up Vanderbilt's Atlantic fleet and took over the complete interocean route, expanding its capital and opening up steamship service to China. By the early 1870s, however, the transcontinental railroad—completed in 1869—was eating into its business. Although the company came to rely mainly on its Far Eastern service, because its rates were about half the rail fare from New York to California, Atlantic and Pacific Mail Steamship hung on as the "poor man's" alternative mode of travel to San Francisco for a few years beyond the mid-1870s.

—*Charles Phillips*

PACIFIC NORTHWEST INDIAN WARS

The major warfare between whites and Native Americans in the Pacific Northwest occurred between 1847 and 1876, beginning with the so-called Whitman Massacre and concluding with the Bannock War. The principal conflicts were the Rogue River War (1855 to 1856), the Yakima War (1855 to 1856), the Coeur d'Alene (or Spokan) War (1858), the Modoc War (1872 to 1873), the Nez Percé War (1877), and the Bannock War (1878).

In the wake of the Whitman Massacre

During the winter of 1847, a deadly measles epidemic devastated Cayuse settlements along the Oregon coast. Marcus Whitman, a Presbyterian missionary to the Indians in the vicinity of Waiilatpu, had earned the enmity and resentment of many Cayuse Indians in the region because of his arrogance and contempt for their beliefs. Some came to believe that Whitman was responsible for bringing the measles plague upon them (in fact, he worked indefatigably to care for the sick), and on November 29, 1847, two Cayuse Indians, Tomahas and Chief Tiloukaikt (whose daughter had died earlier that day) called on Whitman. Tomahas struck the missionary down, and he and other Cayuse Indians murdered him. General mayhem ensued, in which about a dozen whites (accounts vary) were slain, including Whitman's wife Narcissa and Helen Meek, the daughter of mountain man JOSEPH LAFAYETTE MEEK.

In the wake of the massacre, Joe Meek prevailed on his cousin-in-law, President JAMES K. POLK, to organize Oregon as a U.S. territory, thereby making it eligible for federal protection. Even more immediately, a firebrand self-appointed colonel of militia, Cornelius Gilliam, led 550 Oregon militiamen on a punitive expedition. No attempt was made to distinguish hostile Indians from the many who had not taken part in the massacre. Gilliam attacked the first Indian camp he found, killed more than twenty Indians, and suffered five casualties among his own number. He then boycotted a peace commission organized by Oregon's new territorial governor and continued indiscriminately killing Cayuse Indians and "appropriating" their livestock. He was soon killed in battle—not by a Cayuse bullet, but by his own clumsiness—when his rifle became entangled in a rope and he self-inflicted a mortal wound. Oregon militia forces continued to stalk the Cayuse Indians during the fall of 1848 and roused the hostility of Walla Wallas, Umatillas, Palouses, and Nez Percés. Fortunately, the militiamen's enthusiasm petered out before full-scale war could erupt.

Isaac Stevens, governor of the Washington Territory in the mid-1850s, played a major role in the hostilities between Native American tribes of the Pacific Northwest and white settlers greedy for Indian lands. *Courtesy Library of Congress.*

Rogue River War

By 1854, violent conflict between Indians and whites in Oregon and extreme northern California had become a terrible routine. General JOHN ELLIS WOOL, commander of the Department of the Pacific, was charged with policing the region. Favoring moderation and reconciliation, he resisted the demands of local citizens to resolve the crisis by annihilating the Indians. Wool's efforts notwithstanding, the violence continued to escalate. Settlers near the Oregon-California border called the local Takelma and Tutuni Indians "rogues" because they frequently attacked travelers along the Siskiyou Trail. In August 1855, a party of drunken "rogues" killed ten or eleven miners along the Klamath River. Local settlers retaliated by killing about twenty-five Indians—although the killers of the miners were not among them; they had fled.

The initial killing and retribution triggered the Rogue River War by September. The army found itself in an unusual position at the outbreak of this conflict—protecting Indians from indiscriminate white hostility. Captain Andrew Jackson Smith, commander of Fort Lane north of the present-day California-Oregon state line, opened the fort to local Indians but not in time to save them from attack by settlers, who killed twenty-three old men, women, and children on October 16. Retribution was swift; the next day, Indian war parties killed twenty-seven settlers in the Rogue Valley and burned the settlement of Gallice Creek.

Captain Smith could do little more than defend his fort and keep it from being overrun. General Wool, with the bulk of army forces, was engaged in fighting the Yakimas. The holding-action strategy—a strategy of necessity rather than intention—proved effective enough. By the spring of 1856, the "rogues," led by chiefs known to the whites as Limpy, Old John, and George, had grown weary of fighting and agreed to surrender at Big Meadows. Whether by design or because they suddenly had a change of heart, the chiefs decided to attack instead of surrender. They threw some two hundred warriors against Captain Smith's fifty

Chikchikam Lupatkue-latko, known to whites as Scarfaced Charley, led an assault against army troops on April 26, 1873. Although the U.S. Army lost several officers and men in the skirmish, it spurred the army on to a relentless pursuit of the Modoc people. *Courtesy National Archives.*

dragoons and thirty infantrymen. Fortunately for Smith, two Indian women informed him of the impending attack, and he was able to take a hilltop position. Nevertheless, in the two days of combat, Smith suffered twenty-five casualties before he was relieved by the eleventh-hour arrival of reinforcements under Captain Christopher C. Augur. Routed, the "rogues" withdrew. Within a month, they surrendered to military authority and submitted to life on a reservation.

The Yakima War

In May 1855, Isaac Stevens, the young and aggressive governor of the Washington Territory, promised the tribes east of the Cascades—the Nez Percés, Cayuses, Umatillas, Walla Wallas, and Yakimas—homes, schools, livestock, and annuities in exchange for the cession of vast tribal lands. A key proviso was that white settlement of the ceded lands would be delayed two or three years after signing the agreement. Representatives of a majority of the tribes involved signed the Stevens treaty, but a minority, including Yakima Chief Kamiakin, refused to sign and protested the folly of placing faith in Stevens's word. Kamiakin did not have to wait long for vindication of his position. A mere twelve days after the treaty was concluded, Governor Stevens threw open the ceded lands to settlement.

Although Indian war leaders are often portrayed as making desperate gestures of resistance, the most common Native American war strategy was to assemble markedly superior numbers before attacking. That is precisely what Kamiakin set about doing. He forged an alliance among the Walla Wallas, Umatillas, Cayuses, and the Yakimas and then set about organizing and planning. Unfortunately for Kamiakin's plan, his young nephew, Qualchin, led a group of five hotheaded braves against a miner's camp and killed six prospectors in September 1855. A. J. Bolen, the local Indian agent who was sent to investigate the incident, was likewise killed.

The murders forced Kamiakin's hand. Instead of expressing contrition, he issued a warning that a similar fate would befall any whites who trespassed east of the Cascades. In October, a force of 84 U.S. Army regulars with a single howitzer under Major Granville O. Haller marched out of Fort Dalles (on the south bank of the Columbia River) and ventured onto the east face of the mountains. Haller intended to coordinate a pincers action against the Indians in concert with a force of fifty men out of Fort Steilacoom (located just below Seattle), led by Lieutenant W. A. Slaughter. Five hundred warriors under Kamiakin ambushed Haller's troops, killed five, and forced the soldiers to retreat to the fort so hastily that they abandoned their artillery piece. For his part, Slaughter received warning of the action and made a night march back to Puget Sound.

With the army on the run, the Yakima coalition raided a settlement along the White River just above Seattle and killed nine settlers. The survivors of the raid fled to Seattle and erected a crude stockade in anticipation of a siege. Slaughter led his men out of hiding and engaged the Indians repeatedly until they finally broke off their attack on Seattle. Slaughter perished in the action.

Governor Stevens, occupied with making more treaties in Montana, received hysterical reports about the Yakima and Rogue River Wars. He quickly dashed through hostile territory back to Washington and threw together a militia company made up of friendly Spokan Indians, which he dubbed the "Spokane Invincibles," and he took personal command of a militia unit of white settlers called the "Stevens Guards." The grandiose names notwithstanding, the combined forces mustered no more than fifty men. Kamiakin's warriors were held at bay by the repeated, albeit inept, ambush attempts of Major Gabriel Rains, commanding a mixed force of regulars and volunteers.

At about this time, Colonel James Kelley led a militia unit into the Walla Walla homelands along the Walla Walla and Touchet rivers. He encountered Walla Walla Chief Peo-Peo-Mox-Mox, who had just burned an abandoned Hudson's Bay Company facility named Fort Walla Walla. The two agreed to a peace parley, and Peo-Peo-Mox-Mox sent one of his men back to the village, ostensibly to communicate the peace terms to the people there. Apparently, however, the messenger was sent with an order to attack. Kelley had anticipated such a move, and, for that reason, held Peo-Peo-Mox-Mox and six other chiefs as voluntary hostages. When what Kelley subsequently described as "hordes" of Indians attacked, he ordered Peo-Peo-Mox-Mox and the others to be bound. "No tie men; tie dogs and horses," the chief protested. According to Kelley's troops, Peo-Peo-Mox-Mox and his captors engaged in a scuffle, the chief produced a dagger, and the militiamen responded by beating out his brains.

In the meantime, the battle consumed four days before the attackers at last fled. The triumphant Oregon militiamen severed the head of the slain Peo-Peo-Mox-Mox and proudly displayed it as a trophy. This brazen act incited the Umatillas and Cayuses to raid local settlements. Raiding activity on February 23 along the lower Rogue River destroyed more than sixty homes and left thirty-one settlers dead. Approximately 130 survivors took refuge near Gold Beach, where they endured a month-long siege as turbulent waters and heavy surf repeatedly foiled rescue attempts by sea.

During all these engagements, Governor Stevens and Oregon's governor, George Curry, argued with General Wool over the conduct of the war. After the governors repeatedly protested that the settlers wanted nothing less than the extermination of all Indians, Wool sent Colonel George H. Wright with five hundred regulars to attack the forces of Chief Kamiakin. By the time Wright caught up with Kamiakin, however, the war fever seems to have subsided.

While the regulars talked of peace, a force of volunteers under militia colonel Benjamin Franklin Shaw soundly defeated Walla Walla and Cayuse warriors in the Grand Ronde Valley. Yet, for Governor Stevens, the final victory of the Yakima War was the removal of General Wool. In May 1857, responding to Stevens's pleas, the War Department removed the old general from command of the Department of the Pacific. Citing his lack of initiative in "punishing" the Indians, the War Department replaced him with Newman S. Clarke.

Coeur d'Alene War

Kamiakin was not finished fighting. He transferred his activities east of the Columbia River and, during 1857 and 1858, attempted to incite a general uprising against settlers and prospectors in the region. Circulating among the Coeur d'Alene and Spokan Indians, Kamiakin told them that the whites were building a great road—the Missouri-to-Columbia Road—directly through their lands. That news was enough to spark another war.

It began with sporadic raids late in 1857. Prospectors at Colville, Washington, petitioned for protection by federal troops. The army responded in May 1858 by dispatching 158 regulars out of Fort Walla Walla under Lieutenant Colonel Edward J. Steptoe. The army action was mainly a public-relations gesture to placate the miners, and Steptoe's men were issued obsolescent arms and marginal supplies. Twenty miles south of the present-day city of Spokane, one thousand warriors intercepted the force and told Steptoe to go home. He was quite willing to comply. But, through the rest of

A family of Bannocks in front of their grass tent in Idaho photographed by William Henry Jackson in 1872—six years before the hostilities between an union of Bannocks, Shoshones, and so-called Sheepeaters and the U.S. Army. *Courtesy National Archives.*

the day and the next, the warriors followed his column and continually taunted the men. On May 17, the Indians killed two officers. Steptoe led his soldiers to a hilltop, where he deployed his only real defensive assets, a few howitzers.

At nightfall, Steptoe realized that his situation was desperate. He met with his surviving officers and told them that he was resolved to fight to the finish. They suggested an alternative strategy: escape. Leaving their artillery behind, the regulars crept in darkness down the hill, circled behind the Indian camp, and marched to the safety of Fort Walla Walla.

Steptoe's humiliation enraged General Clarke, who ordered Colonel Wright to prosecute a vigorous punitive campaign against the hostiles. Some six hundred warriors met Wright (whose forces were augmented by friendly Nez Percés) on Spokane Plain on September 1, 1858, and at Four Lakes on September 5. At such open combat the army regulars excelled, and the Indians were defeated. Wright next sent Major Garnett with a detachment of men, who went from one Indian camp to another to demand the surrender of those who had led the attack on Steptoe. In all, Garnett hanged fifteen Indians and made prisoners of others. In the meantime, Kamiakin, wounded in the Battle of Spokane Plain, escaped to British Columbia. His brother-in-law, Owhi, approached Wright for a parley, only to be taken prisoner. He was forced to summon his son, the war leader Qualchin, whom Wright summarily hanged before his father's eyes. Owhi himself was shot and killed in an escape attempt. The brutality of the retribution for the Steptoe affair thoroughly dispirited the Columbia Basin tribes, who shortly retired to the reservations prescribed by Isaac Stevens's treaties.

Modoc War

The Modocs were a small tribe of perhaps four to five hundred individuals living in the Lost River valley of northern California and southern Oregon. During the 1850s, they harassed emigrants along the Applegate Trail, but by the Civil War, under the influence of Kintpuash—known to the whites as CAPTAIN JACK—they wanted peace and trade with the miners who had come into the region. On one point they would not yield, however. They would not move to the reservation selected for them by white authorities—a reservation already occupied by the Klamath Indians, with whom they were fundamentally incompatible. Through most of the 1860s, the Modocs' refusal to move presented no real conflict, for the lava beds of the Lost River area near Tule Lake were remote and did not attract settlers. But, toward the end of the 1860s, as the pace of settlement dramatically increased, pressure mounted for the removal of the Modocs, and, in December 1869, Superintendent of Indian Affairs Alfred B. Meacham persuaded Captain Jack to move to the reservation.

Within three months, Captain Jack and sixty or seventy Modoc families returned to the Lost River. Meacham's successor as superintendent of Indian affairs, the Reverend Thomas B. Odeneal, recommended removing the Modocs by force. Accordingly, on November 29, 1872, Captain James Jackson led three officers and forty men into Captain Jack's camp to disarm the Indians. A scuffle ensued, resulting in the death of one Modoc and two troopers and the wounding of others. But the Modocs did not move. The army called the exchange the Battle of Lost River.

In the meantime, a group of impatient ranchers decided to take the issue of removal into their own hands and attacked the camp of a Modoc leader known as Hooker Jim. Two ranchers were killed and a third was wounded. The incident prompted Hooker Jim to unite with Captain Jack in resisting the whites, and their combined forces—perhaps sixty warriors—holed up in the lava beds south of Tule Lake, a place the Indians called the "Land of Burnt-Out Fires" and the white authorities now dubbed Captain Jack's "Stronghold."

The army dispatched a force of 225 regulars and 100 militiamen under Lieutenant Colonel Frank Wheaton to attack the Stronghold at dawn on January 17, 1873. Nine troopers were killed, and twenty-eight were wounded. Yet no soldier had even seen the enemy. President Ulysses S. Grant then sent a group of peace commissioners to meet Captain Jack and his followers during March and the beginning of April of 1873. When that action failed to secure peace, Brigadier General EDWARD RICHARD SPRING CANBY, commander of the Department of the Columbia, formed a new peace commission consisting of himself, Methodist minister Eleaser Thomas, former Indian affairs superintendent Meacham, and another official, L. S. Dyar. Negotiations quickly stalled. Captain Jack pointed out that no white would ever want to settle in the lava beds—a point that was true enough, but Canby would not concede victory to the Modocs.

Before negotiations resumed on April 11, 1873, the Modoc wife of Canby's interpreter warned Canby that his life was in danger. He brushed aside the warning. When Canby remained adamant on the issue of removal, Captain Jack shot him at point-blank range. He fell, dead—the only general of the regular army killed during the Indian Wars. Meacham was wounded and the Reverend Thomas slain, but Dyar escaped unharmed.

The murders brought outrage throughout the army, and General-in-Chief WILLIAM TECUMSEH SHERMAN directed that "any measure of severity to the savages will be sustained." Canby's immediate superior, General John M. Schofield, sent a large infantry force under Colonel Alvin C. Gillem to attack, capture, or destroy the Modocs. A concerted attack from April 15 to 17 failed to dislodge the Modocs despite a heavy howitzer assault. The army doggedly pursued the Modocs deeper into the lava beds. On April 26, a party of five officers, fifty-nine men, and twelve Indian scouts was ambushed by twenty-two Modoc braves under Scarfaced Charley. All five officers were killed, as were twenty other men; sixteen lay wounded. "All you fellows that ain't dead," Charley shouted, "had better go home. We don't want to kill you all in one day."

Although the morale of the army suffered, its unrelenting pursuit took a toll on the Modocs. Through the balance of April and May, they were routed out and surrendered. On May 26, Hooker Jim, captured earlier, led a cavalry detachment to the hiding place of Captain Jack, his family, and the balance of the Modoc warriors. Thirty-seven individuals surrendered, but Captain Jack fled. He and his family were captured on June 3 as they hid in a cave. Captain Jack and others—Boston Charley, Black Jim, and Schonchin John—were tried, convicted of murder, and hanged.

Nez Percé War

In 1855, at the so-called Walla Walla Council, Washington's territorial governor Isaac Stevens proposed to the Nez Percés a treaty offering homes, schools, and annuities in exchange for tribal lands. Chief Joseph (the Elder) refused to sign and thereby became leader of a Nez Percé faction known as the nontreaty Nez Percés. A second treaty, in 1863, reduced tribal lands further, and, once again, Chief Joseph refused to sign or to vacate the disputed lands. Few whites were interested in the Wallowa Valley, however, and the nontreaty Nez Percés were left in peace. In 1873, two years after the death of Joseph the Elder, President Ulysses S. Grant set aside part of the Wallowa Valley as a legitimate Nez Percé reservation. However, Grant yielded to pressure from ranchers who wanted the Wallowa Valley as grazing land, and he reopened the region to settlement.

Civil War hero General Oliver Otis Howard headed a negotiating committee charged with convincing the nontreaty Nez Percés to move to the reservation. When negotiations broke down on November 15, 1876, Howard gave the Nez Percés one month to move or face removal by force. Believing war to be fruitless, Chief Joseph the Younger began leading his people to the reservation. However, on June 13 and 14, a group of young and dispirited warriors, bound for the reservation, killed four whites. The incident panicked local settlers, who persuaded Captain David Perry to lead one hundred cavalry troopers to intercept the Nez Percés. At dawn on June 17, as Perry's troopers rested at White Bird Canyon, a delegation of Nez Percés approached under a flag of truce. Despite the flag, a party of volunteers attached to Perry's command opened fire, and a battle began, resulting in the deaths of one-third of Perry's force.

In response to that humiliating defeat, General Howard dispatched some four hundred troopers in pursuit of the Nez Percés. In almost every encounter, the army was outmaneuvered and fought to exhaustion. On August 9, Colonel John Oliver Gibbon, with fifteen officers and nearly two hundred enlisted regulars and volunteers, surprised a Nez Percé camp at Big Hole River, Montana. Led by Looking Glass, the Indians counterattacked, seized the initiative, and killed two of Gibbon's officers, twenty-two of his men, and six civilians. Although Looking Glass lost eighty-nine men, his forces raided the surrounding countryside, fled through the newly established Yellowstone National Park, and terrorized tourists there.

Howard pressed the chase, and the Nez Percés sought haven among the Crow Indians, only to discover that the Crows had served as Howard's scouts. Continuing toward Canada, they came to rest on September 30, 1877, at the edge of the Bear Paw Mountains, just forty miles south of the border. That day, approximately four hundred men under Colonel Nelson Appleton Miles attacked, laying siege to the Nez Percé positions over six snowy, frigid days. Shortly after Looking Glass was felled by a sniper's bullet, Chief Joseph surrendered with a heartbreaking speech concluding, "Hear me, my chiefs! I am tired; my heart is sick and sad. From where the sun now stands, I will fight no more forever." But on July 1, 1877, a combined force of militia and army regulars attacked Looking Glass's camp near the forks of the Clearwater Creek in Idaho.

Bannock War

What caused the Bannock War? That was a question once asked of General George Crook after hostilities were concluded. "Hunger," he answered. "Nothing but hunger."

On May 30, 1878, a Bannock man shot and wounded two settlers. Dutifully, the Bannocks, Shoshones, and so-called Sheepeaters, all assigned to the Lemhi Reservation (and therefore collectively called Lemhis), reported to their agencies, fearful of retribution. But Buffalo Horn, a Bannock who led about two hundred warriors, including Bannocks, Northern Paiutes, and Umatillas, launched a raid in southern Idaho that resulted in the deaths of ten whites. On

June 8, a party of volunteers engaged Buffalo Horn and his warriors near Silver City, southwest of Boise and killed Buffalo Horn. The leaderless warriors retreated to Steens Mountain, Oregon, where they united with Northern Paiutes under a medicine man known as Oytes and a chief called Egan. Together, the new force consisted of some 450 warriors.

General Howard, determined to perform more effectively against these hostiles than he had against the Nez Percés, prepared for a full-scale, vigorous pursuit. To his credit, however, he enlisted the aid of SARAH WINNEMUCCA, daughter of the esteemed Paiute chief, to attempt a negotiation. Inflamed with war fever, the warriors under Oytes and Egan sent Sarah Winnemucca and her father fleeing from Steens Mountain.

What followed was not so much a war as it was a punishing pursuit of scattered forces over some of the most rugged terrain on the North American continent. On September 12, 1878, the last engagement was fought—in Wyoming. Even that did not end all hostile activity. Renegade Sheepeaters, numbering probably no more than thirty-five warriors, continued to raid prospectors' camps in the Salmon River Mountains of Idaho. They were not rounded up until early October, although a number of them, along with many Bannocks, successfully evaded capture and presumably found refuge on the Lemhi Reservation.

—Alan Axelrod

SEE ALSO: Native American Peoples: Peoples of the Pacific Northwest; Whitman, Marcus and Narcissa

SUGGESTED READING:

Axelrod, Alan. *Chronicle of the Indian Wars: From Colonial Times to Wounded Knee.* New York, 1993.

Beal, Merrill D. *"I Will Fight No More Forever": Chief Joseph and the Nez Percé War.* Seattle, Wash., 1963.

Brown, Dee. *Bury My Heart at Wounded Knee: An Indian History of the American West.* New York, 1970.

Debo, Angie. *A History of the Indians in the United States.* Norman, Okla., 1977.

Josephy, Alvin M., Jr. *The Nez Percé Indians and the Opening of the Northwest.* New Haven, Conn., 1965.

Lavender, David. *Land of Giants: The Drive to the Pacific Northwest.* Lincoln, Nebr., 1958.

Murray, Robert M., and Wilcomb E. Washburn. *Indian Wars.* New York. Reprint. Boston, 1977.

Utley, Robert M. *Frontier Regulars: United States Army and the Indian, 1866–1891.* New York, 1973.

PAGE LAW OF 1875

The Page Law of 1875 reflected the anti-Chinese movement, which was rooted in the West but had attracted national support in Congress by the 1870s. Sponsored by Congressman Horace F. Page of California, the act forbade the entry of three groups of immigrants to the United States: Asian laborers suspected of being brought involuntarily to the United States; women brought for the purposes of prostitution; and felons convicted of nonpolitical crimes. While the act had little effect on male Chinese laborers, recent scholarship suggests that it did curb the immigration of Chinese women—both the wives of Chinese laborers and prostitutes. As a result, the law slowed the growth of families in Chinese American communities.

—Lucy E. Salyer

SEE ALSO: Chinese Americans; Chinese Exclusion; Immigration Law

SUGGESTED READING:

Act of March 3, 1875 (18 Stat. 477).

Chan, Sucheng. "The Exclusion of Chinese Women, 1870–1943." In *Entry Denied: Exclusion and the Chinese Community in America, 1882–1943.* Edited by Sucheng Chan. Philadelphia, 1992.

Peffer, George Anthony. "Forbidden Families: Emigration Experiences of Chinese Women under the Page Law, 1875–1882." *Journal of American Ethnic History* 6 (1986): 28–46.

PAIUTE INDIANS

SEE: Native American Peoples: Peoples of the Great Basin

PALACE OF THE GOVERNORS (NEW MEXICO MUSEUM)

The Palace of the Governors was originally constructed as part of Las Casas Reales (the royal houses), with the establishment of Santa Fe as New Mexico's capital in 1610. The building served as the residence and office for sixty-six Spanish governors from 1610 until 1821. Between 1680 and 1693, the royal houses, which lined the town's plaza, were occupied by Pueblo Indians, when they converted the structure into a multistoried pueblo with two plazas. In the late eighteenth century, the royal houses were converted into *el presidio real* (the royal fort), with a parade ground, soldier's quarters, supply rooms, and stables. The new fort extended to the back and west of the present Palace of the Governors.

With Mexican independence in 1821, the old royal fort housed government offices; the governor's residence became *el palacio del gobierno* (the government palace). Seventeen Mexican governors worked in the building. American traders soon mistranslated the name to the "governor's palace."

In 1850, New Mexico became a territory of the United States, and the palace became home and workplace to twenty-three territorial governors. For a period of around six weeks, the palace was occupied by Confederate soldiers during the Civil War.

In 1909, the territorial legislature designated the palace as a museum. The building already housed the School of American Research and the Historical Society of New Mexico. By 1913, the building was remodeled to its current appearance. Today, the Palace of the Governors is the state's history museum with artifact, manuscript, print, and photographic collections spanning New Mexico and Southwestern history. The museum includes galleries, a research library, photographic archives, and a print shop. Programs include lectures, demonstrations, tours, dances, and the portal (porch) venders. The portal-venders program is an Indian-only market where Indian venders sell their handmade goods.

—*Thomas E. Chávez*

SUGGESTED READING:

Arnold, Carrie. "The Museum's Adobe Palace." *El Palacio* 90 (1984).

Shishkin, J. K. *The Palace of the Governors.* Santa Fe, N. Mex., 1972.

PALMER, WILLIAM JACKSON

Founder of the DENVER AND RIO GRANDE RAILROAD, William Jackson Palmer (1836–1909) was born on Kinsale Farm near Leipsic in Kent County, Delaware, and was raised as a Quaker. His antislavery sentiments resulted in his raising the Anderson Troop of cavalry at the beginning of the Civil War. The troop soon expanded to become the Fifteenth Pennsylvania Cavalry.

Leaving the war as a brevet brigadier general, Palmer served as treasurer and a director during the Kansas Pacific Railroad's construction from Wyandotte, Kansas, to Denver, Colorado. Upon his arrival in Denver in 1870, Palmer formed the Denver and Rio Grande Railway, which connected with the Union Pacific at Ogden, Utah, in 1883. The railroad evolved into the Denver and Rio Grande Western Railroad.

William Jackson Palmer. *Courtesy Denver Public Library, Western History Department.*

Along the line of the railroad in Colorado and Utah, Palmer actively founded towns and companies. The most prominent were Colorado Springs and Durango, Colorado, the Colorado Fuel and Iron Company, and the Utah Fuel and Iron Company.

—*Brit Allan Storey*

SEE ALSO: Railroads

SUGGESTED READING:

Fisher, John S. *A Builder of the West: The Life of General William Jackson Palmer.* Caldwell, Idaho, 1939.

Storey, Brit Allan. "William Jackson Palmer: A Biography." Ph.D. diss., University of Michigan, 1969.

PANAMA-PACIFIC INTERNATIONAL EXPOSITION

The 1915 Panama-Pacific International Exposition in San Francisco was a noteworthy successor to its predecessors in London (1851), Paris (1889), Chicago

(1893), and St. Louis (1904). Before its gates closed, it attracted an audience numbering nearly fifteen million and left an indelible imprint on the cultural life of the American West.

As was the case with earlier and subsequent fairs, the San Francisco exposition was organized by an alliance of local civic and corporate leaders with backing from the state and federal government. Prominent exposition sponsors included major railroad corporations, banks, and utilities. The exposition's board of directors, including William H. Crocker, son of one of the builders of the transcontinental railroad, placed overall direction of the fair in the hands of an engineer, Charles C. Moore. Two future U.S. presidents played important roles in promoting the fair: HERBERT HOOVER helped build European interest in the exposition, while Franklin D. Roosevelt served on the national commission set up by Congress to oversee the federal government's involvement in the fair.

Exposition builders saw the fair as the capstone of the effort to rebuild San Francisco after its devastating 1906 earthquake. They also saw the fair as an opportunity to celebrate the opening of the Panama Canal and to promote San Francisco's fortunes as a port of entry for canal traffic. Fair promoters also regarded the exposition as an opportunity to promote tourism to California and to the American West generally. Exposition authorities saw in the Panama-Pacific International Exposition an opportunity to advertise their vision of San Francisco as the apex of a Pacific Rim triangle that entailed closer economic relations with Latin American and Asian countries. Finally, and perhaps most importantly, the civic leaders who underwrote the fair, saw the exposition as a powerful statement about the triumph of Western civilization and the march of national progress across the United States.

The fair included numerous attractions. Dominating the exposition skyline was the Tower of Jewels, with one hundred thousand dangling jewels illuminated by incandescent light. Other architectural features included BERNARD RALPH MAYBECK's Palace of Fine Arts and a stunning array of exhibit palaces devoted to manufacturing, transportation, electricity, mining, and education. In addition, the exposition also included an amusement section, called the "Zone," that featured mechanical rides, ethnic villages, and erotic—by Victorian standards—shows like the "Dream of Venus."

As a window on the evolving history of the American West, the fair provided compelling evidence that the future of the West would be at once urban, international, and closely linked to America's developing culture of consumerism. At the same time, the fair provided equally compelling evidence that the future of the West would be steeped in nostalgia, romance, and hierarchical ways of thinking about people and culture.

—*Robert W. Rydell*

SUGGESTED READING:

Benedict, Burton. *The Anthropology of World's Fairs.* Berkeley, Calif., and London, 1984.

Rydell, Robert. *All the World's a Fair.* Chicago, 1984.

PANAMINT CITY, CALIFORNIA

SEE: Ghost Towns

PANICS

SEE: Financial Panics

PANTHERS

SEE: Mountain Lions

PAPAGO INDIANS

SEE: Native American Peoples: Peoples of the Southwest

PARK, ALICE

A feminist, birth-control advocate, and devout pacifist, Alice Park (1861–1961) was born in Boston, Massachusetts. She attended the Rhode Island Normal School and received her teaching certificate in 1879. In 1884, she and her husband moved west; in 1906, they settled in Palo Alto, California. A Quaker and a Unitarian, Park became an absolute pacifist, joining her first organized peace movement in 1898 to protest the Spanish-American War. She believed organization was the best way to exert moral suasion and used this policy not only in the peace movement but also in the fight for WOMEN'S SUFFRAGE. Traveling in the West and using the forums of the WOMAN'S CHRISTIAN TEMPERANCE UNION in each town she visited, she organized discussion groups on feminism and pacifism. She served as a delegate for the Women's Peace Society as well as on the board of directors of the Women's International League of Peace and Freedom. At times, she seemed to be directing the entire Western peace movement from her home in Palo Alto. When the Unitarian church refused to oppose the United States's entry into World War I, she renounced her membership and joined the Socialist party. She continued to espouse the cause that defined her life until her death.

—*Kurt Edward Kemper*

PARKER, CYNTHIA ANN

An Indian captive from the Texas frontier, Cynthia Ann Parker (ca. 1827–1864) was born in Illinois. Her family moved to Texas in 1833 and eventually settled near present-day Grosbeck in Limestone County, Texas. She was approximately nine years old when the family's fort was attacked on May 19, 1836, by a force of more than five hundred Comanches. Her father was killed, and she was captured, along with her brother and three other survivors of the attack. Her mother and two other siblings escaped. Her brother, John Parker, died in captivity, but she was adopted by the Indians and grew up to marry a Comanche Chief, Pete Nocona. They had two children, a daughter, Prairie Flower, and a son, Quanah Parker, who became one of the leading chiefs of the Comanches.

Over the years, Cynthia Ann Parker was spotted in Indian camps by different Texas frontiersmen but always refused to return to white culture. In 1860, at the battle of Pease River, she and Prairie Flower were captured by Texas forces. Although, except for blue eyes and fair complexion, she resembled other Indians, she was recognized by Captain Lawrence Sullivan Ross, a future governor of Texas, and taken to Fort Cooper where she was identified by her uncle, Isaac Charles Parker.

Cynthia Ann Parker never became reconciled to her new culture and tried to escape several times. She was given a pension by the Texas legislature in 1861 and lived at her brother Silas's home in Anderson County. Shortly after her daughter died in 1864, she followed her in death, grieving both for her daughter and her husband, as well as her lost son.

In 1909, the United States Congress authorized one thousand dollars to be spent on a monument in her memory, due to the efforts of her son Quanah Parker, and the remains of both Cynthia Ann Parker and Prairie Flower were moved to Post Oak Cemetery on the reservation in Oklahoma in 1910. For many, she was a symbol of the captivity myth, and her life was the source for several plays, books, and movies.

—*Patrick H. Butler, III*

SEE ALSO: Literature: Indian Captivity Narratives; Quanah Parker

SUGGESTED READING:
Hacker, Margaret Schmidt. *Cynthia Ann Parker.* El Paso, Tex., 1990.

PARKER, ISAAC CHARLES

The celebrated "hanging judge" of the Indian Territory, Isaac Charles Parker (1838–1896) was the son of strict Methodist parents and was raised on an Ohio farm. He studied law and began his practice at the age of twenty-one. After a political career in Missouri, he was appointed judge of the court of the Western District of Arkansas at Fort Smith in 1875 by President Ulysses S. Grant. The court had jurisdiction over the vast Indian Territory (now Oklahoma), which was overrun by fugitives and desperadoes. No judge in American history before or since has been faced with the gargantuan task of restoring law to such a huge territory. Parker employed two hundred deputy U.S. marshals to police the Indian Territory; sixty-five of them were murdered by outlaws. He enforced the law with a vengeance. During his twenty-one years on the bench, he handled more than thirteen thousand criminal cases and sentenced 160 killers and rapists to death. Seventy-nine were hanged on the gallows at Fort Smith.

A staunch friend and protector of Native Americans, Parker often criticized the federal government for failing to protect them from the ravages of white

Isaac Charles Parker. *Courtesy National Archives.*

civilization. Never a great judicial intellect, he improperly influenced juries and, in later years, was often overruled on appeal. Nonetheless, he remains perhaps America's greatest trial judge.

—*John Boessenecker*

SUGGESTED READING:

Croy, Homer. *He Hanged Them High*. New York, 1952.
Shirley, Glenn. *Law West of Fort Smith*. New York, 1957.

PARKER, QUANAH

SEE: Quanah Parker

PARKER, ROBERT LEROY

SEE: Cassidy, Butch

PARKMAN, FRANCIS

Historian, author, and horticulturalist Francis Parkman (1823–1893) was born in Boston, Massachusetts, into an affluent family. After graduating from Harvard College in 1844 and its law school two years later, he spent seven months traversing the American West via the Oregon and Santa Fe trails. During the journey, he lived with a band of Oglala Lakota Indians for nearly a month. Upon returning to Boston, he serialized his adventure in the *Knickerbocker* magazine. He later published an account of his exploits as *The California and Oregon Trail* (1849).

Family wealth allowed Parkman to pursue a career as a writer, and he earned his reputation as a historian with the publication of *The Conspiracy of Pontiac* (1851). The book was the forerunner of his multivolume work *France and England in North America* (1865–1892). These volumes detail the history of New France and her subjects' struggles with the English colonies and chronicle the people and events that shaped the struggle for control over America's interior. His career was periodically interrupted by an illness he referred to as "the enemy." Shortly after completing the last volume in the *France and England* series, Parkman's health deteriorated, and he died from peritonitis on November 8, 1893.

Scholars still debate Parkman's place in American colonial and Western history. Critics consider him a literary author, not a historian. They contend that he manipulated, ignored, and, in at least one instance, created documents to fit his framework. Supporters of Parkman emphasize his reliance on primary documents and previously unused repositories. They also note his familiarity with the places he described. His importance to Western Americana centers around his description of the frontier, frontiersmen, and Native Americans of the mid-nineteenth century. Though Parkman never understood his Native American hosts, his descriptions of their customs, ceremonies, and attitudes provide scholars with information not available elsewhere. He borrowed literary forms to construct his history, but his works, when used with caution, are still of use to historians of the West.

Parkman's writings offer three specific legacies for modern scholars. First, his writings offer a view of man and nature different from the view found in the writings of his Boston contemporaries. He rejected his contemporaries' love of nature for its own sake. His works suggest that wilderness and nature are enjoyable only as long as civilization (that is, an urban, literate society) exits as an alternative. Parkman claimed nature reduced man "to his primitive condition."

Second, Parkman's writings show the importance of race, class, and gender in nineteenth-century history and literature. His racist characterizations of Mexicans, Canadians, Catholics, and Native Americans could have come from Know-Nothing politicians in the 1850s or Social Darwinists in the 1870s and 1880s.

Finally, Parkman was one of the first historians to understand the importance of the environment in studying history. He fills his books with descriptions of wildlife, fauna, and geographical information. For these reasons, he remains an imposing and important source of information on the eighteenth- and nineteenth-century West.

—*Michael J. Mullin*

SUGGESTED READING:

Doughty, Howard. *Francis Parkman*. Cambridge, Mass., 1983.
Gayle, Robert L. *Francis Parkman*. New York, 1973.
Jacobs, Wilbur R. *Francis Parkman, Historian as Hero: The Formative Years*. Austin, Tex., 1991.
———. "Some of Parkman's Literary Devices." *New England Quarterly* 31 (1958): 244–252;
Parkman, Francis. *The Conspiracy of Pontiac and the Indian War after the Conquest of Canada*. 2 vols. New York, 1851.
———. *France and England in North America*. 2 vols. Edited by David Levin. New York, 1983.
———. *The Journals of Francis Parkman*. Edited by Mason Wade. Millwood, New York, 1947.

———. *Letters of Francis Parkman.* 2 vols. Edited by Wilbur R. Jacobs. Norman, Okla., 1960.
———. *The Oregon and California Trail Being Sketches of Prairie and Rocky Mountain Life.* New York, 1849.
Pease, Otis A. *Parkman's History: The Historian as Literary Artist.* New Haven, Conn., 1953.
Wade, Mason. *Francis Parkman: Heroic Historian.* Hamden, New York, 1972.

PAROCHIAL SCHOOLS

Strictly speaking, the term *parochial schools* applies to schools supported directly by parishes, but it is generally used to refer to all Catholic schools whether sponsored by parishes or religious orders. Early parochial schools in the West were designed to provide education where none was available and were carried on by lay people. In 1817, Bishop Louis William DuBourg brought direction to the movement by involving the Religious of the Sacred Heart and the Vincentians. Under their direction, the St. Louis area became a center for Catholic education. The Jesuits and the Sisters of Loretto from Kentucky arrived there in 1823.

Early parochial schools generally followed the public-school curriculum in the elementary grades but added religion. As public-school systems developed, parochial schools were viewed as controversial challenges to the public-school philosophy of educating all American children together.

Both public and parochial schools increased in number after the 1850s; parochial schools served a wide region. Spreading out from St. Louis, they went to the Northwest and the Southwest in the 1840s. From then on, the parochial-school system blossomed with schools under a variety of orders in California, New Mexico, and Texas, where the Ursuline Sisters, the Sisters of the Incarnate Word and Blessed Sacrament, and the Sisters of Divine Providence served the Hispanic population and some Anglos. As the populations in states such as Iowa, Kansas, and Minnesota grew, parochial schools spread there. In states where most of the people were Catholic, sisters taught in the public schools.

At a 1894 meeting of all the bishops in the United States, Catholic church leaders ruled that each parish should have a school; the number of schools then increased dramatically. A leading challenge to parochial schools occurred in Oregon in 1922 when the state passed the COMPULSORY SCHOOL BILL, which required all children from the ages of eight to sixteen to attend public schools. In *Pierce* v. *Society of Sisters* (1925), the U.S. Supreme Court struck down the Oregon law on the basis of the due process clause of the Fourteenth Amendment, but there continued to be challenges to parochial schools that received state aid. By 1934, 410,000 children attended parochial schools in the states west of the Mississippi. In 1930, there were 1,786,000 students in all private schools in the nation, so parochial schools in the West amounted to about one-quarter of the total. They formed a significant countercultural system where the state had a near monopoly. They were also significant in showing the determination of CATHOLICS to have what they deemed suitable schools for their children.

—*Catherine Ann Curry*

SUGGESTED READING:

Buetow, Harold. *Of Singular Benefit: The Story of Catholic Education in the United States.* New York, 1970.
Burns, James A., and Bernard J. Kohlbrenner. *A History of Catholic Education in the United States.* New York, 1937.

PARSONS, ELSIE CLEWS

Ethnologist Elsie Clews Parsons (1875–1941) conducted extensive fieldwork among the Native American tribes of the Southwest and wrote classic references to their culture. She was born in New York and received her education at Barnard College. She studied sociology in graduate school at Columbia and received her Ph.D. in 1899. In 1910, she traveled to the Southwest—a trip that spurred her interest in anthropology. Concentrating on rituals, customs, and ceremonies, she studied the Zuni, Hopi, Acoma, Laguna, Isleta, Jemez, and other Tewa groups of the Southwest. She annotated the *Hopi Journal of Alexander M. Stephen* (1936) and published the classic *Pueblo Indian Religion* (1939). Turning her attention to tribes farther south, she studied groups in the Mexican states of Oaxaca and Puebla and in Ecuador. Her book entitled *Mitla, Town of the Souls and other Zapoteco-Speaking Pueblos of Oaxaca, Mexico,* published in 1936, examined the ways in which the Zapotec Indians were acculturated into the Spanish civilization. She also conducted extensive work among the Kiowa tribe. She was the first woman president of the American Anthropological Association and served as associate editor of the *Journal of American Folklore.*

—*Candace Floyd*

SUGGESTED READING:

Babcock, Barbara A. *Daughters of the Southwest, 1880–1980: An Illustrated Catalogue.* Albuquerque, N. Mex., 1988.
Zumwalt, Rosemary Levy. *Wealth and Rebellion: Elsie Clews Parsons, Anthropologist and Folklorist.* Urbana, Ill., 1992.

PASSING WOMEN

In the popular imagination, the American West of the nineteenth century is dominated by stories of cowboys, miners, loggers, soldiers, and pony-express riders—all men doing the "man's job" that built the West. A number of women of the nineteenth century viewed the West as a man's world, too. They dressed as men and worked in jobs only men were employed to do and received much higher wages than those offered to nineteenth-century working women. These passing women often courted other women and married them. Some, in their disguises, participated in the politics of their times and even voted long before women were enfranchised.

From the scattered records now available, the behavior and motives of passing women remain unclear. Reports in contemporary newspapers and journals nearly always portrayed passing women as deceptive and immoral, guilty of committing acts against God, nature, and society. Yet, this label was applied equally to women who dressed as men because they sought the emotional companionship of other women, those who dressed as men of economic necessity, and those who used disguises because they found the traditional roles and behaviors available to women too constraining. Among the latter, passing women could open bank accounts and write checks, own property and houses, and, as mentioned, passing was the only way in which women could vote in local and national elections.

Cora Anderson, a Native American who passed as a man for thirteen years, commented when she was arrested in 1914 in Milwaukee: "Do you blame me for wanting to be a man? . . . In the future centuries, it is probable that woman will be the owner of her own body and the custodian of her own soul. [But] the well-cared for woman [now] is a parasite, and the woman who must work is a slave." The "crime" of these women seems, in truth, to have been that they successfully disguised their true identities from the men they worked with and lived among.

Stories of passing women appeared most frequently in the second half of the nineteenth century. In San Francisco of the 1870s, a disguised Jeanne Bonnet supported herself as a petty thief and shoplifter, but her main work seemed to be in separating prostitutes from the male pimps who lived off their earnings. In her autobiography, *Mountain Charley,* ELSA JANE FOREST GUERIN wrote of her life as a passing woman, a step she took at the age of sixteen, when, as the mother of two children, she was made a widow. BABE BEAN, a newspaper reporter and nurse during the San Francisco earthquake of 1906, lived in Stockton, California, among people who were fully aware of her identity.

Regardless of their various motives or of their diverse experiences as disguised men, passing women seemed to have some characteristics in common. They were certainly active and assertive, and certainly they were determined to set the course of their own lives. That they modeled themselves after the male members of society who were free to behave in these very ways says as much about the social and economic restrictions placed on gender in the nineteenth century as it says about the women who chose to break through the constraints.

—*Patricia Hogan*

SUGGESTED READING:

Katz, Jonathan Ned. *Gay American History: Lesbians and Gay Men in the U.S.A.* 1976 Rev. ed. New York, 1992.

San Francisco Lesbian and Gay History Project. "'She Even Chewed Tobacco': A Pictorial Narrative of Passing Women in America." In *Hidden from History: Reclaiming the Gay and Lesbian Past.* Edited by Martin Bauml Duberman, Martha Vicinus, and George Chauncey, Jr. New York, 1989.

PATTIE, SYLVESTER AND JAMES

Kentucky-born fur trappers James Pattie (1803–1833?) and his father, Sylvester (1782–1828), left Missouri for New Mexico in 1825. After crossing the plains to Taos, they joined a band of trappers, who descended the Gila River as far as the San Pedro River. After the trappers were attacked by Apache Indians, they hid their furs and turned back. Later, when they returned, their cache had been broken into and the furs stolen.

Discouraged, Sylvester Pattie quit trapping and spent the next two years as superintendent of the Santa Rita copper mines. James, however, joined another trapping expedition. He traveled along the Gila and Colorado rivers to the Mojave villages and then turned east to New Mexico. Trouble came his way again: all his furs were confiscated by the governor of New Mexico because he failed to obtain a trapping license.

In his *Personal Narrative,* James Pattie told many stories of his trapping years—some accurate, some garbled, some impossible. His account of the first descent of the Gila can be reconciled with other sources. While his description of a band of Frenchmen who were massacred by Indians is based on a real event, his claim to have been a member of the party is unlikely. His story of an expedition to the Bighorn River, the Yellowstone, and beyond is impossible.

Returning to trapping in 1828, Sylvester joined James and a band of trappers who again descended

An illustration from James Pattie's *Personal Narrative,* published after he completed his 1830 exploration of California. *Courtesy Library of Congress.*

the Gila to the Colorado. There the party divided, with one band ascending the Colorado and the other, led by Sylvester, crossing the desert to California. Once in California, the trappers were arrested and jailed in San Diego where Sylvester, who had collapsed in the desert, died.

James reported that he was later freed to vaccinate Indians during a smallpox epidemic, but that claim is doubtful. California records show no evidence of an epidemic, although they mention a serious outbreak of measles. It is likely that Pattie heard of the spread of that disease and, as he often did, adapted the story for his narrative.

Pattie did travel as far north as San Francisco Bay and Fort Ross. In his *Personal Narrative,* he described California with reasonable accuracy, although he often mixed other people's stories with his own. In 1830, he left California and returned to Kentucky by way of Mexico.

He spent three years in Kentucky and then disappeared. Some stories relate that he later reappeared in California, but none can withstand historical analysis. Although no definite record exists, he undoubtedly died during the severe cholera epidemic that swept Kentucky in 1833.

—Richard Batman

SUGGESTED READING:

Batman, Richard. *American Ecclesiastes: The Stories of James Pattie.* New York and San Diego, 1984.

Pattie, James O. *The Personal Narrative of James O. Pattie.* Original edition edited by Timothy Flint. Cincinnati, Ohio, 1831. Reprint edition edited by Richard Batman. Missoula, Mont., 1988.

Weber, David J. *The Taos Trappers.* Norman, Okla., 1971.

PATWIN INDIANS

SEE: Native American Peoples: Peoples of California

PAUL BUNYAN, LEGEND OF

The first Paul Bunyan tales were published by James MacGillivray in "The Round River Drive" *(Detroit News-Tribune)* on July 24, 1910, and immediately captured public interest. Over the next fifteen years, a number of professional writers took up the Bunyan theme and rapidly transmuted the figure of the giant lumberjack into a national legend. The sources of MacGillivray's original are not clear, but Paul Bunyan did figure in oral traditions of lumbermen in Pennsylvania, Wisconsin, and the Northwest before 1910.

Paul Bunyan is an example of an occupational folk hero, a symbol of largeness, might, a willingness to work hard, and frontier vitality. His exaggerated size is part and parcel of the Western humor tradition, which populated the landscape with beings of gigantic proportions. Bunyan and his companions, Babe the Blue Ox and Johnny Inkslinger, take in stride rainstorms that last for months, mosquitoes of tremendous dimensions, and vast geographical obstacles. Indeed, geography was no problem for Bunyan, who, godlike, created such physical features as lakes and rivers, not to mention Puget Sound, the Grand Canyon, and the Black Hills. Such prodigious creativity generated an enormous appetite, and, we are told, Bunyan's camp

Paul Bunyan. Courtesy *The Bettmann Archive.*

stove covered an acre, and his hot-cake griddle was so vast that it required the service of men using sides of bacon as skates to grease it.

After MacGillivray, the single greatest popularizer of the Paul Bunyan legend was W. B. Laughead, a Minnesota advertising agent who produced a series of pamphlets, spanning 1914 to 1944, to publicize the products of the Red River Lumber Company. Under the influence of the pamphlet series, Esther Shephard wrote a novel entitled *Paul Bunyan* in 1824. Another lumber-company advertising agent, James Stevens, embellished the growing legend in his *Paul Bunyan* of 1925.

Building on this foundation, many authors of juvenile fiction produced versions of the Paul Bunyan legends, and various upper Midwest communities introduced Paul Bunyan festivals to attract tourists to what they characteristically called "Bunyan-land."

The Paul Bunyan tales have found their way into serious literature and art through the poetry of such writers as Robert Frost, Carl Sandburg, and Richard Wilbur and in an operetta with libretto by W. H. Auden and music by Benjamin Britten.

—*Alan Axelrod*

"PAWNEE BILL"

SEE: Lillie, Gordon W.

PAWNEE INDIANS

SEE: Native American Peoples: Peoples of the Great Plains

PAXSON, EDGAR SAMUEL

Artist Edgar Samuel Paxson (1852–1919) is best known for his documentary painting *Custer's Last Stand.* Completed in 1899 after years of painstaking research, the painting is remarkable for its large size (six-by-nine feet) and its attention to authentic detail.

Paxson produced about two thousand oil and water-color paintings in his studio in Butte and later Missoula, Montana. He portrayed Indians, frontiersmen, and frontier scenes based on his own experiences and on historical events. Among his most important works are six historical murals in the Montana State Capitol building and eight in the Missoula County Court House.

Born near Buffalo, New York, Paxson traveled around the West in the 1870s and arrived in Montana in 1877. He worked in an array of adventurous occupations, including scout, hunter, drover, and stagecoach guard, before seriously pursuing a career in painting the West he had known. Paxson had no formal art training. He learned perspective and other artistic techniques as a scenic artist for the many theaters active in booming Montana during the 1880s. The limited influence his contemporaries in Europe and America had on his work, coupled with his extensive frontier experiences, make his work significant among Western art.

—*William E. Paxson, Jr.*

SUGGESTED READING:

Paxson, William Edgar, Jr. *E. S. Paxson: Frontier Artist.* Boulder, Colo., 1984.

PAYNE, DAVID L.

Leader of the Oklahoma "Boomers" and pseudo-founder of Oklahoma City, David L. Payne (1836–1884) was born in Indiana. At the age of twenty-one, he left home for the Kansas prairie and embarked on an adventure that included serving in the Civil War Union Army, in the postwar Kansas legislature, as Leavenworth postmaster, as assistant doorkeeper to the United States House of Representatives, and, finally, as a Kansas farmer. In all of these endeavors, he generally lost more money than he made.

By 1872, Payne was looking for a fresh start. Like other citizens of Kansas and Missouri, he set his sights on settling in the Indian Territory, which due to government treaties with the Cherokees, Choctaws, Chickasaws and others was then off-limits to whites. The would-be settlers were called "Boomers," and Payne shortly took up their cause as his own. By 1879, he was their leader.

Payne argued that the U.S. government, which claimed ownership of the Indian Territory land, had a greater responsibility to U.S. citizens than to Indians. As such, the land could be made subject to the homesteading acts of 1841 and 1862, thereby allowing for white settlement and dispossession of the Indians. Refusing to accept the sovereignty of the Indian nations, Payne saw an opportunity to promote white manifest destiny and make money at the same time. He organized the colony of "Oklahoma" on a membership basis, in which two dollars purchased a quarter section of land and twenty-five dollars purchased a town lot in his proposed capital city.

Payne made his first foray into the forbidden territory on April 26, 1880, and surveyed what would become Oklahoma City. After less than a month, an army detachment discovered and arrested the surveyors but turned them loose at the Kansas border. Undaunted, Payne and his followers made another attempt on July 6; again, they were caught. In all, Payne made at least eight trips into the Indian Territory and pocketed some one hundred thousand dollars from membership fees.

Oklahoma was eventually opened up to the Boomers, but Payne did not live to see it. He died suddenly of a massive heart attack on November 28, 1884, barely a month before he planned to lead another excursion.

—*Kurt Edward Kemper*

SEE ALSO: Homestead Act of 1862; Land Policy; Oklahoma; Oklahoma Land Rush

SUGGESTED READING:

McReynolds, Edwin C. *Oklahoma: A History of the Sooner State.* Norman, Okla., 1965.

Rister, Carl Coke. *Land Hunger: David L. Payne and the Oklahoma Boomers.* Norman, Okla., 1942.

PEACE POLICY

SEE: Grant's Peace Policy; United States Indian Policy

PEALE, TITIAN RAMSAY

Artist and naturalist Titian Ramsay Peale (1799–1885) was the son of portraitist Charles Willson Peale. He received his first instruction in both art and natural history from his father. From the age of fourteen, he worked in his father's museum in Philadelphia where he prepared specimens for display. At the same time, he contributed illustrations to Thomas Say's *American Entomology.* At the age of eighteen, following an expedition to Georgia and Florida, Titian Peale was elected to membership in the Philadelphia Academy of Natural Sciences. The following year, he was selected to accompany Major STEPHEN HARRIMAN LONG's topographical survey of the Rocky Mountains as an assistant to Thomas Say, chief naturalist of the expedition. Returning home to Philadelphia, Peale assisted in the operation of his father's museum and succeeded his brother Franklin as manager in 1833. During this period, he also produced illustrations for Charles Lucien Bonaparte's supplement to Alexander Wilson's *American Ornithology,* issued in four volumes from 1825 to 1833.

With fellow-artists Alfred T. Agate and Joseph Drayton, Peale accompanied the exploratory expedition of the Pacific commanded by CHARLES WILKES from 1838 to 1842. Peale was one of the first Americans to record the topography and landscape of the Hawaiian Islands. On his return to the United States, he settled in Washington, D.C., and, from 1849 to 1873, worked for the U.S. Patent Office. He was again represented in a portfolio of ornithological plates accompanying the reports of the Pacific expedition issued by Wilkes and John Cassin in 1858.

Few of Peale's earlier drawings appeared in the report of the Long Expedition, published by EDWIN JAMES in 1823. According to James, Peale executed more than one hundred drawings during his travels with Long. Of the eight plates illustrating the American edition of Long's report, however, six were credited to SAMUEL SEYMOUR, an English painter who accompanied the expedition as its official artist. Paintings by Seymour and Peale were exhibited in the Peale Museum in Philadelphia. Probably included in the sale of the museum's collections in 1841, they have since become lost.

Original examples of Peale's drawings and water colors are preserved in the collections of the Peabody Museum at Harvard University and the American Philosophical Society in Philadelphia. Included among the latter are some of the earliest known depictions by an Eastern artist of Western wildlife and Plains Indians subjects. Several of Peale's Hawaiian landscapes are owned today by the American Museum of Natural History in New York City and the Bernice P. Bishop Museum in Honolulu.

—*David C. Hunt*

SEE ALSO: Art: Surveys and Expeditions

SUGGESTED READING:

Ewer, John C. *Artists of the Old West, 1850–1900.* Garden City, N.Y., 1965.

Forbes, David. *Encounters with Paradise.* Honolulu, Hawaii, 1992.

Poesch, Jessie. *Titian Ramsay Peale, 1799–1885: And His Journals of the Wilkes Expedition.* Philadelphia, 1976.

Viola, Herman J. *Exploring the West. New* York, 1987.

PECOS BILL, LEGEND OF

Pecos Bill is a semilegendary cowboy-culture hero of the Southwest. The product of journalism rather than of oral tradition, Pecos Bill first appeared in a 1923 article by Edward O'Reilly in *The Century Magazine.* Mody Boatright expanded the story of Bill's adventures in 1934 in three chapters of his *Tall Tales from Texas Cow Camps.* Pecos Bill became a well-known "folk" character, in spite of the fact that during a suit against a writer for using Pecos Bill in a book, O'Reilly admitted that he had invented the character.

Pecos Bill has become the popular super-type of the Texas cowboy. The stories of his exploits depict him as the strongest, meanest cowboy west of the Pecos, the greatest of all ropers, bronc busters, and gunfighters. He invented calf roping and branding and built the first six-shooter. He rode a panther that weighed as much as three steers and a yearling and used a rattlesnake for a quirt. He could ride a cyclone while rolling a cigarette with one hand. He dug the Rio Grande during a year of drought so he could get water from the Gulf of Mexico up to the Pecos. He staked out New Mexico for his ranch spread and used Arizona as a calf pasture. Pecos Bill is the Paul Bunyan of the Southwest.

—*F. E. Abernethy*

SUGGESTED READING:

Boatright, Mody. *Tall Tales from Texas Cow Camps*. Dallas, Tex., 1934.
Botkin, B. A. "The Saga of Pecos Bill." In *A Treasury of American Folklore*. New York, 1944.
Dobie, J. Frank. *Tales of Old-Time Texas*. Boston, 1955.
O'Reilly, Edward. "The Saga of Pecos Bill." *The Century Magazine* 106 (October 1923): 827–833.

PECOS RIVER

The Pecos River originates in Mora County, New Mexico, and, on its five-hundred-mile course, winds its way through the plains of eastern New Mexico into southwestern Texas until it meets the RIO GRANDE north of Del Rio. Like many Western rivers that traverse arid,

Pecos River.

semiarid, or desert lands, the Pecos is a life line and magnet. As it cuts deep into the canyons of eastern New Mexico and the Llano Estacado of West Texas, it forms a large continuous regional aquifer system that includes Roswell and the caverns at Carlsbad, New Mexico. In the desert of lower southwestern Texas, the Pecos becomes more like a stream, yet there it is even more essential to the people who depend on it.

In the desert, prehistoric peoples followed the course of water. Along the banks of the Pecos River are traces of people as early as the Archaic period, eight thousand years ago. The northern Pecos region, near the present-day town of Pecos, New Mexico, had been the easternmost border of the Pueblo world well into the thirteenth century A.D. By 1500, the pueblo of Cicuye (the present-day Pecos National Monument) on the banks of the Pecos River contained two thousand people. In 1541, FRANCISCO VÁSQUEZ DE CORONADO stopped and took guides for his trip to the plains. In 1583, Don Antonio Espejo also departed from Cicuye as he followed the Pecos River back to Mexico. This river, this border, divided the Spanish and Pueblo world from that of Plains Indians.

Because of the harshness of the deserts of eastern New Mexico and the brackish water of the Pecos, Spaniards saw the river as a travel route rather than as a place to establish a mission or presidio. There were no settled Native American communities south of Cicuye and little apparent mineral or other wealth. Spanish presence in the region remained intermittent.

Farther to the south, the Pecos River in western Texas became an important resource for the post–Civil War cattle industry. Besides a source of water, the river was a barrier that separated better grazing land from the rugged mountain deserts of the southwestern corner of Texas. The cattle industry dominated the area around the river, with towns such as Pecos, Texas, developing to cater to the trade. To the west, military outposts such as Fort Stockton and Fort Davis offered protection to ranchers and settlers at the expense of Native Americans.

The Pecos River has a claim on American popular culture. Judge ROY BEAN, who proclaimed himself "law west of the Pecos," had his combination saloon-courthouse near Eagle Nest Canyon in southern Texas, close to where the Pecos meets the Rio Grande. Legendary figures such as Pecos Bill, the quintessential cowboy of myth, also enhance the meaning attached to the river. In reality, the Pecos River, like many rivers in the West, sustained humanity in diverse ecological settings. Its significance is derived as much from what it represents in American culture as from its natural features.

—Hal Rothman

SUGGESTED READING:

Fehrenbach, T. R. *Lone Star: A History of Texas by Texans.* New York, 1968.

PENDERGAST, JAMES

A powerful politician in late nineteenth-century Kansas City, Missouri, James Pendergast (1856–1911) was born in Gallipolis, Ohio. In 1876, at the age of twenty, he arrived in Kansas City to look for work. He labored for a time in a packinghouse and in a few iron foundries. At the racetrack in 1881, he bet his money on a horse named Climax, and when the horse paid out handsomely, Pendergast used his winnings to purchase a hotel and saloon, which he named after the horse that made it possible. The business was successful, and Pendergast eventually purchased two more saloons. He made friends easily and parleyed his popularity into a career in politics, beginning as delegate to the city's Democratic nominating convention in 1884. By 1892, he had won a seat on the city council representing the first ward. In subsequent elections, he proved himself to be the Democratic party's best vote-getter. With each election, Pendergast's influence increased. By 1904, the *Kansas City Star* acknowledged that he ran the city's entire Democratic machine.

He controlled jobs in the police department and the fire department and could usually find employment for friendly voters in the businesses owned by his backers. Placing his younger brother in the position of superintendent of streets gave him access to two hundred more city jobs to dole out. Always championing the causes of workers and the poor and generous with his own money, he supplied groceries, coal, and other necessities to those in need.

By 1910, Pendergast, dying of Bright's disease, had turned his machine, the Jackson County Democratic Club, over to his brother Tom.

—Patricia Hogan

SUGGESTED READING:

Brown, A. Theodore, and Lyle W. Dorsett. *K. C.: A History of Kansas City, Missouri.* Boulder, Colo., 1978.
Dorsett, Lyle W. *The Pendergast Machine.* New York, 1968.

PENDERGAST, TOM

Head of the powerful twentieth-century Pendergast machine of Kansas City, Missouri, Tom Pendergast (1872–1945) received his lessons in Democratic politics from his brother James. Born in St. Joseph, Missouri, Pendergast headed to Kansas City in 1890 to became his brother's bookkeeper and protégé. Groomed in a series of positions—as deputy constable of the first ward, as deputy marshal, as marshal, and as superintendent of streets—Pendergast ran for city alderman in 1910. With the backing of the Irish voters as well as Italians and African Americans, he won his seat, only to resign to look after his business interests and expand his hold on the city's Democratic party. During the next two decades, Pendergast solidified his influence by supplying poor and unemployed voters with food, fuel, and clothing. For the middle-class voters, Pendergast organized political clubs in each of the city's wards. The clubs provided teas and card parties for the ladies and dances, parties, and picnics, for couples. Men of the clubs joined the citywide baseball league and a bowling league during the winter months. The organizations functioned much like the country clubs that middle-class voters could not afford or in which they could not gain membership.

In 1925, Pendergast's power benefited from a new city charter in which the municipal administration was centralized behind a city manager and the city's wards were consolidated into larger districts. Pendergast appointed the loyal Democrat Henry F. McElroy to the new manager's position, and McElroy, in turn, orchestrated control of the city's police force and appointed a friendly police chief. Kansas City, to the horror of some residents, became known as a wide-open town, famous for its night life and nurtured by a new Kansas City style of jazz and illegal alcohol. Most of the city's voters found the new order of things agreeable, and they returned Pendergast's city tickets to office in the elections of the 1930s. These voters were, no doubt, influenced by Pendergast's solution to the hard times of the Great Depression. His Ten-Year Plan of city and county public works projects—most supplied by the Pendergast Ready-Mixed Concrete Company at considerable profit to the owner—fueled building and stadium construction, improved and repaired city streets, and employed some twenty-two thousand voters.

With his influence over the city literally cemented, Pendergast could promise solid city support to any candidate or cause in statewide politics. Thus, by the 1930s, Pendergast's power enveloped the state of Missouri, and he used his machine to back Franklin D. Roosevelt as the Democratic presidential candidate in 1932. As a reward, Roosevelt funneled federal Depression relief funds for the state through Pendergast, and much of the money went to Kansas City.

At the same time, Pendergast fed a compulsive gambling habit that required ever greater sources of income—legal and otherwise. A deal with the state's insurance companies over an increase in premiums put considerable sums into Pendergast's pocket, about which the public and the Internal Revenue Service eventually found out. Tom Pendergast pleaded guilty to income-tax evasion on three hundred thousand dollars in 1939 and served most of a fifteen-month sentence. The most powerful city boss of the twentieth century, after Chicago's Richard Daley, was allowed to return to Kansas City on the promise that he would stay out of politics and away from politicians forever. He died four years later.

—Patricia Hogan

SEE ALSO: City Government; Urban West

SUGGESTED READING:

Brown, A. Theodore, and Lyle W. Dorsett. *K. C.: A History of Kansas City, Missouri.* Boulder, Colo., 1978.

Dorsett, Lyle W. *The Pendergast Machine.* New York, 1968.

Phillips, Charles. *Missouri: Mother of the American West.* Northridge, Calif., 1988.

PEND D'OREILLE INDIANS

SEE: Native American Peoples: Peoples of the Pacific Northwest

PENITENTES

In the far reaches of the Spanish empire today known as the American Southwest, Franciscan friars at mission outposts sought to convert Native Americans and ministered to Hispanic settlers and soldiers. Under lax supervision from Durango, which lay hundreds of miles and months away to the south, the Catholic clergy gave Spanish communicants handwritten prayer books and *alabados* (hymns) and taught them to conduct lay services. As weather, time, and nomadic Indian raiders permitted, the Franciscans, some of them perhaps from the Third Order of St. Francis of Assisi, spread into remote villages and pueblos and took over church rituals. When Mexican liberals secularized the missions in 1828, the Spanish Franciscans departed, and their mostly French replacements rarely visited the isolated foothills and valleys of the North. In the absence of any strong clergy, a lay brotherhood sprang up. Its members called themselves the Brothers of Our Father Jesus, but they were known around New Mexico and southern Colorado as the Los Hermanos Penitentes (The Brotherhood of Penitents).

The Penitentes developed their own liturgy and ceremonies and, like all religious orders, worshipped together guided by those canons. The Catholic church did not recognize them as a bone fide order, although some scholars point to the similarity between the Penitentes' practices and those of the Franciscan Third Order established in 1218, and others argue that the Penitentes were simply a survival of some forgotten medieval organization stemming from Spain. The Catholic church may not have sanctioned the brotherhood, but the Penitentes conducted charitable works in the name of the church nevertheless, helping the sick and the poor, burying the dead, and functioning as something like a mutual-aid society. Perhaps not surprisingly given the blighted borderland world in which they came into existence, the Pentitentes seemed obsessed with the shortness and brutality of human life, its fragility, and its ubiquitous suffering. They punished themselves with extreme penances, whipping each other during Lent to achieve mystical union with the suffering Christ and, in some years, hanging one of their members on a cross on Good Friday until he passed out from pain and exhaustion.

Flagellation was nothing new to the Southwest nor to Catholicism. The church itself had long been ambivalent about such harsh expiation. St. Anthony of Padua, an early thirteenth century flagellant, extolled the virtues of his practice. Organized groups of flagellants spread to northern Italy in the mid-thirteenth century and then to Germany and Holland. Although Pope Clement VI so hated flagellation that he issued papal bulls prohibiting it, many zealots were burned at the stake in the fourteenth century for violating his edicts, and clearly the practice was widespread in Spain shortly before the American conquest. Captain Gasper Peréz de Villagrá first described such penitent rites in New Mexico in 1610 when he reported on the practice approvingly to the king of Spain in a long poem entitled *Historia de la Nueva Mexico (History of New Mexico)*. Members of JUAN DE OÑATE's 1598 expedition celebrated Good Friday that year by whipping themselves in public, and Don Juan scourged himself before the writer in private. The Indians who witnessed these and other extreme acts of contrition thought the Spaniards had gone crazy, and their reaction undercuts the belief that the Penitentes were influenced by Aztec bloodletting and that their secretive *moradas* (chapels) originated with the pueblo kivas, where the Indians held ceremonial meetings closed to outsiders.

The Penitentes hold their Holy Week services in such *moradas* and in village churches, too. Often a procession starts on Ash Wednesday and, led by the *hermano mayor* (head brother), winds through Good Friday from the *morada* to the church, along the Way of the Cross, and sometimes back into remote hills. Beforehand, on Shrove Tuesday, *sangradors* (bleeders) cut long crosses on the backs of the penitents, each of whom has vowed to flagellate himself in imitation of the Roman soldiers who whipped Christ on the way to Golgotha. The cuts help the blood flow more freely and with less pain when the penitents lash their backs with *disciplinas* (yucca-cactus whips, soaked in vinegar or salt water). Sometimes one, sometimes several of the penitents voluntarily drag a heavy wooden cross in imitation of Jesus, and another might also pull a low, heavy, wooden-wheeled *carreta del muerto* (death cart) by rough horsehair ropes tied round his bare shoulders and chest. Death, a skeleton dressed in black, sits in the cart with a bow armed and drawn. A *rezador* (reader) recites prayers from a *cuaderno* (notebook), first written perhaps in the fifteenth or sixteenth century and copied down generation after generation. Dressed only from the waist down in *calzones* (sheer white cotton trousers) and black hoods, the flagellants are ringed on both sides by fully clothed *companeros* (companions), who catch them if they stumble. A *pitero* (flute player) blows windy notes on his *pito* (flute).

On the nights of Maundy Thursday and Good Friday the penitents proceed by lantern and moonlight to the *morada* for *tinieblas* (darkness or Hell), and the villagers join them. When the ceremony is about to begin, the *celabor* (sergeant-at-arms) stands by the door and allows the group to file into a room decorated only with rude holy images and *retablos,* the local folk art originally fashioned by untrained hands in imitation of traditional religious works. A simple table serves as an altar, holding a triangular candelabra or two with twelve *tenebrios* (candlesticks) representing the apostles and a larger candle for Christ. The dirt floor near the altar is covered with broken glass and cactus. The penitents enter near the altar, one carrying a cross, others flagellating themselves with *disciplinas.* Participants devise penances they feel are commensurate with the magnitude of their sins. One might crawl on bare knees across the glass; another might appear with a crown of thorns placed over his temple; still another might embrace tightly the prickly cactus. Some occasionally collapse from exhaustion or loss of blood; they are carried to an adjoining room where the *enfermero* bathes their wounds with rosemary water. Accompanied by a flute player, the *hermano mayor, cuaderno* in hand, conducts the ceremony. The group sings mournful *alabados* and recites psalms and prayers, as one by one the candles are extinguished. When the *morada* plunges into darkness, a brief silence erupts into pandemonium as the crowd rattles chains, beats pots and pans, and shakes *matracas* (rattles). The sounds of slapping whips and wailing women can be heard in the darkness. The noise stops as abruptly as it began, the names of those who have died during the year are called out, and *sudarios* (prayers) or Pater Nosters are recited in response while the twelve candles are relit in reverse order. A final *alabado,* sung by the leading brothers at the altar, closes the ceremony.

Before Anglo-Americans began arriving in the Southwest, the Penitentes practiced their rites more or less openly, but when the newcomers became fascinated with practices so foreign to them that they viewed them not as religious ceremonies but as strange and exotic spectacles, the brothers withdrew into seclusion and prohibited sightseers from attending their activities. The *hermano mayor* would frequently give permission to attend the ceremonies to those who approached him in advance and whom he judged would heed his warnings that the meetings were religious in nature and should be respected as such by spectators who remained silent during the ceremonies. As Protestant missionaries, who were determined to proselytize the "foreigners" and who heartily disapproved of flagellation, moved into the region, many made attempts to discourage, even suppress the brotherhood. Not the least among these was the French Bishop JEAN BAPTISTE LAMY, who headed the Catholic clergy in New Mexico during the early nineteenth century, and whose attacks on the Penitentes was lionized in WILLA CATHER's *Death Comes for the Archbishop* (1927).

Rumors about the Penitentes abounded. Certainly no outsider witnessed the crucifixions that took place, events the Penitentes carefully shielded even from the likes of CHARLES FLETCHER LUMMIS, who first reported in detail on the Penitente rites in *The Land of the Poco Tiempo* (1893). Some—confusing self-inflicted expiation with a tendency toward violence—accused the brothers of killing those who openly opposed them or tried to censure their rituals. In 1936, however, when writer Carl Taylor, shortly after publishing an article on the group, was murdered at his desk in a mountain village called San Antonio east of Albuquerque, the murderer turned out not to be a brother, as many immediately assumed, but Taylor's house boy. Others have long asserted that ambitious politicians, seeking endorsements from New Mexico's northern mountain villages, regularly underwent the Penitente initiation rite, during which a *sangrador* cut three gashes in a initiate's back with a flint knife called a *pedernal:* a religious seal of approval for any aspiring candidate.

"Penitente hunters" sometimes tried to spy on the brothers as they sought out secluded areas in which to carry on their rituals. During Lent, young men and women, many of them college students, would trek out to the mountain villages of northern New Mexico hoping to catch the "drama" of the Penitentes, and sometimes they would be stopped and turned back by armed guards. Most of the stories about shootouts with the brotherhood were apocryphal, although there were occasional incidents of violence between flagellants fanatical about their privacy and determined thrill-seekers, especially back in the days when many New Mexicans went about casually armed. On the other hand, claims that the Penitentes held (and hold) strong political sway over the remote mountain regions of northern New Mexico and southern Colorado were (and, indeed, are) more strongly grounded in truth, not because the brothers are joined together in a secret order, but because in most villages in the area, members of the religious sect are probably in the majority.

—*Charles Phillips*

SEE ALSO: Catholics; Missions: Early Franciscan and Jesuit Missions

SUGGESTED READING:

Campa, Arthur L. *Hispanic Culture in the Southwest.* Norman, Okla., 1979.

Gutiérrez, Ramón A. *When Jesus Came, the Corn Mothers Went Away.* Stanford, Calif., 1991.

Weigle, Marta. *Brothers of Light, Brothers of Blood: The Penitentes of the Southwest.* Albuquerque, N. Mex., 1976.

PEOPLE V. HALL

A California Supreme Court decision of 1854, *People v. Hall* involved the case of George Hall, a white man, who had been convicted of murder on the testimony of Chinese witnesses. Relying on a California law that held that "no Black, or Mulatto person, or Indian shall be allowed to give evidence in favor of, or against a white man," Hall appealed his conviction. In making its decision, the Supreme Court offered the odd argument that, due to the deficiencies of early American ethnological knowledge, lawmakers might have considered "Mongolians" part of the "Indian" race. Using that specious contention to prop up its decree that the word *white* should be interpreted to exclude "all races other than the Caucasian," the Court reversed Hall's conviction, thus denying Chinese Americans the right to testify in California courts.

—*Peggy Pascoe*

PEOPLE'S PARTY

SEE: Populism

PEOPLE'S PARTY OF UTAH

Through the first sixty years of Mormon history, members of the CHURCH OF JESUS CHRIST OF LATTER-DAY SAINTS were admonished to follow the counsel of the prophets. These church leaders directed the lives of their followers in all aspects—social, economic, and political as well as religious. There was no encouragement toward political independence, and most Latter-day Saints generally voted as a bloc, often stimulating opposition.

After more than twenty years of essentially ecclesiastical rule in Utah, the growing number of non-Mormons began to mount challenges, including contesting the election of the delegate to Congress in 1868, even though their candidate garnered only 105 votes. With the coming of the transcontinental railroad and subsequent mining development, many more "Gentiles" entered the territory and combined with dissident MORMONS called "Godbeites" (followers of WILLIAM S. GODBE) to seek more independence from the church. They formed the Liberal party for these purposes.

In response, the Latter-day Saints formed their own People's party. Although most officials of the group during its twenty-year history were not among the highest levels of church leadership, party decision making certainly reflected the wishes of church leaders, particularly GEORGE QUAYLE CANNON, who served as the territorial delegate to Congress for a decade and was a member of the First Presidency of the church.

When prospects for Utah statehood finally improved after the MORMON MANIFESTO of 1890, national political leaders demanded Utah politics be regularized. Church officials encouraged but did not initiate the growth of infant Democrat and Republic parties in the territory. To further that process, they did foster the dissolution of the People's party. The territorial People's party was disbanded on June 10, 1891, and church leaders encouraged former members to embrace the national parties in approximately equal numbers.

—Leo Lyman

PERKINS, CHARLES ELLIOTT

A long-time executive with the Chicago, Burlington and Quincy Railroad, Charles Elliott Perkins (1840–1907) built the line into the leading railroad in the Midwest and pushed the tracks as far west as Billings, Montana. Born in Cincinnati, Perkins was the cousin of JOHN MURRAY FORBES, who was chief among the Boston investors who developed the CB&Q. Perkins joined the company early in its development. Gradually working his way up the corporate ladder, he became general manager of the road in 1873 and began the rapid expansion of the system through the Midwest and into the West. He worked closely with Forbes until the latter retired in 1881; Perkins then became president of the company. He not only enlarged the CB&Q but transformed it into a model of organization and modern railroad management: well planned, flawlessly maintained, and intelligently operated.

Perkins sold the CB&Q to JAMES J. HILL, head of the Great Northern and Northern Pacific Railroads, in 1901 and retired to his estate, The Apple Trees, in Burlington, Iowa. He surfaced from retirement briefly in 1906 to attack THEODORE ROOSEVELT as "the Boss Lunatic in Washington" for having promoted the Hepburn Act, which gave the Interstate Commerce Commission the authority to set maximum rates for railroads. He saw the prospect of such government intervention as a repudiation of the combined enterprise and integrity for which he and his CB&Q had stood.

—Alan Axelrod

SEE ALSO: Interstate Commerce Act of 1887

SUGGESTED READING:
Martin, Albro. *Railroads Triumphant: The Growth, Rejection and Rebirth of a Vital American Force.* New York, 1992.

PÉROUSE, JEAN DE LA

An eighteenth-century French explorer, Jean de la Pérouse (1741–?) sailed around the world and stopped in Alaska, Hawaii, and California (among many other places). He wrote about the journey in *Voyage de La Pérouse autour du Monde* (published posthumously in 1797). He was born in Albi, France, and disappeared in 1788. The date of his death is unknown.

Pérouse entered the French naval academy at an early age and was appointed midshipman on November 19, 1756. He distinguished himself in eight naval campaigns against the English and was promoted to ensign on October 1, 1764, and then to captain on April 11, 1780. He further distinguished himself in battle against the British at Hudson Bay in 1781. Having earned a reputation as a skilled navigator, he was commissioned to undertake a voyage around the world. His two vessels, the *Boussole* and the *Astrolabe*, departed Brest on August 1, 1785, and Pérouse wrote his last letters from Botany Bay, Australia, on January 21, 1788.

A translation of the posthumous collection of his travel letters was published in the United States in 1801. At that early date, detailed information on the California coast, let alone Alaska and Hawaii, was scarce and eagerly sought. Nevertheless, in America, Pérouse sank into obscurity later in the nineteenth century, and interest in him and his voyage was not revived until 1959, when Charles N. Rudkin published *The First French Expedition to California: La Pérouse in 1786.*

—*Alan Axelrod*

SEE ALSO: Exploration: French Expeditions

SUGGESTED READING:

Allen, Edward Weber. *The Vanishing Frenchman: The Mysterious Disappearance of Lapérouse.* Rutland, Vt., 1959.

Rudkin, Charles N. *The First French Expedition to California: La Pérouse in 1786.* Los Angeles, 1959.

PERPETUAL EMIGRATING FUND

The Perpetual Emigrating Fund (PEF) helped finance the migration of members of the CHURCH OF JESUS CHRIST OF LATTER-DAY SAINTS to the West during the last half of the nineteenth century. Organized in Utah in 1849 under the leadership of BRIGHAM YOUNG, the fund was set up to provide revolving loans. While donations would at first provide the means to travel west, travelers' repayment of their transportation costs would finance future migration. The fund first helped Mormon refugees from Illinois; by 1852, it helped MORMONS move to the West from outside the United States—primarily the British Isles and northern Europe. The PEF provided direct assistance to about 26,000 of the 73,000 overseas Mormon immigrants who moved to the West between 1852 and 1887, and to several thousand Mormons moving to the West from elsewhere in the United States. PEF company agents chartered ships; procured ox teams, wagons and supplies; organized travelers into companies; and assigned leaders for each company. Prospective travelers were expected to pay as much of their own expenses as possible.

The PEF was governed by a board of directors and a president. Brigham Young presided from 1849 to 1870; Horace Eldredge from 1870 to 1873; and Albert Carrington from 1873 to 1887.

The Mormons actively promoted migration to the West, and in response to a torrent of requests for assistance in the mid-1850s, PEF agents stretched the fund's resources to the utmost. But cash was scarce in Utah. Repayments and donations lagged far behind expenditures; by 1857, indebtedness overwhelmed the PEF. From then on, overall migration arrangements were under the auspices of the Mormon church rather than the PEF. During the 1860s, the church sent wagons and ox teams from Utah to meet its incoming emigrants at outfitting posts. The travelers signed promissory notes to repay the PEF for the costs involved; the PEF was then to repay the church. Nearly 16,500 people benefited from this arrangement.

By the 1870s, Mormons emigrated entirely by steamship and railroad and needed cash to pay for the trip. Private aid then exceeded PEF assistance. Still, through special fundraising drives, the PEF helped more than one hundred emigrants each year between 1868 and 1881.

Under the provisions of the EDMUNDS-TUCKER ACT OF 1887, the PEF was dissolved, and federal agents seized its assets. They found little except uncollectable promissory notes. The Mormon church had spent all the PEF's resources and many of its own in supporting Mormon migration.

—*Richard L. Jensen*

SEE ALSO: Mormon Trail

SUGGESTED READING:

Arrington, Leonard J. *Great Basin Kingdom.* Cambridge, Mass., 1958.

Jensen, Richard L. "Steaming Through: Arrangements for Mormon Emigration from Europe, 1869–1887." *Journal of Mormon History* 9 (1982): 3–23.

Mulder, William. *Homeward to Zion: The Mormon Migration from Scandinavia.* Minneapolis, Minn., 1957.

Taylor, P. A. M. *Expectations Westward: The Mormons and the Emigration of their British Converts in the Nineteenth Century.* Ithaca, N.Y., 1966.

PERSHING, JOHN JOSEPH

U.S. Army officer John Joseph Pershing served as a commander of the American Punitive Expedition in pursuit of FRANCISCO ("PANCHO") VILLA from 1916 to 1917. He was born in Laclede, Linn County, Missouri, the son of John Frederick and Anne E. Thompson Pershing.

At the age of eighteen, Pershing began teaching at a black school in Laclede. Within a short time, he transferred to Prairie Mound, an all-white school. Continuing his education at the Missouri State Normal School, he received his bachelor's degree in elementary didactics in June 1880.

Young and ambitious, Pershing applied for admission to the U.S. Military Academy at West Point.

Accepted as a cadet in 1882, he did not excel in his academic performance, but he clearly demonstrated an unusual ability for leadership. He was elected president of his class and captain of cadets.

After graduating and receiving his commission as a second lieutenant, Pershing was assigned to the U.S. Sixth Cavalry in New Mexico and South Dakota. He later joined the faculty of the University of Nebraska at Lincoln where he taught military science and served as commandant of the corps of cadets from 1891 to 1895. While at the university, he was promoted to first lieutenant and obtained a bachelor's degree in law.

Pershing returned to the Military Academy in 1897 as a tactical officer. His exactness and demanding discipline along with his earlier experiences with the BUFFALO SOLDIERS, African American soldiers in the West, earned him the nickname "Nigger Jack" or "Black Jack." He served in the Philippines during the Spanish-American War on three separate occasions. In 1905, he was promoted from captain to brigadier general.

After leading the expedition against Pancho Villa, Pershing was appointed commander-in-chief of the American Expeditionary Forces in Europe during World War I. He was promoted to army chief of staff in 1921.

Pershing retired in 1924 to devote his remaining years to directing the American Battle Monuments Commission and to writing his memoirs, *My Experiences in the World War* (1931), a book that was awarded a Pulitzer Prize.

—*Fred L. Koestler*

SEE ALSO: Mexican Border Conflicts

SUGGESTED READING:

Vandiver, Frank E. *Black Jack: The Life and Times of John J. Pershing*. 2 vols. College Station, Tex., 1977.

PESTICIDES

Hydraulic societies, such as that dominating much of the trans-Mississippi West in the late nineteenth century, highly centralized cultures based on the large-scale irrigation of arid or semiarid lands, are often—as Donald Worster points out—ideal breeding grounds for pests given the warm moist environments created by the waterworks typical of such societies. Pests appeared early in the "reclaimed" West, and farmers in the region quickly became advocates of pest control. In 1872, an imported scale insect that fed off tree sap attacked California's citrus groves, and the state responded by introducing the Australian lady bug, a beetle that fed on scale insects. Such clever use of biological methods of control, though not uncommon, frequently gave way, in the twentieth century, to technological controls, most of them deadly new chemical pesticides developed by a burgeoning science industry. Although the avid use of chemical pesticides was a widespread phenomena in the American West, and corn-growing Iowa farmers were quite as addicted to them as those raising fruit and vegetables in California, Western irrigation farmers turned almost exclusively to a series of deadly compounds. Especially after World War II, they became some of the first and the best customers for companies producing new pesticides such as DDT.

From 1962 to 1974, pesticide use doubled in the nation as a whole and then doubled again in the next eight years, and it was the irrigated West that set the pace of the escalating chemical attacks on pests. California was consistently the leading user of chemical pesticides. In 1978, the state spent $1 billion on pesticides—insecticides, rodenticides, HERBICIDES, fungicides—nearly 20 percent of the American total. And that was almost two decades after Rachel Carson had revealed in *Silent Spring* (1962) the deadly impact of chlorinated hydrocarbons such as DDT on the wildlife refuges and the human communities surrounding reclamation lands. Their use continued even after consumers began to worry about the dangerous residues on the fruits and vegetables they ate. The poisons were linked by scientific studies to health problems ranging from liver and blood diseases to cancer, and traces of them appeared in the fatty tissues of nearly all Americans.

It was not as if Western farmers were unaware of the potential harm pesticides could cause. Farm workers in particular, hired to do the actual spraying and dusting of cauliflower, peaches, lettuce, strawberries, and the like, suffered from blisters, inflamed skin, and reddened eyes, symptoms afflicting workers entering the sprayed fields to pick produce even a month after spraying. Between 1950 and 1961, more than three thousand farm workers were poisoned by pesticides in California, with twenty-two adults and sixteen children dying from what one University of California biophysicist labeled the greatest occupational hazard of any type of work in the state. Although few may have had any premonition of the consequences of chemical pesticides in the beginning, even after their dangers became known, it proved difficult to shake off their use. DDT was banned in 1972, but other chlorinated hydrocarbons continued in use—heptachlor, aldrin, dieldren, chlordane, and endrin—as well as such organic phosphates as parathion, malathion, DNCP, EBD, benzine, hexachloride, and toxaphene. Pests developed immunities with each application and then re-

quired stronger doses, which, in turn, often served to swell the number of pests by killing off their natural predators.

As farmers sprayed codling moths in the apple orchards of the Yakima Valley, pink boll weevils infesting cotton in Arizona and the Imperial Valley, aphids crawling on cantaloupes in Colorado, or spider mites swarming alfalfa fields in the San Joaquin Valley, chemical pesticides sometimes threatened water supplies, and consumers and urbanites began to protest the use of pesticides. Agricultural interests, fearful of the very collapse of the irrigation economy, exercised their financial might in Western statehouses and in Washington, D.C. By the late twentieth century, the use of pesticides sometimes resembled chemical warfare. Around Los Angeles, for example, helicopters swarmed overhead during medfly invasions and sprayed the entire region for days, while large numbers of the urban population huddled anxiously in homes they were warned not to leave by media announcers as, all the while, government spokespersons assured them that the danger was minimal.

— *Charles Phillips*

SEE ALSO: Carson, Rachel, and *Silent Spring*

SUGGESTED READING:

Bosch, Robert van den. *The Pesticide Conspiracy.* Garden City, N.Y., 1980.

Carson, Rachel. *Silent Spring.* Boston, 1962.

Dunlap, Thomas. *DDT.* Princeton, N.J., 1981.

Perkins, John. *Insects, Experts, and the Insecticide Crisis.* New York, 1982.

PETROLEUM

SEE: Oil and Gas Industry

PEYOTE RELIGION

SEE: Native American Church

PHELAN, JAMES DUVAL

California politician and banker, James Duval Phelan (1861–1930) was born in SAN FRANCISCO to wealthy Irish-immigrant parents. He graduated from St. Ignatius College (San Francisco) in 1881, studied law, and entered his father's banking business. He never married.

Active in civic organizations, Phelan quickly established himself as a political reformer by attacking municipal corruption. A Democrat, he was elected mayor of San Francisco three times and served from 1897 to 1901. As mayor, he secured a new charter and promoted new schools, parks, and hospital facilities. During a bitter strike in 1901, he allowed city police to protect strikebreakers and thereby incurred the wrath of organized labor; he did not seek reelection.

Leader of the California Democratic party throughout the Progressive era, Phelan merged politics, business affairs, and civic activities. He gave generously of his fortune, especially for civic beautification, libraries, and charities. He served briefly as regent for the University of California beginning in 1898. After the 1906 earthquake, he led the private organization that dispensed relief to victims of the disaster. Throughout his career, in public office or not, Phelan argued that utility monopolies would inevitably corrupt city politics and that the only alternative was municipal ownership of electric, gas, water, and streetcar systems. He worked persistently to secure the Hetch Hetchy Valley as a reservoir for San Francisco's water supply. From 1906 to 1909, as a private citizen, he helped fund the San Francisco Graft Prosecution, an investigation of the alleged boss ABRAHAM (ABE) RUEF, corrupt city officeholders, and the business leaders who bribed them.

In 1914, Phelan won election to the U.S. Senate, where he made little mark aside from his efforts to exclude Asian immigrants. Insisting that "this is a white man's country," he asserted that Asians could not be assimilated and would undermine wage levels and democratic government. He was not reelected in 1920.

—*Robert W. Cherny*

SEE ALSO: City Government; Progressivism

SUGGESTED READING:

Issel, William, and Robert W. Cherny. *San Francisco, 1865–1932: Politics, Power, and Urban Development.* Berkeley and Los Angeles, Calif., 1986.

Starr, Kevin. *Americans and the California Dream, 1850–1915.* New York, 1973.

Walsh, James P., and Timothy J. O'Keefe. *Legacy of a Native Son: James Duval Phelan and Villa Montalvo.* Los Gatos, Calif., 1993.

PHILLIPS, BERT G.

SEE: Taos School of Artists

PHILLIPS, FRANK

Financier, oil man, and art collector Frank Phillips (1873–1950) was born in Scotia, Nebraska, and grew

up in Creston, Iowa, where he became a banker before moving to the Indian Territory in 1903 to join the booming OIL AND GAS INDUSTRY. Organizing the Phillips Petroleum Company in 1917, he became the first president of the company and ran the operation for most of his life. Quite a wealthy man by the 1920s, Phillips avidly pursued an interest in the culture and natural heritage of the American West. He established a wildlife preserve at his Woolaroc Ranch and stocked it with elks, deer, and buffaloes. An aviation buff as well, he built a small museum on the property to house and display a monoplane that he sponsored in a race between Oakland, California, and Honolulu held in 1927, the same year Charles A. Lindbergh first flew across the Atlantic. From this seed grew an enlarged building for his expanding number of guns, paintings, sculptures, and other Western memorabilia. After funding an excavation of prehistoric Indian mounds through the University of Oklahoma, Phillips used his contacts on the dig to hire a professional museum director in 1941 to run the Woolaroc Museum, which today houses one of the larger private collections in the Southwest and displays such Western artists a O. E. Berninghaus and Joseph Henry Sharp. Another Phillips family estate, one belonging to Frank's brother, Waite Phillips, became Tulsa's Philbrook Art Center, home of the American Indian Artists' Annual Festival.

—*Charles Phillips*

PHOENIX, ARIZONA

Phoenix was a late-comer to the Southwestern urban frontier. In 1867, a few pioneers from the small mining camp of Wickenburg moved fifty miles southeast into the Salt River valley in central ARIZONA. Admiring the remains of the canal system of the ancient Hohokam Indian civilization, these pioneers sensed the agricultural possibilities of the area. Homesteading land near the Salt River, clearing out old irrigation ditches and building new ones, planting crops, and negotiating supply contracts with nearby military posts and mining camps, these first settlers, soon followed by others, created a viable economic base.

In 1870, the settlers, numbering about two hundred, selected a town site near the geographic center of the valley. Realizing that they were revitalizing the land of an ancient agricultural people, the settlers named the new town Phoenix, in their view a fitting symbol of life rising anew from the remains of the past. Growth was slow but steady; by 1872, the valley was home to 1,000 residents, one-third of whom lived in Phoenix. Observers predicted a bright future for Phoenix, by then the seat of Maricopa County.

In 1887, a branch line of the SOUTHERN PACIFIC RAILROAD, the Maricopa and Phoenix, connected Phoenix, an Anglo-dominated desert oasis, to the outside world. Two years later, the importance of the city was recognized by the legislature when it moved the territorial capital from Prescott to Phoenix; the move proved to be permanent. In 1895, another branch railroad, the Santa Fe, Prescott and Phoenix, connected with the Santa Fe main line running across North Arizona and provided the city access to two transcontinental outlets. Boosters called Phoenix the future metropolis of Arizona, but growth continued to be slow and steady; by 1900, the population reached 5,544.

Among other beneficial services to Phoenix, the railroads provided transportation for the increasing number of health-seekers and winter tourists seeking relief and relaxation in the Arizona sun. Phoenix promoters supported hospitals and hotels, but they recognized that progress was doomed unless they solved the desert valley's WATER problem. Deciding that a water-storage system was the answer, they formed the Salt River Valley Water Users' Association, an organization that took advantage of the NEWLANDS RECLAMATION ACT OF 1902 and supported the federal government in the construction of nearby Roosevelt Dam (completed in 1911). This endeavor and others brought vital stability, allowed IRRIGATION control, and ensured agricultural growth.

With the development of a stable water-supply and distribution system, the valley bloomed, and Phoenix boomed. The population of the city reached 11,134 in 1910, and the following decade, it almost tripled to 29,053. By 1920, Phoenix had surpassed Tucson in official population, and it was the largest and most important urban center in Arizona. The demands of American participation in World War I and a "cotton craze" in the valley contributed to the boom. In addition, as a service center, the oasis city continued to serve the expanding Phoenix population as well as a vast hinterland of small towns, farms, ranches, and mines.

In the 1920s, the four C's—CLIMATE, cotton, cattle, and copper—continued to contribute to the advancement of Phoenix and the Salt River valley. The climate made the area one of the most inviting winter-resort centers in the country, and affluent visitors flocked to the Westward Ho, the Arizona Biltmore, and other luxury hotels. The city "where winter never comes" became known as "Delightful Phoenix, the Garden Spot of the Southwest." The desert oasis also became more accessible with the arrival of the Southern Pacific main line in 1926 and the inauguration of scheduled airline service in 1927; these means of transportation made it easier for people to respond to the opportunities and amenities available in the Phoenix

area. Phoenix remained an Anglo-dominated city over the years. Mexicans and Mexican Americans made up the largest minority group; they numbered 7,293 or 15.2 percent of the population in 1930. At that time, Phoenix was a regional urban center of 48,118 inhabitants, the largest city in the Southwest between El Paso and Los Angeles, and local leaders felt justified in calling it the "vital hub" of the state.

By 1930, Phoenix had established itself as a leading urban center of the Southwest and exerted an important influence on the development of the region. During the 1930s, Phoenix suffered less from the Great Depression than many of its counterparts elsewhere, and during and following World War II, it experienced an economic boom and population explosion that thrust it toward metropolis status.

—Bradford Luckingham

SEE ALSO: Urban West

SUGGESTED READING:

Johnson, G. Wesley. *Phoenix: Valley of the Sun.* Tulsa, Okla., 1982.

Luckingham, Bradford. *Phoenix: The History of a Southwestern Metropolis.* Tucson, Ariz., 1989.

———. "Trouble in a Sunbelt City." *Journal of the Southwest* 33 (Spring 1991): 52–67.

———. *The Urban Southwest: A Profile History of Albuquerque, El Paso, Phoenix, and Tucson.* El Paso, Tex., 1982.

PHOTOGRAPHY

Before the advent of the daguerreotype—a photograph produced on a copper plate coated with silver—in 1839, Easterners interested in the American West depended for their information about the region on the frequently fanciful paintings of romantic artists, the sometimes exaggerated tales of popular writers, and the occasionally inaccurate or misguided descriptions of flamboyant and often amateur explorers. Photographs offered the potential for accurate, true-to-life images, and they were hailed as "mirrors with a memory" for those fascinated with the Far West, especially in the wake of the California gold rush a decade later. By 1851, San Francisco photographer Robert H. Vance had brought to New York an exhibit of some three hundred daguerreotypes that depicted for excited urbanites gold mines, Forty-niners, California Indians, and the already legendary business leaders spawned by the rush. During the United States–Mexican War, typesetters accompanying General JOHN ELLIS WOOL's campaign to Saltillo made panoramic views of the region from daguerreotypes. Soon, photographs of the West were all the rage, and commercial photographers rushed to the region to capture anything they could find—Indians, Indian camps and villages, rivers, U.S. Army outposts, early towns and villages, steamboats, and some amazing natural phenomena and incredible landscapes—to hawk to Eastern customers.

By the 1850s, it had become standard operating procedure for Western expeditions to document their work with daguerreotypes. Artists often doubled as photographers, as did Solomon Nuñes Caravalho when he accompanied JOHN CHARLES FRÉMONT on his fifth and final expedition to the American West in 1853. Governor I. I. Stevens took JOHN MIX STANLEY on his 1853 survey of a potential transcontinental rail route, and the artist produced a number of photographs as well as sketches and paintings. The same year, photographers were with Captain F. W. Landers exploration, which surveyed a proposed road from Salt Lake City

Technological advances in photography in the 1860s enabled photographers to accompany government-sponsored expeditions to the West. The images they brought back of Western lands and peoples captivated the American public. This nineteenth-century engraving suggests the rigors of the Western photographer's life, contending with weather and the elements while trying to shoot and develop his delicate images. *Courtesy Library of Congress.*

For a perfect shot of the Yosemite Valley, William Henry Jackson set up his camera on Glacier Point above a 3,254-foot drop. *Courtesy Denver Public Library, Western History Department.*

east through the South Pass of the Rocky Mountains. Although the American Civil War brought a halt to such expeditions, the work of Mathew Brady andothers in photographing the war itself advanced the art of photography and its use in the field. The use of glass-plate negatives and paper prints, introduced in 1851, became widespread, and army cameramen developed horse-drawn field darkrooms to transport the heavy equipment used in early photography. After the war, some familiar with photography themselves settled in the rapidly developing West, while itinerant commercial photographers traveled the region with their mobile darkrooms. Doubling as apothecaries, booksellers, medicine-show men, and opticians, photographers set up studios, which captured the people as well as the places of the West, a few of them young women persuaded to pose for "art" paintings and dressed in diaphanous robes when they were dressed at all, which brought a vaguely unsavory reputation to the commerce as a whole.

Accomplished photographers documented the postwar occupation of the North American continent by the United States. Civil War photographer Alexander Gardner followed the quick settlement of Kansas after the war in the wake of the new Homestead Act. Alfred A. Hart and Andrew J. Russell captured on glass the building of the transcontinental railroad from opening ceremonies at Sacramento and Omaha until the final spike was driven at Promontory Summit, Utah. A slew of talented government photographers—TIMOTHY H. O'SULLIVAN, John K. Hillers, James Fennemore, E. O. Beaman, and the dean of them all, WILLIAM HENRY JACKSON—continued to document the work of federal expeditions in the West, which once more began in earnest after the war with CLARENCE KING's three expeditions into the Rocky Mountains in the late 1860s

In about 1872, John K. Hillers, a photographer accompanying John Wesley Powell's excursions, took a photograph of himself at work with his negatives while camped on the Aquarius Plateau, Utah Territory. *Courtesy National Archives.*

The West provided an endless number of majestic vistas. In 1874, William Henry Jackson recorded Harry Yount, forest manager, posed in the Yellowstone Valley. *Courtesy National Archives.*

The photographer recorded settlement and community growth. An unknown photographer documented Deadwood, Dakota Territory, in its gold-rush days of 1876. *Courtesy Nebraska State Historical Society.*

and FERDINAND VANDEVEER HAYDEN's explorations of the 1870s. Not merely the natural landscape, the Grand Canyon and the Colorado River, but also the Native American inhabitants of the region became favorite subjects for these photographers as they had once been for portraitists such as GEORGE CATLIN and for earlier daguerreotype photographers. William Henry Jackson created an immense catalog of Indian portraits; William Soule produced a rare visual record of the Southern Plains Indians during his stay at Fort Sill in the Indian Territory between 1869 and 1874; W. H. Illingworth worked with GEORGE ARMSTRONG CUSTER; V. T. McGillicuddy photographed Sioux and Cheyenne Indians in the Black Hills of the Dakotas in 1874 and 1875; John K. Hillers produced pictures that later provided ethnographers with indispensable information about the Paiutes, Mojaves, and Havasupais; A. F. Randall, Ben Wittick, and A. C. Vroman turned their cameras on the Pueblos, Navajos, Hopis, Zunis, Apaches, and other tribes along the Rio Grande and in the Southwest. The trend toward hiring photographers for almost every branch of government continued well into the twentieth century, when Dorothea Lange, for example, documented the Midwest's Dust Bowl for the Farm Security Administration.

Many photographers not on the government payroll also captured the building of the trans-Mississippi

West in the second half of the nineteenth century. Erwin Smith, G. F. Swearingen, and William S. Prettyman documented the great cattle drives across Texas, Oklahoma, and Kansas, while SOLOMON D. BUTCHER captured the hard essence of homesteading on the Nebraska plains. Darius Kinsey and a German immigrant named Wilhelm Hester made a record of the Pacific Northwest's loggers and Puget Sound sawmills. Trained by Mathew Brady, Stanley J. Morrow took pictures of the steamboats, forts, and Indians of the Dakota Territory around Yankton, including soon famous ones of the Little Bighorn battlefield shortly after the fighting had ended. Charles R. Savage, who roamed the region from the Mississippi to the Pacific, recorded the building of Salt Lake City. A century of growth in San Diego, California, was captured on film by the likes of Charles Fessenden, Herbert R. Fitch, Henry Payne, the Parker brothers, and John A. Sheriff. San Francisco boasted a wealth of talented photographers: a former whaler named I. W. Taber, George Fiske, and Eadward Muybridge. The city's Carleton Watkins loved to photograph the Yosemite Valley; William Henry Rulofson was fascinated by portraits; Arnold Genthe became known for his photographs of San Francisco's Chinatown.

Almost every Western community and every Western industry of any size would create photographic archives for the works of these photographers and others who recorded the region's development. Among the better known of the Western photograph archives are the Bancroft Library, the HUNTINGTON LIBRARY, ART COLLECTIONS, AND BOTANICAL GARDENS, the California Historical Society, the LOS ANGELES COUNTY MUSEUM OF NATURAL HISTORY, the OAKLAND MUSEUM OF CALIFORNIA, the University of Washington, Denver Public Library, Colorado State Historical Society, University of Wyoming, ARIZONA HISTORICAL SOCIETY, Kansas State Historical Society, University of Oklahoma Library, NATIONAL COWBOY HALL OF FAME AND WESTERN HERITAGE CENTER, Buffalo Bill Historical Center, MUSEUM

Timothy H. O'Sullivan's image of Cottonwood Canyon in the Wasatch Mountains, about 1869. *Courtesy National Archives.*

of New Mexico, and the San Diego Historical Society, plus such federal agencies as the Smithsonian Institution, the Library of Congress, and the National Archives.

As the images held by these institutions testify, great nineteenth-century landscape photographers abounded in the West—Watkins, Fiske, Muybridge, Vroman, and Jackson, as well as F. J. Haynes of Montana and Wyoming and Ashael Curtis of the Washington Territory—a tradition that continued in Western photography far into the twentieth century with the likes of Edward Weston and Ansel Adams. Dragging eighty pounds of bulky equipment into remote regions and setting up their tripods and cameras draped with black cloths wherever the angles seemed promising, the nineteenth-century photographers worked with syrupy and smelly chemicals and fragile coated glass under the hot sun and in bad weather to produce for their government and paying customers images that proved, in the long run, to hold as much fascination as any romantic painting had earlier in the century and that in their own ways—staged and cropped—could be just as misleading as romanticized paintings. The impact of Western photography was perhaps greater than that of the early paintings and lithographs. The photographic albums government photographers such as William Henry Jackson turned over to Congress sparked an interest in national reserves and parks. Published photographs of the West provided viewers with images they felt comfortable in believing were true representations of the region, from railroads triumphant to the Wounded Knee Massacre, from the gleaming accomplishment of the Hoover Dam to the shameful internment of Japanese Americans during World War II, images that told the story of the region and at the same time promoted the sense of a shared nationhood and a deeper connection to the West even among those who had never traveled beyond the Mississippi.

—*Charles Phillips*

Photographers chronicled the lives of Native Americans encountered in the West, although often images were staged or contrived for effect. Americans back East perhaps thought they were receiving photographs of Indians as they had always been, but usually, by the time photographers captured the lives and leaders of Native Americans, they were already under white domination. On the left, a Paiute and his daughter in front of their dwelling in 1872. *Courtesy National Archives.* On the right, Poison, a one-hundred-year-old Cheyenne women posed for the camera in 1888. *Courtesy National Archives.*

John K. Hillers documented Dancer's Rock, Walpi, Arizona, part of a Hopi pueblo, in 1879. *Courtesy National Archives.*

SEE ALSO: Art; Exploration: United States Expeditions; Transcontinental Railroad Surveys

SUGGESTED READING:
Naef, Weston J., et al. *Era of Exploration: The Rise of Landscape Photography in the American West, 1860–1885.* Buffalo, N. Y., 1975.
Sandweiss, Martha A., ed. *Photography in Nineteenth-Century America.* Fort Worth, Tex., 1991.

PICKETT, BILL

The first black cowboy star and creator of the modern RODEO event of bulldogging or steer wrestling, Bill (William) Pickett (1870–1932) was the son of former slaves. He was born in the Jenks Branch Community near Austin, Texas. He left school after the fifth grade to become a cowboy. Copying the dogs used locally to herd cattle, Pickett learned to subdue steers by biting their upper lips; he also became an excellent roper and rider.

In 1888, Pickett and his brothers established a business in Taylor, Texas, and performed at the county fair where he bulldogged steers. He jumped from his horse to a steer's back, bit its lip, and threw it to the ground by twisting its horns. After touring the West with his brothers, Pickett achieved sensational national publicity with his bulldogging exhibition at the 1904 Cheyenne Frontier Days. His appearance at the event led to a contract with the famous MILLER BROTHERS 101 RANCH AND WILD WEST SHOW and performances across the United States and abroad with his horse Spradley. As the "Dusky Demon," he also starred in western films. He might have been a big rodeo winner had racism not frequently barred him from competing. Pickett lived and worked at the 101 Ranch with his wife and nine children until his accidental death. The tragedy stunned fellow performers and brought accolades from the great Will Rogers among others.

Pickett was the first black honoree at the National Rodeo Hall of Fame at Oklahoma City, Oklahoma, and he has also been honored by the Prorodeo Hall of Fame and Museum of the American Cowboy at Colorado Springs, Colorado. During the 1990s, the Bill Pickett Rodeo Tour also honored his legacy and that

of other African American Western cowboys. Thanks to Bill Pickett, bulldogging is a major rodeo contest.

—*Mary Lou LeCompte*

SUGGESTED READING:

Hanes, Bailey C. *Bill Pickett: Bulldogger.* Norman, Okla., 1977.
White, Evelyn C. "Paul Stewart's Romance with the West." *Smithsonian* 20 (August 1989): 58–71.

PICO, PÍO DE JESUS

The last governor of Mexican California, Pío de Jesus Pico (1801–1894) was born at the mission of San Gabriel when Alta California was the far northwestern frontier of Spain's American empire. By the time he died in Los Angeles, California had passed from Spanish sovereignty to that of Mexico and then to the United States.

Pico was perhaps the most vocal of the Mexican revolutionaries during a period when, for many Californios (native-born Californians of Hispanic descent), political activism was defined by challenging the existing government. The coup he headed in 1831 led to his first term as governor, which was short-lived, as was typical during these turbulent years. Pico was a member of the territorial assembly from 1828 until 1841 or 1842. He became governor again in February 1845 and served until August 1846 when Los Angeles, the capital, was captured by the American invasion force. After unsuccessfully seeking aid in Mexico to repulse the Americans, Pico returned to adapt to American rule in his homeland.

During the second half of his life, he engaged in several business ventures that earned him substantial wealth and was active in civic affairs. He embodied the "American" values and believed in opportunity, capitalism, and progress. Nonetheless, he lived to witness his own financial ruin, caused by prejudicial treatment of Californios at the hands of unscrupulous people and a biased judicial system. In one of the most shameful of American land cases (*Pico* v. *Cohn,* 1892), the state Supreme Court stripped Pico of all his property, despite acknowledging that perjured testimony and forged documents helped the court formulate its judgment.

Although Pico's life is not well known to the general public, his name is familiar to Californians because of the many places named in honor of him and other members of his family.

—*Janet R. Fireman*

SUGGESTED READING:

Barrows, Henry D. "Pío Pico: A Biographical and Character Sketch of the Last Mexican Governor of Alta California." *Annual Publications of the Historical Society of Southern California* 3 (1894): 55–66.
Cole, Martin, and Henry, Welcome. *Don Pío Pico's Historical Narrative.* Glendale, Calif., 1973.

PICOTTE, SUSAN LAFLESCHE

Indian physician, reformer, and civic leader Susan LaFlesche Picotte (1866–1915) was born on the Omaha reservation in Nebraska. The daughter of Joseph LaFlesche, "progressive" chief of the Omaha Indians, and his wife Mary Gale, Susan LaFlesche was educated at the reservation mission school, a young ladies' academy in New Jersey, and Hampton Institute in Virginia. With the help of the Connecticut branch of the WOMEN'S NATIONAL INDIAN ASSOCIATION, a philanthropic reform group, she then attended the Woman's Medical College in Philadelphia, from which she graduated in March 1889 as the first Indian woman physician in the United States.

Susan LaFlesche Picotte. *Courtesy Nebraska Historical Society.*

After her graduation, she returned to the Omaha reservation where she planned to open a hospital. In 1894, she married Henry Picotte, a French Sioux, with whom she had two sons; after her husband died in 1905, she moved to the newly incorporated town of Walthill, Nebraska.

Picotte created for herself a unique role as civic leader, doctor, missionary, and spokesperson for the Omaha Indians. She was an avid supporter of prohibition; a founder of Walthill's Presbyterian church; president of the local board of health; and a member of the local women's club, the Thurston County Medical Association, the State Medical Society, and the Nebraska Federation of Women's Clubs. Her major satisfaction, however, always came from her work for the Omahas. In addition to treating as many as one hundred patients a month, she assisted countless people with financial or personal problems. She made maximum use of her contacts to cut through government red tape and always blended her concrete assistance with advice firmly rooted in Protestant Christianity and Victorian morality.

In 1913, Picotte saw her dream realized when the Presbyterian Board of Home Missions established a hospital in Walthill. When she died two years later at the age of forty-nine, the hospital was renamed in her honor.

—*Peggy Pascoe*

SUGGESTED READING:

Mathes, Valerie Sherer. "Dr. Susan LaFlesche Picotte: The Reformed and the Reformer." In *Indian Lives: Essays on Nineteenth- and Twentieth-Century Native American Leaders.* Edited by L. G. Moses and Raymond Wilson. Albuquerque, N. Mex., 1985.

Pascoe, Peggy. *Relations of Rescue: The Search for Female Moral Authority in the American West, 1874–1939.* New York, 1990.

PICTURE BRIDES

The seemingly exotic practice of "picture bride" marriages, in which Japanese men living in the United States in the early 1900s married Japanese women known only from photographs, actually combined traditions of Japanese culture with modern technology. Picture bride marriages allowed single Japanese men to find wives and begin families in their adopted homeland without returning to Japan, an undertaking that was too expensive for some and that posed the threat of forced military service for others. The practice built on traditions back home in Japan, where marriages were arranged by the families who worked through a go-between to find suitable mates in terms of background, health, age, and wealth. When a Japanese immigrant was ready to marry, he would send home a photograph of himself with a request that his family find him a wife. When a wife had been found, a marriage ceremony took place in Japan—even though the husband was not present—and the wife's name was entered into the husband's family registry. The wife then set sail for the United States to join her husband.

Japanese picture brides aboard the liner *Shinyu Maru,* arriving in San Francisco, California, in 1920. *Courtesy The Bettmann Archive.*

The picture bride, herself, arriving on the West Coast, after an often grueling voyage, faced a barrage of medical examinations and immigration inspections. There on the docks, she met her husband for the first time. Some Japanese women were distressed to find that the men they had married were much older than their doctored photographs and not so rich as their letters suggested. Other picture brides were bewildered by the forced trip to the clothing store to purchase Western dresses and the rush to forsake their traditional garb. The majority of picture brides, however, made the most of their new lives.

The arrival of thousands of picture brides alarmed American activists, who sensationalized the practice in order to garner support for Japanese exclusion movements. That the marriages produced a number of Nisei

On July 25, 1920, a special delegation of U.S. congressmen inspect the passports of arriving Japanese picture brides at Angel Island in San Francisco. *Courtesy The Bettmann Archive.*

(second-generation, native-born Japanese) offspring was cited as proof in the eyes of prejudicial Americans of how immoral the Japanese people were. Critics of Japanese immigration, led by JAMES DUVAL PHELAN, then U.S. senator from California, saw picture brides as a violation of the GENTLEMEN'S AGREEMENT of 1908, which barred most Japanese from entry into the United States. Under pressure, the Japanese government, by 1920, ceased issuing passports to Japanese women.

—Patricia Hogan

SEE ALSO: Child Rearing: Asian American; Japanese Americans

SUGGESTED READING:

Chan, Sucheng. *Asian Americans: An Interpretive History.* Boston, 1991.

Ichioka, Yuji. *The Issei: The World of the First Generation Japanese Immigrants, 1885–1924.* New York, 1988.

PIERCE, ABEL HEAD ("SHANGHAI")

Texas rancher Abel Head ("Shanghai") Pierce (1834–1900) was born on a family farm near Little Compton, Rhode Island. After a rudimentary education and a brief apprenticeship to his uncle, a Virginia merchant, Pierce stowed away on a ship bound for Texas. He reached Matagorda County in 1854, where he took a job splitting rails and herding cattle for rancher William Bradford Grimes.

While still in Grimes's employ, Pierce began his own herd and increased it rapidly by branding mavericks (unmarked calves on the open range). Along the way he acquired the nickname "Shanghai," fitting for a man destined to become one of the West's most colorful cowmen and sharpest traders.

Pierce served without distinction in the Confederate Army during the Civil War. He married in 1865 and entered into a ranching partnership with his brother Jonathan in Wharton County, Texas. The Pierce brothers supplied the New Orleans market with beef until the Chisholm Trail opened a new road to profit in Kansas.

Following the death of his wife and infant son in 1870 and legal difficulties arising from the hanging of some rustlers the following year, Pierce sold his herds and briefly relocated in Kansas. Returning to Texas, he remarried and became a partner in the 250,000-acre Pierce-Sullivan Pasture Company.

Pierce also invested in railroads, banks, and farms. Although incurring heavy losses due to bank failure, unwise railroad investment, and the Galveston hurricane of 1900, Pierce's assets exceeded $1 million at the time of his death from a cerebral hemorrhage. His investigations into the causes of tick fever later led to the widespread importation of Brahman cattle.

—B. Byron Price

Abel Head ("Shanghai") Pierce. *Courtesy Western History Collections, University of Oklahoma Library.*

SUGGESTED READING:
Emmitt, Chris. *Shanghai Pierce: A Fair Likeness.* Norman, Okla., 1953.
Siringo, Charles A. *A Texas Cowboy.* Chicago, 1885.

PIKE, ALBERT

Albert Pike (1809–1891), soldier, Mason, author, and lawyer, was born in Boston, Massachusetts, the son of Benjamin and Sarah Andrews Pike. He attended school in Newburyport and at Harvard. He then traveled to the West, visited Santa Fe, and settled in Arkansas. He purchased the *Arkansas Advocate* in Little Rock in 1835 and studied law, specializing in Indian affairs and a tangled banking disaster in Arkansas. He fought in the United States–Mexican War and afterward in a duel with John S. Roane. He negotiated treaties with some tribes in the Indian Territory. A supporter of secession, he was commissioned a Confederate brigadier general in the Civil War and took part in the Battle of Pea Ridge. After quarreling with General T. C. Hindman and T. H. Holmes, who placed him under arrest, he resigned his commission. He returned to Arkansas and served on the state's Supreme Court. After the war, he was indicted for treason, and charges that the Indians under his command at Pea Ridge had scalped Union troops haunted him. He was pardoned and returned to the practice of law. He served as editor the *Memphis Appeal* from 1867 to 1868 before settling in Washington, where he died.

Pike's "Hymn to the Gods," published in *Blackwood's Edinburgh Magazine* (1839), made his reputation as a poet. His *Prose Sketches and Poems Written in the Western Country* (1834) secured his place in the Southwest School of literature. He spent his later life writing *Morals and Dogma of the Ancient and Accepted Scottish Rite of Freemasonry* (1872).

—*Michael B. Dougan*

SUGGESTED READING:
Boyden, W. L. *Bibliography of the Writings of Albert Pike: Prose, Poetry, Manuscript.* Washington, D.C., 1921.
Duncan, Robert L. *Reluctant General: The Life and Times of Albert Pike.* New York, 1961.

PIKE, ZEBULON MONTGOMERY

Born in Lamberton, New Jersey, Zebulon Montgomery Pike (1779–1813) served as an army officer and explorer until his death. As a teen-ager, Pike joined his

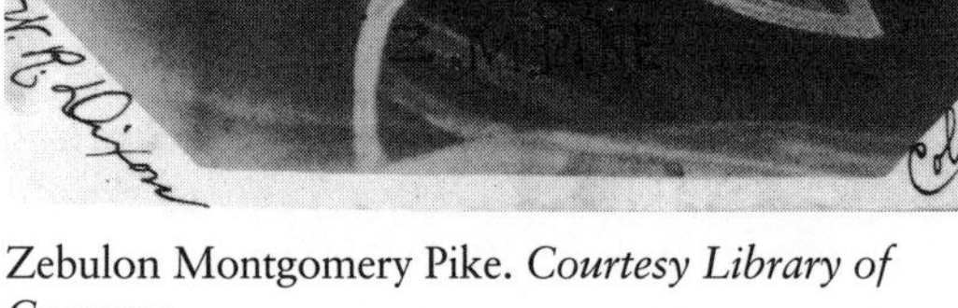

Zebulon Montgomery Pike. *Courtesy Library of Congress.*

father's army unit as a cadet, and in March 1799, he was promoted to the rank of second lieutenant. For the next few years, he served at isolated Western outposts. His chance to prove his competence came in 1805 when General JAMES WILKINSON ordered him to explore the upper Mississippi Valley. The orders directed him to gather geographical data, meet with the Indians, survey potential sites for military garrisons, and investigate the activities of British traders in the region. On August 9, 1805, Pike led his twenty-man command up the Mississippi. The explorers worked their way upstream slowly, stopping to negotiate with Indians and to examine the river valley. Winter set in before the soldiers reached their objective—the headwaters of the Mississippi. Pike then abandoned the party's keelboat, and his men dragged their supplies and equipment overland on sleds. On February 1, 1806, they reached Leech Lake. Erroneously, Pike declared it to be the source of the Mississippi River. He then led his men back downstream, and on April 30, 1806, they arrived in St. Louis. On the nine-month journey, the expedition had traveled nearly five thousand miles, but it had accomplished few of its objectives. The explorers missed the headwaters of the Mississippi, failed to achieve any long-term agreements with the Indians, and had little impact on British trading or diplomatic activities in the region.

Shortly after his return to St. Louis, Pike received new orders. This time General Wilkinson commanded him to lead a party west to locate the headwaters of the Arkansas and Red rivers. On July 15, 1806, Pike led the command of twenty-one soldiers, an interpreter, and a physician out of St. Louis. They moved west across Kansas and then followed the Arkansas River to the Rocky Mountains. There they were unsuccessful in their attempt to climb what is now Pikes Peak and explored the Royal Gorge region of Colorado. Winter overtook the expedition, and with supplies running short, the soldiers built a small stockade for the sick before heading south. Crossing into Spanish New Mexico, the explorers built a larger shelter at the Rio Conejos. There Spanish soldiers took them into custody and led them south to Santa Fe.

Authorities in Santa Fe suspected Pike of spying, a reasonable assumption, and sent him south into Chihuahua for further questioning. The officials treated Pike well, but they seized his maps and journals. When President THOMAS JEFFERSON demanded the Americans' speedy return, the local authorities released them and had the soldiers escorted east across Texas to Louisiana. Pike returned on June 30, 1807, but instead of a hero's welcome, he found his name linked to the questionable actions of General Wilkinson and Aaron Burr in the BURR CONSPIRACY; the explorer apparently had no knowledge of these schemes. In 1810, his published journals gave Americans their first descriptions of the Southern Plains and the Rockies.

Pike's explorations ended with the ill-fated 1806 expedition, but he continued to serve at a variety of Western posts until the War of 1812. In March 1813, he became a brigadier general, but he died a month later while leading troops at the capture of York (Toronto) Canada.

—*Roger L. Nichols*

SUGGESTED READING:

Hollon, W. Eugene. *The Lost Pathfinder: Zebulon Montgomery Pike.* Norman, Okla., 1949.

Jackson, Donald, ed. *Journals of Zebulon Montgomery Pike.* Norman, Okla., 1966.

PIKE'S PEAK EXPRESS COMPANY

The Leavenworth and Pike's Peak Express began service between Leavenworth, Kansas, and Denver, Colorado, on April 18, 1850. It was the brainchild of freighter WILLIAM HEPBURN RUSSELL, who believed that a stagecoach express route serving the newly discovered Pikes Peak gold fields would be profitable, even in the absence of the usual federal subsidies. His regular business partners, WILLIAM BRADFORD WADDELL and ALEXANDER MAJORS, lacked his faith and opposed the venture. Accordingly, Russell took freighter John S. Jones as his partner to create Jones, Russell and Company.

The freighters surveyed a route between the Santa Fe and Oregon trails and deployed 108 men along twenty-seven way stations spread 25 miles apart over a total distance of 680 miles. In May 1859, Jones, Russell and Company acquired J. M. Hockaday and Company's contract to carry the mail from St. Joseph, Missouri, to Salt Lake City. Despite this acquisition, revenues were well below what the partners had anticipated, largely due to the premature failure of the Pikes Peak boom. Waddell and Alexander, fearful that their own ongoing partnership with Russell would be in jeopardy, bought out the faltering company in October 1859. It was reorganized as the Central Overland California and Pike's Peak Company. Again, despite the acquisition of a semimonthly mail-delivery contract forfeited by rival freighter GEORGE CHORPENNING, the reorganized company operated at a loss. One disgruntled employee, whom the company had failed to pay, declared that COC&PP Express stood for "Clear Out of Cash and Poor Pay."

In 1861, the company became a subcontractor of the OVERLAND MAIL COMPANY, which had secured a lucrative mail contract. By 1862, however, the property of the Central Overland and Pike's Peak Express was offered at auction and purchased by master freighter BEN HOLLADAY.

—*Alan Axelrod*

PIMA INDIANS

SEE: Native American Peoples: Peoples of the Southwest

PINCHOT, GIFFORD

Gifford Pinchot (1865–1946) introduced the first systematic forest management in the United States at Biltmore, the George W. Vanderbilt estate outside of Asheville, North Carolina. He established the national forest system and generally promoted forest conservation and regulation.

Born in Simsbury, Connecticut, he was the oldest son of James W. Pinchot, a prosperous New York and Pennsylvania manufacturer. Gifford Pinchot was educated in Paris and New York City. He also attended Phillips Exeter Academy in New Hampshire and Yale

University. After graduating from Yale in 1889, he set out to become a professional forester. Because the profession was unknown in this country at that time, he went to France to study at the Forest School in Nancy. He then toured model forests in France, Switzerland, and Germany before returning to the United States at the end of 1890.

His first major American assignment came in February 1892 when he was hired to manage the forest lands on the Biltmore estate. After setting up a planned forestry program there, he opened an office in New York City in December 1893 and offered his services as a consulting forester. From 1893 to 1898, he developed management plans for privately owned forests in the Adirondacks, Pennsylvania, and New Jersey, and in the course of this work, he established the principles and guidelines for academic forestry instruction in the United States.

In 1896, Pinchot was appointed to the National Forestry Commission, a body charged with formulating national forest policy. This led to his appointment the next year as special agent for the U.S. Department of the Interior and then, in 1898, to the post of chief of the U.S. Department of Agriculture's Division of Forestry, forerunner of the UNITED STATES FOREST SERVICE. Pinchot engaged the enthusiastic support of the conservation-minded president THEODORE ROOSEVELT in formulating a cooperative forest-management program to aid private forest owners. More significantly, Pinchot established the national forest system and generally promulgated forest conservation and regulation. These efforts culminated in the landmark 1908 White House conference on forest conservation and regulation—a conference that created the National Conservation Commission. Named chairman of the commission, Pinchot then undertook the first comprehensive inventory of the nation's natural resources.

Pinchot founded the Society of American Foresters in 1900 and the National Conservation Association in 1909, and he served on many conservation commissions—including the Public Lands Commission, Inland Waterways Commission, and the Commission on Country Life—that had a strong effect on land-use policy in the West and elsewhere. Not everyone in the conservation community greeted Pinchot's efforts warmly. JOHN MUIR, who called for complete federal protection of public forest lands, accused Pinchot of being a scientific exploiter of the nation's natural heritage. The dispute between Muir and Pinchot came to a head in the HETCH HETCHY CONTROVERSY. The city of San Francisco wanted to build a dam in the Hetch Hetchy Valley of Yosemite Park to create a municipal reservoir, and Pinchot agreed to this use of a portion of the national park. Muir and the newly formed SIERRA CLUB opposed the proposal but lost to the combined efforts of the San Francisco city fathers and the federal government in 1913.

After 1910, however, Pinchot was no longer chief forester. During the long Hetch Hetchy battle, Pinchot accused Secretary of the Interior Richard A. Ballinger of having aided private interests in acquiring Alaskan coal lands. President William Howard Taft removed Pinchot as head of the Forest Service when he attacked Ballinger directly in January 1910. The BALLINGER-PINCHOT CONTROVERSY not only made headlines, it split the Republican party wide open and prompted Theodore Roosevelt to begin a third-party campaign aimed at defeating Taft in his bid for reelection in 1912.

Pinchot remained president of the National Conservation Association after he was fired from the Forest Service and ran unsuccessfully for the Senate in 1920 and 1926. He was twice elected governor of Pennsylvania and served from 1922 to 1927 and from 1931 to 1935. He was also a prolific author, whose works include *Biltmore Forest* (1893), *The Adirondack Spruce* (1898), *A Primer of Forestry* (Part 1, 1899; Part 2, 1905), *The Fight for Conservation* (1909), *The Training of a Forester* (1914, 1937), and a highly polemical autobiography, *Breaking New Ground,* published posthumously in 1947.

—*Alan Axelrod*

SUGGESTED READING:

McGeary, M. Nelson. *Gifford Pinchot: Forester-Politician.* Princeton, N.J., 1960.

Pinkett, Harold T. *Gifford Pinchot: Private and Public Forester.* Champaign-Urbana, Ill., 1970.

PINKERTON NATIONAL DETECTIVE AGENCY

Founded in the 1850s, the Pinkerton National Detective Agency grew into America's largest private police force, working on contract with businesses that needed detection and security services. The Pinkerton "operatives" pursued labor anarchists, murderers, Confederate spies, and bank and train robbers and investigated employees suspected of dishonesty. Watchmen from the Pinkerton Protective Patrol guarded businesses. These agency emphases have gradually changed; today, 98 percent of Pinkerton business is providing plant protection.

Allan Pinkerton and his wife left Scotland in 1842 and settled in Dundee, Illinois, where Pinkerton started his detective work. They moved to Chicago, and in 1855, he founded the North West Police Agency, with

a contract to check the honesty of railroad employees. In 1860, he added another large client, the Adams Express Company, and renamed his business Pinkerton's National Detective Agency.

The Pinkertons later gained wide publicity by pursuing notorious train and bank robbers, but the foundation of the business lay in the need of railroads and other rapidly expanding companies to control their workers. The Pinkertons spied on employees and chased professional criminals as well; their detectives could work anywhere, whereas city police and county sheriffs had limited jurisdictions. Not until the twentieth century did public police agencies enjoy regional and national authority.

Allan Pinkerton began by investigating many cases personally and developing his own techniques. He had a talent for selecting good people. George H. Bangs, his first employee, became the general manager. Timothy Webster spied on the Confederates and was captured and hanged. Kate Warne became the first female detective. Charles Angelo Siringo wrote about his twenty-two years as a Pinkerton agent. Tom Horn, a cowboy detective subsequently hanged for murder, and Dashiell Hammett, an author of detective stories, worked as operatives.

Allan Pinkerton headed the agency until his death in 1884, although sons William and Robert were effectively in charge after their father suffered a severe stroke. The main office stayed in Chicago; new ones opened in New York and Philadelphia in 1865 and 1866 and in Denver in 1886. Boston, Kansas City, Portland, St. Paul, and St. Louis were added by 1893. A typical office consisted of the superintendents, the clerical staff, the criminal department with its rogues' gallery, and the detectives. General operatives did undercover work and tracked criminals while secret operatives served as labor spies. Occasional special operatives dealt with minor cases. All training was informal.

Pinkerton techniques included shadowing or spying on employees, infiltrating organizations, gaining the confidence of criminal suspects, and paying informants. The rogues' gallery of photographs and descriptions of lawbreakers was continually expanded and updated, its contents shared with law enforcement agencies elsewhere. The Pinkerton motto became "The Eye That Never Sleeps."

Allan Pinkerton thwarted a plot to assassinate Abraham Lincoln before his inauguration. From 1861 to 1862, he broke up a Confederate spy ring that centered around Washington socialite Rose Greenhow. Pinkerton's agents gathered information from behind Confederate lines. After the Civil War, he chased the Renos, train and bank robbers, until vigilantes lynched them. When Jesse and Frank James held up the bank in Richmond, Missouri, the Pinkertons followed their trail. One detective died while trying to infiltrate the James brothers gang, and another died in a shootout with the Younger brothers. During an attack on a cabin thought to be a hideout of the James boys, Pinkerton agents killed the outlaws' younger half brother and badly injured their mother. After their disastrous Northfield, Minnesota, bank robbery, the James brothers vanished, but the Pinkertons kept after them. Jesse was murdered in 1882; Frank James surrendered later that year.

The Pinkertons trailed outlaw Sam Bass until a gun battle with Texas Rangers ended his career. When night riders in New Mexico tried assassination, operative Charles Siringo infiltrated a lawless Hispanic organization, Las Gorras Blancas, or the White Caps, until he determined that they were not responsible. Governor Thornton employed the Pinkertons for two months when another prominent New Mexican, Albert Jennings Fountain, disappeared. That case remained unsolved. The Pinkertons pursued Butch Cassidy's Wild Bunch after the Montpelier, Idaho, bank heist in 1896. In 1901, Cassidy, the Sundance Kid, and their lady friend Etta Place sailed to Argentina, where operative Frank Dimaio chased them for a couple of months.

The Pinkertons were probably at their best in gathering undercover information. They also earned a good reputation for recovering stolen loot from train and bank robberies. Detective James McParlan joined the Molly Maguires in the Pennsylvania coal mines and helped to send thirteen terrorists to the gallows. The company gained the hatred of organized labor after the Burlington Railroad Strike in 1888, when the Pinkerton agency provided scabs, or strikebreakers. At Homestead, Pennsylvania, Pinkerton guards were met with gunfire by striking steelworkers. Three guards and ten of the strikers died. This virtually ended the Pinkertons' involvement with strikebreaking.

At Coeur d'Alene in northern Idaho, the local miners' union made undercover agent Charles Siringo their recording secretary. Rioting broke out after the mine owners imported scab laborers, and National Guard and federal troops were then called in to restore order. Siringo helped convict eighteen union rioters. Labor troubles in Idaho and Colorado became something of a speciality for the Denver office, especially after the Industrial Workers of the World, or Wobblies, gained prominence.

Following Robert Pinkerton's death in 1907, his son Allan Pinkerton, II, took over the New York office and changed the emphasis to security and property protection. In the 1930s, Allan's son Robert Allan Pinkerton became the last descendant of Allan

Pinkerton to head the business. Labor spying had disappeared by 1940, and detective work gave way to the guarding of property. In January 1988, California Plant Protection paid $95 million to American Brands for Pinkerton's, Inc., and renamed the firm Pinkerton's. By the 1990s, Pinkerton's was headquartered in Van Nuys, California, and the company had forty-three thousand employees and annual revenues of more than $700 million.

—*John P. Wilson*

SEE ALSO: Gorras Blancas, Las

SUGGESTED READING:

Horan, James D. *Desperate Men: Revelations from the Sealed Pinkerton Files*. New York, 1949.

———. *The Pinkertons: The Detective Dynasty That Made History.* New York, 1967.

Morn, Frank. *"The Eye That Never Sleeps": A History of the Pinkerton National Detective Agency.* Bloomington, Ind., 1982.

Schlax, Julie, "The New Pinkerton Man." *Forbes* 146 (September 17, 1990): 46, 48.

Siringo, Charles A. *A Cowboy Detective: A True Story of Twenty-Two Years with a World-Famous Detective Agency.* Lincoln, Nebr., 1988.

PINKLEY, FRANK ("BOSS")

Frank ("Boss") Pinkley (1880–1940) served as superintendent of the Southwestern National Monuments, a far-flung collection of historical, archaeological, and natural park areas under federal administration. Born in Missouri, he moved to Arizona in 1900 and settled at the CASA GRANDE RUINS RESERVATION in 1901. For the next thirty-nine years, Pinkley ran an empire by force of will; he cajoled appropriations from recalcitrant federal officials, created services for visitors, and maintained an odd collection of parks and people by applying initiative, charisma, and a set of uncompromising standards. When he began, little systematic administration had been applied to the cultural features of the Southwest. By the time he died of a heart attack at the opening session of his school for national monument personnel, he had established a network of interrelated parks, procedures and practices for their management, and a tight group of people who had loyalty to him and his organization.

Within the NATIONAL PARK SERVICE, Pinkley was something of a gadfly. In the 1920s, as he put together his system, the emphasis of the agency was on the large scenic national parks. In an era of limited funding, Pinkley believed his parks were slighted by a lack of substantive appropriations, and comparisons of figures bore out his contentions. This led to conflict with the national leadership and, for Pinkley, a kind of marginal status within the agency.

Pinkley typified the entrepreneurial generation that created Western institutions between 1900 and 1930. He learned that the future lay not in the individualism of the past but in a cooperative relationship between local people and state and federal government.

—*Hal Rothman*

SUGGESTED READING:

Rothman, Hal. *Preserving Different Pasts: The American National Monuments.* Urbana, Ill., 1989.

PIONEER LIFE

Euro-American Pioneer Life
Patrick H. Butler, III

Mormon Pioneer Life
Dean L. May

Spanish and Mexican Pioneer Life
Patrick H. Butler, III

EURO-AMERICAN PIONEER LIFE

The character of the Euro-American family in the trans-Mississippi West was shaped by the complexity of the frontier—with its varied physical geography—a mix of more than thirty Indian groups, three major national groups (English, French, and Spanish), many different European and African ethnic groups, and citizens of the new United States. Traditional sources of authority were present but often weak and distant. The West offered opportunities for great wealth through a mix of extractive, agricultural, herding, manufacturing, and commercial enterprises, and in such opportunities lay the attraction for those families moving westward.

For settlers moving to the West, the land had been organized in a grid system based on the principles of the Ordinance of 1785 and which began on the western boundary of Pennsylvania and continued to the Pacific. Government followed the structure prescribed by the Ordinance of 1787, the NORTHWEST ORDINANCE, which provided for the metamorphosis from unsettled frontier to territory and to state.

Often, particularly in the years between the 1780s and the Civil War, family groups moved westward, leaving property behind in the hands either of a stranger or another family member. Families used the proceeds

from the sale of their property back East to acquire much more land at cheaper prices in the West. This expansion followed the course of opening transportation networks, including rivers, roads, and, eventually, railroads. While agriculture usually provided the impetus for the first families to settle in a region, the commercial production of the farms, which was always the focus of the capitalist American families, soon led to the creation of urban centers to serve the needs of the farm families, both as markets and as supply centers.

The expanding West, whether on the prairies of the Great Plains or in the farms of the Pacific Northwest, included substantial numbers of American-born migrants from the East who had often moved West in generational steps. As the nineteenth century passed, increasing numbers of immigrants arrived directly from Europe. With most settlers, traditional preferences in agriculture were often replaced by crops that suited the environment or the market. Within the domestic environment, however, traditional foodways and customs continued for generations. In some instances, imported agricultural preferences introduced new crops, such as grapes, or reappeared after a generation when the family enterprise was stabilized.

The life of the farm family centered on work. In general, roles of men and women were divided between the fields and the home. The husband's work focused on the fields and herds, the primary source of income for the family. No matter the cultural background, the wife was usually responsible for cleaning, food preparation and preservation, manufacture and care of clothing, and other domestic tasks. In addition, the wife usually worked in the garden, often cared for the barnyard animals, milked cows, and churned cream and thus provided hard currency through the sale of these goods. At harvest, the wife would help out, either feeding the hands or sometimes working in the field. Finally, the wife supervised the children. For the most part, despite the gradual mechanization of domestic tasks during the nineteenth century, most housewives had little access to labor-saving devices, particularly before the development of the great mail-order houses of Montgomery Ward and Sears, Roebuck and Company in the last quarter of the century.

Children, who were at least half the household in 72 percent of northern frontier households and 83 percent of southern frontier households were central to the life of the family. They usually supplied essential labor on the farms. With children in a family, the homestead was not quite as lonely as is often described, and the place of family interaction, both within the family and without, among the friends of the children, was as important to the life of the family as the stereotypical polarized roles, which were often less pronounced in actual practice.

While the stereotype described above represented the norm, approximately 15 percent of the farm homes in the West were headed by women in the late nineteenth century. Often, these women were widowed, and to them alone fell the responsibility for maintaining the farm or losing the investment.

Although the farm on the Great Plains is the strongest image of the pioneer frontier for the Euro-Americans, the complex of communities included ranches, mining camps, and small urban centers. The character of life in the different types of communities varied greatly, depending on the resources available and the economic basis of the community. Life on smaller ranches, often established in frontier areas before the arrival of the great cattle companies in the last third of the nineteenth century, were similar, in many respects, to life on the small farms. Because ranching required vast tracts of lands for herding, the domestic life of the ranch family was isolated, and often, because more of the household was made up of itinerant cowboys, ranch life was male-dominated. If ranchers prospered, particularly in the last third of the century, the operation became a complex business with strong ties to urban centers for all members of the family.

Mining towns and CATTLE TOWNS, created for the transshipment of stock by rail, were more complex social groupings, which evolved as the towns' population shifted from primarily male to one of balanced households. During the years after the Civil War, life in the West changed, more in perception than in reality, as images of wide-open cow towns and mining camps found their way into popular culture. In these communities, class differences were most obvious, particularly among women. Women who were devoted to family and the stabilizing institutions of home, church, and school were sharply differentiated from the prostitutes and dance-hall women, who associated with miners and cowboys. As communities stabilized, the class differences became even more dramatic, and it became clear, in towns from Virginia City to Abilene, that the women who associated with the drifters were no longer wanted in the community. With the development of the small urban communities at rail centers that served the ranches, farms, and the extractive industries, the standards imposed were those of the Eastern United States. Institutions of church, school, and civil authority developed.

There was no single style of family in the trans-Mississippi west. Affected by economic circumstance, physical geography, ethnic background, and changing social roles, the character of the individual family could be unique. However, there was a pattern

of change in family life over the course of the century. Particularly in the years before the Civil War, extended families often moved West in groups, sharing economic goals and supporting one another in a variety of entrepreneurial efforts. After the Civil War, however, single families more often made the trek West. In the West of the 1880s and 1890s, the family was restructured. Families were characterized by a companionate relationship between spouses and less by ties to other family members, who may have stayed at home, whether in the East or in Europe.

—Patrick H. Butler, III

SEE ALSO: Child Rearing: Euro-American; Cult of True Womanhood; Farming: Fertility on the Frontier; Homesteading; Mining: Mining Camps and Towns

SUGGESTED READING:

Conzen, Kathleen Neils. "A Saga of Families." In *The Oxford History of the American West.* Edited by Clyde A. Milner, Carol A. O'Connor, Martha A. Sandweis. New York, 1994.

Jeffrey, Julie Roy. *Frontier Women: The Trans-Mississippi West, 1840–1880.* New York, 1979.

Myres, Sandra L. *Westering Women and the Frontier Experience, 1800–1915.* Albuquerque, N. Mex., 1982.

Nelson, Paula M. *After the West Was Won: Homesteaders and Town Builders in Western South Dakota, 1900–1917.* Iowa City, Iowa, 1986.

Underwood, Kathleen. *Town Building on the Colorado Frontier.* Albuquerque, N. Mex., 1987.

In the late 1880s, two Mormon women and their children pose in front of a dairy in a settlement known as Mormon Lake, Arizona. *Courtesy National Archives.*

MORMON PIONEER LIFE

Pioneer life among the MORMONS was greatly different from pioneer life elsewhere in the West. The overarching ideology of a radical and reformist religious faith entered into all aspects of early Mormon culture. Mormon leaders dwelt upon the need for unity and harmony in society; railed against the divisiveness of prevailing systems of ethnicity, class, gender roles, and capitalistic endeavor; and actively pursued alternatives that affected Mormon society profoundly.

In Willamette Valley, large kin groups created tightly knit nodes of social and economic interaction. In contrast, pioneers in Mormon country had usually been severed from old kin and community networks through their conversion and migration to the Great Basin. New social ties were made to church leaders and to fellow "Saints" in a village or church community. In those villages, a communal social ethic was formed and has endured, and a communal economic ethic tempered capitalistic enterprise for a time.

Thus early Mormons were not quite rural in the sense commonly understood. Most did not live on isolated farmsteads; instead, they built their residences within a village and commuted to farm lands on the outskirts. Because of that settlement pattern, Mormon men and women became deeply engaged in organizing and participating in social and cultural institutions, including drama and debating societies, town library committees, choirs, bands, orchestras, relief societies, and numerous other activities that made the social character of their communities more like that of urban than of rural people.

Voluntary positions filled in the rural Mormon village of Alpine, Utah, between 1860 and 1880 totaled 111 percent of the average number of men and women in the community. In the rural district of non-Mormon Middleton, Idaho, the number was 14 percent. As a result of their intense social interaction, Mormon pioneers were strongly attached to place. In Alpine, 32 percent of the 1870 population was still living there in 1900. In Middleton, only 4 percent remained.

In the nineteenth century, most Mormons lived in small, rural communities away from the three cities of

Salt Lake City, Ogden, and Provo. The 1870 population was 82 percent rural (in villages of fewer than 2,500 people). The proportion of rural residents dropped each decade until 1900, when it was 62 percent. Still, because the character of social life seems to have been very similar in village and city, the rural-urban distinction is of less analytical value among Mormons than elsewhere in the West.

Ethnic identity was also altered by the central ideology. Mormon missions in England, Wales, and Denmark were especially successful. During most of the nineteenth century, there were twice as many foreign-born adults in Utah as there were American-born. There were instances of interethnic rivalry and tension, with the Scandinavians particularly subject to discrimination and stereotyping, but the broader experience was one of very rapid assimilation. In fact, British, Scandinavian, and even American converts underwent a process of ethnic transformation in Utah that had the effect of suppressing language and other aspects of former nationality and fusing the people not so much to an American as to a Mormon identity.

Gender manifested an unusual character in Mormon country as well. The Mormon institution of plural marriage (polygamy) affected relationships between women and men. Initiated by JOSEPH SMITH, JR., in the 1840s, polygamy became widespread in the Great Basin by the 1870s and 1880s, with upwards of 25 percent of men, women, and children in many Mormon localities being members of polygamous households. When the strain of maintaining these marriages (or monogamous ones) became too great, church leaders were quick to grant divorces to women (but not to men) on grounds of incompatibility.

Contrary to what many have imagined, Mormon polygamy may have been a liberating force in the lives of many women. Those who were less domestic in inclination found in their sister wives a source of support and encouragement that made it possible to pursue other interests. Mormon women were more evident in the workplace and in public roles than in many parts of the West. In Alpine, Utah, women filled 37 percent of the volunteer offices, while in Middleton, Idaho, women filled 18 percent. BRIGHAM YOUNG encouraged Mormon women to take work outside the home, including in the professions. Martha Hughes Cannon, a medical doctor, was elected state senator in 1897, the first woman in the United States to hold such an office. Phoebe W. Couzins and Georgie Snow were admitted to the Utah bar in 1872. Utah was the first state or territory to give women the vote (in 1870).

Polygamy affected broader family relationships as well. Clearly, many polygamous marriages were based on obligation and mutual advantage more than on romantic love. Although the great majority of men had only one additional wife, the absences of fathers dividing their time between families must have affected children as well as wives. Certainly polygamy quickly built large family networks, which, with the high stability of Mormon villages, led to a rapid rebirth of the family and kin consciousness that had been lost through conversion. The church community nonetheless remained the umbrella institution in the society.

Polygamy also quickly dissipated family fortunes, as inheritances were distributed among large numbers of children, and prevented the establishment of a patrician class based on wealth. In Utah, elites were recognized and set apart more by church position than by financial status. And finally, polygamy had the effect of making Mormons pariahs in the broader American society, distancing them from other Americans and accentuating their separateness and cohesiveness.

Polygamy was officially abandoned under federal pressure in 1890, but church leaders continued to perform a few new polygamous marriages until 1904. Thereafter, many polygamous households remained intact, and federal officials looked away, assuming that, with no new church-sanctioned polygamous marriages, the institution would gradually die out.

Mormon economic practices also were distinctive. All Mormons were asked to "consecrate," or deed, their possessions to the church in the 1850s; to support retail and producers' cooperatives in the 1860s; and to become part of the UNITED ORDER OF ENOCH, an anticapitalist communal effort of the 1870s. Thereafter, at various times, church-sponsored boards of trade attempted to regulate prices and wages.

Although the federal government was outwardly successful in its campaign to eradicate many practices of Mormon pioneer life, the ideological core sustaining those practices remains a vital part of the group's consciousness and religious conduct.

—Dean L. May

See also: Polygamy: Polygamy among Mormons

SUGGESTED READING:

Arrington, Leonard J., and Davis Bitton. *The Mormon Experience: A History of the Latter-day Saints.* New York, 1979.

Arrington, Leonard J., Feramorz Y. Fox, and Dean L. May. *Building the City of God: Community and Cooperation among the Mormons.* 2d ed. Urbana and Chicago, 1992.

May, Dean L. *Three Frontiers: Family, Land, and Society in the American West, 1850–1900.* Cambridge and New York, 1994.

Van Wagoner, Richard S. *Mormon Polygamy: A History.* Salt Lake City, 1989.

SPANISH AND MEXICAN PIONEER LIFE

The culture of the Hispanic pioneer family developed out of the unique experience of the Spanish frontier, isolated from the primary colonial center of Mexico, at the end of supply lines stretching over hundreds of miles of difficult terrain, and in close contact with the Indians of the region. While, as in all colonial outposts, the goal may have been to recapture the life style of Spanish metropolitan settings, the rigors of the frontier simplified and modified the intent of the governments in Spain and Mexico City.

Community patterns in the Hispanic Southwest were shaped by existing geography, small populations, economic necessity, and the community's relationship to the Indians. In New Mexico, Arizona, California, and, to some extent, Texas, the communities were influenced by the difference between the requirements of the missions and those of secular society. The missionaries, primarily Franciscans, hoped to keep their missions separate from the European settlements. In New Mexico, and to a lesser degree, elsewhere, they took advantage of the existing Indian pueblo communities and established their churches in the pueblos, separating themselves from the potentially unruly settlers who might corrupt the new Christians. In their isolation, the missions were often in danger and vulnerable to attack by Indians. All along the frontier—from the early seventeenth century through the PUEBLO REVOLT of 1680 to the massacre at San Saba in 1758 and uprisings in the California missions in 1775—missions were destroyed. Gradually, missions became mixed with the secular Spanish community and, particularly at San Antonio in Texas, the missions became secular Spanish churches during the eighteenth century.

The Spanish secular communities in the border colonies began as military posts to support the missions but were separate from them. The military posts, called *presidios,* were occasionally relocated because of the demands of various defense regulations, particularly in the 1770s. The presidios were, in the eyes of visiting Spanish officials, poorly designed, built, and maintained. Officials noted, for example, that the fortifications near the mission of San Saba simply fell apart.

Civilian settlement in the Southwest usually began in urban centers called *villas,* communities that were smaller than cities but larger than villages. Santa Fe and San Antonio typify these centers. Laid out on a European grid according to the Laws of the Indies published in 1573, the cities included a main plaza with primary structures on it, as in Santa Fe and San Antonio, plus subsidiary open spaces reserved as common land for grazing. The cities had in place plans for the orderly allocation of land within the grid. Only one community—Los Angeles, which was laid out in 1781—included a plan for twelve streets emanating from the plaza. Usually, however, as in San Antonio, the small population built wherever it chose. Communities were often compared to impoverished villages, as was San Antonio with its dirt streets, loose animals, and small buildings in 1778. At the end of the Spanish period, the populations of the frontier urban centers were small, Los Angeles had 850 residents; Santa Fe, 6,000; and San Antonio, 1,500.

As the Indian threat declined, particularly in New Mexico, the population began to disperse to small farms and ranches, often fortified, along the upper Rio Grande and later, in Texas, along the San Antonio River. Management of farms and herds required families to live outside the administrative centers. Often they came to town only for church and shopping on weekends.

Ethnicity and class were inextricably tied together on the Spanish frontier, although isolation blurred the lines over time. At the top of the order were the *peninsulares,* Spaniards born in Spain who usually held key colonial offices. *Criollos,* children of Spaniards who were born in America, were on the second level. These individuals were pure ethnic Spaniards or *españoles.* Below these were mestizos (part *español* and part Indian, mulatto, Hispanicized Indian, and freed or enslaved black).

In the frontier colonies of New Spain, only a small part of the initial population was *español*, exemplified by San Jose and San Francisco, where only one-third of the men and one-fourth of the women in the initial settlements claimed to be Spanish. Because record keeping was lax on the frontier, racial identity was often not noticed or declarations of identity were taken at face value. As a result, the populations became more Spanish over time as those of mixed blood described themselves as Spanish to improve social status. Often, upward mobility came through military service, the only occupation on the frontier offering hard currency, thanks to military payrolls. Individuals who had been convict conscripts made their way up the military ranks to achieve a level of wealth and status not available through agriculture. Often, status was reflected in wardrobe, with items such as mantles, worn even in the summer, distinguishing the Spaniards from the Indians. Because fine clothing was passed down through generations, the fashions became outdated, charmingly so to many visitors. As clothing and shoes became worn, the less prosperous adopted local garb, represented by the Indian-style moccasins, which replaced shoes and boots.

Convention in terms of gender roles and status also varied on the frontier. Under Spanish law, women could hold property while married and pass it on to their

heirs. Life for women could be hard, dominated by regular routines of household management. On the frontier, the high death rates of women in childbirth balanced the high death rates among men caused by accidents, wars, and other the dangers of frontier life. Thus, after the early generations of settlement, the ratio of men to women was almost equal. Often, Indian women married Hispanic men, and efforts to use marriage to maintain racial purity failed simply because there were not enough *españoles* for the elite to perpetuate itself. Below the level of the elite, a large percentage of couples ignored the institution of marriage and lived together. Having no property or honor, in the Spanish sense of racial purity or class status, they were more concerned with the relationship than with its formal legitimacy. Among the upper classes, it was not uncommon for men to have mistresses, but there is little evidence that the rate of adultery or concubinage was higher than in Spain. As in other aspects of life, distance between the small ranches or other settlements permitted a level of independence not found in more ordered or populated parts of the Spanish empire. Despite the protests of priests and others, this independence was an important aspect of life on the frontier.

The Spanish frontier may have seemed a pale imitation of more settled parts of the Spanish empire. Yet, despite proximity to the Indians, intermarriage, and the adoption of some Indian foodways, clothing patterns, and other elements of material culture, Spanish institutions remained intact, although the level of influence was affected by class and degree of isolation. In general, the Spanish were models for the aspirations of Indians, particularly those who had become Christians. Spanish settlement patterns and, with it, Spanish land law shaped development along the frontier until the arrival of large numbers of Anglo-Americans in the middle and late nineteenth century. Even then, elements of Spanish tradition remained important within the Hispanic community through much of the twentieth century.

—Patrick H. Butler, III

SEE ALSO: Mexican Settlement; Spanish and Mexican Towns; Spanish Law; Spanish Settlement

SUGGESTED READING:

Griswold del Castillo. *La Familia: Chicano Families in the Urban Southwest, 1848 to the Present.* Notre Dame, Ind., 1984.

———. *The Los Angeles Barrio, 1850–1890: A Social History.* Berkeley, Calif., 1979.

Reps, John. *The Forgotten Frontier: Urban Planning in the American West before 1890.* Columbia, Mo., 1981.

Taylor, Lonn, and Dessa Bokides. *New Mexican Furniture: 1600–1940.* Santa Fe, N. Mex., 1987.

Weber, David J. *The Spanish Frontier in North America.* New Haven, Conn., 1982.

PISTOL LAWS

Colonial Americans were permitted to carry FIREARMS for hunting and defense, thus relieving the King of England of considerable military expense and making America one of the few societies in which citizens were privileged to bear weapons. But in frontier areas, the high percentage of males and the widespread indulgence in drinking and GAMBLING frequently induced violent encounters, thus prompting states by the early 1800s to enact statutes against the carrying of knives, pistols, or other concealed weapons. The traditions of drinking, gambling, and violence were passed on to the West; firearms were greatly improved; and the traditional legal sanctions against concealed weapons also were continued. But the states had enacted contradictory laws reinforcing the constitutional right to bear arms, which suggested a military privilege rather than a common civilian practice. Indeed, a lawsuit challenged Tennessee's statutory restrictions on the carrying of concealed weapons by appealing to the state constitution's guarantee of the right to keep and bear arms. The concealed weapons restriction was upheld on the grounds that the constitutional "right to keep and bear arms . . . is of a *general* and *public* nature, to be exercised by the people in a body for their *common* defence, so the arms, the right to keep which is secured, are those which are usually employed in civilized warfare, and that constitute the ordinary military equipment. . . . They need not . . . the use of those weapons which are efficient only in the hands of the robber and the assassin."

Western states enacted legislation restricting the carrying or use of concealed weapons. A North Dakota law prohibited the carrying of concealed weapons but said nothing about carrying them openly, while the Arizona Territory's law forbade the concealment of weapons only in towns (in the late twentieth century, Arizona allowed pistols to be carried openly anywhere). Enforcement of concealed-weapons provisions was lax, and in 1890, nine states (California, Colorado, Kansas, Nebraska, Nevada, North Dakota, South Dakota, Utah, and Washington) provided no minimum sentence (usually just a fine). Minimum fines ranged from no prescribed low amounts in several states to five dollars (Wyoming) or ten dollars (Montana, New Mexico, and Oregon); the maximum fine was five hundred dollars (California, Nevada, North Dakota, South Dakota, and Wyoming). The relatively few states that ordered minimum jail sentences for the offense

prescribed five to twenty days, while maximum sentences ranged from twenty days to one year (North and South Dakota).

When Western communities incorporated, it was common practice to reinforce state laws with local ordinances against the carrying of concealed weapons, or at least against the discharge of firearms within city limits. In 1875, the carrying of weapons without special permission was prohibited in San Francisco, but soon hundreds of applicants sought and received special permission. During the rowdy era of the Kansas CATTLE TOWNS, city fathers had to strike a balance between the recreational desires of fun-loving cowboys and the need to maintain sufficient order for the security of Eastern cattle buyers. Local statutes banned gambling, prostitution, intoxication, fighting, disorderly conduct, and disturbing the peace, along with the carrying and discharge of firearms. Law officers ignored these statutes as roistering cowboys fueled local economies—with revolvers belted around their waists. When a sign ordering visitors to check their revolvers at police headquarters was posted outside Wichita, it was shot to splinters by cowboys. Throughout the West, there was abundant legislation restricting the use of revolvers, but in practice, Westerners had ready access to handguns.

—Bill O'Neal

SEE ALSO: Law and Order

SUGGESTED READING:

Dykstra, Robert R. *The Cattle Towns.* New York, 1970.

Jordan Philip D. *Frontier Law and Order.* Lincoln, Nebr., 1970.

Prassel, Frank Richard. *The Western Peace Officer.* Norman, Okla., 1972.

PISTOLS

SEE: Firearms

PLATTE RIVER

The Platte River, its name derived from the French word for broad, flat, or shallow, has been described as "a thousand miles long and six inches deep." The Platte proper begins in North Platte, Nebraska, where the North Platte River—whose headwaters arise in the Rocky Mountains—and the South Platte—which originates on the eastern slopes of the Continental Divide some fifty miles southwest of Denver—meet. The North Platte flows across central Colorado through the Northgate Canyon into Wyoming and Nebraska. The South Platte, sometimes fed by waters cascading down the ten-thousand-foot-high mountain wall behind it, emerges from the mountains fifteen miles south of Denver and flows through the city on its way toward Greeley and then east across the High Plains to the North Platte. Not quite five-hundred-miles long, the South Platt drops one thousand feet per mile near its source but levels out to eight feet per mile by the time it reaches Nebraska. The main Platte, a sandy, shallow stream studded with islands, meanders eastward toward Omaha. Fed by underground and surface flows from the north, the Platte follows no permanent channel, but changes for periods of time from one to any of several others, an erratic flow made more erratic by diversions for irrigation and water power.

Sighted by FRANCISCO VÁSQUEZ DE CORONADO's explorers in the 1540s as they searched north across the plains from Quivira for cities of gold, the Platte was first fully explored and opened for trade in furs by French voyageurs in the early eighteenth century. Fiercely defended by Native Americans, the Platte region witnessed few European or Euro-American settlements before the mid-1800s, when the overland travelers to Oregon and the gold miners of California used the Platte as the main highway to the American Far West. Offering a more or less direct route from points in Iowa and Missouri at which westering pioneers collected to the South Pass through the Rocky Mountains, the Platte—although useless for navigation and therefore an obstacle to be crossed—did provide water and forage for horses, mules, oxen, and cattle and trees and shrubs for fuel for the trekkers themselves. Two essentially independent routes developed, one originating at Council Bluffs, Iowa, and Omaha, Nebraska, crossing the river at its mouth and traveling west along the north bank, the other starting at Independence or Westport Landing, Missouri, up the Republican River to Fort Kearney, and then northwest to the Platte. OVERLAND TRAVEL fostered local outposts, both of settlers and fur traders, and led to the building of Fort Laramie where the North Platte met Laramie Creek. From there, the grade was easy to South Pass, and after gold was discovered in California, so many thousands used the route to cross the Continental Divide and head for the Pacific Coast that the trail became permanently rutted and, in places, remained visible to late twentieth-century tourists.

As a major thoroughfare to the West, the Platte attracted overland stage and mail operations, the Pony Express, the transcontinental railroad, and ultimately widespread settlement. The discovery of gold near Denver in 1858 launched both the cattle industry on

the High Plains and irrigated vegetable farming, both to feed miners and the soldiers who protected them. The coming of the railroads in the 1870s fed the growing region, which supported two new towns at Longmont and Greeley. By the twentieth century, a major sugar-beet industry had developed, further stimulating irrigated agriculture in the region. Perhaps it should come as no surprise then that the North Platte, in 1903, became the site of one of the newly established Bureau of Reclamation's first irrigation projects, which provided water for extensive farming in eastern Wyoming and western Nebraska. As the region became home to some two million people by the middle of the twentieth century, the Platte River—never the hardiest of waterways—no longer supported the needs of the population. Local water, after the 1940s, came in part from pumped ground water, although the river's flow was also augmented by Colorado River water diverted by a tunnel through the Rocky Mountains for local use.

—*Charles Phillips*

SEE ALSO: California Overland Trails; Oregon Trail

PLEASANT, MARY ELLEN ("MAMMY")

Born a slave in Georgia, Mary Ellen Pleasant (1814–1904) became one of San Francisco's most controversial nineteenth-century figures. Freed from slavery by an abolitionist, she lived in Massachusetts and Louisiana, where she married John James Pleasant; the couple moved to San Francisco in 1851. With profits from a chain of laundries she established, Pleasant invested in fashionable boarding houses for well-to-do San Franciscans and later in stocks and real estate. Some of that fortune was spent in schemes to assist African Americans in their civil rights struggles. She provided financial support for the 1863 campaign of California blacks to gain the right to testify in court cases, and in 1868, she successfully sued a San Francisco streetcar company after a conductor treated her and two black female companions rudely. The case went to the California Supreme Court; the state high court's decision was the first in which an African American won an award for damages.

Much of Pleasant's later life was marred by speculative allegations evolving from her efforts to match a number of single female protégés with powerful and wealthy men. One such effort involved Sarah Althea Hill who charged former Nevada Senator William Sharon with refusing to honor a marriage contract. Pleasant's matchmaking activities generated sensational but unproven allegations in the San Francisco press of voodoo, prostitution and, in one case, murder following the mysterious death, in 1892, of her business associate, banker Thomas Bell. The publicity forced Pleasant into isolation and poverty until her death.

—*Quintard Taylor*

SUGGESTED READING:
Fisher, James A. "The Struggle for Negro Testimony in California, 1851–1863." *Southern California Quarterly* 51 (December 1969): 313–324.
Hudson, Lynn M. "A New Look, or 'I'm Not Mammy to Everybody in California': Mary Ellen Pleasant, a Black Entrepreneur." *Journal of the West* 32 (July 1993): 34–40.

PLEASANT VALLEY WAR

SEE: Graham-Tewksbury Feud

PLENTY COUPS (CROW)

Principal chief among the Crow Indians, Plenty Coups (1848–1932) was an important friend and ally of the government during the War for the Black Hills (from 1876 to 1877). Born near present-day Billings, Montana, he was the son of Medicine Bird, a Crow-Shoshone, and a full-blooded Crow mother. His name (in the Crow language, Aleek-chea-ahoosh) means "many accomplishments."

When he was fourteen years old, he ascended the Crazy Mountains on a vision quest and there dreamed of a chickadee. Relating the dream to tribal elders, he was told that the bird betokened peace with the whites. As a warrior, Plenty Coups fought with all of the Crows' traditional enemies, but he never waged war against the whites, and at the outbreak of the War for the Black Hills in 1876, Plenty Coups supplied Indian scouts to General GEORGE CROOK for his campaign against the forces of SITTING BULL and CRAZY HORSE. Crow warriors fell with GEORGE ARMSTRONG CUSTER at the Battle of Little Big Horn, and Crow scouts served with NELSON APPLETON MILES against CHIEF JOSEPH (the Younger) during the Nez Percé War (1877). Plenty Coups also quelled an incipient uprising among the Crows in 1887.

Fluent in English, Plenty Coups personally represented the Crows in right-of-way negotiations with the Northern Pacific Railroad. He also represented the tribe

in Washington, D.C., where he successfully lobbied for Crow land claims. In 1904, following the death of Pretty Eagle, he was elevated to principal chief of the Mountain Crows. Upon the United States's entry into World War I, Plenty Coups actively encouraged young tribal members to enlist in the armed forces. Recognizing his efforts, the U.S. government named him, in 1921, to represent all Native Americans at the dedication of the Tomb of the Unknown Soldier in Arlington National Cemetery. At the end of the ceremony, Plenty Coups laid his war bonnet and coup stick on the grave.

At the age of eighty, Plenty Coups donated his house and the forty acres surrounding it as a public park. The state of Montana has maintained the site as a park and museum devoted to Crow customs and history. If Plenty Coups was honored by the government, he was also revered by the Mountain Crows, who, upon his death, retired the title of "tribal leader."

—Alan Axelrod

SUGGESTED READING:

Linderman, Frank H. *The Life Story of Plenty Coups*. 1930. Reprint. Lincoln, Nebr., 1962.

PLUMMER, WILLIAM HENRY

Lawman and outlaw Henry Plummer (1832–1864) was born in Maine, moved to California in 1852, and settled in the mining town of Nevada City. There he first worked as a miner, then as a baker. Handsome and gentlemanly, he was popular among the town's rough crowd, and in 1856, he was elected city marshal. Although he was an energetic officer and made many arrests, there is evidence that he was actually in league with the criminal element. In 1857, he ran for the state legislature but was publicly accused of being "the leader of a reckless, rowdy gang of gamblers and loafers." Although that description fit many of those who held political office during the gold rush in California, Plummer lost the election.

In the midst of an affair with a married woman, Plummer shot and killed her husband, John Vedder. Sentenced to ten years in San Quentin for murder, the wily Plummer feigned illness and secured a pardon. After killing Bill Riley in a brawl in a Nevada City brothel, Plummer fled from California. He joined the gold rush in the Montana Territory in 1863 and was elected sheriff in Bannack. There he led a double life and acted as the chief of an organized band of some two dozen road agents who committed various robberies and murders. Plummer had known some of the gang in California, including the notorious Cyrus Skinner. Finally, a vigilance committee sprang up, and from December 1863 to February 1864, the vigilantes hanged twenty-two men in one of America's most prolific lynching sprees. Plummer, with gang members Ned Ray and Buck Stinson, was hanged on the sheriff's own gallows in Bannack. He is perhaps the most famous "Jekyll and Hyde" character in the West and is the archetypical crooked sheriff later portrayed in Western film and fiction. In 1993, an unsuccessful effort was made in Montana to have Plummer pardoned posthumously.

—John Boessenecker

SUGGESTED READING:

Mather, R. E., and F. E. Boswell. *Hanging the Sheriff: A Biography of Henry Plummer.* Salt Lake City, 1987.

Pauley, Art. *Henry Plummer, Lawman and Outlaw.* White Sulpher Springs, Mont., 1980.

POETRY

Poetry has been part of the Western American landscape since Siberian shamans and singers crossed the Bering Straits to populate the continent. In historic times, ALEXANDR BARANOV chanted his dedicatory "Song" in Russian in 1791 in Sitka and later published it in Moscow. The Spanish poem "Al Bello Sesco" was published in California in 1836. The first poem written in English in the West (although published in Boston) was Albert Pike's "The Fall of Poland" (1832). However, the history of Western American poetry, like the history all regional poetry in America, is primarily a record of Euro-American pioneers struggling to synthesize unique and universal experiences with profound understandings in written "American English."

The first serious poetry written in English and published in the West is the BRET HARTE-edited anthology, *Outcroppings: Being a Collection of California Verse* (1865). These, and most Western poems for the next twenty-five years, are small songs from smaller throats. Their authors ignore locale and experience and write ethereal, abstract, romantic, "universal" poems rife with clichéd Victorianisms and inappropriate Old World mythologies.

Despite his lionized transcontinental-and-Atlantic Victorian-era posturings, JOAQUIN MILLER ("The Byron of the Sierras") was not an accomplished poet. Far more successful than Miller was Arizona's Sharlot Hall, who based her poetry on keen observation and clear description a decade before the turn of the century. California's Robinson Jeffers, who began publishing a

decade or so after the turn of the century, is generally considered to be the first great poet in the LITERATURE of the West. Some of Jeffers's work draws on Greek myth, but much of it focuses closely on Western American characters in Western America settings and is written in modern (American) English. Other Western poets whose careers blossomed in the 1910s and 1920s include John Neihardt in Nebraska and, in the Southwest, Mary Austin; Alice Corbin Henderson, *Poetry* magazine coeditor; Peggy Pond Church; Haniel Long; Norman Macleod; and others associated with writers' colonies in Taos and Santa Fe. Contemporaries of these poets and also worthy of mention are Genevieve Taggard (Hawaii and California); Hildegarde Flanner (California); Hazel Hall, Howard McKinley Corning, and H. L. Davis (Oregon); Gwendolen Haste and Grace Stone Coates (Montana); and Nellie Burget Miller and Thomas Hornsby Ferril (Colorado). The second major Western poet and first Western Yale Younger Poets Award winner (1927), Ferril successfully infused biology and geology into short lyrics and longer meditations on Western history and landscape.

If poets need publishers to disseminate their work, critics to evaluate, advise, and encourage, and audiences to adore them, Western poets have been served as well as their peers elsewhere. Many of the aforementioned poets were published by major East Coast firms or by Western commercial, academic, and "small" presses, such as Alan Swallow's. For critics, poets since the 1930s have had full-time academics, often part-time poets, most significantly Yvor Winters (Stanford), Witter Byner (Berkeley), H. G. Merriam (Montana), B. A. Botkin (Oklahoma) Glen Hughes (Washington), Wilson O. Clough (Wyoming), Bernice Slote (Nebraska), Mabel Major (Texas Christian), and T. M. Pearce (New Mexico).

Seeking spiritual sustenance in the Depression era, American readers returned enthusiastically and nostalgically to their roots. In the West, academic and regional poetry anthologies flourished; however, with the advent of World War II, interest in and production of regional poetry not unsurprisingly subsided. After World War II, however, a poetic fleet came home to West Coast ports. San Francisco first berthed native and immigrant "Beats" and other poets—Kenneth Rexroth, Jack Kerouac, Jack Spicer, Lawrence Ferlinghetti, Gregory Corso, Allen Ginsberg, Pulitzer Prize–winner Gary Snyder, Thom Gunn, Michael McClure—and, in the 1960s, "hippie" or Aquarian Age poets typified by Richard Brautigan. The Bay Area was also a safe port during these times for Robert Duncan and William Everson (Brother Antoninus). Northward, to Seattle after the war, Pulitzer Prize–winner Theodore Roethke came to the University of Washington, as did David Wagoner and cofounders of *Poetry Northwest,* Carolyn Kizer and Richard Hugo. To Portland, Oregon, came William Stafford from the Midwest.

In the 1960s, poetic pioneers struck out for hinter and more dangerous lands: John Haines to homestead in Alaska; Ed Dorn to Idaho State University in Pocatello; Hugo to Missoula, Montana; and Charles Bukowski to seedy Los Angeles bars. Meanwhile, Native American poets such as N. Scott Momaday and James Welch began publishing, prefiguring increased interest in Asian American and Hispanic poets. In the last quarter of the century, major concerns of Western poets have been ethnicity, environment, and gender, as attested to by the writings of Simon J. Ortiz, Marnie Walsh, Alberto Rios, Leo Romero, Susan Strayer Deal, Linda Bierds, Barbara Meyn, Ai, Sandra Alcosser, and Dennis Cooper.

—Tom Trusky

SUGGESTED READING:

Ahsahta Press. *Modern and Contemporary Poetry of the American West Series.* Boise, Idaho, 1974.

Western American Literature. Selected issues. Logan, Utah, 1966.

Western Literature Association. *A Literary History of the American West.* Fort Worth, Tex., 1987.

Western Writers Series. Selected titles. Boise Idaho, 1972.

POINDEXTER, MILES

A Republican member of the House of Representatives (from 1909 to 1911) and of the U.S. Senate (from 1911 to 1923) from the state of Washington, Miles Poindexter (1868–1946) was an uncompromising Western Progressive. He championed THEODORE ROOSEVELT's nomination for the presidency in 1912, but after Woodrow Wilson's victory in the election, he supported the new president's Progressive programs. Poindexter advocated an imperialist policy in Latin America and favored American intervention into World War I. He joined the Senate "irreconcilables" to help defeat the Treaty of Versailles. His record during his second term cost him valuable support of Progressives in Washington, and he lost his bid for reelection in 1922. He later served as ambassador to Peru (from 1923 to 1928) and practiced law.

—Howard W. Allen

SUGGESTED READING:

Allen, Howard W. *Poindexter of Washington: A Study in Progressive Politics.* Carbondale, Ill., 1981.

POLITICAL PARTIES AND PRESSURE GROUPS

SEE: Agrarianism; Asiatic Exclusion League; Christian Socialism; Claims Associations; Currency and Silver as Western Political Issues; Greenback Party; Industrial Association of San Francisco; Ku Klux Klan; Ladies' Anti-Polygamy Society; National Woman's Party; Nonpartisan League; People's Party of Utah; Populism; Progressivism; San Francisco Building Trades Council; Sierra Club; Socialism; Temperance and Prohibition; Union Labor Party, San Francisco; Woman's Christian Temperance Union; Women's Suffrage; Workingmen's Party of California

POLK, JAMES K.

James K. Polk. *Courtesy Library of Congress.*

The eleventh president of the United States, James Knox Polk (1795–1849) presided over a period of intensive Western expansion resulting in large part from the resolution of the Oregon boundary dispute with England and the UNITED STATES–MEXICAN WAR. Born in Mecklenburg County, North Carolina, Polk moved with his parents to present-day Maury County, Tennessee. He graduated from the University of North Carolina in 1818. For the next two years, he apprenticed with a lawyer, Felix Grundy, in Nashville, and was admitted to the bar in 1820. He established a practice in Columbia, Tennessee, and, on January 1, 1824, married Sarah Childress. The Polks had no children.

Polk served as a member of the Tennessee legislature from 1823 to 1825. In 1825, he was elected to the first of seven terms in the U.S. House of Representatives. Serving from 1825 to 1839, he established himself as a leader of the Democratic party. He enthusiastically supported ANDREW JACKSON, especially in his battle against the Second Bank of the United States.

Polk served as Speaker of the House from 1835 to 1839, when he was elected governor of Tennessee. During his administration, the Whig party grew in strength, and he was defeated for reelection in 1841 and in 1843. Despite those defeats, Polk was tapped by the Democrats as their likely vice-presidential candidate in 1844 as the running mate of former president Martin Van Buren. Just before the Democratic convention, a letter from Van Buren opposing the annexation of Texas was published, to the great consternation of Democrat expansionists. Even though they were a minority in the party, they blocked Van Buren's nomination by adopting a two-thirds majority requirement for nomination. On the ninth ballot, the nomination fell to Polk, who had earlier backed the American claims to Texas as well as Oregon. He was the first "dark horse" presidential candidate.

Running on a bellicose platform calling for "the reoccupation of Oregon and the reannexation of Texas," Polk defeated his Whig opponent, HENRY CLAY, by a mere 38,000 votes (170 electoral votes to 105). The resolution offering terms of annexation to the Republic of Texas was adopted by Congress in March 1845, even before Polk's inauguration, and the new president began his administration by pledging to govern independently. Accordingly, he announced that he would not seek a second term, and he established explicit goals: reduction of the tariff; reestablishment of the independent treasury system; settlement of the "Oregon Question"; and an additional expansionist step, the acquisition of California.

Managing the tariff reduction proved difficult and divisive, especially within Polk's own party. The Walker Tariff of 1846 reduced import duties and therefore gratified Southern Democrats but was opposed by Northern protectionists. Polk further alienated Northerners by vetoing a rivers-and-harbors bill, which was popular in the Northwest. The Independent Treasury Act, also of 1846, pleased antibanking Democrats but outraged the substantial probanking faction.

Polk's conduct of foreign policy also disturbed Northern Democrats. Publicly, Polk affirmed the popular American claim to the entire Oregon Country up to 54° 40' north latitude—"Fifty-four-forty or fight!" and "All of Oregon!" had been campaign slogans—

but he submitted to the Senate the British offer to settle along the forty-ninth parallel. While the resulting Oregon Treaty of 1846 represented reasonable diplomacy, it was perceived by many as a craven compromise. Yet even as Polk took unpopular steps to avoid war with Britain, he rattled the saber at Mexico. Following the congressional resolution to annex Texas, Mexico broke off diplomatic relations with the United States. Polk responded by dispatching John Slidell to Mexico to propose that the United States would assume the claims of American citizens against Mexico in exchange for recognition of the Rio Grande as the southern boundary of Texas. Polk further authorized Slidell to offer as much as $40 million for the cession of California and New Mexico. The Mexican government refused even to see Slidell.

Polk prepared to present before Congress a declaration of war on the grounds that Mexico refused to pay the claims of American citizens. Yet even before the war message was prepared, Mexican forces had crossed the Rio Grande and had attacked U.S. troops commanded by General ZACHARY TAYLOR. Polk summarily recommended to Congress a declaration of war, which came in May 1846.

The president took a direct and active interest in planning U.S. strategy during the war. Although General Taylor performed well, if cautiously, against Mexican forces, Polk lacked faith in Taylor's ability to force the Mexicans to sue for peace, and he was further loathe to make a military hero of a potential political rival. Accordingly, he dispatched an army under War of 1812 veteran General WINFIELD SCOTT to land at Veracruz (in the first amphibious assault ever attempted by the U.S. Army) and to march on Mexico City, which was occupied in September 1847. Accompanying Scott was NICHOLAS TRIST, chief clerk of the State Department, who was given authority to conclude a peace treaty. Although the Mexican army had been soundly defeated, the negotiations proceeded very slowly. Losing confidence in Trist, Polk ordered his recall just as the negotiations were beginning to yield progress. Scott, who feared that the Mexican government was unstable and would soon collapse, leaving no one in authority with whom to negotiate, urged Trist to ignore the recall and conclude a treaty. He did so, submitted it to Polk, who, with some reluctance, put it before the Senate. The Treaty of Guadalupe Hidalgo (1848) secured the United States's claim to Texas and provided for the cession of California and New Mexico.

The United States–Mexican War had been popular in the expansionist West and in the proslavery South, but it was unpopular in much of the North. The abolitionist Northeast saw the conflict as a scheme to bring additional slave states into the Union. After the war, they moved to bar slavery from the Mexican cession, thereby bitterly inflaming sectional controversy and setting the stage for the Civil War, which was postponed only by the adoption of the COMPROMISE OF 1850. Divisions within the Democratic party were, however, immediate and caused the defeat of Democrat Lewis Cass by his Whig opponent, Zachary Taylor, in the presidential election of 1848. Polk died three months after leaving the White House.

—Alan Axelrod

SUGGESTED READING:

Bergeron, Paul H. *James K. Polk*. New York, 1989.

———. *The Presidency of James K. Polk*. Lawrence, Kans., 1987.

Pletcher, David M. *The Diplomacy of Annexation: Texas, Oregon, and the Mexican War.* Columbia, Mo., 1973.

Sellers, Charles Grier. *James K. Polk, Continentalist, 1843–1846*. Princeton, N.J., 1966.

———. *James K. Polk, Jacksonian, 1795–1843*. Princeton, N.J., 1957.

POLYGAMY

POLYGAMY AMONG MORMONS

Polygamy, or the practice of having more than one spouse at the same time, had a significant influence on the early history of the CHURCH OF JESUS CHRIST OF LATTER-DAY SAINTS, better known as the Mormon church. Although scholars estimate that at the height of its practice, only 20 percent of the church's members practiced plural or "celestial" marriage, as faithful MORMONS called it, the practice of polygamy attracted widespread comment and condemnation during the nineteenth century. (The Mormons actually practiced *polygyny*, the practice of taking more than one wife at a time. *Polygamy* refers to the practice of having more than one spouse at a time.)

Although the Mormon church did not publicly announce the practice until 1852, the doctrine and practice of the plurality of wives among the Mormons had its origins in the time of church founder JOSEPH SMITH, JR., who appears to have taken his first plural wife as early as 1833. In 1842, he announced to his closest associates that he had received a revelation commanding him and other worthy male members of the

The non-Mormon press ridiculed the Mormons for their practice of polygamy. In a contemporary image, Mormon leader Brigham Young, atop a cabinet, watches as his two new brides are attacked by his many wives. A crib full of Young's children add a chorus of howls to the scene. *Courtesy Denver Public Library, Western History Department.*

church to take more than one wife. During the next two years, all but a few of the church's hierarchy entered into polygynous marriages.

At the time of Smith's death in 1844, it is estimated that he had married between thirty-seven and forty-seven women. Although some church leaders had many wives—for example BRIGHAM YOUNG had as many as fifty-five—the majority had only two.

Over the years, church apologists gave many reasons for the practice of plural marriage. The most prominent were: first, that it was a commandment from God; second, in order for Joseph Smith, as a prophet of God, to restore the true church of Jesus Christ to the earth, there had to be a restoration of all things, which included the ancient practice of plural marriage; and, third, members practicing plural marriage were raising up seed to God or, in other words, were creating a special, blessed posterity to help establish the kingdom of God on earth.

Most members of nineteenth-century American society, however, did not agree with the Mormons' defenses of polygamy. Plural marriage was at odds with accepted social practices and Victorian morality. Numerous newspaper articles, pamphlets, and books depicted Mormonism as a moral aberration and an American version of Islam (which also practiced polygyny). Several authors even went as far as to describe Brigham Young as a "lustful Turk" and Mormon households as harems.

Contrary to popular views, Mormon households were, for the most part, well ordered and ruled by a strict sense of morality. Most Mormon men married polygynously with the view of producing more children and building the kingdom of God on earth. Women reluctantly entered into polygynous relationships out of faith in their religion and a sense of duty. Intense sexual feelings were not, for the most part, a catalyst for plural marriage.

As a result of years of persecution and harsh antipolygamy legislation including the EDMUNDS ACT and the EDMUNDS-TUCKER ACT of the 1880s, the Mormon church gradually abandoned the practice. In 1890, church President WILFORD WOODRUFF issued a manifesto, which officially banned Mormons from entering into new plural marriages. However, due to misunderstandings over aspects of the first manifesto, a second manifesto was issued by a later church president in 1904.

Presently, the practice of polygamy is punishable in the Mormon church by excommunication. Although there are estimated to be several thousand people throughout the region between the mountains who still practice plural marriage, many of whom trace their roots to a nineteenth-century Mormonism, they are no longer recognized as members of the LDS church.

—*Craig L. Foster*

SEE ALSO: Mormon Manifesto; Pioneer Life: Mormon Pioneer Life

SUGGESTED READING:

Embry, Jessie L. *Mormon Polygamous Families: A Life in the Principle.* Salt Lake City, 1987.

Foster, Lawrence. *Religion and Sexuality: Three American Communal Experiments of the Nineteenth Century.* New York, 1981.

———. *Women, Family and Utopia: Communal Experiments of the Shakers, the Oneida Community, and the Mormons.* Syracuse, N.Y., 1991.

Hardy, B. Carmon. *Solemn Covenant: The Mormon Polygamous Passage.* Urbana, Ill., 1992.

Van Wagoner, Richard S. *Mormon Polygamy: A History.* Salt Lake City, 1986.

POLYGAMY AMONG NATIVE AMERICANS

Most, but not all, American Indian tribes sanctioned polygamy (or *polygyny,* the correct, but rarely used anthropological term for the practice by which a man took more than one wife at a time). Yet, even in tribes that allowed polygamy, the majority of men had only one wife. Because Indian work roles were gender-specific, a man had to work hard to keep up with two or three wives. Polygamy was therefore most often an option for the wealthiest and most successful men in a tribe. Although an accepted practice, polygamy was still contested, especially by women. Some women liked polygamy because it provided them with fellow workers and close friends. And since warfare led to situations in which women greatly outnumbered men, polygamy enhanced women's opportunities to marry. However, a wife often felt threatened when her husband brought home a new, younger wife. Sometimes the first wife left in anger, or she tried to live with the new wife in a constant struggle over authority and prestige. One solution to this difficulty was sororal polygamy, especially common among Plains Indians. If a man married sisters, the family supposedly experienced less tension and fewer arguments.

Euro-American contact eventually curtailed polygamy among Native Americans. Missionaries and U.S. government officials attacked it as a primitive custom and forced polygamous families to separate. The Courts of Indian Offenses, which the BUREAU OF INDIAN AFFAIRS (BIA) established in 1883, punished polygamists with fines and jail sentences. By the early twentieth century, the BIA had eliminated most Indian polygamy and driven the few remaining practitioners underground.

—*Nancy Shoemaker*

SUGGESTED READING:

Hagan, William T. *Indian Police and Judges: Experiments in Acculturation and Control.* Lincoln, Nebr., 1966.

Shoemaker, Nancy. "Native American Families." In *A Research Guide and Historical Handbook.* Edited by Joseph M. Hawes and Elizabeth I. Nybakken. New York, 1991.

POLYNESIAN PEOPLES

SEE: Native American Peoples: Peoples of Hawaii

PONCA INDIANS

SEE: Native American Peoples: Peoples of the Great Plains

POND, PETER

An explorer and trader for the North West Fur Company, Peter Pond (1740–1807) led expeditions through the Canadian Northwest and provided the first accurate maps of the region. At the age of sixteen, Pond left his Milford, Connecticut, home to join the British colonial army. He saw action in the French and Indian War and later spent six years working in the FUR TRADE near Detroit. At the outbreak of the American Revolution, Pond headed north into Canada and the lush, fur-rich lands of the Northwest country. He hooked up with the North West Company and, in 1778, led a company expedition of sixteen voyageurs into the uncharted regions of the Athabaska River basin. Pond's journey gave the North West Company an advantage in the region over its rival the HUDSON'S BAY COMPANY. Pond had had a falling out with his employer in 1785, when he arrived in New York City, hoping to sell to the Continental Congress his map of a clear-water route to the Arctic Ocean and the suggestion of a NORTHWEST PASSAGE. The sale never happened, and Pond returned to trapping along the Athabaska for another five years. In this time, Pond infused his second-

in-command, Alexander Mackenzie, with a thirst for exploration. Mackenzie went on to greater glory; Pond headed to obscurity and poverty.

—*Patricia Hogan*

SEE ALSO: Explorations: English Expeditions

SUGGESTED READING:

Innis, Harold A. *Peter Pond: Fur Trader and Adventurer.* New York, 1930.

PONY EXPRESS

Inaugurated on April 3, 1860, the trans-Missouri Pony Express delivered mail between St. Joseph, Missouri, and Sacramento, California. RUSSELL, MAJORS AND WADDELL, a well-known freighting firm, sponsored and financed the new express. The company had earlier organized the Central Overland California and PIKE'S PEAK EXPRESS COMPANY to operate a mail and passenger service along a central route in the American West. An intense rivalry had developed between Russell, Majors and Waddell and the OVERLAND MAIL COMPANY, which delivered the mail under a government contract along a circuitous route from West Tennessee and Missouri to Fort Smith, Arkansas, southwestward through Texas, New Mexico, and Arizona, and into southern California and north to San Francisco. Senator WILLIAM GWIN of California, an ardent supporter of government aid to transportation, persuaded WILLIAM HEPBURN RUSSELL that a speedy mail-delivery service on horseback would prove the superiority of the shorter central route and might result in a lucrative mail contract from the government. Gwin also agreed to seek financial reimbursement from Congress for the experiment. ALEXANDER MAJORS and WILLIAM BRADFORD WADDELL doubted the soundness of the business venture, but they reluctantly agreed to undertake it. Public announcement that the Pony Express would deliver letters for five dollars an ounce from Missouri to California within ten days, half the time necessary on the Overland Mail Company route, created great excitement in business circles.

Russell established 190 way stations along the route, a distance of nearly two thousand miles. During the first fifteen months of operation, the stations were between twenty-five and thirty miles apart; the company later reduced the distance between stations to twelve or sixteen miles. Both horses and young riders were chosen for their stamina. They rode day and night in all kinds of weather. A few trips were completed in ten days, or 240 hours, by riders who traveled 8.33 miles per hour. The average trip in the spring, summer, and fall was twelve days, or 288 hours at 6.94 miles per hour. From November to March, however, the trips took fourteen days, or 336 hours at 5.95 miles per hour. Riders wrapped the mail in oiled silk to protect it from the weather and placed it in a leather *mochila* that fitted over their saddles.

Frank E. Webner, Pony Express rider, in 1861. *Courtesy National Archives.*

Most Pony Express trips were between Fort Kearney, Nebraska, and Fort Churchill, Nevada, the terminals of the TELEGRAPH by November 1860. The fastest recorded time over that distance was when riders traveled for six days ten hours and ten minutes and an average speed of 8.95 miles per hour to deliver the news of Abraham Lincoln's election as president.

Although a dramatic success at speedy mail delivery, the Pony Express was a financial failure, costing Russell, Majors and Waddell somewhere between one hundred thousand and two hundred thousand dollars, a loss the company could not afford. Moreover, the partnership did not get the anticipated contract for mail service from the government. The Overland Mail Company, forced to abandoned its route through Texas during the Civil War, was reorganized and transferred its stagecoach service to the central route. On March 2, 1861, the government signed a contact with the Overland Mail Company for daily overland mail delivery and semiweekly Pony Express delivery. Thus, during

A nineteenth-century engraving depicts the hazardous life of a Pony Express rider. In a work called *The Persuit* [*sic*], an expressman faces the consequences of having trespassed on a sacred Indian burial ground. *Courtesy Library of Congress.*

the last third of its eighteen-month existence, the Pony Express enjoyed a government subsidy. Largely under the influence of WELLS, FARGO AND COMPANY, the Overland Mail Company awarded Russell, Majors and Waddell a subcontract to carry both the Pony Express and stage mail on the line eastward from Salt Lake City. West of Salt Lake City, the Overland Mail Company operated the Pony Express, integrating its schedule and services with local pony-express services operated by Wells Fargo in California. The trans-Missouri pony-express service ended in October 1861 with the completion of the overland telegraph. Russell, Majors and Waddell's mounting losses and indebtedness forced it into bankruptcy the following year.

The Pony Express was a great boon to Californians who needed to conduct business negotiations in the Midwest and East. Those who used the service often gained a significant advantage over their competitors. To ensure against the disruption of the service by weather conditions, accidents, or Indian raids, cautious businessmen sent duplicate copies of their communications by regular mail.

The Pony Express has occupied a place in the nation's folklore much larger than its historical significance. Responding to the imagination of recent generations, the media, through motion pictures and television, have created a myth about its importance in the American West greater than the reality.

—*W. Turrentine Jackson*

SUGGESTED READING:

Chapman, Arthur. *The Pony Express.* New York, 1932.

Settle, Raymond W., and Mary L. Settle. *Saddles and Spurs: The Pony Express Saga.* Stanford, Calif., 1955.

POPE, JOHN

A career military man, John Pope (1822–1892) was born to a politically prominent family in Illinois, graduated seventeenth in his class at West Point in 1842, and fought in the United States–Mexican War. He spent most of his early career, however, conducting surveys in Minnesota and the Southwest before the CIVIL WAR, during which he won victories at New Madrid, Missouri, and Island No. 10 in the Mississippi and became commander of the army of Virginia before his defeat at the Second Battle of Bull Run, where his poor showing led to controversy and his removal from field operations. Made commander of the new Department of the Northwest in 1862, Pope launched the campaign against the Santee Sioux, who had begun raiding in Minnesota in August of that year, and sent major expeditions to fight the Sioux in the Dakotas in both 1863 and 1864. Impressed by Pope's administrative capabilities, General Ulysses S. Grant appointed him commander of the Division of Missouri, which

John Pope. *Courtesy National Archives.*

included most of the Great Plains. In 1865, Pope organized the Powder River Campaign against the Sioux and the Cheyennes and oversaw the reorganization of his command into the Department of Missouri before he was reassigned, this time to the South during Reconstruction. Returning to the Department of the Missouri in 1870, Pope remained its commander until 1883. In the West, Pope led several columns during the Red River War in 1874 and 1875, and afterward, he played a central role in the United States's efforts to control the Apaches—including the "renegade" GERONIMO—in New Mexico. Suppressing the Utes and policing the Indian Territory to keep out "Boomers" in the late 1870s and early eighties, Pope had, by 1883, taken command of the Division of the Pacific, which put him in charge of the entire trans-Mississippi West except for Texas. An outspoken critic of GRANT'S PEACE POLICY and a proponent of military control over Indian affairs, Pope nevertheless encouraged missionary work on the reservations, insisted that Indians be treated well, and shared with the liberals of the day the hope of assimilating Native Americans into white society. In 1886, he was forced to retire due to his age and wrote extensively about his army experience before dying of "nervous prostration" in Sandusky, Ohio, at the quarters of his brother-in-law, who ran the Ohio Soldier's and Sailor's Home.

—*Patricia Hogan*

SEE ALSO: Sioux Wars; Texas Frontier Indian Wars

SUGGESTED READING:
Axelrod, Alan. *Chronicle of the Indian Wars: From Colonial Times to Wounded Knee.* New York, 1993.
Utley, Robert. *Frontier Regulars: The United States Army and the Indian, 1866–1890.* Lincoln, Nebr., 1984.
———. *Frontiersmen in Blue: The United States Army and the Indian, 1848–1865.* Lincoln, Nebr., 1981.

POPULAR SOVEREIGNTY

SEE: Compromise of 1850; Kansas-Nebraska Act

POPULISM

Spawned by widespread economic, political, and social discontent in the West and South in the late nineteenth century, Populism was the greatest mass challenge to industrializing America, a social movement offering an alternative vision of democratic politics and radical economics. Ultimately, its political manifestation, the People's Party, suffered the customary defeat of third parties in American history, and its larger vision failed to survive a combination of organizational obstacles, political and economic conservatism, and cultural resistance embedded in sectionalism, racism, and tradition.

The origins of Populism in the West were complex. Particularly important was the rush of settlement in the 1880s onto the Great Plains, a land rush stimulated by railroad expansion and Eastern investment capital as well as by the hopes of millions of settlers. The land boom created a substantial rural population possessing limited resources, dependent on credit advances and favorable weather, and enmeshed in the commercial agriculture of staple crops and market exchanges. When the boom collapsed at the end of the 1880s because of drought, low commodity prices, plummeting land values, and crippling debt, many farmers demanded reforms to protect and improve their dwindling interests.

Their proposals were intended to revise the credit system by passing both state laws to reduce interest rates and liberalize foreclosure provisions and national laws to end the credit monopoly of national banks and increase short-term agricultural credits. In order to reduce the burden of debt and increase farm prices, they favored monetary inflation, through both an expanded greenback currency and unlimited silver coinage (or free silver). They called for antimonopoly laws in general and railroad regulation in particular.

To their consternation, farmers soon learned that the Republican party, dominant in the Western states, could not be relied on to support reform legislation, for the party's leadership and ideology promoted untrammeled business development. As one Kansas Republican later admitted, "Republican legislatures of Kansas simply obeyed the orders of the railroad companies."

To overcome this political obstacle to relief and reform, farmers turned to several organizations that soon propelled them into independent political action. The most important was the National Farmers' Alliance and Industrial Union, which spread across the West and South. Also working to mobilize popular discontent were the Northwestern Farmers' Alliance, the Farmers' Mutual Benefit Association, the Patrons of Husbandry, and a number of labor organizations, especially the Knights of Labor. Labor groups were particularly significant farther west, from the Rocky Mountain region to the Pacific Coast. Miners, suffering from dangerous working conditions and declining opportunity as their industry came under the control of Eastern mining corporations, organized unions to campaign for protective labor legislation. Railroad workers, another large group exploited by corporate

employers, were organized by the Knights of Labor and also demanded reform. Despite their different emphases and structures, these groups held important ideas in common. The most significant were antimonopoly, economic cooperation, and greenbackism, the concept that the government should manipulate the currency supply to promote economic democracy.

The discontented farmers and workers of the West engaged in independent political action in 1890, establishing state parties to replace the indifferent Republicans with more responsive officeholders. Political reforms, such as direct election of senators, were added to their earlier economic objectives. The Kansas People's Party was formed on June 12, 1890, at a convention composed of forty-one Alliancemen, twenty-eight Knights of Labor, ten FMBA members, seven Grangers, and four single-taxers—a good indication of the groups that formed the coalition. The same forces nominated other third-party tickets under various names in most other Western states. Ultimately, all such third party advocates were called "Populists," the name derived from their persistent evocation of the rights of the people.

In these state campaigns, a number of memorable Populist leaders emerged. Rural editors such as William A. Peffer of the *Kansas Farmer* and Henry Loucks of the *Dakota Ruralist* proved especially effective mobilizers of popular discontent. Spellbinding orators crisscrossed the region: in Kansas, MARY ELIZABETH CLYENS LEASE, famous for urging farmers "to raise less corn and more *hell,*" and "Sockless" JERRY SIMPSON, a caustic agitator; in Minnesota, the brilliant IGNATIUS DONNELLY and Eva McDonald, described by an admirer as unequaled "on an improvised stove-box platform on the street corner, speaking earnestly to her toil-hardened brother Knights of Labor." Joining these were others such as Omer Kem of Nebraska, John Rogers of Washington, Curtis Castle of California, and Ella Knowles, the Populist candidate for attorney general of Montana.

In the West, these initial campaigns achieved much success. Populists elected congressmen in Kansas, Nebraska, and Minnesota, and United States senators in Kansas and South Dakota. They captured control of the legislatures in Nebraska and Kansas and gained the balance of power in others. In the South, however, Alliance members were reluctant to break from the Democratic party, which dominated the region and symbolized white supremacy. Most Alliancemen thus worked within the Democratic party, trying to turn it to reform, but they had little success.

Western Populists then took the lead in organizing a national People's Party in May 1891 at a conference in Cincinnati. After holding a series of other meetings to generate additional support, the Populists held their first national nominating convention in Omaha, Nebraska, on July 4, 1892. The Populist party nominated JAMES BAIRD WEAVER, a former Greenback congressman from Iowa, but the famous Omaha Platform they adopted captured their enthusiasm and idealism more than did their presidential nominee. The platform eloquently summarized the economic and political demands of the reform groups that had coalesced to form the party, but it did little to attract others to the cause. In the 1892 election, the Populists did carry Kansas, Idaho, and Nevada and garnered more than one million popular votes, but they made few inroads in the South, where fraud, intimidation, and racism obstructed their potential constituency, or in the industrial East, where voters remained bound by traditional political allegiances.

But the Populists nonetheless achieved important victories at the state level in the West, often by cooperating or "fusing" with Democrats on a common ticket. More Populists were elected to Congress, and both Colorado and Kansas elected Populists as governors—the flamboyant Davis Waite and the scholarly Lorenzo Lewelling. In both states, however, divided political control enabled Republicans, entrenched in the legislatures, to block most reforms. Despite such political obstacles, Populists did eventually enact important reforms in several Western states. They were largely responsible for such democratic political reforms as WOMEN'S SUFFRAGE, which passed in Colorado and Idaho, and the initiative and referendum, which they introduced in South Dakota. They also enacted numerous laws regulating railroads, banks, and insurance companies, protecting labor unions, and improving working conditions.

But most Populist objectives required national, not state, action. Although forty-eight Populists were elected to Congress, most prominently Peffer, Simpson, William Allen of Nebraska, and John Bell of Colorado, they were effectively stymied by their minority status, the hostility of both Democrats and Republicans to radical change, and congressional procedures that marginalized them and suppressed their efforts at reform legislation.

To achieve national success, Populists such as Allen, Simpson, and Weaver, who had all cooperated with Democrats in their own states in order to defeat the Republicans, began advocating a policy of fusion with major political parties. This course was facilitated by the gradual transformation of the Populist national and state committees, as party officials emphasized "practical politics" rather than reform principles. Fusionists played down the radical features of the Omaha Platform, such as the nationalization of railroads, and in-

stead emphasized the issue of free silver, which was believed to have wide appeal among both Democrats and Republicans, especially during the serious depression that began in 1893. Electoral defeats of Populists in 1894 encouraged the tendency toward fusion among party officials. Despite opposition from the rank and file and from Populist editors, most of whom favored independent action and a comprehensive reform program, the Populist National Committee postponed the party's 1896 nominating convention until after both the Republicans and the Democrats had met. The National Committee members expected the two old parties to nominate conservative candidates on evasive platforms. The Populists would then be able to attract the disappointed silverites of each party and sweep to victory. The Republicans did as expected, nominating William McKinley and endorsing the gold standard. The Democratic party, however, came under the control of its own silver advocates and nominated WILLIAM JENNINGS BRYAN of Nebraska on a free-silver platform.

The Populists now faced a sobering choice. Bryan had often worked with Populists in Nebraska, and many Western Populists urged the party to nominate Bryan as well, creating a solid coalition for the silver issue they had labored to promote. Other Populists, especially those in the South, who considered Democrats violent enemies rather than friendly allies, insisted that the party retain its autonomy by adopting a comprehensive reform platform and nominating a Populist rather than being submerged in a Democratic silver campaign. Warning that a separate ticket would split the reform vote and guarantee McKinley's election, the fusionists carried the debate, and the party nominated Bryan for president. As a concession to Southern Populists, the convention nominated Thomas Watson of Georgia for vice-president, expecting the Democrats to reciprocate by replacing their own candidate for vice-president with Watson.

Not only did the convention end in disharmony, but the Democrats refused to endorse Watson. Most Western Populists were indifferent to the issue, and their state conventions nominated electoral tickets pledged to the Democratic nominees, often in exchange for Democratic endorsement of Populist candidates for state office. Populists in the South also arranged fusions, but on some state tickets, they fused with Republicans rather than with the hated Democrats, and some Populists even voted for McKinley on the national ticket as well. In the chaos of the fusion campaign, Populism nearly came to an end. Watson explained: "Populists cannot denounce the sins of the two old parties, and yet go into political copartnership with them. The moment we make a treaty the war must cease . . . and when we cease our war upon the two old parties, we have no longer any excuse for living."

In any event, the Populists played only a secondary role in the 1896 campaign and election. Despite subordinating their party and its principles to the Democrats, the election brought them no success, for Bryan was soundly defeated. The fusion campaigns did produce numerous state-level victories in the West, but they were dying gasps, and the disappointing performances of fusionist governors and legislatures further disillusioned the rank and file. Populist candidates lost almost everywhere in the 1898 elections, and squabbles between party officials and antifusion Populists split the national party. Disintegrating, the party made only a few more nominations before disappearing completely.

Many factors explained the decline of Populism. The gradual return of prosperity in the late 1890s certainly undermined the Populist appeal. The rise of issues like expansionism also diverted attention from those the Populists emphasized. But the primary reason for the twisted course and ultimate failure of Populism and the People's Party was their inability to overcome the limitations of American politics, particularly the two-party system, which was institutionalized in the electoral process. It was that obstacle that prompted party officials to favor fusion, but to many Populists, fusion seemed a betrayal of their purpose. As one maintained, "We did not leave the corrupt Republican party to hobnob with the rotten Democratic party." Moreover, since only the weaker of the two major parties had any reason to fuse with a third party, the political sectionalism of the period meant that Populists fused with Democrats in the West and Republicans in the South. This further complicated the tasks of party officials, alienated much of the rank and file, and diminished the national viability of the People's Party. Finally, Republican legislatures in Western states began to enact antifusion laws that not only divided their opponents but seriously restricted the possibility of third parties in general and the Populists in particular, ultimately forcing the party off the ballot and out of electoral consideration.

Despite the practical failures and the decline of the Populists, however, their movement had considerable political significance and an important, and perhaps continuing, impact. That significance and impact have been viewed variously over the years by different generations of historians. Early professional historians, best represented by John D. Hicks in *The Populist Revolt* (1931), presented Populism as a pragmatic response of small farmers to economic distress and Populists as the direct precursors of Progressives, responsible for introducing the reform agenda of the twentieth cen-

tury. Consensus historians of the 1950s, such as Richard Hofstadter, reversed this positive portrait and viewed Populists as irrational and nativistic reactionaries who were the forerunners of such later movements as McCarthyism. This interpretation, overdrawn and poorly substantiated, was in turn countered by a new generation of historians who again emphasized the economic rationality of the Populists and praised them for fashioning political and cultural attitudes and institutions that, while not adopted in the twentieth century, represented important themes in American history and constituted democratic alternatives to the course of industrial capitalism.

—Peter H. Argersinger

SEE ALSO: Currency and Silver as Western Political Issues

SUGGESTED READING:

Argersinger, Peter H. "A Place on the Ballot: Fusion Politics and Antifusion Laws." *American Historical Review* 85 (1980): 287–306.

———. *Populism and Politics: W. A. Peffer and the People's Party.* Lexington, Ky., 1974.

Goodwyn, Lawrence. *Democratic Promise: The Populist Moment in America.* New York, 1976.

Hicks, John D. *The Populist Revolt: A History of the Farmers' Alliance and the People's Party.* Minneapolis, Minn., 1931.

Hofstadter, Richard. *The Age of Reform.* New York, 1955.

Larson, Robert W. *Populism in the Mountain West.* Albuquerque, N. Mex., 1986.

McMath, Robert C. *American Populism: A Social History, 1877–1898.* New York, 1993.

Miller, Worth Robert. "A Centennial Historiography of American Populism." *Kansas History* 16 (1993): 54–69.

Ridge, Martin. *Ignatius Donnelly: The Portrait of a Politician.* Chicago, 1962.

Wright, James E. *The Politics of Populism: Dissent in Colorado.* New Haven, Conn., 1974.

PORTLAND, OREGON

Founded in 1845 when Asa Lovejoy and Francis Pettygrove of Oregon City staked out a new town site on 640 acres that Lovejoy had claimed in 1843, Portland was situated on a clearing on the west bank of the Willamette River halfway between the HUDSON'S BAY COMPANY post at Fort Vancouver and the American settlement at Oregon City. Massachusetts-born Lovejoy and Maine-born Pettygrove flipped a coin to decide whether the new town would be called "Portland" or "Boston."

The small settlement prospered by selling Oregon wheat and lumber to gold-seekers in California after 1849. The town fought off rivals along the lower Willamette by constructing a plank road to tap the farms of what is now Washington County and by securing regular steamship service to San Francisco. In 1850, approximately two hundred women and six hundred men lived in the town. When five New England women passed through town in 1851 on their way to teaching jobs in Oregon City, one noted that "the one-sided community was exceedingly interested." By 1860, Portland's population was 2,900, with a strong New York and New England influence among the emerging civic leadership of lawyers and merchants.

Over the next decades, Portland boomed as the gateway between the Columbia River basin and markets in California and the East. The discovery of gold in Idaho in 1860 brought a rush of prospectors through the city. The OREGON STEAM NAVIGATION COMPANY, controlled by Portland businessmen, carried settlers and gold-seekers up the Columbia and brought the products of the "Inland Empire" to Portland wharves and warehouses for shipment to world markets. Railroad connections supplemented Portland's water-borne trade in the 1880s and made the city the focal point of the transportation network in the Pacific Northwest. A railroad to California was completed in 1882; a transcontinental connection via the Northern Pacific opened in 1883; and a second eastward connection via the Union Pacific opened the following year.

In the last decades of the nineteenth century, Portland was a city of immigrants, and most visible was the city's Chinese population. Most Chinese immigrants had come to Oregon originally to build the railroads and had settled permanently in Portland when construction jobs dried up in the depression of the 1890s. With 7,800 residents in 1900, Portland's Chinatown was second in size only to San Francisco's. The city's population of Asian immigrants was supplemented at the turn of the century by 1,200 Japanese. The most prominent groups of European immigrants were Scandinavians, Italians, and Jews from Poland and Russia.

Neighborhood patterns at the turn of the century reflected the increasing social distance between rich and poor, immigrant and native born. The Chinese clustered near the waterfront on the edge of the downtown business district. Single men and transient workers populated one of the nation's largest skid-row districts on the north waterfront, with its saloons, cheap hotels, flop houses, employment offices, and missions. The upper class moved to spacious houses on the high land that rose from downtown toward the West Hills. Skilled workers and Portlanders with white-collar jobs took advantage of the first three bridges across the Willamette River (constructed in 1888, 1891, and 1894) to build and buy new houses in the streetcar

A view of Front Avenue and Stark Street, Portland, Oregon, in 1852. The mast of the brig *Henry* can been seen docked at the end of the street. *Courtesy Oregon Historical Society.*

suburbs of the east side. In 1891, the city of Portland, previously confined to the west side of the Willamette, consolidated with the east side municipalities of Albina and East Portland to form a single, unified city.

The twentieth century brought three periods of rapid growth. In 1905, Portland staged the Lewis and Clark Centennial Exposition and Oriental Fair, the first world's fair on the West Coast. The exposition helped usher in a decade of prosperity. The continued development of agriculture, lumbering, and stock raising in Portland's hinterland fueled the city's economy. Population surged from 90,000 in 1900 to an estimated 225,000 in 1913. Downtown was rebuilt in a "metropolitan" style. Portlanders responded to concerns about high taxes and political corruption in 1913 by adopting the popular commission form of municipal government as developed in Galveston, Texas. Eighty years later, Portland remains the last large city in the United States to operate under the commission system.

After its raucous beginnings as a jumping-off point for mining rushes and land booms, Portland settled into a comfortable role as a regional metropolis in the twentieth century. Its cultural institutions were solid but not outstanding. Its tycoons and their children focused their lives on family rather than on flashy display and doled out their wealth sparingly. The most important exception—the endowment of Reed College in 1911—created an institution that has never been quite at home in the conservative city. As one journalist commented in the early 1930s, the easiest way to predict how Portland would respond to a particular situation was to ask what Calvin Coolidge would do.

World War II brought whirlwind change. Henry J. Kaiser built three huge shipyards in Portland and Vancouver from 1941 to 1942. The Kaiser yards and other defense contractors employed a total of 140,000 workers by 1943. Federal war contracts totaled $2.4 billion for a thousand Liberty ships, tankers, escort carriers, and other ocean-going ships. The population in the Portland area grew from 501,000 to 661,000 in three years as workers poured in from the rural West, the East Coast, and the South. The newcomers included nearly 20,000 African Americans (the city's prewar population of African Americans numbered only 2,100). The temporary community of defense workers in Vanport, with more than 40,000 residents, was one of the largest planned communities ever built in the United States.

The dismantling of the shipyards after World War II returned Portland to the slower pace and more conservative values of the 1920s and 1930s. Between 1950 and 1970, Portlanders watched Seattle consolidate its lead as the economic and cultural center of the Pacific Northwest. The years since 1970, however, brought a renewed vitality to the metropolitan area with the expansion of the electronics industry (creating a "silicon forest" in the western suburbs) and the continued importance of the city as a Pacific port. In recent years, Portland has been best known for the quality of local planning and the preservation of a livable community through the conservation of older neighborhoods, revitalization of a pedestrian-oriented downtown, creation of a strong system of public transportation, and management of suburban sprawl under the land-use planning system adopted by the state in 1973.

—*Carl Abbott*

Suggested reading:

Abbott, Carl. *Portland: Planning, Politics, and Growth in a Twentieth Century City.* Lincoln, Nebr., 1983.

MacColl, E. Kimbark. *The Growth of a City: Power and Politics in Portland, Oregon, 1915–50.* Portland, Oreg., 1979.

———. *Merchants, Money, and Power: The Portland Establishment, 1843–1913*. Portland, Oreg., 1988.
Vaughan, Thomas, and Virginia Ferriday, eds. *Space, Style and Structure: Building in Northwest America*. Portland, Oreg., 1974.

POSADAS, LAS

Las Posadas, or The Inns, is a Christmas-season folk drama staged by Hispanic Catholics in the American Southwest as part of the religious and social celebrations beginning on December 15 and continuing through the Epiphany on January 6. Telling the story of Mary and Joseph and their failed search for lodging at the inns of Bethlehem, Las Posadas was traditionally more miracle than morality play, concentrating on the devil's design to deny the holy couple shelter. Originally presented during the course of nine nights that culminated on Christmas Eve, the customary presentation of Las Posadas was modified over time to occupy Christmas Eve alone. While the traditional nine-evening celebration continued to be observed in California, where the nights were warm, in the mountain villages of New Mexico, the celebrants compensated for limiting the drama to one night by stopping at nine different homes on the way to the scene at the manger. Singers, directed by window candles, stopped at each house to request lodging only to have their melodious pleas rejected by the "devil" hidden behind the door of each home. In the contemporary Southwest and in Mexico, Las Posadas celebrations feature the singing of the traditional Spanish melody, but the enactment has dropped the emphasis on the devil. In Mexico, Las Posadas events often become social gatherings with music, dancing, and cocktails. During the Christmas season, in Mexico City's nightclubs, orchestras weave a popular waltz into Las Posadas melodies.

—*Charles Phillips*

POSTON, CHARLES DEBRILLE

An early Arizona promoter, Charles Debrille Poston (1825–1902) is called the "father of Arizona" because of his work to secure territorial status for Arizona. Born near Elizabethtown, Kentucky, Poston acquired a law degree before moving to San Francisco in 1851 to become chief clerk in the customs house. In the summer of 1854, he represented a syndicate interested in mines and railroads and headed a group that explored the GADSDEN PURCHASE. Poston helped organize the Sonora Exploring and Mining Company and, in 1856, brought a train from San Antonio to Tubac, south of Tucson, where he supervised silver mines until 1861. Poston lobbied Congress to create the Arizona Territory (February 24, 1863), served as the territory's first Indian superintendent and, in 1864, was its first territorial delegate to Congress. From 1866 to 1877, he traveled abroad and then held various federal jobs in Arizona: land-office registrar at Florence from 1877 to 1879; consular agent at Nogales from 1886 to 1887; and a writer on the Western irrigation surveys in early 1890s. Poston published three books and numerous pioneer reminiscences.

—*Harwood P. Hinton*

SUGGESTED READING:

Gressinger, A. W. *Charles D. Poston: Sunland Seer.* Globe, Ariz., 1961.

POTTERY

SEE: Native American Pottery, Southwestern

POWELL, JOHN WESLEY

A geologist, ethnologist, and anthropologist, John Wesley Powell (1834–1902) explored the Grand Canyon and the Colorado River, became director of the UNITED STATES GEOLOGICAL SURVEY, and developed a useful classification system of American Indian languages. He was born in Mount Morris, New York.

Before Powell turned to science and exploration, he served in the Union Army during the Civil War and attained the rank of major. He fought with great gallantry and, at the Battle of Shiloh, lost his right arm. After the war, he became a professor of geology at Illinois Wesleyan University in 1865 and at Illinois Normal College in 1867. Powell did not remain within the confines of the classroom for long. In 1867 and 1868, he led field trips into the Rocky Mountains, where the Ute Indians called him Karpurats—"one-arm man." In May and August 1869, having secured support from the Smithsonian Institution and an appropriation from Congress, he led eleven others in the first expedition down the Colorado River and through the Grand Canyon. The expedition faced both natural and human hazards; three of the party were killed by hostile Paiutes.

The expedition brought funding from the Department of the Interior for a "U.S. Geographical and Geological Survey of the Rocky Mountain Region" from 1871 to 1879. In 1871 and 1874, Powell personally

John Wesley Powell. *Editors' collection.*

led expeditions, which not only added vastly to the information on public lands in the Rocky Mountains, but provided photographer John K. Hillers with the opportunity to document the Grand Canyon in a spectacular series of images. Laying the groundwork for a vast part of the national park system, Powell's reports and Hillers's photographs sparked interest in preserving the Grand Canyon as a national scenic area. Remarkably, while undertaking geological studies, Powell also conducted ethnological work among the Native Americans of the region. He published *An Introduction to the Study of Indian Languages* in 1877, a pioneering effort in the linguistic and ethnological classification of Indian languages and dialects, which organized them into fifty-six well-defined linguistic families. Powell also led expeditions into Utah and Arizona and charted large tracts in the region.

In 1879, the so-called Powell Survey, the Hayden Survey (conducted by FERDINAND VANDEVEER HAYDEN), and the King Survey (led by CLARENCE KING) were merged into the U.S. Geological Survey under the aegis of the Department of the Interior. King served as the survey's first director and was succeeded by Powell in 1881. Also in 1879, Powell became the first director of the Smithsonian Institution's Bureau of Ethnology (renamed the Bureau of American Ethnology in 1894). As director of the Geological Survey, Powell was dynamic and energetic but also generally heedless of politics. He built the U.S. Geological Survey into a well-organized, well-funded, and powerful federal agency, which produced a large volume of scientific information through the publication series Powell instituted: the Bulletin series (from 1883), the Monograph series (from 1890), and the folio atlas series (begun in 1894). As early as his *REPORT ON THE LANDS OF ARID REGIONS* in 1878, Powell had advocated government-funded irrigation and RECLAMATION projects, and in 1888, as a result of his work at the Geological Survey, Congress began authorizing funds. However, his unbending advocacy of these government-regulated irrigation projects, coupled with his insistence on stringent forest preservation measures, caused great consternation among Western landowners and capitalists, who pressured Congress into forcing Powell to resign from the survey in 1894.

Powell continued as director of the Bureau of Ethnology until his death. He directed expeditions to study the Zunis of New Mexico and the Pueblo Indians of the Southwest. He brought into the Bureau of Ethnology the leading anthropologists of the day, including ADOLPH ALPHONSE BANDELIER, FRANK HAMILTON CUSHING, James Owen Dorsey, JESSE WALTER FEWKES, William Henry Holmes, Washington Matthews, James Mooney, MATILDA COXE STEVENSON, and William Orrie Tuggle.

Powell's reports on his early geological studies were published in 1875 as *Explorations of the Colorado River of the West and Its Tributaries,* which was revised and enlarged in 1885 as *Canyons of the Colorado.* Not only were these works invaluable for what they revealed about the Southwest, they also developed much of the terminology and many of the concepts used by geologists to this day.

—*Alan Axelrod*

SUGGESTED READING:

Darrah, William Culp. *Powell of the Colorado.* Princeton, N.J., 1951.

Stegner, Wallace. *Beyond the Hundredth Meridian.* Boston, 1954.

Terrell, John Upton. *The Man Who Rediscovered America: A Biography of John Wesley Powell.* New York, 1969.

PRAIRIE

From the forests of the Eastern seaboard to the semiarid Great Plains west of the Missouri River stretches an area known as the prairie. It is distinguished by a thick grass cover, deep root networks, and a lack of

timber cover. But it is wrong to think of the prairie as a vast monotonous expanse. The prairie is a region rich in species of grasses and flowers, changing according to soil type, climate, and available moisture.

More than 640 million acres of tall-grass prairies dominated the midlands of the United States—from Indiana in the east to the eastern fringes of Nebraska and Kansas in the west, from southern Minnesota in the north to parts of Oklahoma in the south. This vast area was once a sweeping panorama of prairie that sometimes frightened the Euro-American settlers accustomed to the forested regions to the east.

Scientists do not agree about the origins of the prairie as a landform. Many are convinced that a warming trend following the recession of glaciers was responsible for their formation. Others believe that some types of soil are more conducive to prairie development than others. All agree, however, that the elements of FIRE and relatively low rainfall levels are essential ingredients.

Prairies are usually identified by the plants that make up their vegetation cover. They are often grouped into such categories as "tall-grass prairie," "short-grass prairie," "wetland prairie," "hill prairie," "sand prairie," and others. Characteristic grasses include big bluestem, little bluestem, Indian grass, switchgrass, sideoats grama, prairie dropseed, and porcupine grass. There are at least seventy-two species of grasses in the prairie environment. Prairie grasses often grow to be six feet or more in height, and settlers commonly said that a man on horseback could not see over it.

In addition to grasses, hundreds of varieties of flowers are found on prairies. More than fifty species of daisies and more than twenty-five species of peas are common. Many species of mint, sedge, and parsley are also present. Common types of flowers also include shooting star, spiderwort, aster, goldenrod, downy gentian, compass plant, and ox eye.

The roots of the grasses branch into a dense mat that may penetrate as much as six feet underground. By contrast, roots of grass on the Great Plains are shallow, and the grass itself is shorter on the prairies. The root network, present for centuries, creates the high organic content of the soil and accounts for its fertility. There is a dichotomy in that however. The fertility of the prairie soil attracted Euro-American farmers, but the root network was so dense that ordinary farm implements could not cultivate the soil. Not until the invention of the so-called breaking plow was it possible to plow the prairie sod and plant domestic crops. Specialized equipment and operators handled that part of the work, and people at the time often remarked that the ripping sound made by the plowshare tearing up the root network sounded like a cry of pain from the earth itself.

The vegetation creates a heavy litter at the end of each growing season. After accumulating for several years, the layer of litter begins to decompose, but, at the same time, it hinders new growth. The natural methods of disposing of this layer of litter is fire. Each year or two, prairie fires burned off the old growth, making for more vigorous new growth. Such burning also prevented the spread of shoots and sprouts of trees, keeping the timber from encroaching on the prairie. Even after the settlement of Euro-Americans, prairie fires continued to be a technique for managing the prairie grasses, as well as an ominous threat to the buildings and lives of settlers. Only after the prairie was plowed up was the danger of fire, and the natural uses of it, ended.

In recreated prairie environments, burning as a management tool is used regularly. Burning many be done annually or every two of three growing seasons. The results are the same whether the plot involved is an acre or a larger expanse.

Prairies tend to be level or gently rolling. Water courses may meander through them, but other than the wetland prairies, they tend to be rather dry. Animals, both large and small, lived in the presettlement prairies areas. BUFFALOES, deer, COYOTES, rabbits, prairies dogs, and other kinds of animals lived on and were a part of the environment. Birds such as prairie chickens, partridges, quail, pheasant, larks, hawks, vultures, and various songbirds were also found. Once the habitat of those animals and birds was disturbed by farming and other human activities, they decreased in number, and some became almost extinct. A few types of birds and animals adjusted to the density of human population, but the WILDLIFE observed by the explorers and first settlers is now unknown.

The prairie changes dramatically with the seasons. As soon as the snow disappears in the spring, the plants appear, and grasses and flowers continue to grow, flower, and seed until the first killing frost of fall. The rich colors are always present but change from time to time. Pasqueflowers and shooting stars are the first to bloom in spring. These pale colors change to bright yellow and purple during the hottest part of the summer. The season ends with masses of goldenrod and blazing stars.

Although the prairie was first thought to be an obstacle to Euro-American settlement, technology and changing attitudes quickly made it a desirable place to live. People accustomed to the forest thought that land was most fertile where trees grew. Moreover, trees were necessary to provide fuel, fencing, and housing. The first settlers laid claim to the wooded areas. Latecomers were left with the prairies, and they soon found that they actually had the best of the deal. Centuries of

decomposing prairie-grass roots and stalks had created a rich soil, sometimes with topsoil as much as two feet deep.

Many travelers recorded their impressions of the prairie. Keturah Belknap wrote in 1848: "We traveled thru part of Ohio and across Indiana and Illinois and crossed the Mississippi at Fort Madison into Iowa; was four weeks on the way and saw prairie to our hearts content, and verily we thought the half had never been told." Susan Amelia Cranston wrote in 1851: "The country thus far . . . is very rolling. The eye scans the open distance in vain to find an object upon which it may rest." Mariette Foster Cummings wrote that the prairie was "as smooth as a house floor." Father PIERRE-JEAN DE SMET, a Roman Catholic missionary, recalled that "nearly the whole of this territory is of an undulating form, and the undulations resemble the billows of the sea when agitated by the storm."

—*Loren N. Horton*

SUGGESTED READING:

Madson, John. *Where the Sky Began: Land of the Tallgrass Prairies.* Ames, Iowa, 1982. Reprint, 1995.

Thompson, Jannette R. *Prairies, Forests, and Wetlands.* Iowa City, Iowa, 1992.

PRAIRIE DOGS

It is difficult to estimate the enormous number of prairie dogs *(Cynonomys ludovicianus)* that once occupied the grasslands west of the Mississippi River to the Pacific Ocean and from southern Canada to Mexico. In 1901, Vernon Bailey of the Bureau of Biological Survey described a prairie-dog town that was more than 250 miles long and almost a 100 miles wide and contained, he estimated, four million prairie dogs. Seven subspecies of prairie dogs are found in the West. White-tailed prairie dogs are found in higher elevations in foothills and mountain parks, while the more common and numerous black-tailed prairie dogs are found on the plains and prairies. Prairie dogs are rodents and are related to rats, mice, woodchucks, beavers, and porcupines. These large ground-burrowing squirrels may reach a weight of three pounds and a length of seventeen inches. They may live for up to five years and bear one litter of up to five pups each year. Their vegetarian diet is varied and includes Russian thistle seedlings, grass seeds, cactus plants, and the roots of many perennial plants and diverse forbs.

Social animals, they live together in large communities. Each pair has a well-developed underground burrow with elaborate interlacing tunnels shared with other members of the community. Tunnels up to eighty-six feet long and more than six feet deep have been found. The constant burrowing of prairie dogs improves the fertility of the soil by bringing minerals to the surface and making the soil less compact. Packed mounds of earth often characterize the entrance to their burrows. The entrance mounds provide some protection from flooding and serve as observation posts and sunning sites. When approached, prairie dogs warn other members of the community with their characteristic bark. Their constant harvesting of grasses and forbs creates a unique habitat for other animals. The conquest of the prairie by cow and plow doomed the great prairie-dog communities, which were once a fundamental part of the ecosystem. From the last quarter of the nineteenth century until World War II, they were systematically removed from much of their former range so that ranching and farming could be practiced.

—*Phillip Drennon Thomas*

SUGGESTED READING:

Costello, David F. *The World of the Prairie Dog.* Philadelphia and New York, 1970.

Hall, E. Raymond, and Keith R. Kelson. *The Mammals of North America.* 2 vols. New York, 1959.

PRAIRIE SCHOONERS

SEE: Conestoga Wagons

PRATT, ORSON

A leading Mormon missionary, editor, pioneer, and pamphleteer, Orson Pratt (1811–1881) was born in Hartford, New York, the younger brother of Parley P. Pratt, a noted Mormon preacher and publicist. Converted and baptized by his brother, Orson Pratt began a remarkable missionary effort that included trips to New York, Ohio, all other Eastern states, Canada, England, Scotland, the continent of Europe, and Washington, D.C. In all, he crossed the Atlantic Ocean sixteen times. He was ordained an apostle in 1835.

Pratt was editor of the *Latter-day Saints' Millennial Star,* published in Liverpool from 1848 to 1851, and the *Seer,* published in Washington, D.C., in 1852. As a missionary in England and Scotland from 1848 to 1851, he wrote and published sixteen pamphlets in defense of Mormon doctrines; from 1856 to 1857, he produced eight more pamphlets on specific gospel principles. His pamphlets, plus the approximately one hundred sermons that were printed for distribution, were all carefully reasoned and prepared and were effective in bringing in thousands of Mormon converts. His

extended arguments and proofs of the central tenets of Mormon theology were based on the revelations and pronouncements of Mormonism's founding prophet JOSEPH SMITH, JR. Because some of Pratt's interpretations were different from those of BRIGHAM YOUNG, there was sometimes tension between the two men.

Pratt was also a pioneer colonizer. A member of the advance company that left the Missouri River valley in 1847, he was the first to enter the Salt Lake Valley, surveyed Salt Lake City, was elected to the territorial legislature, and served seven terms as Speaker of the Utah House of Representatives.

Young chose Pratt to make the first public announcement of the Mormon practice of plural marriage. Pratt later served as official church historian and recorder. In this capacity, he divided modern Mormon scriptures (the BOOK OF MORMON, *Doctrine and Covenants,* and *Pearl of Great Price)* into chapters and verses and provided cross references with the Bible.

—*Leonard J. Arrington*

SEE ALSO: Church of Jesus Christ of Latter-day Saints; Mormons

SUGGESTED READING:

England, Breck. *The Life and Thought of Orson Pratt.* Salt Lake City, 1989.

Lyon, T. Edgar. "Orson Pratt, Pioneer and Proselyter." *Utah Historical Quarterly* 24 (1956): 261–273.

PRATT, RICHARD HENRY

U.S. Army officer and educator Richard Henry Pratt (1840–1924) founded and served as superintendent of Carlisle Indian Industrial School in Carlisle, Pennsylvania, which operated from 1879 to 1918.

A Civil War veteran, Pratt reentered the army in 1867 as an officer with the Tenth Cavalry (BUFFALO SOLDIERS) stationed in the Southwest. After the Red River War in 1875, he was ordered to supervise a group of Cheyenne, Kiowa, and Comanche prisoners detained at Fort Marion, Florida. Believing that "civilization" offered an answer to the so-called Indian problem, Pratt persuaded the Indian Bureau to retain some of the prisoners in the East for schooling. In 1879, he opened a school specifically for Indians at Carlisle, Pennsylvania. His institution soon became a focal point for the government's assimilation program.

Pratt's school operated on the then-popular notion that Indians could be rapidly incorporated into American society. To accomplish that goal, Indian children needed to be removed from the reservation setting and trained in the ways of white society. The school slogan, "To Civilize the Indian, Get Him Into Society. To Keep Him Civilized, Let Him Stay," succinctly stated its outlook. Students, both male and female, learned to speak English, adopt the Anglo-Saxon work ethic, follow Christian moral beliefs, and become "Americanized." With such training, Pratt believed that Indian children would lead their people to integrate with mainstream society. They were, accordingly, trained for occupations as laborers, farmers, and domestic servants. By 1890, Carlisle Indian School, under Pratt's leadership, had attained considerable fame and enrolled more than five hundred students each year. Some twenty-five off-reservation industrial schools modeled after the Carlisle system had also opened across the West by 1900. Despite the illusion of progress, however, Pratt's program became increasingly controversial. His determination to put students directly into mainstream society, rather than prepare them to return to their own people, seemed misplaced. In fact, most students chose to return to the reservation, where they found their schooling of little value. Pratt's belligerent personality also produced friction as he vigorously attacked anyone opposed to his ideas.

In 1904, Pratt was forced to leave Carlisle. Thereafter, he continued to defend his ideas in the public arena. In 1918, Carlisle itself closed, partly a victim of wartime priorities, but also because its approach to Indian education had become outdated.

Throughout his life, Pratt championed the cause of the American Indian. His school shaped the federal approach to Indian education at a time when ethnocentric ideas prevailed. Perhaps more idealistic than realistic, his educational philosophy—requiring the destruction of Indian culture as a necessary prelude to assimilation—failed to produce significant results and created bitter resentment among some Native Americans.

—*Robert A. Trennert*

SEE ALSO: Americanization Programs; Indian Schools: Indian Schools off the Reservation; United States Indian Policy: Civilization Programs

SUGGESTED READING:

Eastman, Elaine Goodale. *Pratt: The Red Man's Moses.* Norman, Okla., 1935.

Pratt, Richard Henry. *Battlefield and Classroom: Four Decades with the American Indian, 1867–1904.* Edited by Robert M. Utley. New Haven, Conn., 1964.

PREEMPTION ACT OF 1841

The Preemption Act of 1841 provided for the purchase of 160-acre tracts of surveyed public lands by settlers

who inhabited the tract, made certain improvements, and paid at least $1.25 per acre. Preceded by numerous special preemption acts and one general preemption act, the 1841 measure was the first to allow prospective preemption—that is, settlement prior to purchase. The law is generally regarded as one of the most important land laws ever enacted. It shifted LAND POLICY away from public lands as a source of government revenue and toward free homesteads, thus hastening westward settlement and democratizing the system of public-land distribution by favoring small but aspiring farmers over large land owners and speculators.

—Stanford J. Layton

SUGGESTED READING:

Robbins, Roy M. *Our Landed Heritage: The Public Domain, 1776–1936.* Princeton, N.J., 1942.

PRESBYTERIANS

SEE: Protestants

PRESBYTERIAN WOMAN'S BOARD OF HOME MISSIONS

Founded in 1878 and initially named the Woman's Executive Committee of Home Missions of the Presbyterian Church, the Woman's Board of Home Missions was intended to unify women's efforts to support home missions. Church leaders had originally envisioned that the Woman's Board would support the work of male home missionaries on the fringe areas of white settlement. However, Presbyterian women quickly adopted an agenda that enhanced the role of women in the church; they constructed and supported mission schools staffed by women. This interest in education was spurred, in part, by requests from missionaries, who found that, in non-Protestant communities, schools were more welcome than churches. One such request provided the impetus behind the organization of the board; it came in 1867 from Amanda McFarland, the wife of a missionary stationed in Santa Fe, New Mexico. She pleaded with her counterparts in the East to help her open a school.

While technically subordinate to the male-dominated Board of Home Missions, the Woman's Board took on as its special project the evangelization of "exceptional populations," which included Hispanic CATHOLICS, Native Americans (both in the West and in Alaska), and MORMONS. Chinese immigrants were later added to the list, as were mountain whites in the Southeast, Italian and Eastern European immigrants (in the 1890s), and Puerto Ricans and Cubans (following the Spanish-American War).

Under its first president, Mary James, who served from 1885 to 1908, the Woman's Board was particularly concerned that those groups, whom they considered to be "embryo citizens," receive Protestant religious instruction to counteract what they believed to be the negative influences of Catholicism, Mormonism, and native religions. They concentrated their efforts in education and opened a network of schools—both day and boarding—in mission fields. Generally single and widowed Anglo-Protestant women, recruited from throughout the United States, staffed the schools. The board proved very flexible in its endeavors. Schools were opened and closed as conditions warranted. Boarding schools, considered to be a better vehicle for both evangelization and Americanization, were given preference over day schools.

The second president, Katherine J. Bennett, diversified the board's activities and emphasized the delivery of a variety of social services during her tenure from 1909 to 1923. As public-school systems developed more fully, the board shifted its efforts to the opening of community centers. Never very successful at persuading client populations to convert, the board did find them receptive to secular services.

The board ceased to exist as an independent agency of the Presbyterian church in 1924. From its modest beginnings in 1879, when it employed fourteen teachers and raised $2,287 to support its activities, the board had grown enormously. In 1924, the board had 421,656 members in its missionary and young people's groups, employed 451 missionaries, and had a budget of $1,120,000. It administered twenty-four boarding schools and twenty-one day schools that served four thousand pupils, twenty-eight community stations from which eighteen thousand home visits were made, as well as eight medical centers that treated forty-nine thousand patients.

—Susan M. Yohn

SUGGESTED READING:

Boyd, Lois, and Douglas Brackenridge. *Presbyterian Women in America: Two Centuries of Quest for Status.* Westport, Conn. 1983.

Verdesi, Elizabeth. *In But Still Out: Women in the Church.* Philadelphia, 1976.

PREUSS, CHARLES

A topographer, map-maker, and artist, Charles Preuss (1803–1854) was born in Hohscheid in the German

principality of Waldeck. He began his career as a surveyor for the Prussian government. After immigrating to the United States in 1834, he joined the United States Coast and Geodetic Survey, where he worked for Frederick Hassler, the project's Swiss-born head. Hassler introduced him to a young protégé, the future explorer JOHN CHARLES FRÉMONT.

Preuss is remembered today solely because he accompanied Frémont on three expeditions. The surveying reports and sketches he made during those forays into the American wilderness were superb. The red-haired Preuss was, however, morose, moody, and highly argumentative. He kept a secret diary in which he wrote, in German, scathing denunciations of Frémont and his other traveling companions. The manuscript was found in 1954 stored in a trunk in an East German attic.

Preuss was the major cartographer on Frémont's first, second, and fourth expeditions into the Far West. The first expedition, from Chouteau's Landing to the Wind River Mountains and back to St. Louis, lasted from June 4, 1842, to October 2, 1842. A second venture, covering much of the same territory, took place from May 30, 1843 to July 15, 1844. Preuss, angry and irritated with Frémont for a variety of reasons, did not accompany him on a third expedition (1845 to 1846) to California; however, he did join a disastrous fourth expedition through the rugged Sangre de Cristo Mountains in midwinter and on to Taos, New Mexico. On that hazardous venture, from December 15, 1848, to February 12, 1849, the expedition lost one-third of its men, and charges of cannibalism surfaced.

Although invited to join Frémont's fifth, and last, expedition in 1853, Preuss refused. Instead he accompanied R. S. Williamson's exploring party on one of several Pacific Railroad Surveys. A despondent Preuss never seemed to recover from the travails he encountered during his Western travels. He hanged himself in 1854.

—*Andrew Rolle*

SUGGESTED READING:

Gudde, Erwin, and Elizabeth Grude, eds. *Exploring with Frémont: The Private Diaries of Charles Preuss.* Norman, Okla., 1958.

Rolle, Andrew. *John Charles Frémont: Character as Destiny.* Norman, Okla., 1991.

PRICE, STERLING

Missouri politician and Confederate Army officer Sterling Price (1809–1867) was born in Prince Edward County, Virginia. After attending college for a year and studying law, he migrated with his parents to Missouri in 1830. There, the family settled on seven hundred acres in Chariton County.

After establishing himself as a merchant in Keytesville, Price became involved in local Democratic politics. From 1836 to 1838 and from 1840 to 1844, he served in the Missouri General Assembly. During his last term, he was Speaker of the assembly. In 1844, the assembly selected him to serve in the U.S. House of Representatives but, two years later, failed to renominate him. In August 1846, with the help of Senator THOMAS HART BENTON, Price secured appointment as colonel in a Missouri regiment headed for New Mexico. After serving with STEPHEN WATTS KEARNY and Colonel ALEXANDER WILLIAM DONIPHAN in New Mexico, Price led a force to Chihuahua in March 1948, secured the surrender of the Chihuahua governor, and set himself up as provisional military governor. His capture of Chihuahua took place after most of the hostilities in the United States–Mexican War had ended, but it may have influenced the Mexican authorities to ratify the Treaty of Guadalupe Hidalgo more quickly than they might have.

After the war, Price returned to Missouri where he resumed his operation of a tobacco plantation and his interest in politics. Siding with the proslavery wing of the Democratic party, he was elected governor in 1852.

Price was chair of the Missouri secession convention, which decided that Missouri would not leave the Union. In the spring of 1861, however, he accepted the command of the Missouri state guard, which was victorious over the Union forces at Wilson's Creek and Lexington. In March 1862, most of his state guard was brought into the Confederate Army, and Price was named major general. He and his troops fought in Mississippi and Arkansas between 1862 and 1864. In September 1864, he attempted to split the Union force of General WILLIAM TECUMSEH SHERMAN by conducting a raid into Missouri. At the end of the CIVIL WAR, he retreated to Mexico and remained there in exile for a year and a half.

In January 1867, Price returned to St. Louis, but his health was broken and he soon died.

—*Candace Floyd*

SUGGESTED READING:

Shalhope, Robert E. *Sterling Price: Portrait of a Southerner.* Columbia, Mo., 1971.

PRISONS

SEE: Jails and Prisons

PROCTOR, ALEXANDER PHIMISTER (A. P.)

A Canadian by birth, sculptor Alexander Phimister (A. P.) Proctor (1860–1950) grew up in the United States and received his first instruction in art in Denver, Colorado, from an itinerant illustrator. In 1885, Proctor traveled to New York City to study at the National Academy of Design and later at the Art Students League. He returned often to Colorado to hunt and sketch wild animals. In 1893, he received a commission to produce several large animal figures for the World's Columbian Exposition in Chicago. While studying abroad in Paris the following year, he met American sculptor Augustus St. Gaudens, who proposed that Proctor model the horse for an equestrian statue St. Gaudens had been commissioned to produce for Chicago's Grant Park. Proctor subsequently collaborated with St. Gaudens on other equestrian monuments, and on his own, he produced decorative sculptures for public buildings in New York City and Washington, D.C. He was elected an associate member of the national Academy of Design in 1895.

Proctor became widely known for the monumental sculptures he produced for the American Pavilion at the Paris International Exposition in 1900, the Pan-American Exposition in Buffalo, New York, in 1901, and the Louisiana Purchase Exposition in St. Louis, Missouri, in 1904. Always on the move, he eventually settled with his family in Seattle, Washington, although he continued to make frequent trips to New York and California while working on various commissions. His last large work, entitled *The Mustangs,* was completed in 1948 for the University of Texas at Austin. Proctor is represented today by public sculptures in cities throughout the United States.

—David C. Hunt

SUGGESTED READING:

Broder, Patricia Janis. *Bronzes of the American West.* New York, 1973.

Proctor, A. P. *Alexander Phimister Proctor: Sculptor in Buckskin, an Autobiography.* With an introduction by Vivian Paladin. Norman, Okla., 1971.

PROGRESSIVISM

Although the term *Progessivism* is impossibly broad and imprecise, the movement itself had fairly specific beginnings amid great promise in Chicago in the fall of 1889, when Jane Addams and Ellen Gates Starr established the social settlement called Hull House. Their pioneering social work attracted writers, thinkers, and muckraking journalists, who publicized the social problems associated with late nineteenth-century industrial development and discussed practical solutions to those problems. This network of social workers, intellectuals, and journalists soon constituted a loose "movement" that spawned a campaign for good government in American cities. The movement captured the imagination of politicians such as Wisconsin's Robert M. La Follette and THEODORE ROOSEVELT, and its political fortunes were made. When Roosevelt was inaugurated as president of the United States in 1901, the movement had in the country's "bully pulpit" a national hero capable of reforming the entire country on those days when he was willing.

Historians have argued at length about whether Progressive reform derived from the earlier Populist movement or was a new phenomenon spawned primarily by middle-class society. In truth, Progressivism, especially in the American West, was a uneasy blend of both. In those states where POPULISM had flourished—in, say, Texas and Kansas—Progressivism bore a strong agrarian and radical flavor. In those states—such as Oregon and California, for example—where what some historians have called the "Western Civil War of Incorporation" was dominated by aggressive Republican capitalists who sought to "tame" a wide-open society and create a stable environment for new investment, Progressivism had an urban and upper- and middle-class focus.

Roosevelt's brand of Progressivism tended toward the latter end of the spectrum, and the Progressives who came to national power at the dawn of the twentieth century with his assumption of the presidency were part of a countrywide political movement that transcended party but not class. Born of the decay of Populism, the growing emphasis on social work among upper- and middle-class women, the sensational writings of muckraking journalists, and the involvement of America's churches in matters of public morality, Progressives reacted to the growing power of labor, the revolutionary demands of America's intellectual radicals, and the changing racial and ethnic composition of American cities in the late nineteenth century with a moral "uplift" program of managerial reform intended to check the excesses of capitalism while in general preserving it.

Progressive leaders were largely upper- and middle-class reformers and developers, business and religious leaders, and the more successful newspapermen. Interested in economic growth and clean government, they talked in lofty terms of "progress," "civic reform," and "modernization." They attacked mere politicians,

especially those elected officials more interested in patronage than patriotism, in political power than honest government, in vote getting than moral decay. Their crusade for good government called for the initiative and referendum, public control of the railroads and utilities, a certain amount of trust busting, primary elections, the popular election of senators, WOMEN'S SUFFRAGE, and—tellingly—prohibition.

But for all the Progressives owed to late nineteenth-century Populist reform, they did not much care for the underdog. Their leaders did not speak for the urban poor, racial and ethnic minorities, or labor radicals, all of whom Progressives tended to view as morally decadent at best, viciously criminal at worst. Not surprisingly, during the Progressive era, America's urban working class came under attack in the Progressive campaign against big-city machines. Progressive leaders, from their country clubs and comfortable homes, reached out to destroy the saloons and brothels where working men relaxed and talked politics. They launched a Red Scare to purge from American society the political agitators and intellectuals who took up the cause of the oppressed and to purge all working-class institutions of "alien"—meaning immigrant—influence. They used social unrest and the crisis of World War I as opportunities to attack ethnic cultures and to homogenize and "standardize" America's white population. The merit system, with which they hoped to replace the spoils system of the urban machines, routinely excluded African Americans and other ethnic minorities from local, state, and FEDERAL GOVERNMENT.

Theodore Roosevelt's national version of Progressive thinking had been developed in newspaper polemics based on his Western experiences of the 1870s and formulated into doctrine by his frontier history *The Winning of the West.* As his world of heroes and villains came to rule the early Progressive movement, it became attractive to elements of the ruling elite and the growing urban middle-class populations of the trans- Mississippi West, whose Victorian good-government movements had sought to tame the wide-open cattle towns and mining camps in the name of middle-class respectability. The bullying reform of prohibition had precedents in the vigilante movements of the West and the gunslingers the "decent" folk hired to keep the lower classes in line. Behind all the talk of moral uplift and civic reform lay a morality play based on Roosevelt's Darwinian version of the frontier myth. In many ways, Western Progressives wanted modern-day gunslingers, military-minded can-do strong men who spoke softly and carried a big stick, to come to town to clean out the rabble—big corporate bandits they called "robber barons" and evil foreign conspirators alike.

The good-government movement experienced early success in the American West, and the very fact that CITY GOVERNMENTS, like those in San Francisco and Los Angeles, could be reformed fed the growth of Western Progressivism, whose major triumphs ultimately came at the state level. Texas and Kansas, two states where the impact of Populism lingered on, passed the first antitrust laws in the United States, and both of them created strong railroad regulatory agencies, aimed in no small measure at protecting their infant OIL AND GAS INDUSTRY against the voracious Standard Oil Trust. Republican reform governors Edward Hoch and Walter Stubbs in Kansas and Democrat Thomas Campbell in Texas launched the Progressive era in these states at the turn of the century, for the most part, by simply continuing the Populist reform efforts of the previous decade. But in the two leading Western Progressive states, Oregon and California, the Populist revolt had played no such major role, and Progressives patterned their crusade after that of Robert La Follette, who as Wisconsin's governor had instituted a full range of reforms, including public administration by nonpartisan civil servants drawn mostly from the University of Wisconsin faculty.

In comparatively middle-class Oregon, reformers led by WILLIAM SIMON U'REN joined with the experienced political hand Jonathan Bourne to take control of the state legislature through the Non-Partisan Direct Legislation League and passed the first general initiative and referendum laws in 1902. Inspired by the "Wisconsin Idea," reformers used these laws as weapons in their crusade to create the "Oregon System," which included the direct primary, the recall vote against corrupt or unresponsive public officials, a corrupt-practices act, and a polling system that allowed Oregon voters to indicate to their legislators their choices for the U.S. Senate, whose members at the time were still appointed by state legislatures. This latter reform constituted an important step in the nationwide movement toward a constitutional amendment calling for the popular election of senators, which Progressives would succeed in passing in 1913. Meanwhile, Oregon proceeded with some basic social reforms, setting a maximum number of work hours per week and the minimum wages that employers could pay women and children.

In California, too, Progressive leaders reflected the upper- and middle-class origins of the state's Progressive reforms, which began in earnest with a crusade against machine politics sparked by Anthony Caminetti, a gadfly opposed to the railroads in a state that was then a virtual fiefdom of the Southern Pacific. In 1906, Caminetti took on the prosecution of San Francisco's political boss, ABRAHAM (ABE)

RUEF, for graft. In 1907, the Progressive leaders of Los Angeles's good-government movement joined Caminetti in calling for the Ruef's ouster. Roosevelt weighed in the fight by sending a federal prosecutor, FRANCIS JOSEPH HENEY, and a federal investigator WILLIAM J. BURNS, to help in the prosecution. In 1910, the Progressive organization created by that battle, the Lincoln-Roosevelt Republican League, nominated HIRAM WARREN JOHNSON for governor. Taking advantage of a new direct-primary law, Johnson captured the statehouse with a promise to "kick the Southern Pacific Railroad out of politics." Once in office, the caustic if brilliant Johnson bulldozed through the legislature a remarkable body of reforms beginning in 1911. Johnson's reforms regulated the railroads and public utilities, introduced a state budget system, and created worker's compensation. Johnson also proposed a number of measures aimed at removing control from party bosses and giving it directly to the people. By 1913, direct primaries, voter initiatives, public referendums, and recall votes gave Californians the power to pass and repeal laws independently of the legislature and immediate control over elected officials. Cross-filing, which allowed a candidate to run for the nomination of more than one party, was a direct attack on party machines. All of these measures weakened the power of political parties, but it was the Democrats who suffered most, since Progressives tended to be Republicans. Progressives held such sway in the early decades of the twentieth century that California became virtually a one-party state. President Roosevelt and Herbert Croly, the major political theorists for Progressivism, both touted California as the leading Progressive state in the nation, a model of nonpartisan government.

The American West became a bastion of Progressivism. In the 1904 election, Roosevelt, the "cowboy" vice-president who had become president when William McKinley was assassinated in 1901, carried every Western state except Texas. The West followed Roosevelt out of the Republican party in 1912 when he became the very willing nominee of a Progressive party formed the year before by La Follette. The Republican candidate, incumbent William Howard Taft managed to carry only Utah in the West in an election marked by the most significant third-party vote in the nation's history. In 1916, when Democrat Woodrow Wilson, a self-proclaimed Progressive reformer, ran for president, he took all but two Western states, Oregon and South Dakota. There were a number of highly individual Western Progressive leaders, whose politics were sometimes characterized by a suspicion of big business: California's Hiram Johnson, Nebraska's United States Senator GEORGE W. NORRIS, Kansas journalists William Allen White and WILLIAM ROCKHILL NELSON, Nevada's United States Senator FRANCIS G. NEWLANDS, and Idaho's U.S Senator WILLIAM E. BORAH. The West figured largely in the three major strands of Progressive reforms—Prohibition, conservation, and women's suffrage. The earliest laws prohibiting the production, sale, and consumption of alcoholic beverages came out of the straight-laced Protestant small towns of the trans-Mississippi Midwest, and along with the South, the West forced national Prohibition on the "wet" cities of the Northeast and Old Northwest. Long before the rest of the country, the West gave women the right to vote, and the region pioneered in women holding political office. Mary Howard became the first female mayor in Kanab, Utah; Bertha Lanes, the first mayor of a major city, Seattle. The nation's first congresswoman was Montana's JEANETTE RANKIN, and its first female governors were Texas's Miriam ("Ma") Ferguson and Wyoming's Nellie Tayloe Ross.

But it was conservation, of all the Progressive-era issues, that had the greatest impact on the West as a region. In many ways, the idea of conservation—that is, the federal protection, regulation, and preservation of natural resources—fit neatly within a Western tradition of dependency on and partnership with the federal government, which had long provided Westerners with federal protection from Indians, federal support of the region's transportation network, and federal largess in the awarding of public lands to settlers and to developing industries. And as long as the Progressives were pushing reclamation projects under the authority of the Newlands Reclamation Act of 1902 (avidly promoted by GIFFORD PINCHOT and adamantly supported by his friend and benefactor Teddy Roosevelt) and under the auspices of the powerful Reclamation Service (later BUREAU OF RECLAMATION), the West was happy, since reform meant federal investment in agriculture and urban development of the region. But when it came to removing public lands from use by private businesses or to protecting the West's forests against the lumber industries, Westerners complained loudly and long about "galling insults" to their sovereignty and the "gross outrages" of a federal overlord intent on keeping the region a colonial possession rather than a full partner in the nation. Such complaints themselves became a Western tradition, as Westerners—with federal help—began in the Progressive era to turn their semiarid land into what Donald Worster has called one of the world's great hydraulic civilizations, a society whose existence depends on the centralized management of water resources.

If, as historians Arthur Link and Richard McCormick note, the "most distinctive aspect of western progressivism was its passion for the more demo-

cratic, antiinstitutional political reforms" and that such reforms were "more common there than anywhere else in the nation," it is also true that the West displayed Progressivism's dark side—its nativism, its antiworking-class bias, and its rough-shod and racist social engineering, all of which reflect the Progressive crusade's upper- and middle-class origins. Idaho's William Borah, for example, first achieved his national reputation not as a Progressive reformer, but as the state's prosecutor of WILLIAM D. ("BIG BILL") HAYWOOD, the personification of radical Western labor.

In California, Progressives pushed through the 1913 law prohibiting Japanese from owning land. In the Pacific Northwest, Progressives were in the vanguard of the anti-immigrant, antiradical laws that would characterize Progressivism, in general, from World War I forward. Northwestern states were among the first to enact criminal syndicalism laws that made it illegal for an immigrant who was not yet a citizen to join a radical labor organization and were foremost among those states issuing language proclamations that insisted on English as the country's official language and, in some cases, banned the use of foreign languages in public discourse. And just as the initiative, the referendum, and the recall created a Western tradition that lingers on today in tax-revolt and environmental-protection propositions, so too did the immigration laws enacted by the Progressives in the 1920s reflect a lasting Western legacy that would reappear in the Japanese internment of World War II and the "illegal alien" laws of the 1980s and 1990s.

—*Charles Phillips*

SEE ALSO: Alien Land Laws; Immigration Law; Owens Valley War; Temperance and Prohibition

SUGGESTED READING:

Cherny, Robert W. *Populism, Progressivism, and the Transformation of Nebraska Politics, 1885–1915*. Lincoln, Nebr., 1981.

Deverell, William, and Tom Sittons, eds. *California Progressivism Revisited*. Berkeley, Calif., 1994.

Goble, Danney. *Progressive Oklahoma: The Making of a New Kind of State*. Norman, Okla., 1980.

Gould, Lewis L. *Progressives and Prohibitionists: Texas Democrats in the Wilson Era*. Austin, Tex., 1973.

Kazin, Michael. *Barons of Labor: The San Francisco Building Trades and Union Power in the Progressive Era*. Urbana, Ill., 1987.

Kolko, Gabriel. *The Triumph of Conservatism*. New York, 1963.

La Forte, Robert Sherman. *Leaders of Reform: Progressive Republicans in Kansas, 1900–1916*. Lawrence, Kans., 1974.

Mowry, George E. *The California Progressives*. Berkeley, Calif., 1951.

The ceremony of the joining the Union Pacific and Central Pacific rail lines at Promontory Summit, Utah, on May 10, 1869. *Courtesy National Archives.*

PROMONTORY SUMMIT

On May 10, 1869, the westering rails of the UNION PACIFIC RAILROAD and eastward bound rails of the CENTRAL PACIFIC RAILROAD were joined at Promontory Summit near Ogden, Utah. GRENVILLE MELLEN DODGE, chief engineer for the Union Pacific, sent a laconic telegram to Oliver Ames, president of the railroad: "You can make affidavit of completion of road to Promontory Summit." Many railroad histories and histories of the West mistakenly identify Promontory Summit as Promontory Point.

—*Alan Axelrod*

PRONGHORNS

Found only in North America, the pronghorn was erroneously called the antelope by early Western settlers and is still commonly called by this name. It is not a member of the antelope family. In 1540, FRANCISCO VÁSQUEZ DE CORONADO was the first European to see a pronghorn. George Ord scientifically identified the species as *Antilocapra americana* from a specimen collected by the Lewis and Clark Expedition of 1804 to 1806. Ord noted that it was a horned, hoofed, even-toed, cud-chewing ungulate and a member of the order *Artiodactlya*. Ranging historically from the southern portions of western Canada to Mexico and from the prairies of western Minnesota to the Pacific, pronghorns numbered between thirty million and sixty million at the beginning of the nineteenth century.

Pronghorns are animals of the prairies and plains and have the physical features that guarantee survival in that environment. Their keen eyesight surpasses that of humans by several factors and enables them to spot

predators and other forms of danger. Speed is their principal weapon of defense, and they are considered, after the cheetah, to be the fastest living animal. Within two weeks of their birth, fawns may run thirty-five miles an hour. Their strong, slender legs and large heart and lungs allow adults to run fifty miles an hour for distances of more than three miles. No North American predator can catch them in open terrain. Standing between thirty-two and forty inches at the shoulders, a male pronghorn weighs between 100 and 140 pounds. Females are smaller. Both sexes have true horns that are shed annually. The pronghorn's rump, body section underneath and half way up the sides, and lower portion of the neck are white, while its legs, upper portion of the torso, and neck are fawn, tan, or reddish-brown. Beneath the head there is a tan collar. Males have a black patch beneath each eye and a dark brown or black mask extending backwards from the nose. The coarse hair of the antelope provides excellent insulation in the winter, but the hide of the animal does not make a good leather.

Pronghorns are primarily browsers whose diet consists of sagebrush, rabbit brush, mountain mahogany, greasewood, Western snowberry, bitter brush, juniper, forbs, and grasses. Sagebrush, in its various forms, is their primary food.

Native Americans hunted pronghorns and celebrated them in numerous tribal myths and traditions. Pronghorn populations were not endangered by traditional hunting practices. For Euro-American settlers on the prairies after the Civil War, pronghorns were an important food source. Meat hunters marketed pronghorn tenderloins in San Francisco in 1857 for twenty-five cents a pound. In Denver in 1865, whole pronghorn carcasses were sold for twenty-five cents. While their hides were difficult to work with and of little value, fifty-five thousand pronghorn hides were shipped from the Yellowstone River region to St. Louis in 1881.

Population declines in Western states were dramatic. Subsistence and market hunting, droughts, blizzards, diseases, and destruction and fragmentation of habitat significantly reduced their numbers. In 1860, Colorado was estimated to have two million pronghorns, but in 1918, the state had fewer than one thousand. In the last decade of the twentieth century, the pronghorn could be found in all Western states and was a significant big-game animal in most of them. In 1994, more than four hundred thousand of the animals were found on their traditional range.

—*Phillip Drennon Thomas*

SUGGESTED READING:

Einarsen, Arthur S. *The Pronghorn Antelope and Its Management.* Washington, D.C., 1948.

Van Wormer, Jan. *The World of the Pronghorn.* Philadelphia and New York, 1969.

PROSPECTORS

SEE: Mining: Prospectors

PROSTITUTION

Prostitution, the act of providing sex in exchange for money or commodities, escalated in the American West throughout the nineteenth century and into the twentieth. Several elements in the regional history of the West contributed to the prevalence of prostitution—uneven power interactions between and among differing cultures, sudden economic growth in a variety of new Western industries, hasty deployment of U.S. Army troops to remote areas, and a general imbalance in the ratio of men to women in urban communities and at military locations.

Western European cultures have tended to link the subject of prostitution to issues of morality. For almost three hundred years, this tendency caused European travelers and explorers to misunderstand the sexual customs of various Native American groups. Men from nonnative cultures tended to label Indian women—whether Navajos or Crows, Pimas or Mandans, Sioux or Paiutes—as "promiscuous prostitutes." Those derogatory European labels crossed culture lines with ease, so that many women of color in the West were, during periods of cultural contact, categorized as "prostitutes" by white society. This inaccuracy, which hindered the development of solid cross-cultural relationships, should be seen as a historical problem distinct from the subject of prostitution itself.

Although it is nearly impossible to estimate the total population of prostitutes in the nineteenth-century West, the number probably surpassed fifty thousand. Western prostitution in the nineteenth century included women from all ethnic and racial categories. The emergence of prostitution among all groups of women living in the West meshed with the appearance of radically changed regional economic patterns. In its most visible forms, Western prostitution was connected to industries, like mining and cattle driving, spawned from the natural resources of the region. These industries, although sometimes rural in nature, centered themselves in hastily built urban areas. Prostitution, along with other "vice" industries, was one response to the social and sexual demands of these towns' largely male populations. For example, in Colorado in 1860, men

In 1885 Denver, two prostitutes of Belle Birnard's "fancy house" await the arrival of their customers. *Courtesy Denver Public Library, Western History Department.*

outnumbered women by two to one, and prostitutes clustered in and around bachelor communities and hoped to divert some of the boom-town prosperity to themselves.

Most communities had demarcated red-light districts, some of which—such as those in San Antonio, Texas; Denver, Colorado; and Boise, Idaho—acquired permanence into the twentieth century. Such brothel districts took on the flavor of Western myth making as America moved into the modern era. Well-known brothels and their back-alley satellites, called "cribs," served as Western tourist attractions. The reminiscences of a few long-lived madams, such as Laura Evans of Denver, reinforced notions of a glamorous "old" West existence for a cadre of young, single, beautiful, and prosperous "soiled doves." This mythic image of prostitutes, though widely promulgated by twentieth-century films and television shows, lacked grounding in reality. Although prostitutes were young (many entered the profession before the age of fifteen), most lived an existence shaped by economic, social, and political deprivation. Drawn from among the poor in the West, which offered limited economic opportunity for women, prostitutes often held other jobs as well. Milliners, seamstresses, laundresses, and waitresses all supplemented skimpy and uneven wages with work in prostitution. Their male customers, largely common laborers, rarely offered generous compensation. A woman might earn anywhere from twenty-five cents to five dollars, but all prostitutes faced various fines and taxes that conspired to keep profits from their wages low. For example, in Tombstone, Arizona, the sheriff collected a monthly fee from each gambling house, brothel, and theater. In Cheyenne, Wyoming, authorities devised a credit system so that jail facilities would not be overcrowded with destitute prostitutes who were unable to meet their weekly fines. In Austin, Texas, prostitutes worked out portions of unpaid fines by doing domestic chores in the jail.

Viewed as a transient population in Western communities, prostitutes enjoyed little political power. Although expected to pay taxes and cooperate with criminal investigations and inquests, they had little recourse in matters of due process. In 1868, an entire Texas regiment demanded the release of two soldiers accused of rape when the public learned their victim was a known prostitute from a nearby town. The quality of protection for rights and personal liberties for prostitutes remained superficial throughout the nineteenth and early twentieth centuries.

Socially, prostitutes rarely gained acceptance within a community. The seeming ribald camaraderie of the earliest days of mining camps or cow towns faded as towns stabilized and was always tainted by a perception of prostitutes as "deviant" women. Even during the heyday of boom communities, men of means or status seldom entered into lasting arrangements with prostitutes. Mining engineers, ranchers, and military officers sent to the East for their brides or married from among the "respectable" families in town. Some prostitutes did marry but usually to husbands from their own economic class. In those marriages, husbands often expected wives to continue their work as prostitutes to add to the family income. Other women who worked as prostitutes struggled as single parents caring for three or four children. The daughters of prostitutes commonly entered the profession at an early age, while the sons became saloon managers, bartenders,

and gamblers. Mrs. Jane Elizabeth Ryan, her three daughters, and one son operated a family prostitution and saloon business in several Colorado mining towns before they settled in Denver around the turn of the century.

There were four main categories of prostitutes: streetwalkers, dance-hall girls, crib residents, and brothel inhabitants. Prostitutes considered life in a brothel the safest, for in them a madam assumed management responsibilities. Western saloons or dance halls hosted a regular assembly of prostitutes, who peddled drinks and danced with customers before taking them to small rooms or tents for business. The unsupervised life of streetwalking or life in cribs or in shacks behind a saloon or brothel had the greatest potential for danger. The divisions among the four main categories were not always rigid, and a woman might move among the levels, depending on her location, the available work arrangements, her connections within the business, her personal health and ethnicity, and the amount of local competition.

Fluidity also marked racial divisions. On some occasions, black and white women worked together, as did Hispanics and Anglos. Of course, many houses welcomed women of only one racial grouping—African American, Anglo, Asian, Hispanic. Caucasian customers, at their pleasure, generally felt free to cross these cultural lines.

Native American prostitutes of the late nineteenth and early twentieth centuries did not typically congregate in the urban areas. Their experiences were closely connected to the U.S. Army, which greatly increased the number of troops in the West after the Civil War. At most military garrisons, soldiers and officers established relationships with indigenous women, often with encouragement from local families anxious for supplies and food. In addition to Native American women, Anglo women, too, lived as camp followers in the hog ranches, post stores, and brothel towns that surrounded military reservations. Within the forts, the residents of the garrison's "Sudsville," military laundresses, whether married to enlisted men or as single women, often earned extra rations through prostitution.

Regardless of where women worked in prostitution or their status within the profession, all chanced certain hazards. Unpredictable violence permeated Western prostitution. Prostitutes encountered violence, both intentional and accidental, from the hands of customers, from each other, and from themselves. Verbal abuse and fights punctuated many relationships with customers and among the women. Prostitutes were easy targets for arrest, and they died at early ages from assault, accidental shootings, alcoholism, laudanum overdose, and suicide.

Because prostitutes left few written records, reconstructing the dynamics of their private lives is difficult. Their strategies for accommodation within society, their pleasures, successes, sorrows, and concerns—all remain shadowy factors, as history has focused on their public demeanor.

Julia Bulette of Virginia City, Nevada; Laura Evans, Mattie Silks, and Jennie Rodgers, all of Denver, Colorado; Squirrel Tooth Alice of Dodge City, Kansas; Baby Doe Tabor of Leadville, Colorado; Josephine Marcus of Tombstone, Arizona—these are among the famous Western prostitutes. Each captured much of the myth of Western prostitution. Some were beautiful, some single, some wealthy. Yet, beneath the surface qualities of their lives lurked the professional difficulties that touched all women—social, economic, and political uncertainty.

As the nation moved into the twentieth century, Americans seemed to view Western prostitution as merely a relic of an earlier age. Reform efforts connected to the Progressive era and World War I diminished the trade, and most Western cities had closed their highly visible red-light districts by 1920. Nonetheless, prostitution continued to flourish around military bases like Fort Bliss, Texas, in urban communities, and anywhere a sudden economic surge recreated the bonanza atmosphere of the nineteenth-century West. The conditions that promoted Western prostitution remained unchanged. Poverty; constraints of race, class, and gender; and the lack of educational opportunity for women in male industrial regions or military encampments help to explain the continuation of prostitution in the American West.

—*Anne M. Butler*

SEE ALSO: Cattle Towns; Violence: Violence against Women; Working-Class Women

SUGGESTED READING:

Butler, Anne M. *Daughters of Joy, Sisters of Misery: Prostitutes in The American West, 1865–1890.* Urbana, Ill., 1985.

Goldman, Marion S. *Gold Diggers and Silver Miners: Prostitution and Social Life on the Comstock Lode.* Ann Arbor, Mich., 1981.

Hirata, Lucie Cheng. "Free, Indentured, Enslaved: Chinese Prostitutes in Nineteenth Century America." *Signs* 5 (1979): 3–29.

Murphy, Mary. "The Private Lives of Public Women: Prostitution in Butte, Montana, 1878–1917." In *The Women's West.* Edited by Susan Armitage and Elizabeth Jameson. Norman, Okla., 1987.

Petrik, Paula. "Capitalists with Rooms: Prostitution in Helena, Montana, 1865–1900." *Montana: The Magazine of Western History* 32 (1981): 28–41.

PROTESTANT HOME MISSIONARY PROGRAMS

By the mid-nineteenth century, every major Protestant denomination in the United States had a home-mission program. The creation of church leaders who feared that westward migration would lead to a decline in religiosity, home-mission programs were originally intended to see to the spiritual needs of Protestant settlers moving west. The Congregational, Presbyterian, Methodist, Baptist, and Episcopal churches all organized home-missions boards to coordinate and oversee the efforts of thousands of smaller local mission societies. The original mandate of these programs was to build churches, support ministers, and, to a lesser extent, establish schools. Over the course of the century, this mandate grew as the churches embraced the idea of MANIFEST DESTINY, thereby linking the triumph of Protestantism over Catholicism with NATIONAL EXPANSION. They also preached the gospel among Western populations deemed "foreign" but living within United States borders, such as Native Americans, Hispanics, and the Chinese. Parallel women's programs, formed after the Civil War, helped expand the scope of home-mission work. In the nineteenth century, women's programs raised money and recruited personnel to support, for instance, the schooling of younger children and rescue homes for young women; in the twentieth century, women's programs sponsored the building of community centers and hospitals.

Home-mission programs were at once religious and political. Their creation reflected sectional rivalries, as Eastern elites feared that the hardships of Western pioneering would lead to lax moral standards; it also reflected religious rivalries between Protestants and CATHOLICS, who had established programs of their own. Checking what Protestants termed *Romanism* was not the only ulterior motive of home MISSIONS; they also promised to stop the spread of others "isms" deemed detrimental to the growth of a Protestant democracy: Mormonism, nihilism, communism, atheism, and what was encompassed by the term *infidelity.* With varying strategies, Protestant churches set out to "save" the West. The Congregational and Presbyterian churches, for example, preferred to establish churches and support full-time ministers, while the Methodist church employed circuit riders.

Home missions were a powerful force in the expansion of Protestantism across the nation. Under their influence, the numbers of Protestants increased; the Methodists were most successful in attracting new members, followed by the Baptists and Presbyterians. Missionaries also played a critical role in the expansion of Western educational opportunities, as the demand for trained ministers gave rise to a network of private colleges throughout the West. In addition, EVANGELISTS expressed concern for the education of younger children and promoted denominational private schools to serve as models for public schools. Male home missionaries working in the West were also among the earliest supporters of women's efforts at social reform. Encouraging the formation of women's home-missionary programs, the male missionaries saw in the women's work an important source of support for their educational efforts.

Home missions proved less successful among those groups their sponsors had labeled "foreign." Converts were so few that successful missionaries learned to promote programs that emphasized secular social services. Among Hispanics, for instance, the schools and hospitals opened by Presbyterians and Methodists proved more popular than religious missions. Because these programs were not explicitly evangelical, however, they often generated controversy within the Protestant churches themselves. Critics charged that home missions had strayed from their religious purpose, while supporters maintained that even the secular aspects of home-mission work were effective efforts at "Americanization" and that they served a nationalist purpose, which would ultimately benefit Protestantism.

—*Susan M. Yohn*

SEE ALSO: American Board of Commissioners for Foreign Missions; Americanization Programs; Presbyterian Woman's Board of Home Missions

SUGGESTED READING:

Drury, Clifford. *Presbyterian Panorama: 150 Years of National Missions History.* Philadelphia, 1952.

Emery, Julia. *A Century of Endeavor 1821–1921: A Record of the First Hundred Years of the Domestic and Foreign Missionary Society of the Protestant Episcopal Church.* New York, 1921.

Goodykoontz, Colin. *Home Missions on the American Frontier.* New York, 1971.

Harwood, Thomas. *History of New Mexico Spanish and English Missions of the Methodist Episcopal Church from 1850 to 1910.* 2 vols. Albuquerque, N. Mex., 1908, 1910.

Pascoe, Peggy. *Relations of Rescue: The Search for Female Moral Authority in the American West, 1874–1939.* New York, 1990.

PROTESTANTS

Protestantism is a set of religious institutions and theological and cultural perspectives deriving from religious

J. J. Methvin, a Methodist missionary, pictured with his Kiowa and Comanche charges in 1894. *Courtesy Western History Collections, University of Oklahoma Library.*

reforms in European Christianity in the sixteenth century. By 1848, when Protestantism had become a permanent part of the trans-Mississippi West, it was already diverse in belief, practice, and polity.

Protestants were a significant minority in the West even before the region was entirely under the dominion of the United States. While Saxon immigrants were settling in Missouri and organizing what would come to be known as the Missouri Synod of the Lutheran church in the 1840s, Finnish, Swedish, and German Lutheran employees of the Russian American Company maintained their own pastor in Sitka, Alaska. Protestants worshipped in the Republic of Texas beginning in 1836, and various denominations were represented among the pre–Civil War settlers in Louisiana, Arkansas, Missouri, Iowa, and Minnesota. The Protestant-derived Church of Jesus Christ of Latter-day Saints moved to the West to reestablish itself next to the Great Salt Lake in 1847. Protestant MISSIONS to various indigenous peoples of the West were also underway before 1848. For example, the AMERICAN BOARD OF COMMISSIONERS FOR FOREIGN MISSIONS sponsored work in Hawaii in 1820 and among the Cayuse and Nez Percé Indians in 1836. Methodists in Oregon supported another major effort in 1834 under JASON LEE.

In the seven decades that followed 1847, Protestants were an integral part of the political, economic, and cultural conquest of the West by Anglo-Americans. The 1849 gold rush to California brought significant numbers of Protestants and their institutions to the Far West. A decade later, a similar rush to Colorado brought Protestantism permanently to the area. The mining rushes illustrated the predominant pattern of the spread of Protestantism throughout the West—home missionaries or frontier EVANGELISTS, usually tied to Eastern-based institutions, established congregations primarily (but not exclusively) among Euro-American migrants soon after an area was occupied.

Many Protestant men and women poured themselves into the home-mission work in the West. Some male missionaries became legends in their own lifetimes. Methodist William Taylor, for example, became famous for his street preaching in San Francisco and California's mining camps, while Presbyterian SHELDON JACKSON traveled some thirty thousand miles annually and established more than 150 churches in the West between 1859 and 1909. Jackson was also an avid supporter in 1878 of what became the PRESBYTERIAN WOMAN'S BOARD OF HOME MISSIONS. Protestant women, whether Presbyterian or not, were less touted than men

in the home-mission movement because of widespread contemporary assumptions that women should be subordinate to male leadership. However, many, perhaps most, Protestant congregations depended on local Ladies Aid societies for their viability, and women founded, funded, and led many Western Protestant institutions, ranging from churches and charity organizations to schools and missionary homes. Women staffed and funded much of the Protestant mission work with Native Americans, Hispanics, Chinese, Japanese, Mormons, and European immigrants. Legendary female missionaries include DONALDINA MCKENZIE CAMERON, the indomitable superintendent of the Presbyterian Chinese Mission Home in San Francisco, and ALICE BLAKE, a Presbyterian teacher, nurse, and community leader among Hispanic New Mexicans.

Protestantism was part of the social and cultural order inherited by the West from the East. Anglo-Americans dominated Protestantism in the nineteenth and early twentieth centuries, and many Protestants in the West assumed that Protestant faith and Anglo-American middle-class society were necessarily bound together. Although Western Protestants' attitudes toward women, people of color, and adherents of other religions were all too often patronizing or destructive, the basic integrity of most Protestants should not be denied. Moreover, Protestants were often prominent and vocal in defending Westerners such as Native Americans, Chinese Americans, and Japanese Americans at a time when these groups had few friends in the United States.

The length of the home-mission phase in a given area of the West depended on the targeted population—its permanence, its racial and cultural composition, and the background and number of new immigrants. In Los Angeles and New Mexico, for example, the well-established Hispanic Roman CATHOLICS frustrated the institutional and cultural goals of Protestants; only when Anglo-Americans became numerous enough to assert cultural dominance did Los Angeles become, for a time in the late nineteenth and early twentieth centuries, an overtly Protestant city. Enough Protestants migrated to the San Francisco Bay area in the latter half of the nineteenth century to enable it to become the institutional center of Protestantism in the Far West. By 1910, several Protestant periodicals were published in San Francisco. Protestant institutions of higher education in the Bay Area included many that have continued to the present: the University of the Pacific (Methodist, 1851), Mills College (nondenominational, 1865), Pacific Theological Seminary (Congregational, 1869, later renamed Pacific School of Religion), San Francisco Theological Seminary (Presbyterian, 1871), Church Divinity School of the Pacific (Episcopal, 1893), Pacific Unitarian School for the Ministry (1904, later renamed Starr King School of the Ministry), and Pacific Coast Baptist Theological Seminary (1905, later renamed American Baptist Seminary of the West). Despite that organizational presence, Protestants in the San Francisco region never achieved the kind of cultural dominance enjoyed by Protestants in the Los Angeles area.

Pluralism, both external and internal to Protestantism, helped make the twentieth-century West a region that has fewer churches and is less Protestant than the other regions of the United States. That does not mean, however, that Protestantism has been insignificant in the history of the modern West. In the Great Plains, for example, the late nineteenth-century dominance of Scandinavian and German Lutherans (in much of North and South Dakota and Minnesota), Mennonites (in parts of Kansas and South Dakota), and Dutch Reformed (in pockets of northwestern Iowa, southwestern Minnesota, South Dakota, and Montana) persists. There also are many examples that serve as reminders that the Protestant faith, if not Euro-American culture, has had and still has loyal adherents among various Western communities of color: Chinese American Presbyterians in San Francisco; Japanese American Methodists in Los Angeles; Native American Reformed in Macy, Nebraska; Hispanic Presbyterians in Las Vegas, New Mexico; African American Baptists in Oakland, California.

Many Protestants have also been significant (if not always critical) leaders and supporters of political and social reform in the West. Examples include the social gospel writings and activities of CHARLES M. SHELDON, who served as pastor of the Central Congregational Church in Topeka, Kansas; the leadership of Protestants in a successful antigambling movement in Wyoming in 1901; the strenuous Protestant support of the legal prosecution of political graft in San Francisco between 1906 and 1909; the campaign and victory of Methodist and Christian Socialist J. Stitt Wilson for the mayor's office in Berkeley, California, in 1911; and the long-term civic leadership in Seattle of Presbyterian pastor Mark Matthews. These people and others, along with evidence of significant support of Western Protestants for voting rights for women and the prohibition of the manufacture and sale of alcohol, indicate that Protestantism has been an underexamined factor in the late nineteenth- and twentieth-century political history of the West.

Some Protestants in the West have been significant religious innovators or exemplars of religious change. Seventh-day Adventism emerged in the East, but Ellen Gould Harmon White, a cofounder of the denomination, retired to California in 1900, reinforcing both

the strength of Adventism in the Far West as well as the reputation of California as a land of health through establishing the group's medical school in Loma Linda in 1909. The holiness movement was a Protestant grouping that not only had an impact on older denominations such as the Methodists, but also spawned new ones through an emphasis on a life of sanctification following conversion. Los Angeles Methodist minister Phineas F. Bresee broke with his denomination in 1895 and helped found and lead what became the Church of the Nazarene, and Denver Methodist Mollie Alma Bridwell White eventually became bishop of the Pillar of Fire denomination that she organized in 1901. Carrie Judd Montgomery helped found another holiness denomination, the Christian and Missionary Alliance, in New York before she moved to Oakland, California, in 1890. From her Western base, she propounded faith healing through her Home of Peace and her newspaper, *Triumphs of Faith*. Moreover, she experienced the gift of speaking in tongues (glossolalia) in 1908 and became a leader in Pentecostalism.

Stressing the millennial renewal of the supernatural gifts of the Holy Spirit, Pentecostalism was a Protestant movement born in the American West. Charles F. Parham began teaching the gift of tongues as the sign of the Spirit's baptism in 1900 at his Bible schools in Topeka and Houston, and his student William J. Seymour, a Louisiana-born son of former slaves, launched Pentecostalism throughout the world when he led widely attended prayer and testimony meetings at the Azusa Street Mission in Los Angeles from 1906 to 1909. Pentecostalism's rootedness in the West was heightened in the 1920s and 1930s by the Los Angeles ministry of AIMEE SEMPLE MCPHERSON, who melded conservative theology with Hollywood style and modern media in her Angelus Temple, Bible school, radio station, and denomination, the International Church of the Foursquare Gospel.

Throughout the twentieth century, Protestantism became increasingly polarized along theological lines. With different understandings of revelation and religious experience, the various denominations held different assumptions about nature, the supernatural, and human society and culture. Moreover, many American Protestants, whether liberal, conservative, or part of the broad middle, found that cultural diversity itself and social interdependence made traditional assertions of moral custodianship and cultural influence increasingly tenuous. The relation of the West to these developments remains to be thoroughly assessed. However, Western Protestantism generally reflected, and perhaps in some cases set the pace for, the broader restructuring of American Protestantism.

The older Protestant denominations became more centralized and bureaucratic, a process that decreased regional variations by the 1930s. The Western Protestant press withered, and the Protestant seminaries in the San Francisco area tended to follow Eastern-based theological centers. Thomas F. Day, for example, exemplified the moderate liberalization of traditional Protestant understandings of the Bible in the West. Initially a Presbyterian home missionary in Mormon Utah, Day accepted a faculty position at the San Francisco Theological Seminary in 1890. He combined newer critical views of the Bible's human origins with a steadfast affirmation of its fundamental divine and revelatory status. While he was forced out of his post in 1912, his successor and some of his fellow professors in the West's Protestant colleges, universities, and seminaries moved in similar or even more liberal directions. Indeed, insofar as the Harvard religious philosopher JOSIAH ROYCE was a self-conscious product of a California Christian (Disciples of Christ) home, Western Protestantism could be said not only to have followed modernizing intellectual trends but also to have shaped them.

The forced removal of Day, though, and the Western connections of the holiness and Pentecostal movements are reminders that, by the 1930s, theological conservatism was well represented in the West. Compared to the liberal end of the Protestant spectrum, in fact, the number of notable representatives of conservative Protestantism in the West during the 1920s and 1930s is striking. Prominent Western theological conservatives of the era include Presbyterians Mark Matthews, a Seattle clergyman; Lyman Stewart and his brother Milton, who founded the Union Oil Company in California and the Bible Institute of Los Angeles (1908, now Biola University) and published a series of booklets entitled *The Fundamentals* (1910–1915); and Henrietta C. Mears, a Bible teacher in Hollywood, who during her career reputedly encouraged some five hundred young men to enter the ministry and who also helped found a publishing firm, Gospel Light, in 1933, and a Christian conference center, Forest Home; Baptists William B. Riley, who founded a Bible school, college, and seminary alongside his First Baptist Church in Minneapolis; and J. Frank Norris, combative pastor of Fort Worth's First Baptist Church; and Methodist Robert P. Shuler, minister of Trinity Methodist Church in Los Angeles and acerbic enough as a preacher, writer, radio broadcaster, and reformer to be nicknamed "Fighting Bob." Further to the theological and political right stood independent Protestant anti-Semite Gerald Burton Winrod, who organized the fundamentalist Defenders of the Christian Faith in Wichita, Kansas, in 1925.

The strength of Protestant conservatism in the West before World War II was due in part to the social and political frustration of many Westerners over the region's dependence on non-Western society and culture. In addition, migrations, especially to southern California, both exacerbated and reinforced the tendency toward conservatism. The "Okie exodus" from the southern Great Plains to California, in particular, tilted the Protestant mosaic in the state further toward conservatism. These two trends—dependence on Eastern social structures and immigration—continue to influence the direction of Protestantism in the West.

—*Douglas Firth Anderson*

SEE ALSO: Campbellites; Progressivism; Temperance and Prohibition

SUGGESTED READING:

Anderson, Douglas Firth. "'We Have Here a Different Civilization': Protestant Identity in the San Francisco Bay Area, 1906–1909." *Western Historical Quarterly* 23 (1992): 199–221.

Banker, Mark T. *Presbyterian Missions and Cultural Interaction in the Far Southwest, 1850–1950.* Urbana, Ill., 1993.

Engh, Michael E. *Frontier Faiths: Church, Temple, and Synagogue in Los Angeles, 1846–1888.* Albuquerque, N. Mex., 1992.

Ernst, Eldon G., with Douglas Firth Anderson. *Pilgrim Progression: Protestants and the California Experience.* Santa Barbara, Calif., 1993.

Etulain, Richard W., comp. *Religion in the Twentieth Century American West: A Bibliography.* Albuquerque, N. Mex., 1991.

Frankiel, Sandra Sizer. *California's Spiritual Frontiers: Religious Alternatives in Anglo-Protestantism, 1850–1910.* Berkeley, Calif., 1988.

Guarneri, Carl, and David Alvarez, eds. *Religion and Society in the American West: Historical Essays.* Lanham, Md., 1987.

Pascoe, Peggy. *Relations of Rescue: The Search for Female Moral Authority in the American West, 1874–1939.* New York, 1990.

Quinn, D. Michael. "Religion in the American West." In *Under an Open Sky: Rethinking America's Western Past.* Edited by William Cronon, George Miles, and Jay Gitlin. New York, 1992.

Singleton, Gregory H. *Religion in the City of Angels: American Protestant Culture and Urbanization, Los Angeles, 1850–1930.* Ann Arbor, Mich., 1979.

Szasz, Ferenc Morton. *The Protestant Clergy in the Great Plains and Mountain West, 1865–1915.* Albuquerque, N. Mex., 1988.

PROVOST, ETIENNE

A fur trader and Western guide, Etienne Provost (1782–1850) was born in Montreal. In 1815, he left Montreal for St. Louis, where he was a partner with Auguste and Pierre Chouteau and Jules de Mun on a two-year expedition to the Upper Arkansas River. Provost and his party were taken prisoner by Mexicans in 1817 for having trespassed on Mexican soil and were imprisoned in Santa Fe. Upon his release, Provost decided to settle in New Mexico after Mexico gained its independence from Spain. During 1823 and 1824, Provost led hunting expeditions into the Colorado Rockies and trapped in the Green River–Uintah Basin region. It is likely that Provost was the first non-Indian to see the Great Salt Lake.

In 1825, Provost participated in the first fur-trapping RENDEZVOUS in the Rocky Mountains. He worked independently and also for the American Fur Company before he retired in 1848. He accompanied the 1837 Fitzpatrick Expedition, the 1839 Nicollet-Frémont Expedition, and the 1843 Audubon Expedition. Provo, Utah, was named in his honor.

—*Alan Axelrod*

SEE ALSO: Chouteau Family; Fur Trade

PROWERS, JOHN WESLEY

Cattleman and entrepreneur John Wesley Prowers (1838–1884) was born near Westport, Jackson County, Missouri. Beginning in the late 1850s, he worked several years as a clerk and teamster for Indian agent Robert C. Miller and trader William Bent. In 1861, he married the daughter of a Southern Cheyenne subchief.

Prowers later became a government freighter and managed the sutler's store at Fort Lyon. In 1868, he became a commissioner of newly formed Bent County, and in 1873, he was elected to the first of two terms in the state legislature.

One of the first permanent ranchers in southeastern Colorado, Prowers eventually controlled more than four hundred thousand acres of range and was among the first to introduce blooded Hereford stock. His diverse economic interests also included a commission and mercantile business and a slaughterhouse. Prowers succumbed to illness in Kansas City, Missouri.

—*B. Byron Price*

SEE ALSO: Cattle Industry

SUGGESTED READING:

Colorado Livestock Record (Denver), Feb. 15, 1884.

Portrait and Biographical Record of the State of Colorado. Chicago, 1899.

Scott, P. G. "John W. Prowers, Bent County Pioneer." *The Colorado Magazine* 7 (September 1930): 183–187.

PUBLIC LANDS COMMISSION OF 1879

The Public Lands Commission of 1879 was constituted by Congress in an effort to bring order to federal land law and to reevaluate conditions in the West. By the end of the 1870s, it was clear that the existing system was inadequate; the rapid pace of westward expansion and the different character of much Western land made earlier LAND POLICY archaic. Beginning with the passage of the HOMESTEAD ACT OF 1862, federal legislators tried to make Western lands available to the public. Such legislation as the TIMBER CULTURE ACT OF 1873, the DESERT LAND ACT OF 1877, and the TIMBER AND STONE ACT OF 1878 typified the process. Each offered lands in the West for almost no cost as long as settlers improved the land.

But myriad problems arose in this process. Western land was rarely as easy to use in agricultural operations as were lands east of the Mississippi River. The GENERAL LAND OFFICE of the Department of the Interior had a reputation for corruption and was poorly staffed. Even when Land Office administrators sought to do their jobs properly, they were hampered by a lack of resources. Speculation in land was rife, and government officials, particularly reform-minded Secretary of the Interior CARL SHURZ, who served from 1877 until 1881, saw the need for change.

The Public Lands Commission reflected Shurz's perspective. It included JOHN WESLEY POWELL, author of the *REPORT ON THE LANDS OF ARID REGIONS* and the author of the Desert Land Act; A. T. Britton, a Washington, D.C., land attorney; and THOMAS CORWIN DONALDSON, who had been responsible for saving GEORGE CATLIN's paintings of the American West. CLARENCE KING, director of the UNITED STATES GEOLOGICAL SURVEY, and General JAMES WILLIAMSON, commissioner of the General Land Office from 1876 to 1881, served as *ex officio* members.

The task these men undertook was daunting. During its one-year term, the commission was asked to make recommendations concerning the codification of land laws, develop a system for classifying public lands into categories of economic use, devise surveys through which land could be parceled out according to its economic uses, and make recommendations about the disposition of the remaining public domain.

The committee's report was a huge document that reflected the seriousness of its charge. With the influential John Wesley Powell playing a major role on the commission, the final report reflected his perspective. But supplanting Powell's radical ideas about public land was a more tempered, middle-of-the-road stance that sought to readjust land law to conditions in the West rather than scrap it altogether. The commission only recommended changes that its members thought would not impede rapid settlement, a position antithetical to Powell's earlier writing.

Despite the efforts of the commission, little change resulted. Caught between the realities of the West and the expectations of the public, Congress simply did not enact the commission's proposals. With this result, a precedent for future land commissions was established. Most subsequent commissions had little more success getting their recommendations implemented.

—*Hal Rothman*

SUGGESTED READING:

Robbins, Roy M. *Our Landed Heritage.* Princeton, N.J., 1942.

Stegner, Wallace. *Beyond the Hundredth Meridian.* Boston, 1954.

PUBLIC SCHOOLS

Public schools in the West owe their existence to the common-school movement, whose advocates sought to provide a modicum of reading, writing, and arithmetic along with nondenominational, but distinctly Protestant, morality to all children, rich and poor, boys and girls. The movement, which began in Massachusetts in 1838, was adapted to Western locations later in the nineteenth century. Western settlers' belief that public schools helped formulate an "American nationality" added to their appeal, and their reputation for "civilizing" behavior was seen as a way to attract a better class of immigrant.

Most Western territorial constitutions authorized the formation of public schools as an essential ingredient in gaining statehood. Territorial and, later, state constitutions encouraged the development of public schools by setting aside lands and establishing perpetual funds. Some went further to standardize certification of teachers, establish normal schools, and appoint state superintendents, but they left the execution and tax raising to local communities. Settlement patterns also facilitated the development of public schools. Rather than living in rural isolation, many Western pioneers settled in or near communities: mining and cattle towns or existing Spanish-speaking pueblos. Yet, expressing interest in education and resolving to support it were different matters, and school development often depended on the appointment of able school superintendents. Residents of the Dakota Territory counted themselves among the fortunate when James F. Foster came West and reorganized the territory's schools in

Seven school boys pose on the back of the cow that transported them to their lessons in the Okanagan, Oregon, schoolhouse in the background. Image by Frank Matsura, 1907. *Courtesy National Archives.*

1864. California's John Swett, educator and editor of a new Western textbook published by HERBERT HOWE BANCROFT in San Francisco, influenced state legislators in 1866 to enact comprehensive school laws. Nevertheless, throughout the West, school funds were often abused or stolen, and poorer counties rarely had the tax revenues to conform to state or territorial mandates. Trying to assist rural and small communities by providing state support for local schools, Washington State initiated a 1895 Barefoot Schoolboy law. Other states passed similar laws, but funding never became totally equitable. Not until the early years of the twentieth century, when state legislatures enacted penalties to accompany their truancy laws, were local districts compelled to finance education.

The earliest teachers were Easterners, men and women, but within a short time, most teachers came from the pool of local girls, many of whom had just finished common school themselves. The cultured young New England schoolmarm who came to tame the West was not so much a myth as a misconception. Often the better educated Eastern teachers were affiliated with Protestant missionary organizations or taught in private schools. Teaching became one of the few professions open to women, and by 1900, an estimated 90 percent of elementary teachers were women. Communities could hire a female teacher for half what it cost to hire a man. Dodge City, Kansas, was typical: in 1880, its male teachers were paid seventy-five dollars per month, while women with more classroom experience earned forty dollars.

From the beginning, politics influenced public-school policy. The controversies that developed reflected the social tensions of the West. There was considerable resistance to government-supported schooling in areas where religious organizations had already established schools through their networks of missions, as among Catholics in former Spanish-speaking territories of New Mexico and Arizona and Protestants in Oregon. In Utah, battles between Mormons and Gentiles over secular tax-supported schools delayed the development of public schools until 1890.

In addition, many areas legislated the segregation of Native American, African American, Latino, and Asian American children, and where no SEGREGATION legislation existed, common practice often led to the exclusion of nonwhites. California segregated African Americans, Chinese Americans, and Native Americans until the 1880s, when African Americans took their case to court and won. The court ruled that blacks and Indians were entitled to attend integrated schools but that Chinese Americans were not. Texas, its institutions more Southern than Western, set up a separate system of education for African Americans after the Civil War. The legislature ignored Spanish-speakers until the 1920s when community leaders demanded public schools. New Mexico neglected the education of many of its Spanish-speaking natives, particularly those who lived in traditional villages, well into the twentieth century. Providing schooling for Indian children was even more problematic. Reformers, often working with missionaries, preferred to set up reservation and off-reservation schools; not until after 1890 did the federal government pay school districts to educate Native Americans in integrated schools.

In some areas, requirements that children attend school conflicted with a family's economic survival. Rural German Russians in North Dakota needed their children's labor and kept them out of school until the truant officer threatened to put the parents in jail. Some ethnic groups offered additional objections; they resisted their children's loss of native languages and cultures, and in areas where one group was dominant, that community might establish its own native-speaking public school. More commonly, immigrants sent their children to public schools but made arrangements with school districts or private organizations to have native-speaking teachers run special language classes after school hours.

The curriculum gave great attention to American culture and ideals. Until the end of the nineteenth century, classrooms in most of the nation relied on *McGuffey's Eclectic Readers,* but in the West, some students used other textbooks. The editors of Bancroft's *Pacific Coast Readers* interspersed stories featuring children with Spanish names, Shasta Indians, and the Pacific Ocean with Shakespearean sonnets, accounts of Andrew Jackson's victory at New Orleans, and stories from the Bible.

Western towns and cities, as their counterparts in the East and, to some extent, in the South, provided most white children with an elementary school education. High schools developed more slowly since they were perceived as extravagances necessary only for elite college-bound children. Beginning in the late nineteenth century, to appeal to wider audiences, educators altered the secondary curriculum by offering clerical courses. Early in the twentieth century, the curriculum also included industrial courses—influenced, in part, by the writings of psychologist G. Stanley Hall and U.S. Children's Bureau Chief Julia Lathrop—as a means of prolonging adolescent schooling. The federal government's involvement came with the 1917 Smith-Hughes Act that provided matching funds for vocational education. Not until the subject matter changed did secondary education appeal to lower-middle-class and working-class parents.

By that time, urban growth, industrialization, immigration, and labor unrest had transformed American society and had created a climate for political and social reform known as PROGRESSIVISM. No institution was as altered by its impulses as public schools.

Progressive reformers introduced a broad range of social services provided under school direction, including kindergartens, lunch programs, after-school playgrounds, health care, day-care centers, and evening classes. In attempts to increase efficiency and professionalization on state and local levels, reformers reorganized school boards based on a corporate model, where, in the ideal, the boards made decisions that were carried out by professional educators—the superintendents. A new elite emerged, composed of public administrators, efficiency experts, professional managers, and social scientists captivated by the vision of a scientifically managed society. Those experts devised methods that they hoped would solve the vexing problems of educating masses of children, many of whom were nonwhite and non-English speaking. They advocated new compulsory-attendance laws, which required students to stay in school up to sixteen years of age, and tried to make secondary education more attractive to older pupils by offering a diversified curriculum. They established intermediate or junior high schools and introduced intelligence testing.

By the twentieth century, the foundations of modern public education were in place, and the Western urban educational system mirrored its counterpart in the East. Western educators incorporated John Dewey's ideas of community and pedagogy. They changed their curricula in ways they thought would better meet the needs of their students. To accommodate the growing school-age population, cities issued bonds to build large impersonal buildings, while in the countryside, most rural children continued to attend one- or two-room schoolhouses. Nevertheless, like their city cousins, rural districts consolidated and became more uniform. After 1917, towns and cities introduced or intensified existing programs to Americanize non-English speaking children. As with earlier reforms, these initiatives were meant to ameliorate some of the inequities of American life and, in immigrant communities, to promote assimilation. Educators and reformers won a hard-fought battle to offer day classes for adults as well as children. Thus, Emily Griffith organized and became principal of Denver's Opportunity School in 1916, and California reformer Mary Simons Gibson introduced the Home Teacher Act in 1915 to bring the English language and American customs to foreign-born mothers in their homes and work places.

In the twentieth century, public schools continued to be seen as civilizers and levelers; indeed, many looked on them as a way to cure society's ills. Schools began to take on responsibilities once reserved for family, church, and community. They offered the promise of upward mobility, but for many, the promise was not kept. Schools also reflected society's racism, as urban school boards, often bowing to community pressure, instituted segregation based on racial quotas and housing covenants. During the 1920s, fiscal conservatives objected to what they saw as excessive spending and tried to dismantle many of the Progressive programs. Nevertheless, some programs flourished, and Progressives had so successfully imposed their reforms that their influence continued to affect schooling to the end of the twentieth century; those reforms were the part and parcel of public education.

—*Judith R. Raftery*

SEE ALSO: Colleges and Universities; Indian Schools; Language Schools; School Life on the Frontier; Teachers on the Frontier

SUGGESTED READING:

Deutsch, Sarah. *No Separate Refuge: Culture, Class, and Gender on an Anglo-Hispanic Frontier, 1880–1940*. New York, 1987.

Haywood, C. Robert. *Victorian West: Class and Culture in Kansas Cattle Towns*. Lawrence, Kans., 1991.

Nelson, Bryce. *Good Schools: The Seattle Public School System, 1901–1930*. Seattle, Wash., 1988.

Raftery, Judith R. *Land of Fair Promise: Politics and Reform in Los Angeles Schools, 1885–1941*. Stanford, Calif., 1992.

San Miguel, Guadalupe. *"Let All of Them Take Heed:" Mexican Americans and the Campaign for Educational Equality in Texas, 1910–1981*. Austin, Tex., 1987.

Swett, John. *Public Education in California*. 1911. Reprint. New York, 1969.

West, Eliott. *Growing up with the Country: Childhood on the Far Western Frontier.* Albuquerque, N. Mex., 1989.

PUEBLO INDIANS

SEE: Native American Peoples: Peoples of the Southwest, Pre-Columbian Peoples

PUEBLO REVOLT

On August 10, 1680, New Mexico's royal governor Antonio de Otermin learned of the murder of Franciscan Father Juan Pio at the hands of the Tewas near the Tesuque Pueblo. Combined with rumors of an uprising by the Indians surrounding the Spanish settlements around Santa Fe, the news led Otermin to call the settlers to arms and gather to put down a possible Indian revolt. Rumors of uprisings, particularly in the northern pueblos, continued to come in, and the settlers fortified Santa Fe against an attack, which came on August 15. Although, on August 20, the Spanish pushed the attackers out of Santa Fe, Otermin recognized that their position was untenable and ordered withdrawal by the survivors to the south. Beginning on the August 21, the Spanish retreated down the river, and by September 19, they had reached the settlements north of El Paso del Norte. In all, Otermin reported that 1,946 survivors, including 155 men and boys capable of bearing arms, retreated to the El Paso area. The roll of dead was estimated at 380, including 73 adult males and 21 of the 40 Franciscans serving in New Mexico. The Spanish presence, established by JUAN DE OÑATE beginning in 1598, was gone and the Indian triumph was complete, the only such instance in the history of European conquest of the Americas.

The causes of the revolt and its success were mixed and reflected the relationship between the Pueblo Indians and the Spanish intruders—a relationship that had developed over eighty years of Spanish presence. Juan de Oñate, establishing the Spanish position with the use of force, offered peace, trade, and the possibility of salvation when he arrived in the early seventeenth century. He also demonstrated the fate of those who resisted the Spanish by destroying the Acoma Pueblo stronghold in 1605.

The coming of the Spanish was a disaster for the native population. Even before the arrival of the Spanish in person, disease vectors were taking their toll. The estimated population of the Pueblo Indians declined from about 130,000 in 1581 to 60,000 in 1600 to 40,000 in 1638 to about 17,000 by 1680. In 1706, it was believed only 6,440 were left. In addition to bringing disease, the Spanish also set the stage for starvation among the Pueblo Indians by efforts to confiscate stored foodstuffs. The impact of this program of confiscation, combined with the *encomienda,* a system of SLAVERY AND INDENTURE IN THE SPANISH SOUTHWEST, led to periods of food shortage and hunger—periods that were particularly bad during the droughts of the early 1670s.

While the Spanish were destroying the native infrastructure, they were also attacking the cultural system of the Pueblo Indians through the activities of the Franciscans, whose apparent success at converting the tribes led to the decision by Felipe III to maintain a Spanish presence in New Mexico despite the failure to find substantial economic resources. The tiny Spanish community, whose only urban center was Santa Fe, remained in place to support the activities of the friars, who attempted to convert the Indians and to destroy the traditions of the medicine men. Although the numbers of converts appeared sufficient to keep the friars in place, the scattered surviving evidence of the continued adherence to Indian values and ceremonies suggests that the Spanish were overly optimistic.

The civil authorities were kept in place to provide support for the missions (and some settlers), but the governors, particularly Juan de Eulate (1618–1625), Luis de Rosas (1637–1641), and Bernardo Lopez de Mendizabal (1659–1662) who were attempting to profit from their appointments, often came into conflict with the Franciscans. These conflicts between civil and religious authorities—combined with failure to understand the language, with limited numbers of priests, and with occasional misconduct by priests—weakened the position of the church.

The 1670s set the stage for the rebellion, although there had been abortive uprisings as early as 1606 and 1607, in 1639, and again in the 1650s. During the late 1660s and early 1670s, continuous droughts and attacks by Apaches and other surrounding tribes placed hardship on the Pueblo Indians. During the governorship of Juan Francisco Trevino, earlier policies of moderation toward Indian customs were reversed, and the Pueblo Indians suffered persecution at a level they had not previously experienced. Medicine men, including Popé, the leader of the revolt, were imprisoned, forty-seven were whipped, and four were ordered to be hanged. Released, Popé fled to the northern pueblos, which were isolated from the Spanish, and began to plan the revolt.

In the aftermath of the 1680 revolt, the Indians, attempting to remove all evidence of the Spanish presence, went through rituals to reverse baptism, gave up Spanish-style marriage, reinstated Indian religious traditions, and attempted to eliminate such products as

All is peaceful. The approach to the Acoma Pueblo in 1882. *Courtesy Museum of New Mexico.*

European plants. Beginning with Popé, however, the Indian leaders followed the precedent of the Spanish governors in their authoritarian rule, which led to heightened conflicts between the traditionally factionalized pueblos.

The Spanish efforts at reconquest were delayed, in part because of the tenuous position of the limited forces available at El Paso del Norte, eight hundred miles beyond the Mexican mining frontier, and in part because of pressures along the northern border of the Spanish empire caused by other Indian revolts and by the presence of the French and the English. During the 1680s, a few expeditions up the Rio Grande were carried out but without success. In 1691, the arrival of a new governor, DIEGO DE VARGAS, who offered to finance the expedition to New Mexico, set the stage for Spain's recovery of the region. The Spanish, after learning during their 1692 expedition that some Pueblo Indians were willing to accept their return, reoccupied Santa Fe the following year. After a period of fighting, Spanish authority was reasserted by 1695, although one last rebellion occurred in 1696 but was quickly put down. The new era of Spanish rule brought on a period of toleration and cooperation between the Spanish and the Pueblo Indians during the eighteenth century. Following the Pueblo Revolt, the *encomienda* system came to an end, the Spanish abandoned forced missionization in the area, and a multiracial society developed more fully in New Mexico.

—*Patrick H. Butler, III*

SUGGESTED READING:

Gutiérrez, Ramón A. *When Jesus Came, the Corn Mothers Went Away: Marriage, Sexuality and Power in New Mexico, 1500-1846* . Stanford, Calif., 1991.

An image of the Acoma Pueblo as it appeared in the 1930s. *Courtesy National Archives.*

John, Elizabeth A. H. *Storms Brewed in Other Men's Worlds: The Confrontation of Indians, Spanish, and French in the Southwest, 1540–1795.* College Station, Tex., 1975.

Knaut, Andrew K. *The Pueblo Revolt of 1680: Conquest and Resistance in Seventeenth-Century New Mexico.* Norman, Okla., 1995.

Weber, David J. *The Spanish Frontier in North America.* New Haven, Conn., 1992.

PULLMAN, GEORGE MORTIMER

An American industrialist, George Mortimer Pullman (1831–1897) invented the Pullman Palace sleeping car, which made long-distance rail travel comfortable and popular. Born in Brocton, New York, Pullman apprenticed as a cabinetmaker before moving to Chicago in 1855, when he saw an opportunity to make money rebuilding and remodeling old railroad coaches. With his partner, Ben Field, he developed the idea of the sleeping car, building the first—called "the Pioneer"—in 1865. The car had a folding upper berth and seat cushions that could be extended to create a lower berth. The design rapidly found favor with the RAILROADS, and in 1867, Pullman organized the Pullman Palace Car Company to manufacture his sleeping cars. He soon developed other types of cars, most notably the dining car in 1868. The Pullman cars made long-distance rail travel practical, comfortable, attractive, and "civilized" and gave great impetus to the ongoing construction of the transcontinental railroad. Pullman controlled the operation of the cars under contract to the railroads.

The Chicago and Alton Railroad touted George Pullman's Palace Cars to attract customers in this nineteenth-century advertisement. *Courtesy Library of Congress.*

Pullman built a factory and company town, Pullman, Illinois, just south of Chicago. The town was designed along utopian lines as a clean and decent place for employees to live. Many employees, however, saw it as a kind of prison. They were compelled to live there, pay rent to Pullman, and redeem their scrip salary at Pullman stores.

The company was the target of the great Pullman strike from May 11 to July 20, 1894. The financial panic of 1893 had prompted the company to slash wages by 25 percent without cutting company-controlled rents or company-store prices. Outraged, local members of the American Railway Union called a general strike. When Pullman refused arbitration, the union's national council, under Eugene V. Debs, mounted a nationwide boycott of Pullman cars. Sympathy strikes were triggered in twenty-seven states. In Chicago, various outbreaks of violence occurred, but the liberal governor of Illinois, John Peter Altgeld, declined to call out the militia. At last, on July 2, U.S. Attorney General Richard Olney bowed to corporate pressure and prevailed upon President Grover Cleveland to mobilize twenty-five hundred federal troops to end the strike.

Paternalistic, authoritarian, and as mean-spirited as he was inventive, Pullman contributed greatly to the development and financial viability of passenger rail operations in the United States and especially over the vast distances of the West. He is buried in an elaborate mausoleum in Chicago's Graceland Cemetery; however, his most enduring physical monument, aside from the Pullman sleeping cars that still traverse America's rails, is the Victorian-Romanesque architecture of his company town, which still stands, largely unchanged, as part of what is now Chicago's South Side.

—*Alan Axelrod*

PUMAS

SEE: Mountain Lions

Q

QUAKER POLICY

SEE: Grant's Peace Policy

QUANAH PARKER (COMANCHE)

Last chief of the Comanches, Quanah Parker was born between 1845 and 1852, son of Chief Peta Nocona and Naduah. The date 1852 is used on his grave marker. His mother, Naduah, was originally CYNTHIA ANN PARKER and had been captured at the age of nine by the Comanches in the May 19, 1836, raid on Fort Parker, Texas. She eventually married Chief Nocona and exhibited no desire to return to the white community whenever attempts were made to bring her back. In 1860, she and her daughter, Prairie Flower, were captured by Texas Rangers. Separated from her husband and her two sons, she never reconciled to her return to the whites and died in 1864, shortly after the death of her daughter.

Quanah Parker grew up within the nomadic culture of the Comanches on the Llano Estacado. After the death of his father and brother in the 1860s, he rose to power among the Comanches and overcame the stigma associated with having a white mother by excelling as a hunter and warrior. Like many other Comanches, he refused to accept the MEDICINE LODGE TREATY OF 1867 (which restricted Kiowas, Comanches, and Kiowa Comanches to a small part of their native range) and withdrew to the Llano Estacado. With the death of Chief Bear's Ear, Quanah Parker became a leader of the Quahada Comanches. In the early 1870s, he fought with the Comanches against the army under RANALD SLIDELL MACKENZIE and refused to go to the reservation. On June 24, 1874, Quanah Parker was a leader of a confederation of tribes who attacked the buffalo hunters' outpost at Adobe Walls in the northern Texas Panhandle. The defeat of the Indians ended the alliance and set the stage for a move to the reservations.

On June 15, 1875, the Quahada Comanches surrendered and were sent to the Indian Territory. Mackenzie held Quanah Parker in high regard for his integrity, and, as a result, the Indian chief and his tribe were treated relatively well by the army. Soon after arriving in the Indian Territory, Quanah Parker visited his mother's family in Texas and then went to Mexico to visit his uncle, John Parker, in Chihuahua.

On the reservation, Quanah Parker's role as a leader expanded, beginning with his leadership of one of the "beef bands," organized to ease distribution of rations. His band became one of the largest, and by 1878, he had three wives. He also was active in bringing back runaways. Some, along with Mackenzie, regarded him highly; others, including Lieutenant Colonel J. W. Davidson, saw him as a man of influence who could lead the Comanches back to war. By 1880, Quanah Parker was well established as the leader of the tribe, performing much of the liaison between the Quahada Comanches and the army.

In the early 1880s, Quanah Parker became involved in leasing reservation land to cattlemen. In addition, he supported the creation of tolls on trails through reservation land. In 1884, in order to garner support for the leasing program, he made his first visit to Washington, D.C., where he was recognized as the principal chief of the Comanches. He held both the Kiowas and Comanches in check during war threats and came to be highly regarded by whites and Indians. The North Texas town of Quanah was named after him. As he prospered, his interests expanded, and he moved into a frame home in 1890, suitable to his position. As a leader of the reservation, he also served as presiding judge of the Indian court from 1886 to 1898. In 1892, he was one of three Indians representing the Oklahoma tribes in negotiations over land leases and allotments. He secured the best deal possible in the transfer of reservation land to the government in the Jerome Agree-

ment, ratified in 1900. In the face of the apparently irreversible tide of white expansion, Quanah Parker resisted white encroachment when possible, negotiated for the best position for Indians when necessary.

Quanah Parker was one of the founders of the Native American Church. Combining traditional Indian ritual and the use of peyote with elements of the Christian tradition, the church took shape between 1875 and the 1890s. He defended the worship tradition, observing, "The white man goes into his church and talks *about* Jesus, but the Indian goes into his tipi and talks *to* Jesus." While a defender of the Native American Church, he opposed the Ghost Dance movement of 1890.

Quanah Parker married seven times and had many children. He died on February 11, 1911 and was buried in the Post Oak Mission Cemetery near Indiahoma, Oklahoma.

—*Patrick H. Butler, III*

Suggested reading:

Fehrenbach, T. R. *Comanches*. New York, 1979.

Hagan, William T. *Quanah Parker: Comanche Chief*. Norman, Okla., 1993.

QUANTRILL, WILLIAM CLARKE

Confederate guerrilla leader William Clarke Quantrill (1837–1865) was born in Canal Dover, Ohio. He went to Kansas early in 1857 and started farming. That summer, he joined a freight outfit and headed west for California. After wandering in the West for two years—as a teamster, gambler, and gold prospector—he returned to Kansas, using the alias "Charlie Hart." He taught school from 1859 to 1860 but soon embarked on a criminal career with James Henry Lane's Jayhawkers. Quantrill was accused of horse theft and several murders in and around Lawrence, Kansas, but he evaded arrest. Mustered into the Confederate army, he fought at Wilson's Creek on August 10, 1861, before forming an independent guerrilla band.

Until the end of the Civil War, his guerrillas burned and looted Union strongholds along the Kansas and Missouri border. The ever-changing cast of his command included such notorious men as William C. ("Bloody Bill") Anderson, George Todd, Cole Younger, David Poole, Kit Dalton, and the James brothers, Frank and Jesse. On August 11, 1862, four days before receiving his commission as a captain in the Confederate army, he captured Independence, Missouri. The following summer, with a combined force of about 450 men, he burned and plundered the abolitionist stronghold at Lawrence, Kansas, on August 21, 1863. His band killed 180 men and boys and caused an estimated $1.5 million in property damage. While on a foraging raid on October 6, 1863, Quantrill dressed his raiders in new Union uniforms and marched them into the Union camp at Baxter Springs, Kansas. At a signal from Quantrill, his guerrillas killed 101 of the 118 Union troops of the Third Wisconsin Cavalry.

In the spring of 1864, Quantrill quarreled with two of his principal deputies, George Todd and "Bloody Bill" Anderson. The guerrilla band subsequently splintered into small units, and Quantrill moved his theater of operations to Kentucky. He was wounded while fleeing an attack by Union troops at James H. Wakefield's farm near Bloomfield, Kentucky, on May 10, 1865. He died a few weeks later at the Union Military Hospital in Louisville.

Quantrill is important in the history of the West because he trained a generation of outlaws who, in the postwar years, used the lessons they had learned as guerrilla fighters to carry out successful bank and train robberies throughout the 1870s.

—*Maurice Law Costello*

See also: Younger Brothers

Suggested reading:

Breihan, Carl W. *Quantrill and His Civil War Guerrillas*. Denver, 1959.

Castel, Albert E. *William Clarke Quantrill: His Life and Times*. New York, 1962.

Jones, Virgil Carrington. *Gray Ghosts and Rebel Raiders*. New York, 1956.

QUAPAW INDIANS

See: Native American Peoples: Peoples of the Great Plains

QUECHAN INDIANS

See: Yuma Revolt

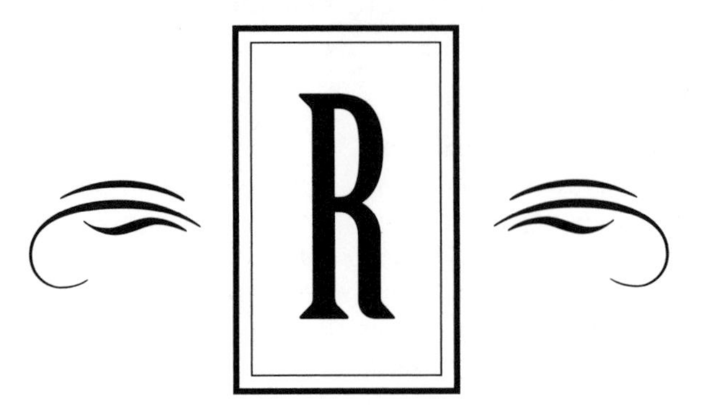

RADIO AND TELEVISION WESTERNS

A nascent broadcasting industry demonstrated the commercial viability of radio in the late 1920s, thus providing a new dramatic medium in time for the Great Depression. Radio, like other delivery systems for popular culture in the 1930s, soon embraced escapist fare for audiences coping with economic distress. The western, a staple in print and cinema during the 1920s and appealing because of its connection to history and heritage no less than because of its emphasis on action and adventure, was ideal escapism; early on, hoof beats were heard in the ether.

Depression-era radio westerns were popular, durable, and influential. "Death Valley Days" (NBC, 1930–1940; CBS, 1941–1945) was a well-produced adult series originally offering dramas drawn from events in Western history; its early success was later reprised on television. "Bobby Benson's Adventures" (CBS, 1932–1936) was a popular juvenile program that was reworked as "Bobby Benson and the B-Bar-B Riders" (Mutual, 1949–1955) for a new generation of children, who would find Bobby Benson comic books at the newsstand. Another juvenile western, "The Tom Mix Ralston Straightshooters" (NBC, 1933–1942), featured fictive adventures of a popular movie cowboy but was otherwise notable for its connection of persona (Mix) with product (Ralston-Purina breakfast cereals) through premium offers available to listeners in return for box tops. Mix died in 1940, but because others had always played his role, the program continued. The Mutual network revived the program in 1944, and it aired until 1950.

The best-remembered Depression-era western was "The Lone Ranger," created for George W. Trendle's Detroit radio station WXYZ in 1933 and picked up by Mutual in 1934. The program went to ABC in 1942 and remained on the air until 1955. Earle Graser played the masked champion of justice until his death in 1941, and thereafter Brace Beemer performed the role. For most of the program's twenty-two-year run, John Todd, an elderly actor from the Shakespearean stage, played the part of the Lone Ranger's "faithful Indian companion" Tonto. As with the Mix program, premium tie-ins with sponsors' products enhanced the show's appeal to children. The radio program inspired a daily comic-strip, comic books, pulp magazines, novels, and motion-picture serials.

Radio westerns proliferated in the 1940s. "The Cisco Kid" and "Red Ryder" began on Mutual in 1942 and enjoyed some success, as did "Hopalong Cassidy" (Mutual, 1949; CBS, 1950–1952), with William Boyd and Andy Clyde continuing their cinematic roles. "Straight Arrow," broadcast on Mutual from 1949 to 1951, was an advertising agency concoction to sell Nabisco Shredded Wheat. Longer-lived, however, were "Gene Autry's Melody Ranch" (CBS, 1940–1956) and "The Roy Rogers Show," which moved between Mutual and NBC four times during its run from 1944 to 1955. Rogers and Autry had huge followings from their films for Republic in the 1930s and 1940s, and radio was a natural medium for the singing cowboys.

Not all radio westerns featured nineteenth-century settings. Two successful contemporary programs were "The Sheriff" (ABC, 1945–1951) and "Sky King" (ABC, 1946–1950; Mutual, 1950–1954). If these programs suggested a break from traditional fare, the programming of the 1950s confirmed the notion, as broadcasters placed greater emphasis on adult themes, psychology, and otherwise atypical material. Radio attempted to answer the challenge of television in the 1950s, and programs had to be innovative to compete with a visual medium that could give form to ideas established by radio. "Sky King" was children's fare, and although it went to television in 1951, it endured for another three years on radio, mainly owing to radio's ability to suggest images that were too expen-

sive for television producers to realize in visual form. Nevertheless, television borrowed heavily from radio: "The Cisco Kid," "The Lone Ranger," and "Death Valley Days" all made the transition, as did "Sergeant Preston of the Yukon" (ABC, 1947–1948 as "Challenge of the Yukon" (Mutual, 1950–1955) and "Tales of the Texas Rangers" (NBC, 1950–1952), to mention but a few. But radio borrowed from television as well; perhaps the best example was "Have Gun, Will Travel," the CBS television series that aired from 1957 to 1963. Richard Boone's television character Paladin became John Dehner's character on CBS radio from 1958 to 1960.

Radio reached the epitome of adult western programming with the premier of "Gunsmoke" on CBS in 1952. It was stark, realistic, violent, and sponsored by a cigarette company. William Conrad was Matt Dillon, marshal of Dodge City, who fought against "the killers and the spoilers" to full orchestral accompaniment and the first-rate sound effects of Ray Kemper, Tom Hanley, and Bill James. The program aired until 1961. CBS, meanwhile, had brought "Gunsmoke" to television in 1955 as a half-hour program continuing the adult orientation of the radio broadcast. When production of the radio program ceased, CBS expanded the television series to one-hour episodes and reran the earlier half-hour versions in prime-time under the title "Marshal Dillon." JOHN WAYNE, the network's first choice to play Dillon, suggested James Arness for the part and appeared on the first television broadcast to introduce Arness to viewers. Arness continued in the role until "Gunsmoke" ended in 1975.

Early television westerns were intended for juvenile audiences. William Boyd bought the rights to his "Hopalong Cassidy" feature films in the 1940s and sold them to television late in the decade. The films were edited to program-length, with Boyd providing narration and occasionally a new scene. NBC broadcast "Hopalong Cassidy" in the New York City market in 1948 and made it a network series from 1949 to 1951, bringing Boyd a fortune from program licensing based on the show's popularity. Other successful juvenile westerns included "The Lone Ranger" (221 episodes, first broadcast on ABC in 1949; last network broadcast in 1961 by NBC), "The Gene Autry Show" (CBS, 1950–1956), and "The Roy Rogers Show" (104 episodes, beginning on NBC in 1951; bought by Rogers and resold to CBS). Network westerns often entered syndication after their original runs, but many 1950s westerns began as syndicated series available to local stations in markets throughout the country. Among the most successful syndicated westerns were "The Cisco Kid" (176 episodes, beginning in 1951) and "Wild Bill Hickok" (120 episodes, beginning in 1952). "The Cisco Kid" was particularly long-lived because it was filmed in color for what was then a black-and-white medium and could survive the transition to color broadcasting.

In the mid-1950s, with the advent of "Gunsmoke" and "The Life and Legend of Wyatt Earp" (ABC, 1955–1961), networks began shifting the orientation of prime-time westerns from juvenile to adult audiences. Network schedules for 1955 carried four and a half hours of western programming, three of which were for children. By 1959, networks carried seventeen hours of prime-time western programming, all of it intended for adults. During the next sixteen years, networks averaged eight and a half hours of western programming in prime-time, ranging from a high of sixteen hours in 1960 to lows of two hours in 1973 and 1975.

"Gunsmoke" was the longest-running television western, in production for twenty years. Other durable programs included "Cheyenne" (ABC, 1955–1963), "Wagon Train" (NBC, 1957–1962; ABC, 1963–1965), "Bonanza" (NBC, 1959–1973), and "The Virginian" (NBC, 1962–1971). "Rawhide" (CBS, 1959–1966) introduced audiences to a young Clint Eastwood, while newcomer Steve McQueen drew attention on "Wanted: Dead or Alive" (CBS, 1958–1961). Whether through recurring roles or guest appearances, television westerns provided opportunities for many actors aspiring to film stardom. Charles Bronson, for example, was a cast regular of "The Travels of Jaimie McPheeters" (ABC, 1963) and appeared in episodes of many other westerns in the late 1950s and early 1960s, including "Gunsmoke," "Have Gun, Will Travel," "Bonanza," "The Virginian," and "Rawhide." Similarly, television was a place for film stars whose Hollywood careers were essentially over, as with Barbara Stanwyck on "The Big Valley" (ABC, 1965–1969) and Lee J. Cobb on "The Virginian."

Television westerns never fully recovered from their decline in the mid-1970s, a decline prompted in part by national concern over violence in the media, especially after the assassinations of Martin Luther King., Jr., and Robert Kennedy in 1968. As well, the public had lost some of its long-standing enthusiasm for westerns, owing to media overexposure of the genre. In the 1980s and 1990s, economic considerations prevented extensive revival of television westerns, inasmuch as contemporary urban crime dramas were cheaper to produce. The success of a miniseries like "Lonesome Dove" (CBS, 1989), however, demonstrated that viewers could still be found.

—*William W. Savage, Jr.*

SEE ALSO: Autry, Gene; Film: The Western; Mix, Tom; Rogers, Roy, and Dale Evans

SUGGESTED READING:
Brooks, Tim, and Earle Marsh. *The Complete Directory to Prime Time Network TV Shows, 1946–Present.* New York, 1979. Subsequent reprints.
Dunning, John. *Tune in Yesterday.* Englewood Cliffs, N.J., 1976.
Grossman, Gary H. *Saturday Morning TV.* New York, 1981.
Harmon, Jim. *Jim Harmon's Nostalgia Catalogue.* Los Angeles, 1973.
Holland, Dave. *From Out of the Past: A Pictorial History of the Lone Ranger.* Granada Hills, Calif., 1988.

RAILROAD LAND GRANTS

Of all the players in the game of Western LAND POLICY in the two decades after the Civil War, none were as important as the railroads. Between 1850 and 1871, the federal government and the individual states gave the railroad corporations some 180 million acres—more than double the acreage made into homesteads during half the time—of public land to encourage construction. The land granted the railroads came not in solid strips, but in alternating sections, like a checkerboard. Still the whole strip was commonly withheld from settlement until the railroad chose its right of way, meaning that great belts of land—at one point or another amounting to three-tenths of the entire country—were placed beyond the reach of the HOMESTEAD ACT OF 1862. Once the tracks were laid, the railroads had, in addition to the alternating sections of public lands along their rights of way, acreage to offer settlers. It was more expensive than the government lands, but it was plentiful and often richer and better watered. Homesteaders could either accept areas remote from the rails or pay the prices the railroads demanded for the land.

The railroads became not only the biggest landowners in the trans-Mississippi West, but its major colonizer. They wanted rapid settlement along their lines. Settlement meant more profits from passenger fares, freight charges, and land sales. And they could offer what the government had not: credit terms, transportation to the site at special rates, advice on farming, and help in settling down for prospective buyers. Railroads—and the states holding their debts—sold settlers six times more land than homesteaders had been able to garner from the government's bounty. Every Western railroad had its own bureau of immigration; every Western line, its agency to advertise—and inevitably to exaggerate—the opportunities out West. The railroads propagandized prairie lands not only throughout the United States, but in Europe as well, and boasted of the availability of millions of Edenic acres to accommodate millions of immigrants. Steamship companies, panting for passenger fares, joined in the campaign abroad. Working with railroad agents, they plastered Europe with posters proclaiming the "Garden of the West" in America. They infected whole countries with "American fever," and from Norway, Sweden, and Denmark, as well as Germany and Ireland, peasants by the millions poured in and headed west, sprinkling Minnesota, Nebraska, and the Dakota Territory with whistlestops and farm villages.

—*Charles Phillips*

RAILROADS

It was the Civil War and the rapid industrialization of the trans-Mississippi West that came in its wake that

"First train from St. Paul, over the last spike en route to Portland, Ore. Sept. 8, 1883." Photograph by F. Jay Haynes. *Courtesy Montana Historical Society.*

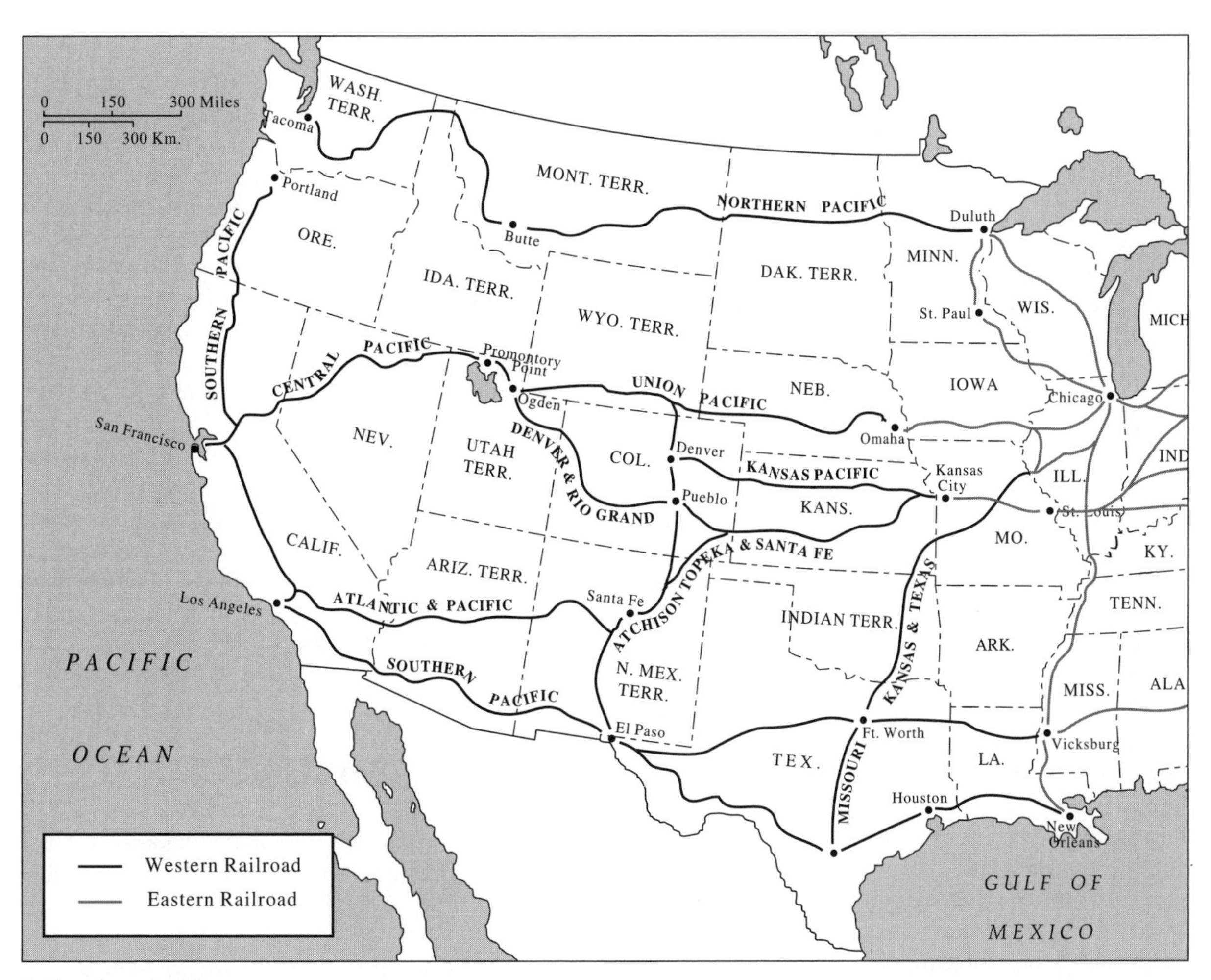

Railroads to the West

made the construction of railroads a top priority for the West. To many it appeared that the Union, having been riven north and south, could only be strengthened by a bond running east and west. The wartime collaboration between business and government had helped teach industrialists and federal authorities not only the value of rail transportation but also how to cooperate in financing and building such transportation. The Pacific Railway Act and subsequent legislation granted huge tracts of land to the railroads, not only for the right of way but also for the railroads to sell in order to finance construction. Railroads would become the biggest land merchants in the West, and they would also eventually become the major promoter of HOMESTEADING. Railroads provided, in addition to lands in the West, cheap transportation there and training in how to farm. Generous loan packages were made available to the railroads, and a transcontinental plan was announced: the CENTRAL PACIFIC RAILROAD would build from west to east; the UNION PACIFIC RAILROAD from east to west. After some false starts, in 1865, U.S. Representative OAKES AMES, at the urging of Abraham Lincoln, put together the financing (and later engendered the scandal surrounding the CRÉDIT MOBILIER OF AMERICA) and GRENVILLE MELLEN DODGE, the engineering leadership to get the transcontinental building launched.

The Union Pacific began laying prodigious lengths of tracks—266 miles in 1866 alone. Through difficult, sometimes all-but impossible terrain and a hostile climate and frequently harassed by Indians, the Union Pacific and Central Pacific pushed their tracks along. And while they built cross-country, local railroad construction boomed as well, making the cry of "railroad through" one recognized by a whole generation. Immigrant laborers, especially the Irish and the Chinese, were hired in unprecedented numbers, and it was largely by dint of their muscle that the project was completed. The graft paid out by the tycoons to government officials and others—so critics claimed—was enormous. Entire towns, wanting to become stops along the road, in turn paid what amounted to huge bribes to the tycoons. Thousands of workers died as Anglo managers, who

cared little for the Irish or the Chinese, cast aside sound construction principles in their rush to lay track and garner bonuses. The great buffalo herds that roamed the plains were decimated by railroaders in order to feed the workers, and a huge new cattle boom was launched toward the same end. The government gave away millions of acres of public land to the railroads as plums. Greed and its handmaiden, corruption, more surely than starry-eyed visions of the future, produced the iron snake that wound its way over mountains, across deserts, and through Indian territory to meet at an obscure site in Utah in 1869. Yet for all the politicking, profiteering, exploitation, waste, rickety financing, and shoddy construction, the line was a remarkable historical accomplishment, and the story of Western railroading became a subject of fascination for generations.

It was a kind of construction and a kind of narrative historically familiar to Americans, who had always valued internal transportation as a life line from frontier wilderness to Eastern civilization, in other words, from the source of raw materials and agricultural goods to developed markets.

The Erie Canal, built between 1817 and 1825 to link New York City with the Great Lakes, was an unqualified success. The nation's other major seaport cities feared losing trade to New York. Philadelphia cobbled together a system of canals and, eventually, railroads in an effort to link its trade to Pittsburgh and the West. Baltimore, however, chose to invest in a railroad rather than canals. Begun in 1828, the Baltimore and Ohio Railroad reached Wheeling—and the Ohio River, the principal artery to the West—by 1852.

At about that time, railroads were also under construction in the Midwest. The Chicago and Rock Island—better known as the Rock Island Line—became the first rail route to the Mississippi River in 1854. By 1856, it bridged the great river and began to branch out through agriculturally rich Iowa. Other Midwestern roads were also beginning to reach beyond the Mississippi, including the Chicago, Burlington and Quincy; the Chicago and Northwestern; and the Chicago, Milwaukee and St. Paul (Milwaukee Road).

By the beginning of the Civil War, the North had a relatively dense network of principal rail lines and short feeder lines stretching from the East through the Midwest. By contrast, the South had only a skeletal rail system. From a Midwestern base, the Union Pacific began construction westward during the Civil War, although work proceeded fitfully until after the war. By the time the UP met the Central Pacific at Promontory Summit in Utah on May 10, 1869, four major Midwestern routes were up and running, ready to link the transcontinental line with the East.

The end of the war brought a quarter-century of westward rail expansion. Following the completion of the Union Pacific–Central Pacific link up, the Atlantic and Pacific Railroad (affiliated with the Atchison, Topeka and Santa Fe Railroad) linked with the Southern Pacific Railroad at Deming, New Mexico, to become the nation's second transcontinental route in 1881. In 1883, the Northern Pacific was completed between Minneapolis–St. Paul and Seattle, Washington. Two years later, the Atchison, Topeka and Santa Fe expanded both east and west from Kansas City to New Orleans and Los Angeles and then northward to San Francisco. From Kansas City, the Santa Fe next was extended to Chicago. From 1887 to 1909, the Milwaukee Road expanded to the West Coast, becoming another direct link between Chicago and the Pacific.

Beginning in 1878, James J. Hill assembled a group of investors to purchase a failing railroad operating out of St. Paul and transform it into a profitable link between the Twin Cities and Manitoba. Slowly, shrewdly, and systematically, Hill purchased or built additional rail links, until, by 1899, his railroad reached the Pacific. He called it the Great Northern, and it became a marvel of efficiency and profitability. It soon effectively merged with the Northern Pacific and the Burlington Route to make it the mightiest and most successful of the transcontinental rail systems.

The last of the transcontinental routes were completed before the end of the 1910s. The Missouri Pacific, Denver and Rio Grande, and the Western Pacific were forged into a single transcontinental system at

A Chicago railroad yard where trains burdened with bales of cotton wait to be unloaded. Chicago became an important city in the railroad shipment of goods between the East and the West. *Courtesy Library of Congress.*

In legend and in reality, train robberies became a part of railroad travel. It was often the contents of the train's express car, pictured above, not the passengers, that the robbers were after. *Courtesy Library of Congress.*

about the same time that the CHICAGO, MILWAUKEE, ST. PAUL AND PACIFIC RAILROAD completed its push to the Pacific in 1909.

The railroads were fueled by Western expansion just as they, in turn, fueled that expansion. Rails carried settlers, goods, and supplies to the West and transported the products of the region—ores and agricultural produce—back East. The railroad made Western agriculture a viable business and gave rise to one of the characteristic fixtures of the Western social landscape, the cattle town—rough-and-tumble rail heads at which the cattle trail met the railroad, and beeves were transported to the hungry East.

On the face of it, railroads would seem to be the great benefactor of the West, tying it together and binding it profitably to the East. Indeed, railroads dominated life in the West through much of the nineteenth century, but Westerners were not always pleased with railroad policies and actions. Perhaps more than any other single force, railroads disrupted the way of life of the Plains Indian tribes and exerted an iron grip on the lives of settlers and farmers. Farmers continually protested that they were the helpless victims of inflated freight rates, and they formed militant agrarian unions—so-called granges—to fight the rates. The granges gave rise to federal Granger laws, the first major steps taken by the FEDERAL GOVERNMENT to regulate private industry.

From the point of view of the railroad operators, however, rates were subject to cutthroat competition and out-and-out wars. Indeed, by the mid-1880s, competition had become so intense that rates fell steadily, sending some rail companies into receivership. That trend was reversed in 1900, when the nation's railroads were swept by a wave of consolidation into so-called communities of interest. In the West, the consolidation was especially dramatic. James J. Hill and EDWARD HENRY HARRIMAN, between them, soon acquired control of the most significant Western lines. Antitrust legislation was enacted, but the rail industry stubbornly resisted attempts to break up concentrations of power, especially in the West. Journalists began to describe the Western lines as the tentacles of a single great "octopus," quite capable of squeezing the life out of the entire region.

Enriched and made more efficient by consolidation, the Western railroads set about improving their lines from 1890 to 1917. Entire routes were re-engineered for greater safety, greater speed, and the ability to handle larger loads. Whereas the nineteenth-century Western railroad had been symbolized by the single track stretching from horizon to horizon, the early twentieth century saw the double tracking of vast stretches of transcontinental routes.

Still, farmers and others protested what they perceived as high freight rates. In fact, while prices in the West rose an average of 50 percent around the turn-of-the century, rail rates rose only 7 percent. Still, the clamor was for federal regulation. The Hepburn Act of 1906 gave the Interstate Commerce Commission authority to fix maximum rates, and the Mann-Elkins Act of 1910 gave the ICC even greater regulatory power, including the authority to suspend or deny rate increases, subject to investigation. The railroads were pressured, too, by labor unions, which demanded wage increases commensurate not with the railroads' profit, but with the rapidly and inexorably escalating cost of living in the West.

A full-scale crisis of finance for the railroads was averted by America's entry into World War I, when the rail carriers were temporarily placed under direct government control. A booming economy carried the Western rail systems back to at least a moderate degree of prosperity after the war, when the companies were returned to private control, but as interstate trucking began to penetrate the West, all but the biggest and strongest Western lines faltered. World War II injected new life into the rail companies, and that prosperity carried over into the immediate postwar years, as rail systems rushed to modernize their lines and convert from steam to diesel locomotive power.

For about a century, the railroad reigned as the supreme mode of long-distance travel, perfectly suited to the vastness of the American West. Freight moved efficiently, smoothly, and directly, while passengers could enjoy the comfort afforded by the Pullman Palace sleeping car. The end of World War II brought a surge in truck freighting, bolstered by the sweeping Interstate Highway Act of 1956, which effectively sub-

sidized the truckers' "right of way." Even more dramatic was the impact of the interstate highway system on long-distance travel by private automobile. And, as if that were not enough to deal a mortal blow to the railroad passenger business, domestic airfares fell steadily during the 1950s. By the early 1960s, jet passenger travel was commonplace and inexpensive. Passenger travel by rail seemed an anachronism.

By 1971, in the West and elsewhere, the federally run national rail corporation, Amtrak, took over the passenger operations other railroads had abandoned. Service was severely cut, and many Western states—let alone Western cities and towns—lost all passenger rail service. Through the 1970s and 1980s, railroads relied on government-guaranteed, low-interest loans to finance the capital improvements necessary to maintain their competitive edge as freight carriers.

If anything, rail-freight operations have fared better in the West than elsewhere in the nation. Long-distance freighting by rail is economical and relatively nonpolluting, and the great Western lines, thanks in no small measure to mergers, remain profitable and powerful businesses.

—Alan Axelrod and Charles Phillips

SEE ALSO: Agrarianism; Booms; Burlington Northern Railroad; Cattle Towns; Denver and Rio Grande Railway Company; Financial Panics; Industrial Workers of the World (IWW); Interstate Commerce Act of 1887; Populism; Pullman Palace Car Company; Labor Movement; Socialism

SUGGESTED READING:

Fogel, Robert W. *The Union Pacific: A Case in Premature Enterprise.* Baltimore, 1960.

Johnson, Arthur M., and Barry E. Supple. *Boston Capitalists and Western Railroads.* Cambridge, Mass., 1967.

Martin, Albro. *James J. Hill and the Opening of the Northwest.* New York, 1976.

Reigel, Robert. *The Story of the Western Railraods.* New York, 1926.

RAIN IN THE FACE (SIOUX)

Rain in the Face—also known as Chasing Enemy (1835 or 1849–1905)—was a Hunkpapa Lakota, a handsome man with regal bearing who, according to JAMES MCLAUGHLIN, U.S. agent at Standing Rock, was a "hereditary chief." Later, as he reluctantly accepted family farming and ranching as ways of life, Rain in the Face said, "I am a chief and a warrior."

Rain in the Face (Sioux). *Courtesy National Archives.*

Rain in the Face first appeared in printed records when he ably supported RED CLOUD at the Fort Sully talks with Governor Newton Edmunds in 1865. On August 4, 1873, Rain in the Face killed a veterinarian named Honzingerm and a sutler named Baliran along the Yellowstone River and, after that, participated in the Battle of Little Bighorn; according to some records, he was the man who killed GEORGE ARMSTRONG CUSTER. With a substantial following, Rain in the Face then accompanied SITTING BULL into exile in Canada, where he brandished a coup stick as he recounted the killing of white soldiers in the Custer fight. Like GALL and Crow King, however, he criticized Sitting Bull for lingering in exile too long to the disadvantage of his people.

Rain in the Face surrendered with his band at Fort Keogh in 1879 and accompanied some seventeen hundred Lakotas to the region around the Standing Rock Agency. There, he laid down his arms, picked up agricultural tools, and made a public display of manual labor. At the agency, he gained recognition with JOHN GRASS among "chiefs" or supervisors of family clusters in an area of Standing Rock jurisdiction labeled "Hunkpapa and Blackfoot" (Siha Sapa) Sioux.

At the Standing Rock Agency, Agent McLaughlin was often suspicious of Rain in the Face. When he vol-

unteered to attend Hampton Institute in Virginia (at the age of thirty-eight) and to join the Coles Circus Company, McLaughlin decided against it. Throughout the 1880s, Rain in the Face vociferously opposed the further cession of land by Lakota people. Yet in the end, he fixed his mark on the Sioux Agreement of March 2, 1889, by which the remaining 12.7 million acres of the 60 million-acre Great Sioux Reservation were divided into six reservations.

Lakotas were reminded of Rain in the Face's leadership by wounds that forced him to walk on crutches in his later years. Although McLaughlin relegated him to a position of secondary importance among recognized "chiefs," the agent praised him for having "more sense and better judgment" about the realities of reservation life than did many other traditionalists. With dignity, he helped Hunkpapa and Blackfoot Lakotas through their greatest trials of adjustment.

—Herbert T. Hoover

SEE ALSO: Little Bighorn, Battle of

SUGGESTED READING:

Eastman, Charles Alexander. *Indian Heroes and Great Chieftains.* Boston, 1918.
National Archives. Record Group 75, Standing Rock Agency.
Wood, Norman Barton. *Lives of Famous Indian Chiefs.* Aurora, Ill., 1906.

RALSTON, WILLIAM CHAPMAN

William Chapman Ralston (1826–1875), mining investor, financier, and founder of the Bank of California, was a native of Ohio. In 1854, he moved to San Francisco as a partner in a steamship company. Ten years later, he and others, including Darius Ogden Mills, established the Bank of California. After becoming president of the bank in 1872, Ralston financed several of the major buildings in San Francisco, including the Palace Hotel. Completed in 1875, the hotel boasted elevators, arc lamps, and an elegant central court. His biggest investment was in the COMSTOCK LODE, the northwestern Nevada mine that produced $300 million in silver and gold between 1860 and 1880.

One of Ralston's most daring investments was in a new water supply for San Francisco. He purchased the Calaveras watershed, which engineers had recommended as a water source for the city, for $100,000 and then acquired stock in the Spring Valley Water Company, which supplied the city with water. Because he lacked the cash needed to acquire the stock outright, he bought it with certificates promising the purchase price plus interest. With control of more than half the company's stock, Ralston then sold the Calaveras watershed to Spring Valley for $1 million—earning him a profit of $900,000. Next he offered to sell Spring Valley to the city for $15 million, but the city supervisors balked at the scheme.

In the meantime, Ralston's other investments proved unsound. A combination of speculative investments, a decline in the value of mining stock, and a general depression caused a run on the Bank of California, which closed for a brief time on August 26, 1875. The directors then asked for his resignation as president. Only a few hours after Ralston resigned, he drowned while swimming in the San Francisco Bay. It has never been determined whether his death was by accident or by suicide.

After his death, Ralston's manipulation of bank funds was questioned and his personal insolvency came to light. After the closing of the bank set off a widespread panic that led to the failure of other banks in the state—including William Workman's bank in Los Angeles—the governor appointed a three-member State Banking Commission to regulate state-chartered financial institutions.

—Candace Floyd

SEE ALSO: Banking

SUGGESTED READING:

Lyman, George D. *Ralston's Ring: California Plunders the Comstock Lode.* New York, 1937.

RANCHING

SEE: Cattle Industry

RANCHO CHICO

Rancho Chico served as a haven to several groups of Northern California Indians. In 1849, General JOHN BIDWELL bought the ranch in northeastern Sacramento Valley (California), the territory of the Northwestern Maidu group of Native Americans. Including more than twenty-two thousand acres, the land grant encompassed the Mechoopda Village of the Maidu. Having used Indians as laborers in his surveying and mining operations, Bidwell again turned to the Indians for agricultural work. The Indians living on the

property were very poor. They had few options for survival because white settlers had seized the most fertile land and the Indians' hunting and gathering grounds.

In 1863, a posse of five hundred white men sought to kill every Native American in Butte County or remove them to the Round Valley Reservation. At that time, the Mechoopda Village on the ranch became a haven for Indians from nine other Maidu villages, as well as for members of the Yana, Pit River, Nome Lacki, Wintu, and Wailacki tribes. The elders among the Maidu people came to call the village Bahapki, which means "unsifted" or "mixed," to reflect the its combination of cultures. While the Indians at Bahapki gained protection and the chance to recreate a village mixing elements from all their cultures, Bidwell gained a source of cheap labor for his ranch.

In 1868, Bidwell married Annie Ellicott Kennedy, a member of a prominent Washington, D.C., family and a reformer. Schooled in the "CULT OF TRUE WOMANHOOD" and the tradition of Protestant women's reform, Annie Bidwell believed it was her duty as a woman and a Christian to "uplift" the Indians she encountered on her husband's ranch. She planned to transform them into "good, upstanding citizens." To accomplish her aims, she taught sewing and reading to Indian women and children and encouraged Indian families to adopt wooden homes. In addition to these material changes, she also sought to root out native religious practices, particularly burial traditions and dances, and to convert the Indians to Christianity. Torn between their need for physical protection and their desire to preserve their culture, the Indians of Bahapki crafted ingenious ways to preserve the integrity of their culture while seeming to meet Mrs. Bidwell's aims. Many of the younger educated Indians used their Christian training as a platform from which to argue for Native American rights. To placate Mrs. Bidwell, the Indians in Bahapki celebrated Christmas and carried out Fourth of July celebrations but imbued them with their own meaning. Despite Mrs. Bidwell's best efforts, the Indians at Rancho Chico succeeded in maintaining the heart of their culture. Today, the city of Chico surrounds the old ranch.

—Margaret D. Jacobs

SEE ALSO: Bidwell, Annie Ellicott Kennedy

SUGGESTED READING:

Azbill, Henry. "Bahapki." *Indian Historian* 4 (Spring 1971): 57.

———. "Maidu Indians of California: A Historical Note." *Indian Historian* 4 (Summer 1971): 21.

Currie, Anne H. "Bidwell Rancheria." *California Historical Society Quarterly* 36 (December 1957): 313–325.

Hill, Dorothy J. *The Indians of Chico Rancheria*. Sacramento, Calif., 1978.

Jacobs, Margaret D. "Resistance to Rescue: The Indians at Bahapki and Mrs. Annie E. K. Bidwell." In *Writing the Range: Race, Class, and Culture in the Women's West*. Edited by Elizabeth Jameson and Susan Armitage. Norman, Okla., 1996.

RANKIN, JEANNETTE

Woman suffragist, pacifist, and the first woman elected to the U.S. Congress, Jeannette Rankin (1880–1973) was born on a ranch near Missoula, Montana. The eldest of seven children, she graduated from the University of Montana in 1902, worked in a settlement house in San Francisco, and studied at the New York School of Philanthropy. After gaining political skills during her work for the National American Woman Suffrage Association in Washington, New York, California, and several other states, she returned to Montana to spearhead its successful WOMEN'S SUFFRAGE campaign in 1914. In 1916, using the political base she had created in the suffrage fight, Rankin ran for the U.S. House of Representatives on the Republican ticket. Her promising political career was arrested by her first vote in the House of Representatives, in which she joined fifty-five other members of Congress who voted against the United States's entry into World War I. Although her position was supported by many Montanans, it ultimately led to her defeat in a 1918 bid for the U.S. Senate.

In 1924, Rankin moved to Georgia and began working as a grassroots peace activist. In 1940, with war again looming on the American horizon, she returned to Montana, where she had continued to own property. Once again, Montanans elected her to the House of Representatives. In 1941, she cast the sole vote against the U.S. declaration of war against Japan, thus becoming the only person in the history of Congress to vote against U.S. entry into both world wars. This vote, which was widely unpopular, put an end to her political career.

Between 1942 and the late 1960s, Rankin led a life of semiretirement. She traveled extensively and studied the philosophy and techniques of pacifism; she was especially influenced by Gandhi. In 1968, she led the Jeannette Rankin Brigade, a phalanx of women protesters, in a march against the Vietnam War. In 1972, the National Organization of Women chose her as the first inductee into the Susan B. Anthony Hall of Fame. Rankin died a year later, having lived a life remarkable for its adherence to principle over political gain.

—Mary Murphy

SUGGESTED READING:
Giles, Kevin S. *Flight of the Dove: The Story of Jeannette Rankin.* Beaverton, Oreg., 1980.
Josephson, Hannah. *Jeannette Rankin, First Lady in Congress: A Biography.* Indianapolis, Ind., 1974.

RATH, CHARLES

Indian trader, buffalo hunter, and entrepreneur Charles Rath (1836–1902) led in the opening of the Panhandle region of Texas and sold supplies to hunters who destroyed the buffalo herds. Born in Urach, Germany, Rath migrated to Sweetwine, Ohio, in 1848. He freighted on the Santa Fe Trail, associated with Bent's Fort, married a Cheyenne woman, ran a road ranch, and hunted buffalo for the railroad. In 1872 with partner Robert M. Wright, he established a store in Dodge City with branches in the western Texas towns of Adobe Walls, Rath City, and Sweetwater, and other sites. Ending his partnership, he centered his interests in Mobeetie. When the railroads by-passed the town, his businesses failed, and he died a pauper.

—*C. Robert Haywood*

SUGGESTED READING:
Rath, Ida Ellen. *The Rath Trail.* Wichita, Kans., 1961.

RATTLESNAKES

Among the most feared animals of the American West, rattlesnakes have been widely commemorated in myth, legend, and scientific reports. As pit vipers, they are members of the family *Crotalidae* and are found primarily in the Americas. They are named and characterized by a unique, singular appendage—the rattle. Formed of keratin, this button is found on the tail of newborn snakes. Each time a snake sheds its skin, a new button is added. Since rattlesnakes shed their skin several times a year, the old folk story that their age can be determined by the number of buttons is false. When agitated, the rattlesnake rapidly shakes its rattle, creating a sinister warning to nearby humans or animals. The explicit purpose of the snake's rattling, which sounds somewhat like a cicada, is not totally understood.

Their fangs are hinged and spring forward only when the snakes are striking. Their venom is chemically complex and varies in biochemical structure from species to species. Rattlesnakes are ovoviviparous (the females produce eggs that are hatched inside their bodies). Some rattlesnakes reach up to seven feet in length. Able to climb trees to heights of four or five feet from the ground and to swim in streams, rivers, and lakes, they have remarkable mobility. Western diamond back rattlesnakes *(Crotalus atrox)* have been captured swimming twenty miles off shore in the Gulf of Mexico.

Rattlesnakes may be found throughout the West, from the Canadian border to Mexico and from the Mississippi and Missouri rivers to the Pacific Ocean. Twelve species of rattlesnakes are found in the West with Arizona containing eleven of them, New Mexico seven, and California six.

Rattlesnakes are a vital part of Western ecosystems and play a valuable role in keeping rodent populations in check.

—*Phillip Drennon Thomas*

SUGGESTED READING:
Klauber, Laurence M. *Rattlesnakes, Their Habits, Life Histories, and Influence on Mankind.* 2 vols. Berkeley and Los Angeles, 1972.
Shaw, Charles E., and Sheldon Campbell. *Snakes of the American West.* New York, 1974.

RAYBURN, SAMUEL TALIAFERRO (SAM)

Speaker of the House of Representatives from 1940 to 1961, Sam Rayburn (1882–1961) was born near Lenoir in East Tennessee. He was one of eleven children whose farmer parents barely eked out enough food to survive. In 1887, he moved with his family to a cotton farm in north-central Texas. Eventually, the family settled in Bonham.

Rayburn attended East Texas Normal College and, at the age of nineteen, was awarded a teaching certificate. He taught school for a few years and then returned to Normal College and received a B.S. degree. Throughout his school years, Rayburn followed the career of his hero, Joseph (Joe) Weldon Bailey, who had been elected to the U.S. House of Representatives in 1890.

In 1906, Rayburn won a seat in the state legislature. He continued his studies at the University of Texas Law School and was admitted to the bar in 1908. He was reelected to the legislature and served as Speaker of the House from 1910 to 1912. That year, he won election to the U.S. House of Representatives. He served under eight presidents for the next forty-eight years and contributed to some of the most significant legislation in modern times. He was the author of the Truth in Security Act, the Public Utilities Holding Company Act, and the Railroad Holding Company Bill, among others. A staunch supporter of the New Deal, he collaborated in the creation of the Federal Communication Commission, the Rural Electrification Act, and

other federal programs. In 1940, he was selected Speaker of the House of Representatives, a position he held until 1961.

A skilled legislative tactician and master politician, Rayburn gained the respect and admiration of his colleagues and of the nation. The Rayburn Library in Bonham, Texas, houses all his papers both public and private.

—*Fred L. Koestler*

SUGGESTED READING:

Dorough, Charles Dwight. *Mr. Sam.* New York, 1962.

RAYNOLDS EXPEDITION

Between 1859 and 1860, U.S. Army Captain William F. Raynolds conducted the last major military exploration of the American West for the CORPS OF TOPOGRAPHICAL ENGINEERS. On April 12, 1859, Raynolds received orders from the War Department to organize and conduct an expedition of the Yellowstone River and the Upper Missouri. The government wanted him to report on the nature of the region, its resources, its Indian tribes, and, perhaps most importantly, the potential for building roads through the Rocky Mountains. With mountain man JAMES (JIM) BRIDGER as a guide and FERDINAND VANDEVEER HAYDEN as a scientific advisor, Raynolds's well-provisioned expeditionary force of seven civilians and thirty soldiers left Fort Pierre on the Missouri at the end of June. He headed west along the Cheyenne River, circled around the Black Hills, followed the Powder River to within about fifty miles of its headwaters, then—sending a small surveying party up O'Fallion's Fork—with his main party followed the Bighorn River to a trading post in the Platte River valley. There, in October, he went into winter quarters. Come spring 1860, Raynold's expedition explored the Bighorn west to the Missouri River's three forks and the Yellowstone to Fort Union.

In all, Raynolds traveled twenty five hundred miles and chartered a region almost one quarter of a million miles square. He documented the Indian tribes of the region and their way of life, the area's mineral resources and agricultural potential, and the best routes for expansion westward. A late and heavy snowfall and the immensely rugged terrain frustrated Raynolds's efforts to explore the region that today makes up the YELLOWSTONE NATIONAL PARK, and he had to take Jim Bridger's word about its strange beauty. Its work completed by September, the expedition disbanded in Omaha on October 14, 1860, fourteen months after it had first set out.

In 1860, Raynolds wrote his report, perhaps the most important report on the West produced by the Corps of Topographical Engineers. In the *Geological Report on the Yellowstone and Missouri Rivers,* which was published in 1868, Raynolds questioned the practicality of building roads in the rugged region he had explored and suggested that the area's aridity would prevent agricultural settlements, but he also noted the region was rich in minerals. Raynolds also produced an area map, which was published in 1864. Together the two documents closed the last major gaps in the understanding of the trans-Mississippi West's geology. Well written, even something of a literary accomplishment, the report did not receive the attention it perhaps deserved at the time because of the Civil War and afterward because a later expedition, led by Henry D. Washburn in 1870, actually explored the lands in the present-day Yellowstone park.

—*Charles Phillips*

SEE ALSO: Exploration: United States Expeditions

SUGGESTED READING:

Goetzmann, William H. *Army Exploration in the American West, 1803–1863.* New Haven, Conn., 1959.

———. *Exploration and Empire: The Explorer and the Scientist in the Winning of the American West.* New York, 1966.

REAVIS, JAMES ADDISON

James Addison Reavis (1843–1914), master swindler and forger, claimed more than 12.7 million acres in Arizona and New Mexico as a Spanish land grant. Railroads, mining companies, and others paid him at least $146,000 for the land until the scheme collapsed.

Born in Missouri, Reavis was a real-estate dealer in 1871 when he met George Willing, an Arizonan with a packet of authentic-looking Spanish documents. Reavis bought out Willing's interest in the vast Peralta land grant in Arizona and New Mexico and filed his claim in 1883. The Arizona surveyor-general disallowed it.

Reavis reappeared in 1887 with his wife, Doña Sophia Micaela Maso Reavis y Peralta de la Cordoba, Baroness of Arizona and heir to the Peralta grant. Reavis filed an amended claim, submitting newly discovered documents. Surveyor-general Royal A. Johnson concluded that the Peralta grant was a fraud.

Reavis, now called Peralta-Reavis, pressed the U.S. Court of Private Land Claims for confirmation. Special counsel Severo Mallet-Prevost made a thorough

investigation, and the justices determined that the Peralta claim was "wholly fictitious and fraudulent" and that the title papers were all forgeries. In 1896, Reavis was sentenced to prison and fined $5,000.

—*John P. Wilson*

SUGGESTED READING:

Cookridge, E. H. *The Baron of Arizona.* New York, 1967.
Powell, Donald M. *The Peralta Grant: James Addison Reavis and the Barony of Arizona.* Norman, Okla., 1960.

RECLAMATION

Historical background

The pioneers who trekked along overland trails to the Far West beginning in the 1840s learned how precious a resource WATER could be, as they carefully portioned it out to ensure they made it through what they believed were the "wastelands" of the GREAT AMERICAN DESERT. For them, the 850 million acres of arid public lands were something to avoid or to escape, not to conquer or to farm.

Even before the Civil War, however, the intrepid explorer JOHN CHARLES FRÉMONT had announced that the "Great American Desert" was a misnomer, and when the United States launched a rapid industrialization of the West after the war, promoters assured potential settlers that all they need do was move out West and begin farming in order for "rain to follow the plow." Railroads, needing buyers for the vast tracts of land granted them by the FEDERAL GOVERNMENT, also promoted the arid and semiarid lands as a potential Eden. They dispensed advice on farming, hired artists to produce idealized images of lush Western landscapes, and recruited settlers from all over the world. Even nature herself seemed to cooperate when the decades during which such promotions were initiated turned out to be unusually free of the West's cyclical droughts. By the 1870s, the desert had taken on a different hue for a few men of vision who imagined there the paradise that an advanced civilization could produce with scientifically sound IRRIGATION projects; in short, with enough money and adequate support from the government, the American "wasteland" could be "reclaimed."

After all, those promoting reclamation pointed out, about one thousand years ago, the Indians of the Southwest had brought water to the desert through long canals. But one need look no farther than the recent example in Salt Lake City, where the Mormons had reclaimed wasteland not only with dirt dams and irrigation ditches, but also with reservoirs for storing the run-off from melting spring snows. With the tremendous success of the Latter-Day Saints as inspiration, the dream took shape. In 1873, Colorado Governor S. H. Elbert invited delegates from Kansas, Nebraska, Wyoming, Utah, and New Mexico to an irrigation conference in Denver, where the nation's first reclamation proposal was produced. A year later, California authorities persuaded the federal government to appropriate funds for investigating the possibility of irrigation in the Central Valley. Then Congress passed the DESERT LAND ACT OF 1877 to encourage the private development of irrigation, ostensibly by small farmers and ranchers.

The act was based on the principle behind Western water laws created by California gold-rush miners for operating placer claims: priority of appropriation. The result was that early filers claimed more than they could use, hoping to sell the surplus, and late filers claimed more than was left in order just to get some water when prior rights were satisfied. If every claimant asserted his rights, the West's few rivers would have been sucked dry, and at least one—the Umatilla in Oregon—suffered such a fate at three different spots during a drought year. Western farmers sat up nights with shotguns, watching their headgates, and Colorado sugar-beet growers made plans to drain the ARKANSAS RIVER, despite the fact that it fed Kansas wheat crops. The controversy created by the misguided law led to demands for federal intervention, which in turn led Congress in 1888 to authorize an irrigation study of the West conducted by the UNITED STATES GEOLOGICAL SURVEY. The study's sponsors, Nevada's U.S. Senator WILLIAM M. STEWART and Colorado's U.S. Senator HENRY M. TELLER, hoped simply to come up with some way to avoid the greedy speculation spawned by the Desert Land Act and to allow private industries and the various states to cooperate in the use of the West's limited water, but they got much more than they bargained for.

The 1888 study was conducted by JOHN WESLEY POWELL, the director of the Geological Survey whose 1878 *REPORT ON THE LANDS OF ARID REGIONS* had made his a powerful voice in the development of the American West. In the arid-lands report, he had already noted that there was only enough accessible water in the arid regions to irrigate some 3 percent of the land, and he had also anticipated the next stage in the evolution of Western irrigation: building reservoirs and setting aside irrigable land to use to encourage as much homesteading as possible. Powell saw this new study as his chance to act on the irrigation policies he had laid out in the report a decade earlier. He called for marking out every possible site for a potential reservoir on public land throughout the West. Then, he suggested, the federal government should reserve these sites *and* the land the future reservoirs could irrigate by withdrawing it from public use by private citizens or enterprises, thus forc-

ing cooperative arrangements among all parties seeking to tap the West's water.

In effect, Powell was suggesting the planned and orderly economic development of the West's hydrographic basins. What Senator Stewart and Senator Teller heard him say, however, was something different. To them, Powell was asking the government to interfere in the private business of their constituencies, which included powerful cattle, mining, and timber interests who feared that Powell's "arbitrary" suggestions might toll the end of their exploitation of the West's natural resources. In 1890, Stewart, Teller, and other Westerners in Congress cut funding drastically for the Geological Survey and terminated the authorization for the irrigation study. Four years later, they finally forced the "autocratic" Powell to resign as the director of the survey. Clearly, Powell was ahead of his time.

Powell may have been gone, but the problem of aridity remained. Private individuals and investment groups had accomplished remarkable feats of irrigation by the 1880s. They had irrigated one million farms and brought into production nearly four million acres by capturing water from running streams. Now, as everyone in the West realized, they needed just the kind of reservoirs Powell was calling for, and construction on such a large scale would indeed seem to require a program of federal funding. The question, a traditional query in the West, was one of how to get the money without losing control, and ELWOOD MEAD—Wyoming's state engineer—had the answer, which he presented to Stewart's Senate Irrigation Committee during the summer of 1889: the cession of land.

Since at least ANDREW JACKSON's day, the federal government had been ceding public lands to the states for one reason or another—to populate territories, to build colleges—and so the idea had a venerable history. Seeing land cession as a means of federal funding that required neither federal financing nor federal management, private enterprise quickly picked up the idea during a new irrigation boom between 1887 and 1893, when businesses were promoting irrigation ventures as a way to expand agricultural production and to feed the huge profits they were making in land speculation. A group of Western politicians—including Senator Stewart, Senator FRANCIS E. WARREN of Wyoming, Congressman FRANCIS G. NEWLANDS of Nevada, and Governor Arthur Thomas of Utah—called for an Irrigation Congress in 1891.

New England journalist WILLIAM E. SMYTHE, who had founded the magazine *Irrigation Age,* became secretary of the Irrigation Congress. Under his evangelical leadership, the Irrigation Congress attempted to get cession adopted as a national irrigation policy. Smythe waxed poetical, always in the name of the small homesteader, about the power of dams, canals, ditches, and sprinklers. He saw the arid West as a challenge that God had put before Americans, to urge them out of their isolated, individual enterprises into the communitywide cooperation needed to build and maintain the dams and ditches necessary to transform the desert into a garden. In 1896, a California lawyer with a background in the Byzantine corridors of water-rights history and a member of the Irrigation Congress named George Maxwell formed his own auxiliary organization called the National Irrigation Association. Maxwell single-handedly turned around the congress's thinking on irrigation. Only the federal government, he argued, had the authority necessary to rule on the question of water rights on interstate streams; only federal construction of storage reservoirs would prevent land monopolies from springing up, as they always seemed to do when the states handled public lands. After he persuaded the Irrigation Congress, especially Congressman Newlands, Maxwell set about persuading, with Newland's help, the U.S. Congress.

Since efficient water management seemed to require healthy watersheds, reclamation also fit right into THEODORE ROOSEVELT's and the GIFFORD PINCHOT's conservation plans. Indeed, American conservationists at the time believed that forests slowed down the run-off from storms and melting snow, thus helping prevent floods and allowing dams to capture more of the run-off in their reservoirs. In short, more water would be available for irrigation if the government protected more of the Western forests. Under this stream-flow theory, conservationists and advocates for reclamation became allies for a time, and their alliance helped give birth to the NEWLANDS RECLAMATION ACT OF 1902. Under this act, the federal government would build dams to irrigate arid land for small family farms whose settlers would repay Uncle Sam the costs of construction over time.

The modern West was born. The federal government, always one of the West's greatest resources, had declared itself ready to solve the problem of aridity, always one of the West's greatest drawbacks. The federal BUREAU OF RECLAMATION grew into perhaps the most powerful agency in the West. The Imperial Valley sprang into existence, producing fruit and vegetables year round. Of course, the small farmers never repaid their debts, and most of the water eventually fed huge agribusinesses and sprawling suburbs. The early diversion of the Truckee River to Nevada farms and ranches caused the Pyramid Lake to wither away and destroyed the remaining economy and spirit of the Paiute Indians. Men such as Fred Eaton, J. B. Lippincott, and WILLIAM MULHOLLAND conspired to

divert all the water from the Owens Valley to whet their interests in Los Angeles, and they did so despite the best efforts of valley residents to hang on to their precious and scarce "commodity." By the Great Depression, the federal reclamation pork-barrel was rolling. With federal funds, HENRY J. KAISER dammed the Colorado and Columbia rivers. Great dams went up everywhere as Bureau of Reclamation commissioners such as Michael Strauss and Floyd Dominy competed with the UNITED STATES ARMY CORPS OF ENGINEERS for ever grander projects. Even when the Teton Dam burst and it became clear that many of the others were eroding, the building went on.

The economy and ecology of reclamation

Some scholars have noted how much of the language used by New Dealers to describe their domestic programs employed military terms and metaphors. And by the late twentieth century, much of the New Deal planning seemed in perspective not unlike a massive counterattack against the Depression and the DUST BOWL, against human greed and an unkind nature. Out West, certainly, nothing so stirred the contemporary imagination and renewed the American people's faith in their ability to endure, to conquer nature, to fund a civilization than the building of Boulder Dam (now called HOOVER DAM). Gleaming white in a blazing desert sun, Boulder Dam was a modern engineering marvel and, as Donald Worster has pointed out, America's answer to the pyramids of Egypt and the ancient Colossus of Rhodes. When it was completed in 1935, it was the biggest structure of its kind anywhere, and it spawned a new age of high-rise dam construction throughout the world, remaking—as Worster wrote—"the face of the earth and altering the distribution of social and economic power" around the globe. Boulder Dam was also an attack on one of the mightiest streams on earth, the COLORADO RIVER.

It was the demand to dominate the Colorado that had first led in the late 1920s to the scheme to build so massive a dam and storage reservoir. Among those clamoring for water from the Colorado was the group of real-estate promoters who had turned Los Angeles from a backwater "adobe outpost of ten thousand people" into a big city with a starry-eyed population of two hundred thousand. Already William Mulholland and his fellow civic salesmen had drained dry the Owens Valley, and now they turned to the Colorado River where, in the 1920s, a few people lived along the river basin in clusters, the biggest of them comprising seven thousand souls up in dusty Las Vegas. Los Angeles boosters, spreading out over the country, promoted a carefree life in the sun along the dry, warm California coast to farmers and factory workers—those the Hollywood movie colony would come to call "the folks." And if the folks came, Los Angeles was certainly going to need water, but the water came before the "need." "If we don't get the water," said Mulholland, "we won't need it. We have to get the water or quit growing."

Los Angeles's demand for the sparkling Colorado water was part of the classic Western real-estate baron's dream: build it, and they will come. But the big-money men who had bought huge stretches of farm land down in the Imperial Valley just north of Mexico wanted the water even more badly, if possible, than the Los Angeles's land speculators. They had their three-thousand-acre "agribusinesses," the advance guard of an army of Chicano migrants who would come north to plant and harvest for them, and railway connections to urban entrepôts for transporting whatever they decided to grow, but they did not have control over the Colorado River, their only source of irrigation. Sometimes the river flooded into their valley and washed away their hopes along with their investments; at other times it refused to give their parched ditches and canals even a taste of water. Lastly there were the Bureau of Reclamation professionals, whose very job description required they undo nature. Bureaucrats grown drunk on New Deal power, they just wanted to build, as one of them said, "the biggest dam ever built by anyone anywhere."

Worster calls all of them—the bureaucrats, the Imperial Valley farmers, the Los Angeles promoters—fanatics, based on philosopher George Santayana's definition of fanatics as "men who redouble their efforts as they lose sight of their aim." For them, Boulder Dam was only the beginning. It was followed by the 1938 Parker Dam, feeding the California Aqueduct into Los Angeles, and in turn by the Imperial Dam and the All-American Canal running down to the Mexican border. Then came the Davis Dam, the Morelos Dam, the Laguna Dam, the Palo Verde Diversion Dam, the Headgate Rock Diversion Dam, the Navajo Dam, the Flaming Gorge Dam, the Seedskadee Dam, the Savery-Pot Hook Dam, the Meeka Cabin Dam, the Vernal Dam, the Bonneville Dam, the Rifle Gap Dam, the Joes Valley Dam, the Paonia Dam, the Blue Mesa Dam, the Morrow Point Dam, the Crystal Dam, the Soap Park Dam, the Crawford Dam, the Silver Jack Dam, the Lemon Dam, the Frying Pan-Arkansas Dam, and on and on until at last and most impressively rose the immense 710-foot high Glen Canyon Dam only a shade shorter than the mother of them all, the Hoover Dam. Backed up, becalmed, bled on every side, the majestic Colorado River in some seasons, Worster says, no longer flowed to the sea; instead it died in a wasteland of salt somewhere in Baja California.

But the dream—Eden from a desert—was intact. From 1900 to 1910, the West's population jumped by 66 percent, while the nation continued to grow by only 21 percent a year. A half-century later, from 1950 to 1960, the states west of the Rockies were still growing by the equivalent of the population of all of New York's five boroughs combined. The new Westerners, like the old Westerners, were a restless and mobile bunch, only now they worked on federal-highway projects, or in federally related industries like aerospace, instead of in the mines, on horseback, or as loggers. For eight decades, they swelled the suburbs around Los Angeles, Phoenix, and Dallas, and they were joined by a growing underclass of poor migrant workers from Mexico who poured into the barrios of the West and hoped, too, to cash in on the benefits of the new hydraulic civilization.

But the truth was that—in part because of reclamation—the West's population had been running ahead of Western resources for some time. In Spokane, Washington, for example, in the 1960s, the farm land southwest of the city enjoyed a surplus of cheap hydroelectric power. The power companies struck a deal with area farmers to install deep-well, electric-powered irrigation systems and to sell the farmers all the power they needed at a discount. Immediately, aluminum refineries and other industries flocked to the region to take advantage of the cheap power, the water surplus disappeared, and the power companies turned to expensive, coal-fired plants and nuclear reactors.

As early as 1927, the subsiding water table in Arizona had caused four-hundred-foot-deep fissures in the earth. With the coming of air-conditioning, the population boomed, and by 1983, there were more than one hundred such cracks. It was, in part, to support this boom that the Colorado River had been dammed from tip to toe. The huge Central Arizona Project, when finished, diverted millions of acre-feet of water from the Colorado River down four hundred miles of aqueducts and dams into Phoenix and Tucson. At the same time, Western cities tapped into water tables at an alarming rate, and the great Ogallala Aquifer that lay underneath the Great Plains—the subject of many competing claims among the various states—grew decade by decade ever closer to total depletion. Its exhaustion would at least mean that the West no longer had water to fight over.

In *Cadillac Desert,* journalist and historian Marc Reisner called the West's dream of reclaiming America's wastelands not so much folly as a kind of hubris, the stuff of tragedy. The dream, he said, seems doomed to glorious failure. As the water runs out, ever more grandiose schemes are hatched. Southern California movers and shakers talk about raiding the Pacific Northwest for water. Bureau of Reclamation contingency plans investigate the feasibility of gargantuan projects to pipe water from the Canadian Rockies into the American Southwest. Rich Texans seriously consider building a canal to divert the Mississippi from its Louisiana delta to the caprock around Lubbock. But in fact, as Reisner pointed out, all the West had managed to do in a century's worth of reclamation was to turn a Missouri-size section of the Great American Desert green at a tremendous cost and to potentially disastrous environmental effect.

—*Charles Phillips*

See also: Central Valley Project; Farming: Farming in the Imperial Valley and the Salton Sea Region; Fruit and Vegetable Growing; Owens Valley War

Suggested reading:

Axelrod, Alan, and Charles Phillips. *The Environmentalists: A Biographical Dictionary from the 17th Century to the Present.* New York, 1993.

Frederic, Kenneth D., and James C. Hanson. *Water for Western Agriculture.* Washington, D.C., 1982.

Green, Donald E. *Land of the Underground Rain: Irrigation on the Texas High Plains, 1910–1970.* Austin, Tex., 1973.

Kahrl, William L. *Water and Power: The Conflict over Los Angeles' Water Supply in the Owens Valley.* Berkeley, Calif., 1982.

Reisner, Marc. *Cadillac Desert: The American West and Its Disappearing Water.* New York, 1986.

Worster, Donald. *Rivers of Empire: Water, Aridity, and the Growth of The American West.* New York, 1985.

———. *Under Western Skies: Nature and History in the American West.* New York, 1992.

RECLAMATION ACT OF 1902

See: Newlands Reclamation Act of 1902

RECREATION

See: Gambling; Hunting; Rodeo

RED CLOUD (SIOUX)

Red Cloud (Makhpyia-luta; 1821 or 1822–1909), noted chief and warrior of the Oglala Sioux, was born probably near the forks of the Platte River in what became the state of Nebraska; the precise facts of his

Red Cloud (Sioux). *Courtesy National Archives.*

birth are obscure. He died on December 10, 1909, at the Pine Ridge Indian Reservation in southwestern South Dakota.

As a young man, Red Cloud developed a reputation for bravery through warfare with the Pawnees, Crows, Utes, and Shoshones and gradually assumed a position of leadership among the Oglalas. By the spring of 1865, as a leading advocate of war against the whites in the West, he directed or participated in attacks on travelers headed for the newly discovered gold fields of Montana.

In the spring of 1866, plied with presents and promises, Red Cloud and others were persuaded to come to Fort Laramie to discuss peace and the opening of the Bozeman Trail to Montana. Red Cloud, however, withdrew in anger when Colonel Henry B. Carrington arrived with troops to protect travelers; for the next two years, the Indians terrorized travelers on the Bozeman Trail. Red Cloud agreed to return to Fort Laramie for further negotiations only after the army abandoned Forts Reno, Phil Kearny, and C. F. Smith, which had been established to protect the trail.

The new Fort Laramie negotiations were conducted with various Sioux tribes throughout the summer and fall of 1868. The Indians agreed, in exchange for presents and the promise of annuities, to abandon war on the whites and to move to a large reservation north of the state of Nebraska and west of the Missouri River. After the forts were abandoned, he went to Fort Laramie in November 1868 and, after three days of inconclusive negotiations, signed the treaty. There is little evidence to suggest that he understood what the treaty meant, or if he did, that he had any intention of abiding by its terms. For the next decade, agents of the government engaged in frustrating and often fruitless efforts—in Washington, D.C., and on the plains—to explain the treaty and to persuade Red Cloud to adhere to it. He desired to remain as near Fort Laramie as possible, and, above all, he did not want to move to the Missouri River, where the government hoped to locate him. Finally, in 1878, he agreed to settle on the Pine Ridge Reservation in western South Dakota. His early years on the reservation were marked by a highly publicized struggle with the agent, Dr. Valentine T. McGillycuddy.

After 1868, Red Cloud kept the peace, although he was under steady pressure from the younger Oglalas to return to the warpath. In the end, he was criticized both for giving in too easily to the government's demands and for obstructing the progress of his people along "the white man's road."

—*James C. Olson*

Suggested reading:
Hyde, George E. *Red Cloud's Folk.* Norman, Okla., 1937.
Olson, James C. *Red Cloud and the Sioux Problem.* Lincoln, Nebr., 1965. Reprint. 1975.

RED RIVER CARTS

A two-wheeled wooden vehicle drawn by oxen, the Red River cart probably originated in the nineteenth century among the French Canadian or the Métis People of Canada's Great Plains. Of simple oak construction, the cart had two large wheels supporting a platform. The wooden rails on either side of the platform held cargo in place. The large wheels allowed the cart to ride high, thus easing travel through rough terrain and streams.

The design and construction of the cart suited its uses. Métis people amassed hundreds of carts for their semiannual buffalo hunts on the Great Plains. Returning to their homes, they cured the hides and prepared pemmican from the buffalo meat. The furs and meat were then loaded on the carts for the trek to trading posts at present-day St. Paul, Minnesota. Heading home

from the posts, the carts carried the merchandise, ammunition, and implements the Métis received in trade.

Red River carts were practical but not necessarily easy to be around. The screech of hundreds of carts—wooden wheels turning on wooden axles—could be heard for miles. One observer likened the sound to "a thousand fingernails drawn across a thousand panes of glass."

—*Patricia Hogan*

RED RIVER WAR

SEE: Central Plains Indian Wars; Texas Frontier Indian Wars

REDWOODS

Ancient redwood trees, some as many as two thousand years old, inhabit small slivers of continental North America. The Big Trees of the Sierra Nevada, *Sequoia-dendron gigantea,* and the coastal redwoods, *Sequoia sempervirens,* are all that remain of a species that covered much of the continent fifty million years ago. The two million acres of coastal redwoods, stretching from south of Monterey, California, across the Oregon border, remained largely intact into the nineteenth century, but the growth of San Francisco and the rest of California in the aftermath of the gold rush of 1849 took a tremendous toll. By the time naturalist JOHN MUIR took up redwoods as a cause in the early 1900s, the East Bay redwoods were gone, and those in Humboldt and Del Norte counties were sold or granted for cutting. The Big Trees of the Sierra Nevada were less desirable; too brittle for use as lumber, they became "earth monuments" in an attempt to give insecure Americans a natural heritage to rival the cultural history of Europe. This cultural nationalism protected the Big Trees because they lacked economic potential and they were too remote for easy cutting. The coastal redwoods did not fare as well; of the two million acres of redwoods in the nineteenth century, only 4 percent remained in the 1990s, preserved in a series of state parks and Redwoods National Park.

Redwoods became a cultural symbol that combined the physical glory of the North American continent with much of antimodern, proregulation sentiment that became Progressivism. Preserving the trees embodied both a backward- and forward-looking impulse, linking preservation with the search for order—two concepts reformers thought would improve American society.

—*Hal Rothman*

SUGGESTED READING:

Schrepfer, Susan. *The Battle to Save the Big Trees: Fight to Save the Redwoods.* Madison, Wis., 1983.

REED, SIMEON GANNETT

Portland businessman Simeon Gannett Reed (1830–1895) was born in East Abingdon (now Rockland), Massachusetts, where he attended public schools and a private academy. In 1852, he went to Portland, Oregon, by way of Panama and California. Hired by pioneer financier William S. Ladd, he soon became Ladd's partner. In 1858, he married Amanda Wood, a woman of substantial wealth. Their marriage was childless. In 1860, Reed joined Robert E. Thompson, John C. Ainsworth, and others in organizing the OREGON STEAM NAVIGATION COMPANY just in time to profit from the gold rush to Idaho. The company, financed almost entirely by Western capital, monopolized steamboat traffic on the Columbia River for two decades. During this time, it paid some $4.6 million in dividends. Reed rose rapidly to vice-president of the OSN. He found further success in railways, both steam and electric, and in mining and real estate. He purchased a three-

Simeon Gannett Reed joined John C. Ainsworth, Robert R. Thompson, and others in organizing the Oregon Steam Navigation Company. *Courtesy Oregon Historical Society.*

thousand-acre farm where he raised imported cattle and sheep and bred racehorses. In 1892, the Reeds moved to Pasadena, California, where Reed died three years later. Although mainly concerned with profits, Reed donated to causes that enhanced Portland's cultural and intellectual life. After her husband's death, Amanda Wood Reed set aside $1.5 million to found Reed College.

—Edwin R. Bingham

RELIEF SOCIETY (LDS)

Founded in the Mormon community of Nauvoo, Illinois, on March 17, 1842, the Female Relief Society of Nauvoo, later the Relief Society, or National Women's Relief Society, was the women's arm of the CHURCH OF JESUS CHRIST OF LATTER-DAY SAINTS. Under the direction of founding prophet JOSEPH SMITH, JR., the organization performed charitable services and fostered the spiritual well-being of its members.

Smith's wife EMMA (SMITH) HALE was the first president of the organization, which during its first two years grew to more than twelve hundred members. Meetings were held only during warm seasons, but welfare work continued year round. The Nauvoo society was disbanded in 1844 because of attempts by Hale to use her position to undermine the nascent practice of plural marriage then promoted by her husband.

In 1854, after the MORMONS had gathered in Utah, a grassroots movement reconstituted the society, this time to provide clothing for Native Americans in the vicinity. BRIGHAM YOUNG, Joseph Smith's successor as president of the church, approved and promoted the concept and encouraged each ward (parish) and settlement to organize a society. Activity was inconsistent over the next decade, until Young called on ELIZA ROXCY SNOW, the most influential woman in the Mormon community, to organize the women churchwide in 1866.

From 1867 to her death in 1887, Snow and her coworkers traveled widely and dictated patterns of procedure and policy to the various chapters. By 1884, more than three hundred chapters were functioning, each with a full cadre of officers. In addition to its mandated responsibilities to the poor and to members, the society established various significant programs for the common good. Society members encouraged sisters to attend medical schools in the Eastern states; on their return, they trained local women in nursing and MIDWIFERY. By 1882, society members had founded the Deseret Hospital in Salt Lake City. They established in 1872 a biweekly newspaper, the *Woman's Exponent,* which continued until 1914. By providing retail outlets, the society encouraged home industry, including, among more common tasks, the culture and manufacture of silk. Local chapters bought land, built their own halls, and often established retail outlets. The women established a grain-storing program and maintained a supply of wheat until after World War I when it was sold to the U.S. government to alleviate a postwar grain shortage. In addition, the National Women's Relief Society sponsored the establishment of churchwide programs for young women and children.

Under society sponsorship, Mormon women organized themselves politically. First in the nation to vote, in January 1870, the Utah women made common cause with the Eastern suffragists, despite the latter group's criticism of the Mormon practice of polygamy. The society was a founding member of the National Council of Women.

In the twentieth century, as its numbers grew and its assets expanded, the society became increasingly corporate and centralized in its operation. From its Salt Lake City offices, first in the Bishop's Building, then in its own structure, society staff supervised programs in infant care, home nursing, adoption, assistance to unwed mothers, indigent care, and public health.

Still viable in the 1990s, under fiscal and curriculum control of the Church of Jesus Christ of Latter-day Saints, the Relief Society meets weekly in each congregation for a forty-five minute lesson and monthly for a project meeting in which all may participate. Each member is visited monthly by "visiting teachers" who ensure her welfare and foster her spiritual well-being.

In 1992, to celebrate its 150th anniversary, members of society in eighteen thousand chapters reached beyond the church membership in a worldwide challenge for community involvement. At the time, Elaine Lowe Jack served as president.

—Maureen Ursenbach Beecher

SUGGESTED READING:

Beecher, Maureen Ursenbach, and Lavina Fielding Anderson. *Sisters in Spirit: Mormon Women in Historical and Cultural Perspective.* Urbana and Chicago, 1987.

Derr, Jill Mulvay, Janath Russell Cannon, and Maureen Ursenbach Beecher. *Women of Covenant: The Story of Relief Society.* Salt Lake City, 1992.

RELIGION

SEE: Asian American Churches; Book of Mormon; Campbellites; Catholics; Church of Jesus Christ of Latter-day Saints; Church of Jesus Christ of Latter-Day Saints, Reorganized; Evangelists; Ghost Dance; Houchen Settlement House; Indian Shaker Church; In-

dustrial Christian Home for Mormon Women; Missions; Mormons; Native American Church; Native American Cultures: Spiritual Life; Penitentes; Presbyterian Woman's Board of Home Missions; Protestant Home Missionary Programs; Protestants; Relief Society (LDS)

REMINGTON, FREDERIC

Although always essentially an Easterner, Frederic Remington (1861–1909) in more than 2,700 paintings, 8 books, illustrations for 142 books by other authors, and 25 bronzes became, with CHARLES MARION RUSSELL, the leading artistic interpreter of the American West in the late nineteenth and early twentieth centuries. Born in Canton, Ohio, Remington was the son of a newspaper owner and editor who served as a captain in the Union forces during the Civil War.

Throughout his life and in much of his art, Remington demonstrated a fascination with men at war. Before enrolling at Yale in 1878, he had attended Highland Military Academy in Worcester, Massachusetts. While at Yale, Remington did not find his studies in fine art challenging, and indeed, he took greater pleasure in playing football. With little support from his family for becoming an artist, Remington withdrew from Yale in 1879 and sought unsuccessfully a career as a clerk in state government.

Remington's first real exposure to the West occurred in 1882 when he used his inheritance to buy a small sheep ranch in Kansas. Raising sheep was hard work, and the twenty-one-year-old Remington sold his ranch two years later without making a profit. His part ownership of a Kansas City saloon was also a failure, and essentially his inheritance was squandered in Kansas. Married to Eva Caten in October 1884, he spent the spring of 1885, traveling through the Southwest as the U.S. Cavalry pursued GERONIMO. He always made sketches as he traveled. At Fort Sill, Oklahoma, he drew Cheyennes, Kiowas, Cherokees, and Apaches. Returning to the East, Remington sought to become an illustrator for the popular magazines. By 1890, more than four hundred of his illustrations had appeared in the ten leading periodicals of the period including *Harper's Weekly, Harper's Monthly, Century Magazine, Scribner's Monthly, St. Nicholas Magazine,* and *Outing.* The authentic feel of his work was acknowledged when THEODORE ROOSEVELT asked him to illustrate his article on ranch life and hunting for *Century Magazine.* By 1889, Remington was beginning to be recognized not only as an illustrator but also as a painter; *A Dash for Timber* was exhibited in the National Academy of Design and *Lull in the Fight* received a silver medal at the Paris Universal Exposition.

Frederic Remington. *Courtesy Library of Congress.*

Frederic Remington's *A Surprise. Courtesy Library of Congress.*

Like his contemporary, Charles Marion Russell, Remington had a profound sense of the transitory nature of the West. His works created a heroic vision of the individual Euro-American men who settled, tamed, and acquired these lands. Until late in his career, landscapes were merely an essential background for his paintings of men confronting the forces of nature, the acts of others, and the challenges of untamed horses. Remington frequently emphasized in his paintings the life of men on horseback, be they cowboys, trappers, cavalrymen, or Indians. Horses were always fundamental components in a Remington painting or sculpture. He was an exceptionally talented artist whose strengths in painting and sculpture have been seldom equaled by artists who focused on the West as a subject of inspiration.

—*Phillip Drennon Thomas*

SEE ALSO: Art: Book and Magazine Illustration, Western Art

SUGGESTED READING:
Dippie, Brian W. *Remington and Russell.* Austin, Tex., 1982.
Hassrick, Peter H. *Frederic Remington.* Fort Worth, Tex., 1973.
McCracken, Harold. *Frederic Remington: Artist of the Old West.* Philadelphia and New York, 1947.
Samuels, Harold, and Peggy Samuels. *Frederic Remington: A Biography.* Garden City, N.Y., 1982.
Taft. Robert. *Artists and Illustrators of the Old West, 1850–1900.* New York, 1963.
Vorpahl, Ben Merchant. *Frederic Remington and the West: With the Eye of the Mind.* Austin, Tex., 1978.

RENDEZVOUS

Rendezvous between the Rocky Mountain fur TRAPPERS and supply trains from St. Louis were held annually between 1825 and 1840. These great trade fairs took place in some of the most remote and beautiful valleys in the Rockies. Selected because of their easy access from the fall and spring hunts, the rendezvous sites also had an abundance of water, wood, and forage.

The rendezvous began with the arrival of a caravan, laden with needed supplies for the trappers, and ended with the return of the caravan, carrying hundreds of packs of beaver pelts, back to St. Louis. As many as four hundred to five hundred men participated in the annual rendezvous, which became the binding force behind the Rocky Mountain FUR TRADE.

The rendezvous of 1825 was an innovation devised by ANDREW HENRY and WILLIAM HENRY ASHLEY. During the winter of 1821 to 1822, Henry and Ashley had formed their Henry-Ashley Fur Company in Saint Louis. Their dream was to capitalize on the fortunes that could be made on the upper Missouri River trading beaver pelts used by the fashion industry in making the popular beaver hats.

While the trans-Mississippi fur trade had begun just after the return of MERIWETHER LEWIS and WILLIAM CLARK in 1806, the industry centered around company-owned trading posts located at strategic positions along

John Edward Borein's *Free Trappers* depicts the mountain men who gathered annually for the rendezvous. *Courtesy National Cowboy Hall of Fame and Western Heritage Center.*

the Missouri River and its major tributaries. Independent trappers and hunters from various Indian tribes brought their furs to the posts to trade for a wide assortment of goods. From his early experiences as part-owner of the St. Louis Missouri Fur Company, which had been actively engaged in the trade between 1809 and 1811, Henry had learned that a company could earn larger profits by hiring its own personnel as trappers than by trading with independent trappers and Indians.

By the late summer of 1823, the company was on the brink of failure. In order to save themselves financially, Henry and Ashley devised a plan whereby their trappers would spend the winter with the friendly Crow Indians near the Wind River Mountains and participate in their winter hunts. After wintering with the Crows, company trappers pushed over South Pass in the spring of 1824 and found abundant beaver in the vast Green, Bear, and Snake river valleys. The company then planned to supply the trappers and retrieve their furs in the mountains. The partners used the Missouri River to ferry supplies to the mountain men, thus enabling the trappers to spend three hundred and sixty five days a year in the mountains.

During the rendezvous era, several legendary figures in American history arose: JEDEDIAH STRONG SMITH, JAMES (JIM) BRIDGER, JAMES CLYMAN, Davy Jackson, William Sublette, THOMAS FITZPATRICK, Osborne Russell, JOSEPH LAFAYETTE MEEK, Warren Ferris, and Daniel Potts. At Rendezvous Creek, Willow Valley, Sweet Lake, Pierre's Hole, Wind River, the Green River valley, and other sites, MOUNTAIN MEN briefly renewed their contacts with the East through letters and newspapers. There they visited with old friends who had traveled west with the fur train and perhaps even met English nobility, missionaries, scientists, artists, government officials, and businessmen, who for various reasons had traveled to the rendezvous sites.

By 1840, economic factors and a change in the fashion industry, which opted for silk rather than beaver as a material for hats, brought the rendezvous era to a close. However, the mountain men had a significant impact on the future of westward expansion. Their knowledge of the Western landscape and the Native Americans helped pave the way for the massive migrations to the West in the following decades.

—Scott Eldredge and Fred R. Gowans

SUGGESTED READING:

Berry, Don. *A Majority of Scoundrels.* New York, 1961.

Gowans, Fred R. *Rocky Mountain Rendezvous.* Layton, Utah, 1986.

Hafen, LeRoy R., ed. *The Mountain Men and the Fur Trade of the Far West.* Vol. 1. Glendale, Calif., 1965.

RENO, NEVADA

Central Pacific Railroad officials designated the town site of Reno, Nevada, in 1868. Situated along the Truckee River in western Nevada with the nearby booming COMSTOCK LODE, the most important Western gold and silver mining site, Reno became a depot for transcontinental rail service to San Francisco and points east. The Virginia and Truckee Railroad connected Reno with the Comstock's Virginia City by 1872. Known as the "tough little town on the Truckee" Reno grew with irrigated agriculture and stock enterprises in the Truckee Meadows as well as with the mines and thriving lumber industry in the nearby Sierra Nevada. The Comstock's failure after 1877 caused hardship for Reno but not catastrophe because the railroad, not mining, was Reno's economic base. By 1900, Reno, with a population of forty-five hundred, was the largest town in Nevada.

Reno prospered along with Nevada's early twentieth-century mining boom, the growth of the state university, and the development of a national IRRIGATION project in nearby Fallon. CITY GOVERNMENT emerged in time to participate in the Progressive-era reforms and to mediate the efforts of reformers in the campaigns to shut down saloons and red-light districts. The legislature outlawed GAMBLING in 1910, and prohibition came in 1918, but under the state's liberal DIVORCE law, Reno continued as the divorce capital of the nation. By 1923, Reno city government fell into the hands of those committed to making it a wide-open town during the decade of the speakeasy. By 1931, at the beginning of the Great Depression, the state made gambling legal again, and Reno openly embraced vice, plus a new six-week-divorce and instant-marriage service, as its economic mainstays. Legal PROSTITUTION remained a fixture in the city until World War II. Gambling boomed with the growth of Harolds Club and Harrah's in downtown Reno.

State "freeport" legislation that protected the warehousing industry aided Reno in becoming a point of reshipment of goods throughout the West. Dramatic growth occurred in the 1970s with the introduction of corporate gambling that enabled out-of-state corporations to invest in Nevada gaming. Growth brought environmental problems to the city, however, as it struggled to maintain adequate sources of water and other city services.

—William D. Rowley

SUGGESTED READING:

Elliott, Russell R. *History of Nevada.* Lincoln, Nebr., 1987.

Rowley, William D. *Reno: Hub of the Washoe Country.* Woodland Hills, Calif., 1985.

REORGANIZED CHURCH OF JESUS CHRIST OF LATTER-DAY SAINTS

SEE: Church of Jesus Christ of Latter-Day Saints, Reorganized

REPORT ON THE LANDS OF ARID REGIONS

In April 1878, JOHN WESLEY POWELL, director of the United States Geographical and Geological Survey of the Rocky Mountain Region, gave to Secretary of the Interior CARL SCHURZ his *Report on the Lands of Arid Regions of the United States, with a More Detailed Account of the Land of Utah*, a radical reform agenda for settling the West. The laws and techniques people used in the humid and subhumid lands, Powell believed, bore little relevance to arid regions, and to continue those practices would bring failed settlements and environmental ruin.

Powell called for completely new federal land policies to meet the challenge of settling the arid West. First, he proposed unifying the four separate geological and geographical surveys of the time under one agency and eliminating the land office and contract surveying. Next, he called for replacing the HOMESTEAD ACT OF 1862 and its provisions for 160-acre farms with regional river-basin planning. The government would classify the land according to function: grazing, timber, or IRRIGATION. People could gain entry to the land only after it had been classified. Farmers could acquire 80 acres for irrigation; ranchers could secure 2,560 acres for pasturage; and timber companies could harvest forests. The people populating the basin regions would cooperatively devise the guidelines for the conservation and use of the most important resource determining their success—WATER.

Author of the *Report on the Lands of Arid Regions*, John Wesley Powell, pictured at camp on an expedition in 1871. *Courtesy National Archives.*

On his own, Powell took the responsibility for writing the report and giving it to Secretary Schurz. The DESERT LAND ACT OF 1877 prompted Powell to complete his report. Powell thought that Congress had made the West susceptible to the machinations of land monopolists with the act and had opened easily damaged soils to ill-advised farming and ranching practices. He believed he had a viable alternative, which was included in his report.

The effects of Powell's ideas were immediate. The prestigious National Academy of Sciences considered the report and recommended that Congress pass the reforms outlined in it. Congressional dickering, however, led to only the consolidation of the four surveys into the UNITED STATES GEOLOGICAL SURVEY. Powell had too many powerful political enemies who still used, for their own business and political purposes, the myth of the unaided individual homesteader bringing civilization and progress to a barren wilderness. Over time, however, regional approaches did become a part of the water-development programs conducted by the BUREAU OF RECLAMATION and the UNITED STATES ARMY CORPS OF ENGINEERS. The elimination of the Land Commission and a regional approach to pasturage and soil conservation came in the TAYLOR GRAZING ACT of 1934 and the Soil Conservation Act of 1935.

Powell's message influenced many Westerners, politicians, and conservationists, such as Stuart Udall and David Brower. Noted writers, such as FREDERICK JACKSON TURNER, WALTER PRESCOTT WEBB, and WALLACE STEGNER, have born the indelible imprint of Powell's thinking. His ideas, if not his reforms, continue to live on.

—*James E. Sherow*

SEE ALSO: Land Policy; Soil Conservation Service

SUGGESTED READING:

Darrah, William C. *Powell of the Colorado*. Princeton, N.J., 1951.

Stegner, Wallace. *Beyond the Hundredth Meridian: John Wesley Powell and the Second Opening of the West*. Boston, 1953.

RESTAURANTS

Early Western travelers and immigrants found the region's food to be monotonous, expensive, and tainted.

A few quality restaurants existed in urban centers such as Denver and San Francisco. More typical, however, were stage stops, tent kitchens in mining camps, lunch stands in cow towns, and saloons. The usual fare consisted of "the four Bs": biscuits, beans, beef, and bacon.

There was no refrigeration unless a town had ice houses. Restaurateurs preserved meat by salting or jerking (drying) it. Bread consisted of bland biscuits made from lard and flour, the latter often infested with insects and containing pieces of grindstone. The absence of fresh vegetables and fruit in some locations resulted in outbreaks of scurvy. Although tinned (canned) fruits and vegetables were available after 1850, they were so expensive that most restaurants could not afford to serve them.

After the Civil War, most urban restaurants were in saloons, hotels, or railroad stations. The saloon was the home of the "free lunch," one of the legends of the American West. To encourage business, saloon owners provided food free to patrons who purchased drinks. In better establishments, customers found fresh oysters, cabbage, slices of porterhouse steak, pastries, chicken, ham and roast pork, turkey, celery, salads, pickled tripe, Swiss cheese, herring, bologna, fish, and stews. Lower-class establishments served stale potato salad, nearly spoiled sardines, heavily salted pickles, and cold cuts. Foods were heavily salted to induce customers to buy more drinks. A counterman posted near serving tables prevented vagrants from helping themselves.

The free lunch was important because the average wage earner brought home less than two dollars per day; meals in boarding houses and hotels cost five to eight dollars a week.

Hotel restaurants ranged from primitive to elegant, depending on the town and clientele. The best establishments in California and Colorado imported European chefs who prepared French and English fare with sauces, fresh vegetables, desserts, and fine wines. They set tables with Irish linen tablecloths and imported china, crystal, and silver. Almost every sizable Western town had at least one hotel aspiring to such a level of service. Successful hotels employed hunters and fishermen who kept their larders stocked with venison, prairie chickens, turkeys, trout, salmon, and exotic meats such as bear. Local farmers delivered vegetables and fruits in season, and farm wives preserved and pickled foodstuffs for sale to restaurants in winter.

Hotel restaurants commonly served steak and chickens, cut vegetables, potatoes, breads, and pies. Several nineteenth-century travel writers noted that the emphasis was on quantity, not quality. Westerners seemed to care less about what they ate than about how much they ate. They masked shortcomings with condiments like mustard, pepper, and Worcestershire sauce.

The English Kitchen, a restaurant on Broadway in Round Pond, Oklahoma, sold meals for twenty cents each in 1894. Photograph by Kennett. *Courtesy National Archives.*

Railroad travel presented few opportunities for fine dining. Vendors on some trains sold boiled eggs, crackers, and stale sandwiches in the days before dining cars. Many passengers carried their own baskets of cheese, tinned meat, and hard bread rather than relying on the poor offerings of track-side eateries.

Railroads scheduled three thirty-minute stops per day so that travelers could dine. Runners met passengers at the trains, banged gongs, waved signs, and all but dragged passengers into adjoining dining houses. The establishments served often unsanitary meals at fifty cents to a dollar each. Tales abound of dishonest conductors who sounded the "all aboard" just as customers began to eat so that restaurant proprietors could serve the same meals over and over. Even the honest railroad restaurants served a monotonous menu of pork chops, beefsteak, green peas, sliced potatoes, and pies.

The quality of Western restaurants improved dramatically after 1876 when Ford Ferguson Harvey opened a string of first-class diners and hotels along the route of the Atchison, Topeka, and Santa Fe Railroad. Harvey Houses became synonymous with quality food and fair prices.

—*Byron A. Johnson*

SEE ALSO: Harvey Girls

SUGGESTED READING:

Conlin, Joseph R. *Bacon, Beans, and Galantines.* Reno and Las Vegas, Nev., 1986.

Johnson, Byron A., and Sharon Peregrine Johnson. *The Wild West Bartender's Guide.* Austin, Tex., 1986.
Van Orman, Richard A. *A Room for the Night.* New York, 1966.

RHODES, EUGENE MANLOVE

Western fiction writer Eugene Manlove Rhodes (1869–1934) was born in Tecumseh, Nebraska. In 1882, he moved to Engle, New Mexico, where he worked as a cowboy. He attended the University of the Pacific in San Jose, California, for two years. He produced a significant body of literature that was greatly influenced by his own experiences as a cowboy and rancher. His masterpiece, the novelette *Paso por Aqui,* was published in 1926. His work includes *Good Men and True, Beyond the Desert,* and six other novels. Although his experiences gave a special spirit to his work, he was sometimes criticized for being too anecdotal. Several of Rhodes's stories were later made into motion pictures.

—*Patrick H. Butler, III*

SUGGESTED READING:

Hutchinson, W. H. *A Bar Cross Man: The Life and Personal Writings of Eugene Manlove Rhodes.* Norman, Okla., 1956.

RICH, CHARLES COULSON

Mormon military leader and pioneer Charles Coulson Rich (1809–1883) was born in Kentucky and moved to Tazewell County in central Illinois in 1829. Baptized a Mormon in 1832, he undertook several proselytizing missions for the church in the Midwest and Upper South and then united with several thousand MORMONS in Caldwell County, Missouri. Plagued by anti-Mormon mobs who resented the "invasion" of the Mormons, the group formed a defense force with the resourceful Rich in command.

After the Mormons were driven out of Missouri in 1838 and moved to Illinois, Rich occasionally engaged in short proselytizing missions and was a cooper and builder. A city councilor, he became a general in the Nauvoo Legion, a branch of the state militia. He remained second in command until 1844, when Mormon leader JOSEPH SMITH, JR., was murdered by a mob. Rich held important responsibilities during the move from Illinois to the Great Basin from 1846 to 1848. In 1849, he became an ecclesiastical leader of the Salt Lake Valley Saints and a member of the Council of Twelve Apostles. He directed the allotment of land, helped distribute the scarce supply of food, fought grasshoppers and crickets, supervised the use of irrigating water, and served in the territorial legislature.

At the beginning of the California gold rush in 1848, Rich led a group to southern California to establish a center for "gathering." He and Apostle Amasa Lyman founded a colony in San Bernardino, California. Rich was elected mayor of the city; once again, he supervised the allotment of land, the distribution of water, the construction of homes, the sharing of food and implements, and the assignment of religious and temporal responsibilities. The colony was abandoned in 1858 as a result of the UTAH EXPEDITION.

In 1860, Rich was called to supervise Mormon missionaries in Europe. Shortly after his return, he was asked to establish and serve as ecclesiastical and temporal leader for settlements in Bear Lake County in present-day Utah and Idaho. He maintained friendly relations with Bannock and Eastern Shoshone Indians, founded sixteen settlements, supervised internal improvements, and adjudicated disputes. Although he lived in Idaho, he continued to serve in the Utah legislature.

—*Leonard J. Arrington*

SUGGESTED READING:

Arrington, Leonard J. *Charles C. Rich: Mormon General and Western Frontiersman.* Provo, Utah, 1974.
———. *History of Idaho.* Moscow, Idaho, 1994.
Evans, John Henry. *Charles Coulson Rich: Pioneer Builder of the West.* Salt Lake City, 1936.

RIDGE, JOHN

John Ridge (1803–1839), a leader of the Cherokee faction that favored removal to the Indian Territory in the 1830s, was born in the Cherokee settlement of Oothcaloga (near present-day Calhoun, Georgia), the second child of The Ridge and Susannah Wickett. Although The Ridge's grandfather was a Scottish trader, he was raised as a warrior and took an active part in the wars against the American settlers in the 1780s and early 1790s. He spoke no English, but in 1792, he staked out land and assumed the role of a Southern planter. John Ridge spoke only Cherokee until his father sent him and his sister in 1810 to the Moravian school at Spring Place. In 1816, the two switched to Brainerd, a school directed by Cyrus Kingsbury, a missionary of the AMERICAN BOARD OF COMMISSIONERS FOR

FOREIGN MISSIONS. Ridge proved too advanced for the curriculum, and in 1818, he followed his cousin Buck Watie, who had taken the name ELIAS BOUDINOT, to the American Board school at Cornwall, Connecticut. There, Ridge continued his education, and although he came to believe in the Christian God, he apparently did not enjoy the experience of conversion as did Boudinot. In 1821, while recuperating from a scrofulous hip that plagued him in his early years, he formed an attachment to Sarah Bird Northrup, the daughter of the school steward. Both sets of parents opposed a marriage but not with the vehemence of either the school officials or the townspeople of Cornwall. The parents relented, and after a suitable delay, Ridge and Northrup were married in 1824. Boudinot's marriage to another Cornwall girl, Harriet Gold, led to the closing of the school.

Back in Cherokee county, Ridge established his family on his father's land at Ridge's Ferry on the Oostanaula and then on land, including a ferry over the Coosa, that he purchased from the estate of Path Killer. He owned five hundred acres and eventually twenty-four slaves. Ridge and his wife had seven children: John Rollin, Clarinda, Susan, Flora, Herman, Aeneas, and Andrew Jackson.

At that point in his life, Ridge strongly favored the acculturation of Indians and the preservation of the tribal domain, but he opposed the removal of the Southeastern tribes to the West. His first foray into public affairs was as adviser to the Creeks. Among his own people, he joined his cousin Boudinot in forming the Moral and Literary Society of the Cherokee Nation (1824), took an active part in the affairs of the Cherokee *Phoenix* (1828), and became clerk of the Cherokee National Council (1829) and president of the National Committee (1830), the administrative body of the tribe.

With Georgia's decision to extend its laws over the Cherokee country and the passage by Congress of the Removal Act in 1830, the Cherokee situation reached a crisis. During one of many meetings with federal authorities in Washington, D.C., in the spring of 1832, Ridge, his father, Boudinot, and Stand Watie (Boudinot's brother) began to revise their views of Cherokee strategy. They soon concluded that the only hope of maintaining the integrity of the Cherokee nation and continuing the move toward civilization was to accept the government's offer to exchange lands in the East for territory in the West. The decision set Ridge and his colleagues squarely against the Cherokee government led by JOHN ROSS and the overwhelming majority of the Cherokee people.

The Ridges formed a faction in favor of removal and broke with the Ross group, which controlled Cherokee public affairs and continued to oppose any change in the location of the tribe. With the Georgia authorities determined to displace the Indians and the refusal of the federal authorities to afford any protection, the Cherokee situation became desperate. The Ridge faction broke the stalemate by enrolling for removal, accepting temporary protection for their property from the Georgia government, and agreeing to meet President ANDREW JACKSON's representative, John F. Schermerhorn, at New Echota for the purpose of signing a treaty. The Cherokee leadership under Ross had already rejected a treaty and had made the tribe's position clear in Washington. The Ridge faction signed the treaty of New Echota on December 29, 1835. (Ridge put his signature to the document in Washington). It was ratified by the Senate on May 12, 1836, by a margin of one vote.

In the fall of 1837, the Ridges and their followers moved to the Indian Territory and settled near Honey Creek. On June 22, 1839, Ridge was murdered in retribution for his stand on removal. Elias Boudinot and The Ridge were killed on the same day.

The Ridges represented the aspiring reformist party among the Cherokees, determined simultaneously to adopt American culture and to retain the unity of Cherokee society. Although the Cherokees shared the cause of tribal unity, they were on the whole reluctant to change their ways and determined to oppose removal.

—*Bernard W. Sheehan*

SEE ALSO: Native American Peoples: Peoples Removed from the East

SUGGESTED READING:

McLoughlin, William C. *Cherokees and Missionaries.* New Haven, Conn., 1984.

———. *Cherokee Renascence in the New Republic.* Princeton, N.J., 1986.

Moulton, Gary E. *John Ross: Cherokee Chief.* Athens, Ga., 1978.

Perdue, Theda, ed. *Cherokee Editor.* Knoxville, Tenn., 1983.

Satz, Ronald N. *American Indian Policy in the Jacksonian Era.* Lincoln, Nebr., 1975.

Wilkins, Thurman. *Cherokee Tragedy: The Ridge Family and the Decimation of the People.* 2d ed. Norman, Okla., 1986.

RIEL, LOUIS DAVID

Sometimes called the "Métis Messiah," Louis David Riel (1844–1885) was the leader of the MÉTIS PEOPLE

of western Canada. Riel's father, also named Louis, had organized a brief rebellion against HUDSON'S BAY COMPANY rule over the Red River Settlement (present-day Manitoba) in 1849 when the boy was not yet five years old, and he grew up surrounded by anti-English, anti-Canadian sentiments. Sent to study for the priesthood in Montreal, the youthful Riel there first showed evidence of the moody, distracted, and quarrelsome personality that would seem to the Métis messianic but would lead the Canadian government to confine him for a while in mental asylums in Quebec. Possibly distraught over the death of his father, Riel gave up the priesthood; scorned by the white parents of his lover when he proposed marriage, Riel returned to the West.

In 1869, the Hudson's Bay Company turned over Rupert's Land, the company's vast holdings in the Canadian West, to the British Crown. When the government launched a survey as the first step in transferring those lands to Canadian jurisdiction, the Métis at Red River reacted with fear and anger. Generally of mixed French and Indian ancestry, the Métis believed, with good cause, that neither their land rights nor the separate culture they had developed over centuries would be respected by the English-speaking Canadians. Given his father's status, Riel quickly became the Métis spokesman after he stood firm against a party of surveyors who were trying to enter the settlement. Under his leadership, the Red River people established the Comité National des Métis, which blocked the region's new Canadian governor, William MacDougal, from entering the territory and seized nearby Fort Garry.

The six thousand Métis turned for help to local English-speaking settlers, four thousand of them also "mixed bloods" with Scottish or English fathers or grandfathers and often lumped together with the Métis by white Canadians as *bois brulé,* or "scorched wood." Since the mixed-blood settlers, too, were leery of the Canadians, they joined with the Métis in a provisional government headed by Riel. In 1870, the Red River settlement negotiated with the Canadian government to become the province of Manitoba. Although both parties came to terms, the agreement was shattered when the rebellious Métis court-martialed and executed some local sympathizers with the Canadian cause for bearing arms against the state. One of them—an obscure Irishman named Thomas Scott who had threatened to kill Riel—became a martyr for white Canadians. Canada's government in Ottawa responded by denying the rebel Métis amnesty, and the rebels fled to Métis settlements on the Saskatchewan River. Riel also fled and ensconced himself in Fort Garry when Ottawa sent Colonel Garnet Wolseley in August to "maintain order" in Manitoba.

In the new province's parliamentary elections of 1873, Riel was elected Manitoba's representative. Denied his seat, he was reelected in 1874, and again the government declined to let him take office. The following year, Riel was banished from all of Canada; between 1876 and 1878 he was thrown into a Quebec mental institution. After he was released, he headed south to Montana, became an American citizen, and began calling himself David—rather that Louis—Riel.

Back in Canada, four members of the Thomas Scott jury were murdered and another was beaten within an inch of his life and left for dead just across the border in the United States. Métis land was appropriated; Métis people were harassed and scorned by white Canadians arriving in the new Canadian West.

Riel had been teaching at a Jesuit mission school near Sun River for several years when the Métis in Saskatchewan appealed to him to return to Canada in 1884 to help them fight off the growing number of English settlers and the Canadian Pacific Railroad, which ominously had begun to survey their lands. Hailed as a Messiah, the perhaps mentally unstable Riel refused all compromise with the Canadians. Turning his back on Canada's legal channels of redress and protest, Riel deliberately provoked Canadian authorities. Growing increasingly suspicious of those around him, including some of his oldest friends, Riel broke with the Catholic Church in the spring of 1885, declared a new Métis provincial government, and enlisted local Indians in his fight against the whites. In March, he defeated a force of NORTH WEST MOUNTED POLICE and attacked settlers along Frog Creek. Canada sent its army out after Riel and defeated the Métis guerrillas at Bartoche on May 12, 1885.

Tried for treason at Regina, Riel refused to plead insanity before an English-speaking jury as his lawyers recommended. The jury found him guilty and sentenced him to hang. After a number of postponements, the government carried out the execution on November 6, 1885, and Riel's death became a national scandal. For the Métis, and for French-speaking Canadians in general, Riel remained a martyred hero, although English-speaking Canadians continued mostly to consider him a madman. Both attitudes remained common even in the late twentieth century, when cultural tension present a century before continued to mar relations among Canada's ethnic groups.

—*Charles Phillips*

SUGGESTED READING:

Giraud, Marcel. *The Métis in the Canadian West.* Trans. by George Woodcock. 2 vols. Lincoln, Nebr., 1986.

Howard, Joseph Kinsey. *Strange Empire: Louis Riel and the Métis People.* Toronto, Ont., 1952. Reprint, 1974.

Sealey, D. Bruce, and Antoine S. Lussier. *The Métis: Canada's Forgotten People.* Winnipeg, Manitoba, 1975.

RIFLES

SEE: Firearms

RIGDON, SIDNEY

A Mormon leader prominent in the days before the Latter-day Saints trekked to Salt Lake City in the late 1840s, Sidney Rigdon (1793–1876) was believed by some to be the true author of the BOOK OF MORMON. Born in Allegheny County, Pennsylvania, Rigdon became a Baptist minister at age twenty-six after a spotty education. In 1819, he moved to Ohio where he soon accepted the millenarian doctrines of the CAMPBELLITES. In November 1830, persuaded by the witness of his friend Parley P. Pratt, Rigdon underwent yet another conversion, this time to Mormonism.

A number of non-Mormon historians have claimed that Rigdon cribbed ideas from a novel by Solomon Spaulding and recast them in a new form. Supposedly JOSEPH SMITH, JR., the founder of the Mormon faith, with Rigdon's help then palmed the plagiarized work off as the Book of Mormon. Other scholars and Mormon historians dismiss the charge as unfounded and as an anti-Mormon slander. Certainly Rigdon grew close to Smith after the former's conversion, and he played a major role in early Mormon history. Although neither man knew Hebrew, Greek, or Latin, both waxed enthusiastic over Smith's plan to create a Mormon translation of the Bible. Rigdon preached the faith widely, promoted Mormonism in exhaustive writings, and helped construct the church's hierarchy. He became first counselor to Joseph Smith before the MORMONS moved from Kirtland, Ohio, to Missouri in 1831.

A determined—some said stubborn—man, Rigdon was given to sudden bursts of anger, to visions, to faith healing, and to speaking in tongues. Some scholars have suggested that he may have been epileptic, since there are descriptions of trances in which he frothed at the mouth. He was evidently a talented speaker, although Smith would later accuse him of being less than faithful to the truth. Without question, he had a major impact on early Mormon theology, perhaps through the "Lectures on Faith" (which—though attributed officially to Smith—most scholars assume he wrote) and certainly through the many habits and beliefs he had picked up as a Campbellite and imported into Mormonism. They include, for example, the emphasis on faith, repentance, baptism, the gift of the Holy Ghost, the restoration of the true word of God, and the coming of the millennium. A proponent of primitive communism, Rigdon influenced the Mormons' communal social experiments, which the Saints, in large measure, ultimately abandoned.

When conflict developed between Smith's followers and Missouri's non-Mormons in 1838, Rigdon was among those imprisoned with the Mormon leader and sentenced to hang. After militia General ALEXANDER WILLIAM DONIPHAN, who had negotiated Smith's surrender, refused to carry out the execution ordered by the subsequent court-martial, Rigdon was freed and made his way east. Arriving in Quincy, Illinois, an exhausted and disheartened Rigdon reluctantly surrendered to Smith's admonishments to join him in the new Mormon Zion at NAUVOO, ILLINOIS. There Rigdon and Smith experienced a parting of the ways, although Rigdon remained prominent in the community as a city councilman, the local postmaster, and church historian. Smith grew ever more certain that Rigdon was plotting against him, especially after Rigdon refused to accept the secret practice of polygamy, which Smith introduced to the Mormon inner circle in the early 1840s. The two men may well have fallen out over Rigdon's daughter Nancy, who heatedly rejected Smith's suggestion that she become one of his wives. Curiously enough, when Smith launched a campaign to become president of the United States in 1844, he chose Rigdon as his running mate, although by then their mutual disenchantment was public knowledge in Nauvoo.

Using the campaign as an excuse, Rigdon fled Nauvoo in June 1844 and planned never to return. But Smith's assassination later that year changed his mind, and he came back hoping to take charge of the church, an ambition quickly dashed by BRIGHAM YOUNG and other apostles. Instead of becoming the Mormon's "guardian," Rigdon was excommunicated on September 8, 1844. Claiming that Smith's successors were destroying the true church, Rigdon led a small group of like-minded Mormons to Pittsburgh, where he formed a new organization, the Church of Christ, and disavowed the Western Mormons. Declaring himself a seer and prophet in the mold of Joseph Smith, Rigdon predicted the fall of Nauvoo. Over the years, however, membership in the new sect declined until it had all but disappeared, and Rigdon lived out his last days in rural New York.

—*Patricia Hogan*

SEE ALSO: Church of Jesus Christ of the Latter-day Saints; Polygamy: Polygamy Among Mormons

RILEY, JAMES M.

SEE: Middleton, "Doc"

RINGO, JOHN PETERS

Outlaw John Ringo (1850–1882) was born in Greenfork, Indiana. He joined his family on a wagon train headed for California in 1864. In Wyoming, his father, Martin Ringo, accidentally killed himself. The rest of the family continued on to San Jose, California. In 1869, young Ringo went to Texas, where he was caught up in Mason County's "Hoodoo War." He joined a rustler gang led by Scott Cooley and was involved in two murders.

In 1879 in Safford, Arizona, Ringo tried to kill gambler Louis Hancock over a drink. This incident and the two Texas killings are the only recorded instances of gunplay by Ringo.

In southeastern Arizona, Ringo joined the "CURLY" BILL BROCIUS–Old Man Clanton rustler gang, whose members ruled Cochise County, rustled Mexican cattle, and sold them in Arizona. When Wyatt Earp, his brothers Virgil and Morgan, and JOHN HENRY ("DOC") HOLLIDAY arrived in Tombstone, the line was drawn between the law and order element and the outlaws. The result was the celebrated gunfight at O.K. Corral on October 6, 1881. Ringo did not participate in the shoot-out. He committed suicide near Tombstone the following summer.

—*Jack Burrows*

Rio Grande.

SEE ALSO: Earp Brothers; O.K. Corral, gunfight at

SUGGESTED READING:

Burrows, Jack. *John Ringo: The Gunfighter Who Never Was.* Tucson, Ariz., 1987.

The Journal of Mrs. Mary Ringo. (Privately printed by Frank Myrle Cushing.) Santa Ana, Calif., 1956.

RIO GRANDE

The fifth longest river in North America, the Rio Grande, "the great river," flows through a semiarid region and drains approximately 172,000 square miles, an area smaller than its length would suggest. At least half of its drainage is in Mexico. From its beginnings at more than 12,500 feet near Stony Pass in the snow-covered peaks of the San Juan Mountains in southwestern Colorado, it flows first eastward from the Continental Divide, passes through the broad, high desert terrain of the San Luis Valley, and begins its southern course just east of Alamosa, Colorado. Beyond the Colorado–New Mexico boundary, the river enters a deep and narrow canyon through which it flows for a hundred miles before it enters that broad valley that is so significant in the history of New Mexico. It reaches the Gulf of Mexico at Brownsville, Texas. The primary tributaries of the eighteen-hundred-mile long river are the Pecos, Devils, Chama, and Puerco rivers in the United States and the Salado, San Juan, and Conchos rivers in Mexico.

The Rio Grande was the first major Western river discovered by Europeans, and in 1598, JUAN DE OÑATE gave it its name. Spanish colonization of New Mexico indelibly engraved the imprint of Hispanic culture along the banks of the Rio Grande. American penetration of the region did not occur until the early decades of the nineteenth century. Mountain men at Taos initiated the exploitation of animal resources and trade, but those activities did not lead to substantial settlement. While ZEBULON MONTGOMERY PIKE's 1806 expedition provided the United States with some knowledge of the potential of the region, it was not until the conclusion of the war with Mexico, that this land was incorporated in the United States and substantial American settlement occurred. The development of the SANTA FE AND CHIHUAHUA TRAIL stimulated economic growth in the region. As established by the International Boundary Commission in 1854, for thirteen hundred miles, the river serves as the international boundary between the United States and Mexico

From its headwaters to the gulf, the Rio Grande nourishes agriculture, which is practiced along its banks irregularly. In New Mexico, Pueblo tribes and their

ancestors have used the Rio Grande for irrigation for more than a millennium. Irrigation grew rapidly from 1850 until 1880 when it reached its peak. Although the river appears not have enough water to meet the constant demands on it, it has still been subject to flooding. Between 1882 and 1962, sixteen major floods devastated life and agriculture along its banks. Efforts were made to address this problem. In 1915, Elephant Butte Reservoir near Truth or Consequences, New Mexico, was completed to lessen the dangers of flooding and to provide water for seasonal irrigation. Much of the region through which the Rio Grande flows receives less than fifteen inches of rain a year. In this sun-baked domain, water is always at a premium and demands on water resources are extensive and subject to intense debate and litigation between two nations and among three American and four Mexican states. Navigation is restricted to only the lowest reaches of the river.

—Phillip Drennon Thomas

SUGGESTED READING:

Fergusson, Harvey. *Rio Grande.* New York, 1945.
Gilpin, Laura. *The Rio Grande, River of Destiny.* New York, 1949.
Horgan, Paul. *Great River, The Rio Grande in North American History.* New York, 1954.

RIPLEY, EDWARD PAYSON

One of the more successful Western railroad executives, Edward Payson Ripley (1845–1920) resurrected the bankrupt and nearly defunct Santa Fe Railroad. Born in Dorchester, Massachusetts, Ripley was trained as a lawyer. He entered the railroad business as the New England agent for a number of Western lines. He performed so well in this capacity that he was hired by the Burlington railroad system as an executive in the traffic department and became general traffic manager by 1888. He next moved to the Chicago, Milwaukee and St. Paul (later called the CHICAGO, MILWAUKEE, ST. PAUL AND PACIFIC RAILROAD, or simply the Milwaukee Road) as vice-president and served in that capacity until the turn of the century, when he was offered the presidency of the ATCHISON, TOPEKA AND SANTA FE RAILROAD.

The appointment was no plum, for the Santa Fe had barely emerged from bankruptcy in the early 1890s and had been floundering ever since. Overhauling and rebuilding the line, Ripley hammered it into one of the more efficient, prosperous, and prestigious railroads in the nation. He accomplished this in part by creatively working with government regulators and supporting the Hepburn Act of 1906, which gave the government the authority to fix maximum railroad rates in cases where carriers and shippers could not agree. Ripley believed that the act would facilitate rail expansion and promote sustained profitability. When the railroads were seeking substantial rate increases to match high levels of inflation in 1910, the Hepburn Act was brought to bear. Ripley was dismayed by what he saw as the government's intransigence. He was nominated by all of the Western railroads to represent them before the Interstate Commerce Commission, which, however, failed to grant the requested rate increases. Ripley, in effect, then threw up his hands in disgust and stepped down from his role as the railroads' emissary to the government.

—Alan Axelrod

SUGGESTED READING:

Martin, Albro. *Railroads Triumphant: The Growth, Rejection, and Rebirth of a Vital American Force.* New York, 1992.
Waters, Lawrence L. *Steel Trails to Santa Fe.* Lawrence, Kans., 1950.

RIVERMEN

Rivermen manned the varied river craft of the Ohio, Mississippi, and Missouri valleys from the time of the American Revolution through the age of the steamboat. They formed a vital element in the emerging folklore and legends of the American West.

In the tradition of Native American canoemen, rivermen along the Ohio, Mississippi, and Missouri worked the waters before and after the invention of the steamboat in 1811. On board their flatboats, keelboats, and rafts, they carried pork, flour, corn, animal skins, fruit and vegetables, whiskey, and other produce down, and sometimes up, the Western rivers. Keelboatmen manned sleek, sixty-foot-long, low-draft vessels, most of which were replaced by steamers after 1811. Some keelboatmen, however, continued to ply tributary streams and the Upper Missouri fur-trading region well into the nineteenth century. Raftsmen assembled and sailed log and lumber rafts throughout the years before the Civil War. Flatboatmen worked the fifty-foot-long, flat-bottomed, box-shaped craft whose cheapness and abundance enabled them to making a good living until their vessels were finally eclipsed by steamboats and railroads and their trade was disrupted by the Civil War. After the war, both flatboats and rafts became "tows," trailing in the wake of steamboats. Rivermen with nonsteam vessels were forced to find new work.

Most rivermen were young Ohio Valley men of predominantly English or Celtic descent (some African

Americans and Franco-Americans manned boats, and rarely, women cooks worked on river boats during the antebellum years). Some rivermen were merchant capitalists and entrepreneurs, but most were frontiersmen and farmers looking for a little adventure and a few dollars in their pockets. The invention of the steamboat revolutionized the rivermen's lives. While early boatmen were a rough, short-lived set of wanderers who braved the dangers of Indian attack and long treks home on the Natchez Trace, boatmen during the steamboat age were more sedate and settled family men, who made quick, safe flatboat trips south and then commuted home on the decks of northbound steamers. More than two hundred thousand men worked on flatboats and rafts from 1811 to 1861; indeed, boating became something of a rite of passage for young Americans of the trans-Appalachian West. While their wages surpassed those of their rural and urban contemporaries, rivermen were frequently unemployed between boat trips, and for most, boating became a temporary or part-time endeavor to supplement income from farming. When steamboats and railroads finally pushed flatboats and rafts out of business after the Civil War, some rivermen went to work on steamers; others left the profession altogether.

Although boating became more and more civilized during the steamboat age, rivermen gained a reputation as "alligator horses"—hard-drinking, straight-shooting, fighting, gambling, promiscuous, swashbuckling river rowdies plying the "Mighty Mississippi" in search of fun and adventure. Folk tales and, later, printed stories of Mike Fink, "King of the River," proliferated in the popular press. A folkloric and literary nemesis of DAVID (DAVEY) CROCKETT, Fink gained fame as a master riverman, sharpshooter, and Indian fighter in action and adventure tales that today smack of racism and violence. Meanwhile, painters such as GEORGE CALEB BINGHAM produced popular images of *The Jolly Flatboatmen,* rivermen characters appeared in plays and minstrel shows, and boatmen's songs were sung on stage. The ultimate depiction of the "alligator horse" riverman came in MARK TWAIN's *Life on the Mississippi* (1874). The riverman thus joined the scout, trapper, cowboy, and soldier as an archetypal Western folk hero embraced by industrial-age Americans nostalgic for the past.

With the decline of steamboating, rivermen retained a small but sturdy role in both American folklore and economic history. They survive today in works that range from Mark Twain's *Life on the Mississippi,* Richard Bissell's *A Stretch of the River* (1950), Walt Disney's film *Davey Crockett and the River Pirates* (1956), and the works of Nashville recording artist and towboatman John Hartford. Meanwhile, rivermen continue to ply the Ohio, Mississippi, and Missouri and their tributaries aboard diesel towboats.

—*Michael Allen*

SUGGESTED READING:

Allen, Michael. *Western Rivermen, 1763–1861: Ohio and Mississippi Boatmen and the Myth of the Alligator Horse.* Baton Rouge, La., 1990.

Baldwin, Leland D. *The Keelboat Age on Western Waters.* Pittsburgh, Pa., 1941.

Curry, Jane. *The River's in My Blood: Riverboat Pilots Tell Their Story.* Lincoln, Nebr., 1983.

Haites, Eric, James Mak, and Gary Walton. *Western River Transportation.* Baltimore, 1975.

Hunter, Louis C. *Steamboats on the Western Rivers: An Economic and Technological History.* Cambridge, Mass., 1949.

RIVER TRANSPORTATION

Three rivers figure prominently in the history of transportation in the West: the Ohio, the Mississippi, and the Missouri. The Ohio was a great highway for exploration, migration, and commerce with the trans-Appalachian West of colonial times. For many years, it was the Indian dugout that chiefly plied the Ohio. The European explorers and traders of the late seventeenth century and the early to mid-eighteenth century sailed in such vessels. By the Revolutionary War, flatboats and keelboats had replaced the canoe as the vessel of choice for commerce and the transportation of troops and materiel. A few years after the war, Pittsburgh swelled into a bustling community where westering families boarded flatboats known as "broadhorns" for the trip downriver to new homes. The broadhorns used the river not only as an artery but as an engine; the river current carried the vessels, which were dismantled when they reached their destination; the precious wood of their hulls was then used for building.

As Ohio River commerce continued to develop, Pittsburgh became the transfer point for cargo to such points as Cincinnati and Louisville. The Ohio joins the Mississippi at the southern tip of the present-day state of Illinois, and Pittsburgh cargoes were carried down the Mississippi as far as New Orleans. For the long hauls (the journey from Pittsburgh to New Orleans consumed almost two months), the flatboat was increasingly supplanted by the keelboat during the early nineteenth century. This vessel was both capacious (80 feet or so in length, with a beam of 12 feet) and, by comparison with the rude flatboat, elegant, sporting a

sharp keel, a shaped hull, and a bow and stern that were rounded. The keelboat commonly was equipped with a mast and sail. Unlike the early broadhorns, keelboats made the round trip. During the return upstream, crews used long poles to push the boat against the current. Sometimes, they grabbed hold of willow branches along the banks to tug the boat onward. In places, crews took a towline ashore and pulled the vessel along.

The 1810s saw the apogee of keelboat traffic on the Ohio and Mississippi. In 1815, there were some 300 major keelboats plying the waters carrying staple commodities, such as flour and salt, and building materials—iron and brick—west, and returning with produce and ores, including molasses, coffee, sugar, animal hides, and lead.

As early as 1787, John Fitch had demonstrated a steam-powered vessel on the Delaware River at Philadelphia, and within three years, he established the world's first steamboat passenger service, between Philadelphia and Trenton. It was not until 1807, with the spectacular demonstration of Robert Fulton's *North River Steamboat* (later renamed the *Clermont),* on the Hudson River, that the river steamboat became commercially practical. The first western steamboat was the *New Orleans,* a 138-foot-long craft with a beam of 26 feet, which sailed from 1811 to 1814 mainly on the lower Mississippi. Other steamboats followed on the Ohio and Mississippi, most notably the 400-ton, double-decked *Washington* in 1816, which set the pattern for subsequent Western steamboats: flat bottom, shallow draft, high-pressure engine, twin smokestacks on either side of a pilothouse, and a stern-mounted paddle wheel.

While steam made inroads on the Ohio and the lower Mississippi and largely replaced keelboats for passenger service by the early 1820s, human-powered vessels continued to ply the side rivers for another decade. Boatyards in Pittsburgh, Cincinnati, and Louisville (the early hub of boat-building activity) turned out about 60 vessels in 1820; by 1850, at least 740 steamboats were operating on the Ohio and Mississippi rivers. The Mississippi in particular became a royal road of commerce, its passenger vessels having evolved

The *Far West,* a Missouri River steamboat, about 1870. *Courtesy National Cowboy Hall of Fame and Western Heritage Center.*

Top: The steamer, pictured here in 1894, *Expansion* worked the Yellowstone River in Montana. *Courtesy National Archives.*

Bottom: The *Rosebud,* on the Missouri River, in 1878. *Courtesy National Archives.*

into what some have described as floating palaces and others as river-borne bordellos: four-deckers, replete with elaborate imported carpeting and furniture, offering elegantly appointed staterooms, dining rooms, gaming rooms, and even barber shops and nursery facilities. Like ocean-going ships, steamboats offered various classes of passage, ranging from an opulent first class, down to the equivalent of steerage, where immigrants, laborers, and farmers shared lower-deck space with livestock and cargo.

The upper Mississippi did not see steamboats until 1823, when the *Virginia* first went into service. By the 1830s, steamboats were plying the river between St. Louis and the lead mines of Wisconsin, and in 1858, St. Paul, Minnesota, saw more than 1,000 steamboat arrivals. During this period, however, the upper Mississippi still floated vigorous rafting traffic. Flatboats and log rafts often brought timber downstream from the North Woods to mills at Burlington and Muscatine, Iowa, and St. Louis, Missouri.

The Missouri River was dominated by keelboat commerce from the 1820s through much of the 1850s. These extremely shallow-draft vessels were well suited to the Missouri, which was shallower and muddier even than the Mississippi. Moreover, settlement during this period was generally too thin to warrant extensive investment in steamboats. Human-powered keelboats were sufficient for transporting furs downstream and trade goods up. However, in 1830, the American Fur Company built its *Yellowstone,* a steamboat displacing 144 tons, and by the 1850s, the lower Missouri saw a lively steamboat traffic as the river towns of Independence and St. Joseph, Missouri, and Council Bluffs, Iowa, became wagon and stagecoach terminals for the overland trek to the Far West. The upper Missouri, too, was served by a few small, very shallow-draft stern-wheel "mountain boats," which plied the remote waters when spring freshets gave the water sufficient depth for passage. During the 1860s, when gold discoveries brought an army of prospectors to Montana, steamboating on the upper Missouri boomed. Cabin passengers paid an extraordinary $300 fare, and freight commanded more than twelve cents per pound. The river was treacherous—replete with shoals and snags—and the fragile vessels themselves were subject to the ever-present plague of river steamboating, devastating boiler explosion. Few upper Missouri steamboats lasted more than three years. In any event, between 1870 and 1885, the advancing Northern Pacific Railroad eclipsed steamboat commerce on the upper river.

The reign of the palatial steamboats of the Mississippi was interrupted by the general river blockade during the Civil War, and by the time the war was over, railroads were making vast inroads into the river-borne commerce. Two decades after the war, the golden age of the Mississippi and Missouri steamboat was at an end. By the beginning of the twentieth century, it was virtually dead. A bulk-shipping commerce developed on the Mississippi, however, and continues to this day, carried in great barges—often several lashed together—and pulled by diesel towboats.

—*Alan Axelrod*

SUGGESTED READING:

Hunter, Louis C. *Steamboats on the Western Rivers: An Economic and Technological History.* Cambridge, Mass., 1949.

Lass, William E. *A History of Steamboating on the Upper Missouri River.* Lincoln, Nebr., 1962.

MacMullen, Jerry. *Paddle Wheel Days in California.* Palo Alto, Calif., 1944.

ROADS AND HIGHWAYS

The federal government's involvement in road building began as early as 1802, when the enabling act for the admission of Ohio into the Union provided for 5 percent of the income from the sale of public land to be used for opening and constructing roads to and in the new state. The accumulated funds were used to survey a national road from Cumberland, Maryland, to Wheeling, Virginia, on the Ohio River. The UNITED STATES ARMY CORPS OF ENGINEERS and later the CORPS OF TOPOGRAPHICAL ENGINEERS were placed in charge of surveys and construction. Future enabling acts provided funds for constructing roads, ostensibly for military purposes, but also used extensively by Western pioneers.

The historical Western trails were in no way roads in the modern sense. Pioneers headed for the Great Basin, Oregon, and California initially followed the river valleys. Settlers traveling in wagon trains sought the lowest mountain passes in the Rockies and Sierra Nevada, established traces, eliminated obstacles in their paths, and marked trails. Both the Pacific Wagon Road program and the railroad surveys of the 1850s were attempts by the federal government to shorten and improve these routes.

Military roads were extensively constructed in the territories west of the Mississippi River. One road ran from Fort Snelling, Minnesota, to Fort Bent, Colorado; a second from Fort Smith, Arkansas, to Albuquerque, New Mexico, and on to the Colorado River; and another from San Antonio toward San Diego.

In the 1850s, Western settlers, primarily on the Pacific Slope, became impatient with the inactivity of the federal government in improving transportation and communication. Following the railroad surveys, politicians could not agree on the location of the first transcontinental railroad. Moreover, the army engineers were thought to be too slow and thorough in making surveys. In response to a petition from Californians demanding action, Congress established the Pacific Wagon Road Office to survey and construct roads located, in general, along routes already surveyed and used. Congress placed the program in the hands of civilian road builders rather than under army supervision. One route ran from Fort Snelling, Minnesota, to South Pass and connected with a central route from Fort Kearny to the California border. A southern route ran from El Paso to Fort Yuma. In general, the program was a disappointment largely because political appointees proved incompetent and engaged in fraud.

The army established FORTS throughout the West along the various routes the emigrants used. In 1861, the federal government established the Emigrant Escort Service to ensure protection in isolated areas. One of the more extensively used military roads was constructed by Lieutenant John Mullan from Fort Walla Walla on the Columbia River across the Continental Divide to the head of navigation on the Missouri River in the Montana Territory. The road was completed just in time to be used by the gold-seekers rushing into the Pacific Northwest. The Topographical Engineers made plans to build along the BOZEMAN TRAIL, but Indian opposition forced its abandonment.

By 1890, lands distant from the transcontinental railroads had been settled, and farmers demanded roads that could be traveled all year to the nearest railroad junction. During that period, bicycle use became a fad. Local organizations of bicyclists formed the League of American Wheelmen in 1880 and began a campaign to improve roads. Farmers and bicyclists joined forces

Top: Construction workers on a military road from Fort Washakie to Buffalo Fork in the Wyoming Territory, 1898. *Courtesy National Archives.*

Bottom: The overland stage road between Ogden and Helena "crossing the Beaver Head River . . . by means of a plank bridge." Photograph by Jackson, 1871. *Courtesy National Archives.*

to established the National League for Good Roads in 1892 and, shortly thereafter, the National Good Roads Association. The federal government then established the Office of Road Inquiry in the Department of Agriculture to study the various methods of making roads, to publish information, and to construct pilot projects. Two million miles of rural highways were constructed in the United States in the 1890s. Most were dirt roads, but approximately one hundred thousand miles had surfaces of gravel or crushed stone that could be used year-round. States soon began to give financial assistance to counties and local efforts at road building.

The introduction of the first gasoline automobile in 1893 made the expansion and improvement of roads imperative. By 1900, there were eight thousand automobiles in the United States, and by 1925, there were twenty-four million motor vehicles on the nation's roads and streets. Thirty-eight states were involved in the planning, construction, and maintenance of highways between 1900 and 1915. In 1916, Congress passed the Federal Aid Road Act to provide funds to states that established a program considered effective by the federal government. Appropriations were distributed among the states on the basis of their comparative areas, populations, and mileage of rural mail routes. The states were expected to make surveys, plan improvements, and supervise construction. The Bureau of Public Roads in the Department of Commerce acted for the federal government. In 1921, a system evolved whereby state roads were welded into a national network.

During World War I, the value of motor-truck transportation was recognized. In subsequent decades, transportation of equipment and supplies throughout the American West by motor truck was integrated with the railway network, and roads and highways were expanded and improved to carry the heavy loads.

TOURISM was initially encouraged by railroad owners who developed resorts near the scenic wonders on their lines. The railroads extended branch lines to many of the national parks and constructed resort hotels. During the 1920s, the use of the passenger car was transformed from a Sunday afternoon recreational activity to long-distance travel for weekend relaxation and vacations. Railroad resorts began to lose their patrons with the widespread use of automobiles for long-distance travel. Highways and roads soon led to national parks, dude ranches, historical places, and wilderness areas. Following the opening of the national parks to automobiles in 1913, visitors increased enormously: from 199,000 in 1910 to 920,000 in 1920 and 2,775,000 in 1930.

By 1930, the automobile had become a business necessity. As speeds increased and trucks became bigger and carried heavier loads, highways had to be rebuilt to provide more durable surfaces and multiple lanes. Around congested urban communities, the tremendous volume of traffic necessitated the establishment of expressways and parkways. Entrances and exits were provided only at specific places, and high ways were divided by strips or barriers to separate cars going in opposite directions. Nowhere was the modern highway more important than in the trans-Mississippi West where great distances had to be traversed. The modern economy of the American West was totally dependent on improved communication and transportation.

—*W. Turrentine Jackson*

SEE ALSO: Transcontinental Railroad Surveys

SUGGESTED READING:

Gregory, John W. *The Story of the Road from the Beginning to the Present Day.* London, 1938.

Hill, Forest G. *Roads, Rails, and Waterways.* Norman, Okla., 1957.

Jackson, W. Turrentine. *Wagon Roads West.* Berkeley and Los Angeles, 1952.

Labatut, Jean, and Wheaton J. Lane. *Highways in Our National Life.* Princeton, N.J., 1950.

Winther, Oscar O. *The Transportation Frontier.* New York, 1964.

ROBERTS, BRIGHAM HENRY

Brigham Henry Roberts (1857–1933) was a journalist and newspaper editor before becoming a high official in the CHURCH OF JESUS CHRIST OF LATTER-DAY SAINTS. He published extensively on church history and theology, led church missionary efforts, and became a controversial figure in local and national politics. He was father of fifteen children by three plural wives.

Born in the manufacturing town of Warrington, Lancashire, England, Roberts migrated to the United States in 1866 to join his mother, who had left her husband after converting to the Mormon faith. He grew up in Davis County, north of Salt Lake City. While working as an apprentice blacksmith, he attended the Deseret University (now the University of Utah). After graduating with teaching credentials in 1878, he worked at teaching and blacksmithing for a time. He eventually turned to journalism and became the editor of the *Salt Lake Herald.*

Roberts was ordained a Seventy (a Mormon priesthood office then charged with missionary work) in

1877, and from 1880 to 1882, he worked as a missionary in Iowa, Nebraska, and Tennessee. In early 1883, he was appointed to preside over the Southern states mission, where he remained until the end of 1884. In 1886, he was sent to England to escape prosecution under federal antipolygamy laws. There he worked as assistant editor of the *Millennial Star.* He returned to the United States in 1888 and was appointed to a leading quorum in the Latter-day Saints hierarchy, called the First Council of Seventy.

In 1889, Roberts was convicted and imprisoned for four months for polygamy. Shortly after his release, he became active in organizing the Democratic party in Utah and served in the state's constitutional convention. He lost a bid for the U.S. Congress in 1895 but won in 1898, only to be denied his seat by the U.S. House of Representatives because he continued to live with his plural wives and children.

Roberts is perhaps best remembered for the scholarly work he did after the turn of the century. In 1909, he began publishing in the *Americana* a history of the Mormon church that ran monthly until 1915. The whole work was published in 1930 in six volumes as *A Comprehensive History of the Church of Jesus Christ of Latter-day Saints* and remains in print as a valuable reference resource.

It is perhaps due to the unflinching integrity in Roberts' work that liberal Mormon scholars claim he seriously questioned the traditional story of the origins of Mormonism. More conservative scholars present persuasive evidence that he carefully scrutinized all attacks on the traditional story in order to refute them and died a believing and committed member of the faith. He was, without question, a pioneer in scholarly historical study of Mormonism.

—Dean L. May

SUGGESTED READING:

Madsen, Truman G. *Defender of the Faith: The B. H. Roberts Story.* Salt Lake City, 1980.

Malan, Robert H. *B. H. Roberts: A Biography.* Salt Lake City, 1966.

Roberts, B. H. *The Autobiography of B. H. Roberts.* Salt Lake City, 1990.

ROBERTSON, ALICE MARY

Educator, businesswoman, and politician Alice Mary Robertson (1854–1931) was born into a family of distinguished Presbyterian missionaries at Tullahassee Mission in the Indian Territory. Her grandfather, Samuel Austin Worcester, and her mother, Ann Eliza Worcester Robertson, had translated the Bible into the Cherokee and Creek languages.

Robertson attended Elmira College in New York for two years before financial need forced her to accept clerical positions, first at the Indian Office in Washington, D.C., then as secretary to Captain RICHARD HENRY PRATT at the Indian School in Carlisle, Pennsylvania. When her father died in 1880, she returned to the Indian Territory, assumed leadership of the family, and began a successful fundraising campaign to build Nuyaka Mission School near Okmulgee, Oklahoma, for her older sister to administer. Robertson herself supervised another school, the Minerva Home for Indian girls, in Muskogee. That school, combined with others, evolved into the University of Tulsa.

At the Lake Mohonk Friends of the Indian conferences, Robertson developed a warm friendship with THEODORE ROOSEVELT. During the Spanish-American War, she told him of students who wanted to join the Rough Riders; she provided each volunteer with a kit of personal supplies and a Bible. Roosevelt in turn helped Robertson secure appointments as federal supervisor of Creek schools until 1905 and then postmistress of Muskogee until 1913.

Robertson also directed a successful farm in Muskogee. The produce supplied a luncheonette, which she expanded into a full-time cafeteria for businessmen. During World War I, she dispensed free coffee and snacks to servicemen and directed a Red Cross canteen, which served as a model for others in the state.

At the age of sixty-six, Robertson ran for the Second District seat to the House of Representatives; her election in 1920 made her the second women to serve in Congress. Political office was a new departure for her. Before then, she had held office in the Oklahoma Anti-Suffrage League and opposed female involvement in politics. Her tenure in Congress was highly unsuccessful. Manipulated by the conservative wing of the Republican party, she alienated her constituency by voting against major legislation on behalf of veterans, women, and children. She lost her bid for reelection in 1922. When her cafeteria business failed, she was left without any income, and for the remainder of her life, she survived on the charity of friends. The career of this educator, businesswoman, and politician shows both the public activism characteristic of unmarried women in the late nineteenth century and the fragile nature of their economic viability.

—Linda Reese

SUGGESTED READING:

Stanley, Ruth Moore. "Alice M. Robertson, Oklahoma's First Congresswoman." *The Chronicles of Oklahoma* 45 (1967): 276–278.

ROBIDOUX BROTHERS

Joseph Robidoux, III

Joseph Robidoux, III (1783–1868), a Missouri fur trader and pioneer of the Santa Fe trade, is the most important historically of four generations of that name in St. Louis. In 1799, at the age of sixteen, Joseph was engaged in trading in northwestern Missouri with the nearly extinct Missouri Indians. In 1806, on their return journey, MERIWETHER LEWIS and WILLIAM CLARK met "Mr. Robideau on his way to the Pawnees and Mahas." Joseph masterminded field operations of his family's business: while his brothers moved up the Kansas, Platte, and Upper Missouri rivers with their trade goods. Joseph's post at the Black Snake Hills became family headquarters from which bales of furs were sent downriver to St. Louis. His post later became the city of St. Joseph, Missouri.

In about 1820, a second Robidoux post was established on the Missouri River above present-day Omaha, a few miles below the original Council Bluffs. Ultimately Robidoux's "territory" went far beyond that authorized by his government trading license. In 1823, he dispatched his brothers to Santa Fe, having learned of the riches to be gained there. In 1830, his son Joseph E., traveled in a caravan up the north side of the Platte to seek a share of the rich beaver harvest first discovered and exploited by the rival Rocky Mountain Fur Company.

The city of St. Joseph and its founder and patriarch, Joseph Robidoux, prospered with the advent of the great westward migrations to Oregon and California. In 1849 and 1850, the Robidouxs had a trading post at Scotts Bluffs on the Oregon-California Trail in western Nebraska. Emigrant diaries vividly describe this last trading post in Robidoux Pass.

Antoine Robidoux

Antoine Robidoux (1794–1860), a brother of Joseph Robidoux, III, played a unique role, beginning in 1823, as a promoter of the trade centered at Taos and Santa Fe. Born in Florissant, a suburb of St. Louis, Antoine became a Mexican citizen, married the daughter of a Mexican army captain, and achieved high office in the municipal government of Santa Fe. He also led seasonal caravans along the SANTA FE AND CHIHUAHUA TRAIL and the Missouri River to Joseph's trading post below Fort Atkinson, Nebraska, and his later post in Missouri's Black Snake Hills.

Seeking to expand his trade in furs, Antoine became the earliest known American explorer of the western slope of the central Rocky Mountains. He established two trading posts, Fort Robidoux, on the Gunnison River near the mouth of the Uncomphagre River in western Colorado, and Fort Uintah in southeastern Utah.

Increasing hostilities by impoverished Indian tribes of the Great Basin and diminished returns induced Antoine to abandon both forts as well as his trading operations in Santa Fe. In 1845, he returned to Joseph Robidoux's Black Snake Hills post, which had become St. Joseph.

In 1846, Colonel STEPHEN WATTS KEARNY hired Antoine as guide and interpreter on a campaign to end Mexican rule in the Southwest and California. At the battle of San Pasqual near Los Angeles, Antoine was severely wounded by a *caballero*'s lance. After a long painful recovery in Monterey, he returned via the Isthmus of Panama and New Orleans to St. Joseph. There is evidence in diaries of travelers along the Oregon-California Trail that Antoine, however handicapped, was later one the several Robidoux family members at, or en route to, the family trading post at Scotts Bluffs, Nebraska.

Louis Robidoux

Louis Robidoux (1796–1868) achieved renown as a partner of his brother Joseph in the fur trade, as a prominent Spanish-speaking citizen and merchant in Santa Fe, and as a big rancher in southern California, where his memory is preserved by Mount Robidoux, near Riverside.

Born in Florissant, Louis traveled to Santa Fe with his brother Antoine in 1823. There he became Joseph's agent for caravans traveling both ways along the Santa Fe Trail, and he occasionally returned to his former headquarters in Missouri. He became enamored of the Southwest ambience, quickly became a Mexican citizen and, while running various enterprises, was elected to the city council. He also married a Spanish woman, Guadaloupe Garcia, and the couple had eight children. In the regional fur trade, Louis served as Antoine's agent to organize pack trains for the mountains.

After the Texas Revolution of 1836, Mexican-American relations in Sante Fe deteriorated, causing Louis, in 1848, to make the long journey to southern California. There he bought three ranches and made his residence at Rancho Jurupa on the Santa Ana river, west of Los Angeles. In 1844, he returned to Santa Fe to move his big family to the "perfect paradise."

In 1846, when American forces under Colonel Stephen Watts Kearny conquered southern California, Louis remained on the sidelines. It is not known if he subsequently learned that his brother Antoine had been severely wounded at the battle of San Pasqual. Louis

himself was threatened during a brief counterrevolt in the Los Angeles area.

While California generally enjoyed increasing prosperity under American rule, Louis's fortunes declined from "flood, drought, earthquakes, grasshoppers, Indian attacks, and costly litigation." Crippled by a fall from his horse and dreaming of his earlier great enterprises, "Don Luis" died peacefully at his ranch home and was buried nearby.

—*Merrill J. Mattes*

SUGGESTED READING:

Mattes, Merrill J. "Joseph Robidoux." In *Mountain Men and the Fur Trade of the Far West.* Vol 8. Edited by LeRoy Hafen. Glendale, Calif., 1971.

———. "Joseph Robidoux's Family: Fur Traders and Trail Blazers." *Overland Journal* 6:3 (1988).

———. "Robidoux's Trading Post at Scotts Bluffs, and the California Gold Rush." *Nebraska History* 30 (June 1949).

Wallace, William. "Antoine Robidoux." In *Mountain Men Fur Trade of the Far West.* Vol 4. Edited by LeRoy Hafen. Glendale, Calif., 1966.

Weber, David J. "Louis Robidoux." In *Mountain Men of the Fur Trade of the Far West.* Vol. 8. Edited by LeRoy Hafen. Glendale, Calif. 1971.

ROBINSON, CHARLES

The first governor of the state of Kansas, Charles Robinson (1818–1894) was born in Massachusetts. After trying his luck in the California gold rush, he returned to Massachusetts in 1851, practiced medicine, and managed a weekly newspaper. He was committed to the abolition of slavery and became involved in the work of the New England Emigrant Aid Company. He led the first party of settlers sent by the organization to Lawrence, Kansas, in July 1854. Elected governor on the Republican ticket in December 1859, he took office on February 9, 1861, about ten days after Kansas was admitted to the Union. His political rival, JAMES HENRY LANE, instigated impeachment proceedings against Robinson for selling state bonds at rates lower than those established by the legislature. While he was acquitted of the charge, his former supporters turned against him in his bid to seek renomination. During the remainder of his life, he remained politically active, serving as a state senator and in various minor posts in state government.

—*Candace Floyd*

SUGGESTED READING:

Socolofsky, Homer E. *Kansas Governors.* Lawrence, Kans., 1990.

ROBINSON, JOSEPH TAYLOR

Joseph Taylor Robinson (1872-1937), U.S. Senator from Arkansas, was born near Lonoke, Arkansas. He attended the University of Arkansas and studied law. In 1894, he entered the state legislature and served one term. He was elected to Congress in 1902 and served five terms before being elected governor in 1912. He resigned from office to enter the U.S. Senate. In 1923, he became the Democratic leader in the Senate, and he accepted the nomination for vice-president in 1927 on the ticket with Al Smith. A supporter of Woodrow Wilson and Franklin Roosevelt, he labored behind the scenes to defeat a plan for a hydroelectric development in the Arkansas River valley, and he maintained ties to the South's planter elite. Promised a Supreme Court seat, he worked for Roosevelt's court-packing plan.

—*Michael B. Dougan*

ROCHE, JOSEPHINE ASPINWALL

Josephine Aspinwall Roche (1886–1976) devoted her life to many social causes. Her professional life included careers in social service, public office, and coal-mine operation. Born in Nebraska, Roche graduated from Vassar in 1908 and received an M.A. from Columbia in 1910. While studying at Columbia, she met Frances Perkins, who would later be appointed secretary of labor by President Franklin D. Roosevelt. Their friendship lasted years and helped Roche establish her political career.

Following college, Roche worked in the Denver, Colorado, Juvenile Court. She became involved with antichild-labor legislation campaigns and developed alliances with the National Consumers League and the U.S. Children's Bureau. She worked for both organizations years later.

In 1927, Roche inherited a large block of Rocky Mountain Fuel Company stock. She used her position to assist the United Mine Workers in unionizing the company's coal workers. That agreement was the first contract for an industrial union west of the Mississippi. In 1934, she narrowly lost the Colorado Democratic primary for the office of governor, but her political career received a boost when President Franklin D. Roosevelt appointed her assistant secretary of the treasury. Roche helped shape the Social Security Act while in office. She resigned from her treasury position in 1937 and became the president of the National

Consumer's League, a post she held until 1944. Between 1947 and 1971, she directed the United Mine Workers Union Welfare and Retirement Fund.

—Joanne L. Goodwin

SUGGESTED READING:

Ware, Susan. *Beyond Suffrage, Women in the New Deal.* Cambridge, Mass., 1981.

ROCKEFELLER, WINTHROP

Governor of Arkansas from 1967 to 1971 and the son of John D. Rockefeller, Jr., Winthrop Rockefeller (1912–1973) moved from New York to Arkansas in 1953 to escape his playboy reputation. He created a model farm, began a lifelong career of philanthropy, and chaired the new Arkansas Industrial Development Commission. After an unsuccessful challenge to Orval Faubus in 1964, he won the governorship in 1966 when Faubus retired. He was reelected in 1968. A Democratic General Assembly opposed to the state's first Republican governor since Reconstruction blocked most of his Progressive legislative program, but he succeeded in ending open gambling and improving race relations. He was defeated in 1970 by Democrat Dale Bumpers. Rockefeller left an influential legacy of moderate reform in Arkansas politics.

—T. Harri Baker

SUGGESTED READING:

Dillard, Tom. "Winthrop Rockefeller." In *The Governors of Arkansas: Essays in Political Biography.* Edited by Timothy P. Donovan and Willard B. Gatewood, Jr. Fayetteville, Ark., 1981.

Urwin, Cathy Kunzinger. *Agenda for Reform: Winthrop Rockefeller as Governor of Arkansas.* Fayetteville, Ark., 1991.

Ward, John L. *The Arkansas Rockefeller.* Baton Rouge, La., and London, 1978.

ROCKWELL, ORRIN PORTER

Utah pioneer, plainsman, and reputed Mormon "Destroying Angel," Orrin Porter Rockwell (1813–1878) was characterized in newspapers and journals of his day as a notorious gunman and religious zealot. Born in Belcher, Hampshire County, Massachusetts, Rockwell was one of the early converts to the CHURCH OF JESUS CHRIST OF LATTER-DAY SAINTS. As a settler in Jackson County, Missouri, in the mid-1830s, he was caught up in the so-called Mormon War of 1838 when Missourians, acting under the Extermination Order issued by Governor Lilburn W. Boggs, drove the MORMONS from the state. During that turbulent period, Rockwell became identified with the DANITES, a short-lived but secret band of Mormon stalwarts sworn to defend their church against its enemies. In 1842, Rockwell was accused of attempting to assassinate Boggs, the man responsible for the Mormon expulsion four years earlier. Boggs survived the shooting. After months in Missouri jails, Rockwell was released when no indictment was brought against him. It was on his return to NAUVOO, ILLINOIS (where the church had relocated), that Rockwell, on Christmas Day of 1843, became the subject of an astonishing prophecy by Mormon leader JOSEPH SMITH, JR. So long as Rockwell remained loyal and true to his faith, Smith predicted, he need fear no enemy: "Cut not thy hair and no bullet or blade can harm thee!"

When Smith and his brother, Hyrum, were murdered by a mob in Carthage, Illinois, in 1844, the attack spurred a Mormon exodus from Nauvoo. In that time of prolonged upheaval, Rockwell shot and killed Frank A. Worrell, who was menacing Hancock County Sheriff Jacob Backenstos. Rockwell had been deputized only moments before the shooting. The incident further inflamed anti-Mormon violence when it was learned the dead man had been responsible for protecting Joseph Smith when the Mormon prophet was assassinated the year before. Rockwell's already notorious reputation as an "avenger" was forever sealed.

Under the leadership of BRIGHAM YOUNG, the Mormons crossed the plains in 1847 to settle in the Great Salt Lake Valley. Rockwell was one of the territory's first lawmen (deputy marshal for the Provisional State of Deseret in 1849, later to become the Utah Territory). When President JAMES BUCHANAN named Alfred Cumming to succeed Brigham Young as Utah's governor in 1857, he also authorized a large expedition of federal troops to escort the new appointee to his mountain offices. Rockwell was among a number of Mormon dependables selected by Brigham Young to annoy, harass, and otherwise vex the UTAH EXPEDITION, which Young considered nothing less than an invasion "by a hostile force who are evidently assailing us to accomplish our overthrow and destruction."

While the people of the Utah Territory and the nation teetered on the brink of war, Rockwell was involved in an attack on the Aiken party, a half-dozen California adventurers planning to reach the U.S. troops wintering at Fort Bridger, a trading post in present-day Wyoming. (Twenty years later, Rockwell would be indicted on two counts of first-degree murder in the deaths of John and William Aiken.)

In the spring of 1858, President Buchanan offered amnesty to the "rebellious Mormons," and Brigham Young accepted. The Utah Expedition commanded by Brigadier General Albert Sidney Johnston went on to establish Camp Floyd south of Great Salt Lake City. After the outbreak of the Civil War, Colonel PATRICK E. CONNOR marched to Utah with seven companies of his Third Regiment of California Volunteers to "protect the mails from Indian depredations." He employed Rockwell as a guide and scout for infantry and cavalry in an action against a band of Shoshones on Bear River near present-day Preston, Idaho, in January 1863.

In his lifetime, Rockwell attracted celebrity-seekers, the curious, and the myth-makers. To journalists, authors, and world-travelers, he was as well known as Brigham Young. A rough-and-ready frontiersman, scout, marksman, and man of iron nerve and unswerving loyalty, he was the stuff of legend. Smith's 1843 prophecy followed Rockwell. The long-haired "Samson of the Mormons" could not be killed by bullet or blade. He died of natural causes in 1878 in Salt Lake City while awaiting trial on the Aiken murder charges. His notorious reputation dogged him to the grave. *The Salt Lake Tribune* editorialized that he "participated in at least a hundred murders."

—*Harold Schindler*

SUGGESTED READING:

Schindler, Harold. *Orrin Porter Rockwell: Man of God, Son of Thunder.* Salt Lake City, 1966. Reprint. 1983.

Stegner, Wallace. *The Gathering of Zion: The Story of the Mormon Trail.* New York, 1964.

ROCKY MOUNTAIN FUR COMPANY

The Rocky Mountain Fur Company (1830–1834) bought the fur-trading partnership of JEDEDIAH STRONG SMITH, David Jackson, and William Sublette in 1830. A group of young men—THOMAS FITZPATRICK, JAMES (JIM) BRIDGER, Milton Sublette, HENRY FRAEB, and Jean Baptist Gervais—all experience traders, were partners in the company. They operated in one of the most colorful eras of fur-trading history in the American West.

In spite of the success of its predecessors, the Rocky Mountain Fur Company was not a business success, largely due to the ineptitude of the partners and the increasing competition from independent traders and JOHN JACOB ASTOR'S AMERICAN FUR COMPANY. No supplies reached the rendezvous in 1831, and the company's trappers started their fall hunt with no way to transport their pelts back to St. Louis. The partners were forced to make a deal with William Sublette for supplies for the following year. In July 1832, Sublette obtained an additional contract with the company that gave him control of the company's finances as long as it existed.

The company struggled against numerous rivals including agents of small companies. NATHANIEL JARVIS WYETH was at the 1832 rendezvous with his 27 followers; Captain BENJAMIN LOUIS EULALIE DE BONNEVILLE, financed by New York capital, had 110 trappers in the field; traders from the St. Louis firm of Gantt and Blackwell and others also competed with the Rocky Mountain Fur Company. The company dealt with these competitors, but the American Fur Company continued as a serious competitor in 1832.

At the rendezvous of 1833, the Rocky Mountain Fur Company brought in the same number of beaver packs as the American Fur Company, despite having only half the number of men in the field. At the meeting, the American Fur Company made a contract with Wyeth for his annual supply of goods at the rendezvous of 1834. That company also intrigued with the previously friendly Crow Indians to rob the Rocky Mountain Fur Company trappers of their skins and horses. At the Green River rendezvous of 1834, William Sublette demanded full payment from the company for supplies purchased earlier, and the partners were unable to buy needed supplies from Wyeth. Sublette then bought the company.

—*W. Turrentine Jackson*

SEE ALSO: Fur Trade; Sublette Brothers

SUGGESTED READING:

Billington, Ray Allen. *Westward Expansion: A History of the American Frontier.* New York, 1974.

Chittenden, Hiram M. *The American Fur Trade of the Far West.* New York, 1935.

Dodds, Gordon B. *Hiram Martin Chittenden: His Public Career.* Lexington, Ky., 1973.

ROCKY MOUNTAINS

West of the Great Plains, America turns into a craggy land. The Rocky Mountains, a diverse range stretching across two nations, dominate the horizon. Created during the Precambrian Age and carved by glaciers during the Pleistocene Age, the Southern Rockies run from northern New Mexico across Colorado into southern Wyoming; the Middle Rockies cover most of central Wyoming; and the Northern Rockies extend far into Canada.

Albert Bierstadt's *Lander's Peak* in the Rocky Mountains. *Courtesy Metropolitan Museum of Art, Rogers Fund.*

The Southern Rockies are a series of high warps, thrust upwards, their cores made of hard granite. In New Mexico, widespread volcanoes and erosion combined to deform colorful sedimentary rocks into a picturesque if rugged landscape, but far more typical of the entire range are the austere mountains of central Colorado. The Front Range of the Southern Rockies, west of Denver, shoots up six thousand feet to rolling meadows that lie between 11,000 and 12,000 feet above sea level. Perched above these meadows, the mountain peaks look like low hills, and although Colorado has some fifty-three mountains higher than 14,000 feet, none of them ever reach 14,500 feet. The Northern Rockies are more varied, their backbone made up of masses of molten rock that cooled slowly before being thrust upward by geologic faults. These batholiths eroded into very ragged mountains, which make much of Idaho, for example, bleak and desolate indeed. East of the batholiths and parallel with the Great Plains, faults folded and thrust sediment rock into a series of ranges—an extension of the spectacular Canadian Rockies—that run in a line north to south. In general, the Northern Rockies are lower than the mountains in Colorado; Idaho's highest peak falls short of 10,000 feet. The Middle Rockies in many ways resemble the granite monoliths of Colorado, but there the faults and volcanoes produced a varied and strange-looking country, much of it running through the GRAND TETON NATIONAL PARK and the YELLOWSTONE NATIONAL PARK. Not all of the Middle Rockies are mountainous; long stretches of basins and plains run through them, their floors filled with an immense amount of sediment eroded from the surrounding mountains. It was through these gaps in the Rockies that all major routes westward were destined to funnel, from the Oregon Trail to the Union Pacific Railroad to the United States's interstate highways.

Collecting huge amounts of snow and water, the Rocky Mountains are the source of all the WATER for the American Southwest. The Arkansas and the North and South Platte rivers run down the eastern side of the mountains; the RIO GRANDE tumbles southward; the COLORADO RIVER swirls and rushes west. But the combined flow of all these rivers is less than that of

either the Missouri or the Yellowstone alone, and both the Clark Fork and the Spokane rivers, which drain the far western slope, have more water than the Colorado. Late in the nineteenth century, JOHN WESLEY POWELL warned that the water pouring into the arid West from the Rockies was quite limited, but Westerners intent on settling in the region saw the great rushes of water and ignored him.

The Americans established their earliest settlements on the rivers at the base of the Rockies, mostly as mining camps and towns or lumber camps, although a number of Westerners took up ranching in the shadow of the mountains. MERIWETHER LEWIS and WILLIAM CLARK crossed the Rockies on their expedition from 1805 to 1806 by traveling up the Missouri River to the Continental Divide, which runs along the eastern part of the Northern Rockies, then backtracking to what became the Clark Fork and cutting through to the Spokane and Columbia rivers in the West. MOUNTAIN MEN trekked the Rockies from the 1820s into the 1840s, discovering streams, rivers, valleys, canyons, and passageways, but complete exploration of the region did not really begin until gold was discovered in the gravel of the streambeds left at the foot of the mountains by retreating glaciers. These explorations led to the discovery of other extractable minerals—silver, copper, lead—which in turn prompted the construction of narrow-gauge railroads through the mountains to new mining towns.

By the early twentieth century, urban centers like BUTTE, MONTANA, and DENVER, COLORADO, born of mining booms, threatened the delicate ecology of the mountains, and conservationists, chief among them author and publicist Enos A. Mills, began urging Congress to establish a national park that would preserve the grandeur of the region. In 1915, Congress obliged, creating the Rocky Mountain National Park in Colorado. In the mid-1930s, the Colorado–Big Thompson project, a plan to irrigate Colorado's arid eastern slope with water from the Grand Lake, embroiled the park in controversy. Ranchers and farmers wanted the government to dig a long tunnel under the park from the lake across the Continental Divide to their parched land investments. The BUREAU OF RECLAMATION officials promised that no damage whatsoever would be done to the park, but conservationists did not believe them and worried that the project would set a precedent for other reclamation. Urged on by the conservationists in the SIERRA CLUB and Audubon Society, the NATIONAL PARK SERVICE opposed the plan, and Franklin D. Roosevelt's Secretary of the Interior HAROLD L. ICKES backed the park service. The contest raged, and the conservationists lost. In 1937, Congress approved the plan. Although the Bureau of Reclamation took pains not to mar the scenery when it built the tunnel, the fight marked a split in the alliance between the two groups that had first given birth to large-scale reclamation efforts in the West.

—*Charles Phillips*

SEE ALSO: Copper Mining; Exploration: United States Expeditions; Exploration and Science; Gold Mining; Lead Mining; Mining; Silver Mining

SUGGESTED READING:

Axelrod, Alan and Charles Phillips. *The Environmentalists: A Biographical Dictionary from the 17th Century to the Present.* New York, 1993.

Tyler, Daniel. *The Colorado-Big Thompson Project and the Northern Colorado Water Conservancy District.* Niwot, Colo., 1992.

Zaslowsky, Dyan. *These American Lands: Parks, Wilderness, and the Public Lands.* New York, 1986.

RODEO

The only American sport originating in the Southwest, rodeo is a product of more than four hundred years of history. Individuals of diverse racial, ethnic, and national backgrounds—both men and women—contributed to its development. Rodeo was also the first sport in which a successful strike by athletes enabled them to wrest control from the businessmen who had dominated them. During the 1990s, more than six hundred rodeos in the United States and Canada attracted millions of spectators and television viewers.

There are seven events in rodeo. In bareback- and saddle-bronc riding and bull riding, cowboys try to stay on the backs of the animals for eight seconds. In calf and team roping, steer wrestling (bulldogging), and women's barrel racing, athletes attempt to finish in the fastest time.

The Professional Rodeo Cowboys Association (PRCA) and Womens Professional Rodeo Association (WPRA) govern the sport. Three halls of fame—the National Rodeo Hall of Fame at the National Cowboy Hall of Fame in Oklahoma City, Oklahoma; the Prorodeo Hall of Fame and Museum of the American Cowboy in Colorado Springs, Colorado; and the National Cowgirl Hall of Fame and Western Heritage Center in Fort Worth, Texas—honor past and present stars.

All of the roping and riding events, except barrel racing, originated in the sixteenth through the eighteenth centuries as part of the Mexican sport of *charrería.* Anglo and black cowboys in the United States learned the events from *vaqueros* in the nineteenth cen-

In the 1920s, Barbara ("Tad") Lucas was one of the big names in the rodeo. *Courtesy National Cowboy Hall of Fame and Western Heritage Center.*

tury, and informal contests among ranch hands were popular. Professional rodeo really began with WILLIAM F. ("BUFFALO BILL") CODY's July 4, 1882, celebration in North Platte, Nebraska. The event attracted record crowds and demonstrated the potential for both rodeos and WILD WEST SHOWS.

For more than thirty years, Cody toured the world with his show, Buffalo Bill's Wild West. Cowboys and *vaqueros* who exhibited bronc riding and roping as part of Cody's "Cowboy Fun," became international stars, and other shows followed. At the same time, Western towns began organizing events, often called "Frontier Days," to celebrate their heritage. Those events featured dozens of cowboy and cowgirl contests and enabled women such as Lucille Mulhall and Tillie Baldwin to defeat men at steer roping and Roman racing. Rodeo was the first and only professional sport in which men and women truly competed as equals. Promoters also scheduled special events for Indians from nearby reservations. Native Americans such as Jackson Sundown succeeded in rodeo events, as did Hispanics such as Estivan Clemento and Juan Levias.

Few blacks participated in rodeos or Wild West shows until 1904 when BILL PICKETT appeared at the Cheyenne Frontier Days. He enthralled audiences as he bulldogged steers by jumping from his horse onto the steer's back, grabbing its horns, twisting its neck, and biting the beast's upper lip. He then tucked a horn under his arm and fell backward, thus taking the animal to the ground. Although officials eventually outlawed biting, bulldogging became a standard rodeo event due to Pickett. The first African American cowboy star, he toured for many years with the MILLER BROTHERS 101 RANCH WILD WEST SHOW.

Popular contests through the 1920s included steer roping, bronc riding, trick and fancy roping, and trick riding, with Yakima Canutt, Johnny Mullins, and Chester Byers among the top cowboys. During these years, outdoor Western celebrations like the Cheyenne Frontier Days were the premier rodeos. Producer Guy Weadick's 1912 Calgary Stampede in Canada offered the biggest purse of this time. The same individuals often participated in both rodeos and Wild West shows. Eventually the lone cowboy struggling against a bull or bronc came to symbolize the West and the people who conquered it.

Tex Austin caused a major change when he produced the initial Madison Square Garden Rodeo in New York City in 1922. The first important indoor contest, it quickly became the most prestigious rodeo, and other indoor venues followed. To shorten performances, promoters eliminated trick riding, trick and fancy roping, and racing; bronc riding was the only event left for women in Eastern rodeos.

During the 1920s and early 1930s when Barbara ("Tad") Lucas and Bob Crosby were the biggest rodeo names, there was no governing body to regulate the sport or the contestants. Prize money was poor, and promoters were sometimes crooked. These conditions led to the cowboy strike against the leading producer, Colonel W. T. Johnson, at the 1936 Boston Garden rodeo. Formation of the Cowboys Turtle Association, or CTA (now the PRCA), soon followed. The CTA eventually attained equitable prizes, standard rules and events, and the right to sanction rodeos.

By 1941, new promoters led by movie cowboy GENE AUTRY controlled the Madison Square Garden Rodeo. They made singers the stars and discontinued cowgirl bronc riding, featured since 1922. Soon after this last official cowgirl contest in a major rodeo was dropped, cowgirls formed the Girls Rodeo Association (GRA) in 1948. Now the WPRA, the organization made women's barrel racing a standard contest

nationwide by the late 1950s. By that time, black, Hispanic, and Native American cowboys had almost vanished from big-time rodeo.

Madison Square Garden remained the preeminent rodeo until 1959 when the PRCA began the National Finals Rodeo (NFR). There, the top fifteen money-winners in seven events compete for a week, with NFR prize money added to the year's winnings. The contestant with the highest total winnings is the world's champion of his or her event. The cowboy earning the most money in two or more events is named "All Around Cowboy." The first NFR superstar was Jim Shoulders, who won a record sixteen individual titles between 1949 and 1959. Larry Mahan won six "All Around" titles between 1966 and 1973, and Tom Ferguson, the first million-dollar cowboy, won six "All Around" titles between 1974 and 1979. After the NFR moved to Las Vegas, Nevada, in 1985, it became the world's richest rodeo. Five-time "All Around Cowboy" Ty Murray's annual winnings in the 1990s averaged more than two hundred thousand dollars, six times what Jim Shoulders averaged thirty years earlier.

Women joined the NFR in 1967, but their earnings lagged far behind the cowboys. In 1980, the WPRA successfully demanded that rodeo producers award women equal prize money as a condition for participating in the events. Cowgirls' earnings have since increased significantly. Ten-time WPRA barrel-racing champion Charmayne James Rodman has set numerous records while becoming the world's first million-dollar cowgirl. Today, most cowboys and cowgirls, like Rodman and Murray, still come from the old cattle frontier where rodeo began. Because of them, the cowboy hero and the mythical West maintain a unique place in the collective national consciousness.

—Mary Lou LeCompte

SUGGESTED READING:

Frederiksson, Kristine. *American Rodeo: From Buffalo Bill to Big Business.* College Station, Tex., 1985.

LeCompte, Mary Lou. *Cowgirls of the Rodeo: Pioneer Professional Athletes.* Champaign, Ill., 1993.

Slatta, Richard W. *Cowboys of the Americas.* New Haven, Conn., and London, 1990.

RODRÍGUEZ, CHEPITA

Convicted of murdering a white man, Chepita Rodríguez (?–1863) was the first woman executed by the state of Texas. She arrived in the present-day state of Texas in 1836, accompanying her father on a flight from the dictatorship of Mexican President ANTONIO LÓPEZ DE SANTA ANNA.

The family settled in South Texas, in an Irish settlement known as San Patricio. When some of Santa Anna's troops passed through the area on their way to suppress the Anglo war for independence, they engaged in battle with local volunteer forces; Rodríguez's father fell among the casualties. Some time later, she developed a friendship with an Anglo cowboy, and the relationship produced a son. It also led to heartbreak when the man abducted the infant and disappeared.

Unexpectedly in 1863, two strangers drifted into Rodríguez's camp. One looked strikingly like the young cowboy who years previously had fathered and then stolen her only child. Surely the resemblance indicated that the young cowboy was the baby taken from her years before. Suddenly, the young man stole away, leaving behind his partner bludgeoned with Rodríguez's axe. Covering up for her supposed son, who presumably had committed the crime, Rodríguez and a local feebleminded neighbor, Juan Silvera, dumped the murdered man's body into the Arkansas River.

Within a few days, however, Anglo residents of the region discovered the body when it washed ashore some miles away. Immediately, suspicion fell on Rodríguez, the only person who lived upstream. Talk of a lynching erupted, even though no evidence specifically linked Rodríguez and Silvera to the atrocity. In their trial, the jury found both guilty despite lean evidence and assessed Silvera five years in prison and Rodríguez the death penalty by hanging. The state executed her that same year. Suspicion of killing a white man had been reason enough to put to death a woman who by that time had reached advanced age and posed no threat to society.

—Arnoldo De León

SUGGESTED READING:

De León, Arnoldo. *They Called Them Greasers.* Austin, Tex., 1983.

Vernon Smylie. *A Noose for Chepita.* Corpus Christi, Tex., 1970.

San Angelo *Standard Times.* San Angelo, Tex., September 24, 1978.

RODRÍGUEZ, IN RE

In Re Rodríguez, a federal lawsuit, ended a brief effort on the part of white Americans to define Mexicans as foreigners ineligible for naturalization and thus to deny them the right to vote. In the case of *In Re Rodríguez,* Anglo-Americans in San Antonio sought to prevent Ricardo Rodríguez, and by extension other Mexican Americans in the city, from acquiring naturalization and the right to the franchise. In May 1896, Rodríguez,

originally from Mexico but a resident of Texas since 1883, applied for naturalization papers in the U.S. Circuit Court. Two Anglo attorneys objected. Relying on a U.S. federal statute that limited naturalization to "free white persons" and persons of African nativity or descent, they submitted briefs to the court arguing that Rodríguez failed to qualify as a white person by virtue of the scientific classifications of the times and because society considered the term "white" to exclude Mexicans. In 1897, however, the presiding judge ruled in favor of Rodríguez. Despite the opinions of ethnologists, the jurist noted, United States law extended the right of citizenship to Mexicans if they possessed a good moral character.

—*Arnoldo De León*

SUGGESTED READING:

In Re Rodríguez. The Federal Reporter. Vol. 81. St. Paul, Minn., 1897.

Padilla, Fernando V. "Early Chicano Legal Recognition, 1846–1897." *Journal of Popular Culture* 13 (Spring 1980).

ROGERS, ROY, AND DALE EVANS

Roy Rogers (1911–) and Dale Evans (1912–) were FILM stars and singing cowboys. Rogers, "The King of the Cowboys," was a founding member of the singing group "Sons of the Pioneers" before he struck out on his own as an actor and singer. Born in Cincinnati, Ohio, as Leonard Slye, he first adopted the stage name Dick Weston. Republic Studio signed a contract with the young performer in 1937. His starting salary was seventy-five dollars a week. In 1938, he added a component that further enhanced his popularity, when he included a Palomino he named Trigger in his movies and public appearances. For nearly thirty years, the horse and the rider were synonymous.

When GENE AUTRY entered the military during World War II, Rogers became the most popular singing cowboy in film. He also enjoyed success on his radio show, which premiered in 1944. That year, he appeared in *The Cowboy and the Señorita,* which also starred Dale Evans.

Born Frances Smith in Uvalde, Texas, Dale Evans started her entertainment career as the featured performer at the Chez Paree Night Club in Chicago in 1940. She then appeared in several minor roles for Twentieth Century-Fox and was a regular performer on Edgar Bergen's "Chase and Sanborn Program" on the radio. Shortly after joining Rogers, Evans was crowned "Queen of the Cowgirls" by studio publicists, and she shared billing in nearly a quarter of

Roy Rogers and Dale Evans, by Everett Raymond Kinstler. *Courtesy National Cowboy Hall of Fame and Western Heritage Center.*

Rogers's 104 movies. The two married on December 31, 1947, and they recorded more than five hundred songs, either individually or jointly.

The big production numbers that regularly formed a part of Rogers's and Evans's films allowed the talented pair to work their magic together on screen. They thrilled generations of matinee and radio audiences. By 1951, they started appearing on a television series that ran one hundred episodes. One of their keys to success was extensive merchandising, which promoted products popular among children across the country.

Deeply religious, the couple made several records with songs based on Christian themes. They likewise adopted or otherwise opened their home to many foster children. In addition, Evans has written a number of autobiographical works, including *Angel Unaware* and *Spiritual Diary.* Much of the couple's career and personal life has been preserved in the museum they established in Victorville, California.

—*John P. Langellier*

SEE ALSO: Radio and Television Westerns

SUGGESTED READING:

Rothel, David. *The Roy Rogers Book.* Madison, N.C., 1987.

ROGERS, WILLIAM (WILL) PENN ADAIR

SEE: Humor

ROLPH, JAMES

Mayor of San Francisco and governor of California, James Rolph (1869–1934) was born in San Francisco to middle-class, British-immigrant parents. After secondary school, he gained experience in business and, in 1900, formed his own company, which eventually engaged in shipping, shipbuilding, importing, banking, and insurance. He married Anne Marshall Reid in 1900.

By 1906, Rolph had become prominent in civic activities. In 1911, he ran for mayor in the city's first nonpartisan election. Promising to be mayor of "all the people" and to unify San Francisco, Rolph won 60 percent of the vote. Regularly winning reelection, he served nineteen years in all. In his first term, he worked tirelessly to encourage urban growth and development: he promoted the PANAMA-PACIFIC INTERNATIONAL EXPOSITION in 1915, secured approval for a new city hall, initiated construction of a new water reservoir, completed the first city-owned streetcar line, and added other municipal streetcar lines. He also exemplified the Progressive era's concern for expertise and efficiency.

As mayor, "Sunny Jim" tried to smother class and ethnic antagonisms with his amiable good nature. Although he remained in office until 1931, he experienced an undefined breakdown in 1916 and never again equaled his early accomplishments. His shipbuilding and shipping enterprises suffered serious losses after World War I. Throughout the 1920s, he promoted municipal ownership of streetcars, water, and electricity but without the dynamism of his first administration and with limited success. He did little to enforce prohibition in San Francisco.

Rolph sought the governorship in 1918. Under California's cross-filing system, which permitted candidates to file in as many party primaries as they wished to enter, he won the Democratic nomination; the state Supreme Court ruled, however, that he was ineligible to run because he had not been nominated by his own party, the Republicans. In 1930, he won the Republican nomination for governor and swept to a landslide victory. Ineffective as governor, he did little to influence legislation, and critics accused him of appointing unqualified cronies to state positions.

—Robert W. Cherny

SUGGESTED READING:

Issel, William, and Robert W. Cherny. *San Francisco, 1865–1932: Politics, Power, and Urban Development.* Berkeley and Los Angeles, 1986.

Rischin, Moses. "Sunny Jim Rolph: The First 'Mayor of All the People.'" *California Historical Quarterly* 53 (1974): 165–172.

ROMAN CATHOLIC CHURCH

SEE: Catholics

ROMAN CATHOLIC MISSIONS

SEE: Missions

ROOSEVELT, THEODORE

Rancher, conservationist, and president of the United States, Theodore Roosevelt (1858-1919) was born in New York City. He sought solace from his grief after the death of his first wife Alice Lee through investment in a Dakota cattle ranch. In the West, he tested himself against the harsh elements to regain his sense of purpose and overcome his personal loss. From then on, the West was an important aspect of both his private life and his public career.

Although he stayed in Dakota only three years, Roosevelt experienced adventures that shaped his public reputation. He faced down the taunts of a bully in a hotel. He pursued and captured thieves whom he then brought to justice. Finally, a near-feud with the Marquis de Mores, a rancher from Europe, gained him further attention. By the time Roosevelt returned to the East in 1886, he had transformed himself from an Eastern dude into a respected figure in the West. The financial cost of the Dakota years was high. Roosevelt

Theodore Roosevelt. *Courtesy Library of Congress.*

lost a large part of his inheritance when the cattle market collapsed in 1886 and 1887.

During the 1880s and 1890s, Roosevelt wrote extensively about the West. His most important publication was *The Winning of the West* (published from 1889 to 1896), a multivolume history that treated Western settlement in heroic terms. When the war with Spain broke out in 1898, Roosevelt organized a volunteer regiment, the Rough Riders, composed of Eastern aristocrats and Western cowboys. The combat success of the Rough Riders caught the popular imagination and further solidified Roosevelt's Western image. His appeal in the West helped put him on the Republican ticket in 1900 as William McKinley's vice-presidential candidate. When McKinley was assassinated, Roosevelt became president in September 1901.

Roosevelt emerged as the first chief executive to advocate conservation of natural resources in the West for the use of future generations. Working with his chief forester and close adviser, GIFFORD PINCHOT, Roosevelt used presidential power to create bird refuges, national parks such as Crater Lake and Grand Canyon, and wildlife preserves. He pushed the NEWLANDS RECLAMATION ACT OF 1902 through Congress to promote irrigation in the arid West. He also set up a Public Lands Commission in 1903 to plan for the wise development of the public domain. In 1907, he withstood congressional efforts to diminish his power and established more extensive forest reserves in the West. His emphasis on executive discretion and national power aroused Western opposition among those who wished to develop the region quickly. After he left office, Roosevelt quarreled with his successor, William Howard Taft, over conservation policy in the West during the BALLINGER-PINCHOT CONTROVERSY (from 1909 to 1911) involving coal lands in Alaska.

Using the presidency as a "bully pulpit," Roosevelt was an effective conservation advocate who set a standard for other presidents to follow. For America between 1880 and 1920, Roosevelt also symbolized the West and its potential for personal development and national renewal.

—Lewis L. Gould

SEE ALSO: Financial Panics; National Expansion: The Imperial Impulse; Progressivism; Reclamation; Owens Valley War

SUGGESTED READING:

Cutright, Paul Russell. *Theodore Roosevelt: The Making of a Conservationist.* Urbana, Ill., 1985.

Gould, Lewis L. *The Presidency of Theodore Roosevelt.* Lawrence, Kans., 1991.

Morris, Edmund. *The Rise of Theodore Roosevelt.* New York, 1979.

ROSE, EDWARD (MIXED CHEROKEE)

Interpreter, leader of the Crow Indians, and man of the wilderness, Edward Rose (?-ca. 1833) was a scoundrel or a brave man, a Mississippi River pirate one step ahead of the law or an able guide and a mediator between white people and Native Americans. Most of what is known of Rose comes from no account of his own, but from reports of soldiers, trappers, and adventurers who met him in the wilderness along the Missouri River in the early nineteenth century. Born of a white father and Cherokee–African-American mother, Rose joined MANUEL LISA's fur-trading expedition on the Missouri River in 1807. In 1811, WILSON PRICE HUNT found him among the Arikara Indians, proficient in Indian languages and wise to the ways of the wilds. Wilson hired Rose to guide an ASTORIA-bound expedition through Crow country but, suspecting Rose of treachery, dismissed him with dispatch.

Speculation about Rose's activities during the next ten years abounds. He may have become, as Joshua Pilcher reported, "a celebrated outlaw who left this country in chains some ten years ago." Or, he probably lived among the Crows until his popularity created friction within the tribe. He also lived among the Arikaras, learning their language and customs.

Beginning in 1823, Rose took on a series of assignments as a guide and interpreter: first, to the unfortunate General WILLIAM HENRY ASHLEY, and later to Colonel Henry Leavenworth's punitive expedition against the Arikaras who had attacked Ashley. Leavenworth, impressed with Rose's ability to mediate between whites and the Arikaras, reported the guide was "a brave and enterprising man." Rose accompanied JEDEDIAH STRONG SMITH on his trek through the Northern Plains. Then Rose became an interpreter for the army on its mission to make peace with the Indians along the Missouri.

Rose returned to the Crows and made a name for himself as a temperamental man and a fierce warrior. He earned the name "Five Scalps" when he killed five Blackfoot Indians single-handedly.

Rose died at the hands of the Arikaras during the winter of 1832 to 1833.

—Patricia Hogan

SUGGESTED READING:

Felton, Harold W. *Edward Rose, Negro Trail Blazer.* New York, 1967.

ROSEWATER, EDWARD

Nebraska politician and journalist Edward Rosewater (1841–1906) was born in Bohemia and immigrated to Ohio with his parents in 1854. As a civilian telegraph operator, he served in the Union Army until 1863, when he moved to Omaha to accept a position with the Pacific Telegraph Company. In that position, Rosewater became interested in both politics and journalism. In 1870, he was elected to the Nebraska state legislature and, the following year, was instrumental in bringing impeachment proceedings against the state's first governor, David Butler, for misuse of state funds. While in office, Rosewater founded the *Omaha Daily Bee,* which quickly became one of the most influential papers in the West. Although Rosewater never served in an elected political office after his one term in the legislature, he used the *Bee* to influence politics throughout the last quarter of the nineteenth century.

—*Mark A. Eifler*

SUGGESTED READING:

Federal Writers Project. *Nebraska: A Guide to the Cornhusker State.* Washington, D.C., 1939.

Sheldon, Addison E. *Nebraska, the Land and the People.* Chicago, 1931.

ROSS, ALEXANDER

Fur trader Alexander Ross (1783–1856) migrated to Canada from his native Scotland in 1804. He entered the fur-trade business with JOHN JACOB ASTOR's 1810 expedition to the Pacific Coast by way of South America's Cape Horn. After Astor abandoned his Northwest outpost, Ross became a trader for the North West Company in 1814 and, four years later, established Fort Nez Perces on the Snake River. He ran the fort until 1823.

Ross was in charge of the Flathead Post in western Montana for the HUDSON'S BAY COMPANY (it merged with the North West Company in 1821) when JEDEDIAH STRONG SMITH and some American trappers rescued Ross and his men from an Indian attack. In gratitude, he allowed Smith to visit Flathead House, an act that cost him his job. Company officials replaced Ross when they realized the Americans had probably used the invitation to gather intelligence about the region and its resources. The company sent PETER SKENE OGDEN to succeed Ross and retired him to its Red River settlement.

In his retirement, Ross wrote *Adventures of the First Settlers on the Oregon or Columbian River* (1849) and the two-volume *Fur Hunters of the Far West* (1856); these works offer rich details of the fur trade and accounts of Oregon's early history. His final book, *The Red River Settlement,* appeared in 1856.

—*Patricia Hogan*

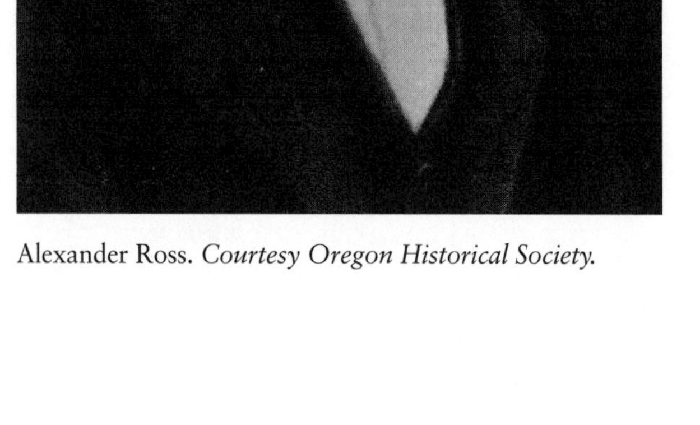

Alexander Ross. *Courtesy Oregon Historical Society.*

ROSS, JOHN (CHEROKEE)

Principal chief of the Cherokee Indians for nearly forty years, John Ross (1790–1866) was born in Turkey Town in the Cherokee Nation (near present-day Center, Alabama). He was the son and grandson of Scottish traders who married Cherokee women. Only one-eighth Cherokee, Ross nonetheless gained the support of the full-blood majority because of his devotion to maintaining the native homeland. For more than fifty years, he labored unceasingly for the survival and unity of his people.

Ross chose first the world of his father and grandfather and went into the merchandising business. At Ross's Landing (present-day Chattanooga, Tennessee), he operated a ferry and warehouse and then moved south to present-day Georgia and took up a planter's life. At Head of Coosa (present-day Rome, Georgia), he built a comfortable home, increased his slave hold-

ings, built a ferry, and worked nearly two hundred acres of choice farmland. By the 1830s, he was one of the wealthiest men in the Cherokee Nation.

While living at Head of Coosa, Ross became involved in Cherokee politics. In 1816, he served as clerk to the Cherokee chiefs and made his first trip to Washington, D.C., as a tribal delegate. Three years later, he became president of the Cherokee national legislature and in 1827 was elected president of the Cherokee constitutional convention and helped write the final document, the first such document among Native American tribes. The following year, he was elected the first principal chief of the new government, a position he held for nearly forty years.

In the 1830s, the Cherokees faced external forces that would deprive them of their lands and internal dissension that would leave them divided. As principal chief, Ross confronted Georgians, backed by their state government, who were pushing onto Cherokee lands. He found courts of little help, and despite landmark decisions like *CHEROKEE NATION v. STATE OF GEORGIA*, the Cherokees got no relief. Ross also found little solace from the federal executive. President ANDREW JACKSON sympathized with Georgia and pressed the Indians to move west. Ross, however, was determined to keep the Cherokees in their homeland, and he had the support of the full-blood majority. But mixed-blood dissenters, led by JOHN RIDGE and others, considered removal the more reasonable solution and signed a treaty to that effect with the United States in 1835.

Ross fought the fraudulent Treaty of New Echota but to no avail. After a military removal of the tribe began in 1838, Ross relented and led his people to the Indian Territory, now Oklahoma. At least one quarter of tribe, perhaps five thousand people, died during the removal and along the Cherokee TRAIL OF TEARS. Afterwards, near civil war erupted as the Cherokees tried to reintegrate. Peace finally returned in 1846 when Ross and others signed a new treaty with the federal government.

The American Civil War renewed factional quarrels, this time on the issues of slavery and of loyalty to the Union. Ross tried to withstand the pressures of Southern agents, but eventually the tribe sided with the South. Ross probably made the decision because of fears of internal division and Confederate invasion. Within a year, he fled east where he lived out the war and worked for the tribe's cause. At war's end, he came back to a defeated nation but turned east one last time to oppose the disintegration of his tribe. Shortly before his death, Ross learned that a new treaty guaranteed that the Cherokee Nation would remain intact. When he died, he was in Washington, D.C., seeking once again to ensure the integrity of the Cherokees.

—*Gary Moulton*

SEE ALSO: Native American Peoples: Peoples Removed from the East

SUGGESTED READING:

Anderson, William L., ed. *Cherokee Removal: Before and After.* Athens, Ga., 1991.

McLoughlin, William G. *Cherokee Renascence in the New Republic.* Princeton, N.J., 1985.

Mooney, James. *Historical Sketch of the Cherokee.* 1900. Reprint. Chicago, 1975.

Moulton, Gary E. *John Ross, Cherokee Chief.* Athens, Ga., 1978.

Moulton, Gary E., ed. *The Papers of Chief John Ross.* 2 vols. Norman, Okla., 1985.

Wilkins, Thurman. *Cherokee Tragedy.* Norman, Okla., 1986.

ROYCE, JOSIAH

One of America's great philosophers and educators, Josiah Royce (1855–1916) was born in Grass Valley, California. His mother, Sarah Eleanor Bayliss Royce, was an intelligent, devout woman, and in the mining camps of California, she imparted some of her earnestness to her only surviving son.

Royce was intellectually precocious. After one year in a San Francisco high school, he was ready for the University of California. He was among the first students who moved from Oakland to the new university site in Berkeley.

Daniel Coit Gilman, president of the university, recognized promise in the young man and secured for him an opportunity to study philosophy in Germany, where young Royce spent a year beginning in 1875. He was invited to join a group of scholars at the new Johns Hopkins University, and Royce received one of the institution's first doctorates. Taking a job for a time at his alma mater in Berkeley, he jumped at the chance to substitute at Harvard for William James, the philosopher of pragmatism. Royce taught at Harvard for the rest of his life.

He was the first native Anglo-Californian to write a history of his state, which appeared in 1886 as *California from the Conquest in 1846 to the Second Vigilance Committee.* It was a sound, documentary study of a formative decade and was steeped in philosophical interpretation. Royce saw the frontier as a place where a community was wrested out of excessive individualism.

An idealist and an absolutist in philosophy, he stood as a polar star to his close friend William James at Harvard. Royce was a brilliant teacher. Among his students were T. S. Eliot, George Santayana, and

Franklin Roosevelt. In a memorable speech late in life, he named his background in the West as the truly significant influence on his thought. He died in Cambridge. His most enduring physical memorial is Royce Hall at the University of California, Los Angeles.

—*Robert V. Hine*

SUGGESTED READING:

Clendenning, John. *The Life and Thought of Josiah Royce.* Madison, Wis., 1985.
Hine, Robert V. *Josiah Royce: From Grass Valley to Harvard.* Norman, Okla., 1992.
Powell, Thomas F. *Josiah Royce.* New York, 1974.

RUEF, ABRAHAM (ABE)

A leader of the UNION LABOR PARTY, in San Francisco, Abe Ruef (1864–1936) was born in San Francisco to middle-class, French-Jewish parents. He graduated from the University of California and Hastings College of Law (San Francisco).

After establishing a law practice in a working-class section of San Francisco, Ruef tried to take over the local Republican party organization in 1901 but failed. That year, police involvement in a major strike led unionists to create the Union Labor Party (ULP) and seek control of City Hall. Ruef persuaded Eugene Schmitz, head of the Musicians' Union, to seek the ULP's nomination for mayor. Schmitz won and was reelected in 1903. Schmitz appointed Ruef attorney for the mayor's office; he quickly became known as the real power in the Schmitz administration and accepted large retainers from companies dealing with the city.

Initially, the ULP won only a handful of offices. In 1905, however, the ULP swept many city offices; newly elected ULP supervisors proved so receptive to bribes that, in what may have been an attempt to insulate the ULP from scandal, Ruef began to act as intermediary. At the urging of FREMONT OLDER, editor of the *San Francisco Bulletin,* federal officials investigated Ruef and the ULP. The "graft prosecution" offered immunity to ULP politicians in return for testimony against Ruef and offered immunity to Ruef for testimony against corporate officials, especially those of the Southern Pacific Railroad. Ruef refused the offer and accused the prosecution of suborning perjury. The prosecution produced many indictments and several convictions, but only Ruef served time in prison. Convicted in 1908, he appealed unsuccessfully and then entered San Quentin penitentiary in 1911 to begin a fourteen-year sentence.

Many people thought the trials confirmed widespread allegations of corruption in politics; along with similar cases across the nation, the San Francisco graft prosecution contributed to the growth of Progressivism. One of Ruef's prosecutors, HIRAM WARREN JOHNSON, having built his reputation as a tenacious opponent of corporate influence in politics, went on to the governorship and the U.S. Senate.

Ruef was paroled in 1915 and pardoned in 1920. Disbarred from practicing law, he turned to real estate and prospered for a time. His business failed in the 1930s, and he died bankrupt.

The graft prosecution painted Ruef as a corrupt boss and the ULP as his political machine, a judgment little challenged by early historians. Recent historians, however, have argued that Ruef was more a twentieth-century influence peddler than a nineteenth-century party boss and have shown that the ULP was a genuine labor party rather than Ruef's personal political machine.

—*Robert W. Cherny*

SUGGESTED READING:

Bean, Walton. *Boss Ruef's San Francisco.* Berkeley, Calif., 1952.
Issel, William, and Robert Cherny. *San Francisco, 1865–1932: Politics, Power, and Urban Development.* Berkeley and Los Angeles, 1986.
Tygiel, Jules. "'Where Unionism Holds Undisputed Sway': A Reappraisal of San Francisco's Union Labor Party." *California History* 62 (1983): 196–215.
Walsh, James P. "Abe Ruef Was No Boss." *California Historical Quarterly* 51 (1972): 3–16.

RUIZ DE BURTON, MARÍA AMPARO

Californio writer María Amparo Ruiz de Burton (1832–1895) was born in Loreto, Baja California. She wrote the first English-language novel to provide the perspective of the conquered Mexican Californio population. Her works included two novels as well as a comedy adaptation of *Don Quixote.* Under the pen name C. Loyal ("loyal citizen" in Spanish), she published *The Squatter and the Don* in 1885. The title page of *Who Would Have Thought It?* (published in 1872) provided no author but is listed under "H.S. Burton and Mrs. Henry S. Burton" by the Library of Congress. Both works are historical romances that highlight social and historical issues. *Who Would Have Thought It?* developed the romance between Lola and Julian and is a bitingly satirical novel on the values and social mores of American society during the pe-

riod of the Civil War. The book takes special acerbic aim at political corruption, religious hypocrisy, and racism. In *The Squatter and the Don,* romance and history also come together; implicit in the love story of Mercedes and Clarence are calls for justice for Californios suffering the consequences of the loss of lands and status brought on by the United States invasion of California.

The author's own life had many traits of historical romance. At the age of fourteen, she met twenty-eight-year-old Henry S. Burton, a U.S. Army captain who had been sent to Baja California with the invasion forces at the onset of the United States–Mexican War. After overcoming several obstacles, not the least of which were her age and religion, the two were married in Monterey, California, in 1849. The couple lived first in San Diego and in 1859 moved to the East Coast. There, as a Union general's wife, Ruiz de Burton moved in Washington's highest social and political circles and came to know the milieu intimately. She drew on her experiences in the East in writing *Who Would Have Thought It?*

Ruiz de Burton's husband died in 1869. The thirty-seven-year-old widow returned to California to do battle in the U.S. courts to retain her lands at Rancho Jamul in southern California. An intelligent and enterprising woman, she also took on several business projects ranging from planting California's first commercial crop of castor beans to setting up the short-lived Jamul Cement Company on her much-litigated ranch lands. She also traveled to Mexico City to defend her claim to lands in Ensenada, Baja California.

Ruiz de Burton's writings trace the complexities and contradictions in late-nineteenth-century political, economic, ethnic, and gender relations as perceived by a witty, acute observer placed by historical circumstances in a subaltern position. Her novels and letters reveal a strong background in the classics, literature, and history as well as a gift for writing and an insightful and critical eye.

—*Beatrice Pita*

SUGGESTED READING:

Ruiz de Burton, María Amparo. *Who Would Have Thought It?* Edited and with an introduction by Rosaura Sánchez and Beatrice Pita. Houston, Tex., 1995.

RUSSELL, CHARLES MARION

Often praised as the "cowboy artist," Charles Marion Russell (1864–1926) chronicled the life of the West in watercolors, oils, and drawings with humor, whimsy, and perceptiveness. His intimate knowledge of the daily life of the West gave him an artistic insight into a region that some artists from the East lacked.

Born in Oak Hill, Missouri, Russell was one of the few prominent nineteenth- or early twentieth-century artists who spent almost all their lives as residents of the West. He had greater intimacy with the life of the cowboy, the nature of early settlements, the fate of the Indian, and the unique wildlife of the region than any other contemporary artist. The West was part of his heritage, for his uncles William, Charles, George, and Robert Bent, had been prominent fur traders on the Upper Missouri and had built Bent's Fort along the Arkansas River. In technical terms, Russell was not the most accomplished Western artist of the period. While his palette was often limited, his compositions contrived, and his technique constrained, his empathy for the people, places, and episodes of the West was unparalleled. Intensely narrative in his art, he sympathetically and humorously portrayed the pleasures and travails of life in a West that was rapidly disappearing before the advance of industrialized America. Among nineteenth-century artists, he was rivaled only by GEORGE CATLIN in his sympathy for the fate and future of the American Indian.

To the dismay of his parents, Russell showed little interest in academic subjects with the exception of history. By the age of sixteen, he had ended his formal education, and in 1880, he set off for Montana to find his future. For the next four and a half decades of his life, he labored in this land as a cowboy and as the "cowboy artist." When he arrived in Montana in the spring of 1880, he was not the first artist to have traveled and painted in this region; George Catlin, KARL (OR CARL) BODMER, JOHN MIX STANLEY, and William Hayes had portrayed subjects and themes from the area. The West that Russell became a part of in the last decades of the nineteenth century was a region and era in transition. GEORGE ARMSTRONG CUSTER had been defeated, the Indian wars were over, and the last of the great herds of buffalo were being reduced by the hide hunters.

Russell began his career in Montana on a sheep ranch in the Judith Basin. Becoming disenchanted with life among the sheep, he then lived for a while with Jake Hoover, a trapper. From Hoover, he gained a knowledge of the wildlife of the Rocky Mountains. In April 1881, he became a night wrangler and took up life as a cowboy on various Montana ranches. Although working primarily with watercolors during this period, he produced in 1885 his first oil on canvas, *Breaking Camp*. Russell took some pride in his ability to include all twenty-one members of his round-up crew

Charles Marion Russell. *Courtesy National Cowboy Hall of Fame and Western Heritage Center.*

although the work was immature in composition. *Breaking Camp* was exhibited at the St. Louis Art Exposition of 1886, the first painting from Montana to be displayed outside of that region. His first sustained recognition as an artist came from a small, simple, watercolor sketch, *Waiting for a Chinook* (1886), which showed the devastation to the range-cattle industry during the blizzard-plagued winter of 1886. During this period, Russell painted for his own pleasure, for the amusement of cowboy companions, and for drinks.

Until 1896 and his marriage to Nancy Cooper, Russell maintained himself by working as a cowboy and by selling a few rather crude and inexpensive paintings each year. His experiences with Hoover and as a cowboy indelibly influenced his selection of subjects and settings for his art; but it was his wife who began to manage his career as an artist. Settling in Great Falls, Montana, Russell, at his wife's urging, began to devote himself to painting. Essentially self-taught, he nevertheless was aware of and influenced by other artists, critics, and developments in painting. His skills matured over time, and he became more adept in all dimensions of his work. Within a decade, he was no longer receiving twenty-five dollars or fifty dollars a painting, but two hundred dollars to four hundred dollars for a single canvas, and on one occasion up to fifteen-hundred dollars. Russell's paintings are intensely narrative and almost always seek to demonstrate clearly and energetically an episode in the lives of the peoples of the West. In the 1890s, his composition was simplified and made stronger by the deletion of unnecessary items. With color and detail, his paintings often focus on one primary, commanding figure, be it man or animal, which is then complemented and supported by subordinate figures. Foreground and background were used by Russell to achieve three-dimensional effects necessary for successful paintings. His greatest strengths as a painter may have been in his superb use of color after 1900 when his palette became lighter and more diverse. While he occasionally worked in sculpture, he never devoted the energy nor achieved the success in that medium that his contemporary FREDERIC REMINGTON received. With passion, humor, good will, and talent, Russell captured in his art a West that he believed was dying. His paintings remain an enduring image of the cowboy's West.

—*Phillip Drennon Thomas*

SEE ALSO: Art: Western Art

SUGGESTED READING:
Dippe, Brian W. *Remington and Russell.* Austin, Tex., 1982.
Hassrick, Peter H. *Charles M. Russell.* New York, 1989.
Linderman, Frank Bird. *Recollections of Charlie Russell.* Norman, Okla., 1963.
McCracken, Harold. *The Charles M. Russell Book: The Life and Work of the Cowboy Artist.* New York, 1957.
Russell, Charles M. *Paper Talk: Charlie Russell's American West.* Edited by Brian N. Dippe. New York, 1979.

RUSSELL, WILLIAM HEPBURN

William Hepburn Russell (1812–1872) was founder of the PONY EXPRESS and a partner in the freighting company of RUSSELL, MAJORS AND WADDELL. Born in Burlington, Vermont, Russell started working as a store clerk in Lexington, Missouri, at the age of sixteen. He married Harriet Elliot Warder in 1835. Three years later, he formed a partnership known as Allen, Russell and Company to operate a store in Lexington; shortly thereafter, he met his future partner, WILLIAM B. WADDELL, when both were promoting a real-estate addition. The store failed in 1845 in part because Russell's time was divided between business ventures and holding public office.

In 1852, Russell and Waddell became partners in a mercantile business and began transporting military supplies to Santa Fe. Two years later, ALEXANDER MAJORS joined them in a partnership known as Russell, Majors and Waddell to engage in the freighting business. The business expanded rapidly, and Russell, always a promoter, entered the stagecoach business. He finally persuaded his reluctant partners to join him in establishing a Pony Express.

Russell was constantly in the public eye, but his days of glory were brief. Going to Washington to obtain funds for his ruinously expensive venture, he became involved in the greatest financial scandal of the time. As a result, Secretary of War John B. Floyd was forced to resign, and Russell was indicted. His transportation empire collapsed in 1862. Over the next ten years, he unsuccessfully engaged in speculative ventures in New York.

—*W. Turrentine Jackson*

SUGGESTED READING:
Bloss, Roy. *Pony Express—The Great Gamble.* Berkeley, Calif., 1959.
Chapman, Arthur. *The Pony Express.* New York, 1932.
Harlow, Alvin. *Old Waybills: The Romance of the Express Companies.* New York, 1934.
Jackson, W. Turrentine. "A New Look at Wells Fargo, Stagecoaches, and the Pony Express." *California Historical Society Quarterly* 45 (1966): 291–324.
———. "Wells Fargo's Pony Expresses." *Journal of the West* 11 (1972): 405–436.
Settle, Raymond W., and Mary L. Settle. *Empire on Wheels.* Stanford, Calif., 1949.
———. *Saddles and Spurs: The Pony Express.* Harrisburg, Pa., 1955.
———. War *Drums and Wagon Wheels.* Lincoln, Nebr., 1966.
Walker, Henry Pickering. *The Wagonmasters.* Norman, Okla., 1966.

RUSSELL, MAJORS AND WADDELL

The freighting partnership of Russell, Majors and Waddell was formed in 1854 to handle a contract from the U.S. Army to supply military posts in the West and Southwest. Previously, military personnel had supervised the supply trains to the army supply depot in Santa Fe, but the army deemed these efforts disorganized and wasteful. William Hepburn Russell and his early partner James H. Brown received the army's first contract for supplies. In 1854, when the quartermaster general decided to make a contract to supply the posts for a two-year period, Russell joined with ALEXANDER MAJORS and WILLIAM B. WADDELL to form a new company that took on the large assignment. The talents of the three men complemented each other: Majors had the field experience; Russell had financial and promotional connections; and Waddell was knowledgeable about trade and business.

The new firm sought to obtain a monopoly of the freighting business through government contracts and private business. From headquarters in Leavenworth, Kansas, the company contracted in 1857 to deliver up to five million pounds of military stores to the forts and depots in Kansas, New Mexico, and Utah.

At the beginning of the 1857 UTAH EXPEDITION in which the government instructed the army to accompany a new presidentially appointed territorial governor to the Utah Territory, the quartermaster at Fort Leavenworth notified Russell, Majors and Waddell that the army expected to ship two and a half million pounds of supplies to Salt Lake, an amount that would make their total shipment greater than specified in the contract. Rather than refuse the additional freight and jeopardize the company's position as prime contractors in

the West, Russell, Majors and Waddell undertook the assignment hoping for reimbursement later. Because of necessary purchases of additional wagons, oxen, and outfits for the train and because of attempts by the Mormons to destroy the U.S. Army's supply line, the freighting partnership lost heavily. The government delayed payment on services beyond the amount specified in the contract, a delay that further weakened the company's financial condition.

In 1858, Russell, Majors and Waddell agreed to haul ten million pounds of freight, twice as much as the company's initial contract, at a new price of $1.30 for every hundred pounds carried one hundred miles in summer, and $4 for the same distance in winter. If additional tonnage up to five million pounds needed to be shipped, the rate would be increased 25 percent because the company would again need to purchase additional oxen and wagons.

Because Russell, Majors and Waddell had purchased much on credit, Russell asked Secretary of War John B. Floyd for permission to issue drafts, known as "acceptances," against the War Department funds. The freighting firm's financial difficulties were further complicated by a decision to organize the Central Overland California and Pike's Peak Express, an express and stagecoach business. To attract national attention to the comparative advantage of the central route over the longer southern route used by the OVERLAND MAIL COMPANY in the trans-Mississippi West, Russell decided to establish the PONY EXPRESS. His partners initially objected but finally agreed.

In 1860, Russell was unable to meet his financial obligations. He used the remaining acceptances authorized by the War Department as security for Indian Trust Fund bonds, held by the Interior Department. When he was unable to raise the cash to redeem the bonds, the whole affair became public. Secretary Floyd was forced to resign, and Russell was arrested. That turn of events brought about the financial ruin of all of the partners in Russell, Majors and Waddell, and the firm failed in 1862.

—*W. Turrentine Jackson*

SUGGESTED READING:

Bloss, Roy. *Pony Express—The Great Gamble.* Berkeley, Calif., 1959.

Chapman, Arthur. *The Pony Express.* New York, 1932.

Harlow, Alvin. *Old Waybills: The Romance of the Express Companies.* New York, 1934.

Jackson, W. Turrentine. "A New Look at Wells Fargo, Stagecoaches, and the Pony Express." *California Historical Society Quarterly* 45 (1966): 291–324.

———. "Wells Fargo's Pony Expresses." *Journal of the West* 11 (1972): 405–436.

Settle, Raymond W., and Mary L. Settle. *Empire on Wheels.* Stanford, Calif., 1949.

———. *Saddles and Spurs: The Pony Express Saga.* Harrisburg, Pa., 1955.

———. *War Drums and Wagon Wheels.* Lincoln, Neb., 1966

Walker, Henry Pickering. *The Wagonmasters.* Norman, Okla., 1966.

RUSSIAN-AMERICAN COMPANY

Czar Peter the Great launched a major scientific exploration in 1741 led by VITUS BERING, in command of the *St. Peter,* and Aleksei Chirikov on the *St. Paul,* to explore eastward from Siberia. Bering reached the Gulf of Alaska, but on his return trip, his ship was partially wrecked, and he died at sea. The surviving crew members returned to Russia with sea-otter pelts and reported about their abundance in Alaska. Private fur traders then made numerous trips through the coastal islands and across the mainland. Grigory Shelikhov, one of the wealthiest merchants in Siberia, and his partner Golikov obtained a monopoly charter in 1799 for the Russian-American Company, a para-governmental organization similar to the British HUDSON'S BAY COMPANY.

Under Shelikhov's management, the company established five Russian outposts. A sixth settlement was established at Kodiak, which was the center of Russian settlement in the Pacific from 1784 to 1804. Sitka became the company's headquarters when ALEKSANDR BARANOV became general manager. The main object of all the Russian settlements was to hunt for fur-bearing animals and to eliminate competition by continuous exploration. Fort Ross on the Spanish California coast was the fifteenth settlement founded by the company.

By diplomatic conventions, the United States, in 1824, and Great Britain, in 1825, forced Russia to restrict exploration and fur hunting north of 54° 40'. Baron Ferdinand von Wrangell, a Russian naval officer and explorer, was in charge of the company between 1830 and 1835. When sea-otter populations began to decline due to overhunting, he renewed exploration on the Yukon and Kuskokwim rivers and inland along the Copper and other streams.

The Russian population remained very small, not exceeding a few hundred people. Many intermarried with the native population of Aleuts. Among the Russians living in Alaska were scientists who made pioneer studies on ethnology and natural history and searched for mineral deposits in the closing decades of company occupation of the region.

By the 1860s, the Russian-American Company was in financial difficulty, and the imperial government was dissatisfied with the cost of holding Alaska. Great Britain was a constant threat through economic pressure and possible annexation, and, most important, Russia's resources were needed to consolidate its position in Siberia along the Chinese border because of the rebellion in China. The United States seized the opportunity in 1867 to purchase Alaska from Russia for seven million dollars plus two hundred thousand dollars for the Russian-American Company.

—*W. Turrentine Jackson*

SEE ALSO: Alaskan Exploration; Exploration: Russian Expeditions

SUGGESTED READING:

Okun, S. B. *The Russian American Company.* New York, 1979.

Sherwood, Morgan, ed. *Alaska and Its History.* Seattle, Wash., 1967.

RUXTON, GEORGE FREDERICK

George Frederick Ruxton (1820–1848) traveled through Mexico and the Mexican-American border region during the United States–Mexican War and then through the U.S. Southwest and the Rocky Mountains. His *Adventures in Mexico and the Rocky Mountains* and *Life in the Far West* provide colorful and important accounts of life in the region.

Ruxton was born in England and was destined by his parents to a career as a soldier. He was educated at Sandhurst, the British military academy, but—eager for adventure—he left in 1837 to enlist as a volunteer in the service of Spain during a period of civil war. He distinguished himself and was decorated by Queen Isabella II.

Subsequently, Ruxton joined a British regiment as an officer and was posted to Canada by 1840. He soon chafed under the tedium of garrison life and resigned his commission. He set off on an abortive trans-African trek and then returned to North America. At the time of the United States–Mexican War, Ruxton ventured into Mexico via Vera Cruz and traveled north to the American Southwest and on to the Rocky Mountain region. In Mexico and the Southwest, he proved himself a keen observer of life. He also recorded the experience of war, chiefly from the perspective of the Mexicans. His wanderings in the Rockies brought him into contact with colorful trappers and mountain men. He also engaged in a series of hunting adventures, which he vividly portrayed in "Life in the Far West," a series of sketches that first appeared in London's *Blackwood's Magazine* and subsequently in book form. The sketches, which deal mainly with a trapper named La Bronté—perhaps a fictional composite—are considered to be among the most vivid and thorough portrayals of life in the Rockies during the waning days of the fur trade.

Ruxton left the United States in July 1847 and reached England in August. He died a year later.

—*Alan Axelrod*

SUGGESTED READING:

Hafen, LeRoy, and Clyde Porter, eds. *Life in the Far West.* Norman, Okla., 1979.

———. *Ruxton of the Rockies.* Norman, Okla., 1979.

RYAN, JOHN DENNIS

John Dennis Ryan's (1864–1933) aggressive leadership of Montana's Anaconda Copper Mining Company (ACM) made him one of the nation's foremost capitalists. A native of the copper country near Houghton, Michigan, Ryan showed little interest in the industry or in college. He clerked in his uncle's store before moving to Denver, Colorado, where he became regional manager for an oil company. In that capacity, he met Montana copper magnate MARCUS DALY, gained the Amalgamated (Anaconda) Copper Company's lucrative account, and won Daly's favor.

After Daly's death in 1900, Ryan moved to Butte, became president of the Daly Bank and Trust Company, and managed the Standard Oil Company's Butte properties. Amazingly, he succeeded in pacifying warring "copper kings" WILLIAM ANDREWS CLARK and FREDERICK AUGUSTUS HEINZE. By 1906, the Amalgamated had purchased the primary Butte holdings of both opponents—thus ending the War of the Copper Kings.

Ryan became president of the Amalgamated (Anaconda) Company in 1909, at the age of forty-four. Under his direction, the corporation consolidated its diverse holdings, expanded to Mexico and South America, and absorbed the American Brass Company, the world's largest consumer of copper. In 1912, Ryan orchestrated the creation of the Montana Power Company (MPC), which soon provided electrical power to much of Montana.

MPC electrified first the Butte, Anaconda and Pacific Railroad in 1913 and, three years later, the 440-mile Rocky Mountain division of the Chicago, Milwaukee, St. Paul and Pacific Railroad (Milwaukee Road). For

years, Ryan served on the MPC board of directors, as well as on the board of its biggest customer, ACM.

After a short term in Washington, D.C., as a corporate volunteer during World War I, Ryan resumed his swift corporate climb and evolved from a Western promoter and executive to a national industrial lord. With the support of Anaconda executive Cornelius F. "Con" Kelley, Ryan shaped ACM into a powerful international organization, specializing in copper, silver, and brass production. A company man who launched profitable personal ventures, he invested in banks, natural gas, mining stocks, and railroads.

At the time of his death, Ryan was the head of an industrial conglomerate he had fashioned with vision, shrewd calculation, formidable negotiating skills, and determination. He was perhaps best characterized by historian Carrie Johnson as a "blend of 'modern' executive and old-fashioned financier."

—David A. Walter

SEE ALSO: Anaconda Mining Company; Copper Kings, War of the

SUGGESTED READING:

Bertie C. Forbes. "John D. Ryan." In *Men Who Are Making the West.* New York, 1923.

Johnson, Carrie. "Electrical Power, Copper, and John D. Ryan," *Montana: The Magazine of Western History* 38: 4 (Autumn 1988): 24–37.

Marcosson, Isaac F. *Anaconda.* New York, 1957.

RYNNING, THOMAS H.

Orphaned in his childhood years in Beloit, Wisconsin, Thomas H. Rynning (1866–1941) came to epitomize the Western rambling man. From the age of twelve when he first headed to Texas, he tried a variety of professions but never managed to stay in one for very long. His first jobs were teamstering and cowboying. By 1885, he had enlisted in the army and was assigned to the Eighth U.S. Cavalry. When the Eighth transferred to Arizona, Rynning saw action against the Navajos and against GERONIMO.

After six years of service, Rynning left the military for WILLIAM F. ("BUFFALO BILL") CODY's Wild West Show. For Cody, he entertained the crowds as a "real-life" cowboy and Indian fighter. Ending his stint in show business, he joined the track crews of the Southern Pacific Railroad, working the lines between Los Angeles and West Texas.

The United States's war with Spain in 1898 caused Rynning to reenlist, joining THEODORE ROOSEVELT's Rough Riders. After the war, he accepted a captain's commission in the ARIZONA RANGERS in 1902. Leaving the rangers, he served as the superintendent of the territorial prison at Yuma. Under his supervision, the prison became a modern and efficient institution.

—Patricia Hogan

SEE ALSO: Wild West Shows

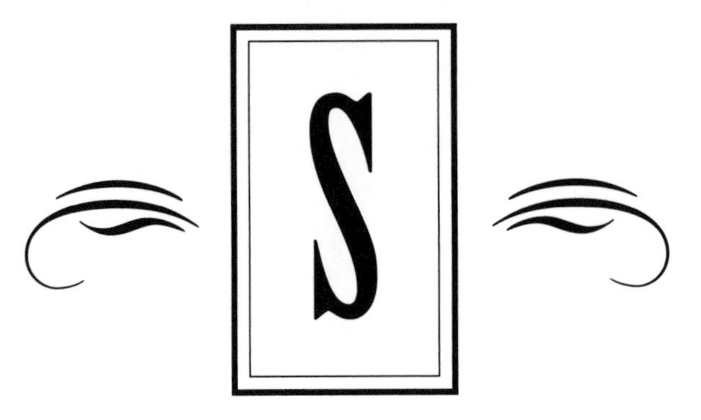

SACAGAWEA (SHOSHONE)

No Native American woman has a more instantly recognizable name in modern times than the young Shoshone Sacagawea (ca. 1788–1812). Her role in the LEWIS AND CLARK EXPEDITION has been celebrated in books, movies, and public monuments. The legend of Sacagawea as guide for MERIWETHER LEWIS and WILLIAM CLARK has grown so large as to obscure what the surviving historical record reveals about her remarkable life.

Born into a band of Lemhi Shoshones, Sacagawea was captured by Hidatsa raiders at the Three Forks of the Missouri sometime around 1800. She and several other female captives were taken to the Hidatsa village of Metaharta on the Knife River in present-day North Dakota. Sometime between 1800 and 1805, Sacagawea and a second Shoshone woman were purchased by French Canadian trader Toussaint Charbonneau. When the Lewis and Clark Expedition reached the Mandan and Hidatsa villages in the fall of 1804, Charbonneau was hired as an interpreter. After learning that Sacagawea knew both Shoshone and Hidatsa and that Charbonneau could translate from Hidatsa to French, Lewis and Clark accepted Sacagawea as member of the expedition, and she became an important asset.

Three controversies have long swirled around Sacagawea. The first involves her precise role on the expedition's journey. Sacagawea was neither a simple tag-along nor a skilled guide. Most of the country traversed by Lewis and Clark was as new to her as it was to them. She did spot important landmarks in southwestern Montana, but her more valuable service was as a translator. Her presence also persuaded many native people that the expedition was not a war party. The Indian woman's name—its spelling and meaning—have also sparked considerable debate. Most scholars now agree that the name should be spelled "Sacagawea," following the various ways Lewis and Clark spelled it in their journals. Linguists believe that the name is not Shoshone but Hidatsa and means something close to "bird woman." Sacagawea's death date and burial place have also prompted some sharp differences of opinion. While a few writers still hold to the outdated view that Sacagawea died in Wyoming's Wind River country in 1884, reliable sources now demonstrate that she died in 1812 and was buried at Fort Manuel on the Missouri River.

—*James P. Ronda*

SUGGESTED READING:

Anderson, Irving W. *A Charbonneau Family Portrait.* Fort Clatsop, Oreg., 1988.

Howard, Harold P. *Sacajawea.* Norman, Okla., 1971.

Ronda, James P. *Lewis and Clark among the Indians.* Lincoln, Nebr., 1984.

SAC AND FOX INDIANS

SEE: Native American Peoples: Peoples Removed from the East

SACRAMENTO, CALIFORNIA

Sacramento, the state capital of CALIFORNIA, developed where the American River joins the Sacramento. Its roots can be traced to the Swiss adventurer JOHN AUGUST SUTTER, who, in 1839, obtained a fifty-thousand-acre grant in California's Central Valley from the Mexican government and attempted to establish a self-sufficient farming and ranching empire. In the early 1840s, his headquarters, Sutter's Fort, on a knoll a mile from the confluence of the American and Sacramento

Johann Hesse's 1850 lithograph of Sacramento. *Courtesy Library of Congress.*

rivers, served as a place of refuge and work for settlers and explorers coming over the Sierra Nevada from the United States. In 1848, gold was discovered on Sutter's land near Coloma; the gold rush that followed overran his holdings. In December 1848, Sutter's son and merchant SAMUEL BRANNAN laid out a town they called Sacramento City on the low ground between Sutter's landing and his fort.

Ninety miles by river from the port of San Francisco, at the head of summer navigation, Sacramento was soon connected by stage line to the mines. As the distribution point for men and materials headed for the mining camps in the Sierra foothills, Sacramento boomed, reaching a population of 6,820 in 1850. In 1854, the California legislature, recognizing the importance of the mining economy, moved the state capital there. And even after gold production slowed, Sacramento continued as a vital transportation center. In 1860, the PONY EXPRESS had its western terminus in Sacramento; the next year, so did the transcontinental TELEGRAPH. Also in 1861, visionary promoter THEODORE DEHONE JUDAH persuaded Sacramento merchants AMASA LELAND STANFORD, CHARLES CROCKER, COLLIS P. HUNTINGTON, and MARK HOPKINS to back the Central Pacific, the western segment of the transcontinental railroad.

But the railroad, which terminated at Oakland, would eventually make Sacramento a tributary to San Francisco. Sutter, fearing floods, had opposed building near the confluence of the rivers; he had been right, for despite extensive systems of levees, annual floods retarded Sacramento's growth. At the end of the nineteenth century, it had a population of only 29,292, sustained primarily by processing and shipping the increasingly valuable agricultural produce of the Sacramento Valley. The city's importance was restored only when the CENTRAL VALLEY PROJECT, begun in 1937, protected Sacramento from flooding while further promoting agricultural production. World War II brought new defense industries, and as the whole state boomed after the war, the state government, which had to expand services to keep up, became Sacramento's economic focus.

From the time that the Swiss-born Mexican citizen John Sutter had employed Hawaiians, Californios, Indians, and Anglo-Americans, the area had been ethnically diverse. Sacramento Valley farms had attracted labor from China, Japan, and Mexico; the railroad yards and processing plants had hired many Eastern Europeans. In 1900, one-fourth of Sacramento's population was foreign-born. World War II brought an

influx of blacks from the South. The rapid suburbanization of the 1950s and 1960s increasingly segregated minority populations, with the result that busing to achieve racial balance in schools was undertaken in the mid-1960s. In the 1970s and 1980s, in a struggle to control growth, Sacramento discouraged some industries from locating there, mandated open space, and limited access to water. In 1990, metropolitan Sacramento had 846,097 residents.

—*Ralph Mann*

See also: California Gold Rush

SUGGESTED READING:

Dana, Julian. *The Sacramento, River of Gold.* New York, 1939.

Holden, Anna. *The Bus Stops Here.* New York, 1974.

Mahan, William E. "The Political Response to Urban Growth: Sacramento and Mayor Marshall R. Beard, 1863–1914." *California History* 69 (1990–1991): 354–371.

SACRAMENTO RIVER

Carrying about a third of all California's run-off, the Sacramento River, flecked with golden sand from the Sierra Nevada foothills, runs from its source in the Klamath range almost four hundred miles southward, where it mingles in a delta with the SAN JOAQUIN RIVER before emptying into San Francisco Bay. The run-off is greater than that of the Colorado, and it flows into the Sacramento from numerous tributaries draining the Cascades and the Sierra Nevada—the most significant of them are the McCloud River, the Pit River, the Feather River, the Yuba River, the Bear River, and the AMERICAN RIVER. Peak flows come from spring snow melts, but sudden floods sometimes occur when unusually warm winter rains fall and create an early melt. The Sacramento drains areas high and low, from the fourteen-thousand-foot high Mount Shasta to points in the delta below sea level. Mild winters and hot summers typify the climate of the Sacramento Valley, where winter fogs quilt the valley floor for weeks on end.

Although the Spanish had tried to penetrate the swampy maze of the delta region for years, it was not until 1817 that Captain Luis Arguello discovered he could cross the Golden Gate by raft and work his way north around San Francisco Bay to the Sacramento. Called by both the Spanish colonials and the Mexicans Rio de San Francisco, it did not become known as the Sacramento until non-Spanish Europeans and Americans picked up on a name that explorer Gabriel Moraga had given one of its branches, El Rio de los Sacramentos, and applied it to the whole river. The first of these Europeans was JOHN AUGUST SUTTER, who settled at the junction of the American and the Sacramento, acquired immense land grants along both rivers, and set up a fort supplying overland emigrants to the Sacramento Valley. It was on Sutter's land that one of his hired hands, John Marshall, made the discovery in 1848 that launched the CALIFORNIA GOLD RUSH. First from Buena Yuba on San Francisco Bay, then from around the world, came prospectors steaming, sailing, and rowing up the Sacramento as far as Marysville and Red Bluff. The miners blasted from the hills tons of silt and sand, which clogged up stream beds, created sand bars, killed fish, and made navigation of the Sacramento, which had been extensive in 1850, nearly impossible by 1860. When U.S. courts banned (in *WOODRUFF V. NORTH BLOOMFIELD, ET AL.*) hydraulic mining in 1884, navigation was limited to low-draft boats.

Miners diverted mountain streams to make sluices and use in hoses to blast the gold free from the foothills, and the dams and canals they created were taken over by bonanza farmers who made the Sacramento Valley into a great wheat-growing region by the end of the century. In 1945, the BUREAU OF RECLAMATION'S CENTRAL VALLEY PROJECT aimed to tame the river and aid the farmers by controlling floods, conserving water, and generating electricity for northern California. The area's biggest utility, Pacific Gas and Electricity, also constructed dozens of dams on the main Sacramento tributaries. In time, not only wheat, but rice, cotton, and other field crops came to depend upon water from the Sacramento, which, at least since mid-century, had become essential to California's hydraulic civilization.

—*Charles Phillips*

SUGGESTED READING:

Dana, Julian. *The Sacramento, River of Gold.* New York, 1939.

SADDLE, STOCK

SEE: Cowboy Tools and Equipment

SAFETY-VALVE THEORY

According to the safety-valve theory, the availability of Western lands provided an opportunity for Eastern factory workers to make a fresh start as independent farmers. As workers left the industrialized East, the labor supply was reduced and wages, therefore, re-

As long as farm land out west was available to Eastern factory workers, according to the saftey-valve theory, the United States could avoid the urban-industrial discontent common to nineteenth-century Europe. Top: Residence of R. L. Rule, Arizona Territory, ca. 1898. *Courtesy National Archives.* Bottom: Two women before a sod house on the Kansas prairie. *Courtesy Kansas State Historical Society.*

mained relatively high. Thus, the urban-industrial discontent that was common in nineteenth-century Europe did not afflict the United States. In short, the frontier acted as a safety valve for urban discontent.

This theory is often attributed to FREDERICK JACKSON TURNER, but he was certainly not the first to present it and did not place much emphasis on it in his 1893 essay, "The Significance of the Frontier in American History." Safety-valve theories were a product of America's agrarian heritage and began to appear more than a century before Turner's frontier thesis. In 1787, THOMAS JEFFERSON declared, "Our governments will remain virtuous . . . as long as there shall be vacant lands in any part of America. When [the people] get piled upon one another in large cities, as in Europe, they will become corrupt as in Europe, and go to eating one another." Numerous European observers in the late eighteenth and nineteenth centuries pointed to the safety valve of Western lands as the factor that made America different from Europe. And, in the antebellum South, defenders of slavery constructed a safety-valve argument in defense of the peculiar institution. They contended that the supply of free land was the only factor guaranteeing a system of free labor in the North and warned that it would soon disappear and the North would have to adopt slavery.

By the 1870s, a number of observers, including social critic HENRY GEORGE and journalist Charles Nordhoff, suggested that the safety valve was closing, and by the 1880s, these expressions of concern were becoming more common. Italian economist Achille Loria, the English lord, James Bryce, and literary realists HAMLIN GARLAND and William Dean Howells pointed to the imminent loss of America's trump card. From this cultural climate, Frederick Jackson Turner's frontier thesis emerged. Turner noted that "each frontier" had furnished "a new field of opportunity, a gate of escape from the bondage of the past" and worried that the frontier era had come to a close. Would America now come to resemble Europe, where there was little social mobility and an abundance of class conflict? That same year the prominent economist Richard T. Ely contended that the closing of the frontier safety valve necessitated population control to prevent a social explosion. Also, in 1893, the Populist leader IGNATIUS DONNELLY declared, "When the valve is closed, swarming mankind every day will increase the danger of explosion."

In the 1880s and 1890s, some advocates of immigration restriction argued that America would be unable to assimilate and Americanize new immigrants without its safety valve of Western lands. And, by the 1930s, the safety-valve theory had become so ingrained in American thinking that it was being used by advocates of large-scale government assistance to those suffering the effects of the Great Depression. Defenders of Franklin Roosevelt's New Deal social programs ar-

gued that the federal government had a responsibility to provide for its citizens now that the safety valve of Western lands had closed.

In the 1930s, scholars were also beginning to question the validity of the safety-valve theory. How, it was argued, could poor Eastern factory workers, earning one or two dollars a day in the mid-nineteenth century, afford to save the approximately fifteen hundred dollars necessary to buy land, seed, and supplies and travel to the Western frontier? In the 1940s, Fred Shannon argued that nineteenth-century farmers moved to the cities in far larger numbers than Eastern workers took up farms. Shannon concluded that the frontier was not a safety valve for urban discontent; in fact, the opposite was true: the city was a safety valve for rural discontent.

As criticism of the safety-valve theory increased in the 1930s and 1940s, Turner's former students were overly defensive of what they mistakenly believed to be a central element of their teacher's frontier thesis. As a result of the intense debates, students will find a mountain of scholarship devoted to the issue of whether the safety valve operated as it was supposed to. While Fred Shannon, in 1945, declared the safety-valve theory to be dead and buried and proclaimed to conduct a post-mortem on it, in the 1960s, some strong defenses were mounted. Ellen von Nardroff, while conceding that the frontier safety valve had not worked directly, contended that it might have worked in more indirect ways. She noted that while Eastern factory workers clearly did not head West to become farmers, Eastern farmers (who might have become factory workers) moved West, and so did large numbers of immigrants. Thus, the frontier benefited wage laborers in the East by siphoning away potential workers whose presence in the job market would have lowered wages—it was an "indirect" safety valve. Furthermore, Nardroff argued, the frontier acted as a "resources" safety valve because the development of natural resources in the West helped keep Eastern wages high. And, finally, she suggested that the frontier served as a "socio-psychological" safety valve. By this, she meant that while most Eastern workers could not afford to start their lives anew on the Western frontier, the presence of a frontier of available land nonetheless held out a certain promise to them; belief in the frontier's limitless opportunity offered a degree of hope.

Since the 1960s, as Western historians have focused more on groups, such as Native Americans, who were displaced by the advancing tide of white settlement and on the destruction of the Western environment, they have been less concerned with whether the frontier acted as a safety valve for urban discontent in the East. New Western historians have shifted attention away from the idea of a frontier process and emphasized instead the West as a geographically defined place. Still, while discussions of the safety-valve theory have little relevance to Western historians today, the notion of poor nineteenth-century Eastern factory workers taking up farms on the Western frontier (inaccurate as it is) still seems to have a hold on the American imagination.

—*David M. Wrobel*

SEE ALSO: Frontier: Frontier Thesis

SUGGESTED READING:

Billington, Ray A. *The American Frontier Thesis: Valid Interpretation of American History?* New York, 1966.

———. *America's Frontier Heritage.* New York, 1966.

Deverell, William F. "To Loosen the Safety Valve: Eastern Workers and Western Lands." *Western Historical Quarterly* 19 (1988): 269–285.

Shannon, Fred A. "A Post-Mortem on the Labor Safety-Valve Theory." *Agricultural History* 19 (1945): 31–37.

Taylor, George Rogers, ed. *The Turner Thesis: Concerning the Role of the Frontier in American History.* Lexington, Mass, 1972.

Von Nardroff, Ellen. "The American Frontier as a Safety Valve—The Life, Death, Reincarnation, and Justification of a Theory." *Agricultural History* 36 (July 1962): 123–142.

Wrobel, David M. *The End of American Exceptionalism: Frontier Anxiety from the Old West to the New Deal.* Lawrence, Kans., 1993.

ST. JOSEPH, MISSOURI

In the summer of 1826, when Joseph Robidoux, II, established a trading post on the MISSOURI RIVER at the doorway to the Platte region, Native American tribes still claimed the territory as their own. By 1836, the trading post was called the town of St. Joseph, and the land-hungry Missourians had taken the Platte from the Indians. Its commerce fed by the stream of Western migration in the 1840s, St. Jo—as the Missourians called the place—grew rapidly throughout the decade. By 1849, when two thousand wagon trains crossed the Missouri, St. Jo challenged Independence and Westport Landing as the state's most popular rendezvous for departing pioneers. The emigrants had to eat, and St. Jo's citizens raised hogs to feed them, thereby establishing the nucleus of a meat-packing industry that played a key role in the town's economy until the 1960s. Even before the Civil War, St. Joseph had become Missouri's second largest city after St. Louis, and the completion of the St. Joseph Railroad in 1859 only made it a more popular jumping-off point than ever.

In fact, since the railroad, the first to span the state, siphoned off Missouri River traffic bound for Chicago through St. Joseph rather than St. Louis, citizens of the latter—notoriously ambitious to become the gateway West and in a traditional bitter rivalry with Chicago—were none too happy to see the rail line completed. The railroad made St. Jo the eastern terminus for the PONY EXPRESS in 1860 and 1861, but that may have been the high point of the town's glory days. After the Civil War, Kansas City, closer to the cattle trails, just as eager to by-pass St. Louis and deal directly with Chicago, stole St. Joseph's thunder as a center for trade and pass-through commerce. St. Joseph failed to get a bridge across the Missouri funded until 1873, and Kansas City's dominance was irreversible. St. Joseph's significance to the history of the trans-Mississippi was a thing of the past.

—*Charles Phillips*

SEE ALSO: Robidoux Brothers; Overland Freight; Overland Travel

SUGGESTED READING:

Phillips, Charles. *Missouri: Mother of the American West.* Northridge, Calif., 1988.

ST. LOUIS, MISSOURI

For centuries, Indians lived near the junction of the Mississippi and Missouri rivers. Indeed, for more than a thousand years, the area around St. Louis had been an urban center when Pierre Laclède, on February 15, 1764, told Auguste Chouteau where to locate their fur trading post. Yet, these Frenchmen knew nothing of the ages-old Native American presence, and in their eyes, they *founded* the trans-Mississippi outpost. On the limestone bluff above the flood levels south of the mouth of the Missouri, the post was to serve as headquarters of the fur-trading monopoly given by Jean Jacques D'Abbadie, the last French governor of Louisiana, to the Maxent-Laclède Company of New Orleans to engage in the Osage Indian fur business. The Osages lived up the Missouri River, then as now the water route into the American West. An earlier Indian culture, which scholars call the Mississippian, had already come and gone, leaving behind great earthen mounds on both sides of the river as mute testimony to their civilization. Laclède called his post "St. Louis," but others called it "Mound City."

Because it was founded shortly after the French lost the French and Indian War, the population of St. Louis swelled with Eastern émigrés, seeking to escape British rule. By 1770, when Laclède died, the population had grown to about five hundred; it would take nearly another twenty years before the number of citizens doubled. After THOMAS JEFFERSON bought the French out of the American West with the LOUISIANA PURCHASE in 1803, the United States made the town the seat of the territorial government. When explorers MERIWETHER LEWIS and WILLIAM CLARK visited the city before they began their Western expedition from 1804 to 1806, more than twenty-five hundred people lived in greater St. Louis—about half the size of the population of Pittsburgh at the same time.

In earlier times, many had believed that other river cities, such as Ste. Genevieve, would grow faster than St. Louis, but when the federal government centered its offices and forts in the St. Louis area, making it a gateway to the West, the city was ensured steady income and growth beyond CHOUTEAU FAMILY enterprises. Lewis and Clark, and other explorers, including ZEBULON MONTGOMERY PIKE and JOHN CHARLES FRÉMONT, confirmed that the West offered a natural bounty. Fur and lead, for decades, remained the two major commodities shipped through St. Louis, and trade along such commercial routes as the Santa Fe Trail increased its commercial importance. Fur traders with JOHN JACOB ASTOR'S AMERICAN FUR COMPANY used the Missouri River to reach the northern Rocky Mountains. MOUNTAIN MEN, competitors of the company's Upper Missouri Outfit, followed the Missouri to the Platte River and went overland to the central Rocky Mountains and the Green River country. As the FUR TRADE declined, hundreds of thousands of pioneers headed

St. Louis on the Mississippi River in 1885, thirty years after the city's incorporation. *Courtesy Library of Congress.*

west on the OREGON TRAIL, and St. Louis businesses provided them with provisions and supplies. First as a great RIVER TRANSPORTATION port, then as a mid-nineteenth century railroad terminus, St. Louis became crucial for people settling in the West and a significant center of transportation and commerce, a legacy it would maintain when the airplane, the automobile, and the truck took their place historically beside the riverboat and the iron horse.

Meanwhile, the city developed other economic mainstays. Early in the nineteenth century, the French fur and lead businesses gave way to manufacturing, and agriculture soon took its place alongside major industries. One of the enigmas of St. Louis has always been its historical disdain for the farm economy that played so important a role in its history. While its industry attracted Mediterranean immigrants, agriculture attracted the Irish, Germans, and other northern Europeans, making the latter more numerous, and later agribusinesses like Ralston-Purina and Monsanto Chemical certainly compared in importance to McDonnell Douglas and Granite City Steel.

The Civil War, for a period, halted the growth of St. Louis and its involvement in the commercial exploitation of the West. After the war, both investment and railroads stayed north, and much of the great, late nineteenth-century immigration from eastern Europe side-stepped St. Louis, making its hated rival, CHICAGO, ILLINOIS, the new gateway to the West. The local population moved away from the river, and St. Louis lost interest in Missouri's historical role as "mother" of the American West. Divisions between urban and suburban groups amplified the deeper divisions that had grown out of the Civil War, leading to racial tensions, ethnic divisions, and commercial in-fighting. The Mississippi and Missouri became boundaries between ethnic and socio-economic groups rather than water routes to commerce and growth.

While the divisions in St. Louis gnawed at its strength, other circumstances began to change its outlook. Twentieth-century wars made river transportation more important. Universities and cultural groups became significant in making life more meaningful for the whole population. TOURISM developed around the new national park on the old St. Louis river front traditionally known for its fur and steamboat traffic. One of the more significant features of St. Louis remained its architecture—from Indian mounds to great commercial and ecclesiastical structures: the Wainwright Building, the Old Cathedral, the Old Courthouse, and Union Station, all near the historic river-front area. With the building of the Gateway Arch and Busch Memorial Stadium, the region developed a new vitality. As St. Louis neared the twenty-first century, many of its leaders were, it seemed, at last coming to grips with its urban-suburban division and its as yet unresolved ethnic issues.

In the long run, St. Louis's history has always been tied to the great rivers that converge nearby, and the great Mississippi flood of 1993 testified to their continuing significance. The river system made transportation of agricultural and extractive products easy and inexpensive. It made shipment of the commodities necessary for settlement inexpensive. Because of the rivers, great commercial enterprises based on agriculture and mining developed in St. Louis, giving it one of the most diverse economies in the nation. The rivers also made St. Louis a center of tourism by spawning a popular interest in old ways of living and the early ethnic roots of the people of St. Louis. In some respects, ethnic difference has made way for ethnic tolerance through exploration of the past. Renewed interest in the West once again made St. Louis a hub for travel throughout North America, and the increased presence of non-English speaking visitors to St. Louis and the Mississippi river front testified to the international interest in the river and in westward expansion.

—*Ray Breun*

SUGGESTED READING:

Chittenden, Hiram Martin. *The American Fur Trade of the Far West.* 2 vols. 1935. Reprint. Lincoln, Nebr., 1986

Dosch, Donald F. *The Old Courthouse: Americans Build a Forum on the Frontier.* St. Louis, Mo., 1979.

Faherty, Barnaby. *The St. Louis Portrait.* Tulsa, Okla., 1979.

Holt, Glen, and Selwyn Troen, eds. *Saint Louis.* New York, 1977.

Phillips, Charles. *Missouri: Mother of the American West.* Northridge, Calif., 1988.

Primm, James Neal. *Lion of the Valley: St. Louis, Missouri.* 1954. Reprint. Boulder, Colo., 1981.

Rodabough, John. *Frenchtown.* St. Louis, Mo., 1980.

Smith, Bruce D., ed. *The Mississippian Emergence.* Washington, D.C., 1990.

Wishart, David J. *The Fur Trade of the American West, 1807-1840.* Lincoln, Nebr., 1979.

ST. LOUIS, MISSOURI, FIRE

About ten o'clock in the evening of Thursday, May 17, 1849, fire began on the steamboat *White Cloud* moored off Cherry Street along the north part of St. Louis's river-front wharf. Sparks from a passing steamer landed on the freshly painted part of the boat, burst into flames, and spread to the steamboat *Edward Bates,* tied up to the rear of the *White Cloud.* Those who spotted the fire on the boats cut them loose from the wharf and pushed into the flow of the Mississippi. Propelled by a strong and unusual wind from the east, the

two burning boats bumped down the row of steamboats and spread the fire. In less than one hour, the entire waterfront was blazing; not only the boats along the wharf but the places of business on the levee caught fire. The fire spread past the levee to the buildings beyond Main Street. The size of the blaze and its concentration along the river made it impossible for the several volunteer fire companies to gain access to the Mississippi's water to fight the fire.

The fire burned all night and into the following morning. More than four hundred buildings, twenty-three steamboats, three barges, a canal boat, and tons of raw and manufactured goods burned. All or part of fifteen square blocks of the old St. Louis river front were destroyed. Captain Thomas B. Targee of the Missouri Volunteer Fire Brigade came up with the idea of using black powder from the nearby federal arsenal to blow up buildings and create a firebreak. His plan worked, but Targee, himself, was blown up in one of the explosions.

In the months after the fire, the city's board of aldermen finally saw to wharf and street improvements, school and health systems, and many types of services—including trained firemen—necessary to make the city safe and habitable. The St. Louis fire was the crucible out of which the modern city of St. Louis emerged.

—*Ray Breun*

SUGGESTED READING:

Dosch, Donald F. *The Old Courthouse: Americans Build a Forum on the Frontier.* St. Louis, Mo., 1979.
Floyd, Candace. *America's Great Disasters.* New York, 1990.
Primm, James Neal. *Lion of the Valley: St. Louis, Missouri.* Boulder, Colo., 1981.

ST. VRAIN, CERAN DE HAULT DE LASSUS

Southwestern fur trader and pioneer of the Santa Fe trade, Ceran de Hault de Lassus St. Vrain (1802–1870) was a native of Missouri. He started his career in merchandising as a clerk in a St. Louis store. In 1824, he obtained goods on credit and pioneered the Santa Fe trade. He quickly prospered in both the Southwestern FUR TRADE and in merchandising. In 1830, for example, he took goods worth three thousand dollars over the SANTA FE AND CHIHUAHUA TRAIL and sold them for ten thousand dollars.

Marrying a New Mexican woman by 1826, he lived in Taos and eventually became a Mexican citizen. In 1831, with partner Charles Bent, he established Bent, St. Vrain, and Company. Three years later, the two men constructed BENT'S FORT on the north bank of the ARKANSAS RIVER. The partners complemented each other admirably in personalities and talents and enjoyed the high regard of their associates. By the early 1840s, only the AMERICAN FUR COMPANY did more business in the Rocky Mountain West. While Bent's Fort remained their headquarters, they also built other trading posts or forts, including one named for St. Vrain.

When Charles Bent was killed in 1847, St. Vrain reorganized the company with William Bent in a partnership that lasted until about 1850. St. Vrain then devoted himself to other enterprises. He was associated with the enterprise that later became the MAXWELL LAND GRANT COMPANY. Owner of a flour mill and sawmills, investor in a Santa Fe bank and the *Santa Fe Gazette,* he dabbled in politics and, in 1861, served briefly as colonel of the First New Mexico Cavalry. St. Vrain died in 1870. His funeral in Mora, his residence since 1855, was a major event in New Mexico.

—*John Porter Bloom*

SEE ALSO: Bent Brothers

SUGGESTED READING:

Hafen, LeRoy R., ed. *The Mountain Men and the Fur Trade of the Far West.* 10 vols. Glendale, Calif., 1965–1972.
Lavender, David. *Bent's Fort.* Garden City, N.Y., 1954.

SALCIDO, ABRÁN

On June 3, 1903, more than thirty-five hundred Mexican miners walked out on strike against the Arizona Copper Company and the Detroit Company in protest over a pay cut. One of the strike leaders was Abrán Salcido, a twenty-six-year-old smelter worker from Chihuahua, Mexico. Salcido's bilingual skills in English and Spanish enabled him to form important political linkages as well as a cultural bond with Mexican and Mexican American miners. These workers believed that the WESTERN FEDERATION OF MINERS, in not accepting Mexicans as members, hindered their earning an equitable wage. Salcido encouraged the strikers to organize and make their demands known. He and the Mexican strikers called for an equitable wage scale for Mexican miners, an end to the *boleta* (scrip) system of pay, to the arbitrary raising of prices in the company store, and to double-standard wages. On June 9, 1903, at least two thousand Mexican workers conducted a one-hour parade through Morenci streets in the rain. The rain turned violent, however, and a flood soon broke out in the Clifton area, ending the strike. Governor Alexander O. Brodie placed the neighboring town

of Morenci under martial law on June 12 to discourage any further strike activity and called for the arrest of strike leaders in the Clifton-Morenci area. Salcido was among those arrested. He was fined one thousand dollars and sentenced to serve two years at the Arizona Territorial Prison in Yuma for his part in agitating the Mexican workers and in helping to lead the Clifton-Morenci strike. Salcido became a folk-hero to the Mexican people, and a *corrido* (folk-song) was written and sung in his honor.

After he was released from prison in the spring of 1906, Salcido returned to the Arizona mining town of Metcalf to continue his labor activities with the Mexican miners there. At the Fifth of May celebration of the Mexicans, Salcido made several inflammatory speeches against Mexican President Porfirio Díaz and his government's policies. After being run out of town by Mexicans who feared violence between pro-Díaz and anti-Díaz sympathizers in the crowd, Salcido went to Douglas, Arizona, where he participated in the formation of the organization known as the "Club Lerdo de Tejada," a three-hundred-member, mutual-aid society for Mexicans committed to the overthrow of Díaz. Salcido was also involved with the Partido Liberal Mexicano. The PLM opposed Díaz's policy of allowing American industrialists to invest in the Mexican economy and, in particular, American investment in the copper-mining industry. Among the symbols of American financial power and foreign encroachment on Mexico's economy were the Cananea Copper Consolidated Company and its owner, William Cornell Greene. Discontent among the Mexicans spread throughout the Cananea camp, and the PLM encouraged a strike against the American company. Abrán Salcido was in Cananea to help the Mexicans organize. On June 1, 1906, the Cananea strike against Greene and his company began. When violence erupted at the lumberyard, Greene called on the Mexican government for assistance. Mounted rural police *(rurales)* arrived in Cananea on the evening of June 2, and their presence put an end to the strike. Although Salcido was not present at the Cananea strike, American officials believed that he had encouraged Mexican miners to walk out.

In early August, just two months after the failed strike at Cananea, Ricardo Flores Magón appointed Salcido to supervise all PLM activities in Arizona. Salcido chose Douglas as his headquarters. He formulated a plan to capture the northern region of Mexico, and he arranged with other PLM supporters to transport arms and munitions across the border into Mexico. With the help of his PLM compatriots, Salcido prepared a military expedition to march into northern Mexico. But a spy employed by the Díaz government infiltrated the PLM and betrayed Salcido and his followers by revealing their plans. Salcido got wind of the betrayal and canceled his invasion. On September 4, 1906, Abrán Salcido was arrested in Douglas by the Arizona Rangers and charged with violating U.S. immigration laws. An American judge found him guilty and ordered his removal from the United States. On September 12, 1906, Abrán Salcido was deported to Hermosillo, Sonora, Mexico. The deportation put an end to his career as a revolutionary for the PLM in Arizona. His role as a labor leader for the Mexican miners in the Clifton-Morenci area, however, became a part of the region's folklore. Abrán Salcido is still celebrated in such songs as "1903 Strike Corrido," written by Lonnie Guerrero:

> These verses that I sing is a corrido/ To remember a hero/ Whose name is Abrán Salcido./ He came to Clifton, Arizona to help his countrymen/ Earn an equal wage like the Americans./ At the height of the tension, a heavy thunderstorm broke./ A massive flood swept over the city./ These verses that I sing is a corrido/ To remember a hero/ Whose name is Abrán Salcido.

—*Christine Marín*

See also: Arizona Mining Strikes; Labor Movement

Suggested reading:
Gálan, Hector, producer. *Los Mineros.* Originally aired on January 28, 1991, for the PBS Series "The American Experience." WGBH Education Foundation, WNET/Thirteen and Galan Productions, Inc.
Park, Joseph E. "The 1903 'Mexican Affair' at Clifton." *Journal of Arizona History* 18 (Summer 1977): 119–148.
Rivera, Antonio G. *La Revolucíon En Sonora.* Hermosillo, Mexico, 1969.
Sonnichsen, C. L. *Colonel Greene and the Copper Skyrocket.* Tucson, Ariz., 1974.

SALISH INDIANS

See: Native American Peoples: Peoples of the Pacific Northwest

SALOONS

The most common commercial enterprise in the frontier West, saloons, or drinking houses, often outnumbered all other businesses combined, and in some areas, most notably in mining camps and cattle towns, they were found in remarkable numbers. In 1879, the

Patrons gathered around the kegs at Kelley's saloon, the Bijou, in Round Pond, Oklahoma Territory, 1894. Photograph by Kennett. *Courtesy National Archives.*

silver mining camp of Leadville, Colorado, had 279 saloons serving a population of about fifteen thousand.

Saloons proliferated in the West because of bountiful supply and prodigious demand. Alcohol was an ideal item of frontier commerce. It did not spoil and could be packed and transported easily over long distances. At its destination, it could be sold in small amounts for a high price. Saloonkeepers often diluted alcohol to increase their profits.

Demand came from the large numbers of men seeking escape and companionship. Before the national prohibition amendment, barrooms were the most prominent male gathering place, especially for the working class. Barrooms provided space for relaxed conversation and games of amusement and provided a chemical product that eased inhibitions and encouraged conviviality—if taken in modest amounts. In many Western communities, men vastly outnumbered women; in some mining camps and towns , males composed 90 percent or more of the population. Lonely, tired, and often depressed over failed dreams, many men found drinking houses to be places of refuge.

Because they were present in such numbers, saloons substituted for other institutions in newly established towns. Saloons served as meeting places for the formation of early governments, the first court sessions, entertainments by traveling troupes, and even a community's first religious services. Mail was deposited and distributed there before the appearance of post offices. Saloonkeepers held the valuables of customers in their safes and cashed checks—at a discount. In desperately crowded boom towns, men found shelter by sleeping on barroom floors. Saloons contributed indirectly to urban development by providing government revenue through licenses. Whatever their positive effects, however, drinking houses also were intimately connected with crime and human misery. The frontier's legendary pace of drinking deepened the level of poverty, helped undermine public health, and encouraged violence, much of which occurred in barrooms.

In larger towns, saloons reflected the population's diversity and class divisions. Many were filthy, drafty shacks, some with only a barrel of whiskey and a few dirty glasses. A few, like Pap Wyman's saloon in Leadville and the Crystal Palace in Tombstone, were grand halls with gaming tables, elaborate entertainments, diamond-dust mirrors, magnificent bars, and private rooms for the wealthy. Despite the apparent promise of success in the liquor trade, intense competition and high local taxes drove most saloonkeepers out of business within a year or two.

In many ways, Western saloons had roles and characteristics no different from barrooms elsewhere in urban America. They were workingmen's social clubs and sites for the rituals of group drinking that were an ancient part of European culture. As such, saloons may be best understood not as a distinctive part of Western life—as shown in films and popular novels—but as one of the most common examples of the pioneers' conservative dedication to bringing their traditions with them to the frontier.

—Elliott West

See also: Mining: Mining Camps and Towns

Suggested reading:
West, Elliott. *The Saloon on the Rocky Mountain Mining Frontier.* Lincoln, Nebr., 1979.

SALT LAKE CITY, UTAH

By the late 1840s, explorers had flooded Americans with information about the Salt Lake Valley. Explorations in the Rocky Mountains by mountain men and by John Charles Frémont acquainted members of the Church of Jesus Christ of Latter-day Saints (LDS) with the twenty-five-by-sixteen-mile valley southeast of the Great Salt Lake. In 1846, the star-crossed Donner Party, bound for California, blazed a trail down Emigration Canyon into the valley.

In 1846, two years after the murder of Joseph Smith, Jr., and following a protracted civil war in Hancock County, Illinois, the Mormons sought refuge in the West. Following a death-dealing winter near Omaha, Nebraska, the vanguard party of Mormon pioneers traveled by wagon, in 1847, to the Rocky Mountains. An advance party led by Orson Pratt, Willard Richards, and George A. Smith followed the Donner route into the Salt Lake Valley on July 22. The next

day, they dammed City Creek and began plowing and planting. BRIGHAM YOUNG entered on July 24, perhaps pronouncing the words, "This is the right place, drive on," at the mouth of Emigration Canyon. Impressed with the fertile soil and abundant resources, the Mormons made their home.

Drawing on Joseph Smith's plan for the city of Zion and on the gridiron system developers had used to lay out many American cities, the Mormons platted Salt Lake City. With blocks of ten acres, streets 132 feet wide, and eight lots on each block, the Saints planned a garden-plot city. In the downtown area, however, the pressure of business enterprise led to smaller lots and closely abutting buildings. Subdividers outside the original plan often left less room for streets and built houses closer together. Still, even today, much of the city presents a rather more open aspect than most American cities.

During the nineteenth century, a number of forces fueled Salt Lake City's growth. Mormon immigration, motivated by the concept of gathering to Zion, served as the principal impetus. Commerce, energized first by the CALIFORNIA GOLD RUSH of 1849 and later by markets on both ends of the overland trail, made Salt Lake a strategic destination even before the linking of Utah with the nation by rail in 1869. After 1869, Salt Lake City became increasingly a mining center. Surrounded by silver-lead, gold, and copper mines in the Wasatch and Oquirrh Mountains and flanked by mills and smelters in the central Salt Lake Valley towns of Murray, Midvale, and Sandy and the western Salt Lake Valley towns of Magna and Garfield, Salt Lake prospered from mining and mineral reduction well before World War I.

As headquarters of the Mormon church, the city became a magnet for pro- and anti-Mormon conflict. Governed first by the local LDS State, Salt Lake came under the domination of Mormon leaders who controlled the elective posts of mayor, aldermen, and councilors. In 1888, impressed with the need to share power with conservative non-Mormons, the Latter-day Saints co-opted several prominent non-Mormons as councilors. In 1890, the anti-Mormon Liberal party captured control of the city government.

After the Mormons divided into national political parties in 1891, city government began to look much like those of other cities until 1905, when voters turned control to the anti-Mormon American party under businessman Ezra Thompson. Under Mayor Thompson and his successor John S. Bransford, Mormon-bashing became the order of the day. By 1911, however, a civic-improvement movement led the Utah legislature to mandate that all large cities adopt nonpartisan commission governments modeled after the Des Moines plan. In addition, several scandals, especially a bunco scheme (con game) that touched Mayor Thompson's supporters and the regulation of prostitution set up during Bransford's term, hurt the American party. Nonpartisan candidates, led by jeweler Samuel C. Park, won the 1911 election. The city continued to operate under a commission system until January 1980 when voters inaugurated a strong mayor system under Ted Wilson.

The city faced its share of problems associated with urban growth. In the late nineteenth century, businesspeople, expecting a profit, provided services such as streetcars, electric lights, and telephones. City-supplied services such as street paving, water supplies, and sewer systems came quite slowly. Even though the city suffered recurrent epidemics of communicable and waterborne diseases like tuberculosis, typhoid, and small pox, Salt Lake was one of the last major cities in the West to establish a health department.

Surrounded by air pollution caused in part by the smelters and in part by coal-burning businesses and homes, city residents coughed their way towards the twentieth century. In the 1890s, however, groups of women began forming clubs, which banded together under the Utah Federation of Women's Clubs. Although organized in part for cultural objectives, clubs—such as the Reapers, the Ladies' Literary Club, and the Utah Congress of Mothers—facilitated the work of civic improvement by Elizabeth M. Cohen, Leah Eudora Dunford Widtsoe, and others. These women attacked smoke pollution in cooperation with some progressive chamber of commerce members (such as GEORGE HENRY DERN) and city engineers (such as Sylvester Q. Cannon and George W. Snow). By the late 1920s, Salt Lake City had reduced the smoke problem largely through business cooperation and the introduction of natural gas. These groups also worked for city beautification in a campaign similar to the nationwide "city-beautiful" movement.

Although immigrants from outside western Europe had come to Salt Lake City at an early date, the large influx of people from Southern and Eastern Europe did not begin until after 1900. Three African Americans had trekked to Salt Lake with the original immigrant party, and Fort Douglas garrisoned African American troops on the eastern fringe of the city. The introduction of the railroad to Salt Lake in 1870 brought African Americans, Chinese, and Japanese to the city. While Italians were the earliest group of southern Europeans to arrive in Salt Lake City, by 1920, Greeks composed the largest percentage of southern Europeans.

Still, by 1930, Salt Lake City was overwhelmingly a city of native-born residents of northern European ancestry. In a population of 140,300, only 681 or about 0.5 percent were African American, and only 18,100

or 12.9 percent were foreign-born. Of these, more than 75 percent came from northern Europe, 6 percent from Greece and Italy, and 2.7 percent from Mexico.

Since 1930, Salt Lake City has experienced swings in fortune. During the 1930s, UTAH, in general, and Salt Lake City with it, suffered from unemployment and deprivation far worse than the rest of the nation. The heavy reliance of Utah's economy on mining and agriculture contributed to the difficulties. During World War II, Salt Lake revived as a major war center, surrounded by military installations and government contractors. Following the war, the heavy reliance on mining and military operations continued into the 1970s, when conditions began to change. By the 1990s, Salt Lake City had emerged as a major financial, service, commercial, high-tech, and educational center in the West.

—*Thomas G. Alexander*

SUGGESTED READING:

Alexander, Thomas G., and James B. Allen. *Mormons and Gentiles: A History of Salt Lake City.* Boulder, Colo., 1984.
McCormick, John S. *Salt Lake City: The Gathering Place.* Woodland Hills, Calif., 1980.

SAN ANDREAS FAULT

The San Andreas Fault, a major geological plate boundary that separates the Pacific and the North American plates, has been a major influence on the formation of the coastal topography of California. The East Pacific Rise, an ocean floor ridge between the two plates, is the origin of the San Andreas Fault. In actuality, the fault is a giant shear zone, composed of a number of parallel faults and stretching nearly seven hundred miles from the Mexican border and the Gulf of California north to, and perhaps beyond, Cape Mendocino. Two years after geologist Andrew Lawson recognized the existence of the fault in 1893, it was named after San Andreas Lake in a "rift" valley on the San Francisco Peninsula. Identifiable from the air as a linear scar along the coast, the San Andreas Fault zone becomes more angular and multidirectional in southern California. Most of the shift caused by movement along the San Andreas zone has been horizontal, the greatest being the twenty feet of horizontal movement near Point Reyes National Seashore during the 1906 SAN FRANCISCO EARTHQUAKE. The San Andreas has been responsible for most of California's major earthquakes: Tejon Pass, 1857; San Jacinto, 1899; San Francisco, 1906; Imperial Valley, 1940; and Loma Prieta, 1989. As the Pacific plate moves northwesterly toward the Aleutian trench and the North American plate heads southeasterly, there is ongoing movement in some areas. Some scientists claim that, in a few million years, San Francisco and Los Angeles will be adjacent cities.

—*Waverly B. Lowell*

SUGGESTED READING:

Hill, Mary. *California Landscape: Origin and Evolution.* Berkeley, Calif., 1984.
Iacopi, Robert. *Earthquake Country.* Menlo Park, Calif., 1971.

SAN ANTONIO, TEXAS

San Antonio, TEXAS, has reflected multiple but intersecting cultures throughout the nineteenth and twentieth centuries. At the turn of the century, San Antonio was not only a city of contrasting nationalities, but one in which the "haciendas met the plantations" and one of extreme social, racial, and economic differences. The nineteenth-century Spanish ambiance continued, but the power and knowledge of the old Spanish-Mexican-Texan elite was just memory in a city that was on the verge of modernization. Because of its different ethnic groups, San Antonio has been known as a multicultural center since the nineteenth century.

In 1718, Martin de Alarcón established the villa and mission that became the city of San Antonio de Bexar. By 1731, Spanish settlers from the Canary Islands immigrated to the settlement and, along with the original settlers from Coahuila and other northeastern Mexican states, contributed to the cultural, political, and economic development of the town. By the end of the eighteenth century, the population of San Antonio had been a mixture of mestizos (mixed-bloods), Mexican Indians, mestizo soldiers, and native Indian women.

By 1810, Mexico declared its independence from Spain, and San Antonio, by 1821, had become a Mexican-Tejano city. With its independence, San Antonio and all of Texas became bicultural, because the Mexicans approved of American immigration and the colonizing settlements led by STEPHEN FULLER AUSTIN. Mexicans also welcomed new German immigrants.

In 1835, the TEXAS REVOLUTION led to independence from Mexico for Anglos, Germans, and Mexican-Tejanos and introduced new institutions, cultural mores, and a new political order. Cultural tensions were almost inevitable, especially with the decline of the Mexican elite.

Friedrich Zizelman, who founded the First Lutheran Church in San Antonio in 1851, reported that the city was a "Babel on a small scale" with its mixture of ethnic groups, languages, and religions. English, German, and Spanish were the most common

languages, and often all three were used on public signs. The city, however, also had a cross-section of African Americans, Chinese, French, and other ethnic groups; in fact, about 50 percent of the population was foreign-born in the nineteenth century.

By the 1930s, for all practical purposes most of the ethnic groups, except the Mexican population (although not the Canary Islanders), had became assimilated into the Anglo community in San Antonio. However, the African American community since its arrival from the other Southern states during Reconstruction had been restricted to the east side of the city. The black population suffered from de jure segregation, and the Mexican population—also considered by many San Antonians as people of color—from de facto segregation. This was not the case for the descendants of the Canary Islanders who were considered Spanish, not Mexican or Indian, or for the German population. The Irish, who had come in the 1840s directly from Ireland and established the section of San Antonio known as the "Irish Flats," like their German and French counterparts, slowly became socially and culturally integrated by the 1940s. Some structures, celebrations, and traditions remained of the Irish, German, Italian, and French cultures.

Overall, there were more than thirty nationalities in San Antonio in the nineteenth century. Only the Mexican and African American communities in the twentieth century remained unassimilated, basically as a result of the considerable immigration of Mexicans in the first three decades of the twentieth century and the continued racism against blacks. The Mexican population in San Antonio increased from 13,722 in 1900 to 82,373 in 1930 and 103,000 in 1940. For non-Mexicans, those figures were 953,321 in 1900; 231,542 in 1930; and 253,854 in 1940.

The existence of the ALAMO in the geographical heart of the city has been a reminder of a curious strain of Texas pride and arrogance complemented by a growing hatred of Mexicans, the largest ethnic group in San Antonio, most of whom reside on the West Side. Since the nineteenth century, the "Latin Quarter" or "Mexican Town," as it was called, had been characterized by low income, low education, high unemployment, deteriorating and dilapidated housing, and, on the whole, harsh socio-economic conditions, although that has changed considerably since the rise of the Mexican middle class in the 1920 and 1930s and the rise of the League of United Latin American Citizens (LULAC) in 1929. However, the city retained, ironically, a pride in its Spanish heritage.

San Antonians welcomed the twentieth century and its "skyline-changing urban mood," as the city became integrated into the rest of the United States. But the old San Antonio still retained the memories and a few traditions of the distinct heritage of a multiplicity of different, but intersecting, ethnic cultures. In 1930, the new urban perspective was reported by the *San Antonio Express,* the morning daily newspaper, when it exclaimed that the city was one of varied and substantial resources, a financial center, a large wholesale and retail trade center, a major livestock center, and the home of cattle barons. Since San Antonio has been a relatively large and well-known center of commerce, trade, and agriculture for more than two centuries, it has also been considered a center for labor. Consequently, its metropolitan culture was the most diverse in Texas. The modernization period from 1900 to 1930 saw not only economic development but also rapid population growth and cultural change.

—*Richard A. Garcia*

SUGGESTED READING:

Broussard, Ray F. *San Antonio during the Texas Republic: A City in Transition.* El Paso, Tex., 1967.

Garcia, Richard A. *Rise of the Mexican American Middle Class: San Antonio, 1929–1941.* College Station, Tex., 1991.

SAND CREEK MASSACRE

The Sand Creek Massacre, a surprise military attack on an unarmed and peaceful Cheyenne camp on November 29, 1864, shocked and outraged many Americans, led to congressional and military investigations, and went down in history as a shameful blight on the often checkered record of the country's treatment of Native Americans.

In 1864, when Colorado's territorial governor JOHN EVANS failed to secure mineral-rich Cheyenne and Arapaho hunting grounds in exchange for reservations, he called upon Colonel JOHN M. CHIVINGTON, military commander of the territory, to sweep the Indians out, even though, of all the Plains tribes, the Cheyennes and Arapahos had given the whites the least excuse for a fight. Chivington was the man Evans wanted for the job. A former Methodist minister, Chivington was known as the "fighting parson," and his hatred of Indians was exuberant in its rabidity. He declared, for example, in an 1864 speech made in Denver that all Indians should be killed and scalped, including infants: "Nits make lice!" was the way he put it.

While the majority of Cheyennes were inclined toward peace, a militant faction, a group of young warriors known as the Hotamitanio, or Dog Soldier Society, provided Chivington with incidents sufficient

Sand Creek Massacre by Robert Lindneux. Note the U.S. flag and the white flag of truce beside Black Kettle's lodge. *Courtesy Colorado Historical Society.*

for him to declare all Cheyennes to be at war. He launched a number of attacks, which provoked Indian counterattacks. During the crisis, Governor Evans and Colonel Chivington formed the Third Colorado Cavalrymen, composed of short-term, hundred-day enlistees drawn mainly from the territory's violence-prone mining camps.

When winter came, however, a large number of Indians, led by BLACK KETTLE, an older chief opposed to the youthful and tempestuous Dog Soldiers, were asking for peace. The sympathetic commander of Fort Lyon in southeastern Colorado, Major Edward Wynkoop, announced the Indians' desire for peace to the governor, who replied: "But what shall I do with the Third Colorado Regiment if I make peace? They have been raised to kill Indians, and they must kill Indians."

Nevertheless, Evans and Chivington met with the Cheyennes and Arapahos and told them that those Indians who wanted peace should "submit to military authority" by laying down their arms at a local fort. The Indians left the meeting and marched to Sand Creek, about forty miles northeast of Fort Lyon, where they planned to talk with Major Wynkoop, who issued rations to them. The army, however, could not seem to tolerate Wynkoop's humane attitude, and on November 5, one of Chivington's command, Major Scott J. Anthony, relieved Wynkoop as commander of the post. Anthony's first action was to cut the Indians' rations and to demand the surrender of their weapons. Apparently out of sheer meanness, he even ordered his men to fire on a group of unarmed Arapahos, who had approached the fort to trade buffalo hides for rations.

By the end of November, most of the Third Colorado had gathered at Fort Lyon. Black Kettle and his Cheyennes, still camping peacefully at Sand Creek, believed that they had abided by Evans's and Chivington's order to submit to military authority and, above all, that they were at peace. Chivington deployed his seven-hundred-man force, which included four howitzers, around the camp. When three of Chivington's officers, Captain Silas Soule and Lieutenants Joseph Cramer and James Conner, protested that an attack on a peaceful village was murder, Chivington barely restrained himself from striking Cramer. "Damn any man who sympathizes with Indians," he was reported as shouting. "I have come to kill Indians, and believe it is right and honorable to use any means under God's heaven to kill Indians."

The presence of a surrounding army alarmed Black Kettle's people. But the chief had faith in Wynkoop and in the honor of what he thought were Wynkoop's like-minded fellow soldiers. Black Kettle sought to calm

his people. At the same time, to signify his loyalty and peaceful intentions, he hoisted an American flag and a white flag of truce over his lodge. In response, the troops opened fire and charged. The unarmed Indians—warriors, old men, women, and children—ran in panic. Unconscionable atrocities were committed: children's brains were beaten out with clubs, women were gutted like fish ("I saw squaw cut open with an unborn child . . . lying by her side," Soule later testified), and warrior corpses were castrated ("I saw the body of White Antelope with the privates cut off," Soule reported, "and I heard a soldier say he was going to make a tobacco pouch out of them"). Two hundred Cheyennes, two-thirds of them women and children, and nine chiefs were killed. Black Kettle escaped.

Far from disheartening the Indians, as Chivington had hoped, the Sand Creek Massacre galvanized their resolve to fight. During late 1864 and early 1865, Southern Sioux, Northern Arapahos, and Cheyennes united in a spasm of revenge raids, called by the U.S. Army the Cheyenne-Arapaho War. Except for Black Kettle, who still desperately hoped for peace, the chiefs as a result of the attack gathered more allies for a quick strike against the military presence in Colorado. On the other hand, news of the massacre and mutilation of men, women, and children shocked and outraged Easterners and caused a wave of condemnation that led to investigations, first by the Congressional Committee on the Conduct of the War, then by a joint committee of the Senate and House, and then by a three-man military commission. Congress and the army brass denounced Chivington, who—having left the army—escaped discipline. The peace offensive in Washington hampered, but did not halt, General John Pope's conduct of war in the field against the Cheyennes and the Arapahos.

—*Alan Axelrod*

See also: Central Plains Indian Wars

Suggested reading:

Axelrod, Alan. *Chronicle of the Indian Wars: From Colonial Times to Wounded Knee.* New York, 1993.

Hoig, Stan. *The Sand Creek Massacre.* Norman, Okla., 1963.

Utley, Robert M. *Frontiersman in Blue: The United States Army and the Indian, 1848–1865.* New York, 1967.

SAN DIEGO, CALIFORNIA

Located at the southwestern tip of the United States, San Diego historically has had both an advantage and a disadvantage because of its geographic position. Bordered on the west by the Pacific Ocean, on the south

San Diego, 1876, a view of Fifth Avenue. *Courtesy San Diego Historical Society.*

San Diego, 1923, a view of Fifth Street, looking north. *Courtesy San Diego Historical Society.*

by Mexico, on the east by mountains and desert, and on the north by Los Angeles, San Diego is relatively isolated—a factor that played a significant role in the way the city and county developed. Despite being the second largest city in CALIFORNIA, San Diego struggled, nonetheless, to compete economically with Los Angeles and San Francisco. Although even the earliest European and American visitors to the area recognized the potential for San Diego's natural landlocked harbor, the region never developed a great commercial seaport, and San Diego lost its late nineteenth-century bid to become the western terminus for a transcontinental railroad line. San Diego's climate as well as its varied topography became its greatest advantage. Miles of coastal beaches, sprawling mesas, valleys, foothills, mountains, and desert could all be reached in a single day and offered dramatic changes in temperature and scenery.

For at least twenty-five hundred years before European contact, four groups of native people made San Diego their home—the Kumeyaays, Luiseños, Cupeños, and Cahuillas. In 1542, JUAN RODRÍGUEZ CABRILLO was the first European explorer to visit San Diego. His epic voyage—from Mexico in search of the Northwest Passage to the Orient—led him to San Diego, where he claimed the region for the Spanish crown. Yet more than two centuries passed before the first overland expedition from Mexico, led by Gaspar de Portolá, Baja California's governor, and Father JUNÍPERO SERRA, a Franciscan missionary, arrived in San Diego. On July 16, 1769, Serra and three other missionaries blessed a site on a hill overlooking the harbor entrance and thus founded the first European settlement in Alta California.

In 1821, California passed from Spanish to Mexican rule, and soldiers and their families began to move down the hill from the old Presidio settlement. By 1835, the pueblo of San Diego had been officially founded. Geographically isolated from the rest of the world, early San Diegans relied heavily on the cattle raised on neigh-

boring ranchos for the lucrative hide trade, which provided necessary supplies and some luxuries for the community. The pueblo of San Diego reflected a mixture of diverse people and goods as ships arrived from the Orient, South America, New England, and Europe.

When California achieved statehood in 1850, San Diego's population stood at 650. Growth continued slowly until San Francisco entrepreneur ALONZO ERASTUS HORTON set in motion his vision to create a great port city. Recognizing the need to relocate the town closer to the harbor, Horton purchased 960 acres of waterfront property and began to build "New Town." Within a few years, his efforts to move San Diego were successful.

In the late 1800s and early 1900s, San Diego experienced a series of economic booms and busts. A population of forty thousand in 1885 dwindled to sixteen thousand by 1889; after that, growth occurred at a slow and steady pace. Surrounding coastal and inland communities, aided by a thriving citrus industry, began to spread through San Diego County. Major hotels and beach resorts were constructed as health-seekers and tourists, attracted by a near ideal climate, flocked to the region. San Diegans planned an international exposition in 1915 to celebrate the opening of the Panama Canal and to showcase San Diego's opportunities for manufacturing and agriculture. San Diegans anticipated that their city, as the closest American port of call to the Panama Canal, would become a major shipping and manufacturing center. San Diego, however, did not become a great commercial port. Its neighbor to the north, Los Angeles, did, and thus a long pattern of rivalry was established and has continued into the late twentieth century.

World War II brought dramatic change to San Diego. Defense companies became the number one employer during the war years. The city's AIRCRAFT INDUSTRY, which had gained international recognition after Charles Lindbergh's historic flight in the *Spirit of St. Louis*—a plane designed and built in San Diego—achieved new records for wartime production. The military had already made the city the nation's chief repair base for destroyers; following the Japanese attack on Pearl Harbor, the U.S. Navy moved its Pacific headquarters from Hawaii to San Diego. The city's population soared, and the geographic isolation that generations of San Diegans had known disappeared forever as the city moved from a sleepy border town to a teeming wartime metropolis. After the war, many former members of the military made San Diego their permanent home.

Since then, San Diego's economic base has been largely related to government and aerospace industries. The U.S. Navy remains a major employer and maintains in San Diego the largest naval air station on the West Coast. TOURISM and agriculture rank high in economic importance, as do marine, biological, and biomedical technologies. The Salk Institute, Scripps Institute of Oceanography, and University of California at San Diego have achieved international status as leaders in scientific research and development. San Diego's proximity to Mexico increasingly fostered opportunities for economic and cultural exchange between the two countries. Many residents of Mexico's border city of Tijuana work and shop in San Diego and sustain many local businesses. According to the 1990 census, immigrants from Mexico increased San Diego's Hispanic population to 20 percent of the county's total number of residents.

—Lucinda Eddy

SUGGESTED READING:

Engstrand, Iris H. W. *San Diego: California's Cornerstone.* Tulsa, Okla., 1980.

———. *San Diego: Gateway to the Pacific.* Houston, Tex., 1992.

MacPhail, Elizabeth C. *The Story of New San Diego and Its Founder, Alonzo E. Horton.* San Diego, Calif., 1979. Reprint. 1989.

Smythe, William A. *History of San Diego, 1542–1908.* San Diego, Calif., 1908.

SANDOZ, MARI

Western writer Mari Sandoz (1896–1966) was born on a homestead in western Nebraska. She is usually remembered primarily for her unromantic portrayal of the West in her 1935 biography *Old Jules.* By the time of her death, she had also established a reputation as a historian of Native Americans, novelist, and chronicler of the trans-Mississippi environment. Her writing was deeply attentive to the relationship between the land and its peoples.

Sandoz is recognized as an early dissenter from the mythic West. *Old Jules,* a biography of her pioneer father Jules Sandoz, startled readers with its frank accounts of domestic violence, political corruption, and extreme poverty. Yet Sandoz also celebrated the Western past; she saw early pioneers and Native Americans as people admirably attuned to the lessons of the landscape. Because of their closeness to nature, she suggested, early societies knew the need for cooperation and democracy even though they eventually succumbed to the overwhelming historical force of competitive capitalism. The themes of greed, class conflict, and incipient fascism dominate Sandoz's fiction, including *Slogum House* (1937) and *Capital City* (1939).

Sandoz derived her political commitments from her childhood exposure to the socialist newspaper *The Appeal to Reason* and from her own experience of poverty and oppression, including beatings by her father and many lean years of odd jobs and occasional college courses before her writing began to sustain her financially. In describing herself as a writer, she said her special interest was in the dispossessed and underprivileged. Her books about Native Americans, including *Crazy Horse: The Strange Man of the Oglalas* (1942) and *Cheyenne Autumn* (1953), denounce the history of U.S. Indian policies and try to recreate for readers the cultures of the two native groups.

As a biographer, Sandoz experimented with idioms to depict language communities; as a historian, she defied emerging conventions of objectivity and employed invented dialogue and evocative descriptions as well as scholarly research to approach her goal of "verisimilitude"; and as an early environmental historian, she dared to include animals as primary characters in her books. Including her widely various works such as the natural history-inspired *Love Song to the Plains* (1961), Sandoz contributed not only to Western history but also, more generally, to the philosophy and practice of writing about the past.

—*Dorothee E. Kocks*

SEE ALSO: Women Writers

SUGGESTED READING:

Sandoz, Mari. *Capital City.* Boston, 1939.
———. *Cheyenne Autumn.* New York, 1953.
———. *Crazy Horse: The Strange Man of the Oglalas.* New York, 1942.
———. *Love Song to the Plains.* New York, 1961.
———. *Old Jules.* Boston, 1935.
———. *Slogum House.* Boston, 1937.
Stauffer, Helen Winter. *Mari Sandoz: Story Catcher of the Plains.* Lincoln, Nebr., 1982.

SAN FRANCISCO

Historical Overview
Robert W. Cherny

City of Immigrants
Robert W. Cherny

HISTORICAL OVERVIEW

The city of San Francisco is located on a great bay, sixty miles long and up to fourteen miles wide, connected to the Pacific Ocean through the Golden Gate, a narrow opening in the high hills that line most of the northern CALIFORNIA coast. The bay has given the city most of its economic reason for existence, as well as its dramatic vistas of sky, land, and water.

The people living in the bay area when the first Europeans arrived were called Costeños (people living along the coast) by the Spanish and Costanoans by early anthropologists. More recently, they have been known as the Ohlone. They lived in small villages and subsisted by hunting, fishing, and gathering.

Spanish explorers first took note of the bay in 1769, and an expedition, in 1776, established a military post (the Presidio) and a mission (San Francisco de Asis—usually called Mission Dolores), but neither thrived. In 1835, a pueblo or village was established and named Yerba Buena ("good herbs") after lush growths of wild mint. Many who settled there were English-speaking entrepreneurs, eager to sell goods to the ships that arrived in the bay and to trade with Bay Area ranchos. When the United States went to war with Mexico in 1846, a naval task force was immediately dispatched to claim the Bay Area. Early in 1847, Washington Bartlett, the naval officer in charge, changed the pueblo's name from Yerba Buena to San Francisco.

In March 1848, the population of San Francisco stood around eight hundred. Then discovery of gold in the interior provoked a massive influx of fortune-seekers. All transportation routes to California were difficult and dangerous, especially the overland route. Most immigrants came by sea and landed at San Francisco, crowding its bay with ships and transforming it into an "instant city." By mid-1849, the city's population had boomed to five thousand, and many residents lived in hastily built shanties and tents. By 1860, the city counted fifty thousand people and had acquired a more substantial appearance.

With the rapid growth of the 1850s came social, economic, and political instability. Many fortune-hunters passed through the city quickly and rushed off to the gold fields. Others hoped to prosper as merchants, but the city's mercantile economy repeatedly boomed and burst due to uncertainties in supply and demand. Some successful merchants moved into BANKING, thus laying the foundation for the city's financial preeminence. Charters in 1850 and 1851 specified the city's formal institutions of government, and a third charter in 1856 consolidated city and county governments. The city's merchants demonstrated their impatience with such formalities by forming in 1851 and 1856 Committees of Vigilance, which operated outside the law to banish or execute those whom they deemed inimical to the city's orderly development.

Economic developments in the 1850s and 1860s marked San Francisco's emergence as financial and commercial center of the West, as well as the region's

In this earliest live visual record of San Francisco, a bustling town and busy seaport crowded with vessels stand where three years before (and prior to the discovery of gold in California) cows grazed and farmers tended their crops. *Courtesy Bancroft Library.*

preeminent port. The transcontinental Telegraph in 1861 and the railroad in 1869 provided reliable connections to the East. As Western mining increasingly required large amounts of capital and technologically advanced equipment, San Francisco banks—in particular the Bank of California, led by William Chapman Ralston—quickly came to dominate much of Western mining, especially the phenomenally rich silver mines of Nevada. The city's foundries produced some of the world's most advanced mining equipment. When large-scale agricultural developments in California's Central Valley demanded extensive capital and elaborate equipment, San Francisco entrepreneurs again led the way. San Francisco's economic leadership was ensured by the time the Central Pacific Railroad (later Southern Pacific Railroad) moved its headquarters there from Sacramento in 1873.

Throughout the late nineteenth century, San Francisco reigned as the metropolis of the West. Corporations with headquarters in the city dominated the economic life of much of the Pacific Coast, the intermountain West, Alaska, and Hawaii. From throughout the West, commerce flowed through the Bay Area—minerals from Western mines, wheat and other agricultural produce from California's Central Valley, timber from the Northwest, salmon from Alaska, sugar from Hawaii. Successful Western entrepreneurs often built luxurious homes in San Francisco, especially on Nob Hill. The Pacific Stock Exchange (founded in 1875), Customs House, and Mint all confirmed the city's prominence. Perhaps the best-known symbol of the city's position as the glittering queen of the West was the Palace Hotel, built in the mid-1870s and modeled after the most modern European luxury hotels. By 1900, San Francisco was the eighth largest city in the nation and also one of the most ethnically diverse, home to large numbers of immigrants from Ireland, Germany, Italy, Great Britain, Scandinavia, and China.

For nearly twenty years after the vigilante actions of 1856, a succession of merchants occupied the mayor's office and dominated the Board of Supervisors, as San Francisco called its city council. From 1877 to 1879, however, a depressed economy contributed to the rise of DENIS KEARNEY and his WORKINGMEN'S PARTY OF CALIFORNIA (WPC). Kearney appealed to Euro-American workers and blamed their misfortunes on the machinations of great capitalists and especially their use of Chinese immigrant laborers, who, Kearney asserted, drove down wage levels for white workers. Such scapegoating was not new to California labor and politics, and anti-Asian agitation formed a staple in most labor and political activity for the next half-century.

The WPC rapidly waned, and the Democratic party—led by CHRISTOPHER AUGUSTINE BUCKLEY, a blind saloonkeeper—dominated CITY GOVERNMENT throughout the 1880s. Charged with corruption, Buckley lost power after 1890. Reformers fought for control of city politics, notably ADOLPH SUTRO, elected to the mayor's office as a Populist in 1894, and JAMES DUVAL PHELAN, a Democrat who won the mayoralty in 1896 and promoted a new, progressive city charter. In 1901, organized labor flexed its political muscle to elect, as mayor, Eugene Schmitz, nominee of the UNION LABOR PARTY (ULP), but charges of corruption brought the downfall in 1906 of Schmitz and ABRAHAM (ABE) RUEF, his close advisor. In 1911, JAMES ROLPH became mayor; a leader in business and civic affairs, he stabilized city politics as he repeatedly won reelection.

Before Rolph came to power, however, the city of San Francisco faced one of its greatest challenges. On April 18, 1906, the city was jolted awake by a powerful earthquake, equivalent to 8.3 on the Richter scale. Fires quickly erupted throughout the city. Hundreds of people died, and thousands of buildings were destroyed, including nearly all of the city's center. The city rebuilt quickly, prompted by business leaders' anxieties that the disaster might erode the city's financial and commercial leadership. In 1915, the city celebrated both the opening of the Panama Canal and its own reconstruction by hosting the PANAMA-PACIFIC INTERNATIONAL EXPOSITION. Despite such efforts, the city's economic prominence inevitably declined as other Western cities matured.

Phelan's reform charter of 1900 had committed the city to acquire ownership of its public utilities, and city politics before the 1930s witnessed repeated efforts to implement those provisions. A city-owned streetcar line, the Municipal Railway, was initiated in 1909, to compete with privately owned lines and was gradually extended. Creation of a city reservoir in the Hetch Hetchy Valley led to the city's acquisition of the company that supplied its water. Several efforts to attain public ownership of the electrical system failed. A new charter in 1932 omitted the public-ownership provision, but high profits on the Municipal Railway during World War II permitted it to purchase all remaining privately owned lines. During the 1930s, the city championed the building of two great bridges, the Golden Gate Bridge north to Marin County and the Bay Bridge to Oakland and the East Bay.

Throughout the first half of the twentieth century, tensions between unions and employers ran high. From 1900 to 1919, the city was one of the most unionized in the nation, but in the 1920s, an antiunion drive by the INDUSTRIAL ASSOCIATION OF SAN FRANCISCO reduced union power and membership. Encouraged by New Deal policies, unions revived in the early 1930s. In 1934, a strike by longshoremen and seafaring unions spawned a brief general strike in San Francisco after police killed two strike supporters. By the late 1930s, San Francisco was again one of the nation's most unionized cities.

During World War II, the Bay Area emerged as the world's leading shipbuilding region. Fed by migrants from across the nation, including many African Americans from the South, the Bay Area's population boomed. After the war, business leaders formulated plans intended to guarantee the city's role as center of the regional economy—including creation of the Bay Area Rapid Transit system, a high-speed rail network centered on downtown San Francisco, and expansion of the financial district through extensive high-rise construction. From the late 1950s through the late 1980s, city politics was usually dominated by a coalition of liberals, unions, and advocates of high-rise development, especially during the mayoralties of Joseph Alioto (from 1968 to 1976) and Dianne Feinstein (from 1978 to 1988). Eventually neighborhood and environmental groups coalesced in 1986 to approve Proposition M, a "slow-growth" initiative that created the nation's most stringent limits on development.

By the 1950s and 1960s, the city had acquired a reputation for toleration of social diversity that attracted both cultural dissidents, notably Beatniks in the 1950s and hippies in the 1960s, and gays and lesbians from at least the 1950s onward. By the 1970s, the city's gay and lesbian communities had become one of the largest in the nation and had begun to make their mark on city politics. Changes in national immigration laws in the 1960s led to increased immigration from Latin America and eastern Asia.

—Robert W. Cherny

SEE ALSO: Booms; California Gold Rush; Hetch Hetchy Controversy; Labor Movement; San Francisco Committee of Vigilance of 1856; San Francisco Earthquake of 1906

SUGGESTED READING:
Issel, William, and Robert W. Cherny. *San Francisco, 1865–1932: Politics, Power, and Urban Development.* Berkeley and Los Angeles, 1986.
LeGates, Richard E. *Left Coast City: Progressive Politics in San Francisco, 1975–1991.* Lawrence, Kans., 1992.
Lotchin, Roger W. *San Francisco, 1846–1856: From Hamlet to City.* New York, 1974.
Wirt, Frederick M. *Power in the City: Decision Making in San Francisco.* Berkeley and Los Angeles, 1974.

CITY OF IMMIGRANTS

San Francisco has been a city of immigrants throughout most of its history. Although sources of immigration have changed over time, large numbers of immigrants have usually been present and have been significant factors in the city's politics and economy.

Even before the CALIFORNIA GOLD RUSH transformed San Francisco into an "instant city," its population was ethnically diverse, including Californios (of Spanish or mestizo ancestry) and merchants and traders of various nationalities. With the gold rush, San Francisco attracted fortune-seekers from much of the United States, Europe, the British Empire, Latin America, and China. In 1850 and 1860, about half the city's residents were foreign-born, with those from the British Empire and Germany most numerous—indeed, first- and second-generation Irish composed nearly one-third of the city's population.

The patterns established by 1860 changed little over the next half-century. Among those San Franciscans who were foreign-born or descended from foreign parents, the Irish remained most numerous, followed closely by Germans. Other sizable European groups included those from the British Empire (other than Ireland), Italy, and the Scandinavian countries. Some groups developed distinctive patterns of residence and occupation. The Irish were concentrated in blue-collar occupations; Scandinavians, in seafaring; Italians, in produce and fishing. Much of the Mission District, a largely working-class neighborhood, was Irish, and the Western Addition included many German Jews. The Latin

Japanese immigrants upon arrival in San Francisco, 1920. *Courtesy The Bettmann Archive.*

Quarter was home to those speaking Spanish, French, and Italian; by the early twentieth century, it had become heavily Italian, especially the North Beach area.

During the nineteenth century, conflicts occasionally flared between or among white ethnic groups. The SAN FRANCISCO VIGILANCE COMMITTEE OF 1856, for example, was largely old-stock and Protestant, and it directed its attacks disproportionately against Irish Catholics. For the most part, however, there was a high level of toleration among Euro-American ethnic groups. In the 1890s, the American Protective Association made little impact in the city, meeting opposition not only from Catholics but also from leading Jews and Protestants.

Social and economic mobility for Euro-Americans was less restricted than in Eastern cities, probably because the gold rush and rapid urban growth created fortunes unrelated to inheritance and in other ways exerted a leveling and homogenizing influence. As early as 1870, Irish Catholics and German Jews ranked among the city's leading bankers and business figures, and Italians began to appear prominently after the 1890s. In politics, too, Catholics and Jews experienced greater success than in major Eastern cities—the city's first Irish Catholic mayor won office in 1867; its first Jewish mayor, in 1894.

San Francisco was considerably less tolerant of non-European ethnic groups. Anti-Chinese agitation formed a staple of political rhetoric and labor agitation throughout the nineteenth and early twentieth centuries. Claims that Chinese immigrant workers drove down wage levels for white workers underlay the appeal of the WORKINGMEN'S PARTY OF CALIFORNIA in the late 1870s and led to the CHINESE EXCLUSION Act of 1882. Anti-Chinese agitation also contributed to the success of the city's labor organizations in uniting Euro-American workers of varying occupations.

In San Francisco, most Chinese immigrants lived in Chinatown, a densely populated ghetto with its own social and economic patterns. As a nearly autonomous enclave, Chinatown developed an system of internal governance through associations. Chinatown was largely male, for immigration officials barred most Chinese women from entering the country. After the Exclusion Act, and especially after the 1890s, the Chinese population declined numerically until the latter half of the twentieth century.

There were never large numbers of Japanese immigrants in San Francisco, but after 1900, they formed a target for the anti-Asian rhetoric of unionists and politicians. President THEODORE ROOSEVELT summoned the city's school board to Washington in 1906 when an international crisis loomed over the board's order for Japanese children to attend the segregated Chinese school. The GENTLEMEN'S AGREEMENT of 1907, eliminating most Japanese immigration, was one result. San Francisco political figures, especially JAMES DUVAL PHELAN, continued to denounce Asian immigration until the Immigration Act of 1924 cut off all immigration from Asia.

The restrictive laws of the 1920s reduced all immigration, leading to a few decades when the proportion of immigrants in the city declined. With changes in immigration laws in 1965 and after, San Francisco once again became a city of immigrants. In 1990, one-third of the city's population was foreign-born, and 80 percent of the foreign-born had arrived since 1965. Available data indicate that the largest numbers have come from Asia and southeast Asia (including Chinese, Filipinos, Japanese, Vietnamese, and Koreans); Latin America, especially Mexico and Central America; and Russia.

—*Robert W. Cherny*

SEE ALSO: Chinatowns; Chinese Americans; Immigration Law; Irish Americans; Italian Americans; Japanese Americans; Jewish Americans

SUGGESTED READING:

Chan, Sucheng. *Asian Californians*. San Francisco, 1991.

Cinel, Dino. *From Italy to San Francisco: The Immigrant Experience*. Stanford, Calif., 1982.

Issel, William, and Robert W. Cherny. *San Francisco, 1865-1932: Politics, Power, and Urban Development*. Berkeley and Los Angeles, 1986.

Nee, Victor G., and Brett de Bary Nee. *Longtime Californ': A Documentary Study of an American Chinatown*. New York, 1972; Stanford, Calif., 1986.

Saxton, Alexander. *The Indispensable Enemy: Labor and the Anti-Chinese Movement in California*. Berkeley and Los Angeles, 1991.

SAN FRANCISCO BUILDING TRADES COUNCIL

Founded in February 1896, the San Francisco Building Trades Council organized workers of the building trades in San Francisco in an attempt to control the industry; for a quarter century, it succeeded in doing so. Made up of the various construction unions in San Francisco, the council included four thousand workers in plumbing, painting, roofing, and related trades. By 1901, when it had incorporated thirty-six component unions and spoke for fifteen thousand members, the council's secretary proudly proclaimed there "was nothing more to organize in the building industry."

Within the council, each member union was given representation relative to the size of its individual membership. Although several individuals served as presi-

dent, the council's greatest gains were made under the domineering Patrick McCarthy. Under McCarthy, the council controlled not only laborers, but also contractors and distributors in the city, allowing the council to by-pass management when necessary. Although the council began to lose ground in the antiunion fervor of World War I, its dominance continued until March 1921. An arbitration ruling mandated a 7.5 percent wage decrease due to the faltering economy. When management ordered a lockout, the council was unable to rally its usual support from contractors and distributors. By the time the ruling was accepted, management had stipulated the open shop as a condition to end the lockout. This failure forced the ouster of McCarthy in January 1922 and signaled the end of the Building Trades Council's power in San Francisco labor relations.

—*Kurt Edward Kemper*

SEE ALSO: Labor Movement

SUGGESTED READING:

Kazin, Michael. *Barons of Labor: The San Francisco Building Trades and Union Power in the Progressive Era.* Urbana, Ill., 1987.

SAN FRANCISCO COMMITTEE OF VIGILANCE OF 1856

The San Francisco Committee of Vigilance was organized on May 14, 1856, following two sensational fatal shootings, that of General William Richardson by gambler Charles Cora and that of James King, crusading editor of the *Daily Evening Bulletin,* by politician James P. Casey. In many respects, the 1856 committee was simply a revival of an earlier vigilance committee of 1851. WILLIAM TELL COLEMAN, who had played a prominent role in the 1851 group, was elected president of the new committee. Most of his fellow merchants joined the committee, as they had done five years earlier. This time, however, they encountered considerable resistance to their campaign to avenge the murders. The *Herald,* the largest newspaper in San Francisco in 1856, editorialized against the committee, and a number of prominent citizens—Mayor James Van Ness, County Sheriff David Scannell, and General WILLIAM TECUMSEH SHERMAN, who commanded the San Francisco district of the California militia—formed an opposition LAW AND ORDER party.

On May 16, 1856, the twenty-eight-year-old governor of California, J. Neely Johnson, arrived in San Francisco and met with Coleman. Johnson, a member of the American or Know-Nothing party, thought that Coleman promised him not to seize Cora and Casey, but some twenty-five hundred vigilantes descended on the county jail and took custody of the two men. The authorities made no effort to resist.

A vigilante tribunal convicted Cora and Casey of murder. On May 22, amid a great public ceremony, both men went to the gallows. While the Law and Order leaders hoped the hangings would mark the end of VIGILANTISM, the committee made more arrests and fortified its headquarters building, nicknamed "Fort Gunnybags." The committee even arrested and tried California State Supreme Court Justice David Terry after he fought with and stabbed a vigilante. The tribunal convicted Terry of assault with intent to kill, but he was released.

Before the committee finished its work, it hanged two more men, Philander Brace and Joseph Hetherington, and banished thirty others from the city. One arrested man committed suicide in his cell. On August 18, the committee held a great parade of several thousand armed vigilantes and then disbanded.

Opinion is greatly divided over the actions of the committee. Effusive in their praise of the vigilantes, nineteenth-century historians, such as John S. Hittell and HUBERT HOWE BANCROFT, argued that the vigilantes' response was appropriate in dealing with crime and corruption in San Francisco. Modern writers, such as Richard Maxwell Brown and Robert M. Senkewicz, suggest that the committee's actions had as much, if not more, to do with a fear of rapidly increasing political and economic power of Irish Catholics in the city as with punishment for crimes.

—*Roger D. McGrath*

SEE ALSO: Violence

SUGGESTED READING:

Bancroft, Hubert Howe. *Popular Tribunals.* San Francisco, 1887.

Brown, Richard Maxwell. *Strain of Violence: Historical Studies of American Violence and Vigilantism.* New York, 1975.

Nunis, Jr., Doyce B., ed. *The San Francisco Vigilance Committee of 1856: Three Views.* Los Angeles, 1971.

Senkewicz, Robert M. *Vigilantes in Gold Rush San Francisco.* San Francisco, 1985.

SAN FRANCISCO EARTHQUAKE OF 1906

The San Francisco earthquake of 1906 was one of the most catastrophic natural disasters in the history of

the American West. The earthquake and subsequent fire devastated the city and caused widespread destruction of property and loss of life.

At 5:12 A.M., Wednesday, April 18, 1906, a low-pitched rumble awakened the people of San Francisco. It was a deafening sound, rising from deep within the earth as the massive Pacific and North American tectonic plates lurched past each other along the SAN ANDREAS FAULT. The lateral movement in plates was an incredible twenty-one feet, an enormous release of pressure that sent shock waves racing through the earth. When the first wave hit San Francisco, the ground began to heave and shake for an agonizing forty-five seconds. After a brief interlude of eerie silence, an even stronger temblor, estimated at 8.3 on the Richter scale, shook the city for another twenty-five seconds. All told, twenty-seven quakes and aftershocks hit the city that day.

Buildings throughout the city collapsed; gaping fissures opened in the streets; sidewalks buckled in grotesque shapes; and water and gas mains snapped. Dennis Sullivan, the city's fire chief, awakened to the sound of an avalanche of brick crashing through his bedroom above the fire station on Bush Street. The chief was blinded by a cloud of mortar dust and fell to his death three stories below. Crowded boarding houses and hotels on the unstable ground south of Market Street crumbled as the earth undulated in sickening waves two or three feet in height. Visiting opera star Enrico Caruso awoke with a start in his room at the Palace Hotel, rushed to his window, and let out what he later said were the grandest notes he had ever sung in his life.

Damage from the earthquake was not limited to San Francisco. Towns on the San Francisco peninsula, sitting directly astride the fault, suffered extensive damage. The business section of Palo Alto and the campus of nearby Stanford University were especially hard hit. Communities in Marin and Sonoma counties, north of San Francisco, also were devastated.

Within an hour of the first temblor, more than fifty fires were raging out of control in San Francisco. The flames spread rapidly and created a huge fire storm with temperatures reaching an estimated 2,000 degrees. Fire-fighters put up a heroic battle, but broken water mains and cracked underground cisterns made their work nearly impossible. The fire burned unchecked for three days and two nights. Fire-fighters succeeded in containing the inferno only by taking the desperate step of dynamiting a wide swath of homes to create a firebreak along Van Ness Avenue.

On Saturday, April 21, a spring shower doused the remaining flames. As the smoke cleared, the magnitude of the disaster was revealed in all its horrible clarity. Four square miles—or 490 city blocks—had been leveled. More than twenty-eight thousand buildings had been destroyed. The official death toll was set at 478, but more recent research has revealed that as many as 3,000 people lost their lives.

The city soon began the mighty task of recovery. San Francisco Mayor Eugene Schmitz, later convicted of extortion and removed from office, moved quickly to begin relief efforts and ensure the maintenance of law and order. Schmitz was joined in the effort by fifteen hundred soldiers under the command of General Frederick Funston from the San Francisco Presidio. Rescue crews dug through the rubble in a desperate search for survivors, while workers pitched two hundred thousand tents at the Presidio and in Golden Gate Park as temporary shelters for those who were left homeless.

Civic and business leaders, eager to counteract the idea that a similar catastrophe could ever destroy the city again, began their own campaign of "damage control." They insisted that the greatest damage was done not by the earthquake, over which human beings had no control, but by the subsequent conflagration whose recurrence could be rendered impossible by improved fire-prevention measures. Within a week of the disaster, the San Francisco Real Estate Board resolved that the phrase "the great earthquake" should no longer be used. The calamity would henceforth be known as "the great fire."

San Franciscans took great pride in their remarkable recovery from the disaster. They invited the world to come and celebrate their recovery at the magnificent PANAMA-PACIFIC INTERNATIONAL EXPOSITION of 1915, and they heralded their triumph by adopting a new emblem for the city, a phoenix rising from the ashes.

—James J. Rawls

SUGGESTED READING:

Hansen, Gladys, and Emmet Condon. *Denial of Disaster: The Untold Story and Photographs of the San Francisco Earthquake and Fire of 1906*. San Francisco, 1989.

Sutherland, Monica. *The Damndest Finest Ruins*. New York, 1959.

Thomas, Gordon, and Max Morgan Witts. *The San Francisco Earthquake*. New York, 1971.

SAN JOAQUIN RIVER

One of two major rivers in California, the San Joaquin drains the southern reaches of the state's great Central Valley. Rising above eleven thousand feet in the Sierra Nevada southeast of YOSEMITE NATIONAL PARK, the river is formed by the juncture of numerous streams. The San Joaquin runs for more than one hundred miles

before it reaches the foothills of the valley. Northeast of Fresno, the Friant Dam today impounds most of the river's waters, but as it heads west and then northwest, the San Joaquin is fed by several tributaries from the Sierra Nevada—the Fresno, Chiwchilla, Merced, Tuolumne, Stanislaus, Calaveras, and Mokelumne rivers being the most important of them. The San Joaquin basin covers thirty-two thousand square miles, one-fifth of California. For three hundred miles, the river runs through mountains and valleys toward its delta, where it mingles with the SACRAMENTO RIVER and flows into San Francisco Bay. The San Joaquin basin gets much more snow than rain, most of it falling from November to April. Run-off, the vast majority of it melting snow, peaks between late spring and summer as the snow line back-peddles up the mountain slopes.

Called Rio de San Francisco by the Spanish priest Father Crespi, who first saw the river on March 30, 1772, it was renamed the San Joaquin by explorer Gabriel Moraga around 1805, perhaps because he called the Sacramento the San Francisco River at that point. Left basically untouched by Europeans and their New World descendants until the California gold rush, the San Joaquin region was not truly developed until the completion of the SOUTHERN PACIFIC RAILROAD in the 1870s. Opening land for settlement, making cattle shipments possible, and creating links to markets for grain, the Southern Pacific held a virtual monopoly over the region's economy until the late 1880s. When the Santa Fe line reached the area, the San Joaquin Valley truly began to prosper. The discovery of oil at the turn of the century only improved an already thriving economy.

In the 1920s and 1930s, California's hydraulic civilization came to the San Joaquin, whose many tributaries had long been turned to the irrigation of crops. In 1933, Stockton completed a deep-water canal, which provided the valley with an ocean port. Deep-water wells allowed area farmers to put in cotton. And in the late 1930s, the CENTRAL VALLEY PROJECT—aimed at controlling the San Joaquin's flow and diverting the Sacramento into the San Joaquin basin—got under way. Late in the twentieth century, some merchants began to make a mark on the valley's economy by outfitting hikers and mountaineers headed for the Sierra Nevada, but for the most part, oil and agriculture dominated the valley's economy and the lives of its citizens as they had since the century began.

—*Charles Phillips*

SUGGESTED READING:

Rose, Gene. *San Joaquin: A River Betrayed.* Fresno, Calif., 1992.

SAN JOSE, CALIFORNIA

The county seat of Santa Clara County, San Jose, CALIFORNIA, was founded in 1777 as California's first pueblo and was incorporated as an American city in 1850, shortly after California became a state. Because San Jose lost out to Sacramento in the bidding to be state capital, its initial growth was slow. In 1860, its population stood at fewer than 5,000 people, and its economy revolved around cattle raising. By the time of the next census, however, the railroad had come to the valley, the population had begun a steady if unspectacular growth, and wheat had replaced cattle as the leading product. Around 1875, wheat gave way to fruit-growing, the area became known as the "Valley of Heart's Delight," and San Jose was on its way to becoming the capital of the most extensive fruit-growing and fruit-processing region in the world. By the 1930s, thousands of acres of prune, apricot, and cherry trees surrounded the city, and one-third to one-half of the world's prune supply came from Santa Clara County alone. As late as 1960, there were 215 fruit-processing operations in the area.

San Jose was also noteworthy for its large population of European immigrants, some of whom brought cuttings that helped launch the fruit industry. In 1930, the largest group had come from Italy—about 20 percent of the more than 57,000 residents of San Jose were first- or second-generation Italian Americans. The changing economy ushered in by World War II opened opportunities outside the fruit industry for the European immigrants and inside the industry for a newer wave of immigrants—Chicanos from the Southwest. Beginning in the 1970s, the city saw an influx from Southeast Asia. By the early 1990s, while the majority of the city's population was white, 27 percent was Hispanic, and 20 percent, Asian.

World-famous for its fruit industry through World War II (as late as the 1950s Soviet leader Nikita Khruschev came to town and received a ceremonial box of prunes), San Jose later became even more celebrated as the capital of the "Silicon Valley." One harbinger of change came when the Food Machinery Corporation, which manufactured heavy equipment for canneries, began to seek defense contracts during the war. With Stanford University's renowned engineering program in its backyard, San Jose and its environs had the human capital to attract firms such as IBM in the 1940s and Lockheed Missiles and Space Company in the 1950s, as well as to produce hundreds of home-grown electronic firms. By the mid-1980s, there were only seven canneries left, and in 1983 alone, the valley's defense contractors manufactured $4 billion worth of goods for the federal government.

The electronics and defense industries produced explosive growth in population, from 95,000 in 1950 to 822,000 in 1993. Because of an aggressive policy of annexation, the city grew in its physical dimensions as well. Yet there was continuity as well as growth and change: in 1930, thousands of European immigrant women constituted the mainstay of the fruit-processing work force. In 1990, tens of thousands of Hispanic and Asian immigrant women made up the preponderance of the electronics-assembly operatives.

—*Glenna Matthews*

SUGGESTED READING:

Arbuckle, Clyde. *History of San Jose.* San Jose, Calif., 1986.

Leonardo, Micaela. *Varieties of Ethnic Experience: Kinship, Class, and Gender among California Italian-Americans.* Ithaca, N.Y., 1984.

Matthews, Glenna. "Ethnicity and Success in San Jose." *Journal of Interdisciplinary History* 7 (1976): 305–318.

Payne, Stephen M. *Santa Clara County: Harvest of Change.* Northridge, Calif., 1987.

SAN RAFAEL RANCH, CALIFORNIA

Originally a Spanish land grant, the San Rafael Ranch lay on the United States–Mexican border east of Nogales, Arizona. In 1882, Colin and Brewster Cameron bought 152,000 acres of the San Rafael from R. R. Richardson only to run into the kind of difficulties typical to Spanish and Mexican grants in the Southwest. Its boundaries poorly defined, the ranch became subject to extended litigation among the Camerons, squatters, and neighboring cattlemen, but at length Colin Cameron received clear title to about one-fourth of the land the Camerons claimed was included under the grant. A progressive cattle-breeder, Colin improved ranching operations and introduced Hereford cattle to the Nogales operation. In 1903, he sold San Rafael to colorful *bon vivant* Colonel William Greene, for $1.5 million, ten times the price the brothers paid in 1882. Greene, who owned mines and ranches in Mexico around Cananea, put Tom Heady, manager of his Mexican ranches, in charge of San Rafael. During the course of the twenty-eight years that Heady ran the San Rafael Ranch, he became one of Arizona's leading Hereford breeders.

—*Patricia Hogan*

SAN SIMEON

SEE: Hearst San Simeon State Historical Monument